Principles of Knowledge Representation and Reasoning:

Proceedings of the Fourth International Conference
(KR '94)

The Morgan Kaufmann Series in Representation and Reasoning
Series editor, Ronald J. Brachman (AT&T Bell Laboratories)

Books

James Allen, James Hendler, and Austin Tate, editors
Readings in Planning (1990)

James F. Allen, Henry A. Kautz, Richard N. Pelavin, and Josh D. Tenenberg
Reasoning About Plans (1991)

Ronald J. Brachman and Hector Levesque, editors
Readings in Knowledge Representation (1985)

Ernest Davis
Representations of Commonsense Knowledge (1990)

Thomas L. Dean and Michael P. Wellman
Planning and Control (1991)

Janet Kolodner
Case-Based Reasoning (1993)

Judea Pearl
Probabilistic Reasoning in Intelligent Systems: Networks of Plausible Inference (1988)

Glenn Shafer and Judea Pearl, editors
Readings in Uncertain Reasoning (1990)

John Sowa, editor
Principles of Semantic Networks: Explorations in the Representation of Knowledge (1991)

Daniel S. Weld and Johan de Kleer, editors
Readings in Qualitative Reasoning about Physical Systems (1990)

David E. Wilkins
Practical Planning: Extending the Classical AI Paradigm (1988)

Proceedings

Principles of Knowledge Representation & Reasoning: Proceedings of the First International Conference (KR '89)
Edited by Ronald J. Brachman, Hector J. Levesque, and Raymond Reiter

Principles of Knowledge Representation & Reasoning: Proceedings of the Second International Conference (KR '91)
Edited by James Allen, Richard Fikes, and Erik Sandewall

Principles of Knowledge Representation & Reasoning: Proceedings of the Third International Conference (KR '92)
Edited by Bernhard Nebel, Charles Rich, and William Swartout

Principles of Knowledge Representation & Reasoning: Proceedings of the Fourth International Conference (KR '94)
Edited by Jon Doyle, Erik Sandewall, and Pietro Torasso

The Frame Problem in Artificial Intelligence: Proceedings of the 1987 Conference
Edited by Frank M. Brown (1987)

Reasoning About Actions and Plans: Proceedings of the 1986 Workshop
Edited by Michael P. Georgeff and Amy L. Lansky (1987)

Theoretical Aspects of Reasoning and Knowledge: Proceedings of the First Conference (TARK 1986)
Edited by Joseph P. Halpern

Theoretical Aspects of Reasoning and Knowledge: Proceedings of the Second Conference (TARK 1988)
Edited by Moshe Y. Vardi

Theoretical Aspects of Reasoning and Knowledge: Proceedings of the Third Conference (TARK 1990)
Edited by Rohit Parikh

Theoretical Aspects of Reasoning and Knowledge: Proceedings of the Fourth Conference (TARK 1992)
Edited by Yoram Moses

Theoretical Aspects of Reasoning and Knowledge: Proceedings of the Fifth Conference (TARK 1994)
Edited by Ronald Fagin

Principles of Knowledge Representation and Reasoning:

Proceedings of the Fourth International Conference (KR '94)

Edited by

Jon Doyle
(Massachusetts Institute of Technology)

Erik Sandewall
(Linköping University)

Pietro Torasso
(Università di Torino)

Morgan Kaufmann Publishers, Inc.
San Francisco, California

These proceedings were managed and produced for the organizers
of the KR '94 conference by Professional Book Center, Denver, Colorado.

The individual papers were submitted in camera-ready form by the contributing authors.

Morgan Kaufmann Publishers, Inc.
340 Pine Street, Sixth Floor
San Francisco, CA 94104

Library of Congress **Cataloging-in-Publication** Data

International Conference on Principles of Knowledge Representation and
    Reasoning (4th : 1994 : Bonn, Germany)
    Principles of knowledge representation and reasoning : proceedings
of the fourth international conference (KR'94), Bonn, Germany, May
24–27, 1994 / edited by Jon Doyle, Erik Sandewall, Pietro Torasso.
        p. cm. — (The Morgan Kaufmann series in representation and
reasoning)
    Includes bibliographical references and index.
    ISBN 1-55860-328-X
    1. Knowledge representation (Information theory)—Congresses.
2. Reasoning—Congresses.   I. Doyle, Jon.   II. Sandewall, Erik.
III. Torasso, Pietro.   IV. Title.   V. Series.
Q387.I59   1994
006.3'3—dc20   94-9421
                                                             CIP

Copyright © 1994 by Morgan Kaufmann Publishers, Inc.
All rights reserved.
Printed in the United States of America

No part of this publication may be reproduced, stored in a retrieval system, or transmitted
in any form or by any means—electronic, mechanical, photocopying, recording, or
otherwise—without the prior written permission of the publisher.

Contents

Preface ix

Acknowledgments x

A Computational Account for a Description Logic of Time and Action 3
   Alessandro Artale and Enrico Franconi (IRST, Italy)

Proofs in Context 15
   Giuseppe Attardi and Maria Simi (Università di Pisa, Italy)

An Integrated Implementation of Simulative, Uncertain and Metaphorical Reasoning about Mental States 27
   J. A. Barnden, S. Helmreich, E. Iverson,
   and G. C. Stein (New Mexico State University, USA)

Reasoning with Minimal Models: Efficient Algorithms and Applications 39
   Rachel Ben-Eliyahu (Technion, Israel)
   and Luigi Palopoli (Universitá della Calabria, Italy)

Spatial Reasoning with Propositional Logics 51
   Brandon Bennett (University of Leeds, UK)

On the Relation Between Default and Modal Consequence Relations 63
   Alexander Bochman (Bar-Ilan University, Israel)

Toward a Logic for Qualitative Decision Theory 75
   Craig Boutilier (University of British Columbia, Canada)

Belief Ascription and Mental-Level Modelling 87
   Ronen I. Brafman (Stanford University, USA)
   and Moshe Tennenholtz (Technion, Israel)

Default Logic as a Query Language 99
   Marco Cadoli (Università di Roma, Italy), Thomas Eiter
   and Georg Gottlob (Technical University of Vienna, Austria)

A Unified Framework for Class-based Representation Formalisms 109
   Diego Calvanese, Maurizio Lenzerini, and Daniele Nardi (Università di Roma, Italy)

Learning the Classic Description Logic: Theoretical and Experimental Results 121
   William W. Cohen and Haym Hirsh (AT&T Bell Laboratories, USA)

Directional Resolution: The Davis-Putnam Procedure, Revisited 134
   Rina Dechter and Irina Rish (University of California, Irvine, USA)

A General Approach to Specificity in Default Reasoning 146
   James P. Delgrande (Simon Fraser University, Canada)
   and Torsten H. Schaub (IRISA, France)

Action Representation for Interpreting Purpose Clauses in Natural Language Instructions 158
   Barbara Di Eugenio (Carnegie Mellon University, USA)

Conditional Objects as Nonmonotonic Consequence Relations: Main Results 170
    Didier Dubois and Henri Prade (Université Paul Sabatier, France)

Tractable Closed World Reasoning with Updates 178
    Oren Etzioni, Keith Golden, Daniel Weld (University of Washington, USA)

A Knowledge-based Framework for Belief Change, Part II: Revision and Update 190
    Nir Friedman (Stanford University, USA)
    and Joseph Y. Halpern (IBM Almaden Research Center, USA)

On the Complexity of Conditional Logics 202
    Nir Friedman (Stanford University, USA)
    and Joseph Y. Halpern (IBM Almaden Research Center, USA)

An Efficient Method for Managing Disjunctions in Qualitative Temporal Reasoning 214
    Alfonso Gerevini (IRST, Italy) and Lenhart Schubert (University of Rochester, USA)

GSAT and Dynamic Backtracking 226
    Matthew L. Ginsberg (University of Oregon, USA)
    and David A. McAllester (Massachusetts Institute of Technology, USA)

Representing Uncertainty in Simple Planners 238
    Robert P. Goldman and Mark S. Boddy (Honeywell Technology Center, USA)

How Far Can We 'C'? Defining a 'Doughnut' Using Connection Alone 246
    N. M. Gotts (University of Leeds, UK)

An Ontology for Engineering Mathematics 258
    Thomas R. Gruber and Gregory R. Olsen (Stanford University, USA)

An Ontology of Meta-Level Categories 270
    Nicola Guarino and Massimiliano Carrara (LADSEB-CNR, Italy)
    and Pierdaniele Giaretta (University of Padova, Italy)

Defeasible Reasoning with Structured Information 281
    Anthony Hunter (Imperial College, UK)

On Positive Occurrences of Negation as Failure 293
    Katsumi Inoue (Toyohashi University of Technology, Japan)
    and Chiaki Sakama (ASTEM Research Institute of Kyoto, Japan)

Probabilistic Reasoning in Terminological Logics 305
    Manfred Jaeger (Max Plank Institut für Informatik, Germany)

On Multiagent Autoepistemic Logic—An Extrospective View 317
    Yuejun J. Jiang (Imperial College, UK)

Refinement Search as a Unifying Framework for Analyzing Planning Algorithms 329
    Subbarao Kambhampati (Arizona State University, USA)

Actions with Indirect Effects (Preliminary Report) 341
    G. Neelakantan Kartha and Vladimir Lifschitz (University of Texas, USA)

An Application of Terminological Logics to Case-based Reasoning 351
    Jana Koehler (German Research Center for Artificial Intelligence [DFKI], Germany)

Risk-Sensitive Planning with Probabilistic Decision Graphs 363
    Sven Koenig and Reid G. Simmons (Carnegie Mellon University, USA)

Easy to be Hard: Difficult Problems for Greedy Algorithms 374
    Kurt Konolige (SRI International, USA)

Complexity Results for First-Order Theories of Temporal Constraints 379
    Manolis Koubarakis (National Technical University of Athens, Greece)

Reasoning in Logic about Continuous Systems 391
    Benjamin J. Kuipers and Benjamin Shults (University of Texas, USA)

Enhancing the Power of a Decidable First-Order Reasoner 403
    Gerhard Lakemeyer and Susanne Meyer (University of Bonn, Germany)

Knowledge, Certainty, Belief, and Conditionalisation (Abbreviated Version) 415
    Philippe Lamarre (IRIN, Université de Nantes, France)
    and Yoav Shoham (Stanford University, USA)

How to Progress a Database (and Why) I. Logical Foundations 425
    Fangzhen Lin and Ray Reiter (University of Toronto, Canada)

Modalities Over Actions, I. Model Theory 437
    L. Thorne McCarty (Rutgers University, USA)

Generating Tests Using Abduction 449
    Sheila McIlraith (University of Toronto, Canada)

Preferential Entailments for Circumscriptions 461
    Yves Moinard (IRISA, France) and Raymond Rolland (IRMAR, France)

A Decision Method for Nonmomotonic Reasoning Based on Autoepistemic Reasoning 473
    Ilkka Niemelä (Helsinki University of Technology, Finland)

A Framework for Part-of Hierarchies in Terminological Logics 485
    Lin Padgham and Patrick Lambrix (Linköping University, Sweden)

Means-End Plan Recognition—Towards a Theory of Reactive Recognition 497
    Anand S. Rao (Australian Artificial Intelligence Institute, Australia)

Terminological Cycles and the Propositional μ-Calculus 509
    Klaus Schild (German Research Center for Artificial Intelligence [DFKI], Germany)

Near-Optimal Plans, Tractability, and Reactivity 521
    Bart Selman (AT&T Bell Laboratories, USA)

Specification and Evaluation of Preferences Under Uncertainty 530
    Sek-Wah Tan and Judea Pearl (University of California, Los Angeles, USA)

Making the Difference: A Subtraction Operation for Description Logics 540
    Gunnar Teege (TU Munich, Germany)

Tractable Databases: How to Make Propositional Unit Resolution Complete Through Compilation 551
    Alvaro del Val (Stanford University, USA)

The Role of Reversible Grammars in Translating Between Representation Languages 562
    Jeffrey Van Baalen (University of Wyoming, USA)
    and Richard E. Fikes (Stanford University, USA)

Constraint Tightness versus Global Consistency 572
    Peter van Beek (University of Alberta, Canada)
    and Rina Dechter (University of California, Irvine, USA)

Honesty in Partial Logic 583
    Wiebe van der Hoek (Utrecht University, Netherlands), Jan Jaspars
    (CWI, Netherlands), and Elias Thijsse (Tilburg University, Netherlands)

Mutual Belief Revision (Preliminary Report) 595
    Ron van der Meyden (NTT Basic Research Labs, Japan)

REVISE: An Extended Logic Programming System for Revising Knowledge Bases 607
    Carlos Viegas Damásio and Luís Moniz Pereira (Università Nova de Lisboa,
    Portugal) and Wolfgang Nejdl (RWTH Aachen, Germany)

Transmutations of Knowledge Systems 619
    Mary-Anne Williams (University of Newcastle, Australia)

INVITED TALKS

Knowledge Representation Issues in Integrated Planning and Learning Systems (*abstract only*) 633
    Jaime Carbonell (Carnegie Mellon University, USA)

Non-Standard Theories of Uncertainty in Knowledge Representation and Reasoning 634
    Didier Dubois and Henri Prade (Université Paul Sabatier, France)

Beyond Ignorance-Based Systems (*abstract only*) 646
    W. A. Woods (Sun Microsystems Laboratories, Inc., USA)

PANELS

Systems vs. Theory vs. ... : KR&R Research Methodologies (*abstract only*) 649
    Moderator: Lin Padgham (Linköping University, Sweden)

Exploiting Natural Language for Knowledge Representation and Reasoning (*abstract only*) 650
    Moderator: Len Schubert (University of Rochester, USA)

Contributions by Topic   653

Author Index   655

Preface

This volume contains the papers presented at the Fourth International Conference on Principles of Knowledge Representation and Reasoning. The KR conferences have established themselves as the leading forum for timely, in-depth presentation of progress in the theory and principles underlying the representation and computational manipulation of knowledge. Following highly successful meetings in Toronto and Cambridge, Massachusetts, the conference convenes this year in Bonn, outside of North America for the first time.

KR '94 continues the tradition of high standards for accepted papers established by the preceding three conferences. We were encouraged by the high quality of the 272 extended abstracts submitted for review and of the 55 chosen for publication. Receiving submissions from every continent, the conference continues to maintain and broaden its international character, with the proceedings presenting the work of authors from 15 countries.

This year's conference continues to move towards a suitable balance between theoretical work and implemented, applied, and experimental work. Many program committee members emphasized this balance in their reviews, and the papers below present excellent examples of such work. Observing great concern about methodological problems among the program committee, we asked Lin Padgham to organize a panel discussion on this topic.

Many areas traditionally attracting strong KR interest remain well represented this year, including deduction and search, description logics, theories of knowledge and belief, nonmonotonic reasoning and belief revision, action and time, planning and decision-making, and reasoning about the physical world. The presence of planning and diagnosis diminished, perhaps due to the appearance of new conferences and workshops devoted to these topics, while the presence of other topics grew, including the relations between KR and other subfields of artificial intelligence. Some papers, including the invited talk by Didier Dubois, concern the integration of numeric and symbolic methods in preference modeling and uncertainty, while others, including the invited talk by Jaime Carbonell, investigate connections between KR and machine learning.

We also sought to strengthen ties between KR and related fields such as philosophy, linguistics, psychology, and economics. While we did not move as far in this direction as hoped, we are glad to include papers along these lines in the program, and were very fortunate to get Len Schubert to organize the panel discussion aimed at identifying ideas from natural language and linguistics for exploitation in KR.

Jon Doyle
Program Co-Chair

Erik Sandewall
Conference Chair

Pietro Torasso
Program Co-Chair

Acknowledgments

KR '94 would not have been possible without the efforts of a great number of dedicated people.

First and foremost was our excellent international program committee, who contributed extraordinary effort in reviewing and comparing 272 papers:

Giuseppe Attardi
  University of Pisa, Italy

Franz Baader
  DFKI, Germany

Fahiem Bacchus
  University of Waterloo, Canada

Philippe Besnard
  IRISA, France

Piero Bonissone
  GE, USA

Craig Boutilier
  UBC, Canada

Ron Brachman
  AT&T, USA

Maurice Bruynooghe
  KUL, Belgium

Anthony Cohn
  University of Leeds, UK

Ernest Davis
  NYU, USA

Rina Dechter
  UC Irvine, USA

Johan de Kleer
  Xerox, USA

Oskar Dressler
  Siemens, Germany

Jennifer Elgot-Drapkin
  Arizona State University, USA

Richard Fikes
  Stanford University, USA

Alan Frisch
  University of York, UK

Hector Geffner
  Simon Bolivar University, Venezuela

Georg Gottlob
  TU Wien, Austria

Pat Hayes
  University of Illinois, USA

Hirofumi Katsuno
  NTT, Japan

Henry Kautz
  AT&T, USA

Sarit Kraus
  Bar-Ilan University, Israel

Maurizio Lenzerini
  University of Rome, Italy

Vladimir Lifschitz
  University of Texas, USA

David Makinson
  Unesco, France

Joao Martins
  IST, Portugal

David McAllester
  MIT, USA

John-Jules Meyer
  University of Amsterdam, Netherlands

Katharina Morik
  University of Dortmund, Germany

Johanna Moore
  University of Pittsburgh, USA

Hideyuki Nakashima
  ETL, Japan

Bernhard Nebel
  University of Ulm, Germany

Hans Juergen Ohlbach
  Max Planck Institut, Germany

Lin Padgham
  Linköping University, Sweden

Peter Patel-Schneider
  AT&T, USA

Ramesh Patil
  USC/ISI, USA

Raymond Perrault
  SRI, USA

David Poole
  UBC, Canada

Henri Prade
  IRIT, France

Anand Rao
  AAII, Australia

Jeff Rosenschein
  Hebrew University, Israel

Stuart Russell
  UC Berkeley, USA

Len Schubert
  University of Rochester, USA

Marek Sergot
  Imperial College, UK

Lokendra Shastri
  ICSI, USA

Yoav Shoham
  Stanford University, USA

Lynn Stein
  MIT, USA

Devika Subramanian
  Cornell University, USA

William Swartout
  USC/ISI, USA

Austin Tate
  AIAI, University of Edinburgh, UK

Peter van Beek
  University of Alberta, Canada

Michael Wellman
  University of Michigan, USA

The program chairs and committee were fortunate to have the assistance of a number of other researchers who offered suggestions and comments concerning the submitted extended abstracts. Many of these people provided help at short notice during the Christmas holidays, for which we are very grateful.

Siegfried Bell
University of Dortmund, Germany

Piero Bonatti
TU Wien, Austria

Dmitri Boulanger
KUL, Belgium

Marco Cadoli
Università di Roma, Italy

Diego Calvanese
Università di Roma, Italy

Giuseppe De Giacomo
Università di Roma, Italy

Marc Denecker
KUL, Belgium

Luc De Raedt
KUL, Belgium

Danny De Schreye
KUL, Belgium

Brian Drabble
University of Edinburgh, UK

Thomas Eiter
TU Wien, Austria

Gerhard Friedrich
Siemens, Austria

Dan Frost
UC Irvine, USA

Alois Haselboeck
Siemens, Austria

Joachim Hertzberg
GMD, Germany

Ian Horswill
MIT, USA

Kalev Kkask
UC Irvine, USA

Volker Klingspor
University of Dortmund, Germany

Jerome Lang
IRIT, France

William J. Long
MIT, USA

Alberto Martelli
Università di Torino, Italy

Igor Mozetic
ARIAI, Austria

Srini Narayanan
ICSI, USA

Daniele Nardi
Università di Roma, Italy

Stephen Omohundro
ICSI, USA

Luigi Portinale
Università di Torino, Italy

Anke Rieger
University of Dortmund, Germany

Irina Rish
UC Irvine, USA

Andrea Schaerf
Università di Roma, Italy

Marco Schaerf
Università di Cagliari, Italy

Klaus Schild
DFKI, Germany

Eddie Schwalb
UC Irvine, USA

Grigori Schwarz
Stanford University, USA

Maria Simi
University of Pisa, Italy

Elizabeth Sonenberg
University of Melbourne, Australia

Marcus Stumptner
TU Wien, Austria

Peter Szolovits
MIT, USA

Mike Uschold
University of Edinburgh, UK

Henk Vandecasteele
KUL, Belgium

We also thank our invited speakers, Jaime Carbonell, Didier Dubois, and William Woods, for their important contributions to the conference, and Lin Padgham and Len Schubert for organizing the panels on KR methodology and natural language opportunities.

We thank Gerhard Lakemeyer for his great effort in handling the logistical matters involved in the conference site, Luzia Sassen-Heβeler for her help in producing the brochure, Christine Harms for handling matters relating to the Stresemann Institut, and our publicity chair, Werner Horn, who worked long hours to spread the word about KR'94 around the globe.

We thank Jim Schmolze, the KR treasurer, for writing the checks needed to keep things moving.

We thank Bernhard Nebel and Ramesh Patil for providing us with a variety of software that helped automate some of the tasks involved in reviewing the submitted papers, and for providing quick answers to desperate questions at all times of the day.

We thank Matt Ginsberg for investigating the US banking system and possible methods for simplifying the payment of registration fees.

As is traditional, the home organizations of the conference organizers provided significant administrative support. We wish to thank MIT and Scott Reischmann personally; the Università di Torino; Linköping University and Lise-Lott Svensson personally; and Institute of Computer Science III, University of Bonn and Martina Fusch personally.

We are happy to be able to continue the tradition of publishing the proceedings through Morgan Kaufmann Publishers, and thank Mike Morgan and Doug Sery for all their help. We also thank Jennifer Ballentine and her staff for organizing the production of the proceedings at Professional Book Center in Denver, Colorado.

We gratefully acknowledge invaluable support from the Gesellschaft für Informatik, the Austrian Society for Artificial Intelligence, the Canadian Society for Computational Studies of Intelligence, the European Coordinating Committee on Artificial Intelligence, the American Association for Artificial Intelligence, and the International Joint Conferences on Artificial Intelligence.

Finally, we thank all the authors who submitted their extended abstracts for review. There would be no conference without them.

Contributed Papers

A Computational Account for a Description Logic of Time and Action

Alessandro Artale* and Enrico Franconi
Knowledge Representation and Reasoning Lab.
IRST, I-38050 Povo TN, Italy
{artale|franconi}@irst.it

Abstract

A formal language for representing and reasoning about time and action is presented. We employ an action representation in the style of Allen, where an action is represented by describing the time course of events while the action occurs. In this sense, an action is defined by means of temporal constraints on the world states, which pertain to the action itself, and on other more elementary actions occurring over time. A distinction between action types and individual actions is supported by the formalism. Plans are seen as complex actions whose properties possibly change with time. The formal representation language used in this paper is a description logic, and it is provided with a well founded syntax, semantics and calculus. Algorithms for the subsumption and recognition tasks – forming the basis for action management – are provided.

1 INTRODUCTION

The goal of this work is to investigate a formal framework that permits dealing with time, actions and plans in a uniform way. As opposed to the most common approaches to modeling actions as state change – e.g., the formal models based on *situation calculus* [McCarthy and Hayes, 1969], the STRIPS-like planning systems [Lifschitz, 1987] – where actions are instantaneous and defined as functions from one state to another, we prefer to explicitly introduce the notion of time by admitting that actions take time, like in [Allen, 1991]. Allen builds a representation based on time, eliminating the notion of state as encoded in the STRIPS-like systems by means of *preconditions* – causes – and *postconditions* – effects. This formalism is not intended to capture any sense of causality, but it represents an action by describing the time course of events while the action occurs. Besides, unlike STRIPS-like systems, an action takes time: then, it is possible to define what is

true while the action is occurring. Different actions can be concurrent or may overlap in time; effects of overlapping actions can be different from the sum of their individual effects; effects may not follow the action but more complex temporal relations may hold. Starting from a formal language able to express temporally related objects, actions are represented through temporal constraints on the world states, which pertain to the action itself, and on other more primitive actions occurring over time. With respect to [Allen, 1991], our formalism has a clear distinction between the language for expressing action types (the conceptual level) and the language for expressing individual actions (the assertional level). Plans are built by temporally relating action types in a compositional way using the temporal constructors available in the language. In this way, since the temporal relationships are proper operators of the basic language, the distinction between actions and plans disappears. As a matter of fact, we do not need distinct languages for objects and states representation, for time representation, for actions representation, and for plans representation.

The basic temporal language we propose is a *concept language* [Nebel, 1990], i.e. a description logic of the KL-ONE family[1], and it is inspired by the work of [Schmiedel, 1990]. The use of a concept language to represent directly action and plan descriptions allows us to exploit the ideas developed in the concept languages family, like procedures for subsumption, classification and instance recognition [Hollunder et al., 1990; Nebel, 1990]. In this paper we present a calculus to check subsumption between actions types, and to recognize which type of action has taken place at a certain time interval from the observation of what is happening in the world. A plan taxonomy based on subsumption can be built, and it can play the role of a plan library to be used for plan retrieval and plan recognition tasks [Kautz, 1991].

Several temporal extensions of a concept language exist in the literature: Claudio Bettini in [Bettini, 1992] and [Bettini, 1993] proposes a variable-free extension

---

*Current address: Ladseb-CNR, I-35020 Padova PD, Italy

[1] Concept languages are also called Frame-Based Description Languages, Term Subsumption Languages, Terminological Logics, Taxonomic Logics or Description Logics.

with both existential and universal temporal quantification; [Devanbu and Litman, 1991] and [Weida and Litman, 1992] – and recently [Weida and Litman, 1994] – propose a loose hybrid integration between concept languages and respectively regular expressions and constraint networks; [Schmiedel, 1990] proposes a very expressive but undecidable language with variables and temporal quantifiers; [Schild, 1993] proposes the embedding of *point*-based tense operators in a propositionally closed concept language – his ideas have been applied in the BACK terminological representation system; [Lambrix and Rönnquist, 1993] study the combination of the temporal logic LITE, where the notion of object is revised from being an indivisible entity into being a temporal structure of *versions*, and a terminological logic. In [Song and Cohen, 1991], temporal constraints between actions and its decomposed subactions – in the context of hierarchical planning – are made explicit from the structure of the plan, in order to improve the results of plan recognition.

Our proposal reduces the expressivity of [Schmiedel, 1990] in the direction of [Weida and Litman, 1992]; in this way, we obtain a decidable logic with a sound and complete subsumption algorithm. However, while [Weida and Litman, 1992] use two different formalisms to represent actions and plans – a non temporal concept language for describing actions and a second formalism to compose plans by adding temporal information – we choose an extension of a description logic where time operators are available directly as term constructors. This view implies an integration of a temporal domain in the semantic structure where terms themselves are interpreted, giving the formal way both for a well-founded notion of subsumption and for proving soundness and completeness of the corresponding algorithm. Moreover, we are able to build *temporal structured* actions – as opposed to atomic actions – describing how the world state changes because of the occurrence of an action. In fact, our language allows for feature representation, as suggested in [Heinsohn et al., 1992], in order to relate actions to states of the world.

The paper is organized as follows. The formal language is first introduced, by presenting its syntax and semantics at both the concept and individual levels. The subsumption and instance recognition problems are formally defined in this framework. Examples of application of the temporal language for action and plan representation and reasoning are presented in section 3. The calculus is finally briefly revealed, by looking first to a normal form for concept expressions, and then to the algorithms for subsumption and instance recognition.

2 THE TEMPORAL LANGUAGE

We introduce in this section the temporal language. Pursuing the ideas of [Schmiedel, 1990], an interval-based temporal extension of concept languages is investigated. A well founded syntax and semantics for the language is given and a formal definition of the subsumption and recognition reasoning tasks is devised.

$$
\begin{aligned}
C, D \rightarrow \ & E \mid & &\text{(non-temporal concept)} \\
& C \sqcap D \mid & &\text{(conjunction)} \\
& C \sqcup D \mid & &\text{(disjunction)} \\
& C@X \mid & &\text{(qualifier)} \\
& C[Y]@X \mid & &\text{(substitutive qualifier)} \\
& \Diamond (X^+)\, \mathit{Tc}^+ .C & &\text{(existential quantifier)} \\
E, F \rightarrow \ & A \mid & &\text{(atomic concept)} \\
& \top \mid & &\text{(top)} \\
& E \sqcap F \mid & &\text{(conjunction)} \\
& E \sqcup F \mid & &\text{(disjunction)} \\
& p \downarrow q \mid & &\text{(agreement)} \\
& p : E & &\text{(selection)} \\
p, q \rightarrow \ & f \mid & &\text{(atomic feature)} \\
& \star g \mid & &\text{(atomic parametric feature)} \\
& p \circ q & &\text{(feature chain)} \\
\mathit{Tc} \rightarrow \ & (X\ (R)\ Y) & &\text{(temporal constraint)} \\
R, S \rightarrow \ & R\ ,\ S \mid & &\text{(disjunction)} \\
& \mathsf{s} \mid \mathsf{mi} \mid \mathsf{f} \mid \ldots & &\text{(Allen's relations)} \\
X, Y \rightarrow \ & \sharp \mid \mathsf{x} \mid \mathsf{y} \mid \ldots & &\text{(temporal variables)}
\end{aligned}
$$

Figure 1: Syntax rules for the temporal language.

Basic types of the language are *concepts*, *individuals*, *temporal variables* and *intervals*. A concept is a description gathering the common properties among a collection of individuals. Concepts can describe entities of the world, states, events. Temporal variables denote intervals bound by temporal constraints, by means of which abstract temporal patterns in the form of constraint networks are expressed. Concepts (resp. individuals) can be specified to hold at a certain interval variable (resp. value) defined by the constraint network. In this way, *action types* (resp. *individual actions*) can be represented in a uniform way by temporally related concepts (resp. individuals).

Concept expressions (denoted by C, D) are built out of *atomic concepts* (denoted by A), *atomic features* (denoted by f), *atomic parametric features* (denoted by $\star g$)[2] and constrained *interval variables* (denoted by X, Y) according to the abstract syntax rules of figure 1[3]. For the basic interval relations we use the same notation as in [Allen, 1991]: before (b), meets (m), during (d), overlaps (o), starts (s), finishes (f), equal (=), after (a), met-by (mi), contains (di), overlapped-by (oi), started-by (si), finished-by (fi).

Temporal variables are introduced by the temporal existential quantifier "$\Diamond$". Variables appearing in temporal constraints should be declared within the same tempo-

---

[2] Names for atomic features and atomic parametric features are from the same alphabet of symbols; the $\star$ symbol is not intended as operator, but only as differentiating the two syntactic types.

[3] The syntax rules are expressed following the tradition of concept languages [Hollunder et al., 1990]. It can be read as, e.g. if C is a concept expression and X is a temporal variable, then $C@X$ is a concept expression.

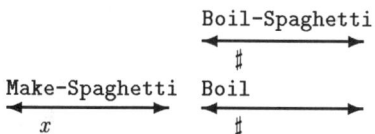

Figure 2: Temporal dependencies in the definition of the Boil-Spaghetti action.

ral quantifier, with the exception of the special variable ♯. Temporal variables appearing at the right hand side of a "@" operator are called *bindable*. Concepts should not include *unbound* (a.k.a. *free*) bindable variables, with the exception of the special variable ♯; a bindable variable is said to be bound in a concept if it is declared at the nearest temporal quantifier in the body of which it occurs. Moreover, in chained constructs of the form $((C[Y_1]@X_1)[Y_2]@X_2\ldots)$ non bindable variables should not appear more than once, with the exception of the special variable ♯.

In this language, unlike [Schmiedel, 1990; Bettini, 1992], it is not possible to express the negated of the existential temporal quantifier: it is argued that the dual of $\Diamond$ – i.e. the universal temporal quantifier $\Box$ – leads the satisfiability problem – and the subsumption – for the language to be undecidable [Halpern and Shoham, 1991; Venema, 1990; Bettini, 1993].

Concept expressions are interpreted in our logic over pairs of *temporal intervals* and *individuals* $\langle i, a \rangle$, meaning that the individual a is in the extension of the concept at the interval i. If a concept is intended to denote an action, then its interpretation can be seen as the set of individual actions of that type occurring at some interval.

Within a concept, the special ♯ variable refers to the generic interval at which the concept itself *holds*[4]; in the case of actions, it refers to the temporal interval at which the action itself *occurs*. A concept holds at an interval X if it is temporally qualified at X – written $C@X$; in this way, every occurrence of ♯ embedded in C is interpreted as the X variable. Since any concept is implicitly temporally qualified at the special ♯ variable, it is not necessary to explicitly qualify concepts at ♯. The temporal existential quantifier introduces interval variables, related each other and possibly to the ♯ variable in a way defined by the set of *temporal constraints*. The informal meaning of a concept with a temporal existential quantification can be understood with the following examples in the action domain [Weida and Litman, 1992].

Boil-Spaghetti $\doteq$
$\Diamond x$ (x b ♯). (Boil ⊓ Make-Spaghetti@x)

Boil-Spaghetti denotes, by definition, any action occurring at some interval such that an event of Boiling occurs at the same time and an event of type Make-Spaghetti occurs at some preceding interval. The ♯ interval could be understood as the occurring time of the action type being defined: referring to it within the definition is an explicit way to temporally relate states and actions occurring in the world with respect to the occurrence of the action itself. The temporal constraint (x b ♯) states that the interval denoted by x should be before the interval denoted by ♯, i.e. the occurrence interval of the action type Boil-Spaghetti. Figure 2 shows the temporal dependencies of the intervals in which the concept Boil-Spaghetti holds.

As a more complex example, let Chef, Make-Spaghetti, Make-Fettuccine and Boil be atomic concepts, ⋆AGENT be an atomic parametric feature and y be a temporal variable. We can describe the class of "*any action of a chef boiling pasta after having made spaghetti or fettuccini*" as:

Boil-Pasta $\doteq$
$\Diamond y$ (y b ♯).
(⋆AGENT : Chef ⊓ Boil ⊓
(Make-Spaghetti ⊔ Make-Fettuccine)@y)

The parametric feature ⋆AGENT plays the role of *formal parameter* of the action type Boil-Pasta, mapping any instance of the action itself to its own agent, independently from time. The occurrence time of the disjunctive action type Make-Spaghetti ⊔ Make-Fettuccine is bound to the y interval, while the occurrence times of ⋆AGENT:Chef, Boil and Boil-Pasta itself are implicitly bound to the ♯ interval. Please note that, whereas the existence and identity of the ⋆AGENT of the action is independent from time, it can be qualified differently in different intervals of time, e.g the fact that it is a Chef is necessarily true only at the ♯ interval.

The temporal substitutive qualifier $C[Y]@X$, renames the variable Y, within C, to X and it is a way of making coreference between two temporal variables in different scopes – i.e. declared in different temporal quantifiers. This is useful when using already defined concept names. As an example, Boil-Pasta could be redefined by simply renaming the temporal variable x within Boil-Spaghetti:

Boil-Pasta $\doteq$
$\Diamond y$ (y b ♯). (⋆AGENT : Chef ⊓
(Boil-Spaghetti[x]@y ⊔
(Boil ⊓ Make-Fettuccine@y)))

The assertion Boil-Pasta(i, a) says that a is an individual action of types Boil-Pasta and Boil at the interval i, while it is either of type Make-Spaghetti or of type Make-Fettuccine at some interval j preceding i. Moreover, the same assertion implies that a is related to an ⋆AGENT, say b, which is of type Chef at the interval i:

Boil-Pasta(i, a) $\Longrightarrow$
$\exists b$. Boil$(i, a) \wedge$ ⋆AGENT$(a, b) \wedge$ Chef$(i, b) \wedge$
$\exists j$. b(j, i) $\wedge$ (Make-Spaghetti(j, a) $\vee$
Make-Fettuccine(j, a))

---
[4]This variable is usually called *NOW*. We prefer not to adopt such a name, because it could be misleading.

$$
\begin{aligned}
(\mathsf{s})^{\mathcal{E}} &= \{\langle[u,v],[u_1,v_1]\rangle \in \mathcal{T}_{\leq}^{\star} \times \mathcal{T}_{\leq}^{\star} \mid \\
&\qquad u = u_1 \wedge v < v_1\} \\
(\mathsf{f})^{\mathcal{E}} &= \{\langle[u,v],[u_1,v_1]\rangle \in \mathcal{T}_{\leq}^{\star} \times \mathcal{T}_{\leq}^{\star} \mid \\
&\qquad v = v_1 \wedge u_1 < u\} \\
(\mathsf{mi})^{\mathcal{E}} &= \{\langle[u,v],[u_1,v_1]\rangle \in \mathcal{T}_{\leq}^{\star} \times \mathcal{T}_{\leq}^{\star} \mid \\
&\qquad u = v_1\} \\
&\ldots \text{(meaning of other Allen's relations)} \\
(R,S)^{\mathcal{E}} &= R^{\mathcal{E}} \cup S^{\mathcal{E}} \\
\langle \overline{X}, \overline{\mathit{Tc}} \rangle^{\mathcal{E}} &= \{\mathcal{V}: \overline{X} \mapsto \mathcal{T}_{\leq}^{\star} \mid \forall (X\ (R)\ Y) \in \overline{\mathit{Tc}}. \\
&\qquad \langle \mathcal{V}(X), \mathcal{V}(Y) \rangle \in (R)^{\mathcal{E}}\}
\end{aligned}
$$

Figure 3: The temporal interpretation function.

2.1 THE FORMAL SEMANTICS

We assume a linear, unbounded and dense temporal structure $\mathcal{T} = \langle \mathcal{P}, < \rangle$, where $\mathcal{P}$ is a set of time points and $<$ is a strict total order on $\mathcal{P}$. The *interval set* of a structure $\mathcal{T}$ is defined as the set $\mathcal{T}_{\leq}^{\star}$ of all closed intervals $[u,v] \doteq \{x \in \mathcal{P} \mid u \leq x \leq v, u \neq v\}$ in $\mathcal{T}$.

An *interpretation* $\mathcal{I} \doteq \langle \mathcal{T}_{\leq}^{\star}, \Delta^{\mathcal{I}}, \cdot^{\mathcal{I}} \rangle$ consists of a set $\mathcal{T}_{\leq}^{\star}$ (the *interval set* of the selected temporal structure $\mathcal{T}$), a set $\Delta^{\mathcal{I}}$ (the *domain* of $\mathcal{I}$) and a function $\cdot^{\mathcal{I}}$ (the *primitive interpretation function* of $\mathcal{I}$). The primitive interpretation is a function giving a meaning to atomic concepts, features and parametric features:

$$A^{\mathcal{I}} \subseteq \mathcal{T}_{\leq}^{\star} \times \Delta^{\mathcal{I}}\ ;$$
$$f^{\mathcal{I}}: (\mathcal{T}_{\leq}^{\star} \times \Delta^{\mathcal{I}}) \stackrel{partial}{\longmapsto} \Delta^{\mathcal{I}}\ ; \quad \star g^{\mathcal{I}}: \Delta^{\mathcal{I}} \stackrel{partial}{\longmapsto} \Delta^{\mathcal{I}}$$

Atomic parametric features are interpreted as partial functions; they differ from atomic features for being independent from time.

To give a meaning to complex temporal and conceptual expression, we introduce the *temporal interpretation function* and the *general interpretation function*.

The *temporal interpretation function* $\cdot^{\mathcal{E}}$ depends on the temporal structure $\mathcal{T}$, and it is defined in figure 3. The labeled directed graph $\langle \overline{X}, \overline{\mathit{Tc}} \rangle$, where $\overline{X}$ is a shorthand for a set of variables – representing the nodes – and $\overline{\mathit{Tc}}$ is a shorthand for a set of temporal constraints – representing the arcs, is called *temporal constraint network*; the temporal interpretation of a temporal constraint network is the set of all assignments of the variables which satisfy the temporal constraints. An *assignment of variables* is a function $\mathcal{V}: \overline{X} \mapsto \mathcal{T}_{\leq}^{\star}$ associating an interval value to each temporal variable. We will write $\langle \overline{X}, \overline{\mathit{Tc}} \rangle^{\mathcal{E}}_{\{x_1 \mapsto t_1, x_2 \mapsto t_2, \ldots\}}$ to denote the subset of $\langle \overline{X}, \overline{\mathit{Tc}} \rangle^{\mathcal{E}}$ where the variable x_i is mapped to the interval value t_i. A temporal constraint network is *consistent* if it admits a non empty interpretation.

A *general interpretation function* $\cdot^{\mathcal{I}}_{\mathcal{V},t,\mathcal{H}}$, based on a interpretation $\mathcal{I}$, an assignment of variables $\mathcal{V}$, an interval t and a set of constraints $\mathcal{H} = \{x_1 \mapsto t_1, \ldots\}$ over the assignments of inner variables, is defined in such a way that the equations of figure 4 are satisfied. The composition should be read from left to right, i.e.

$$
\begin{aligned}
A^{\mathcal{I}}_{\mathcal{V},t,\mathcal{H}} &= \{a \in \Delta^{\mathcal{I}} \mid \langle t, a \rangle \in A^{\mathcal{I}}\} \\
f^{\mathcal{I}}_{\mathcal{V},t,\mathcal{H}} &= \hat{f}_t : \Delta^{\mathcal{I}} \stackrel{partial}{\longmapsto} \Delta^{\mathcal{I}} \mid \\
&\quad \forall a.\ (a \in \mathrm{dom}\,\hat{f}_t \leftrightarrow \\
&\qquad \langle t, a \rangle \in \mathrm{dom}\,f^{\mathcal{I}}) \wedge \\
&\qquad \hat{f}_t(a) = f^{\mathcal{I}}(t, a) \\
\star g^{\mathcal{I}}_{\mathcal{V},t,\mathcal{H}} &= \star g^{\mathcal{I}} \\
\top^{\mathcal{I}}_{\mathcal{V},t,\mathcal{H}} &= \Delta^{\mathcal{I}} \\
(C \sqcap D)^{\mathcal{I}}_{\mathcal{V},t,\mathcal{H}} &= C^{\mathcal{I}}_{\mathcal{V},t,\mathcal{H}} \cap D^{\mathcal{I}}_{\mathcal{V},t,\mathcal{H}} \\
(C \sqcup D)^{\mathcal{I}}_{\mathcal{V},t,\mathcal{H}} &= C^{\mathcal{I}}_{\mathcal{V},t,\mathcal{H}} \cup D^{\mathcal{I}}_{\mathcal{V},t,\mathcal{H}} \\
(p \circ q)^{\mathcal{I}}_{\mathcal{V},t,\mathcal{H}} &= p^{\mathcal{I}}_{\mathcal{V},t,\mathcal{H}} \circ q^{\mathcal{I}}_{\mathcal{V},t,\mathcal{H}} \\
(p : E)^{\mathcal{I}}_{\mathcal{V},t,\mathcal{H}} &= \{a \in \mathrm{dom}\,p^{\mathcal{I}}_{\mathcal{V},t,\mathcal{H}} \mid \\
&\qquad p^{\mathcal{I}}_{\mathcal{V},t,\mathcal{H}}(a) \in E^{\mathcal{I}}_{\mathcal{V},t,\mathcal{H}}\} \\
(p \downarrow q)^{\mathcal{I}}_{\mathcal{V},t,\mathcal{H}} &= \{a \in \mathrm{dom}\,p^{\mathcal{I}}_{\mathcal{V},t,\mathcal{H}} \cap \mathrm{dom}\,q^{\mathcal{I}}_{\mathcal{V},t,\mathcal{H}} \mid \\
&\qquad p^{\mathcal{I}}_{\mathcal{V},t,\mathcal{H}}(a) = q^{\mathcal{I}}_{\mathcal{V},t,\mathcal{H}}(a)\} \\
(C@X)^{\mathcal{I}}_{\mathcal{V},t,\mathcal{H}} &= (C[\sharp]@X)^{\mathcal{I}}_{\mathcal{V},t,\mathcal{H}} \\
(C[Y]@X)^{\mathcal{I}}_{\mathcal{V},t,\mathcal{H}} &= \begin{cases} C^{\mathcal{I}}_{\mathcal{V},t,\mathcal{H}} & \text{if } X = \sharp, Y = \sharp \\ C^{\mathcal{I}}_{\mathcal{V},\mathcal{V}(X),\mathcal{H}} & \text{if } X \neq \sharp, Y = \sharp \\ C^{\mathcal{I}}_{\mathcal{V},t,\mathcal{H} \cup \{Y \mapsto \mathcal{V}(\sharp)\}} & \text{if } X = \sharp, Y \neq \sharp \\ C^{\mathcal{I}}_{\mathcal{V},t,\mathcal{H} \cup \{Y \mapsto \mathcal{V}(X)\}} & \text{if } X \neq \sharp, Y \neq \sharp \end{cases} \\
(\diamondsuit(\overline{X})\overline{\mathit{Tc}}.C)^{\mathcal{I}}_{\mathcal{V},t,\mathcal{H}} &= \{a \in \Delta^{\mathcal{I}} \mid \\
&\quad \exists \mathcal{W}.\ \mathcal{W} \in \langle \overline{X}, \overline{\mathit{Tc}} \rangle^{\mathcal{E}}_{\mathcal{H} \cup \{\sharp \mapsto t\}} \wedge \\
&\quad a \in C^{\mathcal{I}}_{\mathcal{W},t,\emptyset}\}
\end{aligned}
$$

Figure 4: The general interpretation function.

$(p^{\mathcal{I}}_{\mathcal{V},t,\mathcal{H}} \circ q^{\mathcal{I}}_{\mathcal{V},t,\mathcal{H}})(a)$ means $q^{\mathcal{I}}_{\mathcal{V},t,\mathcal{H}}(p^{\mathcal{I}}_{\mathcal{V},t,\mathcal{H}}(a))$. The expression $\mathrm{dom}\,f^{\mathcal{I}}_{\mathcal{V},t,\mathcal{H}}$ (respectively, $\mathrm{dom}\,f^{\mathcal{I}}$) denotes the domain of the partial function $f^{\mathcal{I}}_{\mathcal{V},t,\mathcal{H}}$ ($f^{\mathcal{I}}$) – i.e., a subset of $\Delta^{\mathcal{I}}$ ($\mathcal{T}_{\leq}^{\star} \times \Delta^{\mathcal{I}}$) for which $f^{\mathcal{I}}_{\mathcal{V},t,\mathcal{H}}$ ($f^{\mathcal{I}}$) is defined. Intuitively, the general interpretation of a concept $C^{\mathcal{I}}_{\mathcal{V},t,\mathcal{H}}$ is the set of entities of the domain which are of type C at the time interval t, with the assignment for the free temporal variables in C given by $\mathcal{V}$, and with the constraints for the assignment of variables in the scope of the outermost temporal quantifiers given by $\mathcal{H}$.

In absence of free variables in the concept expression – with the exception of $\sharp$, we introduce the *natural* interpretation function $C^{\mathcal{I}}_t$ being equivalent to the general interpretation function $C^{\mathcal{I}}_{\mathcal{V},t,\mathcal{H}}$ with any $\mathcal{V}$ such that $\mathcal{V}(\sharp) = t$, and $\mathcal{H} = \emptyset$. The set of interpretations $\{C^{\mathcal{I}}_{\mathcal{V},t,\mathcal{H}}\}$ obtained by varying $\mathcal{I}, \mathcal{V}, t$ with a fixed $\mathcal{H}$ is maximal wrt set inclusion if $\mathcal{H} = \emptyset$, i.e. the set of natural interpretations includes any set of general interpretations with a fixed $\mathcal{H}$. In fact, since $\mathcal{H}$ represents a constraint in the assignment of variables, the unconstrained set is the larger one.

An interpretation $\mathcal{I}$ is a *model* for a concept C if $C^{\mathcal{I}}_t \neq \emptyset$ for every t. If a concept has a model, then it is *satisfiable*, otherwise it is *unsatisfiable*. A concept C is *subsumed* by a concept D (written $C \sqsubseteq D$) if $C^{\mathcal{I}}_t \subseteq D^{\mathcal{I}}_t$ for every interpretation $\mathcal{I}$ and every interval t.

Concept definitions are introduced by terminological

axioms of the form $A \doteq C$. An interpretation $\mathcal{I}$ satisfies $A \doteq C$ iff $A_t^\mathcal{I} = C_t^\mathcal{I}$, for every t. A *terminology* (TBox) is a finite set of terminological axioms, with the restriction that an atomic concept may appear at most once in the left-hand side of an axiom in the terminology, and that the terminology may not contain cycles [Nebel, 1990]. An interpretation $\mathcal{I}$ is a model for a TBox iff it satisfies all terminological axioms in the TBox. An *expanded* TBox, i.e. a terminology where each definition does not make use of the other definitions, is obtained by applying an interpretation-preserving expansion procedure[5], i.e. substituting every defined concept occurring in a definition with its defining term.

Please note that concepts in this language are always satisfiable, with the proviso that the temporal constraints introduced by the existential quantifiers are consistent. This can be easily checked, after the reduction of the concept into a *normal form* (see section 4), by checking each resulting temporal constraint network using some standard algorithm [van Beek and Cohen, 1990]. In the following we will consider satisfiable concepts only.

It is interesting to notice that only the relations s, f, mi are really necessary in the concept language, because it is possible to express any temporal relationship between two distinct intervals using only these three relations and their transposes si, fi, m [Halpern and Shoham, 1991]. In fact, the following equivalences hold:

$\Diamond x \ (x \text{ a } \sharp). \ C@x \equiv \Diamond x \ (x \text{ mi } \sharp). \ (\Diamond y \ (y \text{ mi } \sharp). \ C@y)@x$
$\Diamond x \ (x \text{ d } \sharp). \ C@x \equiv \Diamond x \ (x \text{ s } \sharp). \ (\Diamond y \ (y \text{ f } \sharp). \ C@y)@x$
$\Diamond x \ (x \text{ o } \sharp). \ C@x \equiv \Diamond x \ (x \text{ s } \sharp). \ (\Diamond y \ (y \text{ fi } \sharp). \ C@y)@x$
$\Diamond x \ (x = \sharp). \ C@x \equiv C$

Other interesting equivalences are the following:

$C \equiv \Diamond () \ (). \ C$
$C \equiv C@\sharp$
$C@X \equiv C[\sharp]@X$
$(C[X]@Y)[Z]@W \equiv (C[Z]@W)[X]@Y$
$\top \equiv \Diamond (X) \ \overline{T_<}. \ \top$

2.2 THE ASSERTIONAL LANGUAGE

We consider now *assertions*, i.e. predications on temporally qualified individual entities; usually, they are referred to as *ABox statements*. Let $\mathcal{O}$ be the alphabet of symbols denoting *individuals*; an assertion is a statement of one of the following forms $C(i,a)$, $p(i,a,b)$, $\star p(a,b)$, $R(i,j)$, where C is a concept, p is a feature, $\star p$ is a parametric feature, R is a temporal relation, a and b are in $\mathcal{O}$ and denote individuals, i and j denote intervals in $\mathcal{T}_<^\star$.

In order to assign a meaning to the assertions, the interpretation function $\cdot^\mathcal{I}$ is extended to individuals, so that $a^\mathcal{I} \in \Delta^\mathcal{I}$ for each individual $a \in \mathcal{O}$ and $a^\mathcal{I} \neq b^\mathcal{I}$ if $a \neq b$ (Unique Name Assumption). Moreover, we intend $i^\mathcal{E}$ to be an element of $\mathcal{T}_<^\star$. The semantics of the

---
[5]The expansion procedure can be expensive [Nebel, 1990].

$$\text{Make-Spaghetti} \xrightarrow[(before)]{} \text{Boil}$$

Figure 5: The graphical definition of the `Boil-Spaghetti` plan.

assertions is the following: $C(i,a)$ is satisfied by an interpretation $\mathcal{I}$ iff $a^\mathcal{I} \in C_{i^\mathcal{E}}^\mathcal{I}$; $p(i,a,b)$ is satisfied by $\mathcal{I}$ iff $p_{i^\mathcal{E}}^\mathcal{I}(a^\mathcal{I}) = b^\mathcal{I}$; $\star p(a,b)$ is satisfied by $\mathcal{I}$ iff $\star p^\mathcal{I}(a^\mathcal{I}) = b^\mathcal{I}$; and $R(i,j)$ is satisfied by $\mathcal{I}$ iff $\langle i^\mathcal{E}, j^\mathcal{E} \rangle \in R^\mathcal{E}$.

A set Σ of ABox statements and TBox axioms is called a *knowledge base*. An interpretation $\mathcal{I}$ is a *model* of Σ iff every assertion and every terminological axiom of Σ is satisfied by $\mathcal{I}$. If Σ has a model, then it is *satisfiable*. Σ *logically implies* an assertion α (written $\Sigma \models \alpha$) if α is satisfied by every model of Σ. Given a knowledge base Σ, an individual a in $\mathcal{O}$ is said to be an *instance* of a concept C *at the interval* i if $\Sigma \models C(i,a)$.

3 ACTIONS AND PLANS

We show in this section how the temporal language can be applied for action and plan representation using some common domains, like the *cooking* domain [Weida and Litman, 1992] and the *block world* domain [Allen, 1991]. While actions describe how the world is affected by their occurrence, plans are described as a collection of action types constrained by temporal relations. In this way, a plan can be graphically represented as a temporal constraint network, where nodes denote action types. At this level of representation, plans can be seen as *complex actions*: since actions composing a plan can be expanded, plans and actions are not structurally different. This distinction is further elaborated in [Artale and Franconi, 1994], where each action composing a plan is considered as a step referring to a different individual action, and an appropriate function relates a plan to its steps.

3.1 THE COOKING DOMAIN

The plan `Boil-Spaghetti` introduced in section 2 can be depicted as in figure 5.

`Boil-Spaghetti` $\doteq$
  $\Diamond x \ (x \text{ b } \sharp). \ (\text{Boil} \sqcap \text{Make-Spaghetti}@x)$

The definition employs the $\sharp$ interval to denote the occurrence time of the plan itself; in this way, it is possible to describe how different actions or states of the world concurring to the definition of the plan are related to it. This is why the variable $\sharp$ is explicitly present in the definition of `Boil-Spaghetti`, instead of a generic variable: the `Boil` action should take place at the same time of the plan itself.

The definition of a plan can be reused within the definition of other plans; the plan `Boil-Spaghetti` defined above is used in the definition of `Assemble-Spaghetti-Marinara` (see figure 6):

`Assemble-Spaghetti-Marinara` $\doteq$

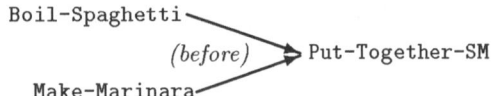

Figure 6: The graphical definition of the Assemble-Spaghetti-Marinara plan.

$\Diamond(y\ z\ w)\ (y\ \text{b}\ w)(z\ \text{b}\ w).\ (\text{Boil-Spaghetti}@y\ \sqcap$
$\text{Make-Marinara}@z\ \sqcap$
$\text{Put-Together-SM}@w)$

In this case, precise temporal relations between the two temporal constraint networks are asserted (figure 7): the action Put-Together-SM takes place after the Boil action. Observe that the occurrence interval of the plan Assemble-Spaghetti-Marinara does not appear in the figure, because it is not temporally related with any other interval.

A plan subsuming Assemble-Spaghetti-Marinara is the plan defined below Prepare-Spaghetti, supposing that the action Make-Sauce subsumes Make-Marinara. This means that among all the individual actions of the type Prepare-Spaghetti there are all the individual actions of type Assemble-Spaghetti-Marinara:

Prepare-Spaghetti $\doteq$
$\Diamond\ (y\ z)\ ().\ (\text{Boil-Spaghetti}@y\ \sqcap\ \text{Make-Sauce}@z)$

Please note that Boil-Spaghetti does subsume neither Prepare-Spaghetti nor Assemble-Spaghetti-Marinara, even if the former is part of the definition of these latter. This could be better explained if we observe how the Prepare-Spaghetti plan is expanded:

Prepare-Spaghetti $\doteq$
$\Diamond\ (x\ y\ z)(x\ \text{b}\ y).\ (\text{Boil}@y\sqcap\text{Make-Spaghetti}@x\ \sqcap$
$\text{Make-Sauce}@z)$

The effect of binding Boil-Spaghetti to the temporal variable y has been that the Boil action occurs at the interval y, which is possibly different from the occurring time of Prepare-Spaghetti; while Boil-Spaghetti and Boil actions take place *necessarily* at the same time. Subsumption between Prepare-Spaghetti and Boil-Spaghetti fails since different temporal relations between the actions composing the two plans and the plans themselves are specified. In particular, we can observe that the plan Boil-Spaghetti denotes a narrower class than the plan

$\Diamond(x\ y)\ (x\ \text{b}\ y).\ (\text{Boil}@y\ \sqcap \text{Make-Spaghetti}@x)$,

which subsumes each of Prepare-Spaghetti, Assemble-Spaghetti-Marinara and Boil-Spaghetti.

3.2 THE BLOCK WORLD DOMAIN

As a further example of the expressive power of the temporal language, we show how to represent the Stack action in the block world, as it is defined in [Allen, 1991]. A stacking action involves two blocks, which should be both clear at the beginning; the central part of the action consists of grasping one block; at the end,

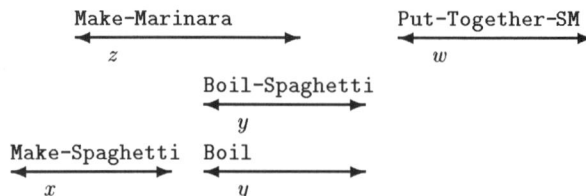

Figure 7: Temporal dependencies in the definition of Assemble-Spaghetti-Marinara.

the blocks are one on top of the other, and the bottom one is no more clear (figure 8).

Our representation borrows from the RAT system [Heinsohn *et al.*, 1992] the intuition of representing action parameters by means of partial functions mapping from the action itself to the involved action parameter. In the language, these functions are called *parametric features*. For example, the action Stack has the parameters ⋆OBJECT1 and ⋆OBJECT2, representing in some sense the objects which are involved in the action independently from time. So, in the assertion "⋆OBJECT1($a, block\text{-}a$)", $block\text{-}a$ denotes the first object involved in the action a at any interval. On the other hand, an assertion involving a (non-parametric) feature, e.g. "ON($i, block\text{-}a, block\text{-}b$)", does not imply anything about the truth value at intervals other than i.

The concept definition makes use of temporal qualified concept expressions, including feature *selections* and *agreements*. The expression (⋆OBJECT2 : Clear-Block)@x means that the second parameter of the action should be a Clear-Block at the interval denoted by x; (⋆OBJECT1∘ON ↓ ⋆OBJECT2)@y indicates that at the interval y the object on which ⋆OBJECT1 is placed is ⋆OBJECT2. The formal definition of the action Stack is:

Stack $\doteq$ $\Diamond(x\ y\ z\ v\ w)$
$(x\ \text{fi}\ \sharp)(y\ \text{mi}\ \sharp)(z\ \text{mi}\ \sharp)(v\ \text{o}\ \sharp)$
$(w\ \text{f}\ \sharp)(w\ \text{mi}\ v).$
$((\text{⋆OBJECT2} : \text{Clear-Block})@x\ \sqcap$
$(\text{⋆OBJECT1}\circ\text{ON} \downarrow \text{⋆OBJECT2})@y\ \sqcap$
$(\text{⋆OBJECT1} : \text{Clear-Block})@v\ \sqcap$
$(\text{⋆OBJECT1} : \text{Hold-Block})@w\ \sqcap$
$(\text{⋆OBJECT1} : \text{Clear-Block})@z)$

The above concept does not state which properties are the prerequisites for the stacking action or which properties must be true whenever the action succeeds. What this action intuitively states is that ⋆OBJECT1 will be on ⋆OBJECT2 in a situation where both objects are clear at the start of the action. Note that the world state described at the intervals denoted by v, w, z is the result of an action of *grasping* a previously clear block:

Grasp $\doteq$ $\Diamond(x\ w\ z)\ (x\ \text{o}\ \sharp)(w\ \text{f}\ \sharp)(w\ \text{mi}\ x)(z\ \text{mi}\ \sharp).$
$((\text{⋆OBJECT1} : \text{Clear-Block})@x\ \sqcap$
$(\text{⋆OBJECT1} : \text{Hold-Block})@w\ \sqcap$
$(\text{⋆OBJECT1} : \text{Clear-Block})@z)$

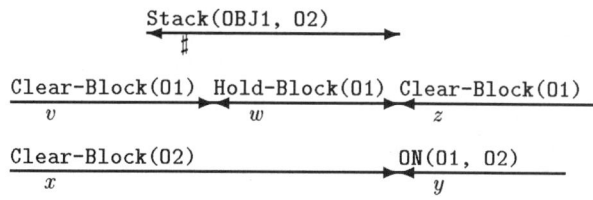

Figure 8: The definition of the Stack action.

We can redefine the Stack action by making use of the Grasp action:

Stack $\doteq$ $\Diamond(x\ y\ u\ v)\ (x\ \text{fi}\ \sharp)(y\ \text{mi}\ \sharp)(u\ \text{f}\ \sharp)(v\ \text{o}\ \sharp).$
$\quad((\star\text{OBJECT2}:\text{Clear-Block})@x \sqcap$
$\quad(\star\text{OBJECT1}\circ\text{ON}\downarrow\star\text{OBJECT2})@y \sqcap$
$\quad(\text{Grasp}[x]@v)@u)$

The temporal substitutive qualifier $(\text{Grasp}[x]@u)$ *renames* within the defined Grasp action the variable x to v and it is a way of making coreference between two temporal variables, while the temporal constraints peculiar to the renamed variable x are inherited by the substituting interval v. The effect of temporally qualifying the grasping action at u is that the $\sharp$ variable associated to the grasping action itself is bound to the interval denoted by u – remember that the variable $\sharp$ used inside an action refers to the occurrence time of the action itself. Because of this binding on the occurrence time of the grasping action, the $\sharp$ variable in the grasping action and the $\sharp$ variable in the stacking action denote different time intervals, so that the grasping action occurs at an interval finishing the occurrence time of the stacking action.

Now we show how from a series of observations in the world we can make action recognition, an inference service which computes if an *individual action* is an instance of an *action type* at a certain interval. Given the following ABox, describing a world where blocks can be clear, grasped and/or on each other and where a generic individual action a is taking place at time interval i_a having the blocks *block-a* and *block-b* as its parameters:

$\star\text{OBJECT1}(a, block\text{-}a),\ \star\text{OBJECT2}(a, block\text{-}b),$
$\text{o}(i_1, i_a),\ \text{Clear-Block}(i_1, block\text{-}a),$
$\text{fi}(i_2, i_a),\ \text{Clear-Block}(i_2, block\text{-}b),$
$\text{mi}(i_3, i_1),\ \text{f}(i_3, i_a),\ \text{Hold-Block}(i_3, block\text{-}a),$
$\text{mi}(i_4, i_a),\ \text{Clear-Block}(i_4, block\text{-}a),$
$\text{mi}(i_5, i_a),\ \text{ON}(i_5, block\text{-}a, block\text{-}b)$

then the system recognizes that in the context of a knowledge base Σ, composed by the above ABox and the definition of the Stack concept in the TBox, the individual action a is an instance of the concept Stack at the time interval i_a, i.e. $\Sigma \models \text{Stack}(i_a, a)$.

4 THE CALCULUS

This section presents a calculus for the temporal concept language. We first look for a *normal form* of con-

- $C@X \sqcap D@X \rightarrow (C \sqcap D)@X$
- $(C@X_1)@X_2 \rightarrow \begin{cases} C@X_1 & \text{if } X_1 \neq \sharp \\ C@X_2 & \text{if } X_1 = \sharp \end{cases}$
- $p:(q:C) \rightarrow (p\circ q):C$
- $\Diamond(\overline{X}_1)\ \overline{Tc}_1.\ (C \sqcap (\Diamond(\overline{X}_2)\ \overline{Tc}_2.\ D)@X) \rightarrow$
  $\Diamond(\overline{X}_1 \uplus \overline{X}_2)\ \overline{Tc}_1 \uplus \overline{Tc}_2[X/\sharp].\ (C \sqcap D_+[X/\sharp])$
- $C \sqcap \Diamond(\overline{X})\ \overline{Tc}.\ D \rightarrow \Diamond(\overline{X})\ \overline{Tc}.\ (C \sqcap D)$
  if C doesn't contain variables

Comment: $\overline{X} \uplus \overline{Y}$ returns the union of the sets $\overline{X}$ and $\overline{Y}$, where all the elements of $\overline{Y}$ occurring in $\overline{X}$ are renamed, except for $\sharp$; Z_+ is intended to be the expression Z where the same renaming has taken place.

Figure 9: Nondeterministic rewrite rules to transform an arbitrary concept into an equivalent existential concept.

cepts, which will be useful for the subsumption and instance recognition algorithms. Since the dimension of the normal form of a concept can be exponential in presence of concept disjunction, a way to compute an effective normal form in the special case of absence of concept disjunction is also devised. Section 4.1 considers the language without concept disjunction; section 4.2 considers the full language.

4.1 NORMAL FORM AND SUBSUMPTION

Let us consider in this section the restricted language without concept disjunction. Every concept of the restricted language in an expanded TBox can be reduced into an equivalent *existential concept* of the form: $\Diamond(\overline{X})\ \overline{Tc}.\ (Q^1@X^1 \sqcap \ldots \sqcap Q^n@X^n)$, where each Q^j is a non-temporal concept, i.e. it does not contain neither temporal quantifiers nor temporal qualifiers – nor concept disjunctions. Figure 9 presents a set of rules for reducing a concept C into the existential form $(ef\ C)$, once concept names and substitutive qualifiers have been expanded in C. A concept in existential form can be seen as a *conceptual temporal constraint network*, i.e. a labeled directed graph $\langle \overline{X}, \overline{Tc}, \overline{Q@X} \rangle$ where arcs are labeled with a set of arbitrary temporal relationships – representing their disjunction – and nodes are labeled with nontemporal concepts.

Proposition 1 (Existential Form) *Every concept can be reduced into an equivalent existential concept by applying the rules of figure 9, i.e. given a concept C, $C^\mathcal{I}_{\mathcal{V},t} = (ef\ C)^\mathcal{I}_{\mathcal{V},t}$ for every interpretation $\mathcal{I}$, every assignment $\mathcal{V}$ and every interval t.*

Given a concept in existential form, the temporal completion of the constraint network is computed:

Definition 1 (Temporal Completion) The temporal completion of a concept in existential form – the Completed Existential Form, CEF – is obtained by sequentially applying the following steps:

- *(Closure)* The transitive closure of the Allen temporal relations in the conceptual temporal constraint network is computed (see e.g. [van Beek and Cohen, 1990]).

- *(parameter introduction)* New information is added to each node because of the presence of parameters, as the following rules show (the $\leadsto$ symbol is intended in such a way that each time the concept expression in the left hand side appears at a top level conjunction in some node of the temporal constraint network then the right hand side represents the concept expression that must be conjunctively added to all the other nodes):

$$\star g_1 \circ \ldots \circ \star g_n \ [\circ \ f \ [\circ \ p]] : C$$
$$\leadsto \star g_1 \circ \ldots \circ \star g_n : \top.$$
$$\star g_1^1 \circ \ldots \circ \star g_n^1 \downarrow \star g_1^2 \circ \ldots \circ \star g_m^2$$
$$\leadsto \star g_1^1 \circ \ldots \circ \star g_n^1 \downarrow \star g_1^2 \circ \ldots \circ \star g_m^2.$$
$$\star g_1^1 \circ \ldots \circ \star g_n^1 \circ f^1 \ [\circ \ p^1] \downarrow \star g_1^2 \circ \ldots \circ \star g_m^2 \circ f^2 \ [\circ \ p^2]$$
$$\leadsto \star g_1^1 \circ \ldots \circ \star g_n^1 : \top \sqcap \star g_1^2 \circ \ldots \circ \star g_m^2 : \top.$$

- *(= introduction)* New temporal constraints with the "=" relation are introduced, if they are not already present, for every variable declared in the constraint network and for the ♯ variable, by applying the following rewrite rule:

$$\Diamond(\overline{X}) \ \overline{T\!c}. \ C \ \rightarrow$$
$$\Diamond(\overline{X}) \ \overline{T\!c} \ (\sharp = \sharp) \ (x = x) \ (y = y) \cdots . \ C$$

- *(= collapsing)* For each equality temporal constraint, collapse the equal nodes by applying the following rewrite rule:

$$\Diamond(\overline{X}) \ \overline{T\!c} \ (x = y). \ C \ \rightarrow \ \Diamond(\overline{X} \setminus \{y\}) \ \overline{T\!c}_{[x/y]}. \ C_{[x/y]}$$
if $x \neq y$ and $y \neq \sharp$ □

Proposition 2 (Equivalence of CEF) *Every concept in existential form can be reduced into an equivalent completed existential concept by applying the above procedure.*

The most relevant properties of a concept in CEF is that all the admissible interval temporal relations are explicit and the concept expression in each node is no more refinable without changing the overall concept meaning; this is stated by the following proposition.

Proposition 3 (Node Independence of CEF) *Let $\langle \overline{X}, \overline{T\!c}, \overline{Q@X} \rangle$ be a conceptual temporal constraint network in its completed form (CEF); for all $Q \in \overline{Q}$ and for all $C \not\sqsupseteq Q$ then $\langle \overline{X}, \overline{T\!c}, \overline{(Q \sqcap C)@X} \rangle^{\mathcal{I}}_{\mathcal{V},t} \neq \langle \overline{X}, \overline{T\!c}, \overline{Q@X} \rangle^{\mathcal{I}}_{\mathcal{V},t}$ for every interpretation $\mathcal{I}$, every assignment $\mathcal{V}$ and every interval t.*

Proof. The proposition states that the information in each node of the CEF is independent from the information in the other nodes. In fact, $\langle \overline{X}, \overline{T\!c}, \overline{(Q \sqcap C)@X} \rangle^{\mathcal{I}}_{\mathcal{V},t} = \langle \overline{X}, \overline{T\!c}, \overline{Q@X} \rangle^{\mathcal{I}}_{\mathcal{V},t}$ if the concept expression in one node implies new information in some other node, since, for nontemporal concepts, adding information means restricting the concept in some way.

We examine the only two cases in which the information stated in a node adds new information in some other node, and we show that these cases are covered by the completion rules.

i. *Nodes related only by means of the equal relations.* The *(= collapsing)* rule provides to collapse two contemporary nodes conjoining the concept expressions of each of them. Note that, thanks to the *(Closure)* rule, all the possible equal temporal relations are made explicit.

ii. *Time-invariant information.* Every time-invariant information should spread over all the nodes. Only parametric features and the $\top$ concept have a time-invariant semantics: by induction, we prove that the only time-invariant concepts are $\top$, $\star g_1 \circ \ldots \circ \star g_n : \top$, $\star g_1 \circ \ldots \circ \star g_n \downarrow \star p_1 \circ \ldots \circ \star p_m$ (with $n, m \geq 1$) or an arbitrary conjunction of these terms. The *(parameter introduction)* rule considers all the possible syntactical cases of deduction concerning time-invariant concept expressions. □

As an example, we show the completed existential form of the previously introduced Stack action:

```
Stack ≐
  ◇(x y v w z)
    (x fi ♯)(y mi ♯)(v mi ♯)(w f ♯)(z o ♯)(y mi x)
    (v mi x)(w f x)(z (o,d,s) x)(v (=,s,si) y)
    (w m y)(z b y)(w m v)(z b v)(w mi z)
    (♯ = ♯)(x = x)(y = y)(v = v)(w = w)(z = z).
    ((*OBJECT2 : Clear-Block ⊓ *OBJECT1 : ⊤)@x ⊓
     (*OBJECT1 : Clear-Block ⊓ *OBJECT2 : ⊤)@y ⊓
     (*OBJECT1∘ON ↓ *OBJECT2)@v ⊓
     (*OBJECT1 : Hold-Block ⊓ *OBJECT2 : ⊤)@w ⊓
     (*OBJECT1 : Clear-Block ⊓ *OBJECT2 : ⊤)@z)
```

As we have seen in section 2.1, a concept subsumes another just in case every possible instance of the second is also an instance of the first, for every time interval. Concept subsumption in the temporal language is reduced to concept subsumption between nontemporal concepts and to subsumption between temporal constraint networks. A similar general procedure was first presented in [Weida and Litman, 1992], where the language for nontemporal concepts is less expressive – it does not include features nor parametric features. Algorithms to compute subsumption between nontemporal concepts – $E_1 \sqsubseteq E_2$ – are well known, see e.g. [Hollunder et al., 1990].

Definition 2 (Variable mapping) A *variable mapping* $\mathcal{M}$ is a total function $\mathcal{M} : \overline{X} \mapsto \overline{X}$ such that $\mathcal{M}(\sharp) = \sharp$. We write $\mathcal{M}(\overline{X})$ to intend $\{\mathcal{M}(X) \mid X \in \overline{X}\}$, and $\mathcal{M}(\overline{T\!c})$ to intend $\{(\mathcal{M}(X) \ (R) \ \mathcal{M}(Y)) \mid (X \ (R) \ Y) \in \overline{T\!c}\}$. □

Definition 3 (Temporal Constraint subsumption) A temporal constraint $(X_1(R_1)Y_1)$ is said to *subsume* a temporal constraint $(X_2(R_2)Y_2)$ under a generic variable mapping $\mathcal{M}$ – written $(X_1(R_1)Y_1) \sqsupseteq_{\mathcal{M}} (X_2 \ (R_2) \ Y_2)$ – if $\mathcal{M}(X_1) = X_2$, $\mathcal{M}(Y_1) = Y_2$ and $(R_1)^{\mathcal{E}} \supseteq (R_2)^{\mathcal{E}}$ for every temporal interpretation $\mathcal{E}$. □

Proposition 4 $(X_1(R_1)Y_1) \sqsupseteq_{\mathcal{M}} (X_2(R_2)Y_2)$ *if and only if* $\mathcal{M}(X_1) = X_2$, $\mathcal{M}(Y_1) = Y_2$ *and the disjuncts in R_1 are a superset of the disjuncts in R_2.*

Proof. Follows from the observation that the 13 temporal relations are mutually disjoint and their union covers the whole interval pairs space. □

Definition 4 (Temporal Constraint Network subsumption) A temporal constraint network $\langle \overline{X}_1, \overline{Tc}_1 \rangle$ subsumes a temporal constraint network $\langle \overline{X}_2, \overline{Tc}_2 \rangle$ under a variable mapping $\mathcal{M} : \overline{X}_1 \mapsto \overline{X}_2$, written $\langle \overline{X}_1, \overline{Tc}_1 \rangle \sqsupseteq_{\mathcal{M}} \langle \overline{X}_2, \overline{Tc}_2 \rangle$, if $\langle \mathcal{M}(\overline{X}_1), \mathcal{M}(\overline{Tc}_1) \rangle^{\mathcal{E}} \supseteq \langle \overline{X}_2, \overline{Tc}_2 \rangle^{\mathcal{E}}$ for every temporal interpretation $\mathcal{E}$. □

Proposition 5 $\langle \overline{X}_1, \overline{Tc}_1 \rangle \sqsupseteq_{\mathcal{M}} \langle \overline{X}_2, \overline{Tc}_2 \rangle$ *iff there exist a variable mapping* $\mathcal{M} : \overline{X}_1 \mapsto \overline{X}_2$ *such that for all* $X_1^i, Y_1^j \in \overline{X}_1$ *exist* $X_2^m, Y_2^n \in \overline{X}_2$ *which satisfy* $(X_1^i (R_1^{i,j}) Y_1^j) \sqsupseteq_{\mathcal{M}} (X_2^m (R_2^{m,n}) Y_2^n)$.

Proof. "$\Leftarrow$" From the definition of interpretation of a temporal constraint network, it is easy to see that each assignment of variables $\mathcal{V}$ in the interpretation of $\langle \overline{X}_1, \overline{Tc}_1 \rangle$ is also an assignment in the interpretation of $\langle \mathcal{M}(\overline{X}_2), \mathcal{M}(\overline{Tc}_2) \rangle$, since for all i,j $(R_1^{i,j})^{\mathcal{E}} \supseteq (R_2^{m,n})^{\mathcal{E}}$.
"$\Rightarrow$" Suppose that we are not able to find such a mapping; then, by hypotheses, for each possible variable mapping there exist some i,j such that $(R_1^{i,j})^{\mathcal{E}} \not\supseteq (R_2^{m,n})^{\mathcal{E}}$. So, for each variable mapping we can build an interpretation $\mathcal{E}^*$ and an assignment $\mathcal{V}^*$ such that $\mathcal{V}^* \in \langle \overline{X}_2, \overline{Tc}_2 \rangle^{\mathcal{E}^*}$ and $\mathcal{V}^* \notin \langle \mathcal{M}(\overline{X}_1), \mathcal{M}(\overline{Tc}_1) \rangle^{\mathcal{E}^*}$. But this contradicts the assumption that $\langle \overline{X}_1, \overline{Tc}_1 \rangle \sqsupseteq_{\mathcal{M}} \langle \overline{X}_2, \overline{Tc}_2 \rangle$. □

Definition 5 (S-mapping) A *s-mapping* from a conceptual temporal constraint network $\langle \overline{X}_1, \overline{Tc}_1, \overline{Q@X}_1 \rangle$ to a conceptual temporal constraint network $\langle \overline{X}_2, \overline{Tc}_2, \overline{Q@X}_2 \rangle$ is a variable mapping $\mathcal{S} : \overline{X}_1 \mapsto \overline{X}_2$ such that the nontemporal concept labeling each node in $\overline{X}_1$ subsumes the nontemporal concept labeling the corresponding node in $\mathcal{S}(\overline{X}_1)$, and $\langle \overline{X}_1, \overline{Tc}_1 \rangle \sqsupseteq_{\mathcal{S}} \langle \overline{X}_2, \overline{Tc}_2 \rangle$. □

The last normalization procedure reduces the graph by eliminating nodes with redundant information. This final normalization step ends up with the concept in the *essential graph form*, that will be the normal form used for checking concept subsumption.

Definition 6 (Essential graph) The subgraph of the CEF of a conceptual temporal constraint network $T = \langle \overline{X}, \overline{Tc}, \overline{Q@X} \rangle$ obtained by deleting the nodes labeled only with time-invariant concept expressions – with the exception of the $\sharp$ node – is called *essential graph* of T: (ess T). □

Proposition 6 (Essential Graph Reduction) *Every conceptual temporal constraint network in completed existential form can be reduced into an equivalent essential graph, i.e. given a conceptual temporal constraint network T, $T_{\mathcal{V},t}^{\mathcal{I}} = (\text{ess } T)_{\mathcal{V},t}^{\mathcal{I}}$ for every interpretation $\mathcal{I}$, every assignment $\mathcal{V}$ and every interval t.*

Definition 7 (Redundant Node) A node K in a conceptual temporal constraint network $\langle \overline{X}, \overline{Tc}, \overline{Q@X} \rangle$ is *redundant* if the network resulting by deleting it is equivalent to the original one: $\langle \overline{X} \setminus K, \overline{Tc}|_{\overline{X} \setminus K}, \overline{Q@X}|_{\overline{X} \setminus K} \rangle_{\mathcal{V},t}^{\mathcal{I}} = \langle \overline{X}, \overline{Tc}, \overline{Q@X} \rangle_{\mathcal{V},t}^{\mathcal{I}}$ for every interpretation $\mathcal{I}$, every assignment $\mathcal{V}$ and every interval t. □

Definition 8 (Mapping-Redundant Set) A set $\overline{K}$ of nodes in a conceptual temporal constraint network $\langle \overline{X}, \overline{Tc}, \overline{Q@X} \rangle$ is a mapping-redundant set if there exists a s-mapping $\mathcal{S}$ from $\langle \overline{K}, \overline{Tc}|_{\overline{K}}, \overline{Q@X}|_{\overline{K}} \rangle_{\mathcal{V},t}^{\mathcal{I}}$ to $\langle \overline{X} \setminus \overline{K}, \overline{Tc}|_{\overline{X} \setminus \overline{K}}, \overline{Q@X}|_{\overline{X} \setminus \overline{K}} \rangle_{\mathcal{V},t}^{\mathcal{I}}$, such that $\forall K_i \in \overline{K}$. $\mathcal{S}(K_i) = X_j \rightarrow \exists Tc \in \overline{Tc}$. $Tc \sqsupseteq_{\text{id}} (K_i = X_j)$.

Proposition 7 *A node in an essential graph is redundant if and only if it is in the maximal – wrt set inclusion – mapping-redundant set of the graph. Moreover, the only other way to add redundant nodes to an essential graph is to add time-invariant nodes.*

The following theorem states that subsumption is decidable and provides a sound and complete procedure to compute it: first reduce the subsumer and the subsumee in essential graph form, then look for a s-mapping between the essential graphs by exhaustive search.

Theorem 1 (Concept subsumption) *A conceptual temporal constraint network $T_1 = \langle \overline{X}_1, \overline{Tc}_1, \overline{Q@X}_1 \rangle$ subsumes a conceptual temporal constraint network $T_2 = \langle \overline{X}_2, \overline{Tc}_2, \overline{Q@X}_2 \rangle$ – $T_1 \sqsupseteq T_2$ – iff there exists a s-mapping from the essential graph of T_1 to the essential graph of T_2.*

Proof. "$\Leftarrow$" Follows from the soundness of TCN subsumption, from the soundness of the algorithm for computing the subsumption between nontemporal concepts and from the semantics of the conceptual temporal constraint networks.

"$\Rightarrow$" Suppose that such a s-mapping does not exist. We can distinguish two main cases.

i) There is not a mapping $\mathcal{M}$ such that $\langle \overline{X}_1, \overline{Tc}_1 \rangle \sqsupseteq_{\mathcal{M}} \langle \overline{X}_2, \overline{Tc}_2 \rangle$. By adding redundant nodes to T_2, we obtain an equivalent conceptual temporal constraint network $T_2^* = \langle \overline{X}_2^*, \overline{Tc}_2^*, \overline{Q@X}_2^* \rangle$. Let us consider the extended network in a way that there exists a variable mapping $\mathcal{M}^*$ such that $\langle \overline{X}_1, \overline{Tc}_1 \rangle \sqsupseteq_{\mathcal{M}^*} \langle \overline{X}_2^*, \overline{Tc}_2^* \rangle$. Now, for all possible $\mathcal{M}^*$, there is a node $X_1^i \in \overline{X}_1$ such that $\mathcal{M}^*(X_1^i) = X_2^j$ with $X_2^j \notin \overline{X}_2$ and $Q_1^i \not\sqsupseteq Q_2^j$, since either Q_1^i is not in a time-invariant node – whereas Q_2^j

- $(C \sqcup D)@X \rightarrow C@X \sqcup D@X$
- $p:(C \sqcup D) \rightarrow p:C \sqcup p:D$
- $(C_1 \sqcup C_2) \sqcap D \rightarrow (C_1 \sqcap D) \sqcup (C_2 \sqcap D)$
- $\Diamond(\overline{X}) \, \overline{Tc}. \, (C \sqcup D) \rightarrow \Diamond(\overline{X}) \, \overline{Tc}. \, C \sqcup \Diamond(\overline{X}) \, \overline{Tc}. \, D$

Figure 10: Nondeterministic rewrite rules for computing the disjunctive form.

is in a time-invariant node – or Q_2^j is in the maximal mapping-redundant set of T_2^* – contradicting the hypothesis that the mapping $\mathcal{M}$ does not exist. Since the construction of $\mathcal{M}^*$ allows for the existence of a unique $\mathcal{V}^6$ for both networks, then we can build an instance of T_2^* which is not an instance of T_1.

ii) For each possible mapping $\mathcal{M}$ such that $\langle \overline{X}_1, \overline{Tc}_1 \rangle \sqsupseteq_\mathcal{M} \langle \overline{X}_2, \overline{Tc}_2 \rangle$ there will be always two nodes X_1^i and X_2^j such that $\mathcal{M}(X_1^i) = X_2^j$ and $Q_1^i \not\sqsupseteq Q_2^j$. Since, from proposition 3, the concept expression in each node is independent from any concept expression of the other nodes, we cannot refine the concept expression Q_2^j, looking for a subsumption relationships with Q_1^i. Besides, Q_1^i can not be eliminated – i.e. generalized to $\top$ – from T_1, since the conditions of proposition 7 hold. So, we can build an instance of T_2 which is not an instance of T_1.

Both cases contradict the assumption that T_1 subsumes T_2. □

4.2 DISJUNCTIVE CONCEPTS

In this section we introduce the disjunction operator and we show how to modify the calculus in order to check subsumption. In the way of computing subsumption, we need a normal form for concepts. The normalization procedure is essentially the same as the one reported in section 4.1. The figure 10 shows the rules dealing explicitly with disjunction. Those, in addition to the rules introduced in figure 9, reduce every concept into an equivalent *disjunctive concept* of the form:

$(\Diamond(\overline{X}_1) \, \overline{Tc}_1. \, G_1) \sqcup \cdots \sqcup (\Diamond(\overline{X}_n) \, \overline{Tc}_n. \, G_n) \sqcup$
$H_1 \sqcup \cdots \sqcup H_m$

where G_i are conjunctions of concepts of the form $H^j@X^k$, and each H does not contain neither temporal quantifiers, nor temporal qualifiers, nor disjunctions.

Given a concept in *disjunctive form*, applying the *temporal completion* rules showed in section 4.1 to each disjunct, we end up with an equivalent concept in *completed disjunctive form* where the *node independence* property is preserved. Then the *essential graph form* is computed, obtaining a concept where each disjunct does not contain time-invariant nodes. At this point, we are able to compute the *disjunctive normal form*

---

[6] Since subsumption is computed with respect to a fixed evaluation time, $\mathcal{V}$ maps the different occurrences of $\sharp$ to the same interval; this justifies the choice that $\mathcal{M}(\sharp) = \sharp$.

(dnf C).

Definition 9 (Disjunctive Normal Form) The *disjunctive normal form* of a concept is computed starting from its *essential graph form* and applying the following nondeterministic rewrite rules to each disjunct:

- (⊔ *introduction*) Transform the conceptual temporal constraint network into an equivalent disjunction of conceptual temporal constraint networks containing only basic temporal relationships:

$\Diamond(\overline{X}) \, (X_1 \, (R,S) \, X_2) \overline{Tc}.C \rightarrow \Diamond(\overline{X})(X_1 \, R \, X_2)\overline{Tc}.C \sqcup$
$\Diamond(\overline{X})(X_1 \, S \, X_2)\overline{Tc}.C$

- (⊔ *elimination*) If the disjunct is unsatisfiable – i.e. the temporal constraint network associated with it is inconsistent – then eliminate it. □

Proposition 8 (Equivalence of DNF) *Every disjunctive essential graph can be reduced into an equivalent disjunctive normal concept by applying the above procedure.*

A concept in *disjunctive normal form* can be seen as the disjunction of several *basic conceptual temporal constraint networks*, where arcs are labeled with basic temporal relationships and nodes are labeled with non-temporal non-disjunctive concepts:

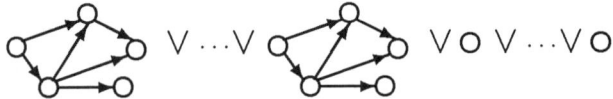

Each basic conceptual temporal constraint network – i.e. a disjunct of the normal form – has some interesting properties, which are crucial for the proofs of the theorem: temporal constraints are always explicit, i.e. any two intervals are related by a basic temporal relation; there is no disjunction, neither implicit nor explicit, neither in the conceptual part nor in the temporal part; the information in each node is independent from the information in the other nodes. The following theorem reduces subsumption between concepts in disjunctive normal form into subsumption of disjunction-free concepts, such that the results of theorem 1 can be applied.

Theorem 2 (Concept subsumption) *Let $C = C_1 \sqcup \cdots \sqcup C_m$ and $D = D_1 \sqcup \cdots \sqcup D_n$ be concepts in disjunctive normal form; then $C \sqsubseteq D$ if and only if $\forall i \exists j. \, C_i \sqsubseteq D_j$.*

Proof. [7] Since it is easy to show that

$C_1 \sqcup \ldots \sqcup C_n \sqsubseteq D$ iff $\forall i. C_i \sqsubseteq D$

we need only to prove the restricted thesis

$C_i \sqsubseteq D_1 \sqcup \cdots \sqcup D_n$ iff $C_i \sqsubseteq D_1 \vee \ldots \vee C_i \sqsubseteq D_n$

---

[7] The proof of this theorem comes from an idea of Werner Nutt.

Every conceptual expression C_i corresponds to an existential quantified formula with one free variable. Moreover, the matrices of such formulas are conjunctions of positive predicates. Let us denote the formula corresponding to a concept C_i as $C_i'(x)$. The functionality of feature concept expressions can be expressed with a set F of definite Horn clauses. The restricted thesis holds – in the binary case – if and only if $F \cup \{C_i''(a)\} \models D_1'(a) \vee D_2'(a)$, where a is a constant substituting the free variable x and $C_i''(a)$ is obtained by skolemizing the existential quantified variables. $F \cup \{C_i''(a)\}$ is equivalent to a set of definite Horn clauses, which are characterized by a *minimal Herbrand model*, say $\mathcal{H_B}$. Then:

$$F \cup \{C_i''(a)\} \models D_1'(a) \vee D_2'(a) \quad \text{iff}$$
$$\mathcal{H_B} \models D_1'(a) \vee D_2'(a)$$

Since we are talking of a single model, $D_1'(a) \vee D_2'(a)$ is valid in $\mathcal{H_B}$ if and only if either $D_1'(a)$ or $D_2'(a)$ is valid in $\mathcal{H_B}$. □

4.3 INSTANCE RECOGNITION

Given a knowledge base Σ, an interval i, an individual a and a concept C, the *instance recognition problem* is to test whether $\Sigma \models C(i, a)$, i.e. the inference task checking if the individual is an instance of the concept at the given time. We will only sketch here the procedure for the instance recognition problem. The algorithm first computes the *most specialized concept expression* – $\texttt{MSC}_i^a$ – for the individual a at the reference interval i. The $\texttt{MSC}_i^a$ is a concept such that it instantiates the individual at the interval i, i.e. $\Sigma \models \texttt{MSC}_i^a(i, a)$, and it is the *most* specific one, i.e. for every concept expression D of the language satisfying $\Sigma \models D(i, a)$ then $\texttt{MSC}_i^a \sqsubseteq D$. The procedure computing the $\texttt{MSC}_i^a$ is a variant of the well known abstraction procedure of concept languages – see e.g. [Nebel, 1990; Lenzerini and Schaerf, 1991; Donini and Era, 1992]. Even if we conjecture the completeness of the procedure computing the $\texttt{MSC}_i^a$, no formal proof is available.

Given the most specialized concept of every individual, the instance recognition problem can be reduced to a subsumption test: $\Sigma \models C(i, a)$ if and only if $\texttt{MSC}_i^a \sqsubseteq C$.

For example, the most specialized concept for the individual action a at the reference interval i_a with respect to the ABox defined in section 3 is the following:

$$\texttt{MSC}_{i_a}^a \doteq \Diamond(x_1\ x_2\ x_3\ x_4\ x_5)$$
$$(x_1 \circ \sharp)(x_2 \text{ fi } \sharp)(x_3 \text{mi } x_1)$$
$$(x_3 \text{ f } \sharp)(x_4 \text{ mi } \sharp)(x_5 \text{ mi } \sharp).$$
$$((\texttt{*OBJECT1}:\texttt{Clear-Block})@x_1 \sqcap$$
$$(\texttt{*OBJECT1}:\texttt{Hold-Block})@x_3 \sqcap$$
$$(\texttt{*OBJECT1}:\texttt{Clear-Block})@x_4 \sqcap$$
$$(\texttt{*OBJECT2}:\texttt{Clear-Block})@x_2 \sqcap$$
$$(\texttt{*OBJECT1} \circ \texttt{ON} \downarrow \texttt{*OBJECT2})@x_5)$$

Since $\texttt{MSC}_{i_a}^a \sqsubseteq \texttt{Stack}$, the individual action a is an instance of the concept $\texttt{Stack}$ at the time interval i_a.

5 CONCLUSIONS

We have shown in this paper a formalism for representing time, actions and plans in a uniform way. The proposed temporal concept language allows for the representation of actions in the style of Allen: an action can have parameters, which are the ties with the temporal evolution of the world, and an action is associated over time with other actions. An action taxonomy based on subsumption can be set up, and it can play the role of a plan library for plan retrieval tasks. From the observation of the evolution of the world state, the type of the involved actions can be understood, for plan recognition purposes.

Currently, the language is able to express a plan as an action having possibly different properties through time – i.e. as a *complex activity*. In [Artale and Franconi, 1994] a decomposition operator is introduced to distinguish the different actions composing a plan. A plan can be viewed as a hierarchical structure whose constituent actions could be seen as its distinct decomposing steps. Further research work within this approach includes the treatment of temporally *homogeneous*, *concatenable* and *countable* concepts[8]. Homogeneity is useful to characterize the temporal behavior of world states [Artale et al., 1994]. The language can be successfully extended in order to cope with problems characterized by *inertial* – or *persistent* – properties. In this larger framework, states can be represented as simple non-temporal homogeneous and persistent concepts [Artale and Franconi, 1994].

Acknowledgments

This paper is a revised and extended version of a working paper presented at two IJCAI-93 workshops [Artale and Franconi, 1993]. This work has been partially supported by the Italian National Research Council (CNR), projects "Sistemi Informatici", "Pianificazione Automatica" and "Robotica". This research was partly done while the first author was visiting IRST from University of Florence, Italy. We would like to thank Claudio Bettini, Paolo Bresciani, Alfonso Gerevini, Werner Nutt, Andrea Schaerf, Luciano Serafini, Achille C. Varzi and two anonymous referees. All the errors of the paper are, of course, our own.

References

[Allen, 1991] James F. Allen. Temporal reasoning and planning. In James F. Allen, Henry A. Kautz, Richard N. Pelavin, and Josh D. Tenenberg, editors, *Reasoning about Plans*, chapter 1, pages 2–68. Morgan Kaufmann, 1991.

---

[8] A concept is *homogeneous* if its instances at some interval are also instances at the subintervals; a concept is *concatenable* if its instances at two meeting intervals are also instances at the union interval; a concept is *countable* if its instances at some interval are not instances at the overlapping intervals.

[Artale and Franconi, 1993] Alessandro Artale and Enrico Franconi. A unified framework for representing time, actions and plans. In F. D. Anger, H. W. Guesgen, and J. van Benthem, editors, *Workshop Notes of the IJCAI Workshop on Temporal and Spatial Reasoning*, pages 193–217, Chambery, France, August 1993. Also in the Workshop Notes of the IJCAI-93 Workshop on Object-Based Representation System; a shorter version appears in the Workshop Notes of the Italian 1993 Workshop on Automatic Planning, Roma Italy, September 1993.

[Artale and Franconi, 1994] Alessandro Artale and Enrico Franconi. Time, actions and plans representation in a description logic. *International Journal of Intelligent Systems*, 1994. To appear.

[Artale et al., 1994] Alessandro Artale, Claudio Bettini, and Enrico Franconi. Homogeneous concepts in a temporal description logic. Forthcoming, 1994.

[Artale, 1994] Alessandro Artale. *Rappresentazione di Tempo ed Azioni e Ragionamento Tassonomico per Object-Oriented Databases nel Contesto dei Linguaggi Terminologici*. PhD thesis, University of Florence, Italy, February 1994. (in italian).

[Bettini, 1992] Claudio Bettini. A formalization of interval-based temporal subsumption in first order logic. In *Workshop Notes of the ECAI Workshop on Theoretical Foundations of Knowledge Representation and Reasoning*, Vienna, Austria, August 1992.

[Bettini, 1993] Claudio Bettini. *Temporal Extensions of Terminological Languages*. PhD thesis, Computer Science Department, University of Milan, Italy, 1993.

[Devanbu and Litman, 1991] Premkumar T. Devanbu and Diane J. Litman. Plan-based terminological reasoning. In *Proc. of the 2nd International Conference on Principles of Knowledge Representation and Reasoning*, pages 128–138, Cambridge, MA, May 1991.

[Donini and Era, 1992] Francesco M. Donini and Angelo Era. Most specific concepts for knowledge bases with incomplete information. In *Proc. of CIKM-92*, pages 545–551, 1992.

[Halpern and Shoham, 1991] J. Y. Halpern and Y. Shoham. A propositional modal logic of time intervals. *Journal of ACM*, 38(4):935–962, 1991.

[Heinsohn et al., 1992] Jochen Heinsohn, Daniel Kudenko, Bernhard Nebel, and Hans-Jürgen Profitlich. RAT: representation of actions using terminological logics. Technical report, DFKI, Saarbrücken, Germany, November 1992.

[Hollunder et al., 1990] B. Hollunder, W. Nutt, and M. Schmidt-Schauß. Subsumption algorithms for concept description languages. In *Proc. of the 9th ECAI*, pages 348–353, Stockholm, Sweden, 1990.

[Kautz, 1991] Henry A. Kautz. A formal theory of plan recognition and its implementation. In James F. Allen, Henry A. Kautz, Richard N. Pelavin, and Josh D. Tenenberg, editors, *Reasoning about Plans*, chapter 2, pages 69–126. Morgan Kaufmann, 1991.

[Lambrix and Rönnquist, 1993] Patrick Lambrix and Ralph Rönnquist. Terminological logic involving time and evolution: A preliminary report. In *Proceedings of ISMIS-93*, 1993.

[Lenzerini and Schaerf, 1991] M. Lenzerini and A. Schaerf. Concept languages as query languages. In *Proc. of AAAI-91*, pages 471–476, Anaheim, CA, 1991.

[Lifschitz, 1987] Vladimir Lifschitz. On the semantics of STRIPS. In *The 1986 Workshop on Reasoning about Actions and Plans*, pages 1–10. Morgan Kaufman, 1987.

[McCarthy and Hayes, 1969] J. McCarthy and P. J. Hayes. Some philosophical problems from the standpoint of Artificial Intelligence. In B. Meltzer and D. Michie, editors, *Machine Intelligence*, volume 4, pages 463–502, Edinburgh, UK, 1969. Edinburgh University Press.

[Nebel, 1990] B. Nebel. *Reasoning and Revision in Hybrid Representation Systems*, volume 422 of *Lecture Notes in Artificial Intelligence*. Springer-Verlag, Berlin, Heidelberg, New York, 1990.

[Schild, 1993] Klaus D. Schild. Combining terminological logics with tense logic. In *Proceedings of the 6th Portuguese Conference on Artificial Intelligence, EPIA'93*, October 1993.

[Schmiedel, 1990] A. Schmiedel. A temporal terminological logic. In *Proc. of AAAI-90*, pages 640–645, Boston, MA, 1990.

[Song and Cohen, 1991] Fei Song and Robin Cohen. Temporal reasoning during plan recognition. In *Proc. of AAAI-91*, pages 247–252, Anaheim, CA, 1991.

[van Beek and Cohen, 1990] P. van Beek and R. Cohen. Exact and approximate reasoning about temporal relations. *Computational Intelligence*, 6:132–144, 1990.

[Venema, 1990] Yde Venema. Expressiveness and completeness of an interval tense logic. *Notre Dame Journal of Formal Logic*, 31(4):529–547, Fall 1990.

[Weida and Litman, 1992] Robert Weida and Diane Litman. Terminological reasoning with constraint networks and an application to plan recognition. In *Proc. of the 3rd International Conference on Principles of Knowledge Representation and Reasoning*, pages 282–293, Cambridge, MA, October 1992.

[Weida and Litman, 1994] Robert Weida and Diane Litman. Subsumption and recognition of heterogeneous constraint networks. In *Proceedings of CAIA-94*, 1994.

Proofs in context

Giuseppe Attardi
Dipartimento di Informatica
Università di Pisa
Corso Italia, 40
I-56125 Pisa, Italy
attardi@di.unipi.it

Maria Simi
Dipartimento di Informatica
Università di Pisa
simi@di.unipi.it

Abstract

An analysis of some formal proofs appeared in recent literature dealing with multiple theories, reveals that they are not always accurate: some steps are not properly accounted for, lifting is use improperly, extra logical constructions or unnecessary assumptions are made. Many such problems appears due to the involved mechanisms of reflection. We show that proof in context can replace the most common uses of reflection principles. Proofs can be carried out by switching to a context and reasoning within it. Context switching however does not correspond to reflection or reification but involves changing the level of nesting of theory within another theory. We introduce a generalised rule for proof in context and a convenient notation to express nesting of contexts, which allows us to carry out reasoning in and across contexts in a safe and natural way.

1 INTRODUCTION

A general notion of relativised truth can be useful for reasoning in and about different theories in a formal setting. For example to reason about the reasoning of different agents, to model temporal evolution of knowledge, to split a large knowledge base into manageable chunks or microtheories that can be related to each other by means of lifting axioms.

There are several approaches to the formalization of a notion of relativised truth: by means of a predicate expressing "provability" like for example $PR(T, P)$ in (Weyhrauch 80) and $demo(T, P)$ in (Bowen-Kowalski 82), or with a notion of truth in context like for example $ist(c, p)$ in (Guha 91, McCarthy 87, McCarthy 93, Buvač-Mason 93) and p^c in (Shoham 91), or with a notion of entailment from a set of assumptions like $in(P, vp)$ (Attardi-Simi 84, Simi 91, Attardi-Simi 93).

Most of these are syntactic approaches where theories can be modeled as collections of *reified sentences* or *sentence names* in First Order Predicate Calculus. The object theory is extended with a meta-theory consisting of sentences about sentences. The relation between general validity and truth relativised to a subtheory is usually expressed by means of a pair of reflection/reification rules. For example, (Kowalski-Kim 91) use the following rules:

$$\frac{T \vdash P}{pr \vdash \mathsf{demo}(T, P)} \qquad (Reification1)$$

$$\frac{pr \vdash \mathsf{demo}(T, P)}{T \vdash P} \qquad (Reflection1)$$

which say that if formula P is derivable from the set of sentences T, then $\mathsf{demo}(T, P)$ is derivable in the meta-theory from theory pr and vice versa, where pr is a theory containing a suitable axiomatisation of the demo predicate.

Unfortunately carrying out proofs dealing with multiple theories is not simple. When reasoning about reasoning, one often needs to carry out some proof steps within a different theory from the current one and then to lift the conclusions back into the original theory. The deductive rules required to carry out these steps involve either *reflection* principles or some other notion of *proof in context*. Reflection principles have to be carefully restricted in order to avoid paradoxes. Such restrictions however limit significantly their usefulness and also defeat intuition while building proofs in context. Standard formulations of the reflection rules also assume explicit knowledge of the theory one reasons about. This is not always the case for theories representing agents or for theories which refer to each other, as those required for expressing common knowledge.

To illustrate some of the subtle issues involved when performing proofs composed of subproofs in different contexts, we examine two examples taken from the recent literature.

The first one is a solution to the three wise men puzzle by Kowalski and Kim presented in (Kowalski-Kim 91) where a rule of *reification* is used to lift a conclusion from the object level to metalevel theory.

The second example was used by John McCarthy (McCarthy 93) to illustrate the power of "lifting axioms", which allow extrapolating facts from one theory to another and transforming them at the same time into a different format. Even though no formal proof theory was provided, the example was meant to suggest the kind of proofs one would like to be able to perform. In this case, things are complicated by the fact that the proof is carried out in a natural deduction setting, so there are pending assumption when switching from one context to another.

The three approaches examined in the paper use three slightly different notations for relativized truth, whose correspondence is shown below:

demo(T, P) Kowalski
ist(T, P) McCarthy
in(P, T) Attardi and Simi

After critically examining the examples, we will discuss the formulation and use of the reflection rules and argue that the meaning of context switching in a natural deduction proof is just nesting or unnesting of contexts. A notation is introduced to write more readable proofs with context switching according to this semantics.

2 DIFFICULTIES WITH PROOFS IN CONTEXT

2.1 INCOMPLETE THEORIES

All standard formulations of the reflection rules require the theory from which one reflects to be completely specified and expressed by means of a term in the meta-language. For instance the conclusion $T \vdash P$ from *Reflection1* would not be meaningful unless T was known.

While there are many useful finite theories that one can handle with such rules, most interesting theories turn out to be infinite or only partially specified. For example theories involving axiom schemata or theories which involve other theories in a mutually recursive fashion. A particular case of the latter are theories used to express common knowledge among several agents, where not only certain facts are known to everybody, but also everybody is aware that everybody knows them, and so on.

In order to deal with incomplete theories one must introduce names for theories and express what is known about them by means of assertions.

For instance one could assert:

demo(T, P)

demo(T, Q)

However, if one wanted to conclude, given $P, Q \vdash R$, that

demo(T, R)

reflection would not be applicable, since theory T in not known. As we will see later, there could be other means to achieve this conclusion.

When mutually recursive theories are allowed in our language, one must account for them in the semantics of the logic. One way to do so is to use non well founded sets (Aczel 88) as denotation for theories and rely on Barwise solution lemma to ensure that solutions to the recursive equations exist.

A different approach is the one pursued in the theory of viewpoints (Attardi-Simi 93), where viewpoints denote recursive set of sentences and the interpretation of in sentences is done in a layer by layer fashion so as to properly account for paradoxical self referential sentences.

Mutually recursive theories appear for instance in the formulation of the three wise men puzzle.

2.1.1 The three wise men puzzle

The statement of this well known puzzle is the following (Kowalski-Kim 91).

> *A king, wishing to determine which of his three wise men is the wisest, puts a white spot on each of their foreheads, and tells them that at least one of the spots is white. The king arranges the wise men in a circle so that they can see and hear each other (but cannot see their own spots) and asks each wise man in turn what is the colour of his spot. The first two say that they don't know, and the third says that his spot is white.*

We analyse the solution this puzzle presented in (Kowalski-Kim 91) in the framework of the amalgamated logic of Bowen and Kowalski (Bowen-Kowalski 82), which is based on a meta-level predicate demo which represent provability, and reflection rules that link the meta-level and the object level.

The reflection rules used there are conservative and safe: actually no additional facts can be proved which could not be derived from the axiomatisation of demo.

The knowledge of each wise man is defined as a theory which includes all the facts that are considered common knowledge. This is done by "initializing" those theories with facts of the form $demo(wise_0, ...)$, where $wise_0$ is meant to represent the theory containing the common knowledge.

Moreover each theory $wise_i$ is equipped with additional "rules" to enable each wise man to perform his reasoning. In particular:

$$demo(T, P) \land agent(T) \Rightarrow P \qquad (Conf)$$

a "confidence" axiom, which makes any agent to believe the conclusions of other agents he's aware of; and three axioms for common knowledge:

$$demo(wise_0, P) \land agent(T) \Rightarrow demo(T, P) \quad (Comm1)$$

$$agent(wise_0) \qquad (Comm2)$$

$$demo(wise_0, P \land agent(T) \Rightarrow demo(T, P)) \quad (Comm3)$$

The last one is used to obtain that everybody knows that everybody knows ... P, for any fact P which is common knowledge.

The proof is performed in two stages: the first part of the reasoning is done in theory $wise_0$ to prove $white_2 \lor white_3$ (i.e. either the second or the third man has a white spot on his head). This conclusion is then lifted to $wise_3$ so that $white_3$ can be proved there.

However $wise_0$ is not an explicit theory, therefore reification could not be used to lift the conclusion into $wise_3$. A workaround for this problem is to build a theory on purpose (let's call it $WISE_0$) from the facts of type $demo(wise_0, x)$ present in $wise_3$. This step remains however external to the logic.

Once $white_2 \lor white_3$ has been proved in $WISE_0$, this fact is lifted to $wise_3$ to complete the proof. The authors justify this lifting step as an application of rule *Reification1*.

However *Reification* does not appear to be used properly here. The conclusion reached in $WISE_0$ can indeed be lifted to $wise_3$, but for a different reason. Since $WISE_0$ contains those facts x for which $wise_3$ knows $demo(wise_0, x)$, then $wise_3$ can repeat the same proof himself, nested within $demo(wise_0, ...)$, by repeated applications of the rule

$$\frac{demo(T, P), P \vdash Q}{demo(T, Q)} \qquad (\text{Proof in context})$$

which is a valid principle in most systems.

This sequence of steps can be generalised and abstracted in the following rule:

$$\frac{\{x \mid demo(T, x)\} \vdash A}{\vdash demo(T, P)} \quad (\text{Generalised proof in context})$$

which can replace reflection in many proofs.

There is however a more serious problem with the formalisation of the puzzle.

In order to ensure that $WISE_0$ is a finite set, the authors use $Comm3$, a strong common knowledge axiom. $Comm3$ allows adding a single finite schema to $WISE_0$ (i.e. $P \land agent(T) \Rightarrow demo(T, P)$) rather than an infinite set of formulae generated recursively by a more standard common knowledge axiom like:

$$demo(wise_0, P) \land demo(wise_0, agent(T)) \Rightarrow demo(wise_0, demo(T, P))$$

But the resulting formulation of common knowledge, forbids the agents to have private beliefs, since anything that is believed would be believed to be believed by anybody else. For example the second wise man could reason that since the first wise man spot is white then the first wise man must know. However, when the first man says "I do not know", he could logically derive anything, or at least become very confused. Formally, in theory $wise_2$:

(1) $white_1$ (after all he can see it!)
(2) $agent(wise_2)$ ($Comm2$, $Conf$)
(3) $P \land agent(T) \Rightarrow demo(T, P)$ ($Comm3$)
(4) $agent(wise_1)$ ($Comm2$, $Conf$)
(5) $demo(wise_1, white_1)$ (1, 4, 3)
(6) $\neg demo(wise_1, white_1)$ ($Comm2$, $Conf$)

The three wise men puzzle is also tackled in (Nakashima, Peters, Schütze, 1991) where a model for the representation of common knowledge is presented in the framework of situation theory.

Oddly, the authors claim that with a *static* (declarative) formalization of problems involving common knowledge in their language it is impossible to build proofs by contradiction, which is the most natural style of reasoning to solve this puzzle. They argue that no private knowledge is possible with their static model and this leads them to develop a procedural model for the representation of common knowledge.

Later we will present a solution to the three wise men puzzle, where common knowledge is grouped in a single theory and lifting rules are provided for each agent to access it. The advantages are a more compact statement of the problem which does not rely on "ad hoc" initialization or on the fly construction of theories by extra logical machinery and a proof which is more carefully accounted for; moreover the formulation of common knowledge is not so strong as to prevent private knowledge and the solution does not make use of the axiom of confidence which is altogether unnecessary.

Several solutions to the three wise men puzzle have appeared in the literature, some of which quite reasonable; so our focus here is in the search for an adequate proof system within a very expressive logic enabling us to carry out proofs with multiple theories in both a sound and intuitive way.

2.2 LIFTING RULES AND NATURAL DEDUCTION

In performing proofs involving multiple theories, one would like to be able to move easily from one theory to another, reason within a theory with traditional means, for instance by natural deduction, and then to carry outside some of the consequences obtained.

One must be careful however, not to leave behind in an innermost context essential assumptions and not to extrapolate to an unrelated context.

We use of the following example, presented in (McCarthy 93), to illustrate these issues.

A fixed theory, called *AboveTheory*, is used to represent the basic facts about the blocks world which do not depend on situations. One would like to make these facts and their consequences available, in the appropriate form, in another theory where situations are accounted for. The correspondence between these theories is established by axioms written in a certain context c.

We use here McCarthy's notation:

$$c : \phi$$

to express that statement ϕ is true in the context c.

Context *AboveTheory*:

(1) $\forall x, y \; on(x,y) \Rightarrow above(x,y)$
(2) $\forall x, y, z \; above(x,y) \land above(y,z) \Rightarrow above(x,z)$

Context c:

(3) $\forall x, y, s \; on(x,y,s) \Leftrightarrow \text{ist}(c(s), on(x,y))$
(4) $\forall x, y, s \; above(x,y,s) \Leftrightarrow \text{ist}(c(s), above(x,y))$
(5) $\forall p, s \; \text{ist}(AboveTheory, p) \Rightarrow \text{ist}(c(s), p)$

An outer context, c_0, is also needed for lifting facts deduced in *AboveTheory* or c, together with the following lifting axioms:

(6) $c_0 : \text{ist}(AboveTheory, x)$ iff $AboveTheory : x$
(7) $c_0 : \text{ist}(c, x)$ iff $c : x$

The example consists in showing that, assuming:

$$c_0 : \text{ist}(c, on(A,B,S_0))$$

one can prove:

$$c_0 : \text{ist}(c, above(A,B,S_0))$$

The proof goes as follows:

(8) $c_0 : \text{ist}(c, on(A,B,S_0))$ (assumption)
(9) $c : on(A,B,S_0)$ (7, 8)

The outer context c_0 and axiom (7) are needed to lift an assumption into c. Context c_0 plays the role of a special context, where the the facts in other useful theories are lifted to do the necessary reasoning.

(10) $c : \text{ist}(c(S_0), on(A,B))$ (9 and 3)
(11) $c(S_0) : on(A,B)$ (10, entering $c(S_0)$)

This last step, apparently, implies a very strong reflection, allowing a fact to be lifted P in a context c' from the fact that $\text{ist}(c', P)$ holds in another context. But the indentation warns us that this is done in the context of some assumptions we should not forget about!

(12) $c : \text{ist}(c(S_0), \forall x, y \; on(x,y) \Rightarrow above(x,y))$

In order to prove the above line in c the fact $\text{ist}(AboveTheory, \forall x, y \; on(x,y) \Rightarrow above(x,y))$ should be lifted into c in order to exploit (5). It is not enough to lift it into c_0. This really requires a strong version of reification, or rather, as we will argue later, an additional axiom.

(13) $c(S_0) : \forall x, y \; on(x,y) \Rightarrow above(x,y)$
(14) $c(S_0) : above(A,B)$ (11 and 13)
(15) $c : \text{ist}(c(S_0), above(A,B))$

A strong reification, apparently. This can be justified only because c is the "enclosing box" in the natural deduction proof; lifting in any context would not be reasonable.

(16) $c : \text{ist}(c(S_0), above(A,B)) \Rightarrow above(A,B,S_0)$ (4)
(17) $c : above(A,B,S_0)$ (15 and 16)
(18) $c_0 : \text{ist}(c, above(A,B,S_0))$ (7)

3 A METHOD FOR PROOFS IN CONTEXT

In order to discuss the problems and subtle issues hinted in the previous sections, we introduce a formal deductive system for proofs in contexts developed in connection with the theory of viewpoints (Attardi-Simi 93).

Viewpoints are sets of reified sentences and the expression $\text{in}('P', vp)$ means that a sentence P is entailed by the set of assumptions represented by vp.[1] The theory of viewpoints is a reflective first order theory allowing

---
[1]More precisely $'P'$ is a term denoting sentence P, vp a viewpoint constant, function or set of reified sentences, and $\text{in}('P', vp)$ is true at a model $\mathcal{M}$ iff P is true in any model of the sentences denoted by vp which is "coherent" with $\mathcal{M}$, i.e. interprets vp as $\mathcal{M}$ does.

us to deal with implicit viewpoints (viewpoint constants and functions). A complete semantic account of viewpoints is presented in (Attardi-Simi 93).

3.1 PROOF THEORY

The proof theory for viewpoints can be conveniently presented in the style of natural deduction.

3.1.1 Inference rules for classical natural deduction

The notation $vp \vdash P$ puts in evidence the pending assumptions in rules where some of the assumptions are discharged, like for instance the rules of implication introduction and negation introduction. When the pending assumptions are the same in the antecedent and consequent of a rule they are left implicit.

The rules for natural deduction are quite standard. For example:

$$\frac{P, Q}{P \wedge Q} \quad (\wedge\ I) \qquad \frac{P \wedge Q}{P, Q} \quad (\wedge\ E)$$

are the rules for conjunction introduction and elimination, respectively, and

$$\frac{vp \cup \{P\} \vdash Q}{vp \vdash (P \Rightarrow Q)} \quad (\Rightarrow I) \qquad \frac{P, P \Rightarrow Q}{Q} \quad (\Rightarrow E)$$

are the rules for implication introduction and elimination. The full set of classical rules used is presented in the appendix.

3.1.2 Metalevel axioms and inference rules

The behaviour of in is characterized by the following axioms and inference rules, which allow classical reasoning to be performed inside any viewpoint.

The first axiom asserts that all the sentences constituent of a viewpoint hold in the viewpoint itself, while the second establishes a principle which could be called *positive introspection*, if we choose an epistemic interpretation for in.

$$\text{in}('P', \{\ldots, 'P', \ldots\}) \qquad (Ax1)$$

$$\text{in}('P', vp) \Rightarrow \text{in}('\text{in}('P', vp)', vp) \qquad (Ax2)$$

Moreover we have a meta-inference rule for each classical natural deduction inference rule. For example:

$$\frac{\text{in}('P', vp), \text{in}('Q', vp)}{\text{in}('P \wedge Q', vp)} \qquad (Meta\ \wedge\ I)$$

$$\frac{\text{in}('P \wedge Q', vp)}{\text{in}('P', vp), \text{in}('Q', vp)} \qquad (Meta\ \wedge\ E)$$

$$\frac{\text{in}('P', vp) \vdash \text{in}('Q', vp)}{\text{in}('P \Rightarrow B', vp)} \qquad (Meta\ \Rightarrow\ I)$$

$$\frac{\text{in}('P', vp), \text{in}('P \Rightarrow Q', vp)}{\text{in}('Q', vp)} \qquad (Meta\ \Rightarrow\ E)$$

The full set of meta-inference rules is presented in the appendix.

3.1.3 Reflection rules

The following are the reflection and reification rules for the theory of viewpoints: they are more powerful than those of (Bowen-Kowalski 82), but still safe from paradoxes as discussed in (Attardi-Simi 91).

$$\frac{vp_1 \vdash \text{in}('P', vp_2)}{vp_1 \cup vp_2 \vdash P} \qquad (Reflection)$$

$$\frac{vp \vdash_C P}{\vdash \text{in}('P', vp)} \qquad (Reification)$$

The notation $\vdash_C$ stands for "classically derivable" or "derivable without using the reflection rules". Reification is a derived inference rule; in fact any proof at the object level can be completely mirrored at the metalevel using the meta-level inference rules. This can be proved by induction on the length of a proof steps, with the base case being provided by $Ax1$.

3.1.4 Derived theorems and rules

As a consequence of reification and $Ax1$, we have:

Theorem 1 $\text{in}('P', vp)$, *for any logical theorem P and viewpoint vp.*

As a consequence of the strong version of reflection, we have:

Theorem 2 $\text{in}('P', \{'Q'\}) \Rightarrow (Q \Rightarrow P)$

Moreover we can prove the following derived rule:

$$\frac{\text{in}('P', vp), P \vdash_C Q}{\text{in}('Q', vp)} \qquad (Proof\ in\ context)$$

which generalises to:

$$\frac{\{x \mid \text{in}(x, vp)\} \vdash_C P}{\vdash \text{in}('P', vp)} \qquad (Generalised\ proof\ in\ context)$$

The antecedent of the rule corresponds to the condition that in order to exploit a proof carried out in another context one must know at least that the premises of the proof are in that context.

Moreover proofs in contexts can be performed at any level of nesting.

3.1.5 Entering and leaving contexts

Another useful mechanism to build proofs in context is the ability to switch contexts and perform natural deduction proofs within viewpoints. The safest way to interpret context switching in the framework of natural deduction proofs is simply to go one level deeper or shallower in nesting, or in other words *unnesting* and *nesting*.

This means for instance that in order to prove a sentence of the form

$$\text{in}('P', vp_1) \qquad (Ax1)$$

one may pretend to move inside vp_1, and perform a proof using those facts which are present in vp_1, i.e. are of the form $\text{in}('Q', vp_1)$. If the formula P is itself of the form $\text{in}('R', vp_2)$ one will have to one level deeper to prove R by using this time just facts of the form $\text{in}('\text{in}('S', vp_2)', vp_1)$.

In their formalization of contexts (Buvač-Mason 93) Buvač and Mason propose rules for context switching which correspond to this idea, and introduce the notation of sequences of contexts to represent the nesting of several contexts. The rule they present is bidirectional and reads as follows:

$$\frac{\vdash_{\overline{k}*k_1} \phi}{\vdash_{\overline{k}} \text{ist}(k_1, \phi)} \qquad (CS)$$

The index $\overline{k}$ represents a sequence of contexts, each one nested within the previous, and the rule expresses that a statement about the truth of ϕ in a series of nested contexts $\overline{k}$ can be turned into the fact ϕ holding in the series of contexts $\overline{k} * k_1$. Keeping track of the level of nesting is crucial for the correctness of the rule.

Later we will provide safe rules for importing and exporting facts in a context.

4 A PROOF METHOD AND NOTATION

Our proofs will become more readable and intuitive with the aid of a graphical notation, which emphasises the boundaries and nesting of contexts. The notation we introduce is an extension of the box notation introduced by Kalish and Montague (Kalish-Montague 64).

4.1 RULES FOR CLASSICAL NATURAL DEDUCTION

We show here some examples of proof schemas for classical natural deduction.

The following schema corresponds to the rule of $\Rightarrow I$ and should be read as: "if assuming P you succeed in proving Q, then you have proved $P \Rightarrow Q$".

$$\boxed{\begin{array}{l} P \quad (assum.) \\ \ldots \\ Q \end{array}}$$

$$P \Rightarrow Q$$

Similarly, the schema corresponding to the inference rule of $\neg I$ is the following:

$$\boxed{\begin{array}{l} P \quad (assum.) \\ \ldots \\ Q \\ \ldots \\ \neg Q \end{array}}$$

$$\neg P$$

The box notation is useful to visualise the scope of the assumptions made during a natural deduction proof. In performing a proof within a box one can use facts proved or assumed in the same box or in enclosing boxes. Facts cannot be exported from within a box to an enclosing or unrelated box.

4.2 RULES FOR PROOFS IN CONTEXT

For proofs in context we introduce a different kind of box, with a double border, to suggest boundaries which are more difficult to traverse. The double box represents a viewpoint, i.e. a theory, whose assumptions, if known, are listed in the heading of the box. If the assumptions are not known the name of the viewpoint is shown. The only two rules for bringing facts in and out of a double box are the rules corresponding to unnesting and nesting.

Importing a fact in a viewpoint:

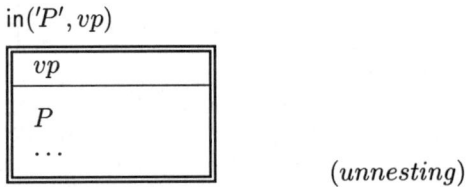

(unnesting)

Exporting a fact from a viewpoint:

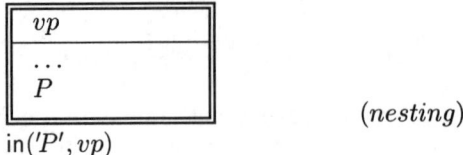

(nesting)

The only way to import a fact P in a double box vp is to have a statement $\text{in}('P', vp)$ in the environment immediately outside the box. Symmetrically you can obtain $\text{in}('P', vp)$ in the environment immediately outside a double box vp if P appears in a line immediately inside the double box (not inside a further single or double box within the double box). Note that to import a fact in nested double boxes an appropriate number of crossing double lines must be justified.

According to $Ax1$, the assumptions of a viewpoint can also be used inside the viewpoint:

$$\boxed{\boxed{\begin{array}{l} \{'P'_1,\ldots,'P'_n\} \\ P_1,\ldots,P_n \\ \ldots \end{array}}}$$

Introducing in, in the case of explicit viewpoints:

$$\boxed{\boxed{\begin{array}{l} \{'P'_1,\ldots,'P'_n\} \\ \ldots \\ P \end{array}}}$$

$$\mathsf{in}('P',\{'P'_1,\ldots,'P'_n\})$$

The meta-inference rules justify the possibility of carrying on regular natural deduction proofs within a double box. For example the $Meta \neg I$ inference rule, for negation introduction in context, justifies the following deduction schema:

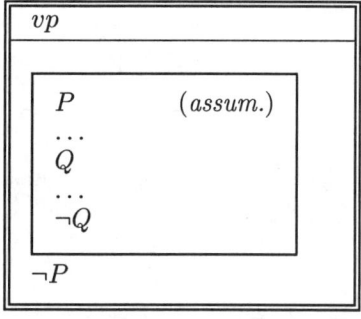

$$\mathsf{in}('\neg P', vp)$$

which is just a combination of the schemas introduced above for classical negation introduction and *nesting*.

Despite the appearances, the justification for this schema is not obvious and it is worth elaboration. The above schema is valid as long as the following deduction schema is valid in the environment outside the box:

$$\begin{array}{c} \mathsf{in}('P', vp) \quad (ass.) \\ \ldots \\ \mathsf{in}('Q', vp) \\ \ldots \\ \underline{\mathsf{in}('\neg Q', vp)} \\ \mathsf{in}('\neg P', vp) \end{array}$$

with the restriction that only facts of the form $\mathsf{in}(\ldots, vp)$, in addition to the assumption, are allowed in the proofs of Q and its negation within vp. In fact the only way to import facts in the double box is by *unnesting*.

Let us therefore suppose that only the facts:

$$\mathsf{in}('P'_1, vp)$$
$$\ldots$$
$$\mathsf{in}('P'_k, vp)$$

where used. Then it is also a fact that

$$\mathsf{in}('P \wedge P_1 \wedge \ldots \wedge P'_k, vp) \vdash \mathsf{in}('Q \wedge \neg Q', vp)$$

But then, by the sound inference rule of $Meta \neg I$, we can derive

$$\mathsf{in}('\neg(P \wedge P_1 \wedge \ldots \wedge P_k)', vp)$$

and, since we also have

$$\mathsf{in}('P_1 \wedge \ldots \wedge P'_k, vp)$$

we can obtain, by proof in context:

$$\mathsf{in}('\neg P', vp)$$

So this schema provides us a mean to carry out proofs by contradiction, as were sought by Nakashima, which we will use in the solution of the three wise men puzzle.

4.3 THE LIFTING EXAMPLE REVISITED

Exploiting the proof method and notation just introduced we can present a rational reconstruction of McCarthy's example, filling in some assumptions which where missing in the original version. To simplify the notation, from now on we will drop the quotation marks used to represent meta-level sentences. The statement of the problem is summarised in Figure 1.

The lifting axiom (1) was missing in the sketch of proof presented by McCarthy (McCarthy 93) but it is necessary in order to lift

$$\mathsf{in}(\forall x, y \; on(x, y) \Rightarrow above(x, y), AboveTheory)$$

from c_0 to c where it can be exploited by axiom (6). Without this additional assumption step (10) below could not be accounted for by any sound rule, producing a case of improper lifting.

The full proof appears in Figure 2.

Generalising from this example, we conjecture that, in any sound system for proof in context, the only way to transfer facts between two unrelated contexts is to exploit lifting axioms in a context which is external to both of them.

Let us call an *autolifting* statement a sentence in a theory T_1 which enables to lift into T_1 all or a group of facts from another theory T_2. An example of *autolifting* could be the statement $\forall p \; \mathsf{in}(p, T_2) \Rightarrow p$. For instance, we might want to use a single axiom within

c_0

(1) $\forall p \; \mathsf{in}(p, AboveTheory) \Rightarrow \mathsf{in}(\mathsf{in}(p, AboveTheory), c)$

> AboveTheory
>
> (2) $\forall x, y \; on(x, y) \Rightarrow above(x, y)$
> (3) $\forall x, y, z \; above(x, y) \land above(y, z) \Rightarrow above(x, z)$

> c
>
> (4) $\forall x, y, s \; on(x, y, s) \Leftrightarrow \mathsf{in}(on(x, y), c(s))$
> (5) $\forall x, y, s \; above(x, y, s) \Leftrightarrow \mathsf{in}(above(x, y), c(s))$
> (6) $\forall p, s \; \mathsf{in}(p, AboveTheory) \Rightarrow \mathsf{in}(p, c(s))$

Figure 1. Statement of the lifting problem

c_0

(7) $\mathsf{in}(on(A, B, S_0), c)$ (assumption)

> c
>
> (8) $on(A, B, S_0)$ (unnesting, 7)
> (9) $\mathsf{in}(on(A, B), c(S_0))$ (8 and 4)
> (10) $\mathsf{in}(\forall x, y \; on(x, y) \Rightarrow above(x, y), AboveTheory)$ (2, nesting, 1, unnesting)
> (11) $\mathsf{in}(\forall x, y \; on(x, y) \Rightarrow above(x, y), c(S_0))$ (proof in context, 6 and 10)
>
> > $c(S_0)$
> >
> > (12) $on(A, B)$ (unnesting, 9)
> > (13) $\forall x, y \; on(x, y) \Rightarrow above(x, y)$ (unnesting, 11)
> > (14) $above(A, B)$ (proof in context, 12 and 13)
>
> (15) $\mathsf{in}(above(A, B), c(S_0))$ (nesting, 14)
> (16) $\mathsf{in}(above(A, B), c(S_0)) \Rightarrow above(A, B, S_0)$ (instance of 5)
> (17) $above(A, B, S_0)$ (proof in context, 15 and 16)

(18) $\mathsf{in}(above(A, B, S_0), c)$

Figure 2. Proof of the lifting problem

context c of McCarthy's example, to enable to transfer there all the facts from *AboveTheory*. This however seems to be possible only when T_1 is an outermost context of T_2, so that a fact p in T_2 can be exported by nesting into $T1$.

We conjecture that, if T_1 and T_2 are not related (as the case of c and *AboveTheory* in the example) no *autolifting* is possible in any reasonable formal system for proof in context. Obviously it is possible to assert in T_1 individual statements taken from T_2, but this would not provide the ability to transfer wholesale a theory into another, which is an essential feature of a general mechanism of contexts.

4.4 THE THREE WISE MEN REVISITED

With the tools just developed, we are able to present a solution to the three wise men puzzle in a fairly straightforward way. Notice that there is no need for axioms like *confidence* or *wiseness* used in other solutions. The following viewpoints are used.

$wise_1$: viewpoint of the first wise man
$wise_2$: viewpoint of the second wise man
$wise_3$: viewpoint of the third wise man
CK: viewpoint including the common knowledge.

The predicate $white_i$ means the color of the spot of wise man i is white. The common knowledge viewpoint is shown in Figure 3.

Two axioms, external to the CK and wise men viewpoints are needed for the wise men to obtain the common knowledge.

(1) $\forall x\ \mathsf{in}(x, CK) \Rightarrow$
$\mathsf{in}(x, wise_1) \wedge \mathsf{in}(x, wise_2) \wedge \mathsf{in}(x, wise_3)$

(2) $\forall x\ \mathsf{in}(x, CK) \Rightarrow$
$\mathsf{in}(\mathsf{in}(x, wise_1) \wedge \mathsf{in}(x, wise_2) \wedge \mathsf{in}(x, wise_3), CK)$

Axioms (1) and (2) provide a proper account of common knowledge, allowing to derive the commonly known facts in any viewpoint, no matter how nested. In particular axiom (2) is used to achieve the appropriate level of nesting in CK, axiom (1) to lift from the CK viewpoint to any other viewpoint. The details of the derivation of common knowledge are omitted from the proof.

We can formally account, as shown in Figure 4, for the reasoning of the third wise man after the first and second one have spoken. The third wise man is in fact able to prove that his spot is white.

A common approach to the representation of nested beliefs is to introduce explicitly a number of different theories according to the different views that an agent has of other agents. In the three wise men puzzle we would have the theory that $wise_3$ has about $wise_2$, the theory that $wise_3$ has about the theory that $wise_2$ has about $wise_1$, ... and so on. The construction of tower of theories, one being "meta" for the one below, is what justifies the use of reflection and reification principles to transfer information between them.

It seems to us very unnatural to be forced to conceive from the beginning an appropriate number of theories according to the number of agents and the nesting level of the reasoning which is required: in this simple puzzle, which requires a nesting level of three, one should theoretically conceive of 27 different theories (even without considering the evolution of time).

Our solution is not radically different but, we believe, more natural. The nesting of viewpoints implicitly takes care of the different perspectives.

5 CONCLUSIONS

We have shown that proofs in contexts are difficult by pointing out delicate or unclear steps in proofs found in the literature. We presented our own, hopefully correct, version of the same proofs. Paradoxically, if our solution were wrong, we would have made this point even stronger.

The constructive part of this paper aims at providing a proof method for checking proofs in context when implicit contexts are allowed. We present a set of inference rules based on the theory of viewpoints and a method for their application which expands on the box notation introduced by Kalish and Montague for natural deduction.

We suggest a reformulation of the reflection rules more suitable to deal with partially specified theories or contexts and give an account of what "entering" and "leaving" a context should be in the setting of natural deduction proofs.

Acknowledgments

We wish to thank the International Computer Science Institute in Berkeley, for providing the support and the right atmosphere to get this work done and Saša Buvač for interesting and useful discussions which helped us to better understand McCarthy's notion of context.

References

P. Aczel (1988). *Non-well-founded sets*, CSLI lecture notes, **12**, Center for the Study of Language and Information, Stanford, California.

G. Attardi and M. Simi (1984). Metalanguage and reasoning across viewpoints, in *ECAI84: Advances in Artificial Intelligence*, T. O'Shea (ed.), Elsevier Science Publishers, Amsterdam.

G. Attardi and M. Simi (1991). Reflections about reflection, in Allen, J. A., Fikes, R., and Sandewall,

(1) $\forall x\ \text{in}(x, CK) \Rightarrow$
    $\text{in}(x, wise_1) \wedge \text{in}(x, wise_2) \wedge \text{in}(x, wise_3)$
(2) $\forall x\ \text{in}(x, CK) \Rightarrow$
    $\text{in}(\text{in}(x, wise_1) \wedge \text{in}(x, wise_2) \wedge \text{in}(x, wise_3), CK)$

CK	
(3) $white_1 \vee white_2 \vee white_3$	(at least one spot is white)
(4) $white_1 \Rightarrow \text{in}(white_1, wise_2) \wedge \text{in}(white_1, wise_3)$	($wise_2$ and $wise_3$ see $wise_1$'s spot)
(4') $\neg white_1 \Rightarrow \text{in}(\neg white_1, wise_2) \wedge \text{in}(\neg white_1, wise_3)$	
(5) $white_2 \Rightarrow \text{in}(white_2, wise_1) \wedge \text{in}(white_2, wise_3)$	($wise_1$ and $wise_3$ see $wise_2$'s spot)
(5') $\neg white_2 \Rightarrow \text{in}(\neg white_2, wise_1) \wedge \text{in}(\neg white_2, wise_3)$	
(6) $white_3 \Rightarrow \text{in}(white_3, wise_1) \wedge \text{in}(white_3, wise_2)$	($wise_1$ and $wise_2$ see $wise_3$'s spot)
(6') $\neg white_3 \Rightarrow \text{in}(\neg white_3, wise_1) \wedge \text{in}(\neg white_3, wise_2)$	
(7) $\neg \text{in}(white_1, wise_1)$	(asserted by first man)
(8) $\neg \text{in}(white_2, wise_2)$	(asserted by second man)

Figure 3. Statement of the problem in the three wise men puzzle

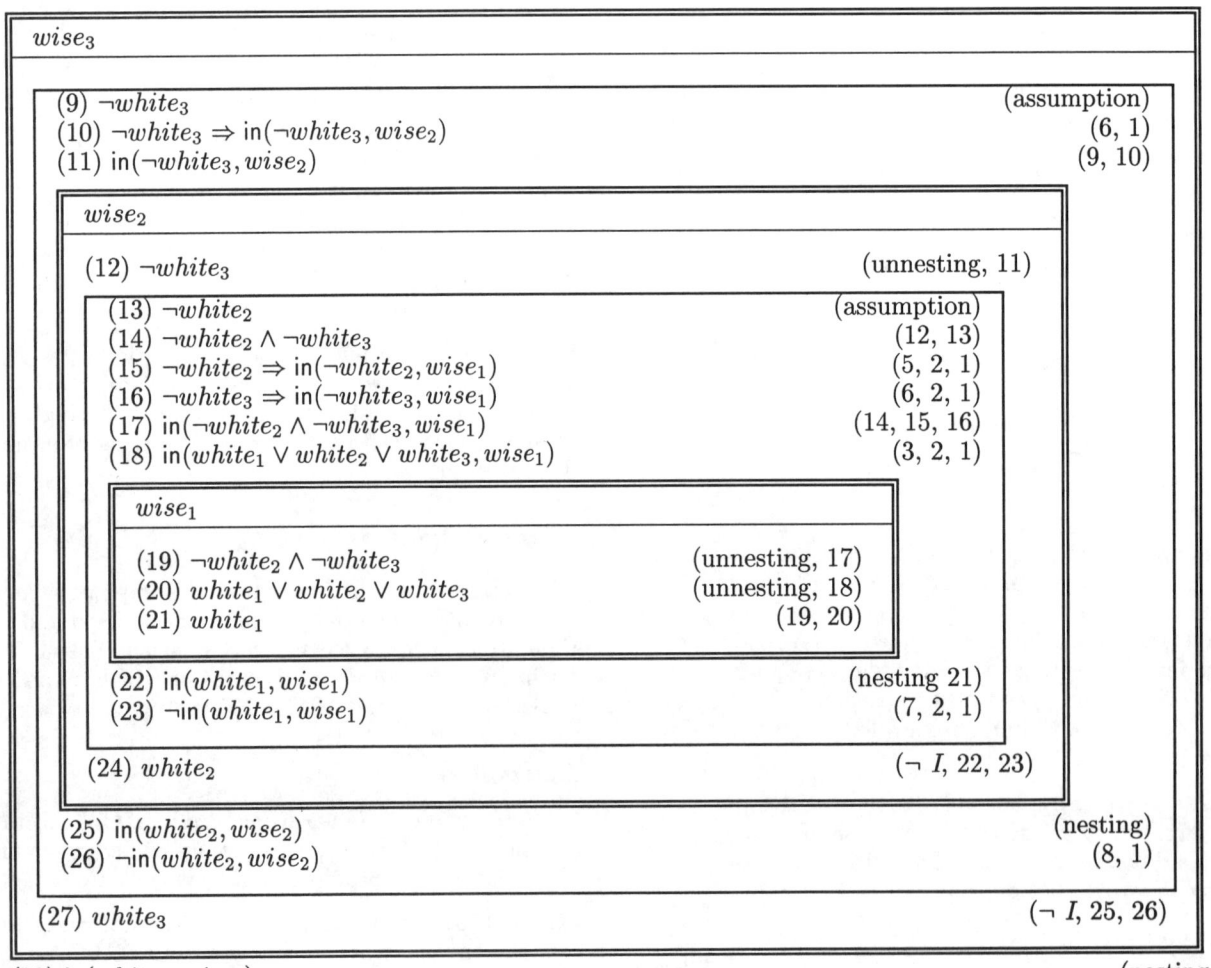

Figure 4. Proof of the three wise men puzzle

E. (eds.) *Principles of Knowledge Representation and Reasoning: Proceedings of the Second International Conference.* Morgan Kaufmann, San Mateo, California.

G. Attardi and M. Simi (1993). A formalisation of viewpoints, TR-93-062, International Computer Science Institute, Berkeley.

K.A. Bowen and R.A. Kowalski (1982). Amalgamating language and metalanguage in logic programming, in *Logic Programming*, K. Clark and S. Tarnlund (eds.), Academic Press, 153-172.

S. Buvač and I.A. Mason (1993). Propositional Logic in Context, *Proc. of the Eleventh AAAI Conference*, Washington DC, 412-419.

R.V. Guha (1991). Contexts: a formalization and some applications, MCC Tech. Rep. ACT-CYC-42391.

R. Kowalski and Kim J.S. (1991). A metalogic programming approach to multi-agent knowledge and belief, in Vladimir Lifschitz (ed.), *Artificial Intelligence and the Mathematical Theory of Computation: Papers in Honor of John McCarthy*, Academic Press, 1991, Academic Press, 231-246.

McCarthy J., Generality in Artificial Intelligence, *Communications of the ACM*, **30**(12), 1987, 1030-1035.

J. McCarthy (1993). Notes on Formalizing Context, *Proceedings of the Thirteenth International Joint Conference on Artificial Intelligence*, Chambery.

D. Kalish and R. Montague (1964). *Logic: techniques of formal reasoning*, New York, Harcourt, Brace & World.

H. Nakashima, S. Peters, H. Schütze (1991). Communication and Inference through situations, *Proc. of 12th International Joint Conference on Artificial Intelligence*, Sidney, Australia.

Y. Shoham (1991). Varieties of contexts, in Vladimir Lifschitz (ed.), *Artificial Intelligence and the Mathematical Theory of Computation: Papers in Honor of John McCarthy*, Academic Press, 393-407.

M. Simi (1991). Viewpoints subsume belief, truth and situations, in *Trends in Artificial Intelligence, Proc. of 2nd Congress of the Italian Association for Artificial Intelligence*, Ardizzone, Gaglio, Sorbello (Eds), Lecture Notes in Artificial Intelligence 549, Springer Verlag, 38-47.

R.W. Weyhrauch (1980). Prolegomena to a theory of mechanized formal reasoning, *Artificial Intelligence*, **13**(1,2):133-170.

A APPENDIX

A.1 Inference rules for classical natural deduction

$$\frac{P,Q}{P \wedge Q} \quad (\wedge\ I)$$

$$\frac{P \wedge Q}{P,Q} \quad (\wedge\ E)$$

$$\frac{vp \cup \{P\} \vdash Q}{vp \vdash (P \Rightarrow Q)} \quad (\Rightarrow I)$$

$$\frac{P, P \Rightarrow Q}{Q} \quad (\Rightarrow E)$$

$$\frac{P}{P \vee Q, Q \vee P} \quad (\vee\ I)$$

$$\frac{vp \vdash P \vee Q, vp \cup \{P\} \vdash C, vp \cup \{Q\} \vdash C}{vp \vdash C} \quad (\vee\ E)$$

$$\frac{vp \cup \{P\} \vdash Q, vp \cup \{P\} \vdash \neg Q}{vp \vdash \neg P} \quad (\neg\ I)$$

$$\frac{\neg\neg P}{P} \quad (\neg\ E)$$

$$\frac{P}{\forall y\ .\ P[y/x]} \quad (\forall\ I)$$

where the notation $P[y/x]$ stands for P with all the free occurrences of variable x substituted by t and y is a new variable not occurring in P.

$$\frac{\forall x\ .\ P}{P[t/x]} \quad (\forall\ E)$$

$$\frac{P[t/x]}{\exists x\ .\ P} \quad (\exists\ I)$$

$$\frac{vp_1 \vdash \exists x\ .\ P, vp_1 \cup P[y/x] \vdash Q}{vp_1 \vdash Q} \quad (\exists\ E)$$

where Q does not contain the newly introduced variable y.

A.2 Metalevel axioms and inference rules

$$\mathsf{in}('P', \{\ldots, 'P', \ldots\}) \quad (Ax1)$$

$$\mathsf{in}('P', vp) \Rightarrow \mathsf{in}('\mathsf{in}('P', vp)', vp) \quad (Ax2)$$

$$\frac{\mathsf{in}('P', vp), \mathsf{in}('Q', vp)}{\mathsf{in}('P \wedge Q', vp)} \quad (Meta \wedge I)$$

$$\frac{\mathsf{in}('P \wedge Q', vp)}{\mathsf{in}('P', vp), \mathsf{in}('Q', vp)} \quad (Meta \wedge E)$$

$$\frac{\text{in}('P', vp) \vdash \text{in}('Q', vp)}{\text{in}('P \Rightarrow Q', vp)} \qquad (Meta \Rightarrow I)$$

$$\frac{\text{in}('P', vp), \text{in}('P \Rightarrow Q', vp)}{\text{in}('Q', vp)} \qquad (Meta \Rightarrow E)$$

$$\frac{\text{in}('P', vp)}{\text{in}('P \vee Q', vp), \text{in}('Q \vee P', vp)} \qquad (Meta \vee I)$$

$$\frac{\begin{array}{c}\text{in}('P \vee Q', vp)\\ \text{in}('P', vp) \vdash \text{in}('R', vp)\\ \text{in}('Q', vp) \vdash \text{in}('R', vp)\end{array}}{\text{in}('R', vp)} \qquad (Meta \vee E)$$

$$\frac{\text{in}('P', vp) \vdash \text{in}('Q \wedge \neg Q', vp)}{\text{in}('\neg P', vp)} \qquad (Meta \neg I)$$

$$\frac{\text{in}('\neg \neg P', vp)}{\text{in}('P', vp)} \qquad (Meta \neg E)$$

$$\frac{\text{in}('P', vp)}{\text{in}('\forall y \,.\, P[y/x]', vp)} \qquad (Meta \forall I)$$

$$\frac{\text{in}('\forall x \,.\, P', vp)}{\text{in}('P[t/x]', vp)} \qquad (Meta \forall E)$$

$$\frac{\text{in}('P[t/x]', vp)}{\text{in}('\exists x \,.\, P', vp)} \qquad (Meta \exists I)$$

$$\frac{\begin{array}{c}vp_1 \vdash \text{in}('\exists x \,.\, P', vp_2)\\ vp_1 \cup \text{in}('P[y/x]', vp_2) \vdash \text{in}('Q', vp_2)\end{array}}{vp_1 \vdash \text{in}('Q', vp_2)} \qquad (Meta \exists E)$$

An Integrated Implementation of Simulative, Uncertain and Metaphorical Reasoning about Mental States

John A. Barnden   Stephen Helmreich   Eric Iverson & Gees C. Stein

Computing Research Laboratory
New Mexico State University, Las Cruces, NM 88003

Abstract

An unprecedented combination of *simulative* and *metaphor based* reasoning about beliefs is achieved in an AI system, ATT-Meta. Much mundane discourse about beliefs productively uses conceptual metaphors such as MIND AS CONTAINER and IDEAS AS INTERNAL UTTERANCES, and ATT-Meta's metaphor-based reasoning accordingly leads to crucial discourse comprehension decisions. ATT-Meta's non-metaphorical mode of belief reasoning includes simulative reasoning (SR). In ATT-Meta, metaphor-based reasoning can block and otherwise influence the course of SR.

1 INTRODUCTION

In spoken and written discourse, mental states and processes are often described with the aid of commonsense models of mind. These models are largely metaphorical, and the metaphorical descriptions often convey information, about the quality of the mental states, that is important for understanding the discourse. In particular, the descriptions can clarify how agents can fail to draw even quite obvious conclusions from their beliefs. Accordingly, as a step towards making mental state reasoning more realistic, refined and powerful, we have developed a system, ATT-Meta, for reasoning about mental states reported in small fragments of discourse, paying attention to metaphorical descriptions. The reasoning part of the system currently has an advanced prototype implementation in Quintus Prolog.

As an example of the phenomena of interest, consider the following passage: *Veronica was preparing for her dinner party. Her brother's recipe had said to fry the mushrooms for one hour. She did this even though in the recesses of her mind she believed the recipe to be wrong.* We claim that this last sentence manifests the conceptual metaphor of MIND AS PHYSICAL SPACE. Under this metaphor, the mind is a physical space within which ideas or thinking events/situations can lie at particular locations. The ideas and thinkings are often themselves conceived metaphorically as physical objects, events or situations. As we will see below, the use of this metaphor in the passage makes a considerable difference to what it can be reasonably taken to convey. It metaphor affects the balance of reasonableness between possible explanations of the disparity between Veronica's following of the recipe and her belief that it was wrong. If no metaphor, or a different one, had been used, then the balance would have been different.

ATT-Meta's main contributions are that it enriches mental state representation/reasoning by bringing in the commonsense models of mental states that people actually use, and it integrates metaphor-based reasoning about mental states with simulative reasoning (SR) about mental states. It thereby constrains SR in useful and novel ways.

The plan of the paper is as follows. Section 2 expands on the role of metaphor in discourse understanding. Section 3 informally sketches the reasoning ATT-Meta does on some example discourse fragments. Sections 4 to 7 provide many representation and reasoning details underlying the account in section 3. The present paper is a natural sequel to Barnden (1989, 1992).

2 METAPHORS OF MIND

Metaphors in discourse affect an understander's task of obtaining a coherent understanding. This is clear from, e.g., Hobbs (1990), Martin (1990) and others. Here we expand on the recipe example given above. Consider the discourse fragment (1), and contrast some possible continuations of it, namely (1a-c):

(1) *Veronica was preparing for her dinner party. Her brother's recipe had said to fry the mushrooms for one hour.*

(1a) *She did this even though she believed the recipe to be wrong.*

(1b) *She did this even though in the recesses of her mind she believed the recipe to be wrong.*

(1c) *She did this even though she thought, "The recipe's wrong."*

Here (1a) contains an ordinary, non-metaphorical mental state description. Sentence (1b) manifests the MIND AS PHYSICAL SPACE conceptual metaphor, explicitly referring to a specific subregion of the whole "space" of the mind. (See, e.g., Lakoff 1993 for the notion of conceptual metaphor as opposed to mere linguistic manifestations of metaphor.) Ideas or thinking episodes in one subregion can be incompatible with ideas in another. For instance, one subregion can contain the thought that a recipe is wrong, whereas another can contain the thought that the recipe is right. Alternatively, thoughts in one subregion can simply be absent from another.

In (1c) we see the conceptual metaphor of IDEAS AS INTERNAL UTTERANCES (following Barnden 1992). A thinking episode is portrayed as inner speech within the agent (or, more rarely, as inner non-speech utterances). The thinking episode is necessarily an occurrent event happening at a particular moment in time (as opposed to a long-term believing), is conscious, is usually a "forefront" thought as opposed to being in the background, and, in cases like 1c, is usually confident as opposed to being tentative. We take IDEAS AS INTERNAL UTTERANCES to be a special case of MIND AS PHYSICAL SPACE, with the internal utterance being an event that takes place within the "space" of the agent's mind. MIND AS PHYSICAL SPACE and IDEAS AS INTERNAL UTTERANCES are two of the metaphors to which we have paid most attention in our work. Two others, MIND PARTS AS PERSONS and IDEAS AS MODELS, are omitted from this paper for brevity, but see Barnden (1989, 1992). There are many commonly-used, important metaphors of mind. See, for example, Lakoff *et al.* (1991) (and Barnden 1989, 1992 for further metaphors and citations).

If one looked only at (1b,c,d) one might dispute the above claims about metaphor, saying that those sentences just involved canned forms of language. However, consider the following productive variants of them:

(1b′) *She did this [i.e. followed the instruction] after forcibly shoving the idea that the recipe was wrong to a murky corner of her mind.*

(1c′) *She did this even while whining to herself, "Oh no, this damned recipe's wrong."*

Consider also the immense potential for further varying these, e.g. using verbs other than "shove" and "whine" or physical location phrases other than "murky corner." The most economical explanation of the sense that (1b′,c′) and their further variants make is that they appeal to the metaphors we mentioned above. Then, for uniformity and continuity, it is a short step to saying that (1b,c) also manifest those metaphors, though in a more pallid way. If one wanted to maintain that (1b) was not metaphorical, one would have to claim, for instance, that "recesses," and the overwhelming majority of, if not all, words that can be used to mean physical subregions of various sorts, also happened to have literal mental meanings. And, one would have to account for why the regularities in the way the words are used to describe the mind are analogous to regularities in their physical usage. An example of such a regularity is that words such as "recesses" and "corner" convey related meanings when applied to the mind, much as they do when applied to physical space. These considerations are similar to the arguments used by Lakoff (1993).

(1c) does differ markedly from (1c′) in not using an ordinary verb of speech. However, we make three observations. First, people commonly experience some thoughts as "inner speech," so that it is fair to take (1c) as saying that Veronica was experiencing inner speech. Secondly, the verb "think" is in fact often used to portray speech in the following way: "Veronica thought aloud that the recipe was wrong." Thirdly, the idea that (1c) really is suggesting speech is reinforced by the effect of introducing the evaluative adjective "damned" into the quotation in (1c). One might question whether (1c) implies inner speech as opposed to inner writing. We plump for speech as being a far more likely implication, given that it is very common to find thought-description sentences using phrases such as "said to himself," "debated within herself", etc., and relatively rare to find ones that convey inner writing; also, the sentence forms used within the quote marks appear to be more typical of speech than writing.

In (1a–c) there is a disparity between Veronica's obeying the recipe and her belief in its incorrectness. The different ways the belief is described lead to different degrees of plausibility for various possible explanations of the disparity. One reasonable interpretation for (1b) is that Veronica's wrong-recipe belief was only minimally involved, if at all, in her conscious thinking, so that she did not consciously think (to any significant degree) that she was following a recipe that was incorrect. By contrast, continuation (1c) places the wrong-recipe belief squarely in her conscious thinking, so it seems much more likely that Veronica deliberately went against her own strong doubts, for some reason. For example, she might have been ordered to follow the recipe. We are not saying that an explanation for (1c) could not hold for (1b), or vice versa. Rather, our point is that the *balance of reasonableness* is different between (1c) and (1b). The non-metaphorical (1a) is vaguer in its implications than (1b,c), but (1c)-type explanations seem more likely than (1b)-type ones.

3 SKETCH OF REASONING

Here we informally and partially outline the main reasoning steps ATT-Meta takes for examples (1–1a), (1–1b) and (1–1c), conveying the rough flavor of its SR and metaphor-based reasoning and of their intimate interaction. We will touch on ATT-Meta's unusual feature of distinguishing conscious belief as an important special case of belief. The section also illustrates the uncertainty and defeasibility of ATT-Meta's reasoning, largely apparent below through the use of the qualifier "presumably."

3.1 OVERALL STRATEGY AND SIMULATIVE REASONING

We take (1–1a) first. It is given that Veronica followed the recipe. (ATT-Meta currently always trusts the discourse sentences to be true.) ATT-Meta infers from this that

(2) *presumably, Veronica consciously believed she was following it*

via a rule that says that if someone does an action then (s)he is, presumably, conscious of doing so. It is also given that Veronica believes the recipe to be wrong. From this ATT-Meta uses simulative reasoning (SR) to infer that

(3) *presumably, she believed it was not good to follow it.*

(We use "not good" here in the sense of "not conducive to achieving the recipe's normal purpose.") The process is basically as follows. In a special Veronica-simulation environment, ATT-Meta adopts the premise that *the recipe is wrong*. We call this environment a *simulation pretence cocoon*. Using a rule that says that if a body of instructions is wrong it is not good to follow it, ATT-Meta infers within the cocoon that

(3′): *it is not good to follow the recipe.*

Concomitantly, ATT-Meta infers (3). Further, within the cocoon ATT-Meta adopts the following premise, because of (2):

(2′): *Veronica follows the recipe.*[1]

Then, within the cocoon ATT-Meta infers the conjunction of (2′) and (3′), namely

(4′): *Veronica follows the recipe AND it's not good to follow the recipe.*

---

[1] Since ATT-Meta is simulating Veronica, it would be better to couch this premise as "I am following the recipe." However, the ATT-Meta implementation does not yet use the treatment of indexicals that we have developed (but do not present here). This deficiency does not get in the way of the issues that are our main concern.

Concomitantly, it infers that, presumably, Veronica believes this conjunction. Notice here that an SR conclusion such as this one or (3) is always qualified by "presumably," reflecting the fact that ATT-Meta merely presumes that the agent does the necessary inferencing.

Now, ATT-Meta has the following rule:

(R.1) IF *someone is following a set of instructions and believes it to be wrong* THEN, presumably, *(s)he consciously believes that.*

Therefore, ATT-Meta infers that Veronica's belief in the wrongness of the recipe was presumably conscious. Thus, both premises used in the simulation cocoon (namely: *the recipe is wrong*; *Veronica follows the recipe*) reflect conscious beliefs of Veronica's. As a result, ATT-Meta presumes that any belief resulting from the simulation is also conscious. Therefore, the main result of the belief reasoning is

(4) *presumably, Veronica* **consciously** *believed that: she follows the recipe AND it's not good to follow the recipe.*

This feeds into a rule that can be paraphrased as follows:

(R.2) IF *agent X does action A and consciously believes that [(s)he does A AND it's not good to do A]* THEN, presumably, *the explanation is that (s)he has a special reason for doing A despite having that conscious belief.*

Thus, ATT-Meta is able to infer the main result of the example, namely:

(5) *presumably, Veronica had a special reason for following the recipe even though consciously believing that [she's following the recipe AND it is not good to follow it].*

3.2 METAPHOR-BASED REASONING

We now turn to (1–1c), which involves simpler reasoning than (1–1b) does. ATT-Meta's general approach to metaphor is to "pretend" to take a metaphorical utterance at face value (i.e literally). That is, in the case of (1c), ATT-Meta pretends that

(P) *there was a real utterance of "The recipe's wrong" within Veronica's mind,*

where also ATT-Meta pretends Veronica's mind was a PHYSICAL SPACE. The pretences are embodied as the adoption of P as a premise within a special environment that we call a *metaphorical pretence cocoon* for Veronica's-IDEAS AS INTERNAL UTTERANCES. Now, the real force of such cocoons is that inference can take place within them, much as within simulation cocoons. This will happen for (1–1b). However, in the present example, the only important action that ATT-Meta bases on the metaphor is to use the following "transfer rule" linking certain metaphorical cocoons to reality:

(TR.1) IF [within a cocoon for agent X's-IDEAS AS INTERNAL UTTERANCES *there is an utterance of a declarative sentence S within X's mind*] THEN, presumably, *X consciously believes the proposition stated by S.*

Thus, ATT-Meta infers that, presumably, Veronica consciously believed the recipe to be wrong. Thus, the remainder of the reasoning is essentially the same as that for (1–1a), and ATT-Meta again constructs the main result (5). (There is a sense in which (5) is more strongly supported in the (1–1c) case than in the (1–1a) case, because of general principles concerning the specificity of inferences. However, this matter is still under investigation.)

Notice that it is only within the metaphorical pretence cocoon that ATT-Meta takes Veronica's mind to be a physical space. ATT-Meta could have information outside the cocoon saying or implying that no mind is a physical space. However, this generalization, as instantiated to Veronica, is overridden by the proposition within the cocoon that Veronica's mind is a physical space. (The reason for this is given below.) Also, propositions about Veronica's mind within the cocoon have no effect on reasoning outside the cocoon unless explicitly exported by a transfer rule. Thus, the within-cocoon proposition that Veronica's mind is a physical space does not cause trouble outside the cocoon.

In case (1–1c), the metaphor-based reasoning was minimal, and furthermore did not interact with SR very much. Things are markedly different in the case of (1–1b). ATT-Meta still tries to do the same SR about Veronica as above. However, one of the steps, namely the one that constructs the conjunction (4') within the simulation cocoon, is blocked from occurring. The reason for this is as follows.

Suppose ATT-Meta comes to a within-cocoon conclusion Q, and that this was directly based on within-cocoon propositions Q1, ..., Qn. ATT-Meta concomitantly sets up the external conclusion that the agent (X) presumably believes Q, as was implied above. However, another action is to record that this conclusion is dependent upon the hypothesis that

(I) *X performs an inference step yielding Q from Q1, ..., Qn.*

This hypothesis is, normally, deemed by ATT-Meta to be *presumably* true. It turns out that for examples (1–1a) and (1–c) there is nothing that defeats this presumption. However, one use of metaphor-based reasoning in ATT-Meta is precisely to defeat presumptions of form (I). If an instance of I is defeated then ATT-Meta abandons the conclusion that X presumably believes Q (unless Q has other support, e.g. other instances of I). If ATT-Meta abandons this conclusion then it concomitantly abolishes Q within the simulation cocoon. Two instances of I are set up in case (1–1b):

(I.1) *Veronica performed an inference step yielding [it is not good to follow the recipe] from [the recipe is wrong];*

(I.2) *Veronica performed an inference step yielding [Veronica follows the recipe AND it is not good to follow the recipe] from [Veronica follows the recipe] and [it is not good to follow the recipe].*

Now, part of ATT-Meta's understanding of the MIND AS PHYSICAL SPACE metaphor is:

(TR.2) *X's performing an inference process yielding Q from Q1, ..., Qn corresponds metaphorically to Q1, ..., Qn* **physically interacting** *within X's mind space to produce Q.* (If n is 1 then Q arises just out of Q1, without an interaction with something else.)

This principle is couched in a set of transfer rules analogous in form to TR.1. In addition, ATT-Meta has a rule *purely about physical interactions* that says

(R.3) IF *some things are spatially separated from each other, rather than being close together,* THEN, presumably, *they do not interact.*

Another purely physical rule is

(R.4) IF *Q1,..., Qn physically interact to produce Q and the Pi are all within a particular region R*, THEN, presumably, *Q is in R.*

Other parts of ATT-Meta's understanding of the metaphor are the following transfer principles:

(TR.3) *X believing P corresponds to the thinking-that-P being at some position in X's mind-space;*

(TR.4) *X consciously believing P corresponds to X's mind having a front region and the thinking-that-P being in that region;*

(TR.5) IF *a thinking occurs in the recesses of X's mind* THEN, presumably, *it is not conscious.*

ATT-Meta sets up a metaphorical pretence cocoon for Veronica's-MIND AS PHYSICAL SPACE. ATT-Meta takes (1b) at face value and adopts the within-cocoon premise that in the recesses of this space there was the thought that the recipe is wrong. As before, ATT-Meta performs the SR step that concludes, within the simulation cocoon, that it is not good to follow the recipe. Hence, by TR.2 it also infers that, within Veronica's mind-space, the thought that the recipe is wrong *physically produced* the thought that it is not good to follow it. By R.4, it follows that the latter thought was also in the *recesses* of Veronica's mind.

However, ATT-Meta infers as in (1–1a) that presumably Veronica consciously believed that she was following the recipe. Hence, by TR.4, the thought that

Veronica follows the recipe was in the *front* of her mind. ATT-Meta takes the front and the recesses to be distant from each other (relative to the size of the mind-space). Therefore, ATT-Meta uses R.3 within the metaphorical pretence cocoon to infer that the thought that Veronica follows the recipe did *not* interact with the thought that it is not good to follow the recipe. Via TR.2, this undermines I.2. As a result, the conjunction (4′) [Veronica follows the recipe AND it is not good to follow the recipe] is abolished from the SR cocoon. Concomitantly, the proposition that Veronica believed this conjunction is abolished. (I.1, on the other hand, is not undermined.)

Recall that in (1–1a) ATT-Meta inferred that, presumably, Veronica *consciously* believed the recipe to be wrong. This inference is attempted also in case (1–1b). However, it is defeated indirectly by the given information that the thought that the recipe was wrong was in the *recesses* of her mind, which supports via TR.5 the hypothesis that the belief was *not* conscious. This support for this hypothesis is judged to be more specific, and therefore stronger, than the support for the hypothesis that the belief was conscious.

All in all, (4) is defeated in case (1–1b) — ATT-Meta does *not* conclude it. In fact, because of a closed-world provision about belief in section 6, ATT-Meta comes to the stronger conclusion that Veronica actually failed to believe the conjunction (4′). This then allows the following rule to proceed:

(R.5) IF *agent X does action A, believes that it's not good to do A, but fails to believe that [X does A AND it's not good to do A]* THEN, presumably, *this failure explains the apparent disparity between X's action and belief*.

Thus, ATT-Meta is able to infer the main result of the example, namely:

(6) *presumably, the explanation for the apparent disparity concerning Veronica is that she failed to believe that [Veronica follows the recipe AND the recipe is wrong]*.

Finally, it turns out that ATT-Meta does arrive at some *weak* support for (6) in cases (1–1a) and (1–1c), and conversely comes up with some weak support for (5) in case (1–1b). This reflects our point in section 2 that the metaphors affect the balance of reasonableness of explanations, and do not totally discount particular explanations.

4 REPRESENTATION SCHEME

ATT-Meta's representations are expressions in a first-order logic with equality and with set description devices (that are syntactic sugar for first-order expressions). The logic is episodic, in that terms can denote "episodes" and sets of them. Our logical representations are similar in spirit to those of Hobbs (1990), Schubert & Hwang (1990) and Wilensky (1991). They are, overall, closest to Wilensky's, but the treatment of belief is similar to Hobbs' and different from those of Wilensky and Schubert & Hwang. In common with Schubert & Hwang, we take an episode to be any sort of situation, event or process. An episode has a time, which can be an instant, a bounded interval, or an unbounded interval. Time instants and time intervals are just objects in the domain (of the intended interpretation), just like any other object. We have no space here to go into the detail of the handling of time or causation, and in any case ATT-Meta's reasoning about time is currently limited. The detail we do give here is just what is most directly relevant to the aim of this paper (i.e. to explain ATT-Meta's mixing of belief reasoning and metaphor-based reasoning).

Objects in the domain can be "non-certain" or "certain." For instance, the episode of John kissing Mary at <some time> could be non-certain. That is, ATT-Meta would not take the kissing to be necessarily real. The basic type of term for denoting an episode is illustrated by:

$$\texttt{\#ep(Kissing, } \tau \texttt{, John, Mary)}.$$

`Kissing` denotes the set of all conceivable kissing episodes. τ is some term denoting a specific time interval, and the other arguments denote particular entities (which can be non-certain). We assume that a kissing episode is uniquely specified by the time interval and the identity of the participants. If a kissing episode has other aspects, for instance a manner, then these can be specified on the side, as i: e = #ep(Kissing, ...) $\wedge$ manner(e) = lovingly, for some constant or variable e.

Episodes with the same time as each other can be compounded by conjunction and disjunction, using function symbols `#ep-conj` and `#ep-disj`. For example, the term

$$\texttt{\#ep-conj(\#ep(Being-Happy, } \tau \texttt{, John),}$$
$$\texttt{\#ep(Being-Sad, } \tau \texttt{, Bill))}$$

denotes the episode of John being happy and Bill being sad at/over τ. Episode disjunction and negation is similar. There is also a way for expressing quantificational episodes, such as the episode of John loving each of his sisters over interval i, or the episode of some person in a given room laughing at John during interval i. The quantificational apparatus is simple, but its design required attention to subtleties raised by having to allow for non-certain episodes and other entities. For instance, the episode of all dogs being happy over interval τ must be defined independently of which entities really are dogs (according to ATT-Meta) but must instead map all conceivable being-a-dog situations to corresponding being-happy situations.

Non-certain entities episodes can have the status of *Possible*, *Suggested* or *Presumed*. *Possible* means that the episode may be real (its negation is not certain). *Suggested* means there is some reason to think the episode is real. *Presumed* means ATT-Meta is presuming the episode is real. These degrees of uncertainty are stated by means of predications such as `#presumed(#ep(Kissing,...))`.[2] Any formulae at the top level in the system are (implicitly) certain — it is only episodes (and other domain entities) that are qualified as to certainty.

We now turn to mental states, concentrating here exclusively on the central case of belief. We have several modes of belief representation, one default mode and various different modes corresponding to different metaphors of mind used in mental state descriptions. The default mode is used, for instance, when a belief is reported non-metaphorically, as in "Bill believes that John was ill on <some date>." Under the default mode, this state of belief is cast as an episode of Bill being in a particular relationship to the episode of John being ill on the date in question. The formula we use is

```
#certain(
  #ep(#Believing-Certain, now, Bill,
      #ep(Being-Ill, John, τ)))
```

where τ denotes the time interval for the specified date, `now` denotes some time interval including the current instant, and `#Certain-Believing` denotes the set of all conceivable episodes of an agent believing something with certainty. Notice the two different layers of certainty qualification: ATT-Meta has one degree of certainty that Bill had the belief, and Bill, if he does have the belief, has his own degree of certainty. The two layers are independent, so that we might alternatively have

```
#suggested(
  #ep(#Believing-Presumed, now, Bill,
      #ep(Being-Ill, John, τ))).
```

Note that we take Bill's being certain of something as implying that he presumes it (i.e. he "believes-presumed" it), and believing-presumed similarly implies believing-suggested. Conscious belief is represented similarly, but using episode kinds `#Consciously-Believing-Certain`, etc.

Finally, we sketch the most important aspect of the representation, which is how ATT-Meta expresses belief states that are described metaphorically in the input discourse. The basic principle here is that of *metaphor-infused representation*. That is, ATT-Meta pretends to take the metaphorical descriptions literally, and uses the ordinary episode kinds that are used within the source domain (or "vehicle") of the metaphor. For example, consider the sentence, *The idea that Sally is clever is in Xavier's mind.* In line with our comments on the productivity of metaphor in section 2, we take this sentence to be a manifestation of MIND AS PHYSICAL SPACE. The encoding of the sentence is

```
[WITHIN Xavier's-MIND AS PHYSICAL SPACE cocoon
#certain(
  #ep-conj(
    #ep(Being-Physical-Object-Type, t, i),
    #ep(Being-Physical-Space, t, m),
    #ep(Being-Mind-Of, t, m, Xavier),
    #ep(Inst-Being-Physically-In, t,i,m),
    #ep(Being-Agent's-Certain-Idea-Of,t,Xavier,i,
        #ep(Being-Clever,t,Sally))).
]
```

where `t`, `i`, etc. are Skolem constants. Here `Inst-Being-Physically-In` is the set of all conceivable situations of an instance of some physical-object type being *physically* in something. The idea (denoted by `i`) of Sally's (certainly) being clever is stated to be a physical-object type, Xavier's mind (`m`) is stated to be a physical space, and and instance of `i` is stated to be physically in `m`.

We therefore do *not* represent the meaning of the sentence by translating the metaphorical input into non-metaphorical internal representations: the internal representations are themselves metaphorical. Note that we are not saying that ATT-Meta really believes that, say, an idea is a physical-object type — in a sense ATT-Meta merely pretends temporarily to believe it, because the representation is within the stated cocoon.

Below, two propositions are *complements* iff one is the negation of the other. Also, a *given proposition* is either a piece of knowledge in ATT-Meta's own knowledge base or is a proposition derived directly from the discourse. In the latter case it has a rating of Certain.

5 REASONING BASICS

ATT-Meta's reasoning is centered on a goal-directed, backwards-chaining usage of production rules that link episodes to episodes (rather than formulae to formulae). Each rule has the form

<LHS> ⟶ [<qualifier>] <RHS>,

where the LHS is a list of episode-denoting terms (typically of the form `#ep(...)` possibly containing free variables, the RHS is one such term, and <qualifier> is one of Suggested, Presumed, or Certain. Also, a term *e*, or a sublist of terms on the LHS, can be embedded in a metaphorical cocoon designator as follows:

---

[2]Elsewhere we have called the Suggested and Presumed ratings by the names PERHAPS and DEFAULT respectively.

[WITHIN-COCOON χ: μ e]. Here χ is an (agent-denoting) term (usually a variable) and μ is the name of a metaphor such as MIND AS PHYSICAL SPACE.

An (unrealistic) example of a rule is

```
#ep(Loving, t, x, y), #ep(Being-Boy, t, x)
⟶ [Presumed] #ep(Being-Hungry, t, x).
```

This says that any boy who loves something at/over some time t is, presumably, hungry at/over t. Suppose ATT-Meta is investigating the proposition that Mark is hungry during a time interval denoted by some term τ. Then it sets up the episode-term #ep(Being-Hungry, τ, Mark) as a subgoal. (We use the term "proposition" loosely to mean an episode-denoting term that has either been given a rating of at least Possible, or is an existing reasoning goal.) It finds the above rule, and instantiates its t and x variables to now and Mark. Suppose ATT-Meta already has the formulae

```
#certain(Loving, τ, Mark, Mary)
#certain(Being-Boy, τ, Mark).
```

As a result, ATT-Meta creates the formula #presumed(#ep(Being-Hungry, τ, Mark)). If there were other rules also providing evidence for the Mark-hungry goal, then the qualifier assigned would be the maximum of the qualifiers suggested by the individual rules, where Suggested is less then Presumed which is less than Certain.

Also, the LHS terms can match with Suggested and Presumed episodes, not just Certain ones as in our example. Then the qualifier suggested by the rule for the RHS episode is the minimum of the certainty levels picked up by the LHS terms and the <qualifier> in the rule itself. So, if is only Suggested that Mark loves Mary, then from the rule it would only get a Suggested rating for Mark being hungry.

When ATT-Meta investigates a goal-episode (e.g. Mark being hungry), it automatically investigates its negation as well. Suppose there are rules that could provide evidence for the negation (so an RHS could have the form #ep-neg(#ep(Being-Hungry, t, x)). Let us say that the maximum of the confidence levels for the original hypothesis is P, and the maximum for the negated hypothesis is N. (Each of N or P is always at least Suggested.) Then ATT-Meta proceeds as follows: If P and N are both Certain, then a genuine error condition has arisen and ATT-Meta halts. Otherwise, if one is Certain, then it prevails and the other goal is deleted. Otherwise, both the original goal and its negation are given ratings by the following *rating reconciliation scheme*: if one or both of P, N are Suggested then they are accepted as the certainty levels of the two hypotheses; and if P, N are both Presumed, then, unless there is reason to prefer one presumption over the other, both hypotheses are "downgraded" by being given a rating of Suggested. Currently, the only way in which a one presumption can be preferred over another is through a *specificity comparison heuristic*.

We are actively investigating the question of how to compare specificity. We describe here one crude, preliminary approach that we are experimenting with. The defined more-specific-than relation is irreflexive and antisymmetric, but it is not transitive and is therefore not a partial order. It is not yet clear how important this deficiency is.

Let R be a rule that contributed a Presumed rating to a proposition P. Then the set of propositions to which R was applied is an *immediate basis* (IB) for P. Also, if P is a given proposition, then one IB for P is just {P}. It may have other IBs because a given proposition may also be supported by rules.

With Q as above, we give prefermce to Q over $\overline{Q}$ if the support for Q is more *Q-specific* than the support for $\overline{Q}$. The support for a proposition S1 is more Q-specific than the support for a proposition S2 *iff* some IB for S1 is more Q-specific than some IB for S2 and not less Q-specific than any IB for S2, *and* any IB for S2 that is more Q-specific than some for S1 is also less Q-specific than some for S1. (Our more-specific-than relation is relative to Q because of condition (b) below. "Q-specific" is synonymous with "$\overline{Q}$-specific."))

IB1 is more Q-specific than IB2 *iff* each proposition P in IB2 is either in IB1 or less Q-specific than IB1 *and* there is a proposition in IB1\IB2 that is not less Q-specific than IB2. Proposition P is less Q-specific than proposition set IB *iff*

(a) P can be derived just from IB but the propositions in IB cannot all be derived just from P; or:

(b) neither of P, IB can be derived just from the other, and some proposition in IB is "closer" to Q than P is (see below); or:

(c) neither of P, IB can be derived just from the other, P is incomparable as to Q-closeness with each proposition in IB, and the support for P is less Q-specific than the support for some proposition in IB.

P1 is *closer* than P2 to Q under the following conditions:

(b1) Q is about (exactly) one agent X's mental state, P1 is about X's mental state, but P2 is not; or

(b2) Q is about one agent X's mental state, P1 is about X, but P2 is not.

Derivability in (a) is examined using heuristically limited techniques; and note that the derivability check is a matter of examining the implementation's inter-proposition dependency links rather than undertaking more reasoning. The recursion introduced by (c) must be limited because of circularities, notably those introduced by {P} being an IB of P when P is a given proposition. Provision (b) is closely tailored to the purposes of ATT-Meta, but it is a special case of a general principle: *if one is trying to establish something, Q, and some proposition P1 is closer in subject matter to Q than some other proposition P2 is, then one should tend to give more weight to P1 than to P2.* In turn, this general principle is a natural generalization of the normal overriding-of-inheritance principle commonly employed in semantic networks. For a given node, closer ancestors are closer in subject matter to the node than more distant ancestors are. Aboutness in (b1,2) is assessed in a simple, crude way.

As an example of the use of the Q-specificity heuristic, consider the hypothesis in the (1–1c) example in section 2 that Veronica consciously believed that she was following the recipe. Let this be Q. Q gets an initial Presumed rating only via rule R.1 from the propositions that (i) she followed the recipe and (ii) she believed the recipe to be wrong. Here (i) is a given proposition (with no rule-based support) and (ii) is derived by one rule application from the given proposition that (iii) she believed in the recesses of her mind that the recipe was wrong. On the other hand, not-Q (i.e. $\overline{Q}$) gets an initial Presumed rating from (iii) via TR.5 only. So, the only IB for Q is {(i),(ii)} and the only IB for not-Q is {(iii)}. Here (ii) is less Q-specific than {(iii)} since (ii) is derivable from just (iii) (but not vice versa). Also, (i) is less Q-specific than {(iii)} by condition (b1) above. It is also easy to see that (iii) is not less Q-specific than {(i),(ii)}. Therefore, $\overline{Q}$'s only IB is more Q-specific than Q's only IB, and only Q is downgraded to Suggested.

Finally, we can only briefly mention an important truth-maintenance algorithm used in the implementation. Because of the common phenomenon of circularities in the inter-hypothesis derivation graph, and because of the above downgrading of Presumed ratings to Suggested, ATT-Meta must sometimes traverse parts of the graph, adjusting confidence ratings in order to satisfy some constraints. The updating is done lazily (i.e., on demand). (Cf. the lazy type of ATMS studied by Kelleher & van der Gaag 1993).

6 BELIEF REASONING

The central, but not the only, mode of belief reasoning in ATT-Meta is simulative reasoning (SR). SR has been proposed by a number of investigators as a relatively efficient technique for reasoning about agents' beliefs (Ballim & Wilks 1991, Chalupsky 1993, Creary 1979, Dinsmore 1991, Haas 1986, Konolige 1986, Moore 1973; although Konolige describes as simulation what we call explicit meta-reasoning, and calls SR a form of "attachment"). An SR system can intuitively be described as going into the agent's belief space, and reasoning within it by means of the system's own inference rules, acting on beliefs in the space; it then counts resulting conclusions as beliefs of the agent (perhaps only defeasibly). SR can also be described as the system pretending temporarily to adopt the agent's beliefs. SR is in contrast to using axioms or rules that constitute a meta-theory of agents' reasoning. The advantages of SR are discussed in some detail in Haas (1986) and Barnden (in press), and include the point that SR allows *any* style of base-level reasoning used by the system for ordinary purposes to be easily attributed to an agent, without the need for a separate meta-theory for each such style of reasoning — abduction, induction, ATT-Meta-style defeasible/uncertain reasoning, or whatever.

ATT-Meta's SR is procedurally complex. We therefore describe it informally, though still precisely. First we give a thumbnail sketch. The SR proceeds in a backwards, goal-directed way. Suppose ATT-Meta is investigating the hypothesis that X believes-ρ_0 P, where ρ_0 is one of the confidence ratings from Possible to Certain. ATT-Meta strips off the "X believes-ρ_0" to get the reasoning goal P within a simulation cocoon for X. In the implementation, placing a proposition within a simulation cocoon consists of tagging it with the identity of the believer, X. In its normal way, ATT-Meta also investigates the complement $\overline{P}$ of P within the cocoon. Hence, the SR might end up concluding that X believes $\overline{P}$ rather than P.

Currently, any of ATT-Meta's own rules can be used within the X-simulation cocoon (i.e. can be applied to X-tagged propositions, yielding X-tagged conclusions). However, in contrast with some other SR schemes, ATT-Meta's own propositions are *not* ascribed (by default) to the believer, i.e. imported into the cocoon. (This reflects a very recent change in our approach. In fact, a provision at the end of this section embodies an opposite to default ascription.) Rather, the only way for a proposition Q to enter the cocoon from outside is via a proposition (outside the cocoon) of the form [X believes-ρ Q] for some ρ. Further, Q cannot be inserted in the cocoon unless ATT-Meta's rating for [X believes-ρ Q] is Presumed or Certain. This is to limit the complexity of reasoning and to boost its definiteness. In practice, ATT-Meta has many rules that can lead to propositions of form [X believes-ρ Q], for general classes of agent. An example is a rule we appealed to in section 3, saying that if an agent X performs an action then, presumably, X consciously believes (s)he does so. (A further rule is needed here to go from conscious belief to belief *simpliciter*.) Notice that conclusions from such rules can be defeated by other information. For instance, the conclusion of the rule just mentioned could be defeated by a given Certain proposition that X does not believe (s)he performs the action. Also, conclusions from SR can defeat the conclusions of such rules, or vice versa (depending on which way specificity comparisons go).

Let Q be P, $\overline{P}$ or a subgoal used in the reasoning within the cocoon towards P or $\overline{P}$. If Q is given rating ρ by reasoning within the cocoon, then the proposition that X believes-ρ Q is given a rating of Presumed outside the cocoon, barring interference from reasoning outside the cocoon.

Now we provide a complete description of the process. It schema instance complex, but, as we will explain, for much of the time in practice only simple special cases arise. With Q as above, the steps of the process applied to Q and $\overline{Q}$ are in outline as follows. After the outline we will provide the detail.

(A): *Simulation proper.* Because the reasoning is backwards, we assume that all reasoning towards Q and $\overline{Q}$ has been done (by recursive application of the process we are now describing), and in particular that their ratings have been reconciled with each other. Notice that one of Q, $\overline{Q}$ may have been eliminated by a Certain rating for the other.

(B): *Externalization.* Q and $\overline{Q}$ are "externalized" to create hypotheses, outside the cocoon, of the following types:

(i)   X believes-ρ' Q
(ii)   not(X believes-ρ' Q)
(iii)   X believes-ρ' $\overline{Q}$
(iv)   not(X believes-ρ' $\overline{Q}$)

for various ratings ρ' related to the ratings for Q and $\overline{Q}$. The propositions of types (i) to (iv) are given particular preliminary ratings.

(C): *Non-simulative phase.* The hypotheses introduced in (B) are now investigated by ordinary reasoning outside the cocoon, using any rules that address those hypotheses. (Of course, some of the hypotheses may coincide with given propositions.) In particular, special rules that mutually constrain propositions of types (i) to (iv) are available. In this phase, a proposition introduced by (B) can have its rating upgraded or downgraded, or can be eliminated altogether.

(D): *Consciousness attribution.* There may be a goal to show that Q is consciously believed by X, not just believed. If so, and Q still exists and resulted within the cocoon from conscious beliefs, then that goal is given support.

(E): *Re-internalization.* If any proposition of form [X believes-ρ Q] still exists and has rating at least Presumed, then the final rating given to Q inside the cocoon is the maximum of the ρ values in such propositions. Similarly for $\overline{Q}$. If no [X believes-ρ Q/$\overline{Q}$] exists anymore, then Q/$\overline{Q}$ (resp.) is eliminated from the cocoon.

The following fleshes out steps (A) to (D) of the above outline. (We use informal IF-THEN descriptions of rules, but they are straightforwardly expressible in the formalism).

(For A) Ratings for Q and $\overline{Q}$ contributed by individual rules are reconciled with each other in the normal way, except that a Certain/Certain clash results only in the SR for X being halted, rather than in a global system error. (A more sophisticated possible action is mentioned below as a future research item.)

(B.1) If Q is still present and has rating ρ, then for each rule that contributed to Q within the cocoon by being applied to some propositions Q_1 to Q_n with ratings ρ_1 to ρ_n, the following goal is set up outside the cocoon, with an initial rating of Presumed:

(I.Q)   X does-inference-step to Q with rating ρ from $Q_1, \ldots, Q_n$ with ratings ρ_1 to ρ_n.

(Cf. schema (I) in section 3.) And, [X believes-ρ Q] is regarded as having been supported by the rule

(R.Q)   IF ...(I.Q) as above ... AND X believes-ρ_1 Q_1 AND ... AND X believes-ρ_n Q_n THEN [Certainly] X believes-ρ Q.

Since, by recursion over the process we are describing, the Q_i do not exist in the cocoon unless X believes them to some degree, [X believes-ρ Q] is given some degree of support by R.Q, using the normal scheme for ratings management in rule application. Normally, I.Q keeps its rating of Presumed, but it is investigated in the normal way and could be upgraded, downgraded or eliminated.

$\overline{Q}$ is dealt with similarly, possibly giving rise to analogous propositions (I.$\overline{Q}$) and rule (R.$\overline{Q}$).

(B.2) Suppose $\overline{Q}$ has rating Suggested inside the cocoon, and this resulted from a downgrade because of conflict with Q. Then ATT-Meta regards the following rules as having been applied, for each (I.Q) produced by step (B) for which ρ = Presumed:

(R'.$\overline{Q}$)   IF ...(I.Q) as above ... AND X believes-ρ_1 Q_1 AND ... AND X believes-ρ_n Q_n THEN [Certainly] not(X believes-Presumed $\overline{Q}$).

Q is treated similarly.

(For C) The special rules mentioned above are defined by the following schemata. ρ and ρ' stand for any ratings where $\rho > \rho' \geq$ Possible.

(RB1)   IF Y believes-ρ B THEN [Certainly] Y believes-ρ' B

(RB1')   IF not(Y believes-ρ' B) THEN [Certainly] not(Y believes-ρ B)

(RB2)   IF Y believes-Certain B THEN [Presumably] not(Y believes-Possible $\overline{B}$)

(RB2')   IF Y believes-Possible B THEN [Presumably] not(Y believes-Certain $\overline{B}$)

(RB3) IF Y believes-Presumed B THEN [Presumably] not(Y believes-Presumed $\overline{B}$).

A Presumed/Presumed clash between X believes-ρ Q′ and not(X believes-ρ Q′), where Q′ is either Q or $\overline{Q}$, is treated in the normal way.

Once the reasoning of this phase is complete, ATT-Meta applies a closed-world assumption to X's belief in Q and X's belief in $\overline{Q}$. If ρ is the maximum rating such that [X believes-ρ Q] has a rating of Presumed or Certain, then ATT-Meta gives a Presumed rating to not[X believesρ' Q] for each ρ' higher than ρ (unless that proposition already has a rating of Presumed or Certain). Similarly for $\overline{Q}$.

(For D) Consciousness attribution is handled in part by a "conscious" counterpart for each rule of type (R.Q) or (R.$\overline{Q}$) as defined in (B.1). This counterpart just has "believes" replaced by "consciously believes" throughout. In addition, ordinary non-simulative reasoning within (C) can lead directly to conclusions of form [X consciously-believes Q], or similarly with $\overline{Q}$. In particular, we have made use of rules such as the following for specific sorts of belief B: IF Y believes-ρ B AND Y is conscious THEN [Presumably] Y consciously-believes-ρ B.

That completes the description of SR. Although the process is quite complicated in general, it is in practice relatively unusual for both (A) and (C) to involve a significant amount of processing. If (A) does do so but (C) does not, then essentially (B) and (D) leave the results of (A) unchanged. Conversely, if (C) involves significant reasoning but (A) and (B) are trivial because Q and $\overline{Q}$ find no support within the cocoon, then essentially (D) just strips off belief layers from positive belief propositions established by (C). Also, the process is optimized by means of special processing steps in the implementation. For instance, the RB... and (R.Q) rules are not explicit in the implementation.

When both (A) and (C) are significant, some interesting effects can arise. In particular, a downgrade during (A) of Q or $\overline{Q}$ because of a Presumed/Presumed clash within the cocoon can be reversed by (C). For example, there might be a given, Certain proposition that X believes-Presumed Q, preventing a downgrade of Q. The prevention happens thus: during (C), that given proposition defeats the Presumed proposition arising from (B.2) that X does not believe-Presumed Q. As a result, during (D), Q is given a rating of Presumed.

During (C), a Presumed/Presumed conflict between a proposition of one of the forms (i) to (iv) and its complement can bring in a specificity comparison, as normal. The rules of form (R.Q), (R.$\overline{Q}$), (R′.Q) and (R′.$\overline{Q}$) allow the comparison to look back to the way that the believings on the LHSs of those rules were established, with the reasoning within the cocoon being invisible to the process.

The SR scheme as described can also be used with SR, allowing nested belief to be handled. However, we have not yet intensively investigated this matter.

ATT-Meta's top-level reasoning goal when faced with discourse fragments like (1–1a/b/c/d) in section 2 is currently set by hand and is to the effect that some disparity in the discourse is resolved because of explanation e, where e is a variable in the goal and is bound as a result of satisfying the goal. Such goals match the RHSs of rules such as R.2 and R.5 in section 2. The disparity is currently not detected by ATT-Meta itself.

7 METAPHORICAL REASONING

Hypotheses of form (I.Q) above (or, of course, I.$\overline{Q}$) introduced by steps (B.1) and (B.2) of SR provide a means whereby meta-reasoning about an agent's individual reasoning steps can be applied to affect the course of SR. Such reasoning might downgrade or upgrade those hypotheses, thus affecting the strength of the conclusions reached by rules such as (R.Q). We have studied metaphor-based reasoning that affects (in fact, only ever downgrades) the hypotheses (I.Q), but, in principle, non-metaphorical reasoning could also do so. In particular, limitations on the amount of reasoning the agent is assumed to be able to do could be brought into the picture.

We concentrate here on the effect of metaphor on hypotheses (I.Q), but a metaphor-based inference can also say something direct about an agent's belief. For instance, in section 3, an IDEAS AS INTERNAL UTTERANCES inference directly produced the conclusion that a particular belief was conscious.

When a hypothesis (I.Q) is created, one sort of rule that might attack it (i.e. support its negation) is a metaphorical "transfer" rule such as TR.2 in section 3. Through the ordinary process of backwards rule usage, this causes subgoals to be set up inside the (X,M) metaphorical pretence cocoon specified by the rule, if that cocoon exists. Here X is the agent and M is the name of the metaphor. A special action is to try to establish whether the cocoon exists. Currently, the cocoon only exists if a metaphorical belief representation (as at the end of section 4) has been set up as a direct result of one the sentences in the input discourse. If the cocoon does not exist, then the transfer rule fails. If the cocoon does exist, then the presence of a proposition P within it is simply noted in the implementation by tagging a copy of P with (X,M). When the cocoon is created, one or more *standard premises* are inserted. For instance, if M is MIND AS PHYSICAL SPACE, then the cocoon will contain the Certain premise that X's mind is a physical space. Also, other premises resulting directly from the input discourse can be inserted. For instance, the discourse might say that a particular idea is in X's mind. We call these *discourse premises for the cocoon*. Currently all such premises are Certain.

Reasoning within the cocoon is as normal, with a small but important change to the rating-reconciliation scheme. The reasoning within the cocoon (i.e. mediating between (X,M)-tagged propositions) can use any of ATT-Meta's rules, but because of its goal-directedness it will ordinarily just use rules peculiar to the vehicle domain of M. Subgoals resulting from within-cocoon rule consideration can also be addressed (supported or attacked) by transfer rules. In turn, these rules can lead to rule consideration entirely outside the cocoon. In this way, metaphor-based reasoning is intimately and context-sensitively combined with non-metaphorical reasoning.

Knowledge outside the cocoon can conflict with knowledge inside, as pointed out in section 3. For instance, ATT-Meta may have the rule (R) that a mind is Certainly not a physical space. This rule's Certain conclusion in X's case would conflict with the standard premise mentioned above as being in the cocoon. To handle this problem, we simply make the following change to the rating-reconciliation scheme as used within the cocoon: when considering a subgoal Q and its complement $\overline{Q}$ where the preliminary rating for the latter is Certain, if Q has support (however indirectly) from a standard cocoon premise, discourse premise for the cocoon, and/or transfer rules, whereas $\overline{Q}$ does not have such support, then the Certain rating for $\overline{Q}$ is first downgraded to Presumed. (Notice that this does not affect cases where both or neither of Q, $\overline{Q}$ have support of the type mentioned.) As a result, the ordinary operation of ATT-Meta's rating reconciliation scheme can cause the downgrading of $\overline{Q}$ to Suggested only, or its elimination. Elimination would happen with Q being that X's mind is a physical space, since this is a standard cocoon premise and therefore Certain. This defeats $\overline{Q}$'s original Certain rating because that is first downgraded to Presumed.

Finally, observe that there may be more than one hypothesis (I.Q) for a given Q, because Q may be supported within SR in more than one way. It could be that metaphor-based reasoning only downgrades one such hypothesis. Then, the rating of the proposition [X believes-ρ Q] supported by rules of form R.Q is not, after all, affected. Also, in principle, an (I.Q) could have completely independent support from non-metaphorical, non-simulative reasoning, and this support might defeat the support from metaphor-based reasoning.

8 CONCLUSION

ATT-Meta differs from other work on belief representation/reasoning mainly by taking account of the important phenomenon of metaphorical descriptions of mental states in discourse. In particular, these descriptions can clarify the way in which an agent believes something (as opposed to specifying what is believed). Such ways of believing can make a major difference in discourse understanding, for instance by explaining how agents can fail to see consequences of their beliefs. Also, ATT-Meta is unique in having a systematic and well-motivated way of constraining the application of SR, namely by integrating it with metaphor-based reasoning. The SR and metaphor-based reasoning are completely integrated into a powerful and practical uncertain/defeasible reasoning framework. The SR is unusual in distinguishing conscious belief as an important special case.

ATT-Meta is one of the few implemented, or detailed theoretical, schemes for significant metaphor-based reasoning. (Others are Hobbs 1990 and Martin 1990.) We integrate metaphor-based reasoning into an uncertain reasoning framework much as Hobbs does, except that he uses abductive framework. In addition, our scheme for metaphor-based reasoning is much like that of Hobbs, in that it usually proceeds by applying concepts and rules from the metaphor vehicle directly to the target items, rather than by translating them into target-domain concepts and rules. Some of the advantages of the approach are discussed in Barnden (1992). ATT-Meta differs from Hobbs' and Martin's work in being concerned only with metaphors of mind. Nevertheless, there is nothing in our approach that is peculiar to metaphors of mind, as opposed to metaphors for other abstract matters. ATT-Meta currently handles only metaphor that is conventional to it. Our work therefore differs from, e.g., that of Fass (1991) and Iverson & Helmreich (1992), who are concerned with working out the nature of novel(to-the-system) metaphors encountered in sentences.

Nevertheless, ATT-Meta can be creative in its use of any given metaphor, because any source-domain fact or rule can be opportunistically used during metaphor-based reasoning. For example, consider the sentence "One part of Veronica was insisting that the recipe was wrong." We take this to exhibit what we call the MIND PARTS AS PERSONS metaphor. Given that a normal inference from the fact that a real person insists something that some interlocutor of that person has said something that conflicts with it, ATT-Meta can conclude (within a metaphorical pretence cocoon) that some non-mentioned part of Veronica has said that the recipe was correct, and therefore presumably believes this. Notice that *there is no need here for any transfer rule to impinge on the notion of insisting.* In this way, all the richness of metaphor vehicle (source) domains is available for use. This point is strengthened by the fact that the knowledge bases we have built up for the metaphor vehicles are not contrived for metaphorical use, but are designed to support ordinary reasoning within those domains. For instance, the physical rules in section 3 are commonsensical rules that are useful for ordinary physical reasoning.

In future work, we hope to address the following issues among others: a formal Q-specification of the intended interpretation of the episodic logic; a more powerful specificity heuristic; and a more sophisticated treatment of Certain/Certain clashes within SR — e.g., one possibility is for the system to *postulate* a MIND AS PHYSICAL SPACE view of the agent, even if this is not directly indicated by the discourse, and then place the clashing propositions in different mind regions. Also, ATT-Meta provides a promising framework for various interesting ways of nesting different types of reasoning. The nesting of metaphor-based within simulative reasoning allows the ascription of metaphorical thinking about mental states to agents. This is a useful addition to ordinary nested belief reasoning. The nesting of belief reasoning, including SR, within metaphor-based reasoning allows SR to be applied to metaphorical "persons" in a metaphor vehicle. The nesting of metaphor-based reasoning inside itself allows the handling of chained metaphor (where aspects of a metaphor vehicle are themselves conceived metaphorically).

In this work we have had to adopt provisional solutions to a number of difficult problems, both in representation and reasoning, aside from SR and metaphor-based reasoning themselves. For example, we have had to deal with the de-dicto/de-re distinction, indexicality in beliefs, complex episodes, representation of time and causality, and defeasible reasoning. Our solutions to these issues are to some extent orthogonal to the main principles of simulative and metaphor-based reasoning that we have adopted, and are subject to change.

Acknowledgements

This work was supported in part by grants IRI-9101354 and CDA-8914670 from the National Science Foundation. We are grateful for extensive help from Kim Gor, Kanghong Li and Jan Wiebe.

References

Ballim, A. & Wilks, Y. (1991). *Artificial believers: The ascription of belief.* Hillsdale, N.J.: Lawrence Erlbaum.

Barnden, J.A. (1989). Belief, metaphorically speaking. In *Procs. 1st Intl. Conf. on Principles of Knowledge Representation and Reasoning* (Toronto, May 1989). San Mateo, CA: Morgan Kaufmann. pp.21–32.

Barnden, J.A. (1992). Belief in metaphor: taking commonsense psychology seriously. *Computational Intelligence, 8* (3), pp.520–552.

Barnden, J.A. (in press). Simulative reasoning, common-sense psychology and artificial intelligence. In M. Davies & A. Stone (Eds), *Mental Simulation,* Oxford: Blackwell.

Chalupsky, H. (1993). Using hypothetical reasoning as a method for belief ascription. *J. Experimental and Theoretical Artificial Intelligence, 5* (2&3), pp.119–133.

Creary, L.G. (1979). Propositional attitudes: Fregean representation and simulative reasoning. *Procs. 6th. Int. Joint Conf. on Artificial Intelligence* (Tokyo), pp.176–181. Los Altos, CA: Morgan Kaufmann.

Dinsmore, J. (1991). *Partitioned representations: a study in mental representation, language processing and linguistic structure.* Dordrecht: Kluwer Academic Publishers.

Fass, D. (1991). met*: A method for discriminating metonymy and metaphor by computer. *Computational Linguistics, 17* (1), pp.49–90.

Haas, A.R. (1986). A syntactic theory of belief and action. *Artificial Intelligence, 28,* 245–292.

Hobbs, J.R. (1990). *Literature and cognition.* CSLI Lecture Notes, No. 21, Center for the Study of Language and Information, Stanford University.

Iverson, E. & Helmreich, S. (1992). Metallel: an integrated approach to non-literal phrase interpretation. *Computational Intelligence, 8* (3), pp.477–493.

Kelleher, G. & van der Gaag, L. (1993). The LazyRMS: Avoiding work in the ATMS. *Computational Intelligence, 9* (3), pp. 239–253.

Konolige, K. (1986). *A deduction model of belief.* London: Pitman.

Lakoff, G. (1993). The contemporary theory of metaphor. In A. Ortony (Ed.), *Metaphor and Thought,* 2nd edition, pp.202–251. Cambridge, U.K.: Cambridge University Press.

Lakoff, G., Espenson, J. & Schwartz, A. (1991). Master metaphor list. Draft 2nd Edition. Cognitive Linguistics Group, University of California at Berkeley, Berkely, CA.

Martin, J.H. (1990). *A computational model of metaphor interpretation.* Academic Press.

Moore, R.C. (1973). D-SCRIPT: A computational theory of descriptions. In *Advance Papers of the Third Int. Joint Conf. On Artificial Intelligence,* Stanford, Calif, pp.223–229. Also in *IEEE TRansactions on Computers, C-25* (4), 1976, pp.366–373.

Schubert, L.K. & Hwang, C.H. (1990). An episodic knowledge representation for narrative texts. Tech. Report 345, Computer Science Department, University of Rochester, Rochester, NY. May 1990.

Wilensky, R. (1991). The ontology and representation of situations. In *Procs. 2nd Int. Conf. on the Principles of Knowledge Representation and Reasoning,* pp.558–569.

Reasoning with minimal models:
Efficient algorithms and applications

Rachel Ben-Eliyahu[*]
Computer Science Department
Technion —
Israel Institute of Technology
Haifa 32000, Israel
rachelb@cs.technion.ac.il

Luigi Palopoli
DEIS
Universitá della Calabria
87036 Rende (CS), Italy
luigi@si.deis.unical.it

Abstract

Reasoning with minimal models is at the heart of many knowledge representation systems. Yet it turns out that this task is formidable, even when very simple theories are considered. In this paper we introduce the *elimination algorithm*, which performs in polynomial time minimal model finding and minimal model checking for a significant subclass of CNF theories which we call head-cycle-free (HCF) theories. We then show how variations of the elimination algorithm can be applied for answering queries posed on disjunctive knowledgebases and disjunctive default theories in an efficient way. Finally, using techniques developed in database theory, we argue that the tractable subsets identified in this paper are quite expressive.

1 Introduction

Computing minimal models is an essential task in many artificial intelligence reasoning systems, including circumscription [McCarthy, 1980, McCarthy, 1986, Lifshitz, 1985], default logic [Reiter, 1980], and minimal diagnosis [de Kleer et al., 1992], and in answering queries posed on logic programs (under stable model semantics [Gelfond and Lifschitz, 1991, Bell et al., 1991]) and deductive databases (under the generalized closed-world assumption [Minker, 1982]). The ultimate goal in these systems is to produce plausible inferences, not to compute minimal models. However, efficient algorithms for computing minimal models can substantially speed up inference in these systems.

Special cases of this task have been studied in the diagnosis literature and, more recently, the logic programming literature. For instance, algorithms used in many diagnosis systems [de Kleer and Williams, 1987, de Kleer et al., 1992] are highly complex in the worst case: to find a minimal diagnosis, they first compute all prime implicates of a theory and then find a minimal cover of the prime implicates. The first task is output exponential, while the second is NP-hard. Therefore, in the diagnosis literature, researchers have often compromised completeness by using heuristic approaches. The work in the logic programming literature (e.g., [Bell et al., 1991]) has focused on using efficient optimization techniques, such as linear programming, for computing minimal models. A limitation of this approach is that it does not address the issue of worst-case and average-case complexities.

Surprisingly, and perhaps due to its inherent difficulty, the problem has received a formal analysis only recently [Papadimitriou, 1991, Cadoli, 1991, Cadoli, 1992, Kolaitis and Papadimitriou, 1990, Eiter and Gottlob, 1993, Chen and Toda, 1993, Ben-Eliyahu and Dechter, 1993]. Given a propositional CNF theory T and an atom A in T, the following tasks (and others) have been considered:

model finding Find a minimal model for T.

model checking Check whether a given interpretation[1] is a minimal model for T.

minimal entailment Is A *true* in all the minimal models of T?

minimal membership Is A *true* in at least one minimal model of T?

Unfortunately, the results of the formal work on the complexities of reasoning with minimal models are very discouraging. It turns out that even when the theory is positive, that is, when the theory has no clause where all the literals are negative, these questions are very hard to answer: model finding is $P^{NP[O(\log n)]}$-hard [Cadoli, 1992] (and positive theo-

---

[*]Part of this work was done while the first author was a student at the Cognitive Systems Lab, Computer Science Department, UCLA, Los Angeles, California, USA.

[1]We take an interpretation to be an assignment of truth values to the atoms in the theory.

ries always have a minimal model!)[2] model checking is co-NP-complete [Cadoli, 1991], minimal entailment is co-NP-complete, and minimal membership is Σ_2^p-complete [Eiter and Gottlob, 1993].

In this paper we introduce a basic property that turns out to characterize classes for which the above problems and other related problems can be solved more efficiently. The property is head-cycle freeness. The idea is simple: a clause[3] can be viewed as having a direction — from the negative to the positive literals. This direction is made explicit in the way clauses are represented in logic programs. We can then associate a dependency graph with each theory: each atom is a node in the graph, and there is an arc directed from A to B iff there is a clause where A appears negative and B positive. Then a theory will be called *head-cycle free* (HCF) iff in its dependency graph there is no directed cycle that goes through two different atoms that appear positive in the same clause. Head-cycle freeness can be checked in quadratic time in the size of the theory.

We will show that for positive HCF theories, most of the above problems are manageable: model finding and model checking can be done in $O(n^2)$ time, where n is the size of the theory, and minimal membership is NP-complete. However, [Eiter, 1993] has shown that for the minimal entailment problem, being HCF does not help — the problem is co-NP-complete even if you restrict the theories to being HCF. Our results can be generalized quite naturally to compute minimal Herbrand models of a significant subclass of first-order CNF theories.

We will also show applications of the results we have on CNF theories for answering queries on knowledgebases that use disjunctive rules. More specifically, we will show an algorithm that computes efficiently a stable model of an HCF stratified disjunctive knowledgebase[4]. If the knowledgebase is propositional, the algorithm computes a stable model in time polynomial in the size of the knowledgebase. We will also demonstrate how we can use this algorithm for answering queries posed on disjunctive default theories.

The last important question that we address is how significant or, in other words, expressive is this class of tractable theories. In database theory, the expressive power of query languages is a much-studied topic. Ideally, we would like to have a language that is easy to compute but yet capable of expressing powerful queries. Using techniques developed in database theory, we argue that the tractable subsets identified in this paper are quite expressive.

2 The elimination algorithm for HCF theories

In this section we introduce the *elimination algorithm* (EA), which can be used to perform both model checking and model finding on an HCF positive propositional theory in polynomial time.

We will refer to a theory as a set of clauses of the form

$$A_1 \wedge A_2 \wedge ... \wedge A_m \supset C_1 \vee C_2 \vee ... \vee C_n \qquad (1)$$

where all the A's and the C's are atoms[5]. The expression to the left of the $\supset$ is called the *body* of the clause, while the expression to the right of the $\supset$ is called the *head* of the clause. We assume that all the C's are different. A theory is called *positive* if for every clause $n > 0$. In this section we deal with positive theories, unless stated otherwise. When $n = 0$ we take it as if the clause is $A_1 \wedge A_2 \wedge ... \wedge A_m \supset$ **false**. When $m = 0$ we take it as if the clause is **true** $\supset C_1 \vee C_2 \vee ... \vee C_n$.

With every theory T we associate a directed graph G_T, called the *dependency graph* of T, in which (a) each atom in T is a node, and (b) there is an arc directed from a node A to a node C iff there is a clause in T in which A is one of the A_i's and C is one of the C_i's.

As mentioned before, model finding for positive theories is $P^{NP[O(\log n)]}$-hard, model checking is co-NP-complete, and minimal membership is Σ_2^p-complete. We will show that most of these problems are easier for the class of HCF theories. A theory T is HCF iff there is no clause of the form (1) in T such that for some C_i and C_j, $i \neq j$, G_T contains a directed cycle involving C_i and C_j. So, for example, the theory $A \supset B$, $B \supset A$, $A \vee B$ is *not* HCF, while the theory $A \supset B$, $B \supset A$, $A \vee C$ *is* HCF.

Fact 2.1 *Head-cycle freeness of a theory of size[6] n can be checked in time $O(n^2)$.*

Clearly, just any model for a positive theory can be found very easily — take, for example, the set of all atoms in the theory. What is difficult is finding a *minimal* model for the theory. Roughly speaking, the idea behind the EA is as follows: we pick a model of the theory and then *eliminate* from this model all the atoms that we know will not be part of one of the minimal

---

[2][Chen and Toda, 1993] have recently characterized the complexity of model finding as a NPMV//OptP[Olog n]-complete task.

[3]In this section, a clause is a disjunction of literals. In the sequel we will use a different syntax.

[4]Stable models and stratified knowledgebases will be defined in the following sections.

[5]Note that the syntax of (1) is a bit unusual for a clause; usually, the equivalent notation $\neg A_1 \vee \neg A_2 \vee ... \vee \neg A_m \vee C_1 \vee C_2 \vee ... \vee C_n$ is used. We chose the first notation because it is closer to the way clauses are represented in knowledgebases.

[6]The size of a theory is the number of symbols it contains.

EA(T)

Input: A positive HCF theory T. **Output:** A minimal model for T.

1. $M :=$ a model of T; $M' := \emptyset$.

2. Let Δ be the set of all clauses in T violated by M' such that for each $\delta \in \Delta$ $|\text{head}(\delta, M)| = 1$.
   If $\Delta = \emptyset$, go to step 3.
   Else, let $X := \bigcup_{\delta \in \Delta} \text{head}(\delta, M)$; $M' := M' + X$; $M := M - X$;
   repeat step 2.

3. Let Δ be the set of all clauses in T violated by M' such that for each $\delta \in \Delta$, $|\text{head}(\delta, M)| \geq 2$.
   If $\Delta = \emptyset$, return M'.
   Else, let $H := \bigcup_{\delta \in \Delta} \text{head}(\delta, M)$ and let $X \subset H$ be a nonempty source of H in the dependency graph of T; let $M := M - X$; go to step 2.

Figure 1: The elimination algorithm for HCF theories

models that are subsets of this model (Hence the name of the algorithm).

Given a directed graph G and a set of nodes Y in the graph, $X \subseteq Y$ will be called a *source of* Y iff (a) all the nodes in X are in the same strongly connected component[7] in G, and (b) for each node A in $Y - X$, there is no directed path in G from A to any of the nodes in X. Intuitively, if X is a source of Y in a dependency graph of some theory, then none of the atoms in $Y - X$ can be used to derive any of the atoms in X. During the execution of the EA, we sometimes need to eliminate from a model that is not minimal a subset of a set of atoms. We always delete a *source* of this set to prevent a situation where atoms that were already eliminated turn out to be part of a minimal model.

A set of atoms *satisfies the body of a clause* iff all the atoms in the body of the clause belong to this set. A set of atoms *violates a clause* iff the set satisfies the body of the clause but none of the atoms in the head of the clause belongs to the set. A set of atoms X is a *model* of a theory if none of its clauses is violated by X. A model X of a theory T is *minimal* if there is no $Y \subset X$ which is also a model of T. Given a set X, $|X|$ denotes the cardinality of X. The EA is shown in Figure 1. It uses the function head(), which is defined as follows: given a clause δ and a set of atoms M, $\text{head}(\delta, M)$ is the set of all atoms in M that belong to the head of δ.

The proof of the next theorem appears in the appendix. The proofs of the rest of the claims appear in the full version of the paper [Ben-Eliyahu and Palopoli, 1993].

---

[7]A strongly connected component C of a directed graph G is a maximal subgraph of G such that for each pair of nodes v_1 and v_2 in C, C contains both a directed path from v_1 to v_2 and a directed path from v_2 to v_1.

Theorem 2.2 (the EA is correct) *The EA generates a minimal model of the input theory.*

Theorem 2.3 (nondeterministic completeness) *If M is a minimal model of an HCF theory T, then there is an execution of the EA that outputs M.*

Theorem 2.4 (complexity) *The EA for HCF theories runs in time $O(n^2)$, where n is the size of the theory.*

The following example demonstrates how the EA works.

Example 2.5 *Suppose we have the theory*

1. $a \vee b$ 2. $b \supset a$ 3. $a \vee c$

And suppose we start the EA with $M = \{a, b, c\}$. At step 1 of the EA, $M' = \emptyset$. At step 2 we get that $\Delta = \emptyset$, because the clauses violated by M' are the first and third clauses, but both atoms in their head belong to M. Since Δ is empty, we go to step 3, and in step 3 we get $\Delta := \{a \vee b, a \vee c\}$. Since $\{b\}$ is a source of $\{a, b, c\}$ (note that $\{c\}$ is also a source), we delete $\{b\}$ from M and are left with $M = \{a, c\}$, and we go to step 2. In step 2 we now get $\Delta = \{a \vee b\}$, so we add $\{a\}$ to M' and delete $\{a\}$ from M, which leaves us with $M' = \{a\}$ and $M = \{c\}$. We then repeat step 2, but this time we get $\Delta = \emptyset$ (because none of the rules is violated by M') and so we go to step 3. In step 3 we also have $\Delta = \emptyset$, so the EA in this case returns $\{a\}$. Indeed, $\{a\}$ is a minimal model for the theory above.

The previous example is of a theory having only one minimal model. In the next example, the theory has several minimal models.

Example 2.6 *Suppose we have the theory*

1. $a \vee b$
2. $c \vee b$
3. $a \vee c$

And suppose we start the EA with $M = \{a, b, c\}$. At step 1 of the EA, $M' = \emptyset$. At step 2, we get that $\Delta = \emptyset$, because although all the clauses are violated by M', all the atoms in their head belong to M. Since Δ is empty, we go to step 3, and in step 3 we get $\Delta := \{\text{all the clauses}\}$. Since both $\{a\}$ and $\{b\}$ and $\{c\}$ are source of $\{a, b, c\}$, we can delete from M any one of them. Suppose we delete $\{b\}$. We are left with $M = \{a, c\}$, and we go to step 2. In step 2, we now get $\Delta = \{a \vee b, b \vee c\}$, so we add $\{a, c\}$ to M' and delete $\{a, c\}$ from M, which leaves us with $M' = \{a, c\}$ and $M = \emptyset$. We then repeat step 2, but this time we get $\Delta = \emptyset$, so we go to step 3. In step 3, we also have $\Delta = \emptyset$, so the EA in this case returns $\{a, c\}$. Indeed, $\{a, c\}$ is a minimal model for the theory above. It is easy to see that the EA could return $\{a, b\}$ or $\{b, c\}$, had we selected $\{c\}$ or $\{a\}$ as a source, respectively.

With minor modifications, the EA can also be used for model checking. This is due to the fact that if we start executing the EA with M initialized to some minimal model, this will be the model that it outputs. Hence:

Theorem 2.7 *The EA solves model checking for positive HCF theories in time $O(n^2)$, where n is the size of the theory.*

Also minimal membership is easier for HCF theories than in general:

Theorem 2.8 *Minimal membership for the class of positive HCF theories is NP-complete[8].*

Before closing this section, we would like to address an important issue raised by [Dechter, 1993]. Instead of representing a theory as a set of clauses of the form (1), we could have represented a theory as a set of clauses of the form

$$A_1 \wedge A_2 \wedge ... \wedge A_m \wedge \neg B_1 \wedge \neg B_2 \wedge ... \wedge \neg B_k \supset C \quad (2)$$

where all the A's, the B's, and the C's are atoms[9]. We could then identify the class of *stratified* theories in a way that is parallel to the way stratified knowledgebases are defined[10]. It is well known that if a logic program is stratified, a minimal model for this program (namely, the one coinciding with its *perfect* model) can be found in linear time [Apt et al., 1988]. Therefore, it is quite immediate that a minimal model for stratified theories can be found also in linear time. But what is the relation between HCF theories and stratified theories? Our conclusion is that HCF theories are strictly more general than stratified theories. By a simple local syntactic transformation, namely, by moving all the B's to the head (as disjunctions), every stratified theory (with no clauses with empty heads) can be converted into a positive HCF theory. For example, the stratified theory $\{\neg a \supset b, \neg b \supset c\}$ is logically equivalent to the HCF theory $\{a \vee b, b \vee c\}$. However, as the following example illustrates, there is no such straightforward local translation of positive HCF theories into stratified theories.[11]

Example 2.9 *Consider the following HCF theory T:*

$$a \vee b, \quad a \supset c \quad b \vee c$$

The following theory, T', is obtained by moving all but one of the atoms from the head of the clause to the body:

$$\neg b \supset a, \quad a \supset c \quad \neg c \supset b$$

However, T' is not stratified.

Moreover, note that while the algorithm for stratified theories will yield one specific model, the EA is capable of generating any minimal model and can also be used for model checking. Another interesting observation is that the class of Horn theories, for which a unique minimal model can be found in linear time [Dowling and Gallier, 1984, Itai and Makowsky, 1987], intersects the class of HCF theories but neither of these classes includes one other[12].

3 The elimination algorithm for first-order HCF theories

In this section we show how we can generalize the EA so that it can be used to perform efficiently both model checking and model finding on a *first-order* positive HCF theory.

One way to go is to write an algorithm that is similar to the one presented in figure 1 but works on first-order theories. If we restrict our attention to positive theories only, such an algorithm would work exactly like the algorithm we present in the next section. In this section, however, we present a different variation of the EA. The version presented here does not require to construct an arbitrary model before finding a minimal one.

We will now refer to a theory as a set of clauses of the form

$$\forall(X_1, ..., X_n) A_1 \wedge A_2 \wedge ... \wedge A_m \supset C_1 \vee C_2 \vee ... \vee C_n \quad (3)$$

where all the A's and the C's are atoms in a *first-order* language with no function symbols, and $X_1, ..., X_n$ are all the variables that appear in the clause. We will often write (3) simply as

$$A_1 \wedge A_2 \wedge ... \wedge A_m \supset C_1 \vee C_2 \vee ... \vee C_n, \quad (4)$$

keeping in mind that all the variables are universally quantified. The definitions of head, body, and positive theories are the same as for propositional theories. In the expression $p(X_1, ..., X_n)$, p is called a *predicate name*.

As in the propositional case, with every theory T we associate a directed graph G_T, called the *dependency graph* of T, in which (a) each predicate name in T is a node and (b) there is an arc directed from a node A to a node C iff there is a clause in T in which A is a

---

[8]Membership in NP was already shown in [Ben-Eliyahu and Dechter, 1992]; we show NP-hardness.

[9][Schaerf, 1993] advocates a semantics for positive disjunctive databases which is based on considering all normal logic programs that can be obtained from the database using this transformation.

[10]For a formal definition of stratification see next section.

[11]Actually, another variation of the elimination algorithm can be used for finding for each HCF theory an equivalent stratified theory that can be obtained by shifting all but one of the atoms from the head to the body.

[12]Consider, for example, the theories $T_1 = \{a\}$, $T_2 = \{\neg a\}$, $T_3 = \{a \vee b\}$: T_1 is both Horn and positive HCF, T_2 is Horn but not positive, and T_3 is positive HCF but not Horn.

EA$_\mathcal{F}$(T)

Input: A safe first-order positive HCF theory T. **Output:** A minimal Herbrand model for T.

1. $M := \emptyset$.
2. Let Δ be the set of all instances of definite clauses in T not satisfied by M. If $\Delta = \emptyset$, go to step 3. Else, let $X := \bigcup_{\delta \in \Delta} \text{head}(\delta)$; $M := M + X$; repeat step 2.
3. Let Δ be the set of all instances of disjunctive clauses in T not satisfied by M. If $\Delta = \emptyset$, return M. Else, let $H := \bigcup_{\delta \in \Delta} \text{name-head}(\delta)$, and let $X \subset H$ be a nonempty source of all the predicate names in H in the dependency graph of T; from each δ in T, delete from the head all atoms with predicate names that appear in X; goto step 2.

Figure 2: The elimination algorithm for safe first-order HCF theories

predicate name in one of the A_i's and C is a predicate name in one of the C_i's.

A theory will be called *safe* if each of its rules is safe. A rule is *safe* iff all the variables that appear in its head also appear in its body. In this section we assume that theories are safe and positive. A theory T is HCF iff there is no clause of the form (3) in T such that for some C_i and C_j, $i \neq j$, G_T contains a directed cycle involving the predicate name of C_i and the predicate name of C_j.

Fact 3.1 *Head-cycle freeness of a theory of size[13] n can be checked in time $O(n^2)$.*

3.1 Model finding

In figure 2 we present a variation of the EA, called EA$_\mathcal{F}$ ($\mathcal{F}$ for "first-order"), that computes a minimal Herbrand model [14] of a positive first-order HCF theory. The algorithm EA$_\mathcal{F}$ uses the functions head() and name-head(). Given a clause δ, head(δ) will return the set of atoms that appear in the head of δ, and name-head(δ) will return the set of predicate names that appear in the head of δ. Thus, for example, if $\delta = a(X) \vee b(X) \leftarrow c(X)$, head($\delta$) = $\{a(X), b(X)\}$, and name-head(δ) = $\{a, b\}$.

A clause is called *definite* iff it contains exactly one atom in the head. We call a clause *disjunctive* iff it contains at least two atoms in the head.

---
[13]The size of a theory is the number of symbols it contains.

[14]The set of all atoms constructed using predicate names and constants from a given theory T is called a Herbrand base of T. A Herbrand model of T is a subset of the Herbrand base that satisfies all the instances of the clauses of the theory.

The proofs for the following claims appear in the full version of the paper [Ben-Eliyahu and Palopoli, 1993].

Theorem 3.2 (EA$_\mathcal{F}$ is correct) *EA$_\mathcal{F}$ generates a minimal Herbrand model of the input theory.*

The following example shows how EA$_\mathcal{F}$ works.

Example 3.3 *Suppose we have the theory*

1. $a(s) \vee b(s)$ 2. $b(X) \supset a(X)$
3. $a(s) \vee c(s)$ 4. $a(X) \supset d(X)$

At step 1 of the EA, $M = \emptyset$. At step 2 we get that $\Delta = \emptyset$, because the clauses that are violated by M are 1 and 3 but they are not definite. Since Δ is empty, we go to step 3, and in step 3 we get $\Delta = \{a(s) \vee b(s), a(s) \vee c(s)\}$. Since $\{b\}$ is a source of $\{a, b, c\}$ (note that $\{c\}$ is also a source), we delete $\{b(s)\}$ from clause 1, and are left with the theory $\{a(s), b(X) \supset a(X), a(s) \vee c(s), a(X) \supset d(X)\}$, and we go to step 2. In step 2 we now get $\Delta = \{a(s)\}$, so we add $a(s)$ to M, and repeat step 2. Since now $M = \{a(s)\}$, the only instance of a clause violated by M is $a(s) \supset d(s)$ (which we get by instantiating X to s in clause 4). So we add $d(s)$ to M and get $M = \{a(s), d(s)\}$. Since there are no more instances of a clause violated by M, the algorithm will stop and return M. Indeed, $\{a(s), d(s)\}$ is a minimal Herbrand model for the theory above.

The complexity of the EA for first-order HCF theories can be analyzed using the same principles by which the *data complexity* of a query language over a relational database under some fixed semantics is defined [Vardi, 1982].

A given safe first-order theory T can be divided into two disjoint sets [Reiter, 1978]: the *intentional* component, which represents the reasoning component of the theory, and the *extensional* component, which represents the collection of facts in the theory. For our purposes, the extensional part of a given theory T, denoted T_E, is the set of all clauses with an empty body and grounded atoms only in the head, and the intentional part of T, denoted T_I, is simply $T - T_E$. For example, in the theory presented in example 3.3, clauses 1 and 3 form the extensional component, and clauses 2 and 4 form the intentional component. If we analyze how the complexity of EA$_\mathcal{F}$ changes when we fix T_I and vary T_E, we discover the following:

Theorem 3.4 *Using the algorithm EA$_\mathcal{F}$, a minimal model of a safe first-order HCF theory $T(T_E) = T_I \bigcup T_E$ can be found in time polynomial in the size of T_E.*

Note that this variation of the EA is not nondeterministically complete, that is, there are some minimal models that cannot be generated by this algorithm.

---

model-check(T, M)

Input: A safe first-order positive HCF theory T, and a Herbrand model M. **Output:** If M is a minimal Herbrand model for T — YES, else — NO.

1. $M' := \emptyset$.
2. Let Δ be the set of all instances of clauses in T violated by M. If $\Delta \neq \emptyset$ return NO (* M is not a model *).
3. Let Δ be the set of all instances of clauses in T violated by M' such that for each $\delta \in \Delta$, $|\text{head}(\delta, M)| == 1$. If $\Delta = \emptyset$, go to step 4.
   Else, let $X := \bigcup_{\delta \in \Delta} \text{head}(\delta, M)$; $M' := M' + X$; repeat step 3.
4. If $M == M'$ return YES; else, return NO.

Figure 3: Model checking for safe first-order HCF theories

Consider, for example, the theory $T = \{a \lor c, b \land c \supset a\}$. Clearly, both $\{a\}$ and $\{c\}$ are minimal models of T, but since $\{c\}$ is a source of $\{a\}$ in the dependency graph of T, the model $\{c\}$ will never be generated by the algorithm in figure 2. Note, however, that both the algorithm in figure 1, and the algorithm in figure 4 (Section 4.1) are nondeterministically complete and that both have an execution that outputs $\{c\}$. We conjecture that algorithm $EA_{\mathcal{F}}$ can generate any minimal model that is also a minimal model of a *stratified* theory which is logically equivalent to the input theory.

3.2 Model checking

The algorithm model-check in figure 3 performs model checking for safe first-order positive HCF theories. Note that in contrast with the EA in figure 1 this algorithm does not use the dependency graph of the theory.

Theorem 3.5 (correctness) *Given an HCF safe theory T and a Herbrand model M, model-check(T, M) will return YES iff M is a minimal Herbrand model of T.*

Again, by distinguishing between the extensional and intentional componenets of the theory, we can show that algorithm model check is efficient.

Theorem 3.6 (complexity) *Model checking for a safe first-order HCF theory $T(T_E) = T_E \bigcup T_I$ can be done in time polynomial in the size of T_E.*

4 Applications of the elimination algorithm

4.1 Application to disjunctive knowledgebases

In this section we will show that a variation of the EA can be used to efficiently answer queries posed on disjunctive knowledgebases. We will refer to a *disjunctive knowledgebase* (DKB) as a finite set of rules of the form

$$C_1 \mid C_2 \mid \ldots \mid C_n \longleftarrow A_1, \ldots, A_m, \text{not } B_1, \ldots, \text{not } B_k \quad (5)$$

where all the A's, the B's, and the C's are atoms over a first-order language with no function symbols. Without loss of generality, we assume that all of the C's are different. The symbol " $\mid$ " is used instead of the classical "$\lor$" in order to emphasize that here disjunction is used in a slightly different manner than in classical logic. The B's are called negative predicates, the A's — positive predicates.

A DKB is a *positive* DKB iff $k = 0$. A DKB will be called *safe* if each of its rules is safe. A rule is *safe* iff all the variables that appear in its head or in negative predicates in its body appear also in positive predicates in its body. So, for example, the rule $b(X) \longleftarrow \text{not } a(X)$ is not safe, while the rule $b(X) \longleftarrow c(X), \text{not } a(X)$ is. In this section we restrict our attention to safe DKBs. The dependency graph of a DKB KB, denoted G_{KB}, is defined similarly to that of a theory: Each predicate name in KB is a node, and there is an arc directed from a node A to a node C iff there is a rule in KB in which A is a predicate name in one of the A_i's and C is a predicate name in one of the C_i's. Note that when we construct the dependency graph, the B_i's in (5) are ignored. A *Head-cycle-free* DKB (HDKB) is also defined in analogy to HCF theories: a DKB KB is HCF iff there is no rule of the form (5) in KB such that for some C_i and C_j, $i \neq j$, G_T contains a directed cycle involving the predicate name of C_i and the predicate name of C_j.

Fact 4.1 *Head-cycle freeness of a DKB of size n can be checked in time $O(n^2)$.*

Following [Przymusinski, 1988], we define a *stratified* DKB (SDKB) to be a DKB where it is possible to partition the set S of predicate names into subsets $\{S_0, \ldots, S_r\}$, called *strata*, such that for each rule δ of the form (5),

1. all the C's that appear in the head of δ have the same stratum index c,
2. the strata indexes associated with the A's are smaller than or equal to c, and
3. the strata indexes associated with the B's are strictly smaller than c.

So, each SDKB KB is associated with at least one partition of its predicate names into strata. For every feasible stratification $\{S_0, \ldots, S_r\}$ of KB's predicate names ($r \geq 1$), we can partition the rules of KB into corresponding subsets $\{KB_1, \ldots, KB_r\}$ such that KB_i contains the rules having in their heads predicates that are in the stratum S_i. (We assume w.l.o.g. that S_0 contains the predicates not appearing in the head of any rule.)

A *model* for a DKB is a subset M of its Herbrand

base[15] having the property that, for every rule in the grounded knowledgebase, if all the atoms in the body of the rule belong to M, then at least one of the atoms in the head of the rule belongs to M.

Several different semantics have been proposed for DKBs [Przymusinski, 1988, Przymusinski, 1991, C. Baral and Minker, 1991, Gelfond and Lifschitz, 1991, Dix, 1992]. Notably, all these semantics agree on identifying the minimal models of a *positive* DKB to define its intended meaning. The same holds for stratified knowledgebases: all the semantics that handle SDKBs agree on identifying the *stable* models of a SKDB as its intended meaning. Intuitively, a model for a DKB is stable if it is minimal and if you can prove each atom in the model using the rules in the knowledgebase. Formally:

Definition 4.2 (stable model)
[Gelfond and Lifschitz, 1991]

Suppose KB is a variable-free DKB. If KB has no occurrence of "not", then the set of all its stable models is the set of all its minimal models.

If "not" occurs in KB, then its stable models are defined as follows: for any subset S of the atoms in KB, define KB^S to be the DKB obtained from KB by deleting

1. *all formulas of the form "not B" where $B \notin S$ from the body of each rule and*
2. *each rule that has in its body a formula "not B" for some $B \in S$.*

If S is one of the minimal models of KB^S (KB^S has no "not"), then we say that S is a stable model of KB. To apply the definition to a DKB with variables, we first have to replace each rule with its grounded instances.

A DKB may have none or several stable models. We claim that sometimes it is enough to compute only one arbitrary stable model of a DKB. For example, consider the following DKB KB that solves the 3-colorability of a graph represented in an obvious way by the relations vertex() and edge() (g, y, and r stands for green, yellow, and red, respectively):

$color(X,g) \mid color(X,r) \mid color(X,y) \longleftarrow vertex(X)$
$\quad ERROR \longleftarrow edge(X,Y), color(X,Z), color(Y,Z)$
$\quad\quad\quad color(X,r) \longleftarrow vertex(X), ERROR$
$\quad\quad\quad color(X,y) \longleftarrow vertex(X), ERROR$
$\quad\quad\quad color(X,g) \longleftarrow vertex(X), ERROR$

The reader can verify that the graph is not 3-colorable iff every stable model of KB contains the atom ERROR, and if the graph is colorable, each of the stable

---

EA*(KB)
Input: An SHDKB KB.
Output: A stable model for KB.

1. Partition KB into strata $KB_1, \ldots, KB_r$.
2. $M := \emptyset$.
3. For $i:=1$ to r, do:
   (a) Let Δ_i be the set of all instances of rules from KB_i that are not satisfied by M.
   (b) Eliminate all the negative literals from the rules in Δ_i.
   (c) $M' := EA(\Delta_i \cup \{P \longleftarrow \mid P \in M\})$.
   If $M' \neq M$, then set $M := M'$ and goto step 3 (a).

Figure 4: The elimination algorithm for SHDKBs

---

models of KB will encode a legal coloring of the graph. Therefore, to solve the 3-colorability of a graph, it is enough to compute an arbitrary stable model of KB.

The previous DKB is not HCF. Here is an example of a HDKB:

Example 4.3 *The CEO of a company decides that a Christmas sweepstakes is to be held, with one prize of 10,000 dollars to be divided among the winners; the only constraint is that no two winners be employed by the same department. Each stable model of the following stratified HDKB encodes a feasible outcome of the sweepstakes, and therefore it is enough to consider one arbitrary stable model of the knowledgebase. The knowledgebase assumes the existence of the 2-place predicate* inDep, *where* inDep(D, X) *is true iff X works in department D*[16].

$eliminate(X) \mid eliminate(Y) \longleftarrow inDep(D,X),$
$\quad\quad\quad\quad\quad\quad\quad\quad\quad\quad\quad\quad\quad inDep(D,Y),$
$\quad\quad\quad\quad\quad\quad\quad\quad\quad\quad\quad\quad\quad X \neq Y$
$\quad\quad\quad candidate(X) \longleftarrow inDep(D,X),$
$\quad\quad\quad\quad\quad\quad\quad\quad\quad\quad\quad\quad\quad not\ eliminate(X)$
$\quad win(X) \mid noWin(X) \longleftarrow candidate(X)$

In figure 4 we show an algorithm called EA*, which computes one arbitrary stable model of a stratified HDKB (denoted SHDKB). The basic idea is to partition the DKB according to its stratification and then call the EA on each subset in the order implied by the stratification.

Note that EA* calls the EA as a subroutine. In fact, any other polynomial algorithm capable of computing one minimal model of a propositional positive HCF

---

[15] Roughly speaking, the Herbrand base of a knowledgebase is the set of all grounded atoms that can be formed out of symbols appearing in the knowledgebase.

[16] In the full paper [Ben-Eliyahu and Palopoli, 1993] we analyze in detail how this knowledgebase performs this task.

theory could be used in place of the EA without influencing any of the properties of EA*. As yet, however, the EA is the only algorithm that we know of that can perform this task in polynomial time on the entire class of propositional positive HCF theories. Properties of EA* are summarized next.

Theorem 4.4 *Let KB be an SHDKB. Then:*

1. *(correctness) EA* generates a stable model of KB.*
2. *(nondeterministic completeness) If M is a stable model of KB, then there is an execution of the EA* that outputs M.*

Corollary 4.5 *Let KB be a nondisjunctive stratified knowledgebase. Then EA*(KB) yields the unique stable model for KB.*

The following example shows how the EA* works.

Example 4.6 *Suppose that we have the following stratified knowledgebase KB:*

1. $a(s) \mid b(s) \longleftarrow$ 2. $c(X) \longleftarrow b(X), not\, a(X)$
3. $a(r) \mid b(r) \longleftarrow$ 4. $d(X) \mid e(X) \longleftarrow c(X)$

Assume we adopt the following stratification: $S_0 = \emptyset$, $S_1 = \{a, b\}$, $S_2 = \{c, d, e\}$. At step 1 of the EA, we compute the rule stratification. In this case, KB_1 consists of the first and third rules, and KB_2 consists of rules 2 and 4. After setting $M = \emptyset$ (step 2), we start the for loop in step 3. In step 3a, Δ_1 is set to KB_1, and it is not changed after step 3b. In step 3c, we apply the EA to Δ_1. Assume that $EA(\Delta_1) = \{a(r), b(s)\}$. Since we get $M' \neq M$, we set M to $\{a(r), b(s)\}$ and go to step 3a. Since now both rules in KB_1 are satisfied by M, nothing is changed in steps 3b and 3c and we repeat the for loop in step 3 with $i = 2$. In step 3a, Δ_2 is instantiated to $\{c(s) \longleftarrow b(s) not\, a(s)\}$. In step 3b, Δ_2 is set to be $\{c(s) \longleftarrow b(s)\}$ (since $a(s)$ is not in M), and in step 3c, the EA is called to find a minimal model of the theory $\{a(r), b(s), c(s) \longleftarrow b(s)\}$. The EA will then return $\{a(r), b(s), c(s)\}$, and since $M' \neq M$ we go to step 3a. Δ_2 will be now set to $\{d(s) \mid e(s) \longleftarrow c(s)\}$, and it will not be changed in step 3b. In step 3c, the EA will be called with the theory $\{a(r), b(s), c(s), d(s) \mid e(s) \longleftarrow c(s)\}$, and suppose that it will return $\{a(r), b(s), c(s), d(s)\}$. Again, we get that $M' \neq M$ and will go to step 3a. This time, Δ_2 will be set to $\emptyset$ in steps 3a and 3b and therefore the algorithm will stop with M unchanged. Indeed, $\{a(r), b(s), c(s), d(s)\}$ is a minimal model of KB. The reader can verify that for every other minimal Herbrand model of KB, there is an execution of EA* that returns this model.*

As in the case of first-order theories (Section 3), a given SHDKB KB can be divided into two disjoint sets [Reiter, 1978]: the *intentional* component, which represents the reasoning component of the knowledge base, and the *extensional* component, which represents the collection of facts in the database. For our purposes, the extensional part of a given KDB KB, denoted KB_E, is the set of body-free rules such that all the predicates that appear in the head are grounded, and the intentional part of KB, denoted KB_I, is simply $KB - KB_E$. If we analyze how the complexity of the EA* changes when we fix KB_I and vary KB_E, we discover the following:

Theorem 4.7 *Using the EA*, a stable model of an SHDKB $KB(KB_E) = KB_I \bigcup KB_E$ can be found in time polynomial in the size of KB_E.*

When applied to *propositional* SHDKBs, EA* is polynomial in the size of the entire knowledgebase:

Theorem 4.8 *Using the EA*, a stable model of a propositional SHDKB can be found in time $O(n^2)$, where n is the size of the knowledgebase.*

4.2 Application to disjunctive default logic

Disjunctive default logic is a generalization of Reiter's default logic introduced by [Gelfond et al., 1991] in order to overcome some of the difficulties that Reiter's default logic has when dealing with disjunctive information. Gelfond et al. define a *disjunctive default theory* as a set of disjunctive defaults. A *disjunctive default* is an expression of the form

$$\frac{\alpha : \beta_1, ..., \beta_n}{\gamma_1 | ... | \gamma_m} \quad (6)$$

where $\alpha, \beta_1, ..., \beta_n$, and $\gamma_1, ..., \gamma_m$ are quantifier-free formulas in some *first-order* language. Gelfond et al. define an extension for a disjunctive default theory Δ to be one of the minimal deductively closed set of sentences E' satisfying the condition[17] that, for any grounded instance of a default (6) from Δ, if $\alpha \in E'$ and $\neg\beta_1, ..., \neg\beta_n \notin E$, then for some $1 \leq i \leq m$, $\gamma_i \in E'$.

Let us now consider the subset of disjunctive default theories that we call *disjunctive default programs*. A *disjunctive default program* (DDP) is a set of defaults of the form

$$\frac{A_1 \wedge ... \wedge A_m : \neg B_1, ..., \neg B_k}{C_1 | ... | C_n} \quad (7)$$

in which each of the A's, the B's, and the C's is an atom with no function symbols and $n > 0$. Each such DDP Δ can be associated with a DKB KB_Δ by replacing each default of the form (7) with the rule $C_1 | ... | C_n \longleftarrow A_1, ..., A_m, not\, B_1, ..., not\, B_k$.

The following theorem implies that all the techniques and complexity results established with respect to DKBs also apply to DDPs.

Theorem 4.9 *[Gelfond et al., 1991] Let Δ be a DDP. The logical closure of E is an extension of Δ iff E is a stable model of KB_Δ.*

---
[17]Note the appearance of E in the condition.

So, in particular, we can conclude that for the class of DDPs computing an extension is $P^{NP[O(\log n)]}$-hard, checking whether a set of atoms is an extension is co-NP-hard, and deciding whether an atom belongs to some extension is Σ_2^p-hard.

Let us call a DDP *completely ordered* iff its corresponding DKB is stratified and head-cycle free[18]. Then, using the results in previous sections, we can identify subclasses of DDPs that are more manageable than the whole class of DDPs.

Theorem 4.10 *Let Δ be a propositional completely ordered DDP, and let n be its size[19]. Then:*
1. *An extension for Δ can be found in time $O(n^2)$.*
2. *We can check whether a set of atoms is an extension of Δ in time $O(n^2)$.*
3. *Deciding whether an atom belongs to some extension of Δ is NP-complete.*

Using the results of [Ben-Eliyahu and Dechter, 1992], one can easily show that each completely ordered DDP Δ corresponds to a default theory Δ' in the sense of Reiter, such that E is an extension of Δ iff it is an extension of Δ'. Using this observation, we show in the full paper how theorem 4.10 leads to the discovery of tractable subsets of Reiter's default theories.

The results of this paper can also be extended to deal with first-order disjunctive default theories, using the same principles by which the EA for CNF propositional theories was generalized to deal with first-order theories.

5 Expressive power of stratified knowledgebases

Since we can compute a stable model of an SHDKB in polynomial time, it is clear that unless we discover that $P = NP$, we cannot encode either NP-hard or co-NP-hard problems in an SHDKB in such a way that any stable model of the SHDKB will provide a solution to the problem. Nevertheless, we will show in this section that the class of SHDKBs (under stable model semantics) is quite expressive. We believe that this indicates that the class of HCF theories identified in Sections 2 and 3 are a significant subclass of all CNF theories.

The expressive power of logic languages has been given a lot of attention in database theory recently (see [Abiteboul and Vianu, 1992] for a survey). Following the database theory approach, we define a (non-deterministic) query to be a generic transformation from an input database to a set of output relations, each of which denotes a possible outcome of the query on the database. For the sake of this exposition, we will assume that a database is a relational database that can be viewed as a knowledgebase in an obvious way (i. e. , each relation is a predicate name, and each tuple $(c_1,\ldots,c_n)$ in the relation P is represented by a body-free rule $P(c_1,\ldots,c_n)\leftarrow$). We can also conversely look at a set of atoms as denoting a relational database, in the obvious way.

A knowledgebase can be viewed as a mapping of an input database into a set of output databases. Given an input database DB and a knowledgebase KB, the set of output databases is defined (under the stable model semantics) to be the set of all stable models of $KB \bigcup DB$. Viewing the knowledgebase as such a mapping, we shall say that an SHDKB KB expresses a query Q (under the stable model semantics) iff, for every database DB, $(R \in Q(DB)) \Leftrightarrow (\exists M$ stable model of $DB \bigcup KB$ such that $R \in M)$. We shall say that an SHDKB KB weakly expresses a query Q (under the stable model semantics) iff, for every database DB, $(R \in Q(DB)) \Rightarrow (\exists M$ stable model of $DB \bigcup KB$ such that $R \in M)$. Less formally, we will say that an SHDKB KB (resp. weakly) expresses a query Q under the stable model semantics iff for every database DB, every (resp. some) stable model(s) of $KB \bigcup DB$ encodes a possible result of the query, and, conversely, each possible result of the query is encoded in some stable model.

Stratified knowledgebases (under the stable model semantics) are capable of expressing all polynomial time computable queries if a total ordering of the domain (the set of all constants in the input database) is provided [Papadimitriou, 1985, Ben-Eliyahu and Palopoli, 1994]. So, in the case where this ordering is available, SHDKB's under stable model semantics would express all polynomial time queries, since the class of SHDKBs is a superset of the class of stratified knowledgebases. However, it is known that stratified knowledgebases are not expressive enough to "construct" an ordering on the domain if the ordering is not available. We leave it open whether SHDKBs are expressive enough to construct such an ordering. In the full paper we show that any polynomial time query can be *weakly* expressed by an SHDKB under the stable model semantics[20]. The above discussion is summarized in the following theorem:

Theorem 5.1

1. *For every polynomial time computable query Q there exists an $SHDKB$ KB that weakly expresses Q under the stable model semantics.*

2. *For every polynomial time computable query Q over an input database with an ordered domain,*

---

[18]In the full paper we define "completely ordered" DDPs directly, i. e. , without first mapping them to their corresponding knowledgebases.

[19]We measure the size of a DDP by the number of symbols it contains.

[20]The proof is based on simulating the well-known *witness* operator [Abiteboul and Vianu, 1992] using an SHDKB.

there exists an $SHDKB$ KB that expresses Q under the stable model semantics.

6 Related work

The class of head-cycle-free DKBs was introduced by [Ben-Eliyahu and Dechter, 1992], where it was shown that queries on propositional HDKBs can be answered by solving the classical satisfiability problem. Cadoli [Cadoli, 1992, Cadoli, 1991] has described a partition of the set of propositional theories into classes for which model finding and model checking is tractable or NP-hard. His partition is based on considering the set of logical relations that correspond to the theory, and it is not clear whether these tractable classes can be identified effectively. Other efficient algorithms for finding minimal models of propositional CNF theories can be found in [Ben-Eliyahu and Dechter, 1993]. The expressive power of the tractable subsets identified in both of the above works was not analyzed yet.

7 Conclusion

The task of computing minimal models is of interest to the AI community as well as to the logic programming community. In circumscription, default logic, diagnosis, and commonsense reasoning in general, the task of computing minimal models has been proven to be crucial to speeding up the reasoning process.

In this paper we have introduced the *elimination algorithm*, which performs in polynomial time minimal model finding and minimal model checking for a significant subclass of CNF theories. We have demonstrated how variations of the elimination algorithm can be applied for answering queries posed on disjunctive knowledgebases and disjunctive default theories in an efficient way, and we have shown that the tractable classes identified in this paper are quite expressive.

It has been argued that sometimes it is useful to use a "vivid" form of the knowledge in order to perform deductions rapidly, where a vivid form of a theory would be some data structure in which the information is stored in a way that enables fast answers to commonly asked queries [Levesque, 1986]. One appealing idea, suggested by [Halpern and Vardi, 1991], [Papadimitriou, 1991], and others, is that a vivid form of a theory need only be a model of the theory. In this case, deduction can be replaced by model checking, which is often the much easier task. Since a theory might have an exponential number of models, only the models that "best" represent the theory, namely, the models that are the closest to the real world, should be selected. One approach, adopted in circumscription, for example, is to select the minimal models of a theory as its vivid form. We argue, as do others [Giannotti et al., 1991, Saccá and Zaniolo, 1990, Abiteboul et al., 1990], that sometimes even only one arbitrary minimal model of a theory can be used for fast query answering. The work presented here is a step toward efficient implementation of such ideas.

Appendix

A Proofs

First, we need to present some definitions and known theorems.

Following [Ben-Eliyahu and Dechter, 1992], we define a *proof* of an atom to be a sequence of clauses that can be used to derive the atom from the theory. Formally, an atom A has a *proof* w.r.t. a set of atoms M and a theory T iff there is a sequence of clauses $\delta_1, ..., \delta_n$ from T such that

1. for each clause δ_i, one and only one of the atoms that appear in its head belongs to M (this atom will be denoted $h_M(\delta_i)$),

2. $A = h_M(\delta_n)$,

3. the body of each δ_i is satisfied by M, and

4. δ_1 has an empty body and, for each $i > 1$, each atom that appears positive in the body of δ_i is equal to $h_M(\delta_j)$ for some $1 \leq j < i$.

The following theorem, by Ben-Eliyahu and Dechter, will be used to prove the correctness of the elimination algorithm:

Theorem A.1 *[Ben-Eliyahu and Dechter, 1992] A set of atoms M is a minimal model of an HCF theory T iff*

1. *M satisfies each clause in T, and*

2. *for each atom A in M, there is a proof of A w.r.t T and M.*

Proof of Theorem 2.2

First, we prove the following Lemma:

Lemma A.2 *The following invariants hold throughout the execution of the algorithm EA:*

1. *Every atom in M' has a proof w.r.t M' and T.*

2. *For each clause violated by M', there is an atom in its head that belongs to M.*

It is easy to observe that claim no. 1 holds – we start the algorithm with $M' = \emptyset$ and whenever we add an atom A to M' it is the case that there is a clause δ in T such that all the atoms in the body of δ belong to M' and A is the only atom in the head of δ which belong to $M \bigcup M'$. Atoms are added to M' only if they belong to M. Therefore, we conclude each atom in M' there is a proof w.r.t T and M'.

Claim no. 2 sure holds when we finish step 1 of the algorithm, because M is a model of T. Now we will show that if the claim holds just before we execute the command "$M := M - X$" in steps 2 and 3, it holds after we execute this command. Suppose we have executed the command $M := M - X$ in step 2. Divide the group of clauses violated by M' before executing the command into two groups: in group A there are all the clauses violated by M' which have and atom from X in their head. In group B there are clauses violated by M' which do not have an atom from X in their head. Since just before executing the command $M := M - X$ in step 2 we did $M' := M' + X$, group A must be empty. Since before executing $M := M - X$ for each clause in group B there was an atom in its head that belonged to M, also after executing $M := M - X$ it must be the case that for each atom in group B there was an atom in its head that belongs to M.

Now, suppose we execute the command $M := M - X$ in step 3. Note that before executing this command it is the case that all the clauses in Δ, the set of all clauses violated by M, has at least two atoms that belong to M. Now, it cannot be the case that there are two atoms from the head of the same clause that belong to X, because T is head-cycle-free and all the atoms in X are in the same strongly connected component in the dependency graph of T. So it must be the case that after executing the command $M := M - X$ in step 3 claim no. 2 holds.

Now to the proof of theorem 2.2:

It is easy to see that the elimination algorithm terminates. It is enough to show then that when the algorithm terminates, M' is a minimal model of T. By Theorem A.1, it is enough to show that when the EA terminates,

1. M' is a model, and
2. every atom in M' has a proof w.r.t M' and T.

We proved in Lemma A.2 that (2) holds. In view of Lemma A.2 (2), it is easy to see that (1) holds as well. Hence, M' is a minimal model of T. □

Acknowledgments

The authors gratefully acknowledge Marco Cadoli, Rina Dechter, Thomas Eiter, Georg (Giorgio) Gottlob, Victor Vianu, and Victoria Zemlyanker for useful suggestions and discussions (some through e-mail). Special thanks to Carlo Zaniolo for numerous discussions about database theory which have been an invaluable source of insight and inspiration. Thanks also to Michelle Bonnice for editing.

The work of the first author was supported in part by grants NSF IRI-88-21444 and AFOSR 90-0136. The second author is supported in part by the Consiglio Nazionale delle Ricerche, Italy.

References

[Abiteboul et al., 1990] Abiteboul, S., Simon, E., and Vianu, V. (1990). Non-deterministic languages to express deterministic transformations. In *Proc. ACM PODS*, pages 218–229.

[Abiteboul and Vianu, 1992] Abiteboul, S. and Vianu, V. (1992). *Expressive power of query languages*. Theoretical Studies in Computer Science. Academic Press.

[Apt et al., 1988] Apt, K., Blair, H., and Walker, A. (1988). Towards a theory of declarative knowledge. In Minker, J., editor, *Foundations of deductive databases and logic programs*, pages 89–148. Morgan Kaufmann.

[Bell et al., 1991] Bell, C., Nerode, A., Ng, R., and Subrahmanian, V. (1991). Computation and implementation of non-monotonic deductive databases. Technical Report CS-TR-2801, University of Maryland.

[Ben-Eliyahu and Dechter, 1992] Ben-Eliyahu, R. and Dechter, R. (1992). Propositional semantics for disjunctive logic programs. In *JICSLP-92: Proceedings of the 1992 joint international conference and symposium on logic programming*, Washington, D.C. To appear in a special issue of *Annals of Mathematics and AI* on disjunctive logic programs.

[Ben-Eliyahu and Dechter, 1993] Ben-Eliyahu, R. and Dechter, R. (1993). On computing minimal models. In *AAAI-93: Proceedings of the 11th national conference on artificial intelligence*, pages 2–8, Washington, DC, USA. submitted for a journal publication.

[Ben-Eliyahu and Palopoli, 1993] Ben-Eliyahu, R. and Palopoli, L. (1993). Reasoning with minimal models: Efficient algorithms and applications. Technical Report R-201, Cognitive Systems Lab, UCLA. In preparation.

[Ben-Eliyahu and Palopoli, 1994] Ben-Eliyahu, R. and Palopoli, L. (1994). On the expressive power of stratified datalog. In preparation.

[C. Baral and Minker, 1991] C. Baral, J. L. and Minker, J. (1991). WF^3: A semantics for negation in normal disjunctive logic programs. In Raz, Z. and Zemankova, M., editors, *Methodologies for intelligent systems*, pages 459–468. Springer.

[Cadoli, 1991] Cadoli, M. (1991). The complexity of model checking for circumscriptive formulae. Technical Report RAP.15.91, Università di Roma "La Sapienza", Dipartimento di Informatica e Sistemistica. To appear in *Information Processing Letters*.

[Cadoli, 1992] Cadoli, M. (1992). On the complexity of model finding for nonmonotonic propositional logics. In Marchetti Spaccamela, A., Mentrasti, P., and Venturini Zilli, M., editors, *Proceedings of the 4th Italian conference on theoretical computer science*, pages 125–139. World Scientific Publishing Co.

[Chen and Toda, 1993] Chen, Z. and Toda, S. (1993). The complexity of selecting maximal solutions. In *Proc. 8th IEEE Int. Conf. on Structures in Complexity Theory*, pages 313–325.

[de Kleer et al., 1992] de Kleer, J., Mackworth, A., and Reiter, R. (1992). Characterizing diagnosis and systems. *Artificial Intelligence*, 56:197–222.

[de Kleer and Williams, 1987] de Kleer, J. and Williams, B. (1987). Diagnosis multiple faults. *Artificial Intelligence*, 32:97–130.

[Dechter, 1993] Dechter, R. (1993). Personal communication.

[Dix, 1992] Dix, J. (1992). Classifying semantics of disjunctive logic programs. In *JICSLP-92: Proceedings of the 1992 joint international conference and symposium on logic programming*, pages 798–812, Washington, D.C.

[Dowling and Gallier, 1984] Dowling, W. F. and Gallier, J. H. (1984). Linear time algorithms for testing the satisfiability of propositional horn formulae. *Journal of Logic Programming*, 3:267–284.

[Eiter, 1993] Eiter, T. (1993). Personal communication.

[Eiter and Gottlob, 1993] Eiter, T. and Gottlob, G. (1993). Complexity results for disjunctive logic programming and application to nonmonotonic logics. In *Proc. of the 1993 International Symposium on Logic Programming*, pages 266–278, Vancouver, Canada.

[Gelfond and Lifschitz, 1991] Gelfond, M. and Lifschitz, V. (1991). Classical negation in logic programs and disjunctive databases. *New Generation Computing*, 9:365–385.

[Gelfond et al., 1991] Gelfond, M., Przymusinska, H., Lifschitz, V., and Truszczyński, M. (1991). Disjunctive defaults. In *KR-91: Proceedings of the 2nd international conference on principles of knowledge representation and reasoning*, pages 230–237, Cambridge, MA, USA.

[Giannotti et al., 1991] Giannotti, F., Pedreschi, D., Saccá, D., and Zaniolo, C. (1991). Non-determism in deductive databases. In *Proc. 2nd Int. Conf. on Deductive and Object Oriented Databases*.

[Halpern and Vardi, 1991] Halpern, J. and Vardi, M. (1991). Model checking vs. theorem proving: a manifesto. In *KR-91: Proceedings of the International conference on principles of knowledge representation and reasoning*, pages 325–334.

[Itai and Makowsky, 1987] Itai, A. and Makowsky, J. A. (1987). Unification as a complexity measure for logic programming. *Journal of Logic Programming*, 4:105–117.

[Kolaitis and Papadimitriou, 1990] Kolaitis, P. G. and Papadimitriou, C. H. (1990). Some computational aspects of circumscription. *J. ACM*, 37:1–14.

[Levesque, 1986] Levesque, H. (1986). Making believers out of computers. *Artificial Intelligence*, 30:81–108.

[Lifshitz, 1985] Lifshitz, V. (1985). Computing circumscription. In *IJCAI-85: Proceedings of the international joint conference on AI*, pages 121–127.

[McCarthy, 1980] McCarthy, J. (1980). Circumscription - a form of non-monotonic reasoning. *Artificial Intelligence*, 13:27–39.

[McCarthy, 1986] McCarthy, J. (1986). Application of circumscription to formalizing common-sense knowledge. *Artificial Intelligence*, 28:89–116.

[Minker, 1982] Minker, J. (1982). On indefinite databases and the closed world assumption. In *Proceedings of the 6th conference on automated deduction, Lecture Notes in Computer Science Vol. 138*, pages 292–308. Springer-Verlag.

[Papadimitriou, 1985] Papadimitriou, C. (1985). A note on the expressive power of prolog. *Bull. of the EATCS*.

[Papadimitriou, 1991] Papadimitriou, C. H. (1991). On selecting a satisfying truth assignment. In *The 32nd annual ACM symposium on foundations of computer science*, pages 163–169, San Juan, Puerto Rico.

[Przymusinski, 1988] Przymusinski, T. (1988). On the declarative semantics of deductive databases and logic programs. In Minker, J., editor, *Foundations of deductive databases and logic programs*, pages 193–216. Morgan Kaufmann.

[Przymusinski, 1991] Przymusinski, T. (1991). Stationary semantics for normal and disjunctive logic programs. In *DOOD-91*. Springer-Verlag.

[Reiter, 1978] Reiter, R. (1978). On closed world databases. In Gallaire, H. and Minker, J., editors, *Logic and databases*, pages 55–76. Plenum Press.

[Reiter, 1980] Reiter, R. (1980). A logic for default reasoning. *Artificial Intelligence*, 13:81–132.

[Saccá and Zaniolo, 1990] Saccá, D. and Zaniolo, C. (1990). Partial models stable models and non-determinism in logic programs with negation. In *Proc. ACM PODS*.

[Schaerf, 1993] Schaerf, M. (1993). Negation and minimality in non-Horn databases. In *Proc. ACM PODS*, pages 147–157.

[Vardi, 1982] Vardi, M. Y. (1982). The complexity of relational query languages. In *STOC-82: Proceedings of the 14th ACM symposium on theory of computing*, pages 137–145.

Spatial Reasoning with Propositional Logics

Brandon Bennett
Division of AI
School of Computer Studies
University of Leeds
Leeds LS2 9JT, England
brandon@scs.leeds.ac.uk

Abstract

I present a method for reasoning about spatial relationships on the basis of entailments in propositional logic. Formalisms for representing topological and other spatial information (e.g. [2] [10] [11]) have generally employed the 1st-order predicate calculus. Whilst this language is much more expressive than 0-order (propositional) calculi it is correspondingly harder to reason with. Hence, by encoding spatial relationships in a propositional representation automated reasoning becomes more effective. I specify representations in both classical and intuitionistic propositional logic, which — together with well-defined meta-level reasoning algorithms — provide for efficient reasoning about a large class of spatial relations.

1 INTRODUCTION

This work has developed out of research done by Randell, Cui and Cohn (henceforth RCC) on formalising spatial and temporal concepts used in describing physical situations [11]. A set of classical 1st-order logic axioms has been formulated in which a large number of spatial and temporal relations can be defined [10]. One problem with this formalism is that computing inferences in the theory is far from easy — see e.g. [12]. Of course one can use any general purpose 1st-order theorem prover, but the complexity of the theory means that for many significant problems this approach is impractical.

In this paper I present an alternative approach to the logical representation of spatial relationships. Whilst the system of relations that are represented is essentially the same as that identified by the RCC work, the way in which they are represented is substantially different. Rather than using 1st-order logic, spatial relations are encoded into purely propositional formulae together with certain meta-level constraints concerning entailments between these formulae. I show first how a limited set of relations can be defined by means of classical propositional logic and then show how by using intuitionistic logic a more expressive representation is obtained.

The main motivation for using this alternative approach is that automated reasoning becomes far more efficient. In fact, given a finite set of spatial relationships characterisable in the propositional representation, there is an effective procedure for deciding whether this set describes a possible situation.

This paper can be regarded as a response to the challenge laid down in [12] (*Computing Transitivity Tables: a challenge for automated theorem provers*). However the approach taken is quite different from that envisaged in [12] in that, rather than enhancing or adapting a 1st-order theorem prover to suit the domain of spatial reasoning, a substantially different logical system is used to reason about this domain.

Since the taxonomy of spatial relations which I represent is identical to a family of relations dealt with in the RCC work, I use the same names to refer to these relations. Figure 1 gives 2-dimensional examples of the set of 8 jointly exhaustive and pairwise-disjoint relations which forms the basis of a lattice of topological relations definable in the RCC formalism (see [10] for more details).

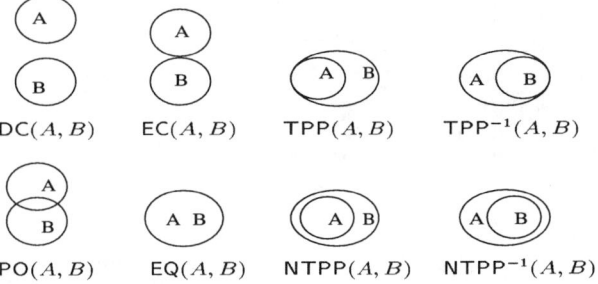

Figure 1: Basic Relations in the RCC Theory

1.1 PRELIMINARY DEFINITIONS

We shall need some precise terminology for referring to topological relationships and expressions describing those relationships:

- A *space* is a non-empty set. (In the intended interpretation the space will be the set of points constituting Cartesian 3 dimensional space.)[1]

- A *situation* is a triple $\langle \mathcal{U}, \Sigma, f \rangle$, where $\mathcal{U}$ is a space, Σ is a set of constant symbols and f is an assignment function which maps each constant in Σ to a subset of $\mathcal{U}$.

- A *situation-description* is a triple $\langle \mathcal{L}, \Sigma, \Theta \rangle$, where $\mathcal{L}$ is a logical language whose vocabulary includes the constant symbols Σ and whose semantics interprets these symbols as denoting sets; Θ is a theory expressed in $\mathcal{L}$.

- A situation $\langle \mathcal{U}, \Sigma, f \rangle$ *exemplifies* a situation-description $\langle \mathcal{L}, \Sigma, \Theta \rangle$ iff the assignment f of subsets of $\mathcal{U}$ to the constants Σ (together with some auxiliary assignment to any non-logical symbols of $\mathcal{L}$ occurring in Θ but not in Σ) satisfies Θ according to the semantics of $\mathcal{L}$.[2]

- A situation-description $\langle \mathcal{L}, \Sigma, \Theta \rangle$ is *impossible* iff it is not exemplified by any situation $\langle \mathcal{U}, \Sigma, f \rangle$.

2 TOPOLOGICAL INTERPRETATION OF PROPOSITIONAL LOGIC

There is a close connection between classical propositional calculus, which I shall refer to as $\mathcal{C}_0$, and set theory [8, p14]. The simplest semantics for $\mathcal{C}_0$ is to take propositions as denoting truth values and to correlate the connectives with truth functions. However, if we interpret propositional letters as denoting arbitrary subsets of some universal set $\mathcal{U}$ and the connectives $\neg$, $\wedge$ and $\vee$ respectively as the set operations *complement*, *intersection* and *union* then the classical tautologies will be those formulae whose value is $\mathcal{U}$ whatever the assignment of set values to propositional letters. To give content to this interpretation one can regard $\mathcal{U}$ as a set of all *possible worlds*. Then propositional letters denote the set of worlds in which they are true.

---
[1] We shall later adopt a richer notion of space: what mathematicians call a *topological space*. This is a pair $\langle \mathcal{U}, i \rangle$, where i is a function which maps subsets of $\mathcal{U}$ to their *interiors*.

[2] This *exemplification* relation is very similar to but slightly more general than the usual *satisfaction* relation between models and theories. It allows one to speak of models as satisfying (*exemplifying*) descriptions given in a number of different formal languages.

This semantics can be formally characterised as follows: a model for the logic $\mathcal{C}_0$ is a structure, $\langle \mathcal{U}, \mathcal{P}, d \rangle$, where $\mathcal{U}$ is a non-empty set, $\mathcal{P}$ is a denumerably infinite set of propositional constants, and d is a denotation function which assigns to each constant in $\mathcal{P}$ a subset of $\mathcal{U}$. The domain of d is extended to all $\mathcal{C}_0$ formulae formed from the propositional constants by stipulating that:

1. $d(\neg P) = \overline{d(P)}$
2. $d(P \wedge Q) = d(P) \cap d(Q)$
3. $d(P \vee Q) = d(P) \cup d(Q)$

where for any set S, $\overline{S}$ is the set of all elements of $\mathcal{U}$ which are not elements of S.

Intuitively, tautologous formulae ought to be true in any possible world; and indeed it can be shown that F is a theorem of $\mathcal{C}_0$ if and only if $d(F) = \mathcal{U}$ in all models.

This interpretation induces a simple correspondence between propositional formulae and *set-terms* — i.e. terms comprised of set-constants combined with the operations: union, intersection and complement. I use the notation $_{\mathcal{C}_0}\rightleftharpoons^{ST}$ to refer to the mapping between propositional formulae and set-terms; thus we can write e.g. $(P \vee \neg Q) \;_{\mathcal{C}_0}\!\!\rightleftharpoons^{ST} (P \cup \overline{Q})$.

I now introduce some further notation in order to state the theorem which provides the foundation for my reasoning system.

- A *universal set-equation* is an expression of the form $\phi = \mathcal{U}$ which asserts that the set-term ϕ denotes the set of all elements in the universe..

- $P_1, \ldots, P_n \models_{\mathcal{C}_0} P_0$ means that in the calculus, $\mathcal{C}_0$, the formula P_0 is entailed by the set of formulae, $\{P_1, \ldots, P_n\}$. (Thus $\models_{\mathcal{C}_0} P$ means that P is a theorem of $\mathcal{C}_0$.)

- $E_1, \ldots, E_n \models_S E_0$, where $E_0, \ldots, E_n$ are set-equation, means that in any model for which the equations $E_1, \ldots, E_n$ hold, the equation E_0 also holds. ($\models_S E$ means that E holds in every model.)

It can then be shown that:

Theorem 1 $P_1, \ldots, P_n \models_{\mathcal{C}_0} P_0$ *if and only if* $\pi_1 = \mathcal{U}, \ldots, \pi_n = \mathcal{U} \models_S \pi_0 = \mathcal{U}$, *where* $P_i \;_{\mathcal{C}_0}\!\!\rightleftharpoons^{ST} \pi_i$ *for each* i.

I first establish that:

Lemma 1 *If* $\models_{\mathcal{C}_0} P$ *then* $\models_S t = \mathcal{U}$, *where* $P \;_{\mathcal{C}_0}\!\!\rightleftharpoons^{ST} t$.

Proof: If P is a tautology then if it is converted to *conjunctive normal form* (CNF) each conjunct will

Table 1: Definitions of Four Topological Relations in $\mathcal{C}_0$

Relation	Description	Set Equation	Model Constraint
$\mathsf{DR}(X,Y)$	X and Y are discrete	$\overline{X \cap Y} = \mathcal{U}$	$\neg(X \wedge Y)$
$\mathsf{P}(X,Y)$	X is part of Y	$\overline{X} \cup Y = \mathcal{U}$	$X \to Y$
$\mathsf{P}^{-1}(X,Y)$	Y is part of X	$X \cup \overline{Y} = \mathcal{U}$	$Y \to X$
$\mathsf{EQ}(X,Y)$	X and Y are equal	$(\overline{X} \cup Y) \cap (X \cup \overline{Y}) = \mathcal{U}$	$X \leftrightarrow Y$

contain a pair of complementary literals (L and $\neg L$). Set-terms can also be converted to an analogous normal form, *intersection normal form* (INF): by means of simple re-write rules any set-term can be expressed as an intersection of unions of set-constants and their complements.

If a set-term corresponds to a tautological proposition then when expressed in INF each union in the expression must contain some pair, τ and $\overline{\tau}$, of a set constant and its complement. So whatever the assignment to the set constants each union and hence the intersection of these unions will have the value $\mathcal{U}$. This ensures that lemma 1 must hold. □

I now return to the proof of theorem 1.

Proof: If $P_1, \ldots, P_n \models_{\mathcal{C}_0} P_0$ then the formula $(P_1 \wedge \ldots \wedge P_n) \to P_0$ must be a tautology; hence, by lemma 1, the equation $\overline{t_1 \cap \ldots \cap t_n} \cup t_0 = \mathcal{U}$ must hold. But in any model satisfying $t_1 = \mathcal{U}, \ldots, t_n = \mathcal{U}$ one must have $\overline{t_1 \cap \ldots \cap t_n} = \emptyset$. Therefore $t_0 = \mathcal{U}$.

On the other hand suppose $P_1, \ldots, P_n \not\models_{\mathcal{C}_0} P_0$; this means that there is some truth-functional assignment, f, under which $P_1, \ldots, P_n$ are all true whilst P_0 is false. Given such an assignment we construct a set assignment, s, such that $s(P) = \mathcal{U}$ if $f(P) = true$ and $s(P) = \emptyset$ if $f(P) = false$. Clearly, the values of complex set-terms under s will correspond directly with the truth values of the associated propositions under f. Hence s is an assignment such that $t_1 = \mathcal{U}, \ldots, t_n = \mathcal{U}$ and $t_0 = \emptyset$. So $t_1 = \mathcal{U}, \ldots, t_n = \mathcal{U} \not\models_s t_0 = \mathcal{U}$. □

This correspondence theorem allows us to use classical propositional formulae to reason about universal set-equations.

2.1 FROM POSSIBLE WORLDS TO SPATIAL CONSTRAINTS

The basis of the topological representation system presented below is to exploit this semantics of propositional logic in terms of sets; but rather than taking $\mathcal{U}$ to be a set of possible worlds, $\mathcal{U}$ will be interpreted as a *space* of points and propositional letters will thus be interpreted as referring to *regions* within that space.

A universal set-equation can be regarded as a constraint on possible models — i.e. possible assignments of subsets of $\mathcal{U}$ to set-constants. If the set-constants denote regions, this allows one to specify relationships between these regions. For example the constraint $\overline{A} \cup B = \mathcal{U}$ will be satisfied by all and only those models in which set A is a subset of set B — i.e. region A is part of region B. In terms of $\mathcal{C}_0$ this constraint could be represented by the formula $\neg A \vee B$ (or equivalently $A \to B$). Thus, if $\mathcal{L}_{use}$ refers to the language whose expressions are all universal set-equations, a set of these equations can form the Θ component of a *situation-description*, $\langle \mathcal{L}_{use}, \Sigma, \Theta \rangle$.

3 DEFINING TOPOLOGICAL RELATIONS

The basic method is as follows: certain constraints associated with topological relationships are represented by propositional formulae; further constraints are then added at the meta-level in terms of restrictions on entailments of these formulae. A topological relation is thus defined by a set of formula called *model constraints* together with a further set of formulae called *entailment constraints*. A situation involving a number of topological relations is possible if and only if the set of model-constraints associated with all of the relations does *not* entail any of the entailment constraint formulae.

3.1 MODEL CONSTRAINTS

Suppose we have a situation in which a region A is part of another region B. Then the union of B with the complement of A must fill the entire space, $\mathcal{U}$. This can be represented by the set equation $\overline{A} \cup B = \mathcal{U}$. Hence because of the correspondence with $\mathcal{C}_0$ we can represent this as $\neg A \vee B$ (or equivalently $A \to B$). This formula is the model constraint associated with the situation A is part of B since in any model $A \to B$ denotes $\mathcal{U}$ if and only if A is part of B.

By means of such formulae four topological relations can be defined as shown in table 1. The relations defined here strictly correspond to the RCC relations of the same names only if we constrain all propositional letters to denote non-null regions. This rules out pathological cases such as where X is part of Y and X and Y are also discrete, which is only possible if X is null. More will be said about null regions below.

3.2 ENTAILMENT CONSTRAINTS

As it stands, our representation is very limited: many simple spatial relations cannot be defined solely by means of universal set-equations specifying model constraints. For example the relation $\mathsf{PP}(X,Y)$, X is a *proper* part of Y cannot be so expressed. Nevertheless, informally this relation can be defined quite straightforwardly as that relation which holds whenever $\mathsf{P}(X,Y)$ is true but not $\mathsf{EQ}(X,Y)$. So it would seem that we can characterise the proper part relation if we can find a way to represent the absence of a relation which we can already define.

We must now ask how the negations of $\mathcal{C}_0$ model constraints should be represented. Take for example $\neg\mathsf{P}(X,Y)$ (X is not part of Y). Suppose we simply negate the model-constraint corresponding to $\mathsf{P}(X,Y)$; we would then get $\neg(X \to Y)$. But this formula corresponds to the set equation $\overline{X} \cup Y = \mathcal{U}$ or equivalently $\overline{X \cap \overline{Y}} = \mathcal{U}$; and this will only hold when $X = \mathcal{U}$ and $Y = \emptyset$. So we see that the negation of a model-constraint formula does not correspond to the absence of the relation enforced by that constraint.

In terms of sets, what we really wanted to represent was $\overline{X} \cup Y \neq \mathcal{U}$ which is the direct negation of the set equation for $\mathsf{P}(X,Y)$. But negating the formula in the propositional representation does not give us this because such a negation is interpreted as a complement operation on the set-term rather than a negation of the whole equation. This means that the absence of the relations defined so far cannot be represented directly as model-constraints.

We need to increase the expressive capabilities of our representation language so we can represent situations in which we specify not only that a number of universal set-equations hold but also that certain such equations do not hold. Thus, we employ the language $\mathcal{L}_{usei}$ of universal set-equations and inequalities. A situation-description in this language is a structure $\langle \mathcal{L}_{usei}, \Sigma, \Theta \rangle$ where Θ is a set of universal set-equations and inequalities which are negations of universal set-equations. Such a situation description can be represented by a pair $\langle \mathcal{M}, \mathcal{E} \rangle$ where $\mathcal{M}$ and $\mathcal{E}$ are sets of $\mathcal{C}_0$ formulae obtained respectively from the set-terms involved in the set-equations and inequalities in Θ according to $\mathcal{C}_0\rightleftharpoons^{ST}$. The language consisting of pairs of sets of $\mathcal{C}_0$ formulae will be called $\mathcal{C}_0^+$.

3.3 CONSISTENCY OF $\mathcal{C}_0^+$ SITUATION DESCRIPTIONS

What we now need is a method of determining from a pair of formula sets, $\langle \mathcal{M}, \mathcal{E} \rangle$, whether the corresponding situation-description, $\langle \mathcal{L}_{usei}, \Sigma, \Theta \rangle$, is possible.

Suppose Θ is a set $\{m_1 = \mathcal{U}, \ldots, m_j = \mathcal{U}, e_1 \neq \mathcal{U}, \ldots, e_k \neq \mathcal{U}\}$ then Θ describes an impossible situation if and only if the following entailment holds:

$$m_1 = \mathcal{U}, \ldots, m_j = \mathcal{U} \models_S e_1 = \mathcal{U} \vee \ldots \vee e_k = \mathcal{U}$$

The r.h.s. is a disjunction of set-equations and as such cannot be translated into a union at the level of set-terms (just as negating a set equation is not equivalent to applying the complement operation to its set term).

However, it can be established that in the domain of sets, entailments of this kind are *convex* [3] in the sense of [9]. A class of entailments is convex iff whenever $\Gamma \models \phi_1 \vee \ldots \vee \phi_n$ then $\Gamma \models \phi_i$, for some i in $1 \ldots n$.

Consider the entailment associated with the impossibility of Θ. Suppose none of the disjuncts on the r.h.s. are entailed by the equations on the l.h.s.. This means that for each disjunct $e_i = \mathcal{U}$ there is a model, $\langle \mathcal{U}_i, \mathcal{P}, d_i \rangle$ in which it is false whilst all the l.h.s. equations are true. We can assume that the universes for each of these models are disjoint. We now construct a new model, $\langle \mathcal{U}_*, \mathcal{P}, d_* \rangle$, such that $\mathcal{U}_* = \bigcup_i \mathcal{U}_i$ and $d_*(X) = \bigcup_i d_i(X)$. The $\mathcal{U}_i$'s thus form discrete sub-spaces of $\mathcal{U}_*$. A consideration of this new model will reveal that it provides a counter-example to the entailment, since it must satisfy all the l.h.s. equations whilst making each of the disjuncts on the r.h.s. false.

Thus the r.h.s. will be entailed if and only if at least one of the disjuncts is individually entailed. So for each e_i we need to check whether

$$m_1 = \mathcal{U}, \ldots, m_j = \mathcal{U} \models_S e_i = \mathcal{U}$$

Thus, because of the equivalence between $\models_S$ and entailment between corresponding $\mathcal{C}_0$ formulae given by Theorem 1, we have the following:

Theorem 2 *A $\mathcal{C}_0^+$ representation $\langle \mathcal{M}, \mathcal{E} \rangle$ corresponds to a possible situation description (specified in $\mathcal{L}_{usei}$) if and only if there is no formula $F \in \mathcal{E}$ such that $\mathcal{M} \models_{\mathcal{C}_0} F$.*

This theorem should make clear why the formulae in the set $\mathcal{E}$ are called entailment constraints.

3.4 THE RCC RELATIONS DEFINED

We can now give $\mathcal{C}_0^+$ representations for a significant sub-class of the RCC relations. Let us first look at how the situation type "A is a proper part of B" is represented. We can say that $\mathsf{PP}(A,B)$ holds when A is part of B but the two regions are not equal. This gives us the equality $\overline{A} \cup B = \mathcal{U}$ and the inequality $(\overline{A} \cup B) \cap (A \cup \overline{B}) \neq \mathcal{U}$. Also as noted above, to rule out cases where either A or B is the null set, we also need $\overline{A} \neq \mathcal{U}$ and $\overline{B} \neq \mathcal{U}$. Equalities are encoded as

---
[3]Note that later in the paper I use the term *convex* with its ordinary sense, as a property of the surface of a region. Hopefully this will not cause too much confusion.

Table 2: A Five Relation Basis Defined in $\mathcal{C}_0^+$

Relation	Model Constraint	Entailment Constraints
DR(X,Y)	$\neg(X \wedge Y)$	$\neg X, \neg Y$
PO(X,Y)	—	$\neg X \vee \neg Y, X \to Y, Y \to X, \neg X, \neg Y$
PP(X,Y)	$X \to Y$	$Y \to X, \neg X, \neg Y$
PP$^{-1}(X,Y)$	$Y \to X$	$X \to Y, \neg X, \neg Y$
EQ(X,Y)	$X \leftrightarrow Y$	$\neg X, \neg Y$

model-constraints and inequalities as entailment constraints so our propositional representation for the relation PP(A,B) is the pair

$$\langle \{A \to B\}, \{A \leftrightarrow B, \neg A, \neg B\} \rangle.$$

The $\mathcal{C}_0^+$ representation allows us to define five jointly exhaustive and pairwise disjoint topological relations from the RCC lattice of spatial relations. The definitions are shown in table 2.

The model constraint associated with a relation is the strongest formula which holds in all models in which the relation holds. The entailment constraints serve to exclude cases which, although consistent with the model constraint are incompatible with the relation. Thus the entailment constraints correspond to model constraints of other relations (plus the non-null constraints). The relation PO has no model constraint and is defined by excluding all of the other relations.

Certain entailment constraints which one might expect to be required can be eliminated or weakened because they are indirectly captured by other constraints. For example, in table 2 the entailment constraint $A \leftrightarrow B$, which occurred in the representation of PP worked out above, is replaced by the weaker formula $B \to A$, since in the presence of the model constraint $A \to B$, $B \to A$ would immediately entail $A \leftrightarrow B$.

4 REASONING WITH $\mathcal{C}_0^+$

By making use of the results obtained so far one can use a $\mathcal{C}_0$ theorem prover as the basis of an effective automated spatial reasoning system. For clarity I concisely summarise the consistency checking algorithm for $\mathcal{C}_0^+$. Given a situation description consisting of a set of relations of the form $R(\alpha, \beta)$, where R is one of the relations characterisable in $\mathcal{C}_0^+$, and α and β are constants denoting regions, the following simple algorithm will decide whether the description describes a possible situation:

- For each relation $R_i(\alpha_i, \beta_i)$ in the situation description find the corresponding propositional representation $\langle \mathcal{M}_i, \mathcal{E}_i \rangle$.
- Construct the overall $\mathcal{C}_0^+$ representation $\langle \bigcup_i \mathcal{M}_i, \bigcup_i \mathcal{E}_i \rangle$.

- For each formula $F \in \bigcup_i \mathcal{E}_i$ use a classical propositional theorem prover to determine whether the entailment $\bigcup_i \mathcal{M}_i \models_{C_o} F$ holds.
- If any of the entailments determined in the last step does hold then the situation is impossible.

For example we may want to know whether the following situation is possible: A, is a proper part of B; B is disjoint with C; and, A is a proper part of C. The $\mathcal{C}_0^+$ representations of the three spatial relations are respectively:

$$\langle \{A \to B\}, \{B \to A, \neg A, \neg B\} \rangle,$$
$$\langle \{\neg(B \wedge C)\}, \{\neg B, \neg C\} \rangle,$$
$$\langle \{A \to C\}, \{C \to A, \neg A, \neg C\} \rangle.$$

So the overall $\mathcal{C}_0^+$ representation is

$$\langle \{A \to B, \neg(B \wedge C), A \to C\},$$
$$\{B \to A, C \to A, \neg A, \neg B, \neg C\} \rangle.$$

We determine that this situation is impossible since

$$A \to B, \ \neg(B \wedge C), \ A \to C \models_{C_o} \neg A.$$

4.1 DETERMINING ENTAILMENTS

Computing inconsistency of situations is a special case of determining entailments between situation descriptions characterisable in $\mathcal{C}_0^+$. To refer to such an entailment, I shall use the notation $\langle \mathcal{M}, \mathcal{E} \rangle \models_{C_o^+} \langle \mathcal{M}', \mathcal{E}' \rangle$. We can express the meaning of this as an entailment between set-equations corresponding to the formulae in the $\mathcal{C}_0^+$ representation:

$$m_1 = \mathcal{U} \wedge \ldots \wedge m_h = \mathcal{U} \wedge e_1 \neq \mathcal{U} \wedge \ldots \wedge e_i \neq \mathcal{U}$$
$$\models_S$$
$$m_1' = \mathcal{U} \wedge \ldots \wedge m_j' = \mathcal{U} \wedge e_1' \neq \mathcal{U} \wedge \ldots \wedge e_k' \neq \mathcal{U}$$

If we then bring the r.h.s. over to the left and move the resulting negation inwards we get:

$$m_1 = \mathcal{U} \wedge \ldots \wedge m_h = \mathcal{U} \wedge e_1 \neq \mathcal{U} \wedge \ldots \wedge e_i \neq \mathcal{U} \wedge$$
$$(m_1' \neq \mathcal{U} \vee \ldots \vee m_j' \neq \mathcal{U} \vee e_1' = \mathcal{U} \vee \ldots \vee e_k' = \mathcal{U}) \models_S$$

To show the validity of this we must show that whichever of the equations in the disjunction is chosen the resulting equation set is inconsistent. This is equivalent to showing that:

for all $p \in \mathcal{M}'$ we have $\langle \mathcal{M}, \mathcal{E} \cup \{p\} \rangle \models_{C_o^+}$
and for all $q \in \mathcal{E}'$ we have $\langle \mathcal{M} \cup \{q\}, \mathcal{E} \rangle \models_{C_o^+}$

Table 3: Composition table for the 5 relation basis

$R(a,b)$ \ $R(b,c)$	DR	PO	EQ	PP	PP^{-1}
DR	*	DR ∨ PO ∨ PP	DR	DR ∨ PO ∨ PP	DR
PO	DR ∨ PO ∨ PP^{-1}	*	PO	PO ∨ PP	DR ∨ PO ∨ PP^{-1}
EQ	DR	PO	EQ	PP	PP^{-1}
PP	DR	DR ∨ PO ∨ PP	PP	PP	*
PP^{-1}	DR ∨ PO ∨ PP^{-1}	PO ∨ PP^{-1}	PP^{-1}	O	PP^{-1}

Another equivalent way of expressing these which is more convenient from the point of view of actually calculating the entailments is the following:

Theorem 3 $\langle \mathcal{M}, \mathcal{E} \rangle \models_{\mathcal{C}_o^+} \langle \mathcal{M}', \mathcal{E}' \rangle$ iff
either $\langle \mathcal{M}, \mathcal{E} \rangle \models_{\mathcal{C}_o^+}$
or (for all $p \in \mathcal{M}'$: $\langle \mathcal{M}, \{p\} \rangle \models_{\mathcal{C}_o^+}$
and for all $q \in \mathcal{E}'$: $\langle \mathcal{M} \cup \{q\}, \mathcal{E} \rangle \models_{\mathcal{C}_o^+}$)

Determining the validity of a $\mathcal{C}_0^+$ entailment has thus been reduced to determining the impossibility of certain situation descriptions derived from the constraints involved; and we already know that a description is impossible iff one of its entailment constraints is entailed by its model constraints.

4.2 COMPUTING LOCI OF COMPOSITION

Given a particular theory Θ supporting a set $\mathcal{B}$ of mutually exhaustive and pairwise disjoint dyadic relations (a *basis* set), for each pair of relations R_1 and R_2 taken from $\mathcal{B}$, the *locus of composition*[4] of R_1 and R_2, $\text{Comp}(R_1, R_2)$, is the disjunction of all relations R_3 in $\mathcal{B}$, such that, for arbitrary individual constants a, b, c, the formula $R_1(a,b) \land R_2(b,c) \land R_3(a,c)$ is consistent with Θ. In other words $\text{Comp}(R_1, R_2)$ is the disjunction of all possible base relations which could hold between a and c. Computing loci of composition for spatial relations is the "challenge for automated theorem provers" proposed in [12].

By using the consistency algorithm described above, the $\mathcal{C}_0^+$ representation enables loci of composition for spatial relations to be computed very efficiently.

---

[4] What is here called the *locus of composition* is the same as what in [12] was referred to as the 'transitive closure' of two base relations. This terminology derives from Allen's 'transitivity table' for temporal intervals [1]. However, 'transitive closure' already has a meaning different from what is intended here, so a new term is required to avoid potential confusion. In describing the more general problem of determining possible values of unknown relations in the context of a partial situation description I have adopted the phrase 'locus of an unspecified relation'. The 'locus of composition' is a special case of such a locus.

Given R_1 and R_2, which are members of some basis set $\mathcal{B}$, one simply checks for all values of R_3 taken from $\mathcal{B}$, whether the situation described by $R_1(a,b), R_2(b,c), R_3(a,c)$ is possible. Table 3 gives the loci of composition for the 5 relation basis $\{\text{DR}, \text{PO}, \text{PP}, \text{PP}^{-1}, \text{EQ}\}$. The symbol '*' stands for the disjunction of all 5 relations. This table was computed in under 6.7 seconds on a SPARC1 workstation.

5 MORE EXPRESSIVENESS WITH INTUITIONISTIC LOGIC

In his paper "Sentential Calculus and Topology" [13] Tarski has shown that the intuitionist propositional calculus (henceforth $\mathcal{I}_0$) can be given an interpretation in which propositional letters correspond to *open* sets within a *topological space*.

The spatial interpretation of intuitionistic logic requires a richer notion of a *space* than the classical. Specifically, whereas before a space was simply a set of elements, a space is now a set of elements for which the notions of *interior* and *closure* are defined for each subset of spatial elements.

A topological space can be described by a structure $\langle \mathcal{U}, i \rangle$, where $\mathcal{U}$ is an arbitrary set of elements whose *topology* is defined by a function i which maps each subset of $\mathcal{U}$ to another subset of $\mathcal{U}$, its *interior*. i must satisfy certain well known axioms (see e.g. [6, p.129]). The closure of a set $c(X)$ is defined as equivalent to $\overline{i(\overline{X})}$.

5.1 INTERPRETATION OF $\mathcal{I}_0$

The topological interpretation of $\mathcal{I}_0$ is very similar to the interpretation of $\mathcal{C}_0$ given above. Again propositional formulae will denote subsets of a space, although admissible subsets will be limited to those which are *open* under the topology of the space. A set X is open if and only if $i(X) = X$.

A model for $\mathcal{I}_0$ is a structure $\langle \mathcal{U}, i, \mathcal{P}, d \rangle$, where $\mathcal{U}$ is a non-empty set, i is a function satisfying the appropriate axioms, which maps subsets of $\mathcal{U}$ to their interiors, $\mathcal{P}$ is a denumerably infinite set of propositional constants, and d is a denotation function which assigns to each constant in $\mathcal{P}$ an *open* subset of $\mathcal{U}$. The domain of d is extended to all $\mathcal{I}_0$ formulae formed from these variables by stipulating that:

1. $d(\sim P) = i(\overline{d(P)}\,)$ [5]
2. $d(P \wedge Q) = d(P) \cap d(Q)$
3. $d(P \vee Q) = d(P) \cup d(Q)$
4. $d(P \Rightarrow Q) = i(\overline{d(P)} \cup d(Q))$

where for any set S, $\overline{S}$ is the set of all elements of $\mathcal{U}$ which are not elements of S.

Just as for the classical logic we can consider the topological interpretation of $\mathcal{I}_0$ as associating each intuitionistic formula with a set-term; but set-terms may now contain the interior operator. I refer to the mapping between $\mathcal{I}_0$ formulae and set-terms induced by this interpretation with the notation $_{\mathcal{I}_0}\rightleftharpoons^{ST}$.

Tarski's "Second Principal Theorem" [13, p.448] establishes that a propositional formula is a theorem of $\mathcal{I}_0$ if and only if the corresponding set-term has the value $\mathcal{U}$ in any topological space under any assignment of open sets to the set constants occurring in the term. The proof of this is fairly involved and is not reconstructed. I use the notation '$\vdash_{\mathcal{I}_0}$' to denote entailment in $\mathcal{I}_0$ and '$\models_T$' to denote topological entailment — i.e. entailment between set-equations which may contain the interior operator, i. Tarski's theorem can then be written formally as:

Theorem 4 $\vdash_{\mathcal{I}_0} P$ *if and only if* $\models_T \pi = \mathcal{U}$, *where* $P_{\mathcal{I}_0}\rightleftharpoons^{ST} \pi$. [6]

In using $\mathcal{I}_0$ to represent spatial relations we shall exploit very similar correspondence relations to those holding between the $\mathcal{C}_0$ and the Boolean algebra of sets. In order to secure the correspondence between entailment in $\mathcal{I}_0$ and entailment between set equations in the topological algebra of sets, we need to generalise Tarski's result to a correspondence between entailments:

Theorem 5 $P_1, \ldots, P_n \vdash_{\mathcal{I}_0} P_0$
if and only if $\pi_1 = \mathcal{U}, \ldots, \pi_n = \mathcal{U} \models_T \pi_0 = \mathcal{U}$

Proof: The positive half is simple:

An $\mathcal{I}_0$ entailment $P_1, \ldots, P_n \vdash_{\mathcal{I}_0} P_0$ holds iff $\vdash_{\mathcal{I}_0} (P_1 \wedge \ldots \wedge P_n) \Rightarrow P_0$, so by Theorem 4 we have

---

[5] Under this interpretation one can see why the law of excluded middle fails in intuitionistic logic. $A \vee \sim A$ is interpreted as $A \cup i(\overline{A})$. But the union of A with its exterior, $i(\overline{A})$, does not exhaust the space, since the points in $c(A) - A$, the *boundary* of A, are neither included in A nor its exterior.

[6] This theorem holds for any topology whatsoever. Adding conditions to the topology would mean the corresponding logic would be stronger. The limiting case is the *discrete* topology corresponding to classical logic.

$\models_T i(\overline{\pi_1 \cap \ldots \cap \pi_n} \cup \pi_0) = \mathcal{U}$. But if a set has $\mathcal{U}$ as its interior then it must be equal to $\mathcal{U}$, so the equation $(\overline{\pi_1 \cap \ldots \cap \pi_n} \cup \pi_0) = \mathcal{U}$ must hold in every model. Thus whenever $\pi_i = \mathcal{U}$ for $i = 1 \ldots n$ we must also have $\pi_0 = \mathcal{U}$ — in other words $\pi_1 = \mathcal{U}, \ldots, \pi_n = \mathcal{U} \models_T \pi_0 = \mathcal{U}$.

Suppose on the other hand $P_1, \ldots, P_n \not\vdash_{\mathcal{I}_0} P_0$. Theorem 4 gives us $\not\models_T i(\overline{\pi_1 \cap \ldots \cap \pi_n} \cup \pi_0) = \mathcal{U}$, which means that there is some model, $\mathcal{M} = \langle \mathcal{U}, i, \mathcal{P}, d \rangle$, in which there is at least one element of $\pi_1 \cap \ldots \cap \pi_n$ which is not an element of π_0. On the basis of this model we now construct a model $\mathcal{M}' = \langle \mathcal{U}', i', \mathcal{P}, d' \rangle$ whose universe, $\mathcal{U}'$ is the set denoted by $\pi_1 \cap \ldots \cap \pi_n$ in $\mathcal{M}$. We set $i'(X) = i(X)$ for all $X \subseteq \mathcal{U}'$ and for all propositional constants P_i we set $d'(P_i) = d(P_i) \cap \mathcal{U}'$. The interpretations of the logical operators given above will ensure that for all formulae F, $d'(F) = d(F) \cap \mathcal{U}'$.

Thus in particular for each $i = 1 \ldots n$, $d'(P_i) = d(P_i) \cap \mathcal{U}' = \pi_i \cap \mathcal{U}' = \mathcal{U}'$; i.e. in the new model all antecedent formulae denote the universe. We also have $d'(P_0) = d(P_0) \cap \mathcal{U}' = \pi_0 \cap \mathcal{U}'$. Furthermore, we know that there is at least one element of $\mathcal{U}'$ which is not an element of π_0. This means that $d'(P_0) \neq \mathcal{U}'$; so $\mathcal{M}'$ provides a counter-example to the entailment. This concludes the proof of theorem 5. □

5.2 $\mathcal{I}_0$ REPRESENTATION OF RCC RELATIONS

We can now translate the topological relations defined by 1st-order logic in the RCC system into a 0-order representation in which intuitionistic formulae represent constraints on possible situations.

The basis of the interpretation is as follows:

- A *region* is identified with an open set of points. (So regions are denoted by propositional letters in the $\mathcal{I}_0$ representation.)
- Regions *overlap* if they share at least one point.
- Regions are *connected* if their *closures* share at least one point.

This interpretation is in accord with that suggested for the RCC theory in [10].

Because the topological interpretation of $\mathcal{I}_0$ involves set-terms containing the interior operator, i, it allows us to make some distinctions which are not possible with the classical calculus. In particular we can now distinguish the case where two non-overlapping regions are connected (i.e. touch at one or more points) from that in which they are totally disconnected. And, in a similar manner, we can specify whether a region which is a proper part of another is a tangential or non-tangential proper part.

Table 4: Some RCC Relations Defined in $\mathcal{I}_0^+$ (including the 8 relation basis)

Relation	Model Constraint	Entailment Constraints
DC(X,Y)	$\sim X \vee \sim Y$	$\sim X, \sim Y$
EC(X,Y)	$\sim(X \wedge Y)$	$\sim X \vee \sim Y, \sim X, \sim Y$
PO(X,Y)	—	$\sim(X \wedge Y), X \Rightarrow Y, Y \Rightarrow X, \sim X, \sim Y$
TPP(X,Y)	$X \Rightarrow Y$	$\sim X \vee Y, Y \Rightarrow X, \sim X, \sim Y$
TPP$^{-1}(X,Y)$	$Y \Rightarrow X$	$\sim Y \vee X, X \Rightarrow Y, \sim X, \sim Y$
NTPP(X,Y)	$\sim X \vee Y$	$Y \Rightarrow X, \sim X, \sim Y$
NTPP$^{-1}(X,Y)$	$\sim Y \vee X$	$X \Rightarrow Y, \sim X, \sim Y$
EQ(X,Y)	$X \Leftrightarrow Y$	$\sim X, \sim Y$
C(X,Y)	—	$\sim X \vee \sim Y, \sim X, \sim Y$
EQ$(X, \mathsf{sum}(Y,Z))$	$X \Leftrightarrow (Y \vee Z)$	$\sim X, \sim Y, \sim Z$

If two regions share no points they cannot overlap (although they may be connected). In such a case the equation $i(\overline{X \cap Y}) = \mathcal{U}$ must hold; this can be represented by the $\mathcal{I}_0$ formula $\sim(X \wedge Y)$. In $\mathcal{I}_0$ (unlike $\mathcal{C}_0$) this formula is not equivalent to $\sim X \vee \sim Y$. The latter corresponds to the set-equation $i(\overline{X}) \cup i(\overline{Y}) = \mathcal{U}$, which says that the union of the exteriors of two regions exhaust the space. If the regions touch at one or more points, then these points of contact will not be in the exterior of either region so this equation will not hold. Hence the second (stronger) formula can be employed as a model constraint to describe situations where two regions are completely disconnected.

5.3 THE $\mathcal{I}_0^+$ REPRESENTATION LANGUAGE

To represent relations using $\mathcal{I}_0$ we can use essentially the same type of encoding as we employed for $\mathcal{C}_0$. As before, restrictions on possible models corresponding to the presence of topological relationships between regions are enforced by means of model constraints and entailment constraints. The role of these two types of constraint in reasoning about situations is exactly as in the classical case. In fact the arguments given in sections 3.2, 3.3 and 4.1 regarding the representation of negative constraints and the correct procedures for reasoning in $\mathcal{C}_0^+$ apply equally when $\mathcal{I}_0$ is employed as a language for representing set equations. Most of the arguments rely only upon the correspondence expressed in theorem 1, so parallel arguments for $\mathcal{I}_0$ can be given on the basis of theorem 5. The convexity property shown in section 3.3 can also be similarly demonstrated for the topological interpretation of $\mathcal{I}_0$. Hence we already have the apparatus for reasoning with the language $\mathcal{I}_0^+$, whose expressions are pairs of sets of $\mathcal{I}_0$ formulae specifying model-constraints and entailment-constraints. Counterparts of theorems 2 and 3 apply to the language $\mathcal{I}_0^+$ as well as to $\mathcal{C}_0^+$.

Table 4 gives the $\mathcal{I}_0^+$ representation of each of the 8 basic relations shown in figure 1. The definition of C plus another example using the RCC function sum are also given. That the model constraints given in this table must hold if the corresponding RCC relation holds is easily verified by considering the interpretation of the formulae given in section 5.1. As with $\mathcal{C}_0^+$, the set of entailment constraints represent negative conditions needed to exclude unwanted situations which are compatible with the model-constraint.

6 IMPLEMENTATION OF A $\mathcal{I}_0^+$ REASONING SYSTEM

A spatial reasoner using this technique has been implemented in Prolog using a Horn clause representation of a restricted Gentzen calculus for $\mathcal{I}_0$ and a look-up table to translate topological relations into the appropriate model and entailment constraints. Running on a SPARC1 workstation the program generated the full *composition table* for the 8 base relations shown in Figure 1 in under 244 seconds.

This is a substantial improvement over the method described in [12]. In generating the table given there, the theorem prover OTTER [7] was used, working with the 1st-order axiomatisation of the RCC theory. OTTER took a total of 2460 seconds to prove the required theorems but some proofs required human assistance (addition of hand chosen lemmas and restriction of the set of axioms used). Furthermore this method involves not only theorem proving but also *model building* in order to ensure the minimality of table entries (see [12]) and this is also computationally intensive. This method cannot really compete with reasoning using the $\mathcal{I}_0^+$ representation, since unlike $\mathcal{I}_0^+$ no decision procedure is known for the 1st-order RCC theory.

6.1 THEOREM PROVING IN $\mathcal{I}_0$

Clearly, to use $\mathcal{I}_0^+$ as a representation language for effective spatial reasoning we need to be able to reason efficiently in $\mathcal{I}_0$. Theorem proving in $\mathcal{I}_0$ is decidable but potentially very hard (see [5]). A proof-theory for the language can be specified in terms of a simple cut-free Gentzen sequent calculus which is only a slight modification of the corresponding classical system. The formalisation I use is essentially the same as that given in [4].

Theorem proving in the $\mathcal{I}_0$ sequent calculus is more complex than that of $\mathcal{C}_0$: in $\mathcal{C}_0$ all connectives can be eliminated deterministically because the rules produce Boolean combinations of sequents which are logically equivalent to the original sequent. However with certain rules in the $\mathcal{I}_0$ calculus the resulting combination of proofs is not necessarily provable even if the original sequent is valid. In other words the rule gives a sufficient but not necessary condition for validity. Consequently theorem proving in $\mathcal{I}_0$ is non-deterministic and involves a much larger search space.

However, given that the representation of many spatial constraints involves only a very limited class of $\mathcal{I}_0$ formulae, much of the potential complexity of theorem proving can be avoided. This is achieved by employing a proof system which, although not complete for the full language of $\mathcal{I}_0$, is complete for sequents containing only formulae used to represent the RCC spatial relations. Specifically, we need handle formulae of the following forms: $\sim X$, $\sim X \vee \sim Y$, $\sim(X \wedge Y)$, $X \Rightarrow Y$, $\sim X \vee Y$.

Given this restriction, the non-deterministic and extremely computationally expensive rule for eliminating implications from the left hand side of a sequent can be replaced by other rules which can be applied deterministically (space does not permit a fuller explanation). Use of this restricted proof system dramatically increases the effectiveness of reasoning in $\mathcal{I}_0^+$.

7 EXTENDING THE REPRESENTATION

In the rest of the paper I indicate how the $\mathcal{I}_0^+$ representation can be extended to incorporate extra concepts which are not directly reducible to $\mathcal{I}_0^+$ but for which we do have a set of axioms specified in the (more expressive) 1st-order classical logic, $\mathcal{C}_1$. To illustrate the method I show how the notions of 'inside' and 'outside' can be represented.

7.1 'INSIDE' AND 'OUTSIDE'

Following the approach taken in [10] I define the relations 'inside' and 'outside' in terms of a *convex-hull* operator which is introduced as a new primitive. The convex-hull, $\mathsf{conv}(X)$, of a region X can be informally defined as that region which would be enclosed by a taught rubber membrane stretched around X.[7] In terms of the relations $\mathsf{P}(x,y)$ (x is a part of y) and $\mathsf{TP}(x,y)$ (x is a tangential part of y) and $\mathsf{C}(x,y)$ (x is connected to y) an axiomatisation of $\mathsf{conv}(x)$, the convex-hull operator can be given in $\mathcal{C}_1$ as follows:

1. $\forall x \mathsf{TP}(x, \mathsf{conv}(x))$
2. $\forall x[\mathsf{conv}(\mathsf{conv}(x)) = \mathsf{conv}(x)]$
3. $\forall x \forall y[\mathsf{P}(x,y) \rightarrow \mathsf{P}(\mathsf{conv}(x), \mathsf{conv}(y))]$
4. $\forall x \forall y[\mathsf{conv}(x) = \mathsf{conv}(y) \rightarrow \mathsf{C}(x,y)]$ [8]

Whether these axioms are indeed faithful in characterising the convex-hull is not completely certain. The first three are very simple and undoubtably true. 4) is more difficult to see. It states that, if two (finite) regions have the same convex-hull they must be connected.

To show this I introduce the notion of the *convex-hull defining points* of a (finite) region. These are points in the closure of a region which do not lie between any two other points in its closure. Such points will always lie on the surface of a region (i.e. $c(X) - X$) and will always be points where the surface is convex.

The convex-hull defining points of a region uniquely determine its convex-hull. Also every convex-hull has a unique set of defining points. Consequently, two regions have the same convex-hull if and only if they have the same defining points. We may also note that an n dimensional region must have at least $n+1$ defining points. From these observations it is clear that if two regions have the same convex-hull then their closures must share certain points; they must have at least the convex-hull defining points in common. This being so, regions with the same convex-hull must be connected.

So there are compelling arguments for the truth of all the axioms given above. What is less certain is whether this axiom set is complete: it is possible that there are properties (expressible in terms of C and conv) of the convex-hull in Euclidean space that are not captured. If this were the case then there would be situation descriptions consistent with the axioms but impossible under the intended interpretation of the conv operator[9].

7.2 RELATIONS DEFINABLE WITH conv

A large number of new binary relations can be defined in terms of the conv together with other RCC relations.

---

[7]More formally, in terms of point sets, $\mathsf{conv}(X)$ is the closure of X with respect to the relation of *betweenness*, that is $\mathsf{conv}(X) = \{x : \exists y \exists z [y \in X \wedge z \in X \wedge B(y,x,z)]\}$, where $B(x,y,z)$ means that point y lies on the straight line between x and z.

[8]Actually this is not necessarily true for infinite regions.

[9]One way to demonstrate adequacy of the axioms would be to show that they are faithful to the interpretation in terms of the betweenness relation, which has a straightforward algebraic definition in a model which is a Cartesian space over the real numbers (see [14]).

For example [10] gives the following definitions:

- INSIDE$(X,Y) \equiv_{def}$ DR$(X,Y) \wedge$ P$(X,$conv$(Y))$
- P-INSIDE$(X,Y) \equiv_{def}$
  DR$(X,Y) \wedge$ PO$(X,$conv$(Y))$
- OUTSIDE$(X,Y) \equiv_{def}$ DR$(X,$conv$(Y))$ [10]

More generally by combining the 8 basic RCC relation with the conv operator we can specify a total of 8^4 relations of the form $R_1(X,Y) \wedge R_2(X,$conv$(Y)) \wedge R_3($conv$(X),Y) \wedge R_4($conv$(X),$conv$(Y))$.

To keep the number of relations dealt with manageable, I identify a set of 18 mutually exclusive relations which are refinements of the DR. Following [10] I represent these by expressions of the form $[\sigma_1, \sigma_2, \tau](X,Y)$, where σ_1 is either 'I', 'P' or 'O' according as either INSIDE(X,Y), P-INSIDE(X,Y) or OUTSIDE(X,Y); σ_2 refers to the corresponding inverse relation (i.e. one of these 3 relations but with the arguments reversed); and τ is either 'D' or 'E' according to whether the regions are completely disconnected or externally connected. Thus, for example, [P,I,E](X,Y) means that P-INSIDE(X,Y), INSIDE(Y,X) and EC(X,Y).

Actually the relation [I,I,D](X,Y) is impossible, since if two regions are both inside each other they must share the same convex-hull and therefore, according to axiom 4., must be connected. Thus we can identify a basis of 23 pairwise disjoint and mutually exhaustive relations consisting of the 17 possible refinements of DR, plus the six remaining relations of the RCC 8 relation basis.

7.3 ENCODING conv IN $\mathcal{I}_0^+$

Suppose we treat the expression conv(Y) simply as referring to an arbitrary region. Then the relation INSIDE(X,Y) as defined above could be represented by two model constraints: $\sim(X \wedge Y)$ and $X \Rightarrow$ conv(Y), corresponding to DR(X,Y), and P$(X,$conv$(Y))$, respectively. So we can assimilate references to convex-hulls into the $\mathcal{I}_0^+$ representation simply by introducing propositional expressions of the form conv(X) into $\mathcal{I}_0$ formulae. But, as regards correct reasoning, this is inadequate, since the meaning of conv(X) relative to X is not fixed — they are just two regions.

This can be remedied by adding extra constraints to $\mathcal{I}_0^+$ situation representations which enforce the axioms given above. This extra information means that situations which are inconsistent in virtue of these axioms can be detected by means of a $\mathcal{I}_0$ theorem prover. In so far as the axioms adequately characterise the intended interpretation of conv this will serve to fix the meaning of the operator.

---

[10] Note that these relations are not purely topological, since they are not preserved by *rubber* deformations of the regions involved.

Axiom 1. can be enforced as follows: for each region X mentioned in the initial situation description, augment the description with extra model and entailment constraints corresponding to the situation TP$(X,$conv$(X))$. Any model which satisfies this extended model will clearly satisfy axiom 1.

Axiom 2. is taken into account implicitly. In enforcing axiom 1. we introduce extra regions into the situation description corresponding to the convex-hulls of each region in the initial description. Axiom 2. tells us that these are the only additional regions we need consider, since iterating the conv functions does not produce any more new regions.

Treatment of axioms 3. and 4. is encompassed by a general procedure which enables enforcement of all axioms of the form:

$$\forall x_1, \ldots, x_n[\Phi(x_1,\ldots,x_n) \rightarrow \Psi(x_1,\ldots,x_n)],$$

where $\Phi(x_1,\ldots,x_n)$ and $\Psi(x_1,\ldots,x_n)$ specify situations which can be described by means of $\mathcal{I}_0^+$.

To test whether a given $\mathcal{I}_0^+$ situation description satisfies such an axiom an iterative fixed-point method can be used:

- Test the $\mathcal{I}_0^+$ description for consistency
- Check whether some instance of the antecedent is entailed by an the initial description. This involves translating $\Phi(\ldots)$ into $\mathcal{I}_0^+$ and substituting all combinations of constants occurring in the description for the free variables.
- If any such $\Phi(\ldots)$ is entailed add the corresponding $\mathcal{I}_0^+$ representation of $\Psi(\ldots)$, under the same substitution, to the situation description.
- Repeat until either the situation description becomes inconsistent or no new information is added by the previous step.

This process must terminate; and if the final situation description is still consistent then clearly the axiom is satisfiable, since for all substitutions either the antecedent is not entailed by the description or the consequent has been explicitly added.

Clearly the convex-hull axioms 3. and 4. are of the form which can be captured in this manner. In fact, since their antecedents are quite simple, they can be enforced quite efficiently.

7.4 AN AUTOMATICALLY GENERATED 23 RELATION COMPOSITION TABLE

Table 5 gives the full composition table (i.e. table of loci of composition) for the basis of 23 relations described in section 7.2. If $R_1(A,B)$ and $R_2(B,C)$, where R_1 is the relation specified in the left hand column and R_2 is specified along the top, the corresponding table entry encodes the possible values of the relation $R_3(A,C)$. Each of the 23 relations is represented

Table 5: Loci of Composition for a Basis of 23 Spatial Relations

Rel.	*Rep.*	1	2	3	4	5	6	7	8	9	10	11	12	13	14	15	16	17	18	19	20	21	22	23
		⋆·· ··· ··· ···	∘·· ··· ··· ···	·∘· ··· ··· ···	·⋆· ··· ··· ···	··⋆ ··· ··· ···	··∘ ··· ··· ···	··· ⋆·· ··· ···	··· ·⋆· ··· ···	··· ·∘· ··· ···	··· ··⋆ ··· ···	··· ··∘ ··· ···	··· ··· ⋆·· ···	··· ··· ∘·· ···	··· ··· ·⋆· ···	··· ··· ·∘· ···	··· ··· ··⋆ ···	··· ··· ··∘ ···	··· ··· ··· ⋆··	··· ··· ··· ∘··	··· ··· ··· ·⋆·	··· ··· ··· ·∘·	··· ··· ··· ··⋆	··· ··· ··· ··∘
1 NTPP	⋆·· ··· ··· ···	⋆·· ··· ··· ···	⋆·· ··· ··· ···	•∘· ⋆•• ••• •••	⋆·· ··· ··· ···	••• ⋆•• ••• •••	•∘· ⋆•• ••• •••	··· ·∘∘ ··· ···	··· ·∘∘ ··· ···	··· ·∘∘ ··· ···	··· ··∘ ··· ···	··· ··∘ ··· ···	··· ·∘∘ ∘∘∘ ∘∘∘	··· ·∘∘ ∘∘∘ ∘∘∘	··· ·∘∘ ·∘∘ ·∘∘	··· ·∘∘ ·∘∘ ·∘∘	··· ··∘ ··∘ ··∘	··· ··∘ ··∘ ··∘	··· ··· ··· ∘∘∘	··· ··· ··· ∘∘∘	··· ··· ··· ·∘∘	··· ··· ··· ·∘∘	··· ··· ··· ··∘	··· ··· ··· ··∘
2 TPP	∘·· ··· ··· ···	⋆·· ··· ··· ···	•·· ··· ··· ···	•∘· ⋆•• ••• •••	∘·· ··· ··· ···	·∘• ⋆•• ••• •••	∘•∘ ⋆•• ••• •••	··· ⋆•• ··· ···	··· ·•• ··· ···	··· ·∘∘ ··· ···	··· ··• ··· ···	··· ··∘ ··· ···	··· ⋆•• ••• •••	··· ·∘∘ ∘∘∘ ∘∘∘	··· ·•• ·•• ·••	··· ·∘∘ ·∘∘ ·∘∘	··· ··• ··• ··•	··· ··∘ ··∘ ··∘	··· ··· ··· •••	··· ··· ··· ∘∘∘	··· ··· ··· ·••	··· ··· ··· ·∘∘	··· ··· ··· ··•	··· ··· ··· ··∘
3 PO	·∘· ··· ··· ···	•∘· ··· ··· ···	•∘· ··· ··· ···	••• ⋆•• ••• •••	·∘· ··· ··· ···	·∘• ⋆•• ••• •••	·∘• ⋆•• ••• •••	·∘• ⋆•• ••• ···	·∘• ⋆•• ••• ···	·∘• ⋆•• ••• ···	·∘• ⋆•• ••• ···	·∘• ⋆•• ••• ···	·∘• ⋆•• ••• •••	·∘• ⋆•• ••• •••	·∘• ⋆•• ••• •••	·∘• ⋆•• ••• •••	·∘• ⋆•• ••• •••	·∘• ⋆•• ••• •••	·∘• ··· ••• •••	·∘• ··· ••• •••	·∘• ··· ••• •••	·∘• ··· ••• •••	·∘• ··· ••• •••	·∘• ··· ••• •••
4 EQ	·⋆· ··· ··· ···	⋆·· ··· ··· ···	∘·· ··· ··· ···	·∘· ··· ··· ···	·⋆· ··· ··· ···	··⋆ ··· ··· ···	··∘ ··· ··· ···	··· ⋆·· ··· ···	··· ·⋆· ··· ···	··· ·∘· ··· ···	··· ··⋆ ··· ···	··· ··∘ ··· ···	··· ··· ⋆·· ···	··· ··· ∘·· ···	··· ··· ·⋆· ···	··· ··· ·∘· ···	··· ··· ··⋆ ···	··· ··· ··∘ ···	··· ··· ··· ⋆··	··· ··· ··· ∘··	··· ··· ··· ·⋆·	··· ··· ··· ·∘·	··· ··· ··· ··⋆	··· ··· ··· ··∘
5 NTPP^{-1}	··⋆ ··· ··· ···	••• ··· ··· ···	·∘• ··· ··· ···	·∘• ··· ··· ···	··⋆ ··· ··· ···	··⋆ ··· ··· ···	··⋆ ··· ··· ···	·∘• ··· ··· ···	·∘• ··· ··· ···	·∘• ⋆•· ••· ···	·∘• ··· ··· ···	·∘• ⋆•• ••• ···	·∘• ··· ··· ···	·∘• ··· •·· ···	·∘• ··· ··· ···	·∘• ··· ••· ···	·∘• ··· ··· ···	·∘• ··· ••• ···	·∘• ··· ··· ···	·∘• ··· •·· •··	·∘• ··· ··· ···	·∘• ··· ••· ••·	·∘• ··· ··· ···	·∘• ··· ••• •••
6 TPP^{-1}	··∘ ··· ··· ···	•∘· ··· ··· ···	∘•∘ ··· ··· ···	·∘• ··· ··· ···	··∘ ··· ··· ···	··⋆ ··· ··· ···	··• ··· ··· ···	·∘• ⋆·· ⋆·· ···	·∘• ⋆⋆· ⋆⋆· ···	·∘• ⋆•· ••· ···	·∘• ⋆⋆⋆ ⋆⋆⋆ ···	·∘• ⋆•• ••• ···	·∘• ··· ⋆·· ···	·∘• ··· •·· ···	·∘• ··· ⋆⋆· ···	·∘• ··· ••· ···	·∘• ··· ⋆⋆⋆ ···	·∘• ··· ••• ···	·∘• ··· ⋆·· ⋆··	·∘• ··· •·· •··	·∘• ··· ⋆⋆· ⋆⋆·	·∘• ··· ••· ••·	·∘• ··· ⋆⋆⋆ ⋆⋆⋆	·∘• ··· ••• •••
7 [IIE]	··· ⋆·· ··· ···	•∘· ··· ··· ···	•∘· ⋆⋆· ··· ···	•∘· ⋆•· ••· ••·	··· ⋆·· ··· ···	··· ··· ∘·· ∘··	··· ⋆·· •·· •··	∘•∘ ⋆·· ··· ···	∘∘· ·•· ··· ···	·∘· ·•· ··· ···	··· ··• ··· ···	··· ··• ··· ···	·∘∘ ··· •·· •··	·∘• ··· •·· •··	·∘· ··· ·•· ·•·	·∘· ··· ·•· ·•·	··· ··· ··• ··•	··· ··· ··• ··•	·∘∘ ··· •·· •··	·∘• ··· •·· •··	·∘· ··· ·•· ·•·	·∘· ··· ·•· ·•·	··· ··· ··• ··•	··· ··· ··• ··•
8 [IPE]	··· ·⋆· ··· ···	•∘· ··· ··· ···	•∘· ·⋆· ··· ···	•∘· ⋆•• ••• •••	··· ·⋆· ··· ···	··· ·∘∘ ∘∘∘ ∘∘∘	··· ⋆•• ••• •••	∘∘· ·•• ··· ···	∘∘· ·•• ··· ···	·∘· ·•• ··· ···	··· ··• ··· ···	··· ··• ··· ···	∘•∘ ⋆•• ••• •••	·∘• ⋆•• ••• •••	∘∘· ·•• ·•• ·••	·∘· ·•• ·•• ·••	··· ··• ··• ··•	··· ··• ··• ··•	·∘∘ ··· ••• •••	·∘• ··· ••• •••	·∘· ··· ·•• ·••	·∘· ··· ·•• ·••	··· ··· ··• ··•	··· ··· ··• ··•
9 [IPD]	··· ·∘· ··· ···	•∘· ·•· ··· ···	•∘· ·•· ··· ···	•∘· ⋆•• ••• •••	··· ·∘· ··· ···	··· ·∘∘ ∘∘∘ ∘∘∘	··· ·∘∘ ∘∘∘ ∘∘∘	•∘· ·•• ··· ···	•∘· ·•• ··· ···	•∘· ·•• ··· ···	··· ··• ··· ···	··· ··• ··· ···	•∘· ⋆•• ••• •••	••• ⋆•• ••• •••	•∘· ·•• ·•• ·••	•∘· ·•• ·•• ·••	··· ··• ··• ··•	··· ··• ··• ··•	·∘· ··· ••• •••	·∘• ··· ••• •••	·∘· ··· ·•• ·••	·∘· ··· ·•• ·••	··· ··· ··• ··•	··· ··· ··• ··•
10 [IOE]	··· ··⋆ ··· ···	•∘· ··· ··· ···	•∘· ·⋆⋆ ··· ···	•∘· ·•• ·•• ·••	··· ··⋆ ··· ···	··· ··∘ ··∘ ··∘	··· ··• ··• ··•	∘∘· ·•• ··· ···	∘∘· ·•• ··· ···	·∘· ·•• ··· ···	··· ··• ··· ···	··· ··• ··· ···	∘∘· ·•• ·•• ·••	·∘· ·•• ·•• ·••	∘∘· ·•• ·•• ·••	·∘· ·•• ·•• ·••	··· ··• ··• ··•	··· ··• ··• ··•	∘•∘ ⋆•• ••• •••	·∘• ⋆•• ••• •••	∘∘· ·•• ·•• ·••	·∘· ·•• ·•• ·••	··· ··• ··• ··•	··· ··• ··• ··•
11 [IOD]	··· ··∘ ··· ···	•∘· ·•• ··· ···	•∘· ·•• ··· ···	•∘· ·•• ·•• ·••	··· ··∘ ··· ···	··· ··∘ ··∘ ··∘	··· ··∘ ··∘ ··∘	•∘· ·•• ··· ···	•∘· ·•• ··· ···	•∘· ·•• ··· ···	··· ··• ··· ···	··· ··• ··· ···	•∘· ·•• ·•• ·••	•∘· ·•• ·•• ·••	•∘· ·•• ·•• ·••	•∘· ·•• ·•• ·••	··· ··• ··• ··•	··· ··• ··• ··•	•∘· ⋆•• ••• •••	••• ⋆•• ••• •••	•∘· ·•• ·•• ·••	•∘· ·•• ·•• ·••	··· ··• ··• ··•	··· ··• ··• ··•
12 [PIE]	··· ··· ⋆·· ···	•∘· ··· ··· ···	•∘· ⋆⋆· ⋆⋆· ···	•∘· ⋆•· ••· ••·	··· ··· ⋆·· ···	··· ··· ∘·· ∘··	··· ··· •·· •··	·∘∘ ··· •·· ···	∘•∘ ⋆•· ••· ···	·∘• ⋆•· ••· ···	·∘∘ ⋆•• ••• ···	·∘• ⋆•• ••• ···	·∘∘ ··· •·· •··	·∘• ··· •·· •··	·∘∘ ··· ••· ••·	·∘• ··· ••· ••·	·∘∘ ··· ••• •••	·∘• ··· ••• •••	·∘∘ ··· •·· •··	·∘• ··· •·· •··	·∘∘ ··· ••· ••·	·∘• ··· ••· ••·	·∘∘ ··· ••• •••	·∘• ··· ••• •••
13 [PID]	··· ··· ∘·· ···	•∘· ⋆•· ••· ···	•∘· ⋆•· ••· ···	•∘· ⋆•· ••· ••·	··· ··· ∘·· ···	··· ··· ∘·· ∘··	··· ··· ∘·· ∘··	·∘· ··· •·· ···	•∘· ⋆•· ••· ···	••• ⋆•· ••· ···	·∘· ⋆•• ••• ···	·∘• ⋆•• ••• ···	·∘· ··· •·· •··	·∘• ··· •·· •··	·∘· ··· ••· ••·	·∘• ··· ••· ••·	·∘· ··· ••• •••	·∘• ··· ••• •••	·∘· ··· •·· •··	·∘• ··· •·· •··	·∘· ··· ••· ••·	·∘• ··· ••· ••·	·∘· ··· ••• •••	·∘• ··· ••• •••
14 [PPE]	··· ··· ·⋆· ···	•∘· ··· ··· ···	•∘· ·⋆· ·⋆· ···	•∘· ⋆•• ••• •••	··· ··· ·⋆· ···	··· ··· ∘∘∘ ∘∘∘	··· ··· ••• •••	·∘· ··· ·•• ···	∘∘· ·•• ·•• ···	·∘· ·•• ·•• ···	·∘· ·•• ·•• ···	·∘· ·•• ·•• ···	·∘∘ ··· ••• •••	·∘• ··· ••• •••	∘•∘ ⋆•• ••• •••	·∘• ⋆•• ••• •••	·∘∘ ⋆•• ••• •••	·∘• ⋆•• ••• •••	·∘∘ ··· ••• •••	·∘• ··· ••• •••	·∘∘ ··· ••• •••	·∘• ··· ••• •••	·∘∘ ··· ••• •••	·∘• ··· ••• •••
15 [PPD]	··· ··· ·∘· ···	•∘· ·•· ·•· ···	•∘· ·•· ·•· ···	•∘· ⋆•• ••• •••	··· ··· ·∘· ···	··· ··· ∘∘∘ ∘∘∘	··· ··· ∘∘∘ ∘∘∘	·∘· ··· ·•• ···	•∘· ·•• ·•• ···	•∘· ·•• ·•• ···	·∘· ·•• ·•• ···	·∘· ·•• ·•• ···	·∘· ··· ••• •••	·∘• ··· ••• •••	•∘· ⋆•• ••• •••	••• ⋆•• ••• •••	·∘· ⋆•• ••• •••	·∘• ⋆•• ••• •••	·∘· ··· ••• •••	·∘• ··· ••• •••	·∘· ··· ••• •••	·∘• ··· ••• •••	·∘· ··· ••• •••	·∘• ··· ••• •••
16 [POE]	··· ··· ··⋆ ···	•∘· ··· ··· ···	•∘· ·⋆⋆ ·⋆⋆ ···	•∘· ·•• ·•• ·••	··· ··· ··⋆ ···	··· ··· ··∘ ··∘	··· ··· ··• ··•	·∘· ··· ·•• ···	∘∘· ·•• ·•• ···	·∘· ·•• ·•• ···	·∘· ·•• ·•• ···	·∘· ·•• ·•• ···	·∘· ··· ·•• ·••	·∘· ··· ·•• ·••	∘∘· ·•• ·•• ·••	·∘· ·•• ·•• ·••	·∘· ·•• ·•• ·••	·∘· ·•• ·•• ·••	·∘∘ ··· ••• •••	·∘• ··· ••• •••	∘•∘ ⋆•• ••• •••	·∘• ⋆•• ••• •••	·∘∘ ⋆•• ••• •••	·∘• ⋆•• ••• •••
17 [POD]	··· ··· ··∘ ···	•∘· ·•• ·•• ···	•∘· ·•• ·•• ···	•∘· ·•• ·•• ·••	··· ··· ··∘ ···	··· ··· ··∘ ··∘	··· ··· ··∘ ··∘	·∘· ··· ·•• ···	•∘· ·•• ·•• ···	•∘· ·•• ·•• ···	·∘· ·•• ·•• ···	·∘· ·•• ·•• ···	·∘· ··· ·•• ·••	·∘· ··· ·•• ·••	•∘· ·•• ·•• ·••	•∘· ·•• ·•• ·••	·∘· ·•• ·•• ·••	·∘· ·•• ·•• ·••	·∘· ··· ••• •••	·∘• ··· ••• •••	•∘· ⋆•• ••• •••	••• ⋆•• ••• •••	·∘· ⋆•• ••• •••	·∘• ⋆•• ••• •••
18 [OIE]	··· ··· ··· ⋆··	•∘· ··· ··· ···	•∘· ⋆⋆· ⋆⋆· ⋆⋆·	•∘· ⋆•· ••· ••·	··· ··· ··· ⋆··	··· ··· ··· ∘··	··· ··· ··· •··	··· ··· ··· •··	∘∘· ⋆•· ••· ••·	·∘· ⋆•· ••· ••·	∘•∘ ⋆•• ••• •••	·∘• ⋆•• ••• •••	··· ··· ··· •··	··· ··· ··· •··	·∘· ··· ••· ••·	·∘· ··· ••· ••·	·∘∘ ··· ••• •••	·∘• ··· ••• •••	··· ··· ··· •··	··· ··· ··· •··	·∘· ··· ••· ••·	·∘· ··· ••· ••·	·∘∘ ··· ••• •••	·∘• ··· ••• •••
19 [OID]	··· ··· ··· ∘··	•∘· ⋆•· ••· ••·	•∘· ⋆•· ••· ••·	•∘· ⋆•· ••· ••·	··· ··· ··· ∘··	··· ··· ··· ∘··	··· ··· ··· ∘··	··· ··· ··· •··	•∘· ⋆•· ••· ••·	•∘· ⋆•· ••· ••·	•∘· ⋆•• ••• •••	••• ⋆•• ••• •••	··· ··· ··· •··	··· ··· ··· •··	·∘· ··· ••· ••·	·∘· ··· ••· ••·	·∘· ··· ••• •••	·∘• ··· ••• •••	··· ··· ··· •··	··· ··· ··· •··	·∘· ··· ••· ••·	·∘· ··· ••· ••·	·∘· ··· ••• •••	·∘• ··· ••• •••
20 [OPE]	··· ··· ··· ·⋆·	•∘· ··· ··· ···	•∘· ·⋆· ·⋆· ·⋆·	•∘· ⋆•• ••• •••	··· ··· ··· ·⋆·	··· ··· ··· ∘∘∘	··· ··· ··· •••	··· ··· ··· ·••	∘∘· ·•• ·•• ·••	·∘· ·•• ·•• ·••	∘∘· ·•• ·•• ·••	·∘· ·•• ·•• ·••	··· ··· ··· •••	··· ··· ··· •••	∘∘· ⋆•• ••• •••	·∘· ⋆•• ••• •••	∘•∘ ⋆•• ••• •••	·∘• ⋆•• ••• •••	··· ··· ··· •••	··· ··· ··· •••	·∘· ··· ••• •••	·∘· ··· ••• •••	·∘∘ ··· ••• •••	·∘• ··· ••• •••
21 [OPD]	··· ··· ··· ·∘·	•∘· ·•· ·•· ·•·	•∘· ·•· ·•· ·•·	•∘· ⋆•• ••• •••	··· ··· ··· ·∘·	··· ··· ··· ∘∘∘	··· ··· ··· ∘∘∘	··· ··· ··· ·••	•∘· ·•• ·•• ·••	•∘· ·•• ·•• ·••	•∘· ·•• ·•• ·••	•∘· ·•• ·•• ·••	··· ··· ··· •••	··· ··· ··· •••	•∘· ⋆•• ••• •••	•∘· ⋆•• ••• •••	•∘· ⋆•• ••• •••	••• ⋆•• ••• •••	··· ··· ··· •••	··· ··· ··· •••	·∘· ··· ••• •••	·∘· ··· ••• •••	·∘· ··· ••• •••	·∘• ··· ••• •••
22 [OOE]	··· ··· ··· ··⋆	•∘· ··· ··· ···	•∘· ·⋆⋆ ·⋆⋆ ·⋆⋆	•∘· ·•• ·•• ·••	··· ··· ··· ··⋆	··· ··· ··· ··∘	··· ··· ··· ··•	··· ··· ··· ·••	∘∘· ·•• ·•• ·••	·∘· ·•• ·•• ·••	∘∘· ·•• ·•• ·••	·∘· ·•• ·•• ·••	··· ··· ··· ·••	··· ··· ··· ·••	∘∘· ·•• ·•• ·••	·∘· ·•• ·•• ·••	∘∘· ·•• ·•• ·••	·∘· ·•• ·•• ·••	··· ··· ··· •••	··· ··· ··· •••	∘∘· ⋆•• ••• •••	·∘· ⋆•• ••• •••	∘•∘ ⋆•• ••• •••	·∘• ⋆•• ••• •••
23 [OOD]	··· ··· ··· ··∘	•∘· ·•• ·•• ·••	•∘· ·•• ·•• ·••	•∘· ·•• ·•• ·••	··· ··· ··· ··∘	··· ··· ··· ··∘	··· ··· ··· ··∘	··· ··· ··· ·••	•∘· ·•• ·•• ·••	•∘· ·•• ·•• ·••	•∘· ·•• ·•• ·••	•∘· ·•• ·•• ·••	··· ··· ··· ·••	··· ··· ··· ·••	•∘· ·•• ·•• ·••	•∘· ·•• ·•• ·••	•∘· ·•• ·•• ·••	•∘· ·•• ·•• ·••	··· ··· ··· •••	··· ··· ··· •••	•∘· ⋆•• ••• •••	•∘· ⋆•• ••• •••	•∘· ⋆•• ••• •••	••• ⋆•• ••• •••

by one of the two symbols '⋆' and '∘' at a certain position in a 3×4 matrix. These representations are shown in the second column. Table entries are constructed by superimposing the representations for each of the possible relations. Where '⋆' and '∘' should both be present in the same position, the symbol '•' is used.

The table was generated using meta-level enforcement of the conv axioms in a Prolog implemented $\mathcal{I}_0^+$ reasoning program. It was produced in 3h 31mins on a SPARC10 workstation. Such a table has hitherto never been computed by a proof oriented method. [3] contains a similar table constructed using a model building approach but it has subsequently been found that the table given there is too strict in that it rules out certain configurations, which are in fact possible for 3D spatial regions. My table has not been found to contain any false entries.

8 CONCLUSIONS

I have shown how a significant family of spatial relations can be represented in a logical representation which is decidable. The computational effectiveness of this representation has been demonstrated by generating tables of loci of composition for a number of sets of spatial relations.

The divergence between expressiveness and tractability of logical languages is perhaps the greatest obstacle to the development of AI systems. I believe that this problem can be mitigated to some extent by ensuring that the expressive power of a representation does not exceed what is really needed. In particular, much of the power of 1st-order logic is unnecessary for reasoning in many domains. Hence, it is likely that encoding information in a (non-classical) propositional logic rather than 1st-order calculus may provide a mechanism for effective reasoning in other areas of knowledge representation.

There are many ways in which the system presented here could be enhanced. The efficiency of the system could be improved by optimising its theorem proving performance. Also expressivity could be increased by developing a more general framework for meta-level enforcement of 1st-order axioms.

I am currently exploring the possibility of using the modal logic $S4$ for spatial reasoning. This may well prove to be better suited to the task than $\mathcal{I}_0$.

Acknowledgements

This work was partially supported by the CEC under the Basic Research Action MEDLAR 2, Project 6471 and by the SERC under grants GR/H 78955 and GR/G 64388.

Thanks to Dr. A.G. Cohn for enthusiasm and helpful comments.

References

[1] ALLEN, J. Maintaining knowledge about temporal intervals. *Comm. ACM 26(11)* (1983).

[2] CLARK, B. A calculus of individuals based on 'connection'. *Notre Dame Journal of Formal Logic, 22(3)* (1985).

[3] COHN, A., RANDELL, D., CUI, Z., AND BENNETT, B. Qualitative spatial reasoning and representation. In *Qualitative Reasoning and Decision Technologies*, P. Carrete and M. Singh, Eds. CIMNE, Barcelona, 1993.

[4] DUMMETT, M. *Elements of Intuitionism*. Oxford Logic Guides. Clarendon Press, Oxford, 1977.

[5] HUDELMAIER, J. An $O(n \log n)$-space decision procedure for intuitionistic propositional logic. *Journal of Logic and Computation 3*, 1 (Feb. 1993), 63–75.

[6] KURATOWSKI, K. *Introduction to Set Theory and Topology*, 2nd ed. Pergamon Press, 1972.

[7] MCCUNE, W. Otter 2.0 users guide. Tech. rep., Argonne National Laboratory, Argonne, Illinois, Mar. 1990.

[8] MOSTOWSKI, A. *Thirty Years of Foundational Studies*. Blackwell, Oxford, 1966.

[9] OPPEN, D. Complexity, convexity and combinations of theories. *Theoretical Computer Science*, 12 (1980), 291–302.

[10] RANDELL, D., CUI, Z., AND COHN, A. A spatial logic based on regions and connection. *Proc. of the 3rd Int. Conf. on Knowledge Representation and Reasoning* (1992).

[11] RANDELL, D. A., AND COHN, A. G. Modelling topological and metrical properties of physical processes. In *Proceedings 1st International Conference on the Principles of Knowledge Representation and Reasoning* (Los Altos, 1989), R. Brachman, H. Levesque, and R. Reiter, Eds., Morgan Kaufmann, pp. 55–66.

[12] RANDELL, D. A., COHN, A. G., AND CUI, Z. Computing transitivity tables: A challenge for automated theorem provers. In *Proceedings CADE 11* (Berlin, 1992), Springer Verlag.

[13] TARSKI, A. Sentential calculus and topology. In *Logic, Semantics, Metamathematics*. Oxford Clarendon Press, 1956, ch. 17. trans. J.H. Woodger.

[14] TARSKI, A. What is elementary geometry? In *The Axiomatic Method (with special reference to geometry and physics)* (Amsterdam, 1959), L. Brouwer, E. Beth, and A. Heyting, Eds., North-Holland, pp. 16–29.

On the Relation Between Default and Modal Consequence Relations

Alexander Bochman
Dept. of Mathematics
Bar-Ilan University
Ramat-Gan, Israel

Abstract

The notion of a default consequence relation is introduced as a generalization of both default and modal formalizations of nonmonotonic reasoning. It is used to study a general problem of correspondence between these two formalisms. As is shown, in many cases each of them can be translated into the other.

1 INTRODUCTION

In this paper we will attempt a systematic study of the relation between default and modal formalizations of nonmonotonic reasoning. To this end, we consider first the reformulation of both default logic and modal nonmonotonic logics as proof systems involving rules, or sequents, with the form

$$a : b \Vdash A,$$

where a and b are finite sets of propositions. The informal interpretation of such sequents will be, "If all propositions from a are assumed (or believed) to hold and no proposition from b is assumed to hold, then infer A." Sets of default sequents satisfying certain conditions will be called *default consequence relations*. Such consequence relations can in fact be considered as a generalization of Reiter's default logic. The main distinctive feature of our formalization is an explicit use of 'meta-rules' allowing to infer new default sequents from given ones. It turns out that for extensions and other 'preferred' objects relevant to our study there are important structural rules that preserve these objects, and hence such rules can be safely added to any consequence relation. Though we do not reach completeness in this way, there are reasons to believe that certain sets of such rules provide a primary characterization of 'logical paradigms' behind different kinds of nonmonotonic reasoning.

As the next step, we introduce the notion of a *modal* default consequence relation. These relations will be defined in a language with a modal operator, but otherwise will involve the same rules as default consequence relations. Modal default consequence relations turn out to be an especially suitable tool for studying modal nonmonotonic reasoning. Thus, both autoepistemic reasoning ([14]) and reasoning with 'negative' introspection ([9,11,13]) acquire a natural characterization in this framework.

As we show in [1], under certain reasonable conditions modal consequence relations can be reduced to the associated nonmodal default consequence relations in a way that in some well-defined sense preserves the basic nonmonotonic objects. These results will be used here in order to establish a two-way correspondence between modal and default formalizations. Thus, for a number of modal nonmonotonic logics that appear in the literature, we will give a representation in terms of modal default consequence relations. We will show also how and under what conditions objective default consequence relations can be faithfully embedded into modal ones. These latter results provide a natural generalization of Truszczyński's results (see [19,20]) concerning modal translation of defaults. Finally, we will demonstrate that the modal logic **K45**, associated with autoepistemic reasoning, is in some strong sense equivalent to a certain nonmodal default consequence relation.

Due to space limitations, proofs of all the new results presented here will appear elsewhere.

2 DEFAULT CONSEQUENCE RELATIONS

In this section, we will introduce the notion of a default consequence relation. It will be defined as a set of default sequents of the above form satisfying certain rules that allow to infer new sequents from given ones. In fact, it is these rules that make a set of defaults a proof system. Defaults as such do not bear information about when and how they can be applied on their heads. For ordinary inference rules, this information can be embodied in the form of 'meta-rules' that produce new inference rules from given ones (this is actually the main idea behind various sequent calculi). Default consequence relations is an attempt to extend this idea on (nonmonotonic) inference rules that involve as their premises not only what is assumed to hold, but also what is assumed not to hold.

We will presuppose that default consequence relations are defined in a propositional language with a predefined notion of a logical (deductive) consequence. In this paper we will assume that it is an ordinary classical consequence. The corresponding deductive consequence operator will be denoted, as usual, by Th.

Definition 2.1 A set of default sequents with the form $a : b \Vdash A$, where a, b are finite sets of propositions and A a proposition, will be called a *default consequence relation* if it satisfies the following two rules

(*Monotonicity*) If $a : b \Vdash A$ and $a \subseteq a'$, $b \subseteq b'$, then $a' : b' \Vdash A$.

(*Deductive Closure*) If $A \in \text{Th}(c)$ and $a : b \Vdash C_i$, for any $C_i \in c$, then $a : b \Vdash A$.

Default consequence relations can indeed be considered as relations, that is relations between pairs of premise sets, on the one hand, and propositions in conclusions, on the other. Propositions from the first premise set will be called *positive premises*, while those from the second premise set—*negative premises*. The rules (Monotonicity) and (Deductive Closure) provide a primary constraint on our understanding of default sequents. (Monotonicity) says, in effect, that default sequents are applicable in *all* contexts in which their premises hold. Note that this immediately distinguish default rules from, e.g., preferential entailment that restrict applicability of rules to 'preferred' contexts in which the premises hold. (Deductive Closure) is less controversial; it says that deductive consequences of provable propositions are also provable.

Though default consequence relations were defined only for finite sets of premises, the definition can be easily extended to arbitrary sets of premises by stipulating that for any possibly infinite sets of propositions u and v,

$$u : v \Vdash A \quad \text{if and only if} \quad a : b \Vdash A,$$

for some finite a, b such that $a \subseteq u$, $b \subseteq v$. This stipulation also ensures that default consequence relations will satisfy the *compactness property*. Hence, in treating infinite sets of premises, we will assume that compactness holds.

The general notion of a default consequence relation is rather uninformative. It is only a frame that can be 'filled' by additional rules that would provide a more tight description of our intuitions about nonmonotonic reasoning. As we will see, there is no single system that reflects adequately *all* our intuitions. In fact, different nonmonotonic constructions admit different, even incompatible, reasoning paradigms. Below we will consider a number of rules and conditions that will form the basis for a subsequent classification of various kinds of default reasoning.

To begin with, we introduce the following rule:

$$(Cut) \quad \frac{a : b \Vdash A \quad a, A : b \Vdash B}{a : b \Vdash B}$$

The rule (Cut) reflects a kind of cumulativity of default reasoning in the sense that it permits the use of inferred propositions as additional positive premises in the proof. As we will see, the rule allows to avoid explicit iterative constructions commonly used in defining nonmonotonic objects. Consequently, a default consequence relation will be called *iterative* if it satisfies (Cut).

The following axiom states that no proposition can serve as both a positive and negative premise in a proof:

$$(Consistency) \qquad A : A \Vdash \bot,$$

where $\bot$ denotes the proposition "False". The axiom implies that consistent pairs of premise sets must be disjoint. Though this requirement is not universally acceptable (it does not hold, for example, in some semantics for logic programming), it will hold for all systems we will consider in this paper.

The following pair of rules reflect the requirement of deductive closure for positive and negative premises, respectively.

(*Positive Closure*)
$$\frac{A \in \text{Th}(a) \quad a, A : b \Vdash B}{a : b \Vdash B}$$

(*Negative Closure*) If $B \in \text{Th}(c)$ and $a : b, C_i \Vdash A$, for any $C_i \in c$, then $a : b, B \Vdash A$.

(Positive Closure) implies that deductive consequences of positive premises can be safely used as additional positive premises, while (Negative Closure) says that if we reject a proposition, we must reject at least one proposition from any set of propositions that implies it deductively.

One of the main consequences of the above rules is the possibility of replacment of deductively equivalent formulas both in positive and in negative premises. Note that, in the classical case, (Negative Closure) can be shown to be equivalent to the following three simple rules[1]:

(1) $\quad \emptyset : \neg\bot \Vdash \bot.$

---

[1] Similar rules can also be given for (Positive Closure) and (Deductive CLosure).

(2) If B follows deductively from A and $a:b, A \Vdash C$, then $a:b, B \Vdash C$.

(3) $\dfrac{a:b, A \Vdash C \quad a:b, B \Vdash C}{a:b, A \wedge B \Vdash C}$.

All the rules and conditions considered so far will hold in all basic systems discussed in the paper. Now we turn to considering rules that make a difference. The first is the following Reflexivity axiom:

(*Reflexivity*) $\quad A : \emptyset \Vdash A$.

Despite its apparent plausibility, the axiom does not hold for some natural interpretations of default sequents (e.g., when the premises represent propositions that are or are not *believed*, while conclusions are assumed to be true). Still, there exists an instance of the axiom that will be assumed to hold:

(*Positive Consistency*)
$$\bot : \emptyset \Vdash \bot.$$

(Positive Consistency) implies, in particular, that consistent pairs of premise sets must include consistent sets of positive premises.

The second controversial rule is a rule that permits 'reasoning by cases'(cf. [16]):

(*Factoring*) $\dfrac{a, B : b \Vdash A \quad a : b, B \Vdash A}{a : b \Vdash A}$.

The rule implies, in effect, that contexts of reasoning are complete (two-valued) with respect to positive and negative assumptions. It turns out to be characteristic of autoepistemic reasoning (see below).

Again, there is an important weaker form of 'factoring' that will hold for all systems considered in the paper.

(*Negative Factoring*)
$\dfrac{a, B : b \Vdash \bot \quad a : b, B \Vdash A}{a : b \Vdash A}$.

The rule says that if it is inconsistent to assume a proposition as a positive premise, then it can be assumed as an additional negative premise. In fact, the rule can be seen as a realization of the 'negation as inconsistency' principle suggested in [5].

What will happen if we accept all the rules given above? Before we answer this question, let us introduce the following definition.

Definition 2.2 A default consequence relation will be called *stable* if it satisfies (Cut), (Consistency), (Reflexivity) and (Factoring).

It can be shown that the above four rules imply both (Positive Closure) and (Negative Closure). Hence, stable consequence relations satisfy all the above rules.

Unfortunately, the following theorem shows that stable default consequence relations constitute a limit case—they are already monotonic. To be more exact, they are equivalent to (monotonic) Scott consequence relations. A binary relation $a \vdash b$ between sets of propositions is called a *Scott consequence relation* (see [4]) if it satisfies the following conditions:

(*Reflexivity*) $\quad A \vdash A$;

(*Monotonicity*) If $a \vdash b$ and $a \subseteq a'$, $b \subseteq b'$, then $a' \vdash b'$;

(*Cut*) $\dfrac{a \vdash b, A \quad a, A \vdash b}{a \vdash b}$.

Theorem 2.1 *Let $\Vdash$ be a stable consequence relation. Define the following consequence relation between sets of propositions:*

$$a \vdash_{\Vdash} b \equiv a : b \Vdash \bot.$$

Then $\vdash_{\Vdash}$ is a Scott consequence relation and $a : b \Vdash A$ if and only if $a \vdash_{\Vdash} b, A$.

A distinctive feature of stable consequence relations, a feature that makes them inappropriate as a basis for nonmonotonic reasonig systems, is the validity of the following rule:

(*Symmetry*) $\dfrac{a:b, B \Vdash A}{a:b, A \Vdash B}$.

It is this rule that actually reduces default-type sequents to monotonic disjunctive, or 'multiple-conclusion', rules. Nevertheless, we will see that stable consequence relations constitute an important 'upper bound' on reasonable nonmonotonic systems. In other words, for reasons that will become clear from what follows, all such systems should contain only rules that are also valid for stable consequence relations.

The main lesson from the theorem is that in order to obtain nontrivial nonmonotonic consequence relations, we must reject one of the four rules constituting the definition of a stable consequence relation. As we will show below, default logic and modal nonmonotonic logics give rise to two basic kinds of reasoning. One of them, which is associated with autoepistemic logic, involve rejection of (Reflexivity) and accept the rest of the rules. The second kind of reasoning is associated with default logic and modal nonmonotonic logics based on 'negative introspection'; it is characterized by rejecting (Factoring). Consequently, we introduce the following definitions:

Definition 2.3 A default consequence relation will be called *autoepistemic* if it satisfies (Cut), (Consistency), (Positive Closure) and (Factoring) and *strongly autoepistemic* if it also satisfies (Positive Consistency).

Definition 2.4 A default consequence relation will be called *reflexive* if it satisfies (Cut), (Consistency), (Reflexivity), (Negative Closure) and (Negative Factoring).

Below we are going to consider these systems in detail[2].

2.1 AUTOEPISTEMIC CONSEQUENCE RELATIONS

The majority of nonmonotonic formalisms have two components. The first component is the logical framework, e.g., some modal logic or a set of defaults. The second component involves a stipulation what sets of propositions we should consider as intended, or 'preferred' ones. For Reiter's default logic these are extensions, while for autoepistemic logic it is stable sets and stable expansions. The relation between these two components is usually more complex than in the monotonic case. In usual, monotonic, logical systems the set of all theories (that is, sets of propositions closed with respect to the rules of the system) determines in turn the source provability relation. Unfortunately, this useful property of mutual determination holds neither for default logic nor for modal nonmonotonic formalisms. In both these cases different systems may determine the same set of 'preferred' objects and hence the same nonmonotonic inference. What complicates matters still further is that, in general, the set of such objects does not change monotonically with the growth of the underlying system. However, we will show that both for default logic and modal nonmonotonic logics there are rules that preserve 'preferred' sets of propositions. Such rules can be considered as providing a primary characterization of 'logical paradigms' behind these systems of nonmonotonic reasoning.

We will begin with autoepistemic logic. Let $\mathbb{C}n(u:v)$ denote the set of all consequences of the pair of sets (u,v), $\overline{u}$ the complement of u. The following definition gives a description of the key concepts involved in autoepistemic reasoning.

Definition 2.5 Let $\Vdash$ be a default consequence relation.

1. A set of propositions u will be called *stable* in $\Vdash$ (or $\Vdash$-stable) if it is deductively closed and satisfies the following condition:
$$\mathbb{C}n(u:\overline{u}) \subseteq u;$$

2. u will be called an *expansion* in $\Vdash$ (or $\Vdash$-expansion) if
$$u = \mathbb{C}n(u:\overline{u}).$$

---
[2] All the results in the next two sections, except for Theorem 2.5, were proved in [1].

As we have said, usually sets of 'preferred' nonmonotonic objects do not change monotonically with the growth of the source system. Still, the following lemma, proved in [1], shows that under certain conditions we may have more regular behavior.

Lemma 2.2 Let $\Vdash_1$ and $\Vdash_2$ be two default consequence relations.

1. If $\Vdash_1 \subseteq \Vdash_2$, then any $\Vdash_2$-stable set is $\Vdash_1$-stable.

2. If $\Vdash_1 \subseteq \Vdash_2$ and $\Vdash_1$ and $\Vdash_2$ have the same stable sets, then any $\Vdash_1$-expansion is a $\Vdash_2$-expansion.

The lemma shows that the set of stable sets diminishes monotonically with the growth of a consequence relation (this indicates that stable sets are actually monotonic objects) and that in any interval in which this set is not changing, the set of expansions grows monotonically with the growth of the consequence relation. These facts make it possible to demonstrate that the rules of autoepistemic consequence relations preserve the objects in question.

For an arbitrary consequence relation $\Vdash$, we let $\Vdash^{ae}$ ($\Vdash^{sae}$, $\Vdash^s$) denote the least autoepistemic (resp., the least strongly autoepistemic and the least stable) consequence relation containing $\Vdash$. These consequence relations can be described alternatively as consequence relations obtained from $\Vdash$ by adding the appropriate rules and axioms.

The following theorem shows that, as far as only stable sets are involved, stable consequence relations form a representative class:

Theorem 2.3 *For any default consequence relation $\Vdash$, $\Vdash^s$ is the greatest consequence relation having the same stable sets as $\Vdash$.*

As we said earlier, stable sets behave essentially as monotonic objects. In fact, they can be considered as sets of propositions that are *closed* with respect to the sequents of a default consequence relation in the sense that if positive premises of a sequent belong to a stable set u and negative premises do not belong to u, then the conclusion must belong to u. In fact, the set of stable sets can be seen as providing a primary characterization of a default consequence relation; adding or deleting rules or sequents that change this set involves a significant change of the information embodied in a consequence relation. This gives rise to a natural constraint on the rules we might consider acceptable in various applications of nonmonotonic reasoning: any such rule should be valid in stable consequence relations. In other words, it must follow from the four basic rules involved in their definition—(Cut), (Consistency), (Reflexivity) and (Factoring).

The next theorem shows that autoepistemic consequence relations in general form a representative class with respect to both stable sets and expansions.

Theorem 2.4 *For any default consequence relation* $\Vdash$,

1. $\Vdash^{ae}$ *has the same stable sets and expansions as* $\Vdash$;

2. $\Vdash^{sae}$ *has the same stable sets and consistent expansions as* $\Vdash$.

As an immediate consequence of Lemma 2.2, we obtain that any consequence relation that contains $\Vdash$ and is included in $\Vdash^{ae}$ has the same stable sets and expansions as $\Vdash$. Consequently, addition of any of the rules involved in the definition of an autoepistemic consequence relation does not change stable sets and expansions. Similarly, (Positive Consistency) does not change stable sets and consistent expansions, and (Reflexivity) does not change stable sets.

It is easy to show that, in any consequence relation satisfying (Reflexivity), expansions coincide with stable sets (since for such relations $u \subseteq \mathbb{C}n(u:v)$, for any u,v). Thus, (Reflexivity) does not preserve expansions. Moreover, even a weaker form of reflexivity, (Positive Consistency), always forces the set of all propositions to be an expansion, though it preserves consistent expansions.

The main conclusion that can be made from the above results is that autoepistemic consequence relations provide an admissible framework for autoepistemic reasoning. In the next section we will present a similar result for default logic.

2.2 DEFAULT LOGIC AND REFLEXIVE CONSEQUENCE RELATIONS

Reiter ([15]) defines a default theory as a pair $\Delta = (W, D)$, where W is a set of propositions and D a set of default rules of the form $A : \mathbf{M}B_1, \ldots, \mathbf{M}B_k / C$. The connection between default theories and default consequence relations can be established by representing propositions from W as sequents $\emptyset : \emptyset \Vdash A$ and default rules from D as sequents

$$A : \neg B_1, \ldots, \neg B_k \Vdash C.$$

This translation will be denoted by $tr(\Delta)$. As can be seen, it agrees with the informal meaning of default sequents given in the Introduction. Note also that the translation is reversible, provided we replace sets of positive premises in default sequents by their conjunctions. In other words, a default sequent $A_1, \ldots, A_n : B_1, \ldots, B_k \Vdash C$ is representable by a default

$$A_1 \wedge \cdots \wedge A_n : \mathbf{M}\neg B_1, \ldots, \mathbf{M}\neg B_k / C.$$

Reiter's default logic is based on the notion of extension. As is well-known, extensions can be defined using a certain iterative construction (see [15], Theorem 2.1). It turns out that this construction can be captured in our system through the use of the rule (Cut) given above. The following definition gives a formalization of the notion of extension in the framework of iterative consequence relations, that is, default consequence relations satisfying (Cut).

Definition 2.6 Let $\Vdash$ be an iterative consequence relation. A set of propositions u will be called an *extension* in $\Vdash$ (or $\Vdash$-extension) if

$$u = \mathbb{C}n(\emptyset : \overline{u}).$$

It can be shown that if $\Vdash$ is an iterative consequence relation, then any $\Vdash$-extension is a $\Vdash$-expansion (and hence a $\Vdash$-stable set). The following theorem shows that iterative consequence relations and $\Vdash$-extensions provide a proper generalization of Reiter's default logic.

Theorem 2.5 *Let Δ be a default theory and $\Vdash_\Delta$ the least iterative consequence relation containing $tr(\Delta)$. Then extensions of Δ coincide with $\Vdash_\Delta$-extensions.*

Just as for the case of expansions, iterative consequence relations are not determined uniquely by their extensions. But the following lemma (also proved in [1]) shows that in cases when the set of stable sets remains the same, the set of extensions also grows with the growth of the consequence relation.

Lemma 2.6 *Let $\Vdash_1$ and $\Vdash_2$ be iterative consequence relations. If $\Vdash_1 \subseteq \Vdash_2$ and $\Vdash_1$ and $\Vdash_2$ have the same stable sets, then any $\Vdash_1$-extension is a $\Vdash_2$-extension.*

The lemma allows us to single out rules that preserve extensions. It turns out that reflexive consequence relations (see Definition 2.4) provide an admissible framework for extension-based default reasoning.

We let $\Vdash^r$ denote the least reflexive consequence relation containing $\Vdash$. In other words, this is a consequence relation obtained from $\Vdash$ by adding the appropriate rules.

Theorem 2.7 *For any iterative consequence relation $\Vdash$, $\Vdash^r$ has the same stable sets and extensions as $\Vdash$.*

It can be shown that the rule (Factoring) does not preserve extensions. On the other hand, as we already mentioned, (Reflexivity) obliterates the distinction between stable sets and expansions. This indicates that expansion- and extension-based kinds of nonmonotonic reasoning are in some sense incompatible—each admits inference steps that are inadmissible in the other. However, the rules common to both autoepistemic and reflexive consequence relations clearly preserve all the objects we have considered, i.e. stable sets, expansions and extensions. This suggests the following definition.

Definition 2.7 An iterative consequence relation will be called *introspective* if it satisfies (Consistency),

(Positive Closure), (Negative Closure), (Positive Consistency) and (Negative Factoring).

Introspective consequence relations 'own' some useful features that are common to autoepistemic and reflexive consequence relations, most important of them being the possibility of replacing deductively equivalent premises, both positive and negative ones (this is a consequence of Positive and Negative Closure). In addition, introspective consequence relations form a representative class with respect to all three kinds of objects we have considered.

3 MODAL DEFAULT CONSEQUENCE RELATIONS

In this section we will introduce the notion of a modal default consequence relation. As we will see, modal default consequence relations provide a natural generalization of modal nonmonotonic logics.

Let $\mathcal{L}_L$ be the set of all propositions in a propositional language with a modal operator L. For any set of propositions u from $\mathcal{L}_L$, we let Lu denote the set of all propositions of the form LA, where $A \in u$. The notation $\neg u$ will have a similar meaning.

Definition 3.1 *A default consequence relation in* $\mathcal{L}_L$ *will be called* modal *if it satisfies the following two modal axioms:*

$$A : \emptyset \Vdash LA \qquad \emptyset : A \Vdash \neg LA.$$

If we interpret L as an operator of belief, the two axioms imply, in effect, that positive premises of any sequent include propositions that are believed and negative premises include propositions that are not believed[3]. Consequently, the following understanding of default sequents $a : b \Vdash A$ in modal default consequence relations will be appropriate: *"If all propositions from a are believed and all propositions from b are not believed, then infer A"*. This interpretation is in agreement with the following strengthening of the notion of a modal consequence relation:

Definition 3.2 *A modal default consequence relation will be called* regular *if it satisfies the following two rules:*

$$\frac{a : b \Vdash LA \quad a, A : b \Vdash B}{a : b \Vdash B},$$

$$\frac{a : b \Vdash \neg LA \quad a : b, A \Vdash B}{a : b \Vdash B}$$

Regular consequence relations admit a natural interpretation similar to an autoepistemic interptretation proposed for autoepistemic logic (see [14]). By an *MD-interpretation* we will mean any consistent deductively

---
[3]Note that any modal default consequence relation satisfies (Consistency).

closed set in $\mathcal{L}_L$. For any MD-interpretation u we define the following two sets:

$$u_L = \{B | LB \in u\} \qquad u^L = \{B | \neg LB \in u\}$$

The set u_L can be naturally interpreted as the set of propositions that are *believed* in u, while u^L as the set of propositions that are *not believed* in u. Note that, in contrast to autoepistemic logic, the interpretation is partial with respect to modal propositions. Now, for any set of MD-interpretations T, we define the following consequence relation, denoted by $\Vdash_T$:

$$(\forall u \in T)(a \subseteq u_L \wedge b \subseteq u^L \Rightarrow A \in u).$$

Informally, a default sequent $a : b \Vdash_T A$ is valid if and only if, for any MD-interpretation u from T, if all propositions from a are believed in u and all propositions from b are not believed in u, then A holds in u.

It is easy to show that $\Vdash_T$ is a regular consequence relation. Moreover, the following theorem shows that such interpretation-based default consequence relations provide a complete characterization of regular modal consequence relations.

Theorem 3.1 *For any regular default consequence relation $\Vdash$ there exists a set of theories T such that $\Vdash = \Vdash_T$.*

As the theorem shows, even regular default consequence relations are determined by arbitrary deductively closed sets of modal formulas. This show, in particular, that modal default consequence relations in general have no 'modal content' in the sense that they impose no restriction whatsoever on the modal operator. However, we will see that additional rules of the kind described earlier correspond to well-known modal axioms for L.

Now we will show that modal default consequence relations can be considered as a generalization of modal nonmonotonic logics. To begin with, note that the modal axioms imply that $\Vdash$-stable sets in modal default consequence relations are stable sets in the usual sense, that is, they are deductively closed sets satisfying the following two conditions:

- If $A \in u$, then $LA \in u$;
- If $A \notin u$, then $\neg LA \in u$.

Let $\Vdash_u$ denote the least modal default consequence relation containing a set of (modal) propositions u (that is, $\emptyset : \emptyset \Vdash A$, for any $A \in u$). Clearly, $\Vdash_u$ is simply the set of all sequents obtained from u by applying the two axioms and two rules of modal default consequence relations. The following simple lemma was proved in [1]:

Lemma 3.2 $a : b \Vdash_u A$ *if and only if* $A \in \text{Th}(u \cup La \cup \neg Lb)$.

As an immediate consequence of this lemma, we obtain that $\Vdash_u$-stable sets are those deductively closed sets of propositions s that satisfy the condition

$$\mathrm{Th}(u \cup Ls \cup \neg L\bar{s}) \subseteq s.$$

Thus, $\Vdash_u$-stable sets are exactly stable sets containing u (see [14]). Similarly, $\Vdash_u$-expansions are sets satisfying the condition

$$s = \mathrm{Th}(u \cup Ls \cup \neg L\bar{s}),$$

and hence they coincide with Moore's stable expansions of u. Thus, Moore's autoepistemic logic can be adequately translated into the framework of modal default consequence relations. Furthermore, applying now Theorem 2.4, we can infer that autoepistemic logic can be faithfully represented by means of modal autoepistemic consequence relations. In the next section we will complete the picture by demonstrating that the latter exactly correspond to consequence relations based on the modal logic **K45**.

Now we will turn to modal nonmonotonic logics in general. It is easy to show that the rule (Cut) in modal default consequence relations implies the following rule:

$$(\textit{Necessitation}) \quad \frac{a : b \Vdash A}{a : b \Vdash LA}$$

(In fact, it can be shown that for regular consequence relations the two rules are equivalent.) Thus, (Cut) captures the effect of the necessitation rule A/LA in modal logics.

Let $\mathcal{S}$ be a modal logic containing the necessitation rule. We will say that a modal default consequence relation is an $\mathcal{S}$-*consequence relation* if it is an iterative consequence relation such that if A is an instance of a modal axiom from $\mathcal{S}$, then $\emptyset : \emptyset \Vdash A$. For any set of propositions u, let $\Vdash_u^\mathcal{S}$ be the least $\mathcal{S}$-consequence relation containing u. This consequence relation can also be described as the set of all sequents obtained from u by using the axioms of $\mathcal{S}$, the axioms and rules of modal default consequence relations and the (Cut) rule. The following lemma was also proved in [1]:

Lemma 3.3 $a : b \Vdash_u^\mathcal{S} A$ *if and only if* $A \in \mathrm{Cn}_\mathcal{S}(u \cup La \cup \neg Lb)$.

As a consequence of the lemma, we obtain that $\Vdash_u^\mathcal{S}$-extensions are sets of propositions satisfying the following condition:

$$s = \mathrm{Cn}_\mathcal{S}(u \cup \neg L\bar{s}).$$

Thus, $\Vdash_u^\mathcal{S}$-extensions coincide with $\mathcal{S}$-expansions of u as defined in [11] (see also [13]). It follows that a modal nonmonotonic reasoning based on 'negative introspection' can be also represented in terms of modal default consequence relations and the notion of $\Vdash$-extension. Moreover, Theorem 2.7 implies that reflexive consequence relations provide an adequate framework for reasoning of this kind. In the next section we will consider how and to what extent various modal axioms influence such a reasoning.

3.1 MODAL CONSEQUENCE RELATIONS VS. MODAL NONMONOTONIC LOGICS

In this section we will consider the correspondence between modal nonmonotonic logics and their associated default consequence relations. It follows from the results described above that in order to provide a characterization of modal consequence relations that can serve as representations of modal nonmonotonic logics, we may restrict our attention to consequence relations that are generated by sets of (modal) propositions.

Definition 3.3 A modal default consequence relation $\Vdash$ will be called *prime* if it coincides with the least iterative consequence relation containing $\mathbb{Cn}(\emptyset : \emptyset)$.

It is easy to show that a modal consequence relation is prime if and only if it is the least iterative consequence relation containing some set of propositions. As has been said, the rule (Cut), that characterizes iterative consequence relations, is equivalent to the modal necessitation rule. Consequently, Lemma 3.3 could be replaced by a more general

Lemma 3.4 $\Vdash$ *is a prime consequence relation if and only if, for any a, b and A, $a : b \Vdash A$ is equivalent to*

$$A \in \mathrm{Cn}_\mathbf{N}(\mathbb{Cn}(\emptyset : \emptyset) \cup La \cup \neg Lb),$$

where $\mathrm{Cn}_\mathbf{N}$ denotes the provability operator of **N**.

The lemma shows that, in general, prime modal default consequence relations correspond to modal nonmonotonic logics based on the pure logic of necessitation **N**, that is, a modal logic that has no proper modal axioms and the necessitation rule as the only additional modal rule (see [3]).

An important consequence of the lemma is the following

Theorem 3.5 *Any prime modal default consequence relation is regular.*

The set $\mathbb{Cn}(\emptyset : \emptyset)$ may include all instances of modal axioms characterizing various modal logics. An important question that arises here is to what extent different modal axioms appearing in $\mathbb{Cn}(\emptyset : \emptyset)$ influence the general properties of the corresponding consequence relation, since, as is well-known, different modal logics may determine the same nonmonotonic inference—see [9]. In the rest of this section we will give representation results for a number of well-known modal nonmonotonic logics. It will turn out that most of them posses a simple and natural characterization in terms of different structural rules that hold in the associated default consequence relations.

We begin with demonstrating that prime **K4**-consequence relations can be characterized as consequence relations that satisfy certain *deduction rules*.

Theorem 3.6 ⊩ *is a prime $K4$-consequence relation if and only if it is iterative, satisfies (Positive Closure) and the following two modal deduction rules:*

(*Positive Deduction*)
$$\frac{A, a : b \Vdash B}{a : b \Vdash LA \to B},$$

(*Weak Negative Deduction*)
$$\frac{a : A, b \Vdash B}{a : b \Vdash \neg L\bot \land L\neg LA \to B}.$$

The theorem gives an example of a correspondence between rules of default consequence relations and usual modal axioms. Note that, given (Positive Deduction), the (Positive Closure) rule can be shown to be equivalent to the modal **K** axiom.

The two deduction rules are rules that permit propositions to be transferred from premises to conclusions. Note that these rules are reversible. Consequently, by successive applications of these rules, any sequent can be transformed to a provable proposition:

Corollary 3.7 *For prime $K4$-consequence relations, any default sequent $A_1, \ldots, A_n : B_1, \ldots, B_m \Vdash C$ is equivalent to a provable formula*
$$LA_1 \land \cdots \land LA_n \land [\land \neg L\bot] \\ \land L\neg LB_1 \land \cdots \land L\neg LB_m \to C.$$

(where the conjunct $\neg L\bot$ is present only if the set of negative premises is not empty).

It can be shown that prime **K4**-consequence relations satisfy all the rules of introspective consequence relations, except (Positive Consistency). Adding the latter amounts to addition of the modal **D** axiom $LA \to \neg L\neg A$.

Theorem 3.8 *The following conditions are equivalent:*

1. ⊩ *is a prime $KD4$-consequence relation;*

2. ⊩ *is iterative, satisfies (Positive Closure), (Positive Deduction) and the following rule:*

   (*Negative Deduction*)
   $$\frac{a : A, b \Vdash B}{a : b \Vdash L\neg LA \to B}.$$

3. ⊩ *is introspective and satisfies (Positive Deduction).*

Prime **KD4**-consequence relations satisfy a more strong rule of negative deduction that does not include the conjunct $\neg\bot$. Note also that, in view of (3), the new rule is actually a consequence of (Positive Deduction) and the rules of introspective consequence relation. Thus, we have

Corollary 3.9 *For prime $KD4$-consequence relations, any sequent $A_1, \ldots, A_n : B_1, \ldots, B_m \Vdash C$ is equivalent to a provable formula*
$$LA_1 \land \cdots \land LA_n \land L\neg LB_1 \land \cdots \land L\neg LB_m \to C.$$

As can be seen, taking into account the correspondence between default sequents and ordinary default rules described earlier as $tr(\Delta)$, the above transformation of default sequents into modal formulas is in fact identical with the modal translation of defaults suggested by Truszczyński in [20]. It should be noted, however, that the above Corollary restricts the applicability of this translation to introspective consequence relations. We will return to this translation below when studying the possibility of embedding default consequence relations into modal ones.

Replacing the **D** axiom by the more strong reflexivity axiom $LA \to A$ amounts to adding the (Reflexivity) rule. Consequently, we obtain the following characterization of prime **S4**-consequence relations:

Theorem 3.10 ⊩ *is a prime $S4$-consequence relation if and only if it is a reflexive consequence relation satisfying (Positive Deduction).*

Now we will consider autoepistemic consequence relations. It turns out that in prime **K4**-consequence relations the rule (Factoring) is equivalent to the modal **5** axiom $\neg LA \to L\neg LA$. Moreover, we have that prime **K45**-consequence relations actually *coincide* with modal autoepistemic consequence relations.

Theorem 3.11 *The following conditions are equivalent:*

1. ⊩ *is a prime $K45$-consequence relation;*

2. ⊩ *is iterative and satisfies (Positive Deduction) and the following rule:*

   (*Strong Negative Deduction*)
   $$\frac{a : A, b \Vdash B}{a : b \Vdash \neg LA \to B}.$$

3. ⊩ *is a modal autoepistemic consequence relation.*

Prime **K45**-consequence relations validate a still more strong rule of negative deduction. Note, however, that, since prime **K45**-consequence relations coincide with autoepistemic consequence relations, this time both (Positive Deduction) and the new negative deduction rule are consequences of the rules of modal autoepistemic consequence relations.

Corollary 3.12 *For prime $K45$-consequence relations, any sequent $A_1, \ldots, A_n : B_1, \ldots, B_m \Vdash C$ is equivalent to a provable formula*
$$LA_1 \land \cdots \land LA_n \land \neg LB_1 \land \cdots \land \neg LB_m \to C.$$

Since (Positive Consistency) is equivalent to the **D** axiom and (Reflexivity) is equivalent to the modal reflexivity axiom, an immediate consequence of the last theorem is the following characterization of strongly autoepistemic and stable consequence relations.

Corollary 3.13 *A* ⊩ *is a prime **KD45**-consequence relation if and only if it is a strongly autoepistemic consequence relation.*

Corollary 3.14 ⊩ *is a prime **S5**-consequence relation if and only if it is a stable consequence relation.*

The equivalence of prime **S5** and stable consequence relations can now be combined with Theorem 2.1, and we obtain that prime **S5**-consequence relations are equivalent to Scott consequence relations. This fact can be seen as the source of nonmonotonic degeneration of modal nonmonotonic reasoning based on **S5** (cf. [18]).

To end this section, we introduce still another important consequence relation.

As has been shown, stable consequence relations are already monotonic. It turns out that there are *two* weaker, nontrivial systems that are in some sense maximal. As was proved by Schwarz in [17], nonmonotonic modal logics based on **KD45** and **SW5** are maximal nonmonotonic logics satisfying certain natural conditions. Schwarz proposed to treat nonmonotonic **SW5** as a plausible candidate for nonmonotonic logic of knowledge.

As we have demonstrated, the first nonmonotonic logic corresponds to strongly autoepistemic consequence relations. It turns out that the characteristic axiom of **SW5**, the so-called 'weak' 5 axiom

$$A \wedge \neg LA \rightarrow L\neg LA,$$

is equivalent in our system to the following rule:

(*Conditional Factoring*)
$$\frac{a, B : b \Vdash A \quad a : b, B \Vdash A}{a : b \Vdash B \rightarrow A}.$$

We will say that a default consequence relation is *strongly reflexive* if it is reflexive and satisfies (Conditional Factoring). We have the following result:

Theorem 3.15 ⊩ *is a prime **SW5**-consequence relation if and only if it is a regular strongly reflexive consequence relation.*

The results of this section show that there is a remarkable correspondence between major structural types of default consequence relations and well-known modal nonmonotonic logics. This correspondence can also be considered as a justification of the claim that particular modal axioms, as distinct from ordinary modal propositions, are important for modal nonmonotonic reasoning only to the extent they influence the structural properties of the associated modal consequence relations.

4 REDUCTIONS AND EMBEDDINGS

We let $\mathcal{L}_o$ denote the subset of $\mathcal{L}_L$ consisting of all propositions without occurrences of L; such propositions will be called *objective*. For any set of propositions u from $\mathcal{L}_L$, we let u_o denote the set $u \cap \mathcal{L}_o$ and $\overline{u}_o$ the set $\mathcal{L}_o \setminus u$. Note that, for any modal default consequence relation ⊩, its restriction to $\mathcal{L}_o$ is clearly an objective default consequence relation having the same structural rules as ⊩. We will denote this objective subrelation by $_o\Vdash$.

All nonmonotonic objects we have considered in this paper were stable sets, and it is well-known that the latter are uniquely determined by their objective subsets (kernels). This suggests a possibility of reducing modal nonmonotonic reasoning to nonmodal one. The only question here is whether the reasoning about the kernels can be accomplished entirely in a nonmodal framework. This was the question we considered in [1]. The main result proved there amounted to demonstrating that if ⊩ is a modal introspective consequence relation and u a stable set, then

- u is a ⊩-stable set iff u_o is a $_o\Vdash$-stable set;
- u is a ⊩-expansion iff u_o is a $_o\Vdash$-expansion;
- u is a ground ⊩-extension if and only if u_o is a $_o\Vdash$-extension.

(*Ground* extensions are extensions which are stably minimal, that is, there is no ⊩-stable set v such that $v_o \subset u_o$.)

These results can be reformulated as saying that, for consequence relations that are introspective, the reduction of modal consequence relations to their objective subrelations provides an adequate translation with respect to stable sets, expansions and ground extensions. As to extensions in general, it was shown that, for any introspective consequence relation ⊩, we can construct an objective strongly autoepistemic consequence relation such that its stable sets coincide with kernels of ⊩-stable sets and its expansions are exactly kernels of ⊩-extensions.

Since introspective consequence relations form a representative class of consequence relations with respect to the key nonmonotonic objects, the above reduction provides, in fact, the crucial step in a general translation from modal nonmonotonic logics to default logics. It shows that objective subrelations of modal introspective consequence relations embody all the essential information about the corresponding modal nonmonotonic objects.

We will consider below the reverse problem, namely the problem of translating, or embedding, objective default consequence relations into the corresponding (prime) modal consequence relations.

It turns out that the maximal 'host' modal logic for objective introspective consequence relations is the logic determined by the following Kripke frames: the set of worlds M is the union of three disjoint sets M_1, M_2 and M_3 (where $M_3 \neq \emptyset$) and the accessibility relation is $[(M_1 \cup M_2) \times (M_2 \cup M_3)] \cup (M_3 \times M_3)$. We will denote this logic by **KD4I**. This logic contains **KD4** and is included in both **S4F** (see [19]) and **KD45**. It is in fact equivalent to the logic **KD4·3B$_3$** in the classification of [2].

Theorem 4.1 *Any objective introspective consequence relation coincides with the objective subrelation of some prime **KD4I**-consequence relation.*

In view of the above mentioned results, the embedding is faithful with respect to stable sets, expansions and ground extensions. Note also that in view of Corollary 3.9, objective sequents in **KD4I**-consequence relations are equivalent to their Truszczyński's translations. Thus, it can be said that Truszczyński's translation of defaults generates an exact translation of objective introspective consequence relations into prime **KD4I**-consequence relations. Moreover, it follows from Theorem 3.8 that prime **KD4**-consequence relations are already introspective. Consequently, any modal logic in the range (**KD4**—**KD4I**) can serve as a host logic for such a translation.

The importance of the above theorem lies not only in demonstrating that defaults can be translated into modal formulas. What is even more important is that it can be used to show that extension of objective introspective consequence relations to modal **KD4I**-consequence relations is *conservative* with respect to provability of objective sequents. In other words, addition of the modal axioms of **KD4I** to an objective introspective consequence relation cannot result in provability of some new objective sequents. Formally, we have

Theorem 4.2 *Let $\hat{s}$ be an arbitrary set of objective sequents, $\Vdash_{\hat{s}}^o$ the least objective introspective consequence relation containing $\hat{s}$, and $\Vdash_{\hat{s}}^I$ the least prime **KD4I**-consequence relation containing $\hat{s}$. Then*

$$\Vdash_{\hat{s}}^o = {}_o\Vdash_{\hat{s}}^I.$$

The theorem says that, given a set of objective sequents $\hat{s}$, an objective sequent is provable from $\hat{s}$ using all the rules and modal axioms that hold in prime **KD4I**-consequence relations if and only if it is provable from $\hat{s}$ using only the basic rules of introspective consequence relations. This result complements the results about reduction of introspective consequence relations to their objective subrelations, discussed earlier in this section, by showing that the latter are autonomous with respect to provability of objective sequents.

Another consequence of the above embedding theorem is the following result for reflexive consequence relations:

Theorem 4.3 *Any objective reflexive consequence relation coincides with the objective subrelation of some prime **S4F**-consequence relation.*

Again, Theorem 3.10 implies that any modal logic in the interval (**S4**—**S4F**) is appropriate for such an embedding.

The next theorem shows that, as can be expected, the logic **SW5** is a modal counterpart of strongly reflexive consequence relations.

Theorem 4.4 *Any objective strongly reflexive consequence relation coincides with the objective subrelation of some prime **SW5**-consequence relation.*

Theorem 3.15 can be used this time to show that **SW5** is the only logic that permits the embedding.

Note that the above two theorems also imply that the corresonding objective consequence relations are conservative with respect to their associated modal consequence relations.

Finally, we will consider autoepistemic consequence relations.

Theorem 4.5 *Any objective (strongly) autoepistemic consequence relation coincides with the objective subrelation of some prime **K(D)45**-consequence relation.*

As the following theorem shows, for autoepistemic consequence relations we have a perfect match between objective and modal variants.

Theorem 4.6 *Two modal autoepistemic consequence relations having the same objective subrelations coincide.*

The theorem implies that there is a one-to-one correspondence between prime **K45**-consequence relations and objective autoepistemic consequence relations. In other words, we have a full-fledged equivalence between autoepistemic logic and a particular kind of objective default consequence relations. In fact, we have more. As Konolige demonstrated, for any set of modal propositions there exists a **K45**-equivalent set of disjunctive clauses without nested occurrences of L (see [6], Proposition 3.9). Now, taking into account the deduction rules that hold for prime **K45**-consequence relations (see Corollary 3.12), any such clause

$$\neg LA_1 \vee \cdots \vee \neg A_n \vee LB_1 \vee \cdots \vee LB_m \vee C$$

can be transformed into an *objective* sequent

$$A_1, \ldots, A_n : B_1, \ldots, B_m \Vdash C.$$

Thus, any set of modal propositions can be assigned an 'autoepistemicaly equivalent' set of objective sequents. For a set of propositions a, let a^s denote the corresponding set of objective sequents. The following theorem shows that provability in **K45** is reducible to provability of objective sequents in autoepistemic consequence relations.

Theorem 4.7 *For any set of modal propositions a and any proposition A, A is provable from a in **K45** if and only if any sequent from $\{A\}^s$ is provable from a^s using the rules of an (objective) autoepistemic consequence relation.*

This result shows, in fact, that *the modal logic **K45** itself is reducible to objective autoepistemic consequence relations*. As a corollary, we also have a reduction of modal logics **KD45** and **S5** to objective strongly autoepistemic and stable consequence relations, respectively.

5 CONCLUSIONS

We see the notion of a default consequence relation as the main contribution of the paper. As the results presented above demonstrate, it can be considered as a natural generalization of default logic, on the one hand, and modal nonmonotonic logics, on the other. Moreover, default consequence relations have given us a convenient 'common ground' for studying the relationship between these two formalizations of nonmonotonic reasoning. It should be noted, that the suggested translation, or embedding, of different kinds of objective default consequence relations into the corresponding modal logics (as well as the reverse reductions described in [1]) have an advantage over earlier attempts in that they are not restricted as such to particular 'preferred' nonmonotonic objects. Rather, they establish a direct correspondence between modal and default-based formalizations of different kinds of nonmonotonic *reasoning*.

Both default and modal nonmonotonic formalisms have advantages of their own. For nonmodal default systems it is mainly conceptual simplicity and avoidance of nested layers of modalities. For modal formalisms it is convenience of working with familar modal constructions, for which the underlying theory and semantics already exist. As the results of the paper show, in most cases we can freely choose each of these formalisms.

There are many other possibilities of using the suggested formalism of default consequence relations. We will mention here only one such possibility. Instead of using a single modal operator both for positive and negative assumptions, we may consider *bimodal* default consequence relations defined in the language with two modal operators, say K and **not** such that, roughly, K is intended to characterize positive assumptions and **not** is 'responsible' for negative assumptions (nonmonotonic systems of this kind were suggested in [7] and [8]). Consequently, the two modal axioms of modal default consequence relations should be replaced by the following pair of axioms:

$$A : \emptyset \Vdash KA \qquad \emptyset : A \Vdash \mathbf{not}\, A.$$

The main distinctive feature of such systems, as compared with ordinary modal default consequence relations, is that the Consistency principle, $A : A \Vdash \bot$, is no longer valid. (As we mentioned, (Consistency) is an immediate consequence of the two original modal axioms.) Such rules as (Cut), (Positive Closure) and (Reflexivity) will characterize now only the K operator, while, e.g., (Negative Closure) will impose a (normality) constraint on **not**. Rules that involve both positive and negative premises, such as (Consistency) and (Factoring), will characterize the relation between the two opertors. Note, for example, that a modal axiom $KA \to \neg\mathbf{not}\, A$ implies (Consistency), while (Factoring) implies $\neg\mathbf{not}\, A \to KA$. Finally, it is interesting to note that rejection of Consistency creates a possibilty of nontrivial systems that use both (Reflexivity) and (Factoring)[4], a possibility that were excluded in the present paper.

---

[4] A system of this kind is suggested, in fact, in [16] as a basic logical paradigm for logic programming.

References

1. A. Bochman (1993) Modal nonmonotonic logics demodalized. *Annals of Mathematics and Artificial Intelligence* (to appear).

2. R. A. Bull and K. Segerberg (1984). Basic modal logic. In D. Gabbay and F. Guenthner (eds.) *Handbook of Philosophical Logic*, 1–88, Dordrecht: D. Reidel.

3. M. C. Fitting, W. Marek, and M. Truszczyński (1992). The pure logic of necessitation. *J. of Logic and Computation* bf 2:349–373.

4. D. M. Gabbay (1976). *Investigations in Modal and Tense Logics*. Dordrecht: D. Reidel.

5. D. M. Gabbay and H. J. Sergot (1986). Negation as inconsistency. *J. of Logic Programming* 1:1–35.

6. K. Konolige (1988). On the relation between default and autoepistemic logic. *Artificial Intelligence* 35:343–382.

7. V. Lifschitz (1991). Nonmonotonic databases and epistemic queries. In J. Myopoulos and R. Reiter (eds.) *Proceedings of International Joint Conference on Artificial Intelligence*, 381–386. San Mateo, Calif.: Morgan Kaufmann.

8. F. Lin and Y. Shoham (1992). A logic of knowledge and justified assumptions. *Artificial Intelligence* 57:271–289.

9. W. Marek, G. F. Shvarts, and M. Truszczyński (1991). Modal nonmonotonic logics: ranges, characterization, computation. In *Proc. Second International Conference on Principles of Knowledge Representation and Reasoning, KR'91*, 395–404. Cambridge, MA: MIT Press. A revised and expanded version appeared in *J. of the ACM* (1993) 40:963–990.

10. W. Marek and M. Truszczyński (1989). Relating autoepistemic and default logics. In *Principles of Knowledge Representation and Reasoning*, 276–288. San Mateo, Calif.: Morgan Kaufmann.

11. W. Marek and M. Truszczyński (1990). Modal logic for default reasoning. *Annals of Mathematics and Artificial Intelligence* 1:275–302.

12. W. Marek and M. Truszczyński (1992). More on modal aspects of default logic. *Fundamenta Informaticae* 17:99–116.

13. D. McDermott (1982). Nonmonotonic logic II: Nonmonotonic modal theories. *Journal of the ACM* 29:33–57.

14. R. C. Moore (1985). Semantical considerations on non-monotonic logic. *Artificial Intelligence* 25:75–94.

15. R. Reiter (1980). A logic for default reasoning. *Artificial Intelligence* 13:81–132.

16. J. S. Schlipf (1992). Formalizing a logic for logic programming. *Annals of Mathematics and Artificial Intelligence* 5:279–302.

17. G. Schwarz (1992). Reflexive autoepistemic logic. *Fundamenta Informaticae* 17:157–173.

18. M. Tiomkin and M. Kaminski (1991). Nonmonotonic default modal logics. *Journal of the ACM* 38:963–984.

19. M. Truszczyński (1991). Modal interpretations of default logic. In J. Myopoulos and R. Reiter (eds.) *Proceedings of International Joint Conference on Artificial Intelligence*, 393–398. San Mateo, Calif.: Morgan Kaufmann.

20. M. Truszczyński (1991). Embedding default logic into modal nonmonotonic logics. In A. Nerode, W. Marek and V. Subramanian (eds.), *Logic Programming and Non-Monotonic Reasoning*, 151–165. Cambridge Mass.: The MIT Press.

Toward a Logic for Qualitative Decision Theory

Craig Boutilier
Department of Computer Science
University of British Columbia
Vancouver, British Columbia
CANADA, V6T 1Z4
email: cebly@cs.ubc.ca

Abstract

We present a logic for representing and reasoning with qualitative statements of preference and normality and describe how these may interact in decision making under uncertainty. Our aim is to develop a logical calculus that employs the basic elements of classical decision theory, namely probabilities, utilities and actions, but exploits qualitative information about these elements directly for the derivation of goals. Preferences and judgements of normality are captured in a modal/conditional logic, and a simple model of action is incorporated. Without quantitative information, decision criteria other than maximum expected utility are pursued. We describe how techniques for conditional default reasoning can be used to complete information about both preferences and normality judgements, and we show how maximin and maximax strategies can be expressed in our logic.

1 Introduction

We typically expect a rational agent to behave in a manner that best furthers its own interests. However, an artificial agent might be expected to act in the best interests of a user (or designer) who has somehow communicated its wishes to the agent. In the usual approaches to planning in AI, a planning agent is provided with a description of some state of affairs, a *goal state*, and charged with the task of discovering (or performing) some sequence of actions to achieve that goal. This notion of goal can be found in the earliest work on planning and persists in more recent work on intention and commitment [10]. In most realistic settings, however, an agent will frequently encounter goals that it cannot achieve. As pointed out by Doyle and Wellman [12] an agent possessing only simple goal descriptions has no guidance for choosing an alternative goal state toward which it should strive.

Straightforward goal-driven behavior tends to be inflexible: an agent told to ensure that part A and part B are at location L by $5PM$ will be unable to do anything if it cannot locate B or if something prevents it from reaching L by 5PM. One might suppose that the agent should at least deliver A to L as close to 5PM as possible. While such partial fulfillment of deadline goals [16] undoubtedly arises frequently is practice, more general mechanisms will often be required. If A and B can't be delivered, perhaps alternate parts C and D should be; or if the 5PM deadline can't be met, the agent should wait until next week. To this end, a recent trend in planning has been the incorporation of decision-theoretic methods for constructing optimal plans [11]. Decision theory provides most of the basic concepts we need for rational decision making, in particular, the ability to specify arbitrary preferences over circumstances or outcomes. This allows desired outcomes or goals (and hence appropriate behaviors) to vary with context.

Most decision-theoretic analysis is set within the framework of *maximum expected utility* (MEU). One impediment to the general use of such decision-theoretic tools is the requirement to have both numerical probabilities and utilities associated with the possible outcomes of actions. It is quite conceivable that such information is not readily available to the agent. We can often expect users to present information in a *qualitative* manner, including qualitative *preferences* over outcomes (one outcome or proposition is preferred to another) and qualitative *probabilities* (describing the relative likelihood of propositions or outcomes). The ability to reason *directly* with such qualitative constraints is therefore crucial. An appropriate knowledge representation scheme will allow the expression of constraints of this form and allow one to logically derive goals and reasonable courses of action, to the extent the given information allows.[1]

---

[1] While the foundations of decision theory are, in fact, based on such qualitative preferences [26, 29], the move to numerical utilities (and probabilities) requires that a preferences and likelihoods be calibrated by means of questions concerning acceptable exchanges between outcomes and lotteries. For an agent behaving according to the preferences of some user, this requires that either a) the user's preferences be so completely specified that such calculations can be made; or b) the user (or the source of preference information) be available to be queried about preference information as the need arises. Furthermore, a complete calibration of just the preference ranking, in the most fortunate circumstances, requires a number of queries at least as large as the number of possible worlds (exponential in the number of propositional atoms). Such a mechanism is also often criticized because the queries re-

In this paper, we describe a logic and natural possible worlds semantics for representing and reasoning with qualitative probabilities and preferences, and suggest several reasoning strategies for qualitative decision making using this logic. We can represent *conditional preferences*, allowing (derived) goals to depend on context. Furthermore, these conditional preferences are *defeasible*: I might have a general preference for the proposition A (e.g., that parts be delivered to customers on time) but have a more specific "defeating" preference for $\neg A$ if a customer's account is past due. Semantically, preferences will be captured by an ordering over possible worlds, corresponding to an ordinal value function. The logic that captures such *default* preferences will exactly match existing conditional logics for default reasoning and belief revision [4, 7, 8]. Furthermore, the component of the logic for capturing qualitative probabilities will be isomorphic, with a (separate) *normality* ordering on worlds representing their relative likelihood.

In order to strengthen possible conclusions, we will also present reasoning strategies for completing information about preferences and likelihoods, in essence, making assumptions about unstated constraints. In addition, we describe several ways of making decisions with such completed information. These decision making strategies are motivated by the fact that the scales of normality and preference on which worlds are ranked are incomparable. This reflects the fact that user specified constraints provide qualitative information about the structure of the two rankings, not their relative magnitudes. We will discuss conditions under which decisions are sound in this framework.

In Section 2, we present the basic logic of preferences and its semantics, and show how existing techniques for conditional default reasoning can be used to make various assumptions about incomplete preference orderings. In Section 3, we add normality orderings to our semantics and describe a logic for dealing with both orderings. We describe the derivation of *ideal goal states*, roughly, the best situations an agent can hope for given certain fixed circumstances. This generalizes the usual notion of a goal in AI, for such goals are context-dependent and defeasible, and can be derived from more basic information rather than simply being asserted directly by a user. Such goals do not take into account the ability of an agent to change the fixed circumstances from which they are derived, nor the potential inability of an agent to achieve a goal. In Section 4, we explore a more realistic notion of goal that accounts for a simple form of ability. In planning, as in the decision theory, the ultimate aim is to derive appropriate actions to be performed that will achieve derived goal states. The ability of an agent to affect the world will have a tremendous impact on the *actual goal states* it attempts to achieve. One feature that becomes clear in our model is that, given incomplete knowledge, various behavioral *strategies* can emerge. We show how these can be expressed in our logic. Finally, in Section 5, we point out some related work, and on-going

---
quire answers to which a user does not have ready access or might be uncertain [13].

investigations into how the trade-offs between utility and probability can be captured in a qualitative manner. We also point out some interesting connections to deontic logic.

2 Conditional Preferences

A *goal* is typically taken to be some proposition that we desire an agent to make true. Semantically, a goal can be viewed as a set of possible worlds, those states of affairs that satisfy the goal proposition [10]. Intuitively, if we ignore considerations of ability, the set of goal worlds should be those considered most desirable by an agent (or its designer). To achieve all goals is to ensure that the actual world lies within this desirable set.

Unfortunately, goals are not always achievable. My robot's goal to bring me coffee may be thwarted by a broken coffee maker. Robust behavior requires that the robot be aware of desirable alternatives ("If you can't bring me coffee, bring me tea"). Furthermore, goals may be defeated for reasons other than inability. It is often natural to specify general goals, but list exceptional circumstances that make the goal less desirable than the alternatives. For instance, a general preference for delivering parts within 24 hours may be overridden when the account is past due (which may in turn be overridden if the customer is important enough). To capture these ideas, we propose a generalization of standard goal semantics. Rather than a categorical distinction between desirable and undesirable situations, we will rank worlds according to their *degree of preference*. The most preferred worlds correspond to goal states in the classical sense. However, when such states are unreachable, a ranking on alternatives becomes necessary. Such a ranking can be viewed as an ordinal value function.

The basic concept of interest will be the notion of *conditional preference*. We write $I(B|A)$, read "ideally B given A," to indicate that the truth of B is preferred, given A. This holds exactly when B is true at each of the most preferred of those worlds satisfying A. From a practical point of view, $I(B|A)$ means that if the agent (only) knows A, and the truth of A is fixed (beyond its control), then the agent ought to ensure B. Otherwise, should $\neg B$ come to pass, the agent will end up in a less than desirable A-world. The statement can be *roughly* interpreted as "If A, do B." We propose a bimodal logic CO for conditional preferences using only unary modal operators. The presentation is brief. Further details can be found in [3, 7].

2.1 The Logic CO

We assume a propositional bimodal language $\mathbf{L}_B$ over a set of atomic propositional variables $\mathbf{P}$, with the usual classical connectives and two modal operators $\Box$ and $\overleftrightarrow{\Box}$. Our possible worlds semantics for preference is based on the class of *CO-models*, of the form $M = \langle W, \leq, \varphi \rangle$, where W is a set of possible worlds, φ is a valuation function, and $\leq$ is a determining a unique set of default conclusions. For instance, System Z is one mechanism for defining a unique normality ordering. However, as with preferences, this assumption is not necessary. We assume (for simplicity of presentation) that $Cl(KB)$ is finitely specifiable and take it to be a single propositional sentence.[8]

An agent ought to act not as if only KB were true, but also as if its default beliefs $Cl(KB)$ were true. Given a model M, as a first approximation of a definition of goal, we define an *ideal goal* (w.r.t. KB) to be any $\alpha \in \mathbf{L}_{CPL}$ such that

$$M \models I(\alpha | Cl(KB))$$

The *ideal goal set* is the set of all such α. Intuitively, the ideal goals are those sentences that must be true if the agent is to find itself in a best possible situation satisfying $Cl(KB)$. In our previous example, where $KB = \{C\}$, we have that $Cl(KB) \equiv C \wedge R$ and the agent's goals are those sentences entailed by $C \wedge R \wedge U$. It should be clear that ideal goals are *conditional* and *defeasible*; for instance, given $C \wedge \overline{R}$, the agent has the ideal goal $\overline{U}$.

This formulation does not provide any indication as to what an agent should *do* in order to achieve these ideal goals. This will require the introduction of actions and ability (see the next section). For instance, notice that the ideal goal set is deductively closed, and we should not expect an agent to have to consider each member of this set individually. The notion of a *sufficient condition* for achieving all ideal goals can be defined in QDT and will prove useful later.

Definition Let X be some proposition. C is a *sufficient condition* given X iff $C \wedge X$ is satisfiable and $M \models \overline{\Box}_P(X \supset \overline{\Box}_P(X \supset \neg C))$.

Intuitively, a sufficient condition C guarantees that an agent is in some best possible X-world. Thus, if X is some fixed, unchangeable context, ensuring proposition C means the agent has done the best it could.

Proposition 2 *Let C be a sufficient condition given X and let $w \models C \wedge X$. Then $v <_P w$ only if $v \not\models X$.*

With respect to $Cl(KB)$, ideal goals are necessary conditions for ensuring the best situation. A sufficient condition C for $Cl(KB)$ guarantees the entire ideal goal set is satisfied.[9]

Proposition 3 *If C is a sufficient condition for $Cl(KB)$, then $M \models C \wedge Cl(KB) \supset \alpha$ for all ideal goals α.*

We will explore a detailed example in the next section. We also examine the "priority" given to defaults over preferences implicit in this scheme, where $Cl(KB)$ is constructed before the preference ranking is consulted.

---

[8] A sufficient condition for this property is that each "cluster" of equally normal worlds in $\leq_N$ corresponds to a finitely specifiable theory. This is the case in, e.g., System Z [3].

[9] Hector Levesque (personal communication) has suggested that sufficiency is the crucial "operator."

4 Ability and Incomplete Knowledge

The definition of an ideal goal given KB embodies the idea that an agent should attempt to achieve the best possible situation consistent with what it knows (as well as what it conjectures by default). However, as we have emphasized, this is suitable only when KB is fixed. If the agent can change the truth of certain elements in KB, ideal goals may be too restrictive. Thus, some notion of action and ability must come into play in goal derivation. Actions must also play a role if we are to derive what an agent should *do*, rather than simply what it should *achieve*. Indeed, the term "goal" is often interpreted in this way. This is especially important when we notice that the set of propositions an agent should achieve will always be deductively closed. Finally, actions must play a role in factoring out unachievable desires. For instance, an agent might prefer that it not rain; but this is something over which it has no control. Though it is an ideal outcome, to call this a goal is unreasonable.

4.1 Controllable Propositions

To capture distinctions of this sort, we introduce a simple model of action and ability and demonstrate its influence on conditional goals. We ignore the complexities required to deal with effects, preconditions and such, in order to focus attention on the structure and interaction of ability and goal determination.

We partition our atomic propositions into two classes: $\mathbf{P} = \mathcal{C} \cup \overline{\mathcal{C}}$. Those atoms $A \in \mathcal{C}$ are *controllable*, atoms over which the agent has direct influence. The only actions available to the agent are $do(A)$ and $do(\overline{A})$, which make A true or false, for every $A \in \mathcal{C}$. To keep the treatment simple, we assume actions have no effects other than to change the truth value of A. The atom U (have umbrella) is an example of a controllable atom. Atoms in $\overline{\mathcal{C}}$ are *uncontrollable*, for example, R (it will rain).

Definition For any set of atomic variables $\mathcal{P}$, let $V(\mathcal{P})$ be the set of truth assignments to this set. If $v \in V(\mathcal{P})$ and $w \in V(\mathcal{Q})$ for disjoint sets $\mathcal{P}$, $\mathcal{Q}$, then $v; w \in V(\mathcal{P} \cup \mathcal{Q})$ denotes the obvious extended assignment.

We can now distinguish three types of propositions:

Definition A proposition α is *controllable* iff, for every $u \in V(\overline{\mathcal{C}})$, there is some $v \in V(\mathcal{C})$ and $w \in V(\mathcal{C})$ such that $v; u \models \alpha$ and $w; u \models \neg \alpha$.

A proposition α is *influenceable* iff, for some $u \in V(\overline{\mathcal{C}})$, there is some $v \in V(\mathcal{C})$ and $w \in V(\mathcal{C})$ such that $v; u \models \alpha$ and $w; u \models \neg \alpha$.

α is *uninfluenceable* iff it is not influenceable.

Intuitively, since atoms in $\mathcal{C}$ are within complete control of the agent, it can ensure the truth or the falsity of any controllable proposition α, according to its desirability, simply by bringing about an appropriate truth assignment. If $A, B \in \mathcal{C}$ then $A \vee B$ and $A \wedge B$ are controllable. If α

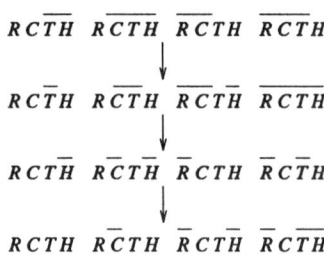

Figure 4: User Preferences

is influenceable, we call the assignment u to $\overline{\mathcal{C}}$ a *context* for α; intuitively, should such a context hold, α can be controlled by the agent. If $A \in \mathcal{C}, X \in \overline{\mathcal{C}}$ then $A \vee X$ is influenceable but not controllable: in context X the agent cannot do anything about the truth of $A \vee X$, but in context $\overline{X}$ the agent can make $A \vee X$ true or false through $do(A)$ or $do(\overline{A})$. Note that all controllables are influenceable. In this example, X is uninfluenceable. The category of controllability into which a proposition falls is easily determined by writing it in minimal DNF. Let $PI(\alpha)$ denote the set of prime implicants of α.

Proposition 4 *a) α is controllable iff each clause in $PI(\alpha)$ contains some literal from $\mathcal{C}$ and some clause contains only literals from $\mathcal{C}$. b) α is influenceable iff some literal from $\mathcal{C}$ appears in $PI(\alpha)$. c) α is uninfluenceable iff no literal from $\mathcal{C}$ appears in $PI(\alpha)$.*

4.2 Complete Knowledge

Given the distinction between controllable and uncontrollable propositions, we want to define goals so that an agent is required to do only those things within its control. A first attempt might simply be to restrict the ideal goal set as defined above to controllable propositions. The following example shows this to be inadequate.

Example Consider five atoms: O, it is overcast; R, it will rain; C, I have coffee; T, I have tea; and H, my office thermostat is set high. My robot has the default information $O \Rightarrow R$. The robot knows $KB = \{O, \overline{H}, \overline{C}, \overline{T}\}$: it is overcast and the thermostat is turned down. Its closure is $Cl(KB) = \{O, R, \overline{H}, \overline{C}, \overline{T}\}$. It can control the three atoms C, T and H. Its preference ordering is designed to respect my preferences: when it's raining I prefer tea when I arrive and the thermostat set high, otherwise I prefer coffee and the thermostat set low. Thus, we have the preference ordering illustrated in Figure 4. (We assume O, R do not contribute directly to preference, and that priority has been given to C and T over H. We also allow the possibility that both C and T together satisfy a preference for either.) The robot has to decide what to do before I arrive at the office.

It should be clear that the robot should not determine its goals by considering the ideal situations satisfying $Cl(KB)$. In such situations, since $\overline{H}$ is known, $\overline{H}$ is true and indeed, it is a simple theorem of QDT that $I(\alpha|\alpha)$. Thus, the robot concludes that $\overline{H}$ *should be true*. This is clearly mistaken, for considering only the best situations in which one's knowledge of controllables is true prevents one from determining whether changing those controllables could lead to a better situation. Since any controllable proposition can be changed if required, we do not require an agent to restrict attention to those situations where KB or $Cl(KB)$ is true. The fact that $\overline{H}$ is known should not unduly influence what are considered to be the best alternatives — H can be made true if that is what's best.

Of course, the goals of an agent must still be constrained by known *uninfluenceable* propositions. The agent should not reject all of its knowledge. For example, if the preference ordering above were modified to reflect my preference for $\overline{R}$, the agent should not base its goals on this preference if it knows R. Making R false is beyond its control, and it goals should determined by restricting attention to $\overline{R}$-worlds. Thus we insist that the best situations satisfying known *uninfluenceable* propositions be considered.

Notice that we should not ignore the truth of controllables when making default predictions. The prior truth value of a controllable might provide some indication of the truth of an uncontrollable; and we *must* take into account these uncontrollables when deciding which alternatives are *possible*, before deciding which are best. In this example, we might imagine that the default $O \Rightarrow R$ doesn't hold, but that $O \wedge H \Rightarrow R$ does: if it is overcast, then the thermostat is set high because I anticipated rain before I left last night. Our agent must use the truth of this controllable atom H to determine the truth of the uncontrollable R, which in turn will influence its decisions.[10] Once accounted for in forming $Cl(KB)$, H can safely be ignored.

This leads to the following formulation of goals that account for ability. We again assume a QDT-model M and sets $\mathcal{C}$, $\overline{\mathcal{C}}$. The *uninfluenceable belief set* of an agent is

$$UI(KB) = \{\alpha \in Cl(KB) : \alpha \text{ is uninfluenceable}\}$$

For the time being, we assume that $UI(KB)$ is complete: the truth value of all uncontrollable atoms is known. This set of beliefs determines an agent's goals.

Definition Proposition α is a *complete knowledge (CK) goal* iff $M \models I(\alpha|UI(KB))$ and α is controllable.

---

[10] If a controllable provides some indication of the truth of an uncontrollable or another controllable, (e.g., $H \Rightarrow R$) we should think of this as an *evidential rule* rather than a *causal rule*. Given our assumption about the independence of atoms in $\mathcal{C}$, we must take all such rules to be evidential (e.g., changing the thermostat will not alter the chance of rain). This can be generalized using a more reasonable conditional representation, and ultimately should incorporate causal structure. Note the implicit temporal aspect here; propositions should be thought of as *fluents*. We can avoid an explicit temporal representation by assuming that preference is solely a function of the truth values of fluents.

As with ideal goals, the set of CK-goals is deductively closed and should be viewed as a set of necessary conditions in any rational course of action. Of course, goals can only be affected by atomic actions, so we will typically be interested in a set of actions that is guaranteed to achieve each CK-goal. An (atomic) *action set* is any set of controllable literals. If $\mathcal{A}$ is such a set we use it also to denote the conjunction of its elements. An *atomic goal set* is any action set $\mathcal{A}$ that guarantees each CK-goal; that is

$$M \models UI(KB) \land \mathcal{A} \supset \alpha$$

for each CK-goal α. Clearly, such any atomic goal set determines a reasonable course of action. Of course, such action sets can be determined by appeal to sufficiency.

Theorem 5 *Let $\mathcal{A}$ be some atomic action set. Then $\mathcal{A}$ is a goal set iff $\mathcal{A}$ is a sufficient condition for $UI(KB)$.*

In our example above, where the robot knows O, possible atomic goal sets are $\{T, H\}$ and $\{C, T, H\}$. Typically, we will be interested in minimal goals sets, since these require the fewest actions to achieve ideality. We may impose other metrics and preferences on goals sets as well (e.g., associating costs with various actions). Notice that the preference for tea does not prevent the robot from bringing coffee. However, such constraints can easily be imposed on the preference ordering. Furthermore, disjunctive goals and "integrity constraints" pose no difficulty. If I have no preference for coffee or tea, but prefer exactly one of the two, the generated atomic goal sets will be $\{C, \overline{T}\}$ and $\{\overline{C}, T\}$. The set $\{\overline{C}, \overline{T}\}$ is not a goal set in this case.

With default information and controllability in place, we can briefly return to the alternative interpretation of preference statements suggested in Section 2. The assertion "I prefer an umbrella when it's raining" can now be interpreted as $I(U|UI(\{R\}))$. Together with the "pure" preferences $I(D|R)$ and $I(\overline{U}|D)$ (and other background information as before), one can conclude $R \Rightarrow \neg D$.

In our goal derivation scheme, a certain priority is given to defaults over preferences. Goals are determined by first constructing the default consequences of KB, and then deciding what to do based on this knowledge as if it were certain. In a truly decision-theoretic setting acting on the basis of uncertain information is a function not only of its likelihood, but also the consequences of being incorrect. For instance, in our framework we might have the default rule $R \Rightarrow S$, if I run across the freeway I will cross safely. If this allows me to arrive at my destination five minutes sooner than had I crossed at a crosswalk, the default assumption S will ensure that I run across the freeway: I won't (by default) get hit by a car and I will arrive sooner. In general, the (drastic) consequences of being wrong in this regard must be traded off against the probability of being right. If the five minutes saved is not worth the risk, then I decide to go to the crosswalk.

To express this tradeoff we must assume that the qualitative scales of preference and normality are calibrated somehow, and nothing in the constraints expressed by the user in our setting allows such an assumption. In the concluding section we discuss "qualitative" ways around this problem. However, the scheme presented here has a certain naive appeal, which may be partly due to the observation that defaults are usually expressed with such considerations in mind [27, 25]. Furthermore, the scheme is conceptually simple in that it embodies a principle analogous to the *separability* of state estimation and control [11]. An agent can calculate what is (probably) true of the world and subsequently and independently base its decisions upon these beliefs. Finally, our scheme is applicable when likelihood and preference information is truly qualitative and explicit calibration of the orderings is not feasible. We can describe some conditions under which the assumption of separability is appropriate.

The logic of conditional normality statements can be given a probabilistic interpretation as described in [7]. In particular, the purely conditional fragment is equivalent to Adam's system of ε-semantics, which has also been applied to the representation of defaults [14]. This means that there is a probability assignment that ensures that every default rule $A \Rightarrow B$ corresponds to an assertion of high conditional probability $P(B|A) > 1 - \varepsilon$, for any $\varepsilon > 0$. Thus, we may assume that a user chooses default rules with such a parameter in mind, and that $P(Cl(KB)|KB) > 1 - \varepsilon$. We can also assume that the preference ordering is "constructed" by clustering together worlds that have actual utility within some reasonably small range, and treating distinct clusters as separated by a reasonably large gap in utility. Thus, the user can treat certain outcomes as having (more or less) indistinguishable utility. Outcomes in different clusters have sufficiently different utilities. To analyze the appropriateness of our goal derivation scheme, we make this assumption precise by assigning a point utility δ_i to each cluster in the preference ordering. Let δ denote the smallest gap $\delta_i - \delta_{i+1}$ between any two adjacent point utilities (the "smallest perceptible change" in utility) and let $\Delta = \delta_0 - \delta_n$ denote the magnitude of the possible range in utility.

Goals (or decisions) are determined with respect to a given KB, which induces a decision problem in the obvious fashion: given $UI(KB)$ what is an optimal action set? Let U^* denote the expected utility of an optimal action under the assumptions above, and let $EU(\mathcal{A})$ denote the expected utility of arbitrary action set $\mathcal{A}$. For any goal set $\mathcal{A}$, we want to compare $EU(\mathcal{A})$ to U^*. We consider a special case first. A *degenerate KB* is one for which every action set applied to $UI(KB)$ leads to an equally desirable outcome — $UI(KB)$ allows no decisions to be distinguished. Since only unlikely circumstances (that contradict default conclusions) can influence the choice of action, our scheme cannot generally be optimal in this case, but the error is bounded by the probability of default violation:

Proposition 6 *If KB induces a degenerate decision problem, then $U^* - EU(\mathcal{A}) \leq \varepsilon\Delta$ for any goal set $\mathcal{A}$.*

Degenerate problems will be rare: we imagine some differentiation among decisions is possible most of the time. If this is the case, then we have $U^* - EU(\mathcal{A}) \leq \varepsilon\Delta - (1-\varepsilon)\delta$.

Proposition 7 *If KB is nondegenerate, any goal set $\mathcal{A}$ is an optimal decision if $\delta(1-\varepsilon) \geq \varepsilon\Delta$.*

This gives some idea of the circumstances under which the assumption of separability is sound. Of course, it is unreasonable to only reason with qualitative constraints that meet these stringent requirements. But they do suggest useful abstractions for ordinary goal derivation, and the degree to which these conditions are approximated gives reasonable assurance of good decisions. Thus, the separability assumption provides a computationally manageable procedure for finding "satisficing" solutions.

4.3 Incomplete Knowledge

The goals described above seem reasonable, in accord with the general maxim "do the best thing possible consistent with your knowledge." We dubbed such goals "CK-goals" because they seem correct when an agent has complete knowledge of the world (or at least of uncontrollable atoms). But CK-goals do not always determine the best course of action if an agent's knowledge is *incomplete*. Consider the preferences in the umbrella example and an agent with an empty knowledge base. For all the agent knows it could rain or not (it has no indication either way). Using CK-goals, the agent ought to $do(\overline{U})$, for the best situation consistent with $KB = \emptyset$ is $\overline{RU}$. Leaving its umbrella is the best choice should it turn out not to rain; but should it rain, the agent has ensured the *worst* possible outcome. It is not clear that $\overline{U}$ should be a goal. Indeed, one might expect U to be a goal, for no matter how R turns out, the agent has avoided the worst outcome.

In the MEU framework, once can deal with such uncertainty easily; but qualitatively, when trying to do as much as possible with strictly ordinal value information, a different approach is required. The scales of preference and normality are unknown and incomparable. It is clear, in the presence of incomplete knowledge, that there are various *strategies* for determining goals. CK-goals form merely one alternative. Such a strategy is opportunistic, or optimistic. Clearly it *maximizes potential gain*, for it allows the possibility of the agent ending up with the best possible outcome. In certain domains this might be a prudent choice (for example, where a cooperative agent determines the outcome of uncontrollables). Of course, another strategy might be the cautious strategy that *minimizes potential loss*.[11] This too can be captured in our logic.

Let a *complete action set* be any complete truth assignment to the atoms in $\mathcal{C}$. These are the alternative courses of action available. To minimize potential loss, we must consider the

---

[11]These alternatives are analogs of the *maximax* and *maximin* decision criteria for decision making without outcome probabilities (under *strict* uncertainty [13]).

worst possible outcome for each alternative, and pick those with the "best" worst outcomes. If $\mathcal{A}_1$, $\mathcal{A}_2$ are complete action sets, $\mathcal{A}_1$ is *as good as* $\mathcal{A}_2$ ($\mathcal{A}_1 \leq \mathcal{A}_2$) iff

$$M \models \widetilde{\Diamond}_P(\mathcal{A}_2 \wedge UI(KB) \wedge \neg\widetilde{\Diamond}_P(\mathcal{A}_1 \wedge UI(KB)))$$

Intuitively, if $\mathcal{A}_1 \leq \mathcal{A}_2$ then the worst worlds satisfying $\mathcal{A}_1$ are at least as preferred as those satisfying $\mathcal{A}_2$ (in the context $UI(KB)$). It is not hard to see that $\leq$ forms a transitive, connected preference relation on action sets. The *best* actions sets are those minimal in this ordering $\leq$. To determine the best action sets, however, we do not need to compare all action sets in a pairwise fashion:

Theorem 8 $\mathcal{A}_i$ *is a best action set iff* $M \models \mathcal{A}_i \leq \neg\mathcal{A}_i$.

This holds because the negation of a complete action set (a complete conjunction of literals) is consistent with any other complete action set. If an agent chooses other than a best action set, it opens the possibility for a worse outcome:

Theorem 9 *Let $\mathcal{A}_i$ be a best action set for KB and $\mathcal{A}_j$ be any complete action set. For any $w \models UI(KB) \wedge \mathcal{A}_i$, there is some $v \models UI(KB) \wedge \mathcal{A}_j$ such that $w \leq_P v$.*

Now, we say α is a *cautious goal* iff

$$\vee\{\mathcal{A}_i : \mathcal{A}_i \text{ is a best action set }\} \models \alpha$$

In this way, if (say) $A \wedge B$ and $A \wedge \neg B$ are best action sets, then A is a goal but B is not. Simply doing A (and letting B run its natural course) is sufficient. This notion of goal has controllability built in (ignoring tautologies). In our example above, U is a cautious goal.

We cannot expect best action sets, in general, to be sufficient in the same sense that CK-goal sets are. The potential for desirable and undesirable outcomes makes it impossible to ensure best outcomes consistent with $UI(KB)$. However, we can show that if there is some action set that is sufficient for KB then all best action sets will be sufficient.

Proposition 10 *If some action set $\mathcal{A}$ for KB is CK-sufficient for KB, then every best action set is CK-sufficient.*

Hence, CK-sufficiency can be applied even in the case of incomplete knowledge. Its applicability implies that possible outcomes of unknown uncontrollables have no influence on preference: all *relevant* factors are known.

The cautious strategy seems applicable in a situation where one expects the worst possible outcome, for example, in a game against an adversary. Once the agent has performed its action, it expects the worst possible outcome, so there is no advantage to discriminating among the candidate (best) action sets: all have equally good worst outcomes. However, it's not clear that this is the best strategy if the outcome of uncontrollables is essentially "random." If outcomes are simply determined by the natural progression of events, then one should be more selective. We think of nature as neither benevolent (a cooperative agent) or malevolent (an adversary). Therefore, even if we decide to be cautious (choosing among *best* action sets), we should account for the fact that a worst outcome might not occur: we should choose the action sets that take advantage of this fact.

Observations

It should be clear that if an agent can *observe* the truth values of certain unknown propositions before it acts, it can improve its decisions. In many cases, it will make the worst outcomes better and change the actions chosen. To continue the "umbrella" example, suppose R and C are unknown. The agent's cautious goal is then U. If it were in the agent's power to determine C or $\overline{C}$ before acting, its actions could change. Observing $\overline{C}$ indicates the impossibility of R, and the agent could then decide to $do(\overline{U})$.

Space limitations preclude a deep discussion, but briefly, we can distinguish two types of uncontrollable atoms: *observables* and *unobservables*. Suppose KB determines a best action set $\mathcal{A}_B$. Intuitively, the observation of some unknown uncontrollable atom O is worthwhile if it can potentially change the agent's goal set. Cautious and optimistic goals must be treated differently. Assume first a cautious strategy. Note that a goal set accounts for some worst outcome which must include either O or $\overline{O}$. Thus, an observation can never be guaranteed to change the agent's decision: it may "validate" its cautious approach. In our example, observing C will not change the agent's decision, but observing $\overline{C}$ will. We say atom O has *value* if $\mathcal{A}_B$ is not a best action set for one of $KB \cup \{O\}$ or $KB \cup \{\overline{O}\}$. In this case, observing O is worthwhile since it *might* (depending on its actual truth value) change the agent's goal set. This is a qualitative analog of *value of information*. Of course, we cannot quantify the potential value of making an observation; but we may compare the relative values of two pieces of information O and P. For simplicity, assume that positive observations O and P are the "improving" outcomes. Let $\mathcal{A}_O$ and $\mathcal{A}_P$ be best action sets for O and P. The value of O is as great as that of P just when

$$M \models \tilde{\diamond}_P(\mathcal{A}_P \wedge UI(KB \cup \{P\})) \wedge \neg \tilde{\diamond}_P(\mathcal{A}_O \wedge UI(KB \cup \{O\})))$$

A similar treatment of optimistic goals can be given, where the valuable observations are *undesired* outcomes that change appropriate action. Observation O has value iff $\neg I(\mathcal{A}_B | UI(KB \cup \{O\}))$ or $\neg I(\mathcal{A}_B | UI(KB \cup \{\overline{O}\}))$ hold.

5 Concluding Remarks

Related Work

Other attempts to define goals using preferences bear some relationship to our system. Doyle and Wellman [12] define goals that exhibit a conditional aspect like ours. Roughly, B is a goal given A just when $A \wedge B$ is preferred to $A \wedge \neg B$ for any *fixed* circumstance. For instance, if such a relationship holds $A \wedge B$ should be preferred given C, given $\neg C$, and so on. Such goals incorporate a *ceteris paribus* assumption: B is preferred to $\neg B$ given A, *all else being equal*. This guarantees that doing B will lead to a better situation whenever A holds. Our conditional goals are much weaker. No such assurances can be provided. Intuitively, if B is a goal given A, then doing B will lead to a better situation, *all else being normal*. However, this permits defeasible goals, affording greater flexibility and naturalness of expression. Only factors directly relevant to utility need be stated, and others are assumed to be irrelevant. In addition, our goals incorporate elements of controllability.

Pearl [24] has proposed a system using much the same underlying logical apparatus as ours. However, conditional statements are taken to impose specific constraints on utility and probability distributions, allowing expected utility calculations (with "order of magnitude" values) to be performed. While this allows stronger conclusions to be reached in general, it makes stronger demands on the input information as well. Thus, the system cannot be construed as truly qualitative, so in a sense the aim here is different. Tan and Pearl [28] introduce a somewhat more qualitative system. It handles quantified conditional desires (adopting the machinery of qualitative probability [14]). To account for likelihood, they adopt our model of closing under default consequence before consulting preferences. Incompletely specified preferences induce a "compact" model where worlds gravitate toward neutrality, but as noted earlier, this is not an obviously useful strategy. Furthermore, conditional preferences are given a *ceteris paribus* interpretation along the lines of Doyle and Wellman. Aside from the unknown impact on the computation of compact rankings, their particular semantics is of questionable value for representing conditional preferences. For example, a preference for A given $A \vee B$ requires that $\neg A \wedge \neg B$ be dispreferred. In our semantics, a conditional preference given any α imposes no constraints on the degree of preference of $\neg \alpha$-worlds.

Our representation of preferences draws much from work on deontic logic, where preference may be determined by some legal or moral code. Indeed, our logic can be applied to such problems [6]. However, the slogan that characterizes ideal goals, "do the best given what you know," is accepted in much work on the derivation of obligations. Just as in the derivation of goals, such a mechanism is not generally appropriate. Some work in deontic logic has recently begun to incorporate, as we do here, default information [20, 1].

Summary

We have presented a logic QDT for representing qualitative preference and likelihood information. We have shown how defeasible conditional preferences can be expressed, and described several methods for goal derivation based on the assumption that priority be given to defaults. There are a number of ways in which this work can be extended. Clearly, the account of action and ability is naive. An object-level characterization of actions with true causal structure can be added to the conditional framework [24] to make goal derivation more realistic.

The assumption of separability and priority of default information must be relaxed in many circumstances. In order to allow reasonable decisions to be made, a logic that allows tradeoffs of likelihood and preference to be expressed in a qualitative fashion is desirable. For instance, if I instruct my robot that it should run across the street (instead of crossing at the crosswalk) to save three minutes while fetching my coffee, it can safely deduce that running across the street is worth the risk if a courier deadline is involved. I have implicitly calibrated part of its preference and normality rankings with each other. We are currently exploring how such mechanisms to reason directly with such qualitative tradeoff information [9]. This can be viewed as a mechanism to deal with *imperatives*, and propagate the implicit knowledge in such commands to other contexts.

Related to this is a fuller investigation of the different forms preference information might take in such a setting. As mentioned earlier, user preferences might be stated independently of typicality information, or might incorporate expected circumstances and controllability information. A well-developed logic for these and other "entangled" constraints is certainly worth pursuing.

References

[1] Carlos E. Alchourrón. Philosophical foundations of deontic logic and the logic of defeasible conditionals. In *Workshop on Deontic Logic in Computer Science*, Amsterdam, 1991.

[2] Craig Boutilier. Conditional logics of normality as modal systems. In *Proc. of AAAI-90*, pages 594–599, Boston, 1990.

[3] Craig Boutilier. Inaccessible worlds and irrelevance: Preliminary report. In *Proc. of IJCAI-91*, pages 413–418, Sydney, 1991.

[4] Craig Boutilier. Normative, subjunctive and autoepistemic defaults: Adopting the Ramsey test. In *Proc. of KR-92*, pages 685–696, Cambridge, 1992.

[5] Craig Boutilier. What is a default priority? In *Proceedings of Canadian Society for Computational Studies of Intelligence Conference*, pages 140–147, Vancouver, 1992.

[6] Craig Boutilier. A modal characterization of defeasible deontic conditionals and conditional goals. In *AAAI Spring Symposium on Reasoning about Mental States: Formal Theories and Applications*, pages 30–39, Stanford, 1993.

[7] Craig Boutilier. Conditional logics of normality: A modal approach. *Artificial Intelligence*, 1994. (in press).

[8] Craig Boutilier. Unifying default reasoning and belief revision in a modal framework. *Artificial Intelligence*, 1994. (in press).

[9] Craig Boutilier and David Poole. Qualitative lotteries: Capturing expected utility calculations in a qualitative framework. Technical report, University of British Columbia, Vancouver, 1994. (Forthcoming).

[10] Philip R. Cohen and Hector J. Levesque. Intention is choice with commitment. *Artificial Intelligence*, 42:213–261, 1990.

[11] Thomas Dean and Michael Wellman. *Planning and Control*. Morgan Kaufmann, San Mateo, 1991.

[12] Jon Doyle and Michael P. Wellman. Preferential semantics for goals. In *Proc. of AAAI-91*, pages 698–703, Anaheim, 1991.

[13] Simon French. *Decision Theory*. Halsted Press, New York, 1986.

[14] Moisés Goldszmidt. Qualitative probabilities: A normative framework for commonsense reasoning. Technical Report R-190, University of California, Los Angeles, October 1992. Ph.D. thesis.

[15] Moisés Goldszmidt, Paul Morris, and Judea Pearl. A maximum entropy approach to nonmonotonic reasoning. In *Proc. of AAAI-90*, pages 646–652, Boston, 1990.

[16] Peter Haddawy and Steve Hanks. Representations for decision-theoretic planning: Utility functions for deadline goals. In *Proc. of KR-92*, pages 71–82, Cambridge, 1992.

[17] Bengt Hansson. An analysis of some deontic logics. *Noûs*, 3:373–398, 1969.

[18] John F. Horty. Moral dilemmas and nonmonotonic logic. *J. of Philosophical Logic*, 1993. To appear.

[19] Richard C. Jeffrey. *The Logic of Decision*. McGraw-Hill, New York, 1965.

[20] Andrew J. I. Jones and Ingmar Pörn. On the logic of deontic conditionals. In *Workshop on Deontic Logic in Computer Science*, Amsterdam, 1991.

[21] Hector J. Levesque. All I know: A study in autoepistemic logic. *Artificial Intelligence*, 42:263–309, 1990.

[22] Barry Loewer and Marvin Belzer. Dyadic deontic detachment. *Synthese*, 54:295–318, 1983.

[23] Judea Pearl. System Z: A natural ordering of defaults with tractable applications to default reasoning. In M. Vardi, editor, *Proceedings of Theoretical Aspects of Reasoning about Knowledge*, pages 121–135. Morgan Kaufmann, San Mateo, 1990.

[24] Judea Pearl. A calculus of pragmatic obligation. In *Proc. of UAI-93*, pages 12–20, Washington, D.C., 1993.

[25] David Poole. Decision-theoretic defaults. In *Proceedings of Canadian Society for Computational Studies of Intelligence Conference*, pages 190–197, Vancouver, 1992.

[26] Frank P. Ramsey. Turth and probability. In R. B. Braithwaite, editor, *The Foundations of Mathematics and Other Logical Essays*, pages 156–198. Kegan Paul, London, 1931.

[27] Yoav Shoham. *Reasoning About Change: Time and Causation from the Standpoint of Artificial Intelligence*. MIT Press, Cambridge, 1988.

[28] Sek-Wah Tan and Judea Pearl. Specification and evaluation of preferences for planning under uncertainty. In *Proc. of KR-94*, Bonn, 1994. To appear.

[29] John von Neumann and Oskkar Morgenstern. *Theory of Gamee and Economic Behavior*. Princeton University Press, Princeton, 1944.

Acknowledgements

Thanks to Carlos Alchourrón, Jon Doyle, Keiji Kanazawa, Judea Pearl, David Poole and Michael Wellman for very valuable discussion of this topic. This research was supported by NSERC Research Grant OGP0121843.

Belief Ascription and Mental-level Modelling

Ronen I. Brafman
Dept. of Computer Science
Stanford University
Stanford, CA 94305
brafman@cs.stanford.edu

Moshe Tennenholtz
Faculty of Industrial Engineering and Management
Technion
Haifa 32000, Israel
moshet@ie.technion.ac.il

Abstract

Models of agents that employ formal notions of mental states are useful and often easier to construct than models at the symbol (e.g., programming language) or physical (e.g., mechanical) level. However, to enjoy these benefits, we must first supply a coherent picture of mental-level models. What is required is a description of the various components of the mental level, their dynamics, their interrelations, and their relations with the agent's behavior. Only then will we have a complete semantics for mental notions. The goal of the first part of this paper is to provide this picture.

The second part of this paper concentrates specifically on belief ascription. We address two fundamental unresolved problems. Our mental-level model addresses the question of *grounding*: where do beliefs come from, i.e., what links a system's symbol or physical level with its beliefs? Our characterization of a class of *goal-seeking agents* goes towards addressing the question of *adequacy*: when can we treat an entity as having beliefs? In addition, we look at general assumptions that can help constrain the set of beliefs an agent can be ascribed. Together, these results supply a basis for agent modelling using mental states.

1 INTRODUCTION

Abstractions play an important role in our reasoning ability. Arguably, the most fundamental abstraction we use involves modelling other entities as having mental states. We use it to model other biological entities and perhaps even ourselves; it may even be used in modelling complex mechanical entities. Indeed, Allen Newel, in a famous paper [Newell, 1980], argues that intelligent systems can be (approximately) described at a level higher than the symbol (e.g., programming language) level and the physical level, which he calls the *knowledge level*.

Having a mental-level model offers many advantages. First, it allows us to describe a system's behavior without a detailed description of its lower-level, e.g., its implementation as machine code, or its physical components. A mental-level model is also much more accessible and intuitive to us. We can, therefore, use it to critique a system by looking at its beliefs and asking ourselves whether they make sense. Similarly, we can examine a system's goals and criticize them. And while a model at the symbol or physical level requires detailed knowledge that is often not available, we can usually construct a mental model of an agent by observing its behavior or by using general knowledge about the typical behaviors of this agent. An understanding of the way this behavior is implemented within this agent is not necessary, as we know from our experience. This makes possible the task of predicting an agent's behavior without access to its program. And as John McCarthy says [McCarthy, 1979],

> (Ascription of mental states) is useful when the ascription helps us understand the structure of the machine, its past or future behavior, or how to repair and improve it. It is perhaps never required even for humans, but expressing reasonably briefly what is actually known about the state of a machine ... may require ascribing mental qualities.

In order to use this abstraction we must provide the foundations required for modelling agents at the mental level. First, we need good models of the mental level, i.e., its components, the way they interact, the way they change over time, the manner in which they determine the agent's behavior and their relation with the lower level descriptions of an agent. This supplies what we call the *grounding* of the mental notions. Secondly, we must find criteria for determining whether an entity can be described at this level. This is the *adequacy* problem. Having answered these questions we can specifically address the theoretical and practical questions of *how to ascribe* a mental state to an entity, based on the available information. Typically this information includes the observable behavior of this entity and additional background information.

In this paper we attempt to address these problems. We develop a formal model of the mental level, which is motivated by work in decision theory [Luce and Raiffa, 1957] and the work of [Rosenschein, 1985] and [Halpern and Moses, 1990] on knowledge ascription. The model is quite simple and intuitive. It uses a number of components: beliefs, utilities, and a decision-strategy to construct a mental-level model. This model relates these components among themselves and with the agent's behavior. It is built upon a lower-level description of the agent, which we will call the *physical level*.

We start with a static model. In this model the agent associates with each possible action a number of plausible outcomes, which depend on the agent's beliefs. The agent assigns a utility to each outcome, representing the relative desirability of this outcome. The agent then uses its decision strategy to choose an action based on the utilities of this action's outcomes. Based on the static model we develop a more dynamic model that also takes into account the issue of belief change, and provide two interesting representation theorems. These theorems relate certain patterns of belief change with a static representation of belief based upon partial and total pre-orders. This model supplies the grounding of the mental notions we use.

With this model at hand we proceed to specifically examine the problem of belief ascription. We show a class of *goal-seeking* agents that can be ascribed belief in our framework, addressing the adequacy problem. Unfortunately, it is often the case that we cannot ascribe an agent unique beliefs based on the available information. We examine this issue and suggest two general heuristics for choosing among multiple candidates. Together these results provide a basis for agent modelling using mental states.

1.1 A MOTIVATING EXAMPLE

To introduce the problem of belief ascription and the motivation behind our proposed solution, we present the following example.

Say we only care about four sets of worlds, described by the propositions *cold* and *rainy*. Our agent, Alice, has an accurate thermostat at home, but no windows. In a $cold \wedge rainy$ world, there are two worlds Alice considers possible: $cold \wedge rainy$ and $cold \wedge \neg rainy$. Because in all her possible worlds *cold* holds, Alice *knows* that it is cold. In general, to determine what Alice knows, we construct her set of possible worlds. [Halpern and Moses, 1990] shows us how we can construct this set given an appropriate description of Alice.

Alice does not *know* that it is rainy, but does she *believe* that it is rainy? It seems, that to answer this question, more information is required. So suppose we see Alice leaving home without an umbrella. This seems to indicate that she does not believe it is rainy, for otherwise she would have taken an umbrella. So based on Alice's action we have deduced her beliefs. However, to do so we implicitly assumed that Alice does not like getting wet and that she had the choice of taking an umbrella. That is, we used information regarding Alice's desires and possible choices of action.

Let's be more precise. The following matrix describes the outcome of Alice's two possible actions.

	$rainy$	$\neg rainy$
take umbrella	dry,heavy	dry,heavy,look stupid
leave umbrella	wet,light	dry,light

Suppose that Alice's preferences are described by the following utility function:

	$rainy$	$\neg rainy$
take umbrella	5	-1
leave umbrella	-4	10

A belief that $\neg rainy$ is the only plausible world would adequately explain Alice's behavior, as it will make the choice of leaving the umbrella the preferred one. Are other beliefs consistent with her behavior? Well, she could not believe $rainy$ to be the only plausible world, for then she would have taken the umbrella. Could she consider both worlds plausible? The answer depends on her *decision criterion*. If she prefers to be on the safe side, employing a *maximin* strategy, which attempts to maximize the worst case outcome, then had she believed both worlds to be plausible, she would have taken the umbrella (with a worst case payoff of -1) rather than leaving it (with a worst case payoff of -4). But if Alice follows the *principle of indifference*, which takes the average payoff across plausible states, belief in both states is consistent, since leaving the umbrella has a better average payoff (3) than taking it (2).

Overview The next section describes a mental-level model based upon the notions of knowledge, belief, decision criteria, and utilities. In Section 3 this model is used to define belief ascription. As we will see, often we cannot ascribe unique beliefs to an agent, and in Section 4 we suggest how one can narrow the choice of appropriate belief ascriptions. In Section 5 we add time to the static model of Section 2, enabling us to investigate the issue of belief change in Section 6. In Section 7, having described a dynamic picture of the mental level, we characterize a class of agents to which belief can be ascribed using this model. Section 8 concludes with a discussion of related work and some of our assumptions.

2 THE FRAMEWORK

Starting with a physical level description of a system containing a single agent and an environment, we review knowledge ascription, following [Halpern and Moses, 1990]. Then, we introduce a number of new elements, beliefs, decision criteria, and utilities, and relate them to the agent's behavior. To make our definitions clear we will accompany them with a simplified version of McCarthy's famous thermostats example.

Example 1 In [McCarthy, 1979], McCarthy shows how we often ascribe mental states to simple devices, thermostats in that case. Our goal is to formalize this informal discussion. We assume that we have a thermostat in a room that controls the flow of hot water into that room's radiator. The thermostat can either turn-on or shut-off the hot water supply to this radiator. It chooses its action based on whether it senses the temperature of the room to be above or below a certain threshold value.

2.1 THE PHYSICAL LEVEL AND KNOWLEDGE

An *agent* is described by a set of possible (local) states and a set of possible actions. The agent functions within an *environment*, which may also be in one of a number of states. We refer to the state of the system, i.e., that of both the agent and the environment as a *global state*. W.l.o.g., we will assume that the environment does not perform actions. The effects of the agent's actions are a (deterministic) function of its state and the environment's state.[1] This effect is described by the *transition function*. Together, the agent and the environment constitute a state machine with two components, with transitions at each state corresponding to the agent's possible actions. It may be the case that not all combinations of an agent's local state and an environment's state are possible. Those global states that are possible are called *possible worlds*.

Definition 1 An **agent** is a pair $\mathcal{A} = \langle L_\mathcal{A}, A_\mathcal{A} \rangle$, where $L_\mathcal{A}$ is the agent's set of **local states** and $A_\mathcal{A}$ is its set of **actions**. $L_\mathcal{E}$ is the environment's set of possible states. A **global state** is a pair $(l_\mathcal{A}, l_\mathcal{E}) \in L_\mathcal{A} \times L_\mathcal{E}$. The set of **possible worlds** is a subset S of the set of global states $L_\mathcal{A} \times L_\mathcal{E}$. A **context**[2] $C = \langle \tau \rangle$, consists of the **transition function**, $\tau : (L_\mathcal{A} \times L_\mathcal{E}) \times A_\mathcal{A} \to (L_\mathcal{A} \times L_\mathcal{E})$.

A context specifies the environment (since $L_\mathcal{E}$ is implicit in τ) and the effects of the agent's actions on the whole system. Later on, when we add time to the picture it will also specify the possible starting points of a system.

Example 1 *(continued):* For our thermostat $L_\mathcal{A} = \{-, +\}$. $-$ corresponds to the case when the thermostat indicates a temperature that is less than the desired room temperature and $+$ corresponds to a temperature greater or equal to the desired room temperature. However, we take into account the fact that the thermostat may be mistaken in its measurement of the room's temperature, which is indeed one of the situations McCarthy considers. The thermostat's actions, $A_\mathcal{A}$, are {turn-on, shut-off}. The environment's states, $L_\mathcal{E}$, are {cold, ok, hot}. We do not assume any necessary relation between the states of the thermostat and the environment. Therefore the set of possible worlds is exactly $L_\mathcal{A} \times L_\mathcal{E}$. We chose the following transition function:

	cold	ok	hot
turn-on	ok	hot	hot
shut-off	cold	ok	ok

In our example, the result of an action does not depend on the state of the thermostat. To simplify matters we assume that the thermostat is not affected by its actions, although this does not matter in this example.

Knowledge can be ascribed to the agent using the notion of a local state. An agent can distinguish between two worlds in S if and only if *its* state in them, is different. Therefore, an agent whose local state is l can rule out as impossible all worlds in which his local state would have been different, but cannot rule out worlds in S in which his local state would have been l. Knowledge corresponds to what holds in all worlds the agent cannot distinguish from the actual world.

Definition 2 The set of **worlds possible at** l, $PW(l)$, is $\{w \in S :$ the agent's local state in w is $l\}$. The agent **knows** φ at $w \in S$ if φ holds in all worlds in $PW(l)$, where l is its local state at w.

Example 1 *(continued):* While the thermostat, by definition, knows its local state, it knows nothing about the room's temperature. This stems from the fact that in our model we allowed for the possibility of a measurement error by the thermostat, making all elements of $L_\mathcal{A} \times L_\mathcal{E}$ possible, e.g., $(-, hot)$ is a possible world.

If truth assignments (for some given language) are attached to each world in S and a world s' is defined to be accessible from s whenever the agent's local states in s and s' are identical, we obtain the familiar $S5$ Kripke structure.

---

[1] A framework in which the environment does act can be mapped into this framework using richer state descriptions and larger sets of states, a common practice in game theory.

[2] Though context is an overloaded term, its use here seems appropriate, following [Fagin et al., 1994].

The agent's observed, or programmed behavior is described by the protocol.

Definition 3 *A* **protocol** *for an agent $\mathcal{A}$ is a function $\mathcal{P}_{\mathcal{A}} : L_{\mathcal{A}} \to A_{\mathcal{A}}$.*

Example 1 *(continued):* Our thermostat follows the following protocol:

state	−	+
action	turn-on	shut-off

2.2 THE AGENCY HYPOTHESIS

What is belief? Belief is part of an abstract description of the agent's state. It sums up the agent's view of the world, and is a basis for decision making. Therefore, we make belief a function of the agent's *local* state, represented by a *belief assignment*, which assigns to each local state a nonempty subset of the set of possible worlds. These worlds are the worlds the agent considers *plausible*.

Definition 4 *A* **belief assignment** *is a function, $B : L_{\mathcal{A}} \to 2^S$, such that for all l : $B(l) \neq \emptyset$ and $B(l) \subseteq PW(l)$.*

Example 1 *(continued):* One possible belief assignment, which would probably make the thermostat's designer happy, is $B(-) = \{-, cold\}$ and $B(+) = \{+, hot\}$. From now on we will ignore the agent's local state in the description of the global state and write, e.g., $B(+) = \{hot\}$.

While knowledge (or $PW(l)$) defines what is theoretically possible, belief defines what, in the eyes of the agent, is the set of worlds that should be taken into consideration. We remark, that (after adding interpretations to each world) this approach yields a $KD45$ belief operator.[3]

However, our view is that belief really makes sense as part of a fuller description of the agent's mental level. In order to describe this mental level and to relate it to the agent's behavior, additional notions are required. We start with the agent's preference order over the set of possible states, represented by a *utility function*. This preference order embodies the agent's desires.

Definition 5 *A* **utility** *function is a function $u : S \to \mathbb{R}$.*

It is well known ([von Neumann and Morgenstern, 1944]) that a utility function can represent preference orders satisfying certain assumptions, which in this paper we will accept. This means that for any two states s_1, s_2: s_1 is preferred over s_2 iff $u(s_1) > u(s_2)$.

Example 1 *(continued):* The goal of our thermostat is for the room temperature to be ok. This can be represented by a utility function which assigns 0 to global states in which the environment's state (i.e., the room temperature) is hot or cold, and which assigns 1 to those states in which the environment's state is ok.

When the exact state of the world is known, the result of following some protocol, $\mathcal{P}$, is also precisely known. (Remember that actions have deterministic effects). We can therefore evaluate a protocol by looking at the utility of the state it would generate at the actual world. However, due to uncertainty about the state of the world, the agent considers a number of states to be possible. It can then subjectively assess $\mathcal{P}$ in a local state l by a vector whose elements are the utilities of the plausible states $\mathcal{P}$ generates, i.e., the worlds generated by using $\mathcal{P}$ at $B(l)$.

Definition 6 *Given a context C and a belief assignment, B, with an arbitrary, fixed, order on the set $B(l)$, for every l; the* **perceived outcome** *of a protocol $\mathcal{P}$ in l is a tuple whose kth element is the utility of the state generated by applying $\mathcal{P}$ in C, starting from the kth state of $B(l)$.* [4]

Example 1 *(continued):* We can construct the following table for the thermostats possible actions:

	cold	ok	hot
turn-on	1	0	0
shut-off	0	1	1

If the thermostat 'knew' the precise state of the world, e.g., that it is cold, it would have no trouble choosing the action turn-on as most preferred. When there is uncertainty, e.g., $B(l) = \{cold, ok\}$, the thermostat associates a perceived outcome of $(1, 0)$ with the action turn-on, and a perceived outcome of $(0, 1)$ with the action shut-off.

While utilities are easily compared, it is not a-priori clear how to compare perceived outcomes, thus, how to choose among protocols. A strategy for choice under uncertainty is required, which depends on e.g., the agent's attitude towards risk. This strategy is represented by the *decision criterion*, a function taking a set of perceived outcomes, returning the *set* of most preferred among them.

Definition 7 *A* **decision criterion** *is a function $\rho : \bigcup_{n \in \mathbb{N}} 2^{\mathbb{R}^n} \to \bigcup_{n \in \mathbb{N}} 2^{\mathbb{R}^n}$ (i.e. from/to sets of*

---

[3] Incidentally, this gives a relation between knowledge and belief similar to the one proposed by Kraus and Lehmann in [Kraus and Lehmann, 1988].

[4] For simplicity we assume a finite number of states. In the general case we use functions instead of tuples, eliminating the need to order $B(l)$.

equal length tuples of reals), such that for all $\mathcal{U} \in \bigcup_{n \in \mathbb{N}} 2^{\mathbb{R}^n} \rho(\mathcal{U}) \subseteq \mathcal{U}$.

Two decision criteria we have encountered are *maximin*, which chooses the tuples in which the worst case outcome is maximal, and the *principle of indifference* which prefers tuples whose average outcome is maximal[5] (A fuller discussion of decision criteria appears in [Luce and Raiffa, 1957, Brafman and Tennenholtz, 1994]).

Returning to the example of Section 1, if Alice considers two worlds plausible, *rainy* and ¬*rainy*, at this order, the perceived outcome of the action *take umbrella* is $(5, -1)$, while the perceived outcome of *leave umbrella* is $(-4, 10)$. If Alice uses *maximin* she prefers $(5, -1)$, with a worst case outcome of -1, over $(-4, 10)$, with a worst case outcome of -4. She will therefore take the umbrella. Under the *principle of indifference*, Alice prefers $(-4, 10)$, with an average utility of 3, over $(5, -1)$, with an average utility of 2, and will leave the umbrella. Notice how the perceived outcome depends on Alice's beliefs. Had Alice believed only ¬*rainy* to be plausible, the perceived outcome of *take umbrella* would be a singleton, (-1).

We remark that decision criteria such as *maximin* can be employed with preference relations satisfying assumptions weaker than those of [von Neumann and Morgenstern, 1944].

We come to a key definition that ties all of the components we have discussed so far.

Definition 8 *The* **agency hypothesis**: *the agent follows a protocol whose perceived outcome is most preferred (according to the agent's decision criterion) among the set of perceived outcomes of all possible protocols.*[6]

The agency hypothesis takes the view of a rational balance among the agent's beliefs, utilities, decision criterion and behavior. It states that the agent chooses actions whose perceived outcome is maximal according to its decision criterion. Thus, the choice of the protocol is dependent upon $B(l)$ and u, which define the perceived outcome, and ρ, which helps choose among the different protocols, based on their perceived outcome. The agency hypothesis states that these components are related via this 'rationality' constraint.

---

[5]With an infinite set of tuples, *maximin* and the *principle of indifference* may not have a set of most preferred tuples. This is fixed by, for example, choosing some cutoff point.

[6]The agent's possible protocols, are implicitly defined by the set of actions $A_\mathcal{A}$ (cf. Def. 1).

3 ASCRIBING BELIEF

We now show how belief can be ascribed according to our framework. We will assume that we are ascribing a complete belief assignment to an agent, i.e., one that is defined in all local states. In many applications one can only ascribe partial belief assignments, e.g., if observations of the agent's actions exist only in some states. It is quite straightforward to generalize our discussion to this case.

Belief can be ascribed once we have certain information regarding the agent. We see this information as putting the agent in some (extended) context, which specifies some of the elements of the rational balance we have just discussed. Our strategy is to look for belief assignments confirming the agency hypothesis. That is, beliefs that would lead an entity satisfying the agency hypothesis to act according to the given protocol when its utilities and decision criterion are as given. This is a process of constraint satisfaction, where our belief assignment is constrained by the given extended context.

Definition 9 *An* **extended context** *is a 3-tuple,* $\mathcal{C} = \langle \tau, u, \rho \rangle$ *(where, τ, u and ρ are as previously defined). Given an extended context $\mathcal{C}$, a belief assignment B is* **consistent with** $\mathcal{A}$**'s protocol,** $\mathcal{P}_\mathcal{A}$, *if it confirms the agency hypothesis regarding* $\mathcal{A}$.

It is clear that this approach could be used to assign other mental states that are part of the agency hypothesis, e.g., we can ascribe goals (i.e., utilities) based on the agent's beliefs, decision criterion, and actions. We have chosen to concentrate on belief assignment. (This choice is discussed in Section 8.) The problem of belief ascription can now be formally stated as:

> In an extended context $\mathcal{C}$, what belief assignments are consistent with the agent's protocol, if any?

Example 1 *(continued):* *Given our knowledge of the thermostat, what beliefs can we assign it? We know the thermostat's protocol and goals. We will assume that its decision criterion simply prefers tuples that are not dominated by another tuple. Given this, we have the following constraints on the thermostat's beliefs:* $B(-) \supseteq \{cold\}$ *and at least one of ok or hot are in* $B(+)$. *If the thermostat's beliefs violate these constraints, the perceived outcome of the action prescribed by its protocol would be strictly less preferred than the perceived outcome of the other action.*

Example 2 A simple game *The following tree describes a one-person decision problem based on a game that appears in [Kreps and Wilson, 1982]:*

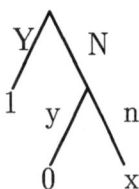

Initially the agent decides whether to choose Y or N. If Y is chosen a payoff of 1 is obtained, otherwise the environment chooses either y, with a payoff of 0 to the agent, or n, with a payoff of $x > 1$. While game theoreticians are mostly concerned with how games should be played when the environment is another rational agent, we ask a simple question: what can we say if we observed the agent's first move to be N? This is an interesting question because it is easy to construct a two person game based on this decision problem, in which N is not a 'rational' move. Such behavior, while perhaps irrational in some sense, can still be understood as rational given certain beliefs, e.g., that the environment will play n.

The following payoff matrix describes the agent's decision problem (the different states of the world correspond to the environment's behavior if N is played):

	y	n
Y	1	1
N	0	x

Having chosen N, if the agent's decision criterion is maximin *then regardless of the value of x, the agent must believe that the environment will play n. Belief that y is plausible is inconsistent with the agent's behavior, since it would imply that Y should be chosen.*

In the case of the principle of indifference, *if $x < 2$, N is chosen only if the agent believes only n to be plausible. If $x \geq 2$ then a belief that both worlds are plausible would also cause N to be preferred.*

Another decision criterion is minmax regret. *The regret of performing action* ACT *in a state* s *is the difference between the best that can be done in state s and the actual payoff of* ACT *in* s. *This decision criterion prefers actions whose maximal regret is minimal. Here is the 'regret' matrix for our decision problem:*

	y	n
Y	0	x-1
N	1	0

For an agent following minmax regret, *if $x < 2$ the agent must believe n to follow N, otherwise it may believe either n or $\{n, y\}$.*

4 CHOOSING AMONG BELIEF ASSIGNMENTS

As we observed in the thermostat example, there are often more than one consistent belief assignment. This is not surprising, as we often require additional assumptions to ascribe unique beliefs to agents, or we may need some lower level, implementation dependent, information. Dennett [Dennett, 1987] paraphrases the Duhemian thesis in this area, saying that belief and desire attribution are under-determined by the available data.

Indeed, one way of obtaining a unique belief assignment in the thermostat example would be to use a better model. That is, by using domain specific information. Assume, for instance, that the thermostat prefers not to change the course of action it is pursuing, if the result is not expected to improve its utility, i.e., if currently it is supplying hot water to the radiator then, all other things being equal, it prefers not to change this and shut-off the water supply. This assumption can be incorporated into our model by adding the course of action pursued into the state description and appropriately changing the utility function to reflect the above consideration. In that case we may be able to limit the number of consistent belief assignments

However, there are also domain *independent* assumptions and preferences that we can make when ascribing beliefs. These assumptions narrow down our choice, without changing the model used. We look at two such assumptions.

A common bias is to favor models that offer adequate explanation of the data. This is the idea behind the following:

Definition 10 *A consistent belief assignment is* **choice complete** *(within an extended context) if for all local states, the decision criterion returns a unique perceived outcome.*

Assume that in all local states no two protocols have the exact same perceived outcome. In that case, given a consistent choice complete belief assignment, no protocol is as preferred as the actual protocol. Thus, the agent will not be indifferent among a number of most preferred protocols. In this sense, a choice complete belief assignment fully explains/justifies the agent's choice of action.

Example 1 *(continued):* We have seen that any belief assignment for state − that includes the state cold is consistent. There are 4 such possibilities. However, only one of them, $B(-) = \{cold\}$ is choice complete. Given this belief assignment the agent must choose the action turn-on, while given any of the other 3 belief assignments, the agent is indifferent to the choice between turn-on and shut-off.

A different modelling bias is toward greater generality. Given a number of belief assignments that explain some behavior *equally well*, the preference is for those making fewer assumptions regarding the agent's beliefs. That is, belief assignments in which fewer worlds are ruled out.

Definition 11 *A belief assignment B is **more general** than B' if $\forall l \in L_A : B'(l) \subseteq B(l)$ and $B \neq B'$. Given a set of belief assignments, $\mathcal{B}$, $B \in \mathcal{B}$ is a most general belief assignment (**mgb**) w.r.t. $\mathcal{B}$ if there is no $B' \in \mathcal{B}$ such that B' is more general than B.*

Example 1 *(continued):* *Any belief assignment that is a non-empty subset of $\{ok, hot\}$ is choice complete for the state $+$. However, the most general choice complete belief assignment for that state is precisely $\{ok, hot\}$.*

In the sequel we will usually assume that either the generality bias is accepted or the combination of both which prefers the most general in the set of consistent, choice complete, belief assignments. As the following lemma shows, in some sense, the latter is the best we can do in terms of assigning beliefs that do not make the agent's actions arbitrary.

Lemma 1 *If B is most general choice complete, the decision criterion satisfies the sure-thing principle[7], and in local state l two protocols have the same perceived outcome, then there is no choice complete belief assignment under which their perceived outcome in l differs.*

Example 1 *(continued):* *To summarize, we have the following unique most general choice complete belief assignment for the thermostat:*

state	−	+
belief	cold	not-cold

5 ADDING TIME

Because we assumed that the thermostat has no memory nor that the environment has some special dynamics, we were able to model them without explicitly introducing time. However, time is essential for reasonably modelling many situation. Indeed the added dimension of time allows us to examine the way the mental state of an agent changes as it obtains new information.

We incorporate time by adding the notion of a *run*, a description of a full history of the system, and the

---

[7]That is, if it chooses v out of $\{v, u\}$ then it chooses $v \circ w$ out of $\{v \circ w, u \circ w\}$, where $\circ$ is the concatenation operator.

notion of an *initial global state*, a state from which the system can start out.

Definition 12 *Let $\mathcal{G}_0 \subseteq L_A \times L_\mathcal{E}$ be the set of **initial (global) states**. A **run** is a sequence of states $s_0, s_1, \ldots$ such that $s_i \in L_A \times L_\mathcal{E}$, $s_0 \in \mathcal{G}_0$ and $(\forall k > 0) (\exists a \in A_A) : \tau(s_{k-1}, a) = s_k$.[8] The **extended system**, $\mathcal{R}$, is the set of all possible runs.*

Having changed from static states to runs, we must redefined some of our basic notions.

Definition 13 *The set of **possible worlds**, $S = \{s | s$ is a global state appearing in a run in $\mathcal{R}\}$. A **context** is redefined as $C = \langle \tau, \mathcal{G}_0 \rangle$ and an **extended context** is redefined as $\mathcal{C} = \langle \tau, \mathcal{G}_0, u, \rho \rangle$. We redefine the utility function as $u : \mathcal{R} \to \mathbb{R}$.*

Applying a protocol $\mathcal{P}$ at a state s will generate a unique run r whose initial state is s, where each state of r is obtained by performing the action prescribed by $\mathcal{P}$ at the previous state. This allows us to maintain the notion of a perceived outcome because we can now associate a utility with each protocol at each state, the utility of the run that this protocol induces at that state.[9]

One last adjustment; we defined a belief assignment as a function $B : L_A \to 2^S$. This definition will make it hard for us to investigate belief change, i.e., the relations between an agent's beliefs at different states of a run. For example, if the agent has a clock, then its local state at two consecutive states of a run will differ, because in each the clock's value would be different; consequently, the states the agent considers plausible at these local states would be disjoint. Rather than add additional atemporal elements, such as an explicit language, we overcome this problem by redefining a belief assignment as assigning *possible runs*, rather than possible worlds, i.e., $B : L_A \to \mathcal{R}$. Because runs are atemporal object, this choice makes the fundamental changes in an agent's beliefs more clearly visible.[10]

6 BELIEF CHANGE

With time added to our model, we must start considering how the agent's mental state changes over time. Belief ascription, as currently defined, allows erratic change across local states. An extreme example would be an agent whose local state changes from l to l', such that $PW(l) = PW(l')$, yet $B(l) \cap B(l') = \emptyset$. Part of

---

[8]Finite runs are modelled by runs in which $\exists n \forall m \ s_n = s_{n+m}$.

[9]Notice the this requires extending the utility function over suffixes of runs. This is quite straightforward given our deterministic model of the environment.

[10]The interested reader may consult [Friedman and Halpern, 1994], where belief change is investigated from this perspective.

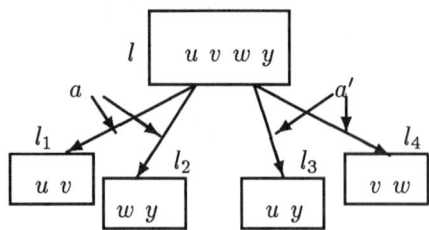

Figure 1: The change in an agent's local state after performing actions a and a', respectively.

our conception of agents involves an expectation that their beliefs should change in a 'sensible' way ([Alchourron et al., 1985]). Constraints on belief change across states are also of immense importance if we are to be able to predict an agent's behavior. Having ascribed beliefs to the agent based on past actions we must have such constraints to deduce the agent's current beliefs. Having deduced the new beliefs, we can use them to predict the agent's choice of action.

We will look at two patterns of belief change that we find reasonable and prove two representation theorems. The theorems show that there are two ways of viewing these restrictions, either as constraints on new beliefs imposed by the previous beliefs and the new information, or as requiring a general static way of representing the agent's beliefs. We can then incorporate these restrictions into our model by requiring a belief assignment to be consistent in the static sense of Definition 9, and to exhibit the desired pattern of belief change. This will redefine the problem of belief ascription for agents that can acquire new information while acting.

In what follows we will assume that the agent has *perfect recall*, i.e., its local state contains all previous local states. This describes agents that do not forget. However, much of the following development also makes sense when the agent has only partial memory of past states. Perfect recall implies that an agent's local state changes from one state to the next. Therefore, any two states on the same run are distinguishable.

6.1 ADMISSIBILITY

Consider the following restriction on belief change: if my new information does not preclude all of the runs I previously considered plausible, I will consider plausible all runs previously considered plausible, that are consistent with this new information.

We can illustrate this using Figure 1. The agent is initially in local state l, where the possible runs are u, v, w and y. Assume that $B(l) = \{u, w\}$. After performing action a the agent finds itself in state l_1. If the agent's beliefs are admissible then $B(l_1) = \{u\}$. However, assume that $B(l) = \{u, v\}$ and the agent arrives at l_2 after performing a. Now we cannot say anything about the agent's beliefs at l_2, even if its beliefs are admissible (except of course $B(l_2) \subseteq \{w, y\}$).

Definition 14 *A belief assignment B is* **admissible**,[11] *if for local states l, l' such that l' follows l on some run: whenever $PW(l') \cap B(l) \neq \emptyset$ then $B(l') = PW(l') \cap B(l)$; otherwise l' is called a* **revision state** *and $B(l') \subseteq PW(l')$ is otherwise not restricted.*

If we were to assume that the worlds here are models of some theory then, in syntactic terms, admissibility corresponds to conjoining the new data with the existing beliefs, whenever this is consistent. It is closely related to the probabilistic idea of conditioning our beliefs upon new information. Most work on belief revision makes additional requirements on beliefs following inconsistent information (what we call a revision state). We will return to this issue in the end of this section.

We can shed additional light on this restriction by the following representation theorem. This theorem shows that we can either ascribe the agent beliefs that change locally in accordance to the admissibility requirement or we can ascribe the agent a more complex static ranking structure that uniquely determines its beliefs in each state. That is at each state l the set $B(l)$ is exactly the set of elements in $PW(l)$ that are minimal w.r.t. this ranking.

Definition 15 *A* **well founded ranking** *r of a set Q is a mapping from Q to a well ordered set $\mathcal{O}$. Given a subset Q' of Q, the elements minimal in Q' are those that have the minimal rank, i.e., are assigned the lowest element of $\mathcal{O}$ by r.*

A ranking of Q associates each member of Q with the group of other members having the same rank and orders these groups according to the rank assigned to them. In general one speaks of a total pre-order with a minimal element. The elements of lower rank are considered to be better, more preferred, or more likely.

Theorem 1 *Assuming perfect recall, a belief assignment B is admissible iff there is a ranking function r (i.e., a total pre-order) on the possible runs such that $B(l) = \{s \in PW(l) : s \text{ is } r\text{-minimal in } PW(l)\}$.*

6.2 WEAK ADMISSIBILITY

The requirement that belief assignments be admissible may seem too strong. A weaker requirement is the following: if my new state is consistent with a run I believed before, I should still believe in that run's possibility. However, unlike when my belief assignment is

---
[11] This is not to be confused with the notion of admissibility in game theory.

admissible, once I learn that a run I considered plausible before is in fact impossible, I may additionally consider plausible runs which I did not consider plausible before. However, if what I learn only reaffirm my previous beliefs, i.e., I only learn that a run I did *not* believe plausible is completely impossible, my beliefs should not change. Formally:

Definition 16 *A belief assignment is* **weakly admissible** *if when a local state l' follows l,*

1. $B(l') \supseteq B(l) \cap PW(l')$.

2. *If* $B(l) \subseteq PW(l')$ *then* $B(l') = B(l)$

Looking at Figure 1 again, if the agent believed in u, w in l and its state changes to l_1 then it may believe either in u or in u, v. However, if the agent only believed u to be plausible in l, then at l_1 its only consistent belief is in u.

Fortunately, we can again relate the ascription of weakly admissible beliefs to that of ascribing a static partially ordered belief structures. Again, this structure determines the agent's beliefs at l by choosing the minimal elements of $PW(l)$ according to this structure.

Definition 17 *A* **partial pre-order** *on Q is a partial subset of $Q \times Q$ that is reflexive and transitive.*

Theorem 2 *The beliefs of an agent with perfect recall are weakly admissible iff there is a partial order $<$ on the set of possible runs, such that its beliefs at l correspond to the minimal runs in $PW(l)$ according to $<$.*

Patterns of beliefs change similar to ours emerge in the work of other researches (e.g., [Friedman and Halpern, 1994, Lamarre and Shoham, 1994]). Indeed, relations between belief revision and belief update, and representations using partial and total pre-orders are well known. It was shown in [Katsuno and Mendelzon, 1991b] that any revision operator that satisfies the AGM postulates ([Alchourron *et al.*, 1985]) can be represented using a ranking of the set of possible states. We require less to obtain the same representation. The reason for this, besides our assumption of perfect recall, is our emphasis on belief ascription, rather than on prescribing belief change. The need for additional requirements arises when counter-factual reasoning has to be accounted for. Then, given a certain state, all ways in which it can be revised must be accounted for. On the other hand, we are not asking the question of how the agent's beliefs would look like if it were to take a different action than the one prescribed by its protocol; we only need to explain the particular actions performed by the agent at different states.

7 EXISTENCE - GOAL SEEKING AGENTS

But when does a belief assignment exist? From the point of view of modelling this question is crucial, and Savage's answer to it ([Savage, 1972]), provides much of the foundation of statistics and economic modelling. In order to model programs, machines, or humans, using the various abstract mental states investigated in AI, it is important to recognize the conditions under which these modelling tools can be used.

Examining Savage's work we see that he is able to ascribe likelihood and utilities by imposing certain consistency restrictions on the agent's actions. We will follow a similar path. We first restrict ourselves to a certain class of extended contexts and then require the agent's protocol to satisfy two restrictions. We will show that an agent satisfying these restrictions and operating in the given class of extended contexts, can be ascribed a unique most general choice complete belief assignment.

The contexts we examine here are of a special kind that is quite natural in many AI applications. Local states are of two types, goal states and non-goal states. Runs are finite and their utility is determined by the last local state, i.e., 1 if it is a goal state, and 0 otherwise. We have a distinguished action, HALT, whose utility (or more precisely, that of its outcome) in a goal state is 1 and 0 otherwise.

We define two rationality postulates on protocols, that embody a notion of a *goal-seeking* agent. The *rational effort* postulate says that the agent must halt whenever it is in a goal state, or when it is impossible to reach a goal state. The *rational despair* postulate says that to halt the agent must either be in the goal or be able to show a possible world under which he can never reach the goal. Notice that these postulates refer to the set $PW(l)$ describing the agent's knowledge, rather than to $B(l)$ (preventing possible circularity later).

Rational Effort Postulate The protocol in a local state l is either HALT or weakly dominates HALT.

Rational Despair Postulate The protocol in a non-goal local state l is HALT only if for some $s \in PW(l)$ there is no protocol that achieves the goal.

We will call an agent satisfying these postulates who operates in the contexts described above and whose decision criterion is consistent with weak dominance (i.e., if v is preferred over v' then v' does not weakly dominate v[12]), a *goal-seeking* agent.

Theorem 3 *If A is a goal seeking agent then it can be ascribed a unique most general admissible belief as-*

---
[12]Let $v(i)$ be the ith element of v. We say that v' *weakly dominates* v if $\forall i\ v'(i) \geq v(i)$ and $\exists i\ v'(i) > v(i)$.

signment and a unique most general choice complete belief assignment.

Many people view rational choice as equivalent to expected utility maximization under some probability distribution. While we find the probabilistic approach most appropriate in many contexts, we do not share this view (see the following discussion). Indeed, we show that, in 0/1 utility contexts any behavior consistent with expected utility maximization under some probability distribution can be attributed belief in our framework. Let us define a *B-type* agent as one whose beliefs are represented by a (subjective) probability assignment, whose preferences are represented by a 0/1 utility function, and whose decision criterion is based on expected utility maximization w.r.t these probability and utility assignments. However, we require that when no action has an expected utility greater than 0 then HALT is performed.

Corollary 1 *An agent that can be modelled as a B-type agent is a goal-seeking agent, and consequently, can be viewed as a perceived outcome maximizer, using some admissible belief assignment and a decision criterion consistent with weak dominance.*

8 DISCUSSION

To conclude we re-examine the work presented in this paper and some related research.

8.1 RE-EXAMINING THE FRAMEWORK

The ability to model agents at the mental level is most likely required for any form of artificial intelligence. However, as an abstraction it is already useful for more mundane modelling tasks. It is extremely important in multi-agent domains, as agents must construct models of other agents, but it is also useful as a means of describing and analyzing systems at an abstract, yet highly intuitive, level. As such, a model of the mental level should strive to be simple and intuitive. Yet, it must also be precisely formulated with sound foundations. We believe that the framework we presented meets these criteria.

Beside presenting a model of the mental level, our work attempts to specifically improve our understanding of belief ascription. Belief, in our framework, represents the agent's subjective information on the outside world that is utilized in decision making. We modelled beliefs as a function of the agent's local state, for otherwise, the actual state of the world would affect its beliefs, without affecting its state. We suggested two methods for narrowing the choice among candidate belief assignments and defined a class of goal-seeking agents that can be ascribed belief in our framework. Additional results, presented in [Brafman and Tennenholtz, 1994], provide conditions under which the criteria for choosing among belief assignments yield a unique belief assignment. Also discussed there are algorithms for ascribing admissible and weakly-admissible beliefs and conditions under which belief ascription is tractable.

One may ask why do we emphasize belief ascription, when the framework supplies the basis for ascribing utilities or a decision criterion. Ascription of these notions is certainly important, but there are a number of reasons for our choice. Belief and knowledge are by far the most extensively researched mental states within AI and philosophy (e.g. [Kripke, 1963, Katsuno and Mendelzon, 1991a, Alchourron *et al.*, 1985, Goldzmidt and Pearl, 1992, Boutilier, 1992, del Val and Shoham, 1992, Lamarre and Shoham, 1994, Friedman and Halpern, 1994]), and it is therefore important to understand where they come from and how to ascribe them. Moreover, mental-level modelling is often used by us to construct rough descriptive models. It is often the case that an agent's goals are known. This suffices to supply rough estimates of utilities. Knowing an agent's decision criteria seems harder, but we have shown that for 'reasonable' protocols in 0/1 utility contexts, beliefs can be ascribed based on the trivial assumption that the agent prefers weakly dominant tuples. These contexts are natural in many CS applications. Additionally, while the plausible worlds for an agent in different situations may be unrelated, the decision criterion is almost constant. Observing an agent's decision criterion in one case seems a good indicator of its decision criterion in other cases. Naturally, in normative applications, such as analysis of protocols, the designer can readily provide all the required information.

8.2 RELATED WORK

There has been some important research on ascribing mental states to agents. One major research area is plan ascription, an important task in discourse understanding and multi-agent systems (e.g.,[Kautz, 1990, Konolige and Pollack, 1989, Pollack, 1990]). The aims of the work on plan ascription is more specific than ours and plans are often ascribed based on utterances (e.g., [Konolige and Pollack, 1989]). More specifically, Konolige ([Konolige, 1990]) has done some theoretical work on explanatory belief ascription. His work looks at the question of how to explain known beliefs of an agent by ascribing this agent additional beliefs. His work implicitly assumes a high-level agent into whose beliefs we have some access, usually through the utterances of that agent. He then explains these beliefs based on other, ascribed, beliefs. This work does not deal with the general problem of belief ascription. Both [Konolige, 1990, Konolige and Pollack, 1989] have a somewhat syntactic flavor, due to the use of argumentation systems and derivational models. In contrast, our framework does not employ some of the stronger techniques used in these papers, but addresses more basic issues and is based upon a more general semantic model of the mental level. We believe that it can provide the foundations for belief ascription based on utterances, if utterances are treated as speech acts [Austin, 1962].

Most influential on our work was the knowledge ascription framework of [Halpern and Moses, 1990]. This work defines a formal notion of knowledge that is grounded in the state space description of a system. The set of possible worlds of an agent then emerges from the notion of a local state. We have built our framework upon their framework. Closely related is the work of [Rosenschein, 1985] on situated automata, which defines knowledge in a similar manner.

The work of Savage [Savage, 1972] on subjective probability and choice theory is closely related to our work. This work shows that given the preferences of an agent over possible actions, where these preferences satisfy certain constraints, the agent can be viewed as acting as an expected utility maximizer under ascribed (probabilistic) beliefs and utilities. This work is extremely elegant, yet it has some limitations from our perspective. First, it is probabilistic, while much work on knowledge and belief within AI, CS, and philosophy is discrete. This means that it cannot provide the foundation for these notions of belief. Secondly, there are serious practical problems with its application to our setting. Savage requires a total pre-order on the set of all possible acts, i.e., *all* functions from initial states to outcomes, many of which are purely fictional acts. This information will not be available to an observer of the system, nor will it be easy for a designer to come up with it. Another assumption is that the state description is rich, i.e., that for any natural n, there exists a partition of the set of states into n subsets, all of which are equally likely. This means that the number of states must be infinite. In addition, expected utility maximization has been criticized as a normatively inadequate decision criterion (see [Kyburg, 1988] and other papers in [Gärdenfors and Sahlin, 1988]). It is certainly inadequate descriptively, as many studies have shown (e.g. extensive work by Tversky cf. [Shafrir and Tversky, 1992]) and is therefore problematic in modelling other agents.

In contrast, we believe that our formalism is better suited for many modelling tasks in AI and CS. Our framework is discrete, thus relevant to the body of work on discrete notions of belief. It also requires much less information. We only assume awareness of the agent's actual protocol (e.g., through observations or as a given specification), and knowledge of the possible alternatives, that is, the agent's set of possible actions. It does not require complete knowledge of the preference relation among other protocols, nor the additional richness assumption on the set of states. Moreover, as we remarked earlier, it is straightforward to apply our ideas when only part of the protocol is known, for example, when we have seen the agent act only in a subset of its set of possible local states.

Another advantage of our framework is that it leaves the decision criterion as a parameter. This gives us added modelling flexibility. On the one hand, our notion of a decision criterion can be easily generalized for our framework to cover expected utility maximization as a special case. On the other hand, decision criteria that allow for notions of preference that do not satisfy the Von Neumann-Morgenstern axioms are possible. This flexibility is useful for descriptive purposes, because we may want to model different classes of entities. But even for normative purposes one may wish to relax these requirements. For example, we may want our agent to act as if some goal's utility is infinitely greater than any other, e.g., the preservation of human life. This can only be done if we relax the Von Neumann-Morgenstern axioms.

We have stressed the problem of grounding before. Research on abstract mental states is certainly important. Yet, notions such as 'beliefs', 'goals','intentions', etc., are more meaningful if they can be embedded in some concrete setting. A major contribution of the work of [Halpern and Moses, 1990, Rosenschein, 1985] is supplying this concrete setting, showing how it arises in distributed systems and in situated agents.

In his 1985 Computers and Thoughts speech [Levesque, 1986b], Levesque spoke about making believers out of computers, thus supplying a concrete interpretation of belief. However, the actions of the systems Levesque is referring to, all have to do with answering queries. This serves as a means of abstracting the constraint that (for a meaningful investigation of knowledge representation schemes) the system's actions depend on the content of the data-structures used to represent knowledge (see also [Levesque, 1986a, p. 258]). This abstract view is extremely fruitful as a means of understanding the task of knowledge representation. However, most systems (computer, mechanical or biological) are situated in some environment. Their goal is usually much more general than correctly representing it, although that may be useful. Their actions range from writing into files to changing the temperature of a room. If we do not de-contextualize beliefs by ignoring the agent's actions, goals, etc., we will be able to obtain a better understanding of these systems. We can ascribe beliefs to a system if it is *acting as though* these are its beliefs. We see our main conceptual contributing in making the notion of belief concrete, by placing it in the context of actions, goals and decisions.

Acknowledgement

We would like to thank Yoav Shoham, Nir Friedman, Daphne Koller, Joe Halpern and Alvaro del Val for their help. Their comments and criticism have greatly helped us improve this work and its presentation. We also wish to thank Robert Aumann and David Kreps who were most helpful in putting this work in perspective.

This work was supported in part by grants from the National Science Foundations, Advanced Research Projects Agency and the Air Force Office of Scientific Research.

References

Alchourron, C. E.; Gärdenfors, P.; and Makinson, D. 1985. On the logic of theory change: partial meet functions for contraction and revision. *Journal of Symbolic Logic* 50:510–530.

Austin, J. L. 1962. *How to do things with words*. Oxford University Press.

Boutilier, C. 1992. Normative, subjective and autoepistemic defaults: Adopting the ramsey test. In *Principles of Knowledge Representation and Reasoning: Proc. Third Intl. Conf. (KR '92)*.

Brafman, R. I. and Tennenholtz, M. 1994. Belief ascription. Technical report, Stanford University.

del Val, A. and Shoham, Y. 1992. Deriving properties of belief update from theories of action. In *Principles of Knowledge Representation and Reasoning: Proc. Third Intl. Conf. (KR '92)*. 584–589.

Dennett, D. C. 1987. *The Intensional Stance*. MIT Press, Cambridge, Mass.

Fagin, R.; Halpern, J. Y.; Moses, Y.; and Vardi, M. Y. 1994. *Reasoning about Knowledge*. MIT Press. to appear.

Friedman, N. and Halpern, J. Y. 1994. A knowledge-based framework for belief change. Part I: Foundations. In *Proc. of the Fifth Conf. on Theoretical Aspects of Reasoning About Knowledge*, Monterey, California. Morgan Kaufmann.

Gärdenfors, P. and Sahlin, N. E., editors 1988. *Decision, Probability, and Utility*. Cambridge University Press, New York.

Goldzmidt, M. and Pearl, J. 1992. Rank-based systems: A simple approach to belief revision, belief update and reasoning about evidence and actions. In *Principles of Knowledge Representation and Reasoning: Proc. Third Intl. Conf. (KR '92)*. 661–672.

Halpern, J. Y. and Moses, Y. 1990. Knowledge and common knowledge in a distributed environment. *J. ACM* 37(3):549–587.

Katsuno, H. and Mendelzon, A. 1991a. On the difference between updating a knowledge base and revising it. In *Principles of Knowledge Representation and Reasoning: Proc. Second Intl. Conf. (KR '91)*. 387–394.

Katsuno, H. and Mendelzon, A. O. 1991b. Propositional knowledge base revision and minimal change. *Artificial Intelligence* 52(3).

Kautz, H. 1990. A circumscriptive theory of plan recognition. In Cohen, P. R; Morgan, J.; and Pollack, M. E., editors 1990, *Intentions in Communication*, Cambridge, Mass. MIT Press. 105–133.

Konolige, K. and Pollack, M. E. 1989. Ascribing plans to agents. In *Proc. Eleventh Intl. Joint Conf. on Artificial Intelligence (IJCAI '89)*. 924–930.

Konolige, K. 1990. Explanatory belief ascription. In *Proc. of the Third Conf. on Theoretical Aspects of Reasoning About Knowledge*, Monterey, California. Morgan Kaufmann. 57–72.

Kraus, S. and Lehmann, D. J. 1988. Knowledge, belief and time. *Theoretical Computer Science* 58:155–174.

Kreps, D. M. and Wilson, R. 1982. Sequential equilibria. *Econometrica* 50(4):863–894.

Kripke, S. 1963. Semantical considerations of modal logic. *Zeitschrift fur Mathematische Logik und Grundlagen der Mathematik* 9:67–96.

Kyburg, H. E. 1988. Bets and beliefs. In Gärdenfors, P. and Sahlin, N. E., editors 1988, *Decision, Probability, and Utility*. Cambridge University Press, New York. chapter 6.

Lamarre, P. and Shoham, Yoav 1994. Knowledge, certainty, belief and conditionalization. In *Proc. of Fourth Intl. Conf. on Principles of Knowledge Representation and Reasoning*.

Levesque, H. J. 1986a. Knowledge representation and reasoning. *An. Rev. Comput. Sci.* 1:255–287.

Levesque, H. J. 1986b. Making believers out of computers. *Artificial Intelligence* 30:81–108.

Luce, R. D and Raiffa, H. 1957. *Games and Decisions*. John Wiley & Sons, New York.

McCarthy, J. 1979. Ascribing mental qualities to machines. In Ringle, M., editor 1979, *Philosophical Perspectives in Artificial Intelligence*, Atlantic Highlands, NJ. Humanities Press.

Newell, A. 1980. The knowledge level. *AI Magazine* 1–20.

Pollack, M. E. 1990. Plans as complex mental attitudes. In Cohen, P. R.; Morgan, J.; and Pollack, M. E., editors 1990, *Intentions in Communication*, Cambridge, Massachusetts. MIT Press. 77–104.

Rosenschein, S. J. 1985. Formal theories of knowledge in AI and robotics. *New Generation Comp.* 3:345–357.

Savage, L. J. 1972. *The Foundations of Statistics*. Dover Publications, New York.

Shafrir, E. and Tversky, A. 1992. Thinking through uncertainty: Nonconsequential reasoning and choice. *Cognitive Psychology* 24(4):449–474.

Neumann, J. von and Morgenstern, O. 1944. *Theory of Games and Economic Behavior*. Princeton University Press, Princeton.

Default Logic as a Query Language

Marco Cadoli
Dipartimento di Informatica e Sistemistica
Università di Roma "La Sapienza"
Via Salaria 113, I-00198 Roma, Italy
cadoli@assi.dis.uniroma1.it

Thomas Eiter   Georg Gottlob
Christian Doppler Laboratory for Expert Systems
Technical University of Vienna
Paniglgasse 16, A-1040 Wien, Austria
{eiter|gottlob}@vexpert.dbai.tuwien.ac.at

Abstract

Research in NMR has focused largely on the idea of representing knowledge about the world via rules that are generally true but can be defeated. Even if relational databases are nowadays the main tool for storing very large sets of data, the approach of using non-monotonic formalisms as relational database query languages has been investigated to a much smaller extent. In this work we propose a novel application of default logic by introducing a *default query language* (DQL) for finite relational databases, which is based on default rules. The main result of this paper is that DQL is as expressive as $SO_{\exists\forall}$, the existential universal fragment of second order logic. This result is not only of theoretical importance: We show queries –which are useful in practice– that can be expressed with DQL and cannot with other query languages based on non-monotonic logics such as $DATALOG^\neg_{stable}$. Another result in this paper concerns the *combined* complexity of DQL, i.e., when it is assumed that the query is part of the input; for this problem, NEXPTIME^{NP}-completeness is shown.

1 INTRODUCTION

For the purpose of Knowledge Representation, non-monotonic reasoning (NMR henceforth) formalisms can be used in two different ways:

- as languages for representing knowledge about the world, via rules that are generally true but can be defeated. Retrieving information from a non-monotonic knowledge base of this kind amounts to prove a theorem.
  As an example, we can use default logic to state that "birds generally fly". In order to prove that Tweety the bird flies we try to prove that a specific formula follows –in the default logic semantics– from the set of general rules plus a set of specific facts;

- as relational database query languages. Retrieving information amounts to computing the set of tuples belonging to an intensional relation, starting from some extensional relations.

As an example, we can query a relational database by means of a DATALOG$^\neg$ program –i.e., a DATALOG program with negated literals in the body of the rules– equipped with a specific semantics for negation.

Research in NMR has focused largely on the former idea, and remarkable results about the computational complexity of several formalisms have been obtained by many authors (cf. [Cadoli and Schaerf, 1993] for a survey on this topic).

Even if relational databases are nowadays the main tool for storing very large sets of data, the latter approach has been investigated to a much smaller extent.

One of the most important aspects of a query language for relational databases is its *expressive power*, i.e., the set of relations that we can compute by querying. The expressive power of relational database query languages has been studied for some twenty years now (cf. [Kannelakis, 1990]). Research has focused mainly on monotonic query languages, i.e., languages such that if the extensional relations grow then the intensional ones grow as well.

Recently some interesting works investigating the expressive power of non-monotonic query languages appeared. Kolaitis and Papadimitriou study in [Kolaitis and Papadimitriou, 1991] the expressive power of two semantics for DATALOG$^\neg$ programs. In particular they prove that DATALOG$^\neg$ with fixpoint semantics is as expressive as $SO_\exists$, the existential fragment of second order logic. Schlipf proves in [Schlipf, 1990] an analogous result for DATALOG$^\neg$ with stable model semantics (DATALOG$^\neg_{stable}$ henceforth). Saccà gives in [Saccà, 1993] further insight on the expressive power of DATALOG$^\neg_{stable}$. Van Gelder analyzes in [Van Gelder,

1989] the expressive power of DATALOG¬ with well-founded semantics. In all these papers, databases are modeled as *finite structures*, i.e., finite interpretations of theories.

In this work we are concerned with *default logic as a query language*. Default logic [Reiter, 1980] is one of the most popular NMR formalisms and has been extensively investigated both from the semantical and the computational point of view. It has also been proposed in [Bidoit and Froidevaux, 1991] as a tool for inferencing in logical databases (i.e., databases which are theories). Anyway the behavior of default logic on finite structures has not been analyzed so far.

Here we propose a novel application of default logic by introducing a *default query language* (DQL) for finite relational databases, which is based on default rules. The main result of this paper is that DQL is more expressive than DATALOG$^¬_{stable}$. In particular DQL is as expressive as SO$_{\exists\forall}$, the existential universal fragment of second order logic. This result is not only of theoretical importance: We show queries –which are useful in practice– that can be expressed with DQL and cannot with DATALOG$^¬_{stable}$. Our queries are taken from the realm of economics.

An alternative way of describing our main result is to say that DQL "captures" the complexity class Σ^p_2 of the polynomial hierarchy, while DATALOG$^¬_{stable}$ "just" captures the class NP. Therefore DQL is more expressive than DATALOG$^¬_{stable}$ provided $\Sigma^p_2 \neq$ NP, i.e., provided the polynomial hierarchy does not collapse –a property that has been widely conjectured and that will be assumed throughout this work.

We remind that Σ^p_2-completeness of credulous propositional default reasoning has been recently proven [Gottlob, 1992; Stillman, 1992]. It is therefore important to remark that the expressive power of a language is not necessarily the same as its complexity. As an example, a language which does not capture NP –even if it has an underlying NP-complete problem– has been shown by Stewart in [Stewart, 1991].

Another result shown in this paper concerns the *combined* complexity of DQL, i.e., when it is assumed that the query is part of the input; in particular, NEXPTIME^{NP}-completeness is proven.

The structure of the paper is the following. In Section 2 we give the definition of the query language DQL, providing syntax, semantics and some simple examples. In Section 3 we give a formal proof of the fact that DQL captures Σ^p_2. In Section 4 we show how to use DQL for expressing queries to a relational database. In particular we show queries relative to a (somewhat simplified) economic world that are expressible in DQL but are not expressible in DATALOG$^¬_{stable}$. In Section 5 we briefly address the issue of combined complexity of DQL, and in Section 6 we draw some conclusions.

2 DEFINITION OF DQL

2.1 SYNTAX

A *database schema* (cf. [Ullman, 1988]) R is a finite set $\{R_1, \ldots, R_n\}$ of relation schemata. A *relation schema* R_i has a name N_i and a finite list of attributes $L_i = \langle A_1, \ldots, A_{l_i}\rangle$. It will sometimes be denoted as $R_i(A_1, \ldots, A_{l_i})$. The number l_i is the arity of the relation schema R_i. We assume that there is an underlying set $\mathcal{U}$ of objects that can be used in relations (the so-called *domain*). The domain $\mathcal{U}$ is arbitrarily large but finite. Given a relation schema R_i, a *relation instance* is a set of tuples of the form $\langle a_1, \ldots, a_{l_i}\rangle$, where $a_j \in \mathcal{U}$ ($1 \leq j \leq l_i$). A *database instance* W is a set of relation instances. The set of objects occurring in a database (the so-called *active domain*) is a subset –possibly not strict– of $\mathcal{U}$.

An *open default* (cf. [Reiter, 1980]) is a sentence of the form

$$\frac{\alpha(\mathbf{x}) : \beta(\mathbf{y})}{\gamma(\mathbf{z})}$$

where $\mathbf{x}, \mathbf{y}$ and $\mathbf{z}$ are (not necessarily disjoint) lists of individual variables and $\alpha(\mathbf{x}), \beta(\mathbf{y}), \gamma(\mathbf{z})$ are quantifier-free formulae of first order logic (without functions) such that the free variables are those in $\mathbf{x}$, $\mathbf{y}$, and $\mathbf{z}$.

A *DQL Input/Output query* Q is a set of open default rules plus a set of *output relation schemata* $S = \{S_1, \ldots, S_m\}$. The set of predicate symbols occurring in the defaults of Q contains all the names of the relation schemata of the database (the *extensional* relations) and possibly other symbols (the *intensional* relations). Output relations are intensional. The intuitive meaning of the query is the following: We want to compute all tuples in the S_i relations which can be inferred under the credulous default semantics. (See the next section for a formal definition.) In particular we apply the credulous default semantics to the propositional instantiation of the open defaults in the query, plus the database.

A *DQL boolean query* is a set of open default rules plus a ground formula γ. The intuitive meaning of the query is the following: We want to know whether γ follows –under the credulous default semantics– from the propositional instantiation of the defaults in the query plus the database.

Example 1: (Tweety flies) We have two relation schemes BIRD and SMALL-WINGS which both have a single attribute NAME. The database instance W_1 is as in the following table:

BIRD	NAME
	Tweety
	Sam
	Fred

SMALL-WINGS	NAME
	Fred

The I/O query is the following set of defaults D_1:

$$\left\{ \frac{bird(x) : \neg abnormal(x)}{flies(x)}, \quad \frac{: \neg abnormal(x)}{\neg abnormal(x)}, \right.$$

$$\left. \frac{bird(x) \wedge small\text{-}wings(x) :}{abnormal(x)} \right\}$$

plus the unary relation FLIES(NAME). The relational database states that Tweety, Sam, and Fred are birds. The query is made out of three open defaults. The first one states that an object that is provably a bird –and that cannot be proven to be abnormal– flies by default. The second default states that objects that cannot be proven to be abnormal should be regarded as not abnormal. The third default states the rule that objects that are provably birds and have small wings are abnormal. The intuitive meaning of the query is that we want to know the set of flying objects.

The boolean query has the same set of defaults, plus the ground formula $flies(Tweety)$. The intuitive meaning of the query is that we want to know whether Tweety flies or not. □

2.2 SEMANTICS

Let W be a database instance over the set of relation schemata $\{R_1, \ldots, R_n\}$. For each relation instance R_i, let $R_i|W$ be the set of tuples in W belonging to R_i. We denote as $COMP(W)$ the *completion* of the database, i.e., the set of the following ground literals:

- $R_i(a_1, \ldots, a_{l_i})$, for each tuple $\langle a_1, \ldots, a_{l_i}\rangle \in R_i|W$;
- $\neg R_i(a_1, \ldots, a_{l_i})$, for each tuple $\langle a_1, \ldots, a_{l_i}\rangle \in \mathcal{U}^{l_i} \setminus R_i|W$.

(This is the standard translation from databases-as-models into databases-as-complete-theories (essentially), as shown for example in [Reiter, 1984]).

Let D be the set of open defaults in a query (either I/O query or boolean query). We denote as $INST(D)$ the *instantiation* of D, i.e., the set of ground defaults obtained in the following way:

- for each open default

$$\frac{\alpha(\mathbf{x}) : \beta(\mathbf{y})}{\gamma(\mathbf{z})}$$

in D there is a set of defaults

$$\frac{\alpha(\xi) : \beta(\tau)}{\gamma(\zeta)},$$

in $INST(D)$, where ξ, τ, and ζ are all possible lists –of the appropriate length– of objects taken from $\mathcal{U}$.

We remark that instantiating the query over the domain is common in databases, and it is assumed in [Schlipf, 1990; Kolaitis and Papadimitriou, 1991].

Let Q be an I/O query, i.e., a set D of defaults plus a set $S = \{S_1, \ldots, S_m\}$ of output relations. Let W be a database on the domain $\mathcal{U}$. The answer to Q is defined as follows. For each relation $S_i \in S$ with arity k_i, the answer is the set of tuples $\langle t_1, \ldots, t_{k_i}\rangle \in \mathcal{U}^{k_i}$ such that $S_i(t_1, \ldots, t_{k_i})$ follows under the credulous default semantics from the ground default theory $\langle INST(D); COMP(W)\rangle$, i.e. it is in at least one of the extensions of such a default theory (cf. [Reiter, 1980] for the definition of extension of a default theory).

The semantics of a boolean query Q is even simpler. Let γ be the distinguished ground formula in Q. If γ follows under the credulous default semantics from the ground default theory $\langle INST(D); COMP(W)\rangle$, then the answer is **yes**; otherwise, the answer is **no**.

We notice that, in the semantics for DQL queries, two sorts of non-monotonic reasoning are involved: first of all, the database is completed ($COMP(W)$), secondly, default rules are applied ($INST(D)$). In fact, the whole mechanism could be made homogeneous by using default rules for obtaining completion of the database as well. One way to achieve this is to use the following method:

- for each extensional relation R_i, introduce a new predicate R'_i (of the same arity) that does not occur elsewhere;
- build a set D' consisting of the following defaults ($1 \leq i \leq n$):

$$\frac{: \neg R'_i(\mathbf{x})}{\neg R'_i(\mathbf{x})}, \quad \frac{R'_i(\mathbf{x}) :}{R_i(\mathbf{x})}, \quad \frac{\neg R'_i(\mathbf{x}) :}{\neg R_i(\mathbf{x})}$$

- define $DB(W)$ as
$R'_i(a_1, \ldots, a_{l_i})$, for each tuple $\langle a_1, \ldots, a_{l_i}\rangle \in R_i|W$.

It can be shown that the default theory $T = \langle INST(D \cup D'); DB(W)\rangle$ provides the same answers (to both boolean and I/O queries) as $\langle INST(D); COMP(W)\rangle$. Intuitively, the R'_i predicates serve to transfer the extension of the input relations to the respective predicate letters R_i. In fact, in any extension of T, R'_i is complete (i.e., every ground atom is true or false) by the first default, and R'_i must coincide with R_i by the second and third default.

Note that if one does not allow occurrence of extensional relations in the conclusions of user defaults (a similar restriction is often made in logical query languages, e.g. in datalog), then also the default theory

$$\langle INST(D \cup \{\, :\neg R_i(\mathbf{x})/\neg R_i(\mathbf{x})\}); W \rangle,$$

where W is seen as $R_i(a_1, \ldots, a_{l_i})$, for each tuple $\langle a_1, \ldots, a_{l_i}\rangle \in R_i$, provides the same answers as $\langle INST(D); COMP(W)\rangle$.

Our semantics for DQL is based on credulous default reasoning, and one may argue if this is the most appropriate way of answering to a query. In general, nothing prevents us from grounding our definitions on *skeptical* default reasoning, i.e. on drawing an inference iff a formula is in *all* the extensions of the relevant default theory. In fact, all forthcoming results about complexity and expressiveness would hold for the complementary complexity classes. As an example, forthcoming Theorem 1 could be rephrased by saying that the boolean (skeptical) DQL queries precisely capture the class Π_2^p.

Let us see how this semantics works in the example shown in the previous subsection.

Example 1 (continued) We assume that the domain is the set $\{Tweety, Sam, Fred\}$, i.e., that the domain is the same as the active domain. Then,

$COMP(W_1) =$

$\{\, bird(Tweety), \neg small\text{-}wings(Tweety),$
$bird(Sam), \neg small\text{-}wings(Sam),$
$bird(Fred), small\text{-}wings(Fred)\,\};$

$INST(D_1) =$

$$\left\{ \frac{bird(Tweety) : \neg abnormal(Tweety)}{flies(Tweety)}, \right.$$

$$\frac{: \neg abnormal(Tweety)}{\neg abnormal(Tweety)},$$

$$\frac{bird(Tweety) \wedge small\text{-}wings(Tweety) :}{abnormal(Tweety)},$$

$$\frac{bird(Sam) : \neg abnormal(Sam)}{flies(Sam)},$$

$$\frac{: \neg abnormal(Sam)}{\neg abnormal(Sam)},$$

$$\frac{bird(Sam) \wedge small\text{-}wings(Sam) :}{abnormal(Sam)},$$

$$\frac{bird(Fred) : \neg abnormal(Fred)}{flies(Fred)},$$

$$\left. \frac{bird(Fred) \wedge small\text{-}wings(Fred) :}{abnormal(Fred)} \right\}$$

The answer to the I/O query is the relation instance:

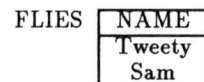

In other words, Tweety and Sam fly, but Fred does not fly. The answer to the boolean query is **yes**. □

3 EXPRESSIVE POWER OF DQL

In the previous section we have seen that default logic is suitable as a query language, i.e., as a language for manipulating relations. A very interesting question is the following: Which relations can be computed by DQL? Which relations cannot? In other words, what is the *expressive power* of DQL? We recall that expressive power of relational database query languages is one of the most studied topics in database theory. One way of presenting a result in this area is to say that a query language can/cannot express a specific relation. For example, it is well-known that relational calculus cannot express the transitive closure of a relation [Aho and Ullman, 1979], while such a relation can be expressed in DATALOG [Ullman, 1988]; the relation of satisfiable propositional clause sets can be computed by a fixed program in $\text{DATALOG}^{\neg}_{stable}$ but not in DATALOG (unless P=NP), cf. [Schlipf, 1990].

Typically, the expressive power of a query language is represented as a set of logical sentences. As an example the expressive power of relational calculus is the set of first order sentences, while the expressive power of $\text{DATALOG}^{\neg}_{stable}$ is $SO_\exists$ [Schlipf, 1990], the existential fragment of second order logic, i.e., the set of sentences

$$(\exists \mathbf{S})\phi(\mathbf{S}),$$

where $\mathbf{S}$ is a list of predicate symbols and $\phi(\mathbf{S})$ is a function-free first order formula in which (among possibly others) the predicates in $\mathbf{S}$ occur. In this section we show that the expressive power of DQL is $SO_{\exists\forall}$, the existential universal fragment of second order logic, on a relational vocabulary, i.e., the set of sentences

$$(\exists \mathbf{S})(\forall \mathbf{T})\phi(\mathbf{S}, \mathbf{T}), \qquad (1)$$

where $\mathbf{S}, \mathbf{T}$ are disjoint lists of predicate symbols and $\phi(\mathbf{S}, \mathbf{T})$ is a function-free first order formula in which at least the predicates in $\mathbf{S}, \mathbf{T}$ occur.

Following the traditional notion of a set of logical sentences *capturing* a complexity class, we can say that the set $SO_\exists$ captures the class NP (cf. [Fagin, 1974]), while the set $SO_{\exists\forall}$ captures Σ_2^p (cf. [Lynch, 1982; Stockmeyer, 1977]). (See [Garey and Johnson, 1979; Johnson, 1990] for a definition of the classes NP and Σ_2^p of the polynomial hierarchy).

We are now ready to prove our main result, which concerns DQL boolean queries. We refer to the following useful lemmas. Let $Cons()$ denote classical deductive closure.

Lemma 1 ([Reiter, 1980, Theorem 2.1]) *Let $\Delta = \langle D, W \rangle$ be a (closed) default theory. A set E is an extension of Δ iff $E = \bigcup_{i=0}^{\infty} E_i$, where $E_0 = W$ and $E_{i+1} = Cons(E_i) \cup \{\gamma | \alpha : \beta/\gamma \in D, \alpha \in E_i, \beta \notin E\}$, for all $i \geq 0$.*

Lemma 2 ([Reiter, 1980, Theorem 2.5]) *Let E be an extension of the default theory $\Delta = \langle D, W \rangle$. Denote by $GD(E, \Delta) = \{\alpha : \beta/\gamma \in D \mid \alpha \in E, \neg\beta \notin E\}$ the generating defaults of E. Then,*

$$E = Cons(W \cup \{\gamma \mid \alpha : \beta/\gamma \in GD(E, \Delta)\})$$

Theorem 1 *The boolean DQL queries precisely capture the Σ_2^p database properties.*

PROOF (sketch): The easy part is to show that every query of DQL can be expressed as a Σ_2^p-recognizable database property. We notice that the semantics of DQL given in Section 2.2 transforms query answering into credulous reasoning in a propositional default theory. The transformation is polynomial in the size of the database, i.e., its data complexity is polynomial. Moreover it has been proven in [Gottlob, 1992; Stillman, 1992] that the problem of credulous inference in propositional default theories is in Σ_2^p, hence this part of the proof is complete.

The more difficult part is to show that each query expressible as a sentence of $SO_{\exists\forall}$ can be expressed in DQL. As we already noticed in the introduction, *we cannot take advantage of the fact that propositional credulous default reasoning is Σ_2^p-hard*, because the expressiveness of a language is not necessarily the same as its complexity (cf. [Stewart, 1991] for a specific example).

Without loss of generality, we assume that sentence (1) is of form

$$(\exists \mathbf{S})(\forall \mathbf{T})(\exists \mathbf{x})(\forall \mathbf{y})\psi(\mathbf{x}, \mathbf{y}), \quad (2)$$

where $\mathbf{S}, \mathbf{T}$ are lists of predicate symbols, $\mathbf{x}, \mathbf{y}$ are lists of individual variables, and ψ is a first order formula in which no function symbol or quantifier occurs. The pass from (1) to (2) is justified in the appendix.

Now we have to show that for each query $Q_{SO_{\exists\forall}}$ of the form (2) there is a DQL query Q_{DQL} such that the two queries give the same answer on all possible database instances W over the unquantified relations in (2).

We outline the idea for Q_{DQL}. The formula $(\exists \mathbf{x})(\forall \mathbf{y})\psi(\mathbf{x}, \mathbf{y})$ is encoded as follows. We use a predicate $<$ that defines a linear order on the set of all $\mathbf{y}$-tuples, together with associated predicates $F(\mathbf{y})$, $S(\mathbf{y}, \mathbf{y}')$, $L(\mathbf{y})$ which state that $\mathbf{y}$ is the first tuple, $\mathbf{y}'$ is the successor of $\mathbf{y}$, and $\mathbf{y}$ is the last tuple in $<$, respectively. Furthermore, we use a predicate $Z(\mathbf{x}, \mathbf{y})$ which intuitively states that for each tuple $\mathbf{y}'$ from the initial segment of $<$ up to $\mathbf{y}$, the formula $\psi(\mathbf{x}, \mathbf{y}')$ is true. A designated propositional letter A indicates

if for some $\mathbf{x}$-tuple $\mathbf{a}$, $Z(\mathbf{a}, \mathbf{b})$ is true, where $\mathbf{b}$ is the last $\mathbf{y}$-tuple. Then, $(\exists \mathbf{x})(\forall \mathbf{y})\psi(\mathbf{x}, \mathbf{y})$ will be true just in case A is derivable. We encode this by default rules, such that in every extension that contains A, a valuation for the $\mathbf{S}$-predicates is defined and for every valuation of the $\mathbf{T}$-predicates some $Z(\mathbf{a}, \mathbf{b})$ is true, i.e., the sentence (2) is true over the underlying database W.

Formally, Q_{DQL} consists of the ground formula A and the set D containing the following open defaults.

- For each predicate P from $\mathbf{S}$ and for $<$:

$$\frac{:P(\mathbf{x})}{P(\mathbf{x})}, \quad \frac{:\neg P(\mathbf{x})}{\neg P(\mathbf{x})}, \quad \frac{:\mathbf{y} < \mathbf{y}'}{\mathbf{y} < \mathbf{y}'}, \quad \frac{:\neg(\mathbf{y} < \mathbf{y}')}{\neg(\mathbf{y} < \mathbf{y}')};$$

- linear order axioms for $<$:

$$\frac{:}{\neg(\mathbf{y} < \mathbf{y}' \wedge \mathbf{y}' < \mathbf{y})},$$

$$\frac{:}{(\mathbf{y} < \mathbf{y}') \vee (\mathbf{y}' < \mathbf{y}) \vee (\mathbf{y} = \mathbf{y}')},$$

$$\frac{:}{(\mathbf{y} < \mathbf{y}'' \wedge \mathbf{y}'' < \mathbf{y}') \rightarrow \mathbf{y} < \mathbf{y}'};$$

- rules for the associated predicates:

$$\frac{\mathbf{y} < \mathbf{y}' :}{\neg F(\mathbf{y}')}, \quad \frac{\mathbf{y} < \mathbf{y}' :}{\neg L(\mathbf{y})},$$

$$\frac{\neg(\mathbf{y} < \mathbf{y}') \vee (\mathbf{y} < \mathbf{y}'' \wedge \mathbf{y}'' < \mathbf{y}') :}{\neg S(\mathbf{y}, \mathbf{y}')};$$

- derivation of A (i.e., checking if $(\exists \mathbf{x})(\forall \mathbf{y})\psi(\mathbf{x}, \mathbf{y})$ is true):

$$\frac{:F(\mathbf{y})}{\psi(\mathbf{x}, \mathbf{y}) \rightarrow Z(\mathbf{x}, \mathbf{y})}, \quad \frac{:S(\mathbf{y}, \mathbf{y}')}{Z(\mathbf{x}, \mathbf{y}) \wedge \psi(\mathbf{x}, \mathbf{y}') \rightarrow Z(\mathbf{x}, \mathbf{y}')},$$

$$\frac{:L(\mathbf{y})}{Z(\mathbf{x}, \mathbf{y}) \rightarrow A}.$$

(Equality between tuples $\mathbf{y} = (y_1, \ldots, y_m)$ and $\mathbf{y}' = (y_1', \ldots, y_m')$, i.e., $(\mathbf{y} = \mathbf{y}')$, is expressed by $((y_1 = y_1') \wedge \cdots \wedge (y_m = y_m'))$.

Let W be any database instance, and denote by Δ the default theory $\langle INST(D); COMP(W) \rangle$.

It is easy to see that Δ has only consistent extensions. (Formally, this can be easily proved by Lemma 2.)

We claim that the atom A belongs to an extension of Δ if and only if $W \models (\exists \mathbf{S})(\forall \mathbf{T})(\exists \mathbf{x})(\forall \mathbf{y})\psi(\mathbf{x}, \mathbf{y})$.

"$\Leftarrow$". Assume that $W \models (\exists \mathbf{S})(\forall \mathbf{T})(\exists \mathbf{x})(\forall \mathbf{y})\psi(\mathbf{x}, \mathbf{y})$. That is,

$$W, \mathbf{S}_0 \models (\forall \mathbf{T})(\exists \mathbf{x})(\forall \mathbf{y})\psi(\mathbf{x}, \mathbf{y}) \quad (3)$$

for some valuation $\mathbf{S}_0$ of the $\mathbf{S}$ predicates. Define a set $\mathcal{F}$ of formulas as follows. Let $<_0$ be an arbitrary linear order of all $\mathbf{y}$-tuples, and let F_0, S_0, L_0 be the associated extensions for F, S, and L. In what follows, let $\mathbf{a}, \mathbf{a}', \mathbf{b}$ denote tuples of appropriate arities over the domain. The set $\mathcal{F}$ contains the following formulas:

$\mathcal{F}_1$: $COMP(W)$
$\mathcal{F}_2$: $\{\mathbf{a} < \mathbf{a}' \mid (\mathbf{a}, \mathbf{a}') \in <_0\} \cup \{\neg(\mathbf{a} < \mathbf{a}') \mid (\mathbf{a}, \mathbf{a}') \notin <_0\}$
$\mathcal{F}_3$: $\{\neg L(\mathbf{a}) \mid \mathbf{a} \notin L_0\}$
$\mathcal{F}_4$: $\{\neg F(\mathbf{a}) \mid \mathbf{a} \notin F_0\}$
$\mathcal{F}_5$: $\{\neg S(\mathbf{a}, \mathbf{a}') \mid (\mathbf{a}, \mathbf{a}') \notin S_0\}$
$\mathcal{F}_6$: $\{P(\mathbf{a}) \mid P \in \mathbf{S}, \mathbf{a} \in P_0\} \cup \{\neg P(\mathbf{a}) \mid P \in \mathbf{S}, \mathbf{a} \notin P_0\}$
$\mathcal{F}_7$: all ground formulas obtained by instantiation of the linear order axioms for $<$ over the domain
$\mathcal{F}_8$: $\{\psi(\mathbf{a}, \mathbf{b}) \to Z(\mathbf{a}, \mathbf{b}) \mid \mathbf{b} \in F_0\}$
$\mathcal{F}_9$: $\{Z(\mathbf{a}, \mathbf{b}) \wedge \psi(\mathbf{a}, \mathbf{b}') \to Z(\mathbf{a}, \mathbf{b}') \mid (\mathbf{b}, \mathbf{b}') \in S_0\}$
$\mathcal{F}_{10}$: $\{Z(\mathbf{a}, \mathbf{b}) \to A \mid \mathbf{b} \in L_0\}$

Claim: $E = Cons(\mathcal{F})$ is an extension of Δ such that $A \in E$. To show this, we first note that E is consistent. Indeed, extend the valuations given by W, $\mathbf{S}_0$, $<_0$, F_0, S_0, L_0 by assigning "true" to A, by letting Z_0 be the set of all possible tuples, and by letting the remaining predicates $\mathbf{T}$ have an arbitrary extension. This valuation satisfies $\mathcal{F}$. Hence, $E = Cons(\mathcal{F})$ is consistent.

Moreover, E is an extension of Δ. This can be easily shown from the iterative characterization of default extensions in Lemma 1. We obtain that

$E_0 = COMP(W) = \mathcal{F}_1$
$E_1 = Cons(E_0) \cup \mathcal{F}_2 \cup \mathcal{F}_6 \cup \mathcal{F}_7 \cup \mathcal{F}_8 \cup \mathcal{F}_9 \cup \mathcal{F}_{10}$
$E_2 = Cons(E_1) \cup \mathcal{F}_3 \cup \mathcal{F}_4 \cup \mathcal{F}_5$
$E_3 = Cons(E_2) = Cons(\mathcal{F})$
$E_4 = E_3$
$\vdots$

Containment of $\mathcal{F}_8$, $\mathcal{F}_9$, and $\mathcal{F}_{10}$ in E_1 holds since for each tuples $\mathbf{b}_0 \in F_0$, $(\mathbf{b}_1, \mathbf{b}_2) \in S_0$, and $\mathbf{b}_3 \in L_0$, we have that $\neg F(\mathbf{b}_0) \notin E$, $\neg S(\mathbf{b}_1, \mathbf{b}_2) \notin E$, and $\neg L(\mathbf{b}_3) \notin E$; this follows immediately from the definition of $\mathcal{F}$ and standard interpolation properties.

Hence, $\bigcup_{i=0}^{\infty} E_i = Cons(\mathcal{F}) = E$. Thus, E is an extension of Δ.

To prove the claim, it remains to show that $A \in E$. Since $E = Cons(\mathcal{F})$, it suffices to show that A is true in every valuation that satisfies $\mathcal{F}$. Consider an arbitrary valuation that satisfies $\mathcal{F}$. Let $\mathbf{T}_0$ be the valuation of $\mathbf{T}$ and Z_0 the valuation of Z. Then, from (3) we have that

$$W, \mathbf{S}_0, \mathbf{T}_0 \models (\exists \mathbf{x})(\forall \mathbf{y}) \psi(\mathbf{x}, \mathbf{y})$$

Let $\mathbf{a}$ be an arbitrary tuple such that

$$W, \mathbf{S}_0, \mathbf{T}_0 \models (\forall \mathbf{y}) \psi(\mathbf{a}, \mathbf{y}) \quad (4)$$

By finite induction on $<_0$ we show that $(\mathbf{a}, \mathbf{b}) \in Z_0$, for all $\mathbf{b}$.

(Basis). Let $\mathbf{b}_0$ be the first tuple of $<_0$. Since $\mathbf{b}_0 \in F_0$, we have $\psi(\mathbf{a}, \mathbf{b}_0) \to Z(\mathbf{a}, \mathbf{b}_0) \in \mathcal{F}$; hence, by (4), $\psi(\mathbf{a}, \mathbf{b}_0)$ is true. Thus, $(\mathbf{a}, \mathbf{b}_0) \in Z_0$.

(Induction). Assume the statement holds for tuple $\mathbf{b}$. We show that it holds also for $\mathbf{b}'$, where $(\mathbf{b}, \mathbf{b}') \in S_0$. We have that $Z(\mathbf{a}, \mathbf{b}) \wedge \psi(\mathbf{a}, \mathbf{b}') \to Z(\mathbf{a}, \mathbf{b}') \in \mathcal{F}$; by the induction hypothesis, $(\mathbf{a}, \mathbf{b}) \in Z_0$, and by (4), $\psi(\mathbf{a}, \mathbf{b}')$ is true. Hence, it follows that $Z(\mathbf{a}, \mathbf{b}')$ is true, i.e., $(\mathbf{a}, \mathbf{b}') \in Z_0$. This shows the induction case.

Since $(\mathbf{a}, \mathbf{b}) \in Z_0$ for all $\mathbf{b}$, in particular we have that $(\mathbf{a}, \mathbf{b}_1) \in Z_0$ where $\mathbf{b}_1$ is the last tuple in $<_0$, i.e., $\mathbf{b}_1 \in L_0$. However, we have that $Z(\mathbf{a}, \mathbf{b}_1) \to A \in \mathcal{F}$; thus, it follows that A has value "true" in the valuation. Consequently, we have shown that $A \in E$.

This concludes the "$\Leftarrow$" part of the proof.

"$\Rightarrow$": Let E be an extension of Δ such that $A \in E$. Notice that E is consistent.

E defines a valuation $\mathbf{S}_0$ for the $\mathbf{S}$ predicates, i.e., for each P from $\mathbf{S}$, we have $P(\mathbf{a}) \in E$ or $\neg P(\mathbf{a}) \in E$ for each tuple $\mathbf{a}$. This follows since the defaults $:P(\mathbf{a})/P(\mathbf{a})$, $:\neg P(\mathbf{a})/\neg P(\mathbf{a})$ are in $INST(D)$. Moreover, E defines a valuation $<_0$ for $<$ such that $<_0$ satisfies the axioms for a linear order of all tuples of the arity of $\mathbf{y}$.

Furthermore, from the instantiated default rules for the predicates associated to $<$, it follows that $\neg F(\mathbf{a}) \in E$ if $\mathbf{a}$ is not the first tuple in $<_0$, that $\neg S(\mathbf{a}, \mathbf{a}') \in E$ if $\mathbf{a}'$ is not the successor of $\mathbf{a}'$ in $<_0$, and that $\neg L(\mathbf{a}) \in E$ if $\mathbf{a}$ is not the last tuple in $<_0$. By the characterization of E in terms of its generating defaults (Lemma 2), it is easy to see that E is consistent with each of $F(\mathbf{a}_0)$, $S(\mathbf{a}_1, \mathbf{a}_2)$, and $L(\mathbf{a}_3)$ such that $\mathbf{a}_0$ is the first tuple in $<_0$, $\mathbf{a}_2$ is the successor of $\mathbf{a}_1$ in $<_0$, and $\mathbf{a}_3$ is the last tuple in $<_0$.

We claim that

$$W, \mathbf{S}_0 \models (\forall \mathbf{T})(\exists \mathbf{x})(\forall \mathbf{y}) \psi(\mathbf{x}, \mathbf{y}) \quad (5)$$

To prove this, assume this is false. Hence, there exists a valuation $\mathbf{T}_0$ of $\mathbf{T}$ such that

$$W, \mathbf{S}_0, \mathbf{T}_0 \models (\forall \mathbf{x})(\exists \mathbf{y}) \neg \psi(\mathbf{x}, \mathbf{y})$$

We extend this valuation to a model of E that has A false. Let for each tuple $\mathbf{a}$ for $\mathbf{x}$ be $m(\mathbf{a})$ the first tuple $\mathbf{b}$ for $\mathbf{y}$ in $<_0$ such that $W, \mathbf{S}_0, \mathbf{T}_0 \models \neg \psi(\mathbf{a}, \mathbf{b})$. Notice that $m(\mathbf{a})$ exists for each $\mathbf{a}$.

Define a valuation Z_0 for Z by

$$Z_0 = \{(\mathbf{a}, \mathbf{b}) \mid \mathbf{b} <_0 m(\mathbf{a})\},$$

assign A the value "false", and complete the partial valuations F_0, S_0, and L_0 of F, S, and L defined by E by letting $\mathbf{a}_0 \in F_0$, $(\mathbf{a}_1, \mathbf{a}_2) \in S_0$, and $\mathbf{a}_3 \in L_0$ for all $\mathbf{a}_0, \mathbf{a}_1, \mathbf{a}_2$, and $\mathbf{a}_3$ such that $\neg F(\mathbf{a}_0) \notin E$, $\neg S(\mathbf{a}_1, \mathbf{a}_2) \notin E$, and $\neg L(\mathbf{a}_3) \notin E$, respectively.

This valuation of the predicates defines a model of E. To prove this, it is by Lemma 2 sufficient to show that the valuation is a model of $COMP(W) \cup G$, where $G = \{\gamma \mid \alpha : \beta/\gamma \in GD(E, \Delta)\}$.

Clearly, the only formulas in G it remains to argue about are those which are conclusions of generating defaults of E with justifications $F(\mathbf{y})$, $S(\mathbf{y},\mathbf{y}')$, and $L(\mathbf{y})$.

- Assume that $\psi(\mathbf{a},\mathbf{b}) \to Z(\mathbf{a},\mathbf{b}) \in G$. Then, $\mathbf{b}$ is the first tuple in $<_0$, and the formula is certainly satisfied.

- Assume that $Z(\mathbf{a},\mathbf{b}) \wedge \Psi(\mathbf{a},\mathbf{b}') \to Z(\mathbf{a},\mathbf{b}') \in G$. Then, $\mathbf{b}'$ is the successor of $\mathbf{b}$ in $<_0$. By considering the three cases (1) $\mathbf{b},\mathbf{b}' <_0 m(\mathbf{a})$, (2) $\mathbf{b}' = m(\mathbf{a}$, and (3) $m(\mathbf{a}) <_0 \mathbf{b},\mathbf{b}'$ it is readily checked from the definition of Z_0 that the formula is satisfied.

- Assume that $Z(\mathbf{a},\mathbf{b}) \to A \in G$. Then, $\mathbf{b}$ is the last tuple in $<_0$. By definition of Z_0, we have that $Z(\mathbf{a},\mathbf{b})$ is false; hence, since A is false, the formula is satisfied.

Thus, the valuation satisfies $COMP(W) \cup G$, and hence also E. Since A is false in this model of E, we have that $A \notin E$. This is a contradiction, however. Hence, claim (5) is proved. Now claim (5) means

$$W \models (\exists \mathbf{S})(\forall \mathbf{T})(\exists \mathbf{x})(\forall \mathbf{y})\psi(\mathbf{x},\mathbf{y}).$$

This concludes the "$\Rightarrow$" part of the proof.

Remark: All defaults in D can be made prerequisite-free by deleting the prerequisite α and rewriting the conclusion γ as $\alpha \to \gamma$. $\square$

In order to give a corresponding result for DQL I/O queries, we need the concept of query recognizability. A query mapping database instances over R into database instances over S is **C**-*recognizable*, **C** a complexity class, if deciding whether a tuple **t** belongs to a certain output relation $S_i \in S$ is in **C** (cf. [Gurevich, 1988]). Using Theorem 1, we can show the following.

Theorem 2 *A database query is Σ_2^p-recognizable if and only if it is definable as a DQL I/O query.*

4 APPLICATIONS AND EXAMPLES

This section is devoted to illustration of queries expressible via DQL.

Example 2: (Strategic companies) Suppose a holding owns some companies. Each company produces a set of products. Each product is produced by at most two companies. The database instance in Table 1 describes a possible situation.

Suppose the holding experiences a crisis and has to sell one company. The holding's policy is to keep on producing all products. This clearly makes it impossible to sell some companies –as an example the company Alpha in the above situation, because it would be impossible to produce wine. Anyway the managers are even more cautious: They know that in the future it may be necessary to sell more companies, and they do not want to get into a situation in which they will not be able to produce all products. More formally, they are interested in the minimal sets of companies that produce all products. A company is *strategic* if it is in at least one of such minimal sets. As an example, both Alpha and Beta are strategic, because {Alpha, Beta} produce all products, while neither {Alpha} nor {Beta} do that. On the other hand Gamma is not strategic. Therefore a query which is very relevant to the managers is whether a company is strategic or not: They prefer to sell a non-strategic company first, because after the transaction the minimal sets of companies that produce all products remain the same.

A manager can easily express a boolean query whose answer tells if a specific company C is strategic or not by writing the set of open defaults D:

$$\frac{produces(x,y,z):}{strat(y) \vee strat(z)} \quad , \quad \frac{:\neg strat(x)}{\neg strat(x)}$$

and the ground formula $strat(C)$. The intuitive meaning of the defaults is that for each product x at least one of the producers y, z are strategic companies, and that companies are non-strategic by default. The answer to the above boolean query is **yes** iff the company C is strategic.

Now let us consider a slightly more complex situation, in which up to three (say) companies can *control* another company. As an example, we assume that the situation is described by means of the relation instance in Table 2.

The meaning of the tuple is that companies Alpha and Beta together have control over Gamma, i.e., the holding cannot own both Alpha and Beta without owning Gamma as well. Further information of this kind completely changes the minimal sets of companies that produce all products. As an example {Alpha, Beta} is no longer such a set, while {Alpha, Beta, Gamma} is. If we add the default

$$\frac{controls(w,x,y,z) \wedge strat(w) \wedge strat(x) \wedge strat(y):}{strat(z)}$$

to D, then the boolean query gives the desired answer.

In the former case –no controlled companies– the problem of deciding whether a company is strategic is in NP (cf. [Cadoli and Lenzerini, 1991]), while in the latter case the same problem is Σ_2^p-complete (cf. [Eiter and Gottlob, 1993]). As a consequence, the former query is expressible in DATALOG$^{\neg}_{stable}$, while the latter is not. In this example we could allow unbounded numbers of producers for each product and controllers for each company, although the queries would get more involved.

Table 1: Database instance of the producers

PRODUCERS	PRODUCT	COMPANY #1	COMPANY #2
	Pasta	Alpha	Beta
	Tomatoes	Gamma	Alpha
	Wine	Alpha	Alpha
	Bread	Beta	Delta

Table 2: Database instance of the controlled companies

CONTROL	CONTROLLED	CONT #1	CONT #2	CONT #3
	Gamma	Alpha	Beta	Beta

Example 3: (Maximal trust) In a finite set of companies it is possible to make agreements. A *trust* is a set T of companies such that each one has an agreement with each other company in T. A *maximal* trust is a trust such that there is no bigger –wrt cardinality– trust. The decision problem "does a company belong to a maximal trust?" is $\text{P}^{\text{NP}[O(\log n)]}$-hard, hence most likely harder than NP.

We can easily represent companies and agreements with a relational database. We can express the query "does a company belong to a maximal trust?" in DQL but we cannot in $\text{DATALOG}^{\neg}_{stable}$. □

5 COMBINED COMPLEXITY OF DQL

The *combined complexity* (cf. [Vardi, 1982]) of Boolean DQL queries amounts to the complexity of deciding a query Q over a database instance W, where the input is arbitrary Q and W.

By the complexity results for propositional default logic [Gottlob, 1992; Stillman, 1992], the combined complexity of Boolean DQL is Σ_2^p-complete if no default is open, i.e., all defaults are already instantiated. The instantiation of a set of open defaults is in general exponentially larger, however; this intuitively suggests an exponential increase of complexity for query answering if open defaults are present. In fact, we can show that it increases to NEXPTIME^{NP}, the problems solvable by a non-deterministic Turing machine in *exponential* time using an NP-oracle (cf. [Johnson, 1990]).

Theorem 3 *The combined complexity of Boolean DQL is* NEXPTIME^{NP}*-complete.*

PROOF (Sketch) The transformation of the semantics of Boolean DQL into credulous reasoning in a propositional default theory is exponential ($O(2^{n^k})$, where k is a constant) in the query size, i.e., the default theory $\langle INST(D), COMP(W) \rangle$ is exponential in the size of D plus W. Credulous reasoning in $\langle INST(D), COMP(W) \rangle$ can be done by a nondeterministic Turing machine with an NP oracle in time polynomial in the size of the input default theory. Therefore, the Boolean DQL query can be decided by a non-deterministic Turing machine in exponential with an NP oracle. This proves membership in NEXPTIME^{NP}.

The hardness proof is too involved to be described here in detail. It gives a reduction from a graph coloring problem (co-CERT3COL$_S$) that can be shown to be NEXPTIME^{NP}-hard, cf. [Eiter *et al.*, 1994]; the reduction is based on advanced complexity upgrading techniques [Balcázar *et al.*, 1992; Papadimitriou and Yannakakis, 1985] and simulation of a Boolean circuit (cf. [Kolaitis and Papadimitriou, 1991]) in DQL.

Problem co-CERT3COL is a follows. An instance I of size n of the problem consists of an undirected graph G on vertices $\{0, \ldots, n-1\}$, whose edges are labeled with a disjunction of two literals where each literal is over the Boolean variables $\{X_{i,j} \mid i, j = 0, \ldots, n-1\}$; I is a Yes-instance if for some truth value assignment t to the Boolean variables, the graph $t(G)$ obtained from G by including only those edges whose labels are true under t is not 3-colorable. I is encoded as a binary string representing a database instance (domain $\{0, \ldots, n-1\}$) over relations describing the edges and the graph labeling.

The succinct version of problem co-CERT3COL, co-CERT3COL$_S$, is NEXPTIME^{NP}-hard, cf. [Eiter *et al.*, 1994]. In the succinct version – instead of a binary string w for I – the input consists of a Boolean circuit C_I with $\log |w|$ input bits, by which each bit i of w can be computed.

The transformation of co-CERT3COL$_S$ to Boolean DQL roughly is as follows. For each instance I of CERT3COL of size n, an equivalent Boolean DQL query on a *fixed* database with domain $\{0, 1\}$ is constructed in polynomial time; elements of the domain are represented by tuples on $\{0,1\}$ of arity $\lceil \log n \rceil$, and each input relation R is computed by a collection of default rules, which simulates the computation of R by a Boolean circuit C_R that is easily constructed from C_I.

Remark: Since the transformation reduces co-CERT3COL to a fixed database, the same result follows for the *expression complexity* of Boolean DQL. □

Notice that NEXPTIME^{NP}-complete problems are *provably* harder than NP-complete problems, since NP $\subset$ NEXPTIME^{NP}; few practical such problems are known.

For the case where Q is fixed, i.e., for the *data complexity*, we immediately obtain from our expressiveness results the following.

Theorem 4 *The data complexity of Boolean DQL is Σ_2^p-complete.*

PROOF (Sketch) From Theorem 1, we have that every Boolean DQL query defines a Σ_2^p database property; this gives the membership part. For the hardness part, we notice that for every $SO_{\exists\forall}$ sentence as in (1), an equivalent sentence of the form (2) in the proof of Theorem 1 can be constructed (cf. Appendix), for which the equivalent default query Q_{DQL} can be easily constructed (even in polynomial time). Consequently, the problem of deciding whether a *fixed* sentence (1) is valid in a given database instance W, which is Σ_2^p-hard, is transformable to a Boolean DQL query in polynomial time. □

Similar results can be derived for DQL I/O queries, measuring the complexity of query recognizability (cf. Section 3).

Theorem 5 *The combined (resp. expression) complexity of DQL I/O queries is NEXPTIME^{NP}-complete and the data complexity is Σ_2^p-complete.*

6 CONCLUSIONS

In this paper we have defined DQL, a query language for relational databases based on default logic. The expressiveness and complexity of DQL have been investigated both for boolean queries and for I/O queries. The results we have shown are not only of theoretical importance: We have presented queries which are useful in practice that can be handled with DQL and cannot with other query languages based on nonmonotonic logics such as DATALOG$^-_{stable}$.

In the definition of query –Section 2.1– open defaults are function- and quantifier-free. While unlimited quantification cannot be allowed without loosing decidability, the impact of allowing functions remains for further investigation. Another interesting question is whether expressiveness of DQL decreases if only normal or semi-normal defaults are allowed.

APPENDIX

The pass from (1) to (2) is justified as follows.

As shown in [Kolaitis and Papadimitriou, 1991, p.130] (cf. also [van Benthem and Doets, 1983, Section 2.5.2]), for every existential second order sentence Ψ over a relational vocabulary σ, there exists an equivalent second order sentence over σ of the form $(\exists \mathbf{T})(\forall \mathbf{x})(\exists \mathbf{y})\phi(\mathbf{x},\mathbf{y})$ over the same vocabulary, where ϕ is a quantifier-free first-order formula; this sentence can be effectively constructed. Consequently, for every universal second order sentence Φ over vocabulary σ, there exists an equivalent second order sentence over σ of the form $(\forall \mathbf{T})(\exists \mathbf{x})(\forall \mathbf{y})\phi(\mathbf{x},\mathbf{y})$, where ϕ is a quantifier-free first-order formula. Let Φ be a universal second order sentence equivalent to $(\forall \mathbf{T})\phi(\mathbf{S},\mathbf{T})$. Let D be any structure for σ. Then,

$$D \models (\exists \mathbf{S})(\forall \mathbf{T})\phi(\mathbf{S},\mathbf{T})$$

iff

$$D, \mathbf{S}_0 \models (\forall \mathbf{T})\phi(\mathbf{S},\mathbf{T})$$

iff

$$D, \mathbf{S}_0 \models \Phi$$

iff

$$D \models (\exists \mathbf{S})\Phi,$$

where $\mathbf{S}_0$ is an appropriate valuation of the $\mathbf{S}$ predicates.

Consequently, the sentence in (1) is equivalent to a sentence of the form (2).

Acknowledgements

The authors are grateful to Torsten Schaub for interesting comments on semantics of DQL. The first author is partially supported by ESPRIT Basic Research Action 6810 COMPULOG II and by *Progetto Finalizzato Informatica* of the CNR (Italian Research Council).

References

[Aho and Ullman, 1979] A.V. Aho and J.D. Ullman. Universality of Data Retrieval Languages. In *Proceedings ACM Symposium on Principles of Programming Languages*, pages 110–117, 1979.

[Balcázar et al., 1992] J.L. Balcázar, A. Lozano, and J. Torán. The Complexity of Algorithmic Problems on Succinct Instances. In R. Baeta-Yates and U. Manber, editors, *Computer Science*, pages 351–377. Plenum Press, New York, 1992.

[Bidoit and Froidevaux, 1991] N. Bidoit and Ch. Froidevaux. General logic databases and programs: Default semantics and stratification. *Information and Computation*, 19:15–54, 1991.

[Cadoli and Lenzerini, 1991] Marco Cadoli and Maurizio Lenzerini. The Complexity of Closed World Reasoning and Circumscription. Technical Report RAP. 17.91, Universitá di Roma "La Sapienza", Dipartimento di Informatica e Sistemistica, September 1991. Preliminary version in *Proc. of AAAI-90*. To appear in *Journal of Computer and System Sciences*.

[Cadoli and Schaerf, 1993] M. Cadoli and M. Schaerf. A Survey of Complexity Results for Non-monotonic Logics. *Journal of Logic Programming*, 17:127–160, 1993.

[Eiter and Gottlob, 1993] T. Eiter and G. Gottlob. Complexity Aspects of Various Semantics for Disjunctive Databases. In *Proceedings of the Twelth ACM SIGACT SIGMOD-SIGART Symposium on Principles of Database Systems (PODS-93)*, pages 158–167, June 1993.

[Eiter et al., 1994] T. Eiter, G. Gottlob, and H. Mannila. Adding Disjunction to Datalog. In *Proceedings of the Thirteenth ACM SIGACT SIGMOD-SIGART Symposium on Principles of Database Systems (PODS-94)*, May 1994. Forthcoming.

[Fagin, 1974] R. Fagin. Generalized First-Order Spectra and Polynomial-Time Recognizable Sets. In R. M. Karp, editor, *Complexity of Computation*, pages 43–74. AMS, 1974.

[Garey and Johnson, 1979] Michael Garey and David S. Johnson. *Computers and Intractability – A Guide to the Theory of NP-Completeness*. W. H. Freeman, New York, 1979.

[Gottlob, 1992] Georg Gottlob. Complexity Results for Nonmonotonic Logics. *Journal of Logic and Computation*, 2(3):397–425, June 1992.

[Gurevich, 1988] Y. Gurevich. Logic and the Challenge of Computer Science. In E. Börger, editor, *Trends in Theoretical Computer Science*, chapter 1. Computer Science Press, 1988.

[Johnson, 1990] David S. Johnson. A Catalog of Complexity Classes. In van Leeuwen [1990], chapter 2.

[Kannelakis, 1990] P. Kannelakis. Elements of Relational Database Theory. In van Leeuwen [1990], chapter 17.

[Kolaitis and Papadimitriou, 1991] Ph. Kolaitis and Ch. H. Papadimitriou. Why Not Negation By Fixpoint ? *Journal of Computer and System Sciences*, 43:125–144, 1991.

[Lynch, 1982] J.F. Lynch. Complexity Classes and Theories of Finite Models. *Mathematical Systems Theory*, 15:127–144, 1982.

[Papadimitriou and Yannakakis, 1985] C.H. Papadimitriou and M. Yannakakis. A Note on Succinct Representations of Graphs. *Information and Computation*, 71:181–185, 1985.

[Reiter, 1980] R. Reiter. A Logic for Default Reasoning. *Artificial Intelligence*, 13:81–132, 1980.

[Reiter, 1984] R. Reiter. Towards a Reconstruction of Logical Databases. In J.W. Schmidt M.L. Brodie, J.L. Mylopoulos, editor, *On Conceptual Modelling*, pages 163–189, New York, 1984. Springer.

[Saccà, 1993] D. Saccà. Multiple Stable Models are Needed to Solve Unique Solution Problems. In *Informal Proceedings of the Second Compulog Net Meeting on Knowledge Bases (CNKBS-93)*, Athens, April 1993.

[Schlipf, 1990] J.S. Schlipf. The Expressive Powers of Logic Programming Semantics. Technical Report CIS-TR-90-3, Computer Science Department, University of Cincinnati, 1990. Preliminary version in *Proc. of PODS-90*. To appear in *Journal of Computer and System Sciences*.

[Stewart, 1991] I. Stewart. Comparing the Expressibility of Languages Formed Using NP-Complete Operators. *Journal of Logic and Computation*, 1(3):305–330, 1991.

[Stillman, 1992] J. Stillman. The Complexity of Propositional Default Logic. In *Proceedings AAAI-92*, pages 794–799, 1992.

[Stockmeyer, 1977] L. J. Stockmeyer. The Polynomial-Time Hierarchy. *Theoretical Computer Science*, 3:1–22, 1977.

[Ullman, 1988] J. D. Ullman. *Principles of Database and Knowledge Base Systems*, volume 1. Computer Science Press, 1988.

[van Benthem and Doets, 1983] Johan van Benthem and Kees Doets. Higher Order Logic. In D. Gabbay and F. Guenthner, editors, *Handbook of Philosophical Logic, Vol.I*, chapter I.4, pages 275–329. D. Reidel Publishing Company, 1983.

[Van Gelder, 1989] A. Van Gelder. The Alternating Fixpoint of Logic Programs With Negation. In *Proceedings PODS-89*, pages 1–10, 1989.

[van Leeuwen, 1990] J. van Leeuwen, editor. Handbook of Theoretical Computer Science. Elsevier Science Publishers B.V. (North-Holland), 1990.

[Vardi, 1982] M. Vardi. Complexity of Relational Query Languages. In *Proceedings 14th STOC*, pages 137–146, 1982.

A Unified Framework for Class-Based Representation Formalisms

Diego Calvanese, Maurizio Lenzerini, Daniele Nardi

Dipartimento di Informatica e Sistemistica
Università di Roma "La Sapienza"
Via Salaria 113, I-00198 Roma, Italy
e-mail: {calvanese,lenzerini,nardi}@assi.dis.uniroma1.it

Abstract

The notion of class is ubiquitous in Computer Science and is central in many knowledge representation languages. In this paper we propose a representation formalism in the style of concept languages, with the aim of providing a unified framework for class-based formalisms. The language we consider is quite expressive and features a novel combination of constructs including number restrictions, inverse roles and inclusion assertions with no restrictions on cycles. We are able to show that such language is powerful enough to model frame systems, object-oriented database languages and semantic data models. As a consequence of the established correspondences, several significant extensions of each of the above formalisms become available. The high expressivity of the language and the need for capturing the reasoning in different contexts forces us to distinguish between unrestricted and finite model reasoning. A notable feature of our proposal is that reasoning in both cases is decidable. For the unrestricted case we exploit a correspondence with propositional dynamic logic and extend it to the treatment of number restrictions. For the finite model case we develop a new method based on the use of linear programming techniques. We argue that, by virtue of the high expressive power and of the associated reasoning techniques on both unrestricted and finite models, our language provides a unified framework for class-based representation formalisms.

1 INTRODUCTION

In many fields of Computer Science we find formalisms for the representation of objects and classes [MM92]. Generally speaking a *class* denotes a subset of the domain of discourse, and a class-based representation formalism allows one to express several kinds of relationships and constraints (e.g. subclass constraints) holding among classes. Moreover, class-based formalisms aim at taking advantage of the class structure in order to provide various information, such as whether an element belongs to a class, whether a class is a subclass of another class, and more generally, whether a given constraint holds between two classes.

Three main families of class-based formalisms can be identified. The first one comes from knowledge representation and in particular from the work on semantic networks and frames (see for example [Leh92, Sow91]). The second one originates in the field of databases and in particular from the work on semantic data models (see for example [HK87]). The third one arises from the work on types in programming languages and object-oriented systems (see for example [KL89]).

In the past there have been several attempts to establish relationships among class-based formalisms. In [BHR90] and [LNS91] a comparative analysis and an attempt to provide a unified view of class-based languages are carried out. The analysis makes it clear that several difficulties arise in identifying a common framework for the formalisms developed in different areas. Some recent papers address this problem. For example, an analysis of the relationships between concept languages and types in programming languages has been carried out in [Bor92], while in [BS92, PSS92] concept languages are used to enrich the deductive capabilities of semantic and object-oriented data models.

The proposed solutions are not fully general and a formalism capturing both the modeling constructs and the reasoning techniques for all the above families is still missing. In this paper we provide a solution to this problem by proposing a class-based representation formalism, called $\mathcal{ALUNI}$, whose main characteristics are:

1. it is quite expressive and features a novel combination of constructs including number restrictions, inverse roles and inclusion assertions with no re-

strictions on cycles;

2. it is equipped with suitable techniques for both unrestricted and finite model reasoning, since it is designed for capturing the reasoning in different contexts;

3. sound and complete reasoning in both unrestricted and finite models can be done in worst-case exponential time.

The first characteristic allows us to show that $\mathcal{ALUNI}$ is powerful enough to provide a unified framework for frame systems, object-oriented languages and semantic data models. We show this by establishing a precise correspondence with the Entity Relationship model [Che76] model and with an object-oriented language in the style of [AK89]. Moreover, we demonstrate that the formalism proposed in this paper provides important features that are currently missing in each family, although their relevance has often been stressed. In this sense, the work reported here may also contribute to significant developments for the languages belonging to all the three families.

With regard to the second point, the two cases of reasoning in both unrestricted and finite models are solved by means of different techniques. For unrestricted satisfiability we exploit the correspondence with dynamic logic [Sch91], by extending it to the treatment of number restrictions which have no direct counterpart in dynamic logics. For finite satisfiability we develop a new method based on linear programming techniques by extending the approach proposed in [CL94]. It is worth noting that the problem of finite reasoning which arises mainly in the field of databases has never been considered in knowledge representation languages, although it seems quite relevant for practical applications.

As for the third point, the expressive power of $\mathcal{ALUNI}$ makes reasoning hard, but nonetheless decidable. We consider this feature very important, because it makes it feasible to regard this language as an actual knowledge representation language and not simply as a formal framework for comparing apparently different approaches. Obviously, there are a number of sublanguages of $\mathcal{ALUNI}$, where, by giving up some of the expressivity, one gains on the comutational complexity. However, this issue is outside the scope of the present paper.

Summarizing, our framework provides an adequate expressive power to account for the most significant features of the major families of class-based formalisms. Moreover, it is equipped with suitable techniques for reasoning in both finite and unrestricted models. Therefore $\mathcal{ALUNI}$ and the associated reasoning capabilities represent the essential core of the class-based representation formalisms belonging to all three families mentioned above.

The paper is organized as follows. In the next section we present our formalism and discuss its relationships with frame languages, semantic data models and object-oriented languages. Section 3 describes the technique for unrestricted model satisfiability and Section 4 the technique for finite model satisfiability. The final section contains some concluding remarks.

2 A UNIFYING CLASS-BASED REPRESENTATION LANGUAGE

In this section, we present $\mathcal{ALUNI}$, a class-based formalism in the style of concept languages, and show that it can be used to formalize knowledge represented with formalisms developed in different fields.

The basic elements of concept languages are *concepts* and *roles*, which denote classes and binary relations, respectively. In $\mathcal{ALUNI}$, concepts and roles are formed by means of the following syntax (A denotes an atomic concept, P an atomic role, C and D arbitrary concepts, R an arbitrary role and m and n positive integers):

$$\begin{aligned} C, D &\longrightarrow \top \mid \bot \mid A \mid \neg A \mid C \sqcap D \mid C \sqcup D \mid \\ & \qquad \forall R.C \mid (\geq m\, R) \mid (\leq n\, R)^1 \\ R &\longrightarrow P \mid P^{-1} \end{aligned}$$

Semantically, concepts are interpreted as subsets of a domain and roles as binary relations over that domain. More precisely, an interpretation $\mathcal{I} = (\Delta^{\mathcal{I}}, \cdot^{\mathcal{I}})$ consists of a set $\Delta^{\mathcal{I}}$ (the *domain* of $\mathcal{I}$) and a function $\cdot^{\mathcal{I}}$ (the *interpretation function* of $\mathcal{I}$) that maps every concept to a subset of $\Delta^{\mathcal{I}}$ and every role to a subset of $\Delta^{\mathcal{I}} \times \Delta^{\mathcal{I}}$ such that the following equations are satisfied: ($\sharp\{\}$ denotes the cardinality of a set)

$$\begin{aligned} \bot^{\mathcal{I}} &= \emptyset \\ \top^{\mathcal{I}} &= \Delta^{\mathcal{I}} \\ (\neg A)^{\mathcal{I}} &= \Delta^{\mathcal{I}} \setminus A^{\mathcal{I}} \\ (C \sqcap D)^{\mathcal{I}} &= C^{\mathcal{I}} \cap D^{\mathcal{I}} \\ (C \sqcup D)^{\mathcal{I}} &= C^{\mathcal{I}} \cup D^{\mathcal{I}} \\ (\forall R.C)^{\mathcal{I}} &= \{a \in \Delta^{\mathcal{I}} \mid \forall b.\, (a, b) \in R^{\mathcal{I}} \to b \in C^{\mathcal{I}}\} \\ (\geq m\, R)^{\mathcal{I}} &= \{a \in \Delta^{\mathcal{I}} \mid \sharp\{b \mid (a, b) \in R^{\mathcal{I}}\} \geq m\} \\ (\leq n\, R)^{\mathcal{I}} &= \{a \in \Delta^{\mathcal{I}} \mid \sharp\{b \mid (a, b) \in R^{\mathcal{I}}\} \leq n\} \\ (R^{-1})^{\mathcal{I}} &= \{(a, b) \in (\Delta^{\mathcal{I}} \times \Delta^{\mathcal{I}}) \mid (b, a) \in R^{\mathcal{I}}\} \end{aligned}$$

In an $\mathcal{ALUNI}$ knowledge base, the knowledge about the classes and the relations is expressed through the use of the so called *inclusion assertions* which have the form

$$A \sqsubseteq C$$

---
[1] We use the shorthand $(= n\, R)$ in place of $(\leq n\, R) \sqcap (\geq n\, R)$.

where A is an atomic and C an arbitrary concept. An interpretation $\mathcal{I}$ *satisfies* the inclusion assertion $A \sqsubseteq C$ if $A^{\mathcal{I}} \subseteq C^{\mathcal{I}}$. An interpretation $\mathcal{I}$ is a *model* of a knowledge base $\mathcal{T}$ if it satisfies all inclusion assertions in $\mathcal{T}$. A *finite model* is a model with finite domain. Number restrictions, inverse roles and inclusion assertions may interact in such a way that a knowledge base is satisfiable only in infinite models. Therefore it is meaningful to distinguish between unrestricted and finite satisfiability (implication): $\mathcal{T}$ is said to be *(finitely) satisfiable* if it admits a (finite) model, and it *(finitely) implies* an inclusion assertion $A \sqsubseteq C$ if the inclusion is satisfied in all (finite) models of $\mathcal{T}$.

Below we discuss three families of class-based formalisms, namely, frame languages, semantic data models, and object-oriented data models, and we show that their basic features are captured by knowledge bases in $\mathcal{ALUNI}$.

2.1 FRAME LANGUAGES

Frame languages are based on the idea of expressing knowledge by means of *frames*, which are structures representing classes of objects in terms of the properties that their instances must satisfy. Such properties are defined by the frame *slots*, that constitute the items of a frame definition. In Figure 1 we present an example of a knowledge base defined by frame languages. The notation is basically the one adopted in [FK85], which is used in the KEE[2] system. The corresponding formalization in $\mathcal{ALUNI}$ is given by:

```
Course     ⊑  ∀ENROLLS.Student ⊓
              (≥ 2 ENROLLS) ⊓ (≤ 30 ENROLLS) ⊓
              ∀TAUGHTBY.(Professor ⊔ Grad) ⊓
              (= 1 TAUGHTBY)
AdvCourse  ⊑  Course ⊓ (≤ 20 ENROLLS) ⊓
              ∀ENROLLS.(Grad ⊓ ¬Undergrad)
BasCourse  ⊑  Course ⊓ ∀TAUGHTBY.(Professor ⊓ ¬Grad)
Grad       ⊑  Student ⊓ ∀DEGREE.String ⊓
              (= 1 DEGREE)
Undergrad  ⊑  Student
```

We observe that inverse roles are not used in the formalization. Indeed, the possibility of referring to the inverse of a slot has been rarely considered in frame knowledge representation systems. However, as recent works show (see [DLNN91]), this is a strong limitation in expressivity. For instance, without inverse roles we cannot specify, in our example, that every student is enrolled in at least 4 courses. In fact, KEE, as well as many practical frame systems, embeds other features, such as attachments and overriding inheritance. Such features cannot be captured in our framework, which

---
[2]KEE is a trademark of Intellicorp.

is intended to deal with the structural and monotonic aspects of these systems.

In [FK85], several reasoning services associated with frames are mentioned, such as: inheritance, cardinality reasoning and consistency checking. For example, one could ask the system whether the knowledge base implies that the filler of a given slot belongs to a certain class. Due to the absence of inverse roles, it is possible to show that if a frame knowledge base is satisfiable, then it admits a finite model. Therefore, the distinction between reasoning in finite and infinite models is not necessary, and all the above mentioned forms of reasoning are captured by unrestricted satisfiability and implication in $\mathcal{ALUNI}$.

```
Frame: Course in KB University
  Subclasses: AdvCourse, BasCourse
  Memberslot: ENROLLS
    ValueClass: Student
    Cardinality.Min: 2
    Cardinality.Max: 30
  Memberslot: TAUGHTBY
    ValueClass: (UNION Grad Professor)
    Cardinality.Min: 1
    Cardinality.Max: 1

Frame: BasCourse in KB University
  Superclasses: Course
  Memberslot: TAUGHTBY
    ValueClass: (INTERSECTION
                 Professor (NOT Grad))

Frame: Professor in KB University

Frame: AdvCourse in KB University
  Superclasses: Course
  Memberslot: ENROLLS
    ValueClass: (INTERSECTION
                 Grad (NOT Undergrad))
    Cardinality.Max: 20

Frame: Student in KB University
  Subclasses: Grad, Undergrad

Frame: Grad in KB University
  Superclasses: Student
  Memberslot: DEGREE
    ValueClass: String
    Cardinality.Min: 1
    Cardinality.Max: 1

Frame: Undergrad in KB University
  Superclasses: Student
```

Figure 1: A KEE Knowledge Base

In the last decade, the research on frame languages concentrated on the definition of concept languages, which are subsets of first-order logics, introduced for the formalization of KL-ONE languages (see [WS92]).

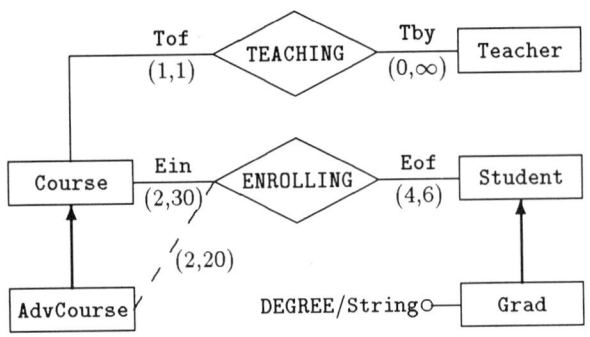

Figure 2: An ER-schema

The only limitation of $\mathcal{ALUNI}$-knowledge bases compared with some of the concept languages appeared in the literature is that inclusion assertions require the left hand side to be an atomic concept. On the other hand, we do not rule out cyclic references in the inclusion assertions, as opposed to most of the approaches to concept languages [Neb91]. Moreover, $\mathcal{ALUNI}$ includes inverse roles, number restrictions and inclusion assertions, whose combination has never been addressed in the literature, and whose decidability (both in unrestricted and finite models) was an open problem.

2.2 SEMANTIC DATA MODELS

Semantic data models were introduced primarily as formalisms for database schema design. They provide means to model databases in a much richer way than traditional data models supported by Database Management Systems, and are becoming more and more important because they are adopted in most of the recent Computer Aided Software Engineering tools.

The most common semantic data model is the Entity-Relationship (ER) model introduced in [Che76]. Figure 2 shows the ER-schema for the same state of affairs represented by the KEE knowledge base in Figure 1. In the ER notation, classes are called *entities* and are represented as boxes, whereas relationships between entities are represented as diamonds. Arrows between entities, called ISA relationships, represent inclusion assertions. The links between entities and relationships represent the ER-*roles*, to which number restrictions are associated. Dashed links are used whenever such restrictions are refined for more specific entities. Finally, elementary properties of entities are modeled by *attributes* (DEGREE in Figure 2).

The ER model does not provide constructs for expressing negation and disjunction, although several recent papers stress their importance in database specification [CL93, CHS91]. Referring to our example, the absence of negation and disjunction makes it impossible to specify that courses are taught by either professors or graduate students. For this purpose, the new entity Teacher has been introduced as an abstraction of professor and graduate student.

An $\mathcal{ALUNI}$ knowledge base that captures exactly the semantics of the schema of Figure 2 is given by the following set of inclusion assertions:

$$
\begin{aligned}
\text{TEACHING} &\sqsubseteq \forall\text{Tof.Course} \sqcap (= 1\,\text{Tof}) \sqcap \\
&\quad \forall\text{Tby.Teacher} \sqcap (= 1\,\text{Tby}) \\
\text{ENROLLING} &\sqsubseteq \forall\text{Ein.Course} \sqcap (= 1\,\text{Ein}) \sqcap \\
&\quad \forall\text{Eof.Student} \sqcap (= 1\,\text{Eof}) \\
\text{Course} &\sqsubseteq \forall\text{Tof}^{-1}.\text{TEACHING} \sqcap (= 1\,\text{Tof}^{-1}) \sqcap \\
&\quad \forall\text{Ein}^{-1}.\text{ENROLLING} \sqcap \\
&\quad (\geq 2\,\text{Ein}^{-1}) \sqcap (\leq 30\,\text{Ein}^{-1}) \\
\text{AdvCourse} &\sqsubseteq \text{Course} \sqcap (\leq 20\,\text{Ein}^{-1}) \\
\text{Teacher} &\sqsubseteq \forall\text{Tby}^{-1}.\text{TEACHING} \\
\text{Student} &\sqsubseteq \forall\text{Eof}^{-1}.\text{ENROLLING} \sqcap \\
&\quad (\geq 4\,\text{Eof}^{-1}) \sqcap (\leq 6\,\text{Eof}^{-1}) \\
\text{Grad} &\sqsubseteq \text{Student} \sqcap \forall\text{DEGREE.String} \sqcap \\
&\quad (= 1\,\text{DEGREE})
\end{aligned}
$$

In order to prove that in general $\mathcal{ALUNI}$ is powerful enough to capture all properties of ER-schemata, we first need formal definitions of their syntax and semantics. In the following, for ease of presentation, we do not consider attributes any more. We point out, however, that their inclusion in the specification is straigtforward, and that even attributes with a predefined domain of a fixed cardinality do not pose special problems with respect to reasoning on the schema.

The definitions make use of the notion of *labeled tuple* over a generic set $\mathcal{D}$, which is a function from a subset of a set $\mathcal{U}$ of ER-roles to $\mathcal{D}$. The labeled tuple T that maps $U_i \in \mathcal{U}$ to $d_i \in \mathcal{D}$, for $i \in 1..k$, is denoted with $\langle U_1{:}d_1,\ldots,U_k{:}d_k\rangle$. We also write $T[U_i]$ to denote d_i.

Definition 2.1 *An ER-schema $\mathcal{S}$ is constituted by:*

- *a set $\mathcal{E}_\mathcal{S}$ of entity symbols, a set $\mathcal{R}_\mathcal{S}$ of relationship symbols and a set $\mathcal{U}_\mathcal{S}$ of role symbols;*

- *a set $\mathcal{S}_{isa}$ of statements of the form $E_1 \preceq E_2$, where E_1 and E_2 are entities; the reflexive transitive closure of $\preceq$ is denoted with $\preceq^*$;*

- *for each relationship symbol $R \in \mathcal{R}_\mathcal{S}$, a labeled tuple over the set of entities[3];*

- *for each relationship $R\langle U_1{:}E_1,\ldots,U_k{:}E_k\rangle$ in S, for $i \in 1..k$ and for each entity $E \in \mathcal{E}$ such that $E \preceq^* E_i$, a non negative integer, $minc(E, R, U_i)$, and a non negative integer or ∞, $maxc(E, R, U_i)$. If not stated otherwise, $minc(E, R, U_i)$ is assumed to be 0 and $maxc(E, R, U_i)$ is assumed to be ∞.*

---

[3]In the following we write $R\langle U_1{:}E_1,\ldots,U_k{:}E_k\rangle$ to denote the relationship R and to specify at the same time that $\langle U_1{:}E_1,\ldots,U_k{:}E_k\rangle$ is the labeled tuple associated to it.

The semantics of an ER-schema can be given by specifying which database states conform to the information structure represented by the schema. Formally, a database state $\mathcal{B}$ is constituted by a nonempty finite set $\Delta^\mathcal{B}$ and a function $\cdot^\mathcal{B}$ that maps

- every entity $E \in \mathcal{E}_\mathcal{S}$ to a subset $E^\mathcal{B}$ of $\Delta^\mathcal{B}$ and
- every relationship $R \in \mathcal{R}$ to a set $R^\mathcal{B}$ of labeled tuples over $\Delta^\mathcal{B}$.

The elements of $E^\mathcal{B}$ and $R^\mathcal{B}$ are called *instances* of E and R respectively.

A database state is considered acceptable if it satisfies all integrity constraints that are part of the schema. This is captured by the definition of legal database state.

Definition 2.2 *A database state $\mathcal{B}$ is said to be* legal *with respect to an ER-schema $\mathcal{S}$, if it satisfies the following conditions:*

- *for each statement $E_1 \preceq E_2 \in \mathcal{S}_{isa}$ it holds that $E_1^\mathcal{B} \subseteq E_2^\mathcal{B}$;*

- *for each relationship $R\langle U_1{:}E_1, \ldots, U_k{:}E_k\rangle$ in $\mathcal{S}$, all instances of R are of the form $\langle U_1{:}\tilde{e}_1, \ldots, U_k{:}\tilde{e}_k\rangle$, where $\tilde{e}_i \in E_i^\mathcal{B}$ for $i \in 1..k$;*

- *for each relationship $R\langle U_1{:}E_1, \ldots, U_k{:}E_k\rangle$ in $\mathcal{S}$, for $i \in 1..k$, for each entity $E \in \mathcal{E}_\mathcal{S}$ such that $E \preceq^* E_i$ and for each instance $\tilde{e}$ of E in $\mathcal{I}$, it holds that*

$$minc(E, R, U_i) \leq \sharp\left\{\tilde{r} \in R^\mathcal{I} \mid \tilde{r}[U_i] = \tilde{e}\right\} \leq$$
$$\leq maxc(E, R, U_i).$$

Notice that the definition of database state reflects the usual assumption in the whole database area that database states are finite structures (see also [CKV90]).

Reasoning in the ER-model includes entity satisfiability and inheritance. Entity satisfiability amounts to checking if a given entity can be populated in some legal database state (see [AP86, LN90]), and corresponds to the notion of concept satisfiability in concept languages. We show that all these forms of reasoning are captured by finite satisfiability and finite implication in $\mathcal{ALUNI}$ knowledge bases. This is done by first defining a mapping Φ from ER-schemas to $\mathcal{ALUNI}$ knowledge bases, and then proving that there is a correspondence between legal database states and finite models of the derived knowledge base.

Definition 2.3 *Let $\mathcal{S}$ be an ER-schema. The $\mathcal{ALUNI}$ knowledge base $\mathcal{K} = \Phi(\mathcal{S})$ is defined as follows:*

- *for each entity $E \in \mathcal{E}_\mathcal{S}$, $\mathcal{K}$ contains an atomic concept $\Phi(E)$;*

- *for each statement $E_1 \preceq E_2 \in \mathcal{S}_{isa}$, $\mathcal{K}$ contains an inclusion assertion $\Phi(E_1) \sqsubseteq \Phi(E_2)$;*

- *for each relationship $R\langle U_1{:}E_1, \ldots, U_k{:}E_k\rangle$ in $\mathcal{S}$, $\mathcal{K}$ contains an atomic concept $\Phi(R)$, k primitive roles $U_{R,1}, \ldots, U_{R,k}$ and the following inclusion assertions:*

$$\Phi(R) \sqsubseteq \forall U_{R,1}.\Phi(E_1) \sqcap \cdots \sqcap \forall U_{R,K}.\Phi(E_k) \sqcap$$
$$(= 1\, U_{R,1}) \sqcap \cdots \sqcap (= 1\, U_{R,k})$$
$$\Phi(E_i) \sqsubseteq \forall U_{R,i}^{-1}.\Phi(R), \quad \text{for } i \in 1..k;$$

- *for each relationship $R\langle U_1{:}E_1, \ldots, U_k{:}E_k\rangle$ in $\mathcal{S}$, for $i \in 1..k$ and for each entity $E \in \mathcal{E}_\mathcal{S}$ such that $E \preceq^* E_i$, if $m = minc(E, R, U_i) \neq 0$, then $\mathcal{K}$ contains the assertion $\Phi(E) \sqsubseteq (\geq m\, U_{R,i}^{-1})$, and if $n = maxc(E, R, U_i) \neq \infty$, then $\mathcal{K}$ contains the assertion $\Phi(E) \sqsubseteq (\leq n\, U_{R,i}^{-1})$;*

- *for each pair of relations R_1 and R_2 in $\mathcal{S}$, $\mathcal{K}$ contains the assertion $\Phi(R_1) \sqsubseteq \neg\Phi(R_2)$, and for each relation R and each entity E it contains the assertion $\Phi(R) \sqsubseteq \neg\Phi(E)$.*

The mapping demonstrates that both inverse roles and number restrictions are necessary in order to capture the semantics of ER-schemata. We observe that binary relations could be treated in a simpler way by mapping them directly to $\mathcal{ALUNI}$-roles. Notice also that the assumption of acyclicity of inclusion assertions is unrealistic when representing ER-schemata. The following theorem ensures that reasoning in the ER-model can be reduced to finite satisfiability and finite implication in $\mathcal{ALUNI}$ knowledge bases.

Theorem 2.4 *An entity $E \in \mathcal{E}_\mathcal{S}$ is satisfiable in an ER-schema $\mathcal{S}$ if and only if $\Phi(\mathcal{S})$ admits a finite model $\mathcal{I}$ in which $E^\mathcal{I} \neq \emptyset$.*

2.3 OBJECT-ORIENTED DATA MODELS

Object-Oriented (OO) data models have been proposed with the goal of devising database formalisms that could be integrated with OO-programming systems (see [Kim90]). They are the subject of an active area of research in the database field, and are based on the following features: (a) in contrast to traditional data models which are value-oriented, they rely on the notion of object identifiers at the extensional level, and on the notion of class at the intensional level; (b) the structure of the classes is specified by means of typing and inheritance.

Figure 3 shows the OO-schema corresponding to a fragment of the KEE knowledge base of Figure 1. The formalization in $\mathcal{ALUNI}$ is given by:

$$
\begin{aligned}
\text{Course} &\sqsubseteq \text{AbstractClass} \sqcap (=1\,\text{VALUE}) \sqcap \\
&\quad \forall \text{VALUE}.(\text{RecType} \sqcap \forall \text{ENROLLS}.\text{SetStud} \sqcap \\
&\quad (=1\,\text{ENROLLS}) \sqcap \\
&\quad \forall \text{TAUGHTBY}.\text{Teacher} \sqcap \\
&\quad (=1\,\text{TAUGHTBY})) \\
\text{SetStud} &\sqsubseteq \text{SetType} \sqcap \forall \text{MEMBER}.\text{Student} \\
\text{Teacher} &\sqsubseteq \text{AbstractClass} \sqcap (\text{Grad} \sqcup \text{Professor}) \\
\text{Grad} &\sqsubseteq \text{AbstractClass} \sqcap \text{Student} \sqcap (=1\,\text{VALUE}) \sqcap \\
&\quad \forall \text{VALUE}.(\text{RecType} \sqcap \forall \text{DEGREE}.\text{String} \sqcap \\
&\quad (=1\,\text{DEGREE})) \\
\text{SetType} &\sqsubseteq \neg \text{AbstractClass} \sqcap \neg \text{RecType} \\
\text{RecType} &\sqsubseteq \neg \text{AbstractClass}
\end{aligned}
$$

The example shows that both classes and type structures of the OO-schema are translated into $\mathcal{ALUNI}$ concepts. We analyze now this correspondence more in detail by providing both the formal definition of the language used for specifying OO-schemata, and the mapping from OO-schemata to $\mathcal{ALUNI}$ knowledge bases. The OO-language is in the style of most popular models featuring complex objects and object identity. In particular, we follow [AK89], although with a slightly different syntax.

An OO-schema $\mathcal{S}$ is constituted by a set of class names, a set of attribute names, and a set of class declarations. Class declarations make use of type expressions over $\mathcal{S}$, which are built according to the following syntax (where C denotes a class name, A_i an attribute name, and T, T_i type expressions):

$$
\begin{aligned}
T, T_1, \ldots, T_k \longrightarrow\ & C\ | \\
& \underline{\text{Union}}\ T_1, \ldots, T_k\ | \\
& \underline{\text{Set-of}}\ T\ | \\
& \underline{\text{Record}}\ A_1{:}T_1; \ldots; A_k{:}T_k\ \underline{\text{End}}
\end{aligned}
$$

The meaning of an OO-schema is given by specifying the characteristics of an instance of the schema. The definition of instance makes use of the notions of object

---

```
Class Course Type-is
    Record
        ENROLLS: Set-of Student;
        TAUGHTBY: Teacher
    End

Class Teacher Type-is
    Union Professor, Grad
End

Class Grad Is-a Student Type-is
    Record
        DEGREE: String
    End
```

Figure 3: An Object-Oriented data schema

---

identifiers and values. Given an OO-schema $\mathcal{S}$ and a finite set $\mathcal{O}$ of *object identifiers* denoting real world objects, the set $\mathcal{V}$ of *values* over $\mathcal{S}$ and $\mathcal{O}$ is inductively defined as follows:

- $\mathcal{O} \subseteq \mathcal{V}$;
- if $v_1, \ldots, v_k \in \mathcal{V}$ then $\{v_1, \ldots, v_k\} \in \mathcal{V}$;
- if $v_1, \ldots, v_k \in \mathcal{V}$ then $[A_1{:}v_1, \ldots, A_k{:}v_k] \in \mathcal{V}$;
- nothing else is in $\mathcal{V}$.

A database instance $\mathcal{I}$ of a schema $\mathcal{S}$ is constituted by a finite set $\mathcal{O}$ of object identifiers, a mapping π that assigns to each class name a subset of $\mathcal{O}$, and a mapping ρ assigning a value in $\mathcal{V}$ to each object in $\mathcal{O}$. The interpretation of type expressions in $\mathcal{I}$ is defined through an *interpretation function* $\cdot^{\mathcal{I}}$ that assigns to each type expression a subset of $\mathcal{V}$ as follows:

$$
\begin{aligned}
C^{\mathcal{I}} &= \pi(C) \\
(\underline{\text{Union}}\ T_1, \ldots, T_k)^{\mathcal{I}} &= T_1^{\mathcal{I}} \cup \cdots \cup T_k^{\mathcal{I}} \\
(\underline{\text{Set-of}}\ T)^{\mathcal{I}} &= \{\{v_1, \ldots, v_k\}\ |\ k \geq 0, \\
& \qquad v_i \in T^{\mathcal{I}}, i \in 1..k\ \} \\
(\underline{\text{Record}}\ A_1{:}T_1;\ \ldots;\ A_k{:}T_k\ \underline{\text{End}})^{\mathcal{I}} &= \\
\{[A_1{:}v_1, \ldots, A_h{:}v_h]\ |\ & h \geq k, v_i \in T_i^{\mathcal{I}}, i \in 1..k, \\
& v_j \in \mathcal{V}, j \in k+1..h\ \}
\end{aligned}
$$

The set of class declarations of an OO-schema is used to specify the structure of the objects in an instance of the database. Each declaration has the form

$$\underline{\text{Class}}\ C\ \underline{\text{Is-a}}\ C_1, \ldots, C_n\ \underline{\text{Type-is}}\ T.$$

The Is-a part of such a declaration allows to specify inclusion between the sets of instances of the involved classes, while the Type-is part specifies the structure allowed for the values assigned to the objects that are instances of the class. This justifies the following definition:

Definition 2.5 *Let $\mathcal{S}$ be an OO-schema. A database instance $\mathcal{I}$ is said to be* legal *with respect to $\mathcal{S}$ if for each declaration*

$$\underline{\text{Class}}\ C\ \underline{\text{Is-a}}\ C_1, \ldots, C_n\ \underline{\text{Type-is}}\ T$$

in $\mathcal{S}$, it holds that $C^{\mathcal{I}} \subseteq C_i^{\mathcal{I}}$ for each $i \in 1..n$, and $\rho(C^{\mathcal{I}}) \subseteq T^{\mathcal{I}}$.

The relationship between $\mathcal{ALUNI}$ and the OO-language presented above is provided by means of a mapping from OO-schemata into $\mathcal{ALUNI}$ knowledge bases. Since the interpretation domain for $\mathcal{ALUNI}$ knowledge bases consists of objects without structures whereas the instances of OO-schemata refer to a structured universe (see the definition of $\mathcal{V}$), we need to explicitly represent some of the notions that underlie the OO-language. In particular, while there is a correspondence between concepts and classes, one must explicitly account for the type structure of each class.

This can be accomplished by introducing the atomic concepts **AbstractClass** to represent the classes in the OO-schema, and **RecType** and **SetType** to represent the corresponding types. The associations between classes and types induced by the class declarations, as well as the basic characteristics of types, are modeled by means of atomic roles: the (functional) role **VALUE** models the association between classes and types, and the role **MEMBER** is used for specifying the type of the elements of a set. Moreover, the concepts representing types are assumed to be mutually disjoint, and disjoint from the concepts representing classes. These constraints are expressed by the following assertions that will be part of the $\mathcal{ALUNI}$ knowledge base $\mathcal{K}$ derived from the schema

$$\texttt{SetType} \sqsubseteq \neg\texttt{AbstractClass} \sqcap \neg\texttt{RecType}$$
$$\texttt{RecType} \sqsubseteq \neg\texttt{AbstractClass}$$

We now define the function Ψ that maps each type expression into an $\mathcal{ALUNI}$ concept expression as follows:

- every class C is mapped into an atomic concept $\Psi(C)$;
- every type expression $\underline{\text{Union}}\ T_1, \ldots, T_k$ is mapped into $\Psi(T_1) \sqcup \cdots \sqcup \Psi(T_k)$;
- every type expression $\underline{\text{Set-of}}\ T$ is mapped into the concept $\texttt{SetType} \sqcap \forall \texttt{MEMBER}.\Psi(T)$;
- every attribute A is mapped into an atomic role $\Psi(A)$, and every type expression $\underline{\text{Record}}\ A_1:T_1;\ldots;A_k:T_k\ \underline{\text{End}}$ is mapped into the concept

$$\texttt{RecType} \sqcap \forall\Psi(A_1).\Psi(T_1) \sqcap (=1\ \Psi(A_1)) \sqcap \cdots \sqcap$$
$$\forall\Psi(A_k).\Psi(T_k) \sqcap (=1\ \Psi(T_k));$$

Definition 2.6 *The $\mathcal{ALUNI}$ knowledge base $\Psi(\mathcal{S})$ corresponding to an OO-schema $\mathcal{S}$ is constituted by*

- *the inclusion assertions that express mutual disjointness of* **AbstractClass**, **RecType**, *and* **SetType**;
- *an inclusion assertion*

$$\Psi(C) \sqsubseteq \texttt{AbstractClass} \sqcap$$
$$\Psi(C_1) \sqcap \cdots \sqcap \Psi(C_n) \sqcap$$
$$\forall\texttt{VALUE}.\Psi(T) \sqcap (=1\ \texttt{VALUE})$$

for each class declaration

$$\underline{\text{Class}}\ C\ \underline{\text{Is-a}}\ C_1, \ldots, C_n\ \underline{\text{Type-is}}\ T$$

in $\mathcal{S}$.

From the above correspondence, we can observe that inverse roles are not necessary for the formalization of OO-data models. Indeed, the possibility of referring to the inverse of an attribute is generally ruled out in such models. However, recent papers (see for example [AGO91]) point out that this strongly limits the expressive power of the data model. Note also that the use of number restrictions is limited to the value 1, which corresponds to existence constraints and functionality, whereas union is used in a more general form than in the KEE system.

The effectiveness of the mapping Ψ is sanctioned by the following theorem.

Theorem 2.7 *For every OO-schema $\mathcal{S}$, there exist two correspondences α, β between instances of a schema $\mathcal{S}$ and interpretations of its translation $\Psi(\mathcal{S})$ such that, for each legal instance $\mathcal{I}$ of $\mathcal{S}$, $\alpha(\mathcal{I})$ is a model of $\Psi(\mathcal{S})$, and, on the converse, for each model $\mathcal{M}$ of $\Psi(\mathcal{S})$, $\beta(\mathcal{M})$ is a legal instance of $\mathcal{S}$.*

The basic reasoning services considered in OO-databases are subtyping (check whether a type denotes a subset of another type in every legal instance) and type checking (check whether an instance is legal). Based on theorem 2.7, it is possible to show that these forms of reasoning are fully captured by finite satisfiability and implication in $\mathcal{ALUNI}$ knowledge bases.

2.4 DISCUSSION

The above subsections should clarify that the language $\mathcal{ALUNI}$ and the associated reasoning capabilities represent the essential core of the class-based representation formalisms belonging to all three families mentioned above. On the other hand, we have shown that the formalism proposed in this paper provides important features that are currently missing in each family, although their relevance has often been stressed. In this sense, the work reported here not only provides a common powerful representation formalism, but may also contribute to significant developments for the languages belonging to all the three families. For this purpose it is essential to develop adequate techniques for reasoning in all of the above contexts. This implies that we have to deal with both unrestricted and finite satisfiability and implication. In the following two sections we present the reasoning methods for the two cases. Due to space limitations, in this paper we concentrate on satisfiability only; a direct extension of the methods provides decision procedures for logical implication too.

3 REASONING IN UNRESTRICTED MODELS

In order to show that the problem of checking unrestricted satisfiability of an $\mathcal{ALUNI}$ knowledge base is decidable, we make use of a correspondence between $\mathcal{ALUNI}$ and a sublanguage of deterministic converse propositional dynamic logic ($\mathcal{CPDL}$). Although this correspondence is similar to the one established in

[Sch91], due to the presence of number restrictions, we cannot directly make use of the known results.

The basic idea of our method is to show that standard reasoning techniques for $\mathcal{CPDL}$ can still be exploited if we perform a preliminary transformation of the knowledge base that allows us to weaken the constraints imposed by number restrictions. We call the knowledge base $\mathcal{K}_{rel}$ resulting from the application of the transformation to a knowledge base $\mathcal{K}$, the *relaxation of* $\mathcal{K}$, defined as follows:

- all number restrictions $(\geq m\,R)$, with $m \neq 1$, and $(\leq n\,R)$ in $\mathcal{K}$ are treated as new symbols for atomic concepts in $\mathcal{K}_{rel}$;
- for each pair of number restrictions $(\geq m\,R)$ and $(\leq n\,R)$ present in $\mathcal{K}$, such that $m > n$, the assertion $(\geq m\,R) \sqsubseteq \neg(\leq n\,R)$ is added to $\mathcal{K}_{rel}$.
- for each number restriction $(\geq m\,R)$, with $m \neq 1$, present in $\mathcal{K}$, the assertion $(\geq m\,R) \sqsubseteq (\geq 1\,R)$ is added to $\mathcal{K}_{rel}$.

The following lemma gives a necessary condition for the satisfiability of an $\mathcal{ALUNI}$ knowledge base.

Lemma 3.1 *If an $\mathcal{ALUNI}$ knowledge base is satisfiable, then its relaxation is also satisfiable.*

In the rest of the section we show that the converse of lemma 3.1 also holds. This is done by exploiting the model preserving transformation of $\mathcal{K}_{rel}$ into a formula ϕ_{rel} of $\mathcal{CPDL}$. Notice that since in $\mathcal{K}_{rel}$ all number restrictions are treated as atomic concepts, the transformation is defined in the same way as in [Sch91]. The resulting formula belongs to a sublanguage of $\mathcal{CPDL}$ which we call $\mathcal{CPDL}^-$. In $\mathcal{CPDL}^-$, programs, denoted with p, q, and formulae, denoted with ϕ, ψ, are built from atomic programs P and atomic formulae A by the following syntax rules:

$$p, q \longrightarrow P \mid P^- \mid p^* \mid p \cup q \mid p; q$$
$$\phi, \psi \longrightarrow \top \mid A \mid \neg A \mid \phi \vee \psi \mid \phi \wedge \psi \mid$$
$$\langle P \rangle \top \mid \langle P^- \rangle \top \mid [p]\phi.$$

We will use the term *basic program* to denote an atomic program or the inverse of an atomic program. The semantics of $\mathcal{CPDL}^-$ is derived from the semantics of $\mathcal{CPDL}$ in a straightforward way (see for example [KT90]).

For an example of a transformation of a knowledge base into a $\mathcal{CPDL}^-$ formula, see Figure 4, showing a knowledge base $\mathcal{K}$, describing the properties of trees in which each node has at least two outgoing edges, the relaxation $\mathcal{K}_{rel}$, and the $\mathcal{CPDL}^-$ formula corresponding to $\mathcal{K}_{rel}$. Note that $(\geq 1\,\text{ARC})$ is transformed into $\langle \text{ARC} \rangle \top$.

In the following, let ϕ_{rel} be the $\mathcal{CPDL}^-$ formula obtained from the relaxation $\mathcal{K}_{rel}$ of $\mathcal{K}$ and let $\mathcal{M}$

$\mathcal{K}$:

Root $\sqsubseteq$ $\forall \text{ARC}^{-1}.\bot \sqcap \forall \text{ARC}.\text{Node} \sqcap (\geq 2\,\text{ARC}) \sqcap \neg \text{Node}$

Node $\sqsubseteq$ $\forall \text{ARC}^{-1}.(\text{Root} \sqcup \text{Node}) \sqcap \forall \text{ARC}.\text{Node} \sqcap$
$(\geq 2\,\text{ARC}) \sqcap (\leq 1\,\text{ARC}^{-1})$

$\mathcal{K}_{rel}$:

Root $\sqsubseteq$ $\forall \text{ARC}^{-1}.\bot \sqcap \forall \text{ARC}.\text{Node} \sqcap (\geq 2\,\text{ARC}) \sqcap$
$\neg \text{Node}$

Node $\sqsubseteq$ $\forall \text{ARC}^{-1}.(\text{Root} \sqcup \text{Node}) \sqcap \forall \text{ARC}.\text{Node} \sqcap$
$(\geq 2\,\text{ARC}) \sqcap (\leq 1\,\text{ARC}^{-1})$

$(\geq 2\,\text{ARC})$ $\sqsubseteq$ $(\geq 1\,\text{ARC})$

$\phi_{rel} = [(\text{ARC} \cup \text{ARC}^-)^*]$
$((\neg \text{Root} \vee ([\text{ARC}^-]\bot \wedge [\text{ARC}]\text{Node} \wedge$
$A_{(\geq 2\,\text{ARC})} \wedge \neg \text{Node})) \wedge$
$(\neg \text{Node} \vee ([\text{ARC}^-](\text{Root} \vee \text{Node}) \wedge [\text{ARC}]\text{Node} \wedge$
$A_{(\geq 2\,\text{ARC})} \wedge A_{(\leq 1\,\text{ARC}^-)})) \wedge$
$(\neg A_{(\geq 2\,\text{ARC})} \vee \langle \text{ARC} \rangle \top))$

Figure 4: An $\mathcal{ALUNI}$ knowledge base, its relaxation, and the corresponding $\mathcal{CPDL}^-$ formula

be a model of ϕ_{rel}. ϕ_{rel} will contain atomic formulae $A_{(\geq m\,R)}$ and $A_{(\leq n\,R)}$ for each number restriction $(\geq m\,R)$ and $(\leq n\,R)$ present in $\mathcal{K}$. We say that a state s of $\mathcal{M}$ *numerically satisfies* $A_{(\geq m\,R)}$ if $\sharp\{t \mid (s,t) \in R^{\mathcal{M}}\} \geq m$. Similarly, s numerically satisfies $A_{(\leq n\,R)}$, if $\sharp\{t \mid (s,t) \in R^{\mathcal{M}}\} \leq n$. According to these definitions, any model $\mathcal{M}$ of ϕ_{rel} is also a model of $\mathcal{K}$ if all states of $\mathcal{M}$ numerically satisfy all atomic formulae corresponding to number restrictions. We show that if ϕ_{rel} is satisfiable then we can construct a model in which this is indeed the case.

[Str82] shows that the *tree model property* holds for $\mathcal{CPDL}$ (see [Str82] for a formal definition of *tree model*). This result carries over immediately to $\mathcal{CPDL}^-$, and therefore every satisfiable $\mathcal{CPDL}^-$ formula admits a model which is a tree, if we view each state as a node and each transition between states as an arc labeled with the corresponding program. However, we can show that for $\mathcal{CPDL}^-$ an even stronger result holds, which is based on the following definition.

Definition 3.2 *A deterministic direct-inverse interpretation is an interpretation $\mathcal{I} = (\Delta^{\mathcal{I}}, \cdot^{\mathcal{I}})$ such that for each state $s \in \Delta^{\mathcal{I}}$ and for each atomic program P, there is at most one state $t \in \Delta^{\mathcal{I}}$ such that $(s,t) \in P^{\mathcal{I}}$ and at most one state $r \in \Delta^{\mathcal{I}}$ such that $(r,s) \in P^{\mathcal{I}}$.*

Lemma 3.3 *Every satisfiable $\mathcal{CPDL}^-$ formula ϕ admits a deterministic direct-inverse tree model.*

Proof (sketch). Since ϕ is satisfiable, by the tree model property it admits a tree model $\mathcal{T}$. Starting from $\mathcal{T}$ we can construct a deterministic direct-inverse tree model $\mathcal{D}$, proceeding by induction on the depth of $\mathcal{T}$ and removing for each state all but one of the arcs incident to that state and labeled with the same basic program. Since the only diamond subformulae of ϕ are of the type $\langle R \rangle \top$, where R is a basic program, we can prove by induction on the structure of ϕ that the root of $\mathcal{D}$ satisfies ϕ. $\square$

Notice that in any deterministic direct-inverse tree model $\mathcal{D}$ all atomic formulae $A_{(\leq n\, R)}$ are already numerically satisfied in all states of $\mathcal{D}$ and no formula $A_{(\geq m\, R)}$ with $m > 1$ is numerically satisfied in any state of $\mathcal{D}$. The following lemma guarantees that we can transform any such model in one in which all atomic formulae are numerically satisfied in all states.

Lemma 3.4 *Let $\mathcal{D}$ be a deterministic direct-inverse tree model of the $\mathcal{CPDL}^-$ formula ϕ_{rel}. Then $\mathcal{D}$ can be transformed into a tree model $\mathcal{T}$ such that all atomic formulae in ϕ_{rel} that correspond to number restrictions are numerically satisfied in all states of $\mathcal{T}$.*

Proof (sketch). We can construct $\mathcal{T}$ in the following way: Initially we set $\mathcal{T}$ equal to $\mathcal{D}$ and then we prooced by induction on the depth of the tree we are constructing. For each state s of $\mathcal{T}$ that we are considering and for each basic program R appearing in ϕ, we consider the atomic formula $A_{(\geq m\, R)}$ with maximum m that is satisfied in s but is not numerically satisfied. The assertions added to $\mathcal{K}_{rel}$ ensure that there is at least one state t connected to s through R. We can take the whole tree structure starting in t and connected to s through R, duplicate it $m-1$ times and connect these $m-1$ trees to s via R. In this way we ensure that $A_{(\geq m\, R)}$ is numerically satisfied in s. Furthermore the assertions added to $\mathcal{K}_{rel}$ guarantee that by proceeding in this way all atomic formulae $A_{(\leq n\, R)}$ are still numerically satisfied in s. $\square$

By combining the results of the previous lemmas we can conclude that the relaxation of a knowledge base in fact captures all relevant properties of the knowledge base itself. This is stated in the following theorem.

Theorem 3.5 *An $\mathcal{ALUNI}$ knowledge base $\mathcal{K}$ is satisfiable if and only if its relaxation $\mathcal{K}_{rel}$ is satisfiable.*

In [VW84] it has been shown that deciding if a $\mathcal{CPDL}$ formula is satisfiable can be done in deterministic exponential time, which also gives the upper bound for satisfiability in $\mathcal{CPDL}^-$. We have seen that $\mathcal{K}_{rel}$ can be transformed in a straightforward way into a formula ϕ_{rel} of $\mathcal{CPDL}^-$ whose size is polynomial in the size of $\mathcal{K}_{rel}$ and which is satisfiable if and only if it is $\mathcal{K}_{rel}$. Therefore we get immediately the following corollary of the previous theorem.

Corollary 3.6 *Unrestricted satisfiability and implication for an $\mathcal{ALUNI}$ knowledge base can be decided in deterministic exponential time.*

4 REASONING IN FINITE MODELS

In this section we sketch a method for verifying finite satisfiability of an $\mathcal{ALUNI}$ knowledge base $\mathcal{K}$. This task requires a quite different approach form the one used for the unrestricted case, since the actual numbers that appear in the number restrictions of $\mathcal{K}$ play a crucial role in the existence of finite models. For this reason we model number restrictions by means of an associated system $\Psi_\mathcal{K}$ of linear disequations, defined in such a way that the existence of a finite model for $\mathcal{K}$ is reflected into the existence of particular solutions of $\Psi_\mathcal{K}$.

The unknowns introduced in $\Psi_\mathcal{K}$ are intended to represent the number of instances of each concept and each role in a possible finite model of $\mathcal{K}$, while the disequations take into account the constraints on the number of instances deriving from number restrictions in $\mathcal{K}$. Because of atomic concepts that may have instances in common, it is not possible to adopt the most natural approach which would be to use one unknown for each atomic concept and role (see [LN90]). We will overcome this problem by introducing the notion of expansion of a knowledge base.

In the sequel we will use the term *literal* for an atomic or negated atomic concept. A concept will be called *simple* if it is of the form: $L \mid L_1 \sqcup L_2 \mid \forall R.L \mid (\geq m\, R) \mid (\leq n\, R)$, where L, L_1 and L_2 are literals. A knowledge base whose inclusion assertions have a simple concept on the right hand side is said to be *simple*. Since a generic knowledge base $\mathcal{K}$ can be transformed in linear time into a simple knowledge base $\mathcal{K}'$ that is finitely satisfiable if and only if it is $\mathcal{K}$ we can restrict our attention to simple knowledge bases.

Therefore in each assertion of a knowledge base $\mathcal{K}$ at most one operator appears on the right hand side. We will denote with $\mathcal{K}_X$, where $X \in \{\sqcup, \forall, \geq, \leq\}$, the subset of assertions involving operator X, and with $\mathcal{K}_{isa}$ those involving only literals.

Let $\mathcal{C}$ be the set of all atomic concepts present in $\mathcal{K}$, together with the symbol $\top$. A *compound concept* is defined as a subset of $\mathcal{C}$ containing $\top$. Intuitively a compound concept $\bar{C}$ represents exactly those elements of the domain that are instances of all atomic concepts in $\bar{C}$ and are not instances of all atomic concepts not in $\bar{C}$. More formally, the extension $\bar{C}^\mathcal{I}$ of $\bar{C}$ is defined as:

$$\bar{C}^\mathcal{I} = \bigcap \{A^\mathcal{I} \mid A \in \bar{C}\} \setminus \bigcup \{A^\mathcal{I} \mid A \in \mathcal{C} \setminus \bar{C}\}$$

Let $\mathcal{R}$ be the set of all atomic roles present in $\mathcal{K}$. We represent explicitly for each such role the association with all possible pairs of compound concepts. This can be accomplished by defining a *compound role* as an indexed pair $\langle \bar{C}_1, \bar{C}_2 \rangle_P$, where $\bar{C}_1$ and $\bar{C}_2$ are compound concepts and P is an atomic role appearing in $\mathcal{K}$. It is interpreted as the restriction of $P^\mathcal{I}$ to pairs whose first and second element belong to $\bar{C}_1^\mathcal{I}$ and $\bar{C}_2^\mathcal{I}$ respectively.

Notice that the way we interpret compound concepts and roles forces them to be disjoint in all interpretations. This property is crucial in order to construct a model from a solution of the system of disequations. The price we have to pay for it is the exponential number of different compound concepts and roles. We are now ready to give the following definition.

Definition 4.1 *The expansion $\bar{\mathcal{K}}$ of an $\mathcal{ALUNI}$ knowledge base $\mathcal{K}$ is constituted by*

- *the set $\bar{\mathcal{C}}$ of all compound concepts of $\mathcal{K}$ and the set $\bar{\mathcal{R}}$ of all compound roles of $\mathcal{K}$;*

- *all assertions of $\mathcal{K}_{isa} \cup \mathcal{K}_\sqcup \cup \mathcal{K}_\forall$;*

- *a set $\mathcal{K}_{num}$ of assertions involving a compound concept on the left hand side and a number restriction on the right hand side, obtained in the following way: for each compound concept $\bar{C}$ and for each role R:*
  - if for some $A \in \bar{C}$ and some positive integer m, $A \sqsubseteq (\geq m\, R)$ is in $\mathcal{K}_\geq$, then $\bar{C} \sqsubseteq (\geq m_{max}\, R)$ is in $\mathcal{K}_{num}$, where
  $m_{max} = \max\{m \mid A \sqsubseteq (\geq m\, R) \in \mathcal{K}_\geq \wedge A \in \bar{C}\}$
  - if for some $A \in \bar{C}$ and some positive integer n, $A \sqsubseteq (\leq n\, R)$ is in $\mathcal{K}_\leq$, then $\bar{C} \sqsubseteq (\leq n_{min}\, R)$ is in $\mathcal{K}_{num}$, where
  $n_{min} = \min\{n \mid A \sqsubseteq (\leq n\, R) \in \mathcal{K}_\leq \wedge A \in \bar{C}\}$.

From the expansion $\bar{\mathcal{K}}$ we can derive a system $\Psi_\mathcal{K}$ of linear disequations, with one unknown $\text{Var}(\bar{C})$ for each compound concept $\bar{C}$, and one unknown $\text{Var}(\bar{R})$ for each compound role $\bar{R}$. The disequations of $\Psi_\mathcal{K}$ are obtained in the following way:

- It is possible to check in polynomial time, with respect to the size of the expansion, whether a compound concept $\bar{C}$ is consistent with $\mathcal{K}_{isa} \cup \mathcal{K}_\sqcup$, i.e. whether there is a model $\mathcal{I}$ of $\mathcal{K}_{isa} \cup \mathcal{K}_\sqcup$ such that $\bar{C}^\mathcal{I}$ is nonempty. In a similar way we can check whether a compound role is consistent with $\mathcal{K}_\forall$. We force to be equal to 0 all those unknowns corresponding to compound concepts and roles that are not consistent respectively with $\mathcal{K}_{isa} \cup \mathcal{K}_\sqcup$ and with $\mathcal{K}_\forall$, and force to be nonnegative all the others.

- We introduce disequations that reflect the number restrictions by relating the unknown corresponding to a compound concept $\bar{C}$ to the sum of the unknowns corresponding to compound roles in which $\bar{C}$ appears. As an example, if $\bar{C} \sqsubseteq (\geq m\, P) \in \mathcal{K}_{num}$, where P is an atomic role, we introduce $m \cdot \text{Var}(\bar{C}) \leq \sum_{\bar{C}_2 \in \bar{\mathcal{C}}} \text{Var}(\langle \bar{C}, \bar{C}_2 \rangle_P)$.

Figure 5 shows the expansion of the simple knowledge base derived from the one of Figure 4 and the corresponding system of disequations. Each unknown is

---

$\bar{\mathcal{C}} = \{\text{R}, \text{N}, \text{O}, \text{RN}, \text{RO}, \text{NO}, \text{RNO}\}$, where
$\quad \text{R} = \{\text{Root}\}, \quad \text{N} = \{\text{Node}\}, \quad \text{O} = \{\text{RootOrNode}\},$
$\quad \text{RN} = \{\text{Root}, \text{Node}\}, \quad \text{RO} = \{\text{Root}, \text{RootOrNode}\},$
$\quad \text{NO} = \{\text{Node}, \text{RootOrNode}\},$
$\quad \text{RNO} = \{\text{Root}, \text{Node}, \text{RootOrNode}\};$
Subset of $\bar{\mathcal{C}}$ consistent with $\mathcal{K}_{isa} \cup \mathcal{K}_\sqcup$: $\{\text{R}, \text{N}, \text{RO}, \text{NO}\}$.

$\bar{\mathcal{R}} = \{\langle \bar{C}, \bar{C}'\rangle_{\text{ARC}} \mid \bar{C}, \bar{C}' \in \bar{\mathcal{C}}\};$
Consistent compound roles:
$\quad \{\langle \text{RO}, \text{N}\rangle_{\text{ARC}}, \langle \text{RO}, \text{NO}\rangle_{\text{ARC}}, \langle \text{NO}, \text{N}\rangle_{\text{ARC}}, \langle \text{NO}, \text{NO}\rangle_{\text{ARC}}\};$

	$\mathcal{K}_{num}$	$\Psi_\mathcal{K}$
R $\sqsubseteq$	$(\geq 2\, \text{ARC})$	$2r \leq 0$
RO $\sqsubseteq$	$(\geq 2\, \text{ARC})$	$2ro \leq arc_{ro,n} + arc_{ro,no}$
N $\sqsubseteq$	$(\geq 2\, \text{ARC})$	$2n \leq 0$
NO $\sqsubseteq$	$(\geq 2\, \text{ARC})$	$2no \leq arc_{ro,n} + arc_{ro,no}$
N $\sqsubseteq$	$(\leq 1\, \text{ARC}^{-1})$	$n \geq arc_{ro,n} + arc_{no,n}$
NO $\sqsubseteq$	$(\leq 1\, \text{ARC}^{-1})$	$no \geq arc_{ro,no} + arc_{no,no}$

Figure 5: The expansion of the knowledge base shown in Figure 4

given the name of the corresponding compound concept or role, but in lower case (for brevity we have not included unknowns corresponding to inconsistent compound concepts and roles). The concept RootOrNode derives from the transformation into a simple knowledge base.

The system of disequations we obtain from the expansion of the knowledge base is linear and homogeneous and admits only nonnegative solutions. The following theorem relates the existence of particular solutions of this system to the existence of finite models for the knowledge base from which the disequations are derived.

We call a solution of $\Psi_\mathcal{K}$ *acceptable* if it assigns a positive value to at least one unknown, and for all compound roles $\bar{R} = \langle \bar{C}_1, \bar{C}_2 \rangle_P$, the value assigned to $\text{Var}(\bar{R})$ is 0 whenever the value assigned to either $\bar{C}_1$ or $\bar{C}_2$ is 0.

Theorem 4.2 *$\mathcal{K}$ is finitely satisfiable if and only if $\Psi_\mathcal{K}$ admits an acceptable integer solution.*

Proof (sketch). Given an acceptable integer solution $\mathcal{X}$ of $\Psi_\mathcal{K}$, it is possible to construct a model of $\mathcal{K}$ such that the number of instances of each compound concept and role is exactly the value assigned by $\mathcal{X}$ to the corresponding unknown. Since $\mathcal{X}$ is nontrivial, the model constructed will be nonempty. Conversely, given a finite model $\mathcal{M}$ of $\mathcal{K}$ it is possible to show that we obtain a solution of $\mathcal{X}$ by assigning to each unknown the number of instances in $\mathcal{M}$ of the corresponding compound concept or role. These can be directly deduced from the interpretations of all concepts and roles. $\square$

In order to make use of this result and show that we

can reason with respect to finite models in $\mathcal{ALUNI}$ knowledge bases, we have to guarantee that verifying the existence of acceptable integer solutions for a system of disequations is decidable. This is indeed the case and, by using linear programming techniques it can be proved that it takes polynomial time in the size of the system. Therefore we can state the following theorem.

Theorem 4.3 *Finite satisfiability and implication for an $\mathcal{ALUNI}$ knowledge base can be decided in deterministic exponential time.*

Proof (sketch). The decidability follows immediately from theorem 4.2 and the previous observation. The exponential upper bound derives from the exponential size of the system of disequations and the polinomial time required for the search of an acceptable solution of the system. □

5 CONCLUSIONS

We have presented a unified framework for representing information about class structures and reasoning about them. We have pursued this goal by looking at various class-based formalisms proposed in different fields of computer science and trying to rephrase them in the framework of concept languages. The resulting language includes a combination of constructs that was not addressed before, although all of the constructs had previously been considered separately.

The major achievement of the paper is the demonstration that class-based formalisms can be given a precise characterization by means of a powerful first-order language where the basic reasoning problems remain decidable, in particular EXPTIME. This has several consequences.

First of all, any of the formalisms considered in the paper can be enriched with constructs originating from other formalisms and treated in the general framework. For example, the usage of inverse roles in concept languages greatly enhances the expressivity of roles, while the combination of ISA, number restrictions and union enriches the reasoning capabilities available in semantic data models.

Secondly, the comparison of class-based formalisms emphasizes the importance of distinguishing between unrestricted reasoning and reasoning in finite models. Although this aspect has seldom been considered in the case of knowledge representation formalisms, the assumption of finiteness seems to be appropriate in most applications, and must be addressed when the representation formalism becomes sufficiently powerful. We have developed a novel technique for finite model reasoning. Although we did not address the problems related to the practical behavior of the method, we point out that, on one hand the constraints imposed on the domain to be modeled make the worst case complexity rarely occur in practice, and on the other hand we can effectively exploit the technology of linear programming for the implementation of real systems.

Finally, it is worth mentioning that the results presented in this paper can be extended to deal both with more general inclusion assertions, and with the extensional level of the knowledge base, where assertions about the instance-of relation between individual objects and classes are specified.

Acknowledgements

This work was partly funded by the ESPRIT BRA Compulog II, and the Italian CNR under Progetto Finalizzato Sistemi Informatici e Calcolo Parallelo, LDR Ibridi.

References

[AGO91] A. Albano, G. Ghelli, and R. Orsini. A relationship mechanism for strongly typed Object-Oriented database programming languages. In *Proc. of the 17th Int. Conf. on Very Large Data Bases VLDB-91*, pages 565–575, Barcelona, 1991.

[AK89] S. Abiteboul and P. Kanellakis. Object identity as a query language primitive. In *Proc. of the ACM SIGMOD Int. Conf. on Management of Data*, pages 159–173, 1989.

[AP86] P. Atzeni and D.S. Parker Jr. Formal properties of net-based knowledge representation schemes. In *Proc. of the 2nd IEEE Int. Conf. on Data Engineering*, pages 700–706, Los Angeles, 1986.

[BHR90] K.H. Bläsius, U. Hedstück, and C.-R. Rollinger, editors. *Sorts and Types in Artificial Intelligence*. Number 418 in Lecture Notes in Artificial Intelligence. Springer-Verlag, 1990.

[Bor92] A. Borgida. From type systems to knowledge representation: Natural semantics specifications for description logics. *Journal of Intelligent and Cooperative Inf. Syst.*, 1(1):93–126, 1992.

[BS92] S. Bergamaschi and C. Sartori. On taxonomic reasoning in conceptual design. *ACM Trans. on Database Syst.*, 17(3):385–422, 1992.

[Che76] P.P. Chen. The Entity-Relationship model: Toward a unified view of data. *ACM Trans. on Database Syst.*, 1(1):9–36, March 1976.

[CHS91] C. Collet, M.N. Huhns, and W. Shen. Resource integration using a large knowledge base in Carnot. *IEEE Computer*, 24(12), 1991.

[CKV90] S.S. Cosmadakis, P.C. Kanellakis, and M. Vardi. Polynomial-time implication problems for unary inclusion dependencies. *Journal of the ACM*, 37(1):15–46, January 1990.

[CL93] T. Catarci and M. Lenzerini. Representing and using interschema knowledge in cooperative information systems. *Journal of Intelligent and Cooperative Inf. Syst.*, 1993. To appear.

[CL94] D. Calvanese and M. Lenzerini. On the interaction between ISA and cardinality constraints. In *Proc. of the 10th IEEE Int. Conf. on Data Engineering*, Houston, 1994. To appear.

[DLNN91] F. M. Donini, M. Lenzerini, D. Nardi, and W. Nutt. Tractable concept languages. In *Proc. of the 12th Int. Joint Conf. on Artificial Intelligence IJCAI-91*, pages 458–463, Sydney, 1991.

[FK85] R. Fikes and T. Kehler. The role of frame-based representation in reasoning. *Communications of the ACM*, 28(9):904–920, 1985.

[HK87] R.B. Hull and R. King. Semantic database modelling: Survey, applications and research issues. *ACM Computing Surveys*, 19(3):201–260, September 1987.

[Kim90] W. Kim. *Introduction to Object-Oriented Databases*. The MIT Press, 1990.

[KL89] W. Kim and F. H. Lochovsky, editors. *Object-Oriented Concepts, Databases, and Applications*. ACM Press and Addison Wesley, New York, 1989.

[KT90] D. Kozen and J. Tiuryn. Logics of programs. In J. Van Leeuwen, editor, *Handbook of Theoretical Computer Science – Formal Models and Semantics*, pages 789–840. Elsevier Science Publishers (North-Holland), Amsterdam, 1990.

[Leh92] F. Lehmann, editor. *Semantic Networks in Artificial Intelligence*. Pergamon Press, Oxford, 1992.

[LN90] M. Lenzerini and P. Nobili. On the satisfiability of dependency constraints in entity-relationship schemata. *Information Systems*, 15(4):453–461, 1990.

[LNS91] M. Lenzerini, D. Nardi, and M. Simi, editors. *Inheritance Hierarchies in Knowledge Representation and Programming Languages*. John Wiley & Sons, Chichester, 1991.

[MM92] R. Motschnig-Pitrik and J. Mylopoulous. Classes and instances. *Journal of Intelligent and Cooperative Inf. Syst.*, 1(1), 1992.

[Neb91] B. Nebel. Terminological cycles: Semantics and computational properties. In John F. Sowa, editor, *Principles of Semantic Networks*, pages 331–361. Morgan Kaufmann, Los Altos, 1991.

[PSS92] B. Piza, K. D. Schewe, and J. W. Schmidt. Term subsumption with type constructors. In Y. Yesha, editor, *Proc. of the Int. Conf. on Information and Knowledge Management CIKM-92*, pages 449–456, Baltimore, 1992.

[Sch91] K. Schild. A correspondence theory for terminological logics: Preliminary report. In *Proc. of the 12th Int. Joint Conf. on Artificial Intelligence IJCAI-91*, pages 466–471, Sydney, 1991.

[Sow91] J. F. Sowa, editor. *Principles of Semantic Networks*. Morgan Kaufmann, Los Altos, 1991.

[Str82] R.S. Street. Propositional dynamic logic of looping and converse is elementarily decidable. *Information and Control*, 54:121–141, 1982.

[VW84] M. Vardi and P. Wolper. Automata-theoretic techniques for modal logics of programs. In *Proc. of the 16th ACM SIGACT Symp. on Theory of Computing STOC-84*, pages 446–455, 1984.

[WS92] W. A. Woods and J. G. Schmolze. The KL-ONE family. In F.W. Lehmann, editor, *Semantic Networks in Artificial Intelligence*, pages 133–178. Pergamon Press, 1992. Published as a special issue of *Computers & Mathematics with Applications*, Volume 23, Number 2–9.

Learning the CLASSIC Description Logic: Theoretical and Experimental Results

William W. Cohen
AI Principles Research Department
AT&T Bell Laboratories
Murray Hill, NJ 07974
wcohen@research.att.com

Haym Hirsh[*]
AI Principles Research Department
AT&T Bell Laboratories
Murray Hill, NJ 07974
hirsh@research.att.com

Abstract

We present a series of theoretical and experimental results on the learnability of description logics. We first extend previous formal learnability results on simple description logics to C-CLASSIC, a description logic expressive enough to be practically useful. We then experimentally evaluate two extensions of a learning algorithm suggested by the formal analysis. The first extension learns C-CLASSIC descriptions from individuals. (The formal results assume that examples are themselves descriptions.) The second extension learns disjunctions of C-CLASSIC descriptions from individuals. The experiments, which were conducted using several hundred target concepts from a number of domains, indicate that both extensions reliably learn complex natural concepts.

1 INTRODUCTION

One well-known family of formalisms for representing knowledge are *description logics*, sometimes also called *terminological logics* or *KL-ONE-type languages*. Description logics have been applied in a number of contexts [Beck *et al.*, 1989; Devanbu *et al.*, 1991; Mays *et al.*, 1987; Wright *et al.*, 1993]; additionally, the complexity of deductive reasoning using description logics is fairly well understood.

Recently we have begun to analyze the complexity of using description logics to support *inductive* reasoning—*i.e.*, learning. Our analysis has focused on determining which description logics are learnable in Valiant's [1984] model of *pac-learnability* [Cohen and Hirsh, 1992b], and with understanding the complexity of the operations necessary to support learning [Cohen *et al.*, 1992].

In this paper, we build on these formal results in several ways. We extend the previous formal results to the description logic C-CLASSIC, which is expressive enough to be practically useful. We also present two extensions of an algorithm suggested by the formal results: the first extension learns descriptions from individuals, and the second learns disjunctions of descriptions from individuals. Finally, we experimentally evaluate these two extensions. Experiments conducted using several hundred naturally occurring concepts from a number of domains support the claim that both extensions can reliably learn complex, naturally-occurring concepts.

2 BACKGROUND

2.1 DESCRIPTION LOGICS

CLASSIC is a knowledge representation system based on a *description logic* (henceforth DL). Some recent surveys of work in description logics can be found in [MacGregor, 1991; Woods and Schmolze, 1992]; however to keep this paper self-contained we will give a brief review below.

Description logics are a family of formalisms for representing knowledge. DLs trace their ancestry back to semantic nets and frame-based languages, but place a stronger emphasis on clear formal semantics and provably tractable inference.

DLs are used to reason about sets of atomic elements called *individuals*; in particular, DLs are used to construct *descriptions* of sets of individuals and then to reason about these descriptions. Descriptions are typically defined compositionally using description *constructors* and building blocks known as *primitives* and *roles*. A *primitive* denotes a specific set of individuals. A *role* denotes a specific binary relation between individuals. Constructors are typically operators like AND or SOME, which we will write in a prefix notation.

Descriptions are built up by specifying constraints on properties an individual must have. As an example, in

---
[*]Also at Computer Science Department, Rutgers University, New Brunswick, NJ 08903.

Table 1: Description Logic Constructors

Constructor	Semantics
AND	$\mathcal{I}((\text{AND } D_1 \ldots D_n)) = \cap_{i=1}^{n} \mathcal{I}(D_i)$
ALL	$\mathcal{I}((\text{ALL } r \text{ D})) = \{x \in \Delta : \forall y \ \langle x,y \rangle \in \mathcal{I}(r) \Rightarrow y \in \mathcal{I}(D)\}$
SOME	$\mathcal{I}((\text{SOME } r)) = \{x \in \Delta : \exists y \ \langle x,y \rangle \in \mathcal{I}(r)\}$
SOMEC	$\mathcal{I}((\text{SOMEC } r \text{ D})) = \{x \in \Delta : \exists y \ \langle x,y \rangle \in \mathcal{I}(r) \wedge y \in \mathcal{I}(D)\}$
AT-LEAST	$\mathcal{I}((\text{AT-LEAST } n \text{ r})) = \{x \in \Delta : |\{y : \langle x,y \rangle \in \mathcal{I}(r)\}| \geq n\}$
AT-MOST	$\mathcal{I}((\text{AT-MOST } n \text{ r})) = \{x \in \Delta : |\{y : \langle x,y \rangle \in \mathcal{I}(r)\}| \leq n\}$
MIN	$\mathcal{I}((\text{MIN } u)) = \{x \in \Delta : x \text{ is a real number and } x \geq u\}$
MAX	$\mathcal{I}((\text{MAX } u)) = \{x \in \Delta : x \text{ is a real number and } x \leq u\}$
ONE-OF	$\mathcal{I}((\text{ONE-OF } I_1 \ldots I_n)) = \{x | x \in \mathcal{I}(I_1) \vee \ldots \vee x \in \mathcal{I}(I_n)\}$
FILLS	$\mathcal{I}((\text{FILLS } r \text{ } I_1 \ldots I_n)) = \{x | \forall j : 1 \leq j \leq n, \exists z \ [\langle x,z \rangle \in \mathcal{I}(r) \wedge z \in I_j]\}$
SAME-AS	$\mathcal{I}((\text{SAME-AS } (a_1 \ldots a_k) \ (b_1 \ldots b_l))) = \{x \in \Delta : \mathcal{I}(a_k) \circ \ldots \circ \mathcal{I}(a_1)(x) = \mathcal{I}(b_l) \circ \ldots \circ \mathcal{I}(b_1)(x)\}$
THING	$\mathcal{I}(\text{THING}) = \Delta$
NOTHING	$\mathcal{I}(\text{NOTHING}) = \emptyset$

a description logic with the constructors AND, ALL and SOME, one might use the description

```
(AND family
    (ALL husband (AND retired (ALL age over-65)))
    (ALL wife employed)
    (SOME child (AND student (ALL school graduate))))
```

to denote the set of families where the husband is retired, the wife is employed, and some child is attending graduate school. In the example, family, retired, over-65, student and graduate are primitives, and husband, wife, child and school are roles.

More formally, a *description* is a representation of a subset of some domain Δ of atomic individuals. A primitive symbol p_i is a description denoting a subset of Δ; we will write this subset as $\mathcal{I}(p_i)$. If $D_1 \ldots D_n$ are descriptions, then (AND $D_1 \ldots D_n$) is a description representing the set

$$\mathcal{I}((\text{AND } D_1 \ldots D_n)) = \cap_{i=1}^{n} \mathcal{I}(D_i)$$

Using the same sort of recursive definition, one can define other constructors easily. Table 1 presents some common constructors, together with their semantics. In the table, r is always a *role*; a role r denotes a subset of $\Delta \times \Delta$, which is written $\mathcal{I}(r)$. I_j is always an *individual*. Finally, n is always an integer and u is always a real number. We assume that Δ contains the real numbers. Note that the semantics of FILLS and ONE-OF, as given in the table, are somewhat nonstandard. For somewhat technical reasons the individuals used as arguments to the FILLS and ONE-OF constructors are defined to be disjoint subsets of the domain, rather than domain elements, as is more usually the case.[1]

---

[1] In a DL with individuals that are domain elements, a description like (AND (ALL Car (ONE-OF Saab Volvo)) (ALL Car Yuppiemobile)) would imply the disjunctive fact that either Saabs or Volvos are Yuppiemobiles. Reasoning with such disjunctive information is intractable. Using the modified semantics Saab and Volvo would stand for two disjoint sets of objects, rather than two distinct

In this paper we focus on a particular description logic called CLASSIC2. CLASSIC2 is a reimplementation and slight extension of CLASSIC1 [Borgida et al., 1989; Brachman, 1990] that contains all of the constructors summarized in Table 1. The main extensions to the logic relative to CLASSIC1 are the MIN and MAX constructors, and the addition of role hierarchies and role inverses; the other constructors are inherited from CLASSIC1.

Most of our results actually concern the DL with the constructors AND, ALL, AT-LEAST, AT-MOST, FILLS, ONE-OF, MIN, and MAX—i.e., CLASSIC2 without the SAME-AS constructor or role hierarchies. In the remainder of this paper we will call this DL C-CLASSIC. A knowledge-based management based on C-CLASSIC has been used for a number of real-world applications (e.g., [Wright et al., 1993]).

2.2 REASONING IN CLASSIC

DLs are primarily used for taxonomic reasoning, and hence an important operation is determining if one description is more general than another. The generality relationship used for descriptions is called *subsumption*: description D_1 is said to *subsume* D_2 if $\mathcal{I}(D_1) \supseteq \mathcal{I}(D_2)$ for every possible definition of the primitives and roles appearing in D_1 and D_2. Subsumption is thus closely related to the familiar notion of set inclusion.

Subsumption in CLASSIC is fairly well understood. The subsumption algorithms for CLASSIC2 are similar to those for CLASSIC1—descriptions are first *normalized* by converting them to a labeled graph structure called a *description graph*, and then subsumption can be efficiently tested by graph-matching operations. Below we will briefly review the special case of description graphs that occur when the standard CLASSIC2

---

objects; tractable and complete inference procedures exist for this modified semantics [Borgida and Patel-Schneider, 1992].

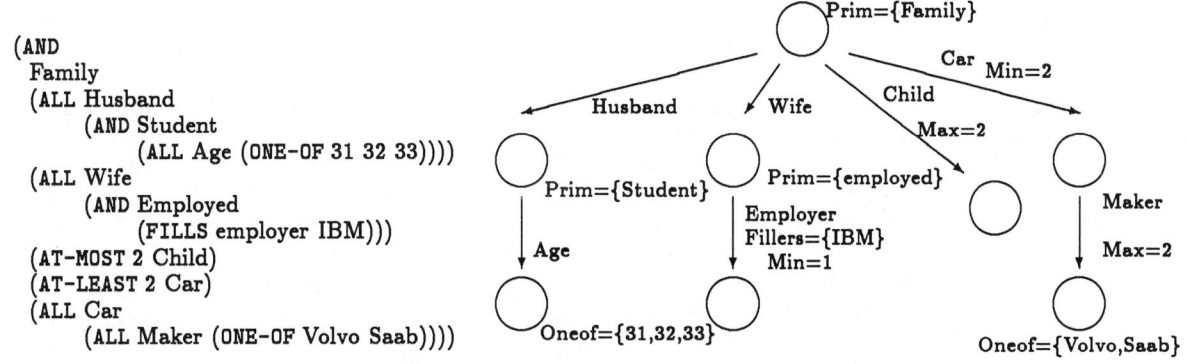

```
(AND
  Family
  (ALL Husband
       (AND Student
            (ALL Age (ONE-OF 31 32 33))))
  (ALL Wife
       (AND Employed
            (FILLS employer IBM)))
  (AT-MOST 2 Child)
  (AT-LEAST 2 Car)
  (ALL Car
       (ALL Maker (ONE-OF Volvo Saab))))
```

Figure 1: A C-CLASSIC Description and Description Graph

algorithms are applied to C-CLASSIC.

For C-CLASSIC, description graphs are always trees. The nodes of *description trees* are labeled with tuples (*dom, prim, mn, mx*). The *dom* component is either a set of individuals $\{I_1, \ldots, I_n\}$, which intuitively represents the constraint that the condition (ONE-OF $I_1 \ldots I_n$) must hold at this vertex, or the special symbol UNIV, which indicates that no ONE-OF restriction is in force. The *mn* and *mx* labels are either real numbers, representing MIN and MAX restrictions, or the symbol NOLIMIT, again representing the absence of any restriction. The *prim* label is a set of primitive concepts.

Each edge in a description graphs is labeled with a tuple (r, *least, most, fillers*). Intuitively *least* is an integer representing an AT-LEAST restriction on the role r, *most* is an integer representing an AT-MOST restriction on r, and *fillers* is a set of individuals representing a FILLS restriction on r. To allow for an absent AT-MOST restriction, *most* can also be the special symbol NOLIMIT.

More formally, given a vertex v from a description tree T, with label (*dom, prim, mn, mx*), a domain element x is defined to be in the *extension of v* iff the following all hold.

- If $dom = \{I_1, \ldots, I_k\}$ (*i.e.*, if $dom \neq$ UNIV) then $x \in \mathcal{I}((\text{ONE-OF } I_1 \ldots I_k))$.
- For each $p_i \in prim$, $x \in \mathcal{I}(p_i)$.
- If $mn \neq$ NOLIMIT, $x \in \mathcal{I}((\text{MIN } mn))$.
- If $mx \neq$ NOLIMIT, $x \in \mathcal{I}((\text{MAX } mx))$.
- For each edge from v to w with label (r, *least, most, fillers*) the following all hold:
  - if y is any domain element such that $(x, y) \in \mathcal{I}(r)$, then y is in the extension of w;
  - $least \leq |\{y|(x, y) \in \mathcal{I}(r)\}|$,
  - if $most \neq$ NOLIMIT then $|\{y|(x, y) \in \mathcal{I}(r)\}| \leq most$,
  - if $fillers = \{I_1, \ldots, I_k\}$, then $x \in \mathcal{I}((\text{FILLS } I_1 \ldots I_k))$

Finally, an individual x is in the extension of the description tree T iff it is in the extension of the root vertex of T.

To normalize a C-CLASSIC description, the description is first converted to a description tree using a simple recursive algorithm. The description tree is then converted into a *canonical form* by further normalization operators: for example, one operator looks for edges labeled (r, *least, most, fillers*) where $|fillers| > least$, and then replaces each such *least* label with $|fillers|$. Figure 1 contains an example of a C-CLASSIC description, and the equivalent canonical description tree. (To simplify the diagram, vacuous labels like *dom*=UNIV and *least*=0 are not shown.) For a more complete discussion of CLASSIC description graphs, and the semantics for CLASSIC, consult Borgida and Patel-Schneider [1992].

2.3 PAC-LEARNABILITY

The problem of inductive learning is to extrapolate a general description of a concept c from a set of *training examples*—things that have been labeled by an oracle as positive if they are elements of c and negative otherwise. To formalize this, let X refer to a *domain*—a set of things that might serve as positive or negative examples. A *concept* c is a subset of X. A *concept class* is a set of concepts; this will designate a constrained set of "target" concepts that could be labeling the training data. Associated with each concept class is a language $\mathcal{L}$ for writing down concepts in that class. In this paper the representation in $\mathcal{L}$ for the concept c will also be denoted c (as it will be clear from context whether we refer to the concept or its representation). We will also assume the existence of some measure for the size of a representation of a concept. Typically this measure will be polynomially related to the number of bits needed to write down a concept.

In learning, the goal is to find the unknown target concept $c \in \mathcal{L}$ (or some reasonable approximation thereof) from a set of labeled examples. Usually examples are elements of the domain X, with $x \in X$ labeled as positive if $x \in c$ and negative otherwise. We will depart from this model here, and instead assume that examples are *concepts* selected from $\mathcal{L}$, and that an example $x \in \mathcal{L}$ will be labeled as positive if c subsumes x, and labeled as negative otherwise. (Thus in learning DLs both examples and target concepts will be descriptions.) This *single-representation trick* [Dietterich et al., 1982] has been used in comparable situations in the computational learning theory literature (*e.g.*, [Haussler, 1989]). In analyzing first-order languages it is particularly useful because there is often no standard representation for instances.

Our model of "efficient learnability" is based on Valiant's model of pac-learnability [Valiant, 1984]. We assume a static probability distribution by which examples are drawn, *i.e.*, some distribution P over the language $\mathcal{L}$. The probability distribution P gives us a natural way of measuring the quality of a hypothesis h; one can simply measure the probability that h's label will disagree with the label of the target concept c on an example chosen according to P. The goal of pac-learning is to produce a hypothesis that will with high probability score well according to this measure—that is, a hypothesis that will be "probably approximately correct"—regardless of the probability distribution P and the target concept $c \in \mathcal{L}$.

More formally, let a *sample of c* be a pair of multisets S^+ and S^- drawn from $\mathcal{L}$ according to P, with S^+ containing the positive examples of c and S^- containing the negative examples. Let $error_{P,c}(h)$ be the probability that h and c disagree on an example x drawn randomly according to P (*i.e.*, the probability that h subsumes x and c does not subsume x, or that c subsumes x and h does not subsume x). Let $\mathcal{L}_n$ denote the set of concepts $c \in \mathcal{L}$ of size no greater than n.

A language $\mathcal{L}$ is said to be *pac-learnable* iff there is an algorithm LEARN and a polynomial function $m(\frac{1}{\epsilon}, \frac{1}{\delta}, n_e, n_t)$ so that for every $n_t > 0$, every $c \in \mathcal{L}_{n_t}$, every $\epsilon : 0 < \epsilon < 1$, every $\delta : 0 < \delta < 1$, and every probability distribution P over $\mathcal{L}_{n_e}$, when LEARN is run on a sample of size $m(\frac{1}{\epsilon}, \frac{1}{\delta}, n_e, n_t)$ or larger it takes time polynomial in the sample size and outputs a concept $h \in \mathcal{L}$ for which $Prob(error_{P,c}(h) > \epsilon) < \delta$.

In other words, even given adversarial choices of n_t, n_e, ϵ, δ, P, and $c \in \mathcal{L}_{n_t}$, LEARN will with high confidence return a hypothesis h that is approximately correct (with respect to the correct hypothesis c and the distribution of examples P), using only polynomial time and a polynomial number of examples. The polynomial bound $m(\frac{1}{\epsilon}, \frac{1}{\delta}, n_e, n_t)$ on the number of examples is called the *sample complexity* of LEARN.

As noted above, this formalization is conventional, except for the assumption that examples are descriptions that are marked positive when subsumed by the target concept. In the discussions below, the *standard pac-learning model* refers to the variant of this model resulting when examples are domain elements.

2.4 RELEVANT PREVIOUS RESULTS

Only a few previous papers have directly addressed the the pac-learnability of description logics. However, a connection can be drawn between pac-learnability and certain previous formal results on the complexity of reasoning in description logics.

For instance, it is known that if $\mathcal{L}$ is pac-learnable in the standard model, then $\mathcal{L} \in P/Poly$ [Schapire, 1990], where $P/Poly$ is the set of languages accepted by a (possibly nonuniform) family of polynomial-size deterministic circuits. This result can be used to obtain a number negative results in our model, such as the following:

Theorem 1 *In the model defined in Section 2.3, if concepts in a language $\mathcal{L}$ can be represented as strings over $\{0, 1\}$ with only a polynomial increase in size, and if subsumption for $\mathcal{L}$ is either NP-hard or coNP-hard, then $\mathcal{L}$ is not pac-learnable unless $NP \subseteq P/Poly$.*

Proof: For any language $\mathcal{L}$ and a concept $c \in \mathcal{L}$, let $\hat{c}$ be a concept that has the same representation as c, but which denotes the set

$$\{d \in \mathcal{L} : d \text{ is subsumed by } c\}$$

Also define $\hat{\mathcal{L}} \equiv \{\hat{c} : c \in \mathcal{L}\}$. It is immediate that $\mathcal{L}$ is pac-learnable in the model of Section 2.3 iff $\hat{\mathcal{L}}$ is pac-learnable in the standard model, and that testing membership for a concept $\hat{c} \in \hat{\mathcal{L}}$ is as hard as testing subsumption for the concept $c \in \mathcal{L}$. By Theorem 7 of Schapire [1990], if $\hat{\mathcal{L}}$ is pac-learnable then $\hat{\mathcal{L}} \in P/Poly$; thus if $\hat{\mathcal{L}}$ is NP-hard ($coNP$-hard) it follows that $NP \subseteq P/Poly$ ($coNP \subseteq P/Poly$). Finally since $P/Poly$ is closed under complementation, $coNP \subseteq P/Poly$ implies that $NP \subseteq P/Poly$. ∎

This theorem immediately establishes the non-learnability of a wide class of DLs, such as $\mathcal{FL}$ [Levesque and Brachman, 1985]; furthermore, it also establishes the non-learnability of many plausible extensions of C-CLASSIC.

Unfortunately, the same method cannot be used to obtain positive results, as the converse of the proposition is false: there are some languages for which subsumption is tractable that are hard to pac-learn. For example, the DL containing only primitives and the AND, ALL and SAME-AS constructors is not pac-learnable, even though a tractable subsumption algorithm for this language exists [Cohen and Hirsh, 1992b]. This negative result can be easily extended to the DLs CLASSIC1 and CLASSIC2, which include the SAME-AS constructor.

```
Function LCS(v_1, v_2):
begin
    let v_LCS be the root of the tree to output
    let the label of v_LCS be (dom, prim, mn, mx) where
        (dom_1, prim_1, mn_1, mx_1) is the label of v_1
        (dom_2, prim_2, mn_2, mx_2) is the label of v_2
        dom = dom_1 ∪ dom_2
        prim = prim_1 ∩ prim_2
        mn = min(mn_1, mn_2)
        mx = max(mx_1, mx_2)
    for each edge from v_1 to w_1 with
    label (r, least_1, most_1, fillers_1)
        if there is an edge from v_2 to w_2
        with label (r, least_2, most_2, fillers_2)
        then
            let least = min(least_1, least_2)
            let most = max(most_1, most_2)
            let fills = fillers_1 ∩ fillers_2
            let w = LCS(w_1, w_2)
            construct an edge from v with w
            with label (r, least, most, fillers)
        endif
    endfor
end LCS function
```

Figure 2: An LCS Algorithm for C-CLASSIC

The principle technique for obtaining a positive result for a language $\mathcal{L}$ is to find a pac-learning algorithm for $\mathcal{L}$. An operation that is frequently useful in learning is finding a least general concept that is consistent with a set of positive examples; thus, we have also studied the complexity of computing *least common subsumers* (LCS) of a set of descriptions. An LCS of a set of descriptions $D_1, \ldots, D_m \in \mathcal{L}$ is simply a most specific description (in the infinite space of all possible descriptions in $\mathcal{L}$) that subsumes all of the D_i's. An LCS can also be thought of as the dual of the intersection (AND) operator, or as encoding the largest expressible set of commonalities between a set of descriptions.

A fairly general method for implementing LCS algorithms is described by Cohen, Borgida and Hirsh [Cohen et al., 1992]. This method can be used to derive an LCS algorithm for any description logic which uses "structural subsumption": this class includes C-CLASSIC, but not full CLASSIC2. An LCS algorithm for C-CLASSIC description trees is shown in Figure 2.[2] This algorithm produces a unique LCS for any set of descriptions, and is tractable in the following sense: if $D_1, \ldots, D_m$ are all C-CLASSIC descriptions of size less than or equal to n_e, their LCS can be computed in time polynomial in m and n_e. We omit proofs of the correctness and tractability of the LCS procedure, and of the uniqueness of the LCS for C-CLASSIC [Cohen and Hirsh, 1992a].

3 C-CLASSIC IS PAC-LEARNABLE

Often it is true that any algorithm that always returns a small hypothesis in $\mathcal{L}$ that is consistent with the training examples will pac-learn $\mathcal{L}$; thus often, if the LCS of a set of examples can be tractably computed for a language $\mathcal{L}$, computing the LCS of all the positive examples is a pac-learning algorithm for $\mathcal{L}$. Unfortunately, this is not the case for C-CLASSIC. As a counterexample, consider the target concept THING, and a distribution that is uniform over the examples (ONE-OF I_1)$^+$, (ONE-OF I_2)$^+$, ... (ONE-OF I_r)$^+$ where the I_j's are distinct individuals. The LCS of any m examples will be the description (ONE-OF $I_{j_1} \ldots I_{j_m}$); in other words, it will simply be a disjunction of the positive examples. It can easily be shown that this does not satisfy the requirements for pac-learning when $r >> m$.

This example suggests that to pac-learn C-CLASSIC one must avoid forming large ONE-OF expressions. The LCSLEARN algorithm is one way of doing this. The LCSLEARN algorithm takes two inputs: a set of positive examples S^+ and a set of negative examples S^-, all of which are normalized CLASSIC2 descriptions. The algorithm behaves as follows.

1. If there are no positive examples, return the empty description NOTHING. Otherwise, let H be the LCS of all of the positive examples, and let $l = 0$.

2. Let H_l be a copy of H in which every ONE-OF label in H that contains more than l individuals is deleted.

3. If H_l does not subsume any negative example e^- in S^-, then return H_l as the hypothesis of LCSLEARN. Otherwise, if $H_l = H$ then abort with failure. Otherwise, increment l and go to Step 2.

The main formal result of this paper is the following.[3]

Theorem 2 *LCSLEARN is a pac-learning algorithm for C-CLASSIC, with a sample complexity of no more*

---

[2] In the code, v_1 and v_2 are roots of two description trees. We also adopt the conventions that $S \cup \text{UNIV} = \text{UNIV} \cup S = \text{UNIV}$ for any set S, and $\max(n, \text{NOLIMIT}) = \min(n, \text{NOLIMIT}) = \text{NOLIMIT}$ for any real number n.

[3] Note that this theorem assumes a size measure on C-CLASSIC concepts. We define the size of a description to be the size of the equivalent canonical description tree, and that the size of a description tree is the sum of the number of vertices, the number of edges, and the sum of the sizes of all the labels, where a label that is a symbol or a real number has size one, and a label that is a set S has size $|S|$.

than

$$m(\frac{1}{\epsilon}, \frac{1}{\delta}, n_e, n_t)$$
$$\equiv \max(\frac{8n_t + 4n_e}{\epsilon} \ln \frac{4n_t + 2n_e}{\sqrt{\delta}}, \frac{32n_e}{\epsilon} \ln \frac{26}{\epsilon})$$
$$\equiv O(\frac{n_t + n_e}{\epsilon} \ln \frac{n_t + n_e}{\sqrt{\delta}} + \frac{n_e}{\epsilon} \ln \frac{1}{\epsilon})$$

regardless of the number of primitive concepts and roles.

Proof: In the proof, we will analyze the behavior of an incremental version of LCSLEARN called INCLCS-LEARN. This will allow us to use proof techniques from mistake-bounded learning [Littlestone, 1988] for part of the proof, thereby achieving a sample complexity independent of the number of roles and primitives.

INCLCSLEARN examines the examples in S^+ and S^- in some randomly chosen order. After examining the i-th example x_i, INCLCSLEARN generates a hypothesis H_i, which is defined to be the hypothesis that LCSLEARN would output from a sample containing the first i examples $x_1, \ldots, x_i$. INCLCSLEARN returns as its hypothesis the first H_i such that

Property 1. $i > \max(\frac{8}{\epsilon} \ln \frac{4}{\delta}, \frac{32n_e}{\epsilon} \ln \frac{26}{\epsilon})$

Property 2. INCLCSLEARN has made no nonboundary errors (defined below) on the $m_j = \frac{2}{\epsilon} \ln \frac{4j^2}{\delta}$ previous examples, where j is the number of previous nonboundary mind changes (defined below) made by INCLCSLEARN.

We will show that INCLCSLEARN is a pac-learner with the stated sample complexity. Since INCLCS-LEARN's hypothesis is the same as LCSLEARN would generate given a subset of the data, this implies that LCSLEARN is also a pac-learner.

Define a *mind change* to be any occasion in which H_i differs from H_{i-1}. A *boundary mind change* is one in which (a) H_i and H_{i-1} have the same number of edges and vertices, (b) for each vertex only the *mn* and *mx* labels change and (c) for each edge only the *least* and *most* labels change. A *nonboundary mind change* is any other sort of mind change. Also define a *prediction error* for an incremental learner to be any occasion in which the i-th hypothesis H_i misclassifies the $(i+1)$-th example x_{i+1}. A *boundary error* is an error in which a positive example x_i is not subsumed by H_i, but it would have been subsumed if every *least* label in H_i were replaced by zero, and every *most*, *mn* and *mx* label by NOLIMIT. A *nonboundary error* is any other sort of error.

The proof begins with two lemmas, the proofs of which are omitted. (The first proof uses a standard Chernoff bound argument; the second is a straightforward application of the main result of Blumer *et. al* [1989], and

a bound of $2d$ on the VC-dimension of the language d-$\mathcal{L}_{\text{RECT}}$.)

Lemma 1 *Let α be some type of prediction error (e.g. a nonboundary error) and let H_i be some hypothesis of an incremental learner that was formed from the examples $x_1, \ldots, x_i$ and that makes no prediction errors of type α on the subsequent examples $x_{i+1}, \ldots, x_{i+m_j}$, where $m_j = \frac{1}{\epsilon} \ln \frac{2j^2}{\delta}$ and j is the number of previous hypotheses of the incremental learner INCLEARN that are different with respect to the type-α errors that they could make. Then with probability at least $1 - \delta$, H_i will have probability less than ϵ of making a type-α prediction error on a randomly chosen example.*

Lemma 2 *Let d-$\mathcal{L}_{\text{RECT}}$ be the set of d-dimensional rectangles whose boundaries are specified by real numbers, and define rectangle R_1 to subsume rectangle R_2 iff the points contained in R_1 are a superset of the points contained in R_2. Then d-$\mathcal{L}_{\text{RECT}}$ is pac-learnable with a sample complexity of*

$$\max(\frac{4}{\epsilon} \ln \frac{2}{\delta}, \frac{16d}{\epsilon} \ln \frac{13}{\epsilon})$$

by any learning algorithm that outputs a rectangle consistent with all of the examples.

With these tools in hand, we can now prove the theorem. By Lemma 1, any hypothesis returned by INCLCSLEARN will with confidence $\frac{\delta}{2}$ have probability less than $\frac{\epsilon}{2}$ of making a nonboundary error on a new random example. Now consider boundary errors. Finding the right values for the *least*, *most*, *mn*, and *mx* labels in a tree of size n is equivalent to finding an accurate hypothesis in $(v + e)$-$\mathcal{L}_{\text{RECT}}$, where v is the number of vertices in the tree and e is the number of edges. Since for any hypothesis tree H_i, $v + e < n_e$, by Lemma 2 any hypothesis that is consistent with

$$\max(\frac{8}{\epsilon} \ln \frac{4}{\delta}, \frac{32n_e}{\epsilon} \ln \frac{26}{\epsilon}) \tag{1}$$

examples will with confidence $\frac{\delta}{2}$ have probability less than $\frac{\epsilon}{2}$ of making a boundary error on a new random example. Thus the hypothesis of INCLCSLEARN will with confidence δ have error less than ϵ.

It remains to bound the number of examples required to satisfy Property 2. The worst case would be to make no nonboundary mind changes on the first $m_1 - 1$ examples, then after a nonboundary mind change on the m_1-th example to make no nonboundary mind changes on the next $m_2 - 1$ examples, and so on. Thus the number of examples required to satisfy Property 2 can be bounded by $\sum_j m_j$. Notice first that the number of nonboundary mind changes can be bounded as follows:

- The hypothesized bound l on *dom* labels can be incremented at most n_t times.

- A set representing a *dom* label can be increased in size to at most n_t, or can be changed from a set to NOLIMIT. Since *dom* labels are initially non-empty, they can be changed at most n_t times (independently of changes to the bound l on *dom* labels.)
- The total number of times that a *prim* or *fillers* label is removed or that an edge or vertex is be removed from the tree is bounded by n_e.

Thus we see that the number of nonboundary errors for INCLCSLEARN is bounded by $2n_t + n_e$. The sum of the m_j's can now be bounded as follows:

$$\sum_{j=1}^{2n_t+n_e} m_j \le (2n_t + n_e)m_{(2n_t+n_e)}$$
$$= \frac{8n_t + 4n_e}{\epsilon} \ln \frac{4n_t + 2n_e}{\sqrt{\delta}}$$

By combining this with Equation 1 we obtain the sample complexity given in the statement of the theorem. ■

This result extends the previous results of Cohen and Hirsh [1992b] to include a larger set of constructors. This result can be also extended to allow a limited use of the SAME-AS constructor by imposing restrictions on the use of SAME-AS analogous to those described by Cohen and Hirsh.

4 EXPERIMENTAL RESULTS

In the formal model described above, examples are assumed to be descriptions, and an example is marked as positive if it is subsumed by the target concept. While convenient for formal analysis, this assumption is not always appropriate; in many cases, it is desirable to use instead *individuals* as examples. The formal results also give only a loose polynomial bound on learning speed.

Thus an experimental investigation of the behavior of LCSLEARN is desirable. In the remainder of this section, we will describe a simple means of extending the LCSLEARN algorithm to learn from individuals, and present some experimental results with the extended algorithm.

4.1 LEARNING FROM INDIVIDUALS

A straightforward way of adapting LCSLEARN to learn from individuals is to provide a preprocessor that *abstracts* an individual I by constructing a very specific description d_I that subsumes I. If one can guarantee that when an individual is an instance of C its abstraction will be subsumed by C, then many of the desirable formal properties of LCSLEARN are preserved.

Suppose, for example, that d_I is always the least general concept that contains I in some sublanguage $\mathcal{L}_0$ of C-CLASSIC. Then applying LCSLEARN to abstracted training examples is a pac-learning algorithm for $\mathcal{L}_0$.

We have experimented with a number of methods to abstract individuals. The simplest of these abstraction methods finds the least general description d_I that (a) contains no SAME-AS restrictions and (b) contains at most k levels of nesting of the ALL constructor, for value of k provided by the user. It is easy to show that this least general concept is unique, and can be found in time polynomial in the size of the knowledge base (but exponential in k). We used this strategy with $k = 3$ in the experiments with the Imacs2 knowledge base (see below), and $k = 5$ for all of the other experiments in this paper.

4.2 RECONSTRUCTING CONCEPT HIERARCHIES

In our first set of experiments, we used LCSLEARN to reconstruct known concept hierarchies from examples. Each concept c in the hierarchy was made a target concept for LCSLEARN, with the instances of c serving as positive examples, and non-instances of c serving as negative examples.

By reconstructing concept hierarchies from a variety of knowledge bases we were able to test LCSLEARN on a large number of naturally occurring concepts—almost 1000 all told. Some of these concepts were simple, but others were quite complex. The largest concept in our benchmark suite has a description more than 10,000 symbols long; for one of the knowledge bases (Prose1) the *average* description size was more than 2000 symbols.

We evaluated the learning algorithm on each knowledge base in two ways. First, we measured the fraction of the concepts in each knowledge base for which the hypothesis of LCSLEARN was equivalent to the true target concept. Somewhat surprisingly, in several of the domains a significant fraction of the hypotheses met this stringent test. Second, we estimated the error rate of each hypothesis using the statistical technique of cross-validation[4] [Weiss and Kulkowski, 1990].

Table 2 contains the results of this experiment. The Wines knowledge base is the one distributed with CLASSIC2. The Imacs1 knowledge base is the one used as a running example by Brachman *et. al* [1992], and Imacs2 is a small knowledge base used to test a real-world application of the system of [Brachman *et al.*, 1992]. Prose1 and Prose2 are knowledge bases used for different hardware configuration tasks [Wright *et al.*, 1993]. KRK, Loan, and Kluster are knowledge bases

---
[4]For problems with 100 or more examples, we used 20 partitions. For problems with less than 100 examples, we used "leave-one-out" cross-validation.

Table 2: Using individuals to reconstruct hierarchies

KB	#Concepts	#Individuals	Equivalent to Target	Error rate LCSLearn	Default
Wines	134	177	37/134	0.49%	3.5%
Imacs1	9	2564	2/9	0.063%	11.1%
Imacs2	74	512	19/74	0.31%	2.1%
Prose1	301	293	1/301	0.031%	0.34%
Prose2	398	202	1/398	0.092%	0.60%
KRK	16	1049	5/16	0.089%	6.4%
Loan	22	1013	3/22	0.031%	15.3%
Kluster	13	16	2/13	7.7%	17.8%
Total	967		70/967		
Average	121.0	728.25		1.15%	6.87%

used to compare LCSLearn with other work in learning first-order concepts. KRK classifies king-rook-king chess positions as legal or illegal [Quinlan, 1990; Pazzani and Kibler, 1992], Loan determines if payment can be deferred on a student loan [Pazzani and Brunk, 1991], and Kluster encodes a pharmacological domain [Kietz and Morik, 1991]. KRK and Loan were translated from Prolog, and Kluster was translated from BACK [Peltason et al., 1991].

To summarize the results, LCSLearn finds very accurate hypotheses in all of the domains except for Kluster, which has few individuals and hence affords little training data for the learning algorithm.

Some of the knowledge bases include many concepts with few instances: for such concepts hypothesizing the empty description NOTHING would also give a low error rate. Thus we also give for each knowledge base the error rate of the *default rule*.[5] LCSLearn outperforms the default rule on all of the knowledge bases, often having an average error rate more than an order of magnitude lower.

4.3 ANALYSIS OF RESULTS

Most implemented learning systems are tested on at most a few dozen learning problems. In the experiments above, however, we have evaluated LCSLearn on several hundred benchmarks. This provides sufficient data to make some general statements about its performance.

In Figure 3, we have plotted one point for each benchmark problem. The x coordinate of each point is the log of the number of positive examples,[6] and the y coordinate is the cross validated error rate of LCSLearn divided by the default error rate; thus $y > 1$ indi-

---

[5]The default rule simply predicts "positive" if more than half of the training examples are positive, and predicts "negative" otherwise.

[6]Logs are used because of the large variation in the amount of training data.

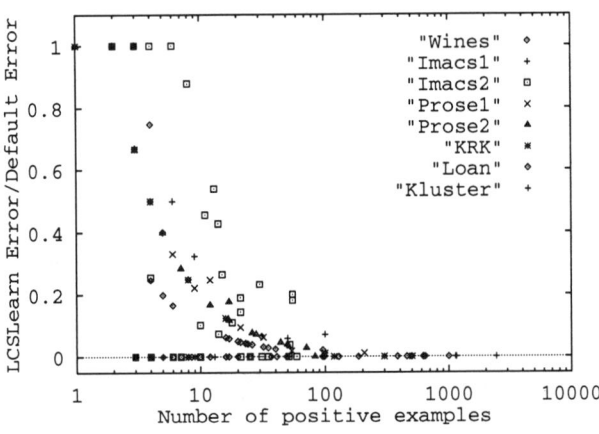

Figure 3: Further analysis of LCSLearn

cates performance worse that the default rule, and $y \approx 0$ indicates performance much better than the default rule. This plot shows in general, the performance of LCSLearn relative to the default rule improves quickly when more positive examples are available. This is unsurprising, when one considers that LCSLearn derives most of its information from the positive examples. Also (on these benchmarks) LCSLearn never performs worse than the default rule, and LCSLearn outperforms the default rule whenever there are more than a handful of positive examples.

One might also expect that when LCSLearn outputs a small hypothesis that is consistent with many examples, that hypothesis is likely to have low error. Figure 4 plots the ratio of number of examples m to hypothesis size n_h, on the x axis, against error rate, on the y axis.[7] Most of the points are clustered near the origin, indicating that for most of the benchmarks

---

[7]For readability, we show only the part of this plot clos-

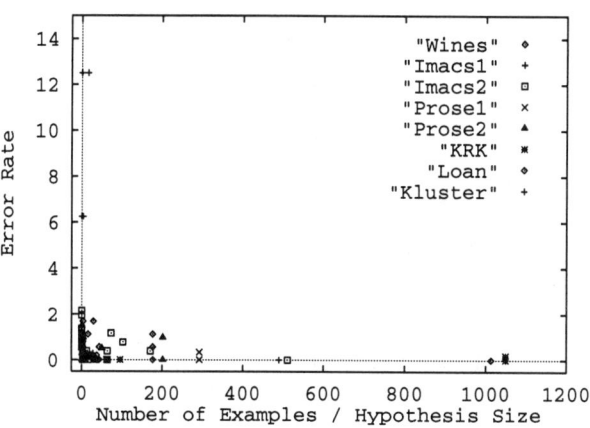

Figure 4: Effect of number of examples on error rate

both the error rate e and the ratio $\frac{m}{n_h}$ are low. The outlying points lie entirely near either the x axis or y axis, showing that error rate e is high only when $\frac{m}{n_h}$ is very low, and conversely that whenever $\frac{m}{n_h}$ high the error rate e is very low.

4.4 RELATIONSHIP TO KLUSTER

This application of LCSLEARN is somewhat similar to an earlier learning system called Kluster [Kietz and Morik, 1991]. Unfortunately, Kluster has not been systematically evaluated over a range of domains, which makes quantitative comparison of Kluster and LCSLEARN difficult. LCSLEARN's performance on the benchmark knowledge based described by Kietz and Morik is given in Table 2; in this section we will comment on the qualitative similarities and differences between LCSLEARN and the learning component of Kluster.

As in the experiments above, Kluster's starting point is a set of individuals which are linked by roles and classified as to the primitive concepts to which they belong.[8] Kluster first heuristically partitions the individuals into disjoint classes, and then learns a description for each class expressed in a subset of the BACK description logic, using as examples the instances and non-instances of the constructed class. Kluster's learning algorithm first uses a sound LCS-like method to learn a description in a sublanguage of descriptions of the form

---

est to the origin.

[8]As CLASSIC allows arbitrary assertions to be made about individuals, more information about individuals can be available for LCSLEARN; however in most of the domains above this is not the case.

(AND (ALL r_1 (AND $p_{1,1} \ldots p_{1,n_1}$))
     (AT-LEAST l_1 r_1) (AT-MOST m_1 r_1)
     $\vdots$
     (ALL r_k (AND $p_{k,1} \ldots p_{k,n_k}$))
     (AT-LEAST l_k r_k) (AT-MOST m_k r_k))

where the r_i's are named roles, the l_i's and m_i's are integers, and the $p_{i,j}$'s are named concepts. To circumvent the restrictiveness of this language, heuristic techniques are then used to introduce new named concepts and named roles. Finally, heuristic techniques are again used to generalize the resulting descriptions.

In contrast, LCSLEARN uses only one heuristic step—the abstraction of individuals—and learns descriptions in CLASSIC2, a language more expressive than the sublanguage above, and incomparable to the full language that is learned by the Kluster technique. CLASSIC2 is more expressive than the subset of BACK used in Kluster in that it includes the MIN, MAX, FILLS, TEST, SAME-AS, and ONE-OF constructors, and allows ALL restrictions to be nested; however, CLASSIC2 does not allow defined roles, and hence it is also in some respects less expressive. To circumvent this limitation it was necessary in the experiments above to add to the original ontology the two roles defined by Kluster.

5 LEARNING DISJUNCTIONS

Because CLASSIC contains only limited disjunction (in the ONE-OF constructor) many target concepts of practical interest can not be expressed by a single CLASSIC2 description. One way to relax this limitation is to consider algorithms that learn a disjunction of descriptions, rather than a single CLASSIC concept; in other words, to learn a target concept $c \equiv d_1 \vee d_2 \vee \ldots \vee d_n$ where each d_i is a CLASSIC2 description.

Learning disjunctions of CLASSIC concepts is somewhat analogous to the problem of "inductive logic programming" (ILP) [Quinlan, 1990; Muggleton and Feng, 1992]. In ILP the target concept is usually assumed to be a single Prolog predicate that is defined by a set of Prolog clauses; such a concept can often be viewed as a disjunction of the sets defined by each clause. Thus one natural approach to learning disjunctions of CLASSIC descriptions is to adapt the techniques used in ILP to learn multi-clause Prolog predicates.

One well-known ILP method for learning multiple clauses is the GOLEM algorithm [Muggleton and Feng, 1992], which is also based on computing least common generalizations. The basic idea behind this algorithm is to use LCS to implement a specific-to-general greedy search for descriptions that cover many positive examples and no negative examples. In GOLEM, these descriptions are then further generalized by a process called *reduction*, and finally disjoined

```
LCSLearnDisj($S^+$,$S^-$)
    $n \leftarrow 0$
    while $S^+$ is nonempty do
        $n \leftarrow n + 1$
        Seed $\leftarrow$ FindSeed($S^+$,$S^-$)
        $d_n \leftarrow$ Generalize(Seed,$S^+$,$S^-$)
        remove from $S^+$ all examples in $d_n$
    endwhile
    return $d_1 \vee \ldots \vee d_n$

FindSeed($S^+$,$S^-$)
    $R \leftarrow c_1$ random elements from $S^+$
    PAIRS $\leftarrow \{$LCS1$(r_i,r_j) : r_i, r_j \in R\}$
    discard from PAIRS all descriptions that
        contain any negative examples $e^- \in S^-$
    return the $p \in$ PAIRS that contains
        the most positive examples $e^+ \in S^+$

Generalize(Seed,$S^+$,$S^-$)
    repeat
        $R \leftarrow c_2$ random elements from $S^+$
            that are not covered by Seed
        GENS $\leftarrow \{$LCS1(Seed,$r_i$) $: r \in R\}$
        discard from GENS all descriptions that
            contain any negative examples $e^- \in S^-$
        if GENS is nonempty then
            Seed $\leftarrow$ the $g \in$ GENS that contains
                the most positive examples $e^+ \in S^+$
        endif
    until GENS is empty
    return Reduce(Seed,$S^-$)

LCS1($d_1$,$d_2$)
    return a copy of LCS($d_1$,$d_2$) with
        all ONE-OF restrictions removed
```

Figure 5: The LCSLearnDisj learning algorithm

```
Reduce(D,N)
    $n \leftarrow 0$
    while $N$ is nonempty do
        $n \leftarrow n + 1$
        $f_n \leftarrow$ the $f \in$ Factors($D$) maximizing $|\{x \in N : x \notin f\}|$
        $N \leftarrow N - \{x \in N : x \notin f_n\}$
    endwhile
    return $f_1 \ldots f_n$

Factors($D$)
    if $D = ($AND $D_1 \ldots D_k)$ then
        return $\cup_{i=1}^{k}$Factors($D_i$)
    elseif $D = ($ALL $r$ $D)$ then
        return $\{($ALL $r$ $f) : f$ is a factor of $D\}$
    elseif $D = ($FILLS $I_1 \ldots I_k)$ then
        return $\{($FILLS $I_1),\ldots,($FILLS $I_k)\}$
    else return $D$
```

Figure 6: Reducing C-Classic Descriptions

to obtain a hypothesis.

Figure 5 gives a brief overview of the algorithm as adapted to Classic.[9] To *reduce* a description D, we first "factor" it into a set of simpler descriptions $\{f_1, \ldots, f_n\}$ such that the intersection of the f_i's is equivalent to D. We then use a greedy set-covering approach to find a small subset of the factors of D that, when conjoined, are consistent with the negative data. The details of the reduction algorithm are given in Figure 6.

Three of the knowledge bases above are useful test cases for this learning algorithm. The KRK and Loan knowledge bases, being adaptations of ILP problems, naturally fall into this category. We ran LCSLearnDisj on these benchmarks and also on some obvious variants of the KRK problem, shown in the table as KBK and KQK.[10]

The third test case is the Wines knowledge base, which contains a set of rules that recommend which wines to serve with which foods. From these rules we derived a number of learning problems. First, we derived 12 disjunctive concepts defining the foods that are acceptable with 12 different types of wines: for example, the disjunctive concept Color-Red-Food contains those foods that can be served with red wine. The training examples for these concepts are just the 33 food individuals in the knowledge base. We also derived a single disjunctive concept containing exactly the (*wine*, *food*) pairs deemed acceptable by the Wine rules. We generated a dataset for the "acceptable pair" concept by choosing a set of (*wine*, *food*) pairs, and then classifying these pairs as acceptable or unacceptable using the rules from the Wines knowledge base; the generated dataset contains all acceptable pairs and a random sample of 10% of the unacceptable pairs.

Table 3 summarizes these experiments; for convenience, the 12 smaller wine problems are also summarized in a single line labeled "Acceptable-Food". LCSLearnDisj is the name given to our learning algorithm; the other points of comparison that we use are Grendel2, a recent version of the ILP learning system Grendel [Cohen, 1992; Cohen, 1993], and the default error rate.[11]

---

[9] In the experiments we used $c_1 = 5$ and $c_2 = 20$. Note that the limited disjunction provided by ONE-OF is no longer needed, as a more general mechanism for disjunction is being provided, hence the use of LCS1 rather than LCS.

[10] The white rook is replaced by a white bishop in KBK-Illegal and by a queen in KQK-Illegal.

[11] Results for Grendel are in each case the best results obtained among a variety of different expressible biases [Cohen, 1993]. Grendel was not applied to the Wines problems

Table 3: Learning disjunctions of CLASSIC concepts

KB	#Examples	Error rate		
		LCSLearnDisj	Default	Grendel2
KRK	100	2.0%	38.0%	3.0%
KBK	100	2.0%	36.0%	54.0%
KQK	100	3.0%	44.0%	55.0%
Loan	100	13.0%	35.0%	2.0%
Acceptable-Pair	320	5.3%	42.5%	—
Acceptable-Foods:				—
Color-White-Food	33	12.2%	33.3%	—
Color-Rose-Food	33	0.0%	6.1%	—
Color-Red-Food	33	6.1%	39.4%	—
Body-Light-Food	33	3.0%	9.1%	—
Body-Medium-Food	33	12.2%	45.5%	—
Body-Full-Food	33	6.1%	36.4%	—
Flavor-Delicate-Food	33	6.1%	21.2%	—
Flavor-Moderate-Food	33	9.1%	39.4%	—
Flavor-Strong-Food	33	9.1%	42.4%	—
Sugar-Sweet-Food	33	3.0%	27.3%	—
Sugar-OffDry-Food	33	3.0%	3.0%	—
Sugar-Dry-Food	33	6.1%	30.3%	—
Average Acceptable-Food	33	6.3%	27.8%	—

The results of Table 3 show that LCSLearnDisj obtains good results, and suggests that it is competitive with existing first-order learning methods. However, it should be noted that both LCSLearnDisj and ILP systems like Grendel are sensitive to the way examples are represented, and ILP systems and LCSLearnDisj necessarily use different representations.

To illustrate the differences in representation, we will briefly discuss our translation of the KRK learning problem. In this domain, the task is to classify king-rook-king chess positions with white to move as legal or illegal. In the formulation of this problem used by Grendel2, a position is represented by six numbers encoding the rank and file position of each of the tree pieces. Illegal positions are recognized by checking arithmetic relationships between pairs and triples of numbers. An an example, the Prolog clause below states that a position is illegal if the white rook and black king are on the same file and the white king does not block the white rook from attacking the black king. (The variables WKR, WKF, WRR, WRF, BKR, and BKF stand for the rank and file of the white king, the rank and file of the white rook, and the rank and file of the black king respectively.)

```
illegal(WKR,WKF,WRR,WRF,BKR,BKF) ←
  WRF=BKF,
  ( WKF=BKF, not between(WRR,WKR,BKR)
  ; not WKF=BKF ).
```

In the C-CLASSIC formulation of the problem, a position has the attributes white-king, white-rook, and black-king, each of which is filled by an individual that must be a piece; a piece has the attribute location, which must be filled by a square; and a square has the attributes rank and file and a role content, which must be filled by one or more pieces. Finally, to encode the spatial relationships among pieces, every piece also has a number of attributes with names like to-white-rook and to-black-king that are filled by vector individuals. A vector individual is related to all the squares between its two endpoints via the role between, and also has a direction attribute. The filler of the *direction* attribute is one of the individuals n, s, e, w, ne, se, nw, or sw, and these individuals are organized in a taxonomy that includes concepts like diagonal-direction and file-direction.

Using this ontology, the Prolog clause above can be translated as the following C-CLASSIC concept.

```
(ALL white-rook
    (ALL to-black-king
        (AND
            (ALL direction file-dir)
            (ALL between (AT-MOST 0 content)))))
```

Both the ILP and C-CLASSIC representations are natural given the choice of languages; however, as the example shows, the representations are also both quite different, and have different strengths and weaknesses. The C-CLASSIC representation makes it possible to concisely describe certain geometric patterns that are difficult to express in the Prolog representation, such as an unobstructed line of attack along a diagonal.

because they are not represented in an ontology conducive to an ILP representation.

The Prolog representation, on the other hand, allows a very compact representation of a position.

To summarize, the differences in the languages greatly complicate comparisons between ILP techniques and learning methods based on description logics: not only does the background knowledge used by the two systems differ, but the representation of the examples themselves is also different. (This is in marked contrast to comparisons among different learning systems based on propositional logic, in which the same representations are typically used for examples.) However, we believe that the experiments above do clearly indicate that LCSLEARN can be competitive with ILP methods, given an appropriate ontology.

6 CONCLUDING REMARKS

The description logic C-CLASSIC has been used in a number of practical systems. In this paper, we have presented a formal result showing that the description logic C-CLASSIC is pac-learnable. The learning algorithm LCSLEARN suggested by this formal result learns descriptions in the C-CLASSIC description logic from examples which are themselves descriptions.

Additionally, we have presented an experimental evaluation of two extensions to the algorithm: one that learns from examples that are individuals (by simply converting each example individual to a very specific concept that includes that individual) and a second that learns disjunctions of descriptions from individuals. Extensive experiments with LCSLEARN using several hundred target concepts from a number of domains support the claim that the learning algorithm reliably learns complex natural concepts, in addition to having behavior that is formally well understood.

Similar experiments with the extension of LCSLEARN that learns disjunctions suggest that it is competitive with existing techniques for learning first-order concepts from examples. This suggests that learning systems based on description logics may prove to be a useful complement to those based on logic programs as a representation language.

Acknowledgments

Thanks are due to Lori Alperin Resnick, for writing the LCS routine for CLASSIC2 and her invaluable help with CLASSIC2, and Deborah McGuinness, for helping me assemble the set of benchmark knowledge bases. Alon Levy also provided valuable comments on a draft of this paper, as did the anonymous reviewers for KR94.

References

(Beck et al., 1989) H. Beck, H. Gala, and S. Navathe. Classification as a query processing technique in the CANDIDE semantic model. In *Proceedings of the Data Engineering Conference*, pages 572–581, Los Angeles, California, 1989.

(Blumer et al., 1989) Anselm Blumer, Andrezj Ehrenfeucht, David Haussler, and Manfred Warmuth. Classifying learnable concepts with the Vapnik-Chervonenkis dimension. *Journal of the Association for Computing Machinery*, 36(4):929–965, 1989.

(Borgida and Patel-Schneider, 1992) A. Borgida and P. F. Patel-Schneider. A semantics and complete algorithm for subsumption in the CLASSIC description logic. AT&T Technical Memorandum. Available from the authors on request, 1992.

(Borgida et al., 1989) A. Borgida, R. J. Brachman, D. L. McGuinness, and L. Resnick. CLASSIC: A structural data model for objects. In *Proceedings of SIGMOD-89*, Portland, Oregon, 1989.

(Brachman et al., 1992) R. J. Brachman, P. G. Selfridge, L. G. Terveen, B. Altman, A. Borgida, F. Halper, T. Kirk, A. Lazar, D. L. McGuinness, and L. A. Resnick. Knowledge representation support for data archaeology. In *Proceedings of the ISMM International Conference on Information and Knowledge Management (CIKM-92)*, pages 457–464, Baltimore, MD, 1992.

(Brachman, 1990) Ron J. Brachman. Living with CLASSIC: when and how to use a KL-ONE-like language. In J. Sowa, editor, *Formal aspects of Semantic Networks*. Morgan Kaufmann, 1990.

(Cohen and Hirsh, 1992a) W. Cohen and H. Hirsh. Learnability of the CLASSIC 1.0 knowledge representation language. AT&T Bell Labs Technical Memorandum. Available from the author on request, 1992.

(Cohen and Hirsh, 1992b) William W. Cohen and Haym Hirsh. Learnability of description logics. In *Proceedings of the Fourth Annual Workshop on Computational Learning Theory*, Pittsburgh, Pennsylvania, 1992. ACM Press.

(Cohen et al., 1992) William W. Cohen, Alex Borgida, and Haym Hirsh. Computing least common subsumers in description logics. In *Proceedings of the Tenth National Conference on Artificial Intelligence*, San Jose, California, 1992. MIT Press.

(Cohen, 1992) William W. Cohen. Compiling knowledge into an explicit bias. In *Proceedings of the Ninth International Conference on Machine Learning*, Aberdeen, Scotland, 1992. Morgan Kaufmann.

(Cohen, 1993) William W. Cohen. Rapid prototyping of ILP systems using explicit bias. In *Proceedings of the 1993 IJCAI Workshop on Inductive Logic Programming*, Chambery, France, 1993.

(Devanbu et al., 1991) P. Devanbu, R. J. Brachman, P. Selfridge, and B. Ballard. LaSSIE: A knowledge-based software information system. *Communications of the ACM*, 35(5), May 1991.

(Dietterich et al., 1982) Thomas Glen Dietterich, Bob London, Kenneth Clarkson, and Geoff Dromey. Learning and inductive inference. In Paul Cohen and Edward A. Feigenbaum, editors, *The Handbook of Artificial Intelligence, Volume III*. William Kaufmann, Los Altos, CA, 1982.

(Haussler, 1989) David Haussler. Learning conjunctive concepts in structural domains. *Machine Learning*, 4(1), 1989.

(Kietz and Morik, 1991) Jorg-Uwe Kietz and Katharina Morik. Constructive induction of background knowledge. In *Proceedings of the Workshop on Evaluating and Changing Representation in Machine Learning (at the 12th International Joint Conference on Artificial Intelligence)*, Sydney, Australia, 1991. Morgan Kaufmann.

(Levesque and Brachman, 1985) Hector Levesque and Ronald Brachman. A fundamental tradeoff in knowledge representation and reasoning (revised version). In *Readings in Knowledge Representation*. Morgan Kaufmann, 1985.

(Littlestone, 1988) Nick Littlestone. Learning quickly when irrelevant attributes abound: A new linear-threshold algorithm. *Machine Learning*, 2(4), 1988.

(MacGregor, 1991) R. M. MacGregor. The evolving technology of classification-based knowledge representation systems. In John Sowa, editor, *Principles of semantic networks: explorations in the representation of knowledge*. Morgan Kaufmann, 1991.

(Mays et al., 1987) E. Mays, C. Apte, J. Griesmer, and J. Kastner. Organizing knowledge in a complex financial domain. *IEEE Expert*, pages 61–70, Fall 1987.

(Muggleton and Feng, 1992) Stephen Muggleton and Cao Feng. Efficient induction of logic programs. In *Inductive Logic Programming*. Academic Press, 1992.

(Pazzani and Brunk, 1991) Michael Pazzani and Clifford Brunk. Detecting and correcting errors in rule-based expert systems: an integration of empirical and explanation-based learning. *Knowledge Acquisition*, 3:157–173, 1991.

(Pazzani and Kibler, 1992) Michael Pazzani and Dennis Kibler. The utility of knowledge in inductive learning. *Machine Learning*, 9(1), 1992.

(Peltason et al., 1991) C. Peltason, A. Schmiedel, C. Kindermann, and J. Quantz. The BACK system revisted. Technical Report KIT-REPORT 75, Technical University of Berlin, 1991.

(Quinlan, 1990) J. Ross Quinlan. Learning logical definitions from relations. *Machine Learning*, 5(3), 1990.

(Schapire, 1990) Robert E. Schapire. The strength of weak learnability. *Machine Learning*, 5(2), 1990.

(Valiant, 1984) L. G. Valiant. A theory of the learnable. *Communications of the ACM*, 27(11), November 1984.

(Weiss and Kulkowski, 1990) Sholom Weiss and Casmir Kulkowski. *Computer Systems that Learn*. Morgan Kaufmann, 1990.

(Woods and Schmolze, 1992) W. A. Woods and J. G. Schmolze. The KL-ONE family. *Computers And Mathematics With Applications*, 23(2-5), March 1992.

(Wright et al., 1993) Jon Wright, Elia Weixelbaum, Gregg Vesonder, Karen Brown, Spephen Palmer, Jay Berman, and Harry Moore. A knowledge-based configurator that supports sales engineering and manufacturing and AT&T network systems. *AI Magazine*, 14:69–80, 1993.

Directional Resolution:
The Davis-Putnam Procedure, Revisited *

Rina Dechter
Information and Computer Science
University of California, Irvine
dechter@ics.uci.edu

Irina Rish
Information and Computer Science
University of California, Irvine
irinar@ics.uci.edu

Abstract

The paper presents algorithm *directional resolution*, a variation on the original Davis-Putnam algorithm, and analyzes its worst-case behavior as a function of the topological structure of the theories. The notions of *induced width* and *diversity* are shown to play a key role in bounding the complexity of the procedure. The importance of our analysis lies in highlighting structure-based tractable classes of satisfiability and in providing theoretical guarantees on the time and space complexity of the algorithm. Contrary to previous assessments, we show that for many theories directional resolution could be an effective procedure. Our empirical tests confirm theoretical prediction, showing that on problems with special structures, like *chains*, directional resolution greatly outperforms one of the most effective satisfiability algorithm known to date, namely the popular Davis-Putnam procedure.

1 Introduction

In 1960, Davis and Putnam [Davis and Putnam, 1960] presented their resolution algorithm. They proved that a restricted amount of resolution, if performed systematically along some order of the atomic formulas, is sufficient for deciding satisfiability. This algorithm, in its original form, has received limited attention, and analyses of its performance have emphasized its worst-case exponential behavior [Galil, 1977, Goerdt, 1992], while neglecting its virtues. This happened, in our view, because the algorithm was immediately overshadowed by a competitor with nearly the same name: *The Davis-Putnam Procedure*. This

---
*This work was partially supported by NSF grant IRI-9157636, by Air Force Office of Scientific Research grant AFOSR 900136, by Toshiba of America, and by a Xerox grant.

competing algorithm, proposed in 1962 by Davis, Logemann, and Loveland [Davis et al., 1962], searches through the space of possible truth assignments while performing unit resolution until quiesience at each step. We will refer to the first algorithm as $DP-elimination$ and to the second as $DP-backtracking$. The latter was presented in [Davis et al., 1962] as a minor syntactic change to the first: the *elimination rule* (rule III in [Davis and Putnam, 1960]) in DP-elimination was replaced by the *splitting rule* (rule III' in [Davis et al., 1962]) in order to avoid the memory explosion encountered when empirically testing DP-elimination. By refraining from an explicit analysis of this exchange (beyond the short comment on memory explosion), the authors of [Davis et al., 1962] may have left the impression that the two algorithms are basically identical. Indeed, from then on, most work on the Davis-Putnam procedure quotes the backtracking version [Goldberg et al., 1982, Selman, 1992], wrongly suggesting that this is the algorithm presented in [Davis and Putnam, 1960].

In this paper, we wish to "revive" the DP-elimination algorithm by studying its virtues theoretically and by subjecting it to a more extensive empirical testing. First, we show that, in addition to determining satisfiability, the algorithm generates an equivalent theory that facilitates model generation and query processing. Consequently, it may be better viewed as a knowledge compilation algorithm. Second, we offset the known worst-case exponential complexities [Galil, 1977, Goerdt, 1992] by showing that the algorithm is tractable for many of the known tractable classes for satisfiability (e.g., $2-cnfs$ and Horn clauses) and for constraint satisfaction problems [Dechter and Pearl, 1987, Dechter and Pearl, 1991] (e.g., causal theories and theories having a bounded induced width). Third, we present a new parameter, called *diversity*, that gives rise to new tractable classes.

On the empirical side, we qualify prior empirical tests in [Davis et al., 1962] by showing that for uniform random propositional theories DP-backtracking outperforms DP-elimination by far. However, for a class of instances having a *chain*-like structure DP-elimination outperforms DP-backtracking by several orders of magnitude.

2 Definition and preliminaries

We denote propositional symbols, also called *variables*, by uppercase letters $P, Q, R, ...$, propositional literals (i.e., $P, \neg P$) by lowercase letters $p, q, r, ...$, and disjunctions of literals, or *clauses*, by $\alpha, \beta, ...$. For instance, $\alpha = (P \vee Q \vee R)$ is a clause. We will sometime denote by $\{P, Q, R\}$ the clause $(P \vee Q \vee R)$. A *unit clause* is a clause of size 1. The notation $(\alpha \vee T)$ will be used as shorthand for the disjunction $(P \vee Q \vee R \vee T)$, and $\alpha \vee \beta$ denotes the clause whose literal appears in either α or β. The *resolution* operation over two clauses $(\alpha \vee Q)$ and $(\beta \vee \neg Q)$ results in a clause $(\alpha \vee \beta)$, thus eliminating Q. *Unit resolution* is a resolution operation when one of the clauses is a unit clause. A formula φ in conjunctive normal form (cnf) is a set of clauses $\varphi = \{\alpha_1, ..., \alpha_t\}$ that denotes their conjunction. The set of *models* of a formula φ is the set of all satisfying truth assignments to all its symbols. A clause α is *entailed* by φ, $\varphi \models \alpha$, iff α is true in all models of φ. A Horn formula is a cnf formula whose clauses all have at most one positive literal. A definite formula is a cnf formula that has exactly one positive literal. A clause is positive if it contains only positive literals and is negative if it contains negative literals only. A k-cnf formula is one whose clauses are all of length k or less.

3 DP-elimination – Directional Resolution

The DP-elimination [Davis and Putnam, 1960] is an ordering-based restricted resolution that can be described as follows. Given an arbitrary ordering of the propositional variables, we assign to each clause the index of the highest ordered literal in that clause. Then we resolve only clauses having the same index, and only on their highest literal. The result of this restriction is a systematic elimination of literals from the set of clauses that are candidates for future resolution. DP-elimination also includes additional steps, one forcing unit resolution whenever possible and another preferring resolution over literals that appear only negatively (called *all-negative*) or only positively (called *all-positive*). There are many other intermediate steps that can be introduced between the basic steps of eliminating the highest indexed variable (i.e., subsumption elimination). However, in this paper, we will focus on the ordered elimination step and will invoke auxiliary steps whenever necessary. Additionally, we will be interested not merely in achieving refutation, but also in the sum total of the clauses accumulated by this process, which constitutes an equivalent theory with useful computational features. Algorithm *directional resolution* (DR) (the core of DP-elimination) is described in Figure 1. We call its output theory, $E_d(\varphi)$, the *directional extension* of φ.

directional-resolution
Input: A cnf theory φ, an ordering $d = Q_1, ..., Q_n$ of its variables.
Output: A decision of whether φ is satisfiable. If it is, a theory $E_d(\varphi)$, equivalent to φ, else an empty directional extension.
1. *Initialize:* generate an ordered partition of the clauses, $bucket_1, ..., bucket_n$, where $bucket_i$ contains all the clauses whose highest literal is Q_i.
2. For $i = n$ to 1 do:
3. Resolve each pair $\{(\alpha \vee Q_i), (\beta \vee \neg Q_i)\} \subseteq bucket_i$. If $\gamma = \alpha \vee \beta$ is empty, return $E_d(\varphi) = \emptyset$, the theory is not satisfiable; else, determine the index of γ and add it to the appropriate bucket.
4. End-for.
5. Return $E_d(\varphi) \Longleftarrow \bigcup_i bucket_i$.

Figure 1: Algorithm *directional resolution*

The algorithm can be conveniently described using a partitioning of the set of clauses of a theory into buckets. Given an ordering $d = Q_1, ...Q_n$, the bucket for Q_i $bucket_i$, contains all the clauses containing Q_i that do not contain any symbol higher in the ordering. Given the theory φ, algorithm *directional resolution* process the buckets in a reverse order of d. When processing $bucket_i$, it resolves over Q_i all possible pairs of clauses in the bucket and insert the resolvents into the appropriate lower buckets.

Theorem 1: (model generation)
Let φ be a cnf formula, $d = Q_1, ..., Q_n$ an ordering, and $E_d(\varphi)$ its directional extension. Then, if the extension is not empty, any model of φ can be generated in time $O(|E_d(\varphi)|)$ in a backtrack-free manner, consulting $E_d(\varphi)$, as follows: Step 1. Assign to Q_1 a truth value that is consistent with clauses in $bucket_1$ (if the bucket is empty, assign Q_1 an arbitrary value); Step i. After assigning a value to $Q_1, ..., Q_{i-1}$, assign to Q_i a value that, together with the previous assignments, will satisfy all the clauses in $bucket_i$. □

Proof: Suppose, to the contrary that during the process of model generation there exists a partial model of truth assignments, $q_1, ..., q_i$ for the first $i-1$ symbols that satisfy all the clauses in the buckets of $Q_1, ..., Q_{i-1}$, and assume that there is no truth value for Q_i that satisfy all the clauses in the bucket of Q_i. Let α and β be two clauses in the bucket of Q_i that clash. Clearly, α and β contain opposite signs of atom Q_i; in one Q_i appears negatively and in the other positively. Consequently, while being processed by directional-resolution, α and β could have been resolved upon, thus resulting in a resolvent that must appear in earlier buckets. Such a clause, if existed, would not have allowed the partial model $q_1, ..., q_i$, thus leading to a contradiction. □

Corollary 1: *[Davis and Putnam, 1960] A theory has a non-empty directional extension iff it is satisfiable.* □

Clearly, the effectiveness of directional resolution both for satisfiability and for subsequent query processing depends on the the size of its output theory $E_d(\varphi)$.

Theorem 2: (complexity)
Given a theory φ and an ordering d of its propositional symbols, the time complexity of algorithm directional resolution is $O(n \cdot |E_d(\varphi)|^2)$, where n is the number of propositional letters in the language.

Proof: There are at most n buckets, each containing no more clauses than the final theory, and resolving pairs of clauses in each bucket is a quadratic operation. □

The bound above, although could be loose, demonstrates the dependence of the algorithm's complexity on the size of its resulting output.

Once $E_d(\varphi)$ is compiled, determining the entailment of a single literal involves checking the bucket of that literal first. If the literal appears there as a unit clause, it is entailed; if not, the negation of that literal should be inserted and the algorithm should be restarted from that bucket. If the empty clause is generated in that process, the literal is entailed. To determine the entailment of an arbitrary clause, each literal of the negated clause must be added to its appropriate bucket and processing restarted from the highest such bucket. This suggests that in knowledge bases, whose queries involve a restricted subset of the alphabet, that subset should be processed last by directional resolution. Namely, the symbols of that subset should appear early in the ordering. In summary,

Theorem 3: *(entailment)*
Given a directional extension $E_d(\varphi)$ and a constant c, the entailment of clauses involving only the first c symbols in d is polynomial in the size of $E_d(\varphi)$. □

4 Tractable classes

Consider the following two examples demonstrating the effect of ordering on $E_d(\varphi)$.

Example 1: Let $\varphi_1 = \{(B, A), (C, \neg A), (D, A), (E, \neg A)\}$. For the ordering $d_1 = (E, B, C, D, A)$, all clauses are initially contained in $bucket(A)$ (highest in the ordering). All other buckets are empty. Following the application of algorithm directional resolution along d_1, we get (note that processing is in the reverse order of d): $bucket(D) = \{(C, D), (D, E)\}$, $bucket(C) = \{(B, C)\}$, $bucket(B) = \{(B, E)\}$.

The directional extension along the ordering $d_2 = (A, B, C, D, E)$ is identical to the input theory, however, and each bucket contains at most one clause.

Example 2: Consider the theory $\varphi_2 = \{(\neg A, B), (A, \neg C), (\neg B, D), (C, D, E)\}$. The directional extensions of φ along the ordering $d_1 = (A, B, C, D, E)$ and $d_2 = (D, E, C, B, A)$ are $E_{d_1}(\varphi) = \varphi$ and $E_{d_2}(\varphi) = \varphi \cup \{(B, \neg C), (\neg C, D), (E, D)\}$, respectively.

In Example 1, A appears in all clauses; hence, it potentially can generate new clauses when resolved upon, unless it is processed last (i.e., put first in the order), as in d_2. This shows that the interactions among clauses play an important role in the effectiveness of the algorithm and may suggest orderings that yield smaller extensions. In Example 2, on the other hand, all atoms have the same type of interaction, each (except E) appearing in two clauses. Nevertheless, D appears positive in both clauses and consequently will not be resolved upon; hence, it can be processed first. Subsequently, B and C appear only negatively in the remaining theory and can, likewise, be processed without generating new clauses. In the following, we will provide a connection between the algorithm's complexity and two parameters: a topological parameter, called *induced width*, and a syntactic parameter, called *diversity*.

Note that directional resolution is tractable for 2-*cnf* theories in all orderings, since 2-*cnf* are closed under resolution (the resolvents are of size 2 or less) and because the overall number of clauses of size 2 is bounded by $O(n^2)$. (In this case, unrestricted resolution is also tractable). Clearly, this algorithm is not the most effective one for satisfiability of 2-*cnfs*. Satisfiability for these theories can be decided in linear time [Even et al., 1976]. However, as noted earlier, DR achieves more than satisfiability, it compiles a theory that allows model generation in linear time. We summarize:

Theorem 4: *If φ is a 2-cnf theory, then algorithm directional resolution will produce a directional extension of size $O(n^2)$, in time $O(n^3)$.* □

Corollary 2: *Given a directional extension $E_d(\varphi)$ of a 2-cnf theory φ, the entailment of any clause involving the first c symbols in d is $O(c^3)$.* □

4.1 Induced width

Let $\varphi = \varphi(Q_1, ..., Q_n)$ be a *cnf* formula defined over the variables $Q_1, ..., Q_n$. The *interaction graph* of φ, denoted $G(\varphi)$, is an undirected graph that contains one node for each propositional variable and an arc connecting any two nodes whose associated variables appear in the same clause. The interaction graph of φ_2 is given in Figure 2a. We can bound the size of all

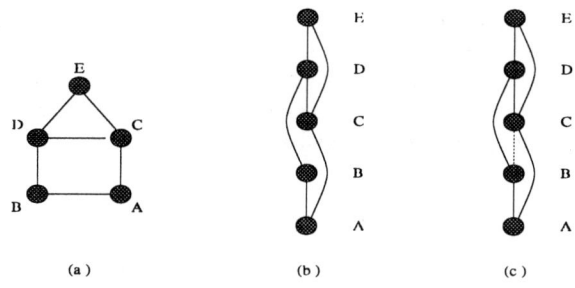

Figure 2: The interaction graph of φ_2

theories having the same interaction graph using some properties of the graph.

Definition 1: Given a graph G and an ordering of its nodes d, the parent set of a node A relative to d is the set of nodes connected to A that precede A in the ordering d. The size of this parent set is the *width* of A relative to d. The width $w(d)$ of an ordering d is the maximum width of nodes along the ordering, and the width w of a graph is the minimal width of all its orderings [Freuder, 1982, Dechter and Pearl, 1987].

Lemma 1: Given the interaction graph $G(\varphi)$ and an ordering d: If A is an atom having $k-1$ parents, then there are at most 3^k clauses in the bucket of A; if $w(d) = w$, then the size of the corresponding theory is $O(n \cdot 3^w)$. □

Proof: The bucket of A contains clauses defined on k literals only. For the set of $k-1$ symbols there are at most $\binom{k-1}{i}$ subsets of i symbols. Each subset can be associated with at most 2^i clauses (i.e., each symbol can appear either positive or negative in a clause), and A can be also positive or negative. Therefore we can have at most

$$2 \cdot \sum_{i=0}^{k-1} \binom{k-1}{i} 2^i = 2 \cdot 3^{k-1}. \qquad (1)$$

clauses. Clearly, if the parent set is bounded by w, the extension is bounded by $O(n \cdot 3^w)$. □

When applied along d to a theory having graph G, algorithm directional resolution adds clauses and, accordingly, the interaction graph changes.

Definition 2: Given a graph G and an ordering d, the graph generated by recursively connecting the parents of G, in a reverse order of d, is called the *induced graph* of G w.r.t. d and is denoted by $I_d(G)$. The width of $I_d(G)$ is denoted by $w*(d)$ and is called the *induced width* of G w.r.t. d.

The graph in Figure 2a, for example, has width 2 along the ordering A, B, C, D, E (Figure 2b). Its induced graph is given in Figure 2c. The induced width of G equals 2.

Lemma 2: Let φ be a theory. Then $G(E_d(\varphi))$, the interaction graph of its directional extension along d, is a subgraph of $I_d(G(\varphi))$.

Proof: The proof is by induction on the symbols along the ordering d. The induction hypothesis is that all the arcs incident to $Q_n, ..., Q_i$ in the $G(E_d(\varphi))$ appear also in $I_d(G(\varphi))$. The claim is true for Q_n, since its connectivity is the same in both graphs. Assume that the claim is true for $Q_n, ..., Q_i$ and we will show that it holds also for Q_{i-1}, namely, if (Q_{i-1}, Q_j) $j < i-1$ is an arc in $G(E_d(\varphi))$, then it is included in $I_d(G(\varphi))$. There are two cases: either Q_{i-1} and Q_j appeared in the same clause of the initial theory, φ, in which case they are connected in $G(\varphi)$ and therefore also in $I_d(G(\varphi))$, or else a clause containing both symbols was introduced during directional resolution. Assume that the clause was introduced while processing bucket $Q_t, t > i-1$. Since Q_{i-1} and Q_j appeared in the bucket of Q_t, each must be connected to Q_t in $G(E_d(\varphi))$ and, by the induction hypothesis, they will also be connected in $I_d(G(\varphi))$. Therefore, Q_{i-1} and Q_j would become connected in $I_d(G(\varphi))$, when connecting the parents of Q_t. □

Theorem 5: Let $\varphi = \varphi(Q_1, ..., Q_n)$ be a cnf, $G(\varphi)$ its interaction graph, and $w*(d)$ its induced width along d; then, the size of $E_d(\varphi)$ is $O(n \cdot 3^{w*(d)})$.

Proof: Since the interaction graph of $E_d(\varphi)$ is a subgraph of $I_d(G)$, and since from lemma 1 the size of theories having $I_d(G)$ as their interaction graph is bounded by $O(n \cdot 3^{w*(d)})$, the result follows. Note that this deduction implicitly assumes that the algorithm eliminates duplicate clauses. □

It is known that if a graph is embedded in a k-tree its induced width is bounded by k [Arnborg et al., 1987]. The definition is recursive.

Definition 3: *(k-trees)*
Step 1: A clique of size k is a k-tree.
Step i: given a k-tree defined over $Q_1, ..., Q_{i-1}$, a k-tree over $Q_1, ..., Q_i$ can be generated by selecting a clique of size k and connecting Q_i to every node in that clique.

Corollary 3: If φ is a formula whose interaction graph can be embedded in a k-tree then there is an ordering d such that the time complexity of directional resolution on that ordering is $O(n \cdot 2^{k+1})$. □

Finding an ordering yielding the smallest induced width of a graph is NP-hard [Arnborg et al., 1987]. However, any ordering d yields a simple bound, $w*(d)$, of $w*$. Consequently, when given a theory and its interaction graph, we will try to find an ordering that yields the smallest width possible. Several heuristic orderings are available (see [Bertele and Brioshi, 1972]). Important special tractable classes are those having $w* = 1$ (namely, the interaction graph is a tree) and

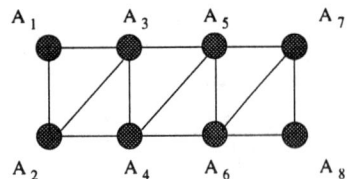

Figure 3: The interaction graph of φ_8 in example 3: $\varphi_8 = \{(A_1, A_2, \neg A_3), (\neg A_2, A_4), (\neg A_2, A_3, \neg A_4), (A_3, A_4, \neg A_5), (\neg A_4, A_6), (\neg A_4, A_5, \neg A_6), (A_5, A_6, \neg A_7), (\neg A_6, A_8), (\neg A_6, A_7, \neg A_8)\}$

those having $w* = 2$, called series parallel networks. These classes can be recognized in linear time. As a matter of fact, given any k, graphs having induced width of k or less can be recognized in $O(exp(k))$.

Example 3: Consider a theory φ_n over the alphabet $\{A_1, A_2, ..., A_n\}$. The theory φ_n has a set of clauses indexed by i, where a clause for i odd is given by $(A_i, A_{i+1}, \neg A_{i+2})$ and two clauses for i even are given by $(\neg A_i, A_{i+2})$ and $(\neg A_i, A_{i+1}, \neg A_{i+2})$. The reader could check that the induced width of such theories along the natural order is 2 and thus the size of the directional extension will not exceed $18 \cdot n$. For this graph, and for the natural ordering the induced graph is identical to the original graph (see figure 3).

4.2 Diversity

The concept of induced width frequently leads to a loose upper bound on the number of clauses recorded by directional resolution. In example 3 for instance, only 8 clauses were generated by directional-resolution when processed in the natural order, even without eliminating subsumption and tautologies in each bucket, while the computed bound is $18 \cdot 8 = 144$. One source for inaccuracy could be that the induced graph is not a tight bound for the interaction graph of $E_d(\varphi)$. Consider, for instance, the two clauses $(\neg A, B), (\neg C, B)$ and the order $d = A, C, B$. When bucket B is processed, no clause is added because B is positive in both clauses, nevertheless, nodes A and C will be connected in the induced graph. In this subsection, we introduce a more refined parameter, called *diversity*, based on the observation that a propositional letter can be resolved upon only when it appears both positively and negatively in different clauses.

Definition 4: (diversity of a theory)
Given a theory φ and an ordering d, let Q_i^+ (or Q_i^-) denote the number of times Q_i appears positively (or negatively) in $bucket_i$ relative to d. The diversity of Q_i relative to d, $div(Q_i)$, is $Q_i^+ \times Q_i^-$. The *diversity of an ordering* d, $div(d)$, is the maximum diversity of its literals w.r.t. the ordering d and the *diversity of a theory*, div, is the minimal diversity over all its orderings.

min-diversity (φ)
1. For $i = n$ to 1 do
2. Step i (after selecting $Q_{i+1}, ..., Q_n$): choose symbol Q having the smallest diversity in $\varphi - \bigcup_{j=i+1}^n bucket_j$, and put it in the i-th position.
3. End.

Figure 4: Algorithm *min-diversity*

Theorem 6: *Algorithm* min-diversity *(Figure 4) generates a minimal diversity ordering of a theory.*

Proof: Let d be an ordering generated by the algorithm and let Q_i be a literal whose diversity equals the diversity of the ordering. If Q_i is pushed up, its diversity can only increase and if pushed down, it must be replaced by a literal whose diversity is either equal to or higher than the diversity of Q_i. □

The concept of diversity yields new tractable classes. If d is an ordering having a zero diversity, algorithm directional resolution will add no clauses to φ along d. Namely,

Theorem 7: *Theories having zero diversity are tractable and can be recognized in linear time.* □

Example 4: Let $\varphi = \{(G, E, \neg F), (G, \neg E, D), (\neg A, F), (A, \neg E) (\neg B, C, \neg E) (B, C, D)\}$. The reader can verify that the ordering $d = A, B, C, D, E, F, G$ is a zero-diversity ordering of φ. Note that the diversity of theories in example 3 along the natural ordering, is 1.

Zero-diversity theories generalize the notion of causal theories defined for general networks of multivalued relations [Dechter and Pearl, 1991]. According to the definition, theories specified in the form of $cnfs$ would correspond to *causal* if there is an ordering of the symbols such that each bucket contains only one clause. Therefore, a causal cnf theory has zero-diversity. Note that even when a general theory is not zero-diversity it is better to put zero-diversity literals last in the ordering (namely they will be processed first). Then, the size of the directional-extension is exponentially bounded in the number of literals having only strictly-positive diversities. In general, however, the parameter of interest is the diversity of the directional extension $E_d(\varphi)$ rather than the diversity of φ.

Definition 5: (induced diversity)
The *induced diversity of an ordering* d, $div^*(d)$, is the diversity of $E_d(\varphi)$ along d, and the *induced diversity of a theory*, $div*$, is the minimal induced diversity over all its orderings.

Since $div*(d)$ bounds the *added* clauses generated from each bucket, we can trivially bound the size of $E_d(\varphi)$ using $div*$: for every d, $|E_d(\varphi)| \leq |\varphi| + n \cdot div*(d)$. The problem is that even for a given ordering d, $div*(d)$ is

not polynomially computable, and, moreover, we did not find an effective upper bound. Still it can be used for some special cases. Clearly, for most theories and most orderings
$div*(d) > div(d)$. A special counter example we observed are the zero diversity theories for which $div*(d) = div(d) = 0$. We next identify a subclass of diversity-1 theories whose div* remains 1.

Theorem 8: *A theory* $\varphi = \varphi(Q_1, ..., Q_n)$, *has* $div* \leq 1$ *and is therefore tractable, if each symbol* Q_i *satisfies one of the following conditions: a. it appears only negatively; b. it appears only positively; c. it appears in exactly two clauses.* □

The set of theories in example 3 has $div* = 2$. Note though, that we can easily create examples with high $w*$ having $div* \leq 1$.

4.3 A diversity graph for Horn theories

It is known that general Horn satisfiability can be determined by unit resolution. Note that when DR is processed in a dynamic ordering (as suggested in the original DP-elimination), namely, when propositional letters that appear in a unit clause are processed first (last in the ordering) and when new unit clauses generated, their buckets are pushed up, we have the essence of unit propagation. When incorporating this *dynamic-ordering* variation to directional resolution, satisfiability will be determined polynomially (for Horn theories) if the algorithm terminates once no unit clauses are available. However, executing the algorithm to full completion may result in long output theories [McAllester]. We now show that definite Horn theories of zero diversity can be given a simple graph interpretation, yielding a more accurate estimate of the extension's size for definite and Horn theories.

One may question the usefulness of this exercise since satisfiability is not a problem for Horn theories. Still, directional resolution achieves more than satisfiability, it compiles the Horn theory into a backtrack-free one which might prove useful in some applications, especially those requiring multiple queries on a small subset of the alphabet. For example, in the context of rule-based programs where the rules represent actions to be taken in real time, preprocessing by directional resolution posts constraints that will not allow the execution of rules leading to future deadends. Also, analysis of Horn theories may guide future extensions to general *cnfs* which are near Horn.

Definition 6: *(diversity graph)*
A Horn theory φ can be associated with a *directed graph* called the *diversity graph* and denoted $D(\varphi)$. $D(\varphi)$ contains a node for each propositional letter and an arc is directed from A to B if there is a Horn clause having B in its head (i.e., B is positive) and A in its

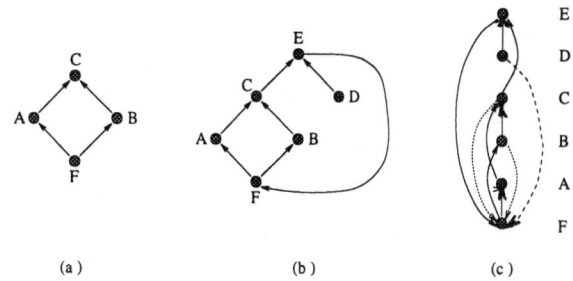

Figure 5: Diversity graphs of Horn theories: a. $D(\varphi_1)$, b. $D(\varphi_2)$, c. the induced diversity graph of φ_2

antecedent (i.e., A is negative). Two special nodes, labeled "true" and "false" are introduced. There is an arc from "true" to A if A is a positive unit clause, and there is an arc from B to "false" if B is included in any negative clause.

Example 5: Consider the following two Horn theories: $\varphi_1 = \{A \wedge B \rightarrow C, F \rightarrow A, F \rightarrow B\}$, $\varphi_2 = \{A \wedge B \rightarrow C, F \rightarrow A, F \rightarrow B, C \wedge D \rightarrow E, E \rightarrow F\}$. The diversity graphs of φ_1 and φ_2 are presented in Figure 5. We see that φ_1 is an acyclic theory (it has an acyclic diversity graph) while φ_2 is cyclic.

Theorem 9: *A definite Horn theory has an acyclic diversity graph iff it has a zero diversity.*

Corollary 4: *If* φ *is an acyclic definite Horn theory w.r.t. ordering* d, *then* $E_d(\varphi) = \varphi$. □

Note that the theorem cannot be extended to full Horn theories. For example, the theory

$$\varphi = \{(A \rightarrow B), (\neg A, \neg B), A\}$$

is a Horn theory whose diversity graph is acyclic. Yet it has a non-zero diversity. Note also that definite theories are always satisfiable and they are closed under resolution. We will now show that the notion of a diversity graph will allow a more refined approximation of the directional extension of definite and Horn theories.

Definition 7: *diversity width (div-width)*
Let D be a directed graph and let d be an ordering of the nodes. The positive width of a node Q, denoted $u_+(Q)$, is the number of arcs emanating from prior nodes, called its positive parents, towards Q. The negative width of Q relative to d, denoted $u_-(Q)$, is the number of arcs emanating from Q towards nodes preceding it in the ordering d, called its negative parents. The *diversity-width (div-width)* of Q, $u(Q)$, relative to d is $max\{u_+(Q), u_-(Q)\}$. The *div-width*, $u(d)$, of an ordering, d, is the maximum div-width of each of its nodes along the ordering, and the *div-width* of a Horn theory is the minimum of $u(d)$ over all orderings that starts with nodes "true" and "false".

Lemma 3: Given a diversity graph of Horn theory $D(\varphi)$, and an ordering d, if A is an atom having k positive parents and j negative parents, then there are at most $O(2^k + j \cdot 2^j)$ non-negative clauses in the bucket of A. □

A minimum div-width of a graph can be computed by a greedy algorithm like the min-diversity algorithm in figure 4, using div-width criteria for node selection.

As in the case of interaction graph, the diversity graph changes when processed by directional resolution and its diversity graph can be *approximated* by graph manipulation as follows:

Definition 8: *(induced diversity graph and width)*
Given a digraph D and an ordering d, such that "true" and "false" appear first, the *induced diversity graph* of D relative to d, denoted $ID_d(D)$, is generated as follows. Nodes are processed from last to first. When processing node Q_i, a directed arc from Q_j to Q_k is added if both nodes precede Q_i in the ordering and if there is a directed arc from Q_j to Q_i and from Q_i to Q_k. The div-width of $ID_d(D)$, denoted by $u*(d)$, is called the *induced diversity width* of D w.r.t. d or *div-width**.

Note that constructing the induced diversity graph is at most $O(n^3)$ when n is the number of vertices.

Example 6: The induced diversity graph of $D(\varphi_2)$ along the ordering $d = F, A, B, C, D, E$ is given in Figure 5. (This is a definite theory, so nodes "true" and "false" are omitted). The added arcs are dotted. The div-width of node E is 2 (its positive div-width is 2 and its negative div-width is 1). In this case, $u(d) = u*(d) = 2$.

We can show:

Lemma 4: Let φ be a Horn theory and d an ordering of its symbols; then the diversity graph of $E_d(\varphi)$, $D(E_d(\varphi))$, is contained in $ID_d(D(\varphi))$ when d is an ordering which starts with "true" and "false". □

We can now bound the size of $E_d(\varphi)$ for a Horn theory φ:

Theorem 10: Let φ be a Horn theory and let d be an ordering of its symbols that starts by "true" and "false", having induced div-width, $u*(d)$ along d; then the size $E_d(\varphi)$ restricted to the non-negative clauses is $O(n \cdot u*(d) \cdot 2^{u*(d)})$ and the size of $E_d(\varphi)$ restricted to the negative clauses is $O(2^{|false|})$, where $|false|$ is the degree of node "false" in the induced diversity graph.

Proof: Follows immediately from Lemma 3 and Lemma 4. □

Note that the bound on the number of negative clauses may be very loose. Sometimes it will be worse than the bound suggested by the width of the undirected interaction graph. The bound on the number of non-negative clauses though is always more accurate. It is easy to see that for any definite theory, φ, and any ordering d, $w*(d) \geq u*(d)$.

Our earlier observation that *acyclic* diversity graphs of definite theories do not change when processed by directional resolution (using an ordering imposed by the graph), suggests that new arcs are *added* only within *strongly connected components* of the diversity graph. We may, therefore, get a tighter bound on the size of the non-negative clauses added to the directional extension (beyond those in the original theory φ) by consulting each strongly connected component separately.

Definition 9: *(Strongly connected components)*
A *strongly connected component* of a directed graph is a maximal set of nodes U such that for every pair A and B in U there is a directed path from A to B and a directed path from B to A. The *component graph* of $G = (V, E)$, denoted $G^{SCC} = (V^C, E^C)$, contains one vertex for each strongly connected component of G, and there is an edge from component A^c to component B^c if there is a directed edge from a node in A^c to a node in B^c in the graph G.

It is well known that the component graph is acyclic and that the strongly connected components can be computed in time linear in the number of vertices and edges of the graph. The connection between the size of the directional extension of a definite theory and its component-based induced div-width is presented in the following theorem. The bound can be extended to Horn theories using the "false" node.

Theorem 11: Let φ be a definite theory having a diversity graph D. Let $S_1, ..., S_t$ be the strongly connected components of G, let $d_1, d_2, ..., d_t$ be orderings of the nodes in each of the strongly connected components, and let d be a concatenation of the orderings $d = d_{i_1}, ..., d_{i_j}, ..., d_{i_t}$ that agrees with the partial acyclic ordering of the components' graph. Let $u*(d_j)$ be the largest induced div-width of any component. Then, the size of $E_d(\varphi) - \varphi$ is $O(n2^{u*(d_j)})$. □

Consequently, we can restrict ourselves to *admissible* orderings only: those that agree with the acyclic structure of the component graph. Hence, we can modify the definition of induced div-width of a digraph along such orderings to coincide with the largest induced div-width among its strongly connected components.

Example 7: Consider again the theory φ_1 in Example 5. Since the graph is acyclic, the strongly connected components contain only one node, and therefore for any admissible ordering d, $u*(d) = 0$. Indeed no clause will be added. For theory φ_2 there are

DP-backtracking(φ)
Input: A *cnf* theory φ.
Output: A decision of whether φ is satisfiable.
1. Unit_propagate(φ);
2. If the empty clause generated return(*false*);
3. else if all variables are assigned return(*true*);
4. else
5. Q = some unassigned variable;
6.   return(DP-backtracking($\varphi \wedge Q$) $\vee$
7.   DP-backtracking($\varphi \wedge \neg Q$))

Figure 6: DP-backtracking algorithm

two components, one including D only and another including the rest of the variables. For the ordering $d = F, A, B, C, E$ on that component, only the arcs $(C, F), (B, F)(A, F)$ will be added, resulting in an induced div-width of 2 (see Figure 5c).

To conclude, the main purpose of the analysis in this section is to determine ahead of time the usefulness of algorithm directional resolution for a given theory and, more importantly, to suggest a good heuristic ordering that may result in a small induced width, small diversity, or small induced div-width for Horn theories. We know that finding an optimal width is NP-hard, and we conjecture that finding an optimal induced div-width is also hard, nevertheless good orderings can be generated using various heuristics (like min-width, min-diversity and min-div-width).

5 Bounded directional resolution

Since algorithm directional resolution is time and space exponential in the worst case, we propose an approximate algorithm called *bounded directional resolution* (BDR). The algorithm records clauses of size k or less when k is a constant. Consequently, its complexity is polynomial in k. Algorithm bounded directional resolution parallels algorithms for directional k-consistency in constraint satisfaction problems [Dechter and Pearl, 1987].

6 Experimental evaluation

DP-backtracking has been implemented in C language as a variant of the Davis-Putnam procedure (see Figure 6).

It has been augmented with the *2-literal clause heuristic* proposed in [Crawford and Auton, 1993] which prefers a variable that would cause the largest number of unit propagations. The number of possible unit propagations is approximated by the number of 2-literal clauses in which the variables appear. The modified version significantly outperforms DP-backtracking without this heuristic

[Crawford and Auton, 1993]. In order to find a solution following DR we ran DP-backtracking using the reverse ordering of variables used by DR, but without the 2-literal clause heuristic. The reason is that we wanted to fix the order of variables. As theory dictates, no deadends occur when DP-backtracking is applied after DR on the same ordering. In this case DP-backtracking takes linear time in the extension size.

Algorithm BDR, since it is incomplete for satisfiability, was followed by DP-backtracking augmented with the 2-literal clause heuristic.

Different orderings of variables were used by the algorithms: input ordering as used by the generator of problems, min-width ordering and min-diversity ordering. Given an interaction graph, min-width ordering selects a variable with the smallest degree, and puts it last in the ordering; the node is eliminated from the graph and the ordering continues recursively. Min-diversity ordering have been described above.

In conjunction with DR we have experimented with both static and dynamic orderings. Static orderings were computed prior to search while dynamic orderings were computed at each step of the search. We report the results on static orderings only since we did not observe any significant difference in DR's efficiency when running the algorithms on both dynamic and static orderings.

Several random generators were used in order to test the algorithms over problems with different structure. To generate *uniform k-cnfs* we used the generator proposed by [Mitchell et al., 1992] taking as input the number of variables n, the number of clauses m, and the number of literals per clause k. We generate each clause randomly choosing k variables from the set of n variables and by determining the polarity of each literal with probability 0.5. Our second generator, called *mixed cnf generator*, generates theories containing clauses of length k_1 and clauses of length k_2. The third generator, called *chains*, first used the *uniform k-cnf* generator to obtain a sequence of n independent random subtheories, and then connected all the subtheories in a chain by generating 2-*cnf* clauses using one variable from the i-th subtheory and one from the $(i + 1)$-th subtheory. Similarly we also connected the n independent subtheories into a tree structure. The obtained results were similar to those on chains, so we report only the result on chains. We experimented also with random *embeddings in k-trees* [Arnborg et al., 1987]. However, we were unable to generate hard instances with more than few deadends. Consequently, the performance of both DR and DP-backtracking was similarly efficient.

We measured CPU time for all algorithms, and the number of deadends for DP-backtracking as characteristics of problems' difficulty. We measured also the number of new clauses generated by DR, the maximal

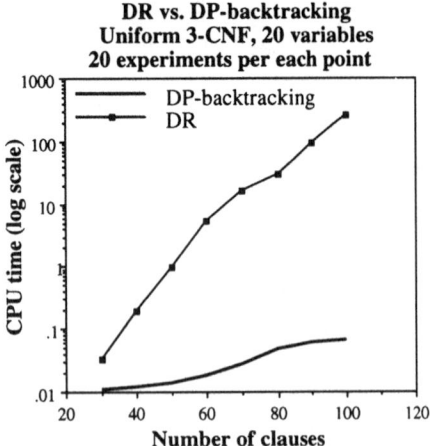

Figure 7: DR and DP-backtracking on 3-$cnfs$

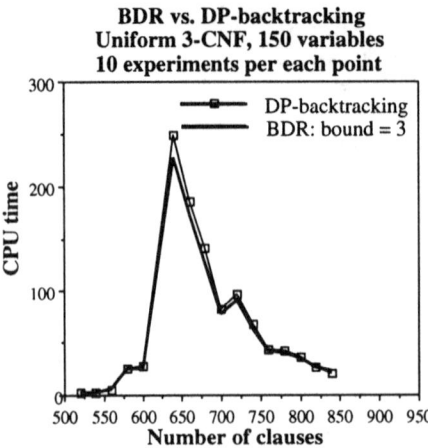

Figure 8: BDR with bound=3 and DP-backtracking on 3-$cnfs$

size of generated clauses, and the induced width. The number of experiments shown in the figures is usually per each point unless stated otherwise.

6.1 Results for Problems with Uniform Structure

We compared DP-backtracking with DR on randomly generated k-$cnfs$ for k=3,4,5 and on mixed theories. In all these cases DP-backtracking significantly outperforms DR. It is observed that the complexity of DR indeed grows exponentially with the size of problems (see Figure 7). We show the results for 3-$cnfs$ with 20 variables only. On larger problems DR often ran out of memory because of the large number of generated clauses.

Since DR was so inefficient for solving uniform k-$cnfs$ we next experimented with Bounded Directional Resolution (BDR) using different bounds. Our experiments show that when the input theory is a uniform k-cnf and BDR uses a bound less than k, almost no new clauses are added. On the other hand, when the bound is strictly greater than k, the preprocessing phase of BDR by itself is considerably worse than DP-backtracking. The only promising case occurs when the bound equals k. We observed that in this case relatively few clauses were added by BDR which therefor ran much faster. Also, DP-backtracking often ran a little bit faster on the generated theory and therefore the combined algorithm was slightly more efficient than DP-backtracking alone (see Figure 8).

6.2 Results for Chains

The behaviour of the algorithms on chains differs dramatically from that on uniform instances. We found extremely hard instances for DP-backtracking, orders of magnitude harder than those generated by the uniform model. In the Table 1 we compare performance of DP-backtracking on uniform 3-cnf problems and on 3-cnf chain problems of the same size. Chain problems contain 25 subtheories with 5 variables and 9 to 23 3-cnf clauses per subtheory, together with 24 2-cnf clauses connecting subtheories in the chain. The corresponding uniform 3-cnf problems have 125 variables and 249 to 599 clauses. We tested DP-backtracking on both classes of problems. The table shows mean values on 20 experiments where the number of experiments is per a constant problem size. We used min-diversity ordering for each instance.

First, we observed extremely hard chain problems with many deadends around the cross-over point for chains, orders of magnitude harder than uniform 3-cnf problems of the same size. Second, we note that the crossover point for chain problems is shifted towards a smaller number of clauses per number of variables.

Table 1: DP on uniform 3-$cnfs$ and on chain problems of the same size: 125 variables

| Num of clauses | Mean values on 20 experiments ||||||
| | Uniform 3-cnfs ||| 3-cnf chains |||
	% Sat	Time 1st solution	Dead ends	% Sat	Time 1st solution	Dead ends
249	100	0.2	0	100	0.3	0
299	100	0.2	0	100	0.4	1
349	100	0.2	3	70	9945.7	908861
399	100	0.2	2	25	2551.1	207896
449	100	0.4	17	15	185.2	13248
499	95	3.7	244	0	2.4	160
549	35	8.5	535	0	0.9	9
599	0	6.6	382	0	0.1	6

On the other hand, DR behaved in a tamed way on the chain problems and was sometimes more than 1000

Table 2: DR and DP on 3-cnf chains: 25 subtheories, 5 variables in each

Min-diversity ordering (static)											
Mean values on 20 experiments											
Num of varia bles	Num of clau ses	% Sat prob lems	Time: 1st solution, DP-back tracking	Number of dead ends	Time: SAT only, DR	Time: 1st solution, DP after DR	Dead ends after DR	Time: SAT+1st solution, DR	Number of new clauses	Size of Max clause	Iduced width
125	249	100	0.34	0.2	0.64	0.30	0.0	1.10	61.4	4.1	5.1
125	299	100	0.41	1.4	1.42	0.32	0.0	1.92	105.2	4.1	5.3
125	349	70	9945.69	908861.2	2.23	0.33	0.0	2.72	130.8	4.0	5.3
125	399	25	2551.09	207896.3	2.79	0.19	0.0	3.08	131.1	4.0	5.3
125	449	15	185.19	13248.1	3.67	0.27	0.0	4.12	135.4	4.0	5.5
125	499	0	2.43	159.6	3.84	0.00	0.0	3.84	116.2	3.9	5.4
125	549	0	0.18	9.4	4.03	0.00	0.0	4.03	99.0	3.9	5.2
125	599	0	0.14	6.1	4.59	0.00	0.0	4.59	93.2	3.6	5.2

times faster than DP-backtracking. In Table 2 we compare DP-backtracking with DR on the same chain problems as in Table 1 for finding one solution and for deciding satisfiability only. A more detailed illustration in Table 3 lists the results on selected hard instances from Table 2 (number of deadend exceeds 4000).

Table 3: DR and DP on hard instances (number of deadends > 4000): 3-cnf chains with 125 variables

Num of cls	SAT: 0 or 1	DP-backtracking		DR
		Time: 1st solution	Dead ends	Time: 1st solution
349	0	41163.8	3779913	1.5
349	0	102615.3	9285160	2.4
349	0	55058.5	5105541	1.9
349	0	21.2	2050	2.4
399	0	74.8	6053	3.6
399	0	87.7	7433	3.1
399	0	149.3	12301	3.1
399	0	37903.3	3079997	3.0
399	0	11877.6	975170	2.2
399	0	52.0	4215	3.3
399	0	841.8	70057	2.9
449	1	655.5	47113	5.2
449	0	60.5	4359	4.7
449	0	2549.2	181504	3.0
449	0	289.7	21246	3.5

As expected, DR significantly outperforms DP-backtracking for instances in which DP-backtracking encountered many deadends. Figure 9a shows that the CPU time of DP-backtracking grows linearly with the numbers of deadends (note, that we use logarithmic scale for CPU time) while in case of DR it remains almost constant. We have displayed CPU time on problem instances hard for DP-backtracking (the number of deadends is greater than 1000).

All the experiments before used min-diversity ordering. When experimenting with different orderings (input and min-width) we observed similar results (Figure 9b,c).

We also experimented a little with the actual code of *tableau* [Crawford and Auton, 1993], Crawford and Auton's implementation of Davis-Putnam procedure with various heuristics. We observed a similar behaviour on chain problems. Although some problem instances hard for our version of DP-backtracking were easy for tableau, others were extremely difficult for both algorithms.

We see that almost all the hard chain problems for DP-backtracking were unsatisfiable. Here is a possible explanation. Suppose there is an unsatisfiable subtheory U in a chain problem whose variables are put at the end of an ordering. If all the other subtheories are satisfiable, then DP-backtracking will try to re-instatiate variables from the satisfiable subtheories each time it encounters a deadend. Not knowing the structure hurts DP-backtracking.

Choosing the right ordering would help but this may be hard to recognize without some preprocessing. Other variants of backtracking that are capable of exploiting the structure like *backjumping* [Dechter, 1990] would avoid useless re-instantiation of variables sometimes performed by DP-backtracking . Experiments with backjumping on the same chain instances as used in Table 2 showed that all the problems that were hard for DP-backtracking were quite easy for backjumping (see Figure 10). Backjumping also outperforms DR.

7 Related work and conclusions

Directional resolution belongs to a family of elimination algorithms first analyzed for optimization tasks in dynamic programming [Bertele and Brioshi, 1972] and later used in constraint satisfaction [Seidel, 1981, Dechter and Pearl, 1987] and in belief networks [Lauritzen and Spigelholter, 1988]. The complexity of all these elimination algorithms can be bounded as a function of the induced width $w*$ of the undirected graph characteristic of each problem instance. Although it is known that determining the $w*$ of an arbitrary graph is NP-hard, useful heuristics for bounding $w*$ are available.

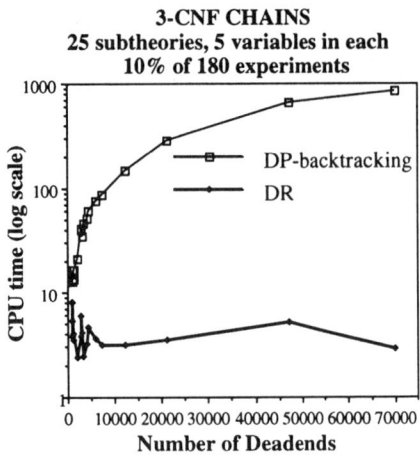

(a) hard instances: more than 1000 deadends

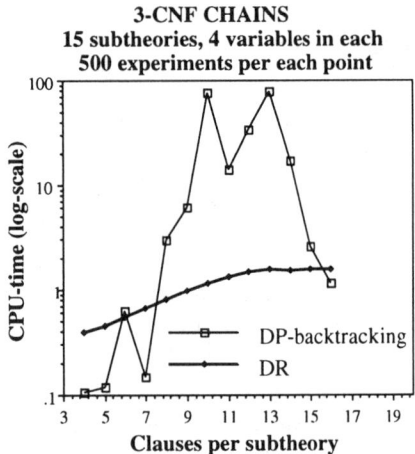

(b) input ordering

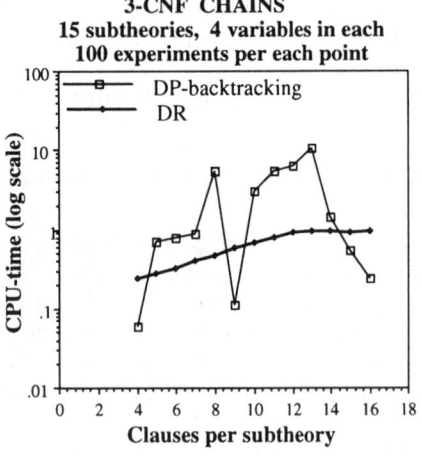

(c) min-width ordering

Figure 9: DR and DP-Backtracking on chains

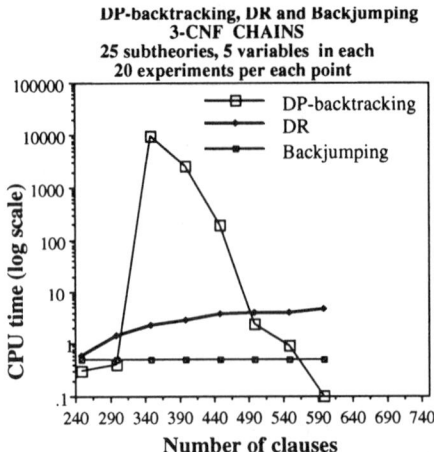

Figure 10: DP-Backtracking, DR and Backjumping on chains: static min-diversity ordering

Since propositional satisfiability is a special case of constraint satisfaction, the induced-width bound could be obtainedby mapping a propositional formula into the relational framework of a constraint satisfaction problem (see [Ben-Eliyahu and Dechter, 1991]), and applying and applying *adaptive consistency*, the elimination algorithm tailored for constraint satisfaction problems [Dechter and Pearl, 1987, Seidel, 1981]. We have recently shown, however, that this kind of pair wise elimination operation as performed by directional resolution is more effective. And, while it can be extended to any row-convex constraint problem [Van Beek and Dechter, 1993] or to every 1-tight relations [Van Beek and Dechter, 1993] it cannot decide consistency for arbitrary multi-valued networks of relations.

Specifically the paper makes three main contributions. First, we revive the old Davis-Putnam algorithm (herein called *directional resolution*). Second, we mitigate the pessimistic analyses of DP-elimination by showing that algorithm *directional resolution* admits some known tractable classes for satisfiability and constraint satisfaction, including *2-cnfs*, Horn clauses, causal networks, and bounded-width networks. In addition, we identify new tractable classes based on the notion of *diversity*, and show a tighter bound for the size of the directional extension of Horn theories based on *induced diversity width*. Finally, Our empirical tests show that, while on uniform theories directional resolution is ineffective, on problems with special structures, like *chains*, namely with low $w*$, directional resolution greatly outperforms DP-backtracking which is one of the most effective satisfiability algorithm known to date.

In conclusion, although directional resolution outperformed DP-backtracking on some classes of problems, it is not advocated as an effective method for general satisfiability problems. Even when the structure is right, there are other structure-exploiting algorithms, like backjumping, that may be more effective in finding a satisfying solution. What we do advocate is that structure-based components should be integrated, together with other heuristics (like unit propagation), into any algorithm that tries to solve satisfiability effectively.

At the same time, we have shown that, for some structured domains, directional resolution is an effective knowledge compilation procedure. It compiles knowledge into a form that facilitates efficient model generation and query processing.

Acknowledgements

We would like to thank Dan Frost for experimenting with backjumping, Eddie Schwalb and Rachel Ben-Eliyahu for comments on this paper.

References

[Arnborg et al., 1987] S. Arnborg, D.G. Corneil and A. Proskurowski, "Complexity of finding embedding in a k-tree", *SIAM Journal of Algebraic Discrete Methods*, 8(2), 1987, pp. 177-184.

[Bertele and Brioshi, 1972] U. Bertele and F. Brioschi, *Nonserial Dynamic Programming*, Academic Press, New York, 1972.

[Ben-Eliyahu and Dechter, 1991] R. Ben-Eliyahu and R. Dechter, "Default logic, propositional logic and constraints", in *Proceedings of the National Conference on Artificial Intelligence* (AAAI-91), July 1991, Anaheim, CA, pp. 379-385.

[Crawford and Auton, 1993] J. Crawford and L. Auton, "Experimental results on the crossover point in satisfiability problems", in *Proceedings of AAAI-93*, 1993, pp 21-27.

[Davis et al., 1962] M. Davis, G. Logemann and D. Loveland, "A machine program for theorem proving", *Communications of the ACM*, 5, 1962, pp. 394-397.

[Davis and Putnam, 1960] M. Davis and H. Putnam, "A computing procedure for quantification theory", *Journal of the ACM*, 7, 1960, pp. 201-215.

[Dechter and Pearl, 1987] R. Dechter and J. Pearl, "Network-based heuristics for constraint satisfaction problems", in *Artificial Intelligence*, 34, 1987, pp. 1-38.

[Dechter and Pearl, 1991] R. Dechter and J. Pearl, "Directed constraint networks: A relational framework for causal models", in *Proceedings of the Twelfth International Joint Conference on Artificial Intelligence* (IJCAI-91), Sidney, Australia, August 1991, pp. 1164-1170.

[Dechter, 1990] R. Dechter, "Enhancement schemes for constraint processing: Backjumping, learning and cutset decomposition", *Artificial Intelligence*, 41, 1990, 273-312.

[Even et al., 1976] S. Even, A. Itai, and A. Shamir, "On the complexity of timetable and multi-commodity flow", *SIAM Journal on Computing*, 5, 1976, 691-703.

[Freuder, 1982] E.C. Freuder, "A sufficient condition for backtrack-free search", *Journal of the ACM*, 29, 1982, 24-32.

[Galil, 1977] Z. Galil, "On the complexity of regular resolution and the Davis-Putnam procedure", *Theoretical Computer Science* 4, 1977, 23-46.

[Goerdt, 1992] A. Goerdt, "Davis-Putnam resolution versus unrestricted resolution", *Annals of Mathematics and Artificial Intelligence*, 6, 1992, 169-184.

[Goldberg et al., 1982] A. Goldberg, P. Purdom and C. Brown, "Average time analysis of simplified Davis-Putnam procedures", *Information Processing Letters*, 15, 1982, 72-75.

[McAllester] D. McAllester, Private communication

[Mitchell et al., 1992] D. Mitchell, B. Selman and H. Levesque, "Hard and Easy Distributions of SAT Problems", in *Proceedings of AAAI-92*, 1992.

[Seidel, 1981] R. Seidel, "A new method for solving constraint satisfaction problems", in *Proceedings of the Seventh international joint conference on Artificial Intelligence* (IJCAI-81), Vancouver, Canada, August 1981, pp. 338-342.

[Selman, 1992] B. Selman, H. Levesque and D. Mitchell, "A new method for solving hard satisfiability problems", in *Proceedings of the Tenth National Conference on Artificial Intelligence* (AAAI-92), San Jose, CA, July 1992.

[Lauritzen and Spigelholter, 1988] S.L. Lauritzen and D.J. Spigelholter, "Local computations with probabilities on graphical structures and their applications to expert systems", *Journal of the Royal Statistical Society, Series, B,* 50, 1988, pp. 65-74.

[Van Beek and Dechter, 1993]
P. van Beek and R. Dechter. On the minimality and decomposability of row-convex constraint networks, June, 1993. Submitted manuscript.

[Van Beek and Dechter, 1993]
P. van Beek and R. Dechter. Constraint tightness vs global consistency November, 1993. Submitted manuscript.

A General Approach to Specificity in Default Reasoning

James P. Delgrande
School of Computing Science
Simon Fraser University
Burnaby, B.C.
Canada V5A 1S6
jim@cs.sfu.ca

Torsten H. Schaub
IRISA
Campus de Beaulieu
35042 Rennes cedex
France
torsten@irisa.fr

Abstract

We present an approach addressing the notion of specificity, or of preferring a more specific default sentence over a less specific one, in commonsense reasoning. Historically, approaches have either been too weak to provide a full account of defeasible reasoning while accounting for specificity, or else have been too strong and fail to enforce specificity. Our approach is to use the techniques of a weak system, as exemplified by System Z, to isolate minimal sets of conflicting defaults. From the specificity information intrinsic in these sets, a default theory in a target language is specified. In this paper we primarily deal with theories expressed (ultimately) in Default Logic. However other approaches would do just as well, as we illustrate by also considering Autoepistemic Logic and variants of Default Logic. In our approach, the problems of weak systems, such as lack of adequate property inheritance and (occasional) unwanted specificity relations, are avoided. Also, difficulties inherent with stronger systems, in particular, lack of specificity are addressed. This work differs from previous work in specifying priorities in Default Logic, in that we obtain a theory expressed in Default Logic, rather than ordered sets of rules requiring a modification to Default Logic.

1 Introduction

A general problem in nonmonotonic reasoning is that *specificity* among default assertions is difficult to obtain in a fully satisfactory manner. Consider for example where birds fly, birds have wings, penguins are birds, and penguins don't fly. We can write this as:

$$B \to F, \ B \to W, \ P \to B, \ P \to \neg F. \qquad (1)$$

From this theory, given that P is true, one would want to conclude $\neg F$ by default. Intuitively, being a penguin is a more specific notion than that of being a bird, and, in the case of a conflict, we would want to use the more specific default. Also, given that P is true one would want to conclude that W is true, and so penguins have wings by virtue of being birds.

Autoepistemic Logic [Moore, 1985], Circumscription [McCarthy, 1980], and Default Logic [Reiter, 1980] are examples of approaches that are overly *permissive*. For example, in the obvious representation of the above theory in Default Logic, we obtain one extension (i.e. a set of default conclusions) in which $\neg F$ is true and another one in which F is true. One is required to use so-called semi-normal defaults[1] to eliminate the second extension. [Reiter and Criscuolo, 1981], for example, gives a list of ways of transforming default theories so that unwanted extensions arising from specific "interactions" are eliminated.

In the past few years there has been some consensus as to what should constitute a basic system of default properties. This, arguably, is illustrated by the convergence (or at least similarity among) systems such as those developed in [Delgrande, 1987; Kraus et al., 1990; Pearl, 1990; Boutilier, 1992a; Geffner and Pearl, 1992], yet which are derived according to seemingly disparate intuitions. A general problem with these accounts however is that they are too weak. Thus in a conditional logic, even though a bird may be assumed to fly by default (i.e. in the preceding theory, we only derive F but not $\neg F$), a green bird cannot be assumed to fly by default (since it is *conceivable* that greenness is relevant to flight). In these systems some mechanism is required to assert that properties not known to be relevant are irrelevant. This is done in conditional logics by meta-theoretic assumptions, and in probabilistic accounts by independence assumptions. In other approaches there are problems concerning property inheritance, and so one may not obtain the inference that a penguin has wings. While various solutions have been proposed, none are entirely satisfactory.

---

[1] See Section 2.2 for a definition of semi-normal defaults and the way they deal with unwanted extensions.

Our approach is to use the specificity information given by a "weak" system to generate a default theory in a "strong" system, where specificity and property inheritance are satisfactorily handled. Hence we address two related but essentially independent questions:

1. How can a (so-called) weak system be used to isolate specific interacting defaults?
2. How can this information be uniformly incorporated in a theory expressed in a (so-called) strong system?

For concreteness, we develop the approach by considering System Z [Pearl, 1990] as an example of a weak system of defeasible reasoning, and Default Logic (DL) [Reiter, 1980] as a strong system; however in Section 6 we consider the application of the approach to other systems. The general idea is to combine the techniques of System Z and DL in a principled fashion to obtain a general hybrid approach for defeasible reasoning.

We begin with a set of default conditionals $R = \{r \mid \alpha_r \rightarrow \beta_r\}$ where each α_r and β_r are arbitrary propositional formulas. By means of System Z we isolate minimally conflicting sets of defaults with differing specificities; intuitively the defaults in such a set should never be simultaneously applicable. Notably we do not use the full ordering given by System Z (which has difficulties of its own, as described in the next section), but rather appeal to the *techniques* of this approach to isolate conflicting subsets of the defaults. In a second step, we use the derived specificity information to produce a set of semi-normal default rules in DL from the rules in R, in such a way that specificity is suitably handled. The framework described here is intended to be a general approach to "compiling" default theories expressed by a set of conditionals, using intuitions from a weak approach (exemplified by System Z), into a strong approach (exemplified by DL). The choice of DL is of course not arbitrary, since it is very well studied and there exist implementations of DL.

The specific approach then can be looked at from two perspectives. First, DL is used to circumvent problems in System Z, including the facts that inheritance isn't possible across conflicting subclasses and that unwanted specificity information may be obtained. Second, System Z is used to address problems in DL that arise from interacting defaults. That is, using System Z, we construct theories in DL wherein specificity is appropriately handled. Hence, this paper might in some respects be looked on as a successor to [Reiter and Criscuolo, 1981], in that the situations addressed here subsume the set of modifications suggested in that paper. Moreover, the present approach provides a justification for these modifications.

Specificity information is thus obtained by appeal to an extant theory of defaults (here, System Z), and not some a priori ordering. In addition, and in contrast to previous approaches, specificity is added to DL without changing the machinery of DL. That is, the resultant default theory is a theory *in* DL, and not a set of ordered default rules requiring modifications to DL. Finally, we do not produce a "global" partial order (or orders) of rules but rather "locally" distinguish conflicting rules. Lastly, specificity conflicts are resolved, leaving unchanged other conflicts (as are found for example in a "Nixon diamond").

In the next section we briefly introduce System Z, Default Logic, and related work. Section 3 introduces and develops our approach, while Sections 4 and 5 provide the formal details. Section 6 considers the application of the approach to other systems. Section 7 gives a brief summary.

2 Background

2.1 System Z

In System Z a set of rules R representing default conditionals is partitioned into an ordered list of mutually exclusive sets of rules $R_0, \ldots, R_n$. Lower ranked rules are considered more normal (or less specific) than higher ranked rules. Rules appearing in lower-ranked sets are *compatible* with those appearing in higher-ranked sets, whereas rules appearing in higher-ranked sets *conflict* in some fashion with rules appearing in lower-ranked sets. One begins then with a set $R = \{r \mid \alpha_r \rightarrow \beta_r\}$ where each α_r and β_r are propositional formulas over a finite alphabet.[2] A set $R' \subseteq R$ *tolerates* a rule r if $\{\alpha_r \wedge \beta_r\} \cup R'$ is satisfiable. We assume in what follows that R is Z-*consistent*,[3] i.e. for every non-empty $R' \subseteq R$, some $r' \in R'$ is tolerated by $R' - \{r'\}$. Using this notion of tolerance, an ordering on the rules in R is defined:

1. First, find all rules tolerated by R, and call this subset R_0.
2. Next, find all rules tolerated by $R - R_0$, and call this subset R_1.
3. Continue in this fashion until all rules have been accounted for.

In this way, we obtain a *partition* $(R_0, \ldots, R_n)$ of R, where $R_i = \{r \mid r \text{ is tolerated by } R - R_0 - \ldots - R_{i-1}\}$ for $1 \leq i \leq n$. More generally, we write R_i to denote the ith set of rules in the partition of a set of conditionals R. A set of rules R is called *trivial* iff its partition consists only of a single set of rules.

The rank of rule r, written $\mathbf{Z}(r)$, is given by: $\mathbf{Z}(r) = i$ iff $r \in R_i$. Every model M of R is given a Z-rank, $\mathbf{Z}(M)$, according to the highest ranked rule it falsifies:

$$\mathbf{Z}(M) = min\{\, n \mid M \models \alpha_r \supset \beta_r,\ \mathbf{Z}(r) \geq n\,\}.$$

---
[2]The inclusion of strict rules is straightforward [Delgrande and Schaub, 1994] but for simplicity is omitted here.

[3]Pearl uses the term *consistent* [Pearl, 1990].

For our initial set of rules in (1), we obtain the ordering

$$R_0 = \{B \to F, B \to W\}, \quad (2)$$
$$R_1 = \{P \to B, P \to \neg F\}. \quad (3)$$

So the **Z** rank of the model in which $B, \neg F, W$, and P are true is 1, since the rule $B \to F$ is falsified. The **Z** rank of the model in which B, F, W, and P are true is 2, since the rule $P \to \neg F$ is falsified.

The rank of an arbitrary formula φ is defined as the lowest **Z**-rank of all models satisfying φ: $\mathbf{Z}(\varphi) = min\{\mathbf{Z}(M) \mid M \models \varphi\}$. Finally we can define a form of default entailment, which is called *1-entailment*, as follows: A formula φ is said to 1-entail ϕ in the context R, written $\varphi \vdash_1 \phi$, iff $\mathbf{Z}(\varphi \wedge \phi) < \mathbf{Z}(\varphi \wedge \neg \phi)$.

This gives a form of default inference that is weaker than Default Logic, yet has some very nice properties. In the preceding example, we obtain that $P \vdash_1 \neg F$, and $P \vdash_1 B$ and so penguins don't fly, but are birds. Unlike **DL**, we cannot infer that penguins fly, i.e. $P \not\vdash_1 F$. Irrelevant facts are also handled well (unlike conditional logics), and for example we have $B \wedge G \vdash_1 F$, so green birds fly. There are two weaknesses with this approach. First, one cannot inherit properties across exceptional subclasses. So one cannot conclude that penguins have wings (even though penguins are birds and birds have wings), i.e. $P \not\vdash_1 W$. Second, undesirable specificities are sometimes obtained. For example, consider where we add to our initial example (1) the default that large animals are calm. We get the **Z**-ordering:

$$R_0 = \{B \to F, B \to W, L \to C\}, \quad (4)$$
$$R_1 = \{P \to B, P \to \neg F\}. \quad (5)$$

Intuitively $L \to C$ is irrelevant to the other defaults, yet one obtains the default conclusion that penguins aren't large, since $\mathbf{Z}(L \wedge \neg P) < \mathbf{Z}(L \wedge P)$.

[Goldszmidt and Pearl, 1990] has shown that 1-entailment is equivalent to *rational closure* [Kraus et al., 1990]; [Boutilier, 1992a] has shown that CO^* is equivalent to 1-entailment and that N [Delgrande, 1987] and $CT4$ are equivalent to the more basic notion of 0-entailment, proposed in [Pearl, 1989] as a "conservative core" for default reasoning. Consequently, given this "locus" of closely-related systems, each based on distinct semantic intuitions, these systems (of which we have chosen System **Z** as exemplar) would seem to agree on a principled minimal approach to defaults.

2.2 Default Logic

In Default Logic, classical logic is augmented by *default rules* of the form $\frac{\alpha:\beta}{\omega}$. Even though almost all "naturally occurring" default rules are normal, i.e. of the form $\frac{\alpha:\beta}{\beta}$, semi-normal default rules, of the form $\frac{\alpha:\beta\wedge\omega}{\beta}$, are required for establishing precedence in the case of "interacting" defaults [Reiter and Criscuolo, 1981] (see below). Default rules induce one or more *extensions* of an initial set of facts. Given a set of facts W and a set of default rules D, any such extension E is a deductively closed set of formulas containing W such that, for any $\frac{\alpha:\beta}{\omega} \in D$, if $\alpha \in E$ and $\neg\beta \notin E$ then $\omega \in E$.

Definition 1 *Let (D, W) be a default theory and let E be a set of formulas. Define $E_0 = W$ and for $i \geq 0$*

$$E_{i+1} = Th(E_i) \cup \left\{ \omega \mid \frac{\alpha:\beta}{\omega} \in D, \alpha \in E_i, \neg\beta \notin E \right\}$$

Then E is an extension for (D, W) iff $E = \bigcup_{i=0}^{\infty} E_i$.

The above procedure is not strictly iterative since E appears in the specification of E_{i+1}.

Consider our birds example (1); in **DL**, it can be expressed as:[4] $\frac{B:F}{F}, \frac{B:W}{W}, \frac{P:B}{B}, \frac{P:\neg F}{\neg F}$. Given that P is true, we obtain two extensions: one in which P, B, W, and F are true and another one in which P, B, W, and $\neg F$ are true. Intuitively we want only the last extension, since the more specific default $\frac{P:\neg F}{\neg F}$ should take precedence over the less specific default $\frac{B:F}{F}$. The usual fix is to establish a precedence among these two interacting defaults by adding the exception P to the justification of the less specific default rule. This amounts to replacing $\frac{B:F}{F}$ by $\frac{B:F\wedge\neg P}{F}$ which then yields the desired result, namely a single extension containing P, B, W, and $\neg F$.

2.3 Related Work

Arguably specificity per se was first specifically addressed in default reasoning in [Poole, 1985], although it has of course appeared earlier. Of the so-called "weak" approaches, as mentioned, we could have as easily used approaches described in [Boutilier, 1992a] or [Kraus et al., 1990] as that of System **Z**; however specificity, as it appears in System **Z** is particularly straightforwardly describable. Other approaches are too weak to be useful here. For example conditional entailment [Geffner and Pearl, 1992] does not support full inheritance reasoning; while [Delgrande, 1988] is unsatisfactory since it gives a syntactic, albeit general, approach in the framework of conditional logics.

In Default Logic, [Reiter and Criscuolo, 1981] considers patterns of specificity in interacting defaults, and describes how specificity may be obtained via appropriate semi-normal defaults. This work in fact may be regarded as a pre-theoretic forerunner to the present approach, since the situations addressed therein all constitute instances of what we call (in the next section) minimal conflicting sets. [Etherington and Reiter, 1983] also considers a problem that fits within the (overall) present framework: specificity information is given by an inheritance network; this network is compiled into a default theory in **DL**.

---

[4] For coherence, we avoid strict implications which might be more appropriate for some of the rules.

Of recent work that develops priority orderings on default theories, we focus on the approaches of [Boutilier, 1992b; Baader and Hollunder, 1993a; Brewka, 1993]. We note however that these approaches obtain specificity by requiring modifications to **DL**. In contrast, we describe transformations that yield classical **DL** theories. Since the last two approaches are also described in Section 5, they are only briefly introduced here.

[Boutilier, 1992b] uses the correspondence between a conditional $\alpha_r \to \beta_r$ of System **Z** and defaults of the form $\frac{:\alpha_r \supset \beta_r}{\alpha_r \supset \beta_r}$ to produce partitioned sets of default rules. For rules in System **Z**, there is a corresponding set of prerequisite-free normal defaults. One can reason in **DL** by applying the rules in the highest set, and working down. Again, however, specificity is obtained by meta-theoretic considerations, in that one steps outside the machinery of **DL**. Also the order in which defaults are applied depends on the original **Z**-order; this order may be "upset" by the addition of irrelevant conditionals.

[Baader and Hollunder, 1993a] addresses specificity in terminological reasoners. In contrast to the present work, this approach does not rely on conflicts between "levels". Rather a subsumption relation between terminological concepts is mapped onto a set of partially ordered defaults in **DL**. [Brewka, 1993] has adopted the idea of minimal conflicting sets described here, but in a more restricted setting. In common with [Baader and Hollunder, 1993a], partially ordered defaults in **DL** are used; however, for inferencing all consistent strict total orders of defaults must be considered.

3 The Approach: Intuitions

As described previously, information in a **Z**-ordering is used to generate a default theory: The **Z**-ordering provides specificity information, and so for example, tells us that $P \to \neg F$ is a more specific rule than $B \to F$. However, we do not use the full **Z**-ordering, since it may introduce unwanted specificities (see Section 2.1). Rather we determine minimal sets of rules that conflict, and use these sets to sort out specificity information. The generated default theory (in **DL**) will be such that some inferences will be blocked (and so a penguin does not fly), while other inferences will go through (and so, penguins have wings).

Consider for example the following theory, already expressed as a **Z**-ordering:

$$R_0 = \{An \to WB, An \to \neg Fe, An \to M\}$$
$$R_1 = \{B \to An, B \to F, B \to Fe, B \to W\}$$
$$R_2 = \{P \to B, P \to \neg F, E \to B, E \to \neg F,$$
$$Pt \to B, Pt \to \neg Fe, Pt \to \neg WB\}$$

That is, in R_0, animals are warm-blooded, don't have feathers, but are mobile. In R_1, birds are animals that fly, have feathers, and have wings. In R_2, penguins and emus are birds that don't fly, and pterodactyls are birds that have no feathers and are not warm-blooded.

First we locate the minimal sets of conditionals, such that there is a non-trivial **Z**-ordering for this set of conditionals. In our example these consist of:

$$C^0 = \{An \to \neg Fe, B \to An, B \to Fe\}$$
$$C^1 = \{B \to F, P \to B, P \to \neg F\} \quad (6)$$
$$C^2 = \{B \to F, E \to B, E \to \neg F\} \quad (7)$$
$$C^3 = \{B \to Fe, Pt \to B, Pt \to \neg Fe\}$$
$$C^4 = \{An \to WB, B \to An, Pt \to B, Pt \to \neg WB\}$$

Any such set is called a *minimal conflicting set* (*MCS*) of defaults. Such a set has a non-trivial **Z**-ordering, but for any subset there is no non-trivial **Z**-ordering. What this in turn means is that if all the rules in such a set are jointly applicable, then, one way or another there will be a conflict.[5] We show below that each such **Z**-ordering of a set C consists of a binary partition (C_0, C_1); furthermore the rules in the set C_0 are less specific than those in C_1. Consequently, if the rules in C_1 are applicable, then we would want to insure that some rule in C_0 was blocked.

Hence, for our initial example (1), we obtain one *MCS*, corresponding to (6), with the following **Z**-order:

$$C_0 = \{B \to F\} \quad (8)$$
$$C_1 = \{P \to B, P \to \neg F\} \quad (9)$$

So there are two issues that need to be addressed:

1. What rules should be selected as candidates to be blocked?
2. How can the application of a rule be blocked?

For the first question, it turns out that there are different ways in which we can select rules. However, arguably the selection criterion should be independent of the default theory in which the rules are embedded, in the following fashion. For default theories R and R', where $R \subseteq R'$, if $r \in R$ is selected, then r should also be selected in R'. Thus, if we wish to block the default $B \to F$ in the case of P in default theory R, then we will also want to block this rule in any superset R'. In the sequel, we do this as follows: For a *MCS* C, we select those defaults in C_0 and C_1 that actually conflict and hence cause the non-triviality of C. The rules selected in this way from C_0 and C_1 are referred to as the *minimal conflicting rules* and *maximal conflicting rules* respectively. Then, the minimal conflicting rules constitute the candidates to be blocked.

Consider where we have a chain of rules, and where transitivity is explicitly blocked, such as may be found in an inheritance network:

$$A \to B_1, B_1 \to B_2, \ldots, B_n \to C \quad \text{but} \quad A \to \neg C.$$

---

[5]If the rules were represented as normal default rules in **DL** for example, one would obtain multiple extensions.

In this case, given A we need only block some rule in $A \rightarrow B_1, B_1 \rightarrow B_2, \ldots, B_n \rightarrow C$ to ensure that we do not obtain an inference from A to C. However, things are typically not so simplistic. Consider instead the MCS C^4 from above, expressed as a Z-ordering:

$$C_0 = \{An \rightarrow WB, B \rightarrow An\} \quad (10)$$
$$C_1 = \{Pt \rightarrow B, Pt \rightarrow \neg WB\}$$

Intuitively An is less specific than Pt. Hence if we were given that An, Pt, $\neg B$ were true, then in a translation into default logic, we would want the default rule corresponding to $Pt \rightarrow \neg WB$ to be applicable over $An \rightarrow WB$, even though the "linking" rule $Pt \rightarrow B$ has been falsified. This in turn means that, for a MCS, we want the more specific rules to be applicable over the less specific conflicting rules, independently of the other rules in the MCS. We do this by locating those rules whose joint applicability would lead to an inconsistency. In the above, this would consist of $An \rightarrow WB$, and $Pt \rightarrow \neg WB$ since $An \wedge WB \wedge Pt \wedge \neg WB$ is inconsistent. Also we have that $An \rightarrow WB \in C_0$ and $Pt \rightarrow \neg WB \in C_1$ and so the rules have differing specificity.

For the second question, we have the following translation of rules into **DL**: The default theory corresponding to R consists of normal defaults, except for those defaults representing minimal conflicting rules, which will be semi-normal. For these latter default rules, the prerequisite is the antecedent of the original rule (as expected). The justification consists of the consequent together with an assertion to the effect that the maximal conflicting rules in the MCS hold.

Consider the set C_0 in (10), along with its minimal conflicting rule $An \rightarrow WB$. We replace $B \rightarrow An$, $Pt \rightarrow B$, $Pt \rightarrow \neg WB$ with $\frac{B:An}{An}$, $\frac{Pt:B}{B}$, $\frac{Pt:\neg WB}{\neg WB}$ respectively. For $An \rightarrow WB$, we replace it with

$$\frac{An : WB \wedge (Pt \supset \neg WB)}{WB},$$

which can be simplified to $\frac{An : WB \wedge \neg Pt}{WB}$. The rule $An \rightarrow WB$ is translated into a semi-normal default since it is the (only) minimal conflicting rule of C^4 (and of no other C^i). On the other hand, the rule $Pt \rightarrow WB$ is translated into a normal default since it does not occur as a minimal conflicting rule elsewhere.

So, for the minimal conflicting rules we obtain semi-normal defaults; all other defaults are normal. Accordingly, we give below only the semi-normal default rules constructed from the MCSs C^0, C^1, C^2, and C^3:

$$C^0 : \quad \frac{An : \neg Fe \wedge \neg B}{\neg Fe}$$
$$C^1 + C^2 : \quad \frac{B : F \wedge (\tilde{P} \supset \neg F) \wedge (E \supset \neg F)}{F} \quad \text{or} \quad \frac{B : F \wedge \neg P \wedge \neg E}{F}$$
$$C^3 : \quad \frac{B : Fe \wedge (Pt \tilde{\supset} \neg Fe)}{Fe} \quad \text{or} \quad \frac{B : Fe \wedge \neg Pt}{Fe}.$$

The conditional $B \rightarrow F$ occurs in C^1 and C^2 as a minimal conflicting rule. In this case we have two MCSs sharing the same minimal conflicting rule, and we combine the maximal conflicting rules of both sets.

So why does this approach work? The formal details are given in the following sections. However, informally, consider first where we have a MCS of defaults C with a single minimal conflicting rule $\alpha_0 \rightarrow \beta_0$ and a single maximal conflicting rule $\alpha_1 \rightarrow \beta_1$. If we are able to prove that α_0 (and so in **DL** can prove the antecedent of the conditional), then we would want β_0 to be a default conclusion—provided that no more specific rule applies. But what should constitute the justification? Clearly, first that β_0 is consistent. But also that "appropriate", more specific, conflicting conditionals not be applicable. Hence we add these more specific conditionals as part of the justification. Now, in our simplified setting, $\alpha_0 \rightarrow \beta_0$ is such that $\{\alpha_0 \wedge \beta_0\}$ is satisfiable, but for the conditional $\alpha_1 \rightarrow \beta_1$, $\{\alpha_0 \wedge \beta_0\} \cup \{\alpha_1 \wedge \beta_1\}$ is unsatisfiable. Hence it must be that $\{\alpha_0 \wedge \beta_0\} \cup \{\alpha_1 \supset \beta_1\} \models \neg \alpha_1$ for these conditionals. Thus if a minimal conflicting rule is applicable, then the maximal rule cannot be applicable.

This suggests that we might simply add the negation of the antecedent of the higher-level conflicting conditional. However the next example illustrates that this strategy does not work whenever a MCS has more than one minimal conflicting rule. Consider for example the following theory, already expressed as a Z-ordering:

$$R_0 = \{A \rightarrow \neg B, C \rightarrow \neg D\} \quad (11)$$
$$R_1 = \{A \wedge C \rightarrow B \vee D\} \quad (12)$$

If we were to represent this as a normal default theory, then with $\{A, C\}$ we would obtain three extensions, containing $\{\neg B, D\}$, $\{B, \neg D\}$, $\{\neg B, \neg D\}$. The last extension is unintuitive since it prefers the two less specific rules over the more specific one in R_1.

Now observe that the rules in $R_0 \cup R_1$ form a MCS with two minimal conflicting rules. In our approach, this yields two semi-normal defaults[6]

$$\frac{A : \neg B \wedge (A \wedge C \supset B \vee D)}{\neg B} \quad \text{or} \quad \frac{A : \neg B \wedge (C \supset D)}{\neg B} \quad \text{and}$$
$$\frac{C : \neg D \wedge (A \wedge C \supset B \vee D)}{\neg D} \quad \text{or} \quad \frac{C : \neg D \wedge (A \supset B)}{\neg D}$$

along with the normal default rule $\frac{A \wedge C : B \vee D}{B \vee D}$. Given $\{A, C\}$, we obtain only the two more specific extensions, containing $\{\neg B, D\}$ and $\{B, \neg D\}$. In both cases, we apply the most specific rule, along with one of the less specific rules.

Note that if we add either only the negated antecedent of the maximal conflicting rule (viz. $\neg A \vee \neg C$) or all remaining rules (e.g. $C \supset \neg D$ and $A \wedge C \supset B \vee D$ in the case of the first default) to the justification of the two semi-normal defaults, then in both cases we obtain justifications that are too strong. For instance, for $A \rightarrow \neg B$ we would obtain either $\frac{A : \neg B \wedge (\neg A \vee \neg C)}{\neg B}$ which simplifies to $\frac{A : \neg B \wedge \neg C}{\neg B}$ or $\frac{A : \neg B \wedge (A \wedge C \supset B \vee D) \wedge (C \supset \neg D)}{\neg B}$

---

[6]We simplify justifications by replacing each occurrence of the prerequisite by true. The correctness for arbitrary prerequisites is shown in [Delgrande and Schaub, 1994].

which also simplifies to $\frac{A\,:\,\neg B\wedge\neg C}{\neg B}$. Given $\{A,C,D\}$ there is, however, no reason why the rule $A \to \neg B$ should not apply. In contrast, our construction yields the default $\frac{A\,:\,\neg B\wedge(C\supset D)}{\neg B}$, which blocks the second semi-normal default rule in a more subtle way, and additionally allows us to conclude $\neg B$ from $\{A,C,D\}$.

One can also show that conflicts that do not result from specificity (as found for example, in the "Nixon diamond") are handled correctly. These and other examples are discussed further following the presentation of the formal details.

4 Minimal Conflicting Sets

In what follows, we consider a Z-consistent set of default conditionals $R = \{r \mid \alpha_r \to \beta_r\}$ where each α_r and β_r are propositional formulas over a finite alphabet. We write $Prereq(R)$ for $\{\alpha_r \mid \alpha_r \to \beta_r \in R\}$, and $Conseq(R)$ for $\{\beta_r \mid \alpha_r \to \beta_r \in R\}$.

For a set of rules R, the set of its MCSs represents conflicts among rules in R due to disparate specificity. Each MCS is a minimal set of conditionals having a non-trivial Z-ordering.

Definition 2 *Let R be a Z-consistent set of rules. $C \subseteq R$ is a minimal conflicting set (MCS) in R iff C has a non-trivial Z-ordering and any $C' \subset C$ has a trivial Z-ordering.*

Observe that adding new rules to R cannot alter or destroy any existing MCSs. That is, for default theories R and R', where $C \subseteq R \subseteq R'$, we have that if C is a MCS in R then C is a MCS in R'.

The next theorem shows that any MCS has a binary partition:[7]

Theorem 1 *Let C be a MCS in R. Then, the Z-ordering of C is (C_0, C_1) for some non-empty sets C_0 and C_1 with $C = C_0 \cup C_1$.*

Moreover, a MCS entails the negations of the antecedents of the higher-level rules:

Theorem 2 *Let C be a MCS in R. Then, if $\alpha \to \beta \in C_1$ then $C \models \neg \alpha$.*

Hence, given the rule set in (1),

$$R = \{B \to F,\ B \to W,\ P \to B,\ P \to \neg F\},$$

there is one MCS

$$C = \{B \to F,\ P \to B,\ P \to \neg F\}.$$

As shown in (8/9), the first conditional constitutes C_0 and the last two C_1 in the Z-order of C. The set $\{B \to F,\ P \to \neg F\}$ for example, is not a MCS since alone it has a trivial Z-order. It is easy to see that $C \models \neg P$.

---
[7]Proofs are omitted for space limitations, but can be found in [Delgrande and Schaub, 1994].

Intuitively, a MCS consists of three mutually exclusive sets of rules: the least specific or *minimal conflicting rules* in C, $min(C)$; the most specific or *maximal conflicting rules* in C, $max(C)$; and the remaining rules providing a minimal inferential relation between these two sets of rules, $inf(C)$. The following definition provides a very general formal frame for these sets:

Definition 3 *Let R be a set of rules and let $C \subseteq R$ be a MCS in R. We define $max(C)$ and $min(C)$ to be non-empty subsets of R such that*

$$\begin{aligned} min(C) &\subseteq C_0 \\ max(C) &\subseteq C_1 \\ inf(C) &= C - (min(C) \cup max(C)) \end{aligned}$$

We observe that min, max, and inf are exclusive subsets of C such that $C = min(C) \cup inf(C) \cup max(C)$. We show below that the rules in $max(C)$ and $min(C)$ are indeed conflicting due to their different specificity. Note however that the following three theorems are independent of the choice of $min(C)$, $inf(C)$, and $max(C)$. Yet after these theorems we argue in Definition 4 for a specific choice for these sets that complies with the intuitions described in the previous section.

First, the antecedents of the most specific rules in $min(C)$ imply the antecedents of the least specific rules in $max(C)$ modulo the "inferential rules":

Theorem 3 *Let C be a MCS in a set of rules R. Then, $inf(C) \cup max(C) \models Prereq(max(C)) \supset Prereq(min(C))$.*

In fact, $inf(C) \cup max(C)$ is the weakest precondition under which the last entailment holds. This is important since we deal with a general setting for MCSs. Observe that omitting $max(C)$ would eliminate rules that may belong to $max(C)$, yet provide "inferential relations". The next theorem shows that the converse of the previous does not hold in general.

Theorem 4 *Let C be a MCS in a set of rules R. Then, for any set of rules R' such that $C \subseteq R'$ and any set of rules $R'' \subseteq min(C)$ such that $R' \cup Prereq(R'')$ is satisfiable, we have: $R' \not\models Prereq(R'') \supset Prereq(max(C))$.*

The reason for considering consistent subsets of $min(C)$ is that its entire set of prerequisites might be equivalent to those in $max(C)$. Then, however, $C \cup Prereq(min(C))$ and so $R' \cup Prereq(min(C))$ is inconsistent. This is, for instance, the case in Equation (11/12). In fact, R' is the strongest precondition under which the above theorem holds. Finally, we demonstrate that these rules are indeed conflicting.

Theorem 5 *Let C be a MCS in a set of rules R. Then, for any $\alpha \to \beta \in max(C)$, we have: $inf(C) \cup \{\alpha\} \models \neg(Conseq(min(C)) \wedge Conseq(max(C)))$.*

As above, $inf(C) \cup \{\alpha\}$ is the weakest precondition under which the last entailment holds. In all, the last three theorems demonstrate that the general framework given for *MCS*s (already) provides an extremely expressive way of isolating rule conflicts due to their specificity.

4.1 Specific Minimal and Maximal Conflicting Rules

As indicated in Section 3, we require further restrictions on the choice of $min(C)$ and $max(C)$ for our translation into **DL**. For a *MCS* $C = (C_0, C_1)$, we have the information that the rules in C_0 are less specific than those in C_1. However we wish to isolate those rules in C_0 whose application would conflict with applications of rules in C_1. Such a set is referred to as a *conflicting core* of a *MCS*. This leads us to the following definition:

Definition 4 *Let $C = (C_0, C_1)$ be a MCS. A conflicting core of C is a pair of least non-empty sets $(min(C), max(C))$ where*

1. $min(C) \subseteq C_0$,
2. $max(C) \subseteq C_1$,
3. $\{\alpha_r \wedge \beta_r \mid r \in max(C) \cup min(C)\} \models \bot$.

This definition specializes the general setting of Definition 3. So, $\alpha_r \to \beta_r$ is in $min(C)$ if its application conflicts with the application of a rule (or rules) in C_1.

In the extended example of Section 3 the conflicting cores are

$$C^0 : \quad (\{An \to \neg Fe\}, \{B \to Fe\})$$
$$C^1 : \quad (\{B \to F\}, \{P \to \neg F\})$$
$$C^2 : \quad (\{B \to F\}, \{E \to \neg F\})$$
$$C^3 : \quad (\{B \to Fe\}, \{Pt \to \neg Fe\})$$
$$C^4 : \quad (\{An \to WB\}, \{Pt \to \neg WB\})$$

respectively. The conflicting core of our initial example in (1) corresponds to the one for C^1. For a complement consider the example given in (11/12), where the conflicting core contains two minimal and one maximal conflicting rules:

$$(\{A \to \neg B, C \to \neg D\}, \{A \wedge C \to B \vee D\}).$$

Note that a conflicting core need not necessarily exist for a specific *MCS*. For example, consider the *MCS* (expressed as a Z-order):

$$C_0 = \{Q \to P, R \to \neg P\}$$
$$C_1 = \{Q \wedge R \to PA\}$$

Thus Quakers are pacifists while republicans are not; Quakers that are republicans are politically active. Here the conflict is between two defaults at the same level (viz. $Q \to P$ and $R \to \neg P$) that manifests itself when a more specific default is given.

We do have the following result however.

Theorem 6 *For MCS C in a set of rules R, if $\{\alpha_r \wedge \beta_r \mid r \in min(C)\} \not\models \bot$ and $\{\alpha_r \wedge \beta_r \mid r \in max(C)\} \not\models \bot$ then C has a conflicting core.*

5 Compiling Specificity into Default Theories

In the previous section, we proposed an approach for isolating minimal sets of rules that conflict because of their different specificity. We also showed how to isolate specific minimal and maximal rules. In this section, we use this information for specifying blocking conditions or, more generally, priorities among conflicting defaults in Default Logic. To this end, we envisage two different possible approaches. First, we could determine a strict partial order on a set of rules R from the *MCS*s in R. That is, for two rules $r, r' \in R$, we can define $r < r'$ iff $r \in min(C)$ and $r' \in max(C)$ for some *MCS* C in R. In this way, $r < r'$ is interpreted as "r is less specific than r'". Then, one could interpret each rule $\alpha \to \beta$ in R as a normal default $\frac{\alpha:\beta}{\beta}$ and use one of the approaches developed in [Baader and Hollunder, 1993a] or [Brewka, 1993] for computing the extensions of ordered normal default theories, i.e. default theories enriched by a strict partial order on rules. These approaches however have the disadvantage that they step outside the machinery of **DL** for computing extensions.

This motivates an alternative approach that remains inside the framework of classical **DL**, where we automatically transform rules with specificity information into semi-normal default theories.

5.1 Z-Default Logic

This section describes a strategy, based on the notions of specificity and conflict developed in the previous section, for producing a standard semi-normal default theory, and which provable maintains this notion of specificity. The transformation is succinctly defined:

Definition 5 *Let R be a set of rules and let $\langle C^i \rangle_{i \in I}$ be the family of all MCSs in R. For each $r \in R$, we define*

$$\delta_r = \frac{\alpha_r : \beta_r \wedge \bigwedge_{r' \in R_r}(\alpha_{r'} \supset \beta_{r'})}{\beta_r} \quad (13)$$

where $R_r = \{r' \in max(C^i) \mid r \in min(C^i) \text{ for } i \in I\}$. We define $D_R = \{\delta_r \mid r \in R\}$.

In what follows, we adopt the latter notation and write $D_{R'} = \{\delta_r \mid r \in R'\}$ for any subset R' of R.

The most interesting point in the preceding definition is the formation of the justifications of the (sometimes) semi-normal defaults. Given a rule r, the justification of δ_r is built by looking at all *MCS*, C^i, in which r occurs as a least specific rule (i.e. $r \in min(C^i)$). Then, the consequent of r is conjoined with the strict counterparts of the most specific rules in the same sets (viz. $(\alpha_{r'} \supset \beta_{r'})$ for $r' \in max(C^i)$). Hence, for the minimal conflicting rules we obtain semi-normal defaults; all other defaults are normal (since then $R_r = \emptyset$). So for any MCS C in R, we transform the rules in $min(C)$ into semi-normal defaults, whereas we transform the rules in $inf(C) \cup max(C)$ into normal defaults, provided that they do not occur elsewhere as a minimal conflicting rule.

As suggested in Section 4.1, we are only interested in minimal and maximal conflicting rules forming a conflicting core. That is, given a MCS C, we stipulate that $(min(C), max(C))$ forms a conflicting core of C. In the extended example of Section 3 the conflicting cores for (6) and (7) are

$$(\{B \to F\}, \{P \to \neg F\}) \text{ and } (\{B \to F\}, \{E \to \neg F\})$$

respectively. According to Definition 5, we get $R_{B \to F} = \{P \to \neg F, E \to \neg F\}$. This results in a single semi-normal default rule

$$\frac{B : F \wedge (P \supset \neg F) \wedge (E \supset \neg F)}{F}, \quad \text{or} \quad \frac{B : F \wedge \neg P \wedge \neg E}{F}.$$

Observe that we obtain $\frac{P:B}{B}$ and $\frac{P:\neg F}{\neg F}$ for $P \to B$, and $P \to \neg F$ since these rules do not occur elsewhere as minimal rules in a conflicting core. Other examples were given at the end of Section 3.

For a more general example, consider the case where, given a rule r, R_r is a singleton set containing a rule r'. Thus r is less specific than r'. This results in the default rules $\frac{\alpha_r : \beta_r \wedge (\alpha_{r'} \supset \beta_{r'})}{\beta_r}$ and $\frac{\alpha_{r'} : \beta_{r'}}{\beta_{r'}}$. Our intended interpretation is that r and r' conflict, and that r is preferable over r' (because of specificity). Thus, assume that β_r and $\beta_{r'}$ are not jointly satisfiable. Then, the second default takes precedence over the first one, whenever both prerequisites are derivable (i.e. $\alpha_r \in E$ and $\alpha_{r'} \in E$), and both β_r and $\beta_{r'}$ are individually consistent with the final extension E (i.e. $\neg \beta_r \notin E$ and $\neg \beta_{r'} \notin E$). That is, while the justification of the second default is satisfiable, the justification of the first default, $\beta_r \wedge (\alpha_{r'} \supset \beta_{r'})$, is unsatisfiable.

In general, we obtain the following results. $GD(E, D)$ stands for the generating defaults of E with respect to D, i.e. $GD(E, D) = \{\frac{\alpha:\beta}{\omega} \in D, | \alpha \in E, \neg \beta \notin E\}$. Note that Theorem 7 is with respect to the general theory of MCSs while Theorem 8 is with respect to the specific development involving conflicting cores.

Theorem 7 *Let R be a set of rules and let W be a set of formulas. Let C be a MCS in R. Let E be a consistent extension of (D_R, W). Then,*

1. *if $D_{max(C)} \cup D_{inf(C)} \subseteq GD(E, D)$ then $D_{min(C)} \nsubseteq GD(E, D)$,*

2. *if $D_{min(C)} \cup D_{inf(C)} \subseteq GD(E, D)$ then $D_{max(C)} \nsubseteq GD(E, D)$.*

Let us relate this theorem to the underlying idea of specificity: Observe that in the first case, where $D_{max(C)} \cup D_{inf(C)} \subseteq GD(E, D)$, we also have

$$Prereq(min(C)) \subseteq E$$

by Theorem 3. That is, even though the prerequisites of the minimal conflicting defaults are derivable, they do not contribute to the extension at hand. This is so because some of the justifications of the minimal conflicting defaults are not satisfied. In this way, the more specific defaults in $D_{max(C)}$ take precedence over the less specific defaults in $D_{min(C)}$. Conversely, in the second case, where $D_{min(C)} \cup D_{inf(C)} \subseteq GD(E, D)$, the less specific defaults apply only if the more specific defaults do not contribute to the given extension.

Theorem 8 *Let R be a set of rules and let W be a set of formulas. Let $(min(C), max(C))$ be a conflicting core of some MCS C in R. Let E be a consistent extension of (D_R, W). Then,*

1. *if $D_{max(C)} \subseteq GD(E, D)$ then $D_{min(C)} \nsubseteq GD(E, D)$,*

2. *if $D_{min(C)} \subseteq GD(E, D)$ then $D_{max(C)} \nsubseteq GD(E, D)$.*

Thus in this case we obtain that the defaults in a conflicting core are not applicable, independent of the "linking defaults" in $D_{inf(C)}$.

Given a set of formulas W representing our world knowledge and a set of default conditionals R, we can apply Definition 5 in order to obtain a so-called **Z-default theory** (D_R, W). The following theorem gives an alternative characterization for extensions of Z-default theories. In particular, it clarifies further the effect of the set of rules R_r associated with each rule r. Recall that in general, however, such extensions are computed in the classical framework of **DL**.

Theorem 9 *Let R be a set of rules, let $D_N = \left\{ \frac{\alpha_r : \beta_r}{\beta_r} \mid \alpha_r \to \beta_r \in R \right\}$, and let W and E be sets of formulas. Define $E_0 = W$ and for $i \geq 0$ (and R_r as in Definition 5)*

$$E_{i+1} = Th(E_i) \cup \left\{ \beta_r \mid \frac{\alpha_r : \beta_r}{\beta_r} \in D_N, \alpha_r \in E_i, \\ E \cup \{\beta_r\} \cup \bigcup_{r' \in R_r} (\alpha_{r'} \supset \beta_{r'}) \nvdash \bot \right\}$$

Then, E is an extension of (D_R, W) iff $E = \bigcup_{i=0}^{\infty} E_i$.

5.2 Properties of Z-Default Theories

We now examine the formal properties of **Z**-default theories. In regular **DL**, many appealing properties are only enjoyed by restricted subclasses. For instance, normal default theories guarantee the existence of extensions and enjoy the property of semi-monotonicity.

Transposed to our case, the latter stipulates that if $R' \subseteq R$ for two sets of rules, then if E' is an extension of $(D_{R'}, W)$ then there is an extension E of

(D_R, W) where $E' \subseteq E$. Arguably, this property is not desirable if we want to block less specific defaults in the presence of more specific defaults. In fact, this property does not hold for **Z**-default theories. For instance, from the rules $B \to F, P \to B$, we obtain the defaults $\frac{B:F}{F}, \frac{P:B}{B}$. Given P, we conclude B and F. However, adding the rule $P \to \neg F$ makes us add the default $\frac{P:\neg F}{\neg F}$ and replace the default $\frac{B:F}{F}$ by $\frac{B:F\wedge P}{F}$. Obviously, the resulting theory does not support our initial conclusions. Rather we conclude now B and $\neg F$, which violates the aforementioned notion of semi-monotonicity.[8]

Also, the existence of extensions is not guaranteed for **Z**-default theories. To see this, consider the rules:

$$A \wedge Q \to \neg P \quad B \wedge R \to \neg Q \quad C \wedge P \to \neg R$$
$$A \to P \quad B \to Q \quad C \to R$$

Each column gives a *MCS* in which the upper rule is more specific than the lower rule. We obtain the rules

$$\frac{A\wedge Q : \neg P}{\neg P} \qquad \frac{B\wedge R : \neg Q}{\neg Q} \qquad \frac{C\wedge P : \neg R}{\neg R}$$
$$\frac{A : P \wedge \neg Q}{P} \qquad \frac{B : Q \wedge \neg R}{Q} \qquad \frac{C : R \wedge \neg P}{R}$$

Given A, B, C, we get no extension.

Arguably, the non-existence of extensions indicates certain problems in the underlying set of rules. [Zhang and Marek, 1990] shows that a default theory has no extension iff it contains certain "abnormal" defaults; these can be detected automatically. However, we can also avoid the non-existence of extensions by translating rules into variants of default logic that guarantee the existence of extensions, as discussed in Section 6.

Another important property is cumulativity. The intuitive idea is that if a theorem is added to the set of premises from which the theorem was derived, then the set of derivable formulas should remain unchanged. This property is only enjoyed by prerequisite-free normal default theories in regular **DL**. It does not hold for **Z**-default theories, as the next example illustrates. Consider the conditionals $\{D \to A, A \to B, B \to \neg A\}$. The last two conditionals form a *MCS*. Transforming these rules into defaults, yields two normal, $\frac{D:A}{A}, \frac{A:B}{B}$, and one (semi-)normal default, $\frac{B:\neg A\wedge(A\supset B)}{\neg A}$, or $\frac{B:\neg A}{\neg A}$. Given D, there is one extension containing $\{D, A, B\}$. Hence this extension contains B. Now, given D and B, we obtain a second extension containing $\{D, \neg A, B\}$. This violates cumulativity.

Note that in this case we obtained a normal default theory from the original set of rules. This is intuitively plausible, since the two conflicting defaults are mutually canceling, i.e. if one applies then the other does not.

---

[8]This differs from the notion of semi-monotonicity described in [Reiter, 1980]. The latter is obtained by replacing R and D_R by D and R' and $D_{R'}$ by D'.

5.3 Exchangeability and Related Work

At the start of this section we described how to extract a strict partial order from a family of *MCS*s for using other approaches (such as [Baader and Hollunder, 1993a; Brewka, 1993]) to compute extensions of ordered default theories, i.e. theories with a strict partial order $<$ on the defaults. In fact, one can view partial orders on rules as general interfaces between approaches. In particular, we can use also our approach for compiling ordered normal default theories into semi-normal default theories. To this end, we have to incorporate the order $<$ into the specification of R_r in Definition 5. We do this by associating with each normal default $\frac{\alpha:\beta}{\beta}$ a rule $\alpha \to \beta$ and define for each such rule r that $R_r^< = \{r' \mid r < r'\}$, where $<$ is a strict partial order on the set of rules. Then, we can use transformation (13) for turning ordered normal default theories into semi-normal default theories.

We can now compare how priorities are dealt with in our and the aforementioned approaches. In both [Baader and Hollunder, 1993a] and [Brewka, 1993] the iterative specification of an extension in **DL** is modified. In brief, a default is only applicable at an iteration step if no more specific (or $<$-greater) default is applicable.[9] The difference between both approaches (roughly) rests on the number of defaults applicable at each step. While Brewka allows only for applying a single default that is maximal with respect to a total extension of $<$, Baader and Hollunder allow for applying all $<$-maximal defaults at each step.

As a first example, consider the default rules $\frac{:A}{A}, \frac{:B}{B}, \frac{B:C}{C}, \frac{A:\neg C}{\neg C}$ (for short $\delta_1, \delta_2, \delta_3, \delta_4$), along with $\delta_4 < \delta_3$, taken from [Baader and Hollunder, 1993b]. With no facts Baader and Hollunder obtain one extension containing $\{A, B, C\}$. Curiously, Brewka obtains an additional extension containing $\{A, B, \neg C\}$. In our approach, we generate from $<$ a single nonempty set $R_{\delta_4}^< = \{\delta_3\}$; all other such sets are empty. Consequently we replace δ_4 by $\frac{A:\neg C\wedge(B\supset C)}{\neg C}$ or $\frac{A:\neg C\wedge \neg B}{\neg C}$. In regular **DL**, the resultant default theory yields only the first extension containing $\{A, B, C\}$.

As a second example, again from [Baader and Hollunder, 1993b], consider the rules $\frac{:A}{A}, \frac{B:\neg A}{\neg A}, \frac{:B}{B}, \frac{A:\neg B}{\neg B}$ (for short $\delta_1, \delta_2, \delta_3, \delta_4$), along with $\delta_1 < \delta_2, \delta_3 < \delta_4$. They show that in Brewka's approach two extensions are obtained, one containing $\{A, \neg B\}$ and another containing $\{\neg A, B\}$. However an additional extension is obtained in Baader and Hollunder's approach, containing $\{A, B\}$. In our approach, we produce from $<$ the nonempty sets $R_{\delta_1}^< = \{\delta_2\}$; and $R_{\delta_3}^< = \{\delta_4\}$; all other such sets are empty. Then, we replace δ_1 and δ_3 by

$$\frac{:A\wedge(B\supset\neg A)}{A} \text{ or } \frac{:A\wedge\neg B}{A} \text{ and } \frac{:B\wedge(A\supset\neg B)}{B} \text{ or } \frac{:B\wedge\neg A}{B},$$

---

[9]In [Baader and Hollunder, 1993a; Brewka, 1993] $<$ is used in the reverse order.

which yields only the first two extensions in **DL**.

Even though these examples appear to be artificial, they can be extended to express reasonable specificity orderings. In all, we observe that in both examples our approach yields the fewer and, in terms of specificity, more intuitive extensions.

Note that the general approach of compiling partial orders into semi-normal default theories makes sense whenever we deal with partial orders that only consider priorities due to specificity where we have *truly conflicting rules*. Otherwise, the resulting default theory may be overly strong. Consider the case where we extract priorities from subsumption relations, as is done in [Baader and Hollunder, 1993a] for terminological logics. Consider terms stating that "birds fly", $B \to F$, and "young birds need special care", $Y \to C$, along with the usual subsumption relation between "birds" and "young birds". This subsumption amounts to a priority between the two rules even though there is no conflict: $(B \to F) < (Y \to C)$. Thus these rules would result in two default rules $\frac{B : F \wedge (Y \supset C)}{F}$ and $\frac{Y : C}{C}$ since the first default would "take priority" over the second, according to the given partial order. Such a priority is unnecessary however as regards avoiding conflicts stemming from more specific information. Obviously, this problem does not arise in the general approach taken by *MCS*s. In this case, in addition to a specificity difference, we also require explicitly conflicting rules. In the above example there is no *MCS* and so we would obtain the two normal rules $\frac{B : F}{F}$ and $\frac{Y : C}{C}$.

Finally we note that the preceding exposition was dominated by the view that rules, like $\alpha \to \beta$, are associated with defaults having prerequisite α and consequent β. This view underlies the approaches in [Baader and Hollunder, 1993a] and [Brewka, 1993]. That is, they rely on the existence of prerequisites. In contrast, we can treat rules also as strict implications, and so compile them into a prerequisite-free defaults, as we show in the next section.

6 Alternative Translations

So far we have focused on translating specificity information into Reiter's default logic. In this section, we show how the specificity information extracted from a family of minimal conflicting sets (or even a strict partial order) can be incorporated into alternative approaches to default reasoning.

As mentioned earlier, we can also interpret a rule $\alpha \to \beta$ as a strict implication, namely $\alpha \supset \beta$. To this end, we turn rules like $\alpha \to \beta$ into prerequisite-free default rules. However, as discussed in [Delgrande et al., 1994], the problem of controlling interactions among such rules is more acute than in the regular case. Consider our initial example (1), translated into prerequisite-free **DL**:

$$\frac{: B \supset F}{B \supset F}, \frac{: B \supset W}{B \supset W}, \frac{: P \supset B}{P \supset B}, \frac{: P \supset \neg F}{P \supset \neg F} \quad (14)$$

Given P, we obtain three extensions, containing $\{P, \neg F, B, W\}$, $\{P, F, B, W\}$, and $\{P, \neg F, \neg B\}$.[10] The first two extensions correspond to the ones obtained in regular **DL**. Clearly, we can apply the techniques developed in the previous sections for eliminating the second extension. The third extension yields also the more specific result in that we obtain $\neg F$. This extension, however, does not account for property inheritance, since we cannot conclude that birds have wings. This is caused by the contraposition of $B \supset F$. That is, once we have derived $\neg F$, we derive $\neg B$ by contraposition, which prevents us from concluding W.

This problem can be addressed in two ways, either by strenthening the blocking conditions for minimal conflicting rules or by blocking the contraposition of minimal conflicting rules. In the first case, we could turn $B \to F$ into $\frac{: (B \supset F) \wedge \neg P}{B \supset F}$ by adding the negated antecedents of the maximal conflicting rules, here $\neg P$. While this looks appealing, we have already seen in Section 3 that this approach is too strong in the presence of multiple minimal conflicting rules. To see this, consider the rules given in (11/12). For $A \to \neg B$, we would obtain $\frac{: (A \supset \neg B) \wedge (\neg A \vee \neg C)}{A \supset \neg B}$ or $\frac{: A \supset (\neg B \wedge \neg C)}{A \supset \neg B}$. However, as argued in Section 3, there is no reason why $A \to \neg B$ should not be applied given the facts $\{A, C, D\}$. Also, in general it does not make sense to address a problem stemming from contrapositions by altering the way specificity is enforced. Rather we should address an independent problem by means of other measures.

So, in the second case, we turn $B \to F$ into $\frac{: (B \supset F) \wedge F \wedge (P \supset \neg F)}{B \supset F}$ or $\frac{: F \wedge \neg P}{B \supset F}$. That is, we add the consequent of $B \to F$ in order to block its contraposition. As before, we add the strict counterparts of the maximal conflicting rules, here $P \supset \neg F$. In the birds example, the resulting justification is strengthened as above. In particular, we block the contribution of the rule $B \supset F$ to the final extension if either $\neg F$ or P is derivable. For $A \to \neg B$ in (11/12), we now obtain, $\frac{: (A \supset \neg B) \wedge \neg B \wedge (A \wedge C \supset B \vee D))}{A \supset \neg B}$ or $\frac{: \neg B \wedge (A \wedge C \supset D)}{A \supset \neg B}$. In contrast to the previous proposal, this rule is applicable to the facts $\{A, C, D\}$. Moreover, this approach is in accord with System **Z**, where rules are classified according to their "forward chaining" behaviour.

So for translating rules along with their specificity into prerequisite-free default theories, we replace the definition of δ_r in Definition 5 by[11]

$$\zeta_r = \frac{: (\alpha_r \supset \beta_r) \wedge \beta_r \wedge \bigwedge_{r' \in R_r}(\alpha_{r'} \supset \beta_{r'})}{(\alpha_r \supset \beta_r)}. \quad (15)$$

---

[10]The third extension would not be present if $P \supset B$ were a strict rule.

[11]Observe that $(\alpha_r \supset \beta_r) \wedge \beta_r$ is equivalent to β_r.

Applying this transformation to our birds example in (1), we obtain:

$$\frac{:F\wedge\neg P}{B\supset F},\quad \frac{:B\supset W}{B\supset W},\quad \frac{:P\supset B}{P\supset B},\quad \frac{:P\supset\neg F}{P\supset\neg F}$$

Now, given P, we obtain a single extension containing $\{P,\neg F, B, W\}$.

Note that blocking the contraposition of minimal conflicting rules is an option outside the presented framework. The purpose of the above transformation is to preserve inheritance over default statements, like $P \to B$. Inheritance over strict statements, like $P \supset B$, however can be done *without* blocking contrapositions. In this case, the following transformation is sufficient:

$$\zeta'_r = \frac{:(\alpha_r \supset \beta_r) \wedge \bigwedge_{r' \in R_r}(\alpha_{r'} \supset \beta_{r'})}{(\alpha_r \supset \beta_r)} \qquad (16)$$

As an example, let us turn the default $P \to B$ into its strict counterpart $P \supset B$. As detailed in [Delgrande and Schaub, 1994], our birds example then yields with transformation (16) the defaults

$$\frac{:(B\supset F)\wedge(P\supset\neg F)}{B\supset F},\quad \frac{:B\supset W}{B\supset W},\quad \frac{:P\supset\neg F}{P\supset\neg F}.$$

Now, given P and $P \supset B$, we obtain a single extension containing $\{P,\neg F, B, W\}$. The details on integrating strict rules are given in [Delgrande and Schaub, 1994].

Transformations (15/16) offer some interesting benefits, since prerequisite-free defaults allow for reasoning by cases and reasoning by contraposition (apart from minimal conflicting rules). That is, such defaults behave like usual conditionals unless explicitly blocked. Nonetheless, the counterexamples for semi-monotonicity, cumulativity, and the existence of extensions carry over to prerequisite-free Z-default theories. Thus none of these properties is enjoyed by these theories in **DL**. Finally, note that this approach differs from [Boutilier, 1992b], where a ranking on defaults is obtained from the original Z-order; this may introduce unwanted priorities due to irrelevant conditionals.

Another alternative is the translation into variants of **DL** that guarantee the existence of extensions [Lukaszewicz, 1988; Brewka, 1991; Delgrande et al., 1994]. This can be accomplished by means of both translation (13) and (15/16). Moreover, the resulting Z-default theories enjoy cumulativity when applying translation (13) and (15/16) in the case of Cumulative Default Logic and when applying (15/16) in the case of Constrained Default Logic. The corresponding results can be found in [Brewka, 1991; Delgrande et al., 1994]. Although none of these variants enjoys semi-monotonicity with respect to the underlying conditionals, all of them enjoy this property with respect to the default rules. As shown in [Brewka, 1991], this may lead to problems in blocking a rule, like $\frac{B:F\wedge\neg P}{F}$, in the case $\neg P$ is a default conclusion. For details on this we refer the reader to [Brewka, 1991].

Similarly we can compile prioritized rules into Theorist [Poole, 1988] or other approaches, such as Autoepistemic Logic [Moore, 1985] or even Circumscription [McCarthy, 1980]. The latter translation is described in a forthcoming paper.

For the translation into Theorist, we refer the reader to [Delgrande et al., 1994], where it is shown that Theorist systems correspond to prerequisite-free default theories in Constrained Default Logic and vice versa. Accordingly, we may obtain a Theorist system from a set of prioritized rules by first applying transformation (15/16) and then the one given in [Delgrande et al., 1994] for translating prerequisite-free default theories in Constrained Default Logic into Theorist.

Autoepistemic Logic [Moore, 1985] aims at formalizing an agent's reasoning about her own beliefs. To this end, the logical language is augmented by a modal operator L. Then, a formula $L\alpha$ is to be read as "α is believed". For a set W of such formulas, an autoepistemic extension E is defined as

$$Th(W \cup \{L\alpha \mid \alpha \in E\} \cup \{\neg L\alpha \mid \alpha \notin E\}).$$

As discussed in [Konolige, 1988], we can express a statement like "birds fly" either as $B \wedge \neg L\neg F \supset F$ or $LB \wedge \neg L\neg F \supset F$. Given B and one of these rules, we obtain in both cases an extension containing F. Roughly speaking, the former sentence corresponds to the default $\frac{:B\supset F}{B\supset F}$ while the latter is close to $\frac{B:F}{F}$.

This motivates the following translations into Autoepistemic Logic. Let R be a set of rules and let $R_r \subseteq R$, for each $r \in R$ we define:

$$\rho_r = \alpha_r \wedge \neg L\neg\big(\beta_r \wedge \bigwedge_{r' \in R_r}(\alpha_{r'} \supset \beta_{r'})\big) \supset \beta_r,$$
$$\varrho_r = L\alpha_r \wedge \neg L\neg\big(\beta_r \wedge \bigwedge_{r' \in R_r}(\alpha_{r'} \supset \beta_{r'})\big) \supset \beta_r.$$

Applying the first transformation to our initial example, we obtain for $B \to F$ the modal sentence

$$B \wedge \neg L\neg(F \wedge(P \supset \neg F)) \supset F \text{ or } B \wedge \neg L\neg(F \wedge \neg P) \supset F,$$

along with $B \wedge \neg L\neg W \supset W, P \wedge \neg L\neg B \supset B$, and $P \wedge \neg LF \supset \neg F$ for $B \to W, P \to B$, and $P \to \neg F$. Now, given P along with the four modal defaults, we obtain a single autoepistemic extension containing $\neg F$ and W. In this way, we have added specificity to Autoepistemic Logic while preserving inheritance.

7 Discussion

This paper has described a hybrid approach addressing the notion of specificity in default reasoning. We begin with a set of rules that express default conditionals, where the goal is to produce a default theory expressed in a "target" formalism, and where conflicts arising from differing specificities are resolved. The approach is to use the techniques of a weak system, as exemplified by System **Z**, to isolate minimal sets of conflicting defaults. From the specificity information intrinsic in these sets, a default theory in a target language (here primarily Default Logic) is derived. In our approach, the problems of weak systems, such as lack of adequate property inheritance and undesirable specificity relations, are avoided. In addition, difficulties inherent in stronger systems, in particular, lack of specificity, are addressed. In contrast to previous work, the approach avoids stepping outside the machinery of **DL**. Thus we do not obtain an explicit global partial order on default rules, but rather a classical default theory where local conflicts are resolved by semi-normal defaults.

This approach is modular, in that we separate the *determination* of conflicts from the *resolution* of conflicts among rules. Thus either module could be replaced by some other approach. For example, one could use an inheritance network to determine conflict relations and then use the mapping described in this paper to obtain a default theory. Alternately, conflicts could be determined using *MCS*s via System **Z**, and then an ordered default theory as described in [Baader and Hollunder, 1993a] could be generated. The approach may be seen as generalising that of [Reiter and Criscuolo, 1981]. Also, for example, [Etherington and Reiter, 1983] and [Brewka, 1993] may be seen as falling into the same general framework.

Acknowledgements

We would like to thank Gerd Brewka for many discussions on the topic. The first author was a visitor at York University and the University of Toronto while this work was being carried out. The first author also acknowledges support from the Natural Science and Engineering Research Council of Canada grant A0884, as well as the Institute for Robotics and Intelligent Systems (IRIS) in the Canadian Networks of Centres of Excellence Program. The second author was supported by the Commission of the European Communities under grant no. ERB4001GT922433.

References

Baader, F. and Hollunder, B. 1993a. How to prefer more specific defaults in terminological default logic. In *Proc. IJCAI-93*, Chambéry, Fr. 669–674.

Baader, F. and Hollunder, B. 1993b. How to prefer more specific defaults in terminological default logic. Technical Report RR-92-58, DFKI.

Boutilier, Craig 1992a. *Conditional Logics for Default Reasoning and Belief Revision*. Ph.D. Dissertation, Department of Computer Science, University of Toronto.

Boutilier, Craig 1992b. What is a default priority? In *Canadian Conference on AI*, Vancouver, B.C.

Brewka, G. 1991. Cumulative default logic: In defense of nonmonotonic inference rules. *Artificial Intelligence* 50(2):183–205.

Brewka, G. 1993. Adding priorities and specificity to default logic. Manuscript.

Delgrande, J. and Schaub, T. 1994. On using system Z to generate prioritised default theories. Technical report, IRISA. Forthcoming.

Delgrande, James P.; Jackson, W. Ken; and Schaub, Torsten 1994. Alternative approaches to default logic. *Artificial Intelligence*. to appear (accepted Feb. 1993).

Delgrande, J.P. 1987. A first-order conditional logic for prototypical properties. *Artificial Intelligence* 33(1):105–130.

Delgrande, J.P. 1988. An approach to default reasoning based on a first-order conditional logic: Revised report. *Artificial Intelligence* 36(1):63–90.

Etherington, D.W. and Reiter, R. 1983. On inheritance hierarchies with exceptions. In *Proc. AAAI-83*. 104–108.

Geffner, Hector and Pearl, Judea 1992. Conditional entailment: Bridging two approaches to default reasoning. *Artificial Intelligence* 53(2-3):209–244.

Goldszmidt, Moisés and Pearl, Judea 1990. On the relation between rational closure and system Z. In *Third International Workshop on Nonmonotonic Reasoning*, South Lake Tahoe. 130–140.

Konolige, K. 1988. On the relation between default theories and autoepistemic logic. *Artificial Intelligence* 35(2):343–382.

Kraus, S.; Lehmann, D.; and Magidor, M. 1990. Nonmonotonic reasoning, preferential models and cumulative logics. *Artificial Intelligence* 44(1-2).

Lukaszewicz, W. 1988. Considerations on default logic: An alternative approach. *Computational Intelligence* 4(1):1–16.

McCarthy, J. 1980. Circumscription – a form of nonmonotonic reasoning. *Artificial Intelligence* 13:27–39.

Moore, R.C. 1985. Semantical considerations on nonmonotonic logic. *Artificial Intelligence* 25:75–94.

Pearl, J. 1989. Probabilistic semantics for nonmonotonic reasoning: A survey. In *Proc. KR-89*, Toronto. Morgan Kaufman. 505–516.

Pearl, J. 1990. System Z: A natural ordering of defaults with tractable applications to nonmonotonic reasoning. In *Proc. of the Third Conference on Theoretical Aspects of Reasoning About Knowledge*, Pacific Grove, Ca. 121–135.

Poole, D. 1985. On the comparison of theories: Preferring the most specific explanation. In *Proc. IJCAI-85*. 144–147.

Poole, D.L. 1988. A logical framework for default reasoning. *Artificial Intelligence* 36(1):27–48.

Reiter, R. and Criscuolo, G. 1981. On interacting defaults. In *Proc. IJCAI-81*, Vancouver, B.C. 270–276.

Reiter, R. 1980. A logic for default reasoning. *Artificial Intelligence* 13:81–132.

Zhang, A. and Marek, W. 1990. On the classification and existence of structures in default logic. *Fundamenta Informaticae* 8(4):485–499.

Action Representation for interpreting Purpose Clauses in Natural Language Instructions

Barbara Di Eugenio
Computational Linguistics, Department of Philosophy
Carnegie Mellon University
Pittsburgh, PA, 15213 USA
dieugeni@lcl.cmu.edu

Abstract

The problem I am concerned with is understanding complex Natural Language instructions, and in particular, instructions containing Purpose Clauses. In this paper, I describe an action representation formalism that encodes both *linguistic* and *planning* knowledge about actions. Such formalism makes use of linguistically motivated primitives, derived from Jackendoff's work on Conceptual Structures [Jackendoff, 1990], and is embedded in the hybrid system CLASSIC [Brachman et al., 1991]. The algorithm that interprets Purpose Clauses crucially exploits CLASSIC's classification algorithm. The output of my algorithm is in turn used in the *Animation from NL* project, that has as its goal the automatic creation of animated task simulations.

1 INTRODUCTION

The analysis of an extensive corpus of naturally occurring Natural Language (NL) instructions, and in particular of those containing Purpose Clauses [Di Eugenio, 1993], highlights some issues that need to be addressed to interpret complex instructions. The one I will concentrate on in this paper is that NL action descriptions only seldom exactly match the knowledge that an agent has about actions and their characteristics. However, in all the work on understanding NL instructions I know of — e.g. [Alterman et al., 1991; Chapman, 1991; Vere and Bickmore, 1990] — the NL form of the utterance is in a sense disregarded: an assumption is made that there is a direct map between the logical form and the knowledge about actions stored in the system's Knowledge Bases. In contrast, I claim that, to model an agent interpreting instructions, we need a flexible action representation, and inference mechanisms that can deal with actions descriptions not necessarily corresponding to the known ones.

I propose a formalism composed of two KBs, both implemented by means of the hybrid system CLASSIC [Brachman et al., 1991]. The first one stores linguistic knowledge about actions: to guarantee that the primitives of the representation are linguistically motivated, those I use derive from Jackendoff's work [1990] on the semantic representation of verbs and actions. The action terms defined in CLASSIC's T-Box are the components of the *recipes*, i.e. *common sense* plans about actions [Pollack, 1986], stored in the *action library*.

In the following, I will first discuss the task I am addressing, thereby justifying the need for the action representation formalism described in the remainder of the paper. Further details on all the topics discussed in the paper can be found in [Di Eugenio, 1993].[1]

2 INFERENCE PROCESSES

The inferences I am interested in stem from interpreting utterances containing *Purpose Clauses*, infinitival *to* constructions as in *Do α to do β*. Given such input instructions, the hearer (H) tries to find the connection between α and β, by exploiting the fact that β describes the goal to be achieved. In computational terms this amounts to:

(1a) use β as an index into the KB;

(1b) find a collection of methods $\mathcal{M}_l$ that achieve β;

(1c) try to **match** α to an action $\gamma_{l,j}$ that appears as a component in $\mathcal{M}_l$.

These are typical *plan recognition* inferences, eg see [Wilensky, 1983; Pollack, 1986; Charniak, 1988; Litman and Allen, 1990]. However, in almost all the work

---

[1]This paper extends both [Di Eugenio, 1992] and [Di Eugenio and White, 1992]: the former discussed using hybrid systems, the latter Conceptual Structure representations of planning knowledge about actions, but the two were not integrated, and recipes were not hierarchically organized.

on plan recognition I know of, with the exception of [Charniak, 1988], *match* in step (1c) is taken to mean that α is *instance-of* $\gamma_{l,j}$. My research has focussed on computing a more flexible notion of match between α and $\gamma_{l,j}$. Another issue that is not addressed in plan inference work is what action ρ_{perf} really has to be performed. In the case of *Do α to do β*, ρ_{perf} can't just be taken to be α. All this is required because of the variability of the NL input, as I will show in the following.

2.1 MATCHING α AND $\gamma_{l,j}$

As mentioned above, action descriptions found in NL instructions don't exactly match the knowledge that an agent has about actions and their mutual relations. The two kinds of discrepancy I have examined so far concern *structural consistency* of descriptions, and *expectations* that have to be computed for a certain relation $\mathcal{R}$ to hold between α and β. I will illustrate them both and I will give a general description of the algorithm and of the general framework of my work, before discussing the knowledge representation formalism.

2.1.1 Structural Consistency

Suppose that H knows a method, call it $\mathcal{M}_{37}$, to create two triangles by *cutting a square in half along the diagonal*:[2]

(2) ACHIEVES(
    [cut(agent,square,in-half,along-diagonal)]$_\gamma$,
    [create(agent,two-triangles)]$_\delta$)

Given the plan recognition paradigm discussed above, $\mathcal{M}_{37}$ would be retrieved through the match of β_k to δ_{37} in all of the following cases:

(3a) *[Cut the square in half along the diagonal with scissors]$_{\alpha_1}$ [to create two triangles]$_{\beta_1}$*.

(3b) *[Cut the square in half]$_{\alpha_2}$ [to create two triangles]$_{\beta_2}$*.

(3c) *[Cut the square in half with scissors]$_{\alpha_3}$ [to create two triangles]$_{\beta_3}$*.

(3d) *[Cut the square in half along a perpendicular axis]$_{\alpha_4}$ [to create two triangles]$_{\beta_4}$*.

Now α_k and γ_{37} have to be compared, to compute the action ρ_{perf} to be performed. More specifically,

1. In (3a), α_1 is more specific than γ_{37}. ρ_{perf} can be taken to be α_1, *after* checking that the added modifier *with scissors* is compatible with γ_{37}. This is the only case that traditional plan inference systems would (possibly) account for.

2. In (3b), α_2 is less specific than γ_{37}, and is therefore compatible with it. That ρ_{perf} should be taken to be γ_{37} is supported by the fact that β_2 exactly matches δ_{37}.

3. α_3, when compared to γ_{37}, lacks the modifier regarding the position where to cut, but adds the instrument modifier *with scissors*, compatible with everything else we know about γ_{37} and β. ρ_{perf} is then inferred to be (and α_3 γ_{37}).

4. Finally, in (3d), α_4 is incompatible with γ_{37}, and therefore ρ_{perf} is Nil.

2.1.2 Expectations About Object Locations

A relation $\mathcal{R}$ different from the structural relations I have illustrated above, such as *generation* or *enablement*,[3] may hold between α and β (or α and $\gamma_{l,j}$). However, sometimes $\mathcal{R}$ holds only under certain expectations $\mathcal{E}$. The ones I have examined so far, in the context of an input such as *Do α to do β*, concern the location of certain objects that β manipulates. Such expectations arise when an action changes the *perceptual space $\mathcal{S}$* H has access to. If α changes $\mathcal{S}$ into $\mathcal{S}$', and α is executed in order to do β, then expect $\mathcal{S}$' to be the site of β. In particular, when α results in H going to a place $\mathcal{S}$' with the purpose of doing β, one can infer $\mathcal{S}$' to be the site of β. If there are objects that β manipulates, expect them to be at $\mathcal{S}$'. Consider

(4a) *[Go into the kitchen]$_{\alpha_1}$ [to get me the coffee urn]$_{\beta_1}$*.

(4b) *[Go into the kitchen]$_{\alpha_2}$ [to wash the coffee urn]$_{\beta_2}$*.

In both cases, H goes to the kitchen, which is then expected to be the location of β_1/β_2. In (4a), but not in (4b), a further expectation that the referent of the coffee urn is in the kitchen is developed. The difference between the two may be explained by appealing to the planning notion of *qualifiers*,[4] conditions that must hold for an action to be relevant, and are not meant to be achieved. Operatively, qualifiers don't give rise to subgoaling. If β has among its qualifiers that an argument be at $\mathcal{S}$' for β to even be relevant, then a locational expectation develops as in (4a). If not, a weaker expectation arises, as in (4b).

---

[2]This is not how knowledge is really represented, but just an approximation — see later.

[3]Intuitively, *generation* holds between α and β if β is done by executing α; while *enablement* holds between α and β if α brings about conditions necessary to execute β. See [Goldman, 1970; Pollack, 1986; Balkanski, 1993]. In [Di Eugenio, 1993] I show that purpose clauses do express generation and enablement.

[4]Also called *applicability conditions* [Schoppers, 1988] or *constraints* [Litman and Allen, 1990].

2.1.3 The Algorithm

As mentioned before, the action representation formalism that I will describe in the rest of the paper is used by an algorithm that implements the inferences discussed above. The algorithm, shown in Fig. 1, is embedded in the *AnimNL (Animation from NL)* system described in [Webber *et al.*, 1992; Webber *et al.*, 1993], and assumes the existence of separate *AnimNL* modules for, among others, parsing the input and providing a logical form, and managing the discourse model and solving anaphora.

The *AnimNL* project has as its goal the automatic creation of animated task simulations from NL instructions. Its agents are animated human figures, and the tasks they are to engage in are *assembly procedures* and *maintenance procedures*. The underlying animation system, *Jack^{TM}*, developed at the Computer Graphics Lab at the University of Pennsylvania, provides articulated, animated human figures — both male and female — capable of realistic motion through model-based inverse kinematics [Badler *et al.*, 1993]. *Jack* agents can be anthropomorphically sized and given different "strengths", so as to vary agents' physical capabilities. Different spatial environments can also be set up and modified, so as to vary the situation in which tasks are carried out. *AnimNL* is intended to support advanced human factors analysis by enabling users of computer-aided design tools to simulate human agents' interactions with the artifacts they are designing.

Going back to Fig. 1, the input to the algorithm is the logical form LF of the input sentence, produced by a parser based on Combinatory Categorial Grammar [White, 1992]. The LF contains one action description α_i, i.e. an instance of a CLASSIC action concept, per clause, plus interclausal connectives.[5] One of the α_i's is designated as Goal, and used to index into the Action Library. The choice of Goal depends on the surface form: e.g. for *Do α to do β*, Goal is β; for *Do α by doing β*, α.

If no Failure is detected,[6] the algorithm produces an initial PlanGraph, representing the intentions and expectations the agent adopts as a consequence of the input instruction and the planning knowledge. The PlanGraph is composed of nodes that contain individual action descriptions, and edges that denote relations such as *generation* and its generalization *is-substep*, *enablement*, and various temporal relations (based on [Allen, 1984]). Edges may have *expectations* associated

---
[5] Basically, each clause describing an action or an event is reified.

[6] Failure can be due to different factors, among them: there is no Recipe whose header is instantiated by Goal; Goal has selected at least one Recipe$_l$, but there is no $\gamma_{l,j}$ such that α_i and $\gamma_{l,j}$ match; the input instruction is inconsistent with the stored knowledge.

with them.

The update step creates the nodes corresponding to the α_i's, and to the $\gamma_{l,j}$'s; and the edges either deriving from the Body and Annotations on the Recipe (see below), or computed during steps 3a and 3b. All these structures are used to update PlanGraph.

The algorithm produces only the initial PlanGraph, namely, it models what intentions the agent adopts simply based on the input instruction and the stored knowledge: the current situation is not taken into account. As an example, consider (4a), *Go into the kitchen to get me the coffee urn*. The algorithm builds a PlanGraph that contains nodes derived from the substeps of the recipe in Fig. 5. This is a first step in the hierarchical expansion of the plan, which will be further expanded e.g. with a step *open the door* if the door to the kitchen is closed — these and other expansion steps are performed by various *AnimNL* modules, up to the point when the instruction becomes executable by the simulator sitting on top of *Jack*.

The algorithm is mainly intended to handle instructions of the form *Do α to do β*. Thus, in step 1 Goal is chosen to be β. The only α_i left is α. I will now illustrate how the action formalism I devised supports the inferences just described.

3 THE REPRESENTATION FORMALISM

3.1 THE ACTION TAXONOMY

From the observations and examples provided so far, it should be clear that

1. It is impossible to define all possible action descriptions a priori, as the number of NL action descriptions is infinite.

2. It must be possible to compare action descriptions among them.

3. It is necessary to represent both linguistic and planning knowledge about actions.

Therefore, an action representation formalism that supports an algorithm such as the one in Fig. 1 must be flexible enough to be able to deal with new action descriptions, and to provide a partial order on descriptions. This is why I propose a hybrid KR system such as CLASSIC [Brachman *et al.*, 1991] as the underlying backbone of my formalism. Hybrid KR systems are composed of a T-Box, that is used to define terms, and an A-Box, used to assert facts or beliefs. The T-Box has its own *term-definition language*, which provides primitives to define *concepts* and *roles*, that express relations between concepts. The T-box is a *virtual* lattice, determined by the *subsumption* relation between concepts. It uses a *concept classifier*, which takes a

INPUT: Logical form LF of input sentence.
OUTPUT: Initial PlanGraph.

1. **(PREPROCESSING)** Choose Goal.

2. **(RETRIEVAL)**
   Retrieve the list of Recipe_l indexed by Goal, i.e. those recipes whose header is instantiated by Goal.

3. FOR each Recipe_l DO
   FOR each $\alpha_i \in \text{LF}$, $\alpha_i \neq \text{Goal}$, DO
   FOR each $\gamma_{l,j} \in \text{Body}(\text{Recipe}_l)$ DO
   (a) **(COMPUTING CONSISTENCY)**
       Check the consistency of α_i and $\gamma_{l,j}$.
   (b) **(COMPUTING EXPECTATIONS)**
       IF α_i and $\gamma_{l,j}$ are consistent
       THEN compute set of expectations $\{\mathcal{E}\}$.
   (c) IF there is **no** $\gamma_{l,j}$ such that α_i and $\gamma_{l,j}$ are consistent
       THEN Failure_l.

4. IF $\forall l\ \text{Failure}_l$
   THEN Signal user *Can't process instruction.* **(SIGNAL)**
   ELSE Choose best interpretation. Update PG. **(UPDATE)**

Figure 1: The Algorithm Top Level

new concept and determines the subsumption relations between it and all the other concepts in a given KB.

Having a virtual lattice allows me not to define all possible action descriptions a priori. The individual action descriptions part of the logical form are asserted into the A-Box, whose recognizer computes the set of types of which such descriptions are instances. After the Recipe_l's have been retrieved, α_k is compared to $\gamma_{l,j}$ by exploiting the hybrid system's classifier, as I will describe in Sec. 4.

If a hybrid system is to be used, its ontology has to include action types. However, just extending the ontology with an *act-type* concept is not enough to provide a linguistically motivated representation of actions. I found that utilizing in the T-Box Conceptual Structure primitives — CSs for short — derived from [Jackendoff, 1990] achieves this goal. CSs are well suited to represent action descriptions, as

- The CS primitives capture generalizations about action descriptions and their relationships to one another, such as that *carry* is *move object* augmented with a specific physical means of moving the object.
- CS representations are particularly amenable to express the logical form of an instruction, as they reveal where information may be missing from an utterance and has to be provided by inference.

The advantages of integrating the two formalisms are: the usage in the T-Box of linguistically sound primitives transforms the T-Box into a real lexicon, or at least, into a KB onto which the logical form can be easily mapped to; on the other hand, a KL-ONE style representation makes it possible to use CSs in a computational framework, by endowing it with a hierarchical organization and with the possibility of extending the lexicon.

Before showing how the T-Box employs CSs, I will illustrate CSs by showing how the CS for *Go into the kitchen* is built. A CS entity may be of ontological type *Thing, Place, Path, Event, State, Manner* or *Property*. The CS for a KITCHEN is shown in (5):

(5) [Thing KITCHEN]

CSs may also contain complex features generated by conceptual functions over other CSs. The conceptual function IN: Thing → Place is used to represent the location *in the kitchen* as shown in (6a) below. Likewise, the function TO: Place → Path describes a path that ends in the specified place, as shown in (6b):

(6a) [Place IN([Thing KITCHEN]$_k$)]$_l$
(6b) [Path TO([Place IN([Thing KITCHEN]$_k$)]$_l$)]$_m$

Finally, by adding GO: Thing × Path → Event, we obtain:

(7)
[Event GO([YOU]$_i$, [Path TO([IN([KITCHEN]$_k$)]$_l$)]$_m$)

Among other functions yielding events, CAUSE will be used in the CLASSIC definition of action:

(8) [Event CAUSE([Thing]$_i$, [Event]$_j$)]

An important notion in CS is that of *semantic field*. Semantic fields, such as Spatial and Possessional, are intended to capture the similarities between sentences like *Jack went into the kitchen* and *The gift went to*

Bill, as shown in (9) below:

(9a) [GO$_{Sp}$([JACK], [TO([IN([KITCHEN])])])]
(9b) [GO$_{Poss}$([GIFT], [TO([AT([BILL])])])]

[Di Eugenio and White, 1992] introduces a new semantic field, called Control. It is intended to represent the functional notion of *having control over* some object. The notion of Control is very relevant to AnimNL's domain, given that any action involving direct physical manipulation requires that the agent have the object to be manipulated under his control.

CSs are readily integrated into CLASSIC, as shown in Figs. 2 and 3, that present part of the T-Box I have implemented. Some comments are in order:

Entity. The taxonomy rooted in *entity* is similar to others used in other KBs.

Place. This subhierarchy encodes conceptual functions of the form F: Thing → Place, such as AT, IN, ON. In Fig. 2, only the concept *spatial-place*, and its subordinate *at-sp-place*, corresponding to the AT conceptual function, are shown. *at-sp-place* has a single role **at-role** with exactly one filler, of type *Entity*.

Path. Concepts belonging to this subhierarchy represent functions yielding *Paths*. There are different kinds of paths (and of places), corresponding to different semantic fields. In Fig. 2 only two of them, *spatial-path* and *control-path*, are represented.[7] Consider *from-to-path-sp(atial)*, defined by means of multiple inheritance from *to-path-sp* and *from-path-sp*. *from-to-path-sp* has two roles, **source** and **destination**, each of which has a filler *place*. The concept *from(at)-to-path-sp* restricts the role **source** inherited from *from-to-path-sp* to be filled by *at-sp-place*. It therefore corresponds to[8]

$$\begin{bmatrix} \text{FROM}([\text{AT}([_{\text{Thing}}])]) \\ \text{TO}([_{\text{Place}}]) \end{bmatrix}$$

Event. Fig. 3 shows part of the action subhierarchy. The intuitive notion of *action* corresponds to the concept *cause-and-acton*. Such definition, possibly puzzling to the reader, is used to maintain the distinction between the *thematic* and *action* tiers that Jackendoff argues for in [1990].

move-sth-swh — for *move something somewhere* — is defined as a subconcept of *cause-and-acton* by imposing the restriction that the filler of the **caused-role** be *go-sp-from-to*, namely, an *act-type* of type *go-spatial*, with a role **path-role** restricted to be *from-to-path-sp*.

---
[7] In CLASSIC the semantic field is represented by defining a role **semfield-role** — not shown in the figures — whose value restriction is the concept *semfield* defined by enumeration.

[8] Semantics fields are not shown.

The **experiencer** of *go-sp-from-to* is the moved object. The definition of *move-sth-swh* reproduces its CS representation, shown in the header in Fig. 5.

3.2 THE ACTION LIBRARY

So far I have only talked about representing *linguistic* action types. *Planning* knowledge is encoded in the Action Library, which contains simple recipes, and is implemented in CLASSIC too.[9] In this way, classification is used to maintain an organized KB of action recipes, and the indexing of recipes through the goal can be performed by exploiting the CLASSIC query language.

Many researchers have noted taxonomies of actions and/or plans as necessary, especially for plan inference. However, they have either just noted that action descriptions form a lattice, but not exploited the power of the virtual lattice as I have here [Balkanski, 1993]; or focussed on representing only planning, and not also linguistic knowledge [Kautz, 1990], [Tenenberg, 1989], even if they do exploit subsumption to deal with hierarchical organizations of complex objects, such as plans [Devanbu and Litman, 1991], [Swartout et al., 1991], [Wellman, 1988], constraint networks [Weida and Litman, 1994], or rules [Yen et al., 1991].

Among the systems that exploit subsumption to deal with plans, CLASP [Devanbu and Litman, 1991] is the closest to my concerns. In CLASP, plans are built out of actions, defined as classic STRIPS planning operators. Plan concept expressions are defined from action and state concepts using operators such as SEQUENCE, LOOP, TEST. The ordinary subsumption algorithm is extended to deal with plan classification. CLASP provides a rich plan language, but linguistic knowledge is absent.

The syntax of my recipes is described as follows:

RECIPE BNF	
RECIPE	→ HEADER BODY QUALIFIER* EFFECT+
HEADER	→ act-type
BODY	→ act-type+ ANNOTATION*
ANNOTATION	→ act-type$_1$ enables act-type$_2$ | act-type$_1$ TEMP-REL act-type$_2$
QUALIFIER	→ state
EFFECT	→ state
TEMP-REL	→ precedes | before | meets ...

Recipes have a *header*, *body*, *qualifiers* and *effects*. The terminology, especially *header* and *body*, is reminiscent of STRIPS, but the relations between these

---
[9] Thus, the distinction between *action taxonomy* and *action library* is conceptual rather than real.

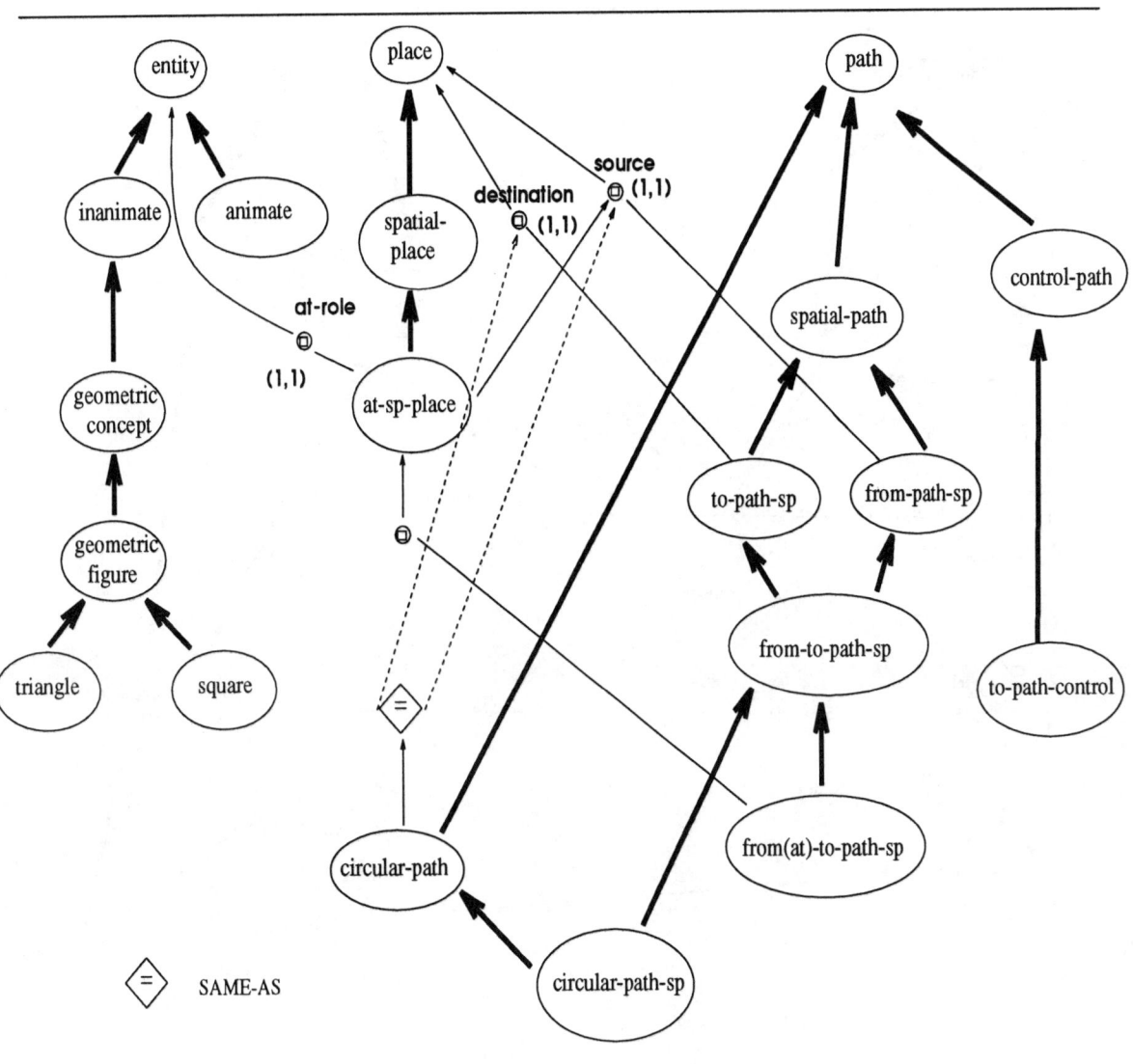

Figure 2: The *Path* Hierarchy

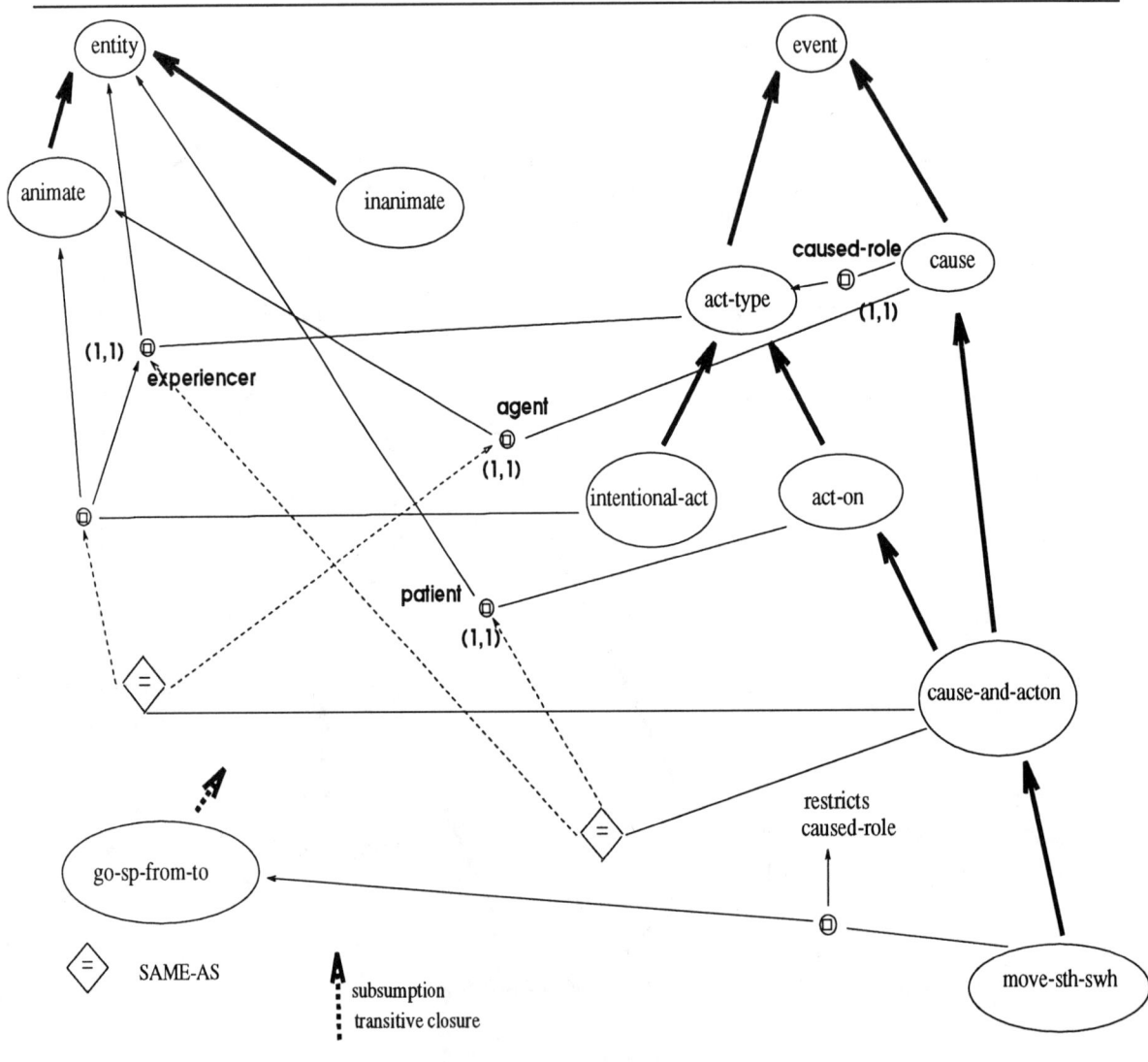

Figure 3: The *Action* Hierarchy

components are expressed in terms of *enablement* and *generation*, e.g. the body *generates* its header.

The representation does not employ preconditions, because it is very difficult to draw the line between what is a precondition and what is part of the body of the action. One could say that the body of a *Move* recipe — see Fig. 5 — simply consists of a *transfer* of an object from one place to another; and that a precondition for a *Move* is having control over that object. However, consider a heavy object: the agent will start exerting force to lift it, and then carry it to the other location. It is not obvious whether the lifting action is still part of achieving the precondition, or already part of the body of the action. The choice of not having preconditions has been more extensively motivated elsewhere in AnimNL [Geib, 1992]. Therefore, action recipes express what is traditionally expressed by means of preconditions by means of actions, which are substeps in the body that generates a certain header. Notice that other functions that preconditions have been used for, such as ordering substeps in a plan, can be performed by means of the annotations. As mentioned earlier, plan expansion is performed by other *AnimNL* modules, that start from the representation I provide and do further processing exploiting representations of actions that become more and more detailed, to take into account the requirements of the simulation system on top of *Jack*.

Other components of a recipe are the *annotations* on the body, that specify the relations between the subactions, e.g. enablement and temporal relations, the latter derived from [Allen, 1984]; *qualifiers*, already discussed in Sec. 2.1.2; and *effects*, what must be true after an action has been executed.

A network representation of *recipe* concepts is shown in Fig. 4. Auxiliary concept definitions, such as *annotation-type*, are not shown; however, SAME-AS constraints, necessary to express coreference, e.g. between the arguments of an annotation and the substeps of the recipe it belongs to, are shown in Fig. 6, the actual CLASSIC definition for the *move-recipe* concept. Fig. 5 shows the same recipe expressed in perhaps more readable CS format.

I make no claims that the *Move* recipe is complete, as neither the qualifier nor the effect list is exhaustive: they both merely list some necessary conditions. I refer the reader to e.g. [Genesereth and Nilsson, 1987] for discussion of the related issues of the *qualification* and *frame* problems in AI. Also notice that such recipe is just one of those possible for moving an object from one location to another.

The most natural way of translating the BNF for *recipe* into CLASSIC would be to define a topmost concept *recipe*, with roles **header, substeps, annotations, qualifiers** and **effects**, properly restricted. For example, **substeps** would be restricted as follows:

(**ALL** substeps intentional-act)
(**AT-LEAST** 1 substeps)

Unfortunately, as CLASSIC doesn't provide for role *differentiation*, it is impossible to express that each substep of *move-recipe* must have a different value restriction, *go-spatial*, *get-control* and *go-spatial-with* respectively. Thus, the *recipe* concept is simply defined as having a *header*, while the substeps appear only on the subconcepts of *recipe*, e.g. *recipe-1-step* and *recipe-3-steps*. Clearly, this way of defining substeps is not particularly perspicuous.[10] One possible solution would be to use a more expressive system that provides role differentiation, such as LOOM [Mac Gregor, 1988]: however, the usual trade-off between expressive power and complexity of the classifier has to be taken into account.

New recipes can be added to the Action Library by exploiting the classifier to maintain the hierarchical organization: for example, a *move-recipe2* concept with further qualifiers, or with a more specific *substep1*, would be correctly classified as a descendant of *move-recipe*. Contrary to CLASP I didn't need to extend subsumption, as the definition of recipe doesn't include complex constructors such as iteration or conditionals. Such extensions are left for future work.

4 INFERENCE IMPLEMENTATION

Just a few words on how steps 3a and 3b in Fig. 1 are implemented. At an abstract level, the matching step can be concisely described as examining the concept (and $\alpha^{conc}\ \gamma$), where α^{conc} is the most specific, possibly virtual concept of which α is an instance.[11] More specifically, the following queries should be posed:

(10a) (and $\alpha^{conc}\ \gamma$) $\stackrel{?}{=} \alpha^{conc}$, i.e., does γ subsume α^{conc}?

(10b) if not, (and $\alpha^{conc}\ \gamma$) $\stackrel{?}{=} \gamma$, i.e., does α^{conc} subsume γ?

(10c) if not, (coherent (and $\alpha^{conc}\ \gamma$))?

(10a) corresponds to consistency as usually embodied in plan recognition algorithms, but the examples in (3) show this is not sufficient. However, the notion of consistency in (10) is purely structural, and it is too restrictive. It has to be relaxed somewhat to allow for some kind of primitive geometric reasoning. Consider $[_{\text{Place}}\ \text{IN}([\text{KITCHEN}_1])]_{\mu_1}$ and $[_{\text{Place}}\ \text{AT}([\text{TABLE}_1])]_{\mu_2}$.

---

[10] For the reader familiar with the CLASP definition of *Action*: there all the required roles, such as **precondition**, can be described in a compact way because the filler is a single state, e.g. (**AND** Off-Hook-State Idle-State). This is clearly impossible to do with **substeps**, which describes actions whose descriptions are mutually exclusive.

[11] It actually has to be computed as it may be more specific than the concept(s) of which the A-Box recognizes that α is an instance.

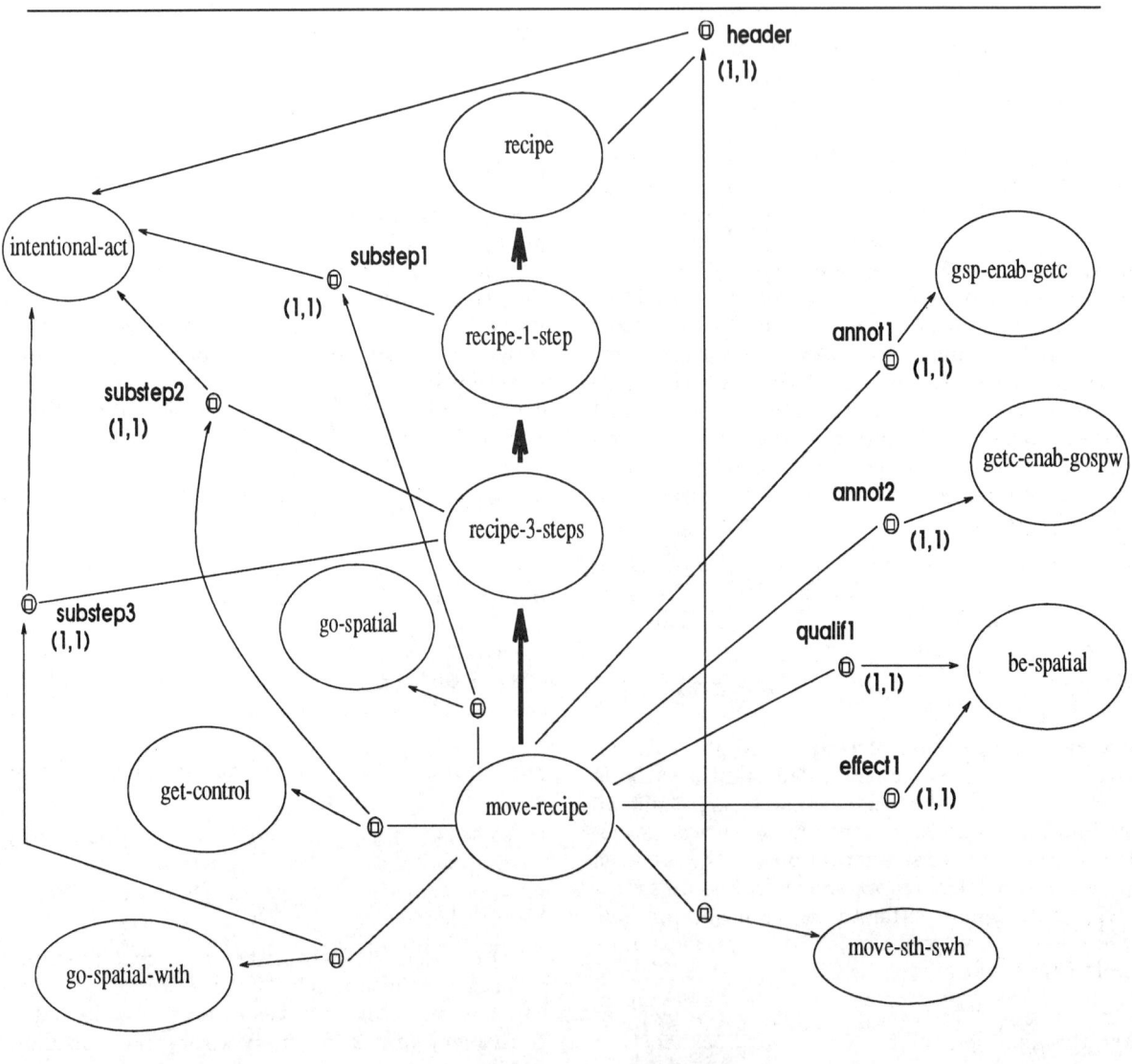

Figure 4: The *Recipe* Hierarchy

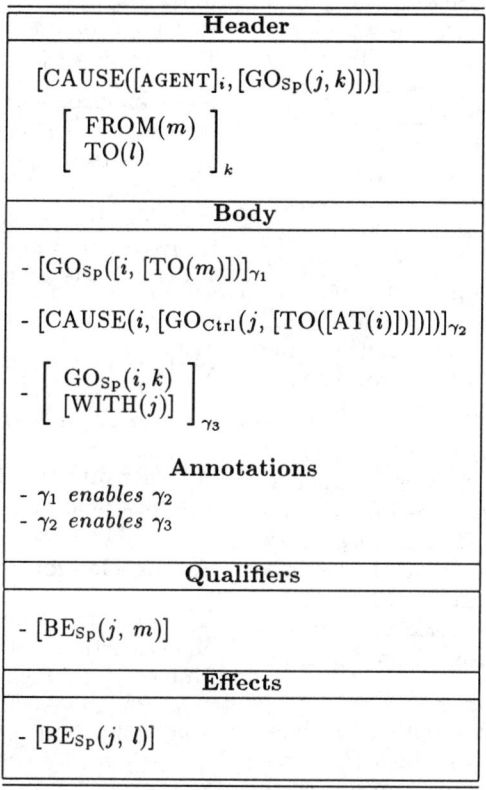

Figure 5: A *Move Something Somewhere* Recipe

```
(cl-define-concept 'move-recipe
    '(and recipe-3-steps
        (all header move-sth-swh)
        (all substep1 go-spatial)
        (all substep2 get-control)
        (all substep3 go-spatial-with)
        (all annot1 gsp-enab-getc)
        (all annot2 getc-enab-gospw)
        (all qualif1 be-spatial)
        (all effect1 be-spatial)
        (same-as (header agent)(substep1 agent))
        (same-as (header agent)(substep2 agent))
        (same-as (header agent)(substep3 agent))
        (same-as (header patient)(substep2 patient))
        (same-as (header patient)(substep3 with-role))
        (same-as (header caused-role path-role source)(substep1 path-role destination))
        (same-as (header caused-role path-role destination)(substep3 path-role destination))
        (same-as substep1 (annot1 ann-arg1))
        (same-as substep2 (annot1 ann-arg2))
        (same-as substep2 (annot2 ann-arg1))
        (same-as substep3 (annot2 ann-arg2))
        (same-as (qualif1 experiencer)(header patient))
        (same-as (effect1 experiencer)(header patient))
        (same-as (qualif1 location)(substep1 path-role destination))
        (same-as (effect1 location)(substep3 path-role destination))
    ))
```

Figure 6: The *Move* Recipe in CLASSIC

While neither of the μ_i's subsumes the other, and (and μ_1 μ_2) is incoherent, they can be considered compatible if TABLE$_1$ is in KITCHEN$_1$. To really understand such compatibilities, a geometric reasoner would be necessary: we are planning to develop one for *AnimNL*, but for the moment I have included only some simple notions of compatibility in the algorithm. Therefore, it is not possible to directly use CLASSIC queries to implement (10), such as (cl-subsumes? α^{conc} γ) for (10b) or (cl-disjoint? γ α^{conc}) for (10c).[12] I have implemented a procedure, (check-real-comp α^{conc} γ), which partly mimics classification, but at the same time provides the more flexible notion of consistency necessary to account for spatial concepts.

No further mechanisms than those already described are needed to implement step 3b,[13] as such expectations arise from what is known about certain parameters within the current Recipe. If such parameters appear more than once in Recipe, in particular in a *qualifier*, they will appear in at least one SAME-AS restriction — see Fig. 6. As check-real-comp checks SAME-AS restrictions as well, expectations "emerge" from the processing.

Apart from concepts of type entity, path and place, the KB comprises 14 state concepts, 44 action concepts, and 9 recipe concepts, which have been used to test about 30 different kinds of examples — where two examples are of a different kind if the action instances involved don't differ just because of fillers that are instances of primitive concepts (such as having different *animate* agents).

5 CONCLUSIONS

I have justified my action representation formalism by means of specific inferences, and I have discussed its three main components, the underlying hybrid system, the CS semantic primitives, and the action library.

Future work includes first of all extending the kind of data that my representation and algorithm account for. I believe that the approach is useful for any kind of instruction, as the need to match input descriptions with stored knowledge will always arise. However, in the case of PCs the problem is simplified by having the goal explicitly given, while precisely the goal has to be inferred in plan recognition algorithms.

The coverage can be very naturally extended to other purpose connectives, such as *so that, such that*, and to Means Clauses, namely, *by* constructions as in *Do α by doing β*: however, to deal with the latter, and

---

[12](10a) is implemented by (cl-instance? α γ).

[13]In fact, the distinction between steps 3a and 3b in Fig. 1 is conceptual rather than real.

to distinguish them from PCs, some more perspicuous treatment of H's mental state, such as in [Balkanski, 1993], is needed.

Some kinds of *negative imperatives*, that I have examined as well [Di Eugenio, 1993], can be dealt with with the same techniques. For example, given a hierarchical representation of *cleaning* actions, it would be easy to recognize that *scrub* and *wet-mop* are not viable alternatives of *cleaning the parquet*: this could lead to learn which are the proper methods for cleaning a parquet.

(11) *Caring for the floor. Dust-mop or vacuum your parquet floor as you would carpeting.* **Do not scrub or wet-mop the parquet.**

Another direction for future work is to devise a more complex plan language in the CLASP style.

Acknowledgements

This research was carried on while the author was at the Department of Computer and Information Science, University of Pennsylvania, and supported by grants DARPA no. N00014-90-J-1863, ARO no. DAAL 03-89-C-0031, NSF no. IRI 90-16592, and Ben Franklin no. 91S.3078C-1. Many thanks to Bonnie Webber for her guidance over the years, to the members of the *AnimNL* group for many discussions over interpreting instructions, and to the two anonymous reviewers for their comments, which greatly improved this paper.

References

[Allen, 1984] J. Allen. Towards a General Theory of Action and Time. *Artificial Intelligence*, 23:123–154, 1984.

[Alterman et al., 1991] R. Alterman, R. Zito-Wolf, and T. Carpenter. Interaction, Comprehension, and Instruction Usage. Technical Report CS-91-161, Dept. of Computer Science, Center for Complex Systems, Brandeis University, 1991.

[Badler et al., 1993] N. Badler, C. Phillips, and B. Webber. *Simulating Humans: Computer Graphics Animation and Control*. Oxford University Press, 1993.

[Balkanski, 1993] C. Balkanski. *Actions, Beliefs and Intentions in Multi-Action Utterances*. PhD thesis, Harvard University, 1993. Technical Report TR-16-93.

[Brachman et al., 1991] R. Brachman, D. McGuinness, P. Patel-Schneider, L. Alperin Resnick, and A. Borgida. Living with CLASSIC: When and How to Use a KL-ONE-like Language. In J. F. Sowa, editor, *Principles of Semantic Networks — Explorations in the Representation of Knowledge*, pages 401–456. Morgan Kaufmann, 1991.

[Chapman, 1991] D. Chapman. *Vision, Instruction and Action*. Cambridge: MIT Press, 1991.

[Charniak, 1988] E. Charniak. Motivation Analysis, Abductive Unification, and Nonmonotonic Equality. *Artificial Intelligence*, 34:275–295, 1988.

[Devanbu and Litman, 1991] P. Devanbu and D. Litman. Plan-Based Terminological Reasoning. In *KR91, Proceedings of the Second International Conference on Principles of Knowledge Representation and Reasoning*, pages 128–138, 1991.

[Di Eugenio and White, 1992] B. Di Eugenio and M. White. On the Interpretation of Natural Language Instructions. In *COLING92, Proceedings of the Fourteenth International Conference on Computational Linguistics*, pages 1147–1151, 1992.

[Di Eugenio, 1992] B. Di Eugenio. Understanding Natural Language Instructions: the Case of Purpose Clauses. In *ACL92, Proceedings of the 30th Meeting of the Association for Computational Linguistics*, pages 120–127, 1992.

[Di Eugenio, 1993] B. Di Eugenio. *Understanding Natural Language Instructions: a Computational Approach to Purpose Clauses*. PhD thesis, University of Pennsylvania, December 1993. Technical Report MS-CIS-93-91 (Also Institute for Research in Cognitive Science report IRCS-93-52).

[Geib, 1992] C. Geib. Intentions in Means/End Planning. Technical Report MS-CIS-92-73, University of Pennsylvania, 1992.

[Genesereth and Nilsson, 1987] M. Genesereth and N. Nilsson. *Logical Foundations of Artificial Intelligence*. Morgan Kaufmann Publishers, 1987.

[Goldman, 1970] A. Goldman. *A Theory of Human Action*. Princeton University Press, 1970.

[Jackendoff, 1990] R. Jackendoff. *Semantic Structures*. Current Studies in Linguistics Series. The MIT Press, 1990.

[Kautz, 1990] H. Kautz. A Circumscriptive Theory of Plan Recognition. In P. Cohen, J. Morgan, and M. Pollack, editors, *Intentions in Communication*. MIT Press, 1990.

[Litman and Allen, 1990] D. Litman and J. Allen. Discourse Processing and Commonsense Plans. In P. Cohen, J. Morgan, and M. Pollack, editors, *Intentions in Communication*. MIT Press, 1990.

[Mac Gregor, 1988] R. Mac Gregor. A Deductive Pattern Matcher. In *AAAI88, Proceedings of the Seventh National Conference on Artificial Intelligence*, 1988.

[Pollack, 1986] M. Pollack. *Inferring Domain Plans in Question-Answering*. PhD thesis, University of Pennsylvania, 1986.

[Schoppers, 1988] M. Schoppers. *Representation and Automatic Synthesis of Reaction Plans*. PhD thesis, University of Illinois at Urbana-Champaign, 1988.

[Swartout et al., 1991] W. Swartout, C. Paris, and J. Moore. Design for a Explainable Expert Systems. *IEEE Expert*, 6(3):58–64, 1991.

[Tenenberg, 1989] J. Tenenberg. Inheritance in Automated Planning. In *KR89, Proceedings of the First International Conference on Principles of Knowledge Representation and Reasoning*, 1989.

[Vere and Bickmore, 1990] S. Vere and T. Bickmore. A Basic Agent. *Computational Intelligence*, 6:41–60, 1990.

[Webber et al., 1992] B. Webber, N. Badler, F. B. Baldwin, W. Becket, B. Di Eugenio, C. Geib, M. Jung, L. Levison, M. Moore, and M. White. Doing What You're Told: Following Task Instructions In Changing, but Hospitable Environments. Technical Report MS-CIS-92-74, University of Pennsylvania, 1992. To appear in *Language and Vision across the Pacific*, Y. Wilks and N. Okada editors.

[Webber et al., 1993] B. Webber, N. Badler, B. Di Eugenio, C. Geib, L. Levison, and M. Moore. Instructions, Intentions and Expectations. Technical Report MS-CIS-93-61, University of Pennsylvania, 1993. To appear in *Artificial Intelligence Journal*, Special Issue on Computational Theories of Interaction and Agency.

[Weida and Litman, 1994] R. Weida and D. Litman. Subsumption and Recognition of Heterogeneous Constraint Networks. In *The Tenth IEEE Conference on Artificial Intelligence for Applications (CAIA-94)*, 1994.

[Wellman, 1988] M. Wellman. *Formulation of Tradeoffs in Planning under Uncertainty*. PhD thesis, Massachusetts Institute of Technology, 1988.

[White, 1992] M. White. Conceptual Structures and CCG: Linking Theory and Incorporated Argument Adjuncts. In *COLING92, Proceedings of the Fourteenth International Conference on Computational Linguistics*, pages 246–252, 1992.

[Wilensky, 1983] R. Wilensky. *Planning and Understanding. A Computational Approach to Human Reasoning*. Addison-Wesley Publishing Company, 1983.

[Yen et al., 1991] J. Yen, R. Neches, and R. MacGregor. CLASP: Integrating Term Subsumption Systems and Production Systems. *IEEE Transactions on Knowledge and Data Engineering*, 3(1), 1991.

Conditional Objects as Nonmonotonic Consequence Relations[1]
—Main Results—

Didier Dubois - Henri Prade
Institut de Recherche en Informatique de Toulouse (I.R.I.T.) – C.N.R.S.
Université Paul Sabatier, 118 route de Narbonne
31062 Toulouse Cedex – France

Abstract

This paper is an investigation of the relationship between conditional objects of the form 'q|p' obtained as a qualitative counterpart to conditional probabilities $P(q|p)$, and nonmonotonic reasoning. Viewed as an inference rule, the conditional object is shown to possess properties of a well-behaved nonmonotonic consequence relation. The basic tool is the 3-valued semantics of conditional objects that differs from the preferential semantics of Lehmann and colleagues and does not require probabilistic semantics. Semantic entailment of a conditional object q|p from a knowledge base made of conditional objects is shown to be equivalent to the inference of the conditional assertion $p \mathrel{\mid\!\sim} q$ in Lehmann's System P. Then a notion of consistency is proposed for a set of conditional objects in the light of the 3-valued semantics; a higher level counterpart of refutation is presented which leads to a procedure for checking that a conditional knowledge base entails a considered conditional object. Modus ponens and resolution-like patterns can be also established for conditional objects and are proved to be useful for inference from conditional objects taking advantage of a disjunctive decomposition of conditional objects.

---

[1] A preliminary version of this paper, entitled "Conditional objects: A three-valued semantics for non-monotonic inference" is in the unpublished Proceedings of the IJCAI'93 Workshop "Conditionals in Knowledge Representation" (Chambéry, France, August 30, 1993), pp. 81-86.

1 INTRODUCTION

The idea of a conditional object corresponds to an attempt to give a mathematical and logical meaning to a conditional relationship between two logical propositions p and q in agreement with the notion of conditional probability $P(q|p)$, but independently of the notion of probability. A conditional object is thus associated to a pair (p,q) of Boolean propositions and denoted q|p which reads "q given p" and is such that $Prob(q|p)$ can indeed be considered as the probability of the entity q|p (and not only as the probability of q, in the context where p is true). This kind of study was pioneered by De Finetti (1937) and Schay (1968). There has been several previously published works along this research line, especially Calabrese (1987), Goodman and Nguyen (1988), Goodman, Nguyen and Walker (1991), Dubois and Prade (1988, 1990).

One way of considering a conditional object q|p is to see it as a defeasible inference rule "if p then q but for exceptions". This point of view is quite in accordance with the usual understanding of a high conditional probability except that no attempt is made to quantify the presence of exceptions. The antecedent p is viewed as a description of a context in which plausible conclusions can be drawn. It differs from the usual notion of inference in the sense that refining the context may invalidate conclusions previously held as plausible. This nonmonotonic behavior is usual in probabilistic reasoning where the probability $P(q|p)$ can be high while simultaneously the probability $P(q|p \wedge r)$ can very well be small.

Following (Dubois and Prade, 1991), the paper mainly deals with the relationships between the logical calculus developed on conditional objects like q|p and nonmonotonic reasoning systems based on the study on nonmonotonic consequence relationships as studied by Gabbay (1985) and more recently by Makinson (1989), Kraus et al. (1990). It is possible to envisage a conditional object as a nonmonotonic consequence relation. Such a suggestion becomes natural if we reconsider a conditional logic proposed by Adams (1975). He interpreted q|p as $P(q|p) \geq 1 - \varepsilon$ where ε is positive but arbitrarily small, developed a conditional logic that supports this semantics and found higher level inference rules that turn out to be exactly those that have later on emerged from the study of nonmonotonic consequence relationships. In the probabilistic camp, Pearl (1988) and his student Geffner (1992) have borrowed Adams' conditional logic to develop a nonmonotonic reasoning system that closely maps the one developed by Lehmann (1989) in the symbolic camp. The former thus claim that the natural semantics for nonmonotonic reasoning is probabilistic, while the latter use complex two-level preferential semantics. The comparative study of conditional objects and nonmonotonic consequence relations proves that a simple 3-valued semantics is enough to capture the core logic of nonmonotonic reasoning. Several proofs of results are omitted for the sake of brevity and can be found in a longer version of the paper available as a report (Dubois and Prade, 1993).

2 CONDITIONAL OBJECTS: THE 3-VALUED SEMANTICS

In the paper we shall consider conditional objects of the form q|p where p and q, are well-formed formulae in a classical propositional language $\mathcal{L}$. $\mathcal{B}$ will denote the Boolean algebra obtained by quotienting $\mathcal{L}$ by the equivalence ($\equiv$) between propositions. The number of propositional variables is assumed to be finite. In order to attach truth-values to conditional objects we adopt a 3-valued semantics related to pioneering works of De Finetti (1937) and Schay (1968), among others, but which has been independently suggested in (Dubois and Prade, 1988).

Let {T, F, U} be the truth-set where T and F mean true and false, and the third value U means undefined or inapplicable. T and F will also denote the ever-true and the ever-false propositions. Classical propositions can only be true or false, i.e., $t(p) \in \{T,F\}, \forall p \in \mathcal{L}$. The truth-assignment of a conditional object q|p is defined as follows:

$$\forall t, t(q|p) = t(q) \text{ if } t(p) = T$$
$$= U \text{ otherwise.}$$

Following Adams (1975), a conditional object is said to be verified by a truth-assignment whenever t(q|p) = T, i.e., t(p) = t(q) = 1 or, if we prefer, $t(p \wedge q) = 1$, and falsified if t(q|p) = F, i.e., $t(\neg p \vee q) = 0$. Otherwise q|p is said to be inapplicable or undefined; another way of interpreting t(q|p) = U, is to say that, whenever p is false the truth-value of q, as determined by p, is unknown. Conditional objects of the form p|T are such that t(p|T) = t(p). Hence any unconditional formula p can be interpreted as a conditional object p|T. Clearly q|p is akin to an inference rule, rather than a classical proposition, and differs as such from the material conditional $p \rightarrow q = \neg p \vee q$ which is such that $t(p \rightarrow q) = T$ whenever t(q|p) = U. Moreover given a conditional object q|p, let $\mathcal{I}(q|p)$ be defined as

$$\mathcal{I}(q|p) = \{\varphi \in \mathcal{L}, \quad t(\varphi) = T \text{ if } t(q|p) = T$$
$$t(\varphi) = F \text{ if } t(q|p) = F\}.$$

where $\vDash$ is the usual notion of semantic entailment. $\mathcal{I}(q|p)$ is the set of classical propositions which coincide with q|p whenever $t(q|p) \neq U$. It is easy to verify that

$$\mathcal{I}(q|p) = \{\varphi | p \wedge q \vDash \varphi \text{ and } \varphi \vDash \neg p \vee q\}.$$

Conversely, given $\varphi, \psi \in \mathcal{L}$ such that $\varphi \vDash \psi$ then $\exists p, q \in \mathcal{L}$ such that $\mathcal{I}(q|p) = \{r | \varphi \vDash r, r \vDash \psi\}$. It means that a conditional object q|p can be interpreted as a set of formulae whose lower bound is $p \wedge q$ and upper bound is $p \rightarrow q$ where $\rightarrow$ denotes the material implication; in other words it is an interval in the Boolean algebra $\mathcal{B}$. Conversely any interval in a Boolean algebra, or equivalently any pair of propositions one of which entails the other gives birth to a conditional object. Namely if $\varphi \vDash \psi$, it corresponds to a conditional object $\varphi|(\psi \rightarrow \varphi)$ since $\varphi \wedge (\psi \rightarrow \varphi) = \varphi$ and $\neg(\psi \rightarrow \varphi) \vee \varphi = \varphi \vee \psi = \psi$.

The above view of conditional objects suggests an ordering relation $\leq$ on {T, F, U} whereby $F \leq U \leq T$, since U is viewed as any element in the set {F,T} when q|p is equated with $\mathcal{I}(q|p)$. It leads to the following extension of the entailment relation

$$q|p \vDash s|r \Leftrightarrow t(q|p) \leq t(s|r).$$

The following property can be obviously checked using the interval $\mathcal{I}(q|p)$

$$q|p \vDash s|r \Leftrightarrow p \wedge q \vDash s \wedge r \text{ and } p \rightarrow q \vDash r \rightarrow s.$$

The conditional object q|p is here meant to represent default rules of the form "if p is true then q generally follows, up to exceptions". The above definition of "meta-entailment" over objects considered as default inference rules makes sense. An interpretation is said to be an *example* of the rule if under this interpretation, the corresponding conditional object is verified; a *counter-example* is an interpretation which falsifies the conditional object. Then $q|p \vDash s|r$ means that any examples of q|p is an example of s|r, and any counter-example of s|r is a counter-example of q|p. Hence s|r is in some sense at least as often valid as q|p insofar as the former has more examples and less counter-examples than q|p. Note that the meta-entailment is reflexive and transitive.

Two conditional objects q|p and s|r are said to be equivalent if and only if both $q|p \vDash s|r$ and $s|r \vDash q|p$ hold. This is clearly equivalent to p ≡ r and $p \wedge q \equiv s \wedge r$, i.e., they have the same context and in this context they are simultaneously verified. For equivalent conditional object we write q|p = s|r. In particular q|p = (p ∧ q) | p = (p → q) | p = (p ↔ q) | p. The meta-entailment verifies some properties, some of which make conditional objects similar to material conditionals, some of which make them quite different:

i) logical equivalence: if $p \leftrightarrow p' \equiv T$ then q|p = q|p'
ii) weakening: if $q \models q'$ then $q|p \models q'|p$.

However, although $p \rightarrow q \models p \land r \rightarrow q$, this is certainly not true for conditional objects, because it is false that $p \land q \models p \land q \land r$. However the two conditional objects q|p and ¬q|p ∧ r cannot be verified together. But a conditional object that is verified in a given context, can be falsified in a more restricted context.

3 CONNECTIVES FOR DEFAULT RULES

Let us turn to the question of connectives. There are several ways of addressing this problem, and various extensions of conjunction and disjunction over to conditional objects have been suggested by Schay (1968), Calabrese (1987), Goodman and Nguyen (1988), but also Adams (1975). Sticking to the 3-valued logic approach, the question comes down to extend truth-tables from {T,F} over to {T, F, U}. Here we shall perform this task with a view to remain consistent with nonmonotonic reasoning applications, but assuming truth-functionality of connectives over {T, F, U}.

In accordance with the idea that a conditional object stands for a default inference rule, a conjunction of conditional objects will stand for a collection of conditional objects forming a rule base K. The problem is thus how to compute a truth-assignment for K entirely, in terms of the rules in K. Let us assume that t(q|p AND s|r) is a function of t(q|p) and t(s|r). The following constraints restrict the possible definitions of the AND, modelled by a binary operation ∗ on {T, F, U}

-) ∗ coincide with usual conjunction ∧ on {T,F}
-) U ∗ U = U.
-) ∗ is commutative
-) U ∗ T ≠ F
-) Bayes conditioning: q|p AND p|T is equivalent to p ∧ q|T.

Let us justify these choices in the light of our view of conditional objects as default rules of inference. Coincidence with classical conjunction accounts for the semantic identity between p and p|T. The property U ∗ U = U is justified by the fact that if in a rule base K, no rule is applicable, then K is considered as not applicable. Commutativity is due to the fact that K is a set. U ∗ T ≠ F sounds natural, namely, when K is falsified, at least one rule in K should be falsified. The last condition says that in order for p ∧ q to be true, it is enough that p be true and q|p verified. But if p is false, p ∧ q is false too. It leads to the constraint F ∗ t(q|p) = F, hence F ∗ U = F. These constraints only leave two choices open for conjunction of conditional objects since only U ∗ T remains incompletely specified:

i) U ∗ T = U. This choice is in complete accordance with the interval understanding of conditional objects since

U ∗ T = {T,F} ∧ T = {T ∧ T, T ∧ F} = {T,F} = U.

The canonicity of this definition has led Goodman and Nguyen (1988) to adopt this definition. It has the merit to be easily generalized to any connective in a systematic way. However, viewing K as a conjunction of default rules, it is then unsatisfactory since K becomes inapplicable as soon as one "rule" is inapplicable. This defect is avoided with the other possible choice.

ii) U ∗ T = T. This corresponds to the following table for ∗

Table 1: Quasi-conjunction

∗	F	U	T
F	F	F	F
U	F	U	T
T	F	T	T

It can be checked that this definition of the conjunction translates in terms of conditional objects into

(q|p) & (s|r) = [(p → q) ∧ (r → s)] | (p ∨ r)

using & for denoting the conjunction of conditional objects based on the above table. It comes down to assuming a different ordering F < T < U where U is the top element, and ∗ is the minimum operator. Using &, a conditional knowledge base becomes applicable as soon as one of its rules applies. This definition has been used by Calabrese (1987) (under a different but equivalent form) and by Adams (1975) who calls it 'quasi-conjunction'. & is clearly associative. It can be checked that & is monotonic with respect to ⊨.

Negation of a conditional object denoted by '−', is naturally defined by requiring that it coincides with the usual negation on {T,F} and that it returns U when applied to U. It leads to

−(q|p) = (¬q) | p,

i.e., the negation of a "rule" is the rule with the opposite conclusion. By De Morgan's duality with respect to &, we obtain the following disjunction, denoted by +, and called 'quasi-disjunction' by Adams (1975)

(q|p) + (s|r) = [(p ∧ q) ∨ (r ∧ s)] | (p ∨ r).

4 CONDITIONAL OBJECTS AND NONMONOTONIC CONSEQUENCE RELATIONS

The following properties were established for conditional objects

$(q|p)$ & $(r|p) \models (r | (p \wedge q))$ (A)
$(q|p)$ & $(r|(p \wedge q)) \models (r|p)$ (B)
$(q|p)$ & $(r|p) \models ((q \wedge r) | p)$ (C)
$(q|p)$ & $(p|q)$ & $(r|q) \models (r|p)$ (D)
$(r|(p \wedge q)) \models ((\neg p \vee r) | q)$ (E)
$(r|p) \wedge (r|q) \models (r | (p \vee q))$.   (F)

and in (Dubois and Prade, 1991) recognized as counterparts of properties of a well-behaved nonmonotonic consequence relation $p \mathrel{|\!\sim} q$, in place of $q|p$. Rational monotony is not satisfied by conditional objects. In fact conditional objects equipped with & and $\models$ enjoy all the properties of the system P (Lehmann, 1989; Kraus et al., 1990), namely it is possible to translate the following properties in the language of conditional events, changing 'and' into & and 'deduce' into $\models$:

Left logical equivalence: from $p \leftrightarrow p' = T$ and $p \mathrel{|\!\sim} q$ deduce $p' \mathrel{|\!\sim} q$
Right weakening: from $q \models q'$ and $p \mathrel{|\!\sim} q$ deduce $p \mathrel{|\!\sim} q'$
Reflexivity: $p \mathrel{|\!\sim} p$
Left OR: from $p \mathrel{|\!\sim} r$ and $q \mathrel{|\!\sim} r$ deduce $p \vee q \mathrel{|\!\sim} r$ (see (F))
Cautious monotony: from $p \mathrel{|\!\sim} q$ and $p \mathrel{|\!\sim} r$ deduce $p \wedge q \mathrel{|\!\sim} r$ (see (A))
Weak transitivity or cut: from $p \wedge q \mathrel{|\!\sim} r$ and $p \mathrel{|\!\sim} q$ deduce $p \mathrel{|\!\sim} r$ (see (B))

and its consequences ('right and' (see (C)), 'reciprocity' (see (D)), half of the deduction theorem (see (E))...). 'Right weakening' and 'left logical equivalence' also hold as indicated in Section 2. Reflexivity holds for conditional objects under the following form: $p|p$ is never falsified.

Let K be a base made of a collection of conditional objects $q_i|p_i$, $i = 1,n$ and $C(K)$ be the object defined as the conjunction of the $q_i|p_i$, i.e., $C(K) = q_1|p_1$ &... & $q_n|p_n$. It is tempting, as done earlier in (Dubois and Prade, 1991) to define entailment from K using $C(K)$ and the ordering $\models$ on conditional objects, i.e., K entails $q|p$ means that $C(K) \models q|p$. However this definition has a serious drawback, pointed out in (Dubois and Prade, 1991), namely we do not have that if $q|p \in K$ then $C(K) \models q|p$. One way of fixing this problem is to define entailment from a conditional knowledge base in a more flexible way:

K *entails* $q|p$, denoted $K \models q|p$, if and only if there exists a subset S of K such that $C(S) \models q|p$.

The case when $C(S) \models q|p$ for $S = \emptyset$ is restricted to conditional objects that can never be falsified, i.e., $q|p$ such that $p \models q$. Hence we always have $K \models p|p$ for any conditional knowledge base K. Now it is easy to check that $\{q|p, s|r\} \models q|p$, and that if $K \models q|p$ then $K \cup \{s|r\} \models q|p$. The entailment of conditional objects from a conditional knowledge base is thus monotonic, reflexive and transitive contrary to the definition in (Dubois and Prade, 1991).

Let $\mathcal{K}$ be the set of conditional assertions $p \mathrel{|\!\sim} q$ corresponding to the set K of conditional objects $q|p$. Let us define a syntactic conditional entailment, denoted by $\vdash$, from a set of conditional assertions, $\mathcal{K}$, as done by Lehmann (1989). Namely,

$\mathcal{K} \vdash p \mathrel{|\!\sim} q$ if and only if $p \mathrel{|\!\sim} q$ can be derived from $\mathcal{K}$ using $p \mathrel{|\!\sim} p$ as an axiom schema and the inference rules of System P.

Then the following representation theorem which is the main result of this paper holds

$\mathcal{K} \vdash p \mathrel{|\!\sim} q$ if and only if $K \models q|p$.

See a proof in Annex. What is obtained here is a formal system for handling exception-tolerant if-then rules, whose (meta) inference rules are exactly those of the system P of Lehmann, but whose semantics is a simple 3-valued extension of the true/false semantics of classical logic; in particular it owes nothing to infinitesimal probabilities (as in Adams conditional logic) nor to partial orderings on possible worlds and the like (as in Kraus, Lehmann and Magidor, 1990). Moreover it opens the road to deduction methods for plausible reasoning based on semantic evaluation. In order to check that $\mathcal{K} \vdash p \mathrel{|\!\sim} q$, where $\vdash$ is the preferential entailment of Lehmann, or equivalently, the p-entailment of Adams (when K contains only conditional objects) also denoted $\vdash_0$ by Pearl (1990) and Geffner (1992), it is enough to check that

$\exists \, S \subseteq K$, $t(C(S)) \leq t(q|p)$

using truth-values, where $t(C(S))$ is computed in a truth-functional way using the table in Figure 1.

Example: Consider the famous penguin case where $K = \{f|b, b|p, \neg f|p\}$ with b = bird, f = fly, p = penguin. It is easy to check that $K \models \neg f|p \wedge b$ using Cautious monotony on $b|p$ and $\neg f|p$. But it is also possible to check that if $S = \{b|p, \neg f|p\}$, $C(S) = b \wedge \neg f|p$ and $t(b \wedge \neg f|p) \leq t(\neg f|p \wedge b)$ since $b \wedge \neg f \wedge p = \neg f \wedge p \wedge b$ and $\neg p \vee (b \wedge \neg f) \models \neg p \vee \neg b \vee \neg f$. Although we did not need any probabilistic view of conditional objects, the above result is not entirely new in the sense that it owes much to Adams' conditional logic and the proofs of the completeness are very similar to (although simpler than) Adams' completeness proof with respect to probabilistic entailment, because for the most part the machinery he used was independent of any probabilistic semantics of conditional objects, although he did not point out this fact in his 1975 book.

5 CONSISTENCY AND REFUTATION

It might also be tempting to define the consistency of a conditional knowledge base K in terms of the quasi-conjunction C(K), namely ascribing that C(K) be not a conditional contradiction, i.e., $\nexists p$, $C(K) \models \neg p|p$, or equivalently $t(C(K)) = T$ for at least one interpretation (i.e., C(K) is verifiable). However, again there might exist situations where $C(K) \models \neg p|p$ for some p, while $C(K \cup \{s|r\})$ is not a conditional contradiction, since $U \wedge T = T$. For instance $t((\neg p|p) \wedge (s|r)) = T$ if $t(p) = F$, $t(s \wedge r) = T$. Hence, contrary to the propositional case, inconsistency can be hidden in a conditional knowledge base by other verified conditional objects. Hence the following definition

> A set of conditional objects K is said to be *consistent* if and only if for no subset $S \subseteq K$ does C(S) entail a conditional contradiction (i.e., $\forall S \subseteq K$, C(S) is verifiable). Otherwise K is said to be inconsistent.

The above definition of consistency also derives from Adams, although he was basically interested in finding a condition ensuring the possibility of attaching arbitrary high conditional probability values to each conditional object in K (what he called p-consistency). He proved that the above definition of consistency was a necessary and sufficient condition for p-consistency.

The next result of the paper relates conditional deduction and inconsistency.

> If K is consistent, then $K \models q|p$ if and only if $K \cup \{\neg q|p\}$ is inconsistent.

The above result can be simply proved using conditional objects. It has actually be noticed in the infinitesimal probability setting by Adams (1975) and Geffner (1992) and established by Lehmann and Magidor (1992) in the framework of conditional assertions. It suggests the use of refutation as a tool for checking conditional entailment.

Pearl (1990) and Geffner (1992) have actually given another definition of consistency of a conditional knowledge base. If q|p is a conditional object, let $p \rightarrow q$ be its material counterpart. Let S* be the set of material counterparts of the conditional objects in S. Then K is consistent if and only if $\forall S \subseteq K$, $\exists q|p \in S$, such that $S^* \cup \{p \wedge q\}$ is consistent. Clearly, this is equivalent to require that C(S) be verified at least for one interpretation, i.e., that one conditional object in S be verified while none of the other is falsified. A conditional object $q|p \in S$ such that $S^* \cup \{p \wedge q\}$ is consistent is called

"tolerated" by S in Pearl (1990). This suggests the use of Pearl's System Z algorithm to check the consistency of a set of conditional objects. Given a consistent set K of conditional objects, checking that $K \models q|p$ comes down to checking the inconsistency of $K \cup \{\neg q|p\}$ using the following algorithm:

$S := K \cup \{\neg q|p\}$
repeat
   if $\neg q|p$ is tolerated by S, then stop; (K does not entail q|p)
   else compute $S' := \{q_i|p_i \in S, q_i|p_i$ not tolerated by S$\}$
     if $S = S'$ stop; (K entails q|p)
     $S := S'$

The algorithm takes advantage of the fact that since K is consistent, the only source of inconsistency is the presence of $\neg q|p$. Once $\neg q|p$ is captured by the tolerance test, the procedure can stop. This consistency-checking method was first hinted in Adams (1975, p. 53). It indicates also that consistency checking, hence deduction, requires at most m classical consistency checking tests, where m is the number of conditional objects in K. It is then easy to estimate the complexity of reasoning with conditional objects.

6 QUASI-CONJUNCTION AND META-RESOLUTION

A conditional object can be decomposed into a disjunction of other conditional objects. Indeed if $q = \vee_i q_i$ and $p = \vee_j p_j$, we have

$$q|p = +_{i,j} q_i|p_j$$

as pointed out by Calabrese (1992) who uses this lemma as a starting point for establishing a counterpart of the disjunctive normal form theorem in Boolean algebra for conditional objects.

This remark can be used conjointly with the following "meta"-resolution rule

$$[((\neg q|p) + (s|r)) \& ((q|p) + (u|t))] \models (s|r) + (u|t).$$

as well as the particular case of the meta-modus ponens $q|p \& (\neg q|p + s|r) \models s|r$ and a meta-deduction theorem:

$$q|p \& s|r \models v|u \text{ if and only if } q|p \models \neg s|r + v|u.$$

It can be checked that the use of inference rules using quasi-disjunction in their expression is compatible with the entailment from a conditional knowledge base K in the sense that, for the meta-modus ponens, if $v|u \in K$ can be decomposed into a disjunction, i.e., $v|u = q|p + s|r$, and $\neg q|p \in K$ then $\exists S = \{v|u, \neg q|p\} \subseteq K$, $C(S) \models s|r$, i.e., $K \models s|r$, and similarly for the meta-resolution. Thus, the decomposition of conditional objects into conditional objects with more focused conclusion-parts and/or context-parts enables us to deduce from a rule of the form *if p or p' then generally q or q'* and from another rule of the form *if p' then ¬q generally*, that *"if p' then q' generally"* or *"if p then q or q' generally"*.

7 TWO MODES OF BELIEF REVISION

The logic developed here is a contribution to the correct handling of plausible reasoning in expert systems. A crucial distinction has been made in expert systems between the "factual base" and the "rule base". The former encodes evidence on a given case, while the latter encodes generic domain-knowledge. In the expert system literature evidence is modeled by instanciated (elementary) formulas, while knowledge is modelled by universally quantified formulas, usually Horn clauses. As a consequence, the handling of exception-tolerant rules proves impossible: either we forget about exceptions and contradictions appear when putting together facts and rules, or we express exceptional situations in the rules and the latter can no longer be triggered in the presence of incomplete information. One solution to this problem is to encode generic domain-knowledge not as first-order formulas but as conditional objects. Then (as suggested in the Penguin example), exception handling becomes imbedded in the inference process. But instead of enriching the factual base as in classical expert systems it is the knowledge base itself that produces new rules until a rule is derived that fits the evidence as a whole. Namely if E contains propositional evidence and K is a conditional knowledge base then the reasoning methodology is to find the set of conclusions r such that $K \models r|E$. While the inference $\models$ is monotonic at the meta level, it is nonmonotonic at the level of plausible (factual) conclusion. The logic presented here has also the merit of displaying the difference between two modes of belief revision: evidence focusing and knowledge expansion that can be defined as follows

- *Evidence focusing*: a new piece of evidence p arrives and makes the available information on the case at hand more complete. Then E is changed into $E \cup \{p\}$ (supposedly consistent). K remains untouched. But the plausible conclusions from K and $E \cup \{p\}$, i.e., r such that $K \models r|E \wedge p$, may radically differ from those derived from K and E.

- *Knowledge expansion*: it corresponds to adding new generic rules tainted with possible exceptions. Insofar as the new knowledge base is consistent it is clear that due to the monotony of inference $\models$, all plausible conclusions derived from K can still be derived from K' since if K is a subset of K' and $K \models r|E$ then $K' \models r|E$. But more conclusions may perhaps be obtained by K'. The case when K' is inconsistent has been recently considered by Boutilier and Goldsmidt (1993).

8 CONCLUSION

The aim of this research is to proceed towards a computationally tractable theory of plausible inference, taking advantage of independent past contributions by Adams, Lewis, Lehmann, Pearl, Zadeh and others, that have significantly contributed to a proper understanding of its basic principles. The thesis advocated here is that the notion of conditional object lies at the core of such a theory. The semantics offered by conditional objects is much simpler than preferential models, and does not need the concept of infinitesimal probability. These results may open the road to semantic deduction techniques for automated reasoning with exception-tolerant knowledge bases. Clearly more research is needed in order to make the logic of conditional objects less conservative. One possible direction in to put together conditional objects, the Z-ordering of defaults (Pearl,1990) and possibilistic logic (e.g., Benferhat et al., 1992).

Acknowledgements

This work is partially supported by the European ESPRIT Basic Research Action No. 6156 "DRUMS-II" (Defeasible Reasoning and Uncertainty Management Systems-II). The authors are grateful to Daniel Lehmann for his remarks.

ANNEX

Lemma 1: The inference rules of preferential entailment are sound with respect to the semantic entailment of conditional objects.

Proof: Left logical equivalence and right weakening correspond to context equivalence and conclusion weakening. The LOR rule, cautious monotony and cut obviously hold for the semantic entailment using Lemma 1 and $C(K) \models q|p \Rightarrow K \models q|p$. Reflexivity holds since p|p is never falsified, and is entailed by any set of conditional objects. Q.E.D.

Soundness theorem: If $\mathcal{K} \vdash p \hspace{0.1em}\vdash\hspace{-0.5em}\sim\hspace{0.1em} q$ then $K \models q|p$.

Proof: Assume $\mathcal{K} \vdash p \hspace{0.1em}\vdash\hspace{-0.5em}\sim\hspace{0.1em} q$. If $p \models q$ then $\mathcal{K} \vdash p \hspace{0.1em}\vdash\hspace{-0.5em}\sim\hspace{0.1em} q$ is always true using reflexivity and RW. $K \models q|p$ also holds because $K \models p|p$ and $p|p \models q|p$. If $p \models q$ is not true then there is a subset $\mathcal{S} \subseteq \mathcal{K}$ such that $\mathcal{S} \vdash p \hspace{0.1em}\vdash\hspace{-0.5em}\sim\hspace{0.1em} q$. The set of conditional assertions that will be effectively used in the derivation of $p \hspace{0.1em}\vdash\hspace{-0.5em}\sim\hspace{0.1em} q$ could include some conditional assertion induced by reflexivity and RW, i.e., assertions of the form $p_i \hspace{0.1em}\vdash\hspace{-0.5em}\sim\hspace{0.1em} q_i$ where $p_i \models q_i$. Let B be the set of the tautological conditional objects that correspond to these supplementary assertions, and $\mathcal{B}$ the set of these assertions. The derivation of $p \hspace{0.1em}\vdash\hspace{-0.5em}\sim\hspace{0.1em} q$ forms an acyclic directed graph whose leaves form the set $\mathcal{S} \cup \mathcal{B}$ and the root is $p \hspace{0.1em}\vdash\hspace{-0.5em}\sim\hspace{0.1em} q$. Due to Lemma 1 we can turn each local derivation $\{r \mid\!\sim s, r' \mid\!\sim s'\} \vdash r'' \mid\!\sim s''$ into (s|r) & (s'|r') $\models$ s"|r". Hence we have C(S ∪ B) $\models$ q|p. It remains to prove that C(S) $\models$ q|p. This is due to the fact that in general, even where r $\models$ s we may have C(S ∪ {s|r}) $\models$ q|p but not C(S) $\models$ q|p, due to the effect of the context of s|r. To check it, it is enough to verify that each time an inference rule is used on a tautological assertion such as $p_i \mid\!\sim q_i$ with $p_i \models q_i$, its counterpart in terms of conditional objects is not needed to ensure the semantic entailment:

- **LOR rule:** if $p \models r$ then r|q $\models$ r|q ∨ p since r ∧ q $\models$ r ∧ (q ∨ p), and ¬q ∨ r $\models$ (¬p ∧ ¬q) ∨ r since the last expression equals ¬q ∨ r due to ¬p ∨ r = T;
- **CM rule:** if $p \models q$ then nothing new follows (up to LLE); hence we can dispense with this case. If $p \models r$ then p ∧ q $\models$ r. Again this result can be obtained only by reflexivity and RW. Hence the CM rule is not applied with any assertion from $\mathcal{B}$;
- **cut rule:** if $p \models q$ then nothing new is produced. If p ∧ q $\models$ r then q|p $\models$ r|p. Indeed p ∧ q $\models$ r implies p ∧ q $\models$ r ∧ p and ¬p ∨ q $\models$ ¬p ∨ r ∨ q = ¬p ∨ r since q $\models$ ¬p ∨ r.

As a consequence not only do we have C(S ∪ B) $\models$ q|p but also C(S) $\models$ q|p, since we can cancel all conditional objects in B when forming the quasi-conjunction in the derivation graph. Hence K $\models$ q|p. Q.E.D.

In order to reach completeness a basic fact is now established, namely a derived inference rule that exactly matches the quasi-conjunction.

Lemma 2: The rule $\{p \mid\!\sim q, p' \mid\!\sim q'\} \vdash p \vee p' \mid\!\sim (p \to q) \wedge (p' \to q')$ can be derived from the rules LLE, RW, RAND, LOR, and reflexivity.

Proof: Again we follow the track of Adams' (1975) study. Note that the following inference rule can be derived $(p \mid\!\sim q) \vdash (r \vee p \mid\!\sim p \to q)$. Indeed from $p \mid\!\sim q$, $p \mid\!\sim p \to q$ follows by RW. By reflexivity r ∧ ¬p $\mid\!\sim$ r ∧ ¬p holds, hence r ∧ ¬p $\mid\!\sim$ p → q from RW. By the LOR rule we get r ∨ p $\mid\!\sim$ p → q. Using the new derived rule on $\{p \mid\!\sim q, p' \mid\!\sim q'\}$, we derive, by letting r = p' and then p, the two conditional objects p ∨ p' $\mid\!\sim$ p → q and p ∨ p' $\mid\!\sim$ p' → q'. By the RAND rule the lemma holds. Q.E.D.

Due to the lemma, we can acknowledge the following derived inference rule in System P:

QAND: $\mathcal{K} \vdash C(\mathcal{K})$.

where $C(\mathcal{K})$ denotes the conditional assertion associated to the quasi-conjunction of the conditional objects associated to the conditional assertions in $\mathcal{K}$.

Completeness theorem: If K $\models$ q|p then $\mathcal{K} \vdash p \mid\!\sim q$

Proof: The first case is when $p \models q$ then $\mathcal{K} \vdash p \mid\!\sim q$ using reflexivity and RW. Assume $p \models q$ does not hold. If K $\models$ q|p then ∃ S ≠ ∅, C(S) $\models$ q|p, where S ⊆ K. Let $\mathcal{S}$ be the set of conditional assertions associated with S. Using QAND we know that $\mathcal{S} \vdash C(\mathcal{S})$. Let $C(\mathcal{S}) = \varphi \mid\!\sim \psi$. C(S) $\models$ q|p means that $\varphi \wedge \psi \models p \wedge q$ and $\varphi \to \psi \models p \to q$. Using reflexivity and RW we can write $\psi \wedge \varphi \mid\!\sim \psi \wedge \varphi, \psi \wedge \varphi \mid\!\sim p \wedge q$. Now, $\{\psi \wedge \varphi \mid\!\sim p \wedge q, \varphi \mid\!\sim \psi\} \vdash_{cut} \varphi \mid\!\sim p \wedge q$, and we can derive both $\varphi \mid\!\sim p$, and $\varphi \mid\!\sim q$ using RW. Now $\{\varphi \mid\!\sim p, \varphi \mid\!\sim q\} \vdash_{CM} \varphi \wedge p \mid\!\sim q$. Besides $\varphi \to \psi \models p \to q$ implies $p \wedge \neg \varphi \models q$ and $\neg \varphi \wedge p \mid\!\sim q$ can be derived from reflexivity and RW. Finally, $\{\varphi \wedge p \mid\!\sim q, \neg \varphi \wedge p \mid\!\sim q\} \vdash_{LOR} p \mid\!\sim q$. Using transitivity of $\vdash$ we get $\mathcal{K} \vdash C(\mathcal{S}) \vdash p \mid\!\sim q$ hence $\mathcal{K} \vdash p \mid\!\sim q$. Q.E.D.

References

E.W. Adams (1975). *The Logic of Conditionals*. Dordrecht: D. Reidel.

S. Benferhat, D. Dubois, and H. Prade (1992). Representing default rules in possibilistic logic. In *Proc. of the 3rd Inter. Conf. on Principles of Knowledge Representation and Reasoning (KR'92)*, Cambridge, Mass., Oct. 26-29, 673-684.

C. Boutilier, and M. Goldszmidt (1993). Revision by conditional beliefs. In *IJCAI Workshop on Conditionals in Knowledge Representation*, Chambéry, France, 42-51.

P. Calabrese (1987). An algebraic synthesis of the foundations of logic and probability. *Information Sciences* **42**:187-237.

P. Calabrese (1992). An extension of the fundamental theorem of Boolean algebra to conditional propositions. Naval Command, Control and Ocean Surveillance Center (NCCOSC), San Diego, CA 92152.

B. De Finetti (1937). La prévision: ses lois logiques, ses sources subjectives. *Ann. Inst. Poincaré* **7**:1-68. Translated in J. Kyburg, and H.E. Smokler (eds.), *Studies in Subjective Probability*, New York: Wiley, 1964.

D. Dubois, and H. Prade (1988). Conditioning in possibility and evidence theories –A logical viewpoint–. In B. Bouchon, L. Saitta, and R.R. Yager (eds.), *Uncertainty and Intelligent Systems*, Berlin: Springer Verlag, 401-408.

D. Dubois, and H. Prade (1990). The logical view of conditioning and its applications to possibility and evidence theories. *Int. J. of Approximate Reasoning* **4**: 23-46.

D. Dubois, and H. Prade (1991). Conditional objects and non-monotonic reasoning. In J. Allen, R. Fikes, and E. Sandewall (eds.), *Proc. of the 2nd Inter. Conf. on Principles of Knowledge Representation and Reasoning (KR'91)*, Cambridge, MA, April 22-25, 175-185.

D. Dubois, and H. Prade (1993). Conditional objects as non-monotonic consequence relationships. *Tech. Report IRIT/93-08-R*, IRIT, Univ. P. Sabatier, Toulouse, France.

D.M. Gabbay (1985). Theoretical foundations for non-monotonic reasoning in expert systems. In K.R. Apt (ed.), *Logics and Models of Concurrent Systems*, Berlin: Springer Verlag, 439-457.

H. Geffner (1992). *Default Reasoning: Causal and Conditional Theories*. Cambridge: MIT Press.

I.R. Goodman, and H.T. Nguyen (1988). Conditional objects and the modeling of uncertainties. In M.M. Gupta, and T. Yamakawa (eds.), *Fuzzy Computing — Theory, Hardware and Applications*, Amsterdam: North-Holland, 119-138.

I.R. Goodman, H.T. Nguyen, and E.A. Walker (1991). *Conditional Inference and Logic for Intelligent Systems: A Theory of Measure-Free Conditioning*. Amsterdam: North-Holland.

K. Kraus, D. Lehmann, and M. Magidor (1990). Nonmonotonic reasoning, preferential models and cumulative logics. *Artificial Intelligence* 44:167-207.

D. Lehmann (1989). What does a conditional knowledge base entail ?. In R.J. Brachman, H.J. Levesque, and R. Reiter (eds.), *Proc. of the 1st Inter. Conf. on Principles of Knowledge Representation and Reasoning (KR'89)*, Toronto, Ontario, Canada, May 15-18, 212-222. Extended version (with M. Magidor), *Artificial Intelligence* 55: 1-60 (1992).

D. Makinson (1989). General theory of cumulative inference. In M. Reinfranck, J. De Kleer, M.L. Ginsberg, and E. Sandewall (eds.), *Non-Monotonic Reasoning* (Proc. of the 2nd Inter. Workshop, Grassau, FRG, June 13-15, 1988), Berlin: Springer Verlag, 1-18.

J. Pearl (1988). *Probabilistic Reasoning in Intelligent Systems: Networks of Plausible Inference*. San Mateo, CA: Morgan Kaufmann.

J. Pearl (1990). System Z: a natural ordering of defaults with tractable applications to nonmonotonic reasoning. In R. Parikh (ed.), *Reasoning About Knowledge* (Proc. of the 3rd Conf. TARK'90, Pacific Grove, March 4-7, 1990), San Mateo, CA: Morgan & Kaufmann, 121-135.

G. Schay (1968). An algebra of conditional events. *J. Math. Anal. & Appl.* 24:334-344

Tractable Closed World Reasoning with Updates

Oren Etzioni   Keith Golden   Daniel Weld
Department of Computer Science and Engineering
University of Washington
Seattle, WA 98195
{etzioni, kgolden, weld}@cs.washington.edu

Abstract

Closed world reasoning is the process of inferring that a logical sentence is false based on its absence from a knowledge base, or the inability to derive it. Previous work on circumscription, autoepistemic logic, and database theory has explored logical axiomatizations of closed world reasoning, and investigated computational tractability for propositional theories. Work in planning has traditionally made the closed world *assumption* but has avoided closed world reasoning. We take a middle position, and describe a tractable method for closed world reasoning over the schematized theories of action used by planning algorithms such as NONLIN, TWEAK, and UCPOP. We show the method to be both sound and tractable, and incorporate it into the XII planner [Golden *et al.*, 1994]. Experiments utilizing our softbot (software robot) demonstrate that the method can substantially improve its performance by eliminating redundant information gathering.

1 INTRODUCTION AND MOTIVATION

Classical planners such as NONLIN [Tate, 1977], TWEAK [Chapman, 1987], or UCPOP [Penberthy and Weld, 1992, Weld, 1994] presuppose correct and complete information about the world. Having complete information facilitates planning since the planning agent need not obtain information from the external world — all relevant information is present in the agent's world model (this is the infamous *closed world assumption* [Reiter, 1978]). However, in many cases, an agent does not have complete information about its world. For instance, a robot may not know the size of a bolt or the location of an essential tool [Olawsky and Gini, 1990]. Similarly, a software agent, such as the UNIX softbot [Etzioni *et al.*, 1993], cannot be familiar with the contents of *all* the bulletin boards, FTP sites, and files accessible through the Internet.[1] Recent work has sketched a number of algorithms for planning with incomplete information (*e.g.*, [Ambros-Ingerson and Steel, 1988, Olawsky and Gini, 1990, Etzioni *et al.*, 1992, Krebsbach *et al.*, 1992, Peot and Smith, 1992]). Because they discard the closed world assumption, none of the above algorithms handle universally quantified goals. The planners cannot satisfy even a simple goal such as "Print all of Smith's postscript files in the /kr94 directory" because they have no way to guarantee that they are familiar with *all* the relevant files. In addition, these planners are vulnerable to *redundant information gathering* when they plan to "sense" information that is already known to the agent [Etzioni and Lesh, 1993]. Since satisfying the preconditions of an information-gathering action can involve arbitrary planning, the cost of redundant information gathering is unbounded in theory and quite large in practice (see Section 4).

To solve this problem we utilize an explicit database of meta-level sentences such as "I know the lengths of all files in /kr94," which encode *local closed world information* (LCW). The information in this database is equivalent to the "closed roles" found in knowledge-representation systems such as CLASSIC [Brachman, 1992] and LOOM [Brill, 1991], to predicate completion axioms [Clark, 1978, Kowalski, 1978], and to circumscription axioms [McCarthy, 1980, Lifschitz, 1985]. Indeed, there is a large body of previous work on the *logic* of closed world reasoning (*e.g.*, [Konolidge, 1982, Etherington, 1988, Reiter, 1982, Moore, 1985, Levesque, 1990]). Work on formal theories of action (*e.g.*, [Ginsberg and Smith, 1988, Katsuno and Mendelzon, 1991, del Val and Shoham, 1993]) has investigated the semantics of theory updates. Formal models of perception have been proposed [Davis, 1988, Davis, 1990], but not made com-

---

[1] Because our work is motivated by the softbot, most of our examples are drawn from the UNIX domain. However, we emphasize that our results are general and corresponding examples are easily found in physical domains as well.

putational. Work in database theory has yielded elegant but intractable approaches, which involve enumerating the possible logical models corresponding to a database (e.g., [Winslett, 1988, del Val, 1992]), or computing the disjunction of all possible results of an update [Keller and Wilkins, 1985]. Similarly, circumscriptive theorem provers of various sorts have been proposed (*e.g.*, [Ginsberg, 1989], and the Minimality Maintenance System [Raiman and de Kleer, 1992]), but remain intractable. Finally, a number of researchers have investigated the computational tractability of closed world reasoning over propositional theories [Cadoli and Schaerf, 1993, Eiter and Gottlob, 1992].

Our contribution is the formulation of a tractable algorithm for closed world reasoning, with updates, over the schematized action representation language utilized by standard planners.[2] Our approach has several novel features:

- We present a sound and tractable calculus for querying and updating local closed world information as the state of the world changes (Sections 2.2 and 3). The update calculus answers questions such as: if a file is deleted from /kr94, is the agent still familiar with the lengths of all files in that directory? What if a file is added to /kr94?

- As described in detail in [Golden et al., 1994], we incorporate our closed world reasoning machinery into the XII partial-order planner, enabling it to satisfy universally quantified goals and avoid redundant information gathering despite the absence of complete information.[3] We measure the impact of the machinery on the planner, using a suite of test problems in the UNIX domain. These preliminary experiments show that the benefit derived by avoiding redundant sensing far outweighs the costs of maintaining the closed world information.

The paper is organized as follows. Section 2 introduces our calculus for answering LCW queries in a static universe. In Section 3 we present our calculus for updating LCW as the world changes. Section 4 provides preliminary experimental confirmation of the efficacy of our techniques. We conclude with related and future work. Appendix A contains a discussion of action semantics, and Appendix B proves that our inference and update rules are sound.

---

[2] Although it might be possible to translate this action representation into a propositional logic, the translation would greatly expand the representation's size, and the computational benefits of the action representation would be lost.

[3] XII is a descendent of UCPOP [Penberthy and Weld, 1992, Weld, 1994], extended to handle incomplete information and to interleave planning with execution.

2 LOCAL CLOSED WORLD INFORMATION

We begin by formalizing the notion of an incomplete world model. At every point in time, the world is in a unique state, w, which may be unknown to the agent. For any ground, atomic sentence φ, either $w \models \varphi$ or $w \models \neg\varphi$ hence the set of ground facts entailed by the world forms a complete logical theory; we use $\mathcal{D}_W$ to denote this theory. Following [Papadimitriou, 1985, Genesereth and Nourbakhsh, 1993] and many others, we formalize an agent's incomplete information with a set of possible world states, $\mathcal{S}$, that are consistent with its information. Since we assume what information the agent *does* have is correct, the current world state, w, is necessarily a member of $\mathcal{S}$. We say that φ is known to the agent (written $\mathcal{S} \models \varphi$) just in case $\forall s \in \mathcal{S}$, $s \models \varphi$. We say that the agent possesses complete information when $\mathcal{S}$ and w entail exactly the same set of facts. Incomplete information means that there are facts such that neither $\mathcal{S} \models \varphi$ nor $\mathcal{S} \models \neg\varphi$; in this case we say φ is unknown to the agent.

We can still salvage a partial notion of complete information, even in the presence of unknown facts. In practice, many sensing actions return exhaustive information which warrants limited or "local" closed world information. For example, scanning with a TV camera shows *all* objects in view, and the UNIX ls -a command lists *all* files in a given directory. After executing ls -a, it is not enough for the agent to record that paper.tex and proofs.tex are in /kr94 because, in addition, the agent knows that *no other* files are in that directory. Note that the agent is not making a closed world *assumption*. Rather, the agent has executed an action that yields closed world *information*.

In general, we say that an agent has *local closed world information* (LCW) relative to a logical sentence Φ if whenever Φ is entailed by the world state w, it is also entailed by the agent's model $\mathcal{S}$. Thus, LCW captures a limited correspondence between $\mathcal{S}$ and w. More precisely:[4]

$$\text{LCW}(\Phi) \equiv \forall \theta \text{ if } w \models \Phi\theta \text{ then } \mathcal{S} \models \Phi\theta \quad (1)$$

For instance, we represent knowing all the files in the directory /kr94 as:[5]

$$\text{LCW}(\text{parent.dir}(f, /\text{kr94}))$$

If the agent knows that paper.tex and proofs.tex are in /kr94 then this LCW sentence is equivalent to the following implication:

---

[4] We use *italics* to denote free variables and write $\Phi\theta$ to denote the result of applying the substitution θ to the sentence Φ.

[5] parent.dir(f,d) means "The parent directory of file f is directory d."

$$\forall f \; \texttt{parent.dir}(f, \; \texttt{/kr94}) \rightarrow$$
$$(f = \texttt{paper.tex}) \vee (f = \texttt{proofs.tex})$$

An LCW sentence can also be understood in terms of circumscription [Lifschitz, 1985]. For the example above, one defines the predicate P(x) to be true exactly when parent.dir(x, /kr94) is true, and circumscribes P in the agent's theory. While our work can be understood within the circumscriptive framework, our implemented agent requires the ability to infer, and update[6] closed world information *quickly*. Thus, we have developed computationally tractable closed world reasoning and update methods, applicable to the restricted representation language used by today's planning algorithms.

2.1 REPRESENTING CLOSED WORLD INFORMATION

Below, we explain how our agent represents its incomplete information about the world, and how it represents LCW in this context. Due to the size of $\mathcal{S}$ (a potentially infinite set of large structures), the agent cannot represent it explicitly. Instead we represent the facts known by the agent with a database $\mathcal{D}_M \subseteq \mathcal{D}_W$; if $\varphi \in \mathcal{D}_M$ then $\mathcal{S} \models \varphi$. In the interest of tractability, we restrict $\mathcal{D}_M$ to ground literals. Since $\mathcal{D}_M$ is incomplete, the Closed World Assumption (CWA) is invalid — the agent cannot automatically infer that any sentence absent from $\mathcal{D}_M$ is false. Thus, the agent is forced to represent false facts in $\mathcal{D}_M$, explicitly, as sentences tagged with the truth value F.

This observation leads to a minor paradox: the agent cannot explicitly represent in $\mathcal{D}_M$ *every* sentence it knows to be false (there is an infinite number of files *not* in the directory /kr94). Yet the agent cannot make the CWA. We adopt a simple solution: we represent closed world information explicitly as a meta-level database, $\mathcal{D}_C$, containing sentences (or "closure axioms") of the form LCW(Φ) that record *where* the agent has closed world information.

We adopt the following procedural semantics for LCW sentences. When asked whether it believes an atomic sentence Φ, the agent first checks to see if it is in $\mathcal{D}_M$. If it is, then the agent responds with the truth value (T or F) associated with the sentence. However, if $\Phi \notin \mathcal{D}_M$ then Φ could be either F or unknown (truth value U). To resolve this ambiguity, the agent checks whether $\mathcal{D}_C$ entails LCW(Φ) (see Section 2.2). If so, the fact is F

[6]Following [Katsuno and Mendelzon, 1991, Keller and Wilkins, 1985] we distinguish between *updating* a database and *revising* it. We assume that our agent's knowledge is correct at any given time point, hence there is no need to revise it. When the world changes, however, the agent may need to update its model to remain in agreement with the world.

otherwise it is U. Note that the agent need not perform inference on $\mathcal{D}_M$ since it contains only ground literals.

2.2 INFERRING LOCAL CLOSED WORLD INFORMATION

An agent requires information about the external world w, but only has direct access to $\mathcal{D}_M$ and $\mathcal{D}_C$. The agent needs to answer queries such as "Do I know all the postscript files in /kr94?" or, more formally, is the following true:

$$\texttt{LCW}(\texttt{parent.dir}(f,/\texttt{kr94}) \wedge \texttt{postscript}(f))$$

Correctly answering LCW queries is not a simple matter of looking up LCW assertions in the $\mathcal{D}_C$ database. For instance, suppose that agent wants to establish whether it is familiar with all the files in /kr94, and it finds that it is familiar with all the files in *all* directories. Then, *a fortiori*, it is familiar with all the files in /kr94. That is:

$$\texttt{LCW}(\texttt{parent.dir}(f,d)) \models$$
$$\texttt{LCW}(\texttt{parent.dir}(f,/\texttt{kr94}))$$

In general, we have:

Theorem 1 (Instantiation Rule) *If Φ is a logical sentence and θ is a substitution, then* LCW(Φ)$\models$LCW($\Phi\theta$).[7]

Moreover, LCW assertions can be combined to yield new ones. For instance, if the agent knows all the group-readable files, and it knows which files are located in /kr94, it follows that it knows the set of group-readable files in /kr94. In general, we have:

Theorem 2 (Conjunction Rule) *If Φ and Ψ are logical sentences then* LCW(Φ) $\wedge$ LCW(Ψ) $\models$ LCW($\Phi \wedge \Psi$).

The intuition behind the rule is simple — if one knows the contents of two sets then one knows their intersection. Note that the converse is invalid. If one knows the group-readable files in /kr94, it does not follow that one knows *all* group-readable files. The rule LCW(Φ) $\models$ LCW($\Phi \wedge \Psi$) is also invalid. For instance, if one knows all the group-readable files, it does not follow that one knows exactly which of these files reside in /kr94.

When $\mathcal{D}_M$ contains the unique value of a variable (*e.g.*, the word count of a file), the agent can infer that it has local closed world information. To state this inference rule in general, we define an instance function, I,

[7]Proofs of the theorems are sequestered in Appendix B.

that returns the set of sentences matching Φ in a given theory:

$$I(\Phi, \mathcal{D}) = \{\Psi \in \mathcal{D} \mid \exists \theta \text{ such that } \Phi\theta = \Psi\} \quad (2)$$

We refer to $I(\Phi,\mathcal{D})$ as the *domain* of Φ in $\mathcal{D}$. When the cardinality of the Φ's domain is the same in $\mathcal{D}_M$ and in the theory induced by w, we can conclude that we have LCW(Φ):[8]

Theorem 3 (Counting Rule (after [Smith, 1983]))
$|I(\Phi, \mathcal{D}_M)| = |I(\Phi, \mathcal{D}_W)| \models \text{LCW}(\Phi)$

To use the Counting Rule in practice, our agent relies on explicit axioms such as

$$\forall f, \; |I(\text{word.count}(f,c), \mathcal{D}_W)| = 1.$$

In the UNIX domain, many predicates encode functions (*e.g.*, file properties such as word count, parent directory, etc.) and the Counting Rule turns out to be quite useful.

To make LCW inference and update tractable, we restrict the sentences in $\mathcal{D}_C$ to conjunctions of positive literals. As a result, we lose the ability to represent LCW statements that contain negation or disjunction such as "I know all the files in /kr94 *except* the files with a .dvi extension," and "If a file is either in /kr94 or is a lisp file then I know its length." However, LCW inference is reduced to the problem of matching a conjunctive LCW query against a database of conjunctive LCW assertions. Although a conjunctive match takes time exponential in the length of the query [Tambe and Rosenbloom, 1989], if we accept a bound k on the number of conjuncts in a query, then the match time is a polynomial of order k in the size of $\mathcal{D}_C$. In the UNIX domain, we have found that LCW queries are typically short ($k \leq 3$) which, with the aid of standard indexing techniques, yields reasonably fast LCW inference in practice (see Section 4).

3 UPDATING CLOSED WORLD INFORMATION

As the agent is informed of the changes to the external world— through its own actions or through the actions of other agents — it can gain and lose LCW. When a file is compressed, for example, the agent loses information about its size; when all postscript files are deleted from a directory, the agent gains the information that it contains no such files. This section presents an efficient algorithm for updating $\mathcal{D}_C$, the agent's store of LCW sentences. The key to our algorithm is the restriction of $\mathcal{D}_M$ to ground literals (Section 2.1). Since domain axioms are banned, we sidestep the ramification problem [Ginsberg and Smith, 1988]; instead, we demand

---
[8] Recall that both $\mathcal{D}_M$ and $\mathcal{D}_W$ are ground.

that updates to $\mathcal{D}_M$ (such as those caused by action execution) explicitly enumerate changes to *every* predicate that is affected. Note that this is standard in the planning literature. For example, a STRIPS operator that moves block A from B to C must delete on(A, B) and also add clear(B) even though clear(B) can be defined as $\forall y \neg \text{on}(y, \text{B})$.

Recall that $\mathcal{D}_M$ is a database of ground atomic sentences each explicitly tagged with a T or F truth value. We signify the atomic update of a single positive literal φ from unknown to true with $\Delta(\varphi, \text{U} \rightarrow \text{T})$ and denote analogous changes in the obvious manner.[9]

$\mathcal{D}_M$ can change due to information gathering on the part of the agent, or when the agent is informed of a change to the state of the external world. We formulate the update policy as a set of rules and state them as theorems since they are sound. Our update rules compute conservative (*i.e.*, sound but incomplete) updates from $\mathcal{D}_C$ to $\mathcal{D}'_C$ based on the changes to w and $\mathcal{D}_M$. By distinguishing between transitions to and from U truth values, $\mathcal{D}_C$ updates can be divided into four mutually exclusive and exhaustive cases which we call information gain, information loss, domain growth, and domain contraction. Below, we consider each case in turn.

3.1 INFORMATION GAIN

An agent gains information when it executes an information-gathering action (*e.g.*, wc or ls), or when a change to the world results in information gain. In general, if the information in the agent's world model increases, the agent cannot lose LCW.

Theorem 4 (Information Gain)
If $\Delta(\varphi, \text{U} \rightarrow \text{T} \vee \text{F})$ then $\mathcal{D}'_C \supseteq \mathcal{D}_C$.

This theorem suggests a simple conservative policy: as long as an action gains information, then $\mathcal{D}_C$ need not be modified. However, by analyzing the form of the information gained and exploiting the assumption of correct information, it is possible to do better. For example, as discussed in Section 2.2, when the agent knows the cardinality of the set of instances matching a sentence, then it can deduce when it has LCW [Smith, 1983].

An agent can obtain local closed world information, even when the cardinality of a domain is variable (*e.g.*, the number of files in a directory) by executing an action with universally quantified effects. For instance, the execution of UNIX chmod * in the directory /kr94

---
[9] Note that, as explained in Section 2.1, if a fact is absent from $\mathcal{D}_M$, the agent determines whether it is F or U by consulting $\mathcal{D}_C$. Thus, updates of the form $\Delta(\varphi, \text{U} \rightarrow \text{F})$ or $\Delta(\varphi, \text{F} \rightarrow \text{U})$ may occur when $\mathcal{D}_C$ changes, even if $\mathcal{D}_M$ does not.

provides information on the protection of *all* files in that directory.

Since a universally quantified effect can change the truth value of an unbounded number of literals, we must extend the update notation to the following general form:

$$\Delta(\text{P}(x), \rightarrow \text{T}) \quad \forall x \text{ satisfying } \text{U}(x)$$

For the example above $\text{U}(x) \equiv \texttt{parent.dir}(x, \texttt{/kr94})$ and $\text{P}(x)$ denotes that x is write protected. With this notation we now define an update policy for universally quantified effects:

Theorem 5 (Forall Rule) *If $\Delta(\text{P}(x), \rightarrow \text{T}) \quad \forall x$ satisfying $\text{U}(x)$ and $\mathcal{D}_\text{C} \models \text{LCW}(\text{U}(x))$ then $\mathcal{D}'_\text{C} \leftarrow \mathcal{D}_\text{C} \cup (\text{P}(x) \wedge \text{U}(x))$.*

The Forall Rule can be extended to handle observational actions which provide LCW on the universe of discourse (*i.e.* the extension of $\text{U}(x)$). In addition it can be combined with the Counting Rule to give LCW in situations where neither rule alone suffices. For example, since each file has exactly one name ($|\text{I}(\texttt{name}(o,n), \mathcal{D}_\text{W})| = 1$), after executing the UNIX action `ls -a bin`, we are able to deduce that we know the names of all files in `bin`:

$$\text{LCW}(\texttt{parent.dir}(o, \texttt{bin}) \wedge \texttt{name}(o,n))$$

For details, see [Golden *et al.*, 1994].

3.2 INFORMATION LOSS

An agent loses information when a literal, previously known to be true (or false), is asserted to be unknown. When a UNIX file is compressed, for example, information about its size is lost. In general, when information is lost about some literal, all LCW statements "relevant" to that literal are lost. To make our notion of relevance precise, we begin by defining the set $\text{PREL}(\varphi)$ to denote the LCW assertions *potentially relevant* to a positive literal φ:[10]

$$\text{PREL}(\varphi) \equiv \{\Phi \in \mathcal{D}_\text{C} \mid \exists x \in \Phi, \exists \theta, x\theta = \varphi\}$$

For example, if an agent has complete information on the sizes of all files in `/kr94`, and a file `lcw.tex` in `/kr94` is compressed ($\varphi = \texttt{size}(\texttt{lcw.tex}, n)$), then the sentence

$$\text{LCW}(\texttt{parent.dir}(f, \texttt{/kr94}) \wedge \texttt{size}(f, c)) \quad (3)$$

---

[10]Since the sentences in $\mathcal{D}_\text{C}$ are conjunctions of positive literals, we use the notation $\varphi \in \Phi$ to signify that φ is one of Φ's conjuncts, and the notation $\Phi - \varphi$ to denote the conjunction Φ with φ omitted.

is in $\text{PREL}(\varphi)$ and should be removed from $\mathcal{D}_\text{C}$. Unfortunately, when a file in the directory `/bin` is compressed, the above LCW sentence is still in $\text{PREL}(\varphi)$ ($x = \texttt{size}(f, c)$) even though the agent retains complete information about the files in `/kr94`. Clearly, LCW sentence 3 ought to remain in $\mathcal{D}_\text{C}$ in this case. To achieve this behavior, we check whether the agent has information indicating that the LCW sentence does not "match" the compressed file. If so, the LCW sentence remains in $\mathcal{D}_\text{C}$. In general, we define the set of LCW assertions *relevant* to a literal φ to be the following subset of $\text{PREL}(\varphi)$:

$$\text{REL}(\varphi) \equiv \{\Phi \in \text{PREL}(\varphi) \mid \forall \phi_i \in (\Phi - x), \neg(\mathcal{D}_\text{C} \wedge \mathcal{D}_\text{M} \models \neg \phi_i \theta)\}$$

where, as in the definition of $\text{PREL}(\varphi)$, $\exists x \in \Phi, \exists \theta$, such that $x\theta = \varphi$.

We can now state our update policy for Information Loss:

Theorem 6 (Information Loss)
If $\Delta(\varphi, \text{T} \vee \text{F} \rightarrow \text{U})$ then $\mathcal{D}'_\text{C} \leftarrow \mathcal{D}_\text{C} - \text{REL}(\varphi)$.

Note that compressing a file `foo` in `/bin` does not remove LCW sentence 3. To see this, set $x = \texttt{size}(f, c)$, $\theta = (\texttt{foo}/f)$, and $\phi_i = \texttt{parent.dir}(f, \texttt{/kr94})$. Since `foo` is in `/bin`, $\mathcal{D}_\text{C} \wedge \mathcal{D}_\text{M}$ entails that $\neg \phi_i \theta$. Hence, $\neg(\mathcal{D}_\text{C} \wedge \mathcal{D}_\text{M} \models \neg \phi_i \theta)$ is false and Φ is not included in $\text{REL}(\varphi)$. Note also that, given our assumptions (correct information, *etc.*), information is only lost when the world's state changes.

3.3 CHANGES IN DOMAIN

Finally, we have the most subtle cases: an agent's model changes without strictly losing or gaining information. For example, when the file `ai.sty` is moved from the `/tex` directory to `/kr94`, we have that the updated $\mathcal{D}'_\text{M} \neq \mathcal{D}_\text{M}$ but neither database is a superset of the other. When the model changes in this way, the domain of sentences containing $\texttt{parent.dir}(f, \texttt{/kr94})$ grows whereas the domain of sentences containing $\texttt{parent.dir}(f, \texttt{/tex})$ contracts. LCW information may be lost in sentences whose domain grew. Suppose that, prior to the file move, the agent knows the word counts of all the files in `/kr94`; if it does not know the word count of `ai.sty`, then that LCW assertion is no longer true. As with Information Loss, we could update $\mathcal{D}_\text{C}$ by removing the set $\text{REL}(\varphi)$. However, this policy is overly conservative. Suppose, in the above file move, that the agent *does* know the word count of `ai.sty`. In this case, it retains complete information over the word counts of the files in `/kr94`, even after `ai.sty` is moved.

More generally, when the domain of an LCW sentence grows, but the agent has LCW on the new element of the domain, then the LCW sentence can be retained.

To make this intuition precise, we define the following "minimal" subset of REL(φ):

$$\text{MREL}(\varphi) = \{\Phi \in \text{REL}(\varphi) \mid \neg(\text{LCW}((\Phi - x)\theta))\}$$

where, as in the definition of PREL(φ), $\exists x \in \Phi, \exists \theta$, such that $x\theta = \varphi$. We can now state our update policy for Domain Growth:

Theorem 7 (Domain Growth)
If $\Delta(\varphi, \text{F} \to \text{T})$ then $\mathcal{D}'_\text{C} \leftarrow \mathcal{D}_\text{C} - \text{MREL}(\varphi)$

When the domain of a sentence contracts, no LCW information is lost. For instance, when a file is removed from the directory /kr94, we will still know the lengths of all the files in that directory.

Theorem 8 (Domain Contraction)
If $\Delta(\varphi, \text{T} \to \text{F})$ then $\mathcal{D}'_\text{C} = \mathcal{D}_\text{C}$.

Note that our update rules cover all possible truth-value transitions. The rules guarantee that $\mathcal{D}_\text{C}$ does not contain invalid LCW assertions, so long as the agent is appraised of any changes to the world state. For the sake of tractability, the rules are conservative — $\mathcal{D}_\text{C}$ may be incomplete. For example, when the word count of ai.sty is unknown in the above example, we could say that we know the word counts of all the files in /kr94 *except* ai.sty . However, that would require us to store negated and disjunctive sentences in $\mathcal{D}_\text{C}$, which would make LCW inference intractable. To see this, consider a singleton LCW query such as LCW(parent.dir(f,/kr94)). If $\mathcal{D}_\text{C}$ contains only positive conjunctions, the query can be answered in sub-linear time — examining only singleton LCW assertions indexed under the predicate parent.dir. If disjunction is allowed, however, then the combination of multiple LCW sentences has to be explored. For instance, by the Conjunction Rule, we have that LCW($\Phi \vee \Psi$) $\wedge$ LCW($\Phi \vee \neg\Psi$)$\models$LCW(Φ). In general, answering a singleton query, in the presence of negation and disjunction, is NP-hard. Since our planner makes numerous such queries, we chose to sacrifice completeness in the interest of speed.

3.4 COMPUTATIONAL COMPLEXITY OF UPDATES

As stated above, our motivation for formulating conservative update rules has been to keep LCW update tractable. We make good on this promise below. We start by considering the complexity of applying single update rules:

- **Information gain:** Theorem 4 implies that no sentences have to be retracted from $\mathcal{D}_\text{C}$. LCW sentences may be added by the Forall Rule (constant time).[11]

- **Information loss:** The agent has to compute the set PREL(Φ), which takes time linear in the size of $\mathcal{D}_\text{C}$ in the worst case. Computing REL(Φ) from PREL(Φ) is linear in the size of PREL(Φ), but also potentially linear in the size of $\mathcal{D}_\text{C}$, since establishing whether $\mathcal{D}_\text{C} \wedge \mathcal{D}_\text{M} \models \neg\phi_i\theta$ may require singleton LCW queries. The agent then removes each element of the set from $\mathcal{D}_\text{C}$, which takes time linear in the size of REL(Φ). In the worst case, the size of PREL(Φ) is linear in the size of $\mathcal{D}_\text{C}$, so the entire update could take time quadratic in the size of $\mathcal{D}_\text{C}$.

- **Domain growth:** The agent has to compute the set REL(Φ) which, as explained above, is quadratic in the size of $\mathcal{D}_\text{C}$. Computing MREL(Φ) from REL(Φ) is linear in the size of REL, but potentially polynomial in the size of $\mathcal{D}_\text{C}$, since additional queries to $\mathcal{D}_\text{C}$ may be involved. The agent then removes each element of the set from $\mathcal{D}_\text{C}$, which takes time linear in the size of the set MREL(Φ). Thus the whole operation is polynomial in the size of $\mathcal{D}_\text{C}$.

- **Domain contraction:** $\mathcal{D}_\text{C}$ remains unchanged in this case.

While the application of each individual update rule is reasonably fast, even in the worst case, we have to consider the possibility of a cascade of $\mathcal{D}_\text{C}$ updates. Will the update rules chain on each other? Are such chains guaranteed to terminate? Fortunately, we can prove that rule chaining is unnecessary. The intuition is as follows. Chaining could potentially occur in one of two ways. First, when $\mathcal{D}_\text{C}$ shrinks, due to Domain Growth or Information Loss, a potentially infinite number of sentences change from F to U. Thus one might think that the Information Loss Rule (Theorem 6) has to be applied to further retract sentences from $\mathcal{D}_\text{C}$. However, careful examination of the definition of REL shows that this is not the case — all relevant LCW sentences have already been excised from $\mathcal{D}_\text{C}$. Second, when $\mathcal{D}_\text{C}$ grows due to Information Gain, a potentially infinite number of sentences changes from U to F. However, by Information Gain, no statements have to be excised from $\mathcal{D}_\text{C}$, and the Forall Rule does not yield new LCW sentences as a consequence.

Thus, in the absence of chaining, the time to perform LCW updates is dominated by the time to retrieve MREL(Φ) which is polynomial in the size of $\mathcal{D}_\text{C}$ in the worst case, but much faster when standard indexing techniques (*e.g.*, hashing on the predicates in Φ) are used. Furthermore, the worst-case polynomial can be reduced to worst-case linear time if the agent updates

---

[11]The Conjunction, Counting, and Instantiation Rules are applied in response to LCW queries, but ignored when $\mathcal{D}_\text{C}$ is updated.

$\mathcal{D}_C$ with the more conservative set PREL instead of taking the time to compute MREL.

3.5 DISCUSSION

The update rules defined above form a sound, efficient algorithm for updating $\mathcal{D}_M$ and $\mathcal{D}_C$. We believe our rules satisfy the update postulates specified in [Katsuno and Mendelzon, 1991] and generalized in [del Val and Shoham, 1993], but we have not yet attempted a proof. Since sentences in $\mathcal{D}_C$ are restricted to positive conjunctions, the algorithm is incomplete. Nevertheless, it is easy to see that our algorithm is better than the trivial update algorithm ($\mathcal{D}'_C \leftarrow \{\}$). In the UNIX domain, for example, our Counting and Forall Rules enable us to derive LCW from a wide range of "sensory" actions, including pwd, wc, grep, ls, finger, and many more. Furthermore, our update rules retain LCW in many cases. For example, changes to the state of one *locale* (such as a directory, a database, an archive, etc.) do not impact LCW on other locales. This feature of our update calculus applies to physical locales as well.

Ultimately, the test of any mechanism for closed world reasoning – conservative or not – is its impact on the agent's performance. Below we describe preliminary experiments that suggest ours is effective in practice, speeding up execution by a factor of ten in some cases.

4 EXPERIMENTAL RESULTS

While we have shown that LCW inference and update are tractable, computational complexity is not always a good predictor of real performance. To test whether our rules perform well in practice (*i.e.*, run quickly and with sufficient completeness for useful results) we added them to the XII partial-order planner [Golden *et al.*, 1994]. We then embedded XII, and our closed world reasoning machinery, inside the UNIX softbot [Etzioni *et al.*, 1993].

Table 1 quantifies the impact of closed world reasoning on the softbot's performance. LCW inference yields a significant performance gain. The tests mostly consist of simple file searches (*e.g.*, find a file with word count greater than 5000, containing the string "theorem," etc.) and relocations. The actions executed in the tests include mv (which can destroy LCW), observational actions such as ls, wc and grep, and more. Each experiment was started from a new lisp session. $\mathcal{D}_M$ and $\mathcal{D}_C$ start out empty, but they are not purged between problems, so for each problem the agent benefits from the information gained in solving the previous problems.

Maintaining $\mathcal{D}_C$ introduced less than 15% overhead per plan explored, and reduced the number of plans explored substantially. In addition, the plans produced were often considerably shorter, since redundant sensing steps were eliminated. Without LCW, the softbot performed 16 redundant ls operations, and 6 redundant pwds in a "typical" file search. With LCW, on the other hand, the softbot performed no redundant sensing. Furthermore, when faced with unachievable goals, the softbot with LCW inference was able to fail quickly; however, without LCW it conducted a massive search, executing many redundant sensing operations in a forlorn hope of observing something that would satisfy the goal. While more experimentation is necessary, these experiments (combined with our analytic results) suggest that LCW inference has the potential to substantially improve performance.

5 RELATED WORK

Since we have already discussed the connection between our work and the broad spectrum of research on autoepistemic logic, circumscription, database theory, and formal theories of action, we now focus on related work in the planning literature. Our research has its roots in the SOCRATES planner, where the problem of redundant information gathering was initially discovered [Etzioni and Lesh, 1993]. Like our planner, SOCRATES relies on the UNIX domain as its testbed and interleaves planning with execution. SOCRATES supports a restricted representation of LCW, which enables it to avoid redundant information gathering in many cases. Our advances over SOCRATES include an improved semantics for the notion of local closed world information, the ability to satisfy universally quantified goals, and our sound and tractable calculi for LCW inference and update.

Some planners count the number of relevant ground propositions in their model, before inserting information-gathering steps into their plans, to check whether the desired information is already known [Olawsky and Gini, 1990]. However, this heuristic, which corresponds directly to the Counting Rule (Section 3 and [Smith, 1983]), is only effective when the number of sought-after facts is known in advance. For example, a bolt has exactly one width, but the number of files in /kr94 is unknown.

Genesereth and Nourbakhsh [Genesereth and Nourbakhsh, 1993] share our goal of avoiding redundant information gathering, but do so using radically different mechanisms, and in the context of state-space search. They derive completeness-preserving rules for pruning the search as well as rules for terminating planning and beginning execution. However, they do not have notions that correspond to LCW, a database like $\mathcal{D}_C$, or our inference and update calculi.

Table 1: Performance of Local Closed World Inference in the UNIX Domain

PROBLEM SET	PLANNER	PLANS EXPLORED	ACTIONS EXECUTED	TOTAL TIME
22 PROBLEMS, 13 SOLVABLE	With LCW	420	55	109
	Without	3707	724	966
14 PROBLEMS, ALL SOLVABLE	With LCW	373	55	94
	Without	1002	140	160

Reasoning about local closed world information (LCW) improves the performance of the softbot on two suites of UNIX problems. Times are in CPU seconds on a Sun Microsystems SPARC-10. Without LCW inference the softbot fails to complete eight of the problems in the first set, and one of the problems in the second set, before reaching a 100 CPU second time bound. With LCW, the softbot completes all the problems. The mean size of $\mathcal{D}_C$ (the agent's store of LCW information) is 155 sentences. The maximum size is 167.

6 FUTURE WORK

Although we have relaxed the assumption of complete information, we still assume correct information. Since we want our agents to cope with exogenous events, we are in the process of relaxing this assumption as well. We are investigating two complementary mechanisms to solve this problem. The first mechanism associates *expiration times* with beliefs. If an agent has a belief regarding φ, which describes a highly dynamic situation (e.g. the idle time of a user on a given machine), then the agent should not keep that belief in $\mathcal{D}_M$ for very long. Thus, after an appropriate amount of time has elapsed, $\Delta(\varphi, T \vee F \rightarrow U)$ occurs automatically.[12] This mechanism is effective when the belief about φ expires before φ changes in the world. However, unless we have extremely short expiration times, we cannot guarantee this to be the case in general.

Thus, an additional mechanism is required that enables the agent to detect and recover from out-of-date beliefs. This is a harder problem, because it involves belief revision, rather than mere update. If executing an action fails, and the action's preconditions are known, it follows that one or more of the preconditions of the action were not satisfied — but which ones? A conservative approach would remove all the preconditions from the agent's model. We are investigating more efficient mechanisms.

7 CONCLUSIONS

Our work was motivated by the problem of eliminating redundant information gathering in planners with incomplete information. To address this problem, we developed a sound and computationally tractable method for representing, inferring, and updating *local closed world information* (LCW) (*e.g.*, "I know the lengths of all the files in /kr94") over a restricted logical theory of the sort used by planning algorithms

such as, NONLIN, TWEAK, and UCPOP. To demonstrate the utility of our approach, we incorporated our closed world reasoning machinery into the UNIX softbot. Preliminary experiments, described in Section 4, indicate that LCW inference can significantly speed up the softbot and drastically reduce the number of actions executed. While computationally tractable, our update and inference rules are conservative. In future work, we hope to identify the precise point at which closed world reasoning becomes intractable (*e.g.*, does introducing disjunction into LCW sentences make it so?).

A ACTION SEMANTICS

We extend ADL, Pednault's [Pednault, 1989, Pednault, 1988, Pednault, 1986] state-transition model of conditional and universally quantified actions, to handle incomplete information. Formally, each action is modeled as a pair, $\langle C, O \rangle$, denoting its causational and observational aspects. Following ADL [Pednault, 1988, p. 357], we define the causational effects, C, of an action as a set of pairs $\langle s_i, s_j \rangle$ — execution of the action in world state s_i yields state s_j.[13]

As defined in Section 2 we model an agent's incomplete knowledge of the actual world state, w, with the set of states $\mathcal{S}$. Since we assume correct information, $w \in \mathcal{S}$. If an agent has incomplete information, then after executing the action it can only conclude that the world is a member of the image of C on $\mathcal{S}$: $\{s_j \mid \langle s_i, s_j \rangle \in C \wedge s_i \in \mathcal{S}\}$.

When the C pairs denote a function, then the effect of execution is unique, but if C specifies a relation (*i.e.*, two pairs share a first element), then the effect of execution is uncertain. Even if the exact initial state is known, precise prediction of the unique final state resulting from execution is impossible with this action model. Flipping a coin and executing compress) are

---

[12]Note that by the Information Loss rule, this update will cause LCW to be retracted as well.

[13]If executed in a state which does not appear as the left member of a C pair, the result of execution is an error.

good examples of actions that require relational C. In contrast to actions which increase uncertainty, if an action's C pairs denote a nonsurjective function, then execution can decrease uncertainty. For example, executing **rm *** reduces the size of S if the contents of the current directory were not known at the time of execution.

Pednault's theory also needs to be extended to handle information gathering actions, *i.e.* effects which change S without changing w. For example, suppose that Φ=turned.on(light53) denotes that the light is on, but S neither entails Φ nor $\neg\Phi$. The act of scanning the room with a TV camera and finding Φ is false doesn't change the world state, but it does allow discarding from S any state s which entails Φ. Syntactically, we describe this action with a UWL **observe** postcondition [Etzioni et al., 1992], but semantically we model the observational effects, O, of an action as a partition over all possible world states. If two states are in different equivalence classes, then the action's observational effects distinguish between them. In other words, O specifies the discriminatory power provided by the execution system — at run time, the execution system reports which equivalence class resulted. Actions with no observational effects can be modeled with O specifying a single equivalence class. The action of detecting whether the light is on (described above) yields a partition with two classes: states entailing Φ and those entailing $\neg\Phi$. More generally, if $A = \langle C, O \rangle$ is an action and S denotes the agent's knowledge of the world state, and $w \in S$ is the actual world state, then after executing A the actual world state will be w' where $\langle w, w' \rangle \in C$ and the agent's state set, S' will be:

$$\{s_j \mid \langle s_i, s_j \rangle \in C \wedge s_i \in S \wedge \exists O \in O, w', s_j \in O\} \quad (4)$$

For example, if $S = \{s_1, s_2\}$, $C = \{\langle s_1, s_3 \rangle, \langle s_2, s_4 \rangle\}$ and $O = \{\{s_1, s_4\}, \{s_2, s_3\}\}$ then by executing the action, the agent should be able to deduce complete information: either S' will equal $\{s_3\}$ or S' will equal $\{s_4\}$.

We close by noting that the $\langle C, O \rangle$ pairs are only a semantic construct. Since there may be an infinite number of these pairs, pragmatics dictates that we describe the actions with a convenient (*e.g.* finite) syntax. A precise definition of the mapping between the syntactic constructs of UWL [Etzioni et al., 1992] and the $\langle C, O \rangle$ pairs is lengthy, but straightforward. For example, suppose $\mathcal{B}$ dennotes the extension of block(x) and a **spray-paint** action has a universally quantified causational effect, $\forall x \in \mathcal{B}$ green(x) then **green** must be true of every block in every state. s_j present in a $\langle s_i, s_j \rangle$ pair in C. Universally quantified observational effects have a similar interpretation. The UNIX **ls -a /kr94** command, for example, provides complete information about *all* files in the **/kr94** directory. This corresponds to a $\langle C, O \rangle$ pair in which each equivalence class in O contains states that agree on the extension of the **parent.dir** predicate so long as **/kr94** is given as the second argument:

$$\forall O \in O \quad \forall s_1, s_2 \in O \quad \forall f$$
$$\text{if } s_1 \models \text{parent.dir}(f, /\text{kr94})$$
$$\text{then } s_2 \models \text{parent.dir}(f, /\text{kr94}) \quad (5)$$

B PROOFS

Proof of Theorem 1 (Instantiation Rule) Let Φ be a logical sentence and suppose LCW(Φ) holds. Let θ be an arbitrary substitution; we need show that LCW($\Phi\theta$) holds. *I.e.*, by definition of LCW (Equation 1) we need show that for all substitutions, σ, if $w \models \Phi\theta\sigma$ then $S \models \Phi\theta\sigma$. But since the composition $\theta\sigma$ of substitutions is a substitution, and since LCW(Φ) we conclude LCW($\Phi\theta$). □

Proof of Theorem 2 (Conjunction Rule) Let Φ and Ψ be logical sentences and suppose LCW(Φ) and LCW(Ψ). Let θ be an arbitrary substitution. We need show $[w \models (\Phi\theta \wedge \Psi\theta)] \rightarrow [S \models (\Phi\theta \wedge \Psi\theta)]$ In other words, we need to show that either S entails the conjunction or w *does not* entail the conjunction. But if $S \models (\Phi \wedge \Psi)\theta$, then the proof is complete; so instead assume that $\neg[S \models (\Phi \wedge \Psi)\theta]$. This implies that either $\neg[S \models \Phi\theta]$ or $\neg[S \models \Psi\theta]$. Then by definition of LCW, either $\neg[w \models \Phi\theta]$ or $\neg[w \models \Psi\theta]$. Thus $\neg[w \models (\Phi \wedge \Psi)\theta]$ so LCW($\Phi \wedge \Psi$) □

Proof of Theorem 3 (Counting Rule) Let Φ be a sentence and suppose that $|I(\Phi, \mathcal{D}_\mathbf{M})| = |I(\Phi, \mathcal{D}_\mathbf{W})|$. We need show that LCW($\Phi$); in other words, we need show that for an arbitrary substitution θ, $\neg[w \models \Phi\theta] \vee [S \models \Phi\theta]$. But if $S \models \Phi\theta$ then the proof is complete, so assume that $\neg[S \models \Phi\theta]$. By the definition of $\mathcal{D}_\mathbf{M}$ and Equation 2, this means that $\Phi \notin I(\Phi, \mathcal{D}_\mathbf{M})$. But the assumption of correct information assures that $I(\Phi, \mathcal{D}_\mathbf{M}) \subseteq I(\Phi, \mathcal{D}_\mathbf{W})$. And since the cardinalities are equal, the sets must be equal. So $\Phi \notin I(\Phi, \mathcal{D}_\mathbf{W})$ and thus $\neg[w \models \Phi\theta]$. Hence, LCW($\Phi$). □

Proof of Theorem 4 (Information Gain) It suffices to prove that for any sentence, Φ, and literal, φ, if LCW(Φ) holds before action A is executed and the sole effect of A is $\Delta(\varphi, \mathbf{U} \rightarrow \mathbf{T} \vee \mathbf{F})$, then LCW($\Phi$) still holds. Suppose LCW(Φ) holds and let θ be an arbitrary substitution. By Equation 1, we know that $[w \models \Phi\theta] \rightarrow [S \models \Phi\theta]$. We need to show that after executing A, $[w' \models \Phi\theta] \rightarrow [S' \models \Phi\theta]$. Note that since A has only observational effects, $w' = w$. As a result, if $\neg[w \models \Phi\theta]$ then the proof is complete, so assume $w \models \Phi\theta$. This means that $S \models \Phi\theta$ which means that $\forall s \in \mathcal{S}$ $s \models \Phi\theta$. But since A has only observational effects, $\mathcal{S}'$ is a subset of $\mathcal{S}$, and $\mathcal{S}' \models \Phi\theta$. □

Proof of Theorem 5 (Forall Rule) Let $A = \langle C, O \rangle$ be an action whose execution leads solely to an update of the form $\Delta(P(x), \to T)$ $\forall x$ such that $U(x)$ and suppose that $LCW(U(x))$. Suppose that A can be legally executed in every state in $\mathcal{S}$, and let w' and $\mathcal{S}'$ denote the result of executing A. Since the only effect of A is on P, forall θ if $s_i \models U(x)\theta$ and $\langle s_i, s_j \rangle \in C$ then $s_j \models U(x)\theta$. Thus

$$\text{if } w' \models U(x)\theta \text{ then } \mathcal{S}' \models U(x)\theta \tag{6}$$

Suppose that a universally quantified *casuational* effect of A was responsible for the quantified update. Then forall $\langle s_i, s_j \rangle \in C$ if $s_i \models U(x)\theta$ then $s_j \models P(x)\theta$ and thus $s_j \models (P(x) \wedge U(x))\theta$. Combining this with Equation 6 yields

$$\text{if } w' \models (P(x) \wedge U(x))\theta \text{ then } \mathcal{S}' \models (P(x) \wedge U(x))\theta$$

So $LCW(P(x) \wedge U(x))$ holds and the update $\mathcal{D}'_C \leftarrow \mathcal{D}_C \cup (P(x) \wedge U(x))$ is sound. On the other hand, if the universally quantified effect is *observational*, then by Equation 4 all states in $\mathcal{S}'$ must belong to one equivalence class $O \in \mathsf{O}$. Furthermore, since the effect is universally quantified, Equation 5 dictates that forall states $s_1, s_2 \in \mathcal{S}'$ and forall substitutions θ of x, if $s_1 \models (P(x) \wedge U(x))\theta$ then $s_2 \models (P(x) \wedge U(x))\theta$. But $w' \in \mathcal{S}'$ so this means that $LCW(P(x) \wedge U(x))$ holds and the update is sound. □

Proof of Theorem 6 (Information Loss) Let Φ be a conjunction of positive literals and suppose that $LCW(\Phi)$. Let φ be a positive literal and let A be an action whose only effect is $\Delta(\varphi, T \vee F \to U)$. We prove the case of $\Delta(\varphi, T \to U)$ but the case of $\Delta(\varphi, F \to U)$ is identical. To prove that the Information Loss Rule is sound in this case, we need to show that if $LCW(\Phi)$ no longer holds after executing A then $\Phi \in REL(\varphi)$. Suppose that $LCW(\Phi)$ *doesn't* hold after executing A; then there exists a substitution, θ such that $[w' \models \Phi\theta] \not\to [\mathcal{S}' \models \Phi\theta]$ even though $[w \models \Phi\theta] \to [\mathcal{S} \models \Phi\theta]$. However, we know that the only positive literal whose proof status changed between w and w' and $\mathcal{S}$ and $\mathcal{S}'$ was φ. Hence $\Phi\theta \models \varphi$. But since Φ is conjunctive, there exists $\phi \in \Phi$ such that $\phi\theta = \varphi$. Since $w' \models \Phi\theta$, and φ was the only literal to change its truth value, the rest of the literals (if any) in Φ must be entailed by w: $\forall \phi_i \in (\Phi - \phi), w \models \phi_i\theta$. Since we assume correct information, this means $\forall \phi_i \in (\Phi - \phi), \neg(\mathcal{S} \models \neg\phi_i\theta)$ Hence Φ satisfies the second part of the definition of $REL(\varphi)$ and we have $\Phi \in REL(\varphi)$. □

Proof of Theorem 7 (Domain Growth) Let Φ be a conjunction of positive literals and suppose that $LCW(\Phi)$. Let φ be a positive literal and suppose A is an action whose only nonderivative effect is $\Delta(\varphi, F \to T)$. Suppose that $LCW(\Phi)$ no longer holds after executing A; then there exists a substitution, θ such that $[w' \models \Phi\theta] \not\to [\mathcal{S}' \models \Phi\theta]$ even though $[w \models \Phi\theta] \to [\mathcal{S} \models \Phi\theta]$. However, we know that the only positive literal whose proof status changed from false to true between w and w' and between $\mathcal{S}$ and $\mathcal{S}'$ was φ. So we have for some $\phi \in \Phi$, $\phi\theta = \varphi$. Since $w' \models \Phi\theta$, and the only literal in $\Phi\theta$ to change its proof status was $\phi\theta$, the rest of the literals in $\Phi\theta$ must be entailed by w: $\forall \phi_i \in (\Phi - \phi)\theta, w \models \phi_i$. Thus $\forall \phi_i \in (\Phi - \phi), \neg(\mathcal{S} \models \neg\phi_i\theta)$, so $\Phi \in REL(\varphi)$. After execution, we have $LCW(\phi\theta)$ (φ changed to T), but not $LCW(\Phi\theta)$. Therefore, by the contrapositive of the Conjunction Rule, $\neg LCW((\Phi - \phi)\theta)$. This leads to $\Phi \in MREL(\varphi)$. □

Proof of Theorem 8 (Domain Contraction) Let φ be a positive literal and suppose A is an action whose only effect is $\Delta(\varphi, T \to F)$. To show that the update rule is sound, it is sufficient to prove that for any Φ, if $LCW(\Phi)$ holds before executing A then $LCW(\Phi)$ holds after executing A. If $LCW(\Phi)$ holds before execution then, for arbitrary θ, we know that $[w \models \Phi\theta] \to [\mathcal{S} \models \Phi\theta]$. We need to show that after executing A $[w' \models \Phi\theta] \to [\mathcal{S}' \models \Phi\theta]$. If $\neg[w' \models \Phi\theta]$ then the proof is complete, so assume $w' \models \Phi\theta$. Since the only effect of A was to make φ *false*, and Φ is a conjunction of *positive* literals. $[w' \models \Phi\theta] \to [w \models \Phi\theta] \to [\mathcal{S} \models \Phi\theta]$ Since the truth value of $\Phi\theta$ did not change between w and w' and since $\mathcal{S} \models \Phi\theta$, it follows that $\mathcal{S}' \models \Phi\theta$. □

Acknowledgments

Tom Dean, Denise Draper, Steve Hanks, Rao Kambhampati, Craig Knoblock, Neal Lesh, Martha Pollack, Rich Segal, Yoav Shoham, Mike Wellman, and Mike Williamson made extremely helpful comments on drafts of this paper. Omid Madani contributed to the formal aspects of the paper, and Rob Spiger contributed to the implementation. This research was funded in part by Office of Naval Research Grants 90-J-1904 and 92-J-1946, by a grant from the University of Washington Royalty Research Fund, and by National Science Foundation Grants IRI-8957302, IRI-9211045, and IRI-9357772. Golden is supported in part by a UniForum Research Award.

References

[Ambros-Ingerson and Steel, 1988]
  J Ambros-Ingerson and S. Steel. Integrating planning, execution, and monitoring. In *Proc. 7th Nat. Conf. on Artificial Intelligence*, pages 735–740, 1988.

[Brachman, 1992] R. Brachman. "Reducing" CLASSIC to Practice: Knowledge Representation Theory Meets Reality. In *Proc. 3rd Int. Conf. on Principles of Knowledge Representation and Reasoning*, October 1992.

[Brill, 1991] D. Brill. *LOOM Reference Manual*. USC-ISI, 4353 Park Terrace Drive, Westlake Village, CA 91361, version 1.4 edition, August 1991.

[Cadoli and Schaerf, 1993] M. Cadoli and M. Schaerf. A survey of complexity results for non-monotonic logics. *Journal of Logic Programming*, 17:127–160, November 1993.

[Chapman, 1987] D. Chapman. Planning for conjunctive goals. *Artificial Intelligence*, 32(3):333–377, 1987.

[Clark, 1978] K. L. Clark. Negation as failure. In H. Gallaire and J. Minker, editors, *Logic and Data Bases*, pages 293–322. Plenum Publishing Corporation, New York, NY, 1978.

[Davis, 1988] E. Davis. Inferring ignorance from the locality of visual perception. In *Proc. 7th Nat. Conf. on Artificial Intelligence*, pages 786–790, 1988.

[Davis, 1990] E. Davis. *Representations of Commonsense Knowledge*. Morgan Kaufmann Publishers, Inc., San Mateo, CA, 1990.

[del Val and Shoham, 1993] Alvaro del Val and Yoav Shoham. Deriving Properties of Belief Update from Theories of Action (II). In *Proceedings of IJCAI-93*, pages 732–737, 1993.

[del Val, 1992] Alvaro del Val. Computing Knowledge Base Updates. In *Proceedings of the Third International Conference on Principles of Knowledge Representation and Reasoning*, pages 740–750, 1992.

[Eiter and Gottlob, 1992] T. Eiter and G. Gottlob. On the complexity of propositional knowledge base revision, updates, and counterfactuals. *Artificial Intelligence*, 57:227–270, October 1992.

[Etherington, 1988] D. Etherington. *Reasoning with Incomplete Information*. Morgan Kaufmann Publishers, Inc., Los Altos, CA, 1988.

[Etzioni and Lesh, 1993] Oren Etzioni and Neal Lesh. Planning with incomplete information in the UNIX domain. In *Working Notes of the AAAI Spring Symposium: Foundations of Automatic Planning: The Classical Approach and Beyond*, pages 24–28, Menlo Park, CA, 1993. AAAI Press.

[Etzioni et al., 1992] O. Etzioni, S. Hanks, D. Weld, D. Draper, N. Lesh, and M. Williamson. An Approach to Planning with Incomplete Information. In *Proc. 3rd Int. Conf. on Principles of Knowledge Representation and Reasoning*, October 1992. Available via anonymous FTP from ~ftp/pub/ai/ at cs.washington.edu.

[Etzioni et al., 1993] Oren Etzioni, Neal Lesh, and Richard Segal. Building softbots for UNIX (preliminary report). Technical Report 93-09-01, University of Washington, 1993. Available via anonymous FTP from pub/etzioni/softbots/ at cs.washington.edu.

[Etzioni, 1993] Oren Etzioni. Intelligence without robots (a reply to brooks). *AI Magazine*, 14(4), December 1993. Available via anonymous FTP from pub/etzioni/softbots/ at cs.washington.edu.

[Genesereth and Nourbakhsh, 1993] M. Genesereth and I. Nourbakhsh. Time-saving tips for problem solving with incomplete information. In *Proc. 11th Nat. Conf. on Artificial Intelligence*, pages 724–730, July 1993.

[Ginsberg and Smith, 1988] M. Ginsberg and D. Smith. Reasoning about action I: A possible worlds approach. *Artificial Intelligence*, 35(2):165–196, June 1988.

[Ginsberg, 1987] M. Ginsberg, editor. *Readings in Nonmonotonic Reasoning*. Morgan Kaufmann, San Mateo, CA, 1987.

[Ginsberg, 1989] M. Ginsberg. A circumscriptive theorem prover. *Artificial Intelligence*, 39(2):209–230, June 1989.

[Golden et al., 1994] K. Golden, O. Etzioni, and D. Weld. To Sense or Not to Sense? (A Planner's Question). Technical Report 94-01-03, University of Washington, Department of Computer Science and Engineering, January 1994. Available via anonymous FTP from ~ftp/pub/ai/ at cs.washington.edu.

[Katsuno and Mendelzon, 1991] H. Katsuno and A. Mendelzon. On the difference between updating a knowledge base and revising it. In *Proc. 2nd Int. Conf. on Principles of Knowledge Representation and Reasoning*, pages 387–394, 1991.

[Keller and Wilkins, 1985] A. Keller and M. Wilkins. On the use of an extended relational model to handle changing incomplete information. *IEEE Transactions on Software Engineering*, SE-11(7):620–633, July 1985.

[Konolidge, 1982] K. Konolidge. Circumscriptive ignorance. In *Proc. 2nd Nat. Conf. on Artificial Intelligence*, pages 202–204, 1982.

[Kowalski, 1978] R. Kowalski. Logic for data description. In H. Gallaire and J. Minker, editors, *Logic and Data Bases*, pages 77–103. Plenum Publishing Corporation, New York, NY, 1978.

[Krebsbach et al., 1992] K. Krebsbach, D. Olawsky, and M. Gini. An empirical study of sensing and defaulting in planning. In *Proc. 1st Int. Conf. on A.I. Planning Systems*, pages 136–144, June 1992.

[Levesque, 1990] H.J. Levesque. All I know: A study in autoepistemic logic. *Artificial Intelligence*, 42(2–3), 1990.

[Lifschitz, 1985] V. Lifschitz. Closed-World Databases and Circumscription. *Artificial Intelligence*, 27:229–235, 1985.

[McCarthy, 1980] J. McCarthy. Circumscription - a form of non-monotonic reasoning. *Artificial Intelligence*, 13(1,2):27–39, April 1980.

[Moore, 1985] R. Moore. A Formal Theory of Knowledge and Action. In J. Hobbs and R. Moore, editors, *Formal Theories of the Commonsense World*. Ablex, Norwood, NJ, 1985.

[Olawsky and Gini, 1990] D. Olawsky and M. Gini. Deferred planning and sensor use. In *Proceedings, DARPA Workshop on Innovative Approaches to Planning, Scheduling, and Control*. Morgan Kaufmann, 1990.

[Papadimitriou, 1985] C. Papadimitriou. Games against nature. *Journal of Computer and Systems Sciences*, 31:288–301, 1985.

[Pednault, 1986] E. Pednault. *Toward a Mathematical Theory of Plan Synthesis*. PhD thesis, Stanford University, December 1986.

[Pednault, 1988] E. Pednault. Synthesizing plans that contain actions with context-dependent effects. *Computational Intelligence*, 4(4):356–372, 1988.

[Pednault, 1989] E. Pednault. ADL: Exploring the middle ground between STRIPS and the situation calculus. In *Proceedings Knowledge Representation Conf.,*, 1989.

[Penberthy and Weld, 1992] J.S. Penberthy and D. Weld. UCPOP: A sound, complete, partial order planner for ADL. In *Proc. 3rd Int. Conf. on Principles of Knowledge Representation and Reasoning*, pages 103–114, October 1992. Available via anonymous FTP from ~ftp/pub/ai/ at cs.washington.edu.

[Peot and Smith, 1992] M. Peot and D. Smith. Conditional Nonlinear Planning. In *Proc. 1st Int. Conf. on A.I. Planning Systems*, pages 189–197, June 1992.

[Raiman and de Kleer, 1992] O. Raiman and J. de Kleer. A Minimality Maintenance System. In *Proc. 3rd Int. Conf. on Principles of Knowledge Representation and Reasoning*, pages 532–538, October 1992.

[Reiter, 1978] R. Reiter. On closed world databases. In H. Gallaire and J. Minker, editors, *Logic and Data Bases*, pages 55–76. Plenum Press, 1978. Reprinted in [Ginsberg, 1987].

[Reiter, 1982] R. Reiter. Circumscription implies predicate completion (sometimes). *Proc. 2nd Nat. Conf. on Artificial Intelligence*, pages 418–420, 1982.

[Smith, 1983] D. Smith. Finding all of the solutions to a problem. In *Proc. 3rd Nat. Conf. on Artificial Intelligence*, pages 373–377, 1983.

[Tambe and Rosenbloom, 1989] Milind Tambe and Paul Rosenbloom. Eliminating expensive chunks by restricting expressiveness. In *Proc. 11th Int. Joint Conf. on Artificial Intelligence*, 1989.

[Tate, 1977] A. Tate. Generating project networks. In *Proc. 5th Int. Joint Conf. on Artificial Intelligence*, pages 888–893, 1977.

[Weld, 1994] D. Weld. An introduction to least-commitment planning. *AI Magazine*, To appear Summer or Fall 1994. Available via anonymous FTP from ~ftp/pub/ai/ at cs.washington.edu.

[Winslett, 1988] M. Winslett. Reasoning about action using a possible models approach. In *Proc. 7th Nat. Conf. on Artificial Intelligence*, page 89, August 1988.

A Knowledge-Based Framework for Belief Change, Part II: Revision and Update

Nir Friedman
Department of Computer Science
Stanford University
Stanford, CA 94305-2140
nir@cs.stanford.edu

Joseph Y. Halpern
IBM Almaden Research Center
650 Harry Road
San Jose, CA 95120-6099
halpern@almaden.ibm.com

Abstract

The study of *belief change* has been an active area in philosophy and AI. In recent years two special cases of belief change, *belief revision* and *belief update*, have been studied in detail. In a companion paper [FH94b] we introduced a new framework to model belief change. This framework combines temporal and epistemic modalities with a notion of plausibility, allowing us to examine the changes of beliefs over time. In this paper we show how belief revision and belief update can be captured in our framework. This allows us to compare the assumptions made by each method and to better understand the principles underlying them. In particular, it allows us to understand the source of Gärdenfors' triviality result for belief revision [Gär86] and suggests a way of mitigating the problem. It also shows that Katsuno and Mendelzon's notion of belief update [KM91a] depends on several strong assumptions that may limit its applicability in AI.

1 INTRODUCTION

The study of *belief change* has been an active area in philosophy and AI. The focus of this research is to understand how an agent should change his beliefs as a result of getting new information. Two instances of this general phenomenon have been studied in detail. *Belief revision* [AGM85, Gär88] focuses on how an agent revises his beliefs when he adopts a new belief. *Belief update* [KM91a], on the other hand, focuses on how an agent should change his beliefs when he realizes that the world has changed. Both approaches attempt to capture the intuition that an agent should make minimal changes in his beliefs in order to accommodate the new belief. The difference is that belief revision attempts to decide what beliefs should be discarded to accommodate a new belief, while belief update attempts to decide what changes in the world led to the new observation.

In [FH94b] we introduce a general framework for modeling belief change. We start with the framework for analyzing knowledge in multi-agent systems, introduced in [HF89], and add to it a notion of plausibility ordering at each situation. We then define belief as truth in the most plausible situations. The resulting framework is very expressive; it captures both time and knowledge as well as beliefs. The representation of time allows us to reason in the framework about changes in the beliefs of the agent. It also allows us to relate the beliefs of the agent about the future with his actual beliefs in the future. Knowledge captures in a precise sense the non-defeasible information the agent has about the world he is in, while belief captures defeasible information. The framework allows us to represent a broad spectrum of notions of belief change. In this paper we show how belief revision and update can be represented. Doing this allows us to compare the assumptions implicit in each method and to understand the principles underlying them.

The explicit representation of time allows us to investigate some of the subtle differences between revision and update. For example, in the literature, belief revision has been described (in [KM91a], for example) as a process of changing beliefs about a *static world*, but this is slightly misleading. In fact, what is important for revision is not that the world is static, but that the propositions used to describe the world are static, i.e., their truth value does not change over time.[1] For example, "At time 0 the block is on the table" is a static proposition, while "The block is on the table" is not, since it implicitly references the *current* state of affairs. Belief update, on the other hand, deals with propositions whose truth depends on the current situation. It allows any proposition to change its truth value, and treats this as a change in the world rather than as a change in the agent's beliefs about the world.

---
[1] This assumption is not unique to belief revision. Bayesian updating, for example, makes similar assumptions.

This distinction allows us to better understand Gärdenfors' triviality result [Gär86]. This result states that the belief revision postulates cannot be applied to belief states that contain *Ramsey conditionals* of the form $\varphi > \psi$ with the interpretation "revising by φ will lead to a state where ψ is believed". Technically, this is because the AGM framework includes a postulate of *persistence*: if φ is consistent with the current beliefs, then no beliefs should be discarded to accommodate φ. Since the truth value of a Ramsey conditional depends on the current state of the agent, it is inappropriate to assume that it persists when that state changes. It should thus be no surprise that assuming persistence of such formulas leads to triviality. Indeed, this observation was essentially already made by Levi [Lev88]. Our solution to the triviality result is somewhat different from others that have been considered in the literature (e.g., [Rot89, Fuh89, LR92, Bou92]) in that it shifts the focus from postulates for the revision process to considerations of the appropriate logic of conditionals.

We then turn our attention to belief update. Our treatment enables us to identify implicit assumptions made in the update process. In particular, it brings out how update prefers to defer abnormalities to as late a time as possible. This allows us to clarify when update is appropriate. Essentially, it is appropriate if the agent always receives enough information to deduce the exact change in the state of the world, a condition unlikely to be met in most AI applications.

We are certainly not the first to provide semantic models for belief revision and update. For example, [AGM85, Gro88, GM88, Rot91, Bou92, Rij92] deal with revision and [KM91a, dVS92] deal with update. In fact, there are several works in the literature that capture both using the same machinery [KS91, GP92] and others that simulate belief revision using belief update [GMR92, dVS94]. Our approach is different from most in that we did not construct a specific framework to capture one or both belief change paradigms. Instead, we start from a natural framework to model how an agent's knowledge changes over time [HF89] and add to it machinery that captures a defeasible notion of belief. As we shall see, our framework allows us to clearly bring out the similarities and differences between update and revision. We believe that the insights gained into revision and update using our approach—particularly in terms of the assumptions that each makes about how an agent's plausibility ordering changes over time—provide further justification as to the usefulness of having such a framework.

2 THE FRAMEWORK

We now review the framework of [HF89] for modeling knowledge in multi-agent systems, and our extension of it [FH94b] for dealing with belief change.

The key assumption in this framework is that we can characterize the system by describing it in terms of a *state* that changes over time. Formally, we assume that at each point in time, the agent is in some *local state*. Intuitively, this local state encodes the information the agent has observed thus far. There is also an *environment*, whose state encodes relevant aspects of the system that are not part of the agent's local state. A *global state* is a tuple (s_e, s_a) consisting of the environment state s_e and the local state s_a of the agent. A *run* of the system is a function from time (which, for ease of exposition, we assume ranges over the natural numbers) to global states. Thus, if r is a run, then $r(0), r(1), \ldots$ is a sequence of global states that, roughly speaking, is a complete description of what happens over time in one possible execution of the system. We take a *system* to consist of a set of runs. Intuitively, these runs describe all the possible behaviors of the system, that is, all the possible sequences of events that could occur in the system over time.

Given a system $\mathcal{R}$, we refer to a pair (r, m) consisting of a run $r \in \mathcal{R}$ and a time m as a *point*. If $r(m) = (s_e, s_a)$, we define $r_a(m) = s_a$ and $r_e(m) = s_e$. We say two points (r, m) and (r', m') are *indistinguishable* to the agent, and write $(r, m) \sim_a (r', m')$, if $r_a(m) = r'_a(m')$, i.e., if the agent has the same local state at both points. Finally, Halpern and Fagin define an *interpreted* system $\mathcal{I}$ to be a tuple $(\mathcal{R}, \pi)$ consisting of a system $\mathcal{R}$ together with a mapping π that associates with each point a truth assignment to the primitive propositions. In an interpreted system we can talk about an agent's knowledge: the agent knows φ at a point (r, m) if φ holds in all points (r', m') such that $(r, m) \sim_a (r', m')$. However, we can not talk about the agent's (possibly defeasible) beliefs at (r, m).

To remedy this deficiency, in [FH94b] we added plausibility orderings to interpreted systems. We can then say that the agent believes φ if φ is true at all the most plausible worlds. Formally, a *plausibility space* is a tuple $(\Omega, \preceq)$, where Ω is a set of points in the system, and $\preceq$ is a preorder (i.e., a reflexive and transitive relation) over Ω. As usual, we write $(r', m') \prec (r'', m'')$ if $(r', m') \preceq (r'', m'')$ and it is not the case that $(r'', m'') \preceq (r', m')$. Intuitively, $(r', m') \prec (r'', m'')$ if (r', m') is strictly more plausible than (r'', m'') according to the plausibility ordering. An *(interpreted) plausibility system* is a tuple $(\mathcal{R}, \pi, \mathcal{P})$ where, as before, $\mathcal{R}$ is a set of runs and π maps each point to a truth assignment, and where $\mathcal{P}$ is a *plausibility assignment function* mapping each point (r, m) to a plausibility space $\mathcal{P}(r, m) = (\Omega_{(r,m)}, \preceq_{(r,m)})$. Intuitively, the plausibility space $\mathcal{P}(r, m)$ describes the relative plausibility of points from the point of view of the agent at (r, m). In this paper we assume that $\Omega_{(r,m)}$ is a (possibly empty) subset of $\{(r', m') | (r, m) \sim_a (r', m')\}$. Thus, the agent considers plausible only situations that are possible according to his knowledge. We also assume that the plausibility space is a function of the agent's local state. Thus, if $(r,m) \sim_a (r',m')$ then $\mathcal{P}(r,m) = \mathcal{P}(r',m')$.[2]

We define the logical language $\mathcal{L}^{KPT}(\Phi)$ to be a propositional language over a set of primitive propositions Φ with the following modalities: $K\varphi$ (the agent knows φ is true), $\bigcirc\varphi$ (φ is true in the next time step), and $\varphi \rightarrow \psi$ (in all most-plausible situations where φ is true, ψ is also true).[3] We recursively assign truth values to formulas in $\mathcal{L}^{KPT}(\Phi)$ at a point (r,m) in a plausibility system $\mathcal{I}$. The truth of primitive propositions is determined by π, so that

$(\mathcal{I}, r, m) \models p$ if and only if $\pi(r,m)(p) = \text{true}$.

Conjunction and negation are treated in the standard way, as is knowledge: The agent knows φ at (r,m) if φ holds at all points that he cannot distinguish from (r,m). Thus,

$(\mathcal{I}, r, m) \models K\varphi$ if $(\mathcal{I}, r', m') \models \varphi$ for all $(r',m') \sim_a (r,m)$.

$\bigcirc\varphi$ is true at (r,m) if φ is true at $(r, m+1)$. Thus,

$(\mathcal{I}, r, m) \models \bigcirc\varphi$ if $(\mathcal{I}, r, m+1) \models \varphi$.

We would like $\varphi \rightarrow \psi$ to be true at (r,m) if the most plausible points in $\Omega_{(r,m)}$ that satisfy φ also satisfy ψ. The actual definition that we use, which is standard in the literature (see [Lew73, Bur81, Bou92]), captures this desideratum if there are most plausible points that satisfy φ (in particular, if $\Omega_{(r,m)}$ is finite), and also deals with the more general case where there may be a sequence of increasingly more plausible points, with none being most plausible, i.e., $\ldots s_3 \prec_{(r,m)} s_2 \prec_{(r,m)} s_1$. The actual definition says that $\varphi \rightarrow \psi$ is true at a point (r,m) if for every point (r_1, m_1) in $\Omega_{(r,m)}$ satisfying φ, there is another point (r_2, m_2) such that (a) (r_2, m_2) is at least as plausible as (r_1, m_1), (b) (r_2, m_2) satisfies $\varphi \wedge \psi$, and (c) each point satisfying φ that is at least as plausible as (r_2, m_2) also satisfies ψ.

$(\mathcal{I}, r, m) \models \varphi \rightarrow \psi$ if for every $(r_1, m_1) \in \Omega_{(r,m)}$ such that $(\mathcal{I}, r_1, m_1) \models \varphi$, there is a point $(r_2, m_2) \preceq_{(r,m)} (r_1, m_1)$ such that $(\mathcal{I}, r_2, m_2) \models \varphi \wedge \psi$, and there is no $(r_3, m_3) \preceq_{(r,m)} (r_2, m_2)$ such that $(\mathcal{I}, r_3, m_3) \models \varphi \wedge \neg\psi$.

We now define a notion of *belief*. Intuitively, the agent believes φ if φ is true in all the worlds he considers most plausible. Formally, we define $B\varphi \Leftrightarrow true \rightarrow \varphi$. In [FH94b] we prove that, in this framework, knowledge is an S5 operator, belief is a KD45 operator, and the interactions between knowledge and belief are captured by the axioms $K\varphi \Rightarrow B\varphi$ and $B\varphi \Rightarrow KB\varphi$.

In a plausibility system, the agent's beliefs change from point to point because his plausibility space changes. The general framework does not put any constraints on how the plausibility space changes. In this paper, we identify the constraints that correspond to belief revision and update.

3 BELIEF CHANGE SYSTEMS

In the rest of this paper, we focus on a certain class of systems that we call *belief change systems*, in which we can capture both belief revision and belief update. These systems describe agents that change their local state at each round according to new information they receive (or learn). Both revision and update assume that this information is described by a formula.[4] Thus, they describe how the agent's beliefs change when the new information is captured by a formula φ. Implicitly they assume that φ is the only factor that affects the change. We now make this assumption precise.

We start with some language $\mathcal{L}(\Phi)$ that describes the worlds. We assume that $\mathcal{L}(\Phi)$ contains the propositional calculus and has a consequence relation $\vdash_{\mathcal{L}}$ that satisfies the deduction theorem. The set Φ denotes the primitive propositions in the $\mathcal{L}(\Phi)$. We can think of $\vdash_{\mathcal{L}}$ as a description of *state constraints* that govern the language. We assume that the agent is described by a *protocol*. The protocol describes how the agent changes state when receiving new information. Formally, a protocol is a tuple $P = (S, s_0, \tau)$, where S is the set of local states the agent can attain, s_0 is the *initial state* of the agent, and τ is a transition function that maps a state and a formula in $\mathcal{L}(\Phi)$ to another state. We take $\tau(s, \varphi)$ to be the local state of the agent after learning φ in local state s. We sometimes write $s \cdot \varphi$ instead of $\tau(s, \varphi)$.

To clarify the concept of protocol, we examine a rather simple protocol that we use below in our representation of update. The protocol P^* is defined as follows: The agent's local state is simply the sequence of observation made. Thus, S is the set of sequences of formulas in $\mathcal{L}(\Phi)$. Initially the agent has not made any observations, so $s_0 = \langle \rangle$. The transition function simply appends the new observation to the agent's state: $\tau(\langle \varphi_0, \ldots, \varphi_n \rangle, \psi) = \langle \varphi_0, \ldots, \varphi_n, \psi \rangle$. This simple definition describes an agent that remembers all

---

[2] The framework presented in [FH94b] is more general than this, dealing with multiple agents and allowing the agent to consider several plausibility spaces in each local state. The simplified version we present here suffices to capture belief revision and update.

[3] It is easy to add other temporal modalities such as until, eventually, since, etc. These do not play a role in this paper.

[4] This is a rather strong assumption, since it implies that the language in question can capture, in a precise manner, the information content of the change. Our framework can also be used to describe situations where this assumption does not hold.

his observations.[5]

Given a protocol P, we define $\mathcal{R}(P)$ to be the system consisting of all runs in which the agent runs P as follows. Recall that in our framework we need to describe the local states of the agent and the environment at each point. We use the environment state to represent which of the propositions in Φ is true and what observation the agent makes. We represent a truth assignment over Φ by the set Ψ of propositions that are true. We say that a truth assignment Ψ is *consistent* according to $\vdash_{\mathcal{L}}$ if for every $\varphi_1, \ldots \varphi_n \in \Psi$ and $\psi_1 \ldots \psi_m \notin \Psi$, it is not the case that $\vdash_{\mathcal{L}} \neg(\bigwedge_{i=1} n\varphi_i \wedge \bigwedge_{i=m} k\neg\psi_i)$. Formally, we take the environment state to be a pair $r_e(m) = \langle \Psi, \varphi \rangle$, such that $\Psi \subseteq \Phi$ is a consistent truth assignment to Ψ and φ is the observation that the agent makes in the transition from (r, m) to $(r, m+1)$. If $r_e(m) = \langle \Psi, \varphi \rangle$, then we define $world(r, m) = \Psi$ and $obs(r, m) = \varphi$.

We take $\mathcal{R}(P)$ to be the set of all runs satisfying the following conditions for all $m \geq 0$:

- $r_a(m) \in S$
- $r_e(m) = \langle \Psi, \varphi \rangle$, where $\Psi \subseteq \Phi$ is consistent according to $\vdash_{\mathcal{L}}$ and $\varphi \in \mathcal{L}(\Phi)$
- $r_a(0) = s_0$
- $r_a(m+1) = \tau_a(r_a(m), obs(r, m))$.

Notice that because $\mathcal{R}(P)$ contains all runs that satisfy these conditions, for each sequence of world states $\Psi_0, \ldots, \Psi_m$ and observations $\varphi_0, \ldots \varphi_m$ there is a run in $\mathcal{R}(P)$ such that $r_e(i) = \langle \Psi_i, \varphi_i \rangle$ for all $0 \leq i \leq m$.

We introduce propositions that allow us to describe the observations the agent make at each step. More formally, let Φ^* be the set of primitive propositions obtained by augmenting Φ with all primitive propositions of the form $learn(\varphi)$, where $\varphi \in \mathcal{L}(\Phi)$. Intuitively, $learn(\varphi)$ holds if the agent has just learned (or observed) φ. We now define a truth assignment π on the points in $\mathcal{R}(P)$ in the obvious way: For $p \in \Phi$, we define $\pi(r, m)(p) = \textbf{true}$ if and only if $p \in world(r, m)$. Since the formula $learn(\varphi)$ is intended to denote that the agent has just learned φ, we define $\pi(r, m)(learn(\varphi)) = \textbf{true}$ if and only if $obs(r, m) = \varphi$.

These definitions set the background for our presentation of belief revision and belief update. Our description is still missing a plausibility assignment function that describes the plausibility ordering of the agent at each point. This function requires a different treatment for revision and update. Indeed, the plausibility function is the main source of difference between the two notions.

---

[5]We remark that P^* is similar to protocols used to model knowledge bases in [FHMV94].

4 REVISION

Belief revision attempts to describe how a rational agent incorporates new beliefs. As we said earlier, the main intuition is that as few changes as possible should be made. Thus, when something is learned that is consistent with earlier beliefs, it is just added to the set of beliefs. The more interesting situation is when the agent learns something inconsistent with his current beliefs. He must then discard some of his old beliefs in order to incorporate the new belief and remain consistent. The question is which ones?

The most widely accepted notion of belief revision is defined by the AGM theory [AGM85, Gär88]. The agent's epistemic state is represented as a *belief set*, that is, a set of formulas in $\mathcal{L}(\Phi)$ closed under deduction. There is also assumed to be a revision operator $\circ$ that takes a belief set A and a formula φ and returns a new belief set $A \circ \varphi$, intuitively, the result of revising A by φ. The following AGM postulates are an attempt to characterize the intuition of "minimal change":

(R1) $A \circ \varphi$ is a belief set
(R2) $\varphi \in A \circ \varphi$
(R3) $A \circ \varphi \subseteq Cl(A \cup \{\varphi\})$[6]
(R4) If $\neg \varphi \notin A$ then $Cl(A \cup \{\varphi\}) \subseteq A \circ \varphi$
(R5) $A \circ \varphi = Cl(false)$ if and only if $\vdash_L \neg \varphi$
(R6) If $\vdash_L \varphi \Leftrightarrow \psi$ then $A \circ \varphi = A \circ \psi$
(R7) $A \circ (\varphi \wedge \psi) \subseteq Cl(A \circ \varphi \cup \{\psi\})$
(R8) If $\neg \psi \notin A \circ \varphi$ then $Cl(A \circ \varphi \cup \{\psi\}) \subseteq A \circ (\varphi \wedge \psi)$.

The essence of these postulates is the following. After a revision by φ the belief set should include φ (postulates R1 and R2). If the new belief is consistent with the belief set, then the revision should not remove any of the old beliefs and should not add any new beliefs except these implied by the combination of the old beliefs with the new belief (postulates R3 and R4). This condition is called *persistence*. The next two conditions discuss the coherence of beliefs. Postulate R5 states that the agent is capable of incorporating any consistent belief and postulate R6 states that the syntactic form of the new belief does not affect the revision process. The last two postulates enforce a certain coherency on the outcome of revisions by related beliefs. Basically they state that if ψ is consistent with $A \circ \varphi$ then $A \circ (\varphi \wedge \psi)$ is just $A \circ \varphi$ combined with ψ. This ensures that revision is coherent regarding the outcome of revision by similar formulas (e.g., φ and $\varphi \wedge \psi$).

While there are several representation theorems for belief revision, the clearest is perhaps the following [Gro88, KM91b]: We associate with each belief set A a set W_A of possible worlds. Intuitively, the worlds in W_A are all those that are consistent with the agent's

---

[6]$Cl(A) = \{\varphi | A \vdash_{\mathcal{L}} \varphi\}$ is the deductive closure of a set of formulas A.

beliefs, in that W_A consists of all those worlds in which all formulas in A are true. Thus, an agent whose belief set is A believes that one of the worlds in W_A is the real world. An agent that performs belief revision behaves as though in each belief state A he has a *ranking*, i.e., a total preorder, over all possible worlds such that the minimal (i.e., most plausible) worlds in the ranking are exactly those in W_A. The ranking prescribes how the agent revises his beliefs. When revising by φ, the agent chooses the minimal worlds satisfying φ in the ranking and constructs a belief set from them. It is easy to see that this procedure for belief revision satisfies the AGM postulates. Moreover, in [Gro88, KM91b] it is shown that any belief revision operator can be described in terms of such a ranking.

This representation suggests how we can capture belief revision in our framework. We want to define a family of belief systems that captures all the revision operators consistent with the AGM postulates. Since revision assumes that the primitive propositions are static, we assume that world state is constant throughout the run. To capture this, we use a variant of our definition from Section 3: Given P, let $\mathcal{R}^R(P)$ be the runs in $\mathcal{R}(P)$ such that $world(r,m) = world(r,0)$ for all $m \geq 0$.

All that remains to define a plausibility system is to define the plausibility assignment function $\mathcal{P}$. We take $\mathcal{S}^R$ to be the set of systems of the form $(\mathcal{R}^R(P), \pi, \mathcal{P})$ for some protocol P, in which $\mathcal{P}(r,m) = (\Omega_{(r,m)}, \preceq_{(r,m)})$ satisfies the following conditions:

- $\Omega_{(r,m)} = \emptyset$ if $obs(r,m)$ is inconsistent; otherwise $\Omega_{(r,m)} = \{(r',m') : (r,m) \sim_a (r',m')\}$, the set of all points the agent considers possible.
- $\preceq_{(r,m)}$ is a ranking, i.e., for any two point $(r',m'),(r'',m'') \in \Omega_{(r,m)}$, either $(r',m') \preceq_{(r,m)} (r'',m'')$ or $(r'',m'') \preceq_{(r,m)} (r',m')$.
- $\preceq_{(r,m)}$ compares points examining only the state of the world, so that if (r',m') and (r'',m'') are in $\Omega_{(r,m)}$ and $world(r',m') = world(r'',m'')$, then (r',m') and (r'',m'') are equivalent according to $\preceq_{(r,m)}$.
- if $obs(r,m)) = \varphi$ is consistent, then $(r',m'+1)$ is a $\preceq_{(r,m+1)}$-minimal point if and only if (r',m') is a $\preceq_{(r,m)}$-minimal point satisfying φ.

Note that our assumptions correspond closely to those of [Gro88, KM91b]. The difference is that we have time explicitly in the picture and that our states have more structure. That is, in [Gro88, KM91b], a state is just a truth assignment. For us, the truth assignment is still there, as part of the environment's state, but we have also added the agent's local state. Of course, we can associate a belief set with each local state, since an agent's local state determines his beliefs over $\mathcal{L}(\Phi)$. That is, if $r_a(m) = r'_a(m)$, then it is easy to check that $(\mathcal{I},r,m) \models B\varphi$ if and only if $(\mathcal{I},r',m') \models B\varphi$

for any $\varphi \in \mathcal{L}(\Phi)$. Thus, we can write $(\mathcal{I}, s_a) \models B\varphi$, where s_a is the agent's local state $r_a(m)$. Define the belief set $\text{Bel}(\mathcal{I}, s_a)$ to be $\{\varphi \in \mathcal{L}(\Phi) : (\mathcal{I}, s_a) \models B\varphi\}$. It is easy to show that every AGM revision operator can be represented in our framework. Recall that we sometimes write $s_a \cdot \varphi$ for $\tau(s_a, \varphi)$.

Theorem 4.1: *Let $\circ$ be an AGM revision operator. There is a system $\mathcal{I}_\circ \in \mathcal{S}^R$ such that for all $\psi \in \mathcal{L}(\Phi)$, we have*

$$\text{Bel}(\mathcal{I}_\circ, s_a) \circ \psi = \text{Bel}(\mathcal{I}_\circ, s_a \cdot \psi). \quad (1)$$

What about the converse? That is, given a system $\mathcal{I} \in \mathcal{S}^R$, can we define a belief revision operator $\circ_\mathcal{I}$ on belief sets such that (1) holds? The answer is no. In general, $\circ_\mathcal{I}$ would not be well defined: It is not hard to find a system $\mathcal{I} \in \mathcal{S}^R$ and two local states s_a and s'_a such that $\text{Bel}(\mathcal{I}, s_a) = \text{Bel}(\mathcal{I}, s'_a)$, but $\text{Bel}(\mathcal{I}, s_a \cdot \psi) \neq \text{Bel}(\mathcal{I}, s'_a \cdot \psi)$. That is, the agent can believe exactly the same propositional formulas at two points in $\mathcal{I}$ and yet revise his beliefs differently at those points. Our framework makes a clear distinction between the agents' belief state and his local state, which we can identify with his epistemic state. In any $S \in \mathcal{S}^R$, the agent's belief set does not determine how the agent's beliefs will be revised; his local state does.

We could put further restrictions on $\mathcal{S}^R$ to obtain only systems in which the agent's belief state determines how his beliefs are revised. That is, we could consider only systems $\mathcal{I}$, where $\text{Bel}(\mathcal{I}, s_a \cdot \varphi) = \text{Bel}(\mathcal{I}, s'_a \cdot \varphi)$ whenever $\text{Bel}(\mathcal{I}, s_a) = \text{Bel}(\mathcal{I}, s'_a)$. If we restrict to such systems, we can obtain a converse to Theorem 4.1, but this seems to us the wrong way to go. We believe it is inappropriate to equate belief sets with epistemic states in general. For example, the agent's local state determines his plausibility ordering, but his belief set does not. Yet surely how an agent revises his beliefs is an important part of his epistemic state.

We believe that there are two more appropriate ways to deal with this problem. The first is to modify the AGM postulates to deal with epistemic states, not belief sets. The second is to enrich the language to allow richer belief sets. We deal with these one at a time.

We can easily modify the AGM postulates to deal with epistemic states. We now assume that we start with a space of abstract epistemic states, $\circ$ maps an epistemic state and a formula to a new epistemic state, and Bel maps epistemic states to belief sets. We then have analogues to each of the AGM postulates, obtained by replacing each belief set by the beliefs of the corresponding epistemic state. For example, we have:

(R1') $E \circ \varphi$ is an epistemic state

(R2') $\varphi \in \text{Bel}(E \circ \varphi)$

(R3') $\text{Bel}(E \circ \varphi) \subseteq Cl(\text{Bel}(E) \cup \{\varphi\})$

and so on, with the obvious transformation.[7]

There is a clear correspondence between systems in our framework and belief revision functions that use abstract epistemic states. Using this correspondence we show that $\mathcal{S}^R$ captures belief revision according to R1'–R8':

Theorem 4.2: $\mathcal{I} \in \mathcal{S}^R$ *if and only if the corresponding belief revision function satisfies R1'–R8'.*

As we said earlier, there is a second approach to dealing with this problem: extending the language. We defer discussion of this approach to Section 6.

Our representation brings out several issues. The revision literature usually does not address the relations between the agent's beliefs and the "real" world. (This point is explicitly discussed in [Gär88, pp 18–20].) In fact, revision does not assume any correlation between what the agent learns and the state of the world. For example, revision allows the agent to learn (revise by) φ and then learn $\neg\varphi$. Moreover, after learning φ the agent may consider worlds where $\neg\varphi$ is true as quite plausible (although he will not consider them to be the most plausible worlds). In this case, most observations that are not consistent with his beliefs will lead him to believe $\neg\varphi$. These examples are two aspects of a bigger problem: The AGM postulates put very weak restrictions on the ordering that the agent has after a revision step (see [Bou93, DP94]). Essentialy, the only requirement is that after learning φ, the most plausible worlds must be ones where φ is true. While this is an important and reasonable constraint on how beliefs should change, it does not capture all our intuitions regarding how beliefs change in many applications. We believe that by introducing more structure it should be possible to derive reasonable constraints that will make revision a more useful tool.

5 UPDATE

The notion of update originated in the database community [KW85, Win88]. The problem is how a knowledge base should change when something is learned about world, such as "A table was moved from office 1 to office 2". Katsuno and Mendelzon [KM91a] suggest a set of postulates that any update operator should satisfy.

The update postulates are expressed in terms of formulas, not belief sets. This is not unreasonable, since we can identify a formula φ with the belief set $Cl(\varphi)$. Indeed, if Φ is finite (which is what Katsuno and Mendelzon assume) every belief set A can be associated with some formula φ_A such that $Cl(\varphi) = A$; we denote this formula $desc(A)$.

(U1) $\vdash_\mathcal{L} \varphi \diamond \mu \Rightarrow \mu$

(U2) If $\vdash_\mathcal{L} \varphi \Rightarrow \mu$, then $\vdash_\mathcal{L} \varphi \diamond \mu \Leftrightarrow \varphi$

(U3) $\vdash_\mathcal{L} \neg\varphi \diamond \mu$ if and only if $\vdash_\mathcal{L} \neg\varphi$ or $\vdash_\mathcal{L} \neg\mu$

(U4) If $\vdash_\mathcal{L} \varphi_1 \Leftrightarrow \varphi_2$ and $\vdash_\mathcal{L} \mu_1 \Leftrightarrow \mu_2$ then $\vdash_\mathcal{L} \varphi_1 \diamond \mu_1 \Leftrightarrow \varphi_2 \diamond \mu_2$

(U5) $\vdash_\mathcal{L} (\varphi \diamond \mu) \wedge \theta \Rightarrow \varphi \diamond (\mu \wedge \theta)$

(U6) If $\vdash_\mathcal{L} \varphi \diamond \mu_1 \Rightarrow \mu_2$ and $\vdash_\mathcal{L} \varphi \diamond \mu_2 \Rightarrow \mu_1$, then $\vdash_\mathcal{L} \varphi \diamond \mu_1 \Leftrightarrow \varphi \diamond \mu_2$

(U7) If φ is complete then $\vdash_\mathcal{L} (\varphi \diamond \mu_1) \wedge (\varphi \diamond \mu_2) \Rightarrow \varphi \diamond (\mu_1 \vee \mu_2)$[8]

(U8) $\vdash_\mathcal{L} (\varphi_1 \vee \varphi_2) \diamond \mu \Leftrightarrow (\varphi_1 \diamond \mu) \vee (\varphi_2 \diamond \mu)$.

Update tries to capture the intuition that there is a preference for runs where all the observations made are true, and where changes from one point to the next along the run are minimized. To capture the notion of "minimal change from world to world", we use a *distance function* d on worlds.[9] Given two worlds w and w', $d(w, w')$ measures the distance between them. Distances might be incomparable, so we require that d maps pairs of worlds into a *partially ordered* domain with a unique minimal element 0 and that $d(w, w') = 0$ if and only if $w = w'$.

We can now describe how update is captured in our framework. The construction is very similar to the one we used for revision. The major difference is in how the preorders are constructed. For our discussion it is enough to consider agents that follow the simple protocol P^* of Section 3. We take $\mathcal{S}^U$, the set of plausibility systems for update, to consist of all systems of the form $(\mathcal{R}(P^*), \pi, \mathcal{P}_d)$, where $\mathcal{P}_d$ is determined by a distance function d in a manner we now describe. Recall that update has a preference for runs where the observations are all true. We say that a point (r, m), is *consistent* if $obs(r, j)$ is true in the world $world(r, j+1)$, for $0 \leq j < m$. We take $\mathcal{P}(r, m) = (\Omega_{(r,m)}, \preceq_{(r,m)})$, where $\Omega_{(r,m)}$ consists of all points that the agent considers possible that are consistent, and $\preceq_{(r,m)}$ is a preorder defined as follows: suppose $(r', m), (r'', m) \in \Omega_{(r,m)}$.[10] Roughly speaking, we prefer (r', m) to (r'', m) if, at the first point where they differ, r' makes the smaller change. Formally, if $n > 0$ is the first point where r' and r'' have different world states (i.e., the first point where $world(r', n) \neq world(r'', n)$) then $(r', m) \prec_{(r,m)} (r'', m)$ if and only if $d(world(r', n-1), world(r', n)) <$

---

[7]The only problematic postulate is R6. The question is whether R6' should be "If $\vdash_\mathcal{L} \varphi \Leftrightarrow \psi$ then $Bel(E \circ \varphi) = Bel(E \circ \psi)$" or "If $\vdash_\mathcal{L} \varphi \Leftrightarrow \psi$ then $E \circ \varphi = E \circ \psi$". Dealing with either version is straightforward. For definiteness, we use the first definition here.

[8]A belief set A is *complete* when for every $\varphi \in \mathcal{L}(\Phi)$ either $\varphi \in A$ or $\neg\varphi \in A$. A formula φ is *complete* if $Cl(\varphi)$ is complete.

[9]Katsuno and Mendelzon identify a "world" with a truth assignment to the primitive propositions. For us, this is just a component of the environment state.

[10]Note that the definition of P^* implies that if $(r, m) \sim_a (r', m')$ then $m = m'$ since the agent's local state encodes the time m by the length of the sequence.

$d(world(r'', n-1), world(r'', n))$. (Note that this definition is independent of (r, m).) Thus, update focuses on the *first* point of difference. The run that makes the smaller change at that point is preferred, even if later it makes quite abnormal changes. This point is emphasized in the example below. However, we first show that $\mathcal{S}^U$ captures all possible update operators.

Theorem 5.1: $\diamond$ *is a KM update operator if and only if there is a system* $\mathcal{I}_\diamond \in \mathcal{S}^U$ *such that for all* $\psi \in \mathcal{L}(\Phi)$, *we have* $desc(Bel(\mathcal{I}_\diamond, s_a)) \diamond \psi \Leftrightarrow desc(Bel(\mathcal{I}_\diamond, s_a \cdot \psi))$.

Notice that for update, unlike revision, the systems we consider are such that the belief state does determine the result of the update, i.e., if $B(\mathcal{I}, s_a) = B(\mathcal{I}, s'_a)$, then for any φ we get that $B(\mathcal{I}, s_a \cdot \varphi) = B(\mathcal{I}, s'_a \cdot \varphi)$.

How reasonable is the notion of update? As the definition of $\preceq_{(r,m)}$ given above suggests, it has a preference for *deferring abnormal events*. This makes it quite similar to Shoham's *chronological ignorance* [Sho88] (a point already noted by del Val and Shoham [dVS92, dVS93]), and it suffers from some of the same problems. Consider the following story, that we call the *borrowed-car example*.[11] (1) The agent leaves his car in a valet parking lot, (2) sits for an hour in a cafe, (3) returns to the car and starts driving home. Since the agent does not observe the car while he is in the cafe, there is no reason for him to revise his beliefs regarding the car's location. Since he finds it in the parking lot at step (3), he still has no reason to change his beliefs. Now, what should he believe when (4) he notices, during his drive, that the car has been driven 50 miles since he left home? The common sense explanation is that the valet took the car out for a joy ride. But update prefers to defer abnormalities, so it will conclude that the mileage must have jumped, for inexplicable reasons, since he left the parking lot. To see this, note that runs where the valet took the car have an abnormality at time (2), while runs where the car did not move at time (2) but the mileage suddenly changed, have their first abnormality at time (4) and thus are preferred! (See Figure 1.)

We emphasize that the counterintuitive conclusion drawn in this example is not an artifact of our representation, but inherent in the definition of update. We can formalize the example using propositions such as *car-in-lot*, *high-mileage*, etc. The observation of *high-mileage* at step (4) must be explained by some means, and an update operator will explain it in terms of a change that occurred in states consistent with the beliefs at step (3) (i.e., *car-in-lot*, $\neg$*high-mileage*). The exact change assumed will depend on the distance function embodied by the update operator. The key point is that update will not go back and revise the earlier beliefs about what happened between steps (1)

---

[11]This example is based on Kautz's stolen car story [Kau86], and is due to Boutilier, who independently observed this problem [private communication, 1993].

and (2).

In an effort to understand the difficulty here, we look at the belief change process more generally. In a world w, the agent has some beliefs that are described by, say, the formula φ. These beliefs may or may not be *correct* (where we say a belief φ is correct in a world w if φ is true of w). Suppose something happens and the world changes to w'. As a result of the agent's observations, he has some new beliefs, described by φ'. Again, there is no reason to believe that φ' is correct. Indeed, it may be quite unreasonable to expect φ' to be correct, even if φ is correct. Consider the borrowed-car example. Suppose that while the agent was sitting in the cafe, the valet did in fact take the car out for a joy ride. Nevertheless, the most reasonable belief for the agent to hold when he observes that the car is still in the parking lot after he leaves the cafe is that it was there all along.

The problem here is that the information the agent obtains at steps (2) and (3) is insufficient to determine what happened. We cannot expect all the agent's beliefs to be correct at this point. On the other hand, if he does obtain sufficient information about the change and his beliefs were initially correct, then it seems reasonable to expect that his new beliefs will be correct. But what counts as *sufficient* information? In the context of update, we can provide a precise formulation.

We say that φ provides *sufficient information* about the change from w to w' if there is no world w'' satisfying φ such that $d(w, w'') < d(w, w')$. In other words, φ is sufficient information if, after observing φ in world w, the agent will consider the real world (w') one of the most likely worlds. Note that this definition is monotonic, in that if φ is sufficient information about the change then so is any formula ψ that implies φ (as long as it holds at w'). Moreover, this definition depends on the agent's distance function d. What constitutes sufficient information for one agent might not for another. We would hope that the function d is realistic in the sense that the worlds judged closest according to d really are the most likely to occur.

We can now show that update has the property that if the agent had correct beliefs and receives sufficient information about a change, then he will continue to have correct beliefs.

Theorem 5.2: *Let* $\mathcal{I} \in \mathcal{S}^U$. *If the agent's beliefs at* (r, m) *are correct and* $obs(r, m)$ *provides sufficient information about the change from* $world(r, m)$ *to* $world(r, m+1)$, *then the agent's beliefs at* $(r, m+1)$ *are correct.*

As we observed earlier, we cannot expect the agent to always have correct beliefs. Nevertheless, it seems reasonable to require that if the agent does (eventually) receive sufficiently detailed information, then he should realize that his beliefs were incorrect. This is

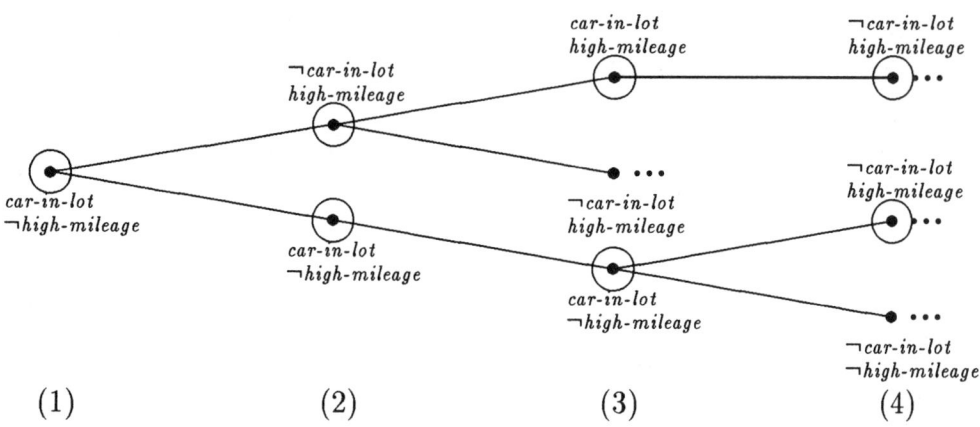

Figure 1: Runs in the borrowed car example. Lower branches are considered more likely than higher ones. The circles mark points that are consistent with the agent's observations at each time step.

precisely what does *not* happen in the borrowed-car example. Intuitively, once the agent observes that the car was driven 50 miles, this should be sufficient information to eliminate the possibility that the car remained in the parking lot. Roughly speaking, because update focuses only on the current state of the world, it cannot go back and revise beliefs about the past.

How can we capture the intuition of a sequence of observations providing sufficient information about the changes that have occurred? Here it is most convenient to take full advantage of our framework with runs. Intuitively, we say that a sequence of observations provides sufficient information about the changes that occurred if, after observing the sequence, the agent will consider as most plausible runs where the real changes occurred. More precisely, we say that a sequence of observations $\varphi_1, \ldots, \varphi_n$ *provides sufficient information about the sequence of changes* $w_0, \ldots, w_n$ if for any run r such that $world(r, i) = w_i$ and $obs(r, i-1) = \varphi_i$ for $i = 1, \ldots, n$, there does not exist a run r' such that $(r, n) \sim_a (r', n)$ and $(r', n) \preceq_{(r,n)} (r, n)$. This definition is a natural generalization of the definition of sufficient information about a single change. We would like to state a theorem similar to Theorem 5.2, i.e., that if the agent has correct beliefs at (r, m) and receives sufficient information about the changes from (r, m) to $(r, m+n)$, then the agent's beliefs at $(r, m+n)$ are correct. However, the problem with update is that once the agent has incorrect beliefs, *no* sequence of observations can ever provide him with sufficient information about the changes that have occurred. More precisely, once the agent has incorrect beliefs, no sequence can satisfy the technical requirements we describe. This is in contrast to our intuition that some sequences (as in the example above) should provide sufficient information about the changes. Note, that this result does not imply that once the agent has incorrect beliefs then he continues to have incorrect beliefs. It is possible that he regains correctness after several observation (for example if the agent is told the exact state of the world). However, it is always possible to construct examples (like the one above) where the agent receives sufficient information about the changes in the rest of the run, and yet has incorrect beliefs in the rest of the run.

Our discussion of update shows that update is guaranteed to be safe only in situations where there is always enough information to characterize the change that has occurred. While this may be a plausible assumption in database applications, it seems somewhat less reasonable in AI examples, particularly cases involving reasoning about action.[12] In Section 7, we discuss how update might be modified to take this observation into account.

6 SYNTHESIS

In previous sections we analyzed belief revision and belief update separately. We provided representation theorems for both notions and discussed issues that are specific to each notion. In this section we try to identify some common themes and points of difference.

Some of the work has already been done for us by Katsuno and Mendelzon [KM91a], who identified three significant differences between revision and update:

1. Revision deals with static propositions, while update allows propositions that are not static. As we noted in the introduction this difference is in the types of propositions that these notions deal with, rather than a difference in the type of situations

---

[12]Similar observations were independently made by Boutilier [Bou94], although his representation is quite different than ours.

that they deal with.

2. Revision and update treat inconsistent belief states differently. Revision allows the agent to "recover" from an inconsistent state after observing a consistent formula. Update dictates that once the agent has inconsistent beliefs, he will continue to have inconsistent beliefs.

3. Revision considers only total preorders, while update allows partial preorders.

How significant are these differences? While the restriction to static propositions may seem to be a serious limitation of belief revision, notice that we can always convert a dynamic proposition to a static one by adding "time-stamps". That is, we can replace a proposition p by a family of propositions p^m that stand for "p is true at time m". Thus, it is possible to use revision to reason about a changing world. (Of course, it would then be necessary to capture connections between propositions of the form p^m, but specific revision operators could certainly do this.)

As far as the other differences go, we can get a better understanding of them, and of the relationship between revision and update, if we return to the general belief change systems described in Section 3 and use a language that allows us to explicitly reason about the belief change process. Although this involves a somewhat extended exposition, we hope the reader will agree that the payoff is worthwhile.

The language we consider for reasoning about the belief change process is called $\mathcal{L}^>(\Phi)$. It uses two modal operators, a binary modal operator $>$ to capture belief change and a unary modal operator B that captures belief, just as before. The formula $\varphi > \psi$ is a *Ramsey conditional*. It is intended to capture the *Ramsey test*: we want $\varphi > \psi$ to hold if ψ holds in the agent's epistemic state after he learns φ.

Formally, we take $\mathcal{L}^>(\Phi)$ be the least set of formulas such that if $\varphi \in \mathcal{L}(\Phi)$ and $\psi, \psi' \in \mathcal{L}^>(\Phi)$ then $B\varphi$, $B\psi$, $\neg \psi$, $\psi \wedge \psi'$, and $\varphi > \psi$ are in $\mathcal{L}^>(\Phi)$. All formulas in $\mathcal{L}^>(\Phi)$ are *subjective*, that is, their truth is determined by the agent's epistemic state. In particular, this means that $\mathcal{L}(\Phi)$ is not a sublanguage of $\mathcal{L}^>(\Phi)$. For example, the primitive proposition p is not in $\mathcal{L}^>(\Phi)$ (although Bp is). Since formulas in $\mathcal{L}^>(\Phi)$ are subjective, this means that all formulas on the right-hand side of $>$ are subjective. This seems reasonable, since we intend these formulas to represent the beliefs of the agent after learning. On the other hand, notice that the only formulas that can appear on the left-hand side of $>$ are formulas in $\mathcal{L}(\Phi)$. This is because only formulas in $\mathcal{L}(\Phi)$ can be learned.[13]

We give formulas in $\mathcal{L}^>(\Phi)$ semantics in interpreted plausibility systems. The semantics for $B\varphi$ is just as

[13] This type of a right-nested language is also considered, for similar reasons, in [Bou93, EG93].

it was before, so all we need to do is define the semantics for $\varphi > \psi$. Notice that since each formula in $\mathcal{L}^>(\Phi)$ is subjective, its truth depends just on the agent's epistemic state. We can give the following natural definition for conditionals with respect to epistemic states, based on our desire to have them satisfy the Ramsey test.

$$(\mathcal{I}, s_a) \models \varphi > \psi \text{ if } (\mathcal{I}, s_a \cdot \varphi) \models \psi.$$

As expected, we then define $(\mathcal{I}, r, m) \models \varphi > \psi$ if and only if $(\mathcal{I}, r_a(m)) \models \varphi > \psi$.

The language $\mathcal{L}^>(\Phi)$ is actually a fragment of $\mathcal{L}^{KPT}(\Phi)$. As the following lemma shows, we can express Ramsey conditionals by using the modal operators for time and knowledge.

Lemma 6.1: *Let $\mathcal{I}$ be a belief change system, let $\varphi \in \mathcal{L}(\Phi)$ and let $\psi \in \mathcal{L}^>(\Phi)$. Then*

$$(\mathcal{I}, r, m) \models \varphi > \psi \Leftrightarrow K(learn(\varphi) \Rightarrow \bigcirc \psi).$$

Despite Lemma 6.1, there is a good reason to consider $\mathcal{L}^>(\Phi)$ rather than $\mathcal{L}^{KPT}(\Phi)$. As we now show, it is the "right" language for capturing the belief change process. Suppose we consider belief sets over the language $\mathcal{L}^>(\Phi)$ rather than $\mathcal{L}(\Phi)$. In analogy to our definition of Bel, define $Bel^>(\mathcal{I}, s_a) = \{\varphi \in \mathcal{L}^>(\Phi) \mid (\mathcal{I}, s_a) \models \varphi\}$.[14] However, this lead to technical We define an *extended belief set* to be any set of the form $Bel^>(\mathcal{I}, s_a)$. The following lemma shows the extended belief set captures exactly the epistemic state of the agent with regard to belief change.

Lemma 6.2: *If $\mathcal{I}, \mathcal{I}'$ are belief change systems, then $Bel^>(\mathcal{I}, s_a) = Bel^>(\mathcal{I}', s'_a)$ if and only if for every sequence $\varphi_1, \ldots, \varphi_n$ it is the case that*

$$Bel(\mathcal{I}, s_a \cdot \varphi_1 \cdot \ldots \cdot \varphi_n) = Bel(\mathcal{I}', s'_a \cdot \varphi_1 \cdot \ldots \cdot \varphi_n).$$

This implies that if two states have the same extended belief set, then they cannot be distinguished by the belief change process.

We can now define the obvious belief change operation on extended belief sets in terms of the Ramsey test:

$$E \cdot \varphi =_{\text{def}} \{\psi \mid \varphi > \psi \in E\}, \qquad (2)$$

for an extended belief sets E. Thus, $\cdot$ maps an extended belief set and a formula to an extended belief set. We have deliberately used the same notation here as for the mapping $\cdot$ ¿From local states and formulas to local states. The following lemma shows that these two mappings are related in the expected way:

[14] We might have defined $Bel^>(\mathcal{I}, s_a)$ as $\{\varphi \in \mathcal{L}^>(\Phi) \mid (\mathcal{I}, s_a) \models B\varphi\}$, which would have been even more in the spirit of our definition of $Bel(\mathcal{I}, s_a)$. This definition agrees with our definition except when $(\mathcal{I}, s_a) \models B(false)$. In this case, our definition does not put all formulas of the form $\varphi > \psi$ into the belief set, which seems to us the more appropriate behavior.

Lemma 6.3: *If $\mathcal{I}$ be a belief change system and $\varphi \in \mathcal{L}(\Phi)$, then $Bel^{>}(\mathcal{I}, s_a \cdot \varphi) = Bel^{>}(\mathcal{I}, s_a) \cdot \varphi$.*

Although the proof of this result is easy, it has important implications. It shows that we have a well-defined notion of belief change on extended belief sets. Thus, it can be viewed as another way of solving the problem raised in Section 4. If we consider systems in $\mathcal{S}^R$, then extended belief sets, unlike belief sets, uniquely determine the outcome of revision.

Our notion of extended belief sets is similar to a notion introduced by Gärdenfors [Gär78, Gär86, Gär88]. He also considers revision of belief sets that contain conditionals of the form $\varphi > \psi$. However, he attempts to apply the AGM revision postulates to these sets (and then obtains his well known triviality result), while we define revision of extended belief sets directly in terms of the Ramsey test. Of course, our notion of belief revision does not satisfy the AGM postulates (although it does when restricted to $\mathcal{L}(\Phi)$). Indeed, we cannot expect it to, given Gärdenfors' triviality result. As we argued in the introduction, this should not be viewed as a defect. We do not want persistence (i.e., R4) to hold for formulas such as Ramsey conditionals whose truth depends on the current state of the agent. Indeed, as we argue in the full paper, other postulates, such as R8, should also not hold for conditional beliefs.

Once we adopt the Ramsey test we can in fact discard postulates R1–R8 altogether, and simply define revision using Eq. (2). That is, we shift the focus from finding a set of postulates for belief revision, as done by previous researchers [AGM85, Gär88, Bou92, Fuh89, Rot89], to that of finding a logical characterization of revision in terms of the properties of $>$.

In [FH94a], it is shown that this general approach of characterizing belief change in terms of characterizing the behavior of the $>$ operator in a class of plausibility structures is relevant for all reasonable notions of belief change, not just belief revision. In particular, this is the case for belief update. The results of [FH94a] enable us to completely characterize the differences between revision and update axiomatically. There is an axiom that holds for revision (and not for update) that captures the fact that revision focuses on total preorders, there is an axiom that holds for update (and not for revision) that captures the intuition that update works "pointwise", and there is an axiom for update that must be weakened slightly for revision because revision can recover from inconsistencies. We refer the reader to [FH94a] for further details.

Thinking in terms of $>$ helps us see connections between revision and update beyond those captured in our axioms. For one thing, it helps us make precise the intuition that both revision and update are characterized by the plausibility ordering at each state. In an arbitrary belief change system, there need be no connections between an agent's beliefs before and after observing a formula φ. We say that the belief change at a point (r, m) in a belief change system is *compatible with the plausibility ordering* if for any $\varphi, \psi \in \mathcal{L}(\Phi)$, we have $(\mathcal{I}, r, m) \models \varphi > B\psi$ if and only if $(\mathcal{I}, r, m) \models \bigcirc\varphi \rightarrow \bigcirc\psi$. That is, the agent believes ψ after learning φ exactly when ψ is true at the next time step in all the most plausible situations in which φ is true at the next time step. The next theorem shows that belief change is compatible with the plausibility ordering in both systems for revision and update (except that in revision, belief change is not compatible with the agent's plausibility ordering at states where the agent's beliefs are inconsistent; this is due to the fact that an agent with inconsistent beliefs may have consistent beliefs again after revision).

Theorem 6.4: *If $\mathcal{I} \in \mathcal{S}^R$ then belief change is compatible with the plausibility ordering at every point (r, m) such that $(\mathcal{I}, r, m) \not\models B(false)$. If $\mathcal{I} \in \mathcal{S}^U$ then belief change is compatible with the plausibility ordering at every point.*

We note that since propositions do not change their values in $\mathcal{S}^R$ we get the following corollary.

Corollary 6.5: *Let $\mathcal{I} \in \mathcal{S}^R$, let $\varphi, \psi \in \mathcal{L}(\Phi)$, and let (r, m) be a point in $\mathcal{I}$ such that $(\mathcal{I}, r, m) \not\models B(false)$. Then $(\mathcal{I}, r, m) \models (\varphi > B\psi) \Leftrightarrow (\varphi \rightarrow \psi)$.*

Consistency provides some connection between $\rightarrow$ and $>$. For example, as this corollary shows, in revision systems they are essentially identical for depth-one formulas. In general, however, they are different. For example, it is not hard to show that $p > (true > Bq)$ is not equivalent to $p \rightarrow (true \rightarrow q)$ in revision systems. Indeed, as noted above while revision guarantees minimal change in propositional (or base) beliefs, it does not put any such restrictions on changes in the ordering at each epistemic state. Thus, there is no necessary connection between $\rightarrow$ and iterated instances of $>$.[15] In our representation of update, on the other hand, we can make such a connection. Indeed, in $\mathcal{S}^U$, $\rightarrow$ completely captures the behavior of $>$.

Lemma 6.6: *Let $\mathcal{I} \in \mathcal{S}^U$. For all sequences of formulas $\varphi_1, \ldots, \varphi_n \in \mathcal{L}(\Phi)$ and all $\psi \in \mathcal{L}(\Phi)$, $(\mathcal{I}, r, m) \models (\varphi_1 > \cdots > \varphi_n > B\psi) \Leftrightarrow ((\bigcirc\varphi_1 \wedge \cdots \wedge \bigcirc^n \varphi_n) \rightarrow \bigcirc^n \psi)$.*

This result can be explained by the fact that in update systems, the plausibility ordering at $s_a \cdot \varphi$ is determined by the plausibility ordering at s_a. More precisely, after learning φ, $\Omega_{(r,m+1)} = \{(r, m+1) | (r, m) \in \Omega_{(r,m)}, (r, m) \models learn(\varphi) \wedge \bigcirc\varphi\}$, and $(r', m+1) \preceq_{(r,m+1)} (r'', m+1)$ if and only if $(r', m) \preceq_{(r,m)} (r'', m)$. (In the terminology of [FH94b], this means that the plausibility space $(r, m+1)$ can be

---
[15] Thus, we use $>$ rather than $\rightarrow$ for belief revision, contrary to the suggestion implicit in [Bou92].

understood as the result of conditioning on the plausibility space at (r, m).)

These results, and those of [FH94a], support the thesis that this language, which lets us reason about plausibility (and thus belief), belief change, time, and knowledge, is the right one with which to study belief change.

7 CONCLUSION

We believe that our framework, with its natural representation of both time and belief, gives us a great deal of insight into belief revision and belief update. Of course, revision and update are but two points in a wide spectrum of possible types of belief change. Our ultimate goal is to use this framework to understand the whole spectrum better and to help us design belief change operations that overcome some of the difficulties we have observed with revision and update. In particular, we want belief change operations that can handle dynamic propositions, while still being able to revise information about the past.

One approach to doing this, much in the spirit of update, would be to use a distance function that relates not just worlds, but sequences of worlds (of the same length). We could then easily modify the definition of update so as to handle the borrowed-car problem correctly. Such a modification, however, comes at a cost. It is much simpler to represent (and do computations with) a distance function that applies to worlds than to sequences of worlds. A natural question to ask is whether we can get away with a simpler distance function (that, perhaps, considers only certain features of the sequence of worlds, rather than the sequence itself). Of course, the answer to this will depend in part on how we make "get away with" precise.

Whether or not this particular approach turns out to be a useful one, it is clear that these are the types of questions we should be asking. We hope that our framework will provide a useful basis for answering them.

Finally, we note that our approach is quite different from the traditional approach to belief change [AGM85, Gär88, KM91a]. Traditionally, belief change was considered as an abstract process. Our framework, on the other hand, models the agent and the environment he is situated in, and how both change in time. This allows us to model concrete agents in concrete settings (for example, diagnostic systems are analyzed in [FH94b]), and to reason about the beliefs and knowledge of such agents. We can then investigate what plausibility ordering induces beliefs that match our intuitions. By gaining a better understanding of such concrete situations, we can better investigate more abstract notions of belief change.

Acknowledgements

The authors are grateful to Craig Boutilier, Ronen Brafman, Adnan Darwiche, Moises Goldszmidt, Adam Grove, Phil Hubbard Alberto Mendelzon, Alvaro del Val, and particularly Daphne Koller and Moshe Vardi, for comments on drafts of this paper and useful discussions relating to this work.

References

[AGM85] C. E. Alchourrón, P. Gärdenfors, and D. Makinson. On the logic of theory change: partial meet functions for contraction and revision. *Journal of Symbolic Logic*, 50:510–530, 1985.

[Bou92] C. Boutilier. Normative, subjective and autoepistemic defaults: Adopting the Ramsey test. In *Principles of Knowledge Representation and Reasoning: Proc. Third International Conference (KR '92)*. 1992.

[Bou93] C. Boutilier. Revision sequences and nested conditionals. In *Proc. Thirteenth International Joint Conference on Artificial Intelligence (IJCAI '93)*, pages 519–525, 1993.

[Bou94] C. Boutilier. An event-based abductive model of update. In *Proc. Tenth Biennial Canadian Conference on Artificial Intelligence (AI '94)*, 1994.

[Bur81] J. Burgess. Quick completeness proofs for some logics of conditionals. *Notre Dame Journal of Formal Logic*, 22:76–84, 1981.

[DP94] A. Darwiche and J. Pearl. On the logic of iterated belief revision. In R. Fagin, editor, *Theoretical Aspects of Reasoning about Knowledge: Proc. Fifth Conference*, pages 5–23. 1994.

[dVS92] A. del Val and Y. Shoham. Deriving properties of belief update from theories of action. In *Proc. National Conference on Artificial Intelligence (AAAI '92)*, pages 584–589, 1992.

[dVS93] A. del Val and Y. Shoham. Deriving properties of belief update from theories of action (II). In *Proc. Thirteenth International Joint Conference on Artificial Intelligence (IJCAI '93)*, pages 732–737, 1993.

[dVS94] A. del Val and Y. Shoham. A unified view of belief revision and update. *Journal of Logic and Computation*, Special issue on Actions and Processes, to appear, 1994.

[EG93] T. Eiter and Gottlob G. The complexity of nested counterfactuals and iterated knowledge base revisions. In *Proc. Thirteenth*

International Joint Conference on Artificial Intelligence (IJCAI '93), pages 526–531, 1993.

[FH94a] N. Friedman and J. Y. Halpern. Conditional logics of belief change. Technical report, 1994. Submitted to AAAI-94.

[FH94b] N. Friedman and J. Y. Halpern. A knowledge-based framework for belief change. Part I: Foundations. In R. Fagin, editor, *Theoretical Aspects of Reasoning about Knowledge: Proc. Fifth Conference*, pages 44–64. 1994.

[FHMV94] R. Fagin, J. Y. Halpern, Y. Moses, and M. Y. Vardi. *Reasoning about Knowledge*. MIT Press, to appear, 1994.

[Fuh89] A. Fuhrmann. Reflective modalities and theory change. *Synthese*, 81:115–134, 1989.

[Gär78] P. Gärdenfors. Conditionals and changes of belief. *Acta Philosophica Fennica*, 20, 1978.

[Gär86] P. Gärdenfors. Belief revision and the Ramsey test for conditionals. *Philosophical Review*, 91:81–93, 1986.

[Gär88] P. Gärdenfors. *Knowledge in Flux*. Cambridge University Press, 1988.

[GM88] P. Gärdenfors and D. Makinson. Revisions of knowledge systems using epistemic entrenchment. In M. Y. Vardi, editor, *Proc. Second Conference on Theoretical Aspects of Reasoning about Knowledge*, pages 83–95. 1988.

[GMR92] G. Grahne, A. Mendelzon, and R. Rieter. On the semantics of belief revision systems. In Y. Moses, editor, *Theoretical Aspects of Reasoning about Knowledge: Proc. Fourth Conference*, pages 132–142. 1992.

[GP92] M. Goldszmidt and J. Pearl. Rank-based systems: A simple approach to belief revision, belief update and reasoning about evidence and actions. In R. Parikh, editor, *Principles of Knowledge Representation and Reasoning: Proc. Third International Conference (KR '92)*, pages 661–672. 1992.

[Gro88] A. Grove. Two modelings for theory change. *Journal of Philosophical Logic*, 17:157–170, 1988.

[HF89] J. Y. Halpern and R. Fagin. Modelling knowledge and action in distributed systems. *Distributed Computing*, 3(4):159–179, 1989.

[Kau86] H. A. Kautz. Logic of persistence. In *Proc. National Conference on Artificial Intelligence (AAAI '86)*, pages 401–405, 1986.

[KM91a] H. Katsuno and A. Mendelzon. On the difference between updating a knowledge base and revising it. In *Principles of Knowledge Representation and Reasoning: Proc. Second International Conference (KR '91)*, pages 387–394. 1991.

[KM91b] H. Katsuno and A. Mendelzon. Propositional knowledge base revision and minimal change. *Artificial Intelligence*, 52(3):263–294, 1991.

[KS91] H. Katsuno and K. Satoh. A unified view of consequence relation, belief revision and conditional logic. In *Proc. Twelfth International Joint Conference on Artificial Intelligence (IJCAI '91)*, pages 406–412, 1991.

[KW85] A. M. Keller and M. Winslett. On the use of an extended relational model to handle changing incomplete information. *IEEE Transactions on Software Engineering*, SE-11(7):620–633, 1985.

[Lev88] I. Levi. Iteration of conditionals and the Ramsey test. *Synthese*, 76:49–81, 1988.

[Lew73] D. K. Lewis. *Counterfactuals*. Harvard University Press, 1973.

[LR92] S. Lindström and W. Rabinowicz. Belief revision, epistemic conditionals and the Ramsey test. *Synthese*, 91:195–237, 1992.

[Rij92] M. de Rijke. Meeting some neighbors. Research Report LP-92-10, University of Amsterdam, 1992.

[Rot89] H. Rott. Conditionals and theory change: revision, expansions, and additions. *Synthese*, 81:91–113, 1989.

[Rot91] H. Rott. Two methods of constructing contractions and revisions of knowledge systems. *Journal of Philosophical Logic*, 20:149–173, 1991.

[Sho88] Y. Shoham. Chronological ignorance: experiments in nonmonotonic temporal reasoning. *Artificial Intelligence*, 36:271–331, 1988.

[Win88] M. Winslett. Reasoning about action using a possible models approach. In *Proc. National Conference on Artificial Intelligence (AAAI '88)*, pages 89–93, 1988.

On the Complexity of Conditional Logics

Nir Friedman
Department of Computer Science
Stanford University
Stanford, CA 94305-2140
nir@cs.stanford.edu

Joseph Y. Halpern
IBM Almaden Research Center
650 Harry Road
San Jose, CA 95120-6099
halpern@almaden.ibm.com

Abstract

Conditional logics, introduced by Lewis and Stalnaker, have been utilized in artificial intelligence to capture a broad range of phenomena. In this paper we examine the complexity of several variants discussed in the literature. We show that, in general, deciding satisfiability is PSPACE-complete for formulas with arbitrary conditional nesting and NP-complete for formulas with bounded nesting of conditionals. However, we provide several exceptions to this rule. Of particular note are results showing that (a) when assuming *uniformity* (i.e., that all worlds agree on what worlds are possible), the decision problem becomes EXPTIME-complete even for formulas with bounded nesting, and (b) when assuming *absoluteness* (i.e., that all worlds agree on all conditional statements), the decision problem is NP-complete for formulas with arbitrary nesting.

1 INTRODUCTION

The study of *conditional* statements of the form "If ... then ..." has a long history in philosophy [Sta68, Lew73, Che80, Vel85]. In recent years these logics have been applied in artificial intelligence to capture nonmonotonic inference [Del88, Bel89, KLM90, Bou92], belief change [Gra91, Bou92], counterfactual reasoning [Gin86], qualitative probabilities [Pea89, GP92], and intentions and desires [Pea93, Bou94]. In general, conditional logics provide a logical language to reason about structures that contain some sort of ordering. In this paper we present complexity results for a family of conditional logics introduced by Lewis [Lew73, Lew74]. We also provide an overview of a completeness proof which substantially simplifies previous proofs in the literature [Bur81].

Lewis's construction starts with a set W of *possible worlds*, each one describing a possible way the world might be. We associate with each possible world $w \in W$ a preorder $\preceq_w$ over a subset W_w of W. Intuitively, W_w is the set of worlds considered possible at w. There are a number of differing intuitions for what is being represented by the $\preceq_w$ relation. For example, in *counterfactual* reasoning, $\preceq_w$ is viewed as capturing a measure of distance from w, so that $w' \preceq_w w''$ if w' is more similar or closer to w than w'' is. In this variant it is usually assumed [Lew73] that the real world is closest to itself. In *nonmonotonic* reasoning the $\preceq_w$ relation captures an agent's plausibility ordering on the worlds, so that $w' \preceq w''$ if w' is more plausible than w'' according to the agent's beliefs in w. Typically (although not, for example, in [FH94a]) it is assumed that the agent's beliefs are the same in all the worlds in W, so that $\preceq_w$ is independent of w. The $\preceq_w$ relation is used to give semantics to conditional formulas of the form $\varphi \rightarrow \psi$; such a formula is taken to be true at a world w if all the $\preceq_w$-minimal worlds satisfying φ also satisfy ψ.

As these examples suggest, we can construct a number of different logics, depending on the assumptions we make about $\preceq_w$. In this paper, we focus on the following assumptions (all of which have been considered before [Lew73, Bur81, Gra91, KS91]), which apply to all $w \in W$:[1]

N *Normality*: $W_w \neq \emptyset$.

R *Reflexivity*: $w \in W_w$.

T *Centering*: w is a minimal element in W_w, i.e., for all $w' \in W_w$, we have $w \preceq_w w'$.[2]

U *Uniformity*: W_w is independent of w, i.e., for all $w' \in W_w$, $W_{w'} = W_w$.

A *Absoluteness*: $\preceq_w$ is independent of w, i.e., for all $w' \in W_w$, $W_{w'} = W_w$ and for all $w_1, w_2 \in W_w$,

---

[1]Whenever possible we adopt the naming scheme used by Lewis [Lew73, pp. 120].

[2]Our notion of centering is that used by Lewis [Lew73]. Other authors [KS91, Gra91] assume the stronger condition of *strict centering*, that is w is the only minimal world in $\preceq_w$. Our results for centering apply with minor technical modifications to strict centering.

we have $w_1 \preceq_{w'} w_2$ if and only if $w_1 \preceq_w w_2$.[3]

C *Connectedness*: all worlds in W_w are comparable according to $\preceq_w$; i.e., for all $w_1, w_2 \in W_w$, either $w_1 \preceq_w w_2$ or $w_2 \preceq_w w_1$.

Notice that centering implies reflexivity, which in turn implies normality. Normality is a minimal assumption, typically made in almost all applications of conditional logics. As we mentioned earlier, centering is typically assumed in counterfactual reasoning, while absoluteness is typically assumed in nonmonotonic reasoning. Uniformity is assumed when, for example, the set of possible worlds is taken to be the set of all logically possible worlds (i.e., the set of all truth assignments). Combinations of these conditions are used in the various applications of conditional logics. For example, Boutilier's [Bou92] work in nonmonotonic reasoning assumes absoluteness and considers variants satisfying connectedness; similar assumptions are made in [KLM90, GP92, Bel89]. Works on counterfactuals (such as Grahne's [Gra91]) typically assume centering and uniformity. Katsuno and Satoh [KS91] consider variants satisfying absoluteness, centering and connectedness.

Completeness results have been obtained for the logics corresponding to various combinations of these constraints [Lew73, Lew74, Bur81]. While we do present completeness proofs here, using a proof that is substantially simpler than that of [Bur81], our focus is on complexity-theoretic issues.

Burgess [Bur81] shows that any satisfiable conditional formula is satisfiable in a finite structure. The structures he obtains are of nonelementary size.[4] To obtain our complexity results we prove that if a formula is satisfiable at all, it can be satisfied in a much smaller structure. We start by showing that a formula without nested conditionals is satisfiable if and only if it is satisfiable in a polynomial-sized structure. Applying the construction for formulas without nested conditionals recursively, we show that, in general, a satisfiable formula with bounded nesting depth is satisfiable in a polynomial-sized structure, and an arbitrary satisfiable formula is satisfiable in an exponential-sized structure. In most variants, this structure takes the form of a tree, where each level of the tree corresponds to one level of nesting. We show that checking whether such a tree-like structure exists can be done in polynomial space, without explicitly storing the whole tree in memory. This gives a PSPACE upper bound for the satisfiability problem for most variants of the logic.[5]

Can we do better? In general, no. We show that an appropriate modal logic (either K, D or T depending on the variant in question) can be embedded in most variants of the logic.[6] The result then follows from results of Ladner [Lad77, HM92] on the complexity of satisfiability for these logics. There are exceptions to the PSPACE results. For one thing, it already follows from our "small model" results that for bounded-depth formulas (in particular, depth-one formulas) satisfiability is NP-complete. Moreover, in the presence of absoluteness, every formula is equivalent to one without nesting, so we can again get NP-completeness. Interestingly, the appropriate modal logic in the presence of absoluteness in the lower bound construction mentioned above is S5, whose satisfiability problem is also NP-complete [Lad77]. On the other hand, while the assumption of uniformity seems rather innocuous, and much in the spirit of absoluteness, assuming uniformity without absoluteness leads to an EXPTIME-complete satisfiability problem, even for formulas with bounded nesting.

Our results form an interesting contrast to those of Eiter and Gottlob [EG92, EG93] and Nebel [Neb91] for a framework for *counterfactual* queries defined by Ginsberg [Gin86], using an approach that goes back to Fagin, Ullman, and Vardi [FUV83]. In this framework a conditional query $p > q$ is evaluated by modifying the knowledge base to include p and then checking whether q is entailed. As shown by Nebel [Neb91] and Eiter and Gottlob [EG92], for formulas without nested conditionals, evaluating such a query is Π_2^p-complete.[7] Roughly speaking, the reason for the higher complexity is that once we prove an analogous small model theorem for this more syntactic approach, checking that a formula is entailed by a theory is co-NP hard, while in our case, checking that a formula is satisfied in a small structure can be done in polynomial time. Eiter and Gottlob [EG93] show that if we restrict to right-nested formulas, without negations of nested conditionals, then queries are still Π_2^p complete. Finally, Eiter and Gottlob show that once we move beyond simple right-nesting, the problem becomes PSPACE-hard; the complexity of queries for the full language is not known. In contrast to these results, we show that the language of simple right-nested conditionals is NP-complete, and when negations are allowed, it becomes

---

[3] Lewis [Lew73] distinguishes between a *local* definition of uniformity and absoluteness and a *global* one. We adopt the local one (i.e., "for all $w' \in W_w$ ...", rather than "for all $w' \in W$ ..."), but it is easy to see that all our results, including the axiomatization, also apply to the global definition with essentially no change.

[4] Roughly speaking, a nonelementary function of n is of the form $2^{2^{\cdot^{\cdot^{\cdot}}}}$, where the height of the stack of 2's is on the order of n.

[5] We assume some familiarity with complexity theory, especially with the complexity classes NP, PSPACE, and EXPTIME. See Section 4 for a review of these complexity-theoretic notions.

[6] We assume some familiarity with modal logic, especially the logics K, D and T. See [HM92] for an overview of these logics and their axiomatizations.

[7] Π_2^p is the complexity class that is characterized by decision problems that can be determined in polynomial time given an NP oracle. This class is believed to be harder than NP, but simpler than PSPACE.

PSPACE-complete.

The rest of the paper is organized as follows: In Section 2 we formally define the logical language and its semantics. In Section 3 we prove small model theorems for the different variants. In Section 4 we prove the complexity results. In Section 5 we provide an axiomatization for each of the logics we consider and sketch a completeness proof.

2 CONDITIONAL LOGIC

The syntax of the logic is simple: we start with a set Φ of primitive propositions, and close off under $\wedge$, $\neg$, and $\rightarrow$ (where $\rightarrow$ is the conditional operator). We call the resulting language $\mathcal{L}^C$. We denote by $\mathcal{L}^C_k$ the sublanguage of $\mathcal{L}^C$ with *bounded nesting*, i.e., formulas in $\mathcal{L}^C$ with no more than k level of nested conditionals. For example, $\mathcal{L}^C_0$ contains propositional formulas without any conditional sentences, and $\mathcal{L}^C_1$ contains $p \rightarrow q$ but not $p \rightarrow (q \rightarrow r)$. Of course, we define the propositional connectives $\vee$, $\Rightarrow$ (material implication), and $\Leftrightarrow$ (logical equivalence) in terms of $\wedge$ and $\neg$ in the standard way.

We use the semantic representation suggested by Lewis to capture conditionals [Lew73, Bur81]: A *structure* M is a tuple (W, π, R), such that W is a set of *possible worlds*, π maps each possible world to a truth assignment over Φ, and R is a ternary relation over W. We think of the possible worlds as different ways the world could be, or the different situations we might be in. The relation R is a preorder on worlds: $(w, u, v) \in R$ if u is as close/preferred/plausible as v when the real world is w. We use the notation $u \preceq_w v$ to denote that $(w, u, v) \in R$. We define $W_w = \{u \mid u \preceq_w v \in R \text{ for some } v \in W\}$; thus, the worlds in W_w are those that are at least as plausible as some world in W according to $\preceq_w$. We require that $\preceq_w$ be a preorder, i.e., a reflexive and transitive relation, on W_w. As usual, we define $u \prec_w v$ if $u \preceq_w v$ and not $v \preceq_w u$.

We now provide semantics for formulas in $\mathcal{L}^C$. The truth of a propositional formula in a world w is determined by the truth assignment $\pi(w)$. The truth of a conditional formula is determined by the ordering $\preceq_w$. The intuition is that $\varphi \rightarrow \psi$ holds at w if all the minimal (e.g., closest, most plausible) φ-worlds satisfy ψ (where a φ-world, of course, is a world where φ is true). Unfortunately, if W is infinite, it may not have minimal φ-worlds. Thus, the actual definition we use, which is standard in the literature (see [Lew73, Bur81, Bou92]), is more complicated. Roughly speaking, $\varphi \rightarrow \psi$ is true if, from a certain point on, whenever φ is true, so is ψ. More precisely, $\varphi \rightarrow \psi$ is true at w if for every φ-world u in W_w, there is another world v such that (a) v is at least as plausible as u, (b) v satisfies $\varphi \wedge \psi$, and (c) each φ-world that is at least as plausible as v is also

a ψ-world. It is easy to see that if W_w is finite, then this is equivalent to saying that the minimal φ-worlds in W_w satisfy ψ.

Formally, we define the truth of $\varphi \in \mathcal{L}^C$ at a world w in a structure $M = (W, \pi, R)$ recursively:

- $(M, w) \models p$, when $p \in \Phi$, if $\pi(w)(p) = \textbf{true}$.
- $(M, w) \models \varphi \wedge \psi$ if $(M, w) \models \varphi$ and $(M, w) \models \psi$.
- $(M, w) \models \neg \varphi$ if it is not the case that $(M, w) \models \varphi$.
- $(M, w) \models \varphi \rightarrow \psi$ if for any world $u \in W_w$, if $(M, u) \models \varphi$ then there is a world v, such that $v \preceq_w u$ and $(M, v) \models \varphi \wedge \psi$ and there is no $v' \preceq_w v$ such that $(M, v') \models \varphi \wedge \neg \psi$.

We say that φ is *valid in M* (resp., *satisfiable in M*) if $(M, w) \models \varphi$ for all worlds w (resp., some world w) in M.

We define the set of all possible structures as $\mathcal{M}$. For each combination of the constraints defined in the introduction, we define the corresponding class of structures satisfying them. For example, $\mathcal{M}^{N,T,U}$ is the class of all structures satisfying normality, centering and uniformity. For $\mathcal{A} \subseteq \{N, R, T, A, U, C\}$, we say that a formula φ is *valid* with respect to $\mathcal{M}^\mathcal{A}$, written $\mathcal{M}^\mathcal{A} \models \varphi$, if φ is valid in every structure $M \in \mathcal{M}^\mathcal{A}$. Similarly, we say that φ is satisfiable in $\mathcal{M}^\mathcal{A}$ if it is satisfiable in some structure $M \in \mathcal{M}^\mathcal{A}$.

3 SMALL MODEL THEOREMS

In this section we provide small model theorems for the logics we examine, showing that if a formula φ is satisfiable, than it is satisfiable in a structure of bounded size. These results play a crucial role in our complexity considerations.

We start with some definitions. Given a formula $\varphi \in \mathcal{L}^C$, we define $Sub(\varphi)$ to be the set of all subformulas of φ and $Sub^+(\varphi) = Sub(\varphi) \cup \{\neg \psi \mid \psi \in Sub(\varphi)\}$. Finally, let $Sub_C(\varphi)$ consist of all formulas in $Sub(\varphi)$ of the form $\varphi \rightarrow \psi$. It is easy to verify that $|Sub(\varphi)|$ (the number of formulas in $Sub(\varphi)$) is at most $|\varphi|$ (the length of φ, viewed as a string of symbols).

We begin by examining formulas without nested conditionals. The first case is when φ is a conjunction of a number of (non-negated) conditional statements and one negated conditional statement. This case will serve as a basis for the general case.

Lemma 3.1: *Let $\varphi = \neg(\psi_0 \rightarrow \psi'_0) \wedge \bigwedge_{i=1}^{k}(\psi_i \rightarrow \psi'_i)$ where $\psi_i, \psi'_i \in \mathcal{L}^C_0$. If φ is satisfiable in $\mathcal{M}$, then φ is satisfiable in a structure in $\mathcal{M}$ with at most $k+1$ worlds which are totally ordered by $\preceq$.*

Proof: Assume we are given $M \in \mathcal{M}$ and w such that $(M, w) \models \varphi$. From the results of [Bur81], it follows that, without loss of generality, we can assume that M

is finite (i.e., that M has only finitely many worlds). Since $(M, w) \models \neg(\psi_0 \to \psi_0')$, there is a a world w_0 such that w_0 is a minimal ψ_0-world in $\preceq_w$ and satisfies $\neg\psi_0'$. Let $\leq$ be a total order over W_w that is compatible with $\preceq_w$, in that if $w_1 \prec_w w_2$ then $w_1 < w_2$, such that $w_0 < w'$ for any $w' \neq w_0$ satisfying ψ_0. (Since $\leq$ is a total order, if $w_1 \neq w_2$, then either $w_1 < w_2$ or $w_2 < w_1$.) Let w_i be the minimal ψ_i-world in W_w according to $\leq$, if there is a ψ_i-world in W_w, and w_0 otherwise.

We now construct a new structure $M' = (W', \pi', R')$. Let $W' = \{w_0, \ldots, w_k\}$, let π' be the restriction of π to W', and let R' be such that for all $w' \in W'$, we have $W'_{w'} = W'$ and $w_i \preceq'_{w'} w_j$ if and only if $w_i \leq w_j$. It is easy to verify that $(M', w') \models \varphi$ for all $w' \in W'$, since if w_i is the minimal ψ_i-world according to $\leq$, then by the construction of $\leq$, it must be a minimal ψ_i-world in M according to $\preceq_{w'}$ and thus must also satisfy ψ_i', while w_0 is the minimal ψ_0-world and thus $(M', w') \models \neg(\psi_0 \to \psi_0')$. ∎

We now use this construction to prove that any formula without nesting is satisfiable if and only if it is satisfiable in a polynomial structure.

Proposition 3.2: *Let $\varphi \in \mathcal{L}_1^C$. If φ is satisfiable in $\mathcal{M}$, then φ is satisfiable in a structure in $\mathcal{M}$ with at most $O(|\text{Sub}_C(\varphi)|^2)$ worlds.*

Proof: Suppose that $M \in \mathcal{M}$ and that $(M, w) \models \varphi$. Again, by Burgess's result, we can assume without loss of generality that M is finite. Our goal is to construct a small structure M' such that for each formula $\psi \in Sub(\varphi)$, we have $(M, w) \models \psi$ if and only if $(M', w) \models \psi$. It clearly suffices to do this for the primitive propositions and the formulas in $Sub_C(\varphi)$. We cannot use the construction of the previous lemma directly, because we may now have to deal with more than one negated conditional. For example, if $(M, w) \models \neg(p \to q) \wedge \neg(p \to \neg q)$, the structure M' we construct must have a minimal p-world satisfying q and a minimal p-world satisfying $\neg q$. This cannot be done by using one total order, as was done in the previous lemma.

We solve the problem by considering the union of several total orders, one for each negated conditional. Let $Neg = \{\psi \to \xi \in Sub_C(\varphi) : (M, w) \models \neg(\psi \to \xi)\}$ and let $Pos = \{\psi \to \xi \in Sub_C(\varphi) : (M, w) \models \psi \to \xi\}$. Suppose $Neg = \{\psi_1^n \to \xi_1^n, \ldots, \psi_k^n \to \xi_k^n\}$. From Lemma 3.1, it follows that for each formula $\psi_i^n \to \xi_i^n \in Neg$, we can construct a structure M_i whose set of worlds W_i has size at most $|Sub_C(\varphi)|$, such that M_i satisfies $\neg(\psi_i^n \to \xi_i^n)$ and all the formulas in Pos. This gives us $|Neg|$ structures, one for each formula in Neg. Without loss of generality, we can assume that the sets W_i are disjoint and do not contain w. The structure we are interested in is essentially the disjoint union of the structures M_i. More precisely, we take $M' = (W', \pi', R')$, where W' is the union of the sets W_i for $1 \leq i \leq |Neg|$, together with w. We define π' to be such that for each world in $w' \in W'$, the truth assignment $\pi'(w')$ is the same as the truth assignment in the structure that w' was drawn from. Finally, we define R' so that for all $w' \in W'$, we have $W'_{w'} = W' - \{w\}$, and $\preceq'_{w'}$ is the union of the orderings in the structure $M_{\psi \in \psi'}$. (We have defined $\preceq'_{w'} = \preceq_w$ for all $w' \in W'$, but this was not necessary. Since we are dealing with depth-one nesting here, all that matters in the proof is the definition of $\preceq_w$. We can redefine $\preceq'_{w'}$ for $w' \neq w$ arbitrarily, without changing the truth value of any formula in $\mathcal{L}_1^C$ at w.) A straightforward induction on the structure of formulas shows that for each formula $\psi \in Sub(\varphi)$, we have $(M, w) \models \psi$ if and only if $(M', w) \models \psi$. In particular, because negated conditionals have an existential nature (i.e., $\neg(p \to q)$ holds if there is a minimal p world satisfying $\neg q$), each negated conditional in Neg is satisfied at (M', w) because it is satisfied in one of the total orders. On the other hand, the conditionals in Pos hold at (M', w) since they hold in each of the total orders. ∎

With minor changes the same construction applies to all the variants we consider.

Corollary 3.3: *Let $\varphi \in \mathcal{L}_1^C$ and let $\mathcal{A}$ be a subset of $\{N, T, U, A, R, C\}$. If φ is satisfiable in $\mathcal{M}^\mathcal{A}$, then φ is satisfiable in a structure in $\mathcal{M}^\mathcal{A}$ with at most $O(|\text{Sub}_C(\varphi)|^2)$ worlds.*

Proof: Suppose $M \in \mathcal{M}^\mathcal{A}$ and $(M, w) \models \varphi$. We now build a structure of the appropriate size satisfying φ. If $\mathcal{A} \subseteq \{U, A\}$, then we can just use the construction of Proposition 3.2, since the structure M' constructed in that proof already satisfies absoluteness (and thus uniformity). If $C \notin \mathcal{A}$, then we can easily modify M' so that it also satisfies whichever of N, T, or R is in $\mathcal{A}$. For example, if $N \in \mathcal{A}$, then M satisfies normality, so W_w is nonempty and we can choose a minimal world in W_w and add it to W'_w as one of the minimal worlds. If $T \in \mathcal{A}$, then we can always choose w as the world to add. If $R \in \mathcal{A}$ but $T \notin \mathcal{A}$, we add w as a maximal world in W'_w.

If $C \in \mathcal{A}$, then we use a different construction. For each formula $\psi \to \psi' \in Sub_C(\varphi)$,

- if $(M, w) \models \psi \to \psi'$, then let $w_{\psi \to \psi'}$ be a minimal ψ-world in W_w if there are ψ-worlds in W_w; otherwise take $w_{\psi \to \psi'}$ to be w.

- if $(M, w) \models \neg(\psi \to \psi')$, then let $w_{\psi \to \psi'}$ be a minimal ψ-world in W_w that satisfies $\neg \psi'$. (There must be such a world since $(M, w) \models \neg(\psi \to \psi')$.)

Let $W' = \{w\} \cup \{w_{\psi \to \psi'} : \psi \to \psi' \in Sub_C(\varphi)\}$, and let $M' = (W', \pi', R')$, where π' is the restriction of π to W' and R' is the restriction of R to W'. By construction, M' has at most $|Sub_C(\varphi)| + 1$ worlds. We leave it to the reader to check that $(M', w) \models \varphi$. This simple construction depends on the properties of connected preorders. In particular, we need the property that any minimal φ-world is strictly more plausible than *all* the non-minimal φ-worlds. This is not true in the general case. ∎

What happens with formulas that have nested conditionals? It turns out that the answer depends on whether we assume absoluteness and/or uniformity. We first consider the situation where we assume absoluteness. The key observation here is that if we assume absoluteness, since the ordering is the same at all worlds, we can get rid of nested conditionals. For example, in structures satisfying absoluteness, the formula $r \rightarrow (q \rightarrow p))$ is equivalent to $((q \rightarrow p) \land (r \rightarrow true)) \lor (\neg(q \rightarrow p) \land (p \rightarrow false))$. In general, the denested formula may be of length exponential in the original formula, but it can be rewritten as a disjunction of formulas each of which does not have too many new conditional subformulas. And since we need to construct a structure satisfying only one of these disjuncts, we conclude that a small structure suffices. More precisely, we have:

Proposition 3.4: *Let $\mathcal{A}$ be a subset of $\{N, T, U, R, C\}$. Given a formula $\varphi \in \mathcal{L}^C$, there are formulas $\varphi_1, \ldots, \varphi_k \in \mathcal{L}_1^C$ such that $\mathcal{M}^{\{A\} \cup \mathcal{A}} \models \varphi \Leftrightarrow \bigvee_{i=1}^{k} \varphi_i$. Moreover, for $i = 1, \ldots, k$, we have $|\text{Sub}_C(\varphi_i)| \leq 5|\text{Sub}_C(\varphi)|$.*

From Proposition 3.4 and Corollary 3.3, we immediately get:

Corollary 3.5: *Let $\mathcal{A}$ be a subset of $\{N, T, U, R, C\}$. If $\varphi \in \mathcal{L}^C$ is satisfiable in $\mathcal{M}^{\{A\} \cup \mathcal{A}}$, then φ is satisfiable in a structure in $\mathcal{M}^{\{A\} \cup \mathcal{A}}$ with at most $O(|\text{Sub}_C(\varphi)|^2)$ worlds.*

In structures that do not satisfy absoluteness, we can still extend the ideas of Proposition 3.2 recursively to get polynomial-sized structures for formulas of bounded-depth nesting, where the polynomial depends on the depth of nesting *provided we do not also assume uniformity*.

Proposition 3.6: *Let $\varphi \in \mathcal{L}_k^C$ and let $\mathcal{A}$ be a subset of $\{N, T, R, C\}$. If φ is satisfiable in $\mathcal{M}^{\mathcal{A}}$, then φ is satisfiable in a structure in $\mathcal{M}^{\mathcal{A}}$ with at most $O(|\text{Sub}(\varphi)|^{2k})$ worlds.*

Proof: We apply the construction of Proposition 3.2 recursively. Roughly speaking, at the top level of the recursion, we treat all nested conditionals as new primitive propositions. Applying the construction of Proposition 3.2 we get the set W'_w. For each $w' \in W'_w$, let $\varphi_{w'}$ be the conjunction of all the propositions (including the nested conditionals) that hold at w'. We note that $\text{Sub}_C(\varphi_{w'}) \subseteq \text{Sub}_C(\varphi)$. We now apply the procedure recursively to w' and $\varphi_{w'}$ to construct $W'_{w'}$.

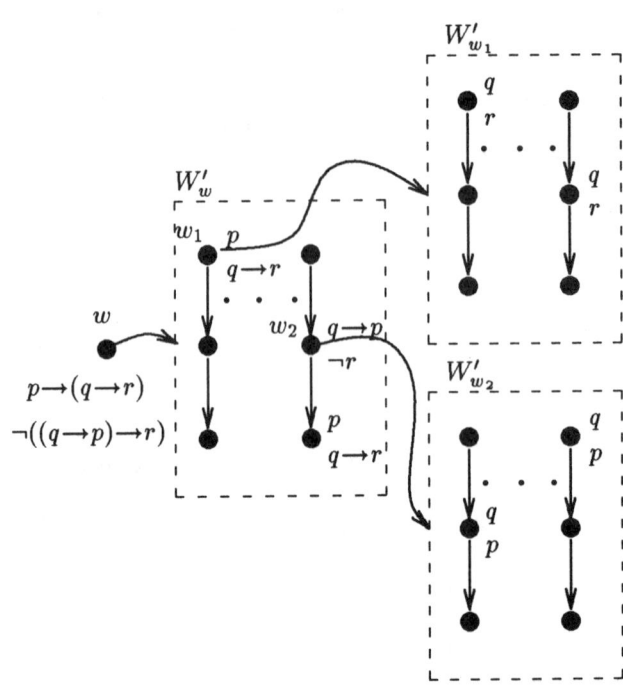

Figure 1: The structure for Proposition 3.6.

We proceed in this manner, constructing a tree-like structure (as shown in Figure 1), dealing with conditionals nested i deep at the ith level of the recursion. Thus, we can stop at the kth level. Note that for w', w'' in the structure, $W'_{w'}$ is disjoint from $W'_{w''}$ if $w' \neq w''$. Thus, this structure does not satisfy uniformity.

We now give a formal description of the construction. We define $Basic_i(\varphi) \subseteq \Phi \cup Sub_C(\varphi)$ as the set of primitive propositions and conditional statements that are subformulas of φ and appear inside exactly i levels of conditional nesting. For example, if φ is $(p \rightarrow (q \rightarrow r)) \land \neg((r \rightarrow q) \rightarrow r)$, then $Basic_0(\varphi) = \{p \rightarrow (q \rightarrow r), (r \rightarrow q) \rightarrow r\}$, $Basic_1(\varphi) = \{p, q \rightarrow r, r \rightarrow q, r\}$ and $Basic_2(\varphi) = \{q, r\}$. We treat formulas in $Basic_{i+1}(\varphi)$ as primitive propositions during the construction of the orderings at level i.

We construct the tree-like structure in the following fashion. The procedure gets as input a structure M, a world w, and a formula φ such that $(M, w) \models \varphi$, and returns a structure M' such that $(M', w) \models \varphi$. Moreover, M' contains at most $O(|Sub_C(\varphi)|^{2k})$ worlds, where k is the depth of nesting in φ. If φ is propositional then the structure M' consists of the single worlds w. If φ contains conditional formulas, then we construct a tree with w as the root. The truth value of any primitive proposition $p \in Basic_0(\varphi)$ is determined at w by π. Thus, we only need to satisfy conditional formulas in $Basic_0(\varphi)$. We apply the procedure described in the proof of Proposition 3.2, treating every formula in $Basic_1(\varphi)$ as a primitive proposition. We get a structure M^w of size $O(|Sub_C(\varphi)|^2)$, such that π^w maps each world $w' \in W_w^w$ to a truth assignment over $Basic_1(\varphi)$. Recall that the construction of M^w is such that each $w' \in W_w^w$ corresponds to a world $f(w')$ in W_w. Moreover, for all $\psi \in Basic_1(\varphi)$, $pi^w(w')(\psi) =$ **true** if and only $(M, f(w')) \models \psi$.

For each $w' \in W_w'$ we define $\varphi_{w'}$ so that it describes the truth value of all formulas in $Basic_1(\varphi)$ at w'. However, since we want to capture conditionals holding in w', we have to be careful; we use the corresponding world $f(w)$ in M to evaluate these conditionals. Formally, $\varphi_{w'}$ is defined as $\bigwedge_{\psi \in Basic_1(\varphi),\ (M,f(w'))\models\psi} \psi \wedge \bigwedge_{\psi \in Basic_1(\varphi),\ (M,f(w'))\models\neg\psi} \neg\psi$. We note that $Sub_C(\varphi_{w'}) \subseteq Sub_C(\varphi)$, $Basic_i(\varphi_{w'}) \subseteq Basic_{i+1}(\varphi)$, and that $\varphi_{w'}$ contains at most $k-1$ levels of conditional nesting. We now recursively apply the tree construction procedure on $(M, f(w'))$ and $\varphi_{w'}$ and get a structure $M^{w'}$ such that $(M^{w'}, w') \models \varphi_{w'}$.

We now construct M'. Let W' contain w and all the worlds in $M^{w'}$ for all $w' \in W_w^w$. Without loss of generality we can assume that the sets of worlds in $M^{w'}$ are disjoint and do not contain w. We define π' to be such that for each world $w' \in W'$, the truth assignment $\pi'(w')$ is the same as the truth assignment in the structure w' is taken from. Finally, we define $\preceq_w$ according to the construction of M^w, and $\preceq_{w'}$ for all $w' \in W' - \{w\}$ to be the same as the ordering $\preceq_{w'}$ in the structure w' is taken from.

It is easy to see that this recursive procedure is well-defined. At i level of recursion the depth of the formula is at most $k - i$, and thus the procedure must terminate. It is also easy to verify, by induction, that $(M', w') \models \varphi$. Finally, we show that the structure M' is not too large. The size of M' is $O(|Sub_C(\varphi)|^2 \cdot |M^{w'}|)$. According to the recursive construction, $|M^{w'}| = O(|Sub_C(\varphi)|^{2(k-1)})$. Thus, the size of M' is $O(|Sub_C(\varphi)|^{2k})$.

The procedure we described constructs structures in $\mathcal{M}$. If $\mathcal{A}$ is not empty we have to modify M' to satisfy the constraints in $\mathcal{A}$. This is done locally at each world in the manner described in the proof of Corollary 3.3. ∎

What happens if we have no bound on the nesting depth? In this case we can get an exponential-sized structure. The result without uniformity follows immediately from Proposition 3.6, since the depth of nesting in a formula φ is clearly bounded by $|\varphi|$. With uniformity, we have to work a little harder; we leave details to the full paper.

Proposition 3.7: *Suppose $\varphi \in \mathcal{L}_k^C$ and $\mathcal{A}$ is a subset of $\{N, T, R, C, U\}$. If φ is satisfiable in $\mathcal{M}^\mathcal{A}$, then φ is satisfiable in a structure in $\mathcal{M}^\mathcal{A}$ with at most* $O(2^{2|Sub_C(\varphi)|})$ *worlds.*

The natural question to ask is whether this the best we can guarantee. The answer is yes. Since the technique for proving this, which depends on the observation that we can embed various modal logics into conditional logic, is also useful for proving lower bounds on complexity, we go into a little detail here.

Let $\mathcal{L}^K$ be the language with a single modal operator K (which intuitively stands for knowledge). As usual, we capture the semantics of knowledge in terms of an accessibility relation, on which we can place various restrictions. Thus, an *epistemic structure* N has the form $(W, \pi, \mathcal{K})$, where W is a set of worlds, π maps each possible world to a truth assignment, and $\mathcal{K}$ is a binary relation. We define $\models$ in the standard way; in particular,

- $(N, w) \models K\varphi$ if $(N, w') \models \varphi$ for all w' such that $(w, w') \in \mathcal{K}$.

Let $\mathcal{N}$ be the class of all epistemic structures. We add superscripts r, s, t, and e, respectively, to denote restrictions on the $\mathcal{K}$ relation to reflexive, serial, transitive, and Euclidean relations, respectively.[8] For each subset $\mathcal{B}$ of $\{r, s, t, e\}$, we let $\mathcal{N}^\mathcal{B}$ denote the class of epistemic structures where the $\mathcal{K}$ relation satisfies the appropriate restrictions.

We can also define modal operators in the context of conditional logic. Let $\Box\varphi$ be an abbreviation for $true \rightarrow \varphi$, and let $\boxdot\varphi$ be an abbreviation for $(\neg\varphi) \rightarrow false$. It is easy to verify that $\Box\varphi$ holds at w exactly if all the minimal worlds according to $\preceq_w$ satisfy φ and that $\boxdot\varphi$ holds at w if all worlds in W_w satisfy φ. Traditionally [Lew73], $\Box$ has been called the *inner* modality and $\boxdot$ has been called the *outer* modality.

As we now show, the inner modality $\Box$ corresponds in a precise sense to K. Under this correspondence, conditions on $\preceq_w$ correspond to conditions on the binary relation $\mathcal{K}$. In particular, conditions N and R both correspond to $\mathcal{K}$ being serial, T corresponds to $\mathcal{K}$ being reflexive, and A corresponds to $\mathcal{K}$ being both transitive and Euclidean. This intuition is made precise by the theorem below.

Proposition 3.8: *Given a formula $\varphi \in \mathcal{L}^K$, let φ^* be the result of replacing each K operator by $\Box$. Let $\mathcal{A}$ be a (possibly empty) subset of $\{N, R, T, A\}$, and let $\mathcal{B}$ be the corresponding subset of $\{e, r, s, t\}$, where s corresponds to N and R, r corresponds to T, and both e and t correspond to A. Finally, let $\mathcal{A}'$ be a subset of $\{C\}$. Then φ is satisfiable in $\mathcal{N}^\mathcal{B}$ in a structure of size k if and only if φ^* is satisfiable in $\mathcal{M}^{\mathcal{A} \cup \mathcal{A}'}$ in a structure of size k.*

---

[8] $\mathcal{K}$ is *serial* if for all w, there exists some w' such that $(w, w') \in \mathcal{K}$; $\mathcal{K}$ is Euclidean if for all u, v, w, if $(u, v) \in \mathcal{K}$ and $(u, w) \in \mathcal{K}$, then $(v, w) \in \mathcal{K}$.

Proof: We show how to map epistemic structures satisfying φ to structures satisfying φ^* and vice versa.

Recall that $\Box \psi$ holds at w exactly when ψ is true in all the minimal worlds in W_w. Assume $(M, w) \models \varphi^*$ for $M = (W, \pi, R)$. Let $N = (W, \pi, \mathcal{K})$ such that $(w_1, w_2) \in \mathcal{K}$ if w_2 is minimal in W_{w_1}. It is easy to check that $(N, w) \models \varphi$. Moreover, if M satisfies normality or reflexivity, then for every w_1 there is at least one minimal w_2, and thus $\mathcal{K}$ is serial. If M satisfies centering, then w_1 is minimal in W_{w_1}, and thus $\mathcal{K}$ is reflexive. If M satisfies absoluteness, then if $w_2 \in W_{w_1}$, then $\preceq_{w_2}$ is the same as $\preceq_{w_1}$. This implies that if $(w_1, w_2) \in \mathcal{K}$ and $(w_2, w_3) \in \mathcal{K}$ then $(w_1, w_3) \in \mathcal{K}$ since w_3 must be minimal in W_{w_1}. Similarly, if $(w_1, w_2), (w_1, w_3) \in \mathcal{K}$ then (w_2, w_3) is also in $\mathcal{K}$. Thus, $\mathcal{K}$ is transitive and Euclidean.

Now assume $(N, w) \models \varphi$ for $N = (W, \pi, \mathcal{K})$. We construct a structure $M = (W, \pi, R)$, where R is such that for each world w, the set W_w consists of all worlds accessible from w according to $\mathcal{K}$, and each of these worlds is equally plausible. This ensures that the minimal worlds according to $\preceq_w$ are precisely the worlds accessible from w, and guarantees that $(N, w) \models K\varphi$ if and only if $(M, w) \models \Box\varphi$. Moreover, if $\mathcal{K}$ is serial, then $W_w \neq \emptyset$ for all w, and thus M satisfies reflexivity (and normality). If $\mathcal{K}$ is reflexive, then w is accessible from w. Thus, $w \in W_w$ in M, and hence minimal (since all worlds in W_w are minimal). Finally, if $\mathcal{K}$ is both transitive and Euclidean, then then it is well known (see [HM92]) that we can assume without loss of generality that the same set of worlds is accessible from each $w \in W$. This implies that the ordering at each world is the same. Thus, M satisfies absoluteness. ∎

In the presence of uniformity we can get similar results. However the reduction is less natural. Since such a reduction does not play a role in our treatment of structures satisfying uniformity, we omit the details here.

Halpern and Moses [HM92] describe formulas in $\mathcal{L}^K$ that can be satisfied only in exponential-sized structures in $\mathcal{N}$, $\mathcal{N}^r$, and $\mathcal{N}^e$. (However, they can be satisfied in polynomial-sized structures in $\mathcal{N}^{et}$.) They also show that once *common knowledge* is added to the language, then there are formulas that have depth of nesting two and can be satisfied only in exponential-sized structures in $\mathcal{N}$, $\mathcal{N}^r$, and $\mathcal{N}^e$. It turns out that the outer modality behaves very much like common knowledge in the presence of uniformity. More precisely, the statement $C\varphi$ ("it is common knowledge that φ") holds exactly when every world that is accessible through repeated applications of K satisfies φ. Similarly, $\Box\varphi$ holds at w when all worlds in W_w satisfy φ. If we assume uniformity, then $\Box\varphi$ implies that all worlds that are accessible by arbitrary level of conditional nesting must satisfy ψ. This is close enough to common knowledge to get the behavior needed for constructing a proof similar to their construction for common knowledge.

When we do not require uniformity, we immediately get the following from the results of Halpern and Moses and Proposition 3.8:

Corollary 3.9: *Let $\mathcal{A}$ be a subset of $\{N, R, T, C\}$. Then for each n, there is a formula $\varphi_n^{\mathcal{A}}$ of size $O(n^2)$ such that $\varphi_n^{\mathcal{A}}$ that is satisfiable in $\mathcal{M}^{\mathcal{A}}$, but only in structures of size at least 2^n.*

When we require uniformity we have to work a bit harder. We can modify the construction Halpern and Moses use for common knowledge to get the following result; we leave the details for the full paper.

Proposition 3.10: *Let $\mathcal{A}$ be a subset of $\{N, R, T, C\}$. Then for each n, there is a formula $\varphi_n^{\mathcal{A}}$ of size $O(n^2)$ and using only depth-two nesting of conditionals such that $\varphi_n^{\mathcal{A}}$ that is satisfiable in $\mathcal{M}^{\mathcal{A} \cup \{U\}}$, but only in structures of size at least 2^n.*

4 COMPLEXITY RESULTS

In this section we examine the inherent difficulty of deciding whether a formula is satisfiable. Checking validity is closely related since φ is valid if and only if $\neg \varphi$ is not satisfiable. We start with an overview of the complexity-theoretic notions we need. For a more detailed treatment of the topic, see [GJ79, HU79].

Complexity theory examines the difficulty of determining membership in a set as a function of the input size. In our case we check if a formula φ is in the set of satisfiable formulas. Difficulty is measured in terms of the time or space required to decide if a formula φ is satisfiable as a function of $|\varphi|$, the length of the formula. The complexity classes we are interested in are NP, PSPACE, and EXPTIME. These classes contain sets such that deciding membership can be done in non-deterministic polynomial time, polynomial space, and exponential time, respectively.

To show that a set is in a complexity class we usually describe a procedure that determine membership in the set and conforms to the time or space restriction of the class. Usually, we also want to show that a set is not in an easier class. To do we show that the set is *hard* in the class. A set A is hard in a class $\mathcal{C}$ if for every set $B \in \mathcal{C}$, an algorithm deciding membership in B can be easily obtained from an algorithm deciding membership in A. A set is *complete* with respect to a complexity class $\mathcal{C}$ if it is both in $\mathcal{C}$ and $\mathcal{C}$-hard.

We now turn to the complexity results. These results are summarized in Table 1 (where each problem is complete for the complexity class listed). For most classes of structures of interest to us, deciding satisfiability is NP-complete for $\mathcal{L}_k^C$ and PSPACE-complete

Table 1: The complexity of the satisfiability problem for $\mathcal{M}^{\mathcal{A}}$.

	$A \in \mathcal{A}$	$A, U \notin \mathcal{A}$	$U \in \mathcal{A}, A \notin \mathcal{A}$
$\mathcal{L}_1^C$	NP	NP	NP
$\mathcal{L}_k^C$	NP	NP	EXPTIME
$\mathcal{L}^C$	NP	PSPACE	EXPTIME

$\mathcal{L}^C$. However, there are several exceptions to this rule: absoluteness makes the problem easier and uniformity makes it harder. Notice that all the other semantic variants do not affect the complexity.

All the logical variants we examine contain the propositional calculus and thus checking satisfiability is NP-hard. For the variants with polynomial-sized structures we see that deciding satisfiability is in NP: We simply nondeterministically choose a structure and then verify that it satisfies the formula. The verification step is easily shown to be in polynomial time, provided the structure is polynomial-sized. Using Proposition 3.2, Corollaries 3.3 and 3.5, and Proposition 3.6 we get the following theorem:

Theorem 4.1: *Let $\mathcal{A}$ be a subset of $\{N, R, T, U, A, C\}$. Then the following problems are NP-complete:*

(a) *the problem of deciding whether a formula in $\mathcal{L}_1^C$ is satisfiable in $\mathcal{M}^{\mathcal{A}}$,*

(b) *the problem of deciding whether a formula in $\mathcal{L}^C$ is satisfiable in $\mathcal{M}^{\mathcal{A}}$, if $\mathcal{A}$ contains A,*

(c) *for a fixed $k > 0$, the problem of deciding whether a formula in $\mathcal{L}_k^C$ is satisfiable in $\mathcal{M}^{\mathcal{A}}$, if $\mathcal{A}$ does not contain U.*

We now turn to the harder cases. As we showed in Corollary 3.9 and Proposition 3.10, in all the remaining variants there are formulas that are satisfiable only in exponential-sized structures. We show that most of these variants, except the ones satisfying uniformity, are PSPACE-complete.

Theorem 4.2: *If $\mathcal{A}$ is a subset of $\{N, T, R, C\}$, the problem of deciding if a formula in $\mathcal{L}^C$ is satisfiable in $\mathcal{M}^{\mathcal{A}}$ is PSPACE-complete.*

Proof: The lower bound is an immediate corollary of Proposition 3.8 and the fact (proved by Ladner [Lad77, HM92]) that checking whether a formula in $\mathcal{L}^K$ is satisfiable in $\mathcal{N}$ (resp., $\mathcal{N}^r$, $\mathcal{N}^e$) is PSPACE-hard.

For the upper bound we use the construction in Proposition 3.7. We describe a polynomial space algorithm that essentially searches through all the tree-like structures of the form described in the proof of Proposition 3.7. In order to simplify the description of this algorithm we rely on the fact that NPSPACE (nondeterministic polynomial space) is equivalent to PSPACE [HU79]. Thus, we describe an algorithm that uses nondeterministic choices and polynomial space.

The algorithm **check-tree** is given a world w and formula φ and returns *true* if there is a tree-like structure containing w such that $w \models \varphi$.

check-tree(w, φ)
  Guess a truth assignment at w to propositions in Φ
  If $\varphi \in \mathcal{L}_0^C$, then
    Let $W_w = \emptyset$
  Else,
    Let $n = |Sub_C(\varphi)|$
    Let $W_w = \{w_{1,1}, \ldots, w_{1,n}, \ldots, w_{n,n}\}$
    Let $w_{i,j} \preceq_w w_{i,k}$ exactly if $j \leq k$
    For each $w_{i,j}$,
      Guess $T_{i,j} \subseteq Basic_1(\varphi)$
      Let $\varphi_{w_{i,j}} = \bigwedge_{\psi \in T_{i,j}} \psi \wedge \bigwedge_{\psi \in Basic_1(\varphi) - T_{i,j}} \neg \psi$
      If **check-tree**$(w_{i,j}, \varphi_{w_{i,j}}) = false$, then
        return *false*.
  Return the evaluation of φ at w (using the ordering $\preceq_w$ and assuming $\varphi_{w_{i,j}}$ is true at $w_{i,j}$).
end.

This algorithm emulates the construction that we used in the proof of Proposition 3.6. It guesses a structure and then checks that φ evaluates to *true* in this structure. It starts by guessing a truth assignment at w. If φ contains conditionals, then the algorithm guesses a structure that contains $|Sub_C(\varphi)|^2$ worlds and defines an ordering $\preceq_w$ over these worlds which is a disjoint union of $|Sub_C(\varphi)|$ total orders. It then guesses a truth assignment in each of these $|Sub_C(\varphi)|^2$ worlds to the formulas in $Basic_1(\varphi)$. According to the proof of Proposition 3.2, if φ is satisfiable (when we consider formulas in $Basic_1(\varphi)$ as propositions), it must be satisfiable in such as structure. The algorithm then verifies that the formulas assigned to each $w_{i,j}$ can be satisfied using a recursive call. Finally, the algorithm verifies that φ evaluates to true at w according to the truth assignment at w and W_w (using $T_{i,j}$ to evaluate formulas at each $w_{i,j} \in W_w$).

We note that the space requirements of the algorithm are the space requirements of all the instances that are active at once. The maximal number of active instances is exactly the recursion depth, i.e., the conditional nesting depth in φ. The space requirements in each instance are $O(|Sub(\varphi)|^3)$ for storing the sets $T_{i,j}$. Thus, the space requirements for **check-tree**(φ, w) are $O(|\varphi|^4)$. ∎

The remaining cases are those satisfying uniformity but not absoluteness. Somewhat surprisingly, these variants are harder than all the others. Roughly speaking, this is because in the presence of uniformity, the outer modality essentially allows us to express common knowledge.

Theorem 4.3: *If $\mathcal{A}$ is a subset of $\{N, T, R, C\}$, the problem of deciding if a formula in $\mathcal{L}^C$ is satisfiable in $\mathcal{M}^{\mathcal{A} \cup \{U\}}$ is EXPTIME-complete.*

Proof: The lower bound is constructed in a similar manner to the lower bound for logics of knowledge and common knowledge of Halpern and Moses [HM92]. The basic idea is that we can simulate the execution of an alternating polynomial-space Turing machine by a sentence φ in $\mathcal{L}^C$, such that φ is satisfiable if only if the machine accepts the input, and φ is of polynomial size.[9] We leave the details of this construction to the full paper.

We prove the upper bound by modifying the algorithm **check-tree** we described in the proof of Theorem 4.2. The basic idea is straightforward: We try to modify the tree-like structure M constructed by **check-tree** to a structure M' over the same set of worlds that satisfies uniformity. The idea is to modify the preference relation so that at each world w, the set W'_w of worlds considered possible consists of all worlds in the tree except the root, and defining $\preceq'_w$ so that the minimal worlds in W'_w are exactly those in W_w. This modification guarantees that if $(M, w) \models \neg(\psi \rightarrow \psi')$ then $(M', w) \models \neg(\psi \rightarrow \psi')$. Since there is a minimal ψ-world in W_w that satisfies $\neg \psi'$, the same world is also a minimal ψ-world in W'_w. Moreover, if $(M, w) \models \psi \rightarrow \psi'$ and there are some ψ-worlds in W_w, then $(M', w) \models \varphi \rightarrow \psi'$ for the same reasons. Unfortunately, this approach runs into problems if there are no ψ-worlds in W_w, so that $\psi \rightarrow \psi'$ holds vacuously at world w in structure M. In that case, if there are some ψ-worlds in W'_w (which is possible), then the conditional $\psi \rightarrow \psi'$ may not be true at (M', w).

To avoid this problem we can decide in advance which conditionals in $Sub_C(\varphi)$ will be satisfied vacuously in M. We initially nondeterministically choose a subset V of $Sub_C(\varphi)$. We then modify **check-tree** so that it searches structures where the only conditionals that hold vacuously are those in V. The modified **check-tree** ensures that no world satisfies ψ for each formula $\psi \rightarrow \psi' \in V$. One side-effect of this change is that we may get new conditionals at each level of recursion, so the algorithm may not terminate. We avoid this by using the fact that there are only an exponential number of formulas of the form $\varphi_{w_{i,j}}$ that can be given as an argument to **check-tree**. We leave details to the full paper. Note that the modified **check-tree** is no longer guaranteed to be in PSPACE. In the full paper we show that it is guaranteed to be in EXPTIME. ■

---

[9]The class of sets recognizable by alternating polynomial-space Turing machines is equal to EXPTIME [CKS81].

4.1 RIGHT-NESTED FORMULAS

As mentioned in the introduction, a similar approach to conditional logic is the framework of counterfactual queries of [FUV83, Gin86]. Eiter and Gottlob [EG93] show that the complexity of evaluating a query of the form $p_1 > (p_2 > \ldots (p_n > q) \ldots)$ is Π_2^p-complete, and the complexity of queries that allow negation on the right-hand side is PSPACE-complete. Since right-nested conditionals also appear in the conditional logic literature [Bou93, FH94b], it seems worth understanding if right-nesting simplifies things here too.

We now define the language $\mathcal{L}_s^C$ of simple right-nested conditionals and the language $\mathcal{L}_r^C$ of (possibly negated) right-nested conditionals. Let $\mathcal{L}_s^C$ be the least language such that if $\varphi, \varphi' \in \mathcal{L}_s^C$ and $\psi, \psi_1, \ldots, \psi_n \in \mathcal{L}_0^C$ ($n \geq 0$), then $\varphi \wedge \varphi'$, $\neg \varphi$, and $\psi_1 \rightarrow \cdots \rightarrow \psi_n \rightarrow \psi$ are in $\mathcal{L}_s^C$. Let $\mathcal{L}_r^C$ be the minimal language such that if $\varphi, \varphi' \in \mathcal{L}_r^C$ and $\psi \in \mathcal{L}_0^C$ then $\psi, \varphi \wedge \varphi'$, $\neg \varphi$, $\psi \rightarrow \varphi$ are in $\mathcal{L}_r^C$. Thus $p \rightarrow q \rightarrow r$ is in both languages, and $p \rightarrow \neg(q \rightarrow r)$ is in $\mathcal{L}_r^C$ but not in $\mathcal{L}_s^C$.

Things are considerably simpler for $\mathcal{L}_s^C$. It is easy to show that the satisfiability problem for $\mathcal{L}_s^C$ is NP-complete for all variants of the logic:

Theorem 4.4: *Let $\mathcal{A}$ be a subset of $\{N, R, T, U, A, C\}$. Then the problem of deciding whether a formula in $\mathcal{L}_s^C$ is satisfiable is NP-complete.*

Proof: Using techniques similar to these of Proposition 3.2, it is easy to show that a formula in $\mathcal{L}_s^C$ is satisfiable if and only if it is satisfiable in a linear-size structure. Thus we get the NP upper bound. The NP-hardness is a result of the fact that $\mathcal{L}_s^C$ contains the propositional calculus. ■

Things get more complicated when we consider the language $\mathcal{L}_r^C$. In many cases this fragment is already as complex as the full language. Recall that the PSPACE lower bound in Theorem 4.2 is proved by a reduction from modal logic. This reduction substitutes the $\Box$ modality for the modal operator K. However $\Box \varphi$ is defined as $true \rightarrow \varphi$. Thus, the reduction maps a modal formula into a formula in $\mathcal{L}_r^C$. (Because modal formulas may be negated, the resulting formula may not be in $\mathcal{L}_s^C$.) Thus, we get the following corollary:

Corollary 4.5: *If $\mathcal{A}$ is a subset of $\{N, T, R, C\}$, the problem of deciding if a formula in $\mathcal{L}_r^C$ is satisfiable in $\mathcal{M}^{\mathcal{A}}$ is PSPACE-complete.*

However, when we consider structures that satisfy uniformity, the satisfiability problem for formulas in $\mathcal{L}_r^C$ is easier than satisfiability of formulas in the full language.

Theorem 4.6: *If $\mathcal{A}$ is a subset of $\{N, T, R, C\}$, the problem of deciding if a formula in $\mathcal{L}_r^C$ is satisfiable in $\mathcal{M}^{\mathcal{A} \cup \{U\}}$ is PSPACE-complete.*

5 AXIOMATIZATION

Several axiom systems for variants of conditional logics appear in the literature [Lew73, Lew74, Che80, Bur81, Bel89, Gra91, KS91]. We present an axiom system for all the variants we introduced based on Burgess's [Bur81] axiomatization. In the full paper, we provide a full completeness proof based on Burgess's techniques, but substantially simpler.

The basic axiom system, AX, contains the following axiom schemata:

A0 All the propositional tautologies
A1 $\varphi \rightarrow \varphi$
A2 $((\varphi \rightarrow \psi_1) \wedge (\varphi \rightarrow \psi_2)) \Rightarrow (\varphi \rightarrow (\psi_1 \wedge \psi_2))$
A3 $(\varphi \rightarrow (\psi_1 \wedge \psi_2)) \Rightarrow (\varphi \rightarrow \psi_1)$
A4 $((\varphi_1 \rightarrow \varphi_2) \wedge (\varphi_1 \rightarrow \psi)) \Rightarrow ((\varphi_1 \wedge \varphi_2) \rightarrow \psi)$
A5 $((\varphi_1 \rightarrow \psi) \wedge (\varphi_2 \rightarrow \psi)) \Rightarrow ((\varphi_1 \vee \varphi_2) \rightarrow \psi)$

and the following inference rules:

MP From φ and $\varphi \Rightarrow \psi$ infer ψ.
RPE From $\varphi_1 \Leftrightarrow \varphi_2$ and ψ infer ψ', where ψ' differs from ψ only by replacing some subformulas of φ of the form φ_1 by φ_2.

The completeness proof works as follows. Given φ and an extension AX′ of AX, we consider all the *maximal consistent* subsets, according to AX′, of $Sub^+(\varphi)$ (where a maximal consistent set is an AX′-consistent set which is not a strict subset of any other AX′-consistent subset of $Sub^+(\varphi)$). We call a such a maximal consistent set an AX'-atom. (We henceforth omit AX′ unless it is relevant to the discussion.) It is easy to verify that each atom is *complete* in the sense that for $\psi \in Sub(\varphi)$, either ψ or $\neg\psi$ must be in the atom. For example, if φ is $p \wedge (q \rightarrow r)$ then $Sub^+(\varphi) = \{p, \neg p, q, \neg q, r, \neg r, q \rightarrow r, \neg(q \rightarrow r), p \wedge (q \rightarrow r), \neg(p \wedge (q \rightarrow r))\}$. The set $\{p, q, \neg r, \neg(q \rightarrow r), \neg(p \wedge (q \rightarrow r))\}$ might be an atom (depending on AX′), but $\{\neg p, q, \neg r, q \rightarrow r, p \wedge (q \rightarrow r)\}$ cannot be an atom since $\neg p$ and $p \wedge (q \rightarrow r)$ are inconsistent. Similarly, $\{p, q\}$ is not atom since it is not maximal. In the following discussion let α, β, and γ stand for atoms and A stand for a set of atoms. We slightly abuse notation and use α both as a set (e.g., $\psi \in \alpha$) and as a formula (e.g., $\alpha \Rightarrow \psi$) which is the conjunction of all members of α.

Given α, β, and A we define $Prefer_{AX'}(\beta, \alpha, A)$ if $\beta \wedge \neg(\alpha \vee \bigvee A \rightarrow \bigvee A)$ is consistent according to AX′. The intuitive account is that a world where β holds is consistent with an ordering that makes worlds where α holds strictly preferred to worlds satisfying one of the atoms in A. We will use this definition to construct all the preorders that are consistent with each possible world.

Given AX′ and φ, we construct a structure $M = (W, \pi, R)$ as follows:

- We set W to be the set of tuples (γ, A) where $\gamma \notin A$. Given $w = (\gamma, A)$ we define $\gamma(w) = \gamma$.
- We set $\pi(w)(p) = \mathbf{true}$ if and only if $p \in \gamma(w)$.
- For any world w, we construct $\preceq_w$ by setting

$$W_w = \{(\gamma, A) \in W | Prefer_{AX'}(\gamma(w), A, \gamma)\}$$

and setting $w' \prec_w w''$ if $w' = (\gamma', A')$, $w'' = (\gamma'', A'')$, and $A'' \cup \{\gamma''\} \subseteq A'$.

The intuition is simple: A world $w = (\gamma, A)$ represents a world satisfying γ that is intended to be strictly preferred to all worlds that satisfy one of the atoms in A. We define π so that it assigns truth values to primitive propositions according their values in γ. The set W_w contains all the worlds (γ', A') such that $Prefer_{AX'}(\gamma, \gamma', A')$, i.e., it is consistent with γ that (γ', A') is strictly preferred to worlds satisfying one of the atoms in A. The definition of $\preceq$ implements this intuition: if $(\gamma', A') \prec_w (\gamma'', A'')$ then $\gamma'' \in A'$. This matches our intuition since (γ', A') is intended to be preferred to worlds satisfying atoms in A'. We also demand that $A'' \subset A'$, this ensures that $\preceq_w$ will be transitive. It implies that if $(\gamma'', A'') \prec_w (\gamma''', A''')$, then $\gamma''' \in A'' \subset A'$ and also $A''' \subset A'' \subset A'$. Thus, $(\gamma', A') \prec_w (\gamma''', A''')$.

We now show that each world w in M satisfies $\gamma(w)$. Since the details of this proof are essentially the same as Burgess's proof [Bur81, p. 82], we leave the details to the full paper.

Lemma 5.1: *Let AX′ be an extension of AX and let $\varphi \in \mathcal{L}^C$. Let M be the structure constructed above. For any $w \in W$ and $\psi \in \mathrm{Sub}^+(\varphi)$, $\psi \in \gamma(w)$ if and only if $(M, w) \models \psi$.*

Using this lemma it is easy to prove the following theorem:

Theorem 5.2: *If $\varphi \in \mathcal{L}^C$, then φ is valid in $\mathcal{M}$ if and only if $\vdash_{AX} \varphi$.*

Proof: It is easy to check the soundness of AX in $\mathcal{M}$. Thus, if $\vdash_{AX} \varphi$, then φ must be valid in $\mathcal{M}$. For the other direction, assume that φ is consistent with AX. Then there is an atom α such that $\varphi \in \alpha$, and from Lemma 5.1 we get that $(M, (\alpha, \emptyset)) \models \varphi$. ∎

We note that this construction is much simpler than Burgess's even though the proof of Lemma 5.1 is almost identical to Burgess's proof. The main difference is that Burgess constructs a tree-like structure of finite but nonelementary size. Our construction, on the other hand, uses the same stock of worlds to construct the ordering for each world. The resulting structure is of doubly-exponential size. (We note that our results from Section 2 show that this can be improved, since only an exponential-sized structure is needed for satisfiability.) The fact that the structure is not tree-like allows us to give completeness proofs for properties such as uniformity and reflexivity that cannot be satisfied in tree-like structures.

The following axioms characterize the various semantic conditions we have considered. These axioms appeared originally in [Lew73] and [Bur81].

AN (Normality) $\neg(true \rightarrow false)$
AR (Reflexivity) $\Box\varphi \Rightarrow \varphi$
AT (Centering) $\Box\varphi \Rightarrow \varphi$[10]
AU (Uniformity) $(\Box\varphi \Rightarrow \Box\Box\varphi) \land (\neg\Box\varphi \Rightarrow \Box\neg\Box\varphi)$
AA (Absoluteness)
$(\varphi \rightarrow \psi \Rightarrow \Box(\varphi \rightarrow \psi)) \land (\neg(\varphi \rightarrow \psi) \Rightarrow \Box\neg(\varphi \rightarrow \psi))$
AC (Connectedness)$(\varphi_1 \lor \varphi_2) \rightarrow \neg\varphi_2 \Rightarrow ((\varphi_1 \lor \psi) \rightarrow \neg\psi) \lor ((\psi \lor \varphi_2) \rightarrow \neg\varphi_2)$

The next results shows that each axiom captures exactly the corresponding condition:

Theorem 5.3: Let $\varphi \in \mathcal{L}$ and let $\mathcal{A}$ be a subset of $\{N, R, T, U, A, C\}$ and A the corresponding subset of $\{AN, AR, AT, AU, AA, AC\}$. Then φ is valid in $\mathcal{M}^{\mathcal{A}}$ if and only if $\vdash_{AXUA} \varphi$.

Proof: In the full paper we provide the details of this proof. The essence of the proof is showing that each axiom forces the constructed structure to satisfy the semantic condition. This is straightforward in the case of absoluteness, uniformity and normality. The other cases require a little more care; we leave details to the full paper. ∎

6 CONCLUSIONS

In this paper we analyzed the complexity problem for conditional logics. As we observed in the introduction, such logics are now being used in many areas of artificial intelligence. The techniques we have introduced in this paper (especially the results in Section 3) can applied to frameworks that combine conditional logics with other modalities. For example, in [FH94a] we use these results to derive complexity results for a logic that contains both conditionals and epistemic modalities.

We did not attempt, in this work, to isolate tractable fragments of the logic. This is certainly an important aspect of any analysis of formal method in artificial intelligence [Lev86, Lev88]. We note that all the logics we examined are intractable because they contain the propositional calculus. It is certainly feasible that there are nontrivial fragments that do not contain the propositional calculus that are tractable (e.g., results in the style of Kautz and Selman's analysis of default logic [KS89]). We plan to pursue this issue in the future. We note that the methods used in this paper are certainly relevant to such an investigation.

Acknowledgements

The authors are grateful to Phil Hubbard, Daphne Koller, Moshe Vardi and the anonymous referees for comments on drafts of this paper.

References

[Bel89] J. Bell. The logic of nonmonotonicity. *Artificial Intelligence*, 41:365–374, 1989.

[Bou92] C. Boutilier. Normative, subjective and autoepistemic defaults: Adopting the Ramsey test. In *Principles of Knowledge Representation and Reasoning: Proc. Third International Conference (KR '92)*. 1992.

[Bou93] C. Boutilier. Revision sequences and nested conditionals. In *Proc. Thirteenth International Joint Conference on Artificial Intelligence (IJCAI '93)*, pages 519–525, 1993.

[Bou94] C. Boutilier. Toward a logic for qualitative decision theory. In *Principles of Knowledge Representation and Reasoning: Proc. Fourth International Conference (KR '94)*. 1994.

[Bur81] J. Burgess. Quick completeness proofs for some logics of conditionals. *Notre Dame Journal of Formal Logic*, 22:76–84, 1981.

[Che80] B. F. Chellas. Basic conditional logic. *Journal of Philosophical Logic*, 4:133–153, 1980.

[CKS81] A. K. Chandra, D. Kozen, and L. J. Stockmeyer. Alternation. *Journal of the ACM*, 28:114–133, 1981.

[Del88] J. P. Delgrande. An approach to default reasoning based on a first-order conditional logic: revised report. *Artificial Intelligence*, 36:63–90, 1988.

[EG92] T. Eiter and Gottlob G. The complexity of propositional knowledge base revision. *Artificial Intelligence*, 57:227–270, 1992.

[EG93] T. Eiter and Gottlob G. The complexity of nested counterfactuals and iterated knowledge base revisions. In *Proc. Thirteenth International Joint Conference on Artificial Intelligence (IJCAI '93)*, pages 526–531, 1993.

[FH94a] N. Friedman and J. Y. Halpern. A knowledge-based framework for belief change. Part I: Foundations. In R. Fagin, editor, *Theoretical Aspects of Reasoning about Knowledge: Proc. Fifth Conference*, pages 44–64. 1994.

---

[10]The axiom for strict centering is $\Box\varphi \Leftrightarrow \varphi$.

[FH94b] N. Friedman and J. Y. Halpern. A knowledge-based framework for belief change. Part II: revision and update. In *Principles of Knowledge Representation and Reasoning: Proc. Fourth International Conference (KR '94)*. to appear, 1994.

[FUV83] R. Fagin, J. D. Ullman, and M. Y. Vardi. On the semantics of updates in databases. In *Proc. 2nd ACM Symp. on Principles of Database Systems*, pages 352–365, 1983.

[Gin86] M. L. Ginsberg. Counterfactuals. *Artificial Intelligence*, 30:35–79, 1986.

[GJ79] M. Garey and D. S. Johnson. *Computers and Intractability: A Guide to the Theory of NP-completeness*. W. Freeman and Co., 1979.

[GP92] M. Goldszmidt and J. Pearl. Rank-based systems: A simple approach to belief revision, belief update and reasoning about evidence and actions. In R. Parikh, editor, *Principles of Knowledge Representation and Reasoning: Proc. Third International Conference (KR '92)*, pages 661–672. 1992.

[Gra91] G. Grahne. Updates and counterfactuals. In *Principles of Knowledge Representation and Reasoning: Proc. Second International Conference (KR '91)*, pages 269–276. 1991.

[HM92] J. Y. Halpern and Y. Moses. A guide to completeness and complexity for modal logics of knowledge and belief. *Artificial Intelligence*, 54:319–379, 1992.

[HU79] J. E. Hopcroft and J. D. Ullman. *Introduction to Automata Theory, Languages and Computation*. Addison-Wesley, 1979.

[KLM90] S. Kraus, D. J. Lehmann, and M. Magidor. Nonmonotonic reasoning, preferential models and cumulative logics. *Artificial Intelligence*, 44:167–207, 1990.

[KS89] H. A. Kautz and B. Selman. Hard problems for simple default logics. In *Proc. First International Conference on Principles of Knowledge Representation and Reasoning (KR '89)*, pages 189–197. 1989.

[KS91] H. Katsuno and K. Satoh. A unified view of consequence relation, belief revision and conditional logic. In *Proc. Twelfth International Joint Conference on Artificial Intelligence (IJCAI '91)*, pages 406–412, 1991.

[Lad77] R. E. Ladner. The computational complexity of provability in systems of modal propositional logic. *SIAM Journal on Computing*, 6(3):467–480, 1977.

[Lev86] H. J. Levesque. Knowledge representation and reasoning. In J. F. Traub, B. J. Grosz, B. W. Lampson, and N. J. Nilsson, editors, *Annual Review of Computer Science, Vol. 1*, pages 255–287. Annual Reviews Inc., 1986.

[Lev88] H. J. Levesque. Logic and the complexity of reasoning. *Journal of Philosophical Logic*, 17(4):355–389, 1988.

[Lew73] D. K. Lewis. *Counterfactuals*. Harvard University Press, 1973.

[Lew74] D. K. Lewis. Intensional logics without iterative axioms. *Journal of Philosophical Logic*, 3:457–466, 1974.

[Neb91] B. Nebel. Belief revision and default reasoning: syntax-based approaches. In *Principles of Knowledge Representation and Reasoning: Proc. Second International Conference (KR '91)*, pages 417–428. 1991.

[Pea89] J. Pearl. Probabilistic semantics for nonmonotonic reasoning: A survey. In *Proc. First International Conference on Principles of Knowledge Representation and Reasoning (KR '89)*, pages 505–516, 1989. Reprinted in *Readings in Uncertain Reasoning*, G. Shafer and J. Pearl (eds.), Morgan Kaufmann, 1990, pp. 699–710.

[Pea93] J. Pearl. From conditional oughts to qualitative decision theory. In *Proc. Ninth Conference on Uncertainty in Artificial Intelligence (UAI '93)*, pages 12–20. 1993.

[Sta68] R. C. Stalnaker. A theory of conditionals. In N. Rescher, editor, *Studies in logical theory*, number 2 in American philosophical quarterly monograph series. Blackwell, Oxford, 1968. Also appears in *Ifs*, (ed., by W. Harper, R. C. Stalnaker and G. Pearce), Reidel, 1981.

[Vel85] F. Veltman. *Logics for conditionals*. PhD thesis, Universiteit van Amsterdam, 1985.

An Efficient Method for Managing Disjunctions in Qualitative Temporal Reasoning

Alfonso Gerevini
Knowledge Representation and Reasoning Lab
IRST, I-38050 Povo Trento, Italy
E-mail: gerevini@irst.it

Lenhart Schubert
Computer Science Department
University of Rochester
Rochester, NY 14627, USA
E-mail: schubert@cs.rochester.edu

Abstract

We provide an efficient method for consistency checking of temporal relations in the Point Algebra (PA-relations) extended by binary disjunctions of PA-relations. Such disjunctions add a great deal of expressive power, including the ability to stipulate disjointness of temporal intervals, which is important in planning applications. The method is based on two main steps: the first preprocesses the initial set of disjunctions reducing it to a logically equivalent subset, while the second performs a search which uses a form of selective backtracking and a "forward propagation" technique to greatly enhance efficiency. The preprocessing phase is worst-case polynomial, and in principle is strong enough to subsume consistency checking for Nebel and Bürckert's ORD-Horn class of interval relations.

Experimental results using a specialized algorithm for binary disjunctions of inequalities show that our method is very efficient especially when the number of disjunctions is limited relative to the number of PA-relations, and that although consistency testing is NP-complete, in practice our algorithms tend to perform polynomially.

1 INTRODUCTION

Reasoning about qualitative temporal information is an important task in many areas of AI. The Interval Algebra (IA) [Allen, 1983] and the Point Algebra (PA) [Vilain et al., 1990; van Beek and Cohen, 1990] are approaches to the representation of qualitative temporal information, based respectively on specifying possible relations between pairs of intervals and pairs of points [van Beek, 1992; Ladkin and Maddux, to appear]. Given a collection of temporal relations, determining the consistency (satisfiability) and find-ing a consistent scenario (interpretation of the time variables) of such a collection are among the main reasoning tasks. These problems are NP-hard for IA, while they are polynomial for PA [Vilain et al., 1990; van Beek and Cohen, 1990; van Beek, 1992; Vilain et al., 1990] and for the ORD-Horn subclass of IA [Nebel and Bürckert, 1993]. The ORD-Horn subclass is particularly attractive from a theoretical perspective because it is a maximal tractable subalgebra of IA, providing substantially greater expressiveness than the "pointizable" part of IA. Still, for many applications (especially in planning and scheduling [Allen, 1991; Allen and Koomen, 1983; Boddy, 1993; Dean et al., 1988; Frederking and Muscettola, 1992; Tsang, 1986; Vere, 1983]) even this subalgebra is too weak, because it does not include some practically essential relations such as disjointness relations.[1] Disjointness is needed, for example, in constraining two actions that require dedicated use of the same resources (agents, tools, pathways, etc.) to be nonoverlapping in time.

We focus on relations in PA (PA-relations) and on a major extension of PA to include binary disjunctions of PA-relations (PA-disjunctions). This extension allows the representation of a large class of interval relations which strictly contains the ORD-Horn subclass[2], the disjointness relations, and many non–binary interval relations such as I before J or after K. For example, the relation I before or after J can be translated into the set $\{I^- < I^+, J^- < J^+, I^+ < J^- \vee J^+ < I^-\}$, where I^- (J^-) and I^+ (J^+) indicate the starting and the end points of the interval I (J).

In [Gerevini and Schubert, 1993a] we show that the problem of determining consistency for a set of PA-

---

[1] The disjointness relations are: I {before, after} J, I {before, met-by} J, I {meets, after} J, I {meets, met-by} J, I {before, after, meets} J, I {before, after, met-by} J, I {before, meets, met-by} J, I {meets, after, met-by} J, I {before, after, meets, met-by} J.

[2] Each of the relations in the ORD-Horn subclass can be translated into a collection of PA-relations and (binary) PA-disjunctions with at most one disjunct in $\{\leq, =\}$ [Nebel and Bürckert, 1993].

disjunctions is NP-complete even when the set contains only relations of the form "x strictly before or strictly after the interval formed by y,z" (where $y < z$). As a consequence, there is no hope for reasoning about disjointness relations in any subclass of PA without losing tractability or compromising completeness (assuming P $\neq$ NP).

In [Gerevini and Schubert, 1993b; Gerevini et al., 1993; Miller and Schubert, 1990] we provide a collection of algorithms for efficiently managing large sets of PA-relations based on *timegraphs*, graphs partitioned into a set of chains on which the search is supported by a metagraph data structure.

In this paper we provide an efficient method for managing PA-disjunctions which uses the timegraph algorithms. In Section 2 we first propose a general algorithm for determining consistency of a set S of PA-relations augmented by a collection of PA-disjunctions. The algorithm effectively exploits the information provided by the timegraph built from S to prune the search. Secondly, we provide a specialized search algorithm for disjunctions of inequalities based on a form of selective backtracking which can be very effective in limiting the number of the backtracks.

The experimental results reported in Section 3 show that our approach is particularly efficient when the timegraph is not very sparse and the number of PA-disjunctions is relatively small compared to the number of PA-relations. For more difficult cases (sparse timegraph with few PA-relations and numerous PA-disjunctions) a "forward propagation" technique can dramatically reduce the number of backtracks. Finally, extensive experiments aimed at investigating the scalability of the proposed method show that in practice our algorithm tends to perform polynomially on average.

2 MANAGING DISJUNCTIONS THROUGH TIMEGRAPHS

A *disjunctive timegraph* ($\mathcal{D}$-timegraph) is a pair $\langle T, D \rangle$ where T is a timegraph and D a set of PA-disjunctions involving only point-variables in T. A $\mathcal{D}$-timegraph $\langle T, D \rangle$ is *consistent* if it is possible to select one of the disjuncts for each PA-disjunction in D in such a way that the resulting collection of selected PA-relations can be consistently added to T. We call this set of selected disjuncts an *instantiation* of D in T, and the task of finding such a set *deciding* D relative to T.

Once we have an instantiation of D, we can easily solve the problem of finding a consistent scenario by adding the instantiation to T and using a topological sort algorithm [van Beek, 1992; Cormen et al., 1990]. Also the task of checking whether a relation R between two time points x and y is entailed by a $\mathcal{D}$-timegraph $\langle T, D \rangle$ can be reduced to the problem of finding an instantiation of D in an augmented version of T. We add the relation $x\overline{R}y$ to T (where $\overline{R}$ negation of R), obtaining a new timegraph T', and then check if (a) T' is consistent, and (b) D can be decided relative to T' (if not empty). The original $\mathcal{D}$-timegraph entails xRy just in case one of (a),(b) does not hold.

In general, in order to decide a set of binary disjunctions we can perform a search in the set of the 2^m possible ways of choosing the disjuncts (for m disjunctions). This search is necessarily exponential in the worst case (assuming P$\neq$NP) since the problem is NP-hard [Gerevini and Schubert, 1993a]. Given a disjunctive timegraph $\langle T, D \rangle$, the algorithm we have developed for deciding D relative to T consists of two main steps:

1. prune the search space by reducing D to a subset D' of D and producing a timegraph T' such that D has an instantiation in T if and only if D' has an instantiation in T'.
2. Search for an instantiation of D' in T' by using backtracking.

We first describe some powerful pruning rules on which the first step is based, and then present an efficient search algorithm for binary disjunctions of inequalities which uses a form of *selective backtracking* [Bruynooghe, 1981; Shanahan and Southwick, 1989].

2.1 PREPROCESSING

The set of disjunctions of a $\mathcal{D}$-timegraph $\langle T, D \rangle$ can be reduced to a significatively smaller subset by applying some *pruning rules* to each disjunction $D(i) = xR_1y \vee wR_2z$ in D (x,y,w, and z time points, R_1, R_2 PA-relations, and $i = 1..m$). These rules detect cases where the timegraph T already entails the disjunction (allowing its removal), or entails the negation of a disjunct (leaving only an ordinary PA-relation). Timegraphs are designed to detect such entailments efficiently.[3]

For example, consider the $\mathcal{D}$-timegraph $H = \langle T, D \rangle$ of Figure 2. H can be transformed into an equivalent $\mathcal{D}$-timegraph $H' = \langle T', D' \rangle$ where T' differs from T by having two additional edges (indicated by dotted arrows) and D' consists of only one of the disjunctions in D. $D(2)$ is redundant because T entails $a < g$; $D(4)$ can be eliminated because it is tautologically true (if we assume the negation of the first disjunct, i.e., $\neg(d < g)$, i.e., $g \leq d$, then we have $c < d$ from the graph and hence the second disjunct, $b < d$, is true); finally neither $f < a$ nor $g \leq a$ can be consistently added to T and hence the second disjuncts of $D(1)$ ($f < d$) and of $D(3)$ ($b \leq f$) must take part in any instantiation of D.

---
[3] In [Gerevini and Schubert, 1993b] we give a worst-case linear time algorithm for querying the strongest entailed relation in a timegraph.

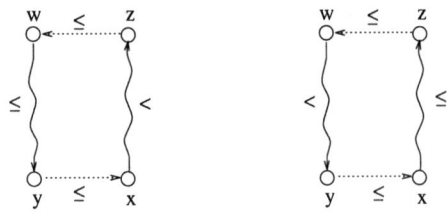

Figure 1: Two cases in which the precondition of Restricted TL-tautology is satisfied. Dotted edges represent the assumed relations. "Wavy" arcs are $\leq$-paths or $<$-paths

More formally, we can define three rules for eliminating a disjunction $D(i) = xR_1y \vee wR_2z$ from D, possibly producing a set Q of PA-relations which must take part in any instantiation of D:

(1) T-derivability
    if $T \vdash xR_1y$ or $T \vdash wR_2z$ then $D := D - \{D(i)\}$

(2) T-tautology
    (2.i) if $T \cup \{x\overline{R}_1y\} \vdash wR_2z$ then $D := D - \{D(i)\}$
    (2.ii) if $T \cup \{w\overline{R}_2z\} \vdash xR_1y$ then $D := D - \{D(i)\}$

(3) T-resolution
    (3.i) if $T \cup \{xR_1y\}$ is consistent and $T \cup \{wR_2z\}$ is inconsistent then $D := D - \{D(i)\}$ and $Q := Q \cup \{xR_1y\}$
    (3.ii) if $T \cup \{wR_2z\}$ is consistent and $T \cup \{xR_1y\}$ is inconsistent then $D := D - \{D(i)\}$ and $Q := Q \cup \{wR_2z\}$
    (3.iii) if both $T \cup \{xR_1y\}$ and $T \cup \{wR_2z\}$ are inconsistent then the $\mathcal{D}$-timegraph $\langle T, D \rangle$ is inconsistent

where $T \vdash xR_iy$ ($i \in \{1,2\}$) is defined according to Theorem 2.2 given in [Gerevini and Schubert, 1993b], $T \cup \{xR_1y\}$ is the timegraph obtained by adding to T the graphical representation of xR_1y (analogously for $T \cup \{wR_2z\}$), $\overline{R}_1$ is the negation of R (analogously for $\overline{R}_2$), Q is initially empty, and the notion of a consistent timegraph is formally given in [Gerevini and Schubert, 1993b].

With respect to the example of Figure 2, $D(2)$ can be eliminated from D by the application of rule (1), $D(4)$ by rule (2) and $D(1)$, $D(3)$ by rule (3). (It is worth noting that if these inferences are made in sequence, and resolvents are *immediately* added to T, then we can also eliminate $D(5)$.)

Rule (1) is a special case of rule (2). We keep them separated because the time required for applying rule (2) may be too great; rule (1) just requires application of the timegraph query algorithms, whereas rule (2) calls for a (temporary) addition to the timegraph. In fact, when one of the disjuncts of the disjunction is an "=" or "<" relation, the addition to the timegraph of the negation of the disjunct can create "implicit <-relations" that have to be made explicit and cycles that have to be collapsed before verifying the entailment of the second disjunct (for more details see [Gerevini and Schubert, to appear]). In these cases a rule weaker than rule (2) may be preferred. In particular, for disjunctions d of the form $x < y \vee w < z$ we can use the following *restricted T-tautology* rule, requiring only timegraph queries:

(2') if $T \vdash (x < z \wedge w \leq y)$ or $T \vdash (x \leq z \wedge w < y)$
     then $D := D - \{d\}$

This rule is sound since if T entails $x < z$ and $w \leq y$, or $x \leq z$ and $w < y$, and we assume the negation of the first disjunct ($y \leq x$) or of the second disjunct ($w \leq z$), the resulting timegraph entails $x < y$ or $w < z$ respectively (see Figure 1). (2') is applied to a disjunction only if it cannot be removed by rule (1), i.e., the timegraph does not contain <-paths from x to y or from w to z. While applying rule (2') is more efficient than applying rule (2), some tautologies may then escape detection. The choice depends on how much effort we want to dedicate to the preprocessing step and how much to the search step.

If both rules (3.i) and (3.ii) can be applied to a disjunction d in D, then there is no instantiation of D because the addition of either disjunct of d makes the resulting timegraph inconsistent. When only one of (3.i) and (3.ii) can be applied to d, the disjunct of d which can be consistently added to the graph is called the T-resolvent of d.[4]

If D contains a disjunct of the form $s < t$ (or $s \leq t$), and T has a $\leq$-path[5] (<-path) from the vertex corresponding to s to the vertex corresponding to t, we say that the $\mathcal{D}$-timegraph contains a *<-quasicycle* (quasicycle hereafter) determined by the disjunct $s < y$ ($s \leq t$). For example, the $\mathcal{D}$-timegraph of Figure 2 contains a quasicycle determined by $g \leq a$ (the first disjunct of $D(3)$). When rule (3) is applied to a disjunction having a disjunct which determines a quasicycle we call this *quasicycle elimination*. The application of rule (3) is an efficient operation especially when the disjuncts are <-relations. In fact, in these cases quasicycle elimination can be applied just by checking the existence of a $\leq$-path in the metagraph of the timegraph [Gerevini and Schubert, 1993b].

The result of applying the pruning rules to all the disjunctions of D is a subset D' of D and a set Q of T-resolvents. The PA-relations of Q can then be added to the original graph producing a new timegraph T'

---
[4]This terminology reflects the strong similarity of T-resolution to a particular form of "Theory Resolution" proposed by Stickel [Stickel, 1985].

[5]A path is a $\leq$-*path* if each label on the edges of the path is $\leq$ or $<$. A $\leq$-path is a $<$-*path* if at least one of these labels is $<$.

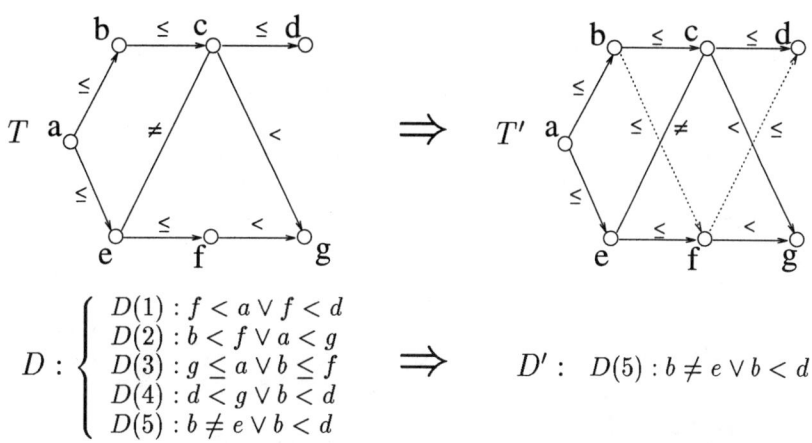

Figure 2: A $\mathcal{D}$-timegraph $\langle T, D \rangle$ and the corresponding $\mathcal{D}$-timegraph $\langle T', D' \rangle$ obtained by applying the pruning rules to the disjunctions in D using T.

which is used by the search step to find an instantiation of D'. In fact, as the following theorem asserts, the original problem of deciding D in T is equivalent to the problem of deciding D' in T'.

Theorem 1 *Given a $\mathcal{D}$-timegraph $\langle T, D \rangle$, D has an instantiation in T if and only if $D - \{d\}$ has an instantiation in T', where d is any disjunction in D which can be eliminated by the application of any pruning rule, $T' = T$ if d is eliminated either by T-derivability, T-tautology or by restricted T-tautology, and $T' = T \cup \{vRw\}$ if d is eliminated by T-resolution and vRw is the T-resolvent of d.*

Proof (sketch). The proof follows from Theorem 2.2 in [Gerevini and Schubert, 1993b] and from the fact that each disjunction is binary. □

Various strategies are possible for preprocessing the set of disjunctions using the pruning rules. Here we have adopted the simplest one in which the rules are applied to each disjunction once and the set of T-resolvents generated is added to the timegraph at the end of the process. This strategy is very efficient since it is based on query algorithms and does not require updating to maintain the timegraph data structures. A more complete strategy, though more computationally expensive, is to add the T-resolvents to the graph as soon as they are produced and to iterate the application of the rules till no further disjunction can be eliminated. In particular, it can be shown that this strategy is complete for ORD-Horn clauses [Nebel and Bürckert, 1993] in which each PA-disjunctions has at most one disjunct in $\{\leq, =\}$ and the others are "$\neq$".

Theorem 2 *There exists a polynomial strategy for applying the pruning rules which is complete for determining the consistency of a $\mathcal{D}$-timegraph $\langle T, D \rangle$, where D is a set of binary ORD-Horn clauses.*

Proof (sketch). The strategy mentioned above is easily seen to take polynomial time. The key point is to show that termination without detection of inconsistency entails consistency of $\langle T, D \rangle$. Let R be the set of PA-relations entailed by T, $\langle T', D' \rangle$ the $\mathcal{D}$-timegraph at termination, and R' the set of PA-relations entailed by T'. Since positive unit resolution is known to be refutation-complete for Horn theories [Henschen and Wos, 1974], it suffices to show that unit resolution applied to $R \cup D \cup ORD_R$, or equivalently to $R' \cup D' \cup ORD_{R'}$, cannot derive any unit clauses (PA-relations) that are not in R' (see [Nebel and Bürckert, 1993] for the definition of ORD_R, the (Horn) theory of "$\leq$" and "$=$" applied to the point variables of R). This follows from the fact the preprocessing already (in effect) performs any possible unit resolutions between PA-relations in R' and any disjunctions in D', and that unit resolvents between R' and $ORD_{R'}$ are already in R'. □

Given a set I of interval relations in the ORD-Horn subclass that can be translated into a set H of ORD-Horn clauses, we write T_I for the timegraph built from the set of the unary clauses of H, and D_I for the set of the remaining (binary) clauses of H.

Theorem 3 *The consistency of a set I of interval relations in the ORD-Horn subclass can be polynomially decided by determining the consistency of T_I and by using the preprocessing step of the algorithm for deciding D_I relative to the timegraph built from T_I.*

Proof (sketch). The proof follows from Theorem 2 and the fact that the clauses in D_I are at most binary [Nebel and Bürckert, 1993]. By Theorem 3.1 in [Gerevini and Schubert, 1993b] consistency checking of the set of unary clauses of H is accomplished in polytime during the construction of T_I. If T_I is consistent then Theorem 2 guarantees that the preprocessing step

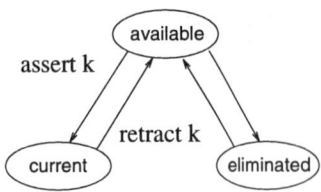

Figure 3: Possible transitions for the status of a disjunct k

of the algorithm for deciding D_I relative to T_I is sufficient for determining the consistency of I. □

2.2 PARTIALLY SELECTIVE BACKTRACKING

Once the initial set of disjunctions has been reduced by the application of the pruning rules, an arbitrary total order is imposed on the remaining disjunctions, and the search for an instantiation of them is activated. In this section we describe an algorithm for binary disjunctions of inequalities. The algorithm can easily be generalized to disjunctions containing $\neq$ relations, while for $\leq$ and $=$ relations some further effort is generally needed in order to maintain the necessary timegraph data structures [Gerevini and Schubert, 1993b; Gerevini and Schubert, to appear].

We first introduce some terminology, part of which is borrowed from [Bruynooghe, 1981], and the general backtracking strategy.

2.2.1 Terminology and backtracking strategy

The two disjuncts of a disjunction $D(j)$ $(1 \leq j \leq m)$ are denoted by $d(j,1)$ and $d(j,2)$. Each disjunct has a status associated with it that can be *available*, *current* or *eliminated*. A disjunct is available if it hasn't been tried yet. Initially all the disjuncts are available. Figure 3 shows the possible transitions for the status of a disjunct. An available disjunct becomes current when it is selected as part of the current (attempted) instantiation of D. At this point the corresponding edge is added to the timegraph, and the disjunction to which it belongs becomes *decided*. A disjunct changes status from available to eliminated when the addition of the corresponding edge to the timegraph would make the resulting graph inconsistent. A disjunction cannot be decided when neither of the edges corresponding to its disjuncts can be consistently added to the timegraph. During backtracking a disjunct can change status from current to available and from eliminated to available. When it changes from current to available the corresponding edge is retracted.

We indicate with T^j the timegraph resulting after deciding $D(j)$.

The set of current disjuncts taking part in a quasicycle determined by an eliminated disjunct $d(i,j)$ is a set of *antagonists* of $D(i)$. Note that a disjunct can determine more than one quasicycle and hence the corresponding disjunction can have more than one set of antagonists. However, we will always consider only one of them: the set of current disjuncts taking part in the $\leq$-path identified by the procedure which checks for the existence of the quasicycle. The *culprit* of an eliminated disjunct $d(i,j)$ (written as $culprit(i,j)$) is the *most recently* decided disjunction responsible for its elimination; i.e., it is the most recently decided disjunction $D(h)$ $(1 \leq h < i)$ such that:

1. one of the disjuncts of $D(h)$ is available;
2. the other disjunct of $D(h)$ is among the antagonists of $D(i)$.

If such a disjunction does not exist there is no culprit for $D(i)$ (i.e. $culprit(i,j)$ is nil).

In order to simplify the explanation of the method, we assume that all the disjuncts are different PA-relations. This assumption can easily be relaxed by checking whenever a disjunction is examined if one of its available disjuncts is equal to the current disjunct of a disjunction already decided, and modifying the relevant data structures accordingly.

The search for an instantiation is conducted by deciding each disjunction in turn, adding the chosen disjunct to the graph, until all disjunctions are decided or an impasse is reached, i.e., the next disjunction $D(i)$ cannot be consistently decided either way (i.e. without adding quasicycles). In the latter case, we backtrack to the culprit of one of the disjuncts of $D(i)$. When both the culprits are null the search proceeds by backtracking chronologically. This is illustrated in the following example.

2.2.2 An example

Let L be a $\mathcal{D}$-timegraph $\langle T, D \rangle$ where T is the timegraph of Figure 4 and D is the set of disjunctions:

$$D(1) : b < f \vee n < g$$
$$D(2) : f < m \vee n < f$$
$$D(3) : c < g \vee m < b$$
$$D(4) : f < b \vee h < e$$
$$D(5) : n < f \vee e < g$$

The graph T_1 shows the state of the disjunctions when the search has reached $D(5)$. Dotted edges correspond to chosen (current) disjuncts. The label on a dotted edge indicates the disjunction to which the disjunct belongs. When the label for a chosen disjunct of a disjunction $D(i)$ has a number in brackets, this means that the other disjunct of $D(i)$ has already been eliminated, and the number indicates the culprit of the examined disjunct.

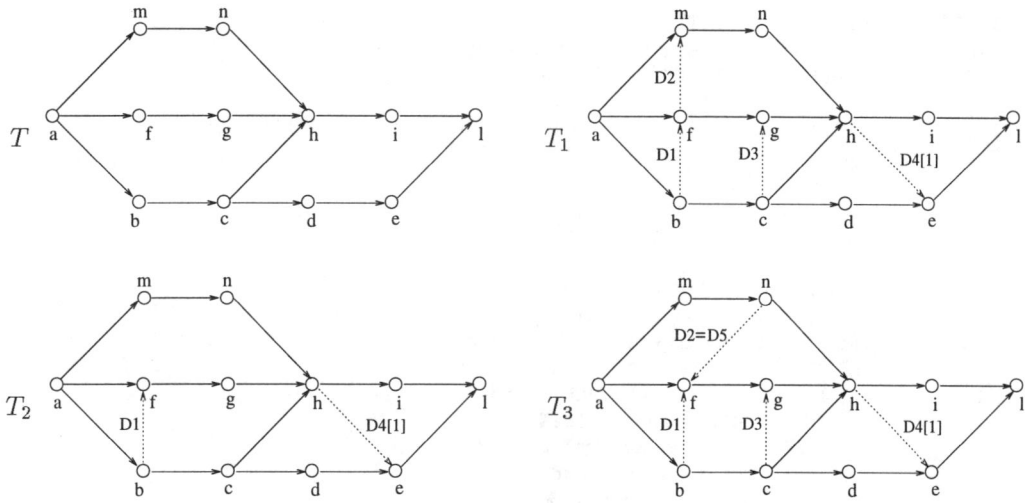

Figure 4: Example of the search for an instantiation of a set of PA-disjunctions

For example, the label D4[1] on the edge from h to e indicates that $D(1)$ is the culprit of $f < b$, the first disjunct of $D(4)$ (when $D(4)$ was decided, the addition of $f < b$ to the graph would have created the cycle b, f, b). Once we have decided $D(4)$, an impasse is reached because $D(5)$ cannot be decided. So, we have to select a decided disjunction for backtracking. Since neither $D(3)$ nor $D(4)$ satisfy conditions 1 and 2, disjunctions $D(1)$ and $D(2)$ are considered because $D(1)$ is the culprit of the eliminated disjunct of $D(4)$, and $D(2)$ is the culprit of $n < f$, the second disjunct of $D(5)$. Redeciding $D(1)$ using $n < g$ will break the cycle b, f, b, while redeciding $D(2)$ using $n < f$ will break the cycle f, m, n, f. $D(2)$ is selected because it has been decided more recently than $D(1)$.

The graph T_2 of Figure 4 shows the state of the search after backtracking. Note that in general the decision for $D(3)$ needs to be reconsidered, whereas we don't have to redecide $D(4)$ since its chosen disjunct involves no new cycles. (Moreover, its culprit remains the same since the other way of deciding $D(4)$ ($f < b$) still creates a quasicycle).

Finally, T_3 shows the instantiation found by the search.

2.2.3 Backtracking algorithm

The basic backtracking algorithm, whose pseudocode is reported in Figure 5, decides (when it is possible) the disjunctions following the arbitrary order imposed earlier. A disjunction $D(j)$ cannot be decided when both its disjuncts take part in a quasicycle determined in T^{j-1}. In this case there are two culprits for $D(j)$, and the one corresponding to the most recently decided disjunction is used to select a disjunction to backtrack to.

A simple chronological backtracking mechanism would always choose as backtrack point the most recently decided disjunction $D(k)$ with an available disjunct, and the status of the disjuncts of all the disjunctions $D(h)$ between $D(k)$ and $D(j)$ would be restored. But exploiting our data structures, if $D(j)$ has an antagonist which is not null, we can use it to jump back directly to the most recently decided disjunction whose current disjunct takes part in a quasicycle determined by the disjunct of $D(j)$. Moreover, not all the disjunctions $D(h)$ between $D(k)$ and $D(j)$ need to be restored, in fact all the disjunctions with an eliminated disjunct $d(p, h)$ ($k < p < j$, $h \in \{1, 2\}$) whose culprit precedes $D(k)$ can be left unchanged. The reason for this is that $D(h)$ can have a value different from the current one (at the moment of backtracking) only if there is a backtrack to a disjunction which is equal to or which precedes $culprit(p, h)$.[6]

This form of selective backtracking can significantly prune the search in comparison with ordinary chronological backtracking. However, since for each eliminated disjunct $d(i, j)$, $culprit(i, j)$ indicates only one disjunction which is responsible for an impasse reached during the search, this technique does not provide complete selective backtracking. In fact, as discussed in [Bruynooghe, 1981; Shanahan and Southwick, 1989], to obtain a complete selective backtracking algorithm we could store for each eliminated disjunct *all* the previously decided disjunctions which are responsible for its elimination (i.e. its set of antagonists) instead of just the latest one. However, the computational space required by the algorithm performing full selective backtracking would then be $O(m^2)$. This bound would be unacceptable for large graphs if the number of disjunctions is comparable to the number n of time points or greater (it can be as high as n^4).

---

[6]In fact, if h precedes $culprit(p, h)$ then the eliminated disjunct of $D(h)$ will continue to determine a quasicycle in each timegraph T^i ($k \leq i < h$), no matter how $D(k)$ and the further disjunctions preceding $D(h)$ will be decided after the backtrack to $D(k)$.

```
ALGORITHM: DECIDE-DISJUNCTIONS
INPUT: a timegraph T and a set D of preprocessed disjunctions
OUTPUT: the vector DSJ if <T,D> is consistent, nil otherwise

1.  i:= 1; fail:= false; done:=false; FOR i = 1 TO m CULPRIT[i]:=nil;
2.  WHILE (fail = false) and (done = false) DO
3.    IF DSJ[i] = 2 THEN {both the disjuncts are available}
4.      IF d(i,1) does not determine a quasicycle THEN
5.        mark d(i,1) current, DSJ[i]:= 1, and CULPRIT[i]:= i
6.      ELSE
7.        BEGIN CULPRIT[i]:= culprit(i,1);
8.        IF d(i,2) does not determine a quasicycle THEN
9.          mark d(i,2) current and DSJ[i]:= 0
10.       ELSE BEGIN
11.         IF culprit(i,2) > CULPRIT[i] THEN CULPRIT[i]:=culprit(i,2);
12.         IF CULPRIT[i] = nil THEN
13.           BEGIN {chronological backtracking}
14.           q:= the highest j such that j < i and DSJ[i] = 1,
                  nil if such a j does not exist;
15.           IF q is not nil THEN
                BEGIN {restore disjunctions between D(q) and D(i)}
16.             CULPRIT[q]:= nil; mark d(q,1) eliminated;
17.             FOR t = q + 1 TO i
18.               IF CULPRIT[t] >= q THEN mark the disjuncts of D(t)
                      available, DSJ[t]:= 2, and CULPRIT[t]:= nil;
19.             i:= q {backtracking to D(q)}
                END
20.           ELSE fail:= true {the D-timegraph is inconsistent}
              END
21.         ELSE {selective backtracking}
22.           q:= CULPRIT[i] and run through steps 16. to 19.
            END
      END
23.   ELSE BEGIN {DSJ[i] = 1, d(i,1) eliminated and d(i,2) available}
24.     CULPRIT[i]:= i;
25.     IF d(i,2) does not determine a quasicycle THEN
26.       mark d(i,2) current, DSJ[i]:= 0
27.     ELSE BEGIN CULPRIT[i]:= culprit(i,2);
28.       IF CULPRIT[i] = nil THEN run through steps 14. to 20.
29.       ELSE q:= CULPRIT[i] and run through steps 16. to 19.
          END
        END
30.   IF NOT fail THEN i:=lowest j such that j>=i and D(j) is undecided;
31.   IF i > m THEN done:= true
      END{WHILE};
32. IF fail = true THEN RETURN nil ELSE RETURN the vector DSJ.
```

Figure 5: Algorithm for deciding a set of m preprocessed disjunctions

In order to guarantee completeness while retaining linear space complexity, whenever an undecidable disjunction $D(j)$ with an empty antagonist is reached, the algorithm performs a chronological backtrack to the first preceding disjunction $D(k)$ ($k < j$) with an available disjunct, and each disjunction between $D(h)$ and $D(k)$ not having an antagonist preceding k is restored. If such a disjunction does not exist, then there is no instantiation of the original set of disjunctions.

The algorithm of Figure 5 uses two main data structure: DSJ and CULPRIT. DSJ is a vector of dimension m in which the status of the disjuncts of the disjunctions is maintained. DSJ$[j]$ is an integer in $\{0, 1, 2\}$ with the following meaning:

- DSJ$[j]$= 2 if $D(j)$ is not decided and both the disjuncts are available;
- DSJ$[j]$= 1 if $D(j)$ is decided and $d(j,1)$ is current;
- DSJ$[j]$= 0 if $D(j)$ is decided and $d(j,2)$ is current.

During the process of deciding a disjunction $D(j)$, when both the disjuncts are available, the disjunct $d(j,1)$ is always tried before the disjunct $d(j,2)$. As a consequence of this when $d(j,2)$ is current $d(j,1)$ is always eliminated.

CULPRIT is a vector of dimension m which is used to

```
ALGORITHM: PROPAGATE
INPUT: a decided disjunction D(i) {i:1..m}
OUTPUT: the lowest j (if any) such that j > i and DSJ[i]=2, or
        m+1 if all the disjunctions are decided, otherwise nil

1.  FOR p = i + 1 TO m
2.     IF DSJ[p]=2 THEN
3.        IF only one disjunct d(p,k) of D(p) does not create a
              quasicycle THEN mark d(p,k) current, CULPRIT[p]:=
              culprit(p,3-k), DSJ[p]:= 2-k, and add p to D-SET[i]
4.        ELSE
5.           IF both d(p,1) and d(p,2) determine a quasicycle THEN
              BEGIN
6.               IF culprit(p,1) = culprit(p,2) = nil THEN
                    BEGIN {chronological backtracking}
7.                  q:= the highest j such that j < i and DSJ[j]=1,
                       or nil if such a j does not exist;
8.                  IF q is not nil THEN
                       BEGIN {restore disjunctions between D(q) and D(i)}
9.                     CULPRIT[q]:= nil; mark d(q,1) eliminated;
10.                    FOR t = q to i
11.                       IF CULPRIT[t] >= q THEN
                             BEGIN
12.                             IF t is not equal to q THEN mark the disjuncts
                                   of D(t) available, DSJ[t]:=2, CULPRIT[t]:=nil;
13.                             FOR EACH h in D-SET[t] mark d(h,1) and d(h,2)
                                   available, DSJ[h]:=2, CULPRIT[h]:=nil,
                                   and D-SET[h]:=nil
                             END
14.                    i:= q {backtrack to D(q)}
                       END
15.                 ELSE RETURN nil {the D-timegraph is inconsistent}
                    END
16.              ELSE
                    BEGIN {selective backtracking}
17.                 CULPRIT[p]:= max(culprit(p,1),culprit(p,2));
18.                 q:= CULPRIT[p]; run through steps 9. to 14.
                    END
19.           RETURN i
              END
20. RETURN the lowest j such that j >= i and DSJ[j] = 2, or
           m + 1 if such a j does not exist.
```

Figure 6: Algorithm for the forward propagation of a decided disjunction

store for each disjunction the CULPRIT of the eliminated disjunct (if any). If $D(j)$ is a decided disjunction without an eliminated disjunct, then CULPRIT$[j]=j$; if $D(j)$ is not yet decided, then CULPRIT$[j]$=nil.

2.2.4 Forward propagation

When the initial timegraph is very sparse, the dearth of constraints imposed by the graph can protract the search for an instantiation of the disjunctions and the algorithm may perform an unacceptable number of backtracks (see Section 3). In order to cope with such cases we have developed a technique which can dramatically reduce the number of backtracks.

Forward propagation of a decided disjunction $D(i)$ consists of checking all disjunctions $D(j)$ not yet decided and following $D(i)$ in the ordering (i.e. such that $i < j \leq m$), to determine whether at least one of the disjuncts of $D(j)$ can be consistently added to T^h ($i < h < j$), where h is the index of the most recently decided disjunction at the moment of checking $D(j)$. If only one disjunct of $D(j)$ determines an inconsistency, then its status is set to eliminated and the other disjunct is made current. If both disjuncts determine a quasicycle then $D(j)$ cannot be decided and we perform a jump back to a selected antagonist of $D(j)$ or, when this is not possible, a chronological backtrack to the first disjunction preceding $D(j)$ with an available disjunct.

Figure 6 shows the algorithm for achieving the forward propagation of a decided disjunction. It uses an additional data structures called D-SET which is a vector of

Table 1: Statistics of DECIDE-DISJUNCTIONS without the forward propagation*

Convex relations	Backtracks			Average CPU-time
	Mean	Deviation	Max.	
30	482.98	3686.99	92424	1160
50	122.17	2143.80	91516	351
75	11.69	311.46	13760	47
100	0.28	3.80	96	19
150	0.019	0.47	20	10
200	0	0	0	6
250	0	0	0	5

* Number of backtracks and average CPU-time for deciding 30 binary disjunctions of <-relations in databases of convex PA-relations constraining 30 points (14,000 problems).

Table 2: Statistics of DECIDE-DISJUNCTIONS with the forward propagation*

Convex relations	Backtracks			Average CPU-time
	Mean	Deviation	Max.	
30	1.13	6.29	142	104
50	0.65	12.27	547	70
75	0.12	0.49	4	29
100	0.03	0.24	3	20
150	0.005	0.09	2	10
200	0	0	0	7
250	0	0	0	5

* Number of backtracks and average CPU-time for deciding 30 binary disjunctions of <-relations in databases of convex PA-relations constraining 30 points (14,000 problems).

dimension m where D-SET$[i]$ is the set I of disjunction indices such that $k \in I$ if $D(k)$ is a disjunction which has been decided by the forward propagation of $D(i)$.

In the search algorithm enhanced by the inclusion of the forward propagation (for a presentation of its pseudocode see [Gerevini and Schubert, to appear]) we restore disjunctions in accordance with the basic algorithm, and in addition for each disjunction $D(i)$ that is updated we also restore the set of decided disjunctions depending on it (i.e. the disjunctions indicated by D-SET$[i]$).

The space complexity overhead introduced by D-SET is negligible because there can never be more disjunction indices stored in all the locations of the vector than the number of disjunctions. Furthermore, since DSJ and CULPRIT are also vectors of dimension m, it follows that the space complexity of the whole algorithm is $O(n+e+m)$, where n is the number of point variables, e the number of PA-relations and m the number of disjunctions.

3 EXPERIMENTAL RESULTS

The algorithms for deciding disjunctions of inequalities has been incorporated into *TimeGraph-II* [Gerevini et al., 1993], a temporal reasoning system written in Common Lisp.[7] This section reports results from large scale tests we have conducted on a SUN SPARCstation 10 with the purpose of (1) exploring the space of the problems of deciding disjunctions of inequalities to identify interesting parameters in terms of which useful heuristics can be formulated, and (2) of testing the scalability of the method proposed.

Tables 1 and 2 report the number of backtracks (the mean, the standard deviation and the maximum value) and the average CPU-time (milliseconds) required for

Table 3: Backtracking Requirements for Sparse Data Sets*

Backtracks	% of $\mathcal{D}$-timegraphs
[0..10]	96.01
(10..50]	1.8
(50..100]	0.53
(100..200]	0.43
(200..300]	0.21
(300..400]	0.12
> 400	0.9

* Distribution of 30,000 $\mathcal{D}$-timegraphs with respect to the number of backtracks performed by the basic search algorithm (30 disjunctions, 20 PA-relations and 30 time points).

deciding a set of 30 disjunctions of form $x < y \vee w < z$ using a timegraph built from a collection of *convex* PA-relations constraining 30 time points.[8] Table 1 pertains to the basic algorithm, while Table 2 pertains to the algorithm performing the forward propagation during the search (see Figure 5) which was applied to the same data sets used for Table 1.

For each number r of convex PA-relations considered, 2000 randomly generated $\mathcal{D}$-timegraphs were built, each of which was created in the following way: first, a consistent set of convex PA-relations S was generated following a method similar to the one used in [Gerevini and Schubert, 1993b] for testing the construction of a timegraph but using the uniform distribution instead of the geometric one in choosing the pair of points to be constrained;[9] second, a timegraph T was con-

---

[7]TimeGraph-II is available by inquiry to the authors.

[8]The convex PA-relations are all the relations of PA except "$\neq$" [Vilain et al., 1990; van Beek and Cohen, 1990]. The reason we haven't considered $\neq$ relations is that for the kind of disjunctions we were dealing with, the information provided by these relations is exploited neither by the preprocessing step nor by the search algorithms.

[9]By choosing the uniform distribution we have relaxed

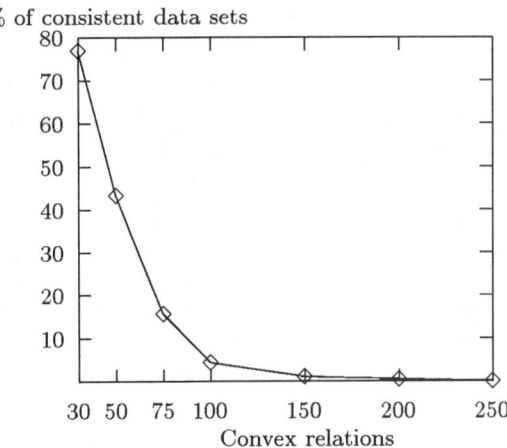

Figure 7: Distribution of the consistent $\mathcal{D}$-timegraphs over 14,000 data sets with 30 binary disjunctions of <-relations and 30 time points

structed from S; finally, a set D of disjunctions of the form $x < y \lor w < z$ was built by randomly generating each of them in such a way that:

- x, y, w and z are point variables taking part in at least one of the relations in S;
- $x \neq y$, $w \neq z$ and the pair (x, y) is different from the pair (w, z);
- neither $x < y$ nor $w < z$ are in S.

It is interesting to observe that the number of backtracks shown in Table 1 decreases dramatically when the number of PA-relations used to build the timegraph is greater than three times the number of time points. The main reason for this is that in general the more constraints are imposed on the timegraph, the more disjunctions are eliminated by the pruning rules, and hence the easier the problem becomes for the backtracking step. For example, with 30 convex PA-relations constraining 30 points only 11% of the disjunctions were eliminated on average, while with 75 convex PA-relations constraining 30 points this percentage was 58.5%.

Figure 7 shows the distribution of the consistent data sets with respect to the number of PA-relations forming the timegraph. This curve indicates that when the timegraph is not particularly sparse the probability of the $\mathcal{D}$-timegraph being consistent is much smaller that the probability of being inconsistent. Since the percentage of consistent data sets generated goes down drastically when the timegraph is not sparse, we have repeated the test of Table 1 by generating only consistent data sets.[10] The results of this experiment are

---

the assumption made in [Gerevini and Schubert, 1993b] that the data sets generated are likely to allow chain formation.

[10] This was obtained by adding to the data set generator the extra requirement that for each disjunction at least one of its disjuncts is consistent.

qualitatively identical to those obtained when consistency is not enforced in the data sets, and so they show that when the timegraph is not particularly sparse our method performs efficiently regardless of whether the information provided is consistent or not.

When the timegraph is sparse, there are some cases in which the basic algorithm performs a large number of backtracks (see Table 1) and hence incurs large CPU-time costs. Fortunately, as shown by the elevated values of the standard deviation when the number of convex PA-relations is between 30 and 75, these computationally expensive cases are relatively rare. This has been further confirmed experimentally by computing their percentage over 30,000 $\mathcal{D}$-timegraphs with 30 time points, 20 convex PA-relations and 30 disjunctions. Table 3 shows that the number of cases for which more than 400 backtracks were performed is limited to 0.9% of all $\mathcal{D}$-timegraph generated, while the percentage of $\mathcal{D}$-timegraphs requiring at most 10 backtracks was 96.01 %.

Table 2 shows that when the timegraph is sparse, the use of forward propagation technique during the search can dramatically reduce the number of backtracks. However, the CPU-time we need for propagating decided disjunctions can be too high for larger data sets. The main reason for this is that quasicycle elimination requires $O(\hat{e})$ time where $\hat{e}$ is the number of metaedges in the timegraph which are a subset of the PA-relations initially provided [Gerevini and Schubert, 1993b]. It follows that a general good heuristic for large data sets is to prefer the use of the forward propagation when the initial timegraph is sparse or when the number of disjunctions to be decided is particularly high with respect to the number of convex PA-relations, and to use the basic algorithm in other cases.

The curves in Figure 8 show the results of other experiments aimed at testing the scalability of the proposed approach. In this experiment we have considered only consistent data sets following the method described above. The two curves of the first graph show the average CPU-time (seconds) required for deciding sets of disjunctions of size n (n number of time points) with $8n$ and $2n \log n$ simple PA-relations (with the logarithm truncated to its integer part). The numbers attached to the points on the curve indicate the percentage of the disjunctions eliminated by preprocessing. While in the case of $8n$ relations this percentage decreases when n increases, for $2n \log n$ relations it tends to be constant (wavering between 88.8 and 91.3).[11]

The curve in the second graph shows the average CPU-time required by more sparse graphs ($4n$ PA-relations) for which forward propagation has been used during

---

[11] In order to simplify the figure these numbers are not shown.

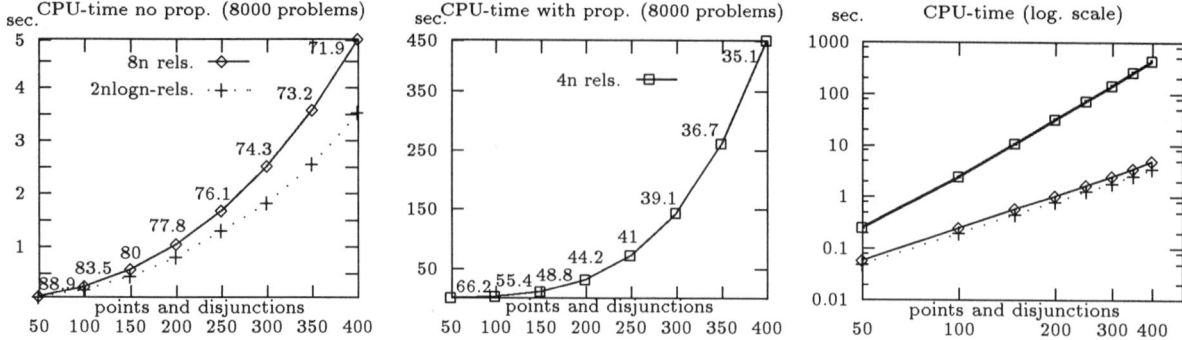

Figure 8: Scalability of the algorithms for deciding consistency

the search.[12]

Finally, the third graph shows that for the 16,000 problems considered our algorithms tend to perform polynomially (quadratic time for the curves of the first graph and cubic time for the curve of the second) since the previous curves approximate straight lines on a log–log scale.

4 CONCLUSIONS

In this paper we have provided an efficient method for managing disjunctions of relations in the Point Algebra, and specialized algorithms for consistency checking of binary disjunctions of inequalities.

The method consists of a preprocessing step and of a search step. The preprocessing step is worst-case polynomial and is based on some pruning rules which exploit the information stored in the timegraph to eliminate disjunctions. There are several polynomial strategies for applying these rules, including one which is complete for checking the consistency of interval relations in the ORD-Horn subclass of IA.

Experimental results show that when the number of PA-disjunctions is relatively small with respect to the number of PA-relations our search algorithms are very efficient, and that although in general the problem addressed is NP-hard, they tend to perform polynomially on average.

Though timegraphs were first proposed for efficient temporal reasoning in story understanding, there are reasons for regarding this approach as well-suited for planning applications. Sets of temporal constraints that were generated in the context of the TRAINS project at Rochester (independently of our work) conformed well with our assumptions [Allen and Schubert, 1991; Yampratoom and Allen, 1993]. In addition, van

---

[12]These experiments were conducted on a Sun SPARCstation 2 and hence a comparison with the results in the previous graph is inappropriate.

Beek [van Beek, 1992] estimated some parameters for sets of IA-relations arising in the kind of constraint-based planning proposed by Allen and Koomen [Allen and Koomen, 1983]. He found that about 25% of the pairs of intervals were constrained by interval relations, and the great majority of these relations were pointizable. These are just the sort of conditions under which our consistency algorithm for $\mathcal{D}$-timegraphs is most efficient.

It is an interesting question whether the preprocessing step by itself can provide a good "approximate" method for determining consistency. Further research in this direction might be aimed at providing approximate consistency-checking algorithms for disjunctive temporal information that operate more efficiently and accurately than current approximate techniques based on constraint propagation.

Acknowledgements

The work of the first author was carried out in part during a visit at the Computer Science Department of the University of Rochester (NY) supported by the Italian National Research Council (CNR), and in part at IRST in the context of the MAIA project and CNR projects "Sistemi Informatici e Calcolo Parallelo" and "Pianificazione Automatica". The second author was supported by Rome Lab Contract F30602-91-C-0010.

References

[Allen and Koomen, 1983] J. F. Allen and J. A. Koomen. Planning using a temporal world model. In *Proceedings of the Eighth International Joint Conference on Artificial Intelligence*, pages 741–747, Karlsruhe, Germany, 1983.

[Allen and Schubert, 1991] J. Allen and L. Schubert. The TRAINS project. Technical Report 91-1, Department of Computer Science, University of Rochester, Rochester, NY, 1991.

[Allen, 1983] J. F. Allen. Maintaining knowledge about temporal intervals. *Communication of the ACM*, 26(1):832–843, 1983.

[Allen, 1991] J. F. Allen. Temporal reasoning and planning. In J. F. Allen, H. Kautz, R. Pelavin, and J. Tenenberg, editors, *Reasoning about Plans*, San Mateo, CA, 1991. Morgan-Kaufmann.

[Boddy, 1993] M. Boddy. Temporal reasoning for planning and scheduling. *SIGART Bulletin*, 4(3), 1993.

[Bruynooghe, 1981] M. Bruynooghe. Solving combinatorial search problems by intelligent backtracking. *Information Processing Letters*, 12(1), 1981.

[Cormen et al., 1990] T. Cormen, C. Leiserson, and R. Rivest. *Introduction to Algorithms*. The MIT Press, 1990.

[Dean et al., 1988] T. Dean, R. J. Firby, and D. Miller. Hierarchical planning involving deadlines, travel time, and resources. *Computational Intelligence*, 4:381–398, 1988.

[Frederking and Muscettola, 1992] R. E. Frederking and N. Muscettola. Temporal planning for transportation planning and scheduling. In *International Conference on Robotics and Automation*, pages 1125–1230, Nice, France, 1992.

[Gerevini and Schubert, 1993a] A. Gerevini and L. Schubert. Complexity of temporal reasoning with disjunctions of inequalities. In *Workshop notes of the IJCAI-93 Workshop on spatial and temporal reasoning*, Chambéry, Savoie, France, 1993. Also available as: Technical Report 9303-01, IRST - Istituto per la Ricerca Scientifica e Tecnologica, 38050 Povo, Trento Italy.

[Gerevini and Schubert, 1993b] A. Gerevini and L. Schubert. Efficient temporal reasoning through timegraphs. In *Proceedings of the Thirteenth International Joint Conference on Artificial Intelligence (IJCAI-93)*, pages 648–654, Chambéry, Savoie, France, 1993.

[Gerevini and Schubert, to appear] A. Gerevini and L. Schubert. Efficient algorithms for qualitative reasoning about time. *Artificial Intelligence*, to appear. Also available as: IRST Technical Report 9307-44, Istituto per la Ricerca Scientifica e Tecnologica, 38050 Povo, Trento Italy.

[Gerevini et al., 1993] A. Gerevini, L. Schubert, and S. Schaeffer. Temporal reasoning in TimeGraph I-II. *SIGART Bulletin*, 4(3):21–25, July 1993.

[Henschen and Wos, 1974] L. Henschen and L. Wos. Unit refutations and Horn sets. *Journal of the Association for Computing Machinery (ACM)*, 21:590–605, 1974.

[Ladkin and Maddux, to appear] P. Ladkin and R. Maddux. On binary constraint problems. *Journal of the Association for Computing Machinery (ACM)*, to appear.

[Miller and Schubert, 1990] S. A. Miller and L. K. Schubert. Time revisited. *Computational Intelligence*, 6:108–118, 1990.

[Nebel and Bürckert, 1993] B. Nebel and H. J. Bürckert. Reasoning about temporal relations: A maximal tractable subclass of Allen's interval algebra. Research Report RR-93-11, German Research Center for Artificial Intelligence (DFKI), Saarbrücken, Germany, March 1993.

[Shanahan and Southwick, 1989] M. Shanahan and R. Southwick. *Search, Inference and Dependencies in Artificial Intelligence*. Ellis Horwood, New York, Chichester, Brisbane, Toronto, 1989.

[Stickel, 1985] M. E. Stickel. Automated deduction by theory resolution. In *Proceedings of the Nineth International Joint Conference on Artificial Intelligence*, pages 1181–1186, Los Angeles, CA, USA, 1985.

[Tsang, 1986] E.P.K. Tsang. Plan generation in a temporal frame. In *Seventh European Conference on Artificial Intelligence* (ECAI), pages 479–493, 1986.

[van Beek and Cohen, 1990] P. van Beek and R. Cohen. Exact and approximate reasoning about temporal relations. *Computational Intelligence*, 6:132–144, 1990.

[van Beek, 1992] P. van Beek. Reasoning about qualitative temporal information. *Artificial Intelligence*, 58(1-3):297–321, 1992.

[Vere, 1983] S. A. Vere. Planning in time: Windows and durations for activities and goals. *IEEE Transactions on Pattern Analysis and Machine Intelligence*, 5(3):246–267, 1983.

[Vilain et al., 1990] M. Vilain, H. Kautz, and P. van Beek. Constraint propagation algorithms for temporal reasoning: a revised report. In *Readings in Qualitative Reasoning about Physical Systems*, pages 373–381. Morgan Kaufmann, San Mateo, CA, 1990.

[Yampratoom and Allen, 1993] E. Yampratoom and J. Allen. Performance of temporal reasoning systems. *SIGART Bulletin*, 4(3), 1993.

GSAT and Dynamic Backtracking

Matthew L. Ginsberg
CIRL
1269 University of Oregon
Eugene, OR 97403

David A. McAllester
MIT AI Laboratory
545 Technology Square
Cambridge, MA 02139

Abstract

There has been substantial recent interest in two new families of search techniques. One family consists of nonsystematic methods such as GSAT; the other contains systematic approaches that use a polynomial amount of justification information to prune the search space. This paper introduces a new technique that combines these two approaches. The algorithm allows substantial freedom of movement in the search space but enough information is retained to ensure the systematicity of the resulting analysis. Bounds are given for the size of the justification database and conditions are presented that guarantee that this database will be polynomial in the size of the problem in question.

1 INTRODUCTION

The past few years have seen rapid progress in the development of algorithms for solving constraint-satisfaction problems, or CSPs. CSPs arise naturally in subfields of AI from planning to vision, and examples include propositional theorem proving, map coloring and scheduling problems. The problems are difficult because they involve search; there is never a guarantee that (for example) a successful coloring of a portion of a large map can be extended to a coloring of the map in its entirety.

The algorithms developed recently have been of two types. *Systematic* algorithms determine whether a solution exists by searching the entire space. *Local* algorithms use hill-climbing techniques to find a solution quickly but are *nonsystematic* in that they search the entire space in only a probabilistic sense.

The empirical effectiveness of these nonsystematic algorithms appears to be a result of their ability to follow local gradients in the search space. Traditional systematic procedures explore the space in a fixed order that is independent of local gradients; the fixed order makes following local gradients impossible but is needed to ensure that no node is examined twice and that the search remains systematic.

Dynamic backtracking [Ginsberg,1993] attempts to overcome this problem by retaining specific information about those portions of the search space that have been eliminated and then following local gradients in the remainder. Unlike previous algorithms that recorded such elimination information, such as dependency-directed backtracking [Stallman and Sussman,1977], dynamic backtracking is selective about the information it caches so that only a polynomial amount of memory is required. These earlier techniques cached a new result with every backtrack, using an amount of memory that was linear in the run time and thus exponential in the size of the problem being solved.

Unfortunately, neither dynamic nor dependency-directed backtracking (or any other known similar method) is truly effective at local maneuvering within the search space, since the basic underlying methodology remains simple chronological backtracking. New techniques are included to make the search more efficient, but an exponential number of nodes in the search space must still be examined before early choices can be retracted. No existing search technique is able to both move freely within the search space and keep track of what has been searched and what hasn't.

The second class of algorithms developed recently presume that freedom of movement is of greater importance than systematicity. Algorithms in this class achieve their freedom of movement by abandoning the conventional description of the search space as a tree of partial solutions, instead thinking of it as a space of total assignments of values to variables. Motion is permitted between any two assignments that differ on a single value, and a hill-climbing procedure is employed to try to minimize the number of constraints violated by the overall assignment. The best-known algorithms in this class are min-conflicts [Minton *et al.*,1990] and GSAT [Selman *et al.*,1992].

Min-conflicts has been applied to the scheduling domain specifically and used to schedule tasks on the Hubble space telescope. GSAT is restricted to Boolean satisfiability problems (where every variable is assigned simply true or false), and has led to remarkable progress in the solution of randomly generated problems of this type; its performance is reported [Selman and Kautz,1993, Selman *et al.*,1992, Selman *et al.*,1993] as surpassing that of other techniques such as simulated annealing [Kirkpatrick *et al.*,1982] and systematic techniques based on the Davis-Putnam procedure [Davis and Putnam,1960].

GSAT is not a panacea, however; there are many problems on which it performs fairly poorly. If a problem has no solution, for example, GSAT will never be able to report this with confidence. Even if a solution does exist, there appear to be at least two possible difficulties that GSAT may encounter.

First, the GSAT search space may contain so many local minima that it is not clear how GSAT can move so as to reduce the number of constraints violated by a given assignment. As an example, consider the CSP of generating crossword puzzles by filling words from a fixed dictionary into an empty frame [Ginsberg *et al.*,1990]. The constraints indicate that there must be no conflict in each of the squares; thus two words that begin on the same square must also begin with the same letter. In this domain, getting "close" is not necessarily any indication that the problem is nearly solved, since correcting a conflict at a single square may involve modifying much of the current solution. Konolige has recently reported that GSAT specifically has difficulty solving problems of this sort [Konolige,1994].

Second, GSAT does no forward propagation. In the crossword domain once again, selecting one word may well force the selection of a variety of subsequent words. In a Boolean satisfiability problem, assigning one variable the value true may cause an immediate cascade of values to be assigned to other variables via a technique known as *unit resolution*. It seems plausible that forward propagation will be more common on realistic problems than on randomly generated ones; the most difficult random problems appear to be tangles of closely related individual variables while naturally occurring problems tend to be tangles of sequences of related variables. Furthermore, it appears that GSAT's performance degrades (relative to systematic approaches) as these sequences of variables arise [Crawford and Baker,1994].

Our aim in this paper is to describe a new search procedure that appears to combine the benefits of both of the earlier approaches; in some very loose sense, it can be thought of as a systematic version of GSAT.

The next section gives a presentation of the original dynamic backtracking algorithm [Ginsberg,1993]. The termination proof is omitted here but can be found in earlier papers [Ginsberg,1993, McAllester,1993]. Section 5 present a modification of dynamic backtracking called *partial-order dynamic backtracking*, or PDB. This algorithm builds on work of McAllester's [McAllester,1993]. Partial-order dynamic backtracking provides greater flexibility in the allowed set of search directions while preserving systematicity and polynomial worst case space usage. Section 6 presents a new variant of dynamic backtracking that is still more flexible in the allowed set of search directions. While this final procedure is still systematic, it can use exponential space in the worst case. Section 7 presents some empirical results comparing PDB with other well known algorithms on a class of "local" randomly generated 3-SAT problems. Concluding remarks are contained in Section 8, and proofs appear in the appendix.

2 CONSTRAINTS AND NOGOODS

We begin with a slightly nonstandard definition of a CSP.

Definition 2.1 *By a* constraint satisfaction problem (I, V, κ) *we will mean a finite set I of variables; for each $x \in I$, there is a finite set V_x of possible values for the variable x. κ is a set of constraints each of the form $\neg[(x_1 = v_1) \wedge \cdots \wedge (x_k = v_k)]$ where each x_j is a variable in I and each v_j is an element of V_{x_j}. A* solution *to the CSP is an assignment P of values to variables that satisfies every constraint. For each variable x we require that $P(x) \in V_x$ and for each constraint $\neg[(x_1 = v_1) \wedge \cdots \wedge (x_k = v_k)]$ we require that $P(x_i) \neq v_i$ for some x_i.*

The technical convenience of the above definition of a constraint will be clear shortly. For the moment, we merely note that the above description is clearly equivalent to the conventional one; rather than represent the constraints in terms of allowed value combinations for various variables, we write axioms that disallow specific value combinations one at a time.

Systematic algorithms attempting to find a solution to a CSP typically work with partial solutions that are then discovered to be inextensible or to violate the given constraints; when this happens, a backtrack occurs and the partial solution under consideration is modified. Such a procedure will, of course, need to record information that guarantees that the same partial solution not be considered again as the search proceeds. This information might be recorded in the structure of the search itself; depth-first search with chronological backtracking is an example. More sophisticated methods maintain a database of some form indicating explicitly which choices have been eliminated and which have not. In this paper, we will use a database consisting of a set of *nogoods* [de Kleer,1986].

Definition 2.2 *A* nogood *is an expression of the form*

$$(x_1 = v_1) \wedge \cdots \wedge (x_k = v_k) \rightarrow x \neq v \qquad (1)$$

A nogood can be used to represent a constraint as an implication; note that (1) is logically equivalent to the constraint

$$\neg[(x_1 = v_1) \wedge \cdots \wedge (x_k = v_k) \wedge (x = v)]$$

There are clearly many different ways of representing a given constraint as a nogood.

One special nogood is the *empty* nogood, which is tautologically false. If this nogood can be derived from the given set of constraints, it follows that no solution exists for the problem being attempted.

The typical way in which new nogoods are obtained is by resolving together old ones. As an example, suppose we have derived the following:

$$\begin{aligned}(x = a) \wedge (y = b) &\rightarrow u \neq v_1 \\ (x = a) \wedge (z = c) &\rightarrow u \neq v_2 \\ (y = b) &\rightarrow u \neq v_3\end{aligned}$$

where v_1, v_2 and v_3 are the only values in the domain of u. It follows that we can combine these nogoods to conclude that there is no solution with

$$(x = a) \wedge (y = b) \wedge (z = c) \qquad (2)$$

Moving z to the conclusion of (2) gives us

$$(x = a) \wedge (y = b) \rightarrow z \neq c$$

In general, suppose we have a collection of nogoods of the form

$$x_{i1} = v_{i1} \wedge \cdots \wedge x_{in_i} = v_{in_i} \rightarrow x \neq v_i$$

as i varies, where the same variable appears in the conclusions of all the nogoods. Suppose further that the antecedents all agree as to the value of the x_i's, so that any time x_i appears in the antecedent of one of the nogoods, it is in a term $x_i = v_i$ for a fixed v_i. If the nogoods collectively eliminate all of the possible values for x, we can conclude that $\bigwedge_j(x_j = v_j)$ is inconsistent; moving one specific x_k to the conclusion gives us

$$\bigwedge_{j \neq k}(x_j = v_j) \rightarrow x_k \neq v_k \qquad (3)$$

As before, note the freedom in our choice of variable appearing in the conclusion of the nogood. Since the next step in our search algorithm will presumably satisfy (3) by changing the value for x_k, the selection of consequent variable corresponds to the choice of variable to "flip" in the terms used by GSAT or other hill-climbing algorithms.

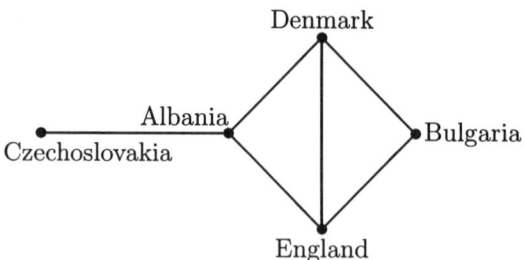

Figure 1: A small map-coloring problem

As we have remarked, dynamic backtracking accumulates information in a set of nogoods. To see how this is done, consider the map coloring problem in Figure 1, repeated from [Ginsberg,1993]. The map consists of five countries: Albania, Bulgaria, Czechoslovakia, Denmark and England. We assume – wrongly – that the countries border each other as shown in the figure, where countries are denoted by nodes and border one another if and only if there is an arc connecting them.

In coloring the map, we can use the three colors red, green and blue. We will typically abbreviate the colors and country names to single letters in the obvious way. The following table gives a trace of how a conventional dependency-directed backtracking scheme might attack this problem; each row shows a state of the procedure in the middle of a backtrack step, after a new nogood has been identified but before colors are erased to reflect the new conclusion. The coloring(s) that are about to be removed appear in boldface. The "drop" column will be discussed shortly.

A	B	C	D	E	add		drop
r	g	**r**			$A = r \rightarrow C \neq r$	1	
r	g	b	**r**		$A = r \rightarrow D \neq r$	2	
r	g	b	**g**		$B = g \rightarrow D \neq g$	3	
r	g	b	b	**r**	$A = r \rightarrow E \neq r$	4	
r	g	b	b	**g**	$B = g \rightarrow E \neq g$	5	
r	g	b	b	**b**	$D = b \rightarrow E \neq b$	6	
r	g	b	**b**		$(A = r) \wedge (B = g)$	7	6
					$\rightarrow D \neq b$		
r	**g**	b			$A = r \rightarrow B \neq g$	8	3,5,7

We begin by coloring Albania red and Bulgaria green, and then try to color Czechoslovakia red as well. Since this violates the constraint that Albania and Czechoslovakia be different colors, nogood (1) in the above table is produced.

We change Czechoslovakia's color to blue and then turn to Denmark. Since Denmark cannot be colored red or green, nogoods (2) and (3) appear; the only remaining color for Denmark is blue.

Unfortunately, having colored Denmark blue, we cannot color England. The three nogoods generated are (4), (5) and (6), and we can resolve these together because the three conclusions eliminate all of the possible colors for England. The result is that there is no solution with $(A = r) \wedge (B = g) \wedge (D = b)$, which we rewrite as (7) above. This can in turn be resolved with (2) and (3) to get (8), correctly indicating that the color of red for Albania is inconsistent with the choice of green for Bulgaria. The analysis can continue at this point to gradually determine that Bulgaria has to be red, Denmark can be green or blue, and England must then be the color not chosen for Denmark.

As we mentioned in the introduction, the problem with this approach is that the set Γ of nogoods grows monotonically, with a new nogood being added at every step. The number of nogoods stored therefore grows linearly with the run time and thus (presumably) exponentially with the size of the problem. A related problem is that it may become increasingly difficult to extend the partial solution P without violating one of the nogoods in Γ.

Dynamic backtracking deals with this by discarding nogoods when they become "irrelevant" in the sense that their antecedents no longer match the partial solution in question. In the example above, nogoods can be eliminated as indicated in the final column of the trace. When we derive (7), we remove (6) because Denmark is no longer colored blue. When we derive (8), we remove all of the nogoods with $B = g$ in their antecedents. Thus the only information we retain is that Albania's red color precludes red for Czechoslovakia, Denmark and England (1, 2 and 4) and also green for Bulgaria (8).

3 DYNAMIC BACKTRACKING

Dynamic backtracking uses a set of nogoods to both record information about the portion of the search space that has been eliminated and to record the current partial assignment being considered by the procedure. The current partial assignment is encoded in the antecedents of the current nogood set. More formally:

Definition 3.1 *An acceptable next assignment for a nogood set Γ is an assignment P satisfying every nogood in Γ and every antecedent of every such nogood. We will call a set of nogoods Γ acceptable if no two nogoods in Γ share the same conclusion and either Γ contains the empty nogood or there exists an acceptable next assignment for Γ.*

If Γ is acceptable, the antecedents of the nogoods in Γ induce a partial assignment of values to variables; any acceptable next assignment must be an extension of this partial assignment. In the above table, for example, nogoods (1) through (6) encode the partial assignment given by $A = r$, $B = g$, and $D = b$. Nogoods (1) though (7) fail to encode a partial assignment because the seventh nogood is inconsistent with the partial assignment encoded in nogoods (1) through (6). This is why the sixth nogood is removed when the seventh nogood is added.

Procedure 3.2 (Dynamic backtracking) To solve a CSP:

$P :=$ any complete assignment of values to variables
$\Gamma := \emptyset$
until either P is a solution or the empty nogood
 has been derived:
  $\gamma :=$ any constraint violated by P
  $\Gamma := \texttt{simp}(\Gamma \cup \gamma)$
  $P :=$ any acceptable next assignment for Γ

To simplify the discussion we assume a fixed total order on the variables. Versions of dynamic backtracking with dynamic rearrangement of the variable order can be found elsewhere [Ginsberg,1993, McAllester,1993]. Whenever a new nogood is added, the fixed variable ordering is used to select the variable that appears in the conclusion of the nogood – the latest variable always appears in the conclusion. The subroutine simp closes the set of nogoods under the resolution inference rule discussed in the previous section and removes all nogoods which have an antecedent $x = v$ such that $x \neq v$ appears in the conclusion of some other nogood. Without giving a detailed analysis, we note that simplification ensures that Γ remains acceptable. To prove termination we introduce the following notation:

Definition 3.3 *For any acceptable Γ and variable x, we define the live domain of x to be those values v such that $x \neq v$ does not appear in the conclusion of any nogood in Γ. We will denote the size of the live domain of x by $|x|_\Gamma$, and will denote by $m(\Gamma)$ the tuple $\langle |x_1|_\Gamma, \ldots, |x_n|_\Gamma \rangle$ where $x_1, \ldots, x_n$ are the variables in the CSP in their specified order.*

The termination proof (which we do not repeat here) is based on the observation that every simplification lexicographically reduces $m(\Gamma)$.

Proposition 3.4 *Any acceptable set of nogoods can be stored in $o(n^2 v)$ space where n is the number of variables and v is the maximum domain size of any single variable.*

It is worth considering the behavior of Procedure 3.2 when applied to a CSP that is the union of two disjoint CSPs that do not share variables or constraints. If each of the two subproblems is unsatisfiable and the variable ordering interleaves the variables of the two subproblems, a classical backtracking search will take time proportional to the product of the times required to search each assignment space separately.[1] In con-

---
[1] This observation remains true even if backjumping techniques are used.

trast, Procedure 3.2 works on the two problems independently, and the time taken to solve the union of problems is therefore the sum of the times needed for the individual subproblems. It follows that Procedure 3.2 is fundamentally different from classical backtracking or backjumping procedures; Procedure 3.2 is in fact what has been called a *polynomial space aggressive backtracking procedure* [McAllester,1993].

4 DYNAMIC BACKTRACKING AS LOCAL SEARCH

Before proceeding, let us highlight the obvious similarities between Procedure 3.2 and Selman's description of GSAT [Selman et al.,1992]:

Procedure 4.1 (GSAT) To solve a CSP:

for $i := 1$ to MAX-TRIES
    $P :=$ a randomly generated truth assignment
    for $j := 1$ to MAX-FLIPS
        if P is a solution, then return it
        else flip any variable in P that results in
            the greatest decrease in the number
            of unsatisfied clauses
        end if
    end for
end for
return failure

The inner loop of the above procedure makes a local move in the search space in a direction consistent with the goal of satisfying a maximum number of clauses; we will say that GSAT follows the local gradient of a "maxsat" objective function. But local search can get stuck in local minima; the outer loop provides a partial escape by giving the procedure several independent chances to find a solution.

Like GSAT, dynamic backtracking examines a sequence of total assignments. Initially, dynamic backtracking has considerable freedom in selecting the next assignment; in many cases, it can update the total assignment in a manner identical to GSAT. The nogood set ultimately both constrains the allowed directions of motion and forces the procedure to search systematically. Dynamic backtracking cannot get stuck in local minima.

Both systematicity and the ability to follow local gradients are desirable. The observations of the previous paragraphs, however, indicate that these two properties are in conflict – systematic enumeration of the search space appears incompatible with gradient descent. To better understand the interaction of systematicity and local gradients, we need to examine more closely the structure of the nogoods used in dynamic backtracking.

We have already discussed the fact that a single constraint can be represented as a nogood in a variety of ways. For example, the constraint $\neg(A = r \wedge B = g)$ can be represented either as the nogood $A = r \to B \neq g$ or as $B = g \to A \neq r$. Although these nogoods capture the same information, they behave differently in the dynamic backtracking procedure because they encode different partial truth assignments and represent different choices of variable ordering. In particular, the set of acceptable next assignments for $A = r \to B \neq g$ is quite different from the set of acceptable next assignments for $B = g \to A \neq r$. In the former case an acceptable assignment must satisfy $A = r$; in the latter case, $B = g$ must hold. Intuitively, the former nogood corresponds to changing the value of B while the latter nogood corresponds to changing that of A. The manner in which we represent the constraint $\neg(A = r \wedge B = g)$ influences the direction in which the search is allowed to proceed. In Procedure 3.2, the choice of representation is forced by the need to respect the fixed variable ordering and to change the latest variable in the constraint.[2] Similar restrictions exist in the original presentation of dynamic backtracking itself [Ginsberg,1993].

5 PARTIAL-ORDER DYNAMIC BACKTRACKING

Partial-order dynamic backtracking [McAllester,1993] replaces the fixed variable order with a *partial* order that is dynamically modified during the search. When a new nogood is added, this partial ordering need not fix a unique representation – there can be considerable choice in the selection of the variable to appear in the conclusion of the nogood. This leads to freedom in the selection of the variable whose value is to be changed, thereby allowing greater flexibility in the directions that the procedure can take while traversing the search space. The locally optimal gradient followed by GSAT can be adhered to more often. The partial order on variables is represented by a set of ordering constraints called *safety conditions*.

Definition 5.1 *A* safety condition *is an assertion of the form $x < y$ where x and y are variables. Given a set S of safety conditions, we will denote by $\leq_S$ the transitive closure of $<$, saying that S is acyclic if $\leq_S$ is antisymmetric. We will write $x <_S y$ to mean that $x \leq_S y$ and $y \not\leq_S x$.*

In other words, $x \leq y$ if there is some (possibly empty) sequence of safety conditions

$$x < z_1 < \ldots < z_n < y$$

---

[2]Note, however, that there is still considerable freedom in the choice of the constraint itself. A total assignment usually violates many different constraints.

The requirement of antireflexivity means simply that there are no two distinct x and y for which $x \leq y$ and $y \leq x$; in other words, $\leq_S$ has no "loops" and $\leq_S$ is a partial order on the variables. In this section, we restrict our attention to acyclic sets of safety conditions.

We now consider some ways of constructing and manipulating sets of safety conditions.

Definition 5.2 *For a set of nogoods Γ, we will denote by S_Γ the set of all safety conditions $x < y$ such that there is a nogood $\gamma \in \Gamma$ with x in the antecedent of γ and y in its conclusion.*

Informally, we require variables in the antecedent of nogoods to precede the variables in their conclusions, since the antecedent variables have been used to determine the live domains of the conclusions.

The state of the partial order dynamic backtracking procedure is represented by a pair $\langle \Gamma, S \rangle$ of a set of nogoods and a set of safety conditions. The states of the procedure described in this section satisfy the following definition.

Definition 5.3 *A pair $\langle \Gamma, S \rangle$ will be called an acceptable pair if Γ is acceptable, S is acyclic and $S_\Gamma \subseteq S$.*

The requirement that $S_\Gamma \subseteq S$ means that the safety conditions encode at least as much ordering information as Definition 5.2 ascribes to the nogoods themselves.

In many cases, we will be interested in only the ordering information about variables that can precede a fixed variable x. If we want to discard the rest of the ordering information, we will do so by discarding all of the safety conditions involving any variable y that follows x, and then recording only that y does indeed follow x. Somewhat more formally:

Definition 5.4 *For any set S of safety conditions and variable x, we define the* weakening *of S at x, to be denoted $W(S, x)$, to be the set of safety conditions given by removing from S all safety conditions of the form $z < y$ where $x <_S y$ and then adding the safety condition $x < y$ for all such y.*

The nogood set $W(S, x)$ is a weakening of S in the sense that every total ordering consistent with S is also consistent with $W(S, x)$. However $W(S, x)$ usually admits more total orderings than S does; for example, if S specifies a total order then $W(S, x)$ allows any order which agrees with S up to and including the variable x. In general, we have the following:

Lemma 5.5 *For any set S of safety conditions, variable x, and total order $<$ consistent with the safety conditions in $W(S, x)$, there exists a total order consistent with S that agrees with $<$ through x.*

We now state the PDB procedure.

Procedure 5.6 To solve a CSP:

$P :=$ any complete assignment of values to variables
$\Gamma := \emptyset$
$S := \emptyset$
until either P is a solution or the empty
        nogood has been derived:
    $\gamma :=$ a constraint violated by P
    $\langle \Gamma, S \rangle := \text{simp}(\Gamma, S, \gamma)$
    $P :=$ any acceptable next assignment for Γ

Procedure 5.7 To compute $\text{simp}(\Gamma, S, \gamma)$

select the conclusion of γ so that $S \cup S_{\{\gamma\}}$ is acyclic
$\Gamma := \Gamma \cup \{\gamma\}$
$x :=$ the variable in the conclusion of γ
remove from Γ each nogood with x in its antecedent
$S := W(S, x) \cup S_\Gamma$
if every value in the domain of x appears in the
        conclusion of a nogood in Γ **then**
    $\rho :=$ the result of resolving all nogoods in Γ with x
        in their conclusion
    $\langle \Gamma, S \rangle := \text{simp}(\Gamma, S, \rho)$
end if
return $\langle \Gamma, S \rangle$

The above simplification procedure maintains the invariant that $\langle \Gamma, S \rangle$ be an acceptable pair – Γ remains acceptable, S remains acyclic, and S_Γ remains a subset of S.

Our implementation uses a sparse representation for S and incremental techniques for ensuring that $S_\Gamma \subseteq S$. The time needed for a single call to simp appears to grow significantly sublinearly with the size of the problem in question (see Section 7). To prove that Procedure 5.6 terminates, we begin with the following definition:

Definition 5.8 *Given a set of safety conditions S and a fixed variable ordering $x_1 < x_2 < \cdots < x_n$ that respects $<_S$, let $m(\Gamma, S, <)$ be the tuple $\langle |x_1|_\Gamma, \ldots, |x_n|_\Gamma \rangle$. We will denote by $m(\Gamma, S)$ that tuple which is lexicographically maximal as $<$ is allowed to vary.*

Theorem 5.9 *If $\langle \Gamma, S \rangle$ is an acceptable pair, γ is a nogood that violates some acceptable next assignment for Γ, and $\langle \Gamma', S' \rangle = \text{simp}(\Gamma, S, \gamma)$, then $m(\Gamma', S')$ is lexicographically smaller than $m(\Gamma, S)$. Hence Procedure 5.6 will always terminate in at most*

$$\prod_i |V_i|$$

steps, where the product ranges over the variables in the problem and $|V_i|$ is the size of the domain for variable i.

As an example, suppose that we return to our map-coloring problem. We begin by coloring all of the countries red except Bulgaria, which is green. The following table shows the total assignment that existed at the moment each new nogood was generated.

A	B	C	D	E	add		drop
r	g	r	r	r	$C = r \to A \neq r$	1	
b	g	r	r	r	$D = r \to E \neq r$	2	
b	g	r	r	g	$B = g \to E \neq g$	3	
b	g	r	r	b	$A = b \to E \neq b$	4	
					$(A = b) \wedge (B = g)$ $\to D \neq r$	5	2
					$D < E$	6	
b	g	r	g	b	$B = g \to D \neq g$	7	
b	g	r	b	b	$A = b \to D \neq b$	8	
					$A = b \to B \neq g$	9	3, 5, 7
					$B < E$	10	6
					$B < D$	11	

The initial coloring violates a variety of constraints; suppose that we choose to work on one with Albania in its conclusion because Albania is involved in three violated constraints. We choose $C = r \to A \neq r$ specifically, and add it as (1) above.

We now modify Albania to be blue. The only constraint violated is that Denmark and England be different colors, so we add (2) to Γ. This suggests that we change the color for England; we try green, but this conflicts with Bulgaria. If we write the new nogood as $E = g \to B \neq g$, we will change Bulgaria to blue and be done. In the table above, however, we have made the less optimal choice (3), changing the coloring for England again.

We are now forced to color England blue. This conflicts with Albania, and we continue to leave England in the conclusion of the nogood as we add (4). This nogood resolves with (2) and (3) to produce (5), where we have once again made the worst choice and put D in the conclusion. We add this nogood to Γ and remove nogood (2), which is the only nogood with D in its antecedent. We also add in (6) a safety condition indicating that D must continue to precede E.

We next change Denmark to green. But now Bulgaria and Denmark are both green; we have to write this new nogood (7) with Denmark in the conclusion because of the ordering implied by nogood (5) above. Changing Denmark to blue conflicts with Albania (8), which we have to write as $A = b \to D \neq b$. This new nogood resolves with (5) and (7) to produce (9).

We drop (3), (5) and (7) because they involve $B = g$, and introduce the two safety conditions (10) and (11). Since E follows B, we drop the safety condition $E > D$. At this point, we are finally forced to change the color for Bulgaria and the search continues.

It is important to note that the added flexibility of PDB over dynamic backtracking arises from the flexibility in the first step of the simplification procedure where the conclusion of the new nogood is selected. This selection corresponds to a selection of a variable whose value is to be changed.

As with the procedure in the previous section, when given a CSP that is a union of disjoint CSPs the above procedure will treat the two subproblems independently. The total running time remains the sum of the times required for the subproblems.

6 ARBITRARY MOVEMENT

Partial-order dynamic backtracking still does not provide total freedom in the choice of direction through the search space. When a new nogood is discovered, the existing partial order constrains how we are to interpret that nogood – roughly speaking, we are forced to change the value of late variables before changing the values of their predecessors. The use of a partial order makes this constraint looser than previously, but it is still present. In this section, we allow cycles in the nogoods and safety conditions, thereby permitting arbitrary choice in the selection of the variable appearing in the conclusion of a new nogood.

The basic idea is the following: Suppose that we have introduced a loop into the variable ordering, perhaps by including the pair of nogoods $x \to \neg y$ and $y \to x$. Rather than rewrite one of these nogoods so that the same variable appears in the conclusion of both, we will view the (x, y) combination as a single variable that takes a value in the product set $V_x \times V_y$.

If x and y are variables that have been "combined" in this way, we can to rewrite a nogood with (for example) x in its antecedent and y in its conclusion so that both x and y are in the conclusion. As an example, we can rewrite

$$x = v_x \wedge z = v_z \to y \neq v_y \qquad (4)$$

as

$$z = v_z \to (x, y) \neq (v_x, v_y) \qquad (5)$$

which is logically equivalent. We can view this as eliminating a particular value for the pair of variables (x, y).

Definition 6.1 *Let S be a set of safety conditions (possibly not acyclic). We will write $x \equiv_S y$ if $x \leq_S y$ and $y \leq_S x$. The equivalence class of x under $\equiv$ will be denoted $\langle x \rangle_S$. If γ is a nogood whose conclusion involves the variable x, we will denote by γ_S the result of moving to the conclusion of γ all terms involving members of $\langle x \rangle_S$. If Γ is a set of nogoods, we will denote by Γ_S is the set of nogoods of the form γ_S for $\gamma \in \Gamma$.*

It is not difficult to show that for any set S of safety conditions the relation $\equiv_S$ is an equivalence relation. As an example of rewriting a nogood in the presence of ordering cycles, suppose that γ is the nogood (4) and let S be such that $\langle y \rangle_S = \{x, y\}$; now γ_S is given by (5).

Placing more than one literal in the conclusions of nogoods forces us to reconsider the notion of an acceptable next assignment:

Definition 6.2 *A cyclically acceptable next assignment for a nogood set Γ under a set S of safety conditions is a total assignment P of values to variables satisfying every nogood in Γ_S and every antecedent of every such nogood.*

We now define a third dynamic backtracking procedure. Note that $W(S, x)$ remains well defined even in the case where S is not acyclic, since $W(S, x)$ drops ordering constraints only on variables y such that $x <_S y$.

Procedure 6.3 To solve a CSP:

$P :=$ any complete assignment of values to variables
$\Gamma := \emptyset$
$S := \emptyset$
until either P is a solution or the empty
  nogood has been derived:
  $\gamma :=$ a constraint violated by P
  $\langle \Gamma, S \rangle := \text{simp}(\Gamma, S, \gamma)$
  $P :=$ any cyclically acceptable next assignment
    for Γ under S

Procedure 6.4 To compute $\text{simp}(\Gamma, S, \gamma)$:

select a conclusion for γ (now an unconstrained choice)
$\Gamma := \Gamma \cup \{\gamma\}$
$x :=$ the variable in the conclusion of γ
remove from Γ each nogood with an element of $\langle x \rangle_S$
  in its antecedent
$S := W(S, x) \cup S_\Gamma$
if the set of conclusions of nogoods in Γ_S rule out all
  possible values for the variables in $\langle x \rangle_S$ **then**
  $\rho :=$ the result of resolving all nogoods in Γ_S whose
    conclusions involve variables in $\langle x \rangle_S$
  $\langle \Gamma, S \rangle := \text{simp}(\Gamma, S, \rho)$
  end if
return $\langle \Gamma, S \rangle$

If the conclusion is selected so that S remains acyclic, the above procedure is identical to the one in the previous section.

Proposition 6.5 *Suppose that we are working on a problem with n variables, that the size of the largest domain of any variable is v, and that we have constructed Γ and S using repeated applications of simp. If the largest equivalence class $\langle x \rangle_S$ contains d elements, the space required to store Γ is $o(n^2 v^d)$.*

If we have an equivalence class of d variables each of which has v possible values then the number of possible values of the "combined variable" is v^d. The above procedure can now generate a distinct nogood to eliminate each of the v^d possible values, and the space requirements of the procedure can therefore grow exponentially in the size of the equivalence classes. The time required to find a cyclically allowed next assignment can also grow exponentially in the size of the equivalence classes. We can address these difficulties by selecting in advance a bound for the largest allowed size of any equivalence class. In any event, termination is still guaranteed:

Theorem 6.6 *Procedure 6.3 will always terminate in at most*

$$\prod_i |V_i|$$

steps, where the product ranges over the variables in the problem and $|V_i|$ is the size of the domain for variable i.

Selecting a variable to place in the conclusion of a new nogood corresponds to choosing a variable whose value is to be changed on the next iteration and is analogous to selecting the variable to flip in GSAT. Since the choice of conclusion is unconstrained in the above procedure, the procedure has tremendous flexibility in the way it traverses the search space. Like the procedures in the previous sections, Procedure 6.3 continues to solve combinations of independent subproblems in time bounded by the sum of the times needed to solve the subproblems individually.

Here are these ideas in use on a Boolean CSP with the constraints $a \to b$, $b \to c$ and $c \to \neg b$. As before, we present a trace and then explain it:

a	b	c	add to Γ		remove from Γ
t	f	f	$a \to b$	1	
t	t	f	$b \to c$	2	
t	t	t	$c \to \neg b$	3	
			$\neg a$	4	1
			$a < b$	5	

The first three nogoods are simply the three constraints appearing in the problem. Although the orderings of the second and third nogoods conflict, we choose to write them in the given form in any case.

This puts b and c into an equivalence class. The nogood (1) requires that the value taken by (b, c) be either (t, t) or (t, f); the nogood (2) disallows (t, f) and (3) disallows (t, t). It follows that the three nogoods can be resolved together to obtain the new nogood given simply by $\neg a$. We add this as (4) above, dropping nogood (1) because its antecedent is falsified.

7 EXPERIMENTAL RESULTS

In this section, we present preliminary results regarding the implemented effectiveness of the procedure we have described. The implementation is based on the somewhat restricted Procedure 5.6 as opposed to the more general Procedure 6.3. We compared a search engine based on this procedure with two others, TABLEAU [Crawford and Auton,1993] and WSAT, or "walk-sat" [Selman et al.,1993]. TABLEAU is an efficient implementation of the Davis-Putnam algorithm and is systematic; WSAT is a modification to GSAT and is not. We used WSAT instead of GSAT because WSAT is more effective on a fairly wide range of problem distributions [Selman et al.,1993].

The experimental data was not collected using the random 3-SAT problems that have been the target of much recent investigation, since there is growing evidence that these problems are not representative of the difficulties encountered in practice [Crawford and Baker,1994]. Instead, we generated our problems so that the clauses they contain involve groups of locally connected variables as opposed to variables selected at random.

Somewhat more specifically, we filled an $n \times n$ square grid with variables, and then required that the three variables appearing in any single clause be neighbors in this grid. LISP code generating these examples appears in the appendix. We believe that the qualitative properties of the results reported here hold for a wide class of distributions where variables are given spatial locations and clauses are required to be local.

The experiments were performed at the crossover point where approximately half of the instances generated could be expected to be satisfiable, since this appears to be where the most difficult problems lie [Crawford and Auton,1993]. Note that not all instances at the crossover point are hard; as an example, the local variable interactions in these problems can lead to short resolution proofs that no solution exists in unsatisfiable cases. This is in sharp contrast with random 3-SAT problems (where no short proofs appear to exist in general, and it can even be shown that proof lengths are growing exponentially on average [Chvátal and Szemerédi,1988]). Realistic problems may often have short proof paths: A particular scheduling problem may be unsatisfiable simply because there is no way to schedule a specific resource as opposed to because of global issues involving the problem in its entirety. Satisfiability problems arising in VLSI circuit design can also be expected to have locality properties similar to those we have described.

The problems involved 25, 100, 225, 400 and 625 variables. For each size, we generated 100 satisfiable and 100 unsatisfiable instances and then executed the three procedures to measure their performance. (WSAT was not tested on the unsatisfiable instances.) For WSAT, we measured the number of times specific variable values were flipped. For PDB, we measured the number of top-level calls to Procedure 5.7. For TABLEAU, we measured the number of choice nodes expanded. WSAT and PDB were limited to 100,000 flips; TABLEAU was limited to a running time of 150 seconds.

The results for the satisfiable problems were as follows. For TABLEAU, we give the node count for successful runs only; we also indicate parenthetically what fraction of the problems were solved given the computational resource limitations. (WSAT and PDB successfully solved all instances.)

Variables	PDB	WSAT	TABLEAU
25	35	89	9 (1.0)
100	210	877	255 (1.0)
225	434	1626	504 (.98)
400	731	2737	856 (.70)
625	816	3121	502 (.68)

For the unsatisfiable instances, the results were:

Variables	PDB	TABLEAU
25	122	8 (1.0)
100	509	1779 (1.0)
225	988	5682 (.38)
400	1090	558 (.11)
625	1204	114 (.06)

The times required for PDB and WSAT appear to be growing comparably, although only PDB is able to solve the unsatisfiable instances. The eventual *decrease* in the average time needed by TABLEAU is because it is only managing to solve the easiest instances in each class. This causes it to become almost completely ineffective in the unsatisfiable case and only partially effective in the satisfiable case. Even where it does succeed on large problems, TABLEAU's run time is greater than that of the other two methods.

Finally, we collected data on the time needed for each top-level call to simp in partial-order dynamic backtracking. As a function of the number of variables in the problem, this was:

Number of variables	PDB (msec)	WSAT (msec)
25	3.9	0.5
100	5.3	0.3
225	6.7	0.6
400	7.0	0.7
625	8.4	1.4

All times were measured on a Sparc 10/40 running unoptimized Allegro Common Lisp. An efficient C implementation could expect to improve either method by approximately an order of magnitude. As mentioned in Section 5, the time per flip is growing sublinearly with the number of variables in question.

8 CONCLUSION AND FUTURE WORK

Our aim in this paper has been to make a primarily theoretical contribution, describing a new class of constraint-satisfaction algorithms that appear to combine many of the advantages of previous systematic and nonsystematic approaches. Since our focus has been on a description of the algorithms, there is obviously much that remains to be done.

First, of course, the procedures must be tested on a variety of problems, both synthetic and naturally occurring; the results reported in Section 7 only scratch the surface. It is especially important that realistic problems be included in any experimental evaluation of these ideas, since these problems are likely to have performance profiles substantially different from those of randomly generated problems [Crawford and Baker,1994]. The experiments of the previous section need to be extended to include unit resolution, and we need to determine the frequency with which exponential space is needed in practice by the full procedure 6.3.

Finally, we have left completely untouched the question of how the flexibility of Procedure 6.3 is to be exploited. Given a group of violated constraints, which should we pick to add to Γ? Which variable should be in the conclusion of the constraint? These choices correspond to choice of backtrack strategy in a more conventional setting, and it will be important to understand them in this setting as well.

A PROOFS

Proposition 3.4 *Any acceptable set of nogoods can be stored in $o(n^2v)$ space where n is the number of variables and v is the maximum domain size of any single variable.*

Proof. This can be done by first storing the partial assignment encoded in Γ using $o(n)$ space. The antecedent of each nogood can now be represented as a bit vector specifying the set of variables appearing in the antecedent, allowing the nogood itself to be stored in $o(n)$ space. Since no two nogoods share the same conclusion there are at most nv nogoods. ∎

Lemma 5.5 *For any set S of safety conditions, variable x and total order $<$ consistent with the safety conditions in $W(S,x)$, there is a total order consistent with S that agrees with $<$ through x.*

Proof. Suppose that the ordering $<$ is given by

$$x_1 < \cdots < x_k = x < y_1 < \cdots < y_m \quad (6)$$

Now let $<'$ be any ordering consistent with S, and suppose that the ordering given by $<'$ on the y_i in (6) is

$$z_1 <' \cdots <' z_m$$

We claim that the ordering given by

$$x_1,\ldots,x_k = x, z_1,\ldots,z_m \quad (7)$$

is consistent with all of S. We will show this by showing that (7) is consistent with any specific safety condition $u < v$ in S.

If both u and v are x_i's, then the safety condition $u < v$ will remain in $W(S,x)$ and is therefore satisfied by (7). If both u and v are z_i's, they are ordered as $u < v$ by $<'$ which is known to satisfy the safety conditions in S. If u is an x_i and v is a z_j, $u < v$ clearly follows from (7).

The remaining case is where $u = z_i$ and $v = x_j$ for some specific z_i and x_j. The safety condition $z_i < x_j$ cannot appear in $W(S,x)$, since it is violated by $<$ in (6). It must therefore be the case that either $z_i >_S x$ or $x_j >_S x$. Since the safety condition $x_j > z_i$ is being assumed to appear explicitly in S, it follows that $x_j >_S x$. But now $W(S,x)$ will include the safety condition $x_j > x$, in conflict with the ordering given by (6). This contradiction completes the proof. ∎

Theorem 5.9 *If $\langle \Gamma, S \rangle$ is an acceptable pair, γ is a nogood that violates some acceptable next assignment for Γ, and $\langle \Gamma', S' \rangle = \mathtt{simp}(\Gamma, S, \gamma)$, then $m(\Gamma', S')$ is lexicographically smaller than $m(\Gamma, S)$. Hence Procedure 5.6 will always terminate in at most*

$$\prod_i |V_i|$$

steps, where the product ranges over the variables in the problem and $|V_i|$ is the size of the domain for variable i.

Proof. Let x be the variable in the conclusion of γ. The first nontrivial step of the procedure simp is $\Gamma := \Gamma \cup \{\gamma\}$. This reduces $|x|_\Gamma$. The next step removes from Γ all nogoods with x in the antecedent. For some variables y with $x <_S y$ this allows $|y|_\Gamma$ to increase. The next step is $S := W(S,x) \cup S_\Gamma$. This introduces new orderings. Let $<$ be any total ordering consistent with $W(S,x) \cup S_\Gamma$. Since $<$ is consistent with $W(S,x)$ there must exist a total ordering $<'$ which is consistent with S such that $<$ and $<'$ agree through x. Since $|x|_\Gamma$ has been reduced, and $|y|_\Gamma$ has increased only for variables y such that $x <_S y$, the tuple associated with $<$ must be lexicographically smaller then the tuple associated with $<'$ at the time the procedure was called. This implies that all tuples allowed after $S := W(S,x) \cup S_\Gamma$ are lexicographically smaller than some tuple allowed at the beginning of the simplification. All tuples after the update are therefore smaller than the maximal tuple before the update. If the simplification performs a resolution and executes a recursive call, then that recursion must continue to decrease the maximum tuple. ∎

Proposition 6.5 *Suppose that we are working on a problem with n variables, that the size of the largest domain of any variable is v, and that we have constructed Γ and S using repeated applications of* simp. *If the largest equivalence class $\langle x \rangle_S$ contains d elements, the space required to store Γ is $o(n^2 v^d)$.*

Proof. We know that the nogood set will be acyclic if we group together variables that are equivalent under $\leq_\Gamma$. Since this results in at most d variables being grouped together at any point, the maximum domain size in the reduced problem is v^d and the maximum number of nogoods stored is thus bounded by nv^d. As previously, the amount of space needed to store each nogood is $o(n)$. ∎

Theorem 6.6 *Procedure 6.3 will always terminate in at most*
$$\prod_i |V_i|$$
steps, where the product ranges over the variables in the problem and $|V_i|$ is the size of the domain for variable i.

Proof. The proof is essentially unchanged from that of Theorem 5.9; we provide only a sketch here. The only novel features of the proof involve showing that the lexicographic size falls as either variables in an equivalence class are combined into a single one or an equivalence class is broken so that the variables it contains are once again handled separately. In order to do this, we extend Definition 5.8 to handle equivalence classes as follows:

Definition A.1 *Given a set of safety conditions S and a fixed variable ordering $x_1 < x_2 < \cdots < x_n$ that respects $<_S$, let $\|x_i\|$ be given by*
$$\|x_i\| = \begin{cases} 1, & \text{if } x_i \equiv x_{i+1}; \\ \prod_{y \in \langle x \rangle_S} |x_i|_\Gamma, & \text{otherwise.} \end{cases} \quad (8)$$

Now denote by $\hat{m}(\Gamma, S, <)$ the tuple $\langle \|x_1\|, \ldots, \|x_n\| \rangle$. We will denote by $\hat{m}(\Gamma, S)$ that tuple which is lexicographically maximal as $<$ is allowed to vary.

This definition ensures that the lexicographic value decreases whenever we combine variables, since the remaining choices for the combined variable aren't counted until the latest possible point. It remains to show that the removal of nogoods or safety conditions does not split an equivalence class prematurely.

This, however, is clear. If removing a nogood with conclusion involving variable z causes two other variables y_1 and y_2 to become not equivalent, it must be the case that $y_1 \equiv y_2 \equiv z$ before the nogood was removed. But note that when the nogood is removed, we must have a variable $x' \in \langle x \rangle_S$ in the antecedent of the nogood, so that $x \equiv x' <_\Gamma z$. It follows that progress has been made on a variable preceding z and there is no harm in splitting z's equivalence class. ∎

Experimental code Here is the code used to generate instances of the class of problems on which our ideas were tested. The two arguments to the procedure are the size s of the variable grid and the number c of clauses to be "centered" on any single variable.

For each variable x on the grid we generated either $\lfloor c \rfloor$ or $\lfloor c \rfloor + 1$ clauses at random subject to the constraint that the variables in each clause form a right triangle with horizontal and vertical sides of length 1 and where x is the vertex opposite the hypotenuse. There are four such triangles for a given x. There are eight assignments of values to variable for each triangle giving 32 possible clauses. Our Common Lisp code for generating these 3-SAT problems is given below. Variables at the edge of the grid usually generate fewer than c clauses so the boundary of the grid is relatively unconstrained.

```
(defun make-problem (s c &aux result xx yy)
  (dotimes (x s)
    (dotimes (y s)
      (dotimes (i (+ (floor c)
                     (if (> (random 1.0)
                            (rem c 1.0))
                         0 1)))
        (setq xx (+ x -1 (* 2 (random 2)))
              yy (+ y -1 (* 2 (random 2))))
        (when (and (< -1 xx) (< xx s)
                   (< -1 yy) (< yy s))
          (push (new-clause x y xx yy s)
                result)))))
  result))

(defun new-clause (x y xx yy s)
  (mapcar
   #'(lambda (a b &aux (v (+ 1 (* s a) b)))
       (if (zerop (random 2)) v (- v))))
   (list x xx x) (list y y yy))
```

References

[Chvátal and Szemerédi,1988] V. Chvátal and E. Szemerédi. Many hard examples for resolution. *JACM*, 35:759–768, 1988.

[Crawford and Auton,1993] James M. Crawford and Larry D. Auton. Experimental results on the crossover point in satisfiability problems. In *Proceedings of the Eleventh National Conference on Artificial Intelligence*, pages 21–27, 1993.

[Crawford and Baker,1994] James M. Crawford and Andrew B. Baker. Experimental results on the application of satisfiability algorithms to scheduling problems. In *Proceedings of the Twelfth National Conference on Artificial Intelligence*, 1994. Submitted.

[Davis and Putnam,1960] M. Davis and H. Putnam. A computing procedure for quantification theory. *J. Assoc. Comput. Mach.*, 7:201–215, 1960.

[de Kleer,1986] Johan de Kleer. An assumption-based truth maintenance system. *Artificial Intelligence*, 28:127–162, 1986.

[Ginsberg et al.,1990] Matthew L. Ginsberg, Michael Frank, Michael P. Halpin, and Mark C. Torrance. Search lessons learned from crossword puzzles. In *Proceedings of the Eighth National Conference on Artificial Intelligence*, pages 210–215, 1990.

[Ginsberg,1993] Matthew L. Ginsberg. Dynamic backtracking. *Journal of Artificial Intelligence Research*, 1:25–46, 1993.

[Kirkpatrick et al.,1982] S. Kirkpatrick, C.D. Gelatt, and M.P. Vecchi. Optimization by simulated annealing. *Science*, 220:671–680, 1982.

[Konolige,1994] Kurt Konolige. Easy to be hard: Difficult problems for greedy algorithms. In *Proceedings of the Fourth International Conference on Principles of Knowledge Representation and Reasoning*, Bonn, Germany, 1994.

[McAllester,1993] David A. McAllester. Partial order backtracking. ftp.ai.mit.edu:/pub/dam/dynamic.ps, 1993.

[Minton et al.,1990] Steven Minton, Mark D. Johnston, Andrew B. Philips, and Philip Laird. Solving large-scale constraint satisfaction and scheduling problems using a heuristic repair method. In *Proceedings of the Eighth National Conference on Artificial Intelligence*, pages 17–24, 1990.

[Selman and Kautz,1993] Bart Selman and Henry Kautz. Domain-independent extensions to GSAT: Solving large structured satisfiability problems. In *Proceedings of the Thirteenth International Joint Conference on Artificial Intelligence*, pages 290–295, 1993.

[Selman et al.,1992] Bart Selman, Hector Levesque, and David Mitchell. A new method for solving hard satisfiability problems. In *Proceedings of the Tenth National Conference on Artificial Intelligence*, pages 440–446, 1992.

[Selman et al.,1993] Bart Selman, Henry A. Kautz, and Bram Cohen. Local search strategies for satisfiability testing. In *Proceedings 1993 DIMACS Workshop on Maximum Clique, Graph Coloring, and Satisfiability*, 1993.

[Stallman and Sussman,1977] R. M. Stallman and G. J. Sussman. Forward reasoning and dependency-directed backtracking in a system for computer-aided circuit analysis. *Artificial Intelligence*, 9(2):135–196, 1977.

Representing Uncertainty in Simple Planners

Robert P. Goldman
Honeywell Technology Center
MN 65-2200
3660 Technology Drive
Minneapolis, MN 55418
goldman@src.honeywell.com

Mark S. Boddy
Honeywell Technology Center
MN 65-2200
3660 Technology Drive
Minneapolis, MN 55418
boddy@src.honeywell.com

Abstract

In this paper, we present an analysis of planning with uncertain information regarding both the state of the world and the effects of actions using a STRIPS- or (propositional) ADL-style representation [4, 17]. We provide formal definitions of plans under incomplete information and conditional plans, and describe PLINTH, a conditional linear planner based on these definitions. We also clarify the definition of the term "conditional action," which has been variously used to denote actions with context-dependent effects and actions with uncertain outcomes. We show that the latter can, in theory, be viewed as a special case of the former but that to do so requires one to sacrifice the simple, single-model representation for one which can distinguish between a proposition and beliefs about that proposition.

1 INTRODUCTION

In this paper, we present an analysis of planning with uncertain information regarding both the state of the world and the effects of actions. Our focus on planning leads us to limit the expressive and inferential power of the formal systems we consider in the interests of efficiency. We do not develop with a full theory of knowledge and action of the sort which has concerned, e.g. Moore [13], Konolige [7], Haas [6], or Morgenstern [14]. In particular, we do not address what Morgenstern calls *knowledge preconditions* for actions and plans: determining when one knows enough to perform an action or successfully execute a plan, respectively. We are concerned only with taming uncertainty about the results of actions or uncertainty about the state of the world in the process of planning with a STRIPS- or (propositional) ADL-style representation [4, 17]. For the sake of computational efficiency, we restrict ourselves to a single model of the world, representing the planner's state of knowledge, rather than a more complex formalization including both epistemic and ground formulas. Our goal in this investigation is an increased understanding of *conditional plans*: plans in which the course of events is dictated by the actual outcome of actions whose effects cannot be predicted *a priori* [19, 5].

We clarify the definition of the term "conditional action." This term has been variously used to denote actions with context-dependent effects and actions with uncertain outcomes. We show that the latter can, in theory, be viewed as a special case of the former. However, we also show that to do so requires one to sacrifice the simple, single-model representation for one which can distinguish between a proposition and beliefs about that proposition. Using this definition, we provide formal definitions of plans under incomplete information and conditional plans.

Section 2 provides some preliminary definitions used in the rest of the paper. Section 3 presents an extension of STRIPS-rule planning to handle cases where the planner has only a partial model of the initial situation, and in which (a restricted kind of) information may be gained and lost through actions. We extend the STRIPS add and delete lists to include three truth values of true, false and unknown, losing in the process the use of negation-as-failure over the propositions that hold in a given situation. The primary limitation of this framework is that it assumes that the planner has sufficient knowledge to completely predict the outcomes of its actions — although one effect of these actions may be to forfeit information. There is no provision for actions with unpredictable outcomes. In Section 5 we remedy this omission, building on the conditional planning work of Peot and Smith.

Following this, we contrast conditional actions with context-dependent actions (Section 7). We show some problems with using context-dependent actions for planning under conditions of partial information. Finally, we compare our work with other work in the area, and present a summary and conclusions.

2 PRELIMINARY DEFINITIONS

We start with a set of *propositions*, $\{P_i\} = \mathcal{P}$. We define a *model*, $\mathcal{M}$ of $\mathcal{P}$, as a triple, $\langle T, F, U \rangle$ which is a partition of the propositions of $\mathcal{P}$ into statements which are true, false and unknown, respectively. A *partial model* is a triple $\langle T, F, U \rangle$ where T, F and U are disjoint subsets of $\mathcal{P}$. A model $\mathcal{M} = \langle T_\mathcal{M}, F_\mathcal{M}, U_\mathcal{M} \rangle$ is an *extension* of a partial model $\pi = \langle T_\pi, F_\pi, U_\pi \rangle$ if $T_\pi \subseteq T_\mathcal{M}$, $F_\pi \subset F_\mathcal{M}$ and $U_\pi \subseteq U_\mathcal{M}$. In the interests of brevity, we speak of a model $\mathcal{M}$ which extends a partial model π as satisfying or entailing π: $\mathcal{M} \vdash \pi$.

We define a set of operators, $\mathcal{O}$, similar to STRIPS operators. Operators are defined as ordered pairs $O = \langle P_O, E_O \rangle$, where P_O (the *preconditions* of O) and E_O (the *postconditions* of O) are both partial models. An operator O defines a partial function from models to models. The function is partial because f_O may only be applied to a model $\mathcal{M}$ which is an extension of P_O: the action represented by O may only be taken in a state where O's preconditions are satisfied.

One could extend the operators to be total functions from models to models by defining $f_O(\mathcal{M}) = \langle \emptyset, \emptyset, \mathcal{P} \rangle$ for any $\mathcal{M}$ that does not satisfy the preconditions of O. As there is little reason to plan to achieve complete ignorance, it makes more practical sense to insist that actions only be performed when their preconditions are satisfied.

We refer to models which entail P_O as satisfying the preconditions of O. For any operator O with effects $E_O = \langle T_E, F_E, U_E \rangle$ and model $\mathcal{M}$ satisfying the preconditions of O, the corresponding function, $f_O(\mathcal{M})$ is defined as follows:

$$f_o(\mathcal{M}) = \left\langle \begin{array}{c} (T_\mathcal{M} - (F_E \cup U_E)) \cup T_E, \\ (F_\mathcal{M} - (T_E \cup U_E)) \cup F_E, \\ (U_\mathcal{M} - (T_E \cup F_E)) \cup U_E \end{array} \right\rangle$$

This definition generalizes the STRIPS assumption to a three-valued logic. For a (possibly partial) model $\mathcal{M}$, let $\text{true}(\mathcal{M}) = T_\mathcal{M}$, $\text{false}(\mathcal{M}) = F_\mathcal{M}$ and $\text{unk}(\mathcal{M}) = U_\mathcal{M}$. Additionally, for an operator $O = \langle P_o, \langle T_o, F_o, U_o \rangle \rangle$, let $\text{precond}(O) = P_o$ (a partial model) and $\text{affected}(O) = T_o \cup F_o \cup U_o$ (a set of propositions).

Note that the U sets represent lack of knowledge on the part of the agent *while the plan is being executed*, rather than the state of knowledge of the planner while it is constructing the plan. For example, a regression planner like McDermott's PEDESTAL [10] will not, in general, project the full state of the world after one of the steps of its plan is done. The planner cannot afford to compute this complete knowledge; it only commits to the truth value of propositions which are needed to ensure that its plan will be successful. However, PEDESTAL's completed plan *could* be used to project a series of complete truth assignments to the propositions describing the world. Once the plan is complete, all uncertainty has been banished. This is not the case in our framework.

3 THE SIMPLE PLANNING PROBLEM

A planning problem is a pair $\langle G, S \rangle$ where G is the *goal* of the planning problem and S is the *initial state*. The initial state S is a complete (i.e., not partial) model of $\mathcal{P}$, while the goal G is a partial model. The solution of a planning problem is a plan whose result satisfies G. In the following paragraphs we describe the result of a plan and how such a plan may be derived.

Following Lifschitz [9], we define a sequence of actions, or plan, as $\alpha = (\alpha_1, \ldots, \alpha_N)$. Assuming that this sequence of actions starts in initial situation $\mathcal{M}_0$, we say the plan is *accepted* by $\mathcal{M}_0$ iff there exists a sequence of models $\mathcal{M}_1 \ldots \mathcal{M}_N$ such that

$$\forall i, 1 \leq i \leq N, \quad f_{\alpha_i}(\mathcal{M}_{i-1}) = \mathcal{M}_i \text{ and} \\ \mathcal{M}_{i-1} \vdash \text{precond}(\alpha_i)$$

We refer to $\mathcal{M}_N$ as the *result* of the plan α.

4 REGRESSION

Regression [24] can be described informally as reasoning backward from the desired effects of an action to what had to be true when the action was executed. One rationale for regression was the need to prove that plan steps used to achieve one goal would not clobber another goal of the same plan. Waldinger suggested a further use for regression: to determine where a step should be added to a linear plan. If a precondition of a new step is threatened by an existing step, put the affected step before the offender, and then *protect* that precondition (i.e., use regression to ensure that any further additions to the plan leave it unchanged). This is the way regression is employed in PEDESTAL [10].

In STRIPS-rule planners, regression only requires verifying that the proposition does not unify with the results of a given operator. Since those results are by definition the sole effect, known or unknown, of applying that operator, the proposition is unaffected by the action. Adding context-dependent effects as in ADL [17] complicates matters. Instead of just verifying that an operator will not affect a given proposition, regression involves deriving the conditions under which the operator will not affect that proposition.

Pednault[17] gives the conditions under which a proposition, p, will hold after the execution of an action a (for the propositional case) as follows:

$$I(a, p) = c_a \vee (p \wedge \neg d_a)$$

where c_A is the condition under which p is on a's add list and d_a is the condition under which p is deleted by

a. More precisely p will hold after act a is performed iff $I(a,p)$ holds before a is performed:

$$f_a(\mathcal{M}) \vdash p \equiv \mathcal{M} \vdash I(a,p)$$

Regression for the operators described here is somewhat more complex; our use of three truth values precludes use of the excluded middle, which can otherwise be used to good effect in simplifying the computation of causation and preservation preconditions. For the language described above, the regression operators are as follows (for p meaning p is true, $\overline{p}$ meaning p is false and $\tilde{p}$ meaning p is unknown):

$$I(a,p) \equiv (p \wedge p \notin \text{affected}(a)) \vee p \in \text{true}(a)$$
$$I(a,\overline{p}) \equiv (\overline{p} \wedge p \notin \text{affected}(a)) \vee p \in \text{false}(a)$$
$$I(a,\tilde{p}) \equiv (\tilde{p} \wedge p \notin \text{affected}(a)) \vee p \in \text{unk}(a)$$

The regression operator $I(a,p)$ may be interpreted as "p will be true following a," and similarly for the other truth values.

5 ACTIONS WITH UNCERTAIN OUTCOMES

In their paper on conditional non-linear planning [19], Peot and Smith extend the STRIPS model of actions to include actions whose outcomes are uncertain. They use these conditional actions to model observation actions. In this section, we extend our operator representation to include conditional actions and provide regression operators for them.

The operator semantics we have defined thus far is insufficient to model the use of observation to gain information. Information may be "gained" in a way analogous to the use of compliant motion for robots: operators may be selected in such a way as to reduce the set of unknown propositions whatever the initial state (e.g., ram into the wall as a way of reducing uncertainty in your position).[1]

The problem is that there is no way to describe an action with uncertain effects. Different effects must be the result of different operators or the same operator with context-dependent effects in different states. As long as the initial state S is a complete model, observations cannot be modelled in this way, because the resulting state is completely determined by the state in which the observation occurs.

Peot and Smith's operators are pairs $O = \langle P_O, O_O \rangle$. As before, P_O, the set of preconditions, is a partial model. O_O is a set of mutually exclusive and exhaustive possible outcomes when an action of type O is performed (i.e., exactly one of the outcomes will be the result of the action). Each outcome is a pair of the form

---
[1]This is the way that BURIDAN handles uncertainty [8].

$\langle \alpha_i, E_{\alpha_i} \rangle$. The α_i's are unique identifiers for outcomes. Let us define $Olabels(O) = \bigcup_i \alpha_i$ (for the sake of tidiness, we require the $Olabels$ sets for different operators to be disjoint). If O is not a conditional operator, then $Olabels(O) = \{\bot\}$. $E_{\alpha_i} = \langle T_{O,\alpha_i}, F_{O,\alpha_i}, U_{O,\alpha_i} \rangle$ is a partial model describing the effects of O in the event of outcome α_i.

We define a new set of partial functions $f'_O : Olabels(O) \times \mathcal{M} \mapsto \mathcal{M}$ to describe the effects of the new operators. If an action of type O is performed in state $\mathcal{M} = \langle T_\mathcal{M}, F_\mathcal{M}, U_\mathcal{M} \rangle$ (which satisfies P_O) and outcome α_i occurs, the effect will be

$$\mathcal{M}' = \left\langle \begin{array}{l} (T_\mathcal{M} - (F_{O,\alpha_i} \cup U_{O,\alpha_i})) \cup T_{O,\alpha_i}, \\ (F_\mathcal{M} - (T_{O,\alpha_i} \cup U_{O,\alpha_i})) \cup F_{O,\alpha_i}, \\ (U_\mathcal{M} - (T_{O,\alpha_i} \cup F_{O,\alpha_i})) \cup U_{O,\alpha_i} \end{array} \right\rangle$$

That is, $f'_O(\alpha_i, \mathcal{M}) = \mathcal{M}'$. For actions that are not conditional, we define $f'_O(\bot, \mathcal{M}) = f_O(\mathcal{M})$. The (partial) functions $f'_O : Olabel(O) \times \mathcal{M} \mapsto \mathcal{M}$ may be mapped straightforwardly to a (still partial) function $f : O \times Olabels \times \mathcal{M} \mapsto \mathcal{M}$, where $Olabels = \bigcup_{O \in \mathcal{O}} Olabels(O)$.

We extend our definition of action sequences, given in section 3 to sequences of action, outcome pairs. Similarly, we may extend our earlier definitions of regression operators to:

$$I(a,\alpha,p) \equiv (p \wedge p \notin \text{affected}(a,\alpha)) \vee p \in \text{true}(a,\alpha)$$
$$I(a,\alpha,\overline{p}) \equiv (\overline{p} \wedge p \notin \text{affected}(a,\alpha)) \vee p \in \text{false}(a,\alpha)$$
$$I(a,\alpha,\tilde{p}) \equiv (\tilde{p} \wedge p \notin \text{affected}(a,\alpha)) \vee p \in \text{unk}(a,\alpha)$$

The conditional actions permit us to describe observation operators. For example, we might want to have a planner which is able to find out what the weather is and plan travel accordingly:

            listen to weather report
preconditions: at(home), unknown(storm)
postconditions:

Olabels	effects
α_1	storm
α_2	not(storm)

Note that it is the need to properly formalize observation operators which forces the third truth value on us. We must insist that unknown(storm) be a precondition of this operator in order that the planner not construct a pathological plan in which it keeps observing the weather over and over again until it gets an observation it likes.

Conditional operators may be used for uncertain actions other than observations. In domains in which actions are fallible, conditional operators allow us to build planners which can plan for contingencies in which actions fail to achieve desired effects. For example, in an image-processing domain, one may have a number of possible operations that can remove noise from an image. These operations are fallible; they do not always succeed in cleaning up the target image. If we describe these operations as conditional actions, we can build plans in which either the operation succeeds, or we must take other, additional actions to clean up the image.

This representation of conditional actions makes it cumbersome to represent and reason about effects that are common to all outcomes of a given operator. One might revise the representation to make this easier, but we do not believe it would repay the effort. In general, conditional actions will be introduced into a plan in the interest of varying outcomes. To take Peot and Smith's example, one might introduce an observation action to determine the state of a road between two points. One would be unlikely to do so simply to expend time (Peot [2] calls for conditional plans to be "without augury").

We view conditional action sequences as action sequences which branch forward in time. A *conditional sequence* is a tree, each of whose nodes corresponds to an action (an instance of an operator). Each edge in the tree will be labeled with an outcome label of the action at the tail of the edge.

More formally, a conditional sequence, $\mathcal{C} \subset \{(n, l, n') | n, n' \in \text{uid}(\mathcal{C}), l \in \textit{Olabels}(\text{op}(n))\}$. $\text{uid}(\mathcal{C})$ is a set of unique identifiers for acts in the conditional sequence $\mathcal{C}$. op is a function mapping uids of acts to the operator of which the act is an instance.

In order to be nonredundant, a conditional sequence must have only one triple (n, l, n') for every pair (n, l).

Unconditional sequences may be drawn from a conditional sequence. Each such unconditional sequence is a rooted path through the tree $\mathcal{C}$. That is, an unconditional sequence, $\mathcal{P}$ is written as $\mathcal{P} = (n_1, l_1) \ldots (n_N, l_N)$ where there must exist an edge $(n_i, l_i, n_{i+1}) \in \mathcal{C}$ and where $n_1 = \text{root}(\mathcal{C})$. In order to be well-formed, an unconditional sequence starting in an initial state $\mathcal{M}_0$ must meet the following conditions:

1. $f(\text{op}(n_i), \mathcal{M}_{i-1}, l_i) = \mathcal{M}_i$ for all $1 \leq i \leq N$.
2. $\mathcal{M}_{i-1} \vdash \text{precond}(\text{op}(n_i))$ for all $1 \leq i \leq N$.

We define $\text{result}(\mathcal{P}) = \mathcal{M}_N$. An unconditional sequence is *complete* if it is a path $\mathcal{P} = (n_1, l_1) \ldots (n_N, l_N)$ for $n_N \in \text{leaves}(\mathcal{C})$.

In order for a conditional sequence, $\mathcal{C}$ to be well-formed, it must be non-redundant and every unconditional path contained in $\mathcal{C}$ must be well-formed. In order to be complete, a conditional sequence must be well-formed and have an out-edge for every pair (n, l) for n an interior (non-leaf) node and l an element of $\textit{Olabels}(\text{op}(n))$ where n corresponds to an instance of operator o. A conditional sequence $\mathcal{C}$ is

---

[2] Personal communication.

a *complete conditional plan* for the planning problem $(\mathcal{M}_0, \mathcal{G}, \mathcal{O})$ if $\mathcal{C}$ is complete and for all complete paths $\mathcal{P} = (n_1, l_1) \ldots (n_N, l_N)$ in $\mathcal{C}$, $\text{result}(\mathcal{P}) \vdash \mathcal{G}$.

6 CNLP AND PLINTH

In this section we briefly discuss two recently-developed conditional planners. The first, CNLP, is a non-linear conditional planner for which conditional actions were developed; our original intent in this research was to clearly understand CNLP. In the course of our investigations, we came to suspect that the case for non-linear planning was less strong for conditional planning than conventional, "classical" planners. The second planner we discuss here, PLINTH, is a *linear* conditional planner which we have developed to investigate the efficiency tradeoffs between linear and nonlinear approaches to conditional planning.

Peot and Smith's CNLP [19] is a conditional, nonlinear planner based on Rosenblitt and MacAllester's SNLP. Like SNLP, CNLP constructs its plans by a series of interleaved goal satisfaction and threat removal operations. CNLP differs in adding conditional actions like those described here.

CNLP augments the SNLP algorithm to accomodate conditional actions. The labels of conditional outcomes are propagated along causal and conditioning links in the plan graph to record to which branch of the plan each action belongs. These conditioning links are added by a new threat-removal operation, "conditioning apart," which is used to assign steps to different contexts. Effectively one resolves a threat to a given step by adding a constraint that the threatener and the threatened step not both be part of the same branch of the plan. As of yet no results have been published concerning the soundness and completeness of CNLP.

Given the current prevalence and popularity of nonlinear planning, our decision to construct a linear conditional planner may require some explanation. In conventional, "classical" planning applications, nonlinear planning is usually an improvement over linear planning because fewer commitments yields a smaller search space, at a relatively minimal added cost to explore each element of that search space [12]. However, it is not clear that this tradeoff operates in the same way for conditional planners. When plans have multiple branches, the savings from considering fewer orderings is likely to be much less and may not repay the cost in the added complexity of individual plan expansion actions. In particular, the domain in which we have applied PLINTH is one in which subgoal interactions are minor, and thus in which a linear planner can be effectively employed. Conditional linear planning is simpler in conception as well as in implementation. In particular, our conditional linear planner can be shown to be sound and complete; we do not yet know of a sound and complete conditional non-linear planner. Finally, the operation which is needed to properly construct branching non-linear plans — resolving clobberers through conditioning apart — is a very difficult operation to direct.

PLINTH's conditional linear planning algorithm is non-deterministic and regressive.[3] Plans are built by manipulating three important data structures: a partial plan, a set of protections and a set of as-yet-unrealized goals. The planner operates by selecting an unrealized goal and nondeterministically choosing an operator to resolve that goal while respecting existing protections. New goals may be introduced when steps are introduced, either to satisfy preconditions or to plan for contingencies introduced by conditional actions. Essentially this algorithm is the same as that of a conventional linear planner. The crucial difference is in the effect of adding a conditional action to the plan.

When adding a conditional action, A, there will be some outcome, O, such that $A - O$ will establish the goal literal (otherwise A would not have been chosen for insertion). This outcome will establish what one can think of as the "main line" of the plan. However, there will also be some set of alternative outcomes, $\{O_i\}$. In order to derive a plan which is guaranteed to achieve the goal, one must find a set of actions which can be added to the plan such that the goals are achieved after $A - O_i$. for all i. This is done by adding new goal nodes to the plan, which are made successors of the other outcomes. The planner will now plan to realize these other goals as well as the "main-line" goal. Note that actions to handle alternative outcomes may be added either before or after the relevant conditional action. Loosely speaking, we can add to our conditional plans either remedial actions or precautionary actions.

PLINTH is described in greater detail elsewhere [5]. We have demonstrated that the algorithm is sound and complete. The algorithm has been implemented in Quintus Prolog. The implementation uses a depth-first iterative-deepening search strategy so it preserves the theoretical properties of soundness and completeness (up to hardware limitations). PLINTH is being applied to planning image processing operations for NASA's Earth Observing System, in collaboration with Nick Short, Jr. and Jacqueline LeMoigne-Stewart of NASA Goddard.

7 UNCERTAINTY AND SECONDARY PRECONDITIONS

In his work on ADL [15, 17], Pednault introduces operators which have context-dependent effects. This might seem to be an attractive method to represent problems of planning under incomplete information. For example, one attempt at representing an observation operator is the following:[4]

Check the road from ?x to ?y.
observe(clear(?x,?y))
preconditions: at(?x), unknown(clear(?x,?y))
effects: clear(?x,?y) ← clear(?x,?y)
not clear(?x,?y) ← not clear(?x,?y)

For those not familiar with ADL: ADL operators are akin to STRIPS operators, but their preconditions are partitioned. STRIPS preconditions are conditions under which the operator can be performed. If the preconditions do not hold when the operator is to be performed, the plan is ill-formed. ADL departs from STRIPS in allowing one to attach additional conditions to the individual effects of operators. For example, one could formalize the action of crossing a bridge by truck as having the preconditions of being at the bridge and in a truck. There might be two possible effects: being on the other side of the bridge, which has as additional precondition that the bridge is sound; and being in the ravine below, which has as additional precondition that the bridge is not sound. We indicate additional preconditions using the "backward chaining arrow," ←. Note that the original ADL syntax uses add lists and delete lists; we use effects instead in the interests of a consistent notation within the body of this paper.

One problem with this representation is apparent in the observation operator given above. Each of the effects has itself as additional precondition! The reason for this paradoxical situation is that planning under uncertainty in this way violates an common planning assumption: that we can treat the planner's model of the world and the state of the world as interchangeable. To handle observations properly, we need to be able to represent and reason about both the state of the world (the road is clear, so when we look, we will find it so) and the planner's state of knowledge (the observation operator makes sense because the planner doesn't know whether the road is clear).

A related problem is that this formalization leads us to an unrealistic model for planning. The obvious way to use an operator like the above is to insert it into one's plan and then continue planning in two contexts: one where the road is clear and one where it is not. But note an undesirable feature of these two contexts: in each of them the road not only is clear, but has always been clear, and the planner should know this. As in the famous problem of Schrodinger's cat, performing the observation seems to cause the entire history of the world to change. Closer to home, this paradox is akin to McDermott's "little Nell" problem [11], in which planning to prevent an action seemed to make planning to prevent it unnecessary. Without explicit

---

[3]Our development of the algorithm was inspired by McDermott's linear planner PEDESTAL [10], hence the name.

[4]We have tried to follow Pednault's notation fairly closely.

representation of belief, ground truth and the relations between them, it is impossible to model the acquisition of information with only deterministic operators.

8 CASSANDRA

Cassandra is a conditional nonlinear planner that uses secondary preconditions for planning under uncertainty [20]. In order to encode uncertainty, certain actions are given secondary preconditions which are unknowable; Cassandra must plan to gain information about these unobservable pseudo-propositions. Reading about Cassandra bears out our conclusions above about the drawbacks of secondary preconditions for encoding uncertainty.

Cassandra is built on top of the nonlinear planner UCPOP [18]. UCPOP is sound and complete, and uses Pednault's ADL for its action representation. In Cassandra, rather than positing conditional actions like those described here, uncertain outcomes are captured by giving actions secondary preconditions which are "unknowable." These unknowable preconditions have multiple outcome labels, like our outcome labels, and like our outcome labels are mutually exclusive and exhaustive. Instead of branching at conditional actions, Cassandra plans branch at *decisions*. Decisions contain condition-action rules which specify the conditions under which the planner should conclude that a given outcome has occurred. When the plan is executed, the execution monitor should perform only those actions labeled consistently with the outcomes of its decisions. These decision rules provide a mechanism for relaxing an assumption common to both CNLP and PLINTH: that the outcomes of conditional actions are always known.

While we find Cassandra's model of uncertainty attractive, it appears to require more expressive power than its ADL action representation provides. It is consequently difficult to say exactly what Cassandra's plans mean. In particular, Cassandra's decisions and their knowledge preconditions cannot be expressed in ADL. Cassandra's decisions have preconditions of the form "knowif(*proposition*)," but such preconditions are beyond its expressive capacity; Cassandra, like the other planners described here, appears to make no distinction between truth in the world and the planner's beliefs about the world. Accordingly, there can be no satisfactory ADL representation for actions which collect information, as we have argued in the previous section.

9 INFORMATION-GATHERING ACTIONS

Recent work on planning under uncertainty done at the University of Washington has brought to the fore a number of issues concerning information-gathering actions [2]. In particular, the UW group has shown that planners must be able to distinguish goals of information-gathering from other goals of achievement. They provide the following persuasive example:

> Suppose that the planner is told that the hidden treasure it is seeking is located behind "the blue door." Painting a door blue does not satisfy the goal of finding "the blue door" — it merely obscures the identity of the appropriate door. [2, p. 116]

In order to capture the distinction between information-gathering goals and achievement goals, the UWL planning language provides goal annotations: **satisfy**, **hands-off** and **find-out**. Satisfy goals are to be achieved as normal planner goals. Hands-off goals, on the other hand, are restricted to information-gathering. If the planner has a goal annotated with (**hands-off** P), it must achieve its other goals without affecting the truth value of P. Finally, (**find-out** P) goals are a hybrid — the planner should prefer to simply observe the truth or falsehood of P, but if the planner must change the value of P for some other reason, that is acceptable. The UW group has developed a conditional planner, SENSp, for UWL, in which the process of matching pre- and post-conditions is altered in order to handle these annotations.[5]

As far as we can tell, the **hands-off** and **find-out** goals are similar encodings of radically different phenomena. The **hands-off** goals are apparently only a special class of preservation goals. They appear different because conventional planning languages are not expressive enough to say "maintain the truth value of P, *whatever it may be now*." and to permit observation of P without modification. Within our framework, we capture this restriction by ruling out the use of operators which would change the truth value of P over part or all of a given plan. We do so by ruling out all operators O such that

$$P \in \text{affected}(O) \wedge \tilde{P} \notin \text{precond}(O)$$

That is, any operator whose use affects the truth value of P with the exception of those operators that simply inform us whether or not P holds. That is the condition captured by the second conjunct of the condition above: observation operators are those that set (reveal) the value of P and that require that the value of P be unknown beforehand. Once the truth value of P has been determined (either given in the initial conditions or established by observation), we may use the conventional planning technique of protecting P, rather than the criterion above.

---

[5]In personal communication, Etzioni reports that two further planners based on the UWL language have been developed since this paper was drafted, both nonlinear and interleaving planning and execution.

The **find-out** goals, on the other hand, do not determine what constitutes a plan that satisfies the specified goals. Rather, they specify a preference over different, but equally valid, plans. This insight suggests that the somewhat cumbersome criterion for satisfaction of **find-out** goals [2, p. 119] might be removed, with the associated preference being expressed instead in the cost function over operators. In most cases, the cost of observations should be lower than the cost of achievement. There are three advantages to factoring this concern into the cost function: first, we avoid further complication of the planning problem; second, the cost information may more readily be used in planning search than the **find-out** criterion and third, the cost mechanism allows us to capture a wider range of tradeoffs.

Distinguishing these two annotations as different phenomena within our framework allows us to considerably simplify their treatment. hands-off goals can be enforced using a slight variation on protection assumptions or preservation preconditions, while find-out annotations are reflected in the planner's search control mechanism.

Note Recent exchanges reveal that in new versions of UWL the **find-out** annotation has been revised from "satisfy without altering if possible" to "satisfy without altering."[6] Our criticisms above apply only to the currently-available paper on UWL [2].

10 OTHER RELATED WORK

Early work on modeling knowledge in AI systems by Moore [13], Haas [6] and Konolige [7] provides a different view on modeling knowledge for planning systems. This early work was primarily concerned with modeling knowledge, rather than the development of planning algorithms. More recent work by Morgenstern [14] and Scherl and Levesque [22] brings such work much closer to the point of constructing working planners. However, these representations are still far more complex than those used by most working planners. In particular, they require the use of complex logical machinery (string manipulations or modal logics) in order to capture the distinction between beliefs and the state of the world. We have attempted to maintain the simplicity of existing approaches and, in particular, maintain the single model approach.

11 POSSIBLE EXTENSIONS

Our extension to the use of a third truth value is intended to model lack of knowledge about a proposition. Another use for three-valued logics has been to allow truth-functional treatment of statements which

---
[6]Oren Etzioni, personal communication.

are meaningless [23], particularly the problem of predicating properties of inexistent objects. We may encounter a prosaic version of this problem in planning under uncertainty. For example, consider the problem of an oil-wildcatter[7] who has the option of taking a core sample before drilling. Imagine that we have three propositions describing mutually exclusive and exhaustive outcomes of such a test: (result os), (result cs), (result ns). What is the truth value of these statements in the initial situation? The truth value of this proposition is not well-defined because the proposition predicates a property of an inexistent object.

We suspect that related issues will arise in Etzioni's work on Unix Softbots [2, 3], which act within the Unix operating system. For example, what is the status of a predication about a file which has yet to be created? We note that Etzioni, et. al. have so far avoided constructing any operators which either create or destroy files. One way of addressing this problem would be to add a fourth "truth value" for propositions that are ill-formed in this way.

For some applications, allowing ADL-style operators with secondary preconditions may make planning more efficient. Such operators allow the planner to defer some commitments to precise methods for achieving goals, in the interests of allowing later reuse of operators for additional goals. We would like to retain this advantage, but doing so will require revision of Pednault's regression operators [16], since many of the identities he uses are not valid in three-valued logic.

12 SUMMARY AND CONCLUSIONS

We have provided a formal analysis of STRIPS-style planning under conditions of incomplete information and where the outcomes of actions are not known with certainty. We have also provided a precise definition of conditional plans. This work provides a unifying theoretical framework and vocabulary for a number of disparate conditional planners such as CNLP, SENSp and PLINTH. In the process of defining this framework, we have clarified the relationship between conditional actions and actions with context-dependent effects, and shown that the latter are not sufficient for modelling information-gathering actions (i.e., observations). We have shown that our analysis simplifies the treatment of information-gathering acts and goals.

Acknowledgements The authors would like to thank Alan D. Christiansen, Oren Etzioni and our two anonymous reviewers for helpful comments.

---
[7]A now-standard problem due to Raiffa [21].

References

[1] Allen, James, Hendler, James, and Tate, Austin, (Eds.), *Readings in Planning*, (Morgan Kaufmann Publishers, Inc., 1990).

[2] Etzioni, Oren, Hands, Steve, Weld, Daniel S., Draper, Denise, Lesh, Neal, and Williamson, Mike, An Approach to Planning with Incomplete Information, Nebel, Bernhard, Rich, Charles, and Swartout, William, (Eds.), *Principles of Knowledge Representation and Reasoning:Proceedings of the Third International Conference*, 1992, 115–125, Morgan Kaufmann Publishers, Inc.

[3] Etzioni, Oren and Segal, Richard, Softbots as Testbeds for Machine Learning, *Proceedings of the 1992 AAAI Spring Symposium on knowledge assimilation*, 1992.

[4] Fikes, Richard E. and Nilsson, Nils J., STRIPS: A new approach to the application of theorem proving to problem solving, *Artificial Intelligence*, 2 (1971) 189–208.

[5] Goldman, Robert P. and Boddy, Mark S., Conditional Linear Planning, *Artificial Intelligence Planning Systems: Proceedings of the Second International Conference*, 1994, Morgan Kaufmann Publishers, Inc., forthcoming.

[6] Haas, Andrew R., A Syntactic Theory of Belief and Action, *Artificial Intelligence*, 28 (1986) 245–292.

[7] Konolige, Kurt, A first-order formalisation of knowledge and action for a multi-agent planning system, Hayes, J.E. and Michie, D., (Eds.), *Machine Intelligence 10*, chapter 2, 41–72, (Halstead, New York, 1982).

[8] Kushmerick, Nicholas, Hanks, Steve, and Weld, Daniel, An Algorithm for Probabilistic Planning, Technical Report 93-06-03, Department of Computer Science and Engineering, University of Washington, June 1993.

[9] Lifschitz, Vladimir, On the Semantics of Strips, In Allen et al. [1], 523–530, Reprinted from *Reasoning about Actions and Plans*.

[10] McDermott, Drew, Regression Planning, *International Journal of Intelligent Systems*, 6(4) (1991) 357–416.

[11] McDermott, Drew V., Planning and acting, *Cognitive Science*, 2 (1978) 71–109.

[12] Minton, Steven, Bresina, John L., and Drummond, Mark, Commitment Strategies in Planning: A Comparative Analysis, *Proceedings of the 12th International Joint Conference on Artificial Intelligence*, Morgan Kaufmann Publishers, Inc., 1991.

[13] Moore, Robert, A Formal Thoery of Knowledge and Action, Hobbs, J., (Ed.), *Formal Theories of the Commonsense World*, (Ablex, Hillsdale, N.J., 1984).

[14] Morgenstern, Leora, Knowledge Preconditions for Actions and Plans, McDermott, John, (Ed.), *Proceedings of the 10th International Joint Conference on Artificial Intelligence*, 1987, 867–874, Morgan Kaufmann Publishers, Inc.

[15] Pednault, Edwin P.D., Extending Conventional Planning Techniques to Handle Actions with Context-dependent effects, *Proceedings of the Seventh National Conference on Artificial Intelligence*, 1988, 55–59, Morgan Kaufmann Publishers, Inc.

[16] Pednault, E.P.D., Synthesizing Plans that contain actions with context-dependent effects, *Computational Intelligence*, 4(4) (1988) 356–372.

[17] Pednault, E.P.D., ADL: Exploring the middle ground between STRIPS and the situation calculus, *First International Conference on Principles of Knowledge Representation and Reasoning*, Morgan Kaufmann Publishers, Inc., 1989.

[18] Penberthy, J. Scott and Weld, Daniel S., UCPOP: A Sound, Complete, Partial Order Planner for ADL, Nebel, Bernhard, Rich, Charles, and Swartout, William, (Eds.), *Principles of Knowledge Representation and Reasoning:Proceedings of the Third International Conference*, 1992, 103–114, Morgan Kaufmann Publishers, Inc.

[19] Peot, Mark A. and Smith, David E., Conditional Nonlinear Planning, Hendler, James, (Ed.), *Artificial Intelligence Planning Systems: Proceedings of the First International Conference*, 1992, 189–197, Morgan Kaufmann Publishers, Inc.

[20] Pryor, Louise and Collins, Gregg, *Cassandra: Planning for Contingencies*, Technical Report 41, The Institute for the Learning Sciences, Northwestern University, June 1993.

[21] Raiffa, Howard, *Decision Analysis: Introductory Lectures on Choices under Uncertainty*, Behavioral Science: Quantitative Methods, (Random House, New York, 1968).

[22] Scherl, Richard B. and Levesque, Hector J., The Frame Problem and Knowledge-producing Actions, *Proceedings of the Eleventh National Conference on Artificial Intelligence*, 1993, 689–695, AAAI Press/MIT Press.

[23] Turner, Raymond, *Logics for Artificial Intelligence*, (Ellis Horwood, Ltd., 1984).

[24] Waldinger, Richard, Achieving Several goals Simultaneously, Elcock, E. and Michie, D., (Eds.), *Machine Intelligence*, volume 8, 94–136, (Ellis Horwood, Edinburgh, Scotland, 1977).

How Far Can We 'C'?
Defining a 'Doughnut' Using Connection Alone

N. M. Gotts
Division of Artificial Intelligence
School of Computer Studies
University of Leeds, Leeds LS2 9JT
ngotts@scs.leeds.ac.uk

Abstract

The paper continues the work of Randell, Cohn and Cui on region-based qualitative representations of spatial properties and relations, built on the 'logic of connection' developed by Clarke. The paper shows how taxonomies of topological properties and relations can be developed, using the single primitive 'C', where $C(x, y)$ indicates that regions x and y are 'connected', meaning that their closures share at least one point. This is done by considering a specific task: deciding whether a region has the topology of a solid torus, or 'doughnut', by asking questions using only terms logically derived from C. It is shown how this task could be performed under a restrictive set of assumptions about the topological properties of regions in general, and the target region in particular. These assumptions are then progressively relaxed. As this is done, the task requires the definition of successive layers of terminology, all derived ultimately from C, providing the basis for successively broader taxonomies of topological properties and relationships.

1 INTRODUCTION

This paper is a continuation of the work of D. Randell, A.G. Cohn, and Z. Cui (henceforth RCC) on a region-based qualitative representation of spatial relations. RCC's work (Randell and Cohn 1989, Randell 1991, Randell, Cui and Cohn 1992, Cohn, Randell and Cui 1994) is based on a modification of Clarke's (Clarke 1981, Clarke 1985) 'calculus of individuals based on connection', and is built on the single primitive binary relation of 'connection' between two spatial, temporal or spatio-temporal regions. This paper was written with spatial regions in mind, but the arguments and examples used would generalize readily to temporal and spatio-temporal ones. That region x is connected to region y is symbolised $C(x, y)$; C is generally given a topological interpretation, but the precise interpretation has varied during the development of RCC's work.

This work forms part of the relatively recent investigation of qualitative representations of spatial relations within AI. Similar work on time has a somewhat longer history, starting with Allen's work (Allen 1981, Allen and Hayes 1985, Allen and Hayes 1989). A much wider range of possible relations must be considered in the spatial case because of the multi-dimensionality of space. In recent papers (Cohn, Randell, Cui and Bennett 1993, Cohn et al. 1994), RCC's main concerns have moved toward computational issues, and the exploitation of an additional primitive concerning convexity introduced in (Randell and Cohn 1989). The purpose of this paper, by contrast, is to investigate the *expressive power* of the C predicate: how much can be expressed using this single predicate? This is most easily done in terms of specific tasks. The one chosen for this paper, as achievable but non-trivial, was to specify the topological properties of a solid torus (the doughnut of the title), in terms of C alone (in (Randell and Cohn 1989) 'toroidalness' was introduced as a primitive). Objects with this topology (illustrated by three examples in figure 1) are common: washers, bracelets, cups, links in chains — and one type of doughnut — and many of these objects perform their functions partly in virtue of their topological properties. A scheme for representing spatial properties and relations should therefore be capable of describing it. Topological description is also a necessary part of the representation of shape, and many of the concepts and techniques developed here to deal with part/whole and region/boundary relationships should be useful in describing non-topological aspects of shape as well.

The work reported is related to that of Casati and Varzi (Casati and Varzi 1993) on holes, but shows that two of their three types of holes (tunnels and internal voids) can be described in terms of C — these authors use C, but introduce the relationship between a hole and its 'host' as an additional primitive. Vieu (Vieu

Figure 1: Three Doughnuts

1993) and her colleagues have also used Clarke's work as a basis for spatial reasoning. RCC's work is concerned with some of the same issues as Hayes (Hayes 1985a, Hayes 1985b), and the Cyc team (Guha and Lenat 1990), insofar as these workers have formalized qualitative aspects of spatial and spatio-temporal representation and reasoning. However, RCC's work is much more sharply focused on these problems, and is based on as few primitives and axioms as possible, in contrast to the wide-ranging and axiom-rich systems preferred by Hayes and the Cyc team; this contrast is briefly discussed in section 6.

In representing either spatial or temporal relations, a decision arises: whether to treat points, extended regions, or both as primitives (in the temporal case, points and regions are often called instants and intervals respectively). In a point-based approach, regions are defined as sets of points; in a region-based approach, points may be defined in terms of sets of regions, or omitted altogether. An advantage of point-based representations is that they can use the extensive work of mathematicians on point-set topology. Three countervailing advantages have been suggested for a region-based ontology: that regions are somehow 'closer to perception' and therefore psychologically primitive; that expressing spatial relations in terms of regions is a useful form of abstraction, paralleling the abstraction from the real-number line to landmark values and intervening intervals exploited in work on qualitative physics (Weld and De Kleer 1990); and that the point-based approach gives rise to counterintuitive distinctions such as that between closed and open regions (those that do and do not include their own boundaries), and weird constructions such as space-filling curves that cross themselves at every point.

The first of these claims is dubious, taking into account the constructive nature of perception: regions, as much as points, are commonsense-theoretical entities in terms of which we interpret information from the senses. The second and third are more substantial, and certainly give sufficient reason to investigate the region-based alternative. So far as the second is concerned, the descriptions of spatial configurations we use in everyday life, and even in technical contexts, are frequently expressed in terms of relations between extended regions, whose extension in terms of points is left unspecified. Turning to the third point, it seems odd (as noted in (Randell et al. 1992)), that two regions can be distinct, yet take up exactly the same part of space, as an open region and its closure do if we allow regions to be either open or closed sets of points. Also, if we take point-sets as fundamental we must allow for those that are neither closed nor open, including *some but not all* of their boundary points, and for oddities such as 2-dimensional point-sets including all those points within an area except those with rational coordinates. Furthermore, if we consider a physical object as occupying a region, is that region closed or open? In the case of a solid object it might seem intuitive to regard the occupied region as containing its boundary, and thus as closed. However, if two such objects touch, this suggests either that one is open and one closed (at least at their common boundary), or that both are closed and share their boundary points. Neither solution is obviously wrong, but both give rise to unease [1].

It is important to consider how relatively unexplored formal representations of spatial relations, such as RCC's, relate to the established mathematical tools in the domain. Otherwise we may rely too much on intuitive understanding of space (which may differ between individuals, and may not be internally consistent), or lean on the Cartesian/point-set approach without acknowledging it. Establishing how the two approaches relate may also highlight problems and possible directions of advance, and allow us to identify the real advantages of the region-based alternative.

Advocacy of region-based rather than point-based spatial and temporal representation has connections with a broader opposition to the view that set theory and predicate logic provide an adequate basis for the formal representation of the world. Those logicians and philosophers who have worked on the alternative or supplementary approaches ('mereology' or 'calculus of individuals') include Whitehead (Whitehead 1929), Leśniewski (originator of the term 'mereology'), Tarski (Tarski 1956), Leonard and Goodman (Leonard and Goodman 1940), Clarke (referred to above), and recently Simons (Simons 1987), Varzi (Varzi 1993), and Smith (Smith 1994). Simons reviews much of the earlier work in this area.

'Individuals' in the sense used in 'calculus of individuals', are whatever singular things we take the world to contain. In this wide context it has been argued (Varzi 1993) that we should allow entities to have the same spatio-temporal extent without being identical or having any parts in common. In the current context, where we are concerned with relations between spatial regions, we shall assume an extensional approach:

---

[1] RCC finesse this problem by dropping the open/closed distinction. Vieu (Vieu 1993), proposes a different region-based solution, also based on Clarke's calculus, using the open/closed distinction to define a notion of 'weak contact', in which two objects touch without being 'connected'.

if all the spatial relations that apply to region x also apply to region y, then x and y are the same region.

2 CLARKE'S LOGIC OF CONNECTION, AND RCC'S VERSION

Clarke's approach (Clarke 1981, Clarke 1985) uses Whitehead's (Whitehead 1929) primitive, 'x is extensionally connected with y', symbolised here as $C(x, y)$. However, Clarke drops Whitehead's informal assumption that each individual is continuous. In his 1981 paper he uses just two axioms. The first asserts that C is reflexive and symmetric, the second makes explicit the assumption of extensionality. Clarke adds a series of definitions of further relations in terms of C. He also adds a definition of the universal region (symbolised here as Us), as that region which connects with every region; and definitions of operators guaranteeing the existence of regions corresponding to the complement of a given region, and to the sum and product of two given regions. These operators are described as 'quasi-Boolean' rather than Boolean because no null region is allowed.

Clarke's formalism is presented as an uninterpreted calculus, but he suggests an informal topological interpretation, in which 'x connects with y' means that the regions x and y share at least one point. The system allows a distinction between the weak relation of connection and the stronger one of overlapping, symbolised $O(x, y)$. O is definable in terms of C, and is interpreted as meaning that x and y share a *region* as a common part. A point is not regarded as a region, nor is a common boundary between regions which is of lower dimensionality than those regions — such as an edge along which two 2-dimensional regions meet. $O(x, y)$ implies $C(x, y)$, but the converse is not the case. This makes it possible to define a relation of external connection, symbolised $EC(x, y)$, meaning that x and y touch, or leave no space for another region between them, but do not share a region as common part. This enhances the expressive power of the calculus.

Clarke's approach allows the definition of the closures and interiors of regions, but not of boundary elements (hence his closure and interior operators are 'quasi-topological' rather than topological). In the 1981 paper there is no commitment either to the existence or nonexistence of atomic regions (regions without proper parts). In his 1985 paper he adds an axiom asserting that every region has a non-tangential (interior) proper part, ruling out the existence of atomic regions.

RCC have developed two successive theories based on Clarke's system; this paper discusses only the second (Randell et al. 1992, Cohn et al. 1994). This differs from Clarke's formulation most significantly in abandoning the distinction between open and closed regions. This was done because of the counterintuitive nature of the open/closed distinction, and to reduce the computational costs of finding proofs.

RCC's basic theory (Randell et al. 1992, section 4) uses two axioms establishing that C is reflexive and symmetric:

$$\forall x C(x, x)$$
$$\forall x, y[C(x, y) \rightarrow C(y, x)],$$

plus metalinguistic definitions of quasi-Boolean functions, guaranteeing the existence of complements of regions, and of the sum, product and difference of ordered pairs of regions (within restrictions explained below). Additional relations are defined in terms of C: $DC(x, y)$ (x is disconnected from y), $P(x, y)$ (x is part of y), $PP(x, y)$ (x is a proper part of y), $EQ(x, y)$ (x is identical with y, also symbolised $x = y$), $O(x, y)$ (x overlaps with y), $PO(x, y)$ (x partially overlaps with y), $DR(x, y)$ (x is discrete from y), $EC(x, y)$ (x is externally connected with y), $TPP(x, y)$ (x is a tangential proper part of y), and $NTPP(x, y)$ (x is a non-tangential proper part of y). P is nonsymmetric, and PP, TPP and NTPP are asymmetric; their inverses will be symbolised here as PI, PPI, TPPI and NTPPI. The eight relations DC, EC, PO, TPP, NTPP, TPPI, NTPPI and EQ constitute a pairwise exclusive and jointly exhaustive set of 'base relations': exactly one of the eight must hold between an ordered pair of regions.

The definitions of the additional relations used in this paper are given below; the remainder can be found in (Randell et al. 1992).

$$DC(x, y) \equiv_{def} \neg C(x, y)$$
$$P(x, y) \equiv_{def} \forall z[C(z, x) \rightarrow C(z, y)]$$
$$PP(x, y) \equiv_{def} P(x, y) \wedge \neg P(y, x)$$
$$EQ(x, y) \equiv_{def} P(x, y) \wedge P(y, x)$$
$$O(x, y) \equiv_{def} \exists z[P(z, x) \wedge P(z, y)]$$
$$EC(x, y) \equiv_{def} C(x, y) \wedge \neg O(x, y)$$
$$TPP(x, y) \equiv_{def} PP(x, y) \wedge \exists z[EC(z, x) \wedge EC(z, y)]$$
$$NTPP(x, y) \equiv_{def} PP(x, y) \wedge \neg \exists z[EC(z, x) \wedge EC(z, y)]$$

The universal region (Us), and a number of quasi-Boolean functions, introduced via explicit metalinguistic definitions in (Randell et al. 1992), are here defined implicitly using additional object-language axioms, which have the same effect: asserting the existence of one region given that of one or more others. The functions concerned are compl(x) (the region-complement of x, defined as a region only when x is not Us); $x+y$ or sum(x, y) (the region-sum of x and y); prod(x, y) (the region-product or intersection of x and y, defined as a region only when $O(x,y)$); and $x - y$ or diff(x, y) (the region-difference of x and y, defined as a region only when $\neg P(x, y)$). These complications are dealt with using a sorted logic, LLAMA (Cohn 1992). The functions compl(x), diff(x, y) and prod(x, y) are partial over the domain of regions, but are rendered total within LLAMA by introducing a sort NULL, disjoint from the sort REGION, and specifying sortal restrictions on the functions' arguments. The axioms below depend on the assumption that these restrictions are applied.

$\forall x \mathsf{EQ}(x, \mathsf{Us}) \equiv \forall y \mathsf{C}(x, y)$
$\forall x, y[[\mathsf{C}(y, \mathsf{compl}(x)) \equiv \neg \mathsf{NTPP}(y, x)] \wedge$
$\quad [\mathsf{O}(y, \mathsf{compl}(x)) \equiv \neg \mathsf{P}(y, x)]]$
$\forall x, y, z[\mathsf{C}(z, \mathsf{sum}(x, y)) \equiv \mathsf{C}(z, x) \vee \mathsf{C}(z, y)]$
$\forall x, y, z[\mathsf{C}(z, \mathsf{prod}(x, y)) \equiv$
$\quad \exists w[\mathsf{P}(w, x) \wedge \mathsf{P}(w, y) \wedge \mathsf{C}(z, w)]]$
$\forall x, y[\mathsf{NULL}(\mathsf{prod}(x, y)) \equiv \mathsf{DR}(x, y)]$
$\forall x, y, z[\mathsf{C}(z, \mathsf{diff}(x, y)) \equiv \mathsf{C}(z, \mathsf{prod}(x, \mathsf{compl}(y)))]$

RCC state in (Cohn et al. 1994) that point-set topology 'may indeed be a model for our formalism, but is not presupposed', and alternatives are suggested. Nevertheless, they do suggest a point-set interpretation: that $\mathsf{C}(x, y)$ is true iff the *closures* of regions x and y share at least one point. RCC do not specify whether the regions themselves are open or closed. Indeed, given the suggested interpretation of C, no predicate defined in terms of it could make this distinction. The axioms and definitions mentioned have models in a very wide range of topological spaces — possibly in *any* topological space (a question currently being investigated). A topological space is a concept much less specific than our intuitive understanding of spatial relations would demand: for example, it is not possible to define a notion of distance in many topological spaces. One aim of current work is to determine what additional axioms on C are needed to capture our spatial intuitions. Here, it will be useful to have a more specific interpretation of regions than RCC's axioms and suggested interpretation determine. It will be assumed that Us is an N-dimensional manifold, where $N > 0$, (an N-dimensional manifold is a set of points, together with a topology which gives each point in the set a neighbourhood homeomorphic to an N-dimensional disc), and that a region is an open set of points belonging to Us, equal to the interior of its closure. This means all regions will be manifolds, but not all manifolds within Us will be regions: every open subset of an N-dimensional manifold is an N-dimensional manifold, but some of these subsets will not be equal to the interior of their own closure — sets with single internal points removed, for example. This interpretation fixes that of the quasi-Boolean functions. For example, $\mathsf{compl}(x)$ becomes, in point-set terms, the complement of the *closure* of x.

All the work reported here has been done within the 'non-atomic' version of RCC's theory, produced (Randell et al. 1992) by adding another axiom to those given above:

$\forall x \exists y[\mathsf{NTPP}(y, x)],$

which establishes that all regions have an NTPP, ruling out atomic regions. This suffices to prove that all regions have an infinite number of NTPPs.

3 DEFINING A DOUGHNUT MADE EASY

Imagine presenting a spatial representation system which knows about 'C' with a task: to decide whether a 'mystery region', which we generally call r, is or is not a 'doughnut' — a region with the topology of a solid torus — by asking questions using only predicates defined in terms of C. The wider the range of topological properties we allow r to have (the less we assume about its topology) the harder this task will be. We can also make the task easier or harder by assuming more or less about the properties of regions in general or of Us. It will be easiest to explain the issues involved by starting with a strong set of (informally-stated) assumptions, then progressively weakening them. The initial set of assumptions is:

1. Us, the universal region, is an infinite 3-dimensional Euclidean space (E^3).

2. The closure of the open set of points corresponding to each region is a *locally Euclidean space* (Fuks and Rokhlin 1984, p.133), that is, each point belonging to this closed set has a neighbourhood homeomorphic *either* to an N-dimensional disc, *or* to half of such a disc (N, again, being the same for all points). This condition rules out a wide range of possibilities, as discussed in section 5 — for example, two open 3-dimensional cubes sharing a corner or an edge, and a disc with a smaller disc removed from it in so that their boundaries share a single point.

3. Any straight line will cut the boundary of any region a finite number of times. This will eliminate 'regions' with 'infinitely convoluted' boundaries, which are also discussed in section 5.

4. Region r is of finite diameter. The implications of this assumption, again, are discussed in section 5.

A self-connected ('CON') region, one which does not divide into two or more DC parts, is easily defined in terms of C (Randell et al. 1992):

$$\mathsf{CON}(x) \equiv_{def} \forall y \forall z[x = y + z \rightarrow \mathsf{C}(y, z)].$$

(In terms of point-set topology, with the interpretation of 'region' used here, this means the *closure* of the region is self-connected.) We can also define the 'separation-number' of a region: the minimum number of CON parts into which it can be divided.

What about connectivity in the sense which distinguishes a simply-connected surface such as a sphere, from a multiply-connected one such as a torus (the *surface* of a doughnut)? A topologist would generally give a definition in terms of the number of closed curves that can be drawn on a surface without dividing it in two — 0 for a sphere, 1 for a torus, 2 for a 2-hole torus, and so forth. It will be useful for us to define connectivity so that it applies to regions of any dimensionality. We could define the connectivity of a CON region as the maximum number of mutually DC subregions, each having two separate boundaries with the rest of the region, which we can remove from it while leaving it CON (see next page). For surfaces without boundary like the sphere and torus, this will be the same as the topologist's connectivity; but it can be applied equally to surfaces with boundary, and to regions of any dimensionality. However, it will in fact be convenient to define a different property, the 'finger-connectivity' of a CON region, which will always be one greater than the connectivity as defined above.

Finger-connectivity is defined in terms of the possible *dissections* of a CON region. A dissection is a division into a finite number of CON, non-overlapping and jointly exhaustive parts. The *dissection-graph* corresponding to a dissection is defined as follows: a node of the graph corresponds to each piece of the dissection, and two nodes are linked iff the corresponding parts are connected. The 'finger-connectivity' of a CON region identifies the largest of a specific family of dissection-graphs which it can host. This family is of graphs with $N + 2$ nodes ($N \geq 1$), with two of the nodes distinguished from the rest. These two are not linked, while each of the other N nodes has a link to each of them, but none to each other. The dissection-graph can be drawn like two N-fingered hands with pairs of corresponding fingertips touching (figure 2). A line-segment, disc or solid ball has finger-connectivity 1, a circle, annulus, torus or doughnut a finger-connectivity of 2, a 2-hole torus or doughnut 3, and so forth.

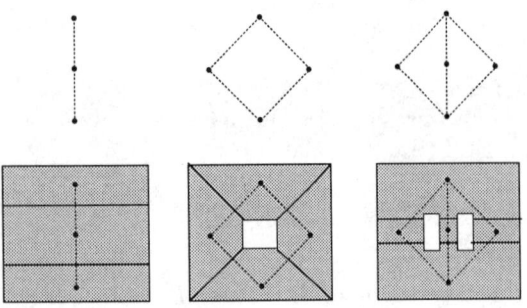

Figure 2: Dissection-Graphs And Dissections: Finger-Connectivities 1, 2 and 3

We can define separation-numbers and finger-connectivity-numbers as high as we need in terms of C. For example, to assert that a region r has separation-number 2 we could assert:

$$\exists s, t[\mathsf{DC}(s,t) \wedge [s + t = r] \wedge \mathsf{CON}(s) \wedge \mathsf{CON}(t)],$$

while to assert that a CON region r has finger-connectivity-number 2 we would assert:

$$[\exists a, b, t, u[[a + b + t + u = r] \wedge \mathsf{CON}(a) \wedge \mathsf{CON}(b) \wedge \\ \mathsf{CON}(t) \wedge \mathsf{CON}(u) \wedge \mathsf{EC}(a,t) \wedge \mathsf{EC}(a,u) \wedge \\ \mathsf{EC}(b,t) \wedge \mathsf{EC}(b,u) \wedge \mathsf{DC}(a,b)) \wedge \mathsf{DC}(t,u))]] \wedge \\ [\neg \exists a, b, t, u, v[[a + b + t + u + v = r] \wedge \\ \mathsf{CON}(a) \wedge \mathsf{CON}(b) \wedge \mathsf{CON}(t) \wedge \mathsf{CON}(u) \wedge \mathsf{CON}(v) \wedge \\ \mathsf{EC}(a,t) \wedge \mathsf{EC}(a,u) \wedge \mathsf{EC}(a,v) \wedge \mathsf{EC}(b,t) \wedge \\ \mathsf{EC}(b,u) \wedge \mathsf{EC}(b,v) \wedge \mathsf{DC}(a,b) \wedge \mathsf{DC}(t,u) \wedge \\ \mathsf{DC}(t,v) \wedge \mathsf{DC}(u,v)]].$$

If we wish to define separation-number for arbitrary regions, and finger-connectivity for arbitrary CON regions, we need to add an axiomatisation of the natural numbers to RCC's theory — although such general definitions are not in fact necessary for the definition of a doughnut. Once having added an axiomatisation of the natural numbers, we can define [2] separation-number as follows (upper-case letters are used to stand for variables ranging over the natural numbers, and '+' has its normal arithmetical meaning when applied to these numbers):

$$\mathsf{SEPNUM}(r, 1) \equiv_{def} \mathsf{CON}(r) \\ \mathsf{SEPNUM}(r, N+1) \equiv_{def} \exists s, t[[r = s+t] \wedge \mathsf{DC}(s,t) \wedge \\ \mathsf{CON}(s) \wedge \mathsf{SEPNUM}(t, N)];$$

and finger-connectivity as follows (leaving the finger-connectivity of a non-CON region undefined):

$$\mathsf{FCON}(r, N) \equiv_{def} \mathsf{CON}(r) \wedge \\ \exists a, x, b[[r = a + x + b] \wedge \mathsf{DC}(a,b) \wedge \mathsf{EC}(a,x) \wedge \\ \mathsf{EC}(x,b) \wedge \mathsf{SEPNUM}(x, N)] \wedge \\ \neg \exists a, y, b[[r = a + y + b] \wedge \mathsf{DC}(a,b) \wedge \mathsf{EC}(a,y) \wedge \\ \mathsf{EC}(y,b) \wedge \mathsf{SEPNUM}(y, N+1)]].$$

Separation-number and finger-connectivity together define a more general notion, region-connectivity, applicable to an arbitrary region. The region-connectivity of a region is described by a 'bag' of integers: a collection in which a member may repeat any number of times (unlike a set, in which each member occurs only once). Each number in the 'bag' rep-

---

[2]Strictly speaking, the formula for SEPNUM, and that given below for RCON, do not have the form of normal definitions, since they are recursive; however, at each point where these defined terms are used in defining a doughnut, they *could* be 'unpacked' to a form using *only* the relation C, and variables ranging over regions.

resents the finger-connectivity of one of the maximal CON components making up the region. For example, the region-connectivity of a region x made up of three separate parts, a 2-hole doughnut (or 2-hole solid torus) and two solid balls, is $[3, 1, 1]$. (We adopt the convention of listing the bag's elements in decreasing order.) We symbolise this RCON($x, [3, 1, 1]$), and also use the form: 'x is a $[3,1,1]$-region'. RCON can be defined more formally as follows (where '$[N]$' means a list containing the single natural number N, 'list' is a list of natural numbers, and '$N :: list$' means a list of natural numbers, the first being N:

RCON$(r, [N]) \equiv_{def}$ CON$(r) \wedge$ FCON(r, N)
RCON$(r, N :: list) \equiv_{def} \exists s, t[[r = s + t] \wedge$ DC$(s, t) \wedge$
FCON$(s, N) \wedge$ RCON$(t, list)$.

The number of boundaries two EC regions share can also now be defined using SEPNUM:

SBNUM$(r, s, N) \equiv_{def}$ EC$(r, s) \wedge$
$\exists x[$PP$(x, r) \wedge$ DC$(r - x, s) \wedge$
SEPNUM$(x, N)] \wedge$
$\neg \exists y[$PP$(y, r) \wedge$ DC$(r - y, s) \wedge$
SEPNUM$(y, N + 1)]$,

and the 'complement-boundary-number of a region (the number of boundaries it shares with its complement) is just a special case of this, except for the case of Us, where this number is defined as 0:

CBNUM$(r, N) \equiv_{def} [$EQ$(r,$ Us$) \wedge N = 0] \vee$
[SBNUM$(r,$ compl$(r), N)]$.

Given the assumptions and definitions above, a doughnut is a region with region-connectivity [2] and complement-boundary-number 1. Neither would be enough on its own: a solid ball embedded in E^3 has complement-boundary-number 1, and a doughnut with a ball-shaped internal void has region-connectivity [2].

4 DEFINING A DOUGHNUT MADE LESS EASY

Weakening the assumptions of section 3 will show how the doughnut can be distinguished among successively larger classes of possibilities. The process is not completed within this paper. The first step, in this section, is to weaken the assumption that Us is E^3. First, replace assumption 1 with assumption 1a:

1a. Us is E^N for some natural number N.

RCC note that their axioms have models in 1, 2, 3 or more dimensions. How can we determine the dimensionality of an arbitrary region r, using C? It is believed the approach outlined here distinguishes the cases where r has 1, 2, 3 or more than 3 dimensions, even if some of the assumptions set out in section 3 are weakened beyond the substitution of 1a for 1, although a full proof is not currently available.

Consider a CON region r, of unknown dimensionality. (Since we insist that a region be a manifold, the dimensionality of a non-CON region is the same as that of any of its CON parts.) Take any 2-piece dissection of r into CON regions s and t with a single boundary s/t (so that SBNUM$(s, t, 1)$). Consider any [1]-region u, such that:

PP$(u, s) \wedge$ SBNUM$(u, t, 1) \wedge$
$\exists v[$PP$(v, t) \wedge$ EC$(v, u) \wedge$ DC$(v, s - u)]$.

This ensures that u has a boundary with t of the same dimensionality as the s/t boundary has *locally*. That is, the u/t boundary will not be a single point in the middle of a linear or higher-dimensional patch of s/t boundary, a linear feature in the midst of a boundary-surface, and so forth. If the s/t boundary has the same dimensionality throughout, as will be the case if r, s and t are all locally Euclidean spaces, this condition ensures that the u/t boundary will be of the same dimensionality. If this is *not* the case, for example if s and t are 3-dimensional and meet in a disclike boundary with a 1-dimensional extension (figure 3), then u/t may also be of non-uniform dimensionality, but its highest dimensionality will be the same as that of the immediately surrounding parts of s/t.

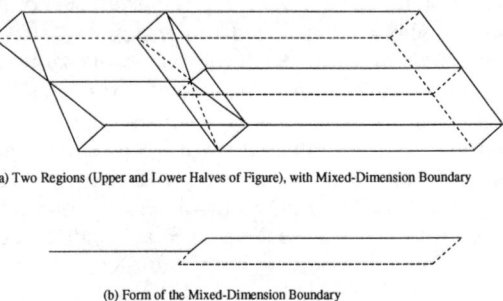

(a) Two Regions (Upper and Lower Halves of Figure), with Mixed-Dimension Boundary

(b) Form of the Mixed-Dimension Boundary

Figure 3: Two 3-D Regions With A Mixed-Dimension Common Boundary

Dissect u into as many parts $(u_1, u_2 ... u_n)$ as possible, such that all the u_i, and all regions that are the region-sum of some set of the u_is, meet the conditions on u above (i.e., each such region is a [1]-region — this implies, among other things, that each pair of the u_i meet in a single boundary — and each has a single boundary with t, meeting the same conditions as u/t). Also, for each pair u_x, u_y, there must be a region $u_{x,y}$ which overlaps (O's) both and is DC to the rest of u, ruling out dissections where the whole of the boundary between any pair of the u_i is also shared by any other of the u_i. Such a forbidden dissection is shown in figure 4: in this case, the whole of the boundary between u_1 and u_3 is also shared with u_2, and u_4 (and conversely, the whole of the u_2/u_4 boundary is also shared with u_1 and u_3). Finally, for any v such that $\mathsf{PP}(v,s)$ and $\mathsf{DC}(v,t)$, there must be a w meeting the same conditions, such that the respective products of the u_i with $u - (v + w)$ meet the same conditions as the u_i themselves. This means that the topological relationships of the u_i are preserved in arbitrarily thin 'skins' of u where it borders t.

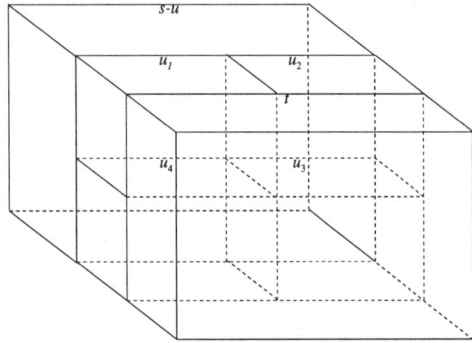

Figure 4: A Forbidden Dissection Of u.

Call the *maximum* number of parts into which u can be divided in this way L. This will be, for example, 1 if the u/t boundary is a single point, 2 if it is a line-segment, 3 if it is disclike, 4 if it is spherical, 7 if toroidal. Now find the *minimum* value of L across all regions meeting the conditions for u; call this minimum M (this will always be 1 if the s/t boundary is 0-dimensional, 2 if it is 1-dimensional, 3 if it is 2-dimensional). Finally, take the *maximum* value of M across all regions meeting the conditions for s. (This takes care of cases such as an r consisting of two lobes joined at a single point, where if s was chosen as one lobe, the value of M would be lower than the dimensionality of r.) This maximum of M will equal the dimensionality of r, at least up to 3, and will be greater than 3 when and only when the dimensionality of r is also greater than 3. (If r is 4-dimensional, the s/t boundary can be 3-dimensional if s is chosen correctly, and if the u/t boundary is a 3-disc, or solid ball, u can be divided into 4 parts in the required fashion (figure 5). (This division gives rise to a total of 15 [1]-regions: the entire ball, the four small regions, and all combinations of these small regions taken two or three at a time.) We then imagine giving each part an arbitrarily small thickness in the fourth dimension, just as we can do if we start with a 2-disc divided into 3 parts and then give them an arbitrarily small thickness in the third dimension.)

We can take the weakening of condition 1 a step further, substituting for 1a:

1b. Us is an N-dimensional orientable manifold.

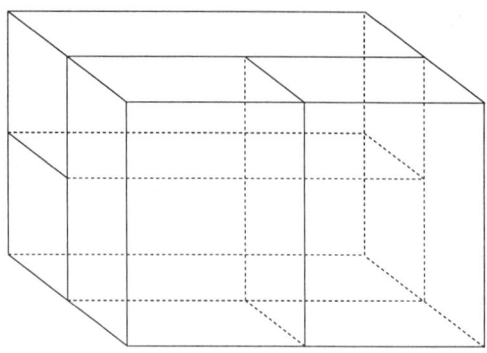

Figure 5: A (Topological) Solid Ball Divided Into Four, Giving Rise To 15 [1]-Regions

It might be thought that this is pointless. If we are interested in 3-dimensional regions, for example, will we not want to assume that Us is E^3? Not necessarily: we might be interested only in the space within some living or mechanical system — such as the electrically conducting parts of the heart (Gotts 1987, Gotts, Hunter, Hamlet and Vincent 1989). Of course, we could always add one more region, consisting of everything we are not interested in, but we would then have a dichotomy between an 'interesting' region, within which spatial relationships are explored, and an 'uninteresting' one, where they are not.

A doughnut can be embedded in any 3-dimensional manifold, because any point in a 3-dimensional manifold has a neighbourhood homeomorphic to a 3-dimensional ball, and a doughnut can be embedded in such a ball. We insist that Us be orientable because, so far, orientability has not been characterised in terms of C, nor is it known whether this is possible. In practice, it is hard to think of areas where one might want to apply a C-based representation to non-orientable manifolds.

If 1b replaces 1a, r may not be identifiable via the same set of questions as when Us was assumed to be E^N. For example, assume that Us itself is a doughnut, and that r is Us. The criterion of section 3 will not work correctly, because r has CBNUM 0. Nor is this the only case where such problems would arise. Suppose r and Us are both doughnuts, topologically speaking, but the relationship of r to Us is equivalent to that of one doughnut in the middle of a stack of doughnuts: r will have CBNUM 2, and so will fail the test.

The problem is that the CBNUM is an *extrinsic* property of a region: that is, dependent on the way it is embedded in Us. We need an *intrinsic* definition of boundary-number — one expressed solely in terms of the way parts of r relate to each other. No intrinsic C-based definition of boundary-number known to apply *whatever* the dimensionality of r has yet been found.

In one dimension, there are only two distinct CON

manifolds that can act as Us: the (topological) circle, and the open line. It does not matter whether the open line is infinite in both directions, a finite open line segment, or an open half-line, infinitely extended in one direction. From the point-set topological point of view, all three are homeomorphic once the boundary-points of the line-segment and half-line are excluded. From our 'region-relation' topological viewpoint, too, there is no way to tell which of these three possibilities corresponds to Us: any configuration of regions can be 'transferred' from any one of the three to any other, using the point-set homeomorphisms between them. Similarly, an open disc is homeomorphic to E^2 and an open ball to E^3. So we want a definition of intrinsic boundary-number (IBNUM) that will assign the same number — 1 — to an infinite line or half-line as to a line-segment; to E^2 minus a disc as to a disc with an internal disc removed (2 in each case); and to E^3 minus M DC solid balls as to a solid ball with M DC interior solid balls removed (M in each case).

If Us is an open line, so are *all* CON regions, and all regions, including Us, have two 'ends', even if one or both are at an infinite distance; if Us is a circle, it has no 'ends'. A way of capturing this difference in terms of C is to say that, for an open line, it is possible to *remove* a maximum of two regions DC from each other, while leaving a remainder with the same RCON as the original (one region is removed from each end of the line). Removing any region from a circle leaves a remainder different from the original.

In the 2-dimensional case, the number of topologically different self-connected manifolds (surfaces) is infinite — although a complete classification is available. If attention is restricted to orientable surfaces, any such surface is homeomorphic to a sphere with H 'handles' (a sphere with no handles is just a sphere, a sphere with 1 handle a torus, a sphere with $H > 1$ handles an H-hole-torus), and B boundary curves. In terms of C, we could define the IBNUM of a surface as the number of mutually DC [2]-regions which can be removed without changing the RCON of the surface: one such region can be removed from around each boundary-curve.

If we start with a '1-dimensional disc' (a line-segment, with RCON [1]), and remove a smaller '1-dimensional disc' from its interior, the result is to produce a [1,1]-region. If we remove a 2-dimensional disc from the interior of a larger 2-dimensional disc (which again is a [1]-region), the remainder is a [2]-region. However, if we remove *any number* of interior 3-dimensional discs (solid balls) from a larger 3-dimensional disc, its region-connectivity is unaffected. The simplest definition of IBNUM for 3-dimensional regions yet found depends on prior definitions of the concepts of a 'firmly tangential proper part' of a region and a 'solid [1]-region'. This definition also works for the 1-dimensional and 2-dimensional cases.

Intuitively, an N-dimensional region x is a firmly-tangential proper part of a region of finite diameter y (symbolised FTPP(x,y)), iff it is a proper part of y, and shares an N-1-dimensional part of its boundary with y: so for example, if y is the area within a circle, x could be the area to one side of a diameter of that circle. However, because we want a definition of IBNUM which assigns the same number to topologically equivalent regions, and because finite diameter is not a topological property, this definition must allow the existence of FTPPs of infinite regions, such as E^2. For example, since we can map the area within a circle onto E^2 in such a way that the part of that area to one side of a diameter is mapped onto half of E^2, this should turn out to be an FTPP of E^2.

The following C-based intrinsic definition works at least for regions with three or fewer dimensions. FTPP(x,y) iff PP(x,y) and it is possible to find a [1]-region w, such that P(w,x), that can be divided into two [1]-regions, one of which is DC from $y - w$, while the other is a 'solid [1]-region'. A 'solid [1]-region' is just a [1]-region with no wholly-internal voids when embedded in E^N, where N is the [1]-region's dimensionality. (An N-dimensional region with B intrinsic boundaries will have $B - 1$ internal voids when embedded in E^N.) All 1-dimensional and 2-dimensional [1]-regions are 'solid', but a ball with an interior ball removed is a [1]-region, but not solid. Unlike a solid ball, it can be divided into two EC [1]-regions, separated by an annular, rather than disclike or spherical boundary. For a 3-dimensional non-solid [1]-region u, there is a dissection into two [1]-regions s, t, such that there is a [2]-region r, where PP(r, s), DC$(t, s - r)$, and there is *no* [1]-region q such that PP(q, r) and DC$(t, s-q)$. For a 3-dimensional solid [1]-region, there is no such dissection. (Solid and non-solid [1]-regions of 4 or more dimensions could, it is thought, be defined recursively, but the details have not been worked out.)

An FTPP (of a region with three or fewer dimensions) can now be formally defined:

FTPP$(x, y) \equiv_{def}$ PP$(x,y) \land$
$\exists u, v, w [$P$(w,x) \land [u + v = w] \land$ EC$(u,v) \land$
DC$(v, y - w) \land$ RCON$(w, [1]) \land$ RCON$(v, [1]) \land$
RCON$(u, [1]) \land$
$\neg \exists r, s, t[[s + t = u] \land$ PP$(r, s) \land$ EC$(s, t) \land$
DC$(t, s - r) \land$ RCON$(r, [2]) \land$
RCON$(s, [1]) \land$ RCON$(t, [1]) \land$
$\neg \exists q[$PP$(q, r) \land$ DC$(t, s - q) \land$
RCON$(q, [1])]]]$.

An *intrinsic* tangential proper part (ITPP) of y can in turn be defined, for regions of three or fewer dimensions, as follows:

ITPP$(x, y) \equiv_{def}$ PP$(x,y) \land$
$\forall w [$PP$(x, w) \land$ PP$(w, y) \land$ DC$(x, y - w) \rightarrow$
FTPP$(w, y)]$

— that is, any PP of y that 'envelopes' x, shielding it from the rest of y, must be an FTPP of y. This definition will always coincide with the definition of a TPP when y is of finite diameter and Us is E^N, but will not always do so in other cases: in particular, Us can have ITPPs - if Us is finite, or its ITPP is infinite. An INTPP can be defined, in three or fewer dimensions, as a PP which is not an ITPP:

$$\text{INTPP}(x, y) \equiv_{def} \text{PP}(x, y) \land \neg \text{ITPP}(x, y).$$

A TPP is always an ITPP, and an INTPP is always an NTPP; but the converses of these statements are not true. Regions that have no intrinsic boundaries (a circle in one dimension, closed surfaces such as a sphere or torus in two dimensions, and their 3-dimensional counterparts such as the 3-sphere), have no FTPPs or ITPPs.

The IBNUM of a region of three or fewer dimensions can now be defined as the greatest SEPNUM of any s such that $\text{PP}(s,r)$, each CON component of s is an ITPP of r, and any ITPP of r connects with s. For a formal definition, it will be convenient to use the predicate MAX-P(x, y) (Cohn et al. 1994), meaning that x is a CON P of y, while any PPI of x which is a P of y is not CON:

$$\text{MAX-P}(x, y) \equiv_{def} \text{CON}(x) \land \text{P}(x, y) \land \\ \neg \exists z [\text{PP}(x, z) \land P(z, y) \land \text{CON}(z)].$$

The predicate IBNUM can now be defined as follows:

$$\text{IBNUM}(r, N) \equiv_{def} [N = 0 \land \neg \exists s[\text{ITPP}(s,r)]] \lor \\ [\exists s[\text{ITPP}(s,r)] \land \\ \exists x[\text{SEPNUM}(x, N) \land \\ \forall z[\text{MAX-P}(z, x) \to \text{ITPP}(z, r)] \land \\ \forall t[\text{ITPP}(t, r) \to C(t, x)]] \land \\ \neg \exists y[\text{SEPNUM}(y, N+1) \land \\ \forall z[\text{MAX-P}(z, y) \to \text{ITPP}(z, r)] \land \\ \forall t[\text{ITPP}(t, r) \to C(t, y)]]]$$

A doughnut can then be defined as a 3-dimensional [2]-region with IBNUM 1.

5 DEFINING A DOUGHNUT MADE HARDER STILL

In this section, we remove or weaken assumptions 2-4, and, since Us is a region, further weaken assumption 1 as we do so.

If we remove assumption 2, allowing regions to have closures that are not locally Euclidean spaces, we are faced with a wide range of 'poorly-connected' regions that have RCON [2] and IBNUM 1, but that do not correspond to the intuitive idea of a doughnut, having a boundary surface that departs from the locally disclike topology we would like that of our doughnut to have.

It is not difficult to define a predicate, ICON (for interior-connected), such that ICON(r) means that r does not divide into two or more parts which are only connected because their closures share a point:

$$\text{ICON}(x) \equiv_{def} \forall y, z[\text{INTPP}(y, x) \land \text{INTPP}(z, x) \to \\ \exists w[\text{CON}(w) \land \text{INTPP}(y, w) \land \text{INTPP}(z, w) \land \\ \text{INTPP}(w, x)]].$$

However, ICON(r) does not rule out all poorly-connected regions. Figure 3 shows one such example, and figure 6 shows cross-sections of two others, both of which can be regarded as 'degenerate doughnuts': 6a is a doughnut 'pinched' to a single point at one place — the darker shading indicates a surface sloping away from the viewer. 6b shows two series of cross-sections through a shape that could be constructed by bringing the sides of the hole 'through' a doughnut together until the hole is contracted to a point halfway through, or by cutting two 4-sided pyramids out of opposite sides of a cuboid so that they share a vertex. The left and right halves of 6b show series of horizontal and vertical cross-sections respectively.

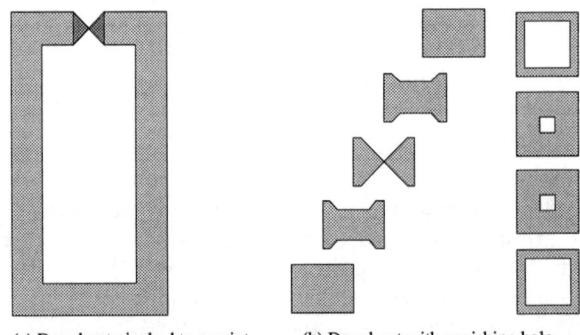

(a) Doughnut pinched to a point   (b) Doughnut with vanishing hole

Figure 6: Degenerate Doughnuts In Cross-Section

We can define a more restrictive predicate, which we call WCON (for 'well-connected'), which appears to deal with all poorly-connected regions — that is, it is believed a 2- or 3-dimensional WCON region will always have a boundary with a locally linear or disclike topology respectively. Given this definition, we can remove assumption 2, and then have the choice of incorporating the conditions ensuring that a region is WCON as an additional axiom, or allowing both WCON and non-WCON regions while being able to distinguish the two. In order to define a WCON region, however, an intermediate definition will be necessary.

A [1]-region s with IBNUM 1 will be called a 'superficial proper part' of another region r — SPP(s, r) — iff s is an ITPP of r, such that for any INTPP of r, say t, there is another INTPP of r, u, such that $s - (t + u)$ is also an [1]-region with IBNUM 1. Formally:

$$\text{SPP}(s,r) \equiv_{def} \text{RCON}(s,[1]) \wedge \text{IBNUM}(s,1) \wedge$$
$$\text{ITPP}(s,r) \wedge \forall t[\text{INTPP}(t,r) \rightarrow \exists u[\text{INTPP}(u,r) \wedge$$
$$\text{RCON}(s-(t+u),[1]) \wedge \text{IBNUM}(s-(t+u),1)]]$$

This same class of [1]-region, 1-IBNUM ITPPs could also be picked out by specifying that s and r share only one patch of intrinsic boundary, and if s and r are N-dimensional, this patch is an N-1-dimensional disc. However, this condition on the form of the patch is redundant if $n \leq 2$. Also, this alternative means of specifying the class of SPPs is more difficult to express in terms of C.

For all the examples of figures 3 and 6, there are SPPs, the removal of which would leave a remainder with a different RCON. At one stage it was thought that this could be used as a way of excluding all poorly-connected regions. However, there are 'regions' which do not have such an SPP, but which are poorly-connected. One such is a solid ball with a smaller solid ball removed from it in such a way that the surfaces of the two balls share a single point. Topologically, such a region could be created by attaching the region of figure 6b to the bottom of a cuboid, so that the depression in the top became an interior hole, meeting the outside at a single point. Such a region has RCON [1] and a single intrinsic boundary, like a solid ball, and removing an SPP cannot change this, as it can for the region of 6b itself, where cutting out the centre so as to leave an ordinary doughnut does the trick.

However, a WCON region can be defined as one with no SPPs of a certain sort. Specifically, a WCON region r has no SPP s which *itself* has an SPP t such that $\text{DC}(t, r-s)$ and such that $s-t$ is not a [1]-region.

$$\text{WCON}(r) \equiv_{def} \forall s, t[\text{SPP}(s,r) \wedge \text{SPP}(t,s) \wedge$$
$$\text{DC}(t, r-s) \rightarrow \text{RCON}(t-s, [1])]$$

Assumption 3 eliminates some dubious 'regions'. These would include, for example, a region bounded by the 'snowflake curve' (Stewart 1987, p.182), and the regions produced by dividing a disc into two parts which spiral around the disc an infinite number of times, decreasing in width toward the edge. Some of the *configurations* of regions such infinitely convoluted boundaries give rise to can certainly be eliminated, if desired, by additional axioms concerning C. For example, the configuration consisting of a disc divided into two 'ever-decreasing spirals' as described above, plus a surrounding region, can be ruled out by the proviso that if x and y are externally connected and their sum is intrinsically bounded, they do not share the entire boundary:

$$\forall x, y[\text{EC}(x,y) \wedge \exists z[\text{ITPP}(z, x+y)]] \rightarrow$$
$$\exists w[\text{ITPP}(w, x+y) \wedge [\text{DC}(w,x) \vee \text{DC}(w,y)]].$$

Many 'regions' that assumption 3 rules out could not be eliminated in this way — including that bounded by the snowflake curve — since assumption 3 makes use of non-topological properties of putative 'regions'. However, it may be that none of those which cannot be excluded using C are *topologically* anomalous.

Assumption 4 means we need not consider regions of infinite diameter when trying to decide whether r is a doughnut. If we remove it, r could be, for example, a doughnut with an infinitely extended, rod-shaped protrusion, provided Us also has an infinite diameter. If Us is E^N, then regions of infinite diameter, and only such regions, can have ITPPs which are also NTPPs, and this fact could be used to distinguish the 'true' doughnut from the doughnut-plus-infinite-rod. An example of such an ITPP, in the case of a doughnut with an infinitely long rod-shaped protrusion, would be an infinitely long rod of smaller diameter, beginning near the doughnut end of the rod-extension and running inside the entire infinite length of that larger diameter rod, nowhere touching its boundary. However, if Us itself is finite but not compact (like an open ball), or can be disconnected by the removal of such a part (like an infinitely long solid cylinder) the same test will eliminate some genuine doughnuts which share part of Us's boundary. We therefore need to know something about Us in order to know which tests to apply to r.

6 Discussion: HOW FAR CAN C TAKE US?

C can be the basis of rich topological classifications of regions and the spatial relations between them. The search for a definition of the doughnut has led to the exploration of a wide range of possibilities, and brought out the distinction between the intrinsic and extrinsic topological properties of a region.

Which of the informally-stated assumptions considered could reasonably be made under which circumstances deserves a brief comment. If the regions we wish to consider correspond to the space occupied by solid or liquid bodies, then we can assume that they are of finite diameter, and that a straight line would intersect their boundaries a finite number of times. We could also assume (assumptions not needed in this paper) that they consist of a finite number of separate pieces, each of finite finger-connectivity. It might also seem that we could assume each region's closure to be 3-dimensional, but this is to ignore the role of *idealization* in spatial reasoning: for many purposes it is useful to regard a piece of paper as 2-dimensional, or a rope as 1-dimensional. Similarly, if we wish to consider something with a cellular structure, such as a piece of plant or animal tissue, or a foam, we may need to consider regions which are best idealized as consisting of one or more 3-dimensional 'lobes' joined at points or along lines rather than at surfaces — contrary to the assumption that regions have closures which are locally-Euclidean spaces.

The exploration of taxonomies of spatial properties and relations based on C is far from complete. Region-connectivity and intrinsic-boundary-number do not distinguish all non-homeomorphic regions, even among manifolds with finite separation-numbers whose closures are locally-Euclidean spaces. In general, this problem is unsolvable (it is known that there is no general method for determining whether 2 N-dimensional manifolds are homeomorphic for $n > 3$) (Stillwell 1980, p.5). Even for finite-diameter manifolds embeddable in E^3, much work on C-based classification remains. In the 2-dimensional case, a way of expressing *orientability* will be sought. In the 3-dimensional case, there are several levels of complexity to consider. First, there may be any number of separate maximal CON parts. CON regions can have any number of surfaces, and each such surface may be a sphere or N-hole torus. So the number and nature of the region's surfaces give a first layer of classification for CON regions, and we can classify non-CON regions by the 'bag' of such CON regions they comprise.

However, this is not the end of the matter. Consider a CON region with two surfaces, each a 1-hole torus (i.e. a doughnut minus a doughnut). The inner surface may be configured relative to the outer so that a sphere could be interposed between the two, or it may be wrapped one or more times round the hole 'through' the doughnut. This example shows that the finger-connectivity of a CON region cannot be calculated simply from those of its boundaries: if a sphere can be interposed between the two surfaces the finger-connectivity of the solid is 3; if not, it is 2 (at least in the simplest case, where the inner torus wraps around the hole through the doughnut once, producing a 'hollow doughnut': a solid like the inner tube of a tyre; more complex cases have still to be checked).

Whether wrapped around the doughnut's hole or not, the inner surface of a 3-dimensional region with two toroidal surfaces may be knotted in any one of an infinite number of ways, or unknotted. Although a knotted torus or doughnut is only extrinsically different from an unknotted one, a solid ball or doughnut *minus* a knotted doughnut *is* intrinsically different from the same containing solid minus an unknotted doughnut.

If a solid has two or more toroidal inner surfaces (whether these are simple — FCON-2 — tori, or are of higher connectivity), a new type of complexity arises, as two or more of these inner surfaces can be *linked* in a variety of ways. (Two or more such surfaces are linked if none of them can be enclosed in a sphere disconnected from all the others.) Finally, two or more of the components of a non-CON region can also be linked — in the same set of possible ways, although in this case the distinctions are extrinsic, not intrinsic.

In the immediate future, investigation of the relationship between RCC's approach and point-set topology will continue, and formal proofs of the assertions made in this paper will be sought. Further work is planned on ways of classifying such multi-surface 3-dimensional regions, drawing on mathematicians' work on algebraic or combinatorial topology — e.g. (Stillwell 1980, Fuks and Rokhlin 1984) — and exploring further the notion of a dissection-graph: if two CON regions have the same finger-connectivity but are not topologically equivalent, can other dissection-graphs be used to distinguish them?

Beyond this, integrating topological and other qualitative aspects of spatial properties and relations is a major task. The work described in this paper needs to be integrated with that on convexity and inside/outside relations done by RCC, and with the work on conceptual neighbourhoods done by Freksa (Freksa 1992), RCC (Cohn et al. 1994) and others.

In conclusion, what are the advantages and disadvantages of the general approach to spatial representation and reasoning developed by RCC and continued here: that of working from a minimal set of primitives and axioms, exploiting their potential as far as possible before adopting any more? The advantages are several: such an approach has a mathematical and philosophical elegance absent from more complex systems of representation, discourages *ad hoc* additions to the system to meet unconsidered problems, and should ensure thorough familiarity with its properties and implications. It should be relatively simple to interface a system of spatial representation using a small number of primitives and axioms with another system — such as a vision module or geographical database. Similarly, it should be easier to investigate in depth the relationship of RCC's approach to point-set topology than would be the case for a more complex system. On the other hand, writing this paper has made it clear to me that expressing what are intuitively quite simple concepts — such as the topological properties of a doughnut — in terms of a single primitive and a few axioms is neither easy nor free of pitfalls. In particular, inability to refer directly to dimensionality, to boundaries, and to the conceptual links between these concepts, gave rise to considerable difficulties. Only by trying to do as much as we can with as little as possible, however, are we likely to discover what representational primitives are likely to be most useful in spatial and qualitative reasoning.

Acknowledgements

The support of the SERC under grant no. GR/H 78955 is gratefully acknowledged. This work was also partially supported by the CEC under the Basic Research Action MEDLAR 2, Project 6471. Thanks are also due to Tony Cohn, Brandon Bennett, John Gooday and two anonymous referees for useful comments and to John for extensive help with the figures.

References

Allen, J. F.: 1981, An interval-based representation of temporal knowledge, *Proceedings 7th IJCAI*, Vancouver, Canada, pp. 221–226.

Allen, J. F. and Hayes, P. J.: 1985, A common sense theory of time, *Proceedings 9th IJCAI*, Los Angeles, USA, pp. 528–531.

Allen, J. F. and Hayes, P. J.: 1989, Moments and points in an interval-based temporal logic, *Computational Intelligence* **5**, 225–238.

Casati, R. and Varzi, A.: 1993, *Holes and Other Superficialities*, MIT Press, Cambridge, MA. To Appear.

Clarke, B. L.: 1981, A calculus of individuals based on connection, *Notre Dame Journal of Formal Logic* **23**(3), 204–218.

Clarke, B. L.: 1985, Individuals and points, *Notre Dame Journal of Formal Logic* **26**(1), 61–75.

Cohn, A. G.: 1992, Completing sort hierarchies, *Computers and Mathematics with Applications* **23**(6-9), 477–491.

Cohn, A. G., Randell, D. A. and Cui, Z.: 1994, Taxonomies of logically defined qualitative spatial relations, in N. Guarino and R. Poli (eds), *Formal Ontology in Conceptual Analysis and Knowledge Representation*, Kluwer. To appear.

Cohn, A. G., Randell, D. A., Cui, Z. and Bennett, B.: 1993, Qualitative spatial reasoning and representation, in N. P. Carreté and M. G. Singh (eds), *Qualitative Reasoning and Decision Technologies*, CIMNE, Barcelona, pp. 513–522.

Freksa, C.: 1992, Temporal reasoning based on semi-intervals, *Artificial Intelligence* **54**, 199–227.

Fuks, D. B. and Rokhlin, V. A.: 1984, *Beginner's Course in Topology: Geometric Chapters*, Springer-Verlag. Translated from the Russian by Andrei Iacob.

Gotts, N. M.: 1987, A qualitative spatial representation for cardiac electrophysiology, in J. Fox, M. Fieschi and R. Engelbrecht (eds), *Lecture Notes in Medical Informatics 33*, Springer-Verlag, pp. 88–95.

Gotts, N. M., Hunter, J. R. W., Hamlet, I. and Vincent, R.: 1989, Qualitative spatio-temporal models of cardiac electrophysiology, *Technical Report AUCS/TR8903*, Dept. of Computing Science, University of Aberdeen.

Guha, R. V. and Lenat, D. B.: 1990, Cyc: a mid-term report, *AI Magazine* **11**(3), 32–59.

Hayes, P. J.: 1985a, Naive physics I: Ontology for liquids, in J. R. Hobbs and B. Moore (eds), *Formal Theories of the Commonsense World*, Ablex, pp. 71–89.

Hayes, P. J.: 1985b, The second naive physics manifesto, in J. R. Hobbs and B. Moore (eds), *Formal Theories of the Commonsense World*, Ablex, pp. 1–36.

Leonard, H. S. and Goodman, N.: 1940, The calculus of individuals and its uses, *Journal of Symbolic Logic* **5**, 45–55.

Randell, D. A.: 1991, *Analysing the Familiar: Reasoning About Space and Time in the Everyday World*, PhD thesis, University of Warwick.

Randell, D. A. and Cohn, A. G.: 1989, Modelling topological and metrical properties of physical processes, in R. Brachman, H. Levesque and R. Reiter (eds), *Proceedings 1st International Conference on the Principles of Knowledge Representation and Reasoning*, Morgan Kaufmann, Los Altos, pp. 55–66.

Randell, D. A., Cui, Z. and Cohn, A. G.: 1992, A spatial logic based on regions and connection, *Proceedings 3rd International Conference on Knowledge Representation and Reasoning*, Morgan Kaufmann, San Mateo, pp. 165–176.

Simons, P.: 1987, *Parts: A Study In Ontology*, Clarendon Press, Oxford.

Smith, B.: 1994, Ontology and the logistic analysis of reality, in N. Guarino and R. Poli (eds), *Formal Ontology in Conceptual Analysis and Knowledge Representation*, Kluwer. To appear.

Stewart, I.: 1987, *The Problems of Mathematics*, Oxford University Press.

Stillwell, J.: 1980, *Classical Topology and Combinatorial Group Theory*, Springer-Verlag, New York.

Tarski, A.: 1956, Foundations of the geometry of solids, *Logic, Semantics, Metamathematics*, Oxford Clarendon Press, chapter 2. trans. J.H. Woodger.

Varzi, A. C.: 1993, On the boundary between mereology and topology, *Procedings 16th Wittgenstein Symposium*.

Vieu, L.: 1993, A logical framework for reasoning about space, in A. U. Frank and I. Campari (eds), *Spatial Information Theory: a Theoretical Basis for GIS*, Vol. 716 of *Lecture notes in computer science*, Springer-Verlag, pp. 25–35. Proceedings of COSIT'93, Elba, Italy, September 1993.

Weld, D. S. and De Kleer, J. (eds): 1990, *Readings in Qualitative Reasoning About Physical Systems*, Morgan Kaufman, San Mateo, Ca.

Whitehead, A. N.: 1929, *Process and Reality*, The MacMillan Company, New York.

An Ontology for Engineering Mathematics

Thomas R. Gruber and **Gregory R. Olsen**
Knowledge Systems Laboratory
Stanford University
701 Welch Road, Building C, Palo Alto, CA 94304
gruber@ksl.stanford.edu

Abstract

We describe an ontology for mathematical modeling in engineering. The ontology includes conceptual foundations for scalar, vector, and tensor quantities, physical dimensions, units of measure, functions of quantities, and dimensionless quantities. The conceptualization builds on abstract algebra and measurement theory, but is designed explicitly for knowledge sharing purposes. The ontology is being used as a communication language among cooperating engineering agents, and as a foundation for other engineering ontologies. In this paper we describe the conceptualization of the ontology, and show selected axioms from definitions. We describe the design of the ontology and justify the important representation choices. We offer evaluation criteria for such ontologies and demonstrate design techniques for achieving them.

1. INTRODUCTION

Engineers use mathematical models, such as sets of equations, to analyze the behavior of physical systems. The conventional notations for formatting mathematical expressions in textbooks and in the engineering literature usually leave implicit many of the details required to understand the equations. For instance, it is not clear from the expression $f = kx+c$ which symbols are variables or constants; whether they represent numbers or physical quantities (e.g., forces, lengths); whether the magnitudes are reals, vectors, or higher-order tensors; whether the quantities are static values, functions of time, or functions of time and space; and how units of measure are treated. The reader must *interpret* these notations using background knowledge and context. This is error-prone for humans and beyond the capability of today's computer agents.

To enable the sharing and reuse of engineering models among engineering tools and their users, it is important to specify a conceptual foundation that makes these distinctions explicit and provides a context- and reader-independent semantics. Toward this end, we have developed a formal ontology for mathematical modeling in engineering, called EngMath. The ontology builds on abstract algebra and measurement theory, adapted to meet the expressive needs of engineering modeling. The specification includes a first-order axiomatization of representational vocabulary that is machine and human readable.

This paper is about the EngMath ontology, and how it exemplifies the design and use of such ontologies in support of agent communication and knowledge reuse. Such an ontology differs from what is found in engineering textbooks and philosophy books in that it is designed as a specification for these knowledge sharing purposes. We begin in Section 2 by describing the role of ontologies as formal specification and the uses of the EngMath ontology. In Section 3, we give define the basic concepts and relations in the ontology. In Section 4, we discuss a series of design decisions and their rationale. In Section 5, we offer design criteria—minimizing ontological commitment and maximizing monotonic extendibility—and demonstrate techniques used to achieve them. In Section 6, we discuss the relationship of the EngMath ontologies to relevant work in philosophy and AI

2. THE PURPOSE OF THE ONTOLOGY

2.1 ONTOLOGY AS FORMAL SPECIFICATION

A body of formally represented knowledge is based on a *conceptualization*: the objects, concepts, and other entities that are assumed to exist in some area of interest and the relationships that hold among them [17]. A conceptualization is an abstract, simplified view of the world that we wish to represent for some purpose. Every knowledge base, knowledge-based system, or knowledge-level agent is committed to some conceptualization, explicitly or implicitly.

For the purpose of knowledge sharing, formal ontologies serve as *specifications of common conceptualizations* [20] among agents. In the philosophy literature, ontology is the systematic account of Existence—aiming to account for all forms and modes of being [5]. For AI systems, what can exist in a conceptualized world is determined by what can be represented.[1] If agents are to communicate in a shared

---

[1] By "what can exist" we mean "anything that can be spoken of," including all of the varieties of existence identified by Hirst [27]. The purpose of our specifications are not to giving ontological status to

language or if a body of formally represented knowledge is to be reused, then there must be some agreement about a universe of discourse. Furthermore, if the shared language includes vocabulary denoting entities and relationships in the conceptualization, there must be some way to specify what can be meaningfully stated in this vocabulary. Ontologies, in the context of knowledge sharing, are a means for making such content-specific agreements.

If we assume a common syntax and semantics for a core representation language, then we can specify conceptualizations by writing definitions of shared vocabulary. That is the strategy proposed by the ARPA Knowledge Sharing Effort [33,35], and is the tack we are taking. A Knowledge Interchange Format (KIF) [16] serves as the language for making assertions and definitions, and ontologies provide axiomatic and textual definitions of relations, functions, and objects. By 'definitions' we mean specifications of the well formed use of the vocabulary. Definitions include axioms that constrain the interpretation.[2] Such an axiomatization specifies a logical theory, but is not intended as a knowledge base. Instead, the ontology serves as a domain-specific representation language in which knowledge is shared and communicated.

In practice, our ontologies define the vocabulary with which queries and assertions are exchanged among interoperating agents, some of which may be passive (e.g., deductive databases). The agents conform to ontological commitments [19,20] which are agreements to use the shared vocabulary in a coherent and consistent manner. An ontological commitment is a guarantee of consistency, but not completeness, with respect to queries and assertions using the vocabulary defined in the ontology (c.f. [23]). Committed agents may "know" things not implied by the shared ontologies, and may not be able to answer queries that follow from the shared ontologies. Furthermore, the "shared knowledge" of these agents can be viewed at the Knowledge Level, as attributed and independent of symbol-level encoding [34]. Thus, the agents may operate on any internal representation desired, as long as they use the shared vocabulary consistently in communication. This model of agent collaboration is being pursued by several groups [9,15,22,32].

2.2 USES OF THE ENGMATH ONTOLOGY

In designing the EngMath ontology, we anticipate three kinds of use, and accept them as requirements. First, the ontology should provide a machine- and human-readable notation for representing the models and domain theories found in the engineering literature. Second, it should provide a formal specification of a shared conceptualization and vocabulary for a community of interoperating software agents in engineering domains. Third, it should provide a foundation for other formalization efforts, including more comprehensive ontologies for engineering and domain-specific languages. In this section we will give examples of each application.

EngMath as a Shared Notation

Engineers use mathematical expressions, such as constraint equations, to describe, analyze, and communicate models of physical devices and their behavior. The quantities represented in these expressions are different from purely numerical values, and the algebra for operating over them must account for extra-numerical considerations such as dimensional consistency, units of measure, and vector and tensor operations. Some form of this 'physical algebra' [31] is taught in nearly every introductory physics or engineering course, and the subject is prominent in the standard texts [26,37]. Students are taught to use dimensional consistency to check for modeling and equation solving errors. A technique called Dimensional Analysis [31] is used in design and to assist in the interpretation of experiments, and is an important area of study itself.

Textbook notations for physical quantities vary by author and leave much implicit—relying on context and background knowledge of the reader for proper interpretation. The problem of implicit notation is revealed when students try to encode engineering models using mathematical support software. Human expertise is required to map expressions about physical quantities to the purely mathematical constructs of current commercial math tools (e.g., Matlab, Mathematica, Maple).

The EngMath ontology is intended to provide a formal language sufficient to express the models in engineering textbooks and to map them to mathematical software tools. We view the latter application as an instance of agent communication, which is the subject of the next section.

EngMath as a Vocabulary for Agent Communication

By providing a declarative, machine readable representation, the EngMath ontologies can enable unambiguous communication between software agents that would otherwise be difficult or impossible.

To illustrate a use of the ontology, consider a simple example of agents exchanging symbolic representations of spring behavior. Agent A is a specialist in the design of springs, and agent B is a specialist in quantity algebra. Agent A needs a solution to a set of equations relating spring and material properties that include the following:

$$k = \frac{d^4 G}{8 D^3 N}, \ G = 11{,}500\,kpsi$$

where k is the spring rate, d is wire diameter, D is spring diameter, N is number of turns, and G is the shear modulus of elasticity.

Agent A can send Agent B these equations as a set of KIF sentences, using the vocabulary of the EngMath ontology:

```
(scalar-quantity k)
(= (physical.dimension k)
   (/ force-dimension length-dimension))
```

---

various modes of being, but to offer a way of representing things in a shared conceptualization.

[2] For the purpose of specifying common conceptualizations, we see no justification for restricting the form of the definitions e.g. to necessary and sufficient conditions, or to require that they be conservative definitions (which make no claims about the world).

```
(scalar-quantity d)
(= (physical.dimension d) length-dimension)
(scalar-quantity Dm)
(= (physical.dimension Dm) length-dimension)
(scalar-quantity N)
(= (physical.dimension N) identity-dimension)
(scalar-quantity G)
(= (physical.dimension G)
   (* force-dimension
      (expt length-dimension -2)))
(= k (/ (* (expt d 4) G) (* 8 (expt Dm 3) N)))
(= G (* 11.5 (expt 10 6) psi))
```

After receiving the equations in this form, agent B can answer questions about the values of the terms such as the diameter (d). The vocabulary used in this interaction, such as the function constant `physical.dimension`, is independent of a domain theory for springs. The sentence simply states an algebraic relationship between quantities and the dimensional characteristics of those quantities. This type of information allows Agent B to perform algebraic manipulations such as solutions of simultaneous equations or numerical evaluations of individual parameters. Because dimensional information is included, the consistency of equations can be checked by the agent and agents are freed from committing to an explicit set of units.

The spring example is typical of problems in introductory engineering textbooks. More complex interactions are required to coordinate commercial design tools on industrial problems.

In the SHADE project [22,32], we have constructed a set of software agents that interact to support collaboration on industrial problems like satellite system design. One SHADE agent is a specialist in rigid body dynamics (RBD), and another is responsible for the geometric layout of satellite components (Layout). Both commit to the EngMath ontology. The RBD agent queries the Layout agent about the inertial characteristics of a particular component. These characteristics include the mass whose value is a scalar quantity and the inertia tensor whose value is a second order tensor. In reply, the Layout agent specifies the inertia tensor with respect to a global reference frame and point. The reference frame is part of the shared domain theory for the two agents; it is not implicit in the representation of the tensor. This allows the RBD agent to translate the inertia into a different reference frame convenient for dynamic analysis.

Most SHADE agents are commercial tools wrapped so that they conform to ontological commitments and communication protocols. These agents are designed to be conformant at the interface, but are not required to represent the ontologies internally. Some agents can assimilate an ontology and use it as input. The Unit Conversion Agent is an example. Its contract is specified entirely by the EngMath ontology. This agent takes KIF expressions over quantities, and performs services such as symbolic simplification, unit conversion, and dimensional consistency verification. It can *read* ontologies that specify of other unit systems, and determine whether the system is complete for the dimensions specified.

EngMath as a Conceptual Foundation

The EngMath ontology was also designed as a conceptual foundation for other ontologies; in its design we needed to anticipate how it would be used in other theories. For example, we are constructing a family of ontologies for representing components and relations among them (e.g., part-subpart relations, connections, association of component features and constraints). One ontology of mechanical components, for instance, is for models in which components have mass properties and associated reference frames and points, but lack complete geometric representations. This theory combines an abstract component ontology, a constraint expression ontology, parts of the EngMath ontology, and a simple geometry theory (that also includes EngMath).

The Compositional Modeling Language (CML) [12] is another example of building on the EngMath ontologies. CML is a modeling language that is intended to synthesize and redesign the various formulations of Compositional Modeling [8,13,14,29] to enable model sharing among research groups. Part of the language design of CML is an ontology about time, continuity, object properties, etc. The semantics of the language are specified axiomatically, using the vocabulary of the CML ontology. The CML ontology builds on the EngMath ontology as a foundation.

3. OVERVIEW OF THE CONCEPTUALIZATION

In this section, we describe the key concepts of the conceptualization specified by EngMath. The ideas will be familiar to many readers. However, since there are multiple ways to formulate the various concepts, it is important to clarify how their synthesis results in a coherent theory.

The entire ontology is too large and complex to present in static, linear form (about 2000 lines of definitions). The complete specification is available on-line on the World Wide Web in cross-indexed, machine-formatted hypertext [21]. To give a flavor for the details, we have included a few axioms from the actual ontologies in this section.

3.1 PHYSICAL QUANTITIES

A mathematical model of a physical system, of the sort we are interested here, consists of a set of constraints on the values of variables. These variables represent physical quantities. A **physical quantity** is a measure of some quantifiable aspect of the modeled world. Quantities "admit of degrees" [11] in contrast to qualities, which are all-or-none (e.g., being pregnant). Physical quantities come in several types, such as the mass of a body (a scalar quantity), the displacement of a point on the body (a vector quantity), the altitude of the particle as a function of time (a unary scalar function quantity), and the stress at a particular point in a deformed body (a second order tensor quantity). For our purposes, what makes quantities "quantifiable" is the ability to combine them with algebraic operations. Physical quantities can be meaningfully added, multiplied, and raised to real-valued exponents. The types of quantities determine the conditions under which operations are allowed and the types of the results. For example, it does not make sense to add a mass quantity and a displacement quantity, and the result of multiplying a length and a length is a third type of quantity—an area. This ontology specifies in detail the conditions under which various algebraic operations on quantities make sense.

Although we use the term "physical quantity" for this generalized notion of quantitative measure, the definition allows for nonphysical quantities such as amounts of money or rates of inflation. However, it excludes values associated with nominal scales, such as Boolean state and part number, because they are not amenable to these algebraic operations.

```
(defrelation PHYSICAL QUANTITY
  (=> (physical-quantity ?x)
      (and (defined (quantity.dimension ?x))
           (physical-dimension
                (quantity.dimension ?x))
           (or (constant-quantity ?x)
               (quantity-function ?x)))))
```

3.2 PHYSICAL DIMENSIONS

The central difference between a physical quantity and a purely numeric entity like a real number is that a quantity is characterized by a physical dimension. The **physical dimension** of a quantity distinguishes it from other types of quantities. The physical dimension of a mass of a body is mass; the physical dimension of a position of a body is length, and the physical dimension of a stress quantity is

```
(* mass (* (expt length -1) (expt time -2)))
```

where `*` is multiplication and `expt` is exponentiation. Nonphysical dimensions are also possible, such as amount of money. Dimensions tell us something intrinsic about the quantity that is invariant over models and measurement. For example, there is no intrinsic difference between a quantity used to describe an altitude and a quantity used to describe a width; both are quantities of the length dimension. A length of three feet and a length of one yard are equal, although we specified them in different units of measure.

Physical dimensions can be composed from other dimensions using multiplication and exponentiation to a real power. It is important for Dimensional Analysis [31] that dimensions have certain algebraic properties. The product of any two physical dimensions is also a physical dimension, and the multiplication operator `*` is associative, commutative, and invertible with an identity element called the identity dimension (i.e., it forms an abelian group with `*`).

```
(define-class PHYSICAL-DIMENSION
  (abelian-group physical-dimension
                 * identity-dimension))
```

Constant quantities whose physical dimension is the identity dimension are called, paradoxically, **dimensionless quantities**. In this ontology, dimensionless quantities include the real numbers and numeric tensors.

```
(defrelation DIMENSIONLESS-QUANTITY
  (<=> (dimensionless-quantity ?x)
       (and (constant-quantity ?x)
            (= (quantity.dimension ?x)
               identity-dimension)))
  (=> (real-number ?x)
      (dimensionless-quantity ?x)))
```

Dimensional homogeneity is a prerequisite to unit conversion and other algebraic operations on quantities. Consider the simplest type of physical quantities, scalar quantities. **Scalar quantities** are constant quantities with real-valued magnitudes, distinguished from higher-order tensors. (We will define the `magnitude` function precisely below.) A physical dimension defines a class of scalars with important algebraic properties. For example, the sum of any two scalars of the same dimension is a scalar of the same dimension. Physical dimensions also provide necessary conditions for *comparing* quantities; two quantities are comparable only if they are of the same physical dimension. It makes sense to quantitatively compare two masses but not a mass and a length.

3.3 COMPARABILITY AND ORDER

Comparability is one way to ground the otherwise algebraic definitions of quantities. Quantities are quantitative measures; a meaningful measure is one that reflects order in the measured (or we would say, modeled) world. Adapting the definition by Ellis [11], we say that the elements of a class Q of (scalar) quantities of the same physical dimension must be *comparable*. According to Ellis, comparability for a quantity type holds if there is as a *linear ordering relationship* in the world given by an equivalence relation $R_=$, and a binary relation $R_<$ that is asymmetric and transitive over Q, such that for any two quantities $q_1, q_2 \in Q$, exactly one of the following must hold: $q_1 R_= q_2$, $q_1 R_< q_2$, or $q_2 R_< q_1$. Using this definition, we can ask whether something we want to call a quantity type or physical dimension should be classified as such. Mass, for instance, is comparable by this definition because one can always order masses. The property of comparability is independent of measurement unit, measurement procedure, scales, or the types of physical objects that are being modeled.

Ellis defines a quantity [type] as exactly that which can be linearly ordered. We needed to depart on two fronts, to accommodate the sorts of quantities we find in engineering models. First, comparability is different for higher-order tensors (see Section 3.5); the tensor order and spatial dimensions of the quantities must be compatible to be able to compare them, and the ordering need not be total. Second, for scalars we insist that the order be dense: one can multiply any scalar quantities of a given physical dimension by a real number and obtain another scalar quantity of that physical dimension. This property also holds for mass, and illustrates that calling something a quantity is a modeling decision. That mass is densely ordered in this way is an assumption of continuum mechanics. It also was a consequence of including the reals as a species of physical quantity. Nonetheless, we depart from writers like Ellis primarily because our goals are slightly different. Our primary responsibility is to explicate a coherent framework that is adequate for expressing the content of engineering models.

The notion of physical dimension is intimately tied up with the notion of physical quantity, and both are primitive concepts ultimately grounded in the comparability of quantities in the world. Thus, from our definitions alone a computer program cannot infer that some entity is a physical quantity unless it defined in terms of other quantities. The practical consequence of including such primitives in a formal ontology is that the types of such entities must be declared.

3.4 FUNCTION QUANTITIES

A physical quantity is either a constant quantity or a function quantity. The mass in our example model is a constant quantity, like 50kg. A function quantity is a function from constant quantities to constant quantities. It is not a function from physical objects to quantities. The altitude of a particle over time is a function quantity, mapping quantities of time to quantities of length. Function quantities can take any finite number of arguments (although in engineering they usually take 1, 3, or 4). For example, the quantities in ordinary differential equation (ODE) models are unary functions mapping scalar quantities (e.g., of time) to scalar quantities. Partial differentials involve functions of several quantities, such as three length quantities and a time quantity. Like all physical quantities, each function quantity has a physical dimension—the dimension of all the elements of the range (a function that maps to quantities of differing ranges is not a function quantity).

3.5 TENSOR QUANTITIES

In the conceptualization, physical quantities include not only scalars but also higher order tensors such as vectors and dyads. Vectors (first order tensors) are distinct from scalars, in that complete specification of a vector constant requires a statement of direction or orientation. A velocity vector, for instance, can be decomposed into a 3-tuple of scalars for a particular choice of reference frame. Mechanical stress is represented by dyad (second order tensor) and instances of it can be mapped to a 3x3 matrix for a given reference frame. Tensors are a useful abstraction, because they possess properties that are invariant across reference frames. Though three dimensional reference frames (or vector spaces) and tensors of order two or less are most common in physical modelling, the concepts generalize to n dimensions and n-orders. Tensors, then, are characterized both in terms of order and spatial dimension, and these distinctions, in turn, imply a set of algebraic restrictions. The EngMath ontology integrates the algebraic properties of tensors with dimensional properties of all physical quantities.

3.6 UNITS OF MEASURE

The identity of quantities does not depend on the process or nature of measurement, or units of measure. A quantity of mass like 50kg is the same thing whether it is measured with a balance beam or a spring, and it is comparable in every way with other mass quantities independently of whether they are specified in kilograms or pounds. However, units are not irrelevant; for example, one cannot specify a constant in an equation without making reference to units of measure.

In our conceptualization, units of measure are quantities themselves (positive, scalar, constant quantities). A unit of measure is an absolute amount of something that can be used as a standard reference quantity. Like all quantities, units have dimensions, and units can be defined as any other scalar quantity. For example, the kilogram is a unit of measure for the mass dimension. The unit called "pound" can be defined as a mass quantity equal to the kilogram times some constant, just as the quantity 50kg is equal to the product of the unit called "kilogram" and the real number 50. What makes the pound special, compared with quantities like 50kg, is a matter of convention. (We will return to the issue of standard units in Section 3.8.) To provide for unit conversion over all physical dimensions, every product and real-valued exponentiation of a unit is also a unit of measure.

```
(defrelation UNIT-Of-MEASURE
  ;; units are scalar quantities
  (=> (unit-of-measure ?u)
      (scalar-quantity ?u))
  ;; units are positive
  (=> (unit-of-measure ?u)
      (forall ?u2
        (=> (and (unit-of-measure ?u2)
                 (= (quantity.dimension ?u)
                    (quantity.dimension ?u2)))
            (positive (magnitude ?u ?u2)))))
  ;; units can be combined using *
  (abelian-group unit-of-measure *
                 identity-unit)
  ;; units can be combined using expt
  (=> (and (unit-of-measure ?u)
           (real-number ?r))
      (unit-of-measure (expt ?u ?r)))
  ;; * is commutative for units and other Qs
  (=> (and (unit-of-measure ?u)
           (constant-quantity ?q))
      (= (* ?u ?q) (* ?q ?u))))
```

3.7 MAGNITUDES

The magnitude of a physical quantity is not a property of the quantity, but is given by a binary function that maps a quantity and unit of measure to a numeric value (a dimensionless quantity). Once it was decided that units were just scalar quantities, it became apparent that the magnitude function is simply a restricted form of scalar division (it is only defined when its first argument is a constant quantity and its second argument is a unit of the same dimension). It is also total for all constant quantities: a constant quantity can be expressed in any unit of the same physical dimension, and the magnitude of a quantity in one unit can be converted to its magnitude in any other comparable unit.

The requirement for dimensional consistency fits our intuition. The magnitude of 50kg in kilograms is 50, but the magnitude of 50kg in meters is undefined. For higher-order tensor quantities, the value of the magnitude function is an ordinary dimensionless tensor. Since units of measure are *scalar* quantities, one can think of the magnitude function as factoring out the physical dimension of a quantity (returning a dimensionless quantity) and producing a value normalized on a scale corresponding to the unit.

Although a unit of measure implicitly determines a measurement scale, units of measure are not the same thing as scales in this conceptualization. Measurement scales are a more general way to map quantities to numeric values, and are described in Section 4.7.

```
(deffunction MAGNITUDE
  (<=> (and (defined (magnitude ?q ?unit))
            (= (magnitude ?q ?unit) ?mag))
       (and (constant-quantity ?q)
            (unit-of-measure ?unit)
            (dimensionless-quantity ?mag)
            (= (quantity.dimension ?q)
               (quantity.dimension ?unit))
            (defined (* ?mag ?unit))
            (= (* ?mag ?unit) ?q))))
;; dimensionless magnitudes can be factored
(forall (?q ?unit ?mag)
  (=> (and (constant-quantity ?q)
           (unit-of-measure ?unit)
           (dimensionless-quantity ?mag)
           (defined (* ?mag ?q)))
      (= (magnitude (* ?mag ?q) ?unit)
         (* ?mag (magnitude ?q ?unit)))))
```

3.8 STANDARD SYSTEMS OF UNITS

Although we do not want to *fix* a set of standard units for the shared ontology, we want to provide the vocabulary with which to define sets of standard units so that agents can share them. For this, the concept of system of units is used. A **system of units** is a class of units defined by composition from a base set of units, such that every instance of the class is the "standard" unit for a physical dimension and every physical dimension has an associated unit.

This is an interesting representation problem, because both the set of units and the space of physical dimensions are conventions, and both are constrained (but not determined) by the background domain theory assumed in a model. The set of dimensions and their mutual relationships are determined by a physical theory, while the choice of units for each dimension is a measurement convention. The relationship between force, mass, length, and time is given by physics. The theory does not need to give fundamental status to any one physical dimension, but it does say that the force dimension is equal to (* (* length mass) (expt time -2)). One system of measurement may take mass, length, and time to be primitive and derive force; another could take force as primitive and derive mass. The same physical laws could be expressed in either system.

The concept of system of units is defined so that commitments to physical theories, sets of fundamental dimensions, and standard units are independent. To define a system of units, the model builder chooses a set of fundamental dimensions that are orthogonal (i.e., not composable from each other). According to this physical theory, mass and time are orthogonal, but force and mass are not. The set of fundamental dimensions determines the space of possible quantities that can be described in this system—those whose physical dimensions are some algebraic combination of the fundamental dimensions. For each of the fundamental dimensions, the model builder chooses a standard unit of that dimension; these are called the base-units of the system. Then every other standard unit in the system is a composition (using * and expt) of units from the base set. For example, the Systeme International (SI) is a system of units that defines a set of seven fundamental dimensions with the base-units meter, kilogram, second, ampere, Kelvin, mole, and candela.

```
(defrelation SYSTEM-OF-UNITS
  (<=> (system-of-units ?s)
       (and (class ?s)
            (subclass-of ?s unit-of-measure)
            ;; The base-units of the system are
            ;; those with fundamental dimens
            (defined (base-units ?s))
            (=> (member ?unit (base-units ?s))
                (instance-of ?unit ?s))
            (orthogonal dimension-set
              (setofall ?dim
                (exists ?unit
                  (and (member ?unit
                               (base-units ?s))
                       (= ?dim
    (quantity.dimension ?unit))
            ;; Every unit in the system is the
            ;; standard unit for its dimension.
            (=> (instance-of ?unit ?s)
                (= (standard-unit
                    ?s
                    (quantity.dimension
?unit))
                   ?unit)))))

(defrelation ORTHOGONAL-DIMENSION-SET
  (<=> (orthogonal-dimension-set ?s)
       (and (set ?s)
            (=> (member ?d ?s)
                (and
                 (physical-dimension ?d)
                 (not
                  (dimension-composable-from
                   ?d
                   (difference ?s
                               (setof ?d)))))))))

(defrelation DIMENSION-COMPOSABLE-FROM
  (<=> (dimension-composable-from ?d ?s)
       (or
        (member ?d ?s)
```

```
        (exists (?d1 ?d2)
         (and
           (dimension-composable-from ?d1 ?s)
           (dimension-composable-from ?d2 ?s)
           (= ?d (* ?d1 ?d2))))
        (exists (?d1 ?real)
         (and
           (dimension-composable-from ?d1 ?s)
           (real-number ?real)
           (= ?d (expt ?d1 ?real))))))
```

3.9 ALGEBRAIC PROPERTIES OF QUANTITIES

We can borrow the well-established theories of algebra for the reals, vectors, and higher-order tensors. To adapt them to physical quantities we must consider physical dimensions in describing the domain and range of operators. We have already seen how dimensional homogeneity is a prerequisite for adding quantities, and physical dimensions establish classes of quantities that are comparable. For each physical dimension, the class of constant scalar quantities of a physical dimension forms an abelian group with the addition operator + and a zero identity element for that dimension (zeros of each dimension are different). The class of all scalars of any dimension, after removing the zero scalars, forms an abelian group with respect to multiplication.

For vector quantities, the sum of the quantities is only defined where the sum of the dimensionless versions of the vectors would be defined (i.e., the spatial dimensions must align). For higher-order tensors, tensor order and spatial dimensions, as well as the physical dimension, must be homogeneous. Analogous restrictions apply for the multiplication of tensors.

For function quantities, the sum or product of two function quantities is another function quantity that is only defined where the domains of the functions are equal. For unary scalar function quantities, the addition and multiplication operators are defined to handle a mix of function quantities and constant quantities. The sum of a constant k and a time-dependent function f, for example, is a function defined everywhere $f(t)$ is defined and is equal to $f(t)+k$. Continuous time-dependent quantities can also be defined from others using a time-derivative function.

Most of the axiomatization in the specialized theories for functions, vectors, and tensors is concerned with specifying the conditions under which algebraic operators apply. This is essential for building agents with guarantees of completeness for some class of quantities.

4. RATIONALE FOR IMPORTANT DISTINCTIONS

There are many possible ways to axiomatize this domain, and the axiomatization makes explicit many things that are implicit in the engineering literature. In this section, we discuss important distinctions that the formalization process forces one to clarify. For each distinction we offer a rationale for the choices made in terms of the purpose of the ontology.

4.1 QUANTITY TYPES VERSUS INSTANCES

Some authors define "a quantity" as a set of values or a property having some order [11]. However, they offer no name for instances of this set, or for the values of this property. Following the AI convention of defining concepts as classes (or equivalently, sets, types, monadic predicates), we define the class physical quantity, and define species of quantities as subclasses of physical quantity. Where some would talk of the unitary concept "the mass quantity," we would say that there is a quantity type whose elements are constant scalars of dimension mass. This allows us to support the common usage in engineering modeling, where specific values such as the length of a beam are called quantities. It also allows us to modularly state properties of quantities, function quantities, scalar quantities, scalar-mass quantities, etc., and have the general properties inherit to the specializations.

4.2 QUANTITIES ARE NOT VARIABLES

Physical quantities and physical dimensions are objects in the universe of discourse, and are not linguistic elements (e.g., "variables" of constraint expressions). Constraints over quantities that are found in engineering models are typically algebraic equations or inequalities, sometimes including the operations of differential calculus. Quantities are very different from linguistic elements. We have built ontologies (for the specification of a configuration design task for elevators—the VT experiment) in which constraint expressions and their constituents (variables and arithmetic operators) are part of the domain of discourse. In that formalization of constraints, constraint expressions are logical sentences with nonlogical constants (not logical variables) denoting physical quantities. The ontological distinction between variables and quantities allowed us to write an ontology in which both the form and denotation of constraint expressions were specified. This is necessary when the committing parties need restrictions on the form of expressions to guarantee completeness.

4.3 QUANTITIES ARE NOT PROPERTIES OF OBJECTS

The identity of quantities is independent of physical objects that might be modeled. For example, let us say that the mass of a body B is the quantity 50kg. 50kg is just a measure of mass; there is nothing intrinsic about 50kg that says it is the mass of B (there is no total function from masses to bodies). Making quantities independent of objects also allows one to state that the mass of B is *equal* to the mass of a different body. It also supports pure parametric models, in which there are no physical objects and only quantities are described.

Of course, the model builder is free to define a function from physical objects to quantities, but this function is not the same thing as a mass quantity. Our formulation of quantities does not preclude such object-to-quantity functions; it provides the language in which to describe the range of those functions. In CML [12], for example, there are functions from objects (e.g. pipes) to time-dependent function quantities. This distinction is central to the semantics of CML, which allows both time-varying and static relations. The object-to quantity functions are time-independent (e.g., the pipe always has a flow rate), but the quantities are functions of time (e.g., the flow rate is a function quantity that has different values throughout a scenario and can be undefined on some values of time).

4.4 QUANTITIES ARE NOT TUPLES

In our ontology, quantities exist as values that are related to, but independent of units and numbers. Quantities can be compared, multiplied, etc., without ever converting to reals or considering units of measure. This independence allows the model builder the flexibility needed to build measurement systems and physical theory independently. Furthermore, although quantities have algebraic properties, they are not purely abstract entities; we have grounded them in the modeled world with the condition of comparability. In contrast, an alternative formulation one often sees is to treat quantities as tuples of numbers and units [2,36], or as simply numbers. Besides the assumption about units that such a formulation makes, we find that it contradicts the conceptualization of quantities in the world made by physicists and philosophers. To reuse a simple example: 3 feet and 1 yard are equal, yet the tuples <3,ft> and <1,yd> are not.

4.5 THERE ARE NO FUNDAMENTAL QUANTITIES

The identity of a physical quantity is also independent of any fundamental quantities. We make no ontological distinction between base and derived quantities. For any pair of comparable physical quantities, their sum and product (if defined) are also physical quantities (the sum will be comparable with the original two; the product may not). This is also independent of scales, which are discussed below.

The rationale for this decision is again to provide generality and flexibility. We know from physics that there is no physical basis for giving some quantities primacy. Measurement theories make a distinction between quantities amenable to fundamental and associative measurement [6]. Again, we have made this distinction irrelevant for engineering models by avoiding the temptation to define quantities in terms of measurement. The analogous argument holds for not giving special status to some units of measure or physical dimensions. Even though it is possible to *compose* units and dimensions, there is no need to stipulate in the shared theory exactly which units and dimensions are fundamental.

4.6 NONPHYSICAL VS. DIMENSIONLESS QUANTITIES

The conceptualization leaves it to the model builder to define the fundamental dimensions for a domain. The definition of physical dimension does not preclude one from defining new dimensions not mentioned in physics texts. We cited the example of amount of money as a possible physical dimension. The ontology also allows for dimensionless quantities, such as real numbers, whose physical dimension is the identity dimension. How does one decide whether to define a new physical dimension for a nonphysical quantity or to make it a dimensionless quantity?

We say that a physical dimension distinguishes a type or class of quantities that can be meaningfully combined with algebraic operations, can undergo unit conversion, and are comparable. Amount of money is a meaningful dimension because one can accumulate sums of money, do currency conversion, and compare relative wealth. Amount of money can be meaningfully combined with other dimensions. A rate of inflation, for example, is computed by dividing an amount of money (a change in price) by a different amount of money (the base price) and dividing the result by a unit of time (a year). The rate is a quantity of dimension (expt time -1). Money is something to be tagged as different in type from other quantities; that's why we see dollar signs (or other units) carried with the numbers in formulae.

As a negative example, consider quantities like number of politicians and number of constituents. We might write a formulae

(= $N_{constituents}$ (* $N_{politicians}$ 1000000)).

In this model, we are making an abstraction; these quantities of humans are being compared as numbers. The = sign implies that the quantities must be of the same physical dimension, which would be, in this case, the identity dimension. Suppose, however, that we wanted to describe the number of molecules in those politicians. There is an international unit for number of molecules, the Mole.[3] In the modern SI system of units, this is not a dimensionless quantity, but a quantity of the dimension amount of substance. Why does amount of substance get special status over number of politicians? Because chemical models need to distinguish amount of substance quantities from other measures. There is something homogeneous about molecules in that it makes sense to measure stuff by counting them. The formula for the average amount of gas in those politicians would use an amount of substance quantity for the amount of gas, and a dimensionless quantity for the number of politicians. This makes sense in the chemist's abstraction of politicians: that they can be viewed as volumes of gas.

4.7 MEASUREMENT SCALES

A measurement scale is a determinative, non-degenerative assignment of numeric values to physical quantities [11]. *Determinative* means that the same quantities are consistently assigned the same numeric values, and *non-degenerative* means that different quantities get different values (ignoring issues of precision). Examples of measurement scales include Mohs scale for the hardness

---

[3]It's actually number of particles, but if you understand that distinction you understand our point here.

of minerals and the Celsius and Kelvin scales for thermodynamic temperature. Using the Coombs [7] classification, the Mohs scale is *ordinal* because it only provides information for inequality comparisons among points on the scale. The Celsius scale is classified as *ordinal-interval* because it supports inequalities between intervals on the scale, and Kelvin is a *ratio* scale because it supports comparisons of the ratio of any two values on the scale. For instance, it makes sense to say that 6 degrees Kelvin is twice as much as 3 degrees Kelvin.

By this mathematical definition, the units of measure in our conceptualization correspond to ratio scales.[4] Each value on the scale is the ratio of the measured quantity to the degree-Kelvin unit. Thus the Kelvin scale can be defined from the degree-Kelvin using the magnitude function:

```
(lambda (?q) (magnitude ?q degree-Kelvin)
```

We don't call Mohs ratings or degrees-Celsius units of measure, because they aren't quantities against which to compare other quantities. Of course one can write a function that does measure any temperature on the Celsius scale, such as

```
(lambda (?q)
   (- (magnitude ?q degree-Kelvin) 273.15))
```

Since there is no principled constraint on the form of such function, we leave it to the model builder to define scales appropriate to a domain.

5. DESIGN AND EVALUATION ISSUES

We view ontologies as designed artifacts, formulated for specific purposes and evaluated against design criteria. In a separate paper [19], we propose a set of ontology evaluation criteria and show examples of their application to this and other domains.

Two of the criteria will be illustrated here: to minimize *ontological commitment* while allowing for *monotonic extendibility*. Minimizing ontological commitment means making as few claims as possible about the world being modeled, allowing the parties committed to the ontology freedom to specialize and instantiate the ontology as needed. Extendibility means an ontology should be crafted so that one can extend and specialize the ontology *monotonically*. In other words, one should be able to define new terms for special uses based on the existing vocabulary, in a way that does not require the revision of the existing definitions. Both of these criteria hold a natural tension with the goal of supporting the knowledge sharing needs of a range of agents with differing abilities and assumptions. Adding vocabulary to handle a broad range of representation needs will increase ontological commitment by adding more constraints on the interpretation, and will make it more likely that some definitions will be incompatible with future representation needs.

---

[4]Ellis (1969) gives no special status to units, saying that they are merely the names for the associated scales. We wanted to allow for agents to commit to unit conversion without committing to a theory of measurement scales.

In this section, we will discuss two techniques in the design of the EngMath ontology that help us meet these two criteria. One is the decomposition of a large ontology into modules. The second is another familiar design technique—parameterization—applied to the problem of representing conventions.

5.1 DECOMPOSING THE ONTOLOGY

The first technique is to decompose a monolithic ontology into a set of loosely coupled sub-ontologies. The EngMath ontology is decomposed into an inclusion lattice of individual ontologies, where each ontology is a set of definitions, and ontology inclusion is set inclusion. If a ontology B *includes* ontology A, then ontology B is the union of the definitions in A with those specific to B. More sophisticated methods for partitioning knowledge bases into modular theories are being explored [25], but set inclusion is sufficient for mutually consistent ontologies in a uniform namespace.

Figure 1 shows the inclusion lattice of theories for the EngMath family. The core ontology of physical quantities includes abstract algebra (evolved from the example in the KIF 3.0 specification [16]) and a theory of objects and relations called the Frame Ontology [20]. The EngMath family includes ontologies for Scalar Quantities, Vector Quantities, and Unary Scalar Functions. The Standard Units ontology defines many of the most common physical dimensions and units, and includes the SI system. Other engineering ontologies that build on the EngMath family—for describing component structure, design tasks, discrete events, and specific analysis domains such as kinematics—are being developed.

Decomposing into loosely coupled ontologies helps minimize ontological commitment by allowing one to commit to a coherent subset of the axioms of the entire ontology. For example, one can commit to scalars but not vectors; unary functions (for ODE models) but not n-ary functions (for PDE models); and static models (no functions). Even an agent that does not include physical

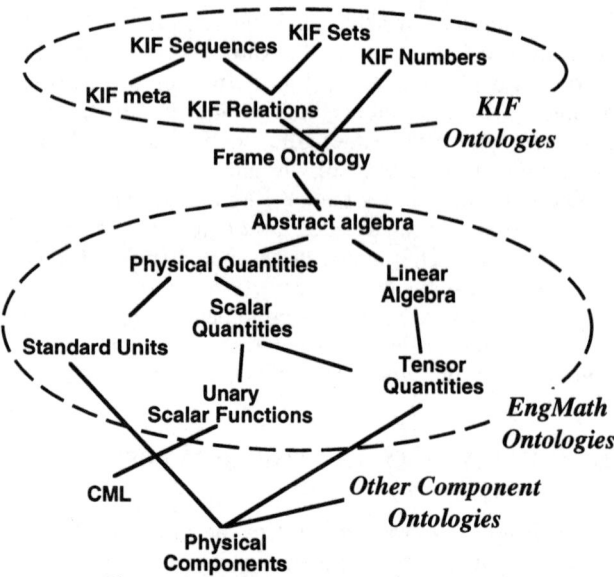

Figure 1: Inclusion lattice of ontologies

dimensions in its conceptualization can be accommodated, since all the real number operations are also defined for quantities, and the reals are quantities.

Decomposition also supports the specialization of monotonically extendible ontologies. For example, the CML ontology inherits the basic commitments of the Unary Scalar Functions ontology and adds notions specific to its needs. Since the definitions in Unary Scalar Functions anticipate the general class of time-dependent functions, the CML extensions were possible without redefining the originals.

Designing a family of coherent ontologies is more difficult than designing a monolithic one, since the designer must anticipate intermodule interactions, such as axioms in several ontologies constraining the same vocabulary. To help manage the extension of vocabulary across ontologies, we borrow a technique from software engineering: *polymorphism*.

Polymorphism allows the same function constant to be defined in several places, where each definition adds axioms about the use of the constant. The +, *, and `expt` functions, for example, are polymorphically extended to each type of quantity and to physical dimensions. The form of a polymorphic definition of a function F is

```
(=> (and (p ?x) (q ?x))
    (=> (= (F ?x ?y) ?z) (r ?x ?y ?z)))
```

where `?x` and `?y` are the arguments of F, `p` and `q` are the domains over which this definition applies (e.g., quantity types), and `r` is the condition that holds for F's arguments and it's value, `?z`.

Due to theory inclusion, the definition of a function is the union of axioms contributed by each theory. For example, the definition of + for the Vector Quantities ontology is the union of the axioms for + for vector quantities, + for scalar quantities, + for physical quantities in general, and + for the reals.

5.2 PARAMETERIZING CONVENTIONS

A second technique to facilitate extendibility and to minimize commitment is the parameterization of conventions. A parameter of a black box system is a representation of assumptions about how the environment interacting with the system will vary. In a computer program, the environment interacts with the program through formal arguments that are bound on invocation (and through the human interface, which is not as neatly parameterized). In the domain of the EngMath ontologies, the environment is the instantiation of the shared vocabulary for particular domain models. We have described several ways in which the domain models vary *by convention*. The choice of fundamental physical dimensions and standard units for a system, and the choice of particular units for individual quantities are conventions.

To minimize ontological commitment, we formulate these choices as parameters of the engineering model, rather than global constants of the shared ontology. To support extendibility, we provide an expressive representational vocabulary for specifying values of parameters. For example, to allow the model builder to specify the choices of fundamental dimensions and standard units, we provide the machinery to define systems of units.

It is in this sense that ontologies are a "coupling mechanism" [18] for knowledge bases and knowledge based agents. Parameters such as the system of units for a domain model are like abstract data types in software, except that the latter are ground and parameters of a domain model can be *theories*. We mentioned that the Unit Conversion agent can take, as inputs, ontologies specifying systems of units. When the other SHADE tools exchange sets of equations they are also exchanging theories. When agents pass around theories, the constraints on what they can pass around is specified in a shared ontology. In this sense, ontologies play a similar role as database schemata, except that ontologies may require a more expressive language for constraints than is typical in database specifications.

6. RELATED WORK
6.1 PHILOSOPHY

The mathematics underlying the EngMath ontologies is drawn from standard textbooks used to teach engineering math [26,31,37], and from the philosophy literature on measurement [6,11]. We had to choose distinctions from the conceptualizations, and modify them to produce the modular, internally coherent ontologies in the EngMath family. The engineering texts assume a conceptualization motivated by abstract algebraic operations, and the philosophy texts explore the grounding of the abstractions.

The aim of the philosophy texts is to describe The World as it Is in its Entirety, and to relate the results to prior writings. For the philosopher, it is important to relate the nature of quantities to the process of measurement and observation, and more generally, to the question of scientific knowledge. For instance, even the very notion that quantities such as mass can be meaningfully expressed as linear ratios of a standard turns out to be a convention, albeit a very useful and familiar one. Ellis [11] argues that the notion of a unit is incomplete without a choice of how such units are combined (which is related to, but not the same as, measurement procedure). We are assuming that there is a shared interpretation to the result of multiplying the meter times the real number 1000.

For our purposes—the sharing and communication of engineering models in machine and human readable forms—it is an *advantage* to be able to isolate the meaning of quantities from the process of measurement. We make no apologies: this is not a sweeping-under-the-rug of relevant issues, but a strategic decoupling of issues. In building ontologies we are writing social contracts. We are free to invent the conceptualization as long as its meaning can be effectively communicated (which is why we use standard terminology and logic). By accepting the KIF language as a foundation, for example, we already commit to including abstract things like sets and relations in the universe of discourse. We add to that an ontology of abstract algebra, and extend it to physical quantities. The philosophical ontologist draws a heavy line when the objects cross from timeless mathematical entities to physical concepts like mass and length. Our agents need no strong boundary; if our engineering model states that a quantity of mass exists and is related to a length quantity by some algebraic expression, it is so for the agent. According to our evaluation criteria [19], clarity and coherence in the specification are paramount, and faithfulness with The World is not an issue.

Nonetheless, we can "share and reuse" the analysis found in philosophy writing, for very pragmatic ends. For example, one of the differences between a casual writing on quantities and a careful one is the treatment of property association. One often sees it stated that quantities are "properties" of "objects" — like qualities but quantitative. However, the careful writer will point out that quantities as we use them are *relational*—they are about comparing objects in some respect, or about relationships among them (e.g., distance between reference points). This informs our design. Departing from the conventional "object oriented" approach, we give independent status to quantities and leave it as a modeling decision to map from objects to quantities. This is, in essence, a decoupling of theories about quantities from theories about model formulation.

Similarly, an understanding of the nature of physical theory and measurement guides us away from the impulse to oversimplify for the sake of computational elegance. For example, it would be simpler from a computational point of view to fix a single basis set of "fundamental" physical dimensions or units of measure, and recursively derive the rest. However, the laws of physics tell us that there are no inherently privileged physical dimensions, and the study of measurement tells us that the choice of basis sets for dimensions and units is a convention. The fact that engineers must deal with at least two systems of units, each of which chooses a different basis set (and which has changed over historical time), motivates us to provide the model builder with the representational machinery to define a system of units as part of the domain model.

Work in Formal Ontology in the philosophy literature that is relevant to knowledge sharing ontologies are found in [4,5], and (combined with papers from AI) in [24].

6.2 OTHER WORK ON ONTOLOGIES

There is a growing body of ontologies appearing in the literature seen by the knowledge representation community, including as a sample [3,10,28,30,39].

The most closely related on engineering ontology is the thesis by Alberts [2]. Alberts describes a formal ontology intended as the basis for building interoperable and reusable knowledge systems for design. His ontology provides a vocabulary for modeling the structure and behavior of systems, based on systems theory [38] and finite element modeling. While the formalization of systems is exemplary, the treatment of quantities in that ontology is simplistic. First, quantities have no status other than as the values of variables with symbolic 'quantity types.' There is no provision for defining new dimensions or describing complex dimensions; the quantity types appear to be those that are anticipated by systems theory (analogs of effort and flow). Second, the values are always unary scalar functions of time, where time is "exceptional" (i.e., outside the range of the model). This prevents vector and tensor models, PDE models, phase-space models where time is not the independent variable, etc. Third, the values of these functions are tuples of numbers and fixed units.

More recent work by Akkermans and Top [1] develops the systems theory methodology to maturity. It proposes engineering ontologies at four levels of description: functional components, physical processes, mathematical relations, and model data. Work on model formulation using the CML language [12] and SHADE engineering agents [32] aims at a suite of ontologies not based on system theory that have similar coverage. Perhaps the ontology presented in this paper can provide a foundation for the mathematical and data level of models in these comprehensive engineering ontologies.

Acknowledgments

The work is supported by ARPA prime contract DAAA15-91-C-0104 through Lockheed subcontract SQ70A3030R, and NASA Grants NCC 2-537 and NAG 2-581 (under ARPA Order 6822). Ideas on knowledge sharing have been shaped by rewarding conversations with Richard Fikes, Mike Genesereth, Pat Hayes, Doug Lenat, Bob Neches, and Marty Tenenbaum. We thank the anonymous KR'94 reviewers, Adam Farquhar, Pat Hayes, and Dan Russell for thoughtful reviews.

References

[1] H. Akkermans & J. Top. Tasks and ontologies in engineering modeling. *Proceedings of the 8th Knowledge Acquisition for Knowledge Based Systems Workshop*, Banff, Canada, 1994.

[2] L. K. Alberts. *YMIR: an ontology for engineering design.* Doctoral dissertation, University of Twente, 1993.

[3] J. A. Bateman, R. T. Kasper, J. D. Moore, & R. A. Whitney. A General Organization of Knowledge for Natural Language Processing: The Penman Upper Model. USC/Information Sciences Institute, Marina del Rey, CA, Technical report 1990.

[4] M. Bunge. *Treatise on Basic Philosophy, Volumes 3-4: Ontology.* D. Reidel Publishing Company, Dordrecht, Holland, 1979.

[5] H. Burkhardt & B. Smith (Eds.). *Handbook of Metaphysics and Ontology.* Philosophia Verlag, Munich, 1991.

[6] N. R. Campbell. *An Account of the Principles of Measurement and Calculations*. Longmans, Green, London, 1928.

[7] C. H. Coombs. The theory and methods of social measurement. In L. Festinger & D. Katz, Ed., *Research*

Methods in the Behavioral Sciences, Dryden Press, New York, 1952.

[8] J. Crawford, A. Farquhar, & B. Kuipers. QPC: A Compiler from Physical Models into Qualitative Differential Equations. *Proceedings of the Eighth National Conference on Artificial Intelligence,* Boston, pages 365-371. AAAI Press/The MIT Press, 1990.

[9] M. Cutkosky, R. S. Engelmore, R. E. Fikes, T. R. Gruber, M. R. Genesereth, W. S. Mark, J. M. Tenenbaum, & J. C. Weber. PACT: An experiment in integrating concurrent engineering systems. *IEEE Computer,* **26**(1):28-37, 1993.

[10] E. Davis. *Representations of Commonsense Knowledge.* Morgan Kaufmann, San Mateo, 1990.

[11] B. Ellis. *Basic Concepts of Measurement.* Cambridge University Press, London, 1966.

[12] B. Falkenhainer, A. Farquhar, D. Bobrow, R. Fikes, K. Forbus, T. Gruber, Y. Iwasaki, & B. Kuipers. CML: A compositional modeling language. Stanford Knowledge Systems Laboratory, Technical Report KSL-94-16, January 1994.

[13] B. Falkenhainer & K. D. Forbus. Compositional modeling: Finding the right model for the job. *Artificial Intelligence,* **51**:95-143, 1991.

[14] K. D. Forbus. Qualitative Process Theory. *Artificial Intelligence,* **24**:85-168, 1984.

[15] M. R. Genesereth. An Agent-Based Framework for Software Interoperability. *Proceedings of the DARPA Software Technology Conference,* Meridian Corporation, Arlington VA, pages 359-366. 1992.

[16] M. R. Genesereth & R. E. Fikes. Knowledge Interchange Format, Version 3.0 Reference Manual. Computer Science Department, Stanford University, Technical Report Logic-92-1, March 1992.

[17] M. R. Genesereth & N. J. Nilsson. *Logical Foundations of Artificial Intelligence.* Morgan Kaufmann Publishers, San Mateo, CA, 1987.

[18] T. R. Gruber. The Role of Common Ontology in Achieving Sharable, Reusable Knowledge Bases. In James A. Allen, Richard Fikes, & Erik Sandewall, Ed., *Principles of Knowledge Representation and Reasoning: Proceedings of the Second International Conference,* Cambridge, MA, pages 601-602. Morgan Kaufmann, 1991.

[19] T. R. Gruber. Toward principles for the design of ontologies used for knowledge sharing. In Nicola Guarino, Ed., *International Workshop on Formal Ontology,* Padova, Italy, 1992. Revised August 1993, to appear in *Formal Ontology in Conceptual Analysis and Knnowledge Representation,* Guarino & Poli (Eds), Kluwer, in preparation.

[20] T. R. Gruber. A Translation Approach to Portable Ontology Specifications. *Knowledge Acquisition,* **5**(2):199-220, 1993.

[21] T. R. Gruber & G. R. Olsen. *The Engineering Math Ontologies.* World Wide Web, URL "http://www-ksl.stanford.edu/knowledge-sharing/README.html", 1994.

[22] T. R. Gruber, J. M. Tenenbaum, & J. C. Weber. Toward a knowledge medium for collaborative product development. In John S. Gero, Ed., *Artificial Intelligence in Design '92,* pages 413-432. Kluwer Academic Publishers, Boston, 1992.

[23] N. Guarino. An ontology of meta-level categories. *KR'94.*

[24] N. Guarino & R. Poli (Eds.). *Formal Ontology in Conceptual Analysis and Knowledge Representation.* Kluwer, in preparation.

[25] R. V. Guha. *Contexts: A formalization and some applications.* doctoral dissertation, Stanford University, 1991.

[26] D. Halliday & R. Resnick. *Physics.* John Wiley and Sons, New York, 1978.

[27] G. Hirst. Ontological assumptions in knowledge representation. KR'89, 1989.

[28] J. R. Hobbs & R. C. Moore (Eds.). *Formal Theories of the Common Sense World.* Ablex, Norwood, NJ, 1985.

[29] Y. Iwasaki & C. M. Low. Model Generation and Simulation of Device Behavior with Continuous and Discrete Changes. *Intelligent Systems Engineering,* **1**(2)1993.

[30] D. B. Lenat & R. V. Guha. *Building Large Knowledge-based Systems: Representation and Inference in the Cyc Project.* Addison-Wesley, Menlo Park, CA, 1990.

[31] B. S. Massey. *Measures in Science and Engineering: Their Expression, Relation, and Interpretation.* Ellis Horwood Limited, 1986.

[32] J. G. McGuire, D. R. Kuokka, J. C. Weber, J. M. Tenenbaum, T. R. Gruber, & G. R. Olsen. SHADE: Technology for knowledge-based collaborative engineering. *Journal of Concurrent Engineering: Applications and Research (CERA),* **1**(2)1993.

[33] R. Neches, R. E. Fikes, T. Finin, T. R. Gruber, R. Patil, T. Senator, & W. R. Swartout. Enabling technology for knowledge sharing. *AI Magazine,* **12**(3):16-36, 1991.

[34] A. Newell. The knowledge level. *Artificial Intelligence,* **18**(1):87-127, 1982.

[35] R. S. Patil, R. E. Fikes, P. F. Patel-Schneider, D. McKay, T. Finin, T. R. Gruber, & R. Neches. The DARPA Knowledge Sharing Effort: Progress report. *Principles of Knowledge Representation and Reasoning: Proceedings of the Third International Conference,* Cambridge, MA, Morgan Kaufmann, 1992.

[36] D. A. Randall & A. G. Cohn. Modelling topological and metrical propoerties in physical processes. *KR'89,* Morgan Kaufmann, 1989.

[37] W. C. Reynolds & H. C. Perkins. *Engineering Thermodynamics.* McGraw-Hill, 1977.

[38] R. C. Rosenberg & D. C. Karnopp. *Introduction to physical system dynamics.* McGraw-Hill, New York, 1983.

[39] Y. Shoham. Temporal logics in AI: Semantical and ontological considerations. *Artificial Intelligence,* **33**:89-104, 1987.

An Ontology of Meta-Level Categories

Nicola Guarino

LADSEB-CNR,
National Research Council,
Corso Stati Uniti, 4
I-35129 PADOVA [Italy]

Massimiliano Carrara

LADSEB-CNR
National Research Council,
Corso Stati Uniti, 4
I-35129 PADOVA [Italy]

Pierdaniele Giaretta

Institute of History of
Philosophy,
University of Padova,
P.zza Capitaniato, 3
I-35100 PADOVA [Italy]

Abstract

We focus in this paper on some meta-level ontological distinctions among unary predicates, like those between concepts and assertional properties. Three are the main contributions of this work, mostly based on a revisitation of philosophical (and linguistic) literature in the perspective of knowledge representation. The first is a formal notion of ontological commitment, based on a modal logic endowed with mereological and topological primitives. The second is a formal account of Strawson's distinction between *sortal* and *non-sortal* predicates. Assertional properties like *red* belong to the latter category, while the former category is further refined by distinguishing *substantial* predicates (corresponding to *types* like *person*) from *non-substantial* predicates (corresponding to *roles* like *student*). The third technical contribution is definition of countability which exploits the topological notion of connection to capture the intended semantics of unary predicates.

1 INTRODUCTION

Most KR formalisms differ from pure first-order logic in their *structuring power*, i.e. their ability to make evident the "structure" of a domain. For example, the advantage of frame-based languages over pure first-order logic is that some logical relations, such as those corresponding to classes and slots, have a peculiar, *structuring* meaning. This meaning is the result of a number of ontological commitments, which accumulate in layers from the very beginning of a knowledge base development process [11]. For a particular knowledge base, such ontological commitments are however implicit and strongly dependent on the particular task being considered, since the formalism itself is in general deliberately *neutral* as concerns ontological choices: in their well-known textbook on AI, Genesereth and Nilsson ([13], p. 13) explicitly state the "essential ontological promiscuity of AI". We have argued elsewhere *against* this neutrality [18,20,21], claiming that a rigorous ontological foundation for knowledge representation can result in better methodologies for conceptual design of data and knowledge bases, facilitating knowledge sharing and reuse. We have shown how theories defined at the (so-called) epistemological level, based on structured representation languages like KL-ONE or order-sorted logics, cannot be distinguished from their "flat" first-order logic equivalents unless we make clear their implicit ontological assumptions. Referring to the classification proposed in [5], we have introduced therefore the notion of *ontological level*, intermediate between the epistemological and the conceptual levels [19]. At the ontological level, formal distinctions are made among logical predicates, distinguishing between (meta-level) categories such as *concepts, roles,* and *assertional properties.*

Such distinctions have three main purposes. First, they allow the knowledge engineer to make clear the *intended meaning* of a particular logical axiomatization, which is of course much more restricted than the set of all its Tarskian models. This is especially important since we are constantly using natural language words within our formulas, relying on them to make our statements readable and to convey meanings not explicitly stated. However, since words are ambiguous in natural language, it may be important to "tag" these words with a semantic category, in association with a suitable axiomatisation, in order to guarantee a consistent interpretation[1]. This is unavoidable, in our opinion, if we want to share theories across different domains [23,16]. A second important advantage of clear ontological distinctions is the possibility of a *method-*

---

[1] Notice that we do not mean that the user is forced to accept some one fixed interpretation of a given word: simply, we want to offer some instruments to help specifying the intended interpretation.

ological foundation for deciding between the various representation choices offered by a KR formalism: for example, within a hybrid terminological framework, for deciding whether a predicate should go in the TBox or ABox, or how a KL-ONE role should be related to a correponding concept. Finally, these distinctions may impact the *reasoning services* offered by a KR formalism: for example, a terminological reasoner can forbid certain kinds of update on the basis of ontological considerations; it may take advantage of the fact that some kinds of concepts form a tree, while in general they do not [31]; it may maintain indices for instances of concepts but not for instances of properties; it may provide domain-checking facilities for properties but not for concepts[1].

We focus in this paper on some fundamental ontological distinctions among unary predicates, refining and extending some previous work [19]. Most of our results come from a revisitation, from the point of view of KR, of philosophical (and linguistic) work largely extraneous to the KR tradition. The main distinction we focus on is that between *sortal* and *non-sortal* predicates, originally introduced by Locke and discussed in more detail e.g. by Strawson [32] and Wiggins [34]. According to Strawson, a sortal predicate (like *apple*) "supplies a principle for distinguishing and counting individual particulars which it collects", while a non-sortal predicate (like *red*) "supplies such a principle only for particulars already distinguished, or distinguishable, in accordance with some antecedent principle or method" [32]. This distinction is (roughly) reflected in natural language by the fact that the former terms are common nouns, while the latter are adjectives and verbs. The issue is also related to the semantic difference between count and non-count (or mass) terms. Philosophers have characterised count terms as denoting integral wholes, whereas entities denoted by mass terms are cumulative and divisive. This criterion has been a matter of lively debate [25], since such semantic-pragmatic distinctions not always correspond to the syntactical "count/mass" distinction, according to which, while mass-terms admit quantifiers like *much*, or *a little* and the indefinite article *some*, count-terms use the quantifiers *each, every, some, few...* and the indefinite article *a*.

Distinctions among unary predicates are also present in the KR literature, where sortal predicates are usually called "concepts", while characterising predicates are called "properties", or sometimes "qualities". The necessity of a distinction between the two kinds of predicates has always been acknowledged by advocates of the logicist approach in KR, as emerges clearly from the following quotation from David Israel [22]:

"There is to be one tree for kinds of things and another for qualities of things. Kinds must be distinguished from qualities: being a cat must be distinguished (in kind, no doubt) from being red"

Within current KR formalisms, however, the difference between the two kinds of predicates is only based on heuristic considerations, and nothing in the semantics of a concept forbids it from being treated like any other unary predicate. Our task here is to formalize such a difference: our job is simpler than that of a linguist, since we do not try to classify a linguistic item as belonging to a particular category, but simply to make explicit its intended meaning when it is used as a predicate symbol with a specific representation purpose.

After giving a simple example showing the necessity of the above distinction, we introduce in section 3 a formal notion of *ontological commitment,* based on a modal logic endowed with mereological and topological primitives. In the philosophical literature, such a term was first used by Quine [27]. According to him, a logical theory is ontologically commited to the entities which it quantifies over. Quine expressed his criterion for ontological commitment with the slogan: "to be is to be the value of a variable". Such criterion was further refined by Church [6] and Alston [1], and finally modified by Searle in order to defend his argument that the ontological commitment of a theory simply coincides with what it asserts. We reject such a position, holding that different theories can share the same ontological commitment. In the AI community, this claim is at the basis of current projects for knowledge sharing and reuse [23]. In the knowledge acquisition literature, the notion of ontological commitment has been introduced by Gruber [16,17] as an agreement to use a shared vocabulary. We focus in this paper on the formal semantic interpretation of such a vocabulary: specifying the ontological commitment of a logical language means offering a way to specify the intended meaning of its vocabulary by constraining the set of its models, giving explicit information about the intended *nature* of the domain elements and relations and their *a priori* relationships. In order to capture such *a priori* knowledge we believe it is necessary to use a modal semantics, in contrast with Quine's view.

The notion of ontological commitment is exploited in section 4 to introduce some meta-level properties of unary predicates such as *countability, temporal stability* and *rigidity*. These properties allow us to establish an ontology meta-level categories of predicates, where the basic sortal/non-sortal distinction is further explored and refined. The impact of these distinctions on the current practice of knowledge engineering is discussed in section 5.

---

[1] The last two examples are due to Bob MacGregor.

2 REDS AND APPLES

Suppose we want to state that a red apple exists. In standard first-order logic, it is a simple matter to write down something like $\exists x.(Ax \wedge Rx)$[1]. If we want to impose some *structure* on our domain, then we may resort to a many-sorted logic. Then, however, we have to decide which of our predicates correspond to sorts: we may write $\exists x:A.Rx$ as well as $\exists x:R.Ax$ (or maybe $\exists(x:A,y:R).x=y$). All these structured formalisations are equivalent to the previous one-sorted axiom, but each contains an implicit structuring choice. How can such a choice be motivated, if the semantics of a primitive sort is the same as that of its corresponding first-order predicate?

A statement like $\exists x:R.Ax$ sounds intuitively odd. What are we quantifying over? Do we assume something like the existence of "instances of redness" that can have the property of being apples? Our position is that structured representation languages like many-sorted logics should be constructed in such a way that predicates can be taken as sorts (or concepts, in KR terminology) only when they satisfy formal, necessary conditions at the meta-level, grounded on common-sense intuitions. According to our previous discussion, a predicate like *red* should not satisfy such conditions, and thus it should be excluded from being used as a sort.

As discussed in the previous section, the introduction of formal, necessary conditions for being a sort has a general ontological motivation. Besides that, ontological distinctions among predicates can be useful to make explicit a particular meaning of a lexical item. For example, compare the statement "a red apple exists" with others where the same term *red* appears in different contexts (Fig. 1):

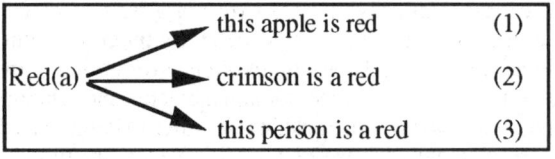

Fig. 1. Varieties of predication.

In case (2) the argument refers to a particular colour gradation belonging to the set of "reds", while in (3) the argument refers to a human-being, meaning for instance that he is a communist. Clearly, *red* is a case of lexical ambiguity. The use of a lexically ambiguous predicate can be specified by stating, for each context, the *intended* meaning. It is interesting, however, that at least for some predicates the possible intended meanings are not simply related to the fact that the arguments belong to different domains: they correspond to different *ways of predication*, i.e. different types of subject-predicate relationships, corresponding to meta-level kinds of predicates. Studying the formal properties of such categories is a matter of *formal ontology*, recently defined by Cocchiarella as "the systematic, formal, axiomatic development of the logic of all forms and modes of being" [9]. In practice, formal ontology can be intended as a theory of *a priori distinctions*:

- among the entities of the world (physical objects, events, processes...);
- among the meta-level categories used to model the world (concepts, properties, states, attributes...).

The latter kind of distinctions are the subject of the present paper.

3 THE FORMAL FRAMEWORK

Instead of trying to give a "universal" definition of the main predicate categories, we shall pursue here a more modest goal: our definitions will be related to a specific first-order theory whose intended meaning we are interested in specifying. This means that the basic building blocks of knowledge are already fixed, being the atomic predicates of the theory itself; our job will be to offer a formal instrument for clarifying their ontological implications, for the specific purposes of knowledge understanding and reuse among users belonging to a single culture. We assume therefore that the intended models of our theory, rather than describing a real or hypothetical situation in a world that has the same laws of nature of ours [10], are states of affairs having an "idealised rational acceptability" [26].

Notation. In the following, we shall use bold capital letters for sets, plain capital letters for predicate symbols and handwritten-style capital letters for relations.

Suppose we have a first-order language **L** with signature $\Sigma = \langle \mathbf{K}, \mathbf{R} \rangle$, where **K** is a set of constant symbols, **R** is a finite set of n-ary predicate symbols and $\mathbf{P} \subseteq \mathbf{R}$ is the set of monadic predicate symbols. Let **T** be a theory of **L**, **D** its intended domain and **M** the set of its models $\mathbf{M} = \langle \mathbf{D}, \mathcal{I} \rangle$, where $\mathcal{I}$ is the usual interpretation function for constants and predicate symbols. We are interested in some formal criteria accounting for those ontological distinctions among the elements of **P** which are considered as relevant to the purposes of **T** as applied to **D**. For example, we are looking for a clear distinction between sortal and non-sortal predicates which can account for the structuring choices implicit in the translation of **T** into an order-sorted theory $\mathbf{T}_S$ with signature $\Sigma_S = \langle \mathbf{K}, \mathbf{S}, \mathbf{Q} \rangle$, where $\mathbf{S} \subseteq \mathbf{P}$ is a set of sortal predicates and $\mathbf{Q} = \mathbf{R} \setminus \mathbf{S}$ a set of ordinary predicates. We shall see how this and other distinctions will be expressed in terms of constraints on the set of models.

---

[1] As usual, predicates are symbolized via the capitalized first letter of the word used in the text.

Our main methodological assumptions here are that (i) we need some notion of tense and modality in order to account for the intended meaning of predicate symbols; (ii) we need mereology and topology in order to capture the *a priori* structure of a domain. In the following, we first extend our first order language by introducing a semantics of tense and modality which satisfies our purposes, then we further extend both the language and the domain on the basis of mereo-topological principles, in order to formalize the notion of *ontological commitment* for the original language applied to the original domain.

Def. 1 Let **L** be a first-order language[1] with signature Σ. The *tense-modal extension* of **L** is the language $\mathbf{L_m}$ obtained by adding to the logical symbols of **L** the usual modal operators $\Diamond$ and $\Box$ and the tense operators $\mathbb{F}$ and $\mathbb{P}$, respectively standing for "sometimes in the future" and "sometimes in the past".

Def. 2 Let **L** be a first-order language with signature $\Sigma = \langle K, R \rangle$, $\mathbf{L_m}$ its tense-modal extension and **D** a domain. A *constant-domain rigid model* for $\mathbf{L_m}$ based on **D** is a structure $M = \langle W, \mathcal{R}, \mathcal{B}, D, \mathcal{F}_K, \mathcal{F}_R \rangle$, where:

- **W** is a set of possible worlds;
- $\mathcal{R}$ and $\mathcal{B}$ are binary relations on **W** such that $\mathcal{B}$ is a union of linear orders and for each $w_i, w_j \in W$ if $\langle w_i, w_j \rangle \in \mathcal{B}$ then $\langle w_i, w_j \rangle \notin \mathcal{R}$.
- $\mathcal{F}_K$ is a function that assigns to each $c \in K$ an element $\mathcal{F}_K(c)$ of **D**.
- $\mathcal{F}_R$ is a mapping that assigns to each $w \in W$ and each n-ary predicate symbol $r_n \in R$ an n-ary relation $\mathcal{F}_R(w, r_n)$ on **D**.[2]

We want to give $\mathcal{R}$ the meaning of an *ontological compatibility* relation: intuitively, two worlds are ontologically compatible if they describe alternative states of affairs which do not disagree on the *a priori* nature of the domain. For instance, referring to the example discussed in the previous section, consider a world where a given individual is an instance of the two relations *apple* and *red* (intended as real world relations, not as predicate symbols). Such a world will be compatible with another where such individual is still an apple but is not red, while it cannot be compatible with a world where *the same individual* is not an apple, since being an apple affects the *identity* of an object. To capture such intuitions, $\mathcal{R}$ must be reflexive, transitive and symmetric (i.e., an equivalence relation), and the corresponding modal theory will be therefore S5.

Def. 3 Let **L** be a first-order language, $\mathbf{L_m}$ its tense-modal extension and **D** a domain. A *compatibility model* for $\mathbf{L_m}$ based on **D** is a constant-domain rigid model for $\mathbf{L_m}$ based on **D**, where $\mathcal{R}$ is the ontological compatibility relation between worlds.

The notion of truth in a model at a world is pretty standard, and it will not defined here in detail because of space limitations. The only slight deviation from standard truth conditions regards formulas that involve tense operators. In particular:

- A formula Φ is necessary in a compatibility model M at a world w (written $M, w \models \Box \Phi$) iff $M, v \models \Phi$ for every v such that $\mathcal{R}(w, v)$;
- $M, w \models \Diamond \Phi$ iff $M, v \models \Phi$ for some v such that $\mathcal{R}(w, v)$;
- $M, w \models \mathbb{F} \Phi$ iff $M, v \models \Phi$ for some v such that $\mathcal{B}(w, v)$;
- $M, w \models \mathbb{P} \Phi$ iff $M, v \models \Phi$ for some v such that $\mathcal{B}(v, w)$.
- Φ is valid in M ($M \models \Phi$) iff $M, w \models \Phi$ for each world w of M.

Given a domain **D**, consider now the set of all compatibility models based on **D** of the tense-modal extension $\mathbf{L_m}$ of a language **L**. In order to account for our ontological assumptions about **D**, we should somehow restrict such a set, excluding those models that allow for non-intended worlds or too large sets of compatible worlds. Within our framework, we can express such constraints by restricting the set of all possible compatibility models of $\mathbf{L_m}$:

Def. 4 A *commitment* for **L** based on **D** is a set **C** of compatibility models for $\mathbf{L_m}$ based on **D**. Such a commitment can be specified by an S5 modal theory of $\mathbf{L_m}$, being in this case the set of all its compatibility models based on **D**. A formula Φ of $\mathbf{L_m}$ is valid in **C** ($C \models \Phi$) iff it is valid in each model $M \in C$.

We shall see in the next section how we can express the constraints mentioned in the example of the red apple by choosing a suitable commitment **C**. Before that, we need first to further extend both $\mathbf{L_m}$ and **D** in order to be able to express our ontological assumptions about **D** itself:

Def. 5 Let **L** be a first order language with signature $\Sigma = \langle K, R \rangle$, and **L'** a language with signature $\Sigma' = \langle K, R' \rangle$, where $R' = R \cup \{<, C\}$, while $<$ and C are two binary predicate symbols used to represent the mereological relation of "proper part" and the topological relation of "connection". The tense-modal extension of **L'** is called the *ontological extension* $\mathbf{L_0}$ of **L**.

---

[1] We assume L as non functional just for the sake of simplicity.
[2] This definition is taken from [12], extended with a relation $\mathcal{B}$ intended to express the temporal precedence relationship between worlds. The latter is a union of linear orders, each of whom represents a possible history. Notice that, due to the fact that $\mathcal{B}$ and $\mathcal{R}$ are disjoint, modal necessity does not imply temporal necessity.

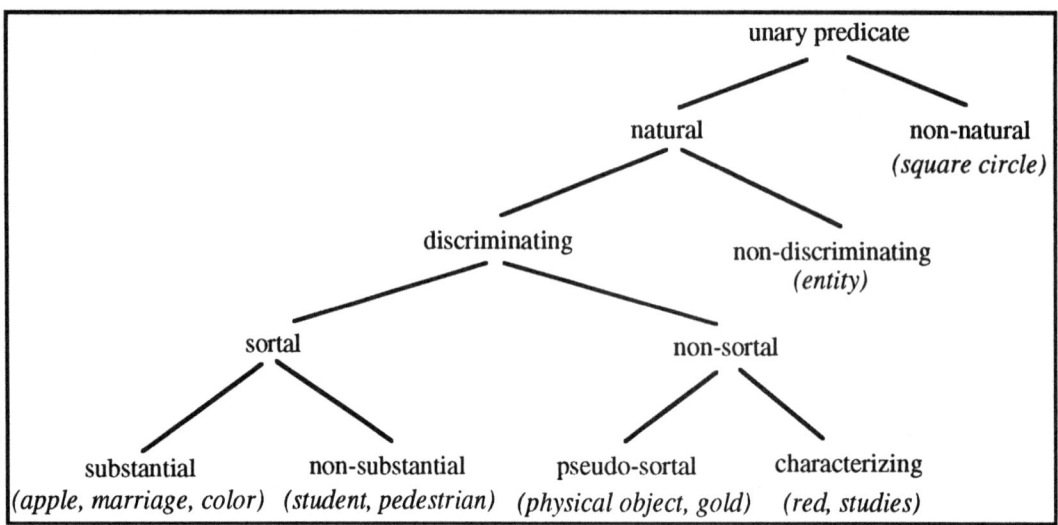

Fig. 2. Preliminary distinctions among unary predicates.

The properties of the part-of relation have been extensively studied in [28]. Connection has been used as a topological primitive in [7] and more recently in [28]. Since our domain is not restricted to topological entities only, the connection relation can have arguments which are physical bodies or events and not only regions as in [28]. We assume here that two entities are spatially connected if *their spatio-temporal extensions* are connected in the sense defined in [28] (i.e. two *regions* are connected if their topological closures share a point). Notice that we do not share with Randell and colleagues the choice to define parthood in terms of connection[1].

Def. 6 The *mereological closure* of a domain **D** is the set D_O obtained by adding to **D** the set of all proper parts of the elements of **D**.

Def. 7 An *ontological commitment* O for L based on D is a commitment for L_O based on D_O, such that the following minimal mereo-topological theory is valid in O^2.

A1 $x < y \supset \neg (y < x)$ (asymmetry)
A2 $x < y \land y < z \supset x < z$ (transitivity)
A3 $x < y \supset \exists z.(z < y \land \neg Ozx)$ (supplementation)
A4 $\forall x.Cxx$ (reflexivity)
A5 $\forall x \forall y.Cxy \supset Cyx$ (symmetry)

D1 $x \leq y =_{def} x < y \lor x = y$ (part)
D2 $Oxy =_{def} \exists z.\ z \leq x \land z \leq y$ (overlap)

4 A BASIC ONTOLOGY OF UNARY PREDICATE TYPES

Let us now stipulate some preliminary distinctions among unary predicates (Fig. 2). Notice that we are interested in very general, purely formal distinctions at the meta-level, completely independent on the nature of the domain. This means that our distinctions are intended to hold not only for standard examples related to the domain of physical objects, but also for predicates such as *color* or *marriage* whose arguments are universals like *red* or temporal entities like a particular marriage event. Analogously, no linguistic assumption is made on the names of predicates, which can be either nouns, adjectives, or verbs.

Within our modal framework, the first fundamental distinction we make among unary predicates regards their "discriminating power". If we want to use a predicate for knowledge-structuring purposes it cannot be necessarily false for each element of the domain, i.e. it must be *natural* in the sense of [8]. Moreover, we are interested in predicates that tell us something non-trivial about the domain, excluding therefore those which are always necessarily true.

Def. 8 Let **L** be a first order language, P a monadic predicate of **L**, and O an ontological commitment for L. P is called *natural* in O iff $O \models \Diamond \exists x.Px$. A natural predicate is *discriminating* in O iff $O \models \Diamond \exists x.\neg Px$.

---
[1] See [33] for a discussion of the relationships between mereology and topology.
[2] Axioms A1-A3 are taken from [29], while A4-A5 from [28].

4.1 COUNTABILITY AND REIDENTIFIABILITY

Among discriminating unary predicates, the relevant distinction is the classical one between sortals and non-sortals. To this end, we introduce two meta-level properties which give a minimal characterization of individuality, and are therefore distinctive of sortal predicates. They bear on two main notions proposed in the philosophical literature: *countability* [15] and temporal *reidentifiability* [34]. The former is bound to the capacity of a predicate to isolate a given object among others: "*this* is a P, this is *another* P, this *is not* a P". In other words, if P is a sortal predicate, then it is possible to answer: "how many Ps are there?" In the literature, various "divisivity" criteria have been proposed to account for the countable/non-countable distinction. Excluding those based on universal quantification on all parts of an object for reasons having to do with the problem of granularity, a quite satisfactory criterion is the one proposed by Griffin [15], which can be formulated in such a way that P is a countable predicate iff $\forall x.(Px \supset \neg \exists z.(z < x \land Pz))$. Such a criterion, however, does not take into account a notion of topological connection which seems to be related to the notion of countability. In our opinion, the main feature of countable predicates is that they cannot be true of an object and of a non-isolated part of it. For example, we think it is natural to consider *piece of wood* as a countable predicate, but it cannot be excluded from being uncountable according to Griffin's definition. The point is that in its ordinary meaning such a predicate does not apply to any part of a single, integral, piece of wood. In order to capture such a structural feature of countable predicates within our formal framework, let us introduce the following definitions within the ontological extension L_0 of a language L:

D3 $\sigma x \phi x =_{def} \iota x \forall y(Oyx \equiv \exists z(\phi z \land Ozy))$[1]
   (sum of all ϕers)

D4 $x-y =_{def} \sigma z.(z \leq x \land \neg Ozy)$
   (mereological difference)

D5 $x <_i y =_{def} x<y \land \neg Cx(y-x)$
   (isolated part)

D6 $x <_c y =_{def} x<y \land Cx(y-x)$
   (connected part)

D7 $\Box_t \phi =_{def} \neg \mathbb{F} \neg \phi \land \phi \land \neg \mathbb{P} \neg \phi$
   (temporal necessity)

Def. 9 A discriminating predicate P is called *countable* in O iff $O \models \forall x. (Px \supset \neg \exists z.(z <_c x \land Pz))$.

In the above definition, we have simply substituted connected part-of to the relation of part-of appearing in Griffin's definition. In other words, a countable predicate P only holds for entities which are "maximally connected" with respect to P, in the sense that they cannot have connected parts which are instances of P. The following theorem follows immediately from the definition:

Theorem 1 A predicate is countable if it only applies to atomic entities, i.e. entities having no parts.

According to Def. 9, the predicate *piece of wood* is countable if (as seems natural) it only applies to isolated pieces of wood, while the monadic predicate *color* turns out to be countable according to theorem 1, assuming that a color has no parts. On the other hand, according to its ordinary sense a predicate like *red* is not countable[2], since while holding for a physical object it can also apply to non-isolated parts of it, such as its surface.

The above definition allows us to consider predicates denoting physical structures like *stack* (of blocks), *chain* or *lump* (of coal) as countable predicates only if it can be claimed, perhaps on the basis of Gestalt-theoretical considerations, that no connected part of a physically realized structure can be a structure of the same kind [30]. In this sense, a substack can be a stack only as an isolated whole. There are some intuitive and practical reasons in favour of this way of thinking. For example, a request to count the chains put in a box is not usually understood as a request to count also the subchains of such chains. Notice that we do not require instances of countable predicates to be isolated entities: for example, we want *arm* to be countable and such that both detached and undetached arms are instances of it[3]. However, it is reasonable to hold that *tube* is countable. It follows that no part of a tube is a tube, otherwise it would violate the assumption of countability. So while arms are instances of *arm* even before a possible detaching event, the same does not hold for halves of tubes. Lack of analogy between the two cases is due to the fact that in the former case the argument of the predicate is connected to something of a different kind.

We may be tempted to conclude now that countability is enough to decide about sortality. Things are not so easy, however. Think of a unary predicate expressed by a verb, like *studies*. It seems to be countable according to our definition, and in fact we can count those entities x such that the statement *x studies* is true, but still it seems odd to consider *studies* as a sortal predicate. The

---

[1] In order to avoid troubles with the satisfiability conditions for modal formulas involving the *iota* operator, we assume that terms built by means of such operator are contextually defined *a la* Russell. For instance, a formula like P($\iota x.\phi x$) is translated in $\exists x(Px \land \phi x \land (\forall y.\phi y \supset y=x))$.

[2] Notice that when we attach an ontological category to a linguistic term we do not imply any *a priori* meaning attribution: we simply assume, for simplicity reasons, the ontological commitment corresponding to the usual meaning of the term (in this case the meaning of case 1 in Fig. 1).

[3] In contrast with [30], we do not assume that detaching an arm is an event such that the arm befor it is not the same arm as the arm after it.

reason is that sortality implies a notion of *reidentifiability* across time, which is not implied by the semantics of a verb. Linguists such as Givòn [14] have pointed out that *temporal stability* can be a useful criterion to distinguish verbs from nouns. We say that a predicate is temporally stable when, if it holds for an object at a given time, then it must hold for the same object at another time[1].

Def. 10 A discriminating predicate P is called *temporally stable* under O iff $O \models \forall x.(Px \supset \mathbb{F}Px \vee \mathbb{P} Px)$.

In conclusion, both mereo-topological and temporal modality are needed to characterize sortal predicates within an ontological commitment:

Def. 11 A discriminating predicate P is called *sortal* in O iff it is both countable and temporally stable in O, and *non-sortal* otherwise.

According to this definition, we have a criterion to distinguish between the two predicates involved in the statement "a red apple exists". *Apple* will be in this case a sortal predicate being countable and temporally stable, while *red* will be non-sortal being not countable under our intended intepretation. Both $\exists x:R.Ax$ and $\exists (x:A, y:R).x=y$ will be therefore excluded from a many-sorted axiomatisation.

4.2 RIGIDITY

Although useful for many purposes, the distinction between sortal and non-sortal predicates discussed above is not fine enough to account for the difference in the interpretation of *red* in cases (2) and (3) of Fig. 1, since in both of them *red* is used as a sortal predicate. Let us therefore further explore the ontological distinctions we can draw among both sortal and non-sortal predicates. An observation that comes to mind, when trying to formalise the nature of the subject-predicate relationship, is that the "force" of this relationship is much higher in "x is an apple" than in "x is red". If x has the property of being an apple, it cannot lose this property without losing its identity, while this does not seem to be the case in the latter example. This observation goes back to Aristotelian essentialism, and can be formalised as follows [2]:

Def. 12 A discriminating predicate P is *ontologically rigid* in O iff $O \models \forall x(Px \supset (\Box Px \wedge \Box_t Px))$.

An immediate theorem following from Definition 10 is the following:

Theorem 2 Any ontologically rigid predicate is also temporally stable.

However, the example above notwithstanding, ontological rigidity is not a sufficient condition for sortality. In fact, there are a number of rigid predicates which should be excluded from being sortals, since no clear distinction criteria are associated with them. Predicates corresponding to certain mass nouns belong to this category (at least if their arguments denote an amount of stuff and not a particular object), as well as "high level" predicates like *physical object*, *individual*, *event*. We call these predicates *pseudo-sortals*[2]. They are all rigid (and therefore stable) but not countable.

Def. 13 Let P be a non-sortal predicate under O. It is a *pseudo-sortal* iff it is ontologically rigid under O, and a *characterising predicate* otherwise.

Rigidity cannot be considered as a necessary condition for sortality, either. According to our definition, sortals include predicates like *student*, which – although not rigid – are still countable and stable enough to guarantee distinguishability and reidentification. Following [34], we call such predicates *non-substantial sortals*[3].

Def. 14 Let P be a sortal predicate under O. It is a *substantial sortal* iff it is ontologically rigid under O, and a *non-substantial sortal* otherwise.

As noticed before, temporal stability plays here a crucial role for distinguishing *student* from *studies*: both are countable and not ontologically rigid, but the latter is not temporally stable and is therefore a characterizing predicate, while the former is a non-substantial sortal.

We are now in a position to exploit the above distinctions in order to specify the ontological commitment of a first order theory: for instance, stating that *red* is a characterizing predicate will clarify its intended meaning in the case (1) of Fig. 1. In case (2), *red* is rigid and countable, since its argument is a colour gradation: it will be therefore a substantial sortal (crimson *has* to be a red: see [24], p. 10). Finally, in case (3), *red* is used as a contingent property of human-beings and hence is not rigid, while it is countable and temporally stable: *red* is therefore a non substantial sortal.

---

[1]This definition is not completely satisfactory, since, according to the intuition, a temporally stable predicate should hold in a *neighbour* of the time where it is true, but this fact cannot be expressed in terms of $\mathbb{F}$ and $\mathbb{P}$. A more accurate definition would require the use of non-standard modal operators.

[2]They are called "super sortals" in [25]. Notice that *physical object* is not intended here in the sense of spatially isolated *thing*.
[3]According to the current terminology used in knowledge representation, substantial sortals should in our opinion correspond to *types* and non-substantial sortals to *roles* (in the sense of [31]), while the terms *class* or *concept* should be reserved to the union of sortal and pseudo-sortal predicates.

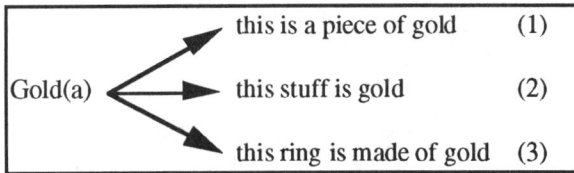

Fig. 3: Different interpretations of mass nouns.

Another interesting example regards the different interpretations of a mass noun like *gold*, reported in Fig. 3 above. In case (1), *gold* is intended as countable, stable but not rigid (since that piece can have been taken from a rock, for instance), and it is used as a non-substantial sortal; in cases (2) and (3) the predicate is non-countable, but in the former case it is rigid (and *gold* is therefore a pseudo sortal), while in the latter it can be assumed as non-rigid, and *gold* becomes a characterizing predicate.

5 ONTOLOGICAL ENGINEERING

We would like to show in this section how the ontological distinctions introduced above can be of concrete utility in the current practice of knowledge engineering. The first result of the formal framework presented above is the possibility to draw a clear distinction between concepts[1] and properties, in the sense usually ascribed to such terms within the KR community. Our proposal is that properties should coincide with what we called characterizing predicates, while all other kinds of unary predicates should be thought of as concepts.

Besides this first important distinction, our meta-level classification of unary predicates allows us to impose some further structure on the set of concepts, usually represented as an oriented graph where arcs denote subsumption relationships. As the size of this graph increases, it may be very useful to isolate a skeleton to be used for indexing and clustering purposes. Substantial sortals are a natural candidate to constitute such a skeleton[2], since their rigidity reduces the "tangleness" of the corresponding graph. However, to effectively use substantial sortals as a skeleton, we must introduce some further constraints to our ontological commitment, which lead to the notion of *well-founded ontological commitment*.

Def. 15 Let P and Q be two natural predicates in **O**. P is *subordinate* to Q in **O** iff **O** $\models \forall x(Px \supset Qx) \land \neg \forall x(Qx \supset Px)$. P and Q are *disjoint* in **O** iff **O** $\models \neg \exists x.Px \land Qx$. A set **P**={$P_1, ..., P_n$} of mutually disjoint natural predicates in **O** is a *domain partition* in **O** iff **O** $\models \forall x.(P_1 x \lor ... \lor P_n x)$.

Def. 16 An ontological commitment **O** based on **D** is *well-founded* iff:

- There is a set $\mathbf{C} \subseteq \mathbf{P}$ of mutually disjoint pseudo-sortal predicates called *categorial predicates*, such that (i) **C** is a domain partition in **O**, and (ii) no element C∈ **C** is subordinate to a discriminating predicate[3].
- For each categorial predicate C∈ **C**, there is a set $\mathbf{S_C}$ of disjoint substantial sortals such that, for each S∈ $\mathbf{S_C}$, S is subordinate to C and there is no substantial sortal S' such that S is subordinate to S'.
- Each non-substantial sortal is subordinate to a substantial sortal.

A well-founded ontological commitment introduces therefore a further subclass of discriminating predicates, i.e. categorial predicates, which belong to the class of pseudo-sortals according to the preliminary distinctions shown in Fig. 2. We call *mass-like predicates* those pseudo-sortals which are not categories; therefore, the final relevant distinctions within a well-founded commitment are those shown in Fig. 4.

Let us briefly motivate our definition of a well-founded ontological commitment. Categorial predicates are intended to represent what traditional ontology would call *summa genera*. A set of categorial predicates useful for a very broad domain is given by *physical object, event, spatial region, temporal interval, amount of matter*[4]. The fact that such predicates are assumed to be pseudo-sortals (and therefore uncountable) underlines their very general nature.
As for the second constraint mentioned in the definition, no particular structure is imposed on substantial sortals within a well-founded commitment[5], except that top-level substantial sortals should specify natural kinds within general categories: therefore, they must be disjoint and cannot overlap general categories. A useful definition related to substantial sortals is the following one:

Def. 17. Let **O** be a well-founded ontological commitment. If a substantial sortal S is subordinate to another substantial sortal T under **O**, then S is called a *kind* of T.

---

[1] The term *concept* is often used interchangeably with *type*, but we deserve to the latter a more specific meaning (see below).

[2] A similar proposal has been made by Sowa [31], which however refers to an unspecified notion of "natural type".

[3] A possible further constraint for categorial predicates could be **O** $\models \forall xy((Cx \land y<x) \supset Cy)$.

[4] These predicates should be characterized by suitable axioms, but such a task is beyond the scope of the present paper.

[5] It may be desirable, both for conceptual and computational reasons, to impose the condition that substantial sortals form a forest of trees; such a conditions seems hohever not obtainable in many cases.

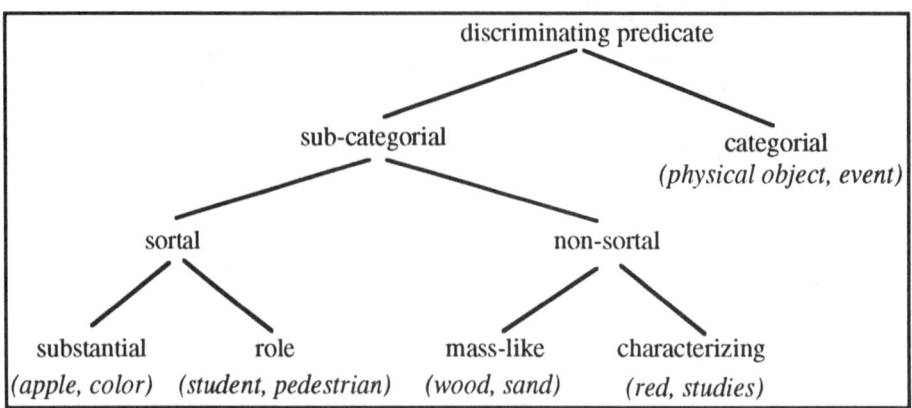

Fig. 4. Basic distinctions among discriminating predicates within a well-founded ontological commitment

Finally, the intuition behind the third constraint in Def. 16 is that in the case of substantial sortals the identity criterion is given by the predicate itself, while for non-substantial sortals it is provided by some superordinate sortal. Under this constraint, non-substantial sortals conform to the notion of "role type" proposed by Sowa, which fits well with the general meaning of the term "role": "Role types are subtypes of natural types in some particular patterns of relationships" [31]. We suggest to adopt the term "role" for non-substantial sortals within the KR community, avoiding to use it at a synonym for an (arbitrary) binary relation as common practice in the KL-ONE circles.[1] A useful theorem following from Def. 16 is the following one:

Theorem 3. Within a well-founded ontological commitment, any two overlapping non-substantial sortals are subordinate to the same substantial sortal.

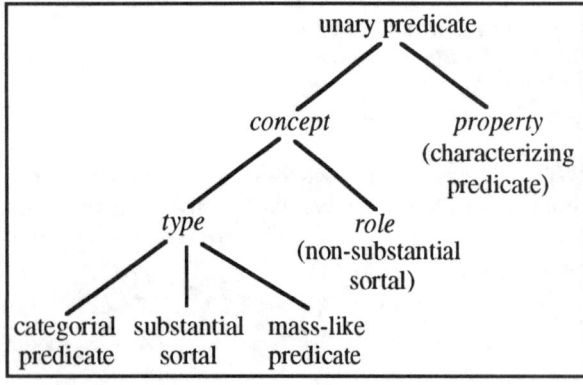

Fig. 5. A terminological proposal for KR formalisms. Commonly used KR terms are shown in italics.

[1] See [18] for a general discussion on roles and attributes. Notice however that the distinctions among unary predicates discussed in that paper have been here drastically revised and simplified; in particular, no notion of ontological foundation is here advocated to distinguish between concepts and properties.

On the basis of the above considerations related to the practice of knowledge engineering, we are now in the position to formulate a terminological proposal regarding the relationship between the terminology currently used in KR formalisms and the philosophical terms we have defined here (Fig. 5 above). Rigid (both countable and uncountable) unary predicates are called *types*, while as noticed before non-substantial sortals correspond to *roles*. Types and roles are collectively called *concepts*, and are distinguished from *properties* since the latter are characterizing predicates, i.e. they are uncountable and non-rigid. Notice that we prefer to speak of *properties* rather than of *qualities*, since it seems more appropriate to adopt the latter term for substantial sortals having universals as arguments, as for instance *color*.

6 CONCLUSIONS

In [3], the authors discussed the example reported in Fig. 6 above. They argued that a question like "How many kinds of rocks are there?" cannot be answered by simply looking at the nodes subsumed by 'rock' in the

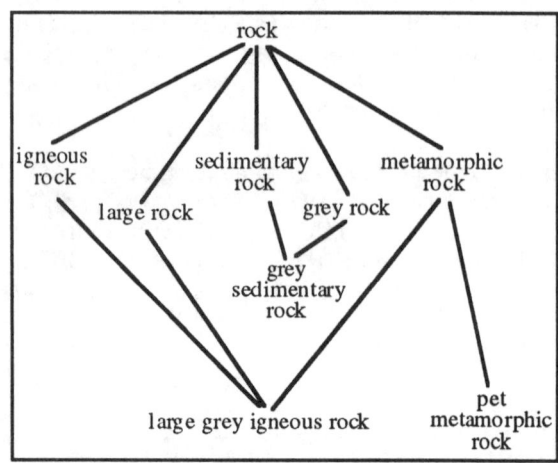

Fig. 6. Kinds of rocks (From [3])

network, since the language allows them to proliferate easily. Hence they give up answering such dangerous questions within a KR formalism, by specifying a functional interface designed to answer "safe" queries about analytical relationships between terms independently of the structure of the knowledge base, like "a large grey igneous rock is a grey rock". On the other hand, the same authors, in an earlier paper [4], stressed the importance of *terminological competence* in knowledge representation, stating for instance that an *enhancement mode transistor* (which is "a *kind* of transistor") should be understood as different from a *pass transistor* (which is "a *role* a transistor plays in a larger circuit").

We hope to have shown in this paper that terminological competence can be gained by formally expressing the ontological commitment of a knowledge base. If, in the example above, predicates corresponding to *rock, igneous-rock, sedimentary-rock* and *metamorphic-rock* are marked as substantial sortals (as they should be according to their ordinary meaning), while all the others are marked as non-substantial sorts (since they are not rigid), then a safe answer to the query "how many kinds of rocks are there?" would be "at least 3".

We think we have still to learn a lot, to understand and represent the *a priori* laws that govern the structure of reality. Bearing on insights coming from the philosophical tradition of formal ontology, we have tried to show that some of these laws are suitable to formal characterization: independently of the particular formalization we have adopted, which can be of course changed or revised, we would like to stress that the ontological distinctions we have introduced can have a profound impact on the current practice of knowledge engineering.

In our opinion, three are the main contributions of this paper. The first one is the formal account of ontological commitment we have given within a modal framework: the use of a modal logic as a tool to constrain the intended semantics of the underlying non-modal theory seems to be unavoidable if we wish to express ontological constraints. The second one is our definition of countability, which seems to solve some of the puzzling cases reported in the literature. The third one is the formalization of Strawson's distinction between sortal and non-sortal predicates, which has been further refined by taking into account Wiggins' distinction between substantial and non-substantial predicates. Far from claiming to have said any definitive word on these issues, we would like to underline here that (i) *some* formal properties which account for distinctions among predicate types can indeed be worked out, even if complete, unproblematic definitions may never be given; (ii) when the semantics of structuring primitives used in KR languages is restricted in such a way as to take into account of such formal distinctions at the ontological level, then potential misunderstandings and inconsistencies due to conflicting intended models are reduced; (iii) further research in this area is needed, and it should be encouraged within the KR community, in cooperation with the philosophical and linguistic communities.

Acknowledgements

We are indebted to Luca Boldrin, Dario Maguolo and Barry Smith for their valuable comments on earlier drafts of this paper.

References

[1] W. P. Alston 1958. Ontological Commitments. *Philosophical Sttudies*, **9**: 8-16.
[2] R. Barcan Marcus 1968. Essential Attribution. *The Journal of Philosophy*, **7**.
[3] R. Brachman, R. Fikes, and H. Levesque 1983. Krypton: A Functional Approach to Knowledge Representation. *IEEE Computer*, October: 67-73.
[4] R. Brachman and H. Levesque 1982. Competence in Knowledge Representation. In *Proceedings of AAAI 82*.
[5] R. J. Brachman 1979. On the Epistemological Status of Semantic Networks. In N. V. Findler (ed.), *Associative Networks: Representation and Use of Knowledge by Computers*. Academic Press.
[6] A. Church 1958. Ontological Commitment. *The Journal of Philosophy*, **55**: 1008-14.
[7] B. L. Clarke 1981. *A Calculus of Individuals Based on "Connection"* **22**.
[8] N. Cocchiarella 1989. Philosophical Perspectives on Formal Theories of Predication. In D. Gabbay and F. Günthner (ed.), *Handbook of Philosophical Logic*. Reidel: 253-326.
[9] N. B. Cocchiarella 1991. Formal Ontology. In H. Burkhardt and B. Smith (ed.), *Handbook of Metaphysics and Ontology*. Philosophia Verlag, Munich.
[10] N. B. Cocchiarella 1993. Knowledge Representation in Conceptual Realism. In N. Guarino and R. Poli (ed.), *Formal Ontology in Conceptual Analysis and Knowledge Representation*. Kluwer (in preparation).
[11] R. Davis, H. Shrobe, and P. Szolovits 1993. What is in a Knowledge Representation? *AI Magazine*, Spring 1993.
[12] M. Fitting 1993. Basic Modal Logic. In D. M. Gabbay, C. J. Hogger and J. A. Robinson (ed.), *Handbook of Logic in Artificial Intelligence and Logic Programming*. Clarendon Press, Oxford.
[13] M. R. Genesereth and N. J. Nilsson 1987. *Logical Foundation of Artificial Intelligence*. Morgan Kaufmann, Los Altos, California.
[14] T. Givón 1979. *On Understanding Grammar*. Academic Press, New-York.
[15] N. Griffin 1977. *Relative Identity*. Oxford University Press, Oxford.

[16] T. Gruber 1993. Toward Principles for the Design of Ontologies Used for Knowledge Sharing. In N. Guarino and R. Poli (ed.), *Formal Ontology in Conceptual Analysis and Knowledge Representation*. Kluwer (in preparation).

[17] T. R. Gruber 1993. A translation approach to portable ontology specifications. *Knowledge Acquisition*, **5**: 199-220.

[18] N. Guarino 1992. Concepts, Attributes and Arbitrary Relations: Some Linguistic and Ontological Criteria for Structuring Knowledge Bases. *Data & Knowledge Engineering*, **8**: 249-261.

[19] N. Guarino 1994. The Ontological Level. In R. Casati, B. Smith and G. White (ed.), *Philosophy and the Cognitive Science*. Hölder-Pichler-Tempsky, Vienna.

[20] N. Guarino and L. Boldrin Formal Ontology and Knowledge Representation. In N. Guarino and R. Poli (ed.), *Formal Ontology in Conceptual Analysis and Knowledge Representation*. Kluwer (in preparation).

[21] N. Guarino and L. Boldrin 1993. Concepts and Relations. In *Proceedings of International Workshop on Formal Ontology in Conceptual Analysis and Knowledge Representation*. Padova, LADSEB-CNR Int. Rep. 01/93.

[22] D. Israel 1983. Interpreting Network Formalisms. *International Journal of Computers and Mathematics*, **9** 1.

[23] R. Neches, R. Fikes, T. Finin, T. Gruber, R. Patil, T. Senator, and W. R. Swartout 1991. Enabling Technology for Knowledge Sharing. *AI Magazine*, : fall.

[24] F. J. Pelletier 1979. Non-Singular References: Some Preliminaries. In F. J. Pelletier (ed.), *Mass Terms: Some Philosophical Problems*. Reidel, Dordrecht: 1-14.

[25] F. J. Pelletier and L. K. Schubert 1989. Mass Expressions. In D. Gabbay and F. Günthner (ed.), *Handbook of Philosophical Logic*. Reidel.

[26] H. Putnam 1981. *Reason, Truth, and History*. Cambridge University Press, Cambridge.

[27] W. O. Quine 1961. *From a Logical Point of View, Nine Logico-Philosophical Essays*. Harvard University Press, Cambridge, Mass.

[28] D. Randell, Z. Cui, and A. Cohn 1992. A spatial logic based on regions and connection. In *Proceedings of KR '92*. San Mateo (CA), Morgan Kaufmann.

[29] P. Simons 1987. *Parts: a Study in Ontology*. Clarendon Press, Oxford.

[30] B. Smith 1992. Characteristica Universalis. In K. Mulligan (ed.), *Language, Truth and Ontology*. Kluwer, Dordrecht: 48-77.

[31] J. F. Sowa 1988. Using a lexicon of canonical graphs in a semantic interpreter. In M. W. Evens (ed.), *Relational models of the lexicon*. Cambridege Univerity Press.

[32] P. F. Strawson 1959. *Individuals. An Essay in Descriptive Metaphysics*. Routledge, London and New York.

[33] A. Varzi 1994. On the Boundary Between Mereology and Topology. In R. Casati, B. Smith and G. White (ed.), *Philosophy and the Cognitive Science*. Hölder-Pichler-Tempsky, Vienna.

[34] D. Wiggins 1980. *Sameness and Substance*. Blakwell, Oxford.

Defeasible reasoning with structured information

Anthony Hunter
Department of Computing, Imperial College
180 Queen's Gate, London, SW7 2BZ, UK
email: abh@doc.ic.ac.uk

Abstract

There is a wide variety of approaches to formalising non-monotonic reasoning, and even though some relationships between formalisms have been established, there is a lack of appropriate general frameworks to support such analyses. There have been some successes such as using general properties of the consequence relation as a framework (Gabbay 1985, Makinson 1989, Kraus 1990), and with argument systems (Lin 1989, Vreeswijk 1991, Simari 1992), but these only provide relatively high level views on the formalisms. We require lower level, higher resolution, frameworks for analysing these logics, and for suggesting new logics that are better suited to practical reasoning. To address this we label formulae in our databases, using this to represent extra information about the formula. The proof rules propagate labels and the consequence relations select preferred inferences according to some preference criteria. Here we show how different non-monotonic logics can be characterized in terms of labelling strategies, algebras for the labels, proof rules, and preference criteria. We also discuss aggregation of preference criteria and compare with Doyle and Wellman (1991).

1 INTRODUCTION

Formalizing non-monotonic reasoning is a significant problem within artificial intelligence. A number of approaches have been proposed, but a clear understanding of the problem remains elusive. Given the diversity of proof theoretic approaches, there is a need for frameworks for elucidating key concepts within non-monotonic reasoning. Here we present a framework to characterize structural information - extra information about formulae that may be implicit or explicit - used in a diverse range of proof-theoretic non-monotonic logics. The framework is based on the approach of Labelled Deductive Systems (Gabbay 1993a, 1993b).

In this framework, formulae are labelled. When proof rules are applied, the labels attached to each formula in the premise are composed to give a label for the consequent. The labelled consequences of the database are called naive inferences, since they constitute weakly justified, tentative, conclusions that can be drawn from the defeasible data. Non-monotonic consequence relations are then defined to select preferred inferences from the naive inferences by using preference criteria over sets of naive inferences.

The framework can be viewed as a significant development of the Argument Systems framework (Lin 1989). The unlabelled language is essentially the same, and our notion of a naive inference corresponds to their notion of an argument, though a naive inference does contain extra information because of the label. In the Argument Systems (AS) framework, default logic, autoepistemic logic, negation-as-failure, and circumscription are special cases. This result can be inherited by our framework.

However, a key aim of our development is to analyse the notion of preference, implicit and explicit, that can be seen in a disparate range of non-monotonic logics. We argue that such preference is based partly on preference of some data over other data, and also on some reasoning strategies over others. In some approaches, such as default logic (Reiter 1980), and negation-as-failure (Reiter 1978) the prioritization is implicit, for other approaches such as inheritance hierarchies (Horty 1987), and ordered logic (Laenens 1990), the prioritization is explicit.

To illustrate implicit preference, take negation-as-failure with a database P. We denote the set of atomic propositions used in the language of P as $A(P)$, and denote the set of complements of $A(P)$ as $C(P)$ where $C(P) = \{\neg\alpha \mid \alpha \in A(P)\}$. We can regard $C(P)$ as the set of default values for atoms. The preference implict for negation-as-failure (NAF) is that for all formulae in

P are preferred over all formulae in C(P). Similarly for normal default logic we consider normal defaults, in a default theory (D,W), of the form $\alpha : \beta/\beta$ as object-level rules of the form $\alpha \to \beta$, and we consider that there is an implicit preference for information from the non-defeasible information over the default information in D.

In Grosof (1991), the wide-ranging role of preference, or priority, in non-monotonic reasoning was identified. The importance of preference has also been reflected in the Abstract Argument Systems framework (Vreeswijk 1991) - another generalization of the AS framework. However, the Abstract Argumentation Systems (AAS) framework does not include explicit labelling of formulae, and does not focus on preference criteria, as we do in this paper, and hence leaves open many interesting questions.

Our framework, as outlined below, is defined in terms of a family of logics called prioritized logics, and for this we define the notion of a database for a prioritized logic in terms of (1) labelling of formulae, and (2) orderings defined over the labelling. Such a database constitutes a structured database. Each member of the family of prioritized logics is defined in terms of consequence relations that can act on the structured databases.

2 STRUCTURED INFORMATION

We assume a set of atomic labels Λ. For example, the set of natural number N can be used as a set of atomic labels. Similarly, the set $\{n \mid n \in \mathbb{N}\}$ can be used as a set of atomic labels.

We define a complex label as follows: (1) If $i \in \Lambda$, then i is a complex label;(2) If i is a complex label, and $j \in \Lambda$, then $i \oplus j$ is a complex label; (3) If $i_1, .., i_n$ are complex labels, and $j \in \Lambda$, then $[i_1, .., i_n] \oplus j$ is a complex label.

We denote the set of complex labels that can be formed from a set Λ as $Tree(\Lambda)$. Let $\oplus$ be an associative function where $\emptyset$ is the identity element. Hence, $(Tree(\Lambda), \oplus)$ is a monoid.

We assume a set of propositional letters $\mathcal{A}$, where $\bot, \top \in \mathcal{A}$, and a set of logical symbols $\{\land, \lor, \neg\}$. The set of classical formulae that can be formed from these is denoted $\mathcal{B}$. We define the set of defeasible rules $\mathcal{R}$, and the set of naive inferences $\mathcal{N}$, as follows, where $Tree(\Lambda)$ is the set of complex labels formed from Λ,

If $\alpha, \beta \in \mathcal{B}$, and $i \in \mathbb{N}$ then $i : \alpha \to \beta \in \mathcal{R}$

If $\alpha \in \mathcal{B}$, and $i \in Tree(\Lambda)$ then $i : \alpha \in \mathcal{N}$

Note that in the proof theory below, we treat the symbols $\{\land, \lor, \neg\}$ classically. However, we treat $\to$ as a default, or synonymously defeasible, implication, and not as strict implication.

We define a structured database as a tuple (Δ, Γ), where $\Gamma = (\Omega, \geq, \sigma)$, $\Delta \subseteq \wp(\mathcal{R})$, $(\Omega, \geq)$ is a poset, and σ is a mapping such that $\sigma : \Lambda \mapsto \Omega$. We assume formulae in Δ are uniquely labelled. Also we assume that Δ is finite, and that $(\Omega, \geq)$ is finite and acyclic. The relation $\geq$ is called the atomic ordering relation. For example, $\Delta = \{i : \alpha \to \beta, j : \top \to \neg\beta\}$, $i, j \in \Omega$, $i \geq j$, and σ is an identity map. To ease notation, we often refer to a structured database (Δ, Γ) as just Δ, and that all functions and relations defined on Δ assume the associated Γ. Also for ease of notation, for any rule $i : \top \to \beta$, we can denote it as $i : \beta$.

We define some subsidiary functions on labels, as follows: The function $Form$ for any $X \subseteq \mathcal{R} \cup \mathcal{N}$ is $Form(X) = \{\alpha \mid i : \alpha \in X\}$, and for any $Y \subseteq \mathcal{B}$ is $Form(Y) = Y$. The function $Head : \mathcal{R} \mapsto \mathcal{B}$ is $Head(i : \alpha \to \beta) = \beta$.

The function $Labels$ for any $X \subseteq \mathcal{R} \cup \mathcal{N}$ is $Labels(X) = \{i \mid i : \alpha \in X\}$. The function $AtomicLabels : Tree(\Lambda) \mapsto \wp(\Lambda)$ is defined for $AtomicLabels(l)$ as the set of atomic labels used in the complex label l. The function $Lastlabel : Tree(\Lambda) \mapsto \Lambda$ is $Lastlabel(i) = i$ if $i \in \Lambda$, and $Lastlabel(i \oplus j) = j$.

The function $Subproofs : Tree(\Lambda) \mapsto \wp(Tree(\Lambda))$ is $Subproofs([i_1,..,i_n] \oplus j) = Subproofs(i_1) \cup \cdots \cup Subproofs(i_n) \cup \{i_1,..,i_n,j\}$, $Subproofs(i \oplus j) = \{i,j\} \cup Subproofs(i)$ if i is a complex label, and $Subproofs(i) = \{i\}$ if $i \in \Lambda$.

3 NAIVE INFERENCES

A naive inference from a structured database Δ is regarded as a plausible, or possible, inference. It is derived by a naive proof theory that manipulates the labelled formulae. The naive proof theory we consider here is defined using the classical consequence relation denoted $\vdash$, where $i_1 : \alpha_1,..,i_n : \alpha_n, i : \alpha \in \mathcal{N}$, and $j : \alpha \to \beta \in \mathcal{R}$. If $\alpha_1,..,\alpha_n \vdash \alpha$ and $\alpha_1,..,\alpha_n \not\vdash \bot$ then

$$\frac{i_1 : \alpha_1,..,i_n : \alpha_n, j : \alpha \to \beta}{[i_1,..,i_n] \oplus j : \beta}$$

$$\frac{i : \alpha, j : \alpha \to \beta}{i \oplus j : \beta}$$

Proofs can be nested. The notation $[i_1,..,i_n]$, denotes a "classical proof" of β from the set of naive inferences $\{i_1 : \alpha_1,..,i_n : \alpha_n\}$. The notation $i \oplus j$ denotes a "defeasible proof" of β using the naive inference labelled i on the defeasible rule labelled j.

Note, this is only one possible naive proof theory. We could for example exchange the labelled consequence relation for a weaker form such as intuitionistic, paraconsistent, or linear. Similarly, we could also strengthen the proof theory to allow an increased manipulation of the rules in the database - such as allowing Contraposition or Or - or to allow manipulation of a richer database language - such as supporting modal operators.

We can consider the naive proof theory as a consequence relation $\vdash_{naive}$. So $\Delta \vdash_{naive} i : \alpha$ means there is a naive proof of $i : \alpha$ from Δ using the above proof rules. Assume that for any Δ, $\top$ follows by $\vdash_{naive}$, and that it is labelled with the identity element - i.e., $\Delta \vdash_{naive} \emptyset : \top$. Let $Naive(\Delta) = \{i \oplus j : \beta \mid j : \alpha \to \beta \in \Delta$ and $\Delta \vdash_{naive} i : \alpha\}$.

We define some subsidiary functions and relations on labels, as follows: The function $Step_\Delta : Tree(\Lambda) \mapsto \wp(\mathcal{N})$, for any $k \in Tree(\Lambda)$, is $Step_\Delta(k) = \{i : \alpha \in Naive(\Delta) \mid i \in Subproofs(k)\}$.

A set of naive inferences X is subproof-complete iff $\forall i : \alpha \in X$ $\forall j : \beta$ [if $j : \beta \in Step_\Delta(i)$ then $j : \beta \in X$]. A set of naive inferences X is consistent iff $Form(X) \not\vdash \bot$.

4 PREFERRED INFERENCES

There are many possible criteria that we could use to prefer some subsets of $\wp(Naive(\Delta))$ over others. In order to capture each useful criterion, we can define a preference relation $\geq_x$ over $\wp(Naive(\Delta))$.

All preference relations are pre-ordering relations. If $\geq_x$ is a preference relation for which anti-symmetry fails, then we use the notation $X \approx_x Y$ for abbreviating the statements $X \geq_x Y$ and $Y \geq_x X$ both holding. For a preference relation $\geq_x$, if $X \not\geq_x Y$ and $Y \not\geq_x X$ hold for some pair X, Y, then we describe X, Y as incomparable with respect to $\geq_x$, and denote this by $X \|_x Y$. Finally, for any $\Phi, \geq_x$, let Top be defined as follows,

$$Top(\Phi, \geq_x) = \{X \subseteq \Phi \mid \neg \exists Y \subseteq \Phi \text{ such that } Y >_x X\}$$

Definitions for preference relations over $\wp(Naive(\Delta))$ include the following where $X, Y \subseteq Naive(\Delta)$: (1) $X \geq_{con} Y$ holds iff X is consistent; and (2) $X \geq_{spc} Y$ holds iff X is subproof-complete. Other preference relations include those definable in terms of subsets of $Naive(\Delta)$ that use more specific information.

An advantage of this approach is that we can compose a useful preference relation by aggregating a selection of simpler preference relations. Let $(\geq_1, .., \geq_n)$ be a tuple of preference relations, let $\mathcal{A} = \wp(Naive(\Delta)) \times \wp(Naive(\Delta))$, and let $Aggregate$ be an n-place function where $Aggregate: \mathcal{A} \times .. \times \mathcal{A} \mapsto \mathcal{A}$. We call $Aggregate$ an aggregation function. We describe $Aggregate(\geq_1, .., \geq_n)$ as an aggregated preference relation of $(\geq_1, .., \geq_n)$, and define $Aggregate$ so that $Aggregate(\geq_1, .., \geq_n)$ is a preference relation. Hence an aggregated preference relation is at least a pre-ordering over $\wp(Naive(\Delta))$.

There are many possible definitions for $Aggregate$ that are of interest. For example, let $Aggregate$ be such that the preference relation $\geq_{ok}$ is defined as follows: For $X, Y \in \wp(Naive(\Delta))$,

$$X \geq_{ok} Y \text{ iff } X \geq_{spc} Y \text{ and } X \geq_{con} Y$$

For example, for $\Delta = \{i : \alpha, j : \neg\alpha, \ p : \neg\alpha \to \beta, q : \alpha \to \neg\beta\}$, $Naive(\Delta) = \{i : \alpha, j : \neg\alpha, i \oplus q : \neg\beta, j \oplus p : \beta\}$, and $Top(Naive(\Delta), \geq_{ok}) = \{\{i : \alpha, i \oplus q : \neg\beta\}, \{j : \neg\alpha, j \oplus p : \beta\}, \{i : \alpha\}, \{j : \neg\alpha\}\}$.

A set of "most preferred" naive inferences, according to a preference relation is considered an "extension" of a structured database. It is called a set of global inferences, since it is identified by taking global considerations into account. The set of all sets of most preferred naive inferences according to a preference relation from $Naive(\Delta)$ is denoted $Global(\Delta)$. There are many possible defintions for $Global$ that are of interest. For example, we could let $Global(\Delta) = Top(Naive(\Delta), \geq_x))$. So if $Top(Naive(\Delta), \geq_x) = \emptyset$, then there is no set of preferred naive inferences. A more skeptical variant is to let $Global(\Delta) = \bigcap Top(Naive(\Delta), \geq_x)$. Another skeptical option is letting $Global(\Delta) = Top(Naive(\Delta), \geq_x)$ if $Top(Naive(\Delta), \geq_x)$ is a singleton set, and letting $Global(\Delta) = \emptyset$ otherwise. For most definitions of $Global$, it seems desirable that all elements of $Global(\Delta)$ are classically consistent.

Once we have accepted a definition for $Global(\Delta)$, then we can identify the global inferences - the most preferred inferences - from Δ. For this we adopt a class of consequence relations $\mid\sim_i$ defined as follows, where $\alpha \in \mathcal{B}$,

$$\Delta \mid\sim_i \alpha \text{ iff } \exists \Phi \in Global(\Delta)$$
$$\text{such that } Form(\Phi) \vdash \alpha$$

Even though we do have a number of choices about how to pick preferred sets of naive inferences from $Naive(\Delta)$, a preference relation does allow us to compare candidates systematically.

5 INFLUENCE RELATIONS

We now consider how we can further use the structural information in the labels to differentiate subsets of $Naive(\Delta)$. For this we define another type of reflexive relation, termed an influence relation, that compares pairs of complex labels. Since the complex label carries a record of the proof of a naive inference, influence relations compare proofs. We use influence relations to define further interesting preference relations.

The following axioms, hold of a number of interesting influence relations $\geq_y$ we consider. For $i, j, \in \Lambda$, and for $p, q \in Tree(\Lambda)$, where $AtomicLabels(p) = \{i_1, \cdots, i_n\}$ and $AtomicLabels(q) = \{j_1, \cdots, j_m\}$

$$\sigma(i) \geq \sigma(j) \text{ iff } i \geq_y j$$

$$p =_y q \text{ iff } \sigma(i_1) = \sigma(j_1) \text{ and } \cdots \text{ and } \sigma(i_n) = \sigma(j_m)$$

We can also extend the axiomatization of the $\oplus$ operator in various ways. For example we can restrict the database so that $(\Omega, \geq)$ is a distributive lattice. If the lattice is distributive, it is guaranteed that there is a greatest lower bound in the lattice for every i and j in the lattice. Hence an influence relation for such a database can be defined in terms of the distributive lattice by as follows. For $p, q \in Tree(\Lambda)$, where $AtomicLabels(p) = \{i_1, \cdots, i_n\}$ $AtomicLabels(q) = \{j_1, \cdots, j_m\}$

$$p \geq_y q \text{ iff } \sigma(i_1) \wedge \cdots \wedge \sigma(i_n) \geq \sigma(j_1) \wedge \cdots \wedge \sigma(j_m)$$

Such an influence relation has application in capturing in the framework variants of default logic such as graded default logic (Froidevaux 1990). Other alternatives include restricting the database to a total ordering, and then defining an algebra $(Tree(\Lambda), \geq_y)$ that is a lexicographic ordering.

6 STRONGFORWARD LOGICS

Here, we consider a particular form of non-monotonic reasoning, namely strongforward reasoning, using a class of prioritized logics, called strongforward logics. In strongforward reasoning arguments 'for' and 'against' each inference are identified.

Informally, a naive inference $i : \alpha$ is a strongforward inference if and only if each subproof of $i : \alpha$ is a strongforward naive inference, and for all inferences $j : \neg \alpha$ that have all their subproofs as strongforward inferences, the rule with head α must have a label preferred to the label on the rule with head $\neg \alpha$. There are a number of closely related variants of this approach, but essentially strongforward reasoning involves assuming that once a formula is a strongforward inference, it is non-defeasible, and that it can then be used for further forward-chaining reasoning. Obviously, when the database is updated, then all inferences need to be re-inferred.

6.1 Argumentation

Argumentation naturally fits into the prioritized logics framework. A naive inference $i : \alpha$ is an argument for α, where the label i is the justification, and influence relations capture notions of preference between arguments. In this way arguments "for" and "against" a conclusion can be compared in order to determine whether the conclusion is valid.

In the following, we consider two types of influence relation, namely "conflicts" and "defeats". Both types are non-transitive binary relations over complex labels.

- The conflicts type of influence relation captures pairwise preference for one complex relation over another, without reference to any other complex relations under consideration.
- The defeats type of influence relation captures pairwise preference for one complex relation over another, with reference to all other complex relations under consideration.

In the remainder of this section we define a particular conflicts influence relation and a particular defeats influence relation, and use them to define the strongforward preference relation.

6.2 The conflict influence relation

There are a number of intuitive ways we can use this framework to capture forms of defeat. Loosely, a naive inference $i : \alpha$ conflicts with $j : \neg \alpha$, if the proof j is not strictly preferred to the proof of i, when only considering the information contained in i and j. Let $Z \subseteq Naive(\Delta)$. Let $conflict_Z$ be the smallest set such that for all $i, j \in Tree(\Lambda)$.

$(i,j) \in conflict_Z$ iff $\quad \exists i : \alpha \in Z$ and $\exists j : \beta \in Z$
and $Lastlabel(i) = p$
and $Lastlabel(j) = q$
and $\sigma(q) \not> \sigma(p)$

Essentially, the $conflict$ influence relation captures the pairwise preference of conflicting arguments on the basis of the last step taken in their respective proofs.

6.3 The defeat influence relation

For $X, Y \subseteq \wp(Naive(\Delta))$, we say $i \ defeats_{(X,Y)} \ j$, if i conflicts with j and i is not defeated itself, when taking the defence of Y into account. Let $Z = X \cup Y$. Also let $defeat_{(X,Y)} = defeat_{(Y,X)}$.

$(i,j) \in defeat_{(X,Y)}$ iff $\quad (i,j) \in conflict_Z$ and
$\forall p : \beta \in Step_\Delta(i)$
$\forall q : \neg \beta \in Defence_\Delta(Y)$
[if $i \in Labels(X)$ then
$(q,p) \notin defeat_{(X,Y)}]$

where $Defence_\Delta(Y) = Y \cup \{v \oplus x : \neg \delta, w \oplus y : \delta \in Naive(\Delta) \mid v : \phi, w : \psi \in Y$ and $[\sigma(x) = \sigma(y)$ or $\sigma(x) \| \sigma(y)]\}$.

Essentially, a conflict between some $i : \alpha \in X$ and some $j : \neg \alpha \in Y$ causes a defeat if one of the following three situations occurs: (1) there is a strict preference for the last step of i over the last step of j, and i is not defeated by the defence for Y; (2) there is another naive proof in X, say $k : \beta$ that defeats a subproof of j, and k is not defeated by the defence for Y; or (3) there is a pair of defeasible rules, say $x : \phi \to \delta$ and

$y : \psi \rightarrow \neg \delta$ in Δ such that x is equally preferred to y, or x is incomparable with y, and there are naive inferences $v : \phi$ and $w : \psi$ in X, and either $v \oplus x$, or $w \oplus y$, defeats a subproof of j without being defeated by the defence for Y.

The third case is when the naive arguments $v \oplus x : \delta$ and $w \oplus y : \neg \delta$ are only defeated by each other. So even though neither can be in the more preferred set of naive inferences, they can defeat other naive inferences.

[Example 1] Let $\Delta = \{i : \alpha, j : \neg \alpha, p : \neg \alpha \rightarrow \neg \beta, q : \alpha \rightarrow \beta\}$, where $\sigma(i) > \sigma(j)$ and $\sigma(p) > \sigma(q)$. So $Naive(\Delta) = \{i : \alpha, j : \neg \alpha, i \oplus q : \beta, j \oplus p : \neg \beta\}$, $conflict_{Naive(\Delta)} = \{(i,j),(j \oplus p, i \oplus q)\}$. Let $X = \{i : \alpha, i \oplus q : \beta\}$, and $Y = \{j : \neg \alpha, j \oplus p : \neg \beta\}$. From this, we obtain $defeat_{(X,Y)} = \{(i,j)\}$.

[Example 2] Let $\Delta = \{i : \alpha, j : \neg \alpha, p : \neg \alpha \rightarrow \neg \beta, q : \alpha \rightarrow \beta, r : \beta \rightarrow \gamma, s : \neg \beta \rightarrow \neg \gamma\}$, where $\sigma(i) > \sigma(j)$ and $\sigma(p) > \sigma(q)$. So $Naive(\Delta) = \{i : \alpha, i \oplus q : \beta, i \oplus q \oplus r : \gamma, j : \neg \alpha, j \oplus p : \neg \beta, j \oplus p \oplus s : \neg \gamma\}$, and $conflict_{Naive(\Delta)} = \{(i,j),(j \oplus p, i \oplus q)(i \oplus q \oplus r, j \oplus p \oplus s)\}$. Let $X = \{i : \alpha, i \oplus q : \beta, i \oplus q \oplus r : \gamma\}$, and $Y = \{j : \neg \alpha, j \oplus p : \neg \beta, j \oplus p \oplus s : \neg \gamma\}$. From this, we obtain $defeat_{(X,Y)} = \{(i,j), (i \oplus q \oplus r, j \oplus p \oplus s)\}$.

[Example 3] Let $\Delta = \{i : \neg \alpha \rightarrow \beta, j : \neg \beta, k : \neg \alpha\}$. Then $Naive(\Delta) = \{k : \neg \alpha, j : \neg \beta, k \oplus i : \beta\}$, and $conflict_{Naive(\Delta)} = \{(k \oplus i, j)\}$. Let $X = \{k : \neg \alpha, k \oplus i : \beta\}$, and $Y = \{j : \neg \beta\}$. From this we obtain $defeat_{(X,Y)} = \{(k \oplus i, j)\}$.

[Example 4] Let $\Delta = \{i : \alpha, j : \neg \alpha\}$, where $\sigma(i) \| \sigma(j)$. So $Naive(\Delta) = \{i : \alpha, j : \neg \alpha\}$, $conflict_{Naive(\Delta)} = \{(i,j),(j,i)\}$. Let $X = \{i : \alpha\}$, and $\{j : \neg \alpha\}$, then $defeat_{(X,Y)} = \{(i,j),(j,i)\}$.

[Example 5] Let $\Delta = \{i : \alpha \rightarrow \alpha, j : \alpha\}$, where $\sigma(i) > \sigma(j)$. So $Naive(\Delta) = \{j : \alpha, j \oplus i : \alpha, j \oplus i \oplus i : \alpha, \cdots\}$, and $conflict_{Naive(\Delta)} = \{\}$.

For some examples of databases there is a cycle in the $defeat_{(X,Y)}$ relation, so that when defeat is propagated through subproofs, a formula eventually conflicts with itself.

[Example 6] Let $\Delta = \{i : \neg \alpha \rightarrow \alpha, j : \neg \alpha\}$, where $\sigma(i) > \sigma(j)$. So $Naive(\Delta) = \{j : \neg \alpha, j \oplus i : \alpha\}$, where $conflict_{Naive(\Delta)} = \{(j \oplus i, j)\}$. Let $X = \{j : \neg \alpha\}$, and $Y = \{j \oplus i : \alpha\}$. Then $(j \oplus i, j) \in defeat_{(X,Y)}$.

[Example 7] Let $\Delta = \{i : \neg \beta \rightarrow \alpha, j : \neg \alpha, p : \neg \alpha \rightarrow \beta, q : \neg \beta\}$, where $\sigma(i) > \sigma(j)$ and $\sigma(p) > \sigma(q)$. So $Naive(\Delta) = \{q \oplus i : \alpha, j : \neg \alpha, j \oplus p : \beta, q : \neg \beta\}$, and $conflict_{Naive(\Delta)} = \{(j \oplus p, q),(q \oplus i, j)\}$. Let $X = \{j : \neg \alpha, j \oplus : \beta\}$, and $Y = \{q : \neg \beta, i \oplus q : \alpha\}$. From this, $(j \oplus p, q) \in defeat_{(X,Y)}$ if and only if $(q \oplus i, j) \in defeat_{(X,Y)}$.

In the next section, we will show how the definition for our preference relations obviates problems raised by examples such as 6 and 7 above.

6.4 The defeat preference relation

First we define the notion of defeatfree. For this we make a restriction to simplify our exposition. Let $X, Y \in \wp(Naive(\Delta))$ such that X and Y are consistent and sub-proof complete.

X is defeatfree iff
$$\forall Y \in \wp(Naive(\Delta))$$
$$\forall i : \alpha \in X \; \forall j : \neg \beta \in Y[(j,i) \notin defeats_{(Y,X)}]$$

Using this, we define the defeat preference relation, denoted $\geq_{defeat}$, as follows,

$$X \geq_{defeat} Y \text{ iff X is defeatfree}$$

[Example 1 cont'd] Let $X = \{i : \alpha, i \oplus q : \beta\}$, and $Y = \{j : \neg \alpha, j \oplus p : \neg \beta\}$, then $X >_{defeat} Y$.

[Example 2 cont'd] Let $X = \{i : \alpha, i \oplus q : \beta, i \oplus q \oplus r : \gamma\}$ and $Y = \{j : \neg \alpha, j \oplus p : \neg \beta, j \oplus p \oplus s : \neg \gamma\}$, then $X >_{defeat} Y$.

[Example 3 cont'd] Let $X = \{k : \neg \alpha, k \oplus i : \beta\}$, and $Y = \{j : \neg \beta\}$, then $X >_{defeat} Y$.

[Example 4 cont'd] No subsets X, Y such that X and Y are consistent, subproof-complete, and $X \geq_{defeat} Y$.

[Example 5 cont'd] $Top(Naive(\Delta)), \geq_{defeat}) = \wp(Naive(\Delta))$.

[Example 6 cont'd] Only $\{j : \neg \alpha\}$ is consistent and subproof-complete.

[Example 7 cont'd] No subsets X, Y such that X is consistent, subproof-complete, and $X \geq_{defeat} Y$.

6.5 The strongforward preference relation

We now use the $\geq_{defeat}$ preference relation in an example of an aggregated preference relation called the strongforward preference relation, denoted $\geq_{sf}$, where $X, Y \in \wp(Naive(\Delta))$.

$X \geq_{sf} Y$ if $X >_{ok} Y$

$X \geq_{sf} Y$ if $X \geq_{ok} Y$ and $X >_{defeat} Y$

$X \geq_{sf} Y$ if $X \geq_{ok} Y$ and $X \approx_{defeat} Y$ and $Y \subseteq X$

When a set of naive inferences, say Φ, is a member of $Top(Naive(\Delta), \geq_{sf})$, then Φ, is a self-contained set of consistent naive inferences that is subproof-complete and defeatfree. Being defeatfree means that for any conflict between Φ and any other set of subproof-complete and consistent naive inferences, say Ψ, the conflict does not result in a defeat for Φ.

In the strongforward preference relation, we consider subproof-completeness and consistency as being essential pre-requisites to argumentation. The preference relation $\geq_{defeat}$ is where the comparison based on the respective proofs is undertaken.

6.6 The strongforward consequence relation

We now assume the definition for the class of consequence relations $\mathrel{\mid\!\sim}_i$ given earlier. We define the strongforward consequence relation $\mathrel{\mid\!\sim}_{sf}$ by letting i be sf and letting $Global(\Delta) = Top(Naive(\Delta), \geq_{sf})$.

[Example 1 cont'd] $\Delta \mathrel{\mid\!\sim}_{sf} \alpha$, $\Delta \mathrel{\mid\!\sim}_{sf} \beta$.

[Example 2 cont'd] $\Delta \mathrel{\mid\!\sim}_{sf} \alpha$, $\Delta \mathrel{\mid\!\sim}_{sf} \beta$, $\Delta \mathrel{\mid\!\sim}_{sf} \gamma$.

[Example 3 cont'd] $\Delta \mathrel{\mid\!\sim}_{sf} \neg\alpha$, $\Delta \mathrel{\mid\!\sim}_{sf} \beta$.

[Example 4 cont'd] There are no $\mathrel{\mid\!\sim}_{sf}$ inferences.

[Example 5 cont'd] $\Delta \mathrel{\mid\!\sim}_{sf} \alpha$.

[Example 6 cont'd] $\Delta \mathrel{\mid\!\sim}_{sf} \neg\alpha$.

[Example 7 cont'd] There are no $\mathrel{\mid\!\sim}_{sf}$ inferences.

Later, we show how a variety of non-monotonic proof theories can be captured by the strongforward consequence relation when using appropriate rewrites of data in these proof theories into structured databases.

6.7 Fixpoint definition of strongforward

In order to further characterize strongforward reasoning, we consider a fixpoint definition. We will show equivalences between the two types of definition.

Let Δ be a structured database. We define Δ as a restricted database iff for all $i : \beta \to \alpha \in \Delta$, α is a literal. We define the strongforward consequence function T_Δ as follows, where Δ is a restricted database. Let $T_\Delta : \wp(\mathcal{B}) \mapsto \wp(\mathcal{B})$, and let $X \in \wp(\mathcal{B})$,

$$T_\Delta(X) = \{\alpha \mid \exists i[proposed(\Delta, X, i, \alpha) \text{ and } unchallenged(\Delta, X, i, \alpha)]\}$$

where

$proposed(\Delta, X, i, \alpha)$ iff $\exists i : \beta \to \alpha \in \Delta$ and $X \vdash \beta$

$unchallenged(\Delta, X, i, \alpha)$
  iff $\forall j : \gamma \to \neg\alpha \in \Delta$,
    $[[\sigma(i) > \sigma(j)]$ or $undercut(\Delta, X, \gamma)]$

$undercut(\Delta, X, \gamma)$
  iff $\forall k : \gamma \in Naive(\Delta)$
    (1)$X \vdash \neg\gamma$
    or (2)$\forall l : \delta \to \gamma \in \Delta\ undercut(\Delta, X, \delta)$
    or (3)$equivocates(\Delta, X, \gamma)$

$equivocates(\Delta, X, \gamma)$ iff
  (1)$proposed(\Delta, X, p, \gamma)$
  and (2)$proposed(\Delta, X, q, \neg\gamma)$
  and (3)$\sigma(p) = \sigma(q)$ or $\sigma(p) \| \sigma(q)$
  and (4)$\forall x : \tau \to \gamma \in \Delta$
    if $\sigma(x) > \sigma(y)$
    then $undercut(\Delta, X, \tau)$
  and (5)$\forall x : \tau \to \neg\gamma \in \Delta$
    if $\sigma(x) > \sigma(y)$
    then $undercut(\Delta, X, \tau)$

Essentially *proposed* ensures that the subproofs for each strongforward inference are strongforward inferences, and *unchallenged* ensures that each counterargument for each proposed inference is either rebutted or undercut. Rebutted is just strict preference for the laststep in the proposed naive argument. Undercut captures the situations where the subproofs for the counterargument are defeated.

6.8 Fixpoint properties

Let F be a function $F : \wp(S) \mapsto \wp(S)$. F is monotonic when for all $X, Y \in \wp(S)$, $X \subseteq Y$ implies $F(X) \subseteq F(Y)$. F is non-inverting when for all $X, Y \in \wp(S)$, $X \subseteq Y$ implies $F(Y) \not\subset F(X)$. F is inflationary when for all $X \in \wp(S)$, $X \subseteq F(X)$. Clearly, T_Δ is inflationary and non-inverting, but not monotonic.

Lemma 1 *For all restricted databases Δ, the function T_Δ is decidable.*

Let F be a function $F : \wp(S) \mapsto \wp(S)$, and let $Fixpoints$ be a function $Fixpoints : ((\wp(S) \mapsto \wp(S)) \mapsto \wp(S))$, where $Fixpoints(F) = \{X \mid F(X) = X\}$. X is a least fixpoint of F iff $X \in Fixpoint(F)$ and $\neg\exists Y \in Fixpoint(F)$ such that $Y \subset X$. Clearly, it is not the case that for any Δ, the function T_Δ has a least fixpoint.

Let an indexed function $F^1(X)$ equal $F(X)$, and let an indexed function $F^{n+1}(X)$ equal $F(F^n(X))$. A normal fixpoint of a function F is a fixpoint that is defined by $F^n(\emptyset)$, where $n \in \mathbb{N}$. Clearly, for all restricted databases Δ, the normal fixpoint of the function T_Δ is unique and computable. In addition, if X is the normal fixpoint of T_Δ, then, there is no $Y \in Fixpoint(F)$ such that $Y \subset X$. In other words, the normal fixpoint of T_Δ is a minimal fixpoint.

Lemma 2 *For all $X \in \wp(\mathcal{B})$, and for all restricted databases Δ, if $X \not\vdash \bot$, then $T_\Delta(X) \not\vdash \bot$.*

Lemma 3 *For all restricted databases Δ, for all i such that $T_\Delta^n(\emptyset)$ and $0 \leq i \leq n$, there is a $\Phi \subseteq Naive(\Delta)$ such that $Form(\Phi) = T_\Delta^i(\emptyset)$, and Φ is subproof-complete and defeatfree.*

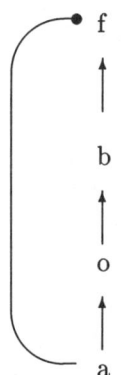

Figure 1: An Inheritance Hierarchy

Theorem 4 *For all restricted databases Δ, if X is a normal fixpoint of T_Δ, and $Top(Naive(\Delta), \geq_{sf}) = \{\Phi\}$, then $Form(\Phi) = X$.*

The strongforward preference relation can be considered as providing a declarative perspective on strongforward reasoning, whereas the strongforward consequence function provides an operational perspective. The above result shows that these two perspectives are equivalent for restricted databases.

7 FRAMEWORK EXAMPLES

In this section we show how a variety of approaches to non-monotonic proof theory can be captured as prioritized logics.

7.1 Inheritance hierarchies

We consider approaches for inheritance hierachies (IHS) - variants including credulous (influenced by Touretzky 1986), skeptical (Horty 1987), ideally skeptical (Stein 1989), and ambiguity propagating (Stein 1989).

For inheritance hierarchies, a database is a set of rules H, where all elements of H are of the form $x \to y$ or $x \operatorname{-\bullet} y$. We assume that H constitutes an acyclic graph. A positive path in H is defined inductively: (1) A rule $x \to y \in H$ is a positive path in H; and (2) if $x_1 \to \cdots \to x_n$ is a positive path, and $x_n \to x_{n+1} \in H$, then $x_1 \to \cdots \to x_n \to x_{n+1}$ is a positive path in H. A negative path in H is defined inductively: (1) A rule $x \operatorname{-\bullet} y \in H$ is a negative path in H; and (2) if $x_1 \to \cdots \to x_n$ is a positive path, and $x \operatorname{-\bullet} y \in H$, then $x_1 \to \cdots \to x_n \operatorname{-\bullet} y$ is a negative path in H. Each x_i in a path corresponds to a node in the graph, and each $\to$ corresponds to an arc. For example, consider Figure 1.

For any inheritance hierarchy database (H, I), where H is a set of rules and I is an individual, the reasoning from (H, I) is such that an "acceptable" path from an individual to a class holds, then the class proposition is a conclusion of (H, I).

The simplest form of IHS is the credulous version of IHS, denoted $\vdash_1$, that can be defined as follows, where α is a positive literal and β is any literal: (1) $(H, I) \vdash_1 \alpha$ iff $[(\alpha \in I)$ or $[(\beta \in I)$ and $(\beta \to \cdots \to \alpha$ is a positive path in $H \cup I)]]$; and (2) $(H, I) \vdash_1 \neg\alpha$ iff $[(\neg\alpha \in I)$ or $[(\beta \in I)$ and $(\beta \to \cdots \operatorname{-\bullet}\alpha$ is a negative path in $H \cup I)]]$. So acceptable paths from I to a class are defined in terms of positive paths and negative paths.

We form a structured database Δ from H as follows: For each rule $x \to y \in H$, we have a clause $i : x \to y$ in Δ, and for each rule $x \operatorname{-\bullet} y$, we have a clause $i : x \to \neg y$ in Δ. Each clause in H is labelled uniquely.

The inheritance hierarchy database for the example in Figure 1 is $\{a \to o, o \to b, b \to f, o \operatorname{-\bullet} f\}$. From this database, we form the following structured database $\{i_1 : a \to o, i_2 : o \to b, i_3 : b \to f, i_4 : o \to \neg f\}$.

For capturing this approach to IHS, we require the following aggregated preference relation, denoted $\geq_{credulous}$. For $X, Y \in \wp(Naive(\Delta))$,

$$X \geq_{credulous} Y \text{ iff } X >_{ok} Y$$
$$X \geq_{credulous} Y \text{ iff } X \approx_{ok} Y \text{ and } Y \subseteq X$$

If we let $Global(\Delta) = Top(\Delta, \geq_{credulous})$, then we can capture the credulous version of IHS by the corresponding $\mathrel{|\!\sim}_i$ consequence relation, which we denote $\mathrel{|\!\sim}_1$.

Theorem 5 *For any literal α, the following equivalence holds, where Δ is the structured database formed from (H,I) according to the above rewrite, then $(H,I) \vdash_1 \alpha$ holds if and only if $\Delta \mathrel{|\!\sim}_1 \alpha$ holds.*

We now consider the skeptical version of inheritance hierachies (Horty 1987). Here an acceptable path is defined in terms of permissible paths. A permissible path π is a positive or negative path from an individual to a class where no node in the path is defeated. Intuitively, for two rules in an inheritance hierarchy that enter into the same node, there is a preference for the rule that eminates from the more specialized sub-class. A node is defeated if no node is defeated in the positive path to the node from the preferred rule.

The consequence relation, denoted $\vdash_2$, is defined as follows, where α is a positive literal and β is any literal: (1) $(H, I) \vdash_2 \alpha$ iff $[(\alpha \in I)$ or $[(\beta \in I)$ and $(\beta \to \cdots \to \alpha$ is a permissible path in $H \cup I)]$; (2) $(H, I) \vdash_2 \neg\alpha$ iff $(\neg\alpha \in I)$ or $[(\beta \in I)$ and $(\beta \to \cdots \operatorname{-\bullet}\alpha$ is a permissible path in $H \cup I)]$

To capture this version in prioritized logics, we order the defeasible rules as follows: For any pair of clauses

$i : \alpha \to \beta$, $i : \gamma \to \delta$ in Δ, if β and δ are complements, or $\beta = \delta$, and $x_1 \to \cdots \to x_n$ is a positive path in i, then i > j holds.

Returning to the example in Figure 1, this gives the following ordering: σ is the identity map, and all labels are incomparable except $i_4 > i_3$.

The following result shows we can capture this consequence relation using the strongforward consequence relation.

Theorem 6 *For any literal α, the following equivalence holds, where Δ is the database formed from (H,I) according to the above rewrite, and $\hspace{-0.2em}\sim$ is the strongforward consequence relation, then $(H,I) \vdash_2 \alpha$ holds if and only if $\Delta \hspace{-0.2em}\sim \alpha$ holds.*

Whilst the skeptical approach to IHS has been well-motivated, it has been criticized as being counter-intuitive in certain cases. An interesting alternative is ideally skeptical inheritance (Stein 1989). We can capture it directly as a prioritized logic by defining an extension as $Global(\Delta) = \bigcap Top(Naive(\Delta), \geq_{credulous})$. A more cautious alternative is ambiguity propagating inheritance (Stein 1989). If we let Φ denote $\bigcap Top(Naive(\Delta), \geq_{credulous})$, then we can define an extension in the ambiguity propagating approach as $Global(\Delta) = Top(\wp(\Phi), \geq_{spc})$.

An immediate benefit of viewing IHS definitions as prioritized logics is we can view an inheritance hierarchy as a logic database. Furthermore, it opens the possibility of generalizing these approaches to allowing any formulae, as opposed to atoms, at nodes in the hierarchies.

7.2 Ordered logic

Ordered logic is conceptually influenced by object-oriented programming languages. It can also be viewed as a generalization of the approach of inheritance hierarchy systems.

Ordered logic is based on a partially ordered structure of logical theories termed objects. An object is a finite set of rules of the form $B \to \alpha$ where B is a finite set of literals, and α is a literal. B is the antecedent and α is the consequent. A knowledgebase is a tuple $\Delta_K = (O, \leq_\kappa, R, \kappa)$ where $(O, \leq_\kappa)$ is a poset of objects, R is a finite set of rules, and $\kappa : O \mapsto \wp(R)$ is a function assigning a set of rules to each object.

The rules and facts that are explicitly represented at an object do not constitute the entire knowledge about an object. A specificity relation (i.e. $\leq_\kappa$) defined on the objects allows for proof rules to infer knowledge at an object on the basis of knowledge higher in the ordering. In particular, the notion of inheritance is supported by allowing knowledge to filter from a higher object to a lower object. Inheritance may be blocked by either being (1) "overruled" by more specific information, that is contradictory, at the lower object; or (2) "defeat" which occurs when an object i inherits contradictory information from two different objects p and q such that there is no preference for one of the objects over the other.

The proof theory is defined in terms of the conclusions that can be proven to hold or proven to not hold at each object. The ordered logic consequence relation $|\!\prec$ is defined as the conclusions that can be proven at the most preferred object.

For example if $\Delta_K = (O, \leq_k, \{\{\beta\} \to \alpha, \{\} \to \neg\alpha, \{\} \to \beta\}, \{(o_1, \{\beta\} \to \alpha), (o_2, \{\} \to \neg\alpha), (o_3, \{\} \to \beta)\})$, where $\{o_1, o_2, o_3\} \subseteq O$, and $o_1 <_k o_2$, and $o_2 <_k o_3$ hold, we can make the inferences $\Delta_K |\!\prec \alpha$ and $\Delta_K |\!\prec \beta$.

For a prioritized logic formulation of ordered logic knowledgebase $\Delta_K = (O, \leq_\kappa, R, \kappa)$, we associate a set of labels for each object $o_i \in O$. Hence for all ordered logic rules $\{\beta_1, \cdots, \beta_i\} \to \alpha \in \kappa(o_i)$, the database rewrite gives formulae of the form $j : \beta_1 \wedge .. \wedge \beta_i \to \alpha \in \Delta$, where j is a unique label, and the function σ defined as $\sigma(j) = o_i$. For the ordering, if $\sigma(i_1) = o_1$ and $\sigma(i_2) = o_2$, and $o_1 \leq_k o_2$, then $\sigma(i_1) \geq \sigma(i_2)$.

For the above example of Δ_K, then $\Delta = \{i_1 : \beta \to \alpha, i_2 : \neg\beta, i_3 : \beta\}$, where $\sigma(i_x) = o_x$, $i_1 > i_2$ and $i_2 > i_3$.

Theorem 7 *For all ordered logic knowledgebases Δ_K, and all ground literals α, if the prioritized logic formulation of Δ_k is Δ, then the following equivalence holds:*

$$\Delta_K |\!\prec \alpha \text{ iff } \Delta \hspace{-0.2em}\sim_{sf} \alpha$$

Negation-as-failure has been shown to be a special case of ordered logic. For all positive literals used in the language for a logic program, a set of negative literals can be formed. An ordered logic knowledgebase is formed by associating the logic program with a more preferred object than the set of negative literals.

7.3 LDR

Defeasible logics such as LDR (Nute 1988) can also be modelled by strongforward reasoning by rewriting each LDR formula as a defeasible rule. The language of LDR is composed of a set of atoms, and the connectives $\{\neg, \Rightarrow, \to, \rightsquigarrow, \wedge\}$. Clauses are formed as follows, where β is a conjunct of literals, and α is a literal: (1) $\beta \to \alpha$ is an absolute rule; (2) $\beta \Rightarrow \alpha$ is a defeasible rule; and (3) $\beta \rightsquigarrow \alpha$ is a defeater rule.

An absolute rule cannot be defeated, and the consequent can be inferred when the antecedent is satisfied. For a defeasible rule, the consequent can be inferred when the antecedent is satisfied, and the rule is not defeated. It is defeated when: (1) the complement of the consequent is inferred from an absolute rule; or (2) the complement of the consequent is inferred from a more specific defeasible rule; or (3) there is a more specific defeater rule that has its antecedent satisfied, and has a consequent that is the complement of the defeasible rule. The defeater rules do not give inferences - they can only defeat defeasible inferences.

The specifcity ordering is determined from the antecedents of the defeasible and defeater rules: If the antecedent to one rule can be used in conjunction with the remainder of the database - i.e. the database minus the two competing rules - to prove the antecedent of the other rule, but not vice versa, then that rule is more specific.

We rewrite an LDR database as a structured database by replacing the connectives $\{\Rightarrow, \rightarrow, \leadsto\}$ with the prioritized logic $\rightarrow$ connective. Furthermore for each defeater rule, of the form $\beta_1 \wedge \cdots \wedge \beta_n \leadsto \alpha$ we provide two formulae:

$$i : \beta_1 \wedge \cdots \wedge \beta_n \rightarrow \alpha$$
$$j : \beta_1 \wedge \cdots \wedge \beta_n \rightarrow \neg\alpha$$

We then order the absolute rules so that they are the most-preferred formulae, and order the other rules according to the specificity of the antecedent. The LDR consequence relation can then be directly reflected by the strongforward consequence relation.

8 FRAMEWORK ISSUES

In the previous section, we illustrated the use of prioritized logics as a framework for non-monotonic proof theories. Elsewhere we have shown how negation-as-failure (Reiter 1978), default logic (Reiter 1980), prioritized default logic (Brewka 1989), graded default logic (Froidevaux 1990), and Theorist (Poole 1988) can be characterized in terms of priorities (Hunter 1992, 1994). We now consider the relationship of the framework to frameworks based on argumentation, model-theory, and belief revision.

8.1 Argumentation frameworks

Argument systems (including Borgida 1984, Loui 1986, Pollock 1987, Simari 1992, Benferhat 1993, Dung 1993, Elvang 1993a, 1993b) can be viewed as frameworks for non-monotonic logics. Furthermore, selecting preferred arguments in some argument system can be reflected directly in some prioritized logic by defining appropriate preference relations.

In the committee-based approach to argument systems (Borgida 1984), a committee C arrives at some conclusion α according to some protocol. The simplest class of protocols is when members of C do not communicate - so some protocols could be: (1) all members support α; (2) at least one member supports α; and (3) at least one member supports α, and no one opposes α

- i.e $\neg\alpha$. More complex protocols include unanimity and democracy. Obviously the committee-based approach can be naturally captured by prioritized logics. We return to this in the section 9.

The work on prioirtized logics presented here complements the algebra of arguments (Simari 1992), which provides a framework of operations that can be defined on arguments. It also complements the theory of acceptability of arguments (Dung 1993) which describes an argument μ as acceptable for an agent Θ if Θ can defend μ from all attacks on μ. Using this basic notion of acceptable, the theory of acceptability incorporates different classes of extension. These different classes of extension can be used to characterize different types of non-monotonic reasoning. However, neither the algebra of arguments nor the theory of acceptability focus on the notion of priority in data or proofs.

8.2 Model-theoretic frameworks

Preference plays a central role in the KLM framework (Kraus 1990) where there is an ordering over possible worlds in the semantics. This ordering is induced by the contraints of satisfying all of the set of the conditional assertions in the database. It is a very weak notion of preference since the logics support no proof-theoretic or semantic means of selecting one inference over another. Though there is the extra-logical option of selecting the conditional assertion with the most specific premises.

However, if we equate the KLM notation for a defeasible rule $\alpha \mathrel{|\!\sim} \beta$ with our notation for a defeasible rule $\alpha \rightarrow \beta$, then the proof theory for manipulating the defeasible rules in KLM is richer then the naive proof theory given above since inference rules such as Or are available.

Another model-theoretic framework characterizing preference is the generalized framework for prioritization (Grosof 1991) that is based on model-minimization. Whilst, it is possible to define "semantics" for indivdual prioritized logics that are based on preferred classical models (by mirroring the proof-theory in the semantics), it is not evident that such semantics are based on notions of model-minimization. Indeed for certain logics it is straightforward to show the contrary. However, the identification of a prioritized logic as the counterpart to the model-theoretic approach of ordered theory presentations (Ryan 1992) does constitute an interesting question.

8.3 Belief-revision frameworks

Explicit ordering has also been used as a means by which formulae can be selected in belief revision (Gardenfors 1988). Whilst the spirit of using prioritiy overlaps with that of prioritized logics, the constraints on the priorities and the means by which the priorities are used creates a significantly different reasoning system to the prioritized logics presented here (Hunter 1994).

Closer to the prioritized logics presented here are the techniques proposed for management of preferences in assumption-based reasoning (Cayrol 1992) where preferences over formulae are used by a system based on voting theory to select a maximally preferred set of inferences. In essence, prioritized logics involve reasoning 'classically' with all the database and then using the priorities to select preferred inferences, whereas the approach of Cayrol *et al* involves using the priorities to select preferred data, and then reasoning classically with the data to the preferred inferences.

9 AGGREGATION PRINCIPLES

As an example of the kind of formal analysis that is facilitated by viewing non-monotonic logics in terms of priorities, we consider the aggregation principles of Doyle and Wellman (1991) proposed for non-monotonic reasoning. These aggregation principles are analogues of Arrow's social choice principles, and were posited as desiderata for aggregating preferences in non-monotonic reasoning.

However, they showed that for $(\geq_1, .., \geq_n)$, if the number of alternatives is greater than 2, and each $\geq_i$ in $(\geq_1, .., \geq_n)$ is a total pre-order, then there is no aggregation function g such that $g(\geq_1, .., \geq_n)$ is a total pre-order over the alternatives and $g(\geq_1, .., \geq_n)$ satisfies their aggregation principles.

We do not believe that, in general, the ordering over $\wp(Naive(\Delta))$ should be total and therefore do not regard their negative result as undermining the argument for using preferences in non-monotonic reasoning. However, we do believe that aggregation principles are of interest, and present the following, where $\geq_x$ be defined by $Aggregate(\geq_1, .., \geq_n)$, and $\geq_i$ and $\geq_j$ are in $(\geq_1, .., \geq_n)$.

(**Collective rationality**) The preference relation $Aggregate(\geq_1, .., \geq_n)$ is a function of the individual preference relations $(\geq_1, .., \geq_n)$.

(**Independence of irrelevant alternatives**) The relation of X and Y according to $Aggregate(\geq_1, .., \geq_n)$ depends only on how the individual preference relations rank those two candidates.

(**Non-dictatorship**) There is no $\geq_i$ such that for all X, Y, $X \geq_x Y$ wherever $X \geq_i Y$, regardless of the other $\geq_j$.

(**Justification**) If for all $\geq_i$, $X \not\geq_i Y$, then $X \not\geq_x Y$

(**Participation**) For all $>_i$, there is an X, Y such that $[X >_i Y$ and $X >_x Y$ and there is a $>_j$ such that $X \not>_j Y]$.

From the perspective of non-monotonic reasoning, rather than the perspective of social choice, these principles can be justified as follows: Collective rationality is part of the definition of Aggregate; Independence of irrelevant alternatives ensures that $(\geq_1, .., \geq_n)$ contains sufficient information to define Aggregate; Non-dictatorship ensures that all $\geq_i$ in $(\geq_1, .., \geq_n)$ are necessary to define Aggregate; Justification ensures that for strict preference to hold, then at least one $\geq_i$ in $(\geq_1, .., \geq_n)$ can justify it; and Participation ensures that no $\geq_i$ in $(\geq_1, .., \geq_n)$ is superfluous.

The principles of collective rationality, independence of irrelevant alternatives, and non-dictatorship are from Doyle and Wellman (1991). The remaining two Doyle and Wellman principles are,

(**Pareto principle**) If $X >_i Y$ for some $>_i$ and there is no $>_j$ such that $Y >_j X$, then $X >_x Y$.

(**Conflict resolution**) If $X \geq_i Y$ for some $\geq_i$, then $X \geq_x Y$ or $Y \geq_x X$.

We reject the Pareto (unanimity) and conflict resolution principles since we allow an unrestricted pre-ordering over the preference relations, and furthermore regard some preference relations, when taken individually, to be insufficient to dictate the aggregated preference.

Using this amended set of principles, we obtain the following result.

Theorem 8 *If each $\geq_i$ in $(\geq_1, .., \geq_n)$ is a pre-ordering, then there is an aggregation function such that $Aggregate(\geq_1, .., \geq_n)$ is a pre-ordering and satisfies the principles collective rationality, independence of irrelevant alternatives, non-dictatorship, justification and participation.*

This result means that given any set of preference criteria, there is an aggregation function that can be used to amalgamate them to give a single pre-ordering. Though, obviously, this result does not mean that the single pre-ordering can always select a single "most preferred extension".

Even though we argue against the relevance of Arrow's theorem to non-monotonic reasoning, there is a valuable literature on voting theory and social choice (for example Fishburn 1973) that needs to be considered with respect to explicit preferences used in non-monotonic reasoning.

10 DISCUSSION

Arguments for investigating formalisms that incorporate explicit ordering are significant. In the short term it offers a conceptual framework for analysing non-monotonic logics and for application in practical artificial intelligence technology.

Explicit ordering is potentially important in machine learning, as a result of the ordering on the clauses being amenable to manipulation by a dynamic, or developing, system. Developments in applying non-monotonic logic to machine learning indicate the value of an explicit representation of preference (Gabbay 1992). It is possible to obtain priorities under certain assumptions, from probabilistic data (Cussens 1991, 1993a), and more significantly, by using statistical inference (Cussens 1993b). Using automated techniques for generating databases overcomes some of the knowledge engineering problems in using non-monotonic logics, and furthermore can enhance the learning process.

The explicit ordering in prioritized logics also provides a useful representation to compare notions of implicit ordering being identified in common sense reasoning, such as specificity (Poole 1985, Nute 1988, Prakken 1993), chronological ignorance (Shoham 1988) and use of certain information (Loui 1986). Furthermore, it is apparent that common-sense principles for ordering are context-dependent. This has also been shown in legal reasoning (Prakken 1994). Aggregated preference relations offer a mechanism for formalizing this type of context-dependency.

In the longer term, viewing non-monotonic proof theories in terms of preference relations could be significant in addressing problems of tractability and viability in non-monotonic reasoning systems. These problems are manifested in prioritized logics in the global constraints necessary in finding the most preferred naive inferences. Yet, preference relations could be defined to order $\wp(Naive(\Delta))$ as successively more accurate/correct extensions of a database. In this way, a balance, potentially, between approximation and viability could be captured.

A further argument for studying prioritized logics is that LDS (the general framework in which prioritized logics reside) is being developed for other frameworks for uncertainty (for example Clark 1993), for applied non-monotonic reasoning/practical reasoning (Barwise 1993, Gabbay 1993b), and for reasoning with inconsistent information (Gabbay 1993c, Elvang 1993b). It is intended that viewing non-monotonic logics within LDS will facilitate bridges to be built between these topics.

Acknowledgements

This work has been funded by the CEC ESPRIT BRA DRUMS2 project, and by UK SERC under grant GR/G 46671.

References

Barwise J and Gabbay D (1993) Situating labelled entailment, Draft paper, Department of Computing, Imperial College, London

Benferhat S, Dubois D and Prade H (1993) Argumentative inference in uncertain and inconsistent knowledge-bases, in Proceedings of the Uncertainty in Artificial Intelligence Conference, (UAI'93), Morgan Kaufmann

Borgida A and Imielinski T (1984) Decision making in committees - a framework for dealing with inconsistency and non-monotonicity, Draft paper, Department of Computer Science, Rutgers University, New Brunswick

Brewka G (1989) Preferred subtheories: An extended logical framework for default reasoning, Proceedings of the Eleventh International Joint Conference on Artificial Intelligence, (IJCAI'89), Morgan Kaufmann

Cayrol C, Royer V and Saurel C (1993) Management of preferences in assumption based reasoning, in Information Processing and the Management of Uncertainty in Knowledge based Systems, (IPMU'92), LNCS 682, Springer

Clarke M and Gabbay D (1993) A logical approach to Dempster Shafer, Draft paper, Department of Computing, Imperial College, London

Cussens J and Hunter A (1991) Using defeasible logic for a window on a probabilistic database: Some preliminary notes, in Kruse R and Siegel P, Symbolic and Quantitaive Approaches to Uncertainty, (ECSQAU'91), LNCS 548, Springer

Cussens J and Hunter A (1993a) Using maximum entropy in a defeasible logic with probabilisitic semantics, in Information Processing and the Management of Uncertainty in Knowledge-based Systems, (IPMU'92), LNCS 682, Springer

Cussens J, Hunter A and Srinivasan A (1993b) Generating explicit orderings for non-monotonic logics, in Proceedings of the National Conference on Artificial Intelligence, (AAAI'93), MIT Press

Doyle J and Wellman M (1991) Impediments to universal preference-based default theories, Artificial Intelligence, 49, 97-128

Dung P (1993) On the acceptability of arguments and its fundamental role in non-monotonic reasoning, logic programming, and human's social and economic affairs, in Proceedings of the Thirteenth International Joint Conference on Artificial Intelligence, (IJCAI'93), Morgan Kaufmann

Elvang-Goransson M, Krause P and Fox J (1993a) Dialectical reasoning with inconsistent information, in Proceedings of the Uncertainty in Artificial Intelligence Conference, (UAI'93), Morgan Kaufmann

Elvang-Goransson M and Hunter A (1993b) Argumentative logics: reasoning with classically inconsistent information, Working Paper, Centre for Cognitive Informatics, Roskilde University

Fishburn P (1973) The Theory of Social Choice,

Princeton University Press

Froidevaux C and Grossetete C (1990) Graded default theories for uncertainty, in Proceedings of the European Conference on Artificial Intelligence, (ECAI'90), Pitman

Gabbay D (1985) Theoretical foundations for non-monotonic reasoning in expert systems in logics and models of concurrent systems, Apt K, Logics and Models of Concurrency, Springer

Gabbay D, Gillies D, Hunter A, Muggleton S, Ng Y, and Richards B (1992) The Rule-based Systems Project: Using confirmation theory and non - monotonic logic in incremental learning, in Inductive Logic Programming, Academic Press

Gabbay D (1993a) Labelled deductive systems: A position paper, in Logic Colloquium '90, Lecture Notes in Logic 2, Springer

Gabbay D (1993b) How to construct a logic for your application, Proceedings of the German Artificial Intelligence Conference (GWAI'92), LNCS 671, 1-30

Gabbay D and Hunter A (1993c) Restricted access logics for inconsistent information, Proceedings of the European Conference on Symbolic and Qualitative Approaches to Reasoning and Uncertainty, (ECSQARU'93), LNCS 747, Springer

Gardenfors P (1988) Knowledge in Flux, MIT Press

Grosof B (1991) Generalizing prioritization, in Principles of Knowledge Representation and Reasoning: Proceedings of the Second International Conference (KR'91), Morgan Kaufmann

Horty J, Thomason R and Touretsky D (1987) A skeptical theory of inheritance in non-monotonic semantic networks, in Proceedings of the National Conference in Artificial Intellligence (AAAI'87) MIT Press

Hunter A (1992) Conceptualizations of priorities in non-monotonic proof theory, D Pearce and G Wagner, Logics in Artificial Intelligence (JELIA'92), LNAI 633, Springer

Hunter A (1994) Prioritized logics for non-monotonic reasoning, Draft report, Imperial College, London

Kraus S, Lehmann D and Magidor M (1990) Non-monotonic reasoning, preferential models, and cumulative logics, Artificial Intelligence, 44, 167 - 207

Laenens E and Vermier D (1990) A fixpoint semantics for ordered logic, J Logic and Computation, 1, 159 - 185

Lin F and Shoham Y (1989) Argument Systems: a uniform basis for non- monotonic reasoning, in Principles of Knowledge Represenation and Reasoning: Proceedings of the First International Conference (KR'89), Morgan Kaufmann

Loui R (1986) Defeat amongst arguments: a system of defeasible inference, Technical report, Department of Computer Science, University of Rochester, New York

Makinson D (1989) A general theory of cumulative inference, in Reinfrank M, Proceedings of Second International Workshop on Non- monotonic Logic, LNCS 346, Springer

Nute D (1988) Defeasible reasoning and decision support systems, Decision Support Systems, 4, 97-110

Pollock J (1987) Defeasible reasoning, Cognitive Science, 11, 481-518

Poole D (1985) On the comparison of theories preferring the most specific explanation, in Proceedings of the Ninth International Joint Conference on Artificial Intelligence (IJCAI'85)

Prakken H (1993) Logical tools for modelling argument, PhD Thesis, Computer/Law Institute, Free University of Amsterdam

Prakken H (1994) Reasoning about priorities in prioritized logics, Draft paper, Computer/Law Institute, Free University of Amsterdam

Reiter R (1978) On the closed-world databases, in Gallaire H and Minker, J, Logic and Databases, Plenum Press

Reiter R (1980) A logic for default reasoning, Artificial Intelligence, 13, 81-13

Ryan M (1992) Representing defaults as sentences with reduced priority, in Principles of Knowledge Represenation and Reasoning: Proceedings of the Third International Conference (KR'92), Morgan Kaufmann

Shoham Y (1988) Reasoning About Change, MIT Press

Simari G and Loui R (1992) Mathematical treatment of defeasible reasoning, Artificial Intelligence, 53, 125-152

Stein L (1989) Skeptical inheritance: computing the intersection of credulous extensions, in Proceedings of the Eleventh International Joint Conference on Artificial Intelligence (IJCAI'89), Morgan Kaufmann

Touretsky D (1986) The Mathematics of Inheritance Systems, Pitman

Vreeswijk G (1991) The feasibility of defeat in defeasible reasoning, in Principles of Knowledge Representation and Reasoning: Proceedings of the Second International Conference (KR'91), Morgan Kaufmann

On Positive Occurrences of Negation as Failure

Katsumi Inoue
Department of Information and Computer Sciences
Toyohashi University of Technology
Tempaku-cho, Toyohashi 441, Japan
inoue@tutics.tut.ac.jp

Chiaki Sakama
ASTEM Research Institute of Kyoto
17 Chudoji Minami-machi,
Shimogyo, Kyoto 600, Japan
sakama@astem.or.jp

Abstract

Logic programs with positive occurrences of negation as failure have recently been introduced as a subset of the logic of minimal belief and negation as failure (MBNF). A unique feature of such programs, which other traditional logic programs lack, is that the minimality of answer sets does not hold. We reveal in this paper that this property is important for applying logic programming to represent abduction and inclusive disjunctions. With its rich expressiveness, however, the computational complexity of such extended programs is shown to remain in the same complexity class as normal disjunctive programs. Through the elimination of negation as failure from programs, computation of such extended programs is realized using bottom-up model generation techniques. A simple translation of programs into autoepistemic logic is also presented.

1 Introduction

Most of semantics of logic programs proposed so far satisfy the *principle of minimality* in some sense. For example, the least model semantics for definite Horn programs, the minimal model semantics for positive disjunctive programs, the prefect model semantics for stratified programs and the stable model semantics for normal programs satisfy the principle in the sense that every canonical model of a logic program is its minimal model. The answer set semantics for extended logic programs by Gelfond and Lifschitz (1991) also satisfies the principle since no answer set of a program is smaller than its other answer set. Hence, it has been argued that the principle of minimality is one of the most important goals that any "commonsense" semantics should obey (Schlipf, 1992).

The situation is similar in research on nonmonotonic formalisms. Circumscription is directly based on minimal models, and (disjunctive) default logic has the property that an extension of a (disjunctive) default theory is not a subset of other extension. While an exception can be seen in *autoepistemic logic* (Moore, 1985), the definition of *stable expansions* has been modified so that each obtainable expansion "rationally" satisfies the principle of minimality. For example, $\{Bp \supset p\}$ has two stable expansions, one containing p and the other not in their objective parts, but only the latter is the moderately (or strongly) grounded expansion (Konolige, 1988).

On the other hand, recent research on the semantics of logic programming and nonmonotonic reasoning has demonstrated that both fields have influenced each other. The logic of *minimal belief and negation as failure* (MBNF) recently proposed by Lifschitz (1992) is a nonmonotonic modal logic that directly allows the negation-as-failure operator *not* in a theory. MBNF is one of the most expressive logics and can serve as a common framework that unifies several nonmonotonic formalisms. As Lifschitz noted, however, MBNF is purely semantical and too intractable to be used directly for representing knowledge. Then, Lifschitz and Woo (1992) investigate a large subset of propositional MBNF called *PL-theories*—theories with "protected literals". The semantics of PL-theories is similar to the answer set semantics for extended disjunctive programs (Gelfond and Lifschitz, 1991), and can be described in terms of sets of objective literals. Moreover, each PL-theory is shown to be replaced with an equivalent set of disjunctions of protected literals. This "logic programming" fragment of MBNF can be expressed as a program consisting of rules of the form:

$$L_1 \mid \ldots \mid L_k \mid \mathit{not}\, L_{k+1} \mid \ldots \mid \mathit{not}\, L_l$$
$$\leftarrow L_{l+1}, \ldots, L_m, \mathit{not}\, L_{m+1}, \ldots, \mathit{not}\, L_n$$

where each L_i is a positive or negative literal. Then, the class of logic programs allowing the above form of rules strictly includes the class of extended disjunctive programs. Interestingly, once *not* appears positively as above, the principle of minimality does not hold any more. For example, the program consisting of the rule

$$p \mid \mathit{not}\, p \leftarrow \qquad (1)$$

has two answer sets: one containing p, and the other including neither p nor $\neg p$.

Then, two criticisms can be made about the use of negation as failure positively in logic programming or MBNF. The first criticism is argued by the fact that one feels a resistance to the existence of non-minimal answer sets. In other words, from the traditional viewpoint, a non-minimal answer set contains a redundant information and is of no use for representing commonsense knowledge. In fact, Lifschitz and Woo also raise a question about the utility of a disjunction of literals and their negations like rule (1), and discuss (Lifschitz and Woo, 1992, page 608):

> It remains to be seen whether rules like this may have applications to knowledge representation.

The second criticism addresses the increase of computational complexity and the difficulty in supplying a procedural semantics in the presence of non-minimal answer sets. Two proof theories for MBNF proposed so far are not sufficient in this respect. Chen (1993) proposes a proof theory for PL-theories, which relies on the proof theory for the logic of only knowing by Levesque, but a procedure would have to deal with modal logic K45. Beringer and Schaub (1993) provide a proof procedure for a subset of MBNF, but this subset neither includes extended disjunctive programs nor allows a positive occurrence of not.

In this paper, we discuss the above two issues on non-minimal answer sets of PL-theories. In the first respect, we reveal that the non-minimality of answer sets is an important property for applying logic programming or MBNF to represent abduction and to interpret disjunctions inclusively. In the second regard, we show that the computational complexity of extended programs with positive occurrences of not is in the same complexity class as normal disjunctive programs. Furthermore, through the elimination of not from programs, computation of such extended programs is shown to be realized using bottom-up model generation theorem proving techniques.

The fact that abduction can be represented by a single logic program is a particularly striking result. Since an abductive program is usually represented by a pair of background knowledge and candidate hypotheses, it is important to know how such meta-level information of hypotheses can be expressed at the object level. Such an expression bridges the gap between abductive and usual (non-abductive) logic programming, and is useful for computational aspect of abduction since we can apply any proof procedure for usual logic programs to programs transformed from abductive frameworks. One of our proposed solutions to Lifschitz and Woo's question about the utility of non-minimal answer sets also appears at this point. Namely, the rule (1), $p \mid not\, p \leftarrow$, can be used to represent the statement that p is a hypothesis.

From the viewpoint of nonmonotonic reasoning, among many nonmonotonic formalisms, Moore's autoepistemic logic can express a stable expansion whose objective part is larger than that of another expansion. We will show that this non-minimal feature of autoepistemic logic is applicable to describe the semantics of logic programming with positive occurrences of not. This result is obtained from a simple translation of programs into autoepistemic logic based on results by Lifschitz and Schwarz (1993) and Chen (1993).

The rest of this paper is organized as follows. In Section 2, we give the answer set semantics for programs with positive occurrences of not. To show practical applications of non-minimal answer sets, abduction and inclusive disjunctions are characterized by positive occurrences of not in Section 3. Section 4 provides complexity results and computation of the answer set semantics, and the connection to autoepistemic logic is shown in Section 5. Some related work is discussed in Section 6, and Section 7 gives a summary.

2 Answer Sets of Programs with Positive Occurrences of not

This section overviews the answer set semantics of logic programs with *positive occurrences of negation as failure* (hereafter called *positive not*). Since a rule with variables stands for the set of ground instances in the semantics of logic programming, we can restrict our attention to ground programs.

A *general extended disjunctive program* (GEDP) is a set of rules of the form
$$L_1 \mid \ldots \mid L_k \mid not\, L_{k+1} \mid \ldots \mid not\, L_l \\ \leftarrow L_{l+1}, \ldots, L_m, not\, L_{m+1}, \ldots, not\, L_n \quad (2)$$
where L_i's are literals and $n \geq m \geq l \geq k \geq 0$. The disjunction in the left of $\leftarrow$ is called the *head* and the conjunction in the right of $\leftarrow$ is called the *body* of the rule. A GEDP is called an *extended disjunctive program* (EDP) when it contains no positive not, i.e., each rule is in the form (2) with $k = l$. An EDP is called (i) an *extended logic program* if for each rule $l \leq 1$; and (ii) a *normal disjunctive program* (NDP) if every L_i is an atom. An NDP is called (i) a *normal logic program* if for each rule $l \leq 1$; and (ii) a *positive disjunctive program* (PDP) if it contains no not, i.e., for each rule $m = n$.

The *answer sets* of a GEDP are defined by the following two steps. First, let P be a *not*-free extended disjunctive program (i.e., for each rule $k = l$ and $m = n$), and $S \subseteq Lit$ where Lit is the set of all ground literals in the language. Then, S is an *answer set* of P iff S is a minimal set satisfying the conditions:

1. S *satisfies* each ground rule from P:
$$L_1 \mid \ldots \mid L_k \leftarrow L_{k+1}, \ldots, L_m,$$

that is, if $\{L_{k+1}, \ldots, L_m\} \subseteq S$, then $L_i \in S$ for some $1 \leq i \leq k$. In particular, for each ground rule $\leftarrow L_1, \ldots, L_m$ from P, $\{L_1, \ldots, L_m\} \not\subseteq S$;

2. If S contains a pair of complementary literals L and $\neg L$, then $S = Lit$.

Secondly, let Π be any general extended disjunctive program, and $S \subseteq Lit$. The *reduct* Π^S of Π *by* S is a *not*-free extended disjunctive program obtained as follows: A rule

$$L_1 \mid \ldots \mid L_k \leftarrow L_{l+1}, \ldots, L_m$$

is in Π^S iff there is a ground rule of the form (2) from P such that

$$\{L_{k+1}, \ldots, L_l\} \subseteq S \text{ and } \{L_{m+1}, \ldots, L_n\} \cap S = \emptyset.$$

For programs of the form Π^S, their answer sets have already been defined. Then, S is an *answer set* of Π iff S is an answer set of Π^S. We say an answer set is *consistent* if it is not *Lit*. An answer set S of a GEDP Π is *minimal* if no other answer set S' of Π satisfies $S' \subset S$; otherwise, it is *non-minimal*.

Note that the above definition of answer sets of a GEDP is given in a way slightly different from that by Lifschitz and Woo (1992) who additionally include in the language two special atoms T and F. When the language does not contain these special atoms, our definition of the reduct is equivalent to that given in (Lifschitz and Woo, 1992, page 606), and thus both definitions of answer sets coincide. Obviously, when a program Π is an extended disjunctive program, the above definition of answer sets reduces to that given by Gelfond and Lifschitz (1991).

An important property of GEDPs, which has been observed by Lifschitz and Woo, is that the minimality of answer sets for EDPs (Lifschitz and Woo, 1992, Theorem 4) no longer holds. For example, the program

$$\{ \; p \mid not\, p \leftarrow, \quad \neg p \mid not\, \neg p \leftarrow \; \}$$

has four answer sets: $\emptyset$, $\{p\}$, $\{\neg p\}$ and *Lit*.

3 Representing Abduction by GEDP

Abduction is a very important form of reasoning not only for various AI problems but also for logic programming. *Abductive logic programming* is an extension of logic programming to perform abductive reasoning (Kakas et al., 1992). In this section, we will show that this extension can be characterized exactly using positive *not* in GEDPs, so that both abductive and non-abductive logic programming have the same expressive power. We will also show that positive *not* is a very useful tool to represent other non-minimal semantics for disjunctive logic programs.

3.1 Belief Sets for Abductive Programs

The semantics of abduction we consider here is based on the *generalized stable model semantics* defined by Kakas and Mancarella (1990) and the *belief set semantics* by Inoue and Sakama (1993), but is extended to handle general extended disjunctive programs.

An *abductive (general extended disjunctive) program* is a pair $\langle P, \Gamma \rangle$, where P is a (general extended disjunctive) program and Γ ($\subseteq Lit$) is a set of ground literals from P called *abducibles*. When P is a normal logic program and Γ is a set of atoms, we will often call an abductive program an *abductive normal logic program*. Let E be a subset of Γ. A set of literals S_E is a *belief set* of $\langle P, \Gamma \rangle$ if it is a consistent answer set of $P \cup E$ and satisfies $E = S_E \cap \Gamma$. A belief set S_E is *minimal* if no belief set $S_{E'}$ satisfies that $E' \subset E$. Note that each belief set reduces to a consistent answer set of P when $\Gamma = \emptyset$. The condition $E = S_E \cap \Gamma$ is necessary since an abducible appearing in the head of a ground rule may become true when other abducibles from E are true. In this way, each belief set S_E is uniquely associated with its "generating" abducibles E.[1]

Let $\langle P, \Gamma \rangle$ be an abductive program, and O a literal. A set $E \subseteq \Gamma$ is an *explanation of* O (*wrt* $\langle P, \Gamma \rangle$) if there is a belief set S_E which satisfies O. An explanation E of O is *minimal* if no $E' \subset E$ is an explanation of O. Without loss of generality, we can assume that an observation O is a non-abducible ground literal. Further, the problem to find explanations is essentially equivalent to find belief sets, since E is a minimal explanation of O wrt $\langle P, \Gamma \rangle$ iff S_E is a minimal belief set of $\langle P \cup \{ \leftarrow not\, O\}, \Gamma \rangle$ (Inoue and Sakama, 1993).

Example 3.1 Consider an abductive program $\langle P, \Gamma \rangle$ where $\Gamma = \{a, b\}$ and

$$P = \{ \; p \leftarrow r, b, not\, q, \quad q \leftarrow a, \quad r \leftarrow \; \}.$$

Then, $S_{E0} = \{r\}$, $S_{E1} = \{r, p, b\}$, $S_{E2} = \{r, q, a\}$ and $S_{E3} = \{r, q, a, b\}$ are the belief sets of $\langle P, \Gamma \rangle$, in which S_{E0} is the only minimal belief set of $\langle P, \Gamma \rangle$. Suppose that p is an observation. Then, $E1 = S_{E1} \cap \Gamma = \{b\}$ is the (minimal) explanation of p. This observation p can be incorporated in the program as

$$P' = P \cup \{ \; \leftarrow not\, p \; \},$$

and the unique belief set of $\langle P', \Gamma \rangle$ is $S_{E1} = \{r, p, b\}$. Note that $E3 = \{a, b\}$ is not an explanation of p because if we would abduce $E3$, q would block to derive p, and $\leftarrow not\, p$ could not be satisfied.

---

[1] Kakas and Mancarella's *generalized stable models* of an abductive normal logic program $\langle P, \Gamma \rangle$ are exactly our belief sets of the program. Note that they require that each abducible must not appear in the heads of rules of P, so that the condition $E = S_E \cap \Gamma$ is always satisfied. They further separate integrity constraints from the background program P, but we include them in P.

3.2 Characterizing Abductive Programs

The most direct way to embed abducibles into a single program is as follows. Let $\langle P, \Gamma \rangle$ be an abductive program. For each abducible γ in Γ, we supply the rule

$$\gamma \mid not\, \gamma \leftarrow . \qquad (3)$$

According to the non-minimality of answer sets of GEDPs, this rule has the effect to augment each answer set of P with either γ or nothing. Given an abductive program $\langle P, \Gamma \rangle$, let P_Γ be the GEDP $P \cup abd(\Gamma)$ where $abd(\Gamma)$ is the set of rules (3) obtained from Γ.

Theorem 3.1 *A set S_E is a belief set of $\langle P, \Gamma \rangle$ iff S_E is a consistent answer set of P_Γ.*

Proof: Since $E = S_E \cap \Gamma$, it holds that $abd(\Gamma)^{S_E} = abd(\Gamma)^E = E = E^{S_E}$. Hence,

S_E is a belief set of $\langle P, \Gamma \rangle$
iff S_E is a consistent answer set of $P \cup E$ and $E = S_E \cap \Gamma$
iff S_E is a consistent answer set of $P^{S_E} \cup E^{S_E}$
  and $E = S_E \cap \Gamma$
iff S_E is a consistent answer set of $P^{S_E} \cup abd(\Gamma)^{S_E}$
iff S_E is a consistent answer set of $P \cup abd(\Gamma)$. □

Given a GEDP Π and a set Γ of ground literals, we say an answer set S of Π is Γ-*minimal* if no other answer set S' of Π satisfies that $S' \cap \Gamma \subset S \cap \Gamma$.

Corollary 3.2 S_E *is a minimal belief set of $\langle P, \Gamma \rangle$ iff S_E is a consistent Γ-minimal answer set of P_Γ.* □

Example 3.2 The abductive program $\langle P', \Gamma \rangle$ given in Example 3.1 is translated into

$$P'_\Gamma = P' \cup \{\ a \mid not\, a \leftarrow,\ \ b \mid not\, b \leftarrow\ \}.$$

Then, $\{r, p, b\}$ is the unique (and hence Γ-minimal) answer set of P'_Γ, which is exactly the (minimal) belief set of $\langle P', \Gamma \rangle$. Notice in this example that there is no non-minimal answer set of P'_Γ. In other words, translating abducibles into rules with positive *not* (3) not only enables us to represent non-minimal belief sets of abductive programs, but plays an important role to obtain a (minimal) explanation.

3.3 Assumptions with Preconditions

In the previous subsections, a set Γ of abducibles in an abductive program $\langle P, \Gamma \rangle$ was defined as a set of literals. Often however, we would like to introduce in Γ an *abducible rule* like

$$\gamma \leftarrow L_1, \ldots, L_m, not\, L_{m+1}, \ldots, not\, L_n, \qquad (4)$$

where γ and L_i's are literals. This abducible rule intuitively means that if the rule is abduced then it is used for inference together with the background rules from P. This kind of extended abductive framework was introduced by Inoue (1991) as a *knowledge system* in which both P and Γ are defined as extended logic programs, and has been shown to be a useful tool for representing commonsense knowledge.

An abducible rule (4) has the effect to introduce the literal γ as an assumption in a particular context in which the body of the rule is true. In this sense, γ in (4) can be considered as an *assumption with preconditions*. On the other hand, each abducible literal γ in an abductive program $\langle P, \Gamma \rangle$ defined in Section 3.1 is viewed as an abducible rule without precondition $\gamma \leftarrow$, and hence can be abduced globally.

An extended abductive framework can be formally defined as a pair $\langle P, \Gamma \rangle$, where P is a GEDP and Γ is now an extended logic program consisting of rules of the form (4). The semantics of this abductive framework is slightly extended from that given in Section 3.1 as follows. Let E be any subset of Γ, and $head(E)$ be the heads of rules in E. A set of literals S_E is a *belief set* of $\langle P, \Gamma \rangle$ if it is a consistent answer set of $P \cup E$ and satisfies that $head(E) = S_E \cap head(\Gamma)$. Clearly, this notion of belief sets reduces to the definition of belief sets in Section 3.1 when Γ is a set of abducible literals without preconditions.

Example 3.3 Suppose that $\langle P, \Gamma \rangle$ is an abductive program where

$$P = \{\ p \leftarrow a,\ \neg p \leftarrow b,\ q \leftarrow c\ \},$$
$$\Gamma = \{\ a \leftarrow,\ b \leftarrow,\ c \leftarrow p\ \}.$$

Then, $\langle P, \Gamma \rangle$ has the four belief sets: $\emptyset$, $\{a, p\}$, $\{a, p, c, q\}$, and $\{b, \neg p\}$. Notice that $\{b, \neg p, c, q\}$ is not a belief set since c can be assumed only when p is true.

The embedding of assumptions with preconditions into GEDPs is a straightforward generalization of that of abducibles without preconditions. Each rule (4) in Γ is replaced with the rule

$$\gamma \mid not\, \gamma \leftarrow L_1, \ldots, L_m, not\, L_{m+1}, \ldots, not\, L_n. \qquad (5)$$

For example, the abducible rules Γ given in Example 3.3 are translated into

$$a \mid not\, a \leftarrow,\ \ b \mid not\, b \leftarrow,\ \ c \mid not\, c \leftarrow p.$$

Corollary 3.3 *Let $\langle P, \Gamma \rangle$ be an abductive framework, and $abd(\Gamma)$ the set of rules (5) obtained from the rules (4) in Γ. A set S_E is a belief set of $\langle P, \Gamma \rangle$ iff S_E is a consistent answer set of $P \cup abd(\Gamma)$.* □

3.4 Inclusive Interpretation of Disjunctions

Another important application of positive *not* is to express an alternative semantics for disjunctive logic programs other than Gelfond and Lifschitz's answer set semantics. Here, we show that the *possible model semantics* for normal disjunctive programs by Sakama and Inoue (1993b) can be characterized by the answer set semantics for GEDPs.

The possible model semantics was initially introduced for positive disjunctive programs to enable one to specify both inclusive and exclusive interpretations of disjunctions (Sakama, 1989; Chan, 1993).[2] Recently, Sakama and Inoue (1994) have presented the equivalence between the possible model semantics for NDPs and the generalized stable model semantics for abductive normal logic programs. Utilizing this result and Theorem 3.1, the embedding of the possible model semantics into GEDPs can be obtained. We show below a direct method to do it based on the embedding of abducible rules into GEDPs in Section 3.3.

For an NDP P, let $disj(P)$ be the disjunctive rules of P, i.e., those rules having more than one atoms in their heads. A *split program* of P is a ground normal logic program obtained from P by replacing each ground disjunctive rule from $disj(P)$ of the form

$$A_1 \mid \ldots \mid A_k \leftarrow A_{k+1}, \ldots, A_m, not\, A_{m+1}, \ldots, not\, A_n \quad (6)$$

($k > 1$) with rules

$$A_i \leftarrow A_{k+1}, \ldots, A_m, not\, A_{m+1}, \ldots, not\, A_n \quad (7)$$

for every $A_i \in S$, where S is some non-empty subset of $\{A_1, \ldots, A_k\}$. Then, a *possible model* of P is an answer set (or *stable model*) of any split program of P (Sakama and Inoue, 1993b). Note that every stable model of P is a possible model of P, but not vice versa. For example, when

$$P = \{\, p \mid q \leftarrow, \quad q \leftarrow p, \quad r \leftarrow not\, p \,\},$$

$\{q, r\}$ is both a stable model and a possible model of P, but another possible model $\{p, q\}$ is not a stable model. Clearly, for normal logic programs, possible models coincide with stable models.

To obtain every possible model, let us consider the translation pm which maps an NDP to a GEDP. Given an NDP P, $pm(P)$ is obtained by replacing every rule from P of the form (6) with $k+1$ rules. The first k rules of them are

$$A_i \mid not\, A_i \leftarrow A_{k+1}, \ldots, A_m, not\, A_{m+1}, \ldots, not\, A_n \quad (8)$$

for $i = 1, \ldots, k$, and the other one is

$$\leftarrow A_{k+1}, \ldots, A_m, not\, A_{m+1}, \ldots, not\, A_n, \\ not\, A_1, \ldots, not\, A_k. \quad (9)$$

Recall that the embedding of abducible rules (4) into GEDPs was based on rules (5). The embedding of possible models is achieved in a similar manner by (8) except that the empty selection from the disjuncts of each disjunction is rejected by (9) in the pm translation.

---
[2] Possible model semantics is also called *possible world semantics* in (Chan, 1993; Sakama and Inoue, 1993b). While Chan (1993) gives a different definition from that by (Sakama, 1989), these notions are proved to be equivalent.

Theorem 3.4 *Let P be an NDP. A set S of atoms is a possible model of P iff S is an answer set of $pm(P)$.*

Proof: Suppose that Γ is the normal logic program obtained from $disj(P)$ by replacing each disjunctive rule (6) with k rules of the form (7) for $i = 1, \ldots, k$, and that IC is the set of rules of the form (9) obtained from the rules of the form (6) in $disj(P)$. Then, a set S of atoms is a possible model of P iff S is a belief set of the abductive program $\langle (P \setminus disj(P)) \cup IC, \Gamma \rangle$ (Sakama and Inoue, 1994). Hence, the theorem follows from Corollary 3.3. □

Example 3.4 (Chan, 1993) Suppose that P consists of rules

$$violent \mid psychopath \leftarrow suspect,$$
$$dangerous \leftarrow violent, psychopath,$$
$$suspect \leftarrow .$$

The first rule is replaced in $pm(P)$ with three rules

$$violent \mid not\, violent \leftarrow suspect,$$
$$psychopath \mid not\, psychopath \leftarrow suspect,$$
$$\leftarrow suspect, not\, violent, not\, psychopath.$$

Then, $\{suspect, violent\}$, $\{suspect, psychopath\}$ and $\{suspect, violent, psychopath, dangerous\}$ are the three answer sets of $pm(P)$, which coincide with the possible models of P. Note that the first and second possible models of P are also the answer sets of P, while the third possible model is not. If we introduce the closed world assumption

$$\neg A \leftarrow not\, A \quad \text{for any atom } A$$

into P, then the answer set semantics entails $\neg dangerous$,[3] which is too strong. The possible model semantics for P (the answer set semantics for $pm(P)$) in this case does not entail $\neg dangerous$.

4 Complexity and Computation

We now show the computational complexity of GEDPs and an algorithm to compute the answer sets of a finite GEDP. These results indicate that positive *not* can be eliminated from programs so that we can use any proof procedure for computing EDPs.

4.1 Reduction to Extended Disjunctive Programs

We first show a polynomial-time transformation from a GEDP to an extended disjunctive program. Let Π be any GEDP. The extended disjunctive program $edp(\Pi)$ is obtained from Π by replacing each rule with positive *not* in Π of the form:

$$L_1 \mid \ldots \mid L_k \mid not\, L_{k+1} \mid \ldots \mid not\, L_l \\ \leftarrow L_{l+1}, \ldots, L_m, not\, L_{m+1}, \ldots, not\, L_n \quad (10)$$

---
[3] The answer set semantics for a program P is said to *entail* a literal L if L is included in all answer sets of P.

($n \geq m \geq l > k \geq 0$) with rules without positive *not*:

$$\lambda_1 \mid \ldots \mid \lambda_k \mid \lambda_{k+1} \mid \ldots \mid \lambda_l \\ \leftarrow L_{l+1}, \ldots, L_m, \text{not } L_{m+1}, \ldots, \text{not } L_n, \quad (11)$$

$$L_i \leftarrow \lambda_i \quad \text{for } i = 1, \ldots, k, \quad (12)$$

$$\lambda_i \leftarrow L_i, L_{k+1}, \ldots, L_l \quad \text{for } i = 1, \ldots, k, \quad (13)$$

$$\leftarrow \lambda_i, \text{not } L_j \quad \begin{array}{l} \text{for } i = 1, \ldots, k \text{ and} \\ j = k+1, \ldots, l, \end{array} \quad (14)$$

$$\leftarrow \lambda_j, L_j \quad \text{for } j = k+1, \ldots, l. \quad (15)$$

Here, λ_i is a new atom not appearing elsewhere in Π and is uniquely associated with each disjunct of a ground rule from Π. In the following, we denote by Lit_Π the set of all ground literals in the language of Π. Thus, Lit_Π includes no new atom λ_i.

Theorem 4.1 *Let Π be a GEDP. A set S is an answer set of Π iff a set Σ is an answer set of $edp(\Pi)$ such that $S = \Sigma \cap Lit_\Pi$.*

Proof: Let S be an answer set of Π. First, consider the reduct Π^S. If a rule

$$L_1 \mid \ldots \mid L_k \leftarrow L_{l+1}, \ldots, L_m \quad (16)$$

is in Π^S, then for the corresponding rule (10) in Π, it holds that $\{L_{k+1}, \ldots, L_l\} \subseteq S$ and $\{L_{m+1}, \ldots, L_n\} \cap S = \emptyset$. In this case, the reduct $edp(\Pi)^S$ includes

$$\lambda_1 \mid \ldots \mid \lambda_k \mid \lambda_{k+1} \mid \ldots \mid \lambda_l \leftarrow L_{l+1}, \ldots, L_m, \quad (17)$$

and the rules (12,13,15), but does not contain the rule (14). Since S satisfies each rule in Π^S, for each rule R of the form (16) such that $\{L_{l+1}, \ldots, L_m\} \subseteq S$, there exists $L_i \in S$ for some $1 \leq i \leq k$. Let

$$\Sigma 1 = \bigcup_{R \in \Pi^S} \{\lambda_i \mid L_i \in S, \; 1 \leq i \leq k\}.$$

Next, suppose that there is a rule (10) in Π such that $\{L_{m+1}, \ldots, L_n\} \cap S = \emptyset$ but $\exists L_j \notin S$ for some $k+1 \leq j \leq l$. In this case, there is no corresponding rule (16) in Π^S, but the rule (17) is present in $edp(\Pi)^S$. $edp(\Pi)^S$ also contains the rules (12,13,15) and the rules $\leftarrow \lambda_i$ for $i = 1, \ldots, k$ (from the rule (14)). Then, for each such rule R' (17) of $edp(\Pi)^S$, let

$$\Sigma 2 = \bigcup_{R' \in edp(\Pi)^S} \{\lambda_j \mid L_j \notin S, \; k+1 \leq j \leq l\}.$$

Now let $\Sigma = S \cup \Sigma 3$, where $\Sigma 3$ is a minimal subset of $\Sigma 1 \cup \Sigma 2$ such that each λ_i or λ_j is chosen in a way that Σ satisfies every rule of the form (17). Obviously, it holds that $S = \Sigma \cap Lit_\Pi$. Because new literals λ_i's never appear within *not*, the program $edp(\Pi)^S$ is exactly the same as $edp(\Pi)^\Sigma$. Then, Σ satisfies all the rules of $edp(\Pi)^\Sigma$, and if $S = Lit_\Pi$ then $Lit_\Pi \subseteq \Sigma$.

To see that Σ is a minimal set satisfying the rules of $edp(\Pi)^\Sigma$, notice that S is a minimal set satisfying the rules of Π^S. From the construction of $\Sigma 3$, it is easy to see that Σ is a minimal set *containing* S and satisfying the rules of $edp(\Pi)^\Sigma$. We thus only need to verify that there is no Σ' such that (i) $\Sigma' \subset \Sigma$, (ii) Σ' satisfies the rules of $edp(\Pi)^\Sigma$, and (iii) $S' \subset S$ for $S' = \Sigma' \cap Lit_\Pi$. Suppose to the contrary that such a Σ' exists. Then, the condition (iii) is satisfied only if there exist rules (12,13) such that $L_i \in S \setminus S'$ and $\lambda_i \in \Sigma \setminus \Sigma'$ for some $1 \leq i \leq k$. For this λ_i, there must be the rule (17) such that $\{L_{l+1}, \ldots, L_m\} \subseteq S'$. By the condition (ii), there is a literal $\lambda_j \in \Sigma'$ for some $k+1 \leq j \leq l$. This λ_j, however, is not included in $\Sigma 2$ by (15), contradicting the condition (i). Therefore, Σ is an answer set of $edp(\Pi)^\Sigma$, and hence an answer set of $edp(\Pi)$.

Conversely, let Σ be an answer set of $edp(\Pi)$, and $S = \Sigma \cap Lit_\Pi$. Since Σ is an answer set of $edp(\Pi)^\Sigma$, for each rule (17) in $edp(\Pi)^\Sigma$, if $\{L_{l+1}, \ldots, L_m\} \subseteq S$, then $\lambda_i \in \Sigma$ for some $1 \leq i \leq l$. There are two cases: (a) If $\lambda_i \in \Sigma$ for some $1 \leq i \leq k$, then $L_i \in S$ by (12) and hence $\{L_{k+1}, \ldots, L_l\} \subseteq S$ by (14). Then, the corresponding rule (16) exists in Π^S and S satisfies it; (b) If $\lambda_i \notin \Sigma$ but $\lambda_j \in \Sigma$ for some $1 \leq i \leq k$ and $k+1 \leq j \leq l$, then $L_j \notin S$ by (15). Then, there is no corresponding rule (16) in Π^S. In either case, S satisfies all rules of Π^S.

Suppose that there is a set S' of literals from Lit_Π such that (i) $S' \subset S$ and (ii) S' satisfies the rules of Π^S. Then, two conditions (i) and (ii) are satisfied only if there is a rule (16) such that $\{L_{l+1}, \ldots, L_m\} \subset S'$ and for some two literals L_{i1} and L_{i2} ($1 \leq i1, i2 \leq k$, $i1 \neq i2$) $L_{i1} \in S'$ but $L_{i2} \in S \setminus S'$. Without loss of generality, we can assume that just one such rule exists in Π^S. Since S and S' contain $L_{k+1}, \ldots, L_l$ in the corresponding rule (10) in Π, $\lambda_{i1}, \lambda_{i2} \in \Sigma$ by (13). Let $\Sigma' = \Sigma \setminus \{L_{i2}, \lambda_{i2}\}$. Then, Σ' satisfies all the rules (17,12,13,15) existing in $edp(\Pi)^\Sigma$. This contradicts the fact that Σ is an answer set of $edp(\Pi)^\Sigma$. Therefore, S is an answer set of Π^S, and hence an answer set of Π. □

We thus see that any GEDP can be reduced to an EDP by eliminating positive *not*. The fact that non-minimal answer sets of GEDPs can be expressed by answer sets of EDPs that must be minimal is a somewhat surprising and unexpected result. The reason why this reduction is possible is that the newly introduced atoms λ_i's have the effect to distinguish each positive *not*, and each answer set of $edp(\Pi)$ becomes minimal by the existence of these new atoms.

Example 4.1 Suppose that a GEDP is given as
$$\Pi = \{\; p \mid \text{not } q \leftarrow, \quad q \mid \text{not } p \leftarrow \;\}.$$
The answer sets of Π are $\{\{p, q\}, \emptyset\}$. Correspondingly,
$$edp(\Pi) = \{\; \lambda_1 \mid \lambda_2 \leftarrow, \quad \lambda_3 \mid \lambda_4 \leftarrow,$$
$$p \leftarrow \lambda_1, \quad \lambda_1 \leftarrow p, q, \quad \leftarrow \lambda_1, \text{not } q, \quad \leftarrow \lambda_2, q,$$
$$q \leftarrow \lambda_3, \quad \lambda_3 \leftarrow q, p, \quad \leftarrow \lambda_3, \text{not } p, \quad \leftarrow \lambda_4, p \;\}$$
has the answer sets $\{\{\lambda_1, \lambda_3, p, q\}, \{\lambda_2, \lambda_4\}\}$.

4.2 Complexity Results

We are now ready to give the complexity results for GEDPs. Since the class of GEDPs includes the class of EDPs and we have shown a polynomial-time transformation from a GEDP to an EDP, the next result follows immediately from the complexity results of EDPs given by Eiter and Gottlob (1993).

Theorem 4.2 *Let Π be a finite propositional GEDP, and L a literal.*
(1) Deciding the existence of an answer set of Π is Σ_2^P-complete.
(2) Deciding whether L is true in some answer set of Π is Σ_2^P-complete.
(3) Deciding whether L is true in all answer sets of Π is Π_2^P-complete. □

Theorem 4.2 demonstrates that allowing positive *not* does not increase the computational complexity of the answer set semantics. Eiter and Gottlob also show that the complexity results for EDPs apply to EDPs without classical negation ¬ as well. Therefore, GEDPs are in the same complexity class as normal disjunctive programs. Furthermore, Theorem 4.2 (2) also applies to the minimal model semantics for positive disjunctive programs. This observation leads us to a further translation in Section 4.3.

Ben-Eliyahu and Dechter (1992) have shown the (co-)NP-completeness of a restricted class of EDPs. According to their notations, a *dependency graph* of a ground EDP P is a directed graph in which its nodes are literals in P and there is an edge from L to L' iff there is a rule in P such that L appears in the body and L' appears in the head of the rule. An EDP is *head-cycle free* if its dependency graph contains no directed cycle that goes through two different literals in the head of the same disjunctive rule. Then, the three problems in Theorem 4.2 for propositional head-cycle free EDPs are reducible to testing satisfiability or provability of propositional formulas in polynomial-time (Ben-Eliyahu and Dechter, 1992). Here, we show such a reduction of complexity results is also possible for a restricted class of GEDPs, by providing a generalization of their results. Given a ground GEDP Π, its *dependency graph* G_Π is defined in the same way as that of an EDP except that an additional edge from L to L' is added for each *not* L and L' in the head of the same rule. Thus, while each *not* L in bodies is ignored, each *not* L in heads constructs an edge in G_Π. A GEDP Π is *head-cycle free* if G_Π contains no directed cycle that goes through two literals L_{i1}, L_{i2} ($1 \leq i1, i2 \leq k$, $L_{i1} \neq L_{i2}$) in any ground rule (10) from Π. The class of head-cycle free GEDPs obviously includes the class of head-cycle free EDPs and the class of extended logic programs, and includes the class of GEDPs each of whose rule permits in the head at most one L' but any number of *not* L's.

Lemma 4.3 *Let Π be a GEDP. Π is head-cycle free iff $edp(\Pi)$ is head-cycle free.*

Proof: An edge from L_j to L_i for $j = k+1,\ldots,l$ and $i = 1,\ldots,k$ in the same rule (10) is in G_Π iff a path from L_j to L_i through rules (13) and (12) is in $G_{edp(\Pi)}$. Then, each directed path from L to L' in G_Π is contained in $G_{edp(\Pi)}$, and vice versa. Hence, any two literals L_{i1}, L_{i2} ($1 \leq i1, i2 \leq k$) in the same rule (10) are contained in a cycle in G_Π iff the literals $\lambda_{i1}, \lambda_{i2}$ in the corresponding rule (11) are contained in a cycle in $G_{edp(\Pi)}$. □

The next result follows from Theorem 4.1, Lemma 4.3 and complexity results of head-cycle free EDPs by (Ben-Eliyahu and Dechter, 1992).

Theorem 4.4 *Let Π be a finite propositional head-cycle free GEDP, and L a literal.*
(1) Deciding the existence of an answer set of Π is NP-complete.
(2) Deciding whether L is true in some answer set of Π is NP-complete.
(3) Deciding whether L is true in all answer sets of Π is co-NP-complete. □

Note that the class of head-cycle free GEDPs includes, as a special case, the class of programs $P \cup abd(\Gamma)$ obtained from abductive programs $\langle P, \Gamma \rangle$ where both P and Γ are extended logic programs (see Section 3.3). This fact and results in Section 3 imply that computational problems for abductive normal logic programs (Kakas and Mancarella, 1990), knowledge systems (Inoue, 1991), and the possible model semantics for normal disjunctive programs (Sakama and Inoue, 1993b) have all the same complexity results as in Theorem 4.4. These results are also stated in (Sakama and Inoue, 1994) based on translations of such programs into normal logic programs.

4.3 Computing Answer Sets of GEDP

To compute the answer set semantics for any GEDP Π, we can apply any proof procedure for extended disjunctive programs to the EDP $edp(\Pi)$ obtained in Section 4.1. To this end, a bottom-up proof procedure for EDPs has been proposed by Inoue et al. (1992) to compute answer sets of EDPs using model generation techniques. Here, we present an essence of the method of (Inoue et al., 1992). First, each EDP P is converted into its *positive form* P^+, which is obtained from P by replacing each negative literal $\neg L$ with a new atom $-L$. Note that P^+ is a normal disjunctive program. We also denote the positive form of a set S of literals as S^+. Next, P^+ is translated into the set $fo(P^+)$ of first-order formulas by completely eliminating *not* as follows. For each rule in P^+ of the form:

$$L_1 \mid \ldots \mid L_k \leftarrow L_{k+1}, \ldots, L_m, \text{not } L_{m+1}, \ldots, \text{not } L_n \tag{18}$$

where L_i's are atoms, $fo(P^+)$ contains the formula:

$$L_{k+1} \wedge \ldots \wedge L_m \supset \\ H_1 \vee \ldots \vee H_k \vee KL_{m+1} \vee \ldots \vee KL_n, \quad (19)$$

where

$$H_i \equiv L_i \wedge \text{-}KL_{m+1} \wedge \ldots \wedge \text{-}KL_n \quad (i=1,\ldots,k),$$

and $fo(P^+)$ contains the formulas:

$$\neg(L \wedge \text{-}KL) \quad \text{for each } L \in Lit_P{}^+, \quad (20)$$

$$\neg(L \wedge \text{-}L) \quad \text{for each pair } L, \text{-}L \in Lit_P{}^+. \quad (21)$$

Here, KL is a new atom which denotes L should be true, and $\text{-}KL$ is the positive form of $\neg KL$. Now, let I be an Herbrand interpretation of $fo(P^+)$, i.e., a set of ground atoms in the language of $fo(P^+)$. We say that I satisfies the stability condition if it holds that

$KL \in I$ implies $L \in I$ for every atom $L \in Lit_P{}^+$.

Lemma 4.5 (Inoue et al., 1992) Let P be an EDP, and $S \subseteq Lit_P$. S is a consistent answer set of P iff M is a minimal Herbrand model of $fo(P^+)$ such that $S^+ = M \cap Lit_P{}^+$ and M satisfies the stability condition. □

The next theorem, which follows from Theorem 4.1 and Lemma 4.5, completely characterizes the consistent answer sets of a GEDP in terms of the above first-order translation.[4]

Theorem 4.6 Let Π be any GEDP, and $S \subseteq Lit_\Pi$. S is a consistent answer set of Π iff M is a minimal Herbrand model of $fo(edp(\Pi)^+)$ such that $S^+ = M \cap Lit_\Pi{}^+$ and M satisfies the stability condition. □

It is well known that for positive disjunctive programs minimal models coincide with answer sets. Then, as the formula (19) can be identified with the rule

$$H_1 \mid \ldots \mid H_k \mid KL_{m+1} \mid \ldots \mid KL_n \leftarrow L_{k+1}, \ldots, L_m,$$

the set $fo(P^+)$ can be viewed as a PDP. We thus now have a polynomial-time transformation from GEDPs to PDPs. Hence, to obtain answer sets of GEDPs, any procedure to compute minimal models of PDPs can be applied as well. There are many techniques for this computation such as (Bell et al., 1992; Inoue et al., 1992; Fernandez and Minker, 1992). In particular, our transformation is suitable for applying a bottom-up model generation procedure to compute answer sets of function-free, range-restricted GEDPs. Since we have characterized abductive programs as GEDPs in Section 3, abduction can also be computed by model generation procedures. Inoue et al. (1993) have developed such a parallel abductive procedure, and Inoue and Sakama (1993) have given a fixpoint semantics that accounts for the correctness of such bottom-up procedures using a similar transformation.

---

[4]Although Theorem 4.6 does not cover the contradictory answer set of Π, the methods used in (Inoue et al., 1992) can be applied to identify the answer set Lit_Π.

Example 4.2 The abductive program $\langle P', \Gamma \rangle$ given in Examples 3.1 and 3.2 is now transformed into $fo(P'_\Gamma)$ that consists of the propositional formulas

$$r \wedge b \supset (p \wedge \text{-}Kq) \vee Kq, \quad a \supset q, \quad r, \quad Kp,$$
$$\lambda_1 \vee \lambda_2, \quad \lambda_1 \equiv a, \quad \lambda_1 \supset Ka, \quad \neg(\lambda_2 \wedge a),$$
$$\lambda_3 \vee \lambda_4, \quad \lambda_3 \equiv b, \quad \lambda_3 \supset Kb, \quad \neg(\lambda_4 \wedge b),$$

and the schema (20).[5] Then, there are five minimal models of $fo(P'_\Gamma)$:

$$M_1 = \{r, Kp, \lambda_1, a, Ka, q, \lambda_3, b, Kb, Kq\},$$
$$M_2 = \{r, Kp, \lambda_1, a, Ka, q, \lambda_4\},$$
$$M_3 = \{r, Kp, \lambda_2, \lambda_3, b, Kb, p, \text{-}Kq\},$$
$$M_4 = \{r, Kp, \lambda_2, \lambda_3, b, Kb, Kq\},$$
$$M_5 = \{r, Kp, \lambda_2, \lambda_4\}.$$

Among these, only M_3 satisfies the stability condition, and corresponds to the belief set $\{r, p, b\}$ of $\langle P', \Gamma \rangle$.

5 Relation to Autoepistemic Logic

Recall that the class of GEDPs is the "logic programming" fragment of propositional MBNF (Lifschitz, 1992). The embedding of the rule (2)

$$L_1 \mid \ldots \mid L_k \mid not\, L_{k+1} \mid \ldots \mid not\, L_l \\ \leftarrow L_{l+1}, \ldots, L_m, not\, L_{m+1}, \ldots, not\, L_n$$

into MBNF is given by Lifschitz and Woo (1992) as the formula

$$BL_{l+1} \wedge \ldots \wedge BL_m \wedge not\, L_{m+1} \wedge \ldots \wedge not\, L_n \\ \supset BL_1 \vee \ldots \vee BL_k \vee not\, L_{k+1} \vee \ldots \vee not\, L_l.$$

Besides MBNF, there are many nonmonotonic formalisms to which EDPs can be embedded. Gelfond et al. (1991) use their disjunctive default logic, and Sakama and Inoue (1993a) show transformations into Reiter's default logic, Moore's autoepistemic logic and McCarthy's circumscription. Since we have presented the reduction of GEDPs to EDPs, these previous results can be directly applied to embed GEDPs into such nonmonotonic formalisms, and they are all well defined. Although these results are all correct, one often wants to see a stronger result such that the logical closure of an answer set is exactly the same as an *extension* of a nonmonotonic formalism and that the set of literals true in an extension is exactly an answer set. In such an extension, the introduction of new literals like λ_i's should be avoided. Then, those formalisms that obey the principle of minimality such as (disjunctive) default logic and circumscription are rejected for this purpose. With this regard, the remaining candidate is autoepistemic logic. Lifschitz and Schwarz (1993) and Chen (1993) have independently provided the correct embedding of EDPs into autoepistemic logic. Moreover, both results are proved in a way applicable to

---

[5]When an EDP P is an NDP, $P^+ = P$ holds and $fo(P)$ need not include the schema (21).

a more general class of programs including consistent PL-theories of (Lifschitz and Woo, 1992). Here, we can take advantage of their proofs.[6]

Given a GEDP Π, its *autoepistemic translation* $ae(\Pi)$ is defined as follows: Each rule of the form (2) in Π is transformed into the following formula in $ae(\Pi)$:

$$(BL_{l+1} \wedge L_{l+1}) \wedge \ldots \wedge (BL_m \wedge L_m)$$
$$\wedge \neg BL_{m+1} \wedge \ldots \wedge \neg BL_n$$
$$\supset (BL_1 \wedge L_1) \vee \ldots \vee (BL_k \wedge L_k)$$
$$\vee \neg BL_{k+1} \vee \ldots \vee \neg BL_l. \quad (22)$$

Recall that given a set A of formulas (called a *premise set*) in autoepistemic logic, T is a *stable expansion* of A iff

$$T = cons(A \cup \{B\varphi \mid \varphi \in T\} \cup \{\neg B\varphi \mid \varphi \notin T\}),$$

where $cons(X)$ denotes the set of propositional consequences of X. It is also well known that for each set F of objective formulas, there is a unique stable set $E(F)$ containing F such that the objective formulas in $E(F)$ are exactly the same as those in $cons(F)$. If a premise set A contains only objective formulas, then $E(A)$ is a unique stable expansion of A. Then, the next result follows from (Lifschitz and Schwarz, 1993, Main Theorem).

Theorem 5.1 *Let Π be a consistent GEDP, and S a set of literals. S is an answer set of Π iff $E(S)$ is a stable expansion of $ae(\Pi)$.* □

The autoepistemic translation $ae(\Pi)$ can be simplified for some class of GEDPs. When Π is a GEDP that consists of rules of the form

$$A_1 \mid not\ A_2 \mid \ldots \mid not\ A_l$$
$$\leftarrow A_{l+1}, \ldots, A_m, not\ A_{m+1}, \ldots, not\ A_n, \quad (23)$$

where $0 \leq l \leq m \leq n$ (A_1 may be empty) and A_i's are atoms, each $(BA_i \wedge A_i)$ for $i = 1$ and $i = l+1, \ldots, m$ in $ae(\Pi)$ can be replaced simply with A_i as

$$A_{l+1} \wedge \ldots \wedge A_m \wedge \neg BA_{m+1} \wedge \ldots \wedge \neg BA_n$$
$$\supset A_1 \vee \neg BA_2 \vee \ldots \vee \neg BA_l. \quad (24)$$

Note that this class of GEDPs is a subset of the class of head-cycle free GEDPs, and includes the class of normal logic programs and programs P_Γ that are translated from abductive normal logic programs $\langle P, \Gamma \rangle$. Let us denote as $ae_n(\Pi)$ the set of autoepistemic formulas obtained from a GEDP Π by replacing each rule of the form (23) with (24). An essential difference between $ae(\Pi)$ and $ae_n(\Pi)$ for a set Π of rules of the form (23) is that, while ae_n may map two different

---

[6]Marek and Truszczyński (1993) also show a different translation of EDPs into *reflexive autoepistemic logic* (Schwarz, 1991). Lifschitz and Schwarz (1993) further prove that reflexive autoepistemic logic can be used for the embedding of consistent PL-theories.

programs with the same answer sets into two autoepistemic theories with different stable expansions, the stable expansions of $ae(\Pi)$ are uniquely determined by the answer sets of Π (Lifschitz and Schwarz, 1993). Nevertheless, we have the following one-to-one correspondence between the answer sets of Π and the stable expansions of $ae_n(\Pi)$.

Corollary 5.2 *Let Π be a consistent GEDP such that Π is a set of rules of the form (23), and S a set of atoms. S is an answer set of Π iff S is the set of objective atoms true in a stable expansion of $ae_n(\Pi)$.*

Proof: Suppose that S is an answer set of Π. By Theorem 5.1, there is a stable expansion E of $ae(\Pi)$ such that $S = E \cap At$ where At is the set of atoms occurring in Π and that

$$E = cons(S \cup \{B\varphi \mid \varphi \in E\} \cup \{\neg B\varphi \mid \varphi \notin E\}).$$

The set $\{B\varphi \mid \varphi \in E\}$ includes BA for each $A \in S$. In the presence of these subjective atoms, all the objective atoms S in E also follows from some stable expansion E' of $ae_n(\Pi)$, and vice versa. Hence, $S = E' \cap At$. The converse direction can also be shown in the same manner. □

The above corollary can also be applied to the embedding of the possible model semantics for a normal disjunctive program P since each rule in the translated GEDP $pm(P)$ is in the form (23).

Theorem 5.3 *Let P be a consistent NDP that consists of rules of the form*

$$A_1 \mid \ldots \mid A_k \leftarrow A_{k+1}, \ldots, A_m, not\ A_{m+1}, \ldots, not\ A_n.$$

A set S of atoms is a possible model of P iff S is the set of objective atoms true in a stable expansion of the set of formulas obtained by translating each above rule in P into the formula

$$A_{k+1} \wedge \ldots \wedge A_m \wedge \neg BA_{m+1} \wedge \ldots \wedge \neg BA_n$$
$$\supset (A_1 \vee \neg BA_1) \wedge \ldots \wedge (A_k \vee \neg BA_k)$$
$$\wedge (BA_1 \vee \ldots \vee BA_k).$$

Proof: The translated formula is equivalent to the conjunction of the ae_n translation of rules (8) and (9) in $pm(P)$. Then, the result follows from Theorem 3.4 and Corollary 5.2. □

Now, let us look again at the embedding of abduction into GEDPs given in Theorem 3.1. The rule (3)

$$\gamma \mid not\ \gamma \leftarrow$$

is translated into

$$(B\gamma \wedge \gamma) \vee \neg B\gamma$$

by the autoepistemic translation, which is then equivalent to

$$B\gamma \supset \gamma. \quad (25)$$

The set consisting of the formula (25) produces two stable expansions, one containing γ and $B\gamma$, the other containing $\neg B\gamma$ but neither γ nor $\neg\gamma$. Historically, the first expansion has been regarded as anomalous since the belief of γ is based solely on the assumption that γ is believed with no other support (Konolige, 1988). However, this situation is most welcome for abduction. The fact that the formula (25) is the archetype to generate hypotheses strongly justifies the correctness of our use of positive *not* in the corresponding rule (3).

Finally, from the relationship between PL-theories and autoepistemic logic, we obtain the next result.

Theorem 5.4 *Let T be a set of propositional combinations of* protected literals, *i.e., formulas of the form* BL *or* $not\,L$ *where L is a literal. Deciding whether T has an MBNF-model is Σ_2^P-complete.*

Proof: Σ_2^P-hardness follows from Theorem 4.2 (1) and the embedding of GEDPs into MBNF. Membership in Σ_2^P is shown by the complexity result for autoepistemic logic (Gottlob, 1992) and a polynomial-time translation of an MBNF formula of the above form into autoepistemic logic (Lifschitz and Schwarz, 1993), which replaces each protected literal BL with $L \wedge BL$ and each protected literal $not\,L$ with $\neg BL$. □

6 Discussion

1. Brewka and Konolige (1993) give another semantics for GEDPs which is different from the answer set semantics in this paper. They allow positive *not* in a program but still obey the principle of minimality. Consequently, their semantics can never represent non-minimal canonical models and its relationship to autoepistemic logic must be different from ours. In this respect, they suggest the use of *moderately grounded expansions* (Konolige, 1988) for the embedding. However, moderately grounded expansions are of no use to characterize the *minimal* answer sets of GEDPs. Instead, *parsimonious stable expansions* (Eiter and Gottlob, 1992) appropriately characterize the minimal answer sets.[7] For example, the GEDP

$$\Pi = \{\ p \mid not\,p \leftarrow,\ \ q \leftarrow p,\ \ \leftarrow not\,q\ \}.$$

has the unique (and hence minimal) answer set $\{p, q\}$, but its autoepistemic translation

$$ae_n(\Pi) = \{\ Bp \supset p,\ \ p \supset q,\ \ Bq\ \}.$$

has no moderately grounded expansion. In fact, $E(\{p,q\})$ is not a minimal stable set that includes

---

[7] A stable expansion of a premise set A is *moderately grounded* if its objective part is not smaller than the objective part of any other stable set that includes A. A stable expansion of A is *parsimonious* if its objective part is not smaller than the objective part of any other stable expansion of A. Note that each moderately grounded expansion is parsimonious but the converse does not necessarily holds.

$ae_n(\Pi)$ since $E(\{q\})$ is a stable set containing $ae_n(\Pi)$ and its objective part is smaller than that of $E(\{p,q\})$. On the other hand, $E(\{p,q\})$ is the unique parsimonious stable expansion. In general, the next result follows from Theorem 5.1 and the definition of parsimonious stable expansions.

Corollary 6.1 *Let Π be a consistent GEDP, and S a set of literals. S is a minimal answer set of Π iff $E(S)$ is a parsimonious stable expansion of $ae(\Pi)$.* □

Recall that our answer set semantics for GEDPs is characterized by stable expansions of the translated autoepistemic theories. From the complexity viewpoint, Eiter and Gottlob have shown that deciding whether an objective formula belongs to some parsimoniously grounded expansion of an autoepistemic theory is Σ_3^P-complete in general (Eiter and Gottlob, 1992), while the same problem for some stable expansion is Σ_2^P-complete (Gottlob, 1992). From their results, it is conjectured that computing with a minimal answer set of a GEDP is strictly harder than computing with its any answer set unless the polynomial hierarchy collapses.

2. An interesting property of the rule (3) $\gamma \mid not\,\gamma \leftarrow$ is that it is *valid* in the sense that every answer set satisfies it, that is, γ is either contained or not contained in it. In autoepistemic logic, the corresponding formula (25) is always contained in any stable expansion. However, the modal axiom schema of the same form

$$T: \quad B\varphi \supset \varphi$$

cannot be put into the premise set without changing its stable expansions (Moore, 1985). Similarly, adding the rule $L \mid not\,L \leftarrow$ to a program allows the literal L to be sanctioned that otherwise would not be, but this may cause literals that are entailed by the program to decrease since the number of answer sets increases. For example, q is entailed by

$$\{\ q \leftarrow not\,p\ \}$$

but once $p \mid not\,p \leftarrow$ is adopted q is no longer entailed. This property is effectively used in Example 3.4 for cautious closed world reasoning. Sometimes such an addition of valid rules may make an incoherent program to get an answer set. For example,

$$\{\ q \leftarrow not\,p,\ \ \neg q \leftarrow\ \}$$

has no answer set, but with the rule $p \mid not\,p \leftarrow$ it obtains the answer set $\{\neg q, p\}$. The schema T in autoepistemic logic and the rule $L \mid not\,L \leftarrow$ in GEDPs can thus be applied to various domains other than abduction such as contradiction resolution, meta-programming and reflection (Konolige, 1992).

3. Gelfond gives another cautious semantics for the closed world assumption in order to treat Example 3.4

properly by introducing the concept of *strong introspection* (Gelfond, 1991). However, unlike Theorem 3.4 for our possible model semantics, this concept cannot be embedded into MBNF (Lifschitz, 1992).

4. Positive *not* can be used to represent conditional rules. For example,

$$p \mid not\ q \leftarrow$$

can be viewed as a conditional formula which states that p is true if q is true. In this sense, the rule is similar to

$$p \leftarrow q.$$

In fact, there is a case that the former rule can be replaced with the latter rule by shifting positive *not* into the body. However, once a "deadlock" loop is constructed with these conditional formulas as Example 4.1, we will have two alternative answer sets, one including every element of the loop and the other including nothing in the loop. We expect that this kind of conditional rules may have interesting applications. On the other hand, a rule having no literals but positive *not* in its head can be used to represent *integrity constraints*. In this case,

$$not\ p \leftarrow q$$

has exactly the same effect as the rule

$$\leftarrow p, q.$$

It may also be interesting to investigate for what class of programs such shifting of positive *not* is possible.

5. Concerning generalizations of the results in this paper, there are a couple of interesting topics. First, the first-order abductive framework $\langle T, \Gamma \rangle$, where T and Γ are sets of first-order formulas, can be translated into the MBNF bimodal formula

$$\bigwedge_{F \in T} \mathrm{B} F \wedge \bigwedge_{G \in \Gamma} (\mathrm{B} G \vee not\ G),$$

or into the set of formulas in autoepistemic logic

$$T \cup \{\ BG \supset G \mid G \in \Gamma\ \}.$$

Secondly, Eiter et al. recently proposed a new nonmonotonic formalism called *curbing* (Eiter et al., 1993) which interprets disjunctions inclusively. Since their *good models* are not necessarily minimal models, it is interesting to see whether MBNF can express curbing or not. In the context of logic programming, it turns out that there is a close relationship between good models and possible models. Thirdly, the computational complexity of propositional MBNF and the possibility of embedding MBNF into autoepistemic logic in general are both left open.

7 Conclusion

This paper has provided a number of new results in the class of general extended disjunctive programs, i.e., disjunctive programs which permit negation as failure and classical negation both positively and negatively. In particular, we have shown in this paper

- an embedding of abductive programs into GEDPs,
- a translation the possible model semantics for NDPs into the answer set semantics for GEDPs,
- a complexity characterization of GEDPs based on a translation of GEDPs into EDPs,
- a computational method for GEDPs based on a translation of GEDPs into PDPs, and
- a relationship between GEDPs and autoepistemic logic.

With these results, we can conclude that the concept of positive occurrences of negation as failure is a useful tool for representing knowledge in various domains in which the principle of minimality is too strong.

The class of GEDPs is a natural extension of previously proposed logic programs, and is an "ultimate" extension with negation as failure. A number of new nonmonotonic logics have recently been proposed in order to cover the growing expressiveness of logic programming. These logics include disjunctive default logic, reflexive autoepistemic logic, and MBNF. On the other hand, existing nonmonotonic formalisms have been tested in various ways whether they are better suited than others for applications to the semantics of logic programming. Circumscription, autoepistemic logic, default logic, and their variants have competed with each other for victory, and winners frequently changed in this decade. We suggest in this paper that, among all these formalisms, autoepistemic logic is one of the best because of its "non-minimal" nature. That is, abduction and inclusive disjunctions in knowledge representation are naturally expressed by this unique feature of autoepistemic logic. Introspective natures involved by autoepistemic logic enable us to believe a certain proposition either from the lack of belief in another proposition or from no additional precondition. These properties can completely describe the meanings of negative and positive occurrences of negation as failure in logic programming.

Acknowledgements

We thank Thomas Eiter and George Gottlob for their comments on complexity results in this paper.

References

C. Bell, A. Nerode, R.T. Ng and V.S. Subrahmanian (1992). Implementing deductive databases by linear programming. In: *Proc. 11th ACM SIGACT-SIGMOD-SIGART Symp. Principles of Database Systems*, San Diego, CA, 283–292.

R. Ben-Eliyahu and R. Dechter (1992). Propositional semantics for disjunctive logic programs. In: *Proc. Joint Int. Conf. Symp. Logic Programming*, Washington, D.C., 813–827, MIT Press.

A. Beringer and T. Schaub (1993). Minimal belief and negation as failure: a feasible approach. In: *Proc. AAAI-93*, Washington, D.C., 400–405.

G. Brewka and K. Konolige (1993). An abductive framework for general logic programs and other nonmonotonic systems. In: *Proc. IJCAI-93*, Chambery, 9–15.

E.P.F. Chan (1993). A possible world semantics for disjunctive databases. *IEEE Trans. Data and Knowledge Engineering*, 5(2):282–292.

J. Chen (1993). Minimal knowledge + negation as failure = only knowing (sometimes). In: *Proc. 2nd Int. Workshop Logic Programming and Non-monotonic Reasoning*, Lisbon, 132–150, MIT Press.

T. Eiter and G. Gottlob (1992). Reasoning with parsimonious and moderately grounded expansions. *Fundamenta Informaticae*, 17(1,2):31–53.

T. Eiter and G. Gottlob (1993). Complexity results for disjunctive logic programming and application to nonmonotonic logics, In: *Proc. 1993 Int. Logic Programming Symp.*, Vancouver, 266–278, MIT Press.

T. Eiter, G. Gottlob and Y. Gurevich (1993). Curb your theory!—a circumscriptive approach for inclusive interpretation of disjunctive information. In: *Proc. IJCAI-93*, Chambery, 634–639.

J.A. Fernandez and J. Minker (1992). Disjunctive deductive databases. In: *Proc. Int. Conf. Logic Programming and Automated Reasoning*, Lecture Notes in Artificial Intelligence, 624, 332–356, Springer-Verlag.

M. Gelfond (1991). Strong introspection. In: *Proc. AAAI-91*, Anaheim, CA, 386–391.

M. Gelfond and V. Lifschitz (1991). Classical negation in logic programs and disjunctive databases. *New Generation Computing*, 9:365–385.

M. Gelfond, V. Lifschitz, H. Przymusinska and M. Truszczynski (1991). Disjunctive defaults. In: *Proc. KR '91*, Cambridge, MA, 230–237, Morgan Kaufmann.

G. Gottlob (1992). Complexity results for nonmonotonic logics. *J. Logic and Computation*, 2(3):397–425.

K. Inoue (1991). Extended logic programs with default assumptions. In: *Proc. 8th Int. Conf. Logic Programming*, Paris, 490–504. An extended version: Hypothetical reasoning in logic programs. *J. Logic Programming*, 18, to appear, 1994.

K. Inoue, M. Koshimura and R. Hasegawa (1992). Embedding negation as failure into a model generation theorem prover. In: *Proc. 11th Int. Conf. Automated Deduction*, Lecture Notes in Artificial Intelligence, 607, 400–415, Springer-Verlag.

K. Inoue, Y. Ohta, R. Hasegawa and M. Nakashima (1993). Bottom-up abduction by model generation. In: *Proc. IJCAI-93*, Chambery, 102–108.

K. Inoue and C. Sakama (1993). Transforming abductive logic programs to disjunctive programs. In: *Proc. 10th Int. Conf. Logic Programming*, Budapest, 335–353, MIT Press.

A.C. Kakas and P. Mancarella (1990). Generalized stable models: a semantics for abduction. In: *Proc. ECAI-90*, Stockholm, 385–391.

A.C. Kakas, R.A. Kowalski and F. Toni (1992). Abductive logic programming. *J. Logic and Computation*, 2(6):719–770.

K. Konolige (1988). On the relation between default and autoepistemic logic. *Artificial Intelligence*, 35:343–382.

K. Konolige (1992). An autoepistemic analysis of metalevel reasoning in logic programming. In: *Proc. 3rd Int. Workshop Meta-Programming in Logic*, Lecture Notes in Computer Science, 649, 26–48, Springer-Verlag.

V. Lifschitz (1992). Minimal belief and negation as failure. An earlier version: Nonmonotonic databases and epistemic queries. In: *Proc. IJCAI-91*, Sydney, 381–386, 1991.

V. Lifschitz and G. Schwarz (1993). Extended logic programs as autoepistemic theories. In: *Proc. 2nd Int. Workshop Logic Programming and Non-monotonic Reasoning*, Lisbon, 101–114, MIT Press.

V. Lifschitz and T.Y.C. Woo (1992). Answer sets in general nonmonotonic reasoning (preliminary report). In: *Proc. KR '92*, Boston, MA, 603–614, Morgan Kaufmann.

W. Marek and M. Truszczynski (1993). Reflexive autoepistemic logic and logic programming. In: *Proc. 2nd Int. Workshop Logic Programming and Non-monotonic Reasoning*, Lisbon, 115–131, MIT Press.

R.C. Moore (1985). Semantical considerations on nonmonotonic logic. *Artificial Intelligence*, 25:75–94.

C. Sakama (1989). Possible model semantics for disjunctive databases. In: *Proc. 1st Int. Conf. Deductive and Object-Oriented Databases*, Kyoto, 337–351.

C. Sakama and K. Inoue (1993a). Relating disjunctive logic programs to default theories. In: *Proc. 2nd Int. Workshop Logic Programming and Non-monotonic Reasoning*, Lisbon, 266–282, MIT Press.

C. Sakama and K. Inoue (1993b). Negation in disjunctive logic programs. In: *Proc. 10th Int. Conf. Logic Programming*, Budapest, 703–719, MIT Press.

C. Sakama and K. Inoue (1994). On the equivalence between disjunctive and abductive logic programs. In: *Proc. 11th Int. Conf. Logic Programming*, Santa Margherita Ligure, to appear, MIT Press.

J.S. Schlipf (1992). Formalizing a logic for logic programming. *Ann. Mathematics and Artificial Intelligence*, 5:279–302.

G.F. Schwarz (1991). Autoepistemic logic of knowledge. In: *Proc. 1st Int. Workshop Logic Programming and Non-monotonic Reasoning*, Washington, D.C., 260–274, MIT Press.

Probabilistic Reasoning in Terminological Logics

Manfred Jaeger
Max-Planck-Institut für Informatik,
Im Stadtwald, D-66123 Saarbrücken

Abstract

In this paper a probabilistic extensions for terminological knowledge representation languages is defined. Two kinds of probabilistic statements are introduced: statements about conditional probabilities between concepts and statements expressing uncertain knowledge about a specific object. The usual model-theoretic semantics for terminological logics are extended to define interpretations for the resulting probabilistic language. It is our main objective to find an adequate modelling of the way the two kinds of probabilistic knowledge are combined in commonsense inferences of probabilistic statements. Cross entropy minimization is a technique that turns out to be very well suited for achieving this end.

1 INTRODUCTION

Terminological knowledge representation languages (concept languages, terminological logics) are used to describe hierarchies of concepts. While the expressive power of the various languages that have been defined (e.g. KL-ONE [BS85] $\mathcal{ALC}$ [SSS91]) varies greatly in that they allow for more or less sophisticated concept descriptions, they all have one thing in common: the hierarchies described are purely qualitative, i.e. only inclusion, equality, or disjointness relations between concepts can be expressed.

In this paper we investigate an extension of terminological knowledge representation languages that incorporate quantitative statements.

A hybrid terminological logic that allows to express both general world knowledge about the relationships between concepts, and information about the nature of individual objects, gives rise to two kinds of quantitative statements: terminological (T-box) axioms may be refined by stating graded or partial subsumption relations, and assertions (A-box statements) can be generalized by allowing to express uncertain knowledge.

Let us illustrate the use of quantitative statements by an example. The following is a simple knowledge base that could be formulated in any concept language:

Example 1.1

T-box:	Flying_bird	$\subseteq$	Bird	(1)
	Antarctic_bird	$\subseteq$	Bird	(2)
A-box:	Opus	$\in$	Bird	(3)

In this purely qualitative description a lot of information we may possess cannot be expressed. The two subconcepts of Bird that are specified, for instance, are very different with regard to the degree by which they exhaust the superconcept. One would like to make this difference explicit by stating relative weights, or conditional probabilities, for concepts in a manner like

$$\text{P(Flying\_bird|Bird)} = 0.95 \quad (4)$$
$$\text{P(Antarctic\_bird|Bird)} = 0.01 \quad (5)$$

Also, it may be desirable to express a degree by which the two concepts Antarctic_bird and Flying_bird, which stand in no subconcept- superconcept relation, intersect:

$$\text{P(Flying\_bird|Antarctic\_bird)} = 0.2 \quad (6)$$

For the A-box, apart from the certain knowledge $Opus \in$ Bird, some uncertain information may be available, that we should be able to express as well. There may be strong evidence, for example, that $Opus$ is in fact an antarctic bird. Hence

$$\text{P}(Opus \in \text{Antarctic\_bird}) = 0.9 \quad (7)$$

could be added to our knowledge base.

It is important to realize that these two kinds of probabilistic statements are of a completely different nature. The former codifies *statistical information* that, generally, will be gained by observing a large number of individual objects and checking their membership of the various concepts. The latter expresses a *degree of belief* in a specific proposition. Its value most often will be justified only by a subjective assessment of "likelihood".

This dual use of the term "probability" has caused a lot of controversy over what the true meaning of probability is: a measure of frequency, or of subjective belief (e.g. [Jay78]). A comprehensive study of both aspects of the term is [Car50]. More recently, Bacchus and Halpern have developed a probabilistic extension of first-order logic that accommodates both notions of probability [Bac90],[Hal90].

Now that we have stressed the differences in assigning a probability to subsets of a general concept on the one hand, and to assertions about an individual object on the other, we are faced with the question of how these two notions of probability interact: how does a body of statistical information affect our beliefs in assertions about an individual?

Among the first to address this problem was Carnap, who formulated the rule of *direct (inductive) inference* [Car50]: if for an object a it is known that it belongs to a class C, and our statistics say that an element of C belongs to another class D with probability p, then our degree of belief in a's membership of D should be just p. Applied to the statements (1),(3) and (4) of our example, direct inference yields a degree of belief of 0.95 in the proposition *Opus* ∈ Flying_bird.

A generalization of direct inference is *Jeffrey's rule* [Jef65]: if all we know about a, is that it belongs to either of finitely many mutually disjoint classes $C_1,\ldots,C_n$, and to each possibility we assign a probability p_i ($\sum_{i=1}^n p_i = 1$), if furthermore, the statistical probability for D given C_i is q_i, then our degree of belief for a being in D should be given by

$$\sum_{i=1}^n p_i q_i.$$

Bacchus et al. have developed a method to derive degrees of belief for sentences in first-order logic on the basis of first-order and statistical information [BGHK92], [BGHK93]. The technique they use is motivated by direct inference, but is of a far more general applicability. However, it does not allow to derive new subjective beliefs given both subjective and statistical information.

In this paper we develop a formal semantical framework that for terminological logics models the influence of statistical, generic information on the assignment of degrees of belief to specific assertions. In order to do this, we will interpret both kinds of probabilistic statements in one common probability space that essentially consists of the set of concept terms that can be formed in the language of the given knowledge base [1]. Defining all the probability measures on the

[1] Different from [Bac90],[Hal90], for instance, where

same probability space allows us to compare the measure assigned to an object a with the generic measure defined by the given statistical information. The most reasonable assignment of a probability measure to a, then, is to choose, among all the measures consistent with the constraints known for a, the one that most closely resembles the generic measure. The key question to be answered, therefore, is how resemblance of probability measures should be measured. We argue that minimizing the cross entropy of the two measures is the appropriate way.

Paris and Vencovská, considering probabilistic inferences very similar in nature to ours, use a different semantical interpretation, which, too, leads them to the minimum cross entropy principle [PV90], [PV92].

Previous work on probabilistic extensions of concept languages was done by Heinsohn and Owsnicki-Klewe [HOK88],[Hei91]. Here the emphasis is on computing new conditional probabilities entailed by the given ones. Formal semantics for the interpretation of probabilistic assertions, which are the main contribution of our work, are not given.

2 SYNTAX

In order to facilitate the exposition of our approach we shall use, for the time being, a very restricted, merely propositional, concept language, which we call $\mathcal{PCL}$. In the last section of this paper an explanation will be given of how the formalism can be extended to more expressive concept languages, notably $\mathcal{ALC}$.

The *concept terms* in our language are just propositional expressions built from a finite set of *concept names* $S_C = \{A, B, C, \ldots\}$. The set of concept terms is denoted by $T(S_C)$. *Terminological axioms* have the form

$$A \subseteq C \text{ or } A = C$$

with $A \in S_C$ and $C \in T(S_C)$. *Probabilistic terminological axioms* are expressions

$$P(C|D) = p,$$

where C and D are concept terms and $p \in]0,1[$. Finally, we have *probabilistic assertions*

$$P(a \in C) = p,$$

where a is an element of a finite set of *object names* S_O, and $p \in [0,1]$.

A knowledge base ($\mathcal{KB}$) in $\mathcal{PCL}$ consists of a set of terminological axioms ($\mathcal{T}$), a set of probabilistic terminological axioms ($\mathcal{PT}$) and a set of probabilistic assertions ($\mathcal{P}_a$) for every object name a:

$$\mathcal{KB} = \mathcal{T} \cup \mathcal{PT} \cup \bigcup \{\mathcal{P}_a | a \in S_O\}.$$

statistical and propositional probabilities are interpreted by probability measures on domains and sets of worlds, respectively

There is a certain asymmetry in our probabilistic treatment of terminological axioms on the one hand, and assertions on the other. While deterministic assertions were completely replaced by probabilistic ones ($a \in C$ has to be expressed by $P(a \in C) = 1$), deterministic terminological axioms were retained, and not identified with 0,1-valued probabilistic axioms (which, therefore, are not allowed in $\mathcal{PT}$).

There are several reasons for taking this approach: First, our syntax for probabilistic terminological axioms is very general in that conditional probabilities for arbitrary pairs of concept terms may be specified. Terminological axioms, on the other hand, are generally required (as in our definition) to have only a concept name on their left hand side. Also, in order to make the computation of subsumption with respect to a terminology somewhat more tractable, usually additional conditions are imposed on $\mathcal{T}$ (e.g. that it must not contain cycles) that we would not want to have on $\mathcal{PT}$ (it may be very important, for instance, to be able to specify both $P(C|D)$ and $P(D|C)$). In essence, it can be said that the non-uniformity of our treatment of deterministic and probabilistic terminological axioms results from our intention to define a probabilistic extension for terminological logics that does not affect the scope and efficiency of standard terminological reasoning in the given logics.

Furthermore, it will be seen that even for actual probabilistic reasoning it proves useful to make use of the deterministic information in $\mathcal{T}$ and the probabilistic information in $\mathcal{PT}$ in two different ways, and it would remain to do so, if both kinds of information were encoded uniformly.

3 SEMANTICS

Our approach to formulating semantics for the language $\mathcal{PCL}$ modifies and extends the usual model-theoretic semantics for concept languages. The terminological axioms $\mathcal{T}$ are interpreted by means of a domain $\mathbf{D}$ and an interpretation function I in the usual way. In order to give meaning to the expressions in $\mathcal{PT}$ and the $\mathcal{P}_a$ ($a \in S_O$), we first have to specify the probability space on which the probability measures described by these expressions shall be defined.

For this probability space we choose the language itself. That is to say, we take the *Lindenbaum algebra*

$$\mathfrak{A}(S_C) := ([T(S_C)], \vee, \wedge, \neg, 0, 1)$$

as the underlying probability space. Here, $[T(S_C)]$ is the set of equivalence classes modulo logical equivalence in $T(S_C)$. The operations $\vee$, $\wedge$, and $\neg$ are defined by performing disjunction, conjunction, and negation on representatives of the equivalence classes. We shall use letters C,D,... both for concept terms from $T(S_C)$ and their equivalence class in $[T(S_C)]$.

An *atom* in a boolean algebra $\mathfrak{A}$ is an element $A \neq 0$, such that there is no $A' \notin \{0, A\}$ with $A' \subset A$ (to be read as an abbreviation for $A' \wedge \neg A = 0$). The atoms of $\mathfrak{A}(S_C)$ with $S_C = \{A_1, \ldots, A_n\}$ are just the concept terms of the form $B_1 \wedge \ldots \wedge B_n$ with $B_i \in \{A_i, \neg A_i\}$ for $i = 1, \ldots, n$. The set of atoms of $\mathfrak{A}(S_C)$ is denoted by $A(S_C)$.

Every element of $\mathfrak{A}(S_C)$, then, is (in the equivalence class of) a finite disjunction of atoms.

On $\mathfrak{A}(S_C)$ probability measures may be defined. Recall that $\mu : \mathfrak{A}(S_C) \to [0,1]$ is a probability measure iff $\mu(1) = 1$, and $\mu(C \vee D) = \mu(C) + \mu(D)$ for all C,D with $C \wedge D = 0$. The set of probability measures on $\mathfrak{A}(S_C)$ is denoted by $\Delta\mathfrak{A}(S_C)$. Note that $\mu \in \Delta\mathfrak{A}(S_C)$ is fully specified by the values it takes on the atoms of $\mathfrak{A}(S_C)$.

The general structure of an interpretation for a vocabulary $S = S_C \cup S_O$ can now be described: a standard interpretation $(\mathbf{D}, I)$ for $\mathcal{T}$ will be extended to an interpretation $(\mathbf{D}, I, \mu, (\nu_a)_{a \in S_O})$, where $\mu \in \Delta\mathfrak{A}(S_C)$ is the *generic* measure used to interpret $\mathcal{PT}$, and $\nu_a \in \Delta\mathfrak{A}(S_C)$ interprets $\mathcal{P}_a$. Hence, we deviate from the standard way interpretations are defined by not mapping $a \in S_O$ to an element of the domain, but to a probability measure expressing our uncertain knowledge of a.

What conditions should we impose on an interpretation to be a model of a knowledge base? Certainly, the measures μ and ν_a must satisfy the constraints in $\mathcal{PT}$ and $\mathcal{P}_a$. However, somewhat more is required when we intend to model the interaction between the two kinds of probabilistic statements that takes place in "commonsense" reasoning about probabilities.

The general information provided by $\mathcal{PT}$ leads us to assign degrees of belief to assertions about an object a that go beyond what is strictly implied by $\mathcal{P}_a$.

What, then, are the rules governing this reasoning process? The fundamental assumption in assigning a degree of belief to a's belonging to a certain concept C is to view a as a random element of the domain about which some partial information has been obtained, but that, in aspects that no observation has been made about, behaves like a typical representative of the domain, for which our general statistics apply.

In the case that $\mathcal{P}_a$ contains constraints only about mutually exclusive concepts this intuition leads to Jeffrey's rule: If

$$\mathcal{P}_a = \{P(a \in C_i) = p_i \mid i = 1, \ldots, n\},$$

where the C_i are mutually exclusive, and, as may be assumed without loss of generality, exhaustive as well, and $\mu \in \Delta\mathfrak{A}(S_C)$ reflects our general statistical knowledge about the domain, then the probability measure that interprets a should be defined by

$$\nu_a(C) := \sum_{i=1}^{n}(p_i \times \mu(C \mid C_i)) \quad (C \in \mathfrak{A}(S_C)).$$

For constraints on not necessarily exclusive concepts we need to find a more general definition for a measure "most closely resembling" the given generic measure μ and satisfying the constraints. Formally, we are looking for a function d that maps every pair (μ, ν) of probability measures on a given (finite) probability space to a real number $d(\mu, \nu) \geq 0$, the "distance" of ν to μ:

$$d: \Delta^n \times \Delta^n \to \mathbf{R}^{\geq 0},$$

where

$$\Delta^n := \{(x_1, \ldots, x_n) \in [0,1]^n \mid \sum_{i=1}^{n} x_i = 1\}$$

denotes the set of probability measures on a probability space of size n.

Given such a d, a subset N of Δ^n and a measure μ, we can then define the set of elements of N that have minimal distance to μ:

$$\pi_N^d(\mu) := \{\nu \in N \mid d(\mu, \nu) = \inf\{d(\mu, \nu') \mid \nu' \in N\}\} \quad (8)$$

Three requirements are immediate that have to be met by a distance function d in order to be used for defining the belief measure ν_a most closely resembling the generic μ:

(i) If N is defined by a constraint-set $\mathcal{P}_a$, then $\pi_N^d(\mu)$ is a singleton.
(ii) If $\mu \in N$, then $\pi_N^d(\mu) = \{\mu\}$.
(iii) If N is defined by a set of constraints on disjoint sets, then $\pi_N^d(\mu)$ is the probability measure obtained by Jeffrey's rule applied to μ and these constraints.

We propose to use the *cross entropy* of two probability measures as the appropriate definition for their distance. For probability measures $\mu = (\mu_1, \ldots, \mu_n)$ and $\nu = (\nu_1, \ldots, \nu_n)$ define:

$$CE(\mu, \nu) := \begin{cases} \sum_{\substack{i=1 \\ \mu_i, \nu_i \neq 0}}^{n} \nu_i \ln \frac{\nu_i}{\mu_i} & \text{if for all } i: \\ & \mu_i = 0 \Rightarrow \nu_i = 0, \\ \infty & \text{otherwise.} \end{cases}$$

This slightly generalizes the usual definition of cross entropy by allowing for 0-components in μ and ν.

Cross entropy often is referred to as a "measure of the distance between two probability measures" [DZ82], or a "measure of information dissimilarity for two probability measures" [Sho86]. These interpretations have to be taken cautiously, however. Note in particular that neither is CE symmetric nor does it satisfy the triangle inequality. All that CE has in common with a metric is positivity:

$$CE(\mu, \nu) \geq 0,$$

where equality holds iff $\mu = \nu$. Hence property (ii) holds for CE. It has been shown that cross entropy satisfies (i) (for any closed and convex set N, provided there is at least one $\nu \in N$ with $CE(\mu, \nu) < \infty$), and (iii) as well ([SJ80], [Wen88]). Therefore, we may define for closed and convex $N \subseteq \Delta^n$ and $\mu \in \Delta^n$:

$$\pi_N(\mu) := \begin{cases} \text{the unique} & \text{if } CE(\mu, \nu) < \infty \\ \text{element in } \pi_N^{CE}(\mu) & \text{for some } \nu \in N \\ \text{undefined} & \text{otherwise.} \end{cases}$$

There are several lines of argument that support the use of cross entropy for forming our beliefs about a on the basis of the given generic μ and a set of constraints.

One is to appeal directly to cross entropy's properties as a measure of information discrepancy, and to argue that our beliefs about a should deviate from the generic measure by assuming as little additional information as possible.

Another line of argument does not focus on the properties of cross entropy directly, but investigates fundamental requirements for a procedure that changes a given probability measure μ to a posterior measure ν in a (closed and convex) set N. Shore and Johnson [SJ80], [SJ83] formulate five axioms for such a procedure (the first one being just our uniqueness condition (i)), and prove that when the procedure satisfies the axioms, and is of the form $\nu = \pi_N^d(\mu)$ for some function d, then d must be equivalent to cross entropy (i.e. must have the same minima).

Paris and Vencovská, in a similar vein, have given an axiomatic justification of the *maximum entropy* principle [PV90], which, when applied to knowledge bases expressing the two types of probabilistic statements in a certain way, yields the same results as minimizing cross entropy [PV92].

With cross entropy as the central tool for the interpretation of $\mathcal{P}_a$, we can now give a complete set of definitions for the semantics of $\mathcal{PCL}$.

Definition 3.1 Let $\mathcal{KB} = \mathcal{T} \cup \mathcal{PT} \cup \bigcup \{\mathcal{P}_a \mid a \in S_C\}$ a $\mathcal{PCL}$-knowledge base. We define for $\mu \in \Delta \mathfrak{A}(S_C)$:

- μ is *consistent with* $\mathcal{T}$ iff $\mathcal{T} \models C = 0 \Rightarrow \mu(C) = 0$;

- μ is *consistent with* $\mathcal{PT}$ iff $P(C|D) = p \in \mathcal{PT} \Rightarrow \mu(C \wedge D) = p \times \mu(D)$;

- μ is *consistent with* $\mathcal{P}_a$ iff $P(a \in C) = p \in \mathcal{P}_a \Rightarrow \mu(C) = p$.

For a given $\mathcal{KB}$, we use the following notation:

$\Delta_{\mathcal{T}}\mathfrak{A}(S_C) :=$
  $\{\mu \in \Delta\mathfrak{A}(S_C) \mid \mu$ is consistent with $\mathcal{T}\}$,
$Gen(\mathcal{KB}) :=$
  $\{\mu \in \Delta\mathfrak{A}(S_C) \mid \mu$ is consistent with $\mathcal{T}$ and $\mathcal{PT}\}$,
$Bel_a(\mathcal{KB}) :=$
  $\{\mu \in \Delta\mathfrak{A}(S_C) \mid \mu$ is consistent with $\mathcal{T}$ and $\mathcal{P}_a\}$.

When no ambiguities can arise, we also write Gen (the set of possible generic measures) and Bel_a (the set of possible belief measures for a) for short.

Definition 3.2 Let $S = S_C \cup S_O$ be a vocabulary. A $\mathcal{PCL}$-interpretation for S is a triple $(\mathbf{D}, I, \mu)$, where $\mathbf{D}$ is a set,

$$I: S_C \to 2^{\mathbf{D}}, \quad I: S_O \to \Delta\mathfrak{A}(S_C),$$

and $\mu \in \Delta\mathfrak{A}(S_C)$. Furthermore, for all concept terms C with $I(C) = \emptyset$: $\mu(C) = 0$ and $I(a)(C) = 0$ ($a \in S_O$) must hold. For $I(a)$ we also write ν_a.

Definition 3.3 Let $\mathcal{KB} = \mathcal{T} \cup \mathcal{PT} \cup \bigcup\{\mathcal{P}_a \mid a \in S_O\}$ be a $\mathcal{PCL}$-knowledge base. Let $(\mathbf{D}, I, \mu)$ be a $\mathcal{PCL}$-interpretation for the language of $\mathcal{KB}$. We define: $(\mathbf{D}, I, \mu) \models \mathcal{KB}$ ($(\mathbf{D}, I, \mu)$ is a *model* of $\mathcal{KB}$) iff

(i) $(\mathbf{D}, I {\restriction} S_C) \models \mathcal{T}$ in the usual sense.

(ii) $\mu \in Gen(\mathcal{KB})$.

(iii) For all $a \in S_O$: $\pi_{Bel_a(\mathcal{KB})}$ is defined for μ, and $I(a) = \pi_{Bel_a(\mathcal{KB})}(\mu)$.

Definition 3.4 Let $J \subseteq [0, 1]$. We write

$$\mathcal{KB} \models P(C|D) \in J$$

iff for every $(\mathbf{D}, I, \mu) \models \mathcal{KB}$: $\mu(C \mid D) \in J$ (if $\mu(D) = 0$, this is considered true for every J). Also, we use the notation

$$\mathcal{KB} \models P(C|D) = J$$

iff $\mathcal{KB} \models P(C|D) \in J$, and J is the minimal subset of [0,1] with this property. Analogously, we use $\mathcal{KB} \models P(a \in C) \in J$, and $\mathcal{KB} \models P(a \in C) = J$.

According to definition 3.2 we are dealing with probability measures on the concept algebra $\mathfrak{A}(S_C)$. An explicit representation of any such measure, i.e. a complete list of the values it takes on $A(S_C)$, would always be of size $2^{|S_C|}$. Fortunately, we usually will not have to actually handle such large representations, though. Since all the probability measures we consider for a specific knowledge base $\mathcal{KB}$ are in $\Delta_{\mathcal{T}}\mathfrak{A}(S_C)$, the relevant probability space for models of $\mathcal{KB}$ only consists of those atoms in $A(S_C)$ whose extensions are not necessarily empty in models of $\mathcal{KB}$:

$$A(\mathcal{T}) := \{C \in A(S_C) \mid \mathcal{T} \not\models C = 0\}$$

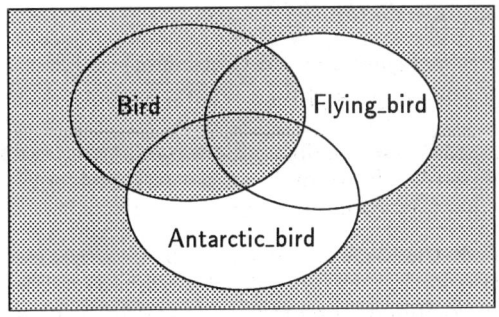

Figure 1: The Algebras $\mathfrak{A}(S_C)$ and $\mathfrak{A}(\mathcal{T})$

Denote the algebra that is generated by these atoms with $\mathfrak{A}(\mathcal{T})$. Technically speaking, $\mathfrak{A}(\mathcal{T})$ is the *relativization* of $\mathfrak{A}(S_C)$ to the element

$$C(\mathcal{T}) := \bigvee A(\mathcal{T})$$

of $\mathfrak{A}(S_C)$. Figure 1 shows the structure of $\mathfrak{A}(S_C)$ for the vocabulary of our introductory example. The shaded area represents the element $C(\mathcal{T})$ for the $\mathcal{T}$ in the example. $\mathfrak{A}(\mathcal{T})$, here, consists of five atoms compared to eight atoms in $\mathfrak{A}(S_C)$.

How much smaller than $\mathfrak{A}(S_C)$ can $\mathfrak{A}(\mathcal{T})$ be expected to be in general? This question obviously is difficult to answer, because it requires a thorough analysis of the structure that $\mathfrak{A}(\mathcal{T})$ is likely to have for real-world instances of $\mathcal{T}$. Here we just mention one property of $\mathcal{T}$ that ensures a non-exponential growth of $|A(\mathcal{T})|$ when new terminological axioms introducing new concept names are added: call $\mathfrak{A}(\mathcal{T})$ *bounded in depth by k* iff every atom in $A(\mathcal{T})$ contains at most k non-negated concept names from S_C as conjuncts. It is easy to see that if $\mathfrak{A}(\mathcal{T})$ is bounded in depth by k, then $|A(\mathcal{T})|$ will have an order of magnitude of $|S_C|^k$ at most. Hence, when new axioms are added to $\mathcal{T}$ in such a way that $\mathfrak{A}(\mathcal{T})$ remains bounded in depth by some number k, then the growth of $|A(\mathcal{T})|$ is polynomial.

The use of the structural information in $\mathcal{T}$ for reducing the underlying probability space from $\mathfrak{A}(S_C)$ to $\mathfrak{A}(\mathcal{T})$ is the second reason for the nonuniform treatment of deterministic and probabilistic terminological axioms that was announced in section 2. If deterministic axioms were treated in precisely the same fashion as probabilistic ones, this would only lead us to handle probability measures all with zeros in the same large set of components, but not to drop these components from our representations in the first place.

Example 3.5 Let $\mathcal{KB}_1$ contain the terminological and probabilistic statements from example 1.1 (the assertion $Opus \in$ Bird being replaced by $P(Opus \in$ Bird$) = 1$). The three statements (4)-(6) in $\mathcal{PT}$ do not determine a unique generic measure μ, but for every $\mu \in Gen(\mathcal{KB}_1)$

$$\mu(\text{Flying\_bird} \mid \text{Antarctic\_bird}) = 0.2$$
$$\text{and } \mu(\text{Flying\_bird} \mid \text{Bird} \wedge \neg\text{Antarctic\_bird}) = 0.958$$

holds: the first conditional probability is explicitly stated in (6), the second can be derived from (4)-(6) by elementary computations.

Since the constraints in $\mathcal{P}_{Opus}$ are equivalent to $P(Opus \in \text{Antarctic\_bird}) = 0.9$ and $P(Opus \in \text{Bird} \wedge \neg\text{Antarctic\_bird}) = 0.1$, and in this case $\pi_{Bel_{Opus}}(\mu)$ is given by Jeffrey's rule,

$$\pi_{Bel_{Opus}}(\mu)(\text{Flying\_bird}) = 0.9 \times 0.2 + 0.1 \times 0.958$$
$$= 0.2758$$

holds for every $\mu \in Gen$. Hence

$$\mathcal{KB}_1 \models P(Opus \in \text{Flying\_bird}) = 0.2758.$$

In the following section we investigate how inferences like these can in general be computed from a $\mathcal{PCL}$-knowledge base.

4 COMPUTING PROBABILITIES

4.1 COMPUTING Gen AND Bel_a

The constraints in $\mathcal{PT}$ and $\mathcal{P}_a$ are linear constraints on $\Delta\mathfrak{A}(S_C)$. When we change the probability space we consider from $\mathfrak{A}(S_C)$ to $\mathfrak{A}(\mathcal{T})$, a constraint of the form $P(C|D) = p$ is interpreted as

$$P(C \wedge C(\mathcal{T}) | D \wedge C(\mathcal{T})) = p.$$

Similarly, $P(a \in C) = p$ must be read as $P(a \in C \wedge C(\mathcal{T})) = p$.

If $|A(\mathcal{T})| = n$, then $\Delta\mathfrak{A}(\mathcal{T})$ is represented by Δ^n. Each of the constraints in $\mathcal{PT}$ or $\mathcal{P}_a$ defines a hyperplane in $\mathbf{R}^n$. $Gen(\mathcal{KB})$ ($Bel_a(\mathcal{KB})$) then, is the intersection of Δ^n with all the hyperplanes defined by constraints in $\mathcal{PT}$ ($\mathcal{P}_a$). Thus, if $\mathcal{PT}$ ($\mathcal{P}_a$) contains k linear independent constraints, $Gen(\mathcal{KB})$ ($Bel_a(\mathcal{KB})$) is a polytope of dimension $\leq n - k$.

Figure 2 shows the intersection of Δ^4 with the two hyperplanes defined by $\{(x_1, x_2, x_3, x_4) \mid x_1 = 0.2(x_1 + x_2)\}$ and $\{(x_1, x_2, x_3, x_4) \mid x_1 = 0.3(x_1 + x_3 + x_4)\}$. The resulting polytope is the line connecting a and b.

A simple algorithm that computes the vertices of the intersection of Δ^n with hyperplanes $H_1, \ldots, H_k$ successively computes $P_i := \Delta^n \cap H_1 \cap \ldots \cap H_i$ ($i = 1, \ldots, k$). After each step P_i is given by a list of its vertices. P_{i+1} is obtained by checking for every pair of vertices of P_i, whether they are connected by an edge, and if this is the case, the intersection of this edge with H_{i+1} (if nonempty) is added to the list of vertices of P_{i+1}.

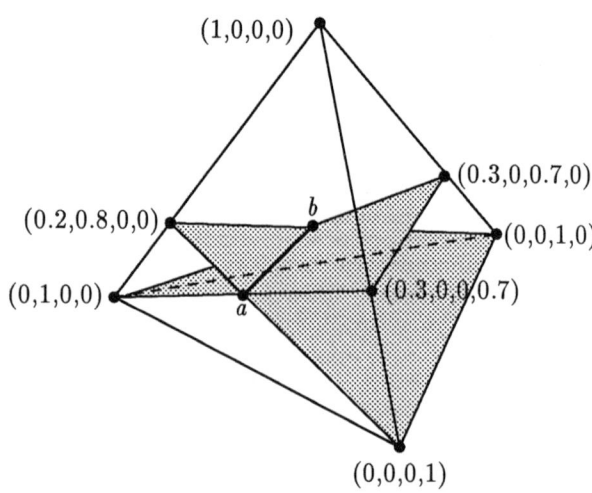

Figure 2: Intersection of Δ^4 With Two Hyperplanes

Example 4.1 The following knowledge base, $\mathcal{KB}_2$, will be used as a running example throughout this section.

$$\mathcal{T}: \quad \mathsf{C} \subseteq \mathsf{A} \wedge \mathsf{B} \qquad (9)$$
$$\mathcal{PT}: \quad P(\mathsf{C}|\mathsf{A}) = 0.1 \qquad (10)$$
$$\phantom{\mathcal{PT}:} \quad P(\mathsf{C}|\mathsf{B}) = 0.9 \qquad (11)$$
$$\mathcal{P}_a \quad P(a \in \mathsf{A}) = 0.5 \qquad (12)$$
$$\phantom{\mathcal{P}_a} \quad P(a \in \mathsf{B}) = 0.5 \qquad (13)$$

The algebra $\mathfrak{A}(\mathcal{T})$ here is generated by the five atoms
$A_1 = \neg\mathsf{A} \wedge \neg\mathsf{B} \wedge \neg\mathsf{C}, \quad A_2 = \neg\mathsf{A} \wedge \mathsf{B} \wedge \neg\mathsf{C},$
$A_3 = \mathsf{A} \wedge \neg\mathsf{B} \wedge \neg\mathsf{C}, \quad A_4 = \mathsf{A} \wedge \mathsf{B} \wedge \neg\mathsf{C},$
$A_5 = \mathsf{A} \wedge \mathsf{B} \wedge \mathsf{C}.$

$Gen(\mathcal{KB}_2)$ is the intersection of Δ^5 with the hyperplanes

$H_1 = \{(x_1, \ldots, x_5) \mid \frac{x_5}{x_3+x_4+x_5} = 0.1\}$ and
$H_2 = \{(x_1, \ldots, x_5) \mid \frac{x_5}{x_2+x_4+x_5} = 0.9\}$,

which is computed to be the convex hull of the three points

$\mu^0 = (1, 0, 0, 0, 0), \qquad \mu^1 = (0, \frac{1}{91}, \frac{81}{91}, 0, \frac{9}{91}),$
$\mu^2 = (0, 0, \frac{80}{90}, \frac{1}{90}, \frac{9}{90}).$

These probability measures represent the extreme ways in which the partial information in $\mathcal{PT}$ can be completed: μ^0 is the borderline case, where (10) and (11) are vacuously true, because of the probabilities of the conditioning concepts being zero. μ^1 and μ^2, on the contrary, both assign probability 1 to $\mathsf{A} \vee \mathsf{B}$, but represent two opposing hypotheses about the conditional probability of A given B. This probability is 1 for μ^2, standing for the case that B is really a subset of A, and 0.9 for μ^1, representing the possibility that A and B intersect only in C.

The set Bel_a is the convex hull of
$\nu^0 = (0.5, 0, 0, 0.5, 0), \quad \nu^1 = (0.5, 0, 0, 0, 0.5),$
$\nu^2 = (0, 0.5, 0.5, 0, 0).$

For the remainder of this paper we will assume that Gen and Bel_a are given explicitly by a list of their vertices, because this allows for the easiest formulation of general properties of $\mathcal{PCL}$. Since the number of vertices in Gen and Bel_a can grow very large, it will probably be a more efficient strategy in practice, to just store a suitable normal form of the sets of linear constraints, and to compute specific solutions as needed.

4.2 CONSISTENCY OF A KNOWLEDGE BASE

The first question about a knowledge base $\mathcal{KB}$ that must be asked is the question of consistency: does $\mathcal{KB}$ have a model? Following (i)-(iii) in definition 3.3, we see that $\mathcal{KB}$ is inconsistent iff one of the following statements (a), (b), and (c) holds:

(a) $\mathcal{T}$ is inconsistent.

(b) $Gen(\mathcal{KB}) = \emptyset$.

(c) For all $\mu \in Gen$ there exists $a \in S_O$ such that $\pi_{Bel_a}(\mu)$ is not defined.

Inconsistency that is due to (a) usually is ruled out by standard restrictions on $\mathcal{T}$: a T-box that does not contain terminological cycles, and in which every concept name appears at most once on the left hand side of a terminological axiom, always has a model. It is trivial to check whether $\mathcal{KB}$ is inconsistent for the reason of $Gen(\mathcal{KB})$ being empty. Also, $\mathcal{KB}$ will be inconsistent if $Bel_a(\mathcal{KB}) = \emptyset$ for some $a \in S_O$, because in this case $\pi_{Bel_a}(\mu)$ is undefined for every μ.

It remains to dispose of the case where $Gen(\mathcal{KB})$ and all $Bel_a(\mathcal{KB})$ are nonempty, but (c) still holds. By the definition of $\pi_{Bel_a}(\mu)$ this happens iff for all $\mu \in Gen(\mathcal{KB})$ there exists $a \in S_O$ such that $CE(\mu, \nu) = \infty$ for all $\nu \in Bel_a(\mathcal{KB})$. Since $CE(\mu, \nu)$ is infinite iff for some index i: $\mu_i = 0$ and $\nu_i > 0$, it is the set of 0-components of μ and ν that we must turn our attention to.

Definition 4.2 Let $\mu \in \Delta^n$. Define
$$Z(\mu) := \{i \in \{1, \ldots, n\} \mid \mu_i = 0\}$$

For a polytope M the notation intM is used for the set of interior points of M; $conv\{\mu^1, \ldots, \mu^k\}$ stands for the convex hull of $\mu^1, \ldots, \mu^k \in \Delta^n$. The next theorem is a trivial observation.

Theorem 4.3 Let $M \subseteq \Delta^n$ be a polytope and $\mu \in int$M. Then for every $\mu' \in$M:
$$Z(\mu) \subseteq Z(\mu').$$
Particularly, $Z(\mu')$=$Z(\mu)$ if $\mu' \in int$M.

With these provisions we can now formulate a simple test for (c):

Theorem 4.4
Let M=$conv\{\mu^1, \ldots, \mu^k\}$ and N=$conv\{\nu^1, \ldots, \nu^l\}$ be polytopes in Δ^n. Define $\bar{\mu} := \frac{1}{k}(\mu^1 + \ldots + \mu^k)$. Then the following are equivalent:

(i) $\forall \mu \in$ M $\forall \nu \in$ N : $CE(\mu, \nu) = \infty$.

(ii) $Z(\bar{\mu}) \not\subseteq Z(\nu^j)$ for $j = 1, \ldots, l$.

Proof: (i) is equivalent to $Z(\mu) \not\subseteq Z(\nu)$ for all $\mu \in$ M and all $\nu \in$ N, which in turn is equivalent to (ii), because by theorem 4.3 $Z(\bar{\mu})$ is minimal in $\{Z(\mu) \mid \mu \in$ M$\}$, and the sets $Z(\nu^j)$ are maximal in $\{Z(\nu) \mid \nu \in$ N$\}$ (i.e. $\forall \nu \in$ N $\exists j \in \{1, \ldots, l\}$ with $Z(\nu) \subseteq Z(\nu^j)$). $\square$

Example 4.5 $\mathcal{KB}_2$ is consistent: $\mathcal{T}$ clearly is consistent, $Gen(\mathcal{KB}_2)$ and $Bel_a(\mathcal{KB}_2)$ are nonempty, and $Z(\bar{\mu}) = \emptyset$ holds for $\bar{\mu} := 1/3(\mu^0 + \mu^1 + \mu^2)$.

4.3 STATISTICAL INFERENCES

Statistical inferences from a knowledge base $\mathcal{KB}$ are computations of sets J for which $\mathcal{KB} \models$ P(C|D)=J.

Definition 4.6 Let $\mathcal{KB}$ be a $\mathcal{PCL}$- knowledge base.
$Gen^*(\mathcal{KB}) :=$
$\{\mu \in Gen(\mathcal{KB}) \mid \forall a \in S_O : \pi_{Bel_a(\mathcal{KB})}(\mu) \text{ is defined}\}$

Thus, $Gen^*(\mathcal{KB})$ is the set of generic measures that actually occur in models of $\mathcal{KB}$. $Gen^*(\mathcal{KB})$ is a convex subset of $Gen(\mathcal{KB})$, which, if $\mathcal{KB}$ is consistent, contains at least all the interior points of $Gen(\mathcal{KB})$. If $\mathcal{KB} \models$ P(C|D)=J we then have

$$J = \{\mu(C \mid D) \mid \mu \in Gen^*(\mathcal{KB}), \mu(D) > 0\}.$$

The following theorem, however, states that J can be essentially computed by simply looking at Gen, rather than Gen^*. Essentially here means that the closure of J (clJ) does not depend on the difference $Gen \setminus Gen^*$.

Theorem 4.7
Let $\mathcal{KB}$ be a consistent $\mathcal{PCL}$-knowledge base, C,D $\in$ T(S_C). Let Gen=$conv\{\mu^1, \ldots, \mu^k\}$, and suppose that $\mathcal{KB} \models$ P(C|D) = J. Then, either $\mu^i(D) = 0$ for $i = 1, \ldots, k$ and J=$\emptyset$, or J is a nonempty interval and
$$\inf J = \min\{\mu^i(C \mid D) \mid 1 \leq i \leq k, \mu^i(D) > 0\} \quad (14)$$
$$\sup J = \max\{\mu^i(C \mid D) \mid 1 \leq i \leq k, \mu^i(D) > 0\} \quad (15)$$

Proof: The proof is straightforward. The continuous function $\mu \mapsto \mu(C \mid D)$ attains its minimal and maximal values at vertices of Gen. From the continuity of this function it follows that for computing the closure of J one can take the minimum and maximum in (14) and (15) over every vertex of Gen, even though they may not all belong to Gen^*. Furthermore, it is easy to see that vertices μ^i with $\mu^i(D) = 0$ need not be considered. The details of the proof are spelled out in [Jae94]. □

Applying theorem 4.4 to the face of *Gen* on which $\mu(C \mid D) = \inf J$ yields a method to decide whether one point of this face is in Gen^*, i.e. whether $\inf J \in J$. Analogously for $\sup J$.

Corollary 4.8 Let $\mathcal{KB} = \mathcal{T} \cup \mathcal{PT}$ and $\mathcal{KB}' = \mathcal{T}' \cup \mathcal{PT}' \cup \bigcup \{\mathcal{P}'_a \mid a \in S_O\}$ be two consistent knowledge bases with $\mathcal{T} = \mathcal{T}'$ and $\mathcal{PT} = \mathcal{PT}'$. For C,D∈T($S_C$) let $\mathcal{KB} \models P(C|D) = J$ and $\mathcal{KB}' \models P(C|D) = J'$. Then $J = clJ'$.

By corollary 4.8 the statistical probabilities that can be derived from a consistent knowledge base are essentially independent from the statements about subjective beliefs contained in the knowledge base. The influence of the latter is reduced to possibly removing endpoints from the interval J that would be obtained by considering the given terminological and statistical information only. This is a very reasonable behaviour of the system: generally subjective beliefs held about an individual should not influence our theory about the quantitative relations in the world in general. If, however, we assign a strictly positive degree of belief to an individual's belonging to a set C, then this should preclude models of the world in which C is assigned the probability 0, i.e. C is seen as (practically) impossible. Those are precisely the conditions under which the addition of a set $\mathcal{P}_a$ to a knowledge base will cause the rejection of measures from (the boundary of) *Gen* for models of $\mathcal{KB}$.

Example 4.9 Suppose we are interested in what $\mathcal{KB}_2$ implies with respect to the conditional probability of C given $A \wedge B$, i.e. we want to compute J with

$$\mathcal{KB}_2 \models P(C|A \wedge B) = J.$$

From $\mu^1(C \mid A \wedge B) = 1$, $\mu^2(C \mid A \wedge B) = 0.9$, and theorem 4.7

$$clJ = [0.9, 1]$$

immediately follows. Since, furthermore, $\mu^1 \in Gen^*(\mathcal{KB}_2)$, and $\mu(C \mid A \wedge B) = 0.9$ also holds for every $\mu \in int\, conv\{\mu^2, \mu^0\} \subset Gen^*(\mathcal{KB}_2)$, we even have

$$J = [0.9, 1]. \tag{16}$$

4.4 INFERENCES ABOUT SUBJECTIVE BELIEFS

Probabilistic inferences about subjective beliefs present greater difficulties than those about statistical relations. If $\mathcal{KB} \models P(a \in C) = J$, then, by definition 3.3 and 3.4,

$$J = \{\pi_{Bel_a}(\mu)(C) \mid \mu \in Gen^*\} =: \pi_{Bel_a}(Gen^*)(C).$$

Theorem 4.10 If $\mathcal{KB} \models P(a \in C) = J$, then J is an interval.

Proof: A simple proof shows that the mapping

$$\pi_{Bel_a} : \Delta^n \to Bel_a$$

is continuous (see [Jae94]). Hence, the codomain $\pi_{Bel}(Gen^*)$ of the connected set Gen^* is connected. Applying another continuous function $\nu \mapsto \nu(C)$ to $\pi_{Bel}(Gen^*)$ yields a subset of [0,1] that again is connected, hence an interval. □

A procedure that computes the sets $\pi_{Bel_a}(Gen^*)(C)$ will certainly have to compute the minimum cross entropy measure $\pi_{Bel_a}(\mu)$ for certain measures μ. This is a nonlinear optimization problem. Generally no closed form solution (like the one given by Jeffrey's rule for the case of constraints on disjoint sets) exists, but an optimization algorithm must be employed to produce a good approximation of the actual solution. There are numerous algorithms available for this problem. See [Wen88] for instance for a C-program, based on an algorithm by Fletcher and Reeves ([FR64]) that implements a nonlinear optimization procedure for cross entropy minimization.

The greatest difficulty encountered when we try to determine $\pi_{Bel_a}(Gen^*)(C)$ does not lie in individual computations of $\pi_{Bel_a}(\mu)$, but in the best choices of μ for which to compute $\pi_{Bel_a}(\mu)$. Unlike the case of statistical inferences, it does not seem possible to give a characterization of $\pi_{Bel_a}(Gen^*)(C)$ in terms of a finite set of values $\pi_{Bel_a}(\mu^i)(C)$ for a distinguished set $\{\mu^1, \ldots, \mu^k\} \subset Gen$.

At present we cannot offer an algorithm for computing $\pi_{Bel_a}(Gen^*)(C)$ any better than by using a search algorithm in Gen^* based on some heuristics, and yielding increasingly good approximations of $\pi_{Bel_a}(Gen^*)(C)$. Such a search might start with elements μ of Gen^* that are themselves maximal (minimal) with respect to $\mu(C)$, and then proceed within Gen^* in a direction in which values of $\pi_{Bel_a}(\cdot)(C)$ have been found to increase (decrease), or which has not been tried yet. The maximal (minimal) values of $\pi_{Bel_a}(\cdot)(C)$ found so far can be used as a current approximation of $\pi_{Bel_a}(Gen^*)(C)$ at any point in the search. The search may stop when a certain number of iterations did not produce any significant increase (decrease) for these current bounds.

Obviously, the complexity of such a search depends on the dimension and the number of vertices of *Gen*. The cost of a single computation of π_{Bel_a} depends on the size of the probability space $\mathfrak{A}(\mathcal{T})$ and the number of constraints in $\mathcal{P}_a$. In the following we show that the search-space Gen^* can often be reduced to a substantially smaller space.

We show that the interval $\pi_{Bel_a}(Gen^*)(C)$ only depends on the restrictions of the measures in Gen^* and Bel_a to the probability space generated by C and the concepts that appear in $\mathcal{P}_a$.

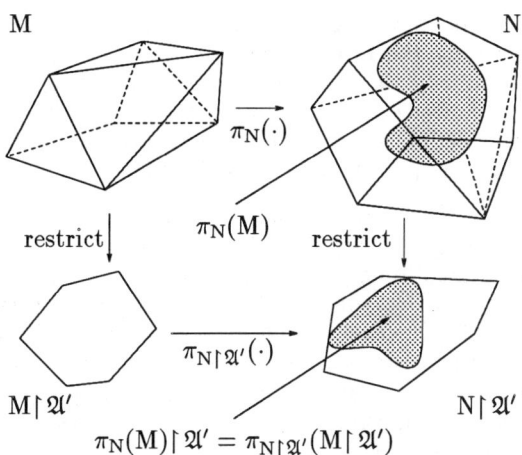

Figure 3: Theorem 4.12

Definition 4.11 Let $\mathfrak{A}$ be an algebra and $\mathfrak{A}'$ a subalgebra of $\mathfrak{A}$. Let $\mu \in \Delta\mathfrak{A}$ and $M \subseteq \Delta\mathfrak{A}$. $\mu \restriction \mathfrak{A}'$ then denotes the restriction of μ to $\mathfrak{A}'$, and $M \restriction \mathfrak{A}'$ is the set $\{\mu \restriction \mathfrak{A}' \mid \mu \in M\}$.

Theorem 4.12 Let $\mathfrak{A}'$ be a subalgebra of the finite algebra $\mathfrak{A}$ generated by a partition $A_1', \ldots, A_k'$ of $\mathfrak{A}$. Let $M, N \subseteq \Delta\mathfrak{A}$, where N is defined by a set of constraints on $\mathfrak{A}'$, i.e.

$$N = \{\nu \in \Delta\mathfrak{A} \mid \nu(C_i) = p_i, \, i = 1, \ldots, l\}$$

for some $p_i \in [0,1]$ and $C_i \in \mathfrak{A}'$. Then:

$$\pi_N(M) \restriction \mathfrak{A}' = \pi_{N \restriction \mathfrak{A}'}(M \restriction \mathfrak{A}').$$

Furthermore, for every $C \in \mathfrak{A}$ and $\mu \in M$:

$$\pi_N(\mu)(C) = \sum_{i=1}^{k} \pi_{N \restriction \mathfrak{A}'}(\mu \restriction \mathfrak{A}')(A_i')\mu(C \mid A_i').$$

Figure 3 illustrates the first part of the theorem.

Proof: The theorem is contained in [SJ81] in a version for probability measures given by density functions, from which the discrete version can be derived. A direct proof for the discrete case on a more elementary level than the one given in [SJ81] is contained in [Jae94]. □

Theorem 4.12 also plays a vital role in the generalization of $\mathcal{PCL}$ to a probabilistic version of $\mathcal{ALC}$ which we turn to in the next section.

Example 4.13 We conclude our discussion of $\mathcal{KB}_2$ by looking at its implications with respect to $P(a \in C)$. Unlike in our previous example 3.5, the probabilistic information about a in $\mathcal{KB}_2$ does not refer to disjoint concepts, so that here Jeffrey's rule can not be used, and cross entropy minimization in its general form must be put to work.

The information about the likelihood for a being in C is particularly ambiguous: the conditional probabilities of C given the two reference classes A and B, that a may belong to with equal probability, are very dissimilar, thereby providing conflicting default information. Also, the generic probability $\mu(A \vee B)$ covers the whole range $[0,1]$ for $\mu \in Gen$. Since assigning a value to $P(a \in A \vee B)$ (which, given the other information in $\mathcal{P}_a$, is equivalent to making up one's mind about $P(a \in A \wedge B)$) is an important intermediate step for a reasonable estimate of $P(a \in C)$, and the result of this step depends on the prior value $\mu(A \vee B)$, this is another reason why it is difficult to propose any narrow interval as appropriate for $P(a \in C)$.

It does not come as a surprise, therefore, that no bounds for $P(a \in C)$ can be derived from $\mathcal{KB}_2$ apart from those that directly follow from $\mathcal{P}_a$: from the information in $\mathcal{P}_a$ alone

$$\mathcal{KB}_2 \models P(a \in C) \in [0, 0.5]$$

is obtained. These bounds can not be substantially improved as computations of $\pi_{Bel_a(\mathcal{KB}_2)}(\mu^\lambda)(C)$ with $\mu^\lambda := \lambda\mu^1 + (1-\lambda)\mu^0$ (with μ^0, μ^1 as in example 4.1) for some $\lambda \in]0,1]$ show. For $\lambda = 1$, $\pi_{Bel_a(\mathcal{KB}_2)}(\mu^1)(C)$ is just $\nu^2(C) = 0$, ν^2 being the only measure in $Bel_a(\mathcal{KB}_2)$ with finite cross entropy with respect to μ^1. With decreasing λ, $\pi_{Bel_a(\mathcal{KB}_2)}(\mu^\lambda)(C)$ is found to increase, having, for example, the value 0.495 at $\lambda = 0.001$. Hence, $\mathcal{KB}_2 \models P(a \in C) = J$ for an interval J with

$$[0, 0.495] \subseteq J \subseteq [0, 0.5].$$

Looking at this result may arouse the suspicion that the whole process of cross entropy minimization really is of little avail, because in the end almost every possible belief measure for a will be in the codomain of $\pi_{Bel_a}(Gen)$. While this can certainly happen, one should not adopt too pessimistic a view based on the current example, where the poor result can really be blamed on the ambiguity of the input. If, for instance, (13) was removed from $\mathcal{KB}_2$, thereby obtaining a smaller knowledge base $\mathcal{KB}_2'$, then the much stronger inference

$$\mathcal{KB}_2' \models P(a \in C) = 0.5 \times 0.1 = 0.05$$

could be made. If, on the other hand, $\mathcal{KB}_2''$ is defined by adding

$$P(a \in A \wedge B) = 0.25 \quad (17)$$

to $\mathcal{KB}_2$, then

$$\mathcal{KB}_2'' \models P(a \in C) = [0.25 \times 0.9, 0.25] = [0.225, 0.25]$$

by our previous result (16).

5 A PROBABILISTIC VERSION OF $\mathcal{ALC}$

5.1 ROLE QUANTIFICATION

The probabilistic concept language $\mathcal{PCL}$ we have described so far does not supply some of the concept-forming operations that are common to standard concept languages. Most notably, role quantification was not permitted in $\mathcal{PCL}$. In this section we show how the formalism developed in the previous sections can be generalized to yield probabilistic extensions for more expressive languages. Our focus, here, will be on $\mathcal{ALC}$, but the results obtained for this language equally apply to other concept languages.

In $\mathcal{ALC}$ the concept-forming operations of section 2 are augmented by role quantification: the vocabulary now contains a set $S_R = \{r, s, \ldots\}$ of role names in addition to, and disjoint from, S_C and S_O. New concept terms can be built from a role name r and a concept term C by *role quantification*

$$\forall r : C \text{ and } \exists r : C.$$

The set of concept terms constructible from S_C and S_R via the boolean operations and role quantification is denoted $T(S_C, S_R)$. This augmented set of concept terms together with the syntax rules for terminological axioms, probabilistic terminological axioms, and probabilistic assertions from section 2 yields a probabilistic extension of $\mathcal{ALC}$ which, unsurprisingly, we call $\mathcal{PALC}$. Note that probabilistic assertions of the form $P((a, b) \in r) = p$ are not included in our syntax.

Example 5.1 Some pieces of information relating the world of birds and fish are encoded in the following $\mathcal{PALC}$-knowledge base $\mathcal{KB}_3$.

$\mathcal{T}$: Herring $\subseteq$ Fish
Penguin $\subseteq$ Bird $\wedge$ $\forall$feeds_on : Herring
$\mathcal{PT}$: P(Penguin|Bird $\wedge$ $\forall$feeds_on : Herring) = 0.2
$\mathcal{P}_{Opus}$: P($Opus \in$ Bird $\wedge$ $\forall$feeds_on : Fish) = 1

The presence of quantification over roles in this knowledge base does not prevent us from forming a subjective degree of belief for the proposition $Opus \in$ Penguin: Since $\forall$feeds_on : Herring is subsumed by $\forall$feeds_on : Fish, we know that the conditional probability of Penguin given Bird $\wedge$ $\forall$feeds_on : Fish must lie in the interval $[0, 0.2]$, but no better bounds can be derived from $\mathcal{T} \cup \mathcal{PT}$. Opus is only known to belong to Bird $\wedge$ $\forall$feeds_on : Fish, so that we would conclude that the likelihood for this individual actually being a penguin is in $[0, 0.2]$ as well.

This example indicates that probabilistic reasoning within the richer language $\mathcal{PALC}$ works in very much the same way as in $\mathcal{PCL}$. In the following section it is shown how the semantics for $\mathcal{PCL}$ can be generalized to capture this kind of reasoning in $\mathcal{PALC}$.

5.2 PROBABILISTIC SEMANTICS FOR $\mathcal{PALC}$

Central to our semantics for the language $\mathcal{PCL}$ were the concepts of the Lindenbaum algebra $\mathfrak{A}(S_C)$ and of the cross entropy of probability measures on this algebra.

The Lindenbaum algebra for $\mathcal{PALC}$ can be defined in precisely the same manner as was done for $\mathcal{PCL}$. The resulting algebra $\mathfrak{A}(S_C, S_R)$ is quite different from $\mathfrak{A}(S_C)$ however: not only is it infinite, it also is nonatomic, i.e. there are infinite chains $C_0 \supset C_1 \supset \ldots$ in $[T(S_C, S_R)]$ with $C_i \neq C_{i+1} \neq 0$ for all i.

The set of probability measures on $\mathfrak{A}(S_C, S_R)$ is denoted $\Delta\mathfrak{A}(S_C, S_R)$. Probability measures, here, are still required to only satisfy finite additivity. $\mathfrak{A}(S_C, S_R)$ not being closed under infinite disjunctions, there is no need to consider countable additivity. Observe that even though $\mathfrak{A}(S_C, S_R)$ is a countable algebra, probability measures on $\mathfrak{A}(S_C, S_R)$ can not be represented by a sequence $(p_i)_{i \in \mathbf{N}}$ of probability values with $\sum_{i \in \mathbf{N}} p_i = 1$ (i.e. a discrete probability measure), because these p_i would have to be the probabilities of the atoms in $\mathfrak{A}(S_C, S_R)$.

Replacing $\mathfrak{A}(S_C)$ with $\mathfrak{A}(S_C, S_R)$ and $\Delta\mathfrak{A}(S_C)$ with $\Delta\mathfrak{A}(S_C, S_R)$ definitions 3.1 and 3.2 can now be repeated almost verbatim for $\mathcal{PALC}$ (with the additional provision in definition 3.2 that role names are interpreted by binary relations on $\mathbf{D}$).

So, things work out rather smoothly up to the point where we have to define what it means for a $\mathcal{PALC}$-interpretation to be a model of a $\mathcal{PALC}$ knowledge base. In the corresponding definition for $\mathcal{PCL}$ (definition 3.3) cross entropy played a prominent role. When we try to adopt the same definition for $\mathcal{PALC}$ we are faced with a problem: cross entropy is not defined for probability measures on $\mathfrak{A}(S_C, S_R)$. While we may well define cross entropy for measures that are either discrete, or given by a density function on some common probability space, measures on $\mathfrak{A}(S_C, S_R)$ do not fall into either of these categories. Still, in example 5.1 some kind of minimum cross entropy reasoning (in the special form of direct inference) has been employed. This has been possible, because far from considering the whole algebra $\mathfrak{A}(S_C, S_R)$, we only took into account the concept terms mentioned in the knowledge base in order to arrive at our conclusions about $P(Opus \in$ Penguin). The same principle will apply for any other, more complicated knowledge base: when it only contains the concept terms $C_1, \ldots, C_n$, and we want to estimate the probability for $P(a \in C_{n+1})$, then we only need to consider probability measures on the finite subalgebra of $\mathfrak{A}(S_C, S_R)$ generated by $\{C_1, \ldots, C_{n+1}\}$.

The following definition and theorem enables us to recast this principle into formal semantics for $\mathcal{PALC}$.

Definition 5.2 Let $\mathfrak{A}'$ be a finite subalgebra of $\mathfrak{A}(S_C, S_R)$ with $\{A'_1, \ldots, A'_k\}$ the set of its atoms. Let $N \subseteq \Delta\mathfrak{A}(S_C, S_R)$ be defined by a set of constraints on $\mathfrak{A}'$ (cf. theorem 4.12). Let $\mu \in \Delta\mathfrak{A}(S_C, S_R)$ such that $\pi_{N \upharpoonright \mathfrak{A}'}(\mu \upharpoonright \mathfrak{A}')$ is defined. For every $C \in \mathfrak{A}(S_C, S_R)$ define

$$\pi^*_N(\mu)(C) := \sum_{i=1}^{k} \pi_{N \upharpoonright \mathfrak{A}'}(\mu \upharpoonright \mathfrak{A}')(A'_i) \mu(C \mid A'_i).$$

Clearly, $\pi_N^*(\mu)$ is a probability measure on $\mathfrak{A}(S_C,S_R)$. The following theorem shows that $\pi_{Bel}^*(\mu)$ realizes cross entropy minimization for every finite subalgebra of $\mathfrak{A}(S_C,S_R)$ containing the concepts used to define Bel.

Theorem 5.3 Let $\mu \in \Delta\mathfrak{A}(S_C,S_R)$, let $Bel \subseteq \Delta\mathfrak{A}(S_C,S_R)$ be defined by a finite set of constraints

$$\{P(C_i) = p_i \mid p_i \in [0,1], C_i \in \mathfrak{A}(S_C,S_R), i=1,\ldots,n\}.$$

Let $\mathfrak{A}'$ be the finite subalgebra generated by $\{C_1,\ldots,C_n\}$, and assume that $\pi_{Bel\restriction\mathfrak{A}'}(\mu\restriction\mathfrak{A}')$ is defined. Then, for every finite $\mathfrak{A}^* \supseteq \mathfrak{A}'$: $\pi_{Bel\restriction\mathfrak{A}^*}(\mu\restriction\mathfrak{A}^*)$ is defined and equal to $\pi_{Bel}^*(\mu)\restriction\mathfrak{A}^*$.

Proof: Substituting $\mathfrak{A}^*$ for $\mathfrak{A}$, $\{\mu\restriction\mathfrak{A}^*\}$ for M, and $Bel\restriction\mathfrak{A}^*$ for N in theorem 4.12 gives

$$\pi_{Bel\restriction\mathfrak{A}^*}(\mu\restriction\mathfrak{A}^*)(C) = \sum_{i=1}^{k} \pi_{Bel\restriction\mathfrak{A}'}(\mu\restriction\mathfrak{A}')(A_i')\mu(C \mid A_i')$$

for every $C \in \mathfrak{A}^*$. The right hand side of this equation is just the definition of $\pi_{Bel}^*(\mu)(C)$. $\square$

With $\pi_{Bel}^*(\mu)$ as the measure that, in a generalized way, minimizes cross entropy with respect to μ in Bel, it is now straightforward to define when a $\mathcal{PALC}$-interpretation $(\mathbf{D}, I, \mu)$ shall be a model of a $\mathcal{PALC}$-knowledge base $\mathcal{KB}$: just replace $\pi_{Bel_a(\mathcal{KB})}(\mu)$ with $\pi_{Bel_a(\mathcal{KB})}^*(\mu)$ in the corresponding definition for $\mathcal{PCL}$ (definition 3.3).

Probabilistic inferences from a $\mathcal{PALC}$-knowledge base $\mathcal{KB}$ can now be made in basically the same manner as in $\mathcal{PCL}$: to answer a query about a conditional probability $P(C|D)$ for two concepts, consider the algebra generated by C, D, and the concept terms appearing in $\mathcal{PT}$. Call this algebra $\mathfrak{M}_{C,D}$. The relativized algebra $\mathfrak{M}_{C,D}(\mathcal{T})$ is defined as above, and $Gen\restriction\mathfrak{M}_{C,D}(\mathcal{T})$ can be computed as in section 4.1. Theorem 4.7, applied to $Gen\restriction\mathfrak{M}_{C,D}(\mathcal{T})$ can then be used to compute the J with $\mathcal{KB} \models P(C|D) = J$.

When J with $\mathcal{KB} \models P(a \in C) = J$ shall be computed, the relevant algebra to be considered is generated by C and the concept terms appearing in $\mathcal{P}_a$. Writing $\mathfrak{N}_{a,C}$ for this algebra,

$$J = \{\pi_{Bel_a\restriction\mathfrak{N}_{a,C}(\mathcal{T})}(\mu)(C) \mid \mu \in Gen\restriction\mathfrak{N}_{a,C}(\mathcal{T})\}$$

then holds. Note that $Gen\restriction\mathfrak{N}_{a,C}(\mathcal{T})$ can not be computed directly in the manner described in section 4.1, because Gen will usually be defined by constraints on concepts not all contained in $\mathfrak{N}_{a,C}$. One way to obtain a representation for $Gen\restriction\mathfrak{N}_{a,C}(\mathcal{T})$ is to first compute $Gen\restriction\mathfrak{B}(\mathcal{T})$, with $\mathfrak{B}$ the algebra generated by C and the concept terms appearing in either $\mathcal{PT}$ or $\mathcal{P}_a$, and then restrict the result to $\mathfrak{N}_{a,C}$.

Example 5.4 Suppose we want to determine J_0 with

$$\mathcal{KB}_3 \models P(\text{Penguin}|\text{Bird} \wedge \forall\text{feeds\_on} : \text{Fish}) = J_0.$$

This query and $\mathcal{PT}$ together contain three different concept terms which generate an algebra $\mathfrak{M}$ whose relativization by $\mathcal{T}$ contains just the four atoms

A_1 : P,
A_2 : B $\wedge$ $\forall$f_o : H $\wedge$ $\neg$P,
A_3 : B $\wedge$ $\forall$f_o : F $\wedge$ $\neg\forall$f_o : H,
A_4 : $\neg$(B $\wedge$ $\forall$f_o : F)

(using suitable abbreviations for the original names). $Gen\restriction\mathfrak{M}(\mathcal{T})$ then is defined by

$$\{(\mu_1,\ldots,\mu_4) \in \Delta^4 \mid \frac{\mu_1}{\mu_1 + \mu_2} = 0.2\}.$$

The value for $\mu_1/(\mu_1 + \mu_2 + \mu_3)$, representing $P(P|B \wedge \forall f\_o : F)$, ranges over the interval $[0,0.2]$ in this set, so the answer to our query is the expected interval.

To compute J_1 with

$$\mathcal{KB}_3 \models P(Opus \in P) = J_1,$$

we consider the even smaller algebra $\mathfrak{N}(\mathcal{T})$ consisting of the atoms

B_1 : P, B_2 : $\neg$P $\wedge$ B $\wedge$ $\forall$f_o : F,
B_3 : $\neg$(B $\wedge$ $\forall$f_o : F).

$Bel_{Opus}\restriction\mathfrak{N}(\mathcal{T})$ then is

$$\{(\nu_1,\nu_2,\nu_3) \in \Delta^3 \mid \nu_1 + \nu_2 = 1\}.$$

It is easy to see that

$$Gen\restriction\mathfrak{N}(\mathcal{T}) = \{(\mu_1,\mu_2,\mu_3) \in \Delta^3 \mid \frac{\mu_1}{\mu_1+\mu_2} \leq 0.2\}.$$

For every $\mu = (\mu_1,\mu_2,\mu_3) \in Gen\restriction\mathfrak{N}(\mathcal{T})$, $(\nu_1,\nu_2,\nu_3) := \pi_{Bel\restriction\mathfrak{N}(\mathcal{T})}(\mu)$ is defined by Jeffrey's rule, so that $\nu_1 = \nu_1/(\nu_1+\nu_2) = \mu_1/(\mu_1+\mu_2)$. Hence,

$$\begin{aligned} J_1 &= \{\nu_1 \mid (\nu_1,\nu_2,\nu_3) \in \pi_{Bel\restriction\mathfrak{N}(\mathcal{T})}(Gen\restriction\mathfrak{N}(\mathcal{T}))\} \\ &= [0,0.2] \end{aligned}$$

in accordance with our intuitive reasoning in example 5.1.

6 CONCLUDING REMARKS

The semantics we have given to probabilistic extensions of terminological logics are designed for soundness rather than for inferential strength. Allowing any generic measure μ consistent with the constraints to be used in a model is the most cautious approach that can be taken. In cases where it seems more desirable to always derive unique values for probabilities $P(C|D)$ or $P(a \in C)$ instead of intervals, this approach can be modified by using the maximum entropy measure in

Gen only (as the one most reasonable generic measure).

Generalizations of the formalism here presented are possible in various directions. It could be permitted, for instance, to also state subjective degrees of belief for expressions of the form $(a,b) \in r$. Since these establish a connection between a and b, it will then no longer be possible to interpret a and b by individual probability measures on $\mathfrak{A}(S_C,S_R)$. Rather, for a language containing object names $\{a_1,\ldots,a_n\}$, a joint probability measure $\nu_{a_1\ldots a_n}$ on the Lindenbaum algebra of all n-ary expressions constructible from $S_C \cup S_R$ will have to be used.

References

[Bac90] F. Bacchus. *Representing and Reasoning With Probabilistic Knowledge*. MIT Press, 1990.

[BGHK92] F. Bacchus, A. Grove, J.Y. Halpern, and D. Koller. From statistics to beliefs. In *Proc. of National Conference on Artificial Intelligence (AAAI-92)*, 1992.

[BGHK93] F. Bacchus, A. Grove, J.Y. Halpern, and D. Koller. Statistical foundations for default reasoning. In *Proc. of International Joint Conference on Artificial Intelligence (IJCAI-93)*, 1993.

[BS85] R.J. Brachmann and Schmolze. An overview of the kl-one knowledge representation system. *Cognitive Science*, 9:171–216, 1985.

[Car50] R. Carnap. *Logical Foundations of Probability*. The University of Chicago Press, 1950.

[DZ82] P. Diaconis and S.L. Zabell. Updating subjective probability. *Journal of the American Statistical Association*, 77(380):822–830, 1982.

[FR64] R. Fletcher and C.M. Reeves. Function minimization by conjugate gradients. *The Computer Journal*, 7:149–154, 1964.

[Hal90] J.Y. Halpern. An analysis of first-order logics of probability. *Artificial Intelligence*, 46:311–350, 1990.

[Hei91] J. Heinsohn. A hybrid approach for modeling uncertainty in terminological logics. In R.Kruse and P.Siegel, editors, *Proceedings of the 1st European Conference on Symbolic an Quantitative Approaches to Uncertainty*, number 548 in Springer Lecture Notes in Computer Science, 1991.

[HOK88] J. Heinsohn and B. Owsnicki-Klewe. Probabilistic inheritance and reasoning in hybrid knowledge representation systems. In W. Hoeppner, editor, *Proceedings of the 12th German Workshop on Artificial Intelligence (GWAI-88)*, 1988.

[Jae94] M. Jaeger. A probabilistic extension of terminological logics. Technical Report MPI-I-94-208, Max-Planck-Institut für Informatik, 1994.

[Jay78] E.T. Jaynes. Where do we stand on maximum entropy? In R.D. Levine and M. Tribus, editors, *The Maximum Entropy Formalism*, pages 15–118. MIT Press, 1978.

[Jef65] R.C. Jeffrey. *The Logic of Decision*. McGraw-Hill, 1965.

[PV90] J.B. Paris and A. Vencowská. A note on the inevitability of maximum entropy. *International Journal of Approximate Reasoning*, 4:183–223, 1990.

[PV92] J.B. Paris and A. Vencowská. A method for updating that justifies minimum cross entropy. *International Journal of Approximate Reasoning*, 7:1–18, 1992.

[Sho86] J.E. Shore. Relative entropy, probabilistic inference, and ai. In L.N. Kanal and J.F. Lemmer, editors, *Uncertainty in Artificial Intelligence*. Elsevier, 1986.

[SJ80] J.E. Shore and R.W. Johnson. Axiomatic derivation of the principle of maximum entropy and the principle of minimum cross-entropy. *IEEE Transactions on Information Theory*, IT-26(1):26–37, 1980.

[SJ81] J.E. Shore and R.W. Johnson. Properties of cross-entropy minimization. *IEEE Transactions on Information Theory*, IT-27(4):472–482, 1981.

[SJ83] J.E. Shore and R.W. Johnson. Comments on and correction to "Axiomatic derivation of the principle of maximum entropy and the principle of minimum cross-entropy". *IEEE Transactions on Information Theory*, IT-29(6):942–943, 1983.

[SSS91] M. Schmidt-Schauß and G. Smolka. Attributive concept descriptions with complements. *Artificial Intelligence*, 48(1):1–26, 1991.

[Wen88] W.X. Wen. Analytical and numerical methods for minimum cross entropy problems. Technical Report 88/26, Computer Science, University of Melbourne, 1988.

On Multiagent Autoepistemic Logic - an extrospective view

Y.J. Jiang*
Department of Computing
Imperial College
London SW7 2BZ, England
yj@uk.ac.ic.doc

Abstract

Moore's autoepistemic logic was only introduced for a *single* agent. Reiter considered the task much harder to extend the logic to *multiagents*. Morgenstern argued that multiagent autoepistemic reasoning is *not* at all *symmetric* with the single agent autoepistemic reasoning. In this paper however, we shall argue for an *extrospective* view of multiagent autoepistemic reasoning that is *symmetric* between the single agent setting and the multiagent setting. In particular, we will present a *multiagent* generalization of McDermott and Doyle's general autoepistemic logical framework. Unlike Morgenstern's *introspective* view which extends Moore's belief operator L to a multiagent setting by indexing the operator with an agent, eg. $L_{John}p$, the proposed extrospective view combines Moore's **L** operator with a multiagent monotonic epistemic logic, eg. **L** Bel(John,p). We shall present two approaches based on the extrospective view of multiagent autoepistemic reasoning. The first approach simply replaces the "base" logic of Moore's autoepistemic logic by an epistemic logic. The second approach allows autoepistemic reasoning within the scope of any nested monotonic epistemic modal operators. On the surface, the two approaches seem to be very different. A closer examination reveals surprisingly that they are essentially equivalent. This suggests that single-agent autoepistemic reasoning and its proof mechanization are in fact readily extendible to multiagents. In particular, we shall show that the extrospective approaches subsume Morgenstern's formulation including its various principles of arrogance.

Keywords : Knowledge Representation, Autoepis-

temic Logic, Epistemic Logic and Multiagent Nonmonotonic Reasoning

1 Introduction

Autoepistemic Logic (AE) [Moore 85] is a nonmonotonic logic about an *implicit* agent who introspects *ideally* about his own beliefs. Despite its connection with epistemic notions, it does not seem to be clear how the logic can be extended to multi-agent nonmonotonic reasoning. Although Lin & Shoham [88] generalizes AE with an epistemic semantics based on posssible-worlds, their logic is still limited to a single agent. Indeed, Reiter [87] claims that "All current nonmonotonic formalisms deal with single agent reasoners. However it is clear that agents must frequently ascribe nonmonotonic inferences to other agents, for example in cooperative planning or speech acts. Such multiagent settings require appropriate formal theories, which currently we lack".

Consider for example the following situation where John and Mary reason about each other's nonmonotonic reasoning capabilities.

> Suppose Mary and John arranged yesterday to meet at John's flat to play tennis at 10am this morning. But it has been raining outside all night. John waited for Mary to 10am. She still has not arrived and it is still raining outside. Since both John and Mary do not have a phone, Mary in fact decided not to come and John also decided to go out after 10am. Mary made her decision by assuming that John knows that raining cannot play tennis and reasons that John would conclude that she will not come after all. John made his decision by assuming that Mary reasons in the above way, so he concludes that Mary will not come and he can then do something else.

Morgenstern [1990] is among the first to tackle multiagent autoepistemic reasoning. She extends Moore's

---

*Advanced Fellow of British Science and Engineering Research Council

AE language by indexing the belief operator **L** in AE with an agent. Multiagent autoepistemic reasoning is achieved in her solution by defining a set of formation rules which are agent-indexed extensions of Moore's stable set formation rules and by defining a set of principles of arrogance which are essential for an agent to reason about another agent's autoepistemic reasoning abilities. Morgenstern argues that these principles are required because multiagent autoepsitemic reasoning is *not at all symmetric* with the single agent case. In the single agent case the given theory was a *complete* description of the mind of some agent. In the multiagent case, agents have at best a *partial* description of other agents' beliefs.

Morgenstern's formulation however suffers a number of drawbacks. First, it lacks a formal semantics. There is no corresponding multiagent fixpoint definition of an AE extension to that of Moore's single agent AE logic. Second, it cannot reason about the principles of arrogance. Instead these principles can only be defined via meta-rules of inferences. Thirdly, it does not have a proper proof theory. Despite the syntactical treatment of Morgenstern's approach, the rules she defined are just like Reiter's default rules [80] which do not constitute a proof method.

In this paper, we shall attempt to address Reiter's concern from an alternative view point. In contrast with Morgenstern's view point which we shall call an *introspective* view point, we shall call the proposed view point an *extrospective* view point. Instead of that an agent introspects his own beliefs, the extrospective view let someone else, eg. God to introspect for the agent. Syntactically, instead of indexing Moore's **L** operator with an agent, the extrospective view keeps the **L** operator intact by changing the *ordinary* part of Moore's AE logic with some epistemic logic which is a *monotonic modal logic of beliefs*.

We shall present two ways of changing the ordinary part of Moore's AE logic to formalize a multiagent autoepistemic logic from an extrospective view point. The first way is to restrict the new multiagent autoepistemic language in such a way that the **L** operator cannot appear in any scope of the Bel operator. The second way is to remove this restriction so that the **L** operator can appear in any scope of the Bel operator. For example, in the first way, **L**Bel(a,p) is allowed but not Bel(a,**L**p) which is howevver additionally allowed in the second way. Intuitively $\neg \mathbf{L}Bel(a, Bel(b,p)) \to Bel(a, Bel(b,q))$ stands for something like "From God's point of view, if he cannot prove (after introspecting its knowledge about a's beliefs) that a believes that b believes p, then God would conclude that a believes b believes q"; while $Bel(a, \neg \mathbf{L}Bel(b,p) \to Bel(b,q))$ intuitively stands for something like "from agent a's point of view, if he cannot prove (after introspecting its knowledge about b's beliefs) that b believes p, then a would conclude that b believes q".

The main objectives of this paper are three-folds. The first is to introduce the above-mentioned two alternatives of multiagent autoepistemic reasoning from an extrospective viewpoint. The second is to show that the two alternatives are essentially equivalent. The third is to show that Morgenstern's approach is subsumed by the proposed extrospective view. Before we achieve these objectives, lets first note several important consequences of the extrospective view.

1. The extrospective view is symmetric between the single agent case and the multiagent case in autoepistemic reasoning. It is no longer the case that the single agent AE will have a complete description of the agent himself. Rather Moore's AE logic is really just a restricted subset of the extrospective view of single agent autoepistemic reasoning.

    Consider the following example. The leftside of ⇒ represents some of the syntactical forms of Moore's AE logic for a single agent. Lets assume that this single agent is John. The right side of ⇒ represents the corresponding syntactical forms of Moore's AE logic under an extrospective view for the single agent John.

$$
\begin{aligned}
p & \Rightarrow & Bel(John, p) \\
q \vee r & \Rightarrow & Bel(John, q \vee r) \\
\neg \mathbf{L}p \to q & \Rightarrow & \neg \mathbf{L}Bel(John, p) \to Bel(John, q) \\
\mathbf{L}p \vee \mathbf{L}q & \Rightarrow & \mathbf{L}Bel(John, p) \vee \mathbf{L}Bel(John, q)
\end{aligned}
$$

    Thus although Moore's AE logic has a corresponding representation $p \vee q$ of $Bel(John, p \vee q)$, however it has no corresponding representation of $Bel(John, p) \vee Bel(John, q)$ which can still be regarded as the belief of a single agent (John in this case) in the extrospective view. This belief is an incomplete description of the mind of John.

2. The fixpoint definition of an AE extension can be readily extended to a multiagent setting in the extrospective view as we shall see later on. In particular, by simply varying the semantics of the monotonic epistemic logic adopted, we can obtain a class of multiagent autoepistemic logics. Here we just use an example to demonstrate the points.

    Consider the AE theory $\{\mathbf{L}p\}$. This theory has *no* AE extension in Moore's autoepistemic logic although it has a *reflexive* AE extension in Schwarz's reflexive AE logic [91] whose ordinary part is the propositional consequence of $\{p\}$. However if we formulate the theory in Morgenstern's introspective view, it will be encoded as something like $\{\mathbf{L}_{John}p\}$ if we assume the single agent that the AE logic is supposed to represent is *John*. This theory however has a stable meaning in Morgenstern's view which has nothing to do with Schwarz's reflexivity.

In contrast, under the extrospective view, the AE theory {**L**p} about John's mind will be represented as {**L**Bel(John,p)}. This theory has precisely the same status as Moore's AE logic and Schwarz's reflexive AE logic. That is, in the former case, the theory has no extension and in the latter case, it has an extension whose ordinary part is the monotonic epistemic logic consequence of {Bel(John,p)}. Furthermore, we can vary the epistemic logic of John to have the semantic structure (eg. transitive and euclidean) of a K45 modal logic. Then given {**L**Bel(John,p)}, we can conclude Bel(John,Bel(John,p)) in the reflexive multiagent setting.

3. There is no longer the need for principles of arrogance. In fact, as we shall see later, the introspection of an agent's beliefs within some nested agents can always be performed by an extrospection from an external agent, say *God*. In particular, different principles of arrogance will be represented as domain axioms in the extrospective view of multiagent autoepistemic reasoning.

Consider for example the multiagent nonmontonic statement "Bill believes that Alex believes that if Alex had an older brother, Alex would know about it " in [Morgenstern 90]. Let Q stand for the sentence: Alex has an older brother. This example would be represented in the extrospective view as follows

$$Bel(Bill, Bel(Alex, Q \rightarrow \mathbf{L}Q))$$

or equivalently as

$$\neg \mathbf{L}Bel(Bill, Bel(Alex, Q))$$
$$\rightarrow Bel(Bill, Bel(Alex, \neg Q))$$

The equivalence of the two representations (as we shall show logically in this paper) might look surprising since it is well known of the property that $Bel(a, p \rightarrow q)$ implies $Bel(a, p) \rightarrow Bel(a, q)$ but not the other way around. In fact this property is still maintained in the proposed logics. However what we claim is that $Bel(a, \mathbf{L}p \rightarrow q)$ is equivalent to $\mathbf{L}Bel(a, p) \rightarrow Bel(a, q)$. This result is now possible since **L**p is strictly stronger than p in this case. For example in Moore's AE logic, the AE theory {**L**p $\rightarrow$ q}, derives q while {p $\rightarrow$ q} does not.

The equivalence of the two representations also removes the need for Morgenstern's principle of moderate arrogance since Bill's reasoning about Alex's autoepistemic reasoning abilities is now performed by the implicit agent God on his behalf. If we want to apply Morgenstern's cautious principle to the above example, we simply represent it as

$$\neg \mathbf{L}Bel(Bill, Bel(Alex, Q)) \land \neg \mathbf{L}Bel(Bill, Q)$$
$$\rightarrow Bel(Bill, Bel(Alex, \neg Q))$$

4. The extrospective view or more precisely the equivalence of the two extrospective approaches naturally extends not just Moore's AE semantics and fixpoint definition of AE extensions, but also the proof methods of the single agent case to the multiagent case.

Instead of designing new methods for the multiagent autoepistemic logics, we simply replace the ordinary proof-theoretic components of the proof method of a single agent autoepistemic logic by a proof method for a monotonic modal logic of beliefs. In particular, by associating different monotonic axiomizations for different (nested) agents, we can obtain different nonmonotonic reasoning capabilities of different (nested) agents without ever changing the basic structure or proof components for the nonmonnotonic parts of the multiagent autoepistemic logics.

The implications of this paper go beyond the topic of the paper. It raises two searching questions to the field of multiagent nonmonotonic reasoning, not just multiagent autoepistemic reasoning. First, is the single agent nonmonotonic reasoning readily extendible to multiagent nonmonotonic reasoning?. Second, can we simply integrate existing nonmonotonic logics with some multiagent monotonic logics to achieve multiagent nonmonotonic reasoning?.

This paper is organized as follows. In Section 2, the preliminaries of Moore''s AE logic and Schwarz's reflexive AE logic are introduced. This is then followed in Section 3 by the development of a simple multiagent autoepistemic logic that replaces the "base" logic of Moore's or Schwatz's AE logic by an epistemic logic. Section 4 conjectures that the simple multiagent AE logic is in fact sufficient for nested multiagent autoepistemic reasoning. It also provides a multiagent generalization of McDermott and Doyle's general autoepistemic logical framework for a single agent. In particular, it outlines how existing proof methods for AE logic can be readily extended to multagent autoepistemic reasoning. In Section 5, a seemingly more powerful multiagent AE logic that allows nonmonotonic reasoning within the scope of any nested agents is presented. Section 6 proves that the logic in fact collapses to the simple multiagent AE logic. Section 7 then goes on to demonstrate that the proposed extrospective approachese in fact subsume Morgenstern's syntactical formulations without any of the drawbacks of her approach mentioned earilier.

2 Autoepistemic Logic

The language of AE is a propositional logic augmented with an autoepistemic modal operator **L**. An AE formula is defined inductively as follows.

1. a propositional atom is an AE formula

2. if ϕ and ψ are AE formulae, so are $\neg\phi, \phi\vee\psi, \phi\wedge\psi$ and $\phi \rightarrow \psi$

3. if ϕ is an AE formula, then $\mathbf{L}\phi$ is an AE formula.

Definition 1 *An AE theory is defined as a set of AE formulae. An ordinary AE formula is an AE formula that does not contain a $\mathbf{L}$ operator.*

An AE theory is stable *[Stalnaker 80] if it is closed under the following rules*

1. *T is closed under ordinary propositional logic consequence*
2. *if $P \in T$, then $\mathbf{L}P \in T$*
3. *if $P \ni T$, then $\neg\mathbf{L}P \in T$*

The *basic* semantics of AE logic is characterized interpretatively in the style of a *list semantics*. Here an AE valuation consists of I and T where I denotes the standard propositional interpretation (a set of propositional letters) and T an AE theory. The satisfiability of an AE formula ϕ in an AE valuation (I,T), indicated by $\models_{(I,T)} \phi$, can be defined inductively as follows:

1. $\models_{(I,T)} p$ iff $p \in I$ where p is a propositional letter.
2. $\models_{(I,T)} \neg\phi$ iff $\neg(\models_{(I,T)} \phi)$
3. $\models_{(I,T)} \phi \vee \psi$ iff $\models_{(I,T)} \phi$ or $\models_{(I,T)} \psi$
4. $\models_{(I,T)} \mathbf{L}\phi$ iff $\phi \in T$
5. Conjunction and implication are defined in the standard way.

Definition 2 *Let A be an AE theory. We define $\models_{(I,T)} A$ iff $\forall \phi \in A, \models_{(I,T)} \phi$. We define $A \models_T \phi$ iff for every I, if $\models_{(I,T)} A$, then $\models_{(I,T)} \phi$. An AE formula is valid iff it is true/satisfied in all AE valuations (I,T). An AE theory is satisfiable iff there exists an AE valuation (I,T) which satisfies all wffs in the theory. Two AE theories are equivalent iff they are true in the same set of AE valuations.*

The basic idea of AE logic is to form an *stable* closure called *extension* over an AE theory. As noted by Levesque [90], this notion is only captured at "meta-level" by Moore [85] through a fixpoint construction that involves the above basic (or "object-level") semantics.

Definition 3 *E is an AE extension of an AE theory A iff it satisfies the following equation:*

$$E = \{\phi \mid A \models_E \phi\}$$

Moore [85] has shown that

Theorem 1 *E is an AE extension of an AE theory A iff it satisfies the following syntactic fixpoint equation:*

$$E = TH(A \cup \{\mathbf{L}\phi \mid \phi \in E\} \cup \{\neg\mathbf{L}\psi \mid \psi \ni E\})$$

where TH(S) denotes the ordinary propositional logical consequence of S.

One possible defect of AE logic is that beliefs of the implicit agent from the *agent point of view* are not regarded as *knowledge* or *true beliefs*. For example, the theory $\{\mathbf{L}p\}$ has no AE extension. Another possible defect is that some AE theories such as $\{\mathbf{L}p \rightarrow p\}$ can have an extension in which p is grounded on the assumption of $\mathbf{L}p$. To solve thses problems, Schwarz [91] proposes a simple variation of Moore's AE logic, called *reflexive* AE logic. The basic semantics of reflexive AE logic is the same as Moore's logic except with the following modification.

$$\models_{(I,T)} \mathbf{L}\phi \text{ iff } \phi \in T \wedge \models_{(I,T)} \phi$$

The fixpoint definition of a reflexive AE extension is then defined in the same way as Moore's definition except with the modified basic semantics.

Schwarz [91] has shown that

Theorem 2 *E is a reflexive AE extension of an AE theory A iff it satisfies the following syntactic fixpoint equation:*

$$E = TH(A \cup \{\phi \equiv \mathbf{L}\phi \mid \phi \in E\} \cup \{\neg\mathbf{L}\psi \mid \psi \ni E\})$$

where TH(S) denotes the ordinary propositional logical consequence of S.

Theorem 3 (Moore 85, Schwarz 91) *Both AE and reflexive AE extensions are stable.*

The reflexive AE extensions and AE extensions of an AE theory in general do not coincide unless we restrict the theory to some form of stratification [Gelfond 87]. For example, both AE theories $\{\mathbf{L}p\}$ and $\{\neg\mathbf{L}p \rightarrow p\}$ have no AE extension but a reflexive AE extension containing p; while $\{\neg\mathbf{L}p \wedge \neg\mathbf{L}q \rightarrow q, \neg\mathbf{L}q \rightarrow p\}$ has only one AE extension containing p but an additional reflexive AE extension containing q. Nevertheless, AE extensions are not subsumed by reflexive AE extensions. For example, the AE theory $\{\mathbf{L}p \rightarrow p\}$ has only one reflexive AE extension but an additional AE extension containing p. Like AE logic, reflexive AE logic does not always produce a fixpoint. For example, $\{\mathbf{L}\neg\mathbf{L}p \rightarrow p\}$ has neither reflexive AE extension nor AE extension.

The key point to note is that the base logic of (cf. reflexive) AE is the *standard propositional logic*. This is evident both in the basic semantics of AE and the syntactic fixpoint equation of a (cf. reflexive) AE extension. To extend the (cf. reflexive) AE logic to multiagents, ideally we would like to achieve this by simply replacing the semantics of the ordinary propositional interpretation of AE logic by a semantics for an epistemic logic, and by replacing TH in the syntactic fixpoint equation of a (cf. reflexive) AE extension by an epistemic logical consequence operator ETH. This provides the motivation for the simple multiagent autoepistemic logic in the next section.

3 A simple multiagent autoepistemic logic AE^{Epis}

An epistemic logic is a *monotonic* modal logic of beliefs. Its language is a propositional logic augmented with a modal operator Bel. Unlike the **L** operator in AE, Bel can be explicitly associated with any agent. For example, we can express the fact that either John believes p or Jim believes p as $Bel(John, p) \vee Bel(Jim, p)$ in epistemic logic. Furthermore, unlike **L**, Bel is not autoepistemic in the sense that its meaning is not context-dependent. For example, given $\{\neg \mathbf{L} p \rightarrow q\}$, AE will derive q; whilst $\{\neg Bel(ag, p) \rightarrow q\}$ will not derive q.

One simple approach to extend AE to a multiagent setting is to replace the base logic of AE by an epistemic logic. In other words the new language, which we call AE^{Epis}, will be exactly the same as the original AE language except that in place of every *ordinary* formula, it will now be an *epistemic* formula. Formally, the AE^{Epis} formulae can be defined inductively as follows:

1. a propositional atom is an AE^{Epis} formula
2. if ϕ and ψ are AE^{Epis} formulae, so are $\neg \phi$, $\phi \vee \psi$, $\phi \wedge \psi$ and $\phi \rightarrow \psi$
3. if ϕ is an AE^{Epis} formula, then $\mathbf{L}\phi$ is an AE^{Epis} formula.
4. if ϕ is an *ordinary* AE^{Epis} formula, i.e. it does not contain a **L** operator, then $Bel(agent, \phi)$ is an AE^{Epis} formula. Here *agent* is a member of the set of agents in AE^{Epis}.

The semantics of AE^{Epis} can be easily defined by substituting the ordinary propositional part of the semantics of AE logic by a possible-worlds semantics. The possible worlds semantics in the spirit of Hintikka [62], is chosen purely for illustration. It should be clear that the general framework defined below can be easily substituted for any specific semantics. The valuation (I,T) of AE^{Epis} is similar to AE's valuation (I,T) with the following differences.

1. The valuation (I,T) of AE^{Epis} will be additionally indexed by a frame structure M=(W,R) where W is a set of possible worlds and R is the accessibility relation between possible worlds for each agent in AE^{Epis}. Each world here is a set of propositional letters.
2. In AE, I is a set of propositional letters. In AE^{Epis}, I is additionally regarded as a possible world of W in M.
3. In AE, T is a set of AE formulae. In AE^{Epis}, T is a set of AE^{Epis} formulae.
4. Since (I,T) of AE^{Epis} is additionally indexed by a frame structure M=(W,R), we can further define some classes of valuations by restricting R. For example, if the class is *reflexive*, then we restrict R of M to be reflexive. There can be many classes of valuations as shown in [Hughes & Cresswell 84]. The default will be valuations whose Rs are not restricted. We will assume that the readers are familiar with modal logics and their axiomatic systems associated with the various classes of valuations. For example, the K system is associated with the default (or unrestricted) class of valuations; the T system is associated with the reflexive class of valuations; while KD45 is associated with the *serial*, *transitive* and *euclidean* class of valuations.

We now define the satisfiability relationship $\models_{(I,T)_M}$ between an AE^{Epis} valuation (I,T) under the frame M=(W,R), and an AE^{Epis} formula.

1. $\models_{(I,T)_M} p$ iff $p \in I$ where p is an atom
2. $\models_{(I,T)_M} \neg\phi$ iff $\neg(\models_{(I,T)_M} \phi)$
3. $\models_{(I,T)_M} \phi \vee \psi$ iff $\models_{(I,T)_M} \phi$ or $\models_{(I,T)_M} \psi$
4.
   - In the case of extending Moore's AE logic to multiagent autoepistemic reasoning $\models_{(I,T)_M} \mathbf{L}\phi$ iff $\phi \in T$
   - In the case of extending Schwarz's reflexive AE logic to multiagent autoepistemic reasoning
     $\models_{(I,T)_M} \mathbf{L}\phi$ iff $\phi \in T$ and $\models_{(I,T)_M} \phi$
5. $\models_{(I,T)_M} Bel(ag, \phi)$ iff $\forall I'(R(ag, I, I') \rightarrow \models_{(I',T)_M} \phi)$
6. Conjunction and implication are defined in the standard way.

Definition 4 *Let A denote an AE^{Epis} theory (which is a set of AE^{Epis} formulae). We define $\models_{(I,T)_M} A$ iff $\forall \phi \in A, \models_{(I,T)_M} \phi$. We define $A \models_{T,Class} \phi$ iff for every M=(W,R) such that R is in the class of Class, and for every I of W, if $\models_{(I,T)_M} A$, then $\models_{(I,T)_M} \phi$. We say A is satisfiable iff there exists an AE^{Epis} valuation $(I,T)_M$ such that, $\models_{(I,T)_M} A$ for some I in W of M. We say an AE^{Epis} formula ϕ is valid iff $\neg \phi$ is not satisfiable.*

Like AE logic, we will also define an *extensional* closure for an AE^{Epis} theory. However, unlike AE logic, a (cf. reflexive) AE^{Epis} extension will be *dependent on the class of valuations*.

Definition 5 *T is a (cf. reflexive) AE^{Epis} extension of class C of an AE^{Epis} theory A iff it satisfies the following equation:*

$$T = \{\phi \mid A \models_{T,C} \phi\}$$

It can be easily shown in parallel with Theorem 1 and Theorem 2 that the following theorem holds.

Theorem 4 *Let ETH^C denote the epistemic logical consequence (or axiomatic system) associated with the class C.*

E is an AE^{Epis} extension of class C of an AE^{Epis} theory A iff it satisfies the following equation:

$$E = ETH^C(A \cup \{\mathbf{L}\phi \mid \phi \in E\} \cup \{\neg \mathbf{L}\psi \mid \psi \ni E\})$$

E is a reflexive AE^{Epis} extension of class C of an AE^{Epis} theory A iff it satisfies the following equation:

$$E = ETH^C(A \cup \{\phi \equiv \mathbf{L}\phi \mid \phi \in E\} \cup \{\neg \mathbf{L}\psi \mid \psi \ni E\})$$

It can be seen that an AE^{Epis}-like logic can be easily obtained by substituting an epistemic logic for the base logic of (cf. reflexive) AE logic. In particular, such an epistemic logic need not be based on a possible worlds semantics. In fact, by generlizing Theorem 4, we can simply replace ETH^C by any epistemic logical consequence operator for any semantics we like. For example, the epistemic semantics can even be one that allows beliefs to have probabilities (eg. [Jiang 92]) in which case ETH^C will be a probabilistic epistemic axiomization (eg. [Jiang 92]).

But is this "replacement" approach enough for multiagent autoepistemic reasoning? This motivates the conjecture in the next section.

4 Conjecture

In AE^{Epis}, we can only perform autoepistemic reasoning outside the scope of a Bel operator, e.g., $(\neg \mathbf{L}Bel(a,p)) \rightarrow Bel(a, Bel(b,q))$. This however raises the question of autoepistemic reasoning inside the scope of a (possibly nested) modal operator Bel, e.g., $Bel(a, (\neg \mathbf{L}p) \rightarrow Bel(b, q))$. The following conjecture however suggests that this worry is unnecessary at least in the *propositional* case. It is not clear if the conjecture still holds in the quantification case. Preliminary works conducted as early as [Jiang 89] seem to suggest otherwise.

Conjecture 1 *Autoepistemic nonmonotonic reasoning performed inside the scope of nested agents can be equivalently performed outside the scope of nested agents. In other words, any multiagent AE formula with a $\mathbf{L}$ operator inside an epistemic modal operator Bel can be equivalently transformed to a mutliagent AE formula that does not have $\mathbf{L}$ inside Bel.*

In this section, we shall attempt to justify this conjecture intuitively. In the next sections, we shall justify the conjecture logically.

The intuitive reasons behind the conjecture are as follows.

1. If each agent is ideal in nonmonotonic reasoning, his reasoning power would be the same as any other agents. In this case, there is no reason why the agent's reasoning cannot be done by a global external agent, say God, in his place.

   For example in a multiagent AE logic, instead of saying that $Bel(a, \neg \mathbf{L}p \rightarrow Bel(b, q))$, we can replace it by $(\neg \mathbf{L}Bel(a, p)) \rightarrow Bel(a, Bel(b, q))$.

2. If an agent's power is different from another agent's in nonmonotonic reasoning, then we can always define the "base" epistemic logic in such a way that different agents will have different sets of axioms and rules of inference. Here the epistemic logic need not be based on the possible worlds semantics of Hintikka [62]. It can be any logic of belief that does not suffer from *logical omniscience* (e.g. the logics of Vardi [86] and Fagin et al [88]), i.e. the problem of "ideal" reasoning.

   For example, we can attribute to John the positive introspective ability with the axiom $Bel(John, p) \rightarrow Bel(John, Bel(John, p))$, whilst to Tom the negative introspective ability with the axiom
   $\neg Bel(Tom, p) \rightarrow Bel(Tom, \neg Bel(Tom, p))$.

The importance of the conjecture is to allow us to keep the development of autoepistemic nonmonotonic reasoning separated from epistemic logics. For example, we can even replace the autoepistemic component by a 3-valued AE logic such as Prymusinksi's [91] or Bonanti's [92]. In fact, both AE logic and reflexive AE logic can be seen as special cases of McDermott and Doyle's general autoepistemic logical framework [80,82] in the following fixpoint definition.

Definition 6 *Let A be an AE theory and S be any monotonic modal logic on the modal operator $\mathbf{L}$. Then E is a S-extension of A iff*

$$E = Th_S(A \cup \{\neg \mathbf{L}\phi \mid \phi \ni E\})$$

where Th_S denote the consequence closure operator of the S modal logic.

Konolige has shown [88] that

Theorem 5 *Let $KD45$ be the modal logic obtained from the $S5$ modal logic by replacing the axiom schema T ($\mathbf{L}\phi \rightarrow \phi$) by the weaker schema D ($\mathbf{L}\phi \rightarrow \neg \mathbf{L}\neg \phi$). Then E is an AE extension of A iff E is a $KD45$-extension of A.*

Schwarz has shown [91] that

Theorem 6 *Let $SW5$ be the modal logic obtained from $S5$ by replacing the 5-axiom schema ($\neg \mathbf{L}\phi \rightarrow \mathbf{L}\neg \mathbf{L}\phi$) by the weaker schema ($\phi \rightarrow (\neg \mathbf{L}\phi \rightarrow \mathbf{L}\neg \mathbf{L}\phi)$). $SW5$ is characterized by the class of valuations with an accessibility relation R being reflexive, transitive and possesses the property that $(R(s,t) \wedge R(s,u)) \wedge s \neq u) \rightarrow$

$R(t,u)$. Then E is a reflexive AE extension of A iff E is a SW5-extension of A.

Clearly, given any modal logics S and U, a S-extension is a U-extension if S is a modal logic contained by U. Schwarz [91] has also shown that $S \in \{KD45, SW5\}$ are the maximal S-extensions that are not collapsed to a monotonic logic as it is the case for S5-extension. This means that instead of using KD45- or SW5- extensions, we can also use any other weaker extensions such as T-extensions based on the modal logic T. To obtain the corresponding multiagent S-extension for a modal logic S on $\mathbf{L}$ operator, we simply add the monotonic axiom schemas on Bel operator of an epistemic logic to the S axiomatic system. We can thus define a multiagent generalization of McDermott and Doyle's autoepistemic logical framework.

Definition 7 *Let A be an AE^{Epis} theory. Let S be any monotonic modal logic on the modal operator $\mathbf{L}$. Let U be any monotonic epistemic logic on the modal operator Bel. Then E is a (S,U)-extension of A iff*

$$E = Th_{(S,U)}(A \cup \{\neg \mathbf{L}\phi \mid \phi \ni E\})$$

where $Th_{(S,U)}$ denote the consequence closure operator of (the S modal axiom schemas) $\cup$ (the U axiom schemas).

Finally, it is worth noting that the conjecture also justifies some of the current approaches in speech act theories (eg. [Appelt & Konolige 89]). In particular, existing proof methods for autoepistemic logics (eg. Moore 88, Marek & Trunsinski 89) can basically remain the same except that we replace the ordinary propositional axiomatic system by an epistemic axiomatic system.

Consider Moore's method [88] which constructs AE extensions of an AE theory in the following steps. First, we enumerate all the truth combinations of $\mathbf{L}\phi$ literals in the theory. For example, for the AE theory $\{\neg \mathbf{L}p \rightarrow q\}$, the possible truth combinations are just the singlton sets $\{(\mathbf{L}p$ is TRUE$)\}$ and $\{(\mathbf{L}p$ is FALSE$)\}$. Then, we use the truth values of a chosen combination to simplify the theory to an *ordinary* theory. For example, the second combination of the above example will reduce the theory to $\{q\}$. Finally, we check if each ϕ of $\mathbf{L}\phi$ literals, that are assigned with the truth value TRUE in the chosen combination, follows from the resultant ordinary theory; and if each ϕ of $\mathbf{L}\phi$ literals, that are assigned with the truth value FALSE in the chosen combination, does not follow from the resultant ordinary theory. If it is so, then the ordinary closure of the resultant theory will form the ordinary core of an AE extension of the original AE theory[1]. For the above example, since p does not follow from $\{q\}$, TH(q) will form the ordinary core of an AE extension of the AE theory $\{\neg \mathbf{L}p \rightarrow q\}$.

To adapt Moore's method to a multiagent AE logic such as AE^{Epis} of any class X, we still perform the truth combinations of $\mathbf{L}\phi$ literals and their simplifications as before. However this time we check if each ϕ of $\mathbf{L}\phi$ literals that are assigned with TRUE (or FALSE) follows (or does not follow) from the resultant *epistemic* theory using the epistemic axiomatic system associated with X. If it is so, then the epistemic closure of the resultant theory will form the epistemic core of an AE^{Epis} extension of class X of the original AE theory.

Now lets try to justify Conjecture 1 logically. We first introduce a multiagent autoepistemic logic that allows autoepistemic reasoning inside the scope of any Bel operators.

5 Another Multiagent Autoepistemic Logic

To draw a parallel with AE^{Epis}, in this section, we shall present a multiagent autoepistemic logic (MAE) in which the epistemic component is also characterized by a possible-worlds semantics. The language of MAE however allows *non-ordinary* formulae inside the scope of a Bel operator. The intended meaning of $\mathbf{L}$ inside a Bel operator of a (nested) agent is to reflect on the beliefs of this agent.

A MAE theory is a set of MAE formulae which can be defined inductively as follows.

1. a propositional atom is a MAE formula
2. if ϕ and ψ are MAE formulae, so are $\neg \phi$, $\phi \vee \psi$, $\phi \wedge \psi$ and $\phi \rightarrow \psi$
3. if ϕ is a MAE formula, then $\mathbf{L}\phi$ is a MAE formula.
4. if ϕ is a MAE formula[2], then Bel(agent,ϕ) is a MAE formula. Here *agent* is a member of the set of agents in MAE.

The semantics of MAE can be defined in a similar way as AE^{Epis}'s valuation (I,T) under a frame structure M=(W,R). However, while T denotes a single AE^{Epis} theory in AE^{Epis}, it would denote a mapping from a sequence of agents $<a_1, ..., a_n>$ to a MAE theory in MAE logic. We also stipulate[3] that

$$Bel(a,\phi) \in T(<a_1,...,a_n>) \text{ iff } \phi \in T(<a_1,...,a_n,a>).$$

for every L-literal $\mathbf{L}\phi$ in the given AE theory. Each combination of assumptions can then be used to simplify the given AE theory. In the case of assuming the equivalence, the equivalence is justified iff ϕ follows from the resultant AE theory.

---

[1]The same method can be applied similarly to construct a reflexive AE extension except that we now only assume either the falsity of a L-literal or the equivlance of $\mathbf{L}\phi \rightarrow \phi$

[2]Note here ϕ is not restricted to be ordinary as AE^{Epis}.

[3]It will be seen that this stipulation is crucial to the proof of the equivalence of the two proposed logics.

Furthermore, the valuation in the MAE semantics is additionally indexed by a sequence of nested agents. The reason for these differences are due to the fact that, in MAE, we additionally allow autoepistemic reasoning within the scope of a Bel operator. As a result, the truth of $\mathbf{L}\phi$ need be defined against the theory associated with the scope of the Bel operator within which the $\mathbf{L}$ operator falls.

We now define the satisfiability relationship $\models_{(I,T)_M, seq\_agents}$ between a MAE formula and a MAE valuation (I,T) at a frame $M=(W,R)$ under the view of seq_agents.

1. $\models_{(I,T)_M, seq\_agents} p$ iff $p \in I$ where p is an atom
2. $\models_{(I,T)_M, seq\_agents} \neg\phi$ iff $\neg(\models_{(I,T)_M, seq\_agents} \phi)$
3. $\models_{(I,T)_M, seq\_agents} \phi \lor \psi$ iff $\models_{(I,T)_M, seq\_agents} \phi$ or $\models_{(I,T)_M, seq\_agents} \psi$
4.
   - In the case of extending Moore's AE logic to multiagent autoepistemic reasoning
     $\models_{(I,T)_M, seq\_agents} \mathbf{L}\phi$ iff $\phi \in T(seq\_agents)$
   - In the case of extending Schwarz's reflexive AE logic to multiagent autoepistemic reasoning
     $\models_{(I,T)_M, seq\_agents} \mathbf{L}\phi$ iff $\phi \in T(seq\_agents)$ and $\models_{(I,T)_M, seq\_agents} \phi$
5. $\models_{(I,T)_M, <a_1,...,a_n>} Bel(ag, \phi)$ iff $\forall I'(R(ag, I, I') \rightarrow \models_{(I',T)_M, <a_1,...,a_n, ag>} \phi)$
6. Conjunction and implication are defined in the standard way.

Definition 8 Let A denote a MAE theory. We define $\models_{(I,T)_M, seq\_agents} A$ iff $\forall \phi \in A$, $\models_{(I,T)_M, seq\_agents} \phi$. We define $A \models_{T, Class, seq\_agents} \phi$ iff for every $M=(W,R)$ such that R is in the class of $Class$, and for every I of W, if $\models_{(I,T)_M, seq\_agents} A$, then $\models_{(I,T)_M, seq\_agents} \phi$. We say A is satisfiable iff there exists a MAE valuation $(I,T)_M$ and a seq_agents such that $\models_{(I,T)_M, seq\_agents} A$ for some I in W of M. We say a MAE formula ϕ is valid iff $\neg\phi$ is not satisfiable.

Like AE^{Epis} logic, we also define an *extensional* closure for a MAE theory. However unlike AE^{Epis} logic which forms a single extension from a God point of view, here we form an *extension* for each sequence of agents. This is because each sequence of agents will denote a scope of epistemic reasoning within which beliefs can be reflected. Before we present the definition of a MAE extension, we first make the following notations.

- Let $\mathbf{Bel}(< a_1, a_2, .., a_n >, \phi)$ denote $Bel(a_1, \mathbf{Bel}(a_2, .., Bel(a_n, \phi)...))$.
- Let $Bel(<>, \phi)$ denote ϕ. Here "$<>$" denotes the empty sequence of agents.
- Let $\Rightarrow$ denote the mapping function.

Definition 9 T is a (cf. reflexive) MAE extension of class C of a MAE theory A iff it satisfies the following equation:

$$T = \{ (seq\_agents \Rightarrow \{\phi \mid A \models_{T,C,<>} Bel(seq\_agents, \phi)\}) \mid seq\_agents \in SA \}$$

where SA denotes the set of all the possible sequences of agents (including the empty sequence) in MAE logic.

Cleary, if SA contains only the empty sequence of agents, a MAE extension simply collapses to that of the single agent AE logic.

Theorem 7 T is a (cf. reflexive) MAE extension of a MAE theory where $SA=\{<>\}$ iff $T(<>)$ is an (cf. reflexive) AE extension of the theory in AE logic.

Furthermore, if we restrict the MAE language to be the same as AE^{Epis}, then a MAE extension simply collapses to that of AE^{Epis} logic.

Theorem 8 T is a (cf. reflexive) MAE extension of a MAE theory where the language of MAE is restricted to AE^{Epis} iff $T(<>)$ is a (cf. reflexive) AE^{Epis} extension of the theory.

The proofs of these theorems are all straighforward. We omit them for space reason.

6 MAE $\equiv AE^{Epis}$

Despite the fact that MAE allows autoepistemic reasoning within the scope of any nested agents, a closer examination will show surprisingly that the logic is essentially equivalent to AE^{Epis}.

Before we prove this result, we prove some basic theorems. We only do this for the MAE logic and the proofs for the reflexive MAE follow similarly.

Theorem 9 $Bel(a, \neg\mathbf{L}\phi \lor \psi) \equiv \neg\mathbf{L}Bel(a, \phi) \lor Bel(a, \psi)$.

Proof We prove the equivalence by expanding the meanings of both sides.

1. $\models_{(I,T)_M, <a_1,...,a_n>} Bel(a, \neg\mathbf{L}\phi \lor \psi)$ iff
   $\forall I'(R(a, I, I') \rightarrow \models_{(I',T)_M, <a_1,...,a_n, a>} (\neg\mathbf{L}\phi \lor \psi))$ iff
   $\forall I'(R(a, I, I') \rightarrow (\models_{(I',T)_M, <a_1,...,a_n, a>} \neg\mathbf{L}\phi$ or $\models_{(I',T)_M, <a_1,...,a_n, a>} \psi))$
   iff $\forall I'(R(a, I, I') \rightarrow (\neg(\phi \in T(<a_1,...,a_n, a>))$ or $\models_{(I',T)_M, <a_1,...,a_n, a>} \psi))$

2. $\models_{(I,T)_M,<a_1,...,a_n>} \neg \mathbf{L}Bel(a,\phi) \vee Bel(a,\psi)$ iff

$\models_{(I,T)_M,<a_1,...,a_n>} \neg \mathbf{L}Bel(a,\phi)$ or
$\models_{(I,T)_M,<a_1,...,a_n>} Bel(a,\psi)$

iff $\neg(Bel(a,\phi) \in T(<a_1,...,a_n>))$ or
$\forall I'(R(a,I,I') \rightarrow \models_{(I',T)_M,<a_1,...,a_n,a>} \psi)$

From the semantics of MAE, we have $Bel(a,\phi) \in T(<a_1,...,a_n>)$ iff $\phi \in T(<a_1,...,a_n,a>)$. In addition, by the classical first order equivalence $\neg \phi \vee \forall x(\psi(x) \rightarrow \alpha(x)) \equiv \forall x(\psi(x) \rightarrow (\neg \phi \vee \alpha(x)))$ where x is not free in ϕ, (2) is equivalent to (1).

Q.E.D

Theorem 10 $Bel(a, \mathbf{L}\phi \vee \psi) \equiv \mathbf{L}Bel(a,\phi) \vee Bel(a,\psi)$.

Proof We prove the equivalence by expanding the meanings of both sides.

1. $\models_{(I,T)_M,<a_1,...,a_n>} Bel(a, \mathbf{L}\phi \vee \psi)$ iff
$\forall I'(R(a,I,I') \rightarrow \models_{(I',T)_M,<a_1,...,a_n,a>} \mathbf{L}\phi \vee \psi)$ iff
$\forall I'(R(a,I,I') \rightarrow (\models_{(I',T)_M,<a_1,...,a_n,a>} \mathbf{L}\phi$ or
$\models_{(I,T),w',<a_1,...,a_n,a>} \psi))$
iff $\forall I'(R(a,I,I') \rightarrow (\phi \in T(<a_1,...,a_n,a>)$ or
$\models_{(I',T)_M,<a_1,...,a_n,a>} \psi))$

2. $\models_{(I,T)_M,<a_1,...,a_n>} \mathbf{L}Bel(a,\phi) \vee Bel(a,\psi)$ iff

$\models_{(I,T)_M,<a_1,...,a_n>} \mathbf{L}Bel(a,\phi)$ or
$\models_{(I,T)_M,<a_1,...,a_n>} Bel(a,\psi)$

iff $Bel(a,\phi) \in T(<a_1,...,a_n>)$ or
$\forall I'(R(a,I,I') \rightarrow \models_{(I',T)_M,<a_1,...,a_n,a>} \psi)$

From the semantics of MAE, we have $Bel(a,\phi) \in T(<a_1,...,a_n>)$ iff $\phi \in T(<a_1,...,a_n,a>)$. In addition, by the classical first order equivalence $\phi \vee \forall x(\psi(x) \rightarrow \alpha(x)) \equiv \forall x(\psi(x) \rightarrow (\phi \vee \alpha(x)))$ where x is not free in ϕ, (2) is equivalent to (1).

Q.E.D

Despite the above equivalence result, it is worth to point out that $Bel(a, \phi \vee \psi)$ is not equivalent to $Bel(a,\phi) \vee Bel(a,\psi)$ in the same spirit that $\mathbf{L}\phi \vee \psi$ is not equivalent to $\phi \vee \psi$ or $\mathbf{L}\phi \vee \mathbf{L}\psi$. All these inequivalencies are confirmed by the semantics of the proposed logics.

Similarly, we can extend the above two theorems in the conjunctive case.

Theorem 11 $Bel(a, \neg \mathbf{L}\phi \wedge \psi) \equiv \neg \mathbf{L}Bel(a,\phi) \wedge Bel(a,\psi)$.

Theorem 12 $Bel(a, \mathbf{L}\phi \wedge \psi) \equiv \mathbf{L}Bel(a,\phi) \wedge Bel(a,\psi)$.

It follows that

Theorem 13 $Bel(a, \neg \mathbf{L}\phi) \equiv \neg \mathbf{L}Bel(a,\phi)$.

Theorem 14 $Bel(a, \mathbf{L}\phi) \equiv (\mathbf{L}Bel(a,\phi)$.

Using these basic theorems, we can now prove the following general result.

Theorem 15 *Every MAE formula A can be equivalently transformed to a MAE formula Trans(A) that does not contain any $\mathbf{L}$ operator inside the scope of any Bel operator.*

Proof We prove the theorem inductively on the complexity of the formula A.

1. Clearly, if A is an ordinary atom, $Trans(A) = A$.

2. Let the induction hypothesis be that the theorem holds for formulae of complexity less or equal than n. In the following, we consider A of complexity n+1.

3. - If A is $\phi \vee \psi$, then by the induction hypothesis, $\phi \equiv Trans(\phi)$ and $\psi \equiv Trans(\psi)$. Therefore, $Trans(A) = Trans(\phi) \vee Trans(\psi)$. Similarly, the result holds for conjunction[4].
   - If A is $\neg \phi$, then by the induction hypothesis, $\phi \equiv Trans(\phi)$. Therefore, $Trans(A) = \neg Trans(\phi)$.
   - If A is $\mathbf{L}\phi$, by the induction hypothesis, $Trans(\phi)$ does not contain any $\mathbf{L}$ operator inside the scope of any Bel operator. Therefore $Trans(A) = \mathbf{L}Trans(\phi)$
   - If A is $Bel(a,\phi)$ where a is any agent, then by the induction hypothsis, $Trans(\phi)$ must have $\mathbf{L}$ outside the scope of any Bel operator. Since $Trans(\phi)$ can only be in one of the four forms: $(\mathbf{L}\alpha)$, $(\neg \mathbf{L}\alpha)$, $(\mathbf{L}\alpha)\diamond \beta$ or $(\neg \mathbf{L}\alpha)\diamond \beta$ where $\diamond \in \{\wedge, \vee\}$, then by the basic theorems and by the induction hypothesis on the fact that $Bel(a,\beta)$'s complexity is at least 1 less than that of $Bel(a,\phi)$, we have the following transformation for the four forms respectively:

$$Trans(A) = \begin{cases} \mathbf{L}Bel(a,\alpha) \\ \neg \mathbf{L}Bel(a,\alpha) \\ \mathbf{L}Bel(a,\alpha)\diamond Trans(Bel(a,\beta)) \\ \neg \mathbf{L}Bel(a,\alpha)\diamond Trans(Bel(a,\beta)) \end{cases}$$

It follows from Theorem 15 of Conjecture 1 for the MAE logic.

Theorem 16 *T is a MAE extension of a MAE theory A iff T is an MAE extension of Trans(A).*

This theorem suggests that MAE is essentially equivalent to AE^{Epis}.

---
[4]We assume that the implication $\rightarrow$ will be expressed in terms of other logical connectives in a standard way.

7 Subsumption of Morgenstern's formulation

The wffs of Morgenstern's multiagent autoepistemic logic (MANML) are defined by the following rules

- if ϕ is an ordinary propositional wff, then ϕ is a MANML wff
- if ϕ is a MANML wff, then $\mathbf{L}_a\phi$ is a MANML wff where a is a constant of the MANML language representing an agent
- if ϕ and ψ are MANML wffs, so are $\phi \wedge \psi$, $\phi \vee \psi$ and $\neg\phi$

Morgenstern did not provide a definition for a MANML extension. Instead, she extends the stability property of AE logic to MANML. A ANML theory T is stable if it is closed under the following syntactical rules where $\vdash$ denotes the ordinary propositional derivability.

1. if $P_1, .., P_n \in T$, $P_1, .., P_n \vdash Q$, then $Q \in T$
2. if $\mathbf{L}_a P_1, .., \mathbf{L}_a P_n \in T$, $P_1, .., P_n \vdash Q, \mathbf{L}_a Q \in T$
3. $\mathbf{L}_a P \in T$ iff $\mathbf{L}_a \mathbf{L}_a P \in T$
4. $\mathbf{L}_a P \not\in T$ iff $\mathbf{L}_a \neg \mathbf{L}_a P \in T$
5. Some commonsense principles of arrogance
    - Principle of Moderated Arrogance (PMA) if $\mathbf{L}_X\mathbf{L}_Y(\mathbf{L}_Y\alpha \wedge \neg\mathbf{L}_Y\beta \to \gamma) \in T$, $\mathbf{L}_X\mathbf{L}_Y\alpha \in T$, and $\mathbf{L}_X\mathbf{L}_Y\beta \not\in T$, then $\mathbf{L}_X\mathbf{L}_Y\gamma \in T$
    - Principle of Cautious Arrogance (PCA) If $\mathbf{L}_X\mathbf{L}_Y(\mathbf{L}_Y\alpha \wedge \neg\mathbf{L}_Y\beta \to \gamma) \in T$, $\mathbf{L}_X\mathbf{L}_Y\alpha \in T$, $\mathbf{L}_X\mathbf{L}_Y\beta \not\in T$, and $\mathbf{L}_X\beta \not\in T$ then $\mathbf{L}_X\mathbf{L}_Y\gamma \in T$

Definition 10 *A MANML wff ϕ is directly in the scope of a wff $\mathbf{L}_X\psi$ if ϕ is contained in ψ and is not contained by a wff $\mathbf{L}_Y\alpha$ which is also contained in ψ.*

In this section, we shall show that Morgenstern's formulation is subsumed by the extrospective approaches presented in this paper. Before we prove this result, we first define a modular transformation $TRAN$ that maps Morgenstern's MANML wffs to MAE wffs. The transformation $TRAN(\psi)$ simply replaces (starting from the inner most scope to the outmost scope of ψ) every MANML wff of the form $\mathbf{L}_a\phi$ in ψ that is not directly in the scope of a wff $\mathbf{L}_a\alpha$ in ψ by $\mathbf{L}Bel(a, \phi)$ and every MANML wff of the form $\mathbf{L}_a\phi$ in ψ that is directly in the scope of a wff $\mathbf{L}_a\alpha$ in ψ by $\mathbf{L}\phi.$. For example, given ψ as $\mathbf{L}_a(p \to \mathbf{L}_a p)$, $TRAN(\psi)$ will be $\mathbf{L}Bel(a, p \to \mathbf{L}p)$.

With the above transformation, we can now show that Morgenstern's Formulation (MF) is subsumed by the K-class of reflexive MAE logics. Here K-class does not put any restriction on the accessablity relationship R in the valuations of MAE logics.

Theorem 17 *Let A be a set of MANML wffs. Let M be the reflexive K-class MAE extension of TRAN(A). Then M satisfies the stability conditions of MF.*

Proof We prove this theorem by proving that every syntactical rule of Morgenstern's Formulation (MF) is satisfied in the K-class reflexive MAE extension M.

1. Since the semantics of a MAE logic satisfies that of the ordinary propositional logic, clearly rule (1) of MF is satisfied.
2. Since $TRAN(\mathbf{L}_a P_i)$ is $\mathbf{L}Bel(a, P_i)$ which is equivalent to $Bel(a, P_i)$ in a reflexive MAE extension, and the possible worlds semantics of the MAE logic satisfies the property that if $Bel(a, P_1), .., Bel(a, P_n)$, $P_1, .., P_n \vdash Q$, $Bel(a, Q)$, rule (2) of MF is thus satisfied.
3. Since $TRAN(\mathbf{L}_a P)$ is $\mathbf{L}Bel(a, P)$ and $TRAN(\mathbf{L}_a\mathbf{L}_a P)$ is $\mathbf{L}Bel(a, \mathbf{L}P)$ which is equivalent to $\mathbf{L}\mathbf{L}Bel(a, P)$ by Theorem 16, and since $\mathbf{L}Bel(a, P)$ is equivlent to $\mathbf{L}\mathbf{L}Bel(a, P)$ in a MAE extension, thus rule (3) of MF is satisfied.
4. Since $TRAN(\mathbf{L}_a P) \not\in M$ is equivalent to $\neg\mathbf{L}\mathbf{L}Bel(a, P) \in M$ in a MAE extension and $TRAN(\mathbf{L}_a\neg\mathbf{L}_a P)$ is $\mathbf{L}Bel(a, \neg\mathbf{L}P)$ which is equivalent to $\mathbf{L}\neg\mathbf{L}Bel(a, P)$ (by Theorem 16) which is equivalent to $\neg\mathbf{L}\mathbf{L}Bel(a, P)$ in a MAE extension, thus rule (4) of MF is satisfied.
5. Morgenstern's principles of arrogance
    - Principle of Moderated Arrogance (PMA) This principle follows implicitly from the MAE logic. That is, in MAE,

    $$\begin{aligned} if \quad & \mathbf{L}Bel(X, \mathbf{L}Bel(Y, \mathbf{L}\alpha \wedge \neg\mathbf{L}\beta \to \gamma)), \\ & \mathbf{L}Bel(X, \mathbf{L}Bel(Y, \alpha)), \\ and \quad & \neg\mathbf{L}\mathbf{L}Bel(X, \mathbf{L}Bel(Y, \beta)), \\ then \quad & \mathbf{L}Bel(X, \mathbf{L}Bel(Y, \gamma)). \end{aligned}$$

    Using theorem 16, this property is equivalent to the following simplified form in a MAE extension,

    $$\begin{aligned} if \quad & \mathbf{L}Bel(X, Bel(Y, \alpha)) \\ & \wedge \neg\mathbf{L}Bel(X, Bel(Y, \beta)) \\ & \to Bel(X, Bel(Y, \gamma)), \\ and \quad & Bel(X, Bel(Y, \alpha)), \\ and \quad & \neg\mathbf{L}Bel(X, Bel(Y, \beta)), \\ then \quad & Bel(X, Bel(Y, \gamma)). \end{aligned}$$

    - Principle of Cautious Arrogance (PCA) This principle is not a property of MAE. However it can be explicitly represented in the given MAE theory due to Theorem 16. For example, we can modify the above simplified form by the following property

    $$if \quad (\mathbf{L}Bel(X, Bel(Y, \alpha))$$

$$\land \neg \mathbf{L} Bel(X, Bel(Y, \beta)) \land$$
$$\neg \mathbf{L} Bel(X, \beta) \land$$
$$\rightarrow Bel(X, Bel(Y, \gamma))),$$
and $\quad \neg \mathbf{L} Bel(X, Bel(Y, \beta)),$
and $\quad \neg \mathbf{L} Bel(X, \beta),$
then $\quad Bel(X, Bel(Y, \gamma)).$

This property is again satisfied in a MAE extension.

The significance of this result are three-folds. First, the K-class reflexive MAE logic provides a semantics and a definition of a MANML AE extension for Morgenstern's syntactical formulation. Second, by the equivalence of the presented two extrospective approaches, the result shows there readily exist a proof method (like the one outlined in Section 4) for Morgenstern's formulation. Thirdly, the result shows that Morgenstern's formulation is only just one class of MAE logics.

Now lets consider Morgenstern's example "Bill believes that Alex believes that if Alex had an older brother, Alex would know about it ". Let Q stand for the sentence: Alex has an older brother. This example would be represented in the extrospective view as follows

$$Bel(Bill, Bel(Alex, Q \rightarrow \mathbf{L}Q))$$

or equivalently (by the Trans function in Theorem 15) as

$$\neg \mathbf{L} Bel(Bill, Bel(Alex, Q)) \rightarrow Bel(Bill, Bel(Alex, \neg Q))$$

Let the formula be the only formula in the given MAE theory. Then $Bel(Bill, Bel(X, \neg Q))$ follows from the MAE logic. In contrast, Morgenstern's theory has to rely on the explicit PMA principle in order to conclude the corresponding result.

Now suppose we want to apply the PCA principle instead in the above example. Then the example should be represented in the first place as follows

$$\neg \mathbf{L} Bel(Bill, Bel(Alex, Q))$$
$$\land \neg \mathbf{L} Bel(Bill, Q)$$
$$\rightarrow Bel(Bill, Bel(Alex, \neg Q))$$

In this way, if the theory contains only the above formula and the formula $Bel(Bill, Q)$, then we will not conclude $Bel(Bill, Bel(Alex, \neg Q))$.

8 Conclusion

In this paper, we have argued for an extrospective view of autoepistemic reasoning in which introspection of an agent's beliefs is performed from an external agent point of view. We have presented two approaches of the extrospective view to formalize a multiagent autoepistemic logic based on Moore's AE logic and Schwarz's reflexive AE logic. The first approach involves the replacement of the "base" logic of AE logic by an epistemic logic so that autoepistemic reasoning can only be performed (implicitly by God) outside the scope of any agent. We have shown that the semantics, extensions and proof methods of this approach can be easily developed on the basis of their counterparts from an AE logic. The second approach allows autoepistemic reasoning within the scope of any nested agents. We have provided a multiagent generalization of McDermott and Doyle's autoepistemic logic framework. We have also both intuitively and logically justified that Moore's and Schwarz's AE logics are in fact readily extedible to multiagents, contrary to Reiter's claim. To demonstrate the generality of our approaches, we have also shown that the proposed extrospective approaches subsume Morgenstern's formulation and at the same time provide a semantic account and proof method for her formulation.

The results developed in this paper have been applied to the formalization of the $DEMO(theory, t)$ notion in metalogic programming in the spirit of Jiang [90] where Clark's *negation as failure* (NAF) [78] is extended for a logic program of beliefs. Under this formalization, $not\ DEMO(theory, t)$ in metalogic programming will be rewritten as $\neg \mathbf{L} Bel(theory, t)$ in AE^{Epis}. The equivalence between MAE and AE^{Epis} enables one to transform the *not* inside the scope of a DEMO predicate to the outside of the scope. For example, $DEMO(th1, q\text{:-}\ not\ DEMO(th2, p))$ can be transformed to

$$DEMO(th1, q)\text{:-}\ not\ DEMO(th1, DEMO(th2, p)).$$

Halpern [93] and Lakmeyers [93] independently proposed multiagent extensions to Levesque's logics of only knowing [90] with similar (but not identical) semantic accounts. However their languages still essentially take Morgenstern's introspective view in the multiagent context. In [Jiang 93c], we have presented an extrospective multiagent extension of Levesque's logic of only knowing (ONL). The general idea is again to replace the ordinary part of Levesque's ONL logic by an epistemic logic in two different formalizations. One is to disallow the modal operators (e. **O, L, N**) of Levesque's ONL logic to appear inside the scope of any Bel operator of the epistemic logic. The other is to relax this restriction.

Unlike the equivalency result demonstrated in this paper, the two formalisms that extend Levesque's ONL logic to multiagents are *not* equivalent. In fact, the second formalism is *strictly* more expressive than the first. For example, from $\{Bel(a, \mathbf{O}p)\}$, we can derive $Bel(a, \mathbf{L}\neg \mathbf{L}q)$; while from $\{\mathbf{O}Bel(a, p)\}$, we can additionally derive $\mathbf{L}\neg \mathbf{L}q$. The inequivalency nevertheless does not contradict what we have argued in this paper since Levesque's ONL logic is strictly more expressive than Moore's AE logic. For example, Levesque's ONL can reason about Moore's *meta-theoretic* AE extensions at an *object level*.

Furthermore, as we have shown in [Jiang 93c], the two formalisms are still *equivalent* if we restrict their languages to wffs that do not contain any **O** and **N** operators. Consequently, if we restrict the languages to the ones mentioned in this paper and close both them by an **O** operator, they would still be equivalent, thus confirming again the conjecture made in this paper. For example, although **O**Bel(a,p) and Bel(a,**O**p) are not quivalent, howevver **OL**Bel(a,p) and **O**Bel(a,**L**p) are.

Acknowledgements

This paper is in many ways inspired by discussions with Bob Kowalski, Barry Richards and Dov Gabbay. I would also like to thank Piero Bonanti (Italy) and Jakko Hintikka (USA) for their useful comments and to J. Halpern and G. Lakemeyer for timely sending their papers which have been helpful. This research is supported by the Compulog project on metareasoning.

References

K. Clark (1978) *Negation as failure* in logic and database eds. H. Galliare and J. Minker, Plenum, New York, 293-322.

M. Gelfond (1987) *On stratified autoepistemic theories* AAAI 87.

R. Fagin, J. Halpern & M. Vardi *A nonstandard approach to the logical omniscience problem* TARK 88.

J. Halpern (1993) *Reasoning about only knowing with many agents* AAAI 93.

J. Hintikka (1962) *Knowledge and Belief* Cornel University Press, 1962.

G. Hughes & M. Cresswell (1984) *A companion to modal logic*, METHUEN.

Y.J. Jiang (1989) *Multiagent Autoepistemic Predicate Logic* 6th Israel Conference on Artificial Intelligence, Dec. 1989.

Y.J. Jiang (1990) *An epistemic model of logic programming* New Generation Computing, No 8.

Y.J. Jiang (1992) *Epistemic Logic, Probability Theory and multiagent nonmonotonic reasoning* Computers and Artificial Intelligence, Vol 11, No.1.

Y.J. Jiang (1993a) *On the autoepistemic reconstruction of logic programming* New Generation Computing, Vol 11.

Y.J. Jiang (1993b) *An intensional epistemic logic* Studia Logica Vol 52, 1993.

Y.J. Jiang (1993c) *All we know about they know* submitted.

G. Lakemeyer (1993a) *All they know: a study in multiagent autoepistemic reasoning* IJCAI 93.

G. Lakemeyer (1993b) *All they know about* AAAI 93.

H. Levesque (1990) *The logic of all I know* AI 1990.

F. Lin & Y. Shoham *Epistemic semantics for fixed-points nonmonotonic logics* TARK 88.

D. McDermott & Doyle (1980) *Nonmonotonic logic I* AI 13.

D. McDermott (1982) *Nonmonotonic logic II* JACM 29.

L. Morgentern (1990) *A theory of multiagent nonmonotonic reasoning* AAAI 90.

R. C. Moore (1985) *Semantic considerations of nonmonotonic logic* AI 25 (1).

R. C. Moore (1986) *Autoepistemic Logic* SRI 3068.

T. Przymusinski (1989) *An algorithm to compute circumscription* AI 38.

R. Reiter (1987) *On nonmonotonic reasoning* Annual Review in Computer Science.

G. Schwarz (1991) *Autoepistemic logic of knowledge* In A. Nerode et al eds, Logic Programming and Nonmontonic Reasoning, MIT.

M. Vardi (1986) *On epistemic logic and logical omniscience* TARK I.

Refinement Search as a Unifying Framework for analyzing Planning Algorithms

Subbarao Kambhampati*
Department of Computer Science and Engineering
Arizona State University, Tempe, AZ 85287-5406
Email: rao@asu.edu

Abstract

Despite the long history of classical planning, there has been very little comparative analysis of the performance tradeoffs offered by the multitude of existing planning algorithms. This is partly due to the many different vocabularies within which planning algorithms are usually expressed. In this paper, I show that refinement search provides a unifying framework within which various planning algorithms can be cast and compared. I will provide refinement search semantics for planning, develop a generalized algorithm for refinement planning, and show that all planners that search in the space of plans are special cases of this algorithm. I will then show that besides its considerable pedagogical merits, the generalized algorithm also (i) allows us to develop a model for analyzing the search space size, and refinement cost tradeoffs in plan space planning, (ii) facilitates theoretical and empirical analyses of competing planning algorithms and (iii) helps in synthesizing new planning algorithms with more favorable performance tradeoffs. I will end by discussing how the framework can be extended to cover other planning models (e.g. state-space, hierarchical), and richer behavioral constraints.

1 Introduction

The idea of generating plans by searching in the space of (partially ordered or totally ordered) plans has been around for almost twenty years, and has received a lot of formalization in the past few years. Much of this formalization has however been limited to providing semantics for plans and actions, and proving soundness and completeness results for planning algorithms. There has been very little effort directed towards comparative analysis of the performance tradeoffs offered by the multitude of plan-space planning

---
*This research is supported in part by an NSF Research Initiation Award IRI-9210997, and ARPA/Rome Laboratory planning initiative under grant F30602-93-C-0039. Special thanks to David McAllester for many enlightening (e-mail) discussions on refinement search, and Bulusu Gopi Kumar for critical comments.

algorithms.[1] Indeed, there exists a considerable amount of disagreement and confusion about the role and utility of even such long-standing concepts as "goal protection", and "conflict resolution" -- not to mention the more recent ideas such as "systematicity."

An important reason for this state of affairs is the seemingly different vocabularies and/or frameworks within which many of the algorithms are usually expressed. The lack of a unified framework for viewing planning algorithms has hampered comparative analyses and understanding of design tradeoffs, which in turn has severely inhibited fruitful integration of competing approaches.

In this paper, I shall show that viewing planning as a refinement search provides a unified framework within which the complete gamut of plan-space planning algorithms can be effectively cast and compared.[2] I will start by characterizing planning as a refinement search, and provide semantics for partial plans and plan refinement operations. I will then provide a generalized algorithm for refinement planning, in terms of which the whole gamut of the so-called plan-space planners can be expressed. The different ways of instantiating this algorithm correspond to the different design choices for plan-space planning. This unified view facilitates separation of important ideas underlying individual algorithms from "brand-names", and thus provides a rational basis for understanding the design tradeoffs and fruitfully integrating the various approaches. I will demonstrate this by using the framework as a basis for analyzing search space size vs. refinement cost trade-offs in plan-space planning, and developing novel planning algorithms with interesting performance tradeoffs.

The paper is organized as follows: Section 2 provides the preliminaries of refinement search, develops a model for

---
[1]The work of Barrett and Weld [1] as well as Minton et. al. [16, 17] are certainly steps in the right direction. However, they do not tell the full story since the comparison there was between a specific partial order and total order planner. The comparison between different partial order planners itself is still largely unexplored.

[2]Although it has been noted in the literature that most existing classical planning systems are "refinement planners," in that they operate by adding successively more constraints to the the partial plan, without ever retracting any constraint, no formal semantics have ever been developed for planning in terms of refinement search.

estimating the size of the search space explored by a refinement search, and introduces the notions of systematicity and strong systematicity. Section 3 reviews the classical planning problem, and provides semantics of plan-space planning in terms of refinement search. Specifically, the notion of candidate set of a partial plan is formally defined in this section, and the ontology of constraints used in representing partial plans is described. Section 4 describes the generalized refinement planning algorithm, discusses its various components, and explains how the existing plan-space planners can all be seen as instantiations of the generalized algorithm. Section 5 discusses the diverse applications of the unifying componental view provided by the generalized algorithm. Specifically, we will see how the unifying view helps in explicating and analyzing the tradeoffs (Section 5.1), facilitating comparative performance analyses (Section 5.2), and synthesizing planning techniques with novel performance tradeoffs (Section 5.3). Section 6 discusses how the generalized algorithm can be extended to handle richer types of goals (e.g. maintenance goals, intermediate goals), and other types of planning models (e.g. HTN planning, state-space planning). Section 7 presents the concluding remarks.

2 Refinement search Preliminaries

A refinement search (or split-and-prune search [18]) can be visualized as a process of starting with the set of *all* potential candidates for solving the problem, and splitting the set repeatedly until a solution candidate can be picked up from one of the sets in *bounded* time. Each search node $\mathcal{N}$ in the refinement search thus corresponds to a set of potential candidates, denoted by $\langle\!\langle \mathcal{N} \rangle\!\rangle$.

A refinement search is specified by providing a set of refinement operators (strategies) **R**, and a solution constructor function sol. The search process starts with the initial node $\mathcal{N}_\emptyset$, which corresponds to the set of all potential candidates (we shall call this set $\mathcal{K}$).

The search progresses by generating children nodes by the application of refinement operators. Refinement operators can be seen as set splitting operations on the candidate sets of search nodes -- they map a search node $\mathcal{N}$ to a set of children nodes $\{\mathcal{N}_i'\}$ such that $\forall i \ \langle\!\langle \mathcal{N}_i' \rangle\!\rangle \subseteq \langle\!\langle \mathcal{N} \rangle\!\rangle$.

Definition 1 *Let* **R** *be a refinement strategy that maps a node* $\mathcal{N}$ *to a set of children nodes* $\{\mathcal{N}_i'\}$. **R** *is said to be* **complete** *if* $\bigcup_i \langle\!\langle \mathcal{N}_i' \rangle\!\rangle = \langle\!\langle \mathcal{N} \rangle\!\rangle$ *(i.e., no candidate is lost in the process of refinement).*

R *is said to be* **systematic** *if* $\forall_{\mathcal{N}_i', \mathcal{N}_j'} \ \langle\!\langle \mathcal{N}_i' \rangle\!\rangle \cap \langle\!\langle \mathcal{N}_j' \rangle\!\rangle = \emptyset$.

The search terminates when a node $\mathcal{N}$ is found for which the solution constructor returns a solution candidate. A solution constructor sol is a 2-place function which takes a search node $\mathcal{N}$ and a solution criterion $S_\mathcal{G}$ as arguments. It will return either one of three values:

1. *fail*, meaning that no candidate in $\langle\!\langle \mathcal{N} \rangle\!\rangle$ satisfies the solution criterion

2. Some candidate $c \in \langle\!\langle \mathcal{N} \rangle\!\rangle$ which satisfies the solution criterion (i.e., c is a solution candidate)

3. $\bot$, meaning that sol can neither construct a solution candidate, nor determine that no such candidate exists.

```
Algorithm: Refinement Search(sol, R)
  Initialize open with N∅, the node with initial
    (null) constraint set
  Begin Loop
  If open is empty, terminate with failure
    Else, non-deterministically pick a node N from open
      If sol(N,G) returns a candidate c,
        Then return it with success
      Else, choose some refinement operator R ∈ R,
        (Not a backtrack point.)
        Generate R(N), the refinements of
          n with respect to R.
        Prune any nodes in R(N) that are inconsistent.
        Add the unpruned nodes in R(N) to open.
  End Loop
```

Figure 1: An algorithm for generic refinement search

In the first case, $\mathcal{N}$ can be pruned. In the second case search terminates with success, and in the third, $\mathcal{N}$ will be refined further. $\mathcal{N}$ is called a **solution node** if the call sol$(\mathcal{N}, S_\mathcal{G})$ returns a solution candidate.

Definition 2 (Completeness of Refinement Search) *A refinement search with the refinement operator set* **R** *and a solution constructor function* sol *is said to be complete if for every solution candidate* c *of the problem, there exists some search node* $\mathcal{N}$ *that results from a finite number of successive refinement operations on* $\mathcal{N}_\emptyset$ *(the initial search node whose candidate set is the entire candidate space), such that* sol *can pick up* c *from* $\mathcal{N}$.

Search nodes as Constraint Sets: Although it is conceptually simple to think of search nodes in terms of their candidate sets, we obviously do not want to represent the candidate sets explicitly in our implementations. Instead, the candidate sets are typically implicitly represented as generalized constraint sets associated with search nodes (c.f. [6]) such that every potential candidate that is *consistent* with the constraints in that constraint set is taken to belong to the candidate set of the search node. Under this representation, the refinement of a search node corresponds to adding new constraints to its constraint set, thereby restricting its candidate set. Anytime the set of constraints of a search node becomes inconsistent (unsatisfiable), the candidate set becomes empty, and the node can be pruned.

Definition 3 (Inconsistent Search Nodes) *A search node is said to be inconsistent if its candidate set is empty, or equivalently, its constraint set is unsatisfiable.*

Search Space Size: Figure 1 outlines the general refinement search algorithm. To characterize the size of the search space explored by this algorithm, we will look at the size of the fringe (number of leaf nodes) of the search tree. Suppose $\mathcal{F}_d$ is the dth level fringe of the search tree explored by the refinement search. Let $\kappa_d \geq 0$ be the average size of the candidate sets of the search nodes in the dth level fringe, and $\rho_d (\geq 1)$ be the redundancy factor, i.e., the average number of search nodes on the fringe whose candidate sets contain a given candidate in $\mathcal{K}$. It is easy to see that $|\mathcal{F}_d| \times \kappa_d = |\mathcal{K}| \times \rho_d$ (where $|.|$ is used to denote the cardinality of a set). If b is the average branching factor of the search, then the size of dth level fringe is also given by b^d. Thus, we have,

$$|\mathcal{F}_d| = b^d = \frac{|\mathcal{K}| \times \rho_d}{\kappa_d} \quad (1)$$

In terms of this model, a minimal guarantee one would like to provide is that the size of the fringe will never be more than the size of the overall candidate space $|\mathcal{K}|$. Trying to ensure this motivates two important notions of irredundancy in refinement search: *systematicity* and *strong systematicity*.

Definition 4 (Systematicity and Strong Systematicity)
A refinement search is said to be **systematic** *if for any two nodes $\mathcal{N}$ and $\mathcal{N}'$ falling in different branches of the search tree, then $\langle\!\langle \mathcal{N} \rangle\!\rangle \cap \langle\!\langle \mathcal{N}' \rangle\!\rangle = \emptyset$ (i.e., the candidate sets represented by $\mathcal{N}$ and $\mathcal{N}'$ are disjoint). Additionally, the search is said to be* **strongly systematic** *if it is systematic and never refines an inconsistent node.*

From the above, it follows that for a systematic search, the redundancy factor, ρ, is 1. Thus, the sum of the cardinalities of the candidate sets of the termination fringe will be no larger than the set of all potential candidates $\mathcal{K}$. For strongly systematic search, in addition to ρ being equal to 1, we also have $\kappa \geq 1$ (since no node has an empty candidate set) and thus $|\mathcal{F}_d| \leq |\mathcal{K}|$. Thus,

Proposition 1 *The fringe size of any search tree generated by a strongly systematic refinement search is strictly bounded by the size of the candidate space (i.e. $|\mathcal{K}|$).*

It is easy to see that a refinement search is systematic if and only if all the individual refinement operations are systematic. To convert a systematic search into a strongly systematic one, we only need to ensure that all inconsistent nodes are pruned from the search. The complexity of the consistency check required to effect this pruning depends upon the nature of the constraint sets associated with the search nodes.

3 Planning as Refinement Search

In this section, we shall develop a formal account of plan-space planning as a refinement search. Whatever the exact nature of the planner, the ultimate aim of (classical) planning is to find a *ground operator sequence*, which when executed in the given initial state, will produce desired *behaviors* or sequences of world states. Most classical planning techniques have traditionally concentrated on the sub-class of behavioral constraints called the goals of attainment [5], which essentially constrain the agent's attention to behaviors that end in world states satisfying desired properties. For the most part, this is the class of goals we shall also be considering in this paper (the exception is Section 6, which shows that our framework can be easily extended to a richer class of goals).

The operators (aka actions) in classical planning are modeled as general state transformation functions. We will be assuming that the domain operators are described in ADL [19, 20] representation with *Precondition* and *Effect* formulas. The precondition and effect formulas are *function-less* first order predicate logic sentences involving conjunction, negation and quantification. The precondition formulas can also have disjunction, but disjunction is not allowed in the effects formula. The subset of this representation where both formulas can be represented as conjunctions of function-less first order *literals*, and all the variables have infinite domains, is called the TWEAK representation (c.f. [2, 10]).[3]

From the above definitions, it is clear that any potential solution for a planning problem must be a ground operator sequence. Thus, viewed as a refinement search, the candidate space, $\mathcal{K}$, of a planning problem, is the set of all ground operator sequences. As an example, if the domain contains three ground actions $a1$, $a2$ and $a3$, then the regular expression $\{a1|a2|a3\}^*$ would describe the candidate space for this domain. We will next define when a ground operator sequence is considered a solution to a planning problem in classical planning:

Definition 5 (Plan Solutions) *A ground operator sequence $S : o_1, o_2, \cdots o_n$ is said to be a* **solution** *to a planning problem $[\mathcal{I}, \mathcal{G}]$, where $\mathcal{I}$ is the initial state of the world, and $\mathcal{G}$ is the specification of the desired behaviors, if the following two restrictions are satisfied:*

1. *S is executable, i.e., $\mathcal{I} \vdash prec(o_1)$, $o_1(\mathcal{I}) \vdash prec(o_2)$ and $o_{n-1}(o_{n-2}\cdots(o_1(\mathcal{I}))) \vdash prec(o_n)$ (where $prec(o)$ denotes the precondition formula of the operator o) and*

2. *The sequence of states $\mathcal{I}$, $o_1(\mathcal{I})$, $\cdots$, $o_n(o_{n-1}\cdots(o_1(\mathcal{I})))$ satisfies the behavioral constraints specified in the goals of the planning problem.*

For goals of attainment, the second requirement is stated solely in terms of the last state resulting from the plan execution: $o_n(o_{n-1}\cdots(o_1(\mathcal{I}))) \vdash \mathcal{G}$. A solution S is said to be **minimal** *if no operator sequence obtained by removing some of the operators from S is also a solution.*

Traditionally, the *completeness* of a planner is measured in terms of its ability to find minimal solutions (cf. [22, 19, 14]):

Definition 6 (Planner Completeness) *A planning algorithm is said to be* **complete** *if it can find all minimal solutions for every solvable problem.*

3.1 Refinement Search Semantics for Partial Plans

When plan-space planning is viewed as a refinement search, the constraint sets associated with search nodes can be seen as defining partial plans (in the following, we will be using the terms "search node" and "partial plan" interchangeably). The candidate set of a partial plan will be defined as all the ground operator sequences that satisfy the partial plan constraints.

The partial plan representation used by refinement planners can be described in terms of a 6-tuple: $\langle T, O, \mathcal{B}, \mathcal{ST}, \mathcal{L}, \mathcal{A} \rangle$ where:

- T is the set of steps in the plan; T contains two distinguished steps t_0 and t_∞.

- $\mathcal{ST}$ is a symbol table, which maps steps to domain operators. The special step t_0 is always mapped to the dummy operator start, and similarly t_∞ is always mapped to fin. The effects of start and the

---
[3]In TWEAK representation, the list of non-negated effects is called the *Add* list while the list of negated effects is called the *Delete* list.

preconditions of fin correspond, respectively, to the initial state and the desired goals (of attainment) of the planning problem.

- O is a partial ordering relation over T.
- $\mathcal{B}$ is a set of codesignation (binding) and non-codesignation (prohibited bindings) constraints on the variables appearing in the preconditions and postconditions of the operators.
- $\mathcal{L}$ is a set of auxiliary constraints. Auxiliary constraints are best seen as putting restrictions on the ground operator sequences being represented by the partial plan (see below).
- $\mathcal{A}$ is the set of preconditions of the plan, which are tuples of the form $\langle c, s \rangle$, where c is a condition that needs to be *made* true before the step $s \in T$. These include the preconditions and secondary preconditions [19] of all the actions introduced during planning process (see Section 4). $\mathcal{A}$ is sometimes referred to as the agenda of the plan.

Informally, the candidate set of a partial plan, $\mathcal{P}$, is the set of all ground operator (action) sequences that are consistent with the step, ordering, binding and auxiliary constraints of $\mathcal{P}$. Before we can formalize this notion, we need a better characterization of auxiliary constraints.

Auxiliary Constraints: Informally, auxiliary constraints should be seen as the constraints that need to be true for a ground operator sequence to belong to the candidate set of a partial plan. They can all be formalized as unary predicates on ground operator sequences. We will distinguish two types of auxiliary constraints: *monotonic* constraints and *non-monotonic* constraints.

Definition 7 (Monotonic Auxiliary Constraints) *An auxiliary constraint C is monotonic if given a ground operator sequence S that does not satisfy C, no operator sequence S' obtained by adding additional ground operators to S will satisfy C.*

Monotonic constraints are useful because of the pruning power they provide. If none of the ground operator sequences matching the ground linearizations of a partial plan satisfy its monotonic constraints, then that partial plan cannot have a non-empty candidate set, and thus can be pruned. For this reason, we will call the set of monotonic auxiliary constraints of a partial plan its **auxiliary candidate constraints** ($\mathcal{L}_c$), and the set of non-monotonic auxiliary constraints of a partial plan are called **auxiliary solution constraints**, ($\mathcal{L}_s$). Although auxiliary solution constraints cannot be used to prune partial plans, they can be used as a basis for selection heuristics during search (see the discussion of MTC-based goal selectors in Section 4.2, and that of filter conditions in 6).

Almost all of the auxiliary constraints employed in classical planning can be formalized in terms of two primitive types of constraints: *interval preservation constraints* (IPCs), and *point truth constraints* (PTCs):

Definition 8 (Interval Preservation Constraint) *An interval preservation constraint, $\langle s_i, c, s_j \rangle$ of a plan $\mathcal{P}$ is said to be satisfied by a ground operator sequence S according to a mapping function $\mathcal{M}$ that maps steps of $\mathcal{P}$ to elements of S, if and only if every operator o in S that comes between $\mathcal{M}(s_i)$ and $\mathcal{M}(s_j)$ preserves the condition c (i.e., if c is true in the state before o, then c will be true in the state after its execution).*[4]

Definition 9 (Point Truth Constraint) *A point truth constraint $\langle c@s \rangle$ is said to be satisfied by a ground operator sequence S with respect to a mapping $\mathcal{M}$ that maps steps of $\mathcal{P}$ to elements of S, if and only if either c is true in the initial state, and is preserved by every action of S occurring before $\mathcal{M}(s)$, or c is made true by some action $S[j]$ that occurs before $\mathcal{M}(s)$, and is preserved by all the actions between $S[j]$ and $\mathcal{M}(s)$.*

It is easy to see that interval preservation constraints are monotonic constraints, while point truth constraints are non-monotonic. In our model of refinement planning, IPCs are used to represent book-keeping (protection) constraints (Section 4.3) while PTCs are used to represent the solution constraints. In particular, given any partial plan $\mathcal{P}$, corresponding to every precondition $\langle C, s \rangle$ on its agenda, the partial plan contains an auxiliary solution constraint $\langle C@s \rangle$.[5]

We are now ready to formally define the candidate set of a partial plan:[6]

Definition 10 (Candidate set of a Partial plan) *Given a partial plan $\mathcal{P} : \langle T, O, \mathcal{B}, \mathcal{ST}, \mathcal{L}, \mathcal{A} \rangle$, a ground operator sequence S is said to belong to $\mathcal{P}$'s candidate set, $\langle\!\langle \mathcal{P} \rangle\!\rangle$, if and only if there exists a mapping function $\mathcal{M}$ (called candidate mapping) that maps steps of $\mathcal{P}$ (excepting the dummy steps t_0 and t_∞) to elements of S, such that S satisfies all the constraints of $\mathcal{P}$ under the mapping $\mathcal{M}$. That is,*

1. *$\mathcal{M}$ is consistent with $\mathcal{ST}$. That is, if $\mathcal{M}$ maps the step s to $S[i]$ (i.e., the ith element in the operator sequence), then $S[i]$ corresponds to the same action as $\mathcal{ST}(s)$.*
2. *$\mathcal{M}$ is consistent with the ordering constraints O and the binding constraints $\mathcal{B}$. For example, if $s_i \prec s_j$, and $\mathcal{M}(s_i) = S[l]$ and $\mathcal{M}(s_j) = S[m]$, then $l < m$.*
3. *S satisfies all the auxiliary candidate constraints ($\mathcal{L}_c$) under the mapping $\mathcal{M}$.*

Definition 11 (Solution Candidate of a Partial Plan) *A ground operator sequence S is said to be a solution candidate of a partial plan $\mathcal{P}$, if S is a candidate of $\mathcal{P}$ and S satisfies all the auxiliary solution constraints of $\mathcal{P}$.*

---

[4] Note that the plan does not have to *make* c true.

[5] Notice that this definition separates that the agenda preconditions from solution constraints. Under this model, the planner can terminate without having explicitly worked on the preconditions in the agenda (as long as the solution constraints are all true). Similarly, it also allows us to post solution constraints that we do not want the planner to explicitly work on (see the discussion about *filter conditions* in Section 6).

[6] Note that by our definition, a candidate of a partial plan may not be executable. It is possible to define candidate sets only in terms of executable operator sequences (or ground behaviors). We will stick with this more general notion of candidates, since coming up with an executable operator sequence can it self be seen as part of planning activity.

Given the definitions above, and the assumption that corresponding to every precondition of the plan, there exists a point truth constraint on the auxiliary solution constraints, we can easily prove the following relation between solution candidates and solutions of a planning problem:

Proposition 2 *Let $\mathcal{I}$ be the effect formula of t_0, and $\mathcal{G}$ be the precondition formula of t_∞ of $\mathcal{P}$. If a ground operator sequence S is a solution candidate of a partial plan $\mathcal{P}$, then S solves the problem $[\mathcal{I}, \mathcal{G}]$ according to Definition 5.*

Example: To illustrate the definitions above, suppose the partial plan $\mathcal{P}$ is given by the constraint set below, where the auxiliary constraints are interval preservation constraints as described above (the agenda field is omitted for simplicity):

$$\left\langle \begin{array}{l} \{t_0, t_1, t_2, t_\infty\}, \{t_0 \prec t_1, t_1 \prec t_2, t_2 \prec t_\infty\}, \emptyset, \\ \{t_1 \to o_1, t_2 \to o_2, t_0 \to \mathtt{start}, t_\infty \to \mathtt{fin}\}, \\ \{\langle t_1, p, t_2 \rangle, \langle t_2, q, t_\infty \rangle\} \end{array} \right\rangle$$

Consider the ground operator sequence $S : o_1 o_3 o_2$. It is easy to see that as long as the action o_3 preserves p, S will belong to the candidate set of $\mathcal{P}$. This is because there exists a candidate mapping, $\mathcal{M} : \{t_1 \to S[1], t_2 \to S[3]\}$ according to which S satisfies all the constraints of $\mathcal{P}$ (the interval preservation constraint $\langle t_1, p, t_2 \rangle$ is satisfied as long as o_3 preserves p). Similarly, the ground operator sequence $S' : o_1 o_2 o_5$ belongs to the candidate set of $\mathcal{P}$ if and only if o_5 preserves q.

Search Space Size: Search space size of a refinement planner can be estimated with the help of Eqn. 1. A minor problem in adapting this equation to planning is that according to the definitions above, both candidate space and candidate sets can have infinite cardinalities even for finite domains. However, if we restrict our attention to minimal solutions, then it is possible to construct finite versions of both. Given a planning problem instance P, let l_m be the length of the longest ground operator sequence that is a minimal solution of P. Let $\mathcal{K}$ be the set of all ground operator sequences of up to length l_m. $|\mathcal{K}|$ provides an upper bound on the number of operator sequences that need to be examined to ensure that all minimal solutions for the planning problem are found. In the rest of the paper, when we talk about the candidate set of a partial plan, we will be concerned about the subset of its candidates that belong to $\mathcal{K}$.

3.2 Candidate sets and Ground Linearizations

Traditionally, semantics for partial plans are given in terms of their ground linearizations (rather than in terms of candidate sets, as is done here).

Definition 12 *A ground linearization (aka completion) of a partial plan $\mathcal{P} : \langle T, O, B, ST, \mathcal{L}, \mathcal{A} \rangle$ is a fully instantiated total ordering of the steps of $\mathcal{P}$ that is consistent with O (i.e., a topological sort) and B.*

A ground linearization is said to be a **safe ground linearization** *if and only if it also satisfies all the auxiliary candidate constraints.*[7]

---
[7]Note that safe ground linearizations do not have to satisfy auxiliary *solution* constraints.

For the example plan discussed above, $t_0 t_1 t_2 t_\infty$ is the only ground linearization, and it is also a safe ground linearization. Safe ground linearizations are related to candidate sets in the following technical sense:

Proposition 3 *Every candidate S belonging to the candidate set of a partial plan $\mathcal{P} : \langle T, O, B, ST, \mathcal{L}, \mathcal{A} \rangle$ is either a minimal candidate, in that it exactly matches a safe ground linearization of $\mathcal{P}$ (except for the dummy steps t_0 and t_∞, and modulo the mapping of ST), or is a safe augmentation of a minimal candidate obtained by adding additional ground operators without violating any auxiliary candidate constraints.*

This proposition follows from the definition of candidate constraints. Consider any candidate (ground operator sequence) S of the plan $\mathcal{P}$. Let $\mathcal{M}$ be the candidate mapping according to which S satisfies the Definition 10. Consider the operator sequence S' obtained by removing from S every element $S[i]$ such that $\mathcal{M}$ does not map any step in $\mathcal{P}$ to $S[i]$. From the definition of candidate set, it is easy to see that S' must match with a ground linearization of $\mathcal{P}$. Further, since S satisfies all the auxiliary candidate constraints, and since candidate constraints are monotonic, it cannot be the case that S' violates them. Thus, S' matches a safe ground linearization of the plan.

For the example plan discussed above, $o_1 o_2$ is a minimal candidate because it exactly matches the safe ground linearization $t_0 t_1 t_2 t_\infty$, under the mapping ST. The ground operator sequence $o_1 o_3 o_2 o_4$, where o_3 does not add or delete p, and o_4 does not add or delete q, is a candidate of this plan. It can be obtained by augmenting the minimal candidate $o_1 o_2$ with the ground operators o_3 and o_4 without violating auxiliary candidate constraints.

During search, it is often useful to recognize and prune inconsistent plans (as they clearly cannot lead to solutions). Proposition 4, which is a direct consequence of Proposition 3, provides a method of checking consistency in terms of safe ground linearizations:

Proposition 4 *A search node in refinement planning is consistent if and only if the corresponding partial plan has at least one safe ground linearization.*

4 A generalized algorithm for Refinement Planning

The algorithms Find-plan and Refine-Plan in Figure 2 instantiate the refinement search within the context of planning. In particular, they describe a generic refinement-planning algorithm, the specific instantiations of which cover the complete gamut of plan-space planners. Table 1 characterizes many of the well known plan-space planners as instantiations of the Refine-Plan algorithm. The algorithms are *modular* in that individual steps can be analyzed and instantiated relatively independently. Furthermore, the algorithms do not assume any specific restrictions on action representation, and can be used by any planner using ADL action representation [19].

The refinement process starts with the partial plan $\mathcal{P}_\emptyset$, which contains the steps t_0 and t_∞, and has its agenda and auxiliary solution constraints initialized to the top level goals of attainment (preconditions of t_∞). The procedure Refine-Plan specifies the refinement operations done by the planning algorithm. Comparing this algorithm to the refinement search algorithm in Figure 1, we note that it uses two broad types of refinements: the establishment refinements (steps 2.1, 2.2); and the tractability refinements (step 3). In each refinement strategy, the added constraints include step addition, ordering addition, binding addition, as well as addition of auxiliary constraints. In the following, we briefly review the individual steps of these algorithms.

4.1 Solution Constructor function

As discussed in Section 3, the job of a solution-constructor function is to look for and return a solution candidate from the candidate set of a partial plan. Since enumerating and checking the full candidate set can be prohibitively expensive, most planners concentrate instead on the safe-ground linearizations of the plan (which bound the candidate set from above; see Proposition 3), and see if any of those correspond to solution candidates. In particular, the following is the default solution constructor used by all existing refinement planners (with respect to which completeness results are proven):

Definition 13 (All-sol) *Given a partial plan $\mathcal{P}$, all-sol returns with success only when $\mathcal{P}$ is consistent, all of its ground linearizations are safe, and each safe ground linearization corresponds to a ground operator sequence that is a solution candidate of $\mathcal{P}$.*

The termination criteria of *all-sol* correspond closely to the notion of necessary correctness of a partially ordered plan, first introduced by Chapman [2]. Existing planning systems implement *All-sol* in two different ways: Planners such as Chapman's TWEAK [2] use the modal truth criterion to explicitly *check* that all the safe ground linearizations correspond to solutions (we will call these the MTC-based constructors). Planners such as SNLP [15] and UCPOP [22] depend on protection strategies and conflict resolution (see below) to indirectly guarantee the safety and necessary correctness required by *all-sol* (we call these protection based constructors). In this way, the planner will never have to explicitly reason with all the safe-ground linearizations.

4.2 Goal Selection and Establishment

The most fundamental refinement operation is the so-called establishment operation. It selects a precondition $\langle C, s \rangle$ of the plan (where C is a precondition of a step s), and refines (i.e., adds constraints to) the partial plan such that different steps act as contributors of C to s in different refinements. Chapman [2] and Pednault [19] provide theories of sound and complete establishment refinement. Pednault's theory is more general as it deals with actions containing conditional and quantified effects.[8] It is possible to limit Refine-Plan to establishment refinements alone and still get a sound and complete (in the sense of Definition 2) planner (using the default solution constructor *all-sol* described earlier).

In Pednault's theory, establishment of a condition c at a step s essentially involves selecting some step s' (either

---

Algorithm Find-Plan$(\mathcal{I}, \mathcal{G})$ **Parameters**: sol: Solution constructor function.

1. Initialize the open list with the null plan $\mathcal{P}_\emptyset$: $\langle \{t_0, t_\infty\}, \{t_0 \prec t_\infty\}, \emptyset, \{t_0 \to \text{start}, t_\infty \to \text{fin}\}, \mathcal{L}_\emptyset, \mathcal{A}_\emptyset \rangle$, where corresponding to each goal $g_i \in G$, $\mathcal{A}_\emptyset$ contains $\langle g_i, t_\infty \rangle$, and $\mathcal{L}_\emptyset$ contains $\langle g_i @ t_\infty \rangle$.
2. Nondeterministically pick a partial plan $\mathcal{P}$ from open.
3. If sol$(\mathcal{P}, \mathcal{G})$ returns a solution, return it, and terminate. If it returns $*fail*$, skip to Step 2. If it returns $\bot$, call Refine-plan$(\mathcal{P})$ to generate refinements of $\mathcal{P}$. Add all the refinements to the open list; Go back to 2.

Algorithm Refine-Plan$(\mathcal{P})$ /*Returns refinements of $\mathcal{P}$ */ **Parameters**: (*i*) pick-prec: the routine for picking the preconditions from the plan agenda for establishment. (*ii*) interacts?: the routine used by pre-ording to check if a pair of steps interact. (*iii*) conflict-resolve: the routine which resolves conflicts with auxiliary candidate constraints.

1. **Goal Selection:** Using the pick-prec function, pick a precondition $\langle C, s \rangle$ (where C is a precondition of step s) from $\mathcal{P}$ to work on. *Not a backtrack point.*

2.1. **Goal Establishment:** Non-deterministically select a new or existing establisher step s' for $\langle C, s \rangle$. Introduce enough ordering and binding constraints, and secondary preconditions to the plan such that (*i*) s' precedes s (*ii*) s' will have an effect C, and (*iii*) C will persist until s (i.e., C is preserved by all the steps intervening between s' and s). *Backtrack point; all establishment possibilities need to be considered.*

2.2. **Book Keeping:** (Optional) Add auxiliary constraints noting the establishment decisions, to ensure that these decisions are protected by any later refinements. This in turn reduces the redundancy in the search space. The protection strategies may be one of *goal protection, interval protection* and *contributor protection* (see text). The auxiliary constraints may be one of point truth constraints or interval preservation constraints.

3. **Tractability Refinements:** (Optional) These refinements help in making the plan handling and consistency check tractable. Use either one or both:

   3.a. **Pre-Ordering:** Impose additional orderings between every pair of steps of the partial plan that possibly interact according to the static interaction metric interacts?. *Backtrack point; all interaction orderings need to be considered.*

   3.b. **Conflict Resolution:** Add orderings, bindings and/or secondary (preservation) preconditions to resolve conflicts between the steps of the plan, and the plan's auxiliary candidate constraints. *Backtrack point; all possible conflict resolution constraints need to be considered.*

4. **Consistency Check:** (Optional) If the partial plan is inconsistent (i.e., has no safe ground linearizations), prune it.

5. **Return** the refined partial plan (if it is not pruned).

Figure 2: *A generalized refinement algorithm for plan-space planning*

---

[8]And also separates checking truth of a proposition from planning to make that proposition true, see [10].

Planner	Soln. Constructor	Goal Selection	Book-keeping	Tractability Refinements
Tweak [2]	MTC-based ($O(n^4)$ for TWEAK rep; NP-hard with ADL)	MTC-based ($O(n^4)$ for TWEAK rep; NP-hard with ADL)	None	None
UA [16]	MTC-based $O(n^4)$	MTC-based $O(n^4)$	None	Unambiguous ordering
Nonlin [26]	MTC (Q&A) based	Arbitrary $O(1)$	Goal Protection via Q&A	Conflict Resolution
TOCL [1]	Protection based $O(1)$	Arbitrary $O(1)$	Contributor protection	Total ordering
Pedestal [14]	Protection based $O(1)$	Arbitrary $O(1)$	Interval Protection	Total ordering
SNLP [15] UCPOP [22]	Protection based $O(1)$	Arbitrary $O(1)$	Contributor protection	Conflict resolution
MP, MP-I [8]	Protection based	Arbitrary	(Multi) contributor protection	Conflict resolution
SNLP-UA (cf. Section 5.3.1)	Protection based $O(1)$/ MTC based/$O(n^4)$	Arbitrary $O(1)$/ Pick if nec. false. /$O(n^4)$	Contributor protection	Unambiguous Ordering

Table 1: Characterization of existing planners as instantiations of Refine-Plan

existing or new), and adding enough constraints to the plan such that (i) $s' \prec s$, (ii) s' causes c to be true and (iii) c is not violated before s. To ensure ii, we need to in general ensure the truth of certain additional conditions before s''. Pednault calls these the *causation preconditions* of s'' with respect to c. To ensure iii, for every step s'' of the plan, we need to either make s'' come before s', or make s'' come after s, or make s'' necessarily preserve c. The last involves guaranteeing truth of certain conditions before s''. Pednault calls these the *preservation preconditions* of s'' with respect to c. Causation and precondition preconditions are called secondary preconditions of the action. These are added to the agenda of the partial plan, and are treated in the same way as normal preconditions. (This includes adding a PTC $\langle c@s \rangle$ to the auxiliary solution constraints, whenever a precondition $\langle c, s \rangle$ is added to the agenda; see Section 3.1).

Goal Selection: The strategy used to select the particular precondition $\langle C, s \rangle$ to be established, (called goal selection strategy) can be arbitrary, can depend on some ranking based on precondition abstraction [24], and/or demand driven (e.g. select a goal only when it is not already necessarily true according to the modal truth criterion [2]). The last strategy, called MTC-based goal selection, involves reasoning about truth of a condition in a partially ordered plan, and can be intractable for general partial orderings consisting of ADL [19] actions (see Table 1, as well as the discussion of pre-ordering strategies in Section 4.5.1.).

4.3 Book Keeping and Protecting establishments

It is possible to do establishment refinement without book-keeping step. Chapman's TWEAK [2] is such a planner. However, such a planner is not guaranteed to respect its previous establishment decisions while making new ones, and thus may have a high degree of redundancy. Specifically such a planner may (i) wind up visiting the same candidate (potential solution) in more than one search branch (in terms of our search space characterization, this means $\rho > 1$), and (ii) wind up repeatedly establishing and clobbering the same precondition. The book-keeping step attempts to reduce these types of redundancy.

At its simplest, the book-keeping may be nothing more than removing each precondition from the agenda of the partial plan once it is considered for establishment. When the agenda of a partial plan is empty, it can be pruned without loss of completeness (this is because the establishment refinement looks at all possible ways of establishing a condition at the time it is considered).

A more active form of book-keeping involves protecting previous establishments in a partial plan, while making new refinements to it. In terms of Refine-Plan, such protection strategies can be seen as posting auxiliary candidate constraints on the partial plan to record the establishment decisions, and ensuring that they are not violated by the later refinements. If they are violated, then the plan can be abandoned without loss of completeness (even if its agenda is not empty). The protection strategies used by classical partial order planners come in two main varieties: interval protection (aka causal link protection, or protection intervals), and contributor protection (aka exhaustive causal link protection [8]). They can both be represented in terms of the interval preservation constraints.

Suppose the planner just established a condition c at step s with the help of the effects of the step s'. For planners using interval protection (e.g., PEDESTAL [14]), the book-keeping constraint requires that no candidate of the partial plan can have p *deleted* between operators corresponding to s' and s. It can thus be modeled in terms of interval preservation constraint $\langle s', p, s \rangle$. Finally, for book keeping based on contributor protection, the auxiliary constraint requires that no candidate of the partial plan can have p either *added* or deleted between operators corresponding to s' and s.[9] This contributor protection can be modeled in terms of the twin interval preservation constraints $\langle s', p, s \rangle$ and $\langle s', \neg p, s \rangle$.

While most planners use one or the other type of protection strategies exclusively for all conditions, planners like NONLIN and O-Plan [26, 27] post different book-keeping constraints for different types of conditions. Finally, the interval protections and contributor protections can also be generalized to allow for multiple contributors supporting a given condition (see [8] for a motivation and formal treatment of this idea).

While all the book-keeping strategies described above avoid considering same precondition for establishment more than once, only the contributor protection eliminates the redundancy of overlapping candidate sets, by making estab-

---

[9]See [7] for a coherent reconstruction of the ideas underlying goal protection strategies.

lishment refinement systematic. Specifically, we have:

Proposition 5 *Establishment refinement with exhaustive causal links is systematic in that partial plans in different branches of the search tree will have non-overlapping candidate sets (thus $\rho = 1$).*

This property can be proven from the fact that contributor protections provide a way of uniquely naming steps independent of the symbol table mapping (see [15, 7]). To understand this, consider the following partial plan (where the agenda and the auxiliary solution constraints are omitted for simplicity):

$$\mathcal{N}: \left\langle \begin{array}{l} \{t_0, t_1, t_\infty\}, \{t_0 \prec t_1, t_1 \prec t_\infty\}, \emptyset, \\ \{t_1 \to o_1, t_0 \to \texttt{start}, t_\infty \to \texttt{fin}\}, \\ \{\langle t_1, p, t_\infty\rangle \langle t_1, \neg p, t_\infty\rangle\} \end{array} \right\rangle$$

where the step t_1 is giving condition p to t_∞, the goal step. Suppose t_1 has a precondition q. Suppose further that there are two operators o_2 and o_3 respectively in the domain which can provide the condition q. The establishment refinement generates two partial plans:

$$\mathcal{N}_1: \left\langle \begin{array}{l} \{t_0, t_1, t_2, t_\infty\}, \{t_0 \prec t_2, t_2 \prec t_1, t_1 \prec t_\infty\}, \emptyset, \\ \{t_1 \to o_1, t_2 \to o_2, t_0 \to \texttt{start}, t_\infty \to \texttt{fin}\}, \\ \{\langle t_1, p, t_\infty\rangle, \langle t_1, \neg p, t_\infty\rangle, \langle t_2, q, t_\infty\rangle, \langle t_2, \neg q, t_\infty\rangle\} \end{array} \right\rangle$$

$$\mathcal{N}_2: \left\langle \begin{array}{l} \{t_0, t_1, t_2, t_\infty\}, \{t_0 \prec t_2, t_2 \prec t_1, t_1 \prec t_\infty\}, \emptyset, \\ \{t_1 \to o_1, t_3 \to o_3, t_0 \to \texttt{start}, t_\infty \to \texttt{fin}\}, \\ \{\langle t_1, p, t_\infty\rangle, \langle t_1, \neg p, t_\infty\rangle \langle t_2, q, t_\infty\rangle \langle t_2, \neg q, t_\infty\rangle\} \end{array} \right\rangle$$

Consider the step t_2 in $\mathcal{N}_1$. This can be identified independent of its name in the following way:

"The step which gives q to the step which in turn gives p to the dummy final step"

An equivalent identification in terms of candidates is:

"The last operator with an effect q to occur before the last operator with an effect p in the candidate (ground operator sequence)"

The contributor protections ensure that this operator is o_2 in all the candidates of $\mathcal{N}_1$ and o_3 in all the candidates of $\mathcal{N}_2$. Because of this, no candidate of $\mathcal{N}_1$ can ever be a candidate of $\mathcal{N}_2$, thus ensuring systematicity of establishment refinement.

4.4 Consistency Check

The aim of the consistency check is to prune inconsistent partial plans (i.e., plans with empty candidate sets) from the search space, thereby improving the performance of the overall refinement search. (Thus, from completeness point of view, consistency check is an optional step.) Given the relation between the safe ground linearizations and candidate sets, the consistency check can be done by ensuring that each partial plan has at least one safe ground linearization. This requires checking the consistency of orderings, bindings and auxiliary constraints of the plan. Ordering consistency can be checked in polynomial time, binding consistency is tractable for infinite domain variables, but is intractable for finite domain variables. Finally, consistency with respect to auxiliary constraints is also intractable for many common types of auxiliary candidate constraints (even for ground partial plans without any variables). Specifically, we have:

Proposition 6 *Given a partial plan whose auxiliary candidate constraints contain interval preservation constraints, checking if there exists a safe ground linearization of the plan is NP-hard.*

This proposition directly follows from the result in [25], which shows that checking whether there exists a conflict-free ground linearization of a partial plan with interval protection constraints is NP-hard.

4.5 Tractability refinements

Since, as observed above, the consistency check is NP-hard in general, each call to `Refine-Plan` is also NP-hard. It is of course possible to reduce the cost of refinement by pushing the complexity into search space size. Specifically, when checking the satisfiability of a set of constraints is intractable, we can still achieve polynomial refinement cost by refining the partial plans into a set of mutually exclusive and exhaustive constraint sets such that the consistency of each of those refinements can be checked in polynomial time, while preserving the completeness and systematicity of the search. This is the primary motivation behind tractability refinements. There are two types of tractability refinements: *pre-ordering* and *conflict resolution*. Both these aim to maintain partial plans all of whose ground linearizations are safe ground linearizations.

4.5.1 Pre-ordering refinements

Pre-ordering strategies aim to restrict the type of partial orderings in the plan such that consistency with respect to auxiliary candidate constraints can be checked without explicitly enumerating all the ground linearizations. Two possible pre-ordering techniques are *total ordering* and *unambiguous ordering* [16]. Total ordering orders every pair of steps in the plan, while unambiguous ordering orders a pair of steps only when one of the steps has an effect c, and the other step either negates c or needs c as a precondition (implying that the two steps *may* interact). Both of them guarantee that in the refinements produced by them, either all ground linearizations will be safe or none will be.[10] Thus, consistency can be checked in polynomial time by examining any one ground linearization.

Pre-ordering techniques can also make other plan handling steps, such as MTC-based goal selection and MTC-based solution constructor, tractable (c.f. [16, 7]). For example, unambiguous plans also allow polynomial check for necessary truth of any condition in the plan. Polynomial necessary truth check can be useful in MTC-based goal selection and termination tests. In fact, unambiguous plans were originally used in UA [16] for this purpose.

4.5.2 Conflict Resolution Refinements

Conflict resolution refines a given partial plan with the aim of compiling the auxiliary constraints into the ordering and binding constraints. Specifically, the partial plan is refined (by adding ordering, binding or secondary preconditions [19] to the plan) until each possible violation of the auxiliary candidate constraint (called conflict) is individually resolved. The definition of conflict depends upon the specific type

---

[10]In the case of total ordering, this holds vacuously true since the plan has only one linearization

of auxiliary constraint. An interval preservation constraint $\langle s_i, p, s_j \rangle$ is violated (threatened) whenever a step s' can possibly come between s_i and s_j and not preserve p. Resolving the conflict involves either making s' not intervene between s_i and s_j (by adding either the ordering $s' \prec s_i$ or the ordering $s_j \prec s'$), or adding secondary (preservation) preconditions of s', required to make s' preserve c [19], to the plan agenda (and the corresponding PTCs to the auxiliary solution constraints; see Section 3.1). When all conflicts are resolved this way, the resulting refinements will have the property that all their ground linearizations are safe. Thus, checking the partial plan consistency will amount to checking for the existence of ground linearizations. This can be done by checking ordering and binding consistency.

5 Applications of the Unified Framework

The componential view of refinement planning, provided by the Refine-Plan algorithm has a variety of applications in understanding and analyzing the performance tradeoffs in the design of plan-space planning algorithms. I will briefly discuss these in this section.

5.1 Explication and analysis of Design Tradeoffs

We have seen that the various ways of instantiating Refine-Plan algorithm correspond to the various choices in designing the plan-space planning algorithms. The model for estimating search space size, developed in Section 2, provides a way of analyzing the search space size vs. refinement cost tradeoffs provided by these different design choices. Understanding these tradeoffs allows us to predict the circumstances under which specific techniques will lead to performance improvements.

If C is the average cost per invocation of the Refine-Plan algorithm, b is the average branching factor and d_e is the effective depth of the search, then the cost of the planning (in a breadth-first regime) is $C \times |\mathcal{F}_{d_e}|$ (where $\mathcal{F}_{d_e}$ is the size of the fringe at $d_e{}^{th}$ level of the search tree. From Section 3 (Eqn. 1), we have

$$\mathcal{F}_{d_e} = \frac{|\mathcal{K}| \times \rho_{d_e}}{\kappa_{d_e}} = b^{d_e}$$

C itself can be decomposed into three main components: $C = C_e + C_c + C_s$, where C_e, is the establishment cost (including the cost of selecting the open goal to work on), C_s is the cost of solution constructor, and C_c is the cost of consistency check. The average branching factor, b can be split into two components, b_e, the establishment branching factor, and b_t the tractability refinement branching factor, such that $b = b_e \times b_t$. b_e and b_t correspond, respectively, to the branching made in steps 2 and 3 of the Refine-Plan algorithm.

This simple model is remarkably good at explaining and predicting the tradeoffs offered by the different ways of instantiating Refine-Plan algorithm. One ubiquitous tradeoff is between that of search space size ($|\mathcal{F}_d|$) and refinement cost (C): *almost every method for reducing C increases $\mathcal{F}_{d_e}$ and vice versa.* For example, consider the MTC-based and protection-based solution constructors discussed in Section 4.1. Protection based constructors have to wait until each precondition of the plan has been considered for establishment explicitly, while the MTC-based constructors can terminate the search as soon as all the preconditions in the partial plan are necessarily correct (according to the modal truth criterion). MTC-based solution constructors can thus allow the search to end earlier, reducing the effective depth of the search, and thereby the size of the explored search space. In terms of candidate space view, such stronger solution constructors lead to larger κ_d at the termination fringe. However, at the same time they increase the cost of refinement C (specifically the C_s factor). For example, MTC-based solution constructor has to reason with all safe ground linearization of the plan explicitly, and can thus be intractable for general partial orderings involving ADL actions [10, 2]. Protection-based constructor, on the other hand need only check that the agenda is empty, and that there are no unresolved conflicts (which can be done in $O(1)$ time).

Book-keeping techniques aim to reduce the redundancy factor ρ_d. This tends to reduce the fringe size, $|\mathcal{F}_d|$. Book keeping constraints do however tend to increase the cost of consistency check. In particular, checking the consistency of a partial plan containing interval preservation constraints is NP-hard even for ground plans in TWEAK representation (c.f. [25]). Tractability refinements primarily aim to reduce the C_c component of refinement cost. In terms of search space size, tractability refinements further refine the plans coming out of the establishment stage, thus increasing the (b_t component of the) branching factor.

This $|\mathcal{F}_d|$ vs. C tradeoff also applies to other types of search-space reduction techniques such as deferment of conflict resolution [21, 7]. Since conflict resolution is an optional step in Refine-Plan, the planner can be selective about which conflicts to resolve, without affecting the completeness or the systematicity of Refine-Plan. Conflict deferment is motivated by the idea that many of the conflicts are ephemeral, and will be resolved automatically during the course of planning. Thus, conflict deferment tends to reduce the search space size by reducing the tractability branching factor b_t. This does not come without a penalty however. Specifically, when the planner does such partial conflict resolution, the consistency check has to once again test for existence of safe ground linearizations, rather than order and binding consistency (making consistency check intractable once again). Using weaker consistency checks, such as order and binding consistency check, can lead to refinement of inconsistent plans, thereby reducing κ_d and increasing $|\mathcal{F}_d|$.

5.1.1 Depth First Search Regimes

Although the above analysis dealt with breadth-first search regimes, the Refine-Plan algorithm also allows us to analyze the performance of different planning algorithms in depth first regimes [7]. Here, the critical factor in estimating the explored search space size is the probability that the planner picks a refinement that contains at least one solution candidate. Even small changes in this probability, which we shall call *success probability*, can have dramatic effects on performance.

To illustrate, let us consider the effect of tractability refinements on the success probability. If we approximate the behavior of all the refinement strategies used by

Refine-Plan as random partitioning of candidate set of a plan into some number of children nodes, then it is possible to provide a quantitative estimate of the success probability. Consider the refinement of a plan $\mathcal{P}$ by Refine-Plan. Suppose that $\mathcal{P}$ has m solution candidates in its candidate set. If b is the average branching factor, then Refine-Plan splits $\mathcal{P}$ into b different children plans. The success probability is just the probability that a random node picked from these b new nodes contains at least one solution candidate. This is just equal to $q(m, b)$ where $q(m, b)$ is the binomial distribution:[11]

$$q(m,b) = \sum_{i=0}^{m-1} \binom{m}{b} \frac{1}{b^{m-i}} \left(1 - \frac{1}{b}\right)^i$$

It can be easily verified that for fixed m, $q(m, b)$, the success probability, monotonically decreases with increasing b. As the success probability reduces, the size of the explored search space increases. Thus, under random partitioning model, the addition of tractability refinements tends to increase the explored search space size even in depth-first search regimes. The only time we will expect reduction in search space size is if the added refinements distribute the solutions in a non-uniform fashion, thereby changing the apparent solution density (c.f. [17]).

5.2 Facilitation of Well-founded Empirical Comparisons

Given the variety of ways in which Refine-Plan can be instantiated, it is important to understand the comparative advantages of the various instantiations. While theoretical analyses of the comparative performances are desirable, sometimes either they are not feasible, or the performance tradeoffs may be critically linked to problem distributions. In such cases, comparisons must inevitably be based on empirical studies.

The unified framework offers help in designing focused empirical studies. In the past, empirical analyses tended to focus on a wholistic "black-box" comparisons of brand-name planning algorithms, such as TWEAK vs. SNLP (c.f. [13]). It is hard to draw meaningful conclusions from such comparisons, since when seen as instantiations of our Refine-Plan algorithm, they differ on a variety of dimensions (see Table 1). A more meaningful approach, facilitated by the unifying framework of this paper, involves comparing instantiations of Refine-Plan that differ only on a single dimension. For example, if our objective is to judge the utility of specific protection (book-keeping) strategies, we could keep everything else constant and vary only the book-keeping step in Refine-Plan. In contrast, when we compare TWEAK [2] with SNLP [15], we are not only varying the protection strategies, but also the goal selection, conflict resolution and termination (solution constructor) strategies, making it difficult to form meaningful hypotheses from empirical results.

In [11], I exploit this experimental methodology to compare the empirical performance of a variety of normalized instantiations of Refine-Plan algorithm. These experiments reveal that the most important cause for the performance differentials among different refinement planners are the differences in the tractability refinements they employ. Although tractability refinements increase the b_t component of the branching factor, they may also indirectly lead to a reduction in the establishment branching factor, b_e. The overall performance of the planner thus depends on the interplay between these two influences. The book-keeping (protection) strategies themselves only act as an insurance policy that pays off in the worst-case scenario when the planner is forced to look at a substantial part of its search space.

5.3 Designing planners with better tradeoffs

By providing a componential view of the plan-space planning algorithms, and explicating the spectrum of possible planning algorithms, the unified framework also facilitates the design of novel planning algorithms with interesting performance tradeoffs. We will look at two examples briefly:

5.3.1 Strong systematicity with polynomial refinement

As we noted earlier, a refinement search is strongly systematic if it is systematic, and never refines an inconsistent node. From Table 1, we see that there exist no partial order planning algorithms which are both strongly systematic and have polynomial time refinement complexity. SNLP, which uses contributor protection, is systematic and can be strongly systematic as long as the consistency check is powerful enough to remove every inconsistent plan from search. However, checking whether a general partially ordered plan is consistent with respect to a set of exhaustive causal links is NP-hard in general [25]. This raises the interesting question: *Is it possible to write a partial order planning algorithm that is both strongly systematic and has a polynomial time refinement cycle?*

Our modular framework makes it easy to synthesize such an algorithm. Table 1 describes a novel planning algorithm called SNLP-UA which uses exhaustive causal links for book-keeping, and uses a pre-ordering refinement whereby every pair of steps s_1 and s_2 such that an effect of s_1 possibly codesignates with a precondition or an effect of s_2, are ordered with respect to each other.[12] Such an ordering converts all potential conflicts into either necessary conflicts, or necessary non-conflicts.[13] This in turn implies that either all ground linearizations are safe or none of them are. In either case, consistency can be checked in polynomial time by examining any one of the ground linearizations. SNLP-UA is thus strongly systematic, maintains partially ordered plans, but still keeps the refinement cost polynomial. It could thus strike a good balance between systematic planners such as SNLP and unsystematic, but polynomial-time refinement

---

[11] $q(m, n)$ is the probability that a randomly chosen urn will contain at least one ball, when m balls are independently randomly distributed into n urns. This is equal to probability that a randomly chosen urn will have all m balls plus the probability that it will have $m - 1$ balls and so on plus the probability that it will have 1 ball.

[12] Note that this definition of interaction is more general than the one used by UA [17]. It is required because of the contributor protections used by SNLP-UA (see [7]).

[13] For actions with conditional effects, a necessary conflict can be *confronted* by planning to make the preservation preconditions true for the interacting step.

planners such as UA. In [11], I provide empirical comparisons between SNLP-UA and other possible instantiations of Refine-Plan.

5.3.2 Polynomial eager solution-constructors

As discussed in Section 4.1, *all-sol*, the solution constructor used in all existing plan-space planners returns with success only when *all* the safe ground linearizations of the partial plan are solutions. Our refinement search paradigm suggests that such solution constructors are over-conservative since the goal of planning is only to find *one* solution. In contrast, *eager* solution constructors, that stop as soon as they find a safe ground linearization that is a solution, will reduce solution depth, increase κ, and there by reduce search-space size. The most eager constructor, which I call *all-eager-constructor*, would stop as soon as the partial plan contains at least *one* safe ground linearization that is a solution. Unfortunately both the *all-sol* and *all-eager-constructor* are NP-hard in general, as the problem of finding necessary and possible truth of a proposition in a partially ordered plan can respectively be reduced to them [10]. This raises the interesting question: *Are there any domain-independent eager solution-constructors that are tractable?* I answer the question in the affirmative by providing a family of tractable eager solution constructors called *k-eager-constructors*:

Definition 14 (k-eager Constructor) *Given a partial plan $\mathcal{P}$, a k-eager-constructor randomly enumerates at most k ground linearizations of $\mathcal{P}$, and returns any one of them that is safe and corresponds to a solution for $\mathcal{P}$.*

The *k-eager-constructors* are tractable since they only enumerate and check at most k different ground linearizations. Based on the value of k, they define a family of solution constructors whose cost increases and effective solution depth reduces with increasing k. Finally, the solution depth of *k-eager-constructor* is guaranteed to lie between that of *all-eager-constructor* and the MTC-based *all-sol* solution constructor, thus providing an interesting balance between the two. Empirical studies are currently under way to assess the practical impact of these constructors.

5.4 Pedagogical explanatory power

The unifying framework also has clear pedagogical advantages in terms of clarifying the relations between many brand-name planning algorithms, and eliminating several long-standing misconceptions. An important contribution of Refine-Plan is the careful distinction it makes between book-keeping constraints or protection strategies (which aim to reduce redundancy), and tractability refinements (which aim to shift complexity from refinement cost to search space size). This distinction removes many misunderstandings about plan-space planning algorithms. For example, it clarifies that the only motivation for total ordering plan-space planners is tractability of refinement. Similarly, in the past it has been erroneously claimed (e.g. [13]) that the systematicity of SNLP *increases* the effective depth of the solution. Viewing SNLP as an instantiation of Refine-Plan template, we see that it corresponds to several relatively independent instantiation decisions, only *one* of which, viz., the use of contributor protections in the book-keeping step, has a direct bearing on the systematicity of the algorithm.

From the discussion in Section 4, it should be clear that the use of exhaustive causal links does not, *ipso facto*, increase the solution depth in any way. Rather, the increase in solution depth is an artifact of the particular solution constructor function, and the conflict resolution and/or preordering strategies used in order to get by with tractable termination and consistency checks. These can be replaced without affecting the systematicity property. Similarly, our framework not only clarifies the relation between the unambiguous planners such as UA [17] and causal-link based planners such as SNLP [15], it also suggests fruitful ways of integrating the ideas in the two planning techniques (cf. SNLP-UA in Section 5.3.1).

6 Extending the framework

In this section, I will discuss how the Refine-Plan framework can be extended to handle a wider variety of behavioral constraints (beyond goals of attainment), as well as other types of planning models.

Maintenance goals are a form of behavioral constraints which demand that a particular condition be maintained (not violated) throughout the execution of the plan (e.g. keep A on B while transferring C to D; avoid collisions while traveling to room R). They can be modeled in the Refine-Plan algorithm simply as auxiliary candidate constraints. For example, we can maintain $On(A, B)$ by adding the interval preservation constraint $\langle t_0, On(A, B), t_\infty \rangle$ to $\mathcal{P}_\emptyset$ in the Find-Plan algorithm in Figure 2.

Intermediate goals are useful to describe planning problems which cannot be defined in terms of the goal state alone. As an example, consider the goal of making a round trip from Phoenix to San Francisco.[14] Since the initial and final location of the agent is Phoenix, this goal cannot be modeled as a goal of attainment, i.e., a precondition of t_∞ (unless time is modeled explicitly in the action representation [23]). However, we can deal with this goal by adding an additional dummy step (say t_D) to the plan such that t_D has a precondition $At(Phoenix)$ and t_∞ has a precondition $At(SFO)$, and $t_0 \prec t_D \prec t_\infty$.

Many refinement planners (especially the so-called task reduction planners) use extensions such as condition-typing [26], time-windows [27] and resource based reasoning [27, 28]. Many of these extensions can be covered with the auxiliary constraint mechanism. Time windows and resource reasoning aim to prune partial plans that are infeasible in terms of their temporal constraints and resource requirements. These can, in principle, be modeled in terms of monotonic auxiliary constraints. Condition typing allows the domain user to specify how various preconditions of an operator should be treated during planning [26]. In particular, some planners use the notion of *filter conditions*, which are the applicability conditions of the operators that should never be explicitly considered for establishment. Filter conditions thus provide a way for the domain writer to *disallow* certain types of solutions (e.g., building an airport in a city for the express purpose of going from there to another city) even if they satisfy the standard definition of plan solutions

---

[14] In the past, some researchers (e.g. [4]) have claimed (mistakenly) that intermediate goals of this type cannot be modeled in classical planning without hierarchical task reduction.

(see Definition 5). Filter conditions can be modeled as point truth constraints, and included in the auxiliary solution constraints (without adding them to the agenda) [12]. Since they are (non-monotonic) solution constraints, they cannot be used to prune partial plans. However, they can be used as a basis for selection heuristics (viz., to prefer partial plans which have already satisfied filter conditions).[15]

Finally, Refine-Plan can also be extended to cover planning models other than plan-space planning. To cover state-space planners (cf. [1]), we need to allow Refine-Plan to use incomplete establishment refinements, and backtrack over goal-selection to make the overall search complete. The HTN planners (cf. [27, 4]) can be modeled by extending the refinement algorithm such that its main refinement operation is task reduction rather than establishment (with establishment refinement being a particular way of reducing tasks); see [12].

7 Conclusion

In this paper, I have shown that refinement search provides a unifying framework for understanding the performance tradeoffs in plan-space planning. I have developed a formalization of plan-space planning in terms of refinement search, and gave a generic refinement search algorithm in which the complete gamut of plan-space planners can be cast. I have shown that this unifying framework facilitates explication and analysis of performance tradeoffs across a variety of planning algorithms. I have also shown that it could help in designing new algorithms with better cost-benefit ratios. Although I concentrated on the plan-space planners solving problems involving goals of attainment, I have shown (Section 6) that the framework can be extended to cover richer types of behavioral constraints, as well as other types of planners (e.g. state-space planners, hierarchical planners).

References

[1] A. Barrett and D. Weld. Partial Order Planning: Evaluating Possible Efficiency Gains. CSE TR 92-05-01, University of Washington, June 1992.

[2] D. Chapman. Planning for conjunctive goals. *Artificial Intelligence*, 32:333--377, 1987.

[3] G. Collins and L. Pryor. Achieving the functionality of filter conditions in partial order planner. In *Proc. 10th AAAI*, 1992.

[4] K. Erol, D. Nau and J. Hendler. Toward a general framework for hierarchical task-network planning. In *Proc. of AAAI Spring Symp. on Foundations of Automatic Planning*. 1993.

[5] M.G. Georgeff. Planning. In *Readings in Planning*. Morgan Kaufmann, 1990.

[6] J. Jaffar and J. L. Lassez. Constraint logic programming. In *Proceedings of POPL-87*, pages 111--119, 1987.

[7] S. Kambhampati. Planning as Refinement Search: A unified framework for comparative analysis of Search Space Size and Performance. Technical Report 93-004, Arizona State University, June, 1993.[16]

[8] S. Kambhampati. Multi-Contributor Causal Structures for Planning: A Formalization and Evaluation. Arizona State University Technical Report, CS TR-92-019, July 1992. (To appear in *Artificial Intelligence*. A preliminary version appears in the Proc. of First Intl. Conf. on AI Planning Systems, 1992).

[9] S. Kambhampati. On the Utility of Systematicity: Understanding tradeoffs between redundancy and commitment in partial order planning. In Proceedings of IJCAI-93, 1993.

[10] S. Kambhampati and D.S. Nau. On the Nature and Role of Modal Truth Criteria in Planning. Tech. Report. ISR-TR-93-30, University of Maryland, March, 1993.

[11] S. Kambhampati. Design Tradeoffs in Partial Order (Plan Space) Planning. Submitted to AIPS-94 and AAAI-94.

[12] S. Kambhampati. HTN Planning: What? Why? and When? ASU Technical Report in preparation, 1994.

[13] C. Knoblock and Q. Yang. A Comparison of the SNLP and TWEAK planning algorithms. In *Proc. of AAAI Spring Symp. on Foundations of Automatic Planning*. 1993.

[14] D. McDermott. Regression Planning. *Intl. Jour. Intelligent Systems*, 6:357-416, 1991.

[15] D. McAllester and D. Rosenblitt. Systematic Nonlinear Planning. In *Proc. 9th AAAI*, 1991.

[16] S. Minton, J. Bresina and M. Drummond. Commitment Strategies in Planning: A Comparative Analysis. In *Proc. 12th IJCAI*, 1991.

[17] S. Minton, M. Drummond, J. Bresina and A. Philips. Total Order vs. Partial Order Planning: Factors Influencing Performance In *Proc. KR-92*, 1992.

[18] J. Pearl. *Heuristics: Intelligent Search Strategies for Computer Problem Solving*. Addison-Wesley (1984).

[19] E.P.D. Pednault. Synthesizing Plans that contain actions with Context-Dependent Effects. *Computational Intelligence*, Vol. 4, 356-372 (1988).

[20] E.P.D. Pednault. Generalizing nonlinear planning to handle complex goals and actions with context dependent effects. In *Proc. IJCAI-91.*, 1991.

[21] M.A. Peot and D.E. Smith. Threat-Removal Strategies for Nonlinear Planning. In *Proc. Eleventh AAAI*, 1993.

[22] J.S. Penberthy and D. Weld. UCPOP: A Sound, Complete, Partial Order Planner for ADL. In *Proc. KR-92*, 1992.

[23] J.S. Penberthy. Planning with continuous change. Ph.D. Thesis. CS-TR 93-12-01. University of Washington. 1993.

[24] E. Sacerdoti. Planning in a Hierarchy of Abstraction Spaces. *Artificial Intelligence*, 5(2), 1975.

[25] D.E. Smith and M.A. Peot. Postponing threats in partial-order planning. In *Proc. Eleventh AAAI*, 1993.

[26] A. Tate. Generating Project Networks. In *Proceedings of IJCAI-77*, pages 888--893, Boston, MA, 1977.

[27] K. Currie and A. Tate. O-Plan: The Open Planning Architecture. *Artificial Intelligence*, 51(1), 1991.

[28] D. Wilkins. *Practical Planning*. Morgan Kaufmann (1988).

---

[15] Some researchers [3] have suggested that filter conditions cannot be used in partial order planning without loss of completeness. I believe that this confusion is mainly a result of seeing filter conditions as filtering out refinement possibilities, as against solutions.

[16] Technical reports available via anonymous ftp from enws318.eas.asu.edu:pub/rao

Actions with Indirect Effects
(Preliminary Report)

G. Neelakantan Kartha
Department of Computer Sciences
University of Texas at Austin
Austin, Texas 78712-1188

Vladimir Lifschitz
Department of Computer Sciences
and Department of Philosophy
University of Texas at Austin
Austin, Texas 78712-1188

Abstract

We define and study a high-level language for describing actions that extends the language $\mathcal{A}$ introduced by Gelfond and Lifschitz. The new language, $\mathcal{AR}_0$, allows us to describe actions with indirect effects (ramifications) and simple forms of nondeterminism. A translation from $\mathcal{AR}_0$ into a formalism based on circumscription is proved to be sound and complete.

1 Introduction

Describing properties of actions and their effects on the state of the world has long been considered one of the central problems in the theory of knowledge representation. The approaches proposed in the literature differ by the temporal ontologies they use (linear or branching time, time points or intervals, situations, events or histories), by the logic used (classical logic, its nonmonotonic extensions, logic programming), and by other details of the formalization (which objects are reified, which circumscription policy is used, etc.).

In this area of research, it turned out to be difficult to discuss the possibilities and limitations of the available methods in a precise and general way. The tradition is to explain every new approach with reference to a few standard examples, such as the blocks world or the "Yale Shooting" story and its enhancements. Competing approaches are evaluated and compared mostly in terms of their ability to handle these examples. Such analysis does not say much about the range of applicability of each method.

Several recent publications, including [Pednault, 1989], [Lifschitz, 1991], [Lin and Shoham, 1991], [Reiter, 1991] and [Sandewall, 1992], attempt to overcome this problem and to discuss representing action in a methodical and theoretically sound way. Gelfond and Lifschitz [1993] address this issue by introducing a simple "high-level" language, called $\mathcal{A}$, designed specifically for describing the effects of actions. Here, for instance, is the "Yale Shooting" domain encoded in $\mathcal{A}$:

$$\begin{aligned}&\textbf{initially } \neg Loaded,\\ &\textbf{initially } Alive,\\ &Load \textbf{ causes } Loaded,\\ &Shoot \textbf{ causes } \neg Alive \textbf{ if } Loaded,\\ &Shoot \textbf{ causes } \neg Loaded.\end{aligned} \quad (1)$$

The first two lines are "value propositions"—they provide information about the values of fluents, such as *Loaded* or *Alive*, at a specific point in time (in this case, in the initial situation). The other three are "effect propositions"—they describe the effects of actions, such as *Load* or *Shoot*. The semantics of $\mathcal{A}$ allows us to determine which value propositions are "entailed" by this domain description. One such proposition, for instance, is

$$\neg Alive \textbf{ after } Load; Wait; Shoot.$$

The available methods for describing actions in logic can be characterized as translations from high-level action languages into monotonic or nonmonotonic logic-based formalisms. The claim that such a method is adequate turns then into a mathematically verifiable property of the corresponding translation. Competing methods can be compared by comparing the high-level languages to which they are applicable.

In [Gelfond and Lifschitz, 1993], for instance, a new method for representing actions in logic programming is specified as a translation from a subset of $\mathcal{A}$ into a logic programming language, and the translation is proved to be sound relative to the semantics of $\mathcal{A}$. In [Kartha, 1993], the methods for formalizing action in classical logic proposed in [Pednault, 1989] and [Reiter, 1991], as well as the use of circumscription in [Baker, 1991], are described as translations from $\mathcal{A}$, and the soundness and completeness theorems for these translations are stated. In the same spirit, $\mathcal{A}$ is translated into abductive logic programming in [Dung, 1993] and [Denecker and De Schreye, 1993], and into equational logic programming in [Thielscher, 1994].

If a theorem prover, or a query evaluation procedure, is available for the target language of such a translation, then it becomes possible to use the translation for the automation of reasoning about action. For example, the logic programming interpreter XOLDT [Chen and Warren, 1992] is put to such use in [Lifschitz et al., 1993], the abductive procedure SLDNFA in [Denecker and De Schreye, 1993], and the theorem prover of [Boyer and Moore, 1988] in [Subramanian, 1993].

In [Thielscher, 1993], the language $\mathcal{A}$ is related to the ideas of [Sandewall, 1992].

In spite of its extremely simple syntax, $\mathcal{A}$ provides a framework for discussing some interesting cases of reasoning about action, including temporal projection with incomplete information about the initial situation, reasoning from the future to the past ("explanation"), and some forms of hypothetical reasoning ("if a different sequence of actions were performed..."). In many ways, however, the expressive possibilities of this language are limited. This has led to the development of a few enhancements of $\mathcal{A}$. Dung [1993] proposed a "relational" version of $\mathcal{A}$, in which fluents and actions may have arguments. In [Denecker and De Schreye, 1993] and [Thielscher, 1994], dialects of $\mathcal{A}$ are outlined in which one can describe actions with nondeterministic effects. Baral and Gelfond [1993] extend $\mathcal{A}$ by an operator for the concurrent execution of a set of actions. The dialect of $\mathcal{A}$ defined in [Lifschitz, 1993b] provides symbols for time intervals.

This paper addresses yet another limitation of $\mathcal{A}$—its inability to represent *domain constraints*. In $\mathcal{A}$, any combination of fluent values represents a possible state of the system. The extension of $\mathcal{A}$ presented below is, in this respect, different. We will be able, for instance, to extend domain description (1) by the constraint

$$\textbf{always } Walking \supset Alive, \qquad (2)$$

where *Walking* is a new fluent name. This constraint tells us that an assignment of truth values to fluents represents a state only if it makes the conditional $Walking \supset Alive$ true.

The domain description consisting of propositions (1) and proposition (2) entails, for instance, the value proposition

$$\neg Walking \textbf{ after } Load; Wait; Shoot.$$

Note that the fluent *Walking* does not occur in the effect propositions. Thus any change in the value of *Walking* is an *indirect effect*, or *ramification*, of the actions that have been performed. The possibility of ramifications is the main feature of the dialect of $\mathcal{A}$ introduced here. We call this language $\mathcal{AR}_0$; $\mathcal{A}$ stands for "actions," $\mathcal{R}$ for "ramifications," and the subscript 0 is used to distinguish this language from the more expressive language $\mathcal{AR}$ that will be defined in the journal version of the paper.

Besides the ability to describe indirect effects, the new language has other expressive possibilities that $\mathcal{A}$ lacks. It allows us to specify not only "fluent preconditions"—the conditions that need to be satisfied in order for an action to affect a specific fluent—but also "action preconditions," which, if violated, make the execution of an action impossible.[1] In $\mathcal{AR}_0$, we can specify a "coordinate frame" in the space of situations, as suggested in [Lifschitz, 1990]; the commonsense law of inertia applies only to the fluents that belong to the frame. Finally, the effects of the actions described in $\mathcal{AR}_0$ can be nondeterministic.

The syntax of the new action language is described in Section 2. Examples illustrating the use of the language are provided in Section 3, and its semantics is defined in Section 4. In Section 5, we show how two well-known properties of first-order logic—the replacement theorem and the theorem on the conservativeness of definitional extensions—can be extended to $\mathcal{AR}_0$. In Section 6, the language $\mathcal{A}$ from [Gelfond and Lifschitz, 1993] is embedded into $\mathcal{AR}_0$.

In Section 7, we use the ideas of [Baker, 1991] to define a translation from $\mathcal{AR}_0$ into the formalism of *nested abnormality theories* [Lifschitz, 1994]. This formalism is based on circumscription, and permits nested applications of the circumscription operator. In this framework, Baker's approach to the frame problem can be presented in a particularly simple form. At the end of the section, a soundness and completeness theorem is stated. It shows that, in the new version, Baker's method is applicable to some examples of nondeterministic actions.

2 Syntax of $\mathcal{AR}_0$

2.1 Formulae and Propositions

To be precise, $\mathcal{AR}_0$, like $\mathcal{A}$, is not a single language, but rather a family of languages. A particular language in this group is characterized by

- a nonempty set of symbols, that are called *fluent names*, or *fluents*,
- a subset of fluent names, that is called the *frame*,
- a nonempty set of symbols, that are called *action names*, or *actions*.

A *formula* is a propositional combination of fluents.

There are four types of *propositions* in $\mathcal{AR}_0$—value propositions, effect propositions, release propositions, and constraints.

A *value proposition* is an expression of the form

$$C \textbf{ after } \overline{A}, \qquad (3)$$

where C is a formula, and $\overline{A}$ is a string of actions. Informally, (3) asserts that C holds after the sequence of actions $\overline{A}$ is performed in the initial situation. For instance,

$$Heads \textbf{ after } Toss$$

is a value proposition, where *Heads* is a fluent and *Toss* is an action.

An *effect proposition* is an expression of the form

$$A \textbf{ causes } C \textbf{ if } P, \qquad (4)$$

---
[1] This terminology belongs to Reiter [1991].

where A is an action, and C and P are formulae. Intuitively, (4) asserts that A, if executed in a situation in which the precondition P is true, makes C true. For instance,

GetOnBoard **causes** *OnBus* **if** *HasTicket*

is an effect proposition, where *GetOnBoard* is an action, and *OnBus* and *HasTicket* are fluents.

A *release proposition* is an expression of the form

$$A \text{ \textbf{releases} } F \text{ \textbf{if} } P, \tag{5}$$

where A is an action, F a fluent which belongs to the frame, and P a formula. Intuitively, (5) says that F is exempt from obeying the commonsense law of inertia when the action A is executed in a situation when the precondition P is true. This is useful for expressing the effects of nondeterministic actions. For instance, the fact that the action *Toss* nondeterministically changes the frame fluent *Heads* is expressed by the release proposition

Toss **releases** *Heads* **if** *True*.

(*True* stands for some standard tautology, and *False* will denote the negation of *True*.)

Finally, a *constraint* is a proposition of the form

$$\textbf{always } C, \tag{6}$$

where C is a formula. Intuitively, (6) asserts that C holds in all possible situations. We will sometimes identify a constraint (6) with the formula C.

A *domain description*, or *domain*, is a set of propositions.

2.2 Notational Conventions

In formulae, we will omit some parentheses, as customary in classical logic. If $\overline{A}$ in a value proposition (3) is empty, we will write this proposition as

initially C.

Otherwise, the members of $\overline{A}$ will be separated by semicolons. An effect proposition (4) will be written as

A **causes** C

if P is *True*, and as

impossible A **if** P

if C is *False*. A release proposition (5) will be written as

A **releases** F

if P is *True*.

3 Examples

In this section we show how some systems involving action and change can be described in $\mathcal{AR}_0$. Our comments on the "models" of these domain descriptions will turn into precise statements after the semantics of $\mathcal{AR}_0$ is described in the next section.

The reader familiar with the language $\mathcal{A}$ from [Gelfond and Lifschitz, 1993] will notice that any domain description in $\mathcal{A}$ can be viewed as a domain description in $\mathcal{AR}_0$ in which all fluents belong to the frame; we only need to agree to identify an effect proposition

A **causes** F **if** $P_1, \ldots, P_n$

in the sense of $\mathcal{A}$ with

A **causes** F **if** $P_1 \wedge \ldots \wedge P_n$.

In Section 6, this will be discussed in more detail.

The following examples illustrate some of the expressive possibilities of $\mathcal{AR}_0$ that $\mathcal{A}$ lacks.

Example 1: Action Preconditions. The door in a hotel room can be opened by inserting the entry card. In the initial situation, the door is closed. We use two propositional fluents *HasCard* and *DoorOpen*, both belonging to the frame. There is one action *InsertCard*. The propositions are

  initially ¬*DoorOpen*,
  InsertCard **causes** *DoorOpen*,
  impossible *InsertCard* **if** ¬*HasCard*.

This domain has two models; in one model, *HasCard* is false in the initial situation, and in the other model it is initially true. In the first model, the action of inserting the card cannot be executed.

Example 2: Nonframe Fluents. There are two switches and a light; the light is on only when the switches are both on or both off [Lifschitz, 1990]. This system can be described using three propositional fluents *Switch1*, *Switch2* and *Light*; only the first two belong to the frame. There are two action names, *Toggle1* and *Toggle2*. The propositions are:

  always $Light \equiv (Switch1 \equiv Switch2)$,
  Toggle1 **causes** ¬*Switch1* **if** *Switch1*,
  Toggle1 **causes** *Switch1* **if** ¬*Switch1*,
  Toggle2 **causes** ¬*Switch2* **if** *Switch2*,
  Toggle2 **causes** *Switch2* **if** ¬*Switch2*.

This domain has 4 models that differ by the initial states of the switches.

It is essential in this example that the fluent *Light* is not included in the frame. Otherwise, the effects of the actions would be indeterminate. For instance, the effect of *Toggle1* would be to change either the values of *Switch1* and *Light* or, surprisingly, the values of *Switch1* and *Switch2*.

Example 3: Ramifications. As discussed in the introduction, this can be illustrated by the domain description consisting of propositions (1) and proposition (2). All fluents are included in the frame. There are two models that differ by the initial value of *Walking*.

Example 4: Nondeterminism. The "Russian Turkey Shoot" [Sandewall, 1992] is the enhancement of the original shooting story in which there is an additional action of spinning the gun's bullet chamber. More precisely, we think of *Spin* as the action of looking to see whether the chamber is empty, inserting a bullet if it is, and then giving it a spin. We extend (1) by the proposition

Spin **releases** *Loaded*.

This domain has infinitely many models. In fact, the set of its models has the cardinality of the continuum. To select a specific model, we need to specify, for every string of actions that ends with *Spin*, whether or not *Loaded* is true after these actions are executed sequentially from the initial situation.

In each of the following two examples, the set of models has the cardinality of the continuum also.

Example 5: Restricted Nondeterminism. A part of a table is painted white, and a part black. There are two actions: picking up a block and dropping it onto the table; the latter may put the block entirely within the white region, or entirely within the black region, or touching both the white and black regions. This example was suggested to us by Ray Reiter (personal communication, March 11, 1992). It can be described in $\mathcal{AR}_0$ using two frame fluents, *White* and *Black*, which express that the block is, at least partially, on the corresponding part of the table:

PickUp **causes** $\neg$*White* $\wedge$ $\neg$*Black*,
Drop **causes** *White* $\vee$ *Black*,
Drop **releases** *White*,
Drop **releases** *Black*.

The second proposition shows that the values of fluents after the execution of *Drop*, although not predetermined by their values in the previous situation, are not totally arbitrary either.

Example 6: Implicit Nondeterminism. Each of two light bulbs is controlled by a switch. The action of turning on the light is nondeterministic, because it is not specified which of the switches is used. In the following description, *Switch1* and *Switch2* belong to the frame, and *Light* does not:

always *Light* $\equiv$ (*Switch1* $\vee$ *Switch2*),
TurnOn **causes** *Light*,
TurnOff **causes** $\neg$*Light*.

There are no release propositions here, and the effect propositions do not include disjunctions; the nondeterminism in this domain description is due entirely to the presence of a constraint.

4 Semantics of $\mathcal{AR}_0$

4.1 States and Transition Functions

In this section, we consider truth-valued functions on the set of fluents. Such a function σ can be extended to arbitrary formulae according to the truth tables of propositional logic.

We say that σ is a *state* of a domain D if it maps every constraint in D to T ("true").

For instance, the domain consisting of propositions (1) and (2) has 6 states; they are the truth-valued functions on

{*Loaded*, *Alive*, *Walking*}

that make the formula *Walking* $\supset$ *Alive* true.

The semantics of $\mathcal{AR}_0$ shows how the effect propositions and release propositions of D define a nondeterministic transition system with this set of states, whose input symbols are actions. We will describe this transition system by a function *Res* that maps an action and a state to a set of states. The elements of $Res(A, \sigma)$ are, intuitively, the states that differ from σ as dictated by the effect propositions for A, but, at the same time, differ from σ as little as possible. In determining the "difference" between σ and the elements of $Res(A, \sigma)$, we will consider only the frame fluents not released by the release propositions for A.

As a preliminary step, define $Res_0(A, \sigma)$ to be the set of states σ' such that, for each effect proposition A **causes** C **if** P in D, $\sigma'(C) = $ T whenever $\sigma(P) = $ T. The set $Res(A, \sigma)$ will be defined as the subset of $Res_0(A, \sigma)$ whose elements are "close" to σ.

In order to make this precise, the following notation is needed. The *distance* $\rho(\sigma_1, \sigma_2)$ between states σ_1 and σ_2 is the set of fluents on which the states differ:

$$\rho(\sigma_1, \sigma_2) = \{F \mid \sigma_1(F) \neq \sigma_2(F)\}.$$

Furthermore, for any action A and any state σ, we define $I(A, \sigma)$ to be the set of frame fluents F such that, for every release proposition A **releases** F **if** P in D, $\sigma(P) = $ F. Intuitively, $I(A, \sigma)$ is the set of frame fluents to which inertia should apply when A is executed in state σ. If D includes no release propositions for A, then $I(A, \sigma)$ is the whole frame. For the domain of Example 4, $I(A, \sigma)$ is the frame {*Loaded*, *Alive*} unless $A = Spin$, in which case $I(A, \sigma) = \{Alive\}$.

Now the transition function *Res* corresponding to D is defined as follows: $Res(A, \sigma)$ is the set of states $\sigma' \in Res_0(A, \sigma)$ for which $\rho(\sigma, \sigma') \cap I(A, \sigma)$ is minimal relative to set inclusion—in other words, for which there is no $\sigma'' \in Res_0(A, \sigma)$ such that $\rho(\sigma, \sigma'') \cap I(A, \sigma)$ is a proper subset of $\rho(\sigma, \sigma') \cap I(A, \sigma)$.

Consider, for instance, the domain of Example 4. We will represent a state σ by the set of fluents F such that $\sigma(F) = $ T. In this notation,

$Res_0(Load, \{Alive\}) = \{\{Loaded\}, \{Loaded, Alive\}\}$,
$Res(Load, \{Alive\}) = \{\{Loaded, Alive\}\}$;

$Res_0(Spin, \{Alive\})$ is the set of all states, and

$Res(Spin, \{Alive\}) = \{\{Alive\}, \{Loaded, Alive\}\}$.

4.2 Models and Entailment

A *structure* is a partial function from strings of actions to states whose domain is nonempty and prefix-closed. If a structure Ψ is defined on a string $\overline{A}$, we say that $\overline{A}$ is *executable* in Ψ. Intuitively, $\Psi(\overline{A})$ represents the state that results from the execution of the members of $\overline{A}$ sequentially from the initial situation.

A value proposition (3) is *true* in a structure Ψ if $\overline{A}$ is executable in Ψ and $\Psi(\overline{A})(C) = \mathsf{T}$.

A structure Ψ is a *model* of a domain D if every value proposition in D is true in Ψ, and, for every string of actions $\overline{A}$ executable in Ψ and every action A,

- if $\overline{A}A$ is executable in Ψ, then
$$\Psi(\overline{A}A) \in Res(A, \Psi(\overline{A})),$$
- otherwise, $Res(A, \Psi(\overline{A})) = \emptyset$.

Consider, for instance, the domain of Example 1. Its states can be represented by subsets of $\{HasCard, DoorOpen\}$. The only action in this domain is *InsertCard*, and its transition function is defined by the equations

$$Res(InsertCard, \sigma) = \begin{cases} \{\sigma \cup \{DoorOpen\}\}, \\ \quad \text{if } HasCard \in \sigma, \\ \emptyset, \quad \text{otherwise.} \end{cases}$$

It is easy to see that this domain has two models. In one model, Ψ_1, the only executable string of actions is the empty string ϵ, and $\Psi_1(\epsilon) = \emptyset$. In the other model, Ψ_2, every string of actions is executable, and

$$\Psi_2(\overline{A}) = \begin{cases} \{HasCard\}, & \text{if } \overline{A} = \epsilon, \\ \{HasCard, DoorOpen\}, & \text{otherwise.} \end{cases}$$

We say that a domain description is *consistent* if it has a model. Two domain descriptions are *equivalent* if they have the same models.

A value proposition is *entailed* by a domain description D if it is true in every model of D.

4.3 Restricted Monotonicity

When an effect proposition, a release proposition, or a constraint is added to a domain description, the set of value propositions entailed by the description often changes in a nonmonotonic fashion: Some of the propositions entailed by the original description are not entailed by the extended one. This cannot happen, however, when a value proposition is added. It is clear from the definition of a model given above that adding a value proposition to a domain description can only make the set of its models smaller, and thus make the set of value propositions entailed by it larger. This is what one would intuitively expect, because an additional value proposition in a domain description expresses merely an additional assumption about the "trajectory" under consideration.

The observation made above is a "restricted monotonicity property" in the sense of [Lifschitz, 1993c]. Propositions of all four types play the role of postulates, and value propositions play the role of sentences, assertions and parameters. A similar fact about the language $\mathcal{A}$ is stated in [Lifschitz, 1993c] as Proposition 3.

5 Two Theorems about Domain Descriptions

In this section, we show how two ideas familiar from classical logic—the "replacement property" and the notion of an explicit definition—can be applied to the language $\mathcal{AR}_0$.

5.1 Replacement

Let T be a set of constraints. We say that formulae A and B are *equivalent* with respect to T if the formula $A \equiv B$ is a propositional consequence of T. If, for instance, T includes the constraint from Example 6, then *Light* is equivalent to *Switch1* $\vee$ *Switch2* with respect to T.

Theorem 1. *Let D be a domain description, let T be a subset of the constraints in D, and let A and B be formulae equivalent with respect to T. If a domain description D' is obtained from D by replacing A by B in some or all occurrences in any value propositions, effect propositions, and constraints that do not belong to T, then D and D' are equivalent.*

This theorem shows, for instance, that the domain of Example 6 is equivalent to

$$\begin{aligned}&\textbf{always } Light \equiv (Switch1 \vee Switch2), \\ &TurnOn \textbf{ causes } Switch1 \vee Switch2, \\ &TurnOff \textbf{ causes } \neg Switch1 \wedge \neg Switch2 \end{aligned} \quad (7)$$

and to

$$\begin{aligned}&\textbf{always } Light \equiv (Switch2 \vee Switch1), \\ &TurnOn \textbf{ causes } Light, \\ &TurnOff \textbf{ causes } \neg Light\end{aligned}$$

(take $T = \emptyset$).

Note that Theorem 1 does *not* allow us to replace a frame fluent F in a release proposition (5) by an equivalent one. In fact, such a replacement can produce a non-equivalent domain. This is shown by the following example:

$$\begin{aligned}&\textbf{always } F_1 \equiv F_2, \\ &A \textbf{ releases } F_1, \\ &A \textbf{ releases } F_2.\end{aligned}$$

Replacing F_1 by F_2 in the second line would change the set of models.

5.2 Explicit Definitions

A constraint in a domain description D is an *explicit definition* of a fluent F if it has the form

$$\textbf{always } F \equiv C, \quad (8)$$

and F

- does not belong to the frame,
- does not occur in C,
- does not occur in any other propositions in D.

For instance, the constraint in (7) is an explicit definition of *Light*.

Theorem 2. *Let D be a domain description that includes an explicit definition of a fluent F, and let D' be the domain description obtained from D by deleting this definition and deleting F from the language. A value proposition that does not contain F is entailed by D if and only if it is entailed by D'.*

Thus in $\mathcal{AR}_0$, as in classical logic, definitional extensions are conservative.

6 Relation to $\mathcal{A}$

We claimed in Section 3 that the language $\mathcal{A}$ from [Gelfond and Lifschitz, 1993] can be viewed as a subset of $\mathcal{AR}_0$. Now this assertion can be given a precise meaning.

In this section, the terms that have different definitions in the languages $\mathcal{A}$ and $\mathcal{AR}_0$, such as "proposition," "structure," "entailed" and "consistent," will be understood in the sense of the language $\mathcal{A}$, unless stated otherwise.

First, we need to review the syntax and semantics of $\mathcal{A}$. We begin with two nonempty sets of symbols, called *fluents* and *actions*. A *fluent expression* is a fluent possibly preceded by ¬. A *value proposition* is of the form

$$F \text{ after } \overline{A}, \tag{9}$$

where F is a fluent expression, and $\overline{A}$ is a string of actions. An *effect proposition* is of the form

$$A \text{ causes } F \text{ if } P_1, \ldots, P_n, \tag{10}$$

where A is an action, and each of $F, P_1, \ldots, P_n$ ($n \geq 0$) is a fluent expression. This proposition is said to *describe the effect of A on F*, and the fluent expressions $P_1, \ldots, P_n$ are said to be its *preconditions*. A *proposition* is a value proposition or an effect proposition. A *domain description* is a set of propositions.

The semantics of $\mathcal{A}$ can be described as follows. A *state* is a truth-valued function on the set of fluents. Given a fluent F and a state σ, we say that F *holds in* σ if $\sigma(F) = \mathsf{T}$; ¬F holds in σ if $\sigma(F) = \mathsf{F}$. A *transition function* is a function from pairs (A, σ), where A is an action and σ is a state, to states. A *structure* is a pair (σ_0, Φ), where σ_0 is a state (the *initial state* of the structure), and Φ is a transition function.

For any structure M and any string of actions $A_1 \ldots A_m$, by $M^{A_1 \ldots A_m}$ we denote the state

$$\Phi(A_m, \Phi(A_{m-1}, \ldots, \Phi(A_1, \sigma_0) \ldots)),$$

where Φ and σ_0 are the transition function and the initial state of M. We say that a value proposition (9) is *true* in M if F holds in the state $M^{\overline{A}}$, and that it is *false* otherwise.

A structure (σ_0, Φ) is a *model* of a domain description D if every value proposition in D is true in (σ_0, Φ), and, for every action A, every fluent F, and every state σ, the following two conditions are satisfied:

(i) if D includes an effect proposition describing the effect of A on F (¬F) whose preconditions hold in σ, then F (¬F) holds in $\Phi(A, \sigma)$;

(ii) otherwise, F holds in $\Phi(A, \sigma)$ if and only if F holds in σ.

As in the case of $\mathcal{AR}_0$, we say that D is *consistent* if it has a model; a value proposition is said to be *entailed* by D if it is true in every model of D.

For a consistent domain description in the language $\mathcal{A}$, there is a simple one-one correspondence between its models as defined here and its models in the sense of Section 4:

Theorem 3. *Let D be a consistent domain description in the language $\mathcal{A}$. If M is a model of D in the sense of $\mathcal{A}$, then the function*

$$\overline{A} \mapsto M^{\overline{A}} \tag{11}$$

is a model of D in the sense of $\mathcal{AR}_0$. Moreover, every model of D in the sense of $\mathcal{AR}_0$ has form (11) for exactly one model M of D.

Corollary. *Let D be a consistent domain description in the language $\mathcal{A}$. A value proposition is entailed by D in the sense of $\mathcal{A}$ if and only if it is entailed by D in the sense of $\mathcal{AR}_0$.*

Without assuming the consistency of D, the assertions of Theorem 3 and of the corollary would be incorrect. For instance, the domain description

$$A \text{ causes } F,$$
$$A \text{ causes } \neg F,$$

although inconsistent in $\mathcal{A}$, has models in the sense of $\mathcal{AR}_0$ (with ϵ as the the only executable string of actions).

7 Translating from $\mathcal{AR}_0$ into Circumscription

In this section, we use $\mathcal{AR}_0$ to study the range of applicability of the approach to representing actions by circumscriptive theories developed in [Baker, 1991]. Baker's method is applied in [Lifschitz, 1991] to a class of reasoning problems characterized in terms of their syntactic form, and in [Kartha, 1993] to the problems expressible in $\mathcal{A}$. Here we further extend that work by showing how the method can be applied to $\mathcal{AR}_0$.

We restrict attention to *finite* domain descriptions, that is, to domain descriptions with finitely many fluents, actions and propositions.

7.1 Nested Abnormality Theories

The formalism of nested abnormality theories is introduced in [Lifschitz, 1994]. Its use is demonstrated there by recasting several familiar applications of circumscription in its framework—inheritance hierarchies, the domain closure assumption, and the causal minimization approach to the frame problem.

The difference between this formalism and earlier uses of circumscription for formalizing knowledge can be characterized as follows. A "circumscriptive theory" is usually defined by a list of axioms $A_1, \ldots, A_n$ that may contain the abnormality predicate Ab, and by a list of predicate and/or function constants[2] $C_1, \ldots, C_m$ that are "described" by the axioms and thus are allowed to vary in the process of circumscribing Ab [McCarthy, 1986]. A possible syntax for such theories is

$$C_1, \ldots, C_m : A_1, \ldots, A_n. \qquad (12)$$

The circumscription operator allows us to translate (12) into the language of classical logic by forming the circumscription of the abnormality predicate Ab relative to the conjunction of the axioms $A_1 \wedge \ldots \wedge A_n$ with $C_1, \ldots, C_m$ allowed to vary; we denote this circumscription by

$$\text{CIRC}[A_1 \wedge \ldots \wedge A_n; Ab; C_1, \ldots, C_m]. \qquad (13)$$

(See [Lifschitz, 1993a] for the definition of the circumscription operator.) Unfortunately, this is not general enough for the purpose of representing defaults, and "prioritized circumscription" is proposed in [McCarthy, 1986] as a more general representation tool. In nested abnormality theories, we generalize (12) in a different way: each A_i in (12) is allowed to be a "block" of form (12), so that axioms become "nested." Intuitively, each block can be viewed as a group of axioms that describes a certain collection of predicates and functions, and the embedding of blocks reflects the dependence of these descriptions on each other.

It is also convenient to replace the predicate constant Ab in (13) by an existentially quantified predicate variable. The abnormality predicate usually plays an auxiliary role in a formalization; what we are actually interested in are the logical consequences of (13) that do not include Ab. To put it differently, if (13) is denoted by $F(Ab)$, and ab is a predicate variable of the same arity as Ab, then what we are interested in are the consequences of the sentence $\exists ab F(ab)$. The effect of this modification in the context of nested abnormality theories is that the abnormality predicate becomes local to the block in which it is used. The syntax of simple abnormality theories is defined in such a way that Ab may even have different arities in different blocks.

We turn now to the formal treatment of the subject. The definitions below are reproduced from [Lifschitz, 1994].

Consider a language L of classical logic which may have variables of several sorts and higher-order variables. We assume that L does not include Ab among its symbols. For any list $\tau_1, \ldots, \tau_k$ of sorts of variables available in L, by $L_{\tau_1 \ldots \tau_k}$ we denote the language obtained from L by adding Ab as a k-ary predicate constant taking arguments of the sorts $\tau_1, \ldots, \tau_k$. Blocks are defined recursively as follows: For any list of sorts $\tau_1, \ldots, \tau_k$ and any list of function and/or predicate constants $C_1, \ldots, C_m$ ($m \geq 0$) of L, if each of $A_1, \ldots, A_n$ ($n \geq 0$) is a formula of $L_{\tau_1 \ldots \tau_k}$ or a block, then

$$\{C_1, \ldots, C_m : A_1, \ldots, A_n\}$$

[2]Object constants are viewed as function constants of arity 0.

is a block. A nested abnormality theory is a set of blocks, called its axioms.

The semantics of nested abnormality theories is characterized by a map φ that translates blocks into formulae. It is convenient to make φ defined also on formulae of the languages $L_{\tau_1 \ldots \tau_k}$. If A is such a formula, then φA stands for the universal closure of A. For blocks we define, recursively:

$$\varphi\{C_1, \ldots, C_m : A_1, \ldots, A_n\} = \exists ab F(ab),$$

where

$$F(Ab) = \text{CIRC}[\varphi A_1 \wedge \ldots \wedge \varphi A_n; Ab; C_1, \ldots, C_m].$$

Note that, for any block A, φA is a sentence not containing Ab.

A sentence A of L will be identified with the block $\{: A\}$. It is easy to see that $\varphi\{: A\}$ is equivalent to A.

For any nested abnormality theory T, φT stands for $\{\varphi A \mid A \in T\}$. A model of T is a model of φT in the sense of classical logic. A consequence of T is a sentence of L that is true in all models of T.

7.2 Language

We will transform a finite domain D in the sense of the language $\mathcal{AR}_0$ into a nested abnormality theory whose language L has variables of three sorts: for fluents, actions and situations. These variables will be denoted respectively by $f, f_1, f_2, \ldots; a, a_1, a_2, \ldots; s, s_1, s_2, \ldots$. In addition, L has predicate variables $\lambda, \lambda_1, \lambda_2, \ldots$ that range over properties of fluents.

The language has the following object constants:

- the fluents of D,
- the actions of D,
- the situation constants S_0 and $\bot$.

It also includes the binary function constant $Result$, which takes an action and a situation as arguments, and produces a situation.

The constant $\bot$ is needed because we want to talk about actions that may not be executable, such as $InsertCard$ in Example 1. Intuitively, $\bot$ represents the value "undefined", so that the assertion that a is not executable in situation s will be represented by

$$Result(a, s) = \bot.$$

Finally, L has two predicate constants:

- the unary predicate $FrameFluent$, whose argument is a fluent,
- the binary predicate $Holds$, whose two arguments are a fluent and a situation.

Note that "formulae" as defined in Section 2.1 are not among the formulae of L. To avoid confusion, we will refer to formulae in the sense of Section 2.1 as "domain formulae." For any domain formula C, by $T(C, s)$ we will denote the formula of L obtained from C as the result of replacing each fluent name F by $Holds(F, s)$. For instance, $T(\neg Alive \land Loaded, s)$ stands for

$$\neg Holds(Alive, s) \land Holds(Loaded, s).$$

For any string of actions $A_1 \ldots A_m$, by $[A_1 \ldots A_m]$ we will denote the ground term

$$Result(A_m, Result(A_{m-1}, \ldots, Result(A_1, S_0), \ldots)).$$

7.3 Law of Inertia and Existence of Situations

Our translation β from $\mathcal{AR}_0$ into nested abnormality theories uses two defaults that play an important role in applications of default reasoning to the frame problem.

According to the *commonsense law of inertia*, the value of a frame fluent normally remains unchanged after performing an action. Formulas describing how actions change the world represent exceptions to this default. The commonsense law of inertia is expressed by the formula

$$FrameFluent(f) \land \neg Ab(f, a, s) \supset$$
$$[Holds(f, Result(a, s)) \equiv Holds(f, s)].$$

This formula will be denoted by *LI*.

According to the *existence of situations principle*, for any assignment of values to fluents, there normally exists a situation in which every fluent takes the assigned value. Recognizing the role of this principle was a major contribution of [Baker, 1991]. Constraints represent exceptions to this default. For instance, the constraint

$$Holds(Walking, s) \supset Holds(Alive, s) \qquad (14)$$

shows that there is no situation in which *Walking* is true and *Alive* is false. The existence of situations principle is expressed by the formula

$$\neg Ab(\lambda) \supset \exists s[s \neq \bot \land \forall f(Holds(f, s) \equiv \lambda(f))].$$

This formula will be denoted by *ES*.

As defined below, the nested abnormality theory βD representing a finite domain D consists of several formulas, including *LI* and *ES*, arranged into a system of blocks. We should not worry about by the fact that *Ab* has three arguments in *LI* and only one argument in *ES*: these formulas will appear in two different blocks.

7.4 Translating Propositions

We will define how to construct, for each proposition P in D, the corresponding formula βP. These formulas will be included in the translation βD of D.

If P is a value proposition (3), then βP is

$$[\overline{A}] \neq \bot \land T(C, [\overline{A}]).$$

The first term expresses that the sequence of actions $\overline{A}$ is executable. For instance, the proposition

Heads **after** *Toss*

is translated as

$$Result(Toss, S_0) \neq \bot \land Holds(Heads, Result(Toss, S_0)).$$

If P is an effect proposition (4), then βP is

$$T(P, s) \land Result(A, s) \neq \bot \supset T(C, Result(A, s)).$$

For instance, the proposition

Shoot **causes** $\neg Alive$ **if** *Loaded*

is translated as

$$Holds(Loaded, s) \land Result(Shoot, s) \neq \bot \supset$$
$$\neg Holds(Alive, Result(Shoot, s)).$$

If P is a release proposition (5), then βP is

$$T(P, s) \supset Ab(F, A, s).$$

This formula will accompany the commonsense law of inertia *LI*, so that the law of inertia will be disabled in application to F when A is executed in the presence of the precondition P. For instance, the proposition

Spin **releases** *Loaded*

is translated as

$$Ab(Loaded, Spin, s)$$

(if we disregard the trivial antecedent $T(True, s)$, which equals *True*).

Finally, if P is a constraint (6), then βP is $T(C, s)$. For instance, (2) is translated as (14).

7.5 Definition of βD

Now we are ready to define the representation βD of a finite domain D as a nested abnormality theory.

By **F** we will denote the set of fluents in the language of D, by **Fr** the set of frame fluents, by **A** the set of actions. Furthermore, let D_v, D_e, D_r and D_c be the parts of D consisting of its value propositions, effect propositions, release propositions and constraints, so that

$$D = D_v \cup D_e \cup D_r \cup D_c.$$

The axioms of βD are as follows.

Group 1. Unique names axioms:

$$F_1 \neq F_2$$

for all pairs of distinct fluents $F_1, F_2 \in \mathbf{F}$,

$$A_1 \neq A_2$$

for all pairs of distinct actions $A_1, A_2 \in \mathbf{A}$, and

$$S_0 \neq \bot.$$

Group 2. Domain closure axioms:
$$\bigvee_{F \in \mathbf{F}} f = F,$$
$$\bigvee_{A \in \mathbf{A}} a = A.$$

Group 3. The universe of situations is assumed to be sufficiently large:
$$\exists s_1, \ldots, s_N \bigwedge_{1 \leq i < j \leq N} s_i \neq s_j,$$
where $N = 2^{|\mathbf{F}|} + 1$.

Group 4. Translations of the value propositions:
$$\beta P \qquad (P \in D_v).$$

Group 5. Characterization of *FrameFluent*:
$$\{FrameFluent :$$
$$FrameFluent(f) \supset Ab(f),$$
$$FrameFluent(F) \qquad (F \in \mathbf{Fr})$$
$$\}.$$

By enclosing the formulae $FrameFluent(F)$ for all F in $\mathbf{Fr}$ in a block along with
$$FrameFluent(f) \supset Ab(f),$$
we express the "closed world assumption" for *FrameFluent*: a fluent satisfies this predicate *only* if it represented by a constant from $\mathbf{Fr}$.

Group 6. Characterization of *Holds* and *Result*:
$$\{Result :$$
$$LI,$$
$$\beta P \qquad (P \in D_r),$$
$$\{Result :$$
$$Result(a, s) = \bot \supset Ab(a, s),$$
$$Result(a, \bot) = \bot,$$
$$\beta P \qquad (P \in D_e),$$
$$\{Holds :$$
$$ES,$$
$$\beta P \qquad (P \in D_c)$$
$$\}$$
$$\}$$
$$\}.$$

The innermost block represents the basic assumption about the universe of situations: for any assignment of truth values to fluents, there exists a situation in which every fluent takes the assigned value, unless such a situation is declared impossible by one of the constraints in D. In the intermediate block, the formula
$$Result(a, s) = \bot \supset Ab(a, s)$$
expresses that, normally, an action is executable. Thus the intermediate block tells us that an action can be executed unless this is prohibited by the propositions in D. The outermost block says that the values of fluents do not change unless this is required by the propositions in D.

The nesting of blocks reflects our intention to decide first what kinds of situations exist, then which actions can be executed, and then what the effects of actions are.

7.6 Soundness and Completeness

Consider a finite domain D. Let Ψ be a model of D, and let M be a model of βD. We say that M is *similar* to Ψ if, for every value proposition P, P is true in Ψ if and only if M satisfies βP.

Theorem 4. *Let D be a finite domain. For any model Ψ of D, there exists a model M of βD similar to Ψ. For any model M of βD, there exists a model Ψ of D such that M is similar to Ψ.*

The following corollary expresses the soundness and completeness of the translation.

Corollary. *For any finite domain D and any value proposition P, βD entails βP if and only if D entails P.*

8 Conclusion

In addition to the expressive possibilities of $\mathcal{A}$, the language $\mathcal{AR}_0$ allows us to represent actions that may be impossible to execute, fluents that are exempt from inertia, actions with indirect effects and simple nondeterministic actions. It has properties similar to the replacement theorem and to the theorem on the conservativeness of definitional extensions familiar from classical logic. There is a sound and complete translation from $\mathcal{AR}_0$ into the language of nested abnormality theories.

The treatment of value propositions in the semantics of $\mathcal{AR}_0$ is analogous to the "filtering" method advocated by Sandewall [1989], [1992]. Indeed, the value propositions included in D do not affect the construction of the corresponding transition function *Res*; they are taken into account only when we define which of the "trajectories" described by this transition function are counted as the models of D. Similarly, in the nested abnormality theory βD, the translations of the value propositions form a separate group of axioms that is not placed in the range of any circumscriptions.

The use of nested abnormality theories, instead of conjunctions of circumscriptions as in [Baker, 1991] and [Lifschitz, 1991], leads to a simpler and more natural presentation of Baker's method. Moreover, the use of conjunctions of circumscriptions along the lines of that earlier work does not seem to lead to satisfactory results when actions can be nondeterministic. This will be discussed in detail elsewhere.

Acknowledgements

We are grateful to Michael Gelfond, Enrico Giunchiglia, Fangzhen Lin, Norman McCain and Hudson Turner for comments on drafts of this paper. This work was partially supported by National Science Foundation under grants IRI-9101078 and IRI-9306751.

References

[Baker, 1991] Andrew Baker. Nonmonotonic reasoning in the framework of situation calculus. *Artificial Intelligence*, 49:5–23, 1991.

[Baral and Gelfond, 1993] Chitta Baral and Michael Gelfond. Representing concurrent actions in extended logic programming. In *Proc. of IJCAI-93*, pages 866–871, 1993.

[Boyer and Moore, 1988] Robert Boyer and J Strother Moore. *A computational logic handbook*. Academic Press, 1988.

[Chen and Warren, 1992] Weidong Chen and David S. Warren. A goal-oriented approach to computing well-founded semantics. In Krzysztof Apt, editor, *Proc. Joint Int'l Conf. and Symp. on Logic Programming*, pages 589–603, 1992.

[Denecker and De Schreye, 1993] Mark Denecker and Danny De Schreye. Representing incomplete knowledge in abductive logic programming. In Dale Miller, editor, *Logic Programming: Proceedings of the 1993 Int'l Symposium*, pages 147–163, 1993.

[Dung, 1993] Phan Minh Dung. Representing actions in logic programming and its applications in database updates. In *Logic Programming: Proceedings of the Tenth Int'l Conf. on Logic Programming*, pages 222–238, 1993.

[Gelfond and Lifschitz, 1993] Michael Gelfond and Vladimir Lifschitz. Representing action and change by logic programs. *The Journal of Logic Programming*, 17:301–322, 1993.

[Kartha, 1993] G. Neelakantan Kartha. Soundness and completeness theorems for three formalizations of action. In *Proc. of IJCAI-93*, pages 724–729, 1993.

[Lifschitz et al., 1993] Vladimir Lifschitz, Norman McCain, and Hudson Turner. Automated reasoning about action: A logic programming approach. In Dale Miller, editor, *Proc. of ILPS-93*, page 641, 1993.

[Lifschitz, 1990] Vladimir Lifschitz. Frames in the space of situations. *Artificial Intelligence*, 46:365–376, 1990.

[Lifschitz, 1991] Vladimir Lifschitz. Towards a metatheory of action. In James Allen, Richard Fikes, and Erik Sandewall, editors, *Proc. of the Second Int'l Conf. on Principles of Knowledge Representation and Reasoning*, pages 376–386, 1991.

[Lifschitz, 1993a] Vladimir Lifschitz. Circumscription. In D.M. Gabbay, C.J. Hogger, and J.A. Robinson, editors, *The Handbook of Logic in AI and Logic Programming*, volume 3, pages 298–352. Oxford University Press, 1993.

[Lifschitz, 1993b] Vladimir Lifschitz. A language for describing actions. In *Working Papers of the Second Symposium on Logical Formalizations of Commonsense Reasoning*, 1993.

[Lifschitz, 1993c] Vladimir Lifschitz. Restricted monotonicity. In *Proc. AAAI-93*, pages 432–437, 1993.

[Lifschitz, 1994] Vladimir Lifschitz. Nested abnormality theories. Manuscript, 1994.

[Lin and Shoham, 1991] Fangzhen Lin and Yoav Shoham. Provably correct theories of action (preliminary report). In *Proc. AAAI-91*, pages 349–354, 1991.

[McCarthy, 1986] John McCarthy. Applications of circumscription to formalizing common sense knowledge. *Artificial Intelligence*, 26(3):89–116, 1986. Reproduced in [McCarthy, 1990].

[McCarthy, 1990] John McCarthy. *Formalizing common sense: papers by John McCarthy*. Ablex, Norwood, NJ, 1990.

[Pednault, 1989] Edwin Pednault. ADL: Exploring the middle ground between STRIPS and the situation calculus. In Ronald Brachman, Hector Levesque, and Raymond Reiter, editors, *Proc. of the First Int'l Conf. on Principles of Knowledge Representation and Reasoning*, pages 324–332, 1989.

[Reiter, 1991] Raymond Reiter. The frame problem in the situation calculus: a simple solution (sometimes) and a completeness result for goal regression. In Vladimir Lifschitz, editor, *Artificial Intelligence and Mathematical Theory of Computation: Papers in Honor of John McCarthy*, pages 359–380. Academic Press, 1991.

[Sandewall, 1989] Erik Sandewall. Filter preferential entailment for the logic of action in almost continuous worlds. In *Proc. of IJCAI-89*, pages 894–899, 1989.

[Sandewall, 1992] Erik Sandewall. Features and fluents: A systematic approach to the representation of knowledge about dynamical systems. Technical Report LiTH-IDA-R-92-30, Linköping University, 1992.

[Subramanian, 1993] Sakthi Subramanian. *A Mechanized Framework for Specifying Problem Domains and Verifying Plans*. PhD thesis, University of Texas, Austin, Department of Computer Science, 1993.

[Thielscher, 1993] Michael Thielscher. An analysis of systematic approaches to reasoning about actions and change. Manuscript, 1993.

[Thielscher, 1994] Michael Thielscher. Representing actions in equational logic programming. In *Proc. ICLP-94*, 1994. To appear.

An Application of Terminological Logics to Case-based Reasoning

Jana Koehler
German Research Center for Artificial Intelligence (DFKI)
Stuhlsatzenhausweg 3,
D-66123 Saarbrücken, Germany
e-mail: koehler@dfki.uni-sb.de

Abstract

A key problem in case-based reasoning is the representation, organization and maintenance of case libraries. While current approaches rely on heuristic and psychologically inspired formalisms, terminological logics have emerged as a powerful representation formalism with clearly defined formal semantics.

This paper demonstrates how the indexing of case libraries can be grounded on terminological logics by using them as a kind of query language to the case library. Indices of cases are represented as concepts in a terminological logic. They are automatically constructed from the symbolic representation of cases with the help of a well-defined abstraction process. The retrieval of cases from the library is grounded on concept classification.

The theoretical approach provides the formal foundation for the fully implemented case-based planning system MRL. The use of terminological logics allows formal proof of properties like the correctness, completeness and efficiency of the retrieval algorithm, which has rarely been done for existing case-based reasoning systems.

1 INTRODUCTION

Reasoning from second principles has emerged as a new research paradigm in problem solving. Instead of searching a solution by reasoning from scratch, this method bases the entire problem-solving process on the reuse and modification of previous solutions.

Current approaches are within the field of *case-based reasoning* which is defined as a general paradigm for reasoning from experience [Slade, 1989]. Approaches to case-based reasoning rely mainly on psychological theories of human cognition and have led to a wide variety of proposals for the representation, indexing and organization of case libraries, cf. [CBR-91, 1991; CBR-93, 1993].

Case-based systems reason by *approximation* and *similarity*. In order to solve a new case by reusing an existing one from a *case library*, several reasoning tasks have to be addressed: First, an *index* is derived from the new case by extracting those of its features that are *abstract enough* to make a case useful in a variety of situations as well as *concrete enough* to be easily recognizable in future situations. In most approaches, the *index vocabulary* is a subset of the vocabulary used for the symbolic representation of cases, cf. [Kolodner, 1993].

The index of the new case is used as a search key on which the *retrieval* of applicable old cases is based. The aim of retrieval is to determine "good cases" *efficiently* in the library—those that make relevant predictions about the current case. Besides the need for an efficient search strategy, the retrieval problem implies the *matching problem*, which is a serious bottleneck for case-based reasoners, cf.[Kolodner, 1993; Slade, 1989; Riesbeck and Schank, 1989]. As we cannot expect that features of different cases coincide completely, so-called *partial matches* have to be computed and cases with *best-matching indices* have to be retrieved. Finally, the set of retrieved cases is ordered according to *ranking heuristics* and the "best" case is determined.

Research in case-based reasoning proposes various solutions to the problems of retrieval, indexing and matching. A common characteristic of these solutions is that they are described in an *informal* way. This makes it difficult to compare the various approaches, to prove their formal properties and to extend them to other applications.

Nevertheless, practice imposes the following requirements on case-based reasoners:

- The behavior of a system should be predictable. It should be possible to verify whether the system implements the intended behavior correctly.

- The derivation of *indexes* should be done automatic instead of "hand-coded", which is still usual in many approaches.
- The retrieval algorithm should find a solution to a new case, if this solution exists in the case library.
- If no direct solution can be determined, the retrieval algorithm should determine the case that best meets the search criterion.

Consequently, this implies the need for case-based reasoning systems with *formal semantics*. The retrieval algorithm should have the following formal properties:

- **Correctness**: The retrieved case is guaranteed to meet the search criterion.
- **Completeness**: Retrieval of existing solutions to new cases from the case library is ensured.
- **Complexity**: The retrieval algorithm is proved to be efficient, i.e. it runs in polynomial time.

A case-based reasoning system with these properties can be expected to meet the challenge of *scaling-up*: The system's behavior remains predictable, sound and efficient even when it is applied to large-scale real-world problems. Surprisingly, it turns out that problems like the correctness and completeness of the retrieval algorithm have not been widely discussed in the literature on case-based reasoning.

The work described in this paper is motivated by research in *case-based planning*. The reuse and modification of plans is a valuable tool for improving the efficiency of planning, because it avoids the repetition of planning effort. Therefore, plans that have been obtained as solutions for planning problems are stored in *plan libraries* for further use. The retrieval of a good plan from a plan library is identified as being a serious bottleneck for plan reuse systems in [Nebel and Koehler, 1993a; Nebel and Koehler, 1993b]. Consequently, efficient and theoretically well-founded retrieval and update procedures for plan libraries have to be developed.

The approach presented in this paper suggests the integration of terminological logics into a hybrid representation formalism for case-based reasoning. Retrieval from and updating of case libraries are grounded on a clearly defined formalism with proper semantics. Their behavior becomes predictable and formal properties like the completeness and soundness of the retrieval algorithm can be proved.

2 THE SOLUTION

While case-based reasoning aims at developing a scientific model of human memory, research in *knowledge representation and reasoning* has led to concept languages of the KL-ONE family [Brachman, 1978], also called *terminological logics*. Terminological logics support a *structured* representation of *abstract* knowledge. In contrast to earlier representation formalisms, terminological logics possess formal semantics. The Tarski style declarative semantics leads them to be considered as sublanguages of predicate logic [Brachmann and Levesque, 1984]. With that, the meaning of expressions within the formalism is clearly defined and it is possible to verify whether or not the knowledge-representation system correctly implements the intended behavior. Furthermore, terminological logics provide special-purpose inference algorithms like *subsumption* and *classification*. These properties of terminological logics clearly suggest their use in case-based reasoning.

2.1 FORMALIZING CASE-BASED REASONING

A *case* represented in a case library consists of three major parts, cf. [Kolodner, 1993]:

- **initial situation**: A state description, *pre*, specifying the preconditions, on which the solution represented in the case relies.
- **resulting situation**: The goal state, *goal*, that is achieved when the solution is carried out.
- **solution**: A solution S that solves the problem specification of the case $C = \langle pre, goal \rangle$.

Case-based reasoning starts with a new case in the form of a problem specification

$$C_{new} = \langle pre_{new}, goal_{new} \rangle$$

for which a solution has to be found in the case library.

- **Given**: a new case C_{new}
- **Wanted**: a solution S_{old} from the case library

To find this solution, a *search key* is derived from the problem specification, which has to reflect the main properties of the problem. Usually, the search is done in the *state space* rather than the solution space. This means, instead of searching the case library directly for solutions, it is searched for *similar* problem specifications. This is justified by the following observation: the solution S_{old} is the result of a previous problem-solving process, i.e. it solves an old case C_{old} in the sense that

$$S_{old} \models C_{old}$$

This means, a solution which is applied in an initial situation satisfying *pre* achieves a resulting situation satisfying *goal*. This suggests a search of the case library for previous problem specifications, i.e. old cases, which entail the problem specification of the new case in the sense that each solution for C_{old} is a solution for C_{new}:

$$C_{old} \models C_{new}$$

If this relationship between C_{old} and C_{new} holds, then the new case has been shown to be an instance of a case from the library. This implies that solving C_{old} is *sufficient* for solving C_{new}. Consequently, the solution S_{old} stored in C_{old} will solve C_{new}.

2.2 REASONING BY APPROXIMATION

Searching a case library according to the $\models$ relationship is obviously too restrictive. Such a search algorithm would only retrieve solutions from the case library. But obviously, a "good" case is one that can be easily adapted to obtain the desired solution. Furthermore, the retrieval process is based on an *index* that is obtained from C_{new} instead of directly taking the specification of C_{new}. Therefore, an *index* of a case is computed with the help of an *encoding scheme* ω mapping the case

$$C_{new} = \langle pre_{new}, goal_{new} \rangle$$

to its index

$$\omega(C_{new}) = \langle \omega(pre_{new}), \omega(goal_{new}) \rangle$$

The encoding scheme formalizes an *abstraction process*: A detailed specification of a particular case is mapped to an abstract index reflecting the main features of that case. The degree of abstraction is determined by the particular encoding scheme, which is used in the case-based reasoning system. This means that different encoding schemes can define different degrees of abstraction in a case-based reasoning system.

The encoding scheme ω has to possess the following formal property:

If $C_{old} \to C_{new}$ then $\omega(C_{old}) \to \omega(C_{new})$

This theorem gives a *monotonicity property* of ω. An existing subset relationship between the models of the cases C_{old} and C_{new} is preserved as a subset relationship between the models of the indices $\omega(C_{old})$ and $\omega(C_{new})$.

If $M[P_{old}] \subseteq M[P_{new}]$ then $M[\omega(P_{old})] \subseteq M[\omega(P_{new})]$

This *monotonicity property* of the encoding scheme ensures that an existing solution can be found by searching the case library along the $\models$ dimension between indices. Note that the inverse of the monotonicity property does not hold in general. A case retrieved from the library, the index of which entails the new index, will not, with certainty, provide a solution to the new case. This reflects *reasoning by approximation*. The retrieval algorithm approximates the $\models$ relationship between the cases when it compares the indices of the cases. Thereby, it extends the solution set computed by the retrieval algorithm.

The definition of a particular encoding scheme depends on three factors:

- the representation formalism for the cases,
- the representation formalism for the indices,
- the application domain.

In Section 3, we illustrate the definition of an encoding scheme for a *case-based planning system*. The representation formalism for the cases is a *temporal planning logic*. The representation formalism for the indices is a *terminological logic*. The application domain comprises planning tasks arising in a subset of the UNIX operating system.

2.3 REASONING BY SIMILARITY

The second aspect of case-based reasoning is *reasoning by similarity*. Case-based systems compute the similarity of cases by comparing the placement of the cases in the abstraction hierarchy or by computing their distance on a qualitative or quantitative scale, cf. [Kolodner, 1993]. A formalization of the notion of *similarity* is beyond the scope of this paper. Nevertheless, the encoding scheme allows to define when a case is more *specific* than another one:

Definition 1 *A case C_1 is defined as being more specific than a case C_2, if $\omega(C_1) \models \omega(C_2)$ holds for their indices.*

Remember, that a case contains three major parts: its initial situation, its resulting situation and the solution. The entailment relation between cases can therefore be reduced to relations between initial and resulting situations. A case is an instance of a stored case if

- the new initial situation entails the old initial situation $pre_{new} \models pre_{old}$, i.e. the solution S_{old} is applicable to the new initial situation,
- the old resulting situation entails the new resulting situation $goal_{old} \models goal_{new}$, i.e. S_{old} solves at least the new problem.

Furthermore, each index $\omega(C) = \langle \omega(pre), \omega(goal) \rangle$ comprises two components, namely the encoding of the initial situation, pre, and the encoding of the resulting situation $goal$. Obviously, testing $\omega(C_{old}) \models \omega(C_{new})$ can be reduced to computing relations between the encodings of both situations:

$\omega(pre_{new}) \models \omega(pre_{old})$ and $\omega(goal_{old}) \models \omega(goal_{new})$

Strong and weak retrieval algorithms can thus be defined. A strong retrieval algorithm determines reusable cases by testing

$\omega(pre_{new}) \models \omega(pre_{old})$ <u>and</u> $\omega(goal_{old}) \models \omega(goal_{new})$

This guarantees that existing solutions can be found in the case library. Furthermore, *more specific* cases are retrieved according to definition 1.

If strong retrieval fails to find a more specific case, the search criterion is replaced by a weaker one: A weak retrieval algorithm can test

$$\omega(pre_{new}) \models \omega(pre_{old}) \underline{\text{ or }} \omega(goal_{old}) \models \omega(goal_{new})$$

Thus, we can ground the retrieval of cases on different well-defined relations between indices that possess formal semantics. This overcomes the problem of defining *partial matches* between cases, the semantics of which remains often unclear.

2.4 HYBRID REPRESENTATION

In this paper, we propose a hybrid representation formalism for case libraries: The major parts of a case, the *case entry*, are represented in a formalism that adequately represents problems and solutions in the underlying application domain, e.g. the planning formalism used by a case-based planner.

The *index* of the case is represented as a *concept* in a terminological logic. The relation $\models$ between indices is determined by computing the *subsumption* relation (denoted with $\sqsubseteq$) between concepts. With that, the retrieval of a reusable case from the case library can be grounded on *concept classification*.

The encoding scheme defines the *degree of abstraction* that is reflected in the indices: a given case is mapped to an index reflecting the main properties of the case. Note that the encoding scheme may map several specific cases to the same index. This means, the index represents a description of an abstract class of specific cases occurring in a particular application domain. The case related to this index represents one possible specific instance of that class.

Terminological logics have the following advantages:

They provide indices with clearly defined semantics. The monotonicity property of the encoding scheme ω can be proved. The encoding scheme implements a representational shift from the vocabulary for the symbolic representation of cases to the indexing vocabulary represented in a terminological logic. This leads to a well-defined abstraction process. Furthermore, the indexing vocabulary can be automatically built by the case-based reasoning system: If the vocabulary for the symbolic representation of cases is a logical formalism, a case will be represented as a formula in this logic. The index of the case is obtained by a transformation of the formula with the help of the encoding scheme. The result is a first-order logic formula that can be interpreted as a concept definition in the terminological logic, cf. Section 3.

The mathematical properties of various terminological logics are well understood. In particular, terminological languages with decidable subsumption relations have been identified. Remember, that retrieval from case libraries must be efficient, i.e. the complexity of the retrieval algorithm must be investigated. The use of a terminological logic with a polynomial subsumption algorithm ensures that the retrieval algorithm runs in polynomial time as well.

Most of the indexing schemes used in case-based reasoning, for example *discrimination networks* [Feigenbaum, 1963], restrict the case library to have a *tree* structure. In using terminological logics, case libraries are indexed on a more general *lattice structure* provided by the subsumption hierarchy.

3 AN EXAMPLE

The MRL system [Koehler, 1994a] is the case-based planning component of the system PHI [Bauer et al., 1993], a logic-based tool for intelligent help systems. PHI integrates plan generation as well as plan recognition. Plan generation can be done from first principles by planning from scratch and from second principles by reusing previously generated plans with MRL [Biundo et al., 1992]. The example application domain of PHI is the UNIX *mail domain* where objects like *messages* and *mailboxes* are manipulated by actions like *read*, *delete*, and *save*.

3.1 THE PLANNING LOGIC

The logical basis of PHI and MRL is the interval-based modal temporal logic LLP [Biundo and Dengler, 1994]. LLP provides the modal operators $\bigcirc$ (next), $\Diamond$ (sometimes), $\square$ (always) and ; (chop), the binary modal operator, which expresses the sequential composition of formulae. As in programming logics, control structures like iterations and conditionals and *local variables* are available, with values that may vary from state to state.

Plans are represented by a certain class of LLP formulae. They may contain, e.g. basic actions which are expressed by the *execute* predicate *ex*, the *chop* operator, which is used to express the sequential composition of plans, and control structures.

The atomic actions available to the planner are the elementary commands of the UNIX mail system. They are axiomatized like assignment statements in programming logics. State changes which are caused by executing an action are reflected in a change of the values of local variables which represent the mailboxes in the mail system. For example, the axiomatization of the *delete*-command which deletes a message x in a mailbox *mbox* reads

$$\forall x\ open\_flag(mbox) = T \land$$
$$delete\_flag(msg(x, mbox)) = F \land$$
$$ex(delete(x, mbox))$$
$$\rightarrow \bigcirc delete\_flag(msg(x, mbox)) = T$$

The state of a mailbox is represented with the help of *flags*. The precondition of the *delete*-command is that the mailbox $mbox$ is open, i.e. its *open_flag* yields the value *true* (T) and that the message x has not yet been deleted, i.e. its *delete_flag* yields the value *false* (F). As an effect, the action sets the *delete_flag* of message x in mailbox $mbox$ to the value *true* in the next state.

Planning problems are represented with the help of formal plan specifications in the logic LLP. They contain the specification of an initial state, the *preconditions* of the plan, and the specification of the *goals* that have to be achieved by executing the plan.

As an example, assume that a plan **P1** for the planning problem "read and delete a message m in the mailbox $mybox$" has to be found. As preconditions, we assume that the mailbox $mybox$ has already been opened and that the message m has not yet been deleted. The formal specification of the preconditions pre_{P1} and the goals $goal_{P1}$ in the logic LLP reads as follows:

pre_{P1}: $open\_flag(mybox) = T \land$
$\qquad delete\_flag(msg(m, mybox)) = F$

$goal_{P1}$: $\Diamond[read\_flag(msg(m, mybox)) = T \land$
$\qquad\quad \Diamond[delete\_flag(msg(m, mybox)) = T]]$

It should be noted that in using the logic LLP in a planning system it becomes possible to specify temporary goals with the help of nested *sometimes* operators, i.e. goals that have to be achieved at some point and not necessarily in the end, something which could not be done in the usual STRIPS or TWEAK type planning systems, cf. [Kautz and Selman, 1992]. In the example, the goal specification requires the message to be read first and then deleted.

The plan **P1**, which solves this planning problem, is a simple sequence containing the actions *type* and *delete*:

P1: $ex(type(m, mybox)); ex(delete(m, mybox))$

To obtain this plan by case-based planning in MRL, appropriate candidate plans have to be retrieved from the plan library. In the example, we assume that the plan library contains the candidate plans **P2** and **P3**:

P2: if $open\_flag(mbox) = T$
$\quad$ then $ex(empty\_action)$
$\quad$ else $ex(mail(mbox))$;
$ex(type(x, mbox)); ex(delete(x, mbox))$

P3: $n := 1$;
$\quad$ while $n < length(mbox)$ do
$\qquad$ if $sender(msg(n, mbox)) = joe$
$\qquad$ then $ex(type(n, mbox))$;
$\qquad\quad ex(delete(n, mbox))$
$\qquad$ else $ex(empty\_action)$;
$\qquad n := n + 1$
od ;

The plan **P2** is an example of a *conditional* plan. It contains a case analysis on the state of the mailbox $mbox$: If the mailbox is open, the message x can be read and deleted. If the mailbox is closed, we first have to open it before the plan can be executed. The case analysis results from incomplete information about the preconditions for plan **P2**:

pre_{P2}: $delete\_flag(msg(x, mbox)) = F$

As a precondition for **P2** we only know that the message has not been deleted, but information about the state of the mailbox not available.

In contrast to the goal specification $goal_{P1}$, the specification of goals in $goal_{P2}$ specifies no temporary goals, but a *conjunctive* goal:

$goal_{P2}$: $\Diamond[read\_flag(msg(x, mbox)) = T \land$
$\qquad\quad delete\_flag(msg(x, mbox)) = T]$

The plan **P3** is an example of an *iterative* plan reading all messages from sender *joe* in the mailbox $mbox$. The specification of its preconditions and goals contains universally quantified formulae:

pre_{P3}: $open\_flag(mbox) = T \land$
$\qquad \forall x\ [sender(msg(x, mbox)) = joe$
$\qquad \rightarrow delete\_flag(msg(x, mbox)) = F]$

$goal_{P3}$: $\Diamond\ [\forall x\ [sender(msg(x, mbox)) = joe$
$\qquad \rightarrow read\_flag(msg(x, mbox)) = T \land$
$\qquad\quad delete\_flag(msg(x, mbox)) = T]]$

Only a very restricted syntactic class of LLP formulae is used for the specification of preconditions and goals. For example, only implicit negation of atomic formulae occurs in implications. Furthermore, atomic formulae are equations assigning constants to terms of a very restricted syntactic structure. The term $msg(x, mbox)$ denotes an arbitrary message in a mailbox. Unary functions like *read_flag* and *delete_flag* represent features of this message. The effects of actions are reflected in changed features.

The plans **P2** and **P3** can be easily adapted in order to obtain the desired plan **P1**:

- **P1** corresponds to the **then**-branch of **P2** when deleting the superfluous *empty_action*.

- **P1** corresponds to the sequential body plan of **P3** when deleting the superfluous iterative control structure and the test on the sender of the message.

Consequently, **P2** and **P3** should both be retrieved from the case library as possible reuse candidates. Furthermore, the retrieval algorithm should differentiate between **P2** and **P3**:

On one hand, both plans **P2** and **P3** are applicable in the initial state specified for **P1** because their preconditions are entailed by pre_{P1}. On the other hand, **P2** is more "similar" to the desired plan than the plan **P3**: it reads and deletes *an arbitrary* message as required in the new case **P1**, while **P3** reads *all* messages from a *particular* sender—an additional condition, which is not required in **P1**.

The identification of **P2** and **P3** as appropriate reusable cases requires *abstraction* from

- specific objects occurring in the specifications,
- temporary subgoal states,
- universally quantified goals.

The effect of actions which reflect in a change of features of a message have to be preserved during the abstraction process.

These requirements are reflected in the definition of the encoding scheme ω, which is used in MRL to map LLP plan specifications to concepts in a terminological logic.

3.2 THE TERMINOLOGICAL LOGIC

The terminological logic $\mathcal{ALC}$ [Schmidt-Schauß and Smolka, 1991] is chosen as a starting point for the terminological part of the representation formalism for case libraries because of its expressiveness and mathematical properties. Concept descriptions in $\mathcal{ALC}$ are built from concepts, intersection, complements and universal role quantifications. The logic possesses a decidable and complete subsumption algorithm which is PSPACE-complete. This means that deciding subsumption in $\mathcal{ALC}$ is intractable. Remember that we required the retrieval algorithm to be efficient, i.e. to run in polynomial time to cope with the scaling-up problem. To obtain polynomial complexity, two solutions can be adopted:

1. Giving up completeness.
2. Restricting the terminological logic.

Giving up completeness in an application system often also implies giving up correctness, because inability to detect existing subsumption relations may lead to incorrect behavior of the system. In particular for case-based systems, the incompleteness of the retrieval algorithm leads to the following problems:

- Existing cases solving the new case may be not found in the case library. This can lead to an undesirable computational overhead in case-based reasoning because the system does not reuse the best available case during problem solving.

- Uncontrolled growth of the case library may occur. Equivalent cases are added to the library because the incomplete subsumption algorithm is unable to recognize the equivalence of indices.

Therefore, the second solution is adopted by restricting concept descriptions to a *normal form* for which a sound, complete and polynomial subsumption algorithm exists. We define a subset of $\mathcal{ALC}$ comprising so-called *admissible concepts* that are consistent concept descriptions in conjunctive normal form. They are only built from *primitive components*, i.e. existential role restrictions of the form $\exists R.C$ and $\exists R.\neg C$ where C is required to be a primitive concept and R is restricted to be a chain of primitive roles. The following subsumption algorithm is defined for admissible concepts $\mathcal{C}_a$:

Definition 2 $SUBS(u,t) : \mathcal{C}_a^2 \longrightarrow \{true, false\}$

$SUBS(u,t)$ *computes its result using the rules:*[1]

$$z \sqsubseteq x, z \sqsubseteq y \rightarrow z \sqsubseteq x \wedge y \quad (1)$$
$$x \sqsubseteq z \rightarrow x \wedge y \sqsubseteq z \quad (2)$$
$$x \sqsubseteq z, y \sqsubseteq z \rightarrow x \vee y \sqsubseteq z \quad (3)$$
$$z \sqsubseteq x \rightarrow z \sqsubseteq x \vee y \quad (4)$$
$$x \sqsubseteq x \quad (5)$$

Theorem 1 *SUBS is sound, complete and decides the subsumption relation in polynomial time for admissible concepts.*

The proof can be found in [Koehler, 1994b].

The expressiveness of admissible concepts is sufficient to adequately represent the mail domain.[2] As an example, consider the LLP formula

$$\Diamond \, read\_flag(msg(x, mbox)) = T$$

The interpretation of this formula is a *message* at a certain *position* in a particular *mailbox* at a certain *world state*, the *read_flag* of which is set to the value

---

[1] This rule set is equivalent to a sound and complete rule set for lattices given in [Givan and McAllester, 1992] that decides the defined inference relation in polynomial time. Note, that $SUBS(u,t)$ is incomplete for arbitrary concept descriptions in $\mathcal{ALC}$.

[2] This property may not generalize to other application domains, see Section 5.

true. Figure 1 illustrates a subset of the primitive concepts and roles representing the mail domain. Starting with the concept STATE, role chains can be composed, which describe the state of a particular message at a particular position in a particular mailbox at a certain world state. Consequently, the admissible concept

$$\exists \, mbox \circ pos \circ mesg \circ read\_flag.T$$

abstracts the LLP example formula.

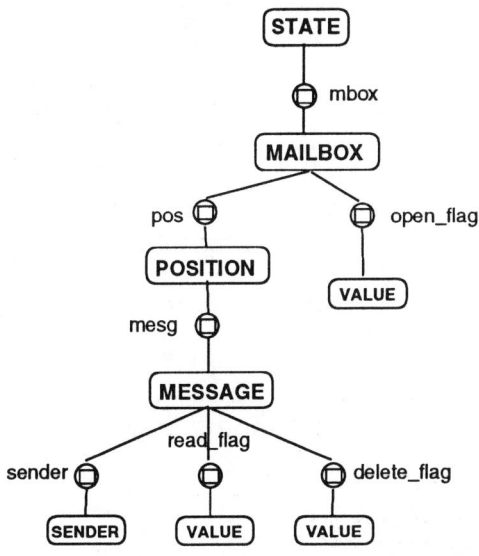

Figure 1: A Subset of the Mail Terminology

3.3 DEFINING THE ENCODING SCHEME

The encoding scheme ω maps LLP plan specifications to indices in $\mathcal{ALC}$ on the basis of the declarative semantics both logics possess. It depends on the source logic LLP as well as on the target logic $\mathcal{ALC}$.

LLP plan specifications are a restricted class of temporal logic formulae containing modal operators. In order to map them to concept descriptions they are translated into first-order predicate logic using the method developed in [Frisch and Scherl, 1991], which has been extended to LLP in [Koehler and Treinen, 1993]. The result of the translation is a formula in a predicate logic with constraints. The constraint theory represents temporal information, e.g. which subgoal has to hold in a particular state. In a next step, the constraint theory is eliminated, preserving the satisfiability of the formula. The elimination of the constraint theory implements a process of temporal abstraction: the temporal information is eliminated from the formula.

The encoding scheme abstracts from specific objects by replacing constants with existentially quantified variables. Furthermore, universal quantification is replaced by the weaker existential quantification. An n-ary function is encoded as an $n+1$-ary relation. Each $n+1$-ary relation is encoded by n binary relations. These abstraction operations are justified by the restricted syntactic structure of terms and formulae.

After the abstraction process has been completed, the conjunctive normal form of preconditions and goals is computed. Of course, the computational effort for this operation grows exponentially with the length of the formulae. But remember that the subsumption algorithm is only complete for concepts in conjunctive normal form. Nevertheless, for pragmatic reasons it is more efficient to compute the normal form only once during the encoding process instead of computing it several times during the classification of an index.

Finally, the remaining set of formulae is syntactically transformed into sets of formulae of the form $\phi_C(x) : \exists y \, P(x,y) \wedge Q(y)$. The declarative semantics of terminological logics allow primitive concepts to be seen as unary predicates and primitive roles to be seen as binary predicates. This identification can be extended to arbitrary concept descriptions, i.e. to every concept C a predicate formula $\phi_C(x)$ can be associated. Consequently, a concept $C : \exists P.Q$ corresponds to the formula $\phi_C(x)$. A model of the formula $\exists x \, \phi_C(x)$ is a model of the concept C and vice versa. In particular, C is unsatisfiable if and only if $\exists x \, \phi_C(x)$ is unsatisfiable [Hollunder et al., 1990].

In the example, the following encoding of preconditions and goals is obtained:[3]

$\omega(pre_{P1})$: $\exists \, mbox \circ open\_flag.T \sqcap$
$\exists \, mbox \circ pos \circ mesg \circ delete\_flag.F$

$\omega(goal_{P1})$: $\exists \, mbox \circ pos \circ mesg \circ read\_flag.T \sqcap$
$\exists \, mbox \circ pos \circ mesg \circ delete\_flag.T$

$\omega(pre_{P2})$: $\exists \, mbox \circ pos \circ mesg \circ delete\_flag.F$

$\omega(goal_{P2})$: $\exists \, mbox \circ pos \circ mesg \circ read\_flag.T \sqcap$
$\exists \, mbox \circ pos \circ mesg \circ delete\_flag.T$

$\omega(pre_{P3})$: $\exists \, mbox \circ open\_flag.T \sqcap$
$[\exists \, mbox \circ pos \circ mesg \circ sender.\neg S \sqcup$
$\exists \, mbox \circ pos \circ mesg \circ delete\_flag.F\,]$

$\omega(goal_{P3})$: $[\exists \, mbox \circ pos \circ mesg \circ sender.\neg S \sqcup$
$\exists \, mbox \circ pos \circ mesg \circ delete\_flag.T\,] \sqcap$
$[\exists \, mbox \circ pos \circ mesg \circ sender.\neg S \sqcup$
$\exists \, mbox \circ pos \circ mesg \circ delete\_flag.T\,]$

3.3.1 Proving the Monotonicity Theorem

To ensure that the retrieval algorithm performs predictably, the monotonicity property has to be proved

---

[3]TRUE is abbreviated to T, FALSE is abbreviated to F, and SENDER is abbreviated to S.

for the encoding scheme used in MRL.

An old plan solving the old planning problem $\langle pre_{old}, goal_{old}\rangle$ is reused as a solution for a new planning problem $\langle pre_{new}, goal_{new}\rangle$ in MRL if

$$pre_{new} \vdash pre_{old} \text{ and } goal_{old} \vdash goal_{new}$$

can be successfully proved in the logic LLP [Koehler, 1994a]. Therefore, we have to prove the following instance of the monotonicity theorem:

Theorem 2
*If $pre_{new} \vdash pre_{old}$ then $\omega(pre_{new}) \sqsubseteq \omega(pre_{old})$ and
if $goal_{old} \vdash goal_{new}$ then $\omega(goal_{old}) \sqsubseteq \omega(goal_{new})$.*

The proof of the theorem can be found in [Koehler, 1994b]. The correctness of the encoding scheme used in MRL relies on the syntactic restrictions which are imposed on terms and formulae. Nevertheless, we believe that the general idea to ground the formalization of abstraction on the definition of an encoding scheme is widely applicable.

3.4 FORMALIZING THE RETRIEVAL

The results of the encoding process are the admissible concepts $\omega(pre)$ and $\omega(goal)$ from which the index of a case is obtained as the pair $\langle \omega(pre), \omega(goal)\rangle$. Now, the *retrieval* of a plan from the plan library is formalized as follows:

Given the description of a new case, the index of this case is computed first. Then, this index is classified in the plan library. Two classification operations are available:

- strong classification
- weak classification

Strong classification classifies the new index by computing the required subsumption relations between encodings of preconditions and goals:

$$\omega(pre_{new}) \sqsubseteq \omega(pre_{old}) \underline{\text{ and }} \omega(goal_{old}) \sqsubseteq \omega(goal_{new})$$

The result of the classification process determines the position of the new index in the plan library. All indices that are subsumed by the new index are considered as potential reuse candidates. The plans belonging to the subsumed indices are assumed to be applicable in the current initial state and to reach all of the current goals.

In the example, *strong classification* of the new index $\langle \omega(pre_{P1}), \omega(goal_{P1})\rangle$ inserts this index at the position shown in Figure 2. Obviously, $\langle \omega(pre_{P2}), \omega(goal_{P2})\rangle$ is subsumed by the new index. According to Definition 1, the planning problem stored in the plan entry related to the index $\omega(P2)$ is more specific than the new planning problem that has to be solved. The plan **P2** is activated as a possible reuse candidate and sent to the plan modification module of MRL [Koehler, 1994a]. The index of plan **P3** does not meet the criteria required by strong classification, since the subsumption test between the goal concepts fails. This plan is not considered as being similar to the desired plan.

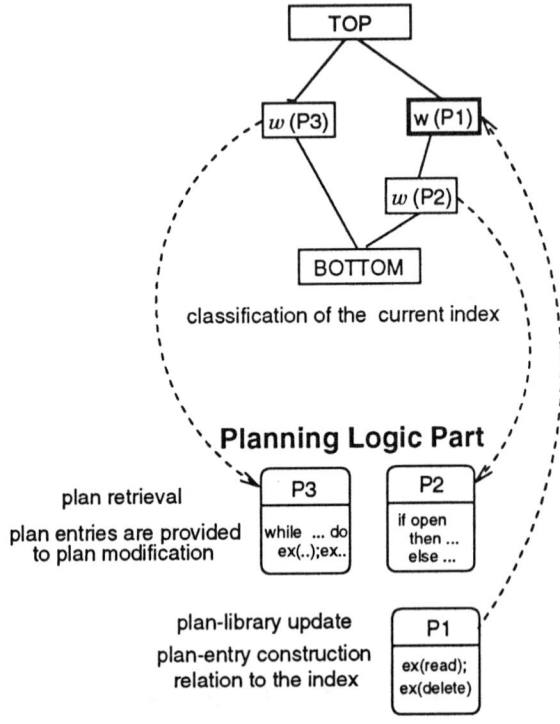

Figure 2: A small Sample Case Library

Weak classification is activated when strong classification *fails* to retrieve a reuse candidate. It is based on a weaker search criterion and can classify according to goals or preconditions:

$$\omega(pre_{new}) \sqsubseteq \omega(pre_{old}) \text{ or } \omega(goal_{old}) \sqsubseteq \omega(goal_{new})$$

Note, that every case that meets the criteria of strong classification also meets the weaker criterion used by weak classification. In the MRL system, plans are reused if they are applicable in the current initial state. Therefore, weak classification in MRL classifies according to preconditions:

$$\omega(pre_{new}) \sqsubseteq \omega(pre_{old})$$

In the example, *weak classification* retrieves **P2** and **P3**, because the subsumption test on the encodings of preconditions is successful. Nevertheless, plan **P3** is considered as being less appropriate for the solution of **P1** than **P2** according to the weaker search criterion.

Figure 2 illustrates the hybrid representation of the plan library in MRL for the example under consideration. The terminological logic part supports the structuring of the plan library. Retrieval and update are grounded on *classification* by computing the subsumption hierarchy of indices. The planning logic part supports the representation of planning knowledge in plan entries.

3.5 RANKING OF CASES

Strong as well as weak classification can retrieve several appropriate reuse candidates from the case library. Consequently, a *ranking* sequence is needed for the candidates in order to find the best one.

Strong classification determines plans from the plan library that are supposed

- to be applicable in the initial state and
- to achieve at least all of the current goals.

This implies that the candidate set retrieved by strong classification may contain plans which achieve superfluous goals, i.e. goals that are currently unnecessary. Actions achieving these goals have to be eliminated from the reused plan by optimizing it. The ranking of the candidates is therefore grounded on an estimation of the *optimization effort* for each candidate. The ranking heuristic estimates the number of superfluous actions that have to be eliminated from the candidate plan.

Observe that the subsumption hierarchy for indices is defined such that a plan $b1$ achieving more atomic goals than a plan $b2$ is placed closer to the *bottom* concept than $b2$. Consequently, the estimated optimization effort for a plan, the index of which is placed closer to the *bottom* concept, is higher than the estimated optimization effort for a plan, the index of which is immediately subsumed by the current index. Therefore, strong classification only adds a case to the solution set, if its index is immediately subsumed by the current index.

The estimation of the optimization effort proceeds as follows:

- The ranking heuristic compares the goal concept of the current index $\omega(goal_{new})$ with the goal concepts of all immediately subsumed indices $\omega(goal_{old_i})$.
- It computes the number of primitive components, which occur in $\omega(goal_{old_i})$, but not in $\omega(goal_{new})$.
- The case with the smallest number is selected as the best candidate according to the ranking heuristic.

The heuristic estimates the number of atomic subgoals that are achieved by a candidate plan but that are not required in the current plan specification. It assumes that this number reflects the minimal number of primitive actions in the candidate plan that have to be eliminated. Therefore, the plan with the smallest number is selected as the best reuse candidate and sent to the plan modification module. If several candidates receive the same ranking value, one of them is selected arbitrarily.

Definition 3 *Let $C_{old_1}, \ldots, C_{old_n}$ be the set of candidates retrieved by strong classification of $\omega(C_{new})$. The goal concepts occurring in the indices of the candidates are $\omega(goal_{old_1}), \ldots, \omega(goal_{old_n})$, the goal concept occurring in the current index is $\omega(goal_{new})$. The set of primitive components that occurs in a concept c is denoted by $\mathsf{PK}[c]$, while their number is denoted by $\mathsf{N}[c]$.*

The optimization effort for each candidate is defined as

$$OPT_{\omega(goal_{old_i})} = \mathsf{N}\Big[\mathsf{PK}[\omega(goal_{old_i})] \setminus \mathsf{PK}[\omega(goal_{new})]\Big]$$

The ranking heuristic $\mathcal{H}_{OPT}$ selects the candidate with the smallest optimization effort:

$$\mathcal{H}_{OPT} = \Big\{ C_{old_i} | OPT_{\omega(goal_{old_i})} = \\ min\Big(OPT_{\omega(goal_{old_1})}, \ldots, OPT_{\omega(goal_{old_n})}\Big)\Big\}$$

Weak classification determines plans from the plan library that are only supposed to be applicable in the initial state.

The goal concepts of the candidate plans can be related to the goal concept of the current case in two ways:

1. $\omega(goal_{new}) \sqsubseteq \omega(goal_{old})$
   This means that we can expect the candidate plan to achieve only a subset of the goals required in the current case.

2. $\omega(goal_{new}) \not\sqsubseteq \omega(goal_{old})$ and $\omega(goal_{old}) \not\sqsubseteq \omega(goal_{new})$
   No subsumption relation holds for the goal concepts of the candidate and the current case. We have to expect that the candidate achieves other goals than those required in the current plan specification.

Therefore, the ranking heuristic for candidates retrieved by weak classification relies on the following assumptions:

- Every candidate is applicable in the current initial state.
- No candidate achieves all of the current goals, i.e. every candidate has to be modified.

Consequently, the heuristic estimates the *modification effort* for each candidate as follows:

- The ranking heuristic compares the goal concept of the current index $\omega(goal_{new})$ with the goal concepts $\omega(goal_{old_i})$ of all indices occurring in the solution set.
- It computes the intersection of the concepts, i.e. the number of primitive components occurring in $\omega(goal_{new})$ as well as in $\omega(goal_{old_i})$.
- This number measures the modification effort by an estimation of the number of current atomic goals that are achieved by each candidate.

The candidate with the biggest number is selected as being the best reuse candidate, because it is assigned the highest "success rate" and therefore its modification effort is estimated as being minimal. Furthermore, the ranking heuristic verifies whether the ranking value of the best candidate exceeds a lower bound: it requires that at least half of the primitive components from $\omega(goal_{new})$ must be contained in $\omega(goal_{old_i})$. If this condition is satisfied, the ranking heuristic assumes that the best candidate achieves at least half of the current atomic goals.[4]

Definition 4 *Let* $C_{old_1}, \ldots, C_{old_n}$ *be the set of candidates retrieved by weak classification of* $\omega(C_{new})$. *The goal concepts occurring in the indices of the candidates are* $\omega(goal_{old_1}), \ldots, \omega(goal_{old_n})$, *the goal concept occurring in the current index is* $\omega(goal_{new})$. *The set of primitive components that occurs in a concept c is denoted by* $\mathsf{PK}[c]$, *while their number is denoted by* $\mathsf{N}[c]$.

The estimated success rate for each candidate is defined as:

$$MOD_{\omega(goal_{old_i})} = \mathsf{N}\Big[\mathsf{PK}[\omega(goal_{old_i})] \cap \mathsf{PK}[\omega(goal_{new})]\Big]$$

The ranking heuristic $\mathcal{H}_{MOD}$ *selects the candidate with the biggest success rate that exceeds the lower bound:*

$$\mathcal{H}_{MOD} = \Big\{ C_{old_i} \mid MOD_{\omega(goal_{old_i})} = \\ max\Big(MOD_{\omega(goal_{old_1})}, \ldots, MOD_{\omega(goal_{old_n})}\Big) \\ and \\ MOD_{\omega(goal_{old_i})} \geq \frac{\mathsf{N}[\omega(goal_{new})]}{2} \Big\}$$

If no candidate receives a ranking value which exceeds the lower bound, all candidates are rejected because their modification effort is too costly. In this situation, case-based planning reports a failure and planning from scratch with the PHI planner is activated.

The ranking heuristics guide the interaction between case-based planning and plan generation, see Figure 3. Plan generation is activated when

---
[4]The definition of an appropriate lower bound may differ for different case-based planning systems.

- no candidate can be retrieved from the library,
- the modification effort is estimated as being too costly for all potential candidates.

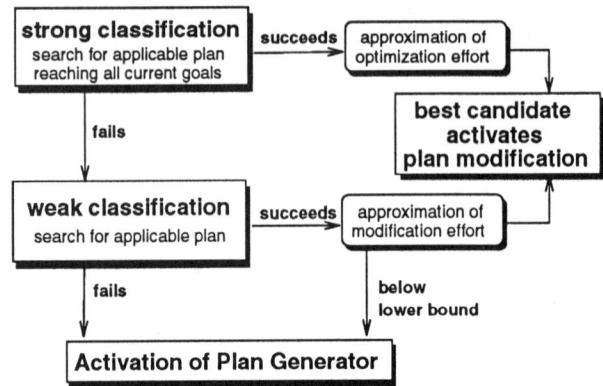

Figure 3: Heuristic Guidance of Case-based Planning

The *update* of the plan library is activated when

- no reusable plan is found and planning from scratch is performed,
- the retrieved plan has to be optimized or modified.

During the update of the plan library a new plan entry is built. Three sources of information are available: the formal plan specification C_{new}, the generated or modified plan S_{new} and the proofs performed during deductive plan generation and plan modification [Koehler, 1994a]. The plan entry is built out of C_{new}, S_{new} and information that is extracted from the proofs. It is related to its index $\omega(P_{new})$ that was already computed and classified during the retrieval process. The index determines the position of the new plan entry in the plan library. It is now available for a subsequent case-based planning process.

4 IMPLEMENTATION

The system MRL has been implemented as an integrated part of the PHI system in SICSTUS Prolog. The plan library can be *static* as well as *dynamic*:

A static library comprises user-predefined typical plans. The system retrieves these plans for reuse, but does not add new plans to the library. A dynamic plan library grows during the lifetime of the system. MRL starts with an empty library and incrementally adds new plan entries to it. The system thus automatically builds a taxonomy of abstract descriptions of typical planning problems that occur in the application domain.

The application of terminological logics leads to remarkable properties of the system:

The mapping of specific planning problems to abstract classes helps to keep the plan library small. Only one representative for each class is added to the plan library. Instances of planning problems which belong to the same class can be solved by instantiation or easy modification of the retrieved candidate plan. Furthermore, the implementation of the representational shift from specific planning problems to abstract problem classes with the help of the encoding scheme requires only marginal computational costs.

The polynomial complexity of the subsumption algorithms leads to an efficient retrieval of candidate plans in polynomial time, cf. [Koehler, 1994b].

The completeness of the subsumption algorithm ensures that existing solutions are found in the plan library. This leads to efficiency gains of the case-based planner compared to the generative planner because the system can reuse any solution that exists in the plan library.

5 RELATED WORK

Recently, the representation of plans based on terminological knowledge-representation systems has led to several approaches, which extend terminological logics with new application-oriented representational primitives for the representation of actions and plans.

One such an extension is the system RAT [Heinsohn et al., 1991] which is based on $\mathcal{KRIS}$ [Baader et al., 1992]. RAT is able to implement reasoning about plans by inferences in the underlying terminological logic. The system simulates the execution of plans, verifies the applicability of plans in particular situations and solves tasks of temporal projection.

An application of terminological logics to tasks of plan recognition is developed in T-REX [Weida and Litman, 1994]. Plans in T-REX may contain conditions and iterations as well as non-determinism in the form of disjunctive actions.

More complex application domains may require the integration of more expressive terminological logics into the hybrid representation formalism for case libraries. A future direction of work is the integration of stochastic approaches and the parallelization of the search. A successful application of a probabilistic method for NP-complete inference problems is described in [Selman et al., 1992]. The usefulness of non-systematic search strategies in planning is demonstrated in [Langley, 1992; Minton et al., 1992].

6 CONCLUSION

We have presented an application of terminological logics as a kind of query language in case-based reasoning. Indices are built from concept descriptions.

The retrieval and update operations working on case libraries are formalized as classification operations over the taxonomy of indices.

An example taken from the field of case-based planning demonstrates the applicability of the theoretical framework. The behavior of the case-based planner becomes predictable and theoretical properties like the correctness, completeness and efficiency of the retrieval algorithm can be proved.

Acknowledgements

I am indebted to Wolfgang Wahlster for his advice and support. I wish to thank Hans-Jürgen Profitlich who helped me test the practical feasibility of the approach with the development of a prototypical plan library in RAT, and Bernhard Nebel and Hans-Jürgen Ohlbach for fruitful discussions regarding the theoretical properties of the formalism. Werner Nutt and the anonymous referees made helpful comments on a draft version of this paper.

References

J.A. Allen, R. Fikes, and E. Sandewall, editors. *Proceedings of the 2nd International Conference on Principles of Knowledge Representation and Reasoning*, Cambridge, MA, April 1991. Morgan Kaufmann.

F. Baader, B. Hollunder, B. Nebel, H.-J. Profitlich, and E. Franconi. An empirical analysis of optimization techniques for terminological representation systems, or making KRIS get a move on. In Nebel et al. 1992, pages 270–281.

M. Bauer, S. Biundo, D. Dengler, J. Koehler, and G. Paul. PHI - a logic-based tool for intelligent help systems. In IJCAI-93, pages 460–466.

S. Biundo and D. Dengler. The logical language for planning LLP. Research Report, German Research Center for Artificial Intelligence, 1994.

S. Biundo, D. Dengler, and J. Koehler. Deductive planning and plan reuse in a command language environment. In Neumann 1992, pages 628–632.

R. Brachman. Structured inheritance networks. In W. Woods and R. Brachman, editors, *Research in Natural Language Understanding*, pages 36–78. Bolt, Beranek, and Newman Inc., Cambridge Mass., 1978.

R. Brachmann and H. Levesque. The tractability of subsumption in frame based description languages. *Proceedings of the 4th National Conference of the American Association for Artificial Intelligence*, pages 34–37, Austin, TX, 1984. MIT Press.

CBR-91 *Proceedings of the 3rd Case-Based Reasoning Workshop*, Washington, D.C., 1991. Morgan Kaufman, San Mateo.

CBR-93 *Proceedings of the AAAI-93 Workshop on Case-Based Reasoning*, number WS-93-01 in AAAI Technical Report, Washington, D.C., 1993. AAAI Press, Menlo Park.

E.A. Feigenbaum. The simulation of natural learning behavior. In E.A. Feigenbaum and J. Feldman, editors, *Computers and Thought*. Mc Graw-Hill, New York, 1963.

A. M. Frisch and R. B. Scherl. A general framework for modal deduction. In Allen et al. 1992, pages 196–207.

R. Givan and D. McAllester. New results on local inference relations. In Nebel et al. 1992, pages 403–412.

J. Heinsohn, D. Kudenko, B. Nebel, and H.-J. Profitlich. Integration of action representation in terminological logics. In C. Peltason, K. Luck, and C. Kindermann, editors, *Proceedings of the Terminological Logic Users Workshop*. KIT–Report 95, TU Berlin, Germany, 1991.

B. Hollunder, W. Nutt, and M. Schmidt-Schauß. Subsumption algorithms for concept description languages. In L.C. Aiello, editor, *Proceedings of the 9th European Conference on Artificial Intelligence*, pages 348–353, Stockholm, Sweden, August 1990. Clays Ltd, England.

IJCAI-93 *Proceedings of the 13th International Joint Conference on Artificial Intelligence*, Chambery, France, August 1993. Morgan Kaufmann.

H. Kautz and B. Selman. Planning as satisfiability. In Neumann 1992, pages 359–363.

J. Koehler and R. Treinen. Constraint deduction in an interval-based temporal logic. In *Working Notes of the AAAI Symposium on Automated Deduction in Nonstandard Logics*. AAAI Press, Menlo Park, 1993.

J. Koehler. Flexible plan reuse in a formal framework. In C. Bäckström and E. Sandewall, editors, *Current Trends in AI Planning*. IOS Press, Amsterdam, Washington, Tokyo, 1994.

J. Koehler. *Reuse of Plans in Deductive Planning Systems*. PhD thesis, University of Saarland, 1994. in German.

J. Kolodner. *Case-Based Reasoning*. Morgan Kaufman, 1993.

P. Langley. Systematic and nonsystematic search strategies. In *Proceedings of the 1st International Conference on Artificial Intelligence Planning Systems*, pages 145–152, Washington, D.C., 1992. Morgan Kaufmann, San Mateo.

S. Minton, M. Drummond, J. Bresina, and A. Philips. Total order vs. partial order planning: Factors influencing performance. In Nebel et al. 1992, pages 83–92.

B. Nebel and J. Koehler. Plan modification versus plan generation: A complexity-theoretic perspective. In IJCAI-93, pages 1436–1441.

B. Nebel and J. Koehler. Plan reuse versus plan generation: A theoretical and empirical analysis. Research Report RR-93-33, German Research Center for Artificial Intelligence (DFKI), 1993.

B. Nebel, W. Swartout, and C. Rich, editors. *Proceedings of the 3rd International Conference on Principles of Knowledge Representation and Reasoning*, Cambridge, MA, October 1992. Morgan Kaufmann.

B. Neumann, editor. *Proceedings of the 10th European Conference on Artificial Intelligence*, Vienna, Austria, August 1992. John Wiley & Sons.

C.K. Riesbeck and R.C. Schank. *Inside Case-based Reasoning*. Lawrence Erlbaum Associates, Hillsdale, New Jersey, 1989.

M. Schmidt-Schauß and G. Smolka. Attributive concept descriptions with complements. *Artificial Intelligence*, 48:1–26, 1991.

B. Selman, H. Levesque, and D. Mitchell. A new method for solving hard satisfiability problems. In *Proceedings of the 10th National Conference of the American Association for Artificial Intelligence*, pages 440–446, San Jose, CA, July 1992. MIT Press.

S. Slade. Case-based reasoning: A research paradigm. *The AI Magazine*, 12(1):43–55, 1989.

R. Weida and D. Litman. Subsumption and recognition of heterogeneous constraint networks. In *Proceedings of the Tenth IEEE Conference on Artificial Intelligence for Applications*, 1994. to appear.

Risk-Sensitive Planning with Probabilistic Decision Graphs

Sven Koenig
School of Computer Science
Carnegie Mellon University
Pittsburgh, PA 15213-3891

Reid G. Simmons
School of Computer Science
Carnegie Mellon University
Pittsburgh, PA 15213-3891

Abstract

Probabilistic AI planning methods that minimize expected execution cost have a neutral attitude towards risk. We demonstrate how one can transform planning problems for risk-sensitive agents into equivalent ones for risk-neutral agents provided that exponential utility functions are used. The transformed planning problems can then be solved with these existing AI planning methods. To demonstrate our ideas, we use a probabilistic planning framework ("probabilistic decision graphs") that can easily be mapped into Markov decision problems. It allows one to describe probabilistic effects of actions, actions with different costs (resource consumption), and goal states with different rewards. We show the use of probabilistic decision graphs for finding optimal plans for risk-sensitive agents in a stochastic blocksworld domain.

1 Introduction

In recent years, numerous planning methods have been developed that are able to deal with stochastic domains.[1] Consider the stochastic domains for which it is easy to construct plans that always reach a given goal for sure (at least, in the limit). Then, one needs a criterion for choosing among these plans. Such a metric is for example the execution cost of the plans: One quantifies the "resource consumption" (for example, time, energy, or money) of an action with a single real number that depends only on the action, the state it is executed in, and the resulting state. Then, the execution cost of a plan is defined to be the sum of the resource consumption costs of all actions executed from the time at which the agent begins until it stops in a goal state.

Since the execution cost of a probabilistic plan can vary from plan execution to plan execution, almost all probabilistic planning methods that take execution cost into account use the *expected* execution cost as ranking criterion: Out of all plans that guarantee to achieve the given goal, they choose the one that minimizes the expected execution cost (when optimizing) or one whose expected execution cost is smaller than a given number (when satisficing). Since they do not take the variance of the execution cost into account, they assume that the agent that executes the plan has a risk-neutral attitude.

However, people are usually not risk-neutral. A risk-seeking agent ("gambler") is willing to accept a plan with a larger expected execution cost if the uncertainty is increased and vice versa for a risk-averse agent ("insurance holder"): If a plan is executed only once (or a small number of times), then — among all plans with the same expected execution cost — the larger the variance of the execution cost, the larger the chance to do much better than average. Of course, the chance to do much worse rises as well.

Imagine, for example, that your task is to design a robot for the annual AAAI robot competition, where it has to complete a given task (for example, "find the coffee pot") in as short a time as possible. You want the robot to win the competition, but — in case it loses — do not care whether it makes second or last place. You know that your robot is not much faster than your competitors' robots, maybe even a bit slower, but cannot assess the capabilities of the other robots in enough detail to use them for determining the utilities of the various task completion times of your robot. In this case, you probably want your robot to take chances, and thus a risk-seeking attitude should be built into the robot's planning mechanism.

It is possible to achieve a risk-sensitive attitude by ranking plans not according to their expected execution costs, but according to their expected execution costs plus or minus a fraction of the variances [Filar et al., 1989] [Karakoulas, 1993], or by searching for plans whose execution costs are optimal in the best or worst case ("nature acts like a friend or enemy") [Heger and Karsten, 1992] [Heger, 1994], see also [Moore and Atkeson, 1993]. However, utility theory [von Neumann and Morgenstern, 1947] — a subfield of decision

---
[1]Examples of probabilistic planning methods include [Smith, 1988], [Bresina and Drummond, 1990], [Christiansen and Goldberg, 1990], [Hansson et al., 1990], [Koenig, 1991], [Dean et al., 1993], [Kushmerick et al., 1993], and many others.

theory — provides a normative framework for making decisions according to a given risk attitude, provided that the agent accepts a few simple axioms and has unlimited planning resources available. The key result of utility theory is that, for every attitude towards risk, there exists a utility function that transforms costs c into real values $u(c)$ ("utilities") such that it is rational to maximize expected utility. Its application to planning problems has been studied by [Etzioni, 1991], [Russell and Wefald, 1991], [Haddawy and Hanks, 1992], [Wellman and Doyle, 1992], [Goodwin and Simmons, 1992], and others. Therefore, we would like to stay within this framework.

In this paper, we describe a planning framework ("probabilistic decision graphs") that can easily be mapped into Markov decision problems and of which cost-annotated decision trees (the kind used in utility theory) are a special case. It allows one to describe probabilistic effects of actions, actions with different costs (resource consumption), and goal states with different rewards (goodness). We show that replacing all costs and rewards with their respective utilities, but leaving the planning mechanism unchanged, usually leads to erroneous results. Furthermore, the best action to execute in a state can depend on the total cost that the agent has already accumulated when deciding on the action.

For utility functions of a certain class, however, planning problems for risk-sensitive agents can be transformed into equivalent planning problems for risk-neutral agents which can then be solved with dynamic programming methods or probabilistic AI planning methods that minimize (or satisfice) expected execution cost. The transformation has the property that the better a plan is for the transformed, risk-neutral planning problem, the better it is for the original, risk-sensitive planning problem as well. Our approach builds on previous work by [Howard and Matheson, 1972] in the context of Markov decision theory. A blocks-world example is used to illustrate our ideas and show how the optimal plan depends on the degree of risk-sensitivity of the agent.

2 The Planning Framework

The following representation of probabilistic planning problems was used in [Koenig, 1991]. A similar framework has recently been used by [Dean et al., 1993] and is commonly used for table-based reinforcement learning.

Planning is done in a state space. S is its finite set of states, $s_0 \in S$ the start state, and $G \subseteq S$ a set of goal states. A plan determines at every point in time which action the agent has to execute in its current state. In a goal state s, the agent receives a (positive or negative) one-time goal reward[2] $r[s]$ and then has to terminate. The goal rewards reflect that different goal states can be of different value

---

[2]From here on, we use the terms "rewards" and "costs" as follows: Rewards can be positive or negative values, but costs are *always* negative values.

to the agent. However, to keep the following discussion simple, we will use only planning examples for which all goal rewards are zero. In a non-goal state s, the agent can choose an action a from a finite set of actions $A(s)$. Nature then determines the outcome of the action with a coin flip: with transition probability $p^a[s, s']$, the agent incurs an action cost $c^a[s, s'] < 0$ and is in successor state s'. Thus, we assume that the outcomes of all action executions are mutually independent given the current state of the agent (Markov property). The action costs reflect the resources consumed, for example, time needed or effort spent. We assume that the values of all parameters are completely known and do not change over time. We do not assume, however, that the planner uses a planning approach that operates in the state space (instead of, say, the space of partial plans).

For a given plan, we define the probability of goal achievement of state s as the probability with which the agent eventually reaches a goal state if it is started in s and obeys the plan. If this probability equals one, we say that the plan solves s. A plan that solves the start state is called admissible. In the risk-neutral case, a plan is evaluated according to the expected total reward of the start state. The expected total reward $v[s]$ of state s for a given plan is the expected sum of the reward of the goal state and the total cost of the actions that are executed from the time at which the agent is started in s until it stops in a goal state (given that it obeys the plan). Similarly, the expected total utility $u[s]$ of state s is the expected utility of the sum of the goal reward and the total cost of the executed actions.

The planning framework described above is very general. For example, one can easily represent goal states in which the agent does not have to stop (that is, goal states that the agent can leave in order to reach a different goal state that has a larger goal reward). This is necessary if one wants unsolvable states to have an expected total reward that is finite instead of minus infinity. One could, for example, allow the agent to stop in *any* state, but penalize it for stopping in a non-goal state. (In this case, all non-goal states must be converted to goal states that have a very small goal reward and can be left again.)

For risk-neutral agents, the planning framework is isomorphic to Markov decision problems [Mine and Osaki, 1970]. A state-action mapping ("stationary, deterministic policy") specifies for every state the action that the agent has to execute when it is in that state. For Markov decision problems, one can restrict plans to state-action mappings without losing optimality.

We use an easier-to-depict representation for probabilistic planning problems here, which we call "probabilistic decision graphs", that resembles the kind of decision trees that are used in utility theory. Its building blocks are shown in Figure 1. Every state corresponds to a (large) circle. The large circle of a non-goal state s contains a decision tree that consists of a decision node (square) followed by chance nodes (small circles), one for every $a \in A(s)$. Transition probabilities and action costs are specified for every

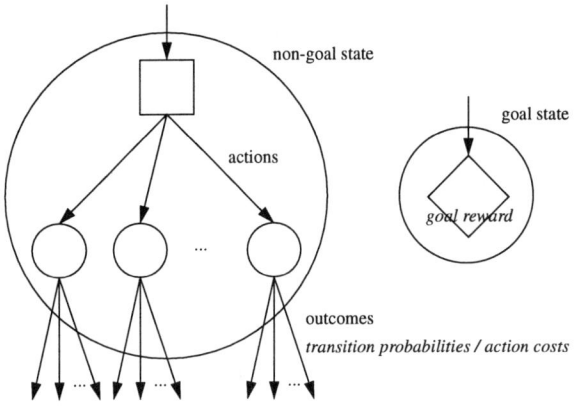

Figure 1: Building Blocks

outcome of the actions. The circle of a goal state contains a value node (diamond) for the goal reward. To represent a planning problem, these building blocks have to be connected so that there are no dangling outcome arrows. In addition, the start state is marked with an incoming arrow that has no source state and is labeled "start."

Note that probabilistic decision graphs can have cycles: cycles do not imply that a decision depends on itself, but that a decision depends on the same decision made at an earlier point in time. In the following, we will distinguish two simplifications of this planning framework, namely *acyclic* probabilistic decision graphs and the even simpler acyclic probabilistic decision graphs *without shared subtrees* ("cost-annotated decision trees"). The last two varieties are commonly used in utility theory.

3 The Problem

We suspect that researchers have largely ignored the question of how to incorporate risk-sensitive attitudes into their planning mechanisms because they assume that by replacing all costs and rewards with their respective utilities (for an appropriate utility function) one can achieve risk-sensitive attitudes without changing the planning mechanisms. In the following, we use acyclic probabilistic decision graphs to demonstrate that this is not necessarily the case after reviewing how to use dynamic programming techniques to determine optimal plans for risk-neutral agents.

3.1 Planning for Risk-Neutral Agents

A risk-neutral agent has to solve planning task PT1: given a complete specification of the planning problem, find a plan for which the start state has the largest expected total reward.

An optimal state-action mapping for planning task PT1 can be determined in polynomial time with dynamic programming techniques. To solve an *acyclic* probabilistic decision graph, we could transform it as follows: First, we propagate the action costs to the value nodes. This amounts to duplicating shared subtrees, since every path from the start state to a goal state needs to have its own value node. The resulting decision tree can then be solved in time linear in its size: the expected total reward of a value node is the sum of its goal reward and the accumulated costs, the expected total reward of a chance node is the average over the expected total rewards of its successor nodes weighted with the transition probabilities, and the expected total reward of a decision node is the maximum of the expected total rewards of its successor nodes. The action that achieves the maximum is the optimal decision for the decision node. The expected total reward $v[s]$ of a (non-goal) state s is equal to the expected total reward of the decision node that it contains, and the optimal action $a[s]$ for the state is the same one that is optimal for its decision node.

The transformation outlined above can be done in linear time if no subtrees are shared. However, if subtrees are shared, it is expensive, since the number of paths — and therefore the size of the transformed decision tree — can be exponential in the number of states of the original tree. Fortunately, it is well known that the following dynamic programming technique ("[averaging-out-and-]folding-back") solves acyclic probabilistic decision graphs for risk-neutral agents on the original tree in linear time, that is, without duplicating shared subtrees.

$$v[s] := \begin{cases} r[s] & \text{for } s \in G \\ \max_{a \in A(s)} \sum_{s' \in S} p^a[s,s'](c^a[s,s'] + v[s']) & \text{otherwise} \end{cases}$$

$$a[s] := \arg\max_{a \in A(s)} \sum_{s' \in S} p^a[s,s'](c^a[s,s'] + v[s'])$$
$$\text{for } s \in S \setminus G$$

Thus, one evaluates every subtree only once and the runtime of the algorithm is linear in the size of the original decision tree. Dynamic programming algorithms, such as this one, can be used to solve planning task PT1, because the Markov property holds for all states: the expected total reward $v[s]$ of every state (and thus the optimal action $a[s]$ for the state) is independent of how the agent reached the state.

3.2 Planning for Risk-Sensitive Agents

A risk-sensitive agent has to solve planning task PT2: given a utility function and a complete specification of the planning problem, find a plan for which the start state has the largest expected total utility.

Planning task PT2 can be solved for probabilistic decision graphs without action costs by first replacing all goal rewards with their respective utilities and then using any planning method for risk-neutral agents. In reality, however, the probabilistic decision graphs of planning task PT2

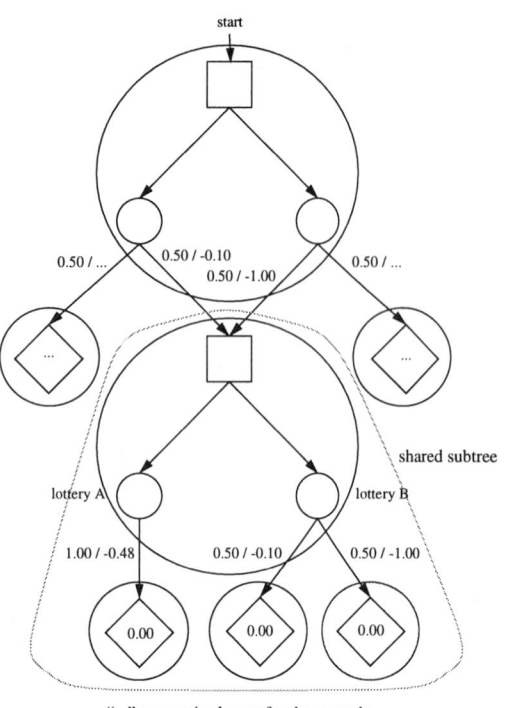
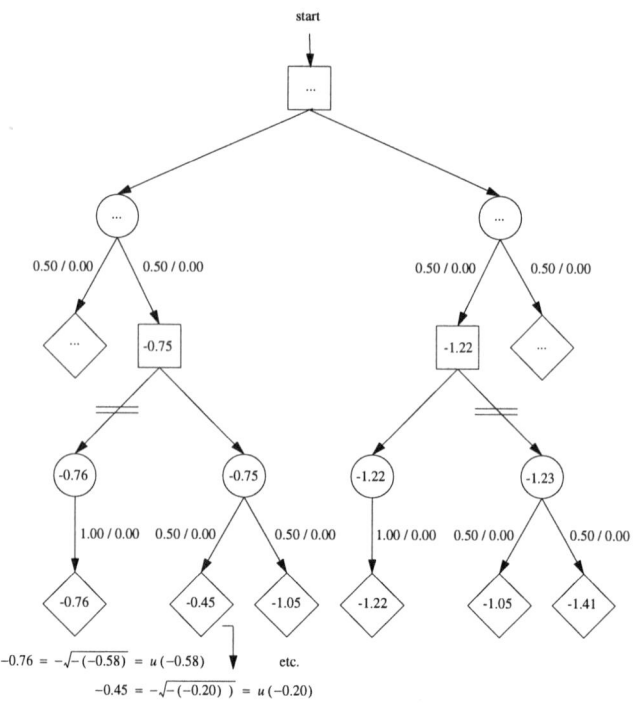

Figure 2: A Planning Problem with a Shared Subtree

Figure 3: Solution for a Risk-Sensitive Agent

do have action costs. Similarly to how we proceeded earlier for risk-neutral agents, we could first propagate the action costs to the value nodes (which involves duplicating shared subtrees if they exist). Next, all rewards at the value nodes are replaced with their respective utilities. Finally, folding-back is used to determine an optimal plan. Remember that this method has an exponential run-time in the worst case (and is not directly applicable to cyclic probabilistic decision graphs). As an example, consider the partly specified planning problem shown in Figure 2. This planning problem contains a shared subtree that represents the choice between a deterministic lottery[3] A (reward -0.48 for sure) and a non-deterministic lottery B (rewards -0.10 and -1.00 with equal probability). The application of folding-back on this planning problem for a risk-seeking agent with utility function $u(c) = -\sqrt{-c}$ (for $c \leq 0$) is shown in Figure 3. (Actions that are sub-optimal are "crossed out" with two horizontal lines.)

It is not optimal to simply replace all costs and rewards with their respective utilities and then use folding-back on the resulting tree, because in general $u(c_1+c_2) \neq u(c_1)+u(c_2)$ for two rewards c_1 and c_2 (that is, the value function is no longer time-additive). In fact, dynamic programming methods can no longer be used *in any way* without considering the total action cost that the agent has already accumulated when

---

[3]"Lottery" is a term from utility theory. A lottery is recursively defined to be either a reward that is received for sure (that is, with probability one) or a probability distribution over lotteries.

deciding on the actions, because the Markov property does not necessarily hold for risk-sensitive agents [Raiffa, 1968].

Consider again the planning problem from Figure 2. As demonstrated in Figure 3 for $u(c) = -\sqrt{-c}$, the agent should choose lottery B if it has already accumulated action costs of -0.10 when deciding between the two lotteries. However, if the accumulated action costs are -1.00, it should prefer lottery A. This can be explained as follows: The agent is risk-seeking, since its utility function $-\sqrt{-c}$ is convex, but the convexity decreases the more negative c gets. The action costs that the agent has already accumulated have to be added to all rewards of a lottery. For example, if the accumulated action costs are -0.10, then lottery B becomes "rewards -0.20 and -1.10 with equal probability." If the agent has already accumulated cost -1.0, then lottery B becomes "rewards -1.10 and -2.00 with equal probability." Thus, the more action costs the agent accumulates, the more negative the total rewards become and the less risk-seeking the agent is. Since the agent accumulates more and more action costs over time, it becomes less and less risk-seeking.

This problem makes planning very inefficient. One can circumvent it with planning methods that have a limited look-ahead. The planner of [Kanazawa and Dean, 1989], for example, determines the plan that generates the largest expected total utility in the first n steps, executes the first action of the plan, and repeats. Such planning methods still duplicate shared subtrees (since they "unroll" the underlying Markov decision problem), but one can now control the amount of work required for one iteration by varying the look-ahead n. These, and related heuristic planning methods, suffer from the limited horizon problem and their success depends critically on the structure of the planning task.

4 A Solution

Our proposed method for incorporating risk-sensitive attitudes involves transforming planning task PT2 into a planning task PT3, which can then be solved with any standard (that is, risk-neutral) planning method. The resulting, optimal plan for planning task PT3 is optimal for the risk-sensitive planning task PT2 as well. The key to accomplishing this task is to utilize utility functions that maintain the Markov property.

Consider utility functions with the following property (called "constant local risk aversion" [Pratt, 1964] or "delta property" [Howard and Matheson, 1972]): if all rewards of an arbitrary lottery are increased by an arbitrary amount, then the certainty equivalent of the lottery is increased by this amount as well. (If the expected utility of a lottery is x, then $u^{-1}(x)$ is called its certainty equivalent.) The only utility functions with this property are the identity function, convex exponential functions $u(c) = \gamma^c$ for $\gamma > 1$, concave exponential functions $u(c) = -\gamma^c$ for $0 < \gamma < 1$, and their strictly positively linear transformations [Watson and Buede, 1987]. Since these utility functions are parameterized with a parameter γ, one can express a whole spectrum of risk-sensitivity, ranging from being strongly risk-averse to being strongly risk-seeking. The larger γ, the more risk-seeking the agent is, and vice versa. For γ approaching infinity, for example, the agent is "extremely risk-seeking": it assumes (wrongly) that nature does not flip coins to determine the outcomes of its actions, but makes the ones happen from which the agent benefits most [Koenig and Simmons, 1993]. Similarly, for γ approaching zero – the other extreme case – the agent thinks that nature hurts it as much as it can. Such "extremely risk-averse agents" believe in Murphy's law: If anything can go wrong, it will. They have recently been studied in the AI literature by [Moore and Atkeson, 1993] and [Heger, 1994].

These utility functions have the advantage that they maintain the Markov property [Howard and Matheson, 1972]: if the agent executes an action in its current state and behaves optimally afterwards, then it faces a lottery. There is one lottery for every action that the agent can execute in its current state. The lottery with the largest expected utility or, equivalently, the largest certainty equivalent identifies the optimal action. Before determining the certainty equivalents, however, one has to add the action costs that the agent has already accumulated to all (goal) rewards of every lottery. This increases the certainty equivalent of every lottery by the same amount (namely, the accumulated action costs), since the utility function has the delta property. Thus, when comparing lotteries, one can ignore the accumulated action costs.

[Howard and Matheson, 1972] apply utility functions with the delta property to Markov decision problems with finite and infinite time horizons. In the later case, they assume a non-goal oriented task, and every state-action mapping has to determine an irreducible (that is, strongly connected) Markov chain. As shown in [Koenig and Simmons, 1994], their analysis can be applied to non-goal oriented planning and reinforcement learning tasks if the agent is risk-sensitive towards variations of the reward that it receives per action execution. Unfortunately, our goal-oriented planning task PT2 does not possess the properties required by Howard and Matheson, and thus we cannot use their methods and proofs unchanged.

4.1 Planning for Risk-Seeking Agents

In the following, we will temporarily restrict our attention to risk-seeking agents with utility function $u(c) = \gamma^c$ (or any strictly positively linear transformation thereof) for risk parameter $\gamma > 1$. For these utility functions, we show how to calculate the expected total utility of a given plan. Then, we will transform the planning problem into one for a risk-neutral agent and show how to solve it.

4.1.1 Calculating the Expected Total Utility of a Plan

Assume that, for some planning problem, a plan (that is, a state-action mapping) is given that assigns action $a[s]$ to non-goal state s. The expected total utility of this plan, that is, the expected total utility $u[s_0]$ of its start state s_0, can recursively be calculated as follows.

The (expected) total utility of a goal state s is $u[s] = u(r[s]) = \gamma^{r[s]}$. After the agent has executed action $a[s]$ in a non-goal state s, it incurs action cost $c^{a[s]}[s, s']$ and is in successor state s' with probability $p^{a[s]}[s, s']$. In state s', it faces a lottery again. This lottery has expected total utility $u[s']$ and certainty equivalent $u^{-1}(u[s']) = \log_\gamma u[s']$. According to the axioms of utility theory, the lottery can be replaced with its certainty equivalent. Then, the agent incurs a total reward of $c^{a[s]}[s, s'] + u^{-1}(u[s'])$ with probability $p^{a[s]}[s, s']$. Thus, the expected total utility of s can be calculated as follows:[4]

$$\begin{aligned}
u[s] &= \sum_{s' \in S} p^{a[s]}[s, s'] u(c^{a[s]}[s, s'] + u^{-1}(u[s'])) \\
&= \sum_{s' \in S} p^{a[s]}[s, s'] \gamma^{c^{a[s]}[s,s'] + u^{-1}(u[s'])} \\
&= \sum_{s' \in S} p^{a[s]}[s, s'] \gamma^{c^{a[s]}[s,s']} \gamma^{u^{-1}(u[s'])} \\
&= \sum_{s' \in S} p^{a[s]}[s, s'] \gamma^{c^{a[s]}[s,s']} u[s'] \\
&= \sum_{s' \in S \setminus G} p^{a[s]}[s, s'] \gamma^{c^{a[s]}[s,s']} u[s']
\end{aligned}$$

---

[4]This corresponds to the policy-evaluation step in [Howard and Matheson, 1972] with the "certain equivalent gain" $\bar{g} = 0$.

$$+ \sum_{s' \in G} p^{a[s]}[s,s'] \gamma^{c^{a[s]}[s,s']} \gamma^{r[s']}$$

This system of linear equations is always uniquely solvable.

4.1.2 Transforming the Planning Problem

To show how every planning task PT2 for a risk-seeking agent can be transformed into an equivalent planning task PT3 for a risk-neutral agent, we assume again that a state-action mapping is given. We use the same symbols for planning task PT3 that we used for PT2, but overline them.

Since (without loss of generality) a risk-neutral agent has utility function $\bar{u}(c) = c$, it holds that $\bar{u}[s] = \bar{v}[s]$. A goal state s has (expected) total utility $\bar{u}[s] = \bar{u}(\bar{r}[s]) = \bar{r}[s]$. The expected total utility of a non-goal state s is

$$\bar{u}[s] = \sum_{s' \in S} \bar{p}^{a[s]}[s,s'] \bar{u}(\bar{c}^{a[s]}[s,s'] + \bar{u}^{-1}(\bar{u}[s']))$$

$$= \sum_{s' \in S} \bar{p}^{a[s]}[s,s'](\bar{c}^{a[s]}[s,s'] + \bar{u}[s'])$$

Comparing these results with the ones in the previous section shows that $\bar{u}[s] = u[s]$ for all states $s \in S$ and all planning problems if and only if three equalities hold: $\bar{r}[s] = \gamma^{r[s]}$ for $s \in G$. Furthermore, $\bar{p}^{a[s]}[s,s'] = p^{a[s]}[s,s']\gamma^{c^{a[s]}[s,s']}$ and $\bar{c}^{a[s]}[s,s'] = 0$ for $s \in S \setminus G$ and $s' \in S$.

Thus, planning task PT2 for a risk-seeking agent with utility function $u(c) = \gamma^c$ is equivalent to the following planning task PT3 for a risk-neutral agent:

> Introduce one additional goal state $\bar{s}$ with goal reward zero. Otherwise, the state space, action space, start state, and goal states remain unchanged. The goal reward of any goal state $s \neq \bar{s}$ is $\gamma^{r[s]}$. When the agent executes action a in a non-goal state s, it incurs an action cost of zero and is in successor state s' with transition probability $p^{a[s]}[s,s']\gamma^{c^{a[s]}[s,s']}$. These probabilities do not sum up to one. With the complementary transition probability $1 - \sum_{s' \in S} p^{a[s]}[s,s']\gamma^{c^{a[s]}[s,s']}$, the agent incurs an action cost of zero and is in successor state $\bar{s}$.

Thus, given γ, one transforms planning task PT2 into the above planning task, for which one then determines the plan with the largest expected total reward. The transformation is trivial and can be done in linear time, since both representations are of the same size.

The only reason for introducing state $\bar{s}$ is to make the probabilities sum up to one. Since its expected total reward is zero, it will not show up in the calculations. The specification of PT3 for the risk-seeking planning problem from Figure 2 is shown in Figure 4. Note that, although they can both be expressed with probabilistic decision graphs of the

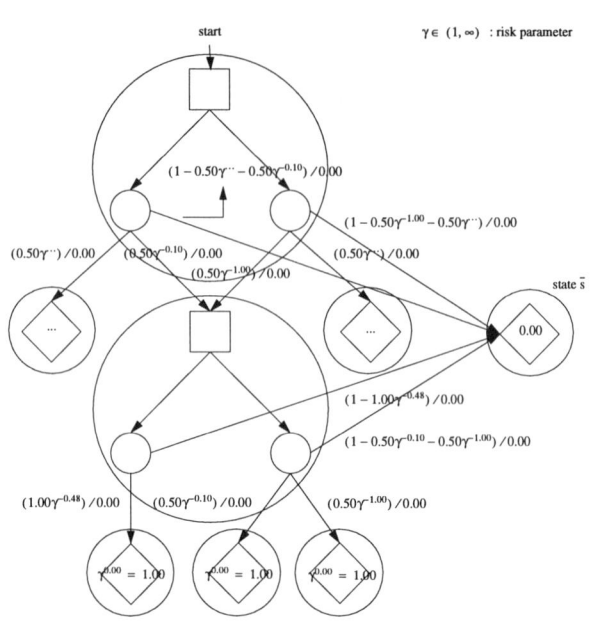

Figure 4: Transformation

same topology, the specification of the planning problem for PT3 differs fundamentally from the one of PT1. For example, an obvious difference is that all actions of planning task PT3 have action cost zero. Therefore, action costs can be ignored for risk-sensitive planning.

4.1.3 Finding Optimal Plans

Planning task PT3 can be solved with probabilistic AI planning methods or, alternatively, with dynamic programming methods, called Markov decision algorithms.

It is interesting to note that the plan with the largest expected total utility is not necessarily admissible even if an admissible plan exists, as shown in Figure 5 for a risk-seeking agent with utility function $u(c) = 2^c$. If the agent chooses action A, then the expected total utility of the plan is $0.50u(-\infty) + 0.50u(-1) = 0.25$, but the plan is not admissible. If the agent chooses action B, then it achieves a total (expected) utility of $1.00u(-3) = 0.125$ and reaches the goal state for sure. Thus, the inadmissible plan results in a larger expected total utility. This cannot happen for risk-neutral agents, since the optimal risk-neutral plan is always admissible if an admissible plan exists. The reason why the plan with the largest expected total utility is no longer guaranteed to be admissible for risk-seeking agents is shown in Table 1: While for risk-neutral agents all inadmissible plans have certainty equivalent minus infinity, this is no longer true for risk-seeking agents. The table also shows that this situation cannot arise for risk-averse agents.

It should be pointed out that, from the standpoint of utility theory, there is absolutely no problem with optimal plans

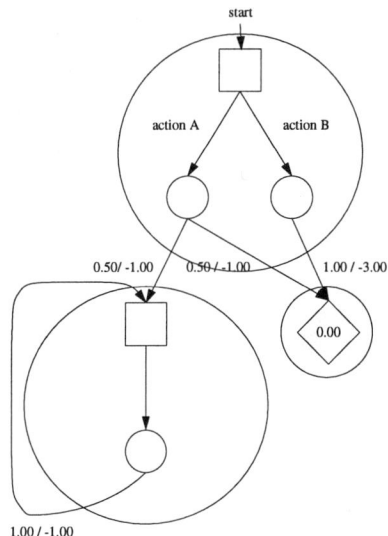

Figure 5: The Optimal Plan is Inadmissible

Table 1: Possible Certainty Equivalents of Plans

agent is ...	certainty equivalent $u^{-1}(u[s_0])$ of ...	
	an admissible plan	an inadmissible plan
risk-neutral	$u^{-1}(u[s_0]) > -\infty$	$u^{-1}(u[s_0]) = -\infty$
risk-seeking	$u^{-1}(u[s_0]) > -\infty$	$u^{-1}(u[s_0]) \geq -\infty$
risk-averse	$u^{-1}(u[s_0]) \geq -\infty$	$u^{-1}(u[s_0]) = -\infty$

(utility function has delta property)

that are inadmissible. However, if one insists on using utility theory only to choose the best plan *among all admissible plans*, one can utilize that the optimal plan for a risk-seeking agent is guaranteed to be admissible if *every* state is solvable.[5] Thus, if some states are unsolvable, one can remove the unsolvable states from the planning problem before solving it [Koenig, 1991]. The optimal plan of the resulting planning problem is then guaranteed to be admissible.

The optimal plan for the transformed planning task PT3 can be determined with dynamic programming algorithms. If the probabilistic decision graph is acyclic, it can be solved in linear time with folding-back. For cyclic probabilistic decision graphs, it can be formulated as Markov decision problem, that can then be solved in polynomial

---

[5] Properties such as this one can easily be proved using the anytime property of Markov decision algorithms such as the policy-iteration algorithm.

time with Markov decision algorithms. The representation as Markov decision problem proves that one can indeed restrict plans to state-action mappings without losing optimality and, furthermore, that there exists at least one state-action mapping that is optimal for all possible start states. It turns out that the Markov decision problems for planning task PT3 have a simpler structure than the ones for PT1 (namely, all state-action mappings determine *absorbing* Markov chains). This simplifies the optimization algorithms.

In order to determine an optimal plan for planning task PT3, one can for example use value-iteration [Bellman, 1957], policy-iteration [Howard, 1964], Q-learning [Watkins, 1989], or linear programming. As an example of such a dynamic programming technique consider a simplified version of Howard's single-chain policy-iteration algorithm [Howard, 1964] [Howard and Matheson, 1972]. One can either use the algorithm on the transformed planning task PT3 or, as we have done here, adapt the algorithm so that it works on the original planning task PT2:

1. Choose an arbitrary state-action mapping $a[s] \in A(s)$ for all $s \in S \setminus G$.

2. (value-determination operation) Solve the system of linear equations

$$u[s] = \sum_{s' \in S \setminus G} p^{a[s]}[s,s']\gamma^{c^{a[s]}[s,s']}u[s']$$
$$+ \sum_{s' \in G} p^{a[s]}[s,s']\gamma^{c^{a[s]}[s,s']}\gamma^{r[s']}$$

for $s \in S \setminus G$.

3. If no $u[s]$ for any $s \in S \setminus G$ has changed in the previous step (from the value that it had in the previous iteration), then stop. An optimal state-action mapping is to select action $a[s]$ in state $s \in S \setminus G$.

4. (policy-improvement routine) Set for every $s \in S \setminus G$

$$a[s] := \arg\max_{a \in A(s)} (\sum_{s' \in S \setminus G} p^a[s,s']\gamma^{c^a[s,s']}u[s']$$
$$+ \sum_{s' \in G} p^a[s,s']\gamma^{c^a[s,s']}\gamma^{r[s']})$$

5. Go to 2.

This algorithm is an anytime algorithm. The term "anytime algorithm" was coined by [Boddy and Dean, 1989]), and [Bresina and Drummond, 1990] first developed an anytime planner. The policy-iteration algorithm is an anytime algorithm in the sense that the expected total utility of no state can decrease from one iteration to the next, but the expected total utility of at least one state strictly increases, until the optimal state-action mapping is found in finite time [Howard, 1964]. Thus, the expected total utility of the currently best plan cannot decrease from iteration to

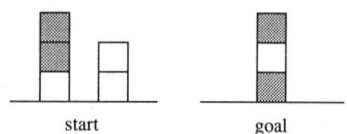

There are seven goal states, all of which are equally preferable.

In every blocks-world state, one can move a block that has a clear top onto either the table or a different block that has a clear top, or paint a block white or black.

Moving a block takes only one minute to execute, but is very unreliable. With probability 0.10, the moved block ends up at its intended destination. With probability 0.90, however, the gripper loses the block and it ends up directly on the table. (Thus, moving a block to the table always succeeds.)

Painting a block takes three minutes and is always successful.

Figure 6: A Blocks-World Problem

iteration. A solved state remains solved in the following iterations and an admissible plan stays admissible. Anytime planning methods can be used to determine — according to decision-theoretic criteria — when to stop planning and start executing the plan, because the possible future increase in plan quality does not justify the effort of planning any further.

However, dynamic programming algorithms are brute-force search algorithms and thus are often impractical, since they do not utilize available domain knowledge such as how different actions interact with each other. AI planning methods, on the other hand, are knowledge-based. Although AI planning methods, such as the ones of [Smith, 1988] or [Dean et al., 1993], are usually not able to guarantee the optimality of their plans, they can be used for risk-seeking planning instead of Markov decision algorithms. The larger the expected total reward of the plan that they determine for planning task PT3, the larger is the expected total utility of the same plan for the corresponding planning task PT2.

4.1.4 Example: A Stochastic Blocks-World

We use the blocks-world problem that is stated in Figure 6 to illustrate this planning method. Figure 7 shows four of the state-action mappings that solve it, and Figure 8 illustrates how the certainty equivalents $u^{-1}(u[s_0]) = \log_\gamma u[s_0]$ of the four plans vary with the natural logarithm of the risk parameter γ.

Plan A, which involves no risk and can be executed in six minutes (that is, has total reward -6.00), has the largest expected total reward of all plans (not just the four plans shown) and will therefore be chosen by a risk-neutral agent. However, plan A is not necessarily optimal for a risk-seeking agent. When executing plan D, for example, the agent can reach a goal state in only three minutes if it is lucky.

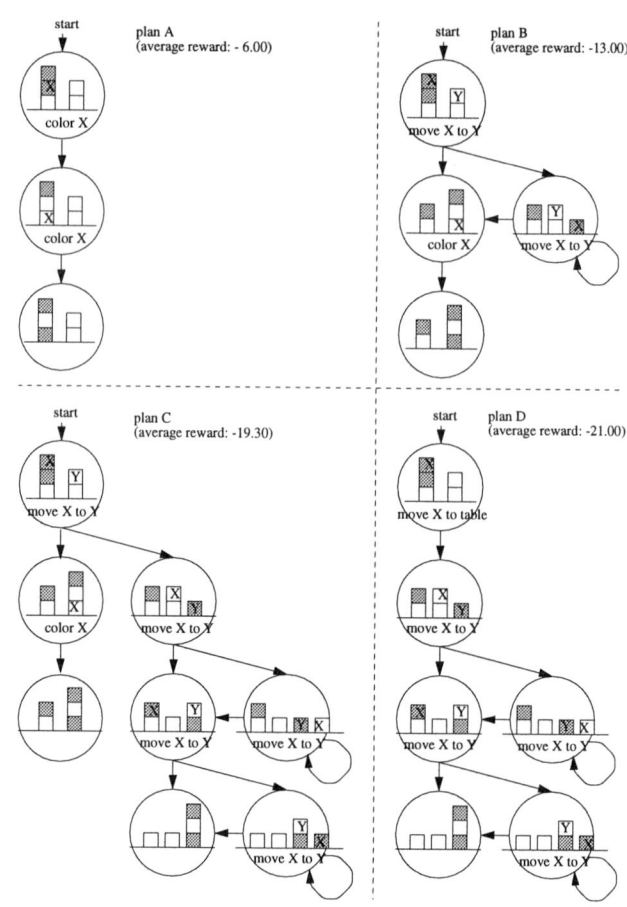

Figure 7: Some Plans for the Blocks-World Problem

The optimal plan for a risk-seeking agent is the one with the largest expected total utility or, equivalently, certainty equivalent. Since Plan A is deterministic, its certainty equivalent equals the (expected) total reward of its start state, no matter what the risk-attitude of the agent is. The other three plans are non-deterministic. Thus, their certainty equivalents increase, the more risk-seeking the agent becomes, and different plans can be optimal for different degrees of risk-seeking attitude. Figure 8 shows that plan A is optimal in the interval $\ln \gamma \in (0.00, 0.93]$. For $\ln \gamma \in [0.94, 4.58]$, plan C is optimal, and plan D should be chosen for $\ln \gamma \in [4.59, \infty)$. (These statements hold for all plans, not just the four plans shown in the figure.)

In order to be able to apply probabilistic planning methods other than Markov decision algorithms, we explicitly transform the planning problem into one for a risk-neutral agent. The original planning problem can for example be expressed with augmented STRIPS-rules [Koenig, 1991], three for the move actions ("move block X from the top of block Y on top of block Z," "stack block X on top of block Y," "unstack block X from block Y") and one for the paint action ("paint block X with color C"). The first move action

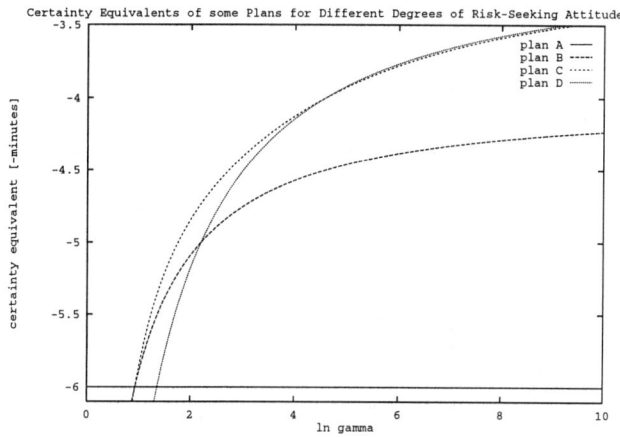

Figure 8: Certainty Equivalents (Risk-Seeking Case)

can be expressed as follows:

```
move(X,Y,Z)
  precond:  on(X,Y), clear(X), clear(Z),
            block(X), block(Y), block(Z),
            unequal(X,Z)
  outcome:
  /* the primary outcome */
  prob:     0.1
  reward:   -1.0
  delete:   on(X,Y), clear(Z)
  add:      on(X,Z), clear(Y)
  outcome:
  /* failure: block X falls down */
  prob:     0.9
  reward:   -1.0
  delete:   on(X,Y)
  add:      clear(Y),on(X,table)
```

The transformation changes the transition probabilities, action costs, and goal rewards. In particular, the STRIPS-rules are transformed as shown in Section 4.1.2. For example, for $\gamma = 2$, the above STRIPS-rule is transformed into the following one:

```
move(X,Y,Z)
  precond:  on(X,Y), clear(X), clear(Z),
            block(X), block(Y), block(Z),
            unequal(X,Z)
  outcome:
  /* the primary outcome */
  prob:     0.05
  reward:   0.0
  delete:   on(X,Y), clear(Z)
  add:      on(X,Z), clear(Y)
  outcome:
  /* failure: block X falls down */
  prob:     0.45
  reward:   0.0
  delete:   on(X,Y)
  add:      clear(Y),on(X,table)
```

With the complementary probability (0.5), the action execution results in the new goal state $\bar{s}$, that has goal reward zero, but is not modeled explicitly. All other goal states (i.e. the goal states of the original, risk-seeking planning problem) get assigned a goal reward of one. Now, one can use any planning method that maximizes expected total reward on the transformed STRIPS-rules to determine an optimal plan for the risk-seeking agent.

4.2 Planning for Risk-Averse Agents

For risk-averse agents, one can proceed as outlined for risk-seeking agents in the previous section. In this case, one has to use a function from the family $u(c) = -\gamma^c$ (or any strictly positively linear transformation thereof) for $0 < \gamma < 1$. Although the values $p^{a[s]}[s,s']\gamma^{c^{a[s]}[s,s']}$ can no longer be interpreted as probabilities (since $\sum_{s' \in S} p^{a[s]}[s,s']\gamma^{c^{a[s]}[s,s']} > 1$), one can use the same methods as in the risk-seeking case if one takes care of one complication: The solution $u[s_0]$ of the system of linear equations from Section 4.1.1 can now be finite even for plans that have expected total utility minus infinity. The planning methods can then erroneously return such plans as optimal solutions. Fortunately, these plans are easy to characterize ("plans that have at least one cycle with 'probability' greater than one"), and one can remedy the problem by either initializing the dynamic programming algorithms more restrictedly or extending them slightly. Details are given in [Koenig and Simmons, 1994].

If there are cycles in probabilistic decision graphs, then — unfortunately — the expected total utilities of admissible plans (and thus their certainty equivalents) can be minus infinity. Imagine for example an extremely risk-averse agent. Thus, given a plan, the agent assumes that nature will try to keep it away from a goal state. The agent assigns a plan an expected total utility of minus infinity if a vicious nature could indeed prevent it from reaching a goal state. In this case, utility theory might no longer be able to distinguish admissible plans from inadmissible ones. Table 1 shows that this problem can not arise for risk-neutral or risk-seeking agents.

As an example, consider again the blocks-world domain from Section 4.1.4. Figure 9 shows how the certainty equivalents of the four plans for the blocks-world problem vary with the natural logarithm of the risk parameter γ if the agent is risk-averse. The optimal plan for such an agent is always plan A, independent of γ. Although the certainty equivalent of plan A is defined for all values of $\ln \gamma$, the certainty equivalents of plans B, C, and D are finite only for

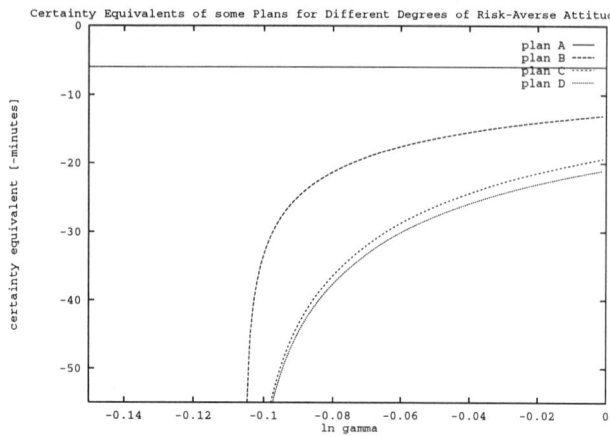

Figure 9: Certainty Equivalents (Risk-Averse Case)

$-0.11 \leq \ln \gamma < 0$ (that is, $0.9 < \gamma < 1$). They are minus infinity for smaller values of $\ln \gamma$.

5 Conclusion

This paper focuses on probabilistic planning for *risk-sensitive* agents, since there are many situations where it is not optimal to determine plans that minimize expected execution cost. We use acyclic and cyclic probabilistic decision graphs as the planning framework and use utility functions that possess the delta property. These utility functions cover a whole spectrum of risk-sensitive attitudes from being strongly risk-averse to being strongly risk-seeking, and fill a gap between approaches previously studied in the AI literature.

We have shown that one can use standard probabilistic planning methods to solve risk-sensitive planning problems. However, it is not enough to replace all costs and rewards with their respective utilities. Instead, one can transform the acyclic probabilistic decision graph into a different probabilistic decision graph of equal size, that one can then optimize for a risk-neutral agent in linear time with dynamic programming methods. Cyclic probabilistic decision graphs can be solved in a similar way in polynomial time with Markov decision algorithms.

This approach to risk-sensitive planning allows one to augment risk-neutral probabilistic AI planning algorithms, since one can use *any* planning method on the transformed planning problem that minimizes (or satisfices) expected execution cost to determine an optimal (or satisficing) plan for a risk-seeking agent. The better a plan is for the transformed planning problem, the better it is for the original planning problem as well. Although the derivation of the transformation requires some knowledge of utility theory and Markov decision theory, the transformation itself is very simple and can be applied without any understanding of the formalisms involved.

We believe that much of the work in operations research or decision theory can be utilized for AI research in a similar way. These disciplines have a different approach to decision making than AI and, consequently, most of their methods might not be interesting from an AI point of view. However, they also offer results that are useful for other problem solving approaches. These results can (and should) be utilized by AI researchers.

Acknowledgements

Thanks (in alphabetical order) to Justin Boyan, Lonnie Chrisman, Matthias Heger, Andrew Moore, Joseph O'Sullivan, Stuart Russell, Jiří Sgall, and Michael Wellman for helpful discussions or comments. This research was supported in part by NASA under contract NAGW-1175. The views and conclusions contained in this document are those of the authors and should not be interpreted as representing the official policies, either expressed or implied, of NASA or the U.S. government.

References

(Bellman, 1957) Bellman, R. 1957. *Dynamic Programming*. Princeton University Press, Princeton (New Jersey).

(Boddy and Dean, 1989) Boddy, M. and Dean, T. 1989. Solving time-dependent planning problems. In *Proceedings of the IJCAI*. 979–984.

(Bresina and Drummond, 1990) Bresina, J. and Drummond, M. 1990. Anytime synthetic projection: Maximizing the probability of goal satisfaction. In *Proceedings of the AAAI*. 138–144.

(Christiansen and Goldberg, 1990) Christiansen, A.D. and Goldberg, K.Y. 1990. Robotic manipulation planning with stochastic actions. In *Proceedings of the DARPA Workshop on Innovative Approaches to Planning, Scheduling, and Control*.

(Dean et al., 1993) Dean, T.; Kaelbling, L.P.; Kirman, J.; and Nicholson, A. 1993. Planning with deadlines in stochastic domains. In *Proceedings of the AAAI*. 574–579.

(Etzioni, 1991) Etzioni, O. 1991. Embedding decision-analytic control in a learning architecture. *Artificial Intelligence* (1-3):129–159.

(Filar et al., 1989) Filar, J.A.; Kallenberg, L.C.M.; and Lee, H.-M. 1989. Variance-penalized Markov decision processes. *Mathematics of Operations Research* 14(1):147–161.

(Goodwin and Simmons, 1992) Goodwin, R. and Simmons, R.G. 1992. Rational handling of multiple goals for mobile robots. In *Proceedings of the First International Conference on AI Planning Systems*. 70–77.

(Haddawy and Hanks, 1992) Haddawy, P. and Hanks, S. 1992. Representation for decision-theoretic planning:

Utility functions for deadline goals. In *Proceedings of the International Conference on Principles of Knowledge Representation and Reasoning*.

(Hansson et al., 1990) Hansson, O.; Mayer, A.; and Russell, S. 1990. Decision-theoretic planning in BPS. In *Proceedings of the AAAI Spring Symposium on Planning*.

(Heger and Karsten, 1992) Heger, M. and Karsten, B. 1992. Risikoloses Reinforcement-Lernen. *KI* 4:26–32.

(Heger, 1994) Heger, M. 1994. Risk and reinforcement learning. Technical report, Computer Science Department, University of Bremen, Bremen, Germany.

(Horvitz, 1988) Horvitz, E.J. 1988. Reasoning under varying and uncertain resource constraints. In *Proceedings of the AAAI*. 111–116.

(Howard and Matheson, 1972) Howard, R.A. and Matheson, J.E. 1972. Risk-sensitive Markov decision processes. *Management Science* 18(7):356–369.

(Howard, 1964) Howard, R.A. 1964. *Dynamic Programming and Markov Processes*. The MIT Press, Cambridge (Massachusetts), third edition.

(Kanazawa and Dean, 1989) Kanazawa, K. and Dean, T. 1989. A model for projection and action. In *Proceedings of the IJCAI*. 985–990.

(Karakoulas, 1993) Karakoulas, G.J. 1993. A machine learning approach to planning for economic systems. In *Proceedings of the Third International Workshop on Artificial Intelligence in Economics and Management*.

(Koenig and Simmons, 1993) Koenig, S. and Simmons, R.G. 1993. Utility-based planning. Technical Report CMU–CS–93–222, School of Computer Science, Carnegie Mellon University, Pittsburgh (Pennsylvania).

(Koenig and Simmons, 1994) Koenig, S. and Simmons, R.G. 1994. Risk-sensitive game-playing, any-time planning, and reinforcement learning. Technical report, School of Computer Science, Carnegie Mellon University, Pittsburgh (Pennsylvania). (forthcoming).

(Koenig, 1991) Koenig, S. 1991. Optimal probabilistic and decision-theoretic planning using Markovian decision theory. Master's thesis, Computer Science Department, University of California at Berkeley, Berkeley (California). (available as Technical Report UCB/CSD 92/685).

(Kushmerick et al., 1993) Kushmerick, N.; Hanks, S.; and Weld, D. 1993. An algorithm for probabilistic planning. Technical Report 93-06-03, Department of Computer Science and Engineering, University of Washington, Seattle (Washington).

(Mine and Osaki, 1970) Mine, Hisashi and Osaki, Shunji 1970. *Markovian Decision Processes*. American Elsevier, New York (New York).

(Moore and Atkeson, 1993) Moore, A.W. and Atkeson, C.G. 1993. The parti-game algorithm for variable resolution reinforcement learning in multidimensional statespaces. In *Proceedings of the NIPS*.

(Pratt, 1964) Pratt, J.W. 1964. Risk aversion in the small and in the large. *Econometrica* 32(1-2):122–136.

(Raiffa, 1968) Raiffa, H. 1968. *Decision Analysis: Introductory Lectures on Choices under Uncertainty*. Addison Wesley, Menlo Park (California).

(Russell and Wefald, 1991) Russell, S. and Wefald, E. 1991. *Do the Right Thing – Studies in Limited Rationality*. The MIT Press, Cambridge (Massachusetts).

(Smith, 1988) Smith, D.E. 1988. A decision-theoretic approach to the control of planning search. Technical Report LOGIC-87-11, Department of Computer Science, Stanford University, Palo Alto (California).

(von Neumann and Morgenstern, 1947) von Neumann, J. and Morgenstern, O. 1947. *Theory of games and economic behavior*. Princeton University Press, Princeton (New Jersey), second edition.

(Watkins, 1989) Watkins, C.J. 1989. *Learning from Delayed Rewards*. Ph.D. Dissertation, King's College, Cambridge University, Cambridge (Great Britain).

(Watson and Buede, 1987) Watson, S.R. and Buede, D.M. 1987. *Decision Synthesis*. Cambridge University Press, Cambridge (Great Britain).

(Wellman and Doyle, 1992) Wellman, M. and Doyle, J. 1992. Modular utility representation for decision theoretic planning. In *Proceedings of the First International Conference on AI Planning Systems*. 236–242.

Easy to be Hard:
Difficult Problems for Greedy Algorithms

Kurt Konolige
Artificial Intelligence Center
SRI International
333 Ravenswood Ave.
Menlo Park, CA 94025
konolige at ai.sri.com

Abstract

Recent advances in hill-climbing satisfiability methods have solved hard classes of problems, which are difficult for existing systematic methods such as Davis-Putnam. In this paper we examine a class of problems derived from crossword puzzles that is difficult for the hill-climbing methods, yet is easily solved by standard forward-checking algorithms. The characteristic feature of this class is its hierarchical nature: clusters of dependent variables, with a small number of connections between the clusters. Although the results are experimental and not theoretical, we speculate that any hierarchical constraint-satisfaction problem with certain characteristics will be difficult for naive greedy algorithms.

1 Introduction

Recently, hill-climbing methods for constraint satisfaction problems (CSPs) have found solutions for some hard problems, including hard scheduling, random 3SAT and random graph-coloring problems. Instances of these methods include min-conflicts [6] and GSAT [10, 9]. Solving a CSP means finding an assignment for all the variables in the CSP that satisfies all the constraints. The common idea behind the hill-climbing methods is to choose an initial assignment for the variables (which almost always does not satisfy all constraints), and then modify the assigment incrementally to satisfy more and more constraints. These methods are nonsystematic, in that they randomly search selected portions of the space.

In this paper we concentrate on GSAT and its variants applied to propositional satisfaction problems. The utility of GSAT for typical AI applications is an open question. There has been some work on toy planning problems using GSAT [5], and the min-conflicts method has been successfully applied to large-scale scheduling for the space shuttle [6, 11]. Still, many AI problems such as diagnosis and planning exhibit structure that is very different from the randomly generated problems that hill-climbing methods seem to be most successful on, and there has been no systematic study of how GSAT performs. There are some reasons for this; the main one is that it is difficult to generate random instances of hard problems that exhibit structure. A second one is that GSAT itself is a moving target. For example, it was reported that assymetric graph coloring [9] and simple planning problems [5] were very difficult for the original version of GSAT. Additional mechanisms enabled GSAT to equal or surpass the performance of systematic algorithms. The main effect of these mechanisms — weights on clauses and random walk — appears to be in moving an assignment out of local minima so it can continue to explore the space.

Many naturally-occurring problems exhibit very deep local minima, and these should cause serious trouble for GSAT. For example, the Tower of Hanoi puzzle is a planning problem that has many such minima, since whenever most of the disks are on the goal peg, they must all be unstacked in order to place the largest disk on the bottom. This problem also is a challenge for other constraint-satisfaction or planning methods, and current GSAT version do as well as the best systematic algorithms. The question then arises: are there classes of problems with deep local minima that are difficult for GSAT but still easy to solve by other methods? The answer given here is "yes" (at least until yet another mechanism is added to GSAT). A general class of satisfiability problems with hierarchical structure is relatively easy to solve by standard foreward-checking algorithms, while GSAT's performance is 3 to 4 orders of magnitude worse. The performance of GSAT appears to be related to the hierarchical nature of the problem, that is, when the structure is collapsed to a flat set of constraints, GSAT's performance improves remarkably.

The next section discusses abductive inference and the conversion to satisfiability. Following this, the problem class and experiments are presented, and an analysis of the results.

2 Graph crosswords

We have experimented with a class of problems generalized from crossword puzzles, which we call graph crosswords (GCWs) because the structure is not necessarily planar. A GCW consists of a set of word instances, each composed of squares containing letters. Letters must combine to form legal words from the dictionary for the GCW. Here is an example of a word instance:

Alphabet: a, b, c, d
Dictionary: bad, cad, cab
Instance w_1: $(w_1 = \text{bad}) \vee (w_1 = \text{cad}) \vee (w_1 = \text{cab})$
   $(w_1 = \text{cad}) \supset (s_1 = c) \wedge (s_2 = a) \wedge (s_3 = d)$
   etc.

The important axioms here are the disjunctions that encode the allowed choices for words instances. For the GCW to be satisfied, each word instance must contain a word from the dictionary.

At the letter level, there are constraints saying that exactly one letter fills each square:

$(s_1 = a) \vee (s_1 = b) \vee (s_1 = c) \vee (s_1 = d)$
$\neg(s_1 = a) \vee \neg(s_1 = b)$
$\neg(s_1 = a) \vee \neg(s_1 = c)$
etc.

Finally, there is a set of connections between the squares of instances, establishing the "cross" part of the crossword, e.g., if s_1 and s_8 are supposed to be the same square, then there are constraints:

$(s_1 = a) \vee \neg(s_8 = a)$
$(s_8 = a) \vee \neg(s_1 = a)$
$(s_1 = b) \vee \neg(s_8 = b)$
$(s_8 = b) \vee \neg(s_1 = b)$
etc.

A complete GCW is specified by the parameters GCW(A,D,W,C), where A is the alphabet, D the dictionary of words over A, W a set of word instances, and C the set of connections between instances. This GCW is solvable if there exists an assignment of letters to squares that satisfies all the axioms. The constraints force each of the word instances in a satisficing assignment to be filled with a dictionary word.

GCW problems exhibit definite structure. Each word instance forms a tight cluster of interdependent variables whose size varies with the length of the instance. Constraints between instances enforce restrictions on pairs of words occupying the connected instances, and so form bridges between the clusters.

3 The experiments

GCWs are a good model for experiments because they have several parameters that can be varied to give different types of problems. For simplicity we consider all words in a given problem to be the same size.

Three parameters control the size of the clusters: the size of word instances (S_i), the alphabet and dictionary size. We fixed the alphabet size at 10 and the dictionary size at 10 (we have also tried experiments with larger values; they do not affect the results reported here). This leaves the single parameter S_i to control cluster size.

The number of clusters is given by the number of word instances N_i. Connectivity between the clusters is controlled by the parameter C_i, the number of connections per instance. For these experiments we used a constant low connectivity of $C_i = 2$.

Experiments were run by setting the parameters N_i and C_i, then generating a random satisfiable instance of GCD(A,D,W,C). 10 random words over A were generated, and N_i of them (with possible repetitions) were chosen to give an assignment so that a satisfiable set of random connections could be generated.[1]

For all experiments, we used version 24C (April 1993) of GSAT. After some experimentation and consultation with GSAT guru Bart Selman, both clause weights and random walk options were used. Random walk was set at -.5 for all experiments; the weight increment was 100, and weights were reset after every 200 flips (sometimes this would increase for harder instances of GCW). The number of flips was either x5 or sometimes x10 for harder instances.

For comparison, we used a systematic method, a version of the Davis-Putnam algorithm called tableau [2]. This method chooses a variable to assign, propagates the results of the assignment using unit resolution, and then repeats the process, backing up when it finds a contradiction. No special effort was made to make tableau more efficient on GCW. There are no parameters to adjust; a simple binary clause count is used as a heuristic for which variable to assign.

The first series of experiments fixed the word size S_i at 6, and varied the number of instances N_i. Data for several runs and problems were averaged and produced the results in Table 1.[2] Runtimes are for a Sparcstation ELC.

GSAT performed relatively poorly on this set of problems. Its runtimes are at least quadratic in the prob-

---

[1] Ordinary crosswords do not have repeated words, but GCW allows them. Additional constraints could be generated to enforce unique usage, but this makes it impossible to generate problems with large N_i over small dictionaries.

[2] Tableau does not have a random component, so only one run was used for each problem instance.

# words	vars	clauses	Time (sec) GSAT	Tableau
2	143	797	1	
4	285	1593	10	
10	711	3981	100	
20	1421	7961	420	
40	2841	15921	*	< 1
100	7101	39801	*	1.5
400	28401	159201	*	13
1000	71001	398001	*	30

Table 1: Results of GSAT and tableau on GCW with a dictionary of 10 6-letter words. An asterisk indicates the time limit of 30 minutes was exceeded.

# words	vars	clauses	Time (sec) GSAT	Tableau
20	62	3481	14	
40	1241	6961	160	< 1
100	3101	17401	717	2
200	6201	34801	10540	3
400	12401	69601	*	7

Table 2: Results of GSAT and tableau on GCW with a dictionary of 10 2-letter words. An asterisk indicates the time limit of 4 hours was exceeded.

lem size, and the cutoff of greater than 30 minutes runtime occurs early, on problems of size 40. By contrast, the tableau method had no trouble with problems as large as 1000, and only memory limitations prevented experiments with higher values. Tableau could solve problems at least 100 times as large as GSAT. These are not hard problems (for example, they are not at a crossover point [7], and there are generally many different satisficing assignments); what is the source of GSAT's difficulties? To test the hypothesis that it is the structure of the GCW, we performed two additional experiments. In the first, we reduced the size of word instances S_i to 2. Data for several problem sizes N_i are shown in Table 2. With just 2-letter words, GSAT shows at least an order of magnitude improvement over the same GCW with 6-letter words, and solves problems 5 times as large. The results for tableau are virtually unchanged, since it is searching essentially the same space.

Finally, we tried an alternate encoding of GCW in which there are no variables for the letters. Instead, all constraints were generated as binary constraints between forbidden word pairs, based on the connections between the instances [4]. So, for example, if word instances 1 and 2 were connected by their second letter, "dog" and "man" would be a forbidden pair for filling them in. Compared to the letter encoding, there are more clauses (quadratic in the dictionary size), but

# words	vars	clauses	Time (sec) GSAT
40	441	7450	6
100	1101	18845	25
200	2201	36966	113
400	4401	74443	232

Table 3: Results of GSAT on GCW with a dictionary of 10 6-letter words, no letter structure.

these is no cluster structure. Data for several values of N_i are given in Table 3. Note that we have used the original word size $S_i = 6$. There is an even more dramatic improvement in GSAT's performance, with solutions to GCW's two orders of magnitude larger than in Table 1.

4 Analysis

Our analysis indicates that it is the hierarchical cluster structure of the GCW problems that determines GSAT's poor performance relative to tableau. These results are dramatic when plotted against each other, in Figure 1. GSAT does very poorly on GCW problems with large clusters; as the clusters get smaller, it does progressively better, although tableau still is the clear winner by at least an order of magnitude. This data is a strong confirmation of the hypothesis that the hierarchical structure of the GCW encoding is difficult for GSAT to cope with. We tried a number of other experiments to eliminate other possible causes of the difference. For example, we varied the number of words in the dictionary and the number of letters in the alphabet; neither had more of an effect on GSAT than on tableau. Also, we raised S_i to 10; as expected, GSAT fared even worse, and we could not find solutions in the maximum time for size 10 problems, while tableau remained unaffected.[3]

The question remains as to why GSAT performs poorly on GCW problems as the size of clusters S_i grows. The number of variables and the number of clause go up linearly with the size of the problem, so GSAT should not be overwhelmed by this. The solutions are relatively easy to find for tableau, involving almost no backtracking, so the constraints lead fairly directly to the solutions: these are not intrinsically hard problems.

Examining the difference between tableau and GSAT helps to pinpoint the factors that make tableau efficient here. Tableau starts by assigning a value to

---

[3]GSAT did about twice as badly on very small problems ($N_i \leq 4$) for values $S_i = 10$ than for $S_i = 6$). The differences at small N_i tend not to be as pronounced because there are very few connections among clusters that have to be satisfied.

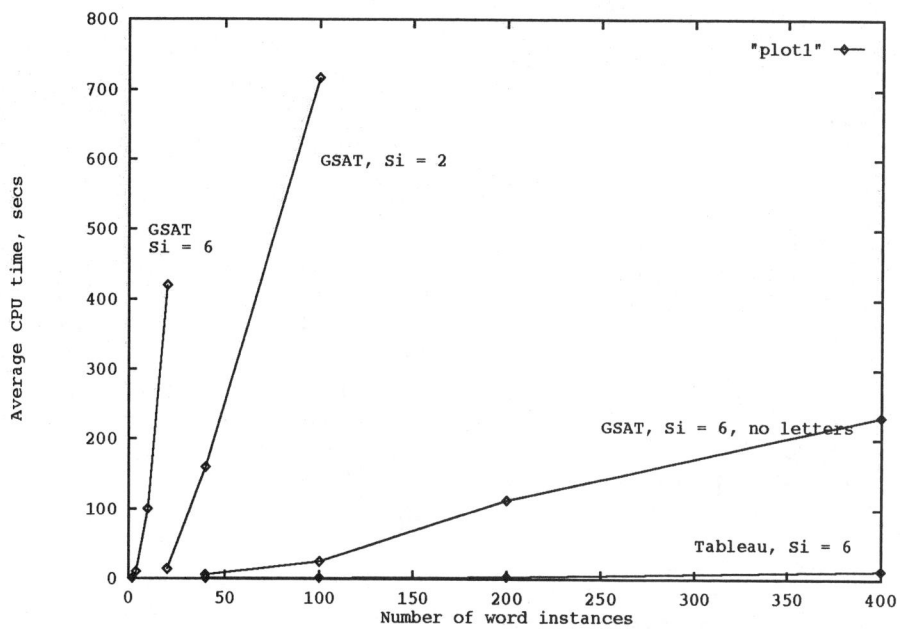

Figure 1: Comparison of runtimes for GSAT with various size of S_i.

some variable, propagating the results by unit resolution, and then finding another variable to instantiate. Whenever a contradiction is detected, it backtracks chronologically, undoing the assignment of the most recent variable. For GCWs, the binary-clause heuristic of tableau generally picks a word-instance variable to assign, since this will generate the most unit resolutions, filling in the letters of the squares and eliminating all competing words and perhaps some choices in connected instances. Then it chooses another word, until the problem is solved or it is forced to backtrack. Relatively few variable assignments are necessary, since they force so many others; tableau searches a relatively small space, on the order of $S_i \times N_i$. It is a very directed search: instantiating a word gives immediate information about the suitability of connecting words.

Once GSAT has settled down from the initial random assignment, it has assigned a unique word to each word instance, along with the corresponding letters. Some of the connections or some of the letters may be inconsistent; it then chooses one of these to flip, and eventually through a series of flips the assignment settles down into an almost satisfied state. GSAT has to perform a number of flips to do this, $2 \times (S_i + 1)$. The problem seems to be that the search for a new low-potential state is not directed enough: in making one connection consistent, GSAT can easily choose a word instance that makes its other connection inconsistent. Haphazardly, it eventually finds an assignment to all word instances that satisfies all connections.

One hypothesis we had was that the size of the alphabet and dictionary domains was critical: there were too many possibilities for words or for letters for words. But increasing these parameters did not change GSAT's performance significantly (nor did it affect tableau). Since the number of unit resolutions performed by tableau goes up at least linearly with the size of the domains, the fact that there were a large number of unit resolutions could not have been the critical factor. Further, the structure of unit resolution is very shallow: there are no long chains of dependent variables that are propagated by tableau. So the presence of unit propagation or chains of unit propagation by itself is not the critical factor, as some have speculated [5]. Also, GSAT performs very well on some problems with large numbers of unit resolutions, such as the N-queens problem.

Our conclusion is that the cluster structure of the problem leads to GSAT's difficulties. The size of the clusters relative to the connection structure is controlled by the parameter S_i, the size of words. As this parameter gets larger, the number of variables that GSAT must change to repair a broken connection grows linearly, and the effect of the connection constraints is diluted, turning the greedy heuristic into an undirected instantiation of clusters that perhaps eventually solves all constraints. But, it is important to note another characteristic of the cluster variables in

GCW: satisficing assignments tend to have large Hamming distances between them. If this were not the case, it would be easy to modify some of the variables to satisfy the connections, without changing the whole cluster.

In terms of the search landscape, the clusters create deep local minima which are hard for GSAT to climb out of; and when it does, the connection constraints do not provide a directed way of finding an assignment to clusters that satisfies more of the connections. The tableau procedure, on the other hand, makes the right moves in the search space, collapsing all of the variables at each cluster to a single choice node.

5 Conclusion

GSAT, even with modifications for random walk and weighted clauses, performs very poorly on easy clustered hierarchical problems such as those in graph crosswords. The characteristic of these clusters is that there is a set of tightly interdependent variables, with a large Hamming distance between satisficing assignments for the variables. The simplicity of the problems comes from having relatively few connections between the clusters. GSAT works best on a level playing field; clusters tend to confuse it.

Hierarchical problems arise naturally in many AI problems, including planning, scheduling, diagnosis, and signal interpretation. On a more abstract level, many AI problems can be recast as abductive inference, e.g., in diagnosis we seek to posit a set of underlying causes that explains the observed symptoms [8, 1]. The structure of such inference is often hierarchical, as we generate intermediate-level hypotheses that account for related observations. If one wants to use GSAT on these problems, then it is helpful to "compile out" as much of the intermediate structure as possible. In general this will lead to an explosion in the number of constraints, as in the case of crossword puzzles. It can also be difficult, since it amounts to performing deductive inference about the unsatisfiability of sets of assignments.

There are two interesting lines of research suggested by these results. One is to adopt forward-checking methods in nonsystematic search. GSAT does poorly because its variable flips are not at the right level of search abstraction; instead, it should be flipping assignments of words and letters simultaneously. We have started to investigate hill-climbing systems that use a limited amount of forward-checking; the difficult problems are deciding when to cut it off, and when to undo it.

Another question to be answered is whether GSAT does worse than systematic methods on CSP's. The data in Figure 1 suggest that tableau is better for simple graph crossword CSP's even when there is no cluster structure, i.e., problem is a binary CSP. Is this the case for harder CSP's near a crossover point? Ginsberg [3] has shown that hard crossword puzzles could be solved by dynamic backtracking, but were impossible for GSAT, although it was an early version without random walk and clause weights. Will GSAT do poorly on hard, randomly-generated CSP's?

References

[1] L. Console and P. Torasso, A spectrum of logical definitions of model-based diagnosis, *Computational Intelligence* **7** (3) (1991) 133–141.

[2] J. M. Crawford and L. D. Auton, Experimental results on the crossover point in satisfiability problems, in: *Proceedings of the National Conference on Artificial Intelligence*, Washington, DC (1993).

[3] M. Ginsberg, Gsat and dynamic backtracking, Unpublished manuscript.

[4] M. Ginsberg, M. Frank, M. P. Halpin, and M. C. Torrance, Search lessons learned from crossword puzzles, in: *Proceedings of the National Conference on Artificial Intelligence*, Boston, MA (1990).

[5] H. Kautz and B. Selman, Planning as satisfiability, in: *Proceedings of the European Conference on Artificial Intelligence*, Vienna, Austria (1992).

[6] S. Minton, M. D. Johnston, A. B. Philips, and P. Laird, Solving large-scale constraint satisfaction and scheduling problems using as heuristic repair method, in: *Proceedings of the National Conference on Artificial Intelligence*, Boston, MA (1990).

[7] D. Mitchell, B. Selman, and H. Levesque, Hard and easy distributions of sat problems, in: *Proceedings of the National Conference on Artificial Intelligence*, San Jose, CA (1992).

[8] D. Poole, A methodology for using a default and abductive reasoning system, *International Journal of Intelligent Systems* **5** (5) (December 1990) 521–548.

[9] B. Selman and H. Kautz, Domain-independent extensions to GSAT: Solving large structured satisfiability problems, in: *Proceedings of the International Joint Conference on Artificial Intelligence*, Chambery, France (199).

[10] B. Selman, H. Levesque, and D. Mitchell, A new method for solving hard satisfiability problems, in: *Proceedings of the National Conference on Artificial Intelligence*, San Jose, CA (1992).

[11] M. Zweben, E. Davis, B. Daun, and M. Deale, Informedness vs. computational cost of heuristics in iterative repair scheduling, in: *Proceedings of the International Joint Conference on Artificial Intelligence*, Chambery, France (1993).

Complexity Results for First-Order Theories of Temporal Constraints

Manolis Koubarakis[*]
Computer Science Division
Dept. of Electrical and Computer Engineering
National Technical University of Athens
Zographou 157 73
Athens GREECE

Abstract

We study the complexity of quantifier elimination and decision in first-order theories of temporal constraints. With the exception of Ladkin, AI researchers have largely ignored this problem. We consider the first-order theories of point and interval constraints over two time structures: the integers and the rationals. We show that in all cases quantifier-elimination can be done in PSPACE. We also show that the decision problem for arbitrarily quantified sentences is PSPACE-complete while for $\exists_k$ sentences it is Σ_k^p-complete. Our results must be of interest to researchers working on temporal constraints, computational complexity of logical theories, constraint databases and constraint logic programming.

1 INTRODUCTION

The study of temporal constraints has recently received much attention from the AI community [All83, LM88, Lad88, VKvB89, vBC90, DMP91, KL91, Mei91, vB92, Kou92, GS93, SD93]. Much of this work draws upon concepts and techniques from the literature of general constraint satisfaction [Mon74, Mac77, DP88]. With the exception of [Lad88], all previous research has concentrated on temporal constraints which are quantifier-free formulas in some first-order theory of time. The problems studied include deciding whether a set of constraints is consistent, computing the minimal network corresponding to a set of constraints, finding one solution, performing variable elimination and enforcing global consistency.

[Lad88] studied the first-order theory of qualitative interval-to-interval relations introduced by Allen

---

[*]Current Address: Planning Applications Research Centre (IC-Parc), Dept. of Computing, Imperial College, London SW7 2BZ, U.K. Email: msk@doc.ic.ac.uk

[All83] and gave a quantifier-elimination (and decision) algorithm. This algorithm works by reducing quantifier-elimination in the given theory to quantifier-elimination in the first-order theory of rational order. The only deficiency of Ladkin's work is that he does not discuss the complexity of his algorithm. He simply assumes that quantifier-elimination in the theory of rational order will be done using standard methods and cites [CK73] as a reference. However [CK73] (as well as any other standard logic text-book) does not take complexity issues very seriously; thus their algorithms are usually inefficient.

In this paper we follow the line of research initiated by [Lad88] and extend it by considering more expressive languages of temporal constraints. Our contributions can be summarized as follows:

1. We study the first-order theory of (qualitative and quantitative) point constraints over the integers. The atomic formulas (i.e., constraints) in this theory are of the form $t \sim c$ or $t_i - t_j \sim c$ where $\sim$ can be $<$, $>$ or $=$ and c is an integer. We show that elimination of quantifiers can be achieved in PSPACE (theorem 4.5) and that the decision problem is PSPACE-complete (theorem 4.1). For $\exists_k$ sentences of this theory the complexity of the decision problem is Σ_k^p-complete (theorem 4.3).

2. We also study the first-order theory of (qualitative and quantitative) point constraints over the rationals. The atomic formulas in this theory are of the form $t \sim c$ or $t_i - t_j \sim c$ where $\sim$ can be $<$, $>$ or $=$ and c is a rational. The complexity results for this theory are similar: elimination of quantifiers can be achieved in PSPACE (theorem 5.5) and the decision problem is PSPACE-complete (theorem 5.1). For $\exists_k$ sentences of this theory the complexity of the decision problem is also Σ_k^p-complete (theorem 5.4).

3. Finally, we briefly turn to the first-order theories of point and interval constraints over the integers (or rationals). As a direct collorary of the above results we point out that the complexity of

quantifier-elimination and decision for these theories does not change due to the introduction of interval constraints (section 6).

The above results will be important for researchers in constraint databases [KKR90] and constraint logic programming [CMT92]. They should also be interesting to the theoretical computer science community in general. This is so because the first-order theory of point constraints over the integers is a subtheory of Presburger arithmetic while the first-order theory of point constraints over the rationals is a subtheory of real addition with order.

The rest of this paper is organized as follows. In section 2 we introduce the theories of point constraints which we will consider. In section 3 we present standard quantifier elimination algorithms for these theories. In sections 4 and 5 we use these standard algorithms as a basis for the development of more sophisticated quantifier elimination algorithms. In section 6 we extend our results to theories of point and interval constraints. Finally, section 7 presents our conclusions.

2 FIRST-ORDER THEORIES OF POINT CONSTRAINTS

In this paper we study the first-order theories of point and interval constraints over two linear and unbounded time structures: the set of integers $\mathbb{Z}$ and the set of rationals $\mathbb{Q}$. In this section we consider *points* to be our only time entities. In the first theory that we consider, points will be identified with the integers. The language *diPCL* (*di*screte *P*oint *C*onstraint *L*anguage) will allow us to make stamements about points in time. diPCL is a first order language with equality defined as follows. The non-logical symbols of diPCL include a countably infinite set of (point or integer) constants, function symbol $-$ of arity 2 and predicate symbol $<$ of arity 2.

The set of *terms* of diPCL are defined as follows:

- Constants and variables are terms.
- If t_1, t_2 are variables or constants then $t_1 - t_2$ is a term.

An *atomic formula* of diPCL is a formula of the form $t \sim c$ or $c \sim t$ where $\sim$ is $<$ or $=$, and t is a term. The set of *well-formed formulas* of diPCL are defined as usual (i.e., they are built up from the atomic formulas using quantifiers and connectives). As usual, we will write $t_1 \leq t_2$ instead of $t_1 = t_2 \vee t_1 < t_2$, $t_2 > t_1$ instead of $t_1 < t_2$, and $t_1 \geq t_2$ instead of $t_1 = t_2 \vee t_1 > t_2$.

The symbols of diPCL are interpreted with respect to the fixed structure $\mathbf{Z}$ which captures our assumptions. The domain of $\mathbf{Z}$ is $\mathbb{Z}$. To each constant symbol, $\mathbf{Z}$ assigns an element of $\mathbb{Z}$. To function symbol $-$, $\mathbf{Z}$ assigns the function $-_{\mathbb{Z}}$ which is the subtraction operation for integers. To predicate symbol $<$, $\mathbf{Z}$ assigns the relation $<_{\mathbb{Z}}$ ("less than") over the integers.

We will take the theory of structure $\mathbf{Z}$ to be *the* theory of point constraints in linear, unbounded and discrete time. This theory will be denoted by $diPC$.[1]

Example 2.1 The following is a diPCL sentence:
$$(\forall x)(\forall y)(x - y \leq 5 \supset (\exists z)(x - z \leq 3 \wedge z \leq 2)).$$

Let us now develop a theory of point constraints which is exactly like diPC except that the time structure is the set of rational numbers. *Points* will again be our only time entities. This time they will be identified with the rationals. The language dePCL (*de*nse *P*oint *C*onstraint *L*anguage) will allow us to make stamements about points in time. dePCL is a first order language with equality defined as follows. The non-logical symbols of dePCL include a countably infinite set of (point or rational) constants, function symbol $-$ of arity 2 and predicate symbol $<$ of arity 2.

The set of *terms* of dePCL are defined exactly as for diPCL. An *atomic formula* of dePCL is a formula of the form $t \sim c$ or $c \sim t$ where $\sim$ is $<$ or $=$, and t is a term. The set of *well-formed formulas* of dePCL are defined as usual.

The symbols of dePCL are interpreted with respect to the fixed structure $\mathbf{Q}$ which captures our assumptions for dense time. The domain of $\mathbf{Q}$ is $\mathbb{Q}$. To each constant symbol, $\mathbf{Q}$ assigns an element of $\mathbb{Q}$. To function symbol $-$, $\mathbf{Q}$ assigns the function $-_{\mathbb{Q}}$ which is the subtraction operation over the rationals. To predicate symbol $<$, $\mathbf{Q}$ assigns the relation $<_{\mathbb{Q}}$ over the rationals.

We will take the theory of structure $\mathbf{Q}$ to be *the* theory of point constraints in linear, unbounded and dense time. This theory will be denoted by $dePC$.

3 NAIVE QUANTIFIER ELIMINATION ALGORITHMS

Let us first define our terminology. The following definition is standard [End72, CK73].

Definition 3.1 *A theory Th admits elimination of quantifiers iff for every formula ϕ there is a quantifier free formula ϕ' such that $Th \models \phi \equiv \phi'$.*

Proposition 3.1 *The theories diPC and dePC admit elimination of quantifiers.*

---
[1] We adhere to the following convention. If a theory is denoted by Th, the language of Th will be denoted by ThL.

Proof: Let us assume that ϕ is a formula of diPCL or dePCL. We can find a quantifier-free formula ϕ' equivalent to ϕ in the following way:

1. Compute the PNF $(Qt_1)\cdots(Qt_m)\psi(t_1,\ldots,t_m)$ of ϕ.

2. Eliminate quantifier (Qt_m) as follows. Let Q be $\exists$ and $\theta_1 \vee \cdots \vee \theta_k$ be the DNF of $\psi(t_1,\ldots,t_m)$. In the case of a dePCL formula, eliminate variable t_m from each θ_i to compute θ_i' using Fourier's algorithm.[2]

   In the case of a diPCL formula, first transform every strict inequality into a weak one and then apply Fourier's algorithm. Fourier's algorithm does not give correct results for arbitrary linear inequalities over the integers but *does work* correctly for diPCL inequalities. The resulting expression is $\theta_1' \vee \cdots \vee \theta_k'$.

   Now let us assume Q is $\forall$ and $\theta_1 \vee \cdots \vee \theta_k$ is the DNF of $\neg\psi(t_1,\ldots,t_m)$. Eliminate variable t_m from each θ_i to compute θ_i' as above. The resulting expression is $\neg(\theta_i' \vee \cdots \vee \theta_k')$.

3. Repeat step 2 to eliminate quantifiers $(Qt_{m-1}),\ldots,(Qt_1)$ to obtain a quantifier-free formula in DNF.

4. Simplify the above DNF formula as follows. Until no other change is possible, substitute $true \wedge \alpha$ by α, $true \vee \alpha$ by $true$, $false \wedge \alpha$ by $false$ and $false \vee \alpha$ by α.

The correctness of the above procedure can be verified easily. For diPC a similar method appears in [Rab77]. ∎

Notation 3.1 If ϕ is a formula then $|\phi|$ denotes the length of ϕ.

Theorem 3.1 *Let ϕ be a diPCL or dePCL formula with K variables and M quantifiers. The quantifier elimination algorithm of proposition 3.1 computes a quantifier-free DNF formula equivalent to ϕ in $O(MK^2|\phi|^{(K(K+1))^M})$ time.*

Proof: There can be at most two types of constraints involving a single variable x or a difference $x_i - x_j$: one giving an upper bound and/or one giving a lower bound. Thus if we have K variables, we can have $K(K+1)$ types of constraints. The formula $\psi(t_1,\ldots,t_m)$ can have at most $|\psi|$ constraints

---
[2]Fourier's algorithm was originally proposed for linear inequalities over the reals [Sch86]. Eliminating a variable x from a conjunction of inequalities using this algorithm can be done as follows. First all inequalities involving x are written in the form $L \leq x$ or $x \leq U$ where L and U do not contain x. Then for every pair of inequalities $L \leq x$ and $x \leq U$, x is eliminated and the resulting inequality $L \leq U$ is returned. Finally, all inequalities which do not involve x are also returned.

of each type. Therefore the DNF form of ψ can contain $O(|\psi|^{K(K+1)})$ disjuncts and each disjunct can contain at most $K(K+1)$ constraints. Finally, after M quantifier eliminations the resulting formula can have $O(|\phi|^{(K(K+1))^M})$ disjuncts. The time to eliminate a variable from a disjunct is $O(K^2)$. The result follows easily. ∎

The above quantifier elimination algorithms are simple but inefficient. The problem with these algorithms is the transformation into DNF; this creates an exponential blow-up in time and space complexity. We will now turn to better algorithms which avoid transformations into DNF.

4 AN IMPROVED QUANTIFIER ELIMINATION ALGORITHM FOR diPC

First, we present a decision procedure for sentences of diPCL. Then we use this procedure for developing a quantifier elimination algorithm for arbitrary diPCL formulas.

Our starting point will be the quantifier elimination technique of [FR75]. The main point of this technique is that "given a particular theory, one gives an elimination of quantifiers procedure, analyzes it to see how *large* constants can grow, and then uses this analysis (...) to limit quantifiers to range over finite sets instead of an infinite domain" [FR75].

We start with a definition from [FR75].

Definition 4.1 *Let i be an integer. We will say that i is limited by the positive integer L, denoted by $i \preceq L$, iff $|i| \leq L$.*

As usual, we will also write $i \succeq j$ when $j \preceq i$. The following definitions introduce additional notation.

Definition 4.2 *Let ϕ be diPCL formula. Then $(\forall z \preceq L)\phi$ is a shorthand for the formula*
$$(\forall z)(z \geq -L \wedge z \leq L \supset \phi)$$
and $(\exists z \preceq L)\phi$ is a shorthand for
$$(\exists z)(z \geq -L \wedge z \leq L \wedge \phi).$$

Definition 4.3 *Let ϕ be a diPCL formula. The expression $maxabs(\phi)$ will denote the maximum absolute value of the integers appearing in ϕ.*

The following lemmas are at the heart of the elimination of quantifiers.

Lemma 4.1 *Let us assume that $\bar{t}$ is a vector of variables, y is a variable, $\phi(\bar{t},y)$ is a diPCL formula with*

K quantifiers and $\overline{\tau}$ is a vector of elements of $\mathbb{Z}$ limited by W. Then $\mathbf{Z} \models (Qy)\phi(\overline{\tau}, y)$ iff

$$\mathbf{Z} \models (Qy \preceq 2^K(maxabs(\phi)+1) + W + 2)\phi(\overline{\tau}, y).$$

If $\bar{t} = ()$, the lemma holds with $W = 0$.

Proof: Let us eliminate quantifiers from ϕ using the procedure of proposition 3.1. After the first quantifier is eliminated, the integer constants in the resulting formula are limited by $2maxabs(\phi) + 1$. With a simple inductive argument, we can show that after all K quantifiers are eliminated the integer constants in the resulting formula $\phi'(\bar{t}, y)$ are limited by $2^K maxabs(\phi) + 2^K - 1$ or (more compactly) by $2^K(maxabs(\phi) + 1)$.

Now let us consider the formula $\phi'(\overline{\tau}, y)$. Every point constraint in this formula can be written in the form $y \sim c$ where $\sim$ is $<, =$ or $>$ and c is limited by $2^K(maxabs(\phi) + 1) + W + 1$. The truth value of $\phi'(\overline{\tau}, y)$ is the same for all y such that $y \succeq 2^K(maxabs(\phi)+1) + W + 2$. Therefore the truth value of $(Qy)\phi'(\overline{\alpha}, \overline{\tau}, y)$ can be determined by simply determining the truth value of $\phi'(\overline{\tau}, y)$ for every integer limited by $2^K(maxabs(\phi) + 1) + W + 2$. ∎

Lemma 4.2 *Let us assume that ϕ is a diPCL sentence. Let $(Q_1 t_1), \ldots, (Q_K t_K)$ be all the quantifiers of ϕ in left to right order of appearance. Then $\mathbf{Z} \models \phi$ iff $\mathbf{Z} \models \phi'$ where ϕ' is the same as ϕ except that $(Q_i t_i)$ is substituted by $(Q_i t_i \preceq 2^{K+i-2}(maxabs(\phi)+1) + i + 1)$ for all $i = 1, \ldots, K$.*

Proof: The sentence ϕ can be written as $(Q_1 t_1)\psi_1(t_1)$ where ψ_1 is a formula with $K - 1$ quantifiers. Thus lemma 4.1 implies that $\mathbf{Z} \models (Q_1 t_1)\psi_1(t_1)$ iff

$$\mathbf{Z} \models (Q_1 t_1 \preceq 2^{K-1}(maxabs(\phi)+1) + 2)\psi_1(t_1).$$

A similar inductive argument gives the result. ∎

Remark 4.1 The models of computation used in the rest of this paper are deterministic and non-deterministic Turing machines with a read-only input tape, a fixed number of read/write work tapes and a write-only output tape where the head can never move left. The *time* of a computation is its length. The *space* of a computation is the number of cells visited on the *work tapes*. Precise definitions of these notions and the associated time and space complexity classes can be found in the standard literature [Joh90].

If $i > 1$ then $\log i$ will denote $\lceil \log_2 i \rceil$. By convention we assume that $\log 1 = 1$.

Formulas will be represented by the standard binary encoding. Integers are written in binary. Rationals are written as fractions of two integers. Variables are chosen from v_0, v_1, v_{10} etc. (i.e., subscripts are written in binary). Finally, the size of all integer constants in a formula ϕ is assumed to be less than $\log |\phi|$.

The following theorem gives the exact complexity of the decision problem for diPC.

Theorem 4.1 *Let ϕ be a diPCL sentence. The problem of deciding whether $\mathbf{Z} \models \phi$ is PSPACE-complete.*

Proof: *Lower bound.* PSPACE-hardness follows from a straightfoward reduction from Quantified Boolean Formulas [Sto77].

Upper bound. It easy to write a recursive algorithm DIPC-EVAL which can be used to decide whether $\mathbf{Z} \models \phi$ using lemma 4.2. DIPC-EVAL can be implemented by a deterministic Turing machine which uses a stack for storing the activation record of each recursive call.

Whenever DIPC-EVAL is called with argument a quantified subformula ϕ' of ϕ, it determines the truth value of ϕ' by cycling through integers limited by $2^{2K-2}(maxabs(\phi) + 1) + K + 1$. Such integers can be written using $O(|\phi|)$ space. Therefore DIPC-EVAL needs $O(|\phi|^2)$ space for keeping track of the current assignment to the quantified variables of ϕ. No more space is required for bookkeeping. Thus deciding if $\mathbf{Z} \models \phi$ can be done in $O(|\phi|^2)$ space. ∎

The reader is invited to compare the above theorem with the following result.

Theorem 4.2 *[Ber80] The problem of deciding a sentence of length n of Presburger Arithmetic is complete for the class $\bigcup_{k>0} TA[2^{2^{n^k}}, n]$.*

The class $TA[t(n), a(n)]$ is the set of all problems solvable by alternating Turing machines using at most $t(n)$ time and $a(n)$ alternations on inputs of length n [Ber80, Joh90].

Let us now consider diPCL sentences with a fixed number of alternations of quantifiers.

Definition 4.4 Let $\mathcal{L}$ be a first-order language and k be a fixed natural number. A $\exists_k$ (resp. $\forall_k$) formula of $\mathcal{L}$ is a formula in prenex normal form with k alternations of quantifiers beginning with an existential (resp. universal) quantifier.

Theorem 4.3 *Let ϕ be a $\exists_k$ sentence of diPCL. The problem of deciding whether $\mathbf{Z} \models \phi$ is Σ_k^p-complete.*

A corresponding Π_k^p bound can be established for $\forall_k$ sentences of diPCL.

It might be interesting to compare the above result with the following result of [RL78].

Theorem 4.4 *There exist constants $d, e > 0$ such that a deterministic Turing machine can decide a sentence with length $n > 4$ and at most K alternations of quantifiers, in the first order theory of integer addition with order, in $O(2^{dn^{K+4}})$ space and $O(2^{2^{en^{K+4}}})$ time.*

4.1 OPEN FORMULAS

We will now present a quantifier elimination algorithm for open formulas of diPCL. Let us assume we have a formula $\phi(\bar{t})$ of diPCL such that $\bar{t}$ is the vector of all the free variables of ϕ. A quantifier free formula ϕ' equivalent to ϕ can be found in the following way. At first, using the techniques presented above, we estimate how large integer constants can grow in the constraints of a quantifier-free formula equivalent to ϕ. Then we use this information to construct a finite partition of the space $\mathbb{Z}^{|\bar{t}|}$ into *regions* with the following properties:

1. Every region can be represented by a conjunction of atomic diPCL formulas.

2. The truth value of the sentence $\phi(\bar{\tau})$ is the same for all points $\bar{\tau}$ in the same region.

Therefore we can check whether *all* points in a region satisfy $\phi(\bar{t})$ by picking a *single* point in the region and checking whether $\mathbb{Z} \models \phi(\bar{\tau})$ is true. The latter check can be done using the algorithm DIPC-EVAL of theorem 4.1. Every conjunction of atomic formulas which represents a region for which this check succeeds becomes a disjunct in the DNF form of ϕ'. Similar techniques have been used in the context of query processing in constraint databases by [KKR90].

The technical tools which we will introduce immediately come from the temporal constraint literature [DMP89]. Similar tools have also been used under various names in [Rev90, CM90] for studying the complexity of query evaluation for Datalog with integer gap-order constraints. Let C be a set (i.e., conjunction) of diPCL inequalities in variables $x_1, \ldots, x_n$. The *binary inequality constraint network* (BICN) associated with C is a labeled directed graph $G = (V, E)$ where $V = \{1, \ldots, n\}$. Node i represents variable x_i and edge (i, j) represents the binary constraints involving x_i and x_j. Let us assume that the constraints on $x_j - x_i$ are $x_j - x_i \leq d_{ij}$ and $x_j - x_i \geq -d_{ji}$ where $-d_{ji} < d_{ij}$. Then the corresponding BICN N will have an edge $i \to j$ labeled by the *convex* interval $N_{ij} = [-d_{ji}, d_{ij}]$. Unary constraints are represented with the introduction of a special variable $x_0 = 0$. The notions of solution set, consistency and minimality are defined as usual [DMP91]. We will also use a function $Constraints(N)$ which gives the set of binary constraints represented by BICN N. The formal definition of $Constraints$ is omitted.

An alternative graph representation will also be useful. Let C be a set of diPCL inequalities in variables $x_1, \ldots, x_n$. The *distance graph* associated with C is a directed labelled graph $G = (V, E)$ where $V = \{1, \ldots, n\}$. Node i represents variable x_i and edge (i, j) represents the binary constraints involving x_i and x_j. If there is a constraint $x_j - x_i \leq d_{ij}$ in C then edge $i \to j$ of the associated distance graph will be labelled by d_{ij}. The concept of *minimal distance graph* can be defined similarly with the concept of minimal network. Given the minimal network associated with a set of weak inequality constraints, it is trivial to construct the associated minimal distance graph (and vice versa). The set of constraints $Constraints(G)$ represented by a distance graph G is defined as for BICN.

Definition 4.5 Let $Z \subseteq \mathbb{Z}$ and $Z \neq \emptyset$. An *integer BICN with bounds from the set Z* is a consistent BICN with all edges labeled with $[c, c], (c, \infty)$ or $(-\infty, c)$ where $c \in Z$.

If an integer BICN has $n+1$ nodes (including the 0-th one which corresponds to variable $x_0 = 0$), we will say that it is of *size n*.

Let us now define the concept of a formula corresponding to a BICN N.

Definition 4.6 Let N be a BICN of size n. The formula with free variables $\bar{x} = (x_1, \ldots, x_n)$ corresponding to N is the diPCL formula $\bigwedge_{\theta \in Constraints(M)} \theta$ where M is the minimal network equivalent to N. This formula will be denoted by $\Phi(N)$.

Definition 4.7 If ϕ is a diPCL formula with K quantifiers and vector of free variables $\bar{t}$ then Z_ϕ will denote the set of integers

$$\{i : i \in \mathbb{Z} \text{ and } |i| \leq |\bar{t}| 2^K (maxabs(\phi) + 1)\}.$$

The following lemma tells us how to partition the answer space into regions.

Lemma 4.3 Let $\phi(\bar{t})$ be a diPCL formula. Then there is a quantifier-free formula $\phi'(\bar{t})$ equivalent to ϕ with the following properties:

1. ϕ' is in DNF

2. Every disjunct of ϕ' is the diPCL formula corresponding to an integer BICN N of size $|\bar{t}|$ with bounds from the set Z_ϕ.

Proof: Let $\phi_1(\bar{t})$ be the quantifier-free formula

$$\psi_1(\bar{t}) \vee \cdots \vee \psi_m(\bar{t})$$

equivalent to ϕ obtained by the algorithm of proposition 3.1. Let us also assume that the only relation symbol appearing in ψ_1 is $\leq$. As in the proof of lemma 4.1, integer constants in ϕ_1 are limited by $2^K(maxabs(\phi) + 1)$.

Let $N_1, \ldots, N_{m_1}$, $(m_1 \leq m)$ be the minimal BICN corresponding to the consistent ψ_i's $(i = 1, \ldots, m)$. Let us create the formula

$$\phi_2(\bar{t}) \equiv \psi'_1(\bar{t}) \vee \cdots \vee \psi'_{m_1}(\bar{t})$$

where
$$\psi'_i = \bigwedge_{\eta \in Constraints(N_i)} \eta, \text{ for all } i = 1, \ldots, m_1.$$

Every integer r, such that $t_k - t_l \leq r$ (or $t_k - t_l = r$) is a conjunct in some ψ'_i, is the length of the shortest (*simple*) path connecting nodes k and l in the minimal distance graph for N_i [DMP91]. The number of edges in a simple path is $|\bar{t}|$ and the label of each edge is limited by $2^K(maxabs(\phi)+1)$. Therefore every integer in ϕ_2 is limited by $|\bar{t}| 2^K(maxabs(\phi) + 1)$.

We can now obtain a formula equivalent to ϕ_2 in the desired form as follows:

1. From every ψ'_i construct a conjuction of disjunctions ψ''_i in the following way.
   (a) For every pair of variables t_k, t_l such that $t_k - t_l = r_1$ is in ψ'_i, add $t_k - t_l = r_1$ to ψ''_i.
   (b) For every pair of variables t_k, t_l such that $t_k - t_l \leq r_1$ and $t_k - t_l \geq r_2$ is in ψ'_i, add
   $$\bigvee_{r_1 \leq r \leq r_2} t_k - t_l = r$$
   to ψ''_i.
   (c) For every pair of variables such that only $t_k - t_l \leq r_1$ is in ψ'_i, add conjunct
   $$t_k - t_l < -\Lambda \vee \bigvee_{-\Lambda \leq r \leq r_1} t_k - t_l = r$$
   to ψ''_i where $\Lambda = |\bar{t}| 2^K(maxabs(\phi) + 1)$.
   (d) For every pair of variables such that only $t_k - t_l \geq r_2$ is in ψ'_i, add conjunct
   $$\bigvee_{r_2 \leq r \leq \Lambda} t_k - t_l = r \vee t_k - t_l > \Lambda$$
   to ψ''_i where Λ is as above.
   (e) For every pair of variables t_k, t_l such that ψ'_i contains no constraint involving t_k and t_l, add conjunct
   $$t_k - t_l < -\Lambda \vee \bigvee_{r_1 \leq r \leq r_2} t_k - t_l = r \vee t_k - t_l > \Lambda$$
   to ψ''_i where Λ is as above.
2. Transform every $\psi''_i(\bar{t})$ in DNF. Let
$$\theta_1(\bar{t}) \vee \cdots \vee \theta_n(\bar{t})$$
be the resulting formula.
3. Let $M_1, \ldots, M_{n_1}$, $(n_1 \leq n)$ be the minimal BICN corresponding to consistent θ_i's $(i = 1, \ldots, n)$. The wanted formula $\phi'(\bar{t})$ is
$$\theta'_1(\bar{t}) \vee \cdots \vee \theta'_{n_1}(\bar{t})$$
where
$$\theta'_i = \bigwedge_{\eta \in Constraints(M_i)} \eta, \text{ for all } i = 1, \ldots, n_1.$$

∎

The following lemmas give some important properties of integer BICN.

Lemma 4.4 *Let $\bar{\tau}$ be an element of $\mathbb{Z}^n$. For any set $Z \subseteq \mathbb{Z}$, there exists a unique integer BICN N with bounds from Z such that $\mathbf{Z} \models \Phi(N)(\bar{\tau})$.*

Proof: Existence is obvious. For the uniqueness part, we simply observe that $N_1 \neq N_2$ implies that $\Phi(N_1) \wedge \Phi(N_2)$ is inconsistent. ∎

The following lemma allows us to verify the truth of a diPCL formula over a region of the answer space by verifying its truth over a *point* in this region.

Lemma 4.5 *Let $\phi(\bar{t})$ be a diPCL formula and N be an integer BICN with bounds from the set Z_ϕ. Then $\mathbf{Z} \models \Phi(N) \supset \phi$ iff $\mathbf{Z} \models \phi(\bar{\tau})$ is true for an arbitrary $\bar{\tau}$ such that $\mathbf{Z} \models \Phi(N)(\bar{\tau})$.*

Proof: The "only if" part is trivial so we consider the "if" part. Let us assume that there is $\bar{\tau} \in \mathbb{Z}^{|\bar{t}|}$ such that $\mathbf{Z} \models \Phi(N)(\bar{\tau})$ and $\mathbf{Z} \models \psi(\bar{\tau})$. Let
$$\phi'(\bar{t}) \equiv \theta'_1(\bar{t})) \vee \cdots \vee \theta'_n(\bar{t})$$
be the diPCL formula equivalent to ϕ computed as in lemma 4.3. Then there exists a single disjunct $\theta_i(\bar{t})$ of ϕ' such that $\mathbf{Z} \models \theta_i(\bar{\tau})$. But then θ_i must be $\Phi(N)$ from lemma 4.4. Therefore $\mathbf{Z} \models \forall(\Phi(N) \supset \phi)$ since $\Phi(N)$ is a disjunct of ϕ'. ∎

Now we are ready to demonstrate the main result of this section.

Theorem 4.5 *Let ϕ be a diPCL formula. A quantifier-free formula equivalent to ϕ in DNF can be computed in PSPACE.*

Proof: Let us assume that $\bar{t}$ is the vector of all free variables of ϕ. We can compute a quantifier-free formula equivalent to ϕ in DNF as follows. We generate one by one all integer BICN of size $|\bar{t}|$ with bounds from Z_ϕ. For every such BICN N, we find a solution $\bar{\tau}$ of N and check whether $\mathbf{Z} \models \phi(\bar{\tau})$ using the algorithm DIPC-EVAL of theorem 4.1. If this check succeeds, the diPCL formula corresponding to N becomes a disjunct of the resulting quantifier-free formula. The correctness of this procedure follows from lemmas 4.3 and 4.5.

Finding a solution of a BICN can be done in the following way. We first compute the minimal network M equivalent to N. Then we find a solution of M using *backtrack-free* search as follows [DMP91]. We initially assign the value 0 to t_0. Then we assign to t_1 any value which satisfies the constraints involving t_1 and t_0. We proceed in the same fashion with t_2, t_3 and so on.

It is not difficult to show that the above procedure can be implemented by a deterministic Turing machine in

PSPACE. A detailed proof can be found in [Kou94a]. ∎

5 AN IMPROVED QUANTIFIER ELIMINATION ALGORITHM FOR dePC

Let us now turn to quantifier elimination and decision for dePCL. We will first develop a decision procedure for sentences of dePCL. Then we will use this procedure for developing a quantifier elimination algorithm for arbitrary dePCL formulas.

At first we show that we can confine our attention to formulas of dePCL involving *only integer* constants. A similar result appears in [Alu91] in the context of checking emptiness of the language of a timed automaton.

Definition 5.1 Let ϕ be a formula of dePCL and $r \in \mathbf{Q}$. Then ϕ_r will denote the formula which is obtained from ϕ by replacing each rational constant c by $r \cdot c$.

Lemma 5.1 *Let ϕ be a formula of dePCL with free variables $\bar{t}$. If $r \in \mathbf{Q}$, $r > 0$ and $\bar{\tau} \in \mathbf{Q}^n$ then*

$$\mathbf{Q} \models \phi[\bar{t} \leftarrow \bar{\tau}] \text{ iff } \mathbf{Q} \models \phi_r[\bar{t} \leftarrow r \cdot \bar{\tau}].$$

Proof: Use induction on the structure of ϕ. ∎

The following definition will be used heavily in the subsequent discussion.

Definition 5.2 A quantifier Qz is limited by the fraction A/B, denoted by $Qz \preceq A/B$, if, instead of ranging over all rational numbers, it ranges over all numbers whose numerator is limited by A and whose denominator *is* B.

Lemma 5.2 *Let ϕ be the following dePCL sentence*

$$(Q_1 t_1) \cdots (Q_K t_K) \psi(t_1, \ldots, t_K).$$

Let us also assume that only integer constants are involved in ϕ. Then $\mathbf{Q} \models \phi$ iff $\mathbf{Q} \models \phi'$ where ϕ' is the same as ϕ except that $(Q_i t_i)$ is substituted by

$$(Q_i \preceq \frac{2^{K+3i-2}(maxabs(\phi)+1)}{2^i})$$

for all $i = 1, \ldots, K$.

Proof: We will use induction on the order of appearance of the quantifier in ϕ. We assume that ϕ is in PNF. Note that the proof still goes through when this assumption is dropped.

Base case, $i = 1$. Let us eliminate quantifiers $(Q_2 t_2), \ldots, (Q_K t_K)$ from ϕ using the procedure of proposition 3.1. The integer constants in the resulting formula $(Q_1 t_1) \phi'(t_1)$ are limited by $2^{K-1}(maxabs(\phi)+$

1) (this can be shown as in lemma 4.1). These integers partition $\mathbf{Q}$ into a set S of $4 \cdot 2^{K-1}(maxabs(\phi)+1)+3$ intervals of the form $(-\infty, r)$ or $[r, r]$ or $(r, r+1)$ or (r, ∞) where $r \preceq 2^{K-1}(maxabs(\phi)+1)$. The truth value of $\phi'(t_1)$ remains the same for all t_1 in the same interval of S. Therefore we can determine the truth value of $(Q t_1) \phi'(t_1)$ in $\mathbf{Q}$ by determining the truth value of $\phi'(t_1)$ while t_1 ranges over a finite set of representatives, one for each interval of S. The set

$$S_{rep} = \{ (t_1+t_2)/2, (t_1+t_2)/2 + 1 : t_1, t_2 \in \mathbb{Z} \text{ and } t_1, t_2 \preceq 2^{K-1}(maxabs(\phi)+1) \}$$

is an appropriate set of such representatives. The elements of S_{rep} are rationals limited by $2^{K+1}(maxabs(\phi)+1)/2$.

Inductive step. Let us now assume that the lemma holds for quantifiers $(Q_1 t_1), \ldots, (Q_i t_i)$. We will show that the lemma holds for $(Q_{i+1} t_{i+1})$ as well. From the induction hypothesis we have $\mathbf{Q} \models \phi$ if and only if $\mathbf{Q} \models \phi_1$ where ϕ_1 is

$$(Q_1 t_1 \preceq \frac{2^{K+1}(maxabs(\phi)+1)}{2}) \cdots$$
$$(Q_i t_i \preceq \frac{2^{K+3i-2}(maxabs(\phi)+1)}{2^i})$$
$$(Q_{i+1} t_{i+1}) \cdots (Q_K t_K) \psi(t_1, \ldots, t_K).$$

Let us eliminate quantifiers $(Q_{i+2} t_{i+2}), \cdots, (Q_K t_K)$ from ϕ_1 using the procedure of proposition 3.1 to arrive at the following formula ϕ_2:

$$(Q_1 t_1 \preceq \frac{2^{K+1}(maxabs(\phi)+1)}{2}) \cdots$$
$$(Q_i t_i \preceq \frac{2^{K+3i-2}(maxabs(\phi)+1)}{2^i})$$
$$(Q_{i+1} t_{i+1}) \psi_1(t_1, \ldots, t_{i+1}).$$

The truth value of ϕ_2 depends on the truth values of all formulas

$$(Q_{i+1} t_{i+1}) \psi_1(\tau_1, \ldots, \tau_i, t_{i+1})$$

where

$$\tau_j \leq \frac{2^{K+3j-2}(maxabs(\phi)+1)}{2^j}, \quad j = 1, \ldots, i.$$

The atomic formulas of $(Q_{i+1} t_{i+1}) \psi_1(\tau_1, \ldots, \tau_i, t_{i+1})$ are of the form $t_{i+1} \sim r$ or $t_{i+1} \sim \tau_j + r$ where $1 \leq j \leq i$, $\sim$ is $<, \leq$ or $=$, τ_j is a rational limited as above and r is an integer limited by $2^{K-(i+1)}(maxabs(\phi)+1)$.

Let us now observe that every rational limited by $2^{K+3j-2}(maxabs(\phi)+1)/2^j$, where $1 \leq j \leq i-1$, is included in the set of rationals limited by $2^{K+3i-2}(maxabs(\phi)+1)/2^i$. Therefore $\tau_j + r$ is a rational limited by $2^{K+3i-1}(maxabs(\phi)+1)/2^i$.

Using an argument similar to the one given for the base case, we can see that the quantifier $(Q_{i+1} t_{i+1})$ can be limited to range over rationals that are the average of two rationals limited by $2^{K+3i-1}(maxabs(\phi)+1)/2^i$, or are one smaller or one larger than all such averages. As a result, $(Q_{i+1} t_{i+1})$ can be limited by

$2^{K+3(i+1)-2}(maxabs(\phi)+1)/2^{i+1}$. The result follows. ∎

Definition 5.3 If ϕ is a dePCL formula then $maxabs(\phi)$ will denote the maximum absolute value of the integers which appear in ϕ as numerators or denominators. If ϕ involves only integer constants then $maxabs(\phi)$ will denote the maximum absolute value of the integers which appear in ϕ.

We are now ready to prove the basic result of this section.

Theorem 5.1 Let ϕ be a dePCL sentence. The problem of deciding whether $\mathbf{Q} \models \phi$ is PSPACE-complete.

Proof: *Lower bound.* PSPACE-hardness follows from a straightfoward reduction from QBF [Sto77].

Upper bound. An algorithm for this problem can proceed as follows. First, we transform ϕ into formula ϕ' which involves only integer constants. This can be done by multiplying every fraction p/q of ϕ by the product of all denominators of fractions in ϕ. Therefore every integer in ϕ' will be limited by $maxabs(\phi)^{|\phi|+1}$. We can conclude that

$$|\phi'| \leq |\phi|(|\phi|+1)\log(maxabs(\phi)) \leq$$
$$2|\phi|^2 \log(maxabs(\phi)) \leq 2|\phi|^2 \log|\phi|$$

and $maxabs(\phi') \leq maxabs(\phi)^{|\phi|+1}$.

Then we can devise a recursive algorithm DEPC-EVAL, similar to DIPC-EVAL, which decides ϕ'. This algorithm will make use of lemma 5.2 to limit quantifiers over finite sets of rationals. Every such rational has a numerator limited by $2^{4K-2}(maxabs(\phi')+1)$ and a denominator limited by 2^K where K is the number of quantifiers in ϕ'. Storing the numerator of each one of these rationals requires

$$4K - 2 + \log(maxabs(\phi') + 1) \leq$$
$$4K - 1 + \log(maxabs(\phi)^{|\phi|+1}) \leq$$
$$4K - 1 + (|\phi|+1)\log(maxabs(\phi)) \leq O(|\phi|\log|\phi|)$$

bits while storing the denominator requires $O(|\phi|)$ bits. Thus DEPC-EVAL needs $O(|\phi|^2 \log|\phi|)$ space for keeping track of the current assignment to the quantified variables of ϕ'. No more space is required for bookkeeping. Therefore the total space requirement of DEPC-EVAL is $O(|\phi|^2 \log|\phi|)$. ∎

It might be interesting to compare the above result with the following theorems. The first one considers a theory which is less expressive than dePC. The second deals with the full first-order theory of real addition with order.

Theorem 5.2 *[FG77] Deciding a sentence of length n in the first order theory of rational order can be done in deterministic space $O(n \log n)$.*

Theorem 5.3 *[Ber80, BM80] The problem of deciding a sentence of length n in the theory of real addition with order is complete for the class $\bigcup_{k>0} TA[2^{n^k}, n]$.*

The next theorem follows easily from the above discussion. It is also a consequence of the fact that deciding a formula of the same form in the first-order theory of real addition with order is also Σ_k^p-complete [Son85].

Theorem 5.4 Let ϕ be $\exists_k$ sentence of dePCL. The problem of deciding whether $\mathbf{Q} \models \phi$ is Σ_k^p-complete.

A corresponding Π_k^p bound can be established for $\forall_k$ sentences of dePCL.

5.1 Open Formulas

We will now present a quantifier elimination algorithm for open formulas of dePCL. We will proceed as in the case of diPCL formulas. The following lemma will allow us to concentrate on dePCL formulas involving only integer constants.

Lemma 5.3 Let ϕ be a formula of dePCL and ϕ' be a quantifier-free formula equivalent to ϕ. If $r \in \mathbf{Q}$ and $r > 0$ then $\phi' \equiv \psi_{r^{-1}}$ where ψ is a quantifier-free formula equivalent to ϕ_r.

Proof: Let $\overline{x}$ be the vector of variables in ϕ'. If $\overline{\chi} \in \mathbf{Q}^{|\overline{x}|}$ then the following equivalences prove the lemma (with help from lemma 5.1):

$\mathbf{Q} \models \phi'[\overline{x} \leftarrow \overline{\chi}]$ iff $\mathbf{Q} \models \phi[\overline{x} \leftarrow \overline{\chi}]$ iff
$\mathbf{Q} \models \phi_r[\overline{x} \leftarrow r \cdot \overline{\chi}]$ iff $\mathbf{Q} \models \psi[\overline{x} \leftarrow r \cdot \overline{\chi}]$ iff
$\mathbf{Q} \models \psi_{r^{-1}}[\overline{x} \leftarrow \overline{\chi}]$.

∎

Now assume we are given a formula ϕ of dePCL. We can find a quantifier-free formula equivalent to ϕ as follows. First we transform ϕ into a formula ϕ_r which has only integer constants by multiplying every fraction by an appropriate integer r. Then we find a quantifier-free formula ψ equivalent to ϕ_r. Finally, we compute $\psi_{r^{-1}}$ which is a quantifier-free formula equivalent to ϕ.

Let us then assume that $\phi(\overline{t})$ is a formula of dePCL which involves only integer constants, and $\overline{t}$ are all the free variables of ϕ. A quantifier free formula ϕ' equivalent to ϕ can be found in the following way. At first, we estimate how large integer constants can grow in the constraints of the answer. Then we use this information to construct a finite partition of the space $\mathbf{Q}^{|\overline{t}|}$ into *regions* with the following properties:

1. Every region can be represented by a conjunction of dePCL-constraints involving only integer constants.

2. The truth value of the sentence $\phi(\overline{\tau})$ is the same for all points $\overline{\tau}$ in the same region.

Therefore we can check whether *all* points in a region satisfy $\phi(\bar{t})$ by picking a *single* point $\bar{\tau}$ in the region and checking whether $\mathbf{Q} \models \phi(\bar{\tau})$ is true. The latter check can be done using the above algorithm DEPC-EVAL. Every conjunction of constraints representing a region for which this check succeeds, becomes a disjunct in the DNF form of ϕ'.

Let us now introduce the machinery required for presenting our method. We first define rational BICN.

Definition 5.4 *A rational BICN with bounds from the set $Z \subseteq \mathbb{Z}$ is a consistent BICN with all edges labeled with $[c,c], (c,d), (c,\infty)$ or $(-\infty, c)$ where $c < d$ and $c, d \in Z$.*

The *size* of a rational BICN is defined as for integer BICN.

Let us now define the concept of a formula corresponding to a rational BICN N.

Definition 5.5 *Let N be a rational BICN of size n. The formula with free variables $\bar{x} = (x_1, \ldots, x_n)$ corresponding to N is the dePCL formula $\bigwedge_{\theta \in Constraints(M)} \theta$ where M is the minimal network equivalent to N. This formula will be denoted by $\Phi(N)$.*

Definition 5.6 *If ϕ is a dePCL formula with K quantifiers and vector of free variables $\bar{t}$ then Z_ϕ will denote the set of integers*

$$\{i : i \in \mathbb{Z} \text{ and } |i| \leq |\bar{t}| 2^K maxabs(\phi)\}.$$

The following lemmas help to establish the main result. The reader can easily notice the similarity with the development of section 4.1. Lemma 5.4 tells us how to partition the answer space into regions. Subsequent lemmas give properties of rational BICN. The proofs of some of the lemmas are omitted.

Lemma 5.4 *Let $\phi(\bar{t})$ be a dePCL formula involving only integer constants. Then there is a quantifier-free formula $\phi'(\bar{t})$ equivalent to ϕ with the following properties:*

1. *ϕ' is in DNF*
2. *Every disjunct of ϕ' is the dePCL formula corresponding to a rational BICN N of size $|\bar{t}|$ with bounds from the set Z_ϕ.*

Proof: First, we transform ϕ into an equivalent quantifier-free formula ϕ_1 using the algorithm of proposition 3.1. Integer constants in ϕ_1 will be limited by $2^K maxabs(\phi)$. Then we proceed as in lemma 4.3. ■

Lemma 5.5 *Let $\bar{\tau}$ be an element of $\mathbb{Q}^n$. For any set $Z \subseteq \mathbb{Z}$, there exists a unique rational BICN N with bounds from Z such that $\mathbf{Q} \models \Phi(N)(\bar{\tau})$.*

Lemma 5.6 *Let $\phi(\bar{t})$ be a dePCL formula involving only integer constants. If N is a rational BICN with bounds from the set Z_ϕ then $\mathbf{Q} \models \Phi(N) \supset \phi$ iff $\mathbf{Q} \models \phi(\bar{\tau})$ for an arbitrary $\bar{\tau}$ such that $\mathbf{Q} \models \Phi(N)(\bar{\tau})$.*

The following theorem gives the main result of this section.

Theorem 5.5 *Let ϕ be a dePCL formula. A quantifier-free formula equivalent to ϕ in DNF can be computed in PSPACE.*

Proof: Let us assume that ϕ has K quantifiers and $\bar{t}$ is the vector of all its free variables. We can find a quantifier-free formula equivalent to ϕ as follows. First, we transform ϕ into a formula ϕ' which involves only integer constants. This can be done as in theorem 5.1: we multiply every fraction of ϕ by the product P of all denominators of fractions in ϕ.

Secondly, we generate, one by one, all rational BICN of size $|\bar{t}|$ with bounds from

$$Z_{\phi'} = \{i : i \in \mathbb{Z} \text{ and } |i| \leq |\bar{t}| 2^K maxabs(\phi)^{|\phi|+1}\}$$

(since $maxabs(\phi') \leq maxabs(\phi)^{|\phi|+1}$). For each BICN N, we find a solution $\bar{\tau}$ of N (using the minimal network M) and check whether $\mathbf{Q} \models \phi'(\bar{\tau})$ using algorithm DEPC-EVAL of theorem 5.1. If this check succeeds then we divide each constant of $\Phi(N)$ by P and use the result to form a disjunct of the returned formula. The correctness of this procedure follows from the previous lemmas. It is not difficult to see that the above algorithm can be implemented by a deterministic Turing machine in PSPACE [Kou94a]. ■

6 THEORIES OF POINT AND INTERVAL CONSTRAINTS

We will now extend the theory diPC to take interval constraints into account. We define the language diTCL (*di*screte *T*emporal *C*onstraint *L*anguage) which is an extension of diPCL. The time entities in this language are points and intervals. Points are identified with the integers while intervals are considered to be pairs of points. diTCL has two sorts: $\mathcal{Z}$ (for points or integers) and $\mathcal{I_Z}$ (for integer intervals). The non-logical symbols of diTCL include a countably infinite set of constant symbols of sort $\mathcal{Z}$ (the point or integer constants), function symbols L and R of sort $(\mathcal{I_Z}, \mathcal{Z})$, function symbol $-$ of sort $(\mathcal{Z}, \mathcal{Z}, \mathcal{Z})$ and predicate symbol $<$ of sort $(\mathcal{Z}, \mathcal{Z})$.

The set of *simple terms* of diTCL are defined by the following rules:

- Constants are simple terms.
- A variable of sort $\mathcal{Z}$ is a simple term.
- If i is a variable of sort $\mathcal{I_Z}$ then i_L and i_R are simple terms.

The set of *terms* of diTCL can now be defined as follows:

- Simple terms are terms.
- If t_1 and t_2 are simple terms then $t_1 - t_2$ is a term.

An *atomic formula* of diTCL is a formula of the form $t \sim c$ or $c \sim t$ where $\sim$ is $<$ or $=$ and t is a term. The set of *well-formed formulas* is defined as usual.

The symbols of diTCL are interpreted with respect to the fixed structure $\mathbf{ZI_Z}$ which captures our assumptions. $\mathbf{ZI_Z}$ assigns to the sort $\mathcal{Z}$ the set of integers $\mathbb{Z}$, and to the sort $\mathcal{I_Z}$ the set of *integer intervals* $Int(\mathbb{Z}) = \{(a,b) : a, b \in \mathbb{Z} \text{ and } a <_{\mathbb{Z}} b\}$. To each constant symbol of sort $\mathcal{Z}$, $\mathbf{ZI_Z}$ assigns an element of $\mathbb{Z}$. To function symbols L and R, $\mathbf{ZI_Z}$ assigns the functions $l, r : Int(\mathbb{Z}) \rightarrow \mathbb{Z}$ such that $l((a,b)) = a$ and $r((a,b)) = b$. These functions map each interval to its left and right endpoint respectively. To function symbol $-$, $\mathbf{ZI_Z}$ assigns the function $-_\mathbb{Z}$ which is the subtraction operation over the integers. To predicate symbol $<$, $\mathbf{ZI_Z}$ assigns the relation $<_\mathbb{Z}$ over the integers.

We will take the theory of structure $\mathbf{ZI_Z}$ to be *the* theory of point and interval constraints in linear, unbounded and discrete time. This theory will be denoted by *diTC*.

In a similar way we can extend dePC to account for time intervals. The corresponding theory will be called *deTC* and its language *deTCL*. Detailed definitions can be found in [Kou94a].

Let us observe that we can introduce all the interval-to-interval relations and point-to-interval relations of [Mei91] as defined relations in these theories.

We can now use the results of sections 4 and 5 and a translation from diTCL to diPCL (as in [Lad88]) to achieve the following results. Details can be found in [Kou94a].

Theorem 6.1 *The decision problem for arbitrary diTCL or deTCL sentences is PSPACE-complete. The decision problem for $\exists_k$ sentences of diTCL or deTCL is Σ_k^p-complete.*

Theorem 6.2 *Let ϕ be a diTCL or deTCL formula. A quantifier-free formula equivalent to ϕ in DNF can be computed in PSPACE.*

7 CONCLUSIONS

In this paper we discussed the complexity of quantifier elimination and decision algorithms for the theory of point constraints over the integers (diPC) and over the rationals (dePC). The theory diPC is a special case of the theory of Presburger arithmetic while dePC is a special case of the theory of real addition with order. We have shown that in both cases quantifier-elimination can be done in PSPACE. We have also shown that the decision problem for arbitrarily quantified sentences is PSPACE-complete while for $\exists_k$ sentences it is Σ_k^p-complete. The bounds for the two theories of point constraints do not change if intervals and interval constraints are introduced.

Our results will be interesting to researchers in constraint databases [KKR90] but also to the theoretical computer science community in general. In [Kou94a, Kou94b] the results of this paper are used to study the complexity of query evaluation in indefinite temporal constraint databases. In related work [Rev90] considered Datalog with integer gap-order constraints ($Datalog^{<_\mathbb{Z}}$). A *gap-order constraint* is a constraint of the form:

$$x = c, \; x = y, \; x < c, \; c < x \text{ or } x - y < g$$

where x, y are variables ranging over $\mathbb{Z}$, $c \in \mathbb{Z}$, $g \in \mathbb{Z}$ and $g \geq 0$. Revesz showed that $Datalog^{<_\mathbb{Z}}$ queries over integer gap-order databases can be evaluated in closed form. In addition recognizing whether a certain tuple is in the answer to a query can be done with PTIME *data complexity*.[3] Independently the above problem has been solved in [CM90] who have also considered gap-order constraints over a dense domain. The only difference with [Rev90] is that [CM90] do not consider data complexity thus the complexity of their query evaluation procedure is EXPTIME.

Acknowledgements

This research is part of the author's Ph.D. thesis. It was initiated at the University of Toronto and was continued at the Institute of Computer Science, FORTH and the National Technical University of Athens. I would like to thank Timos Sellis, John Mylopoulos, Alberto Mendelzon, Stathis Zachos, Yannis Vassiliou, Costas Courcoubetis, Dimitris Plexousakis and Thodoros Topaloglou for their encouragement and support. Financial support was gratefully received from the National Technical University of Athens, the Dept. of Computer Science, University of Toronto the Institute of Computer Science, FORTH. In the final stages of the preparation of this paper, the author was financially supported by the Planning Applications Research Centre, Imperial College.

---

[3]The notion of data complexity was originally introduced in [Var82] in the context of query evaluation for relational databases. When we consider *data complexity*, we measure the complexity of evaluating a query over a database as a function of the database size only; the query program and the database schema are considered *fixed*.

References

[All83] J.F. Allen. Maintaining Knowledge about Temporal Intervals. *Communications of the ACM*, 26(11):832–843, November 1983.

[Alu91] R. Alur. *Techniques for Automatic Verification of Real-Time Systems*. PhD thesis, Dept. of Computer Science, Stanford University, 1991.

[Ber80] L. Berman. The Complexity of Logical Theories. *Theoretical Computer Science*, 11:71–78, 1980.

[BM80] A.R. Bruss and A.R. Meyer. On Time-Space Classes and their Relation to the Theory of Real Addition. *Theoretical Computer Science*, 11:59–69, 1980.

[CK73] C.C. Chang and H.J. Keisler. *Model Theory*. North Holland, 1973.

[CM90] J. Cox and K. McAloon. Decision Procedures for Constraint Based Extensions of Datalog. Technical Report 90-09, Dept. of Computer and Information Sciences, Brooklyn College of C.U.N.Y., 1990.

[CMT92] J. Cox, K. McAloon, and C. Tretkoff. Computational Complexity and Constraint Logic Programing Languages. *Annals of Mathematics and Artificial Intelligence*, 5:163–189, 1992.

[DMP89] Rina Dechter, Itay Meiri, and Judea Pearl. Temporal Constraint Networks. In R. Brachman, H. Levesque, and R. Reiter, editors, *Proceedings of 1st International Conference on Principles of Knowledge Representation and Reasoning*, pages 83–93, Toronto, Ontario, 1989.

[DMP91] Rina Dechter, Itay Meiri, and Judea Pearl. Temporal Constraint Networks. *Artificial Intelligence*, 49(1-3):61–95, 1991. Special Volume on Knowledge Representation.

[DP88] Rina Dechter and Judea Pearl. Network-Based Heuristics for Constraint Satisfaction Problems. *Artificial Intelligence*, 34(1):1–38, 1988.

[End72] H.B. Enderton. *A Mathematical Introduction to Logic*. Academic Press, 1972.

[FG77] J. Ferrante and J.R. Geiser. An Efficient Decision Procedure for the Theory of Rational Order. *Theoretical Computer Science*, 4(2):227–233, 1977.

[FR75] J. Ferrante and C. Rackoff. A Decision Procedure for the First Order Theory of Real Addition with Order. *SIAM Journal on Computing*, 4(1):69–76, 1975.

[GS93] A. Gerevini and L. Schubert. Efficient Temporal Reasoning Through Timegraphs. In *Proceedings of IJCAI-93*, pages 648–654, 1993.

[Joh90] D.S. Johnson. A Catalog of Complexity Classes. In J. van Leeuwen, editor, *Handbook of Theoretical Computer Science*, volume A, chapter 2. North-Holland, 1990.

[KKR90] Paris C. Kanellakis, Gabriel M. Kuper, and Peter Z. Revesz. Constraint Query Languages. In *Proceedings of the 9th ACM SIGACT-SIGMOD-SIGART Symposium on Principles of Database Systems*, pages 299–313, 1990. Long version to appear in Journal of Computer and System Sciences.

[KL91] H. Kautz and P. Ladkin. Integrating Metric and Qualitative Temporal Reasoning. In *Proceedings of AAAI-91*, pages 241–246, 1991.

[Kou92] Manolis Koubarakis. Dense Time and Temporal Constraints with $\neq$. In *Principles of Knowledge Representation and Reasoning: Proceedings of the Third International Conference (KR'92)*, pages 24–35. Morgan Kaufmann, San Mateo, CA, October 1992.

[Kou94a] M. Koubarakis. *Foundations of Temporal Constraint Databases*. PhD thesis, Computer Science Division, Dept. of Electrical and Computer Engineering, National Technical University of Athens, February 1994.

[Kou94b] Manolis Koubarakis. The Complexity of Query Evaluation in Indefinite Temporal Constraint Databases, February 1994. Unpublished paper.

[Lad88] Peter Ladkin. Satisfying First-Order Constraints About Time Intervals. In *Proceedings of AAAI-88*, pages 512–517, 1988.

[LM88] Peter Ladkin and Roger Maddux. On Binary Constraint Networks. Technical Report KES.U.88.8, Kestrel Institute Technical Report, 1988.

[Mac77] A.K. Mackworth. Consistency in Networks of Relations. *Artificial Intelligence*, 8(1):99–118, 1977.

[Mei91] I. Meiri. Combining Qualitative and Quantitative Constraints in Temporal Reasoning. In *Proceedings of AAAI-91*, pages 260–267, 1991.

[Mon74] U. Montanari. Networks of Constraints: Fundamental Properties and Applications to Picture Processing. *Information Sciences*, 7:95–132, 1974.

[Rab77] M.O. Rabin. Decidable theories. In *Handbook of Mathematical Logic*, volume 90 of *Studies in Logic and the Foundations* of Mathematics, pages 595–629. North-Holland, 1977.

[Rev90] Peter Z. Revesz. A Closed Form for Datalog Queries with Integer Order. In *Proceedings of the 3rd International Conference on Database Theory*, pages 187–201, 1990. Long version to appear in Theoretical Computer Science.

[RL78] C.R. Reddy and D.W. Loveland. Presburger Arithmetic with Bounded Quantifier Alternation. In *Proc. of ACM Symposium on the Theory of Computing*, pages 320–325, 1978.

[Sch86] A. Schrijver, editor. *Theory of Integer and Linear Programming*. Wiley, 1986.

[SD93] E. Schwalb and R. Dechter. Coping with Disjunctions in Temporal Constraint Satisfaction Problems. In *Proceedings of AAAI-93*, 1993.

[Son85] E. Sontag. Real Addition and the Polynomial Time Hierarchy. *Information Processing Letters*, 20:115–120, 1985.

[Sto77] L.J. Stockmeyer. The Polynomial-Time Hierarchy. *Theoretical Computer Science*, 3:1–22, 1977.

[Var82] Moshe Vardi. The Complexity of Relational Query Languages. In *Proceedings of ACM SIGACT/SIGMOD Symposium on Principles of Database Systems*, pages 137–146, 1982.

[vB92] Peter van Beek. Reasoning About Qualitative Temporal Information. *Artificial Intelligence*, 58:297–326, 1992.

[vBC90] Peter van Beek and Robin Cohen. Exact and Approximate Reasoning about Temporal Relations. *Computational Intelligence*, 6:132–144, 1990.

[VKvB89] Marc Vilain, Henry Kautz, and Peter van Beek. Constraint Propagation Algorithms for Temporal Reasoning: a Revised Report. In D.S. Weld and J. de Kleer, editors, *Readings in Qualitative Reasoning about Physical Systems*, pages 373–381. Morgan Kaufmann, 1989.

Reasoning in Logic about Continuous Systems

Benjamin J. Kuipers
Computer Science Department
University of Texas at Austin
Austin, TX 78712
kuipers@cs.utexas.edu

Benjamin Shults
Department of Mathematics
University of Texas at Austin
Austin, TX 78712
bshults@math.utexas.edu

Abstract

An intelligent agent, reasoning symbolically in a continuous world, needs to infer properties of the behaviors of continuous systems. A qualitative simulator, such as QSIM, constructs a set of possible behaviors consistent with a qualitative differential equation (QDE) and initial state. This set of behaviors is expressed as a finite tree of qualitative state descriptions. In the case of QSIM, this set is guaranteed to contain the "actual" behavior under certain circumstances. We call this property the "soundness" of QSIM. The behavior tree can then be interpreted as a model for statements in a branching-time temporal logic such as Expressive Behavior Tree Logic (EBTL), which we introduce. Because QSIM is sound, validity of an EBTL proposition (**necessarily** p) implies the corresponding theorem about the dynamical system described by the QDE. Therefore, at least for universals, statements in temporal logic about continuous systems can be proved by qualitative simulation. This allows a hybrid reasoning system to prove such commonsense statements as "what goes up (in a constant gravitational field) must come down", or to do such expert reasoning about dynamical systems as proving the stability of a nonlinear, heterogeneous controller.

1 INTRODUCTION

The world is infinite and continuous. A logical proof is finite and discrete. Nonetheless we want, and reasonably expect, to use logic to draw reliable conclusions about continuous behavior in the world.

A qualitative differential equation (QDE) is a symbolic description expressing a state of incomplete knowledge of the continuous world, and is thus an abstraction of an infinite set of ordinary differential equations. Qualitative simulation, using an algorithm such as QSIM [Kuipers, 86], predicts the set of possible behaviors consistent with a QDE and an initial state.

The QSIM algorithm generates a tree of qualitative states representing a branching-time description of the possible behaviors of the system being described. Qualitative simulation can be viewed as proving a theorem of a very specialized form:

$QSIM \vdash QDE \wedge QState(t_0) \to or(QBeh_1, \ldots QBeh_n)$

where QDE is a qualitative differential equation, $QState(t_0)$ is a qualitative description of an initial state, and each $QBeh_i$ is a sequence of qualitative states. The QSIM Guaranteed Coverage Theorem states that this prediction describes all possible behaviors of all ordinary differential equations which are consistent with the given qualitative differential equation and initial state [Kuipers, 86]. The set of predictions may, however, include spurious predictions, those not corresponding to any real solution.

Building on the basic qualitative simulation algorithm, a variety of methods have been developed for filtering out additional classes of spurious behaviors, obtaining tractable predictions from a wider range of models while retaining the QSIM coverage guarantee. These methods include deeper types of mathematical analysis, application of partial quantitative information, appeal to carefully chosen additional assumptions, and change of the qualitative level of description [Kuipers, 93b].

Since the qualitative model and behavior tree are expressible in logic, we can show that a logical statement Φ follows from the model by showing that it follows from the behavior tree. We do this by showing that the behavior tree can serve as a logical model for Φ.

Since the qualitative behavior tree is a branching-time description of temporal sequences, the appropriate language for such statements Φ is some form of modal temporal logic [Emerson, 90]. Temporal logic augments propositional logic with operators for temporal relations on time-varying truth-values, such as *sometimes*, *always*, *eventually*, and *until*. Modal logic adds operators for relations among truth-values in alternate possible worlds (i.e., alternate behaviors), such as *necessarily* and *possibly*.

We introduce Expressive Behavior Tree Logic (EBTL) as a tool for expressing statements about QSIM behavior trees, and hence about the continuous systems they describe. EBTL is a branching time temporal logic closely related to CTL and CTL* [Emerson, 90]. We describe an algorithm for checking the validity of an EBTL statement against a given QSIM behavior tree.

Based on the QSIM Guaranteed Coverage Theorem, we prove that for any EBTL statement Φ which is *universal* in a sense defined below, if Φ is true for the qualitative behavior tree predicted by QSIM, then the corresponding theorem holds for any ordinary differential equation consistent with the QDE that generated the QSIM behavior tree.

There are a number of applications of model-based reasoning that can profit from reliable inference over the set of all possible behaviors of a continuous system. Since applications – such as monitoring, diagnosis, and design – must often cope with conditions of incomplete knowledge, the ability to reason with all possible behaviors of a system described by a qualitative model is particularly valuable. A discussion of potential applications is provided in [Kuipers, 93a], and a specific application to the validation of heterogeneous controllers is provided in [Kuipers & Åström, 94] and briefly at the end of this paper.

2 BTL AND EBTL

Behavior Tree Logic (BTL) is a branching-time temporal logic. The theory of branching-time temporal logics is described in [Emerson, 90]. BTL is intended to be an extension and customization of Computational Tree Logic (CTL) to work with QSIM behavior trees. We are more interested in its more expressive extension, Expressive Behavior Tree Logic (EBTL), which is similar to CTL* [Emerson, 90]. Customization is necessary because CTL only applies to infinite temporal structures. A QSIM behavior tree is finite although it may be considered to represent an infinite tree. (In this paper, when we say "a QSIM behavior tree" we are referring to the actual output of the QSIM algorithm after finite time. Therefore, although the structure may grow without bound if QSIM were allowed to run indefinitely without memory constraints, a QSIM behavior tree in our discussion is necessarily finite. However, our theorems are applied to the often infinite trees represented by these finite structures.) Therefore, we have modified the logic so that it is applicable to finite QSIM behavior trees. Our definitions are only slight modifications (or complexifications) of Emerson's definitions of CTL and CTL*.

2.1 TERMINOLOGY AND NOTATION

In this section we define the structures related to the theory of Expressive Behavior Tree Logic. QSIM behavior trees are distinguished motivational examples of these structures but EBTL is applicable to a general class of behavior trees. A QSIM behavior tree [Kuipers, 86] can easily be compared to a temporal structure in the sense defined in [Emerson, 90]. This motivates the following general definition.

Definition 1 *In (E)BTL, a behavior tree M is an ordered triple $\langle S, R, L \rangle$ where*

S is a set of states,

R is a binary relation on S, and

L is a labeling which maps each state s to an interpretation of all atomic proposition symbols in s.

It is useful to view a behavior tree as a directed graph with node-set S and arc-set R. Without loss of generality, we can assume that a behavior tree is a *tree* (thus the name), i.e. an acyclic directed graph in which each node has at most one predecessor and there is exactly one root. The root is the only node with the property that it has no predecessor and every node is accessible from it.

It may be helpful for the reader to beware of confusing the structures associated with the logic EBTL (of which QSIM behavior trees are examples) with QSIM structures. The logic EBTL may be applied to structures other than QSIM behavior trees. When we describe the application of EBTL to QSIM trees, many details such as the unwinding method for handling cycle pointers and the labeling of states will be made more explicit. We will try to make it clear when we are referring to the QSIM structures.

We let $\Lambda(x)$ denote the length of a finite ordered set x. A *behavior* $x = \langle s_0, s_1, s_2, \ldots \rangle$ in a behavior tree M is any path in the behavior tree which either terminates at a state with no R-successors or is infinite. In case x is of infinite length, we say $\Lambda(x) = \infty$. By a *path* $x = \langle s_0, s_1, s_2, \ldots \rangle$ we mean that for all $0 \leq i < \Lambda(x) - 1$, $\langle s_i, s_{i+1} \rangle \in R$. If $\Lambda(x) = \infty$ then by $i \leq \Lambda(x) - 1$ we mean i is any nonnegative integer. Notice that the last state in a finite behavior $x = \langle s_0, s_1, s_2, \ldots \rangle$ is $s_{\Lambda(x)-1}$. In this paper we do not require s_0 to be the root of the behavior tree as is customary when referring to QSIM behaviors.

For simplicity we sometimes write $x \in M$ to mean that x is a behavior in M. We say the behavior $x = \langle s_0, s_1, s_2, \ldots \rangle$ starts at the state s_0, and that s_0 is the first state of x. We will say that a behavior $x' \in M'$ *extends* a behavior $x = \langle s_0, s_1, \ldots, s_n \rangle$ in M if the first $n+1$ states in x' are $\langle s_0, s_1, \ldots, s_n \rangle$. When we speak of one tree M being a subset of another tree M' if every behavior in M extends some behavior in M'. We call a behavior *rooted* if it starts at the root of its tree.

We now describe the behavior quantifiers and the basic temporal operators on propositions. We prefer to give the reader a rough description before the formal syntax and semantics are defined. Suppose some state s_0 and behavior x starting at s_0 are given. The two behavior quantifiers are

    (necessarily p), which is true if p is true of *every* behavior starting with s_0, and
    (possibly p), which is true if p is true of *some* behavior starting at s_0.

The elementary temporal operators are (next p) and (until p q).

    (next p) is true of the behavior x if p is true of the behavior obtained from x by deleting its first state, and
    (until p q) is true of x if q is true of some state in x and p is true of every state preceding the first state in which q is true. We may also call this relation strong-until, to distinguish it from weak-until to be defined below.

Let it be stressed that these descriptions are only given in order to give the reader a rough idea. The exact meaning of these operators comes from the formal definition of the syntax and semantics of the logic which are in subsequent sections. We use the following abbreviations:

(eventually p) ≡
    (strong-until true p)
(always p) ≡
    (not (eventually (not p)))
(strict-precedes p q) ≡
    (and (not q)
        (strong-until (not (next q)) p))
(weak-precedes p q) ≡
    (eventually (and p (next (eventually q))))
(strong-precedes p q) ≡
    (and (strict-precedes p q) (eventually q))
(weak-until p q) ≡
    (or (strong-until p q) (always p))
(infinitely-often p) ≡
    (always (eventually p))
(almost-everywhere p) ≡
    (eventually (always p))

These last two expressions seem to presume an infinite tree. The problem of reasoning about the infinite tree represented by a finite QSIM behavior tree is discussed later.

The statement (strict-precedes p q) is true of a behavior if p is true in some state in the behavior and q is not true in any state previous to the first state in which p is true. The statement (weak-precedes p q) is true of a behavior if q is true in some state in the behavior following some state in which p is true. The statement (strong-precedes p q) is true of a behavior if q is true in some state in the behavior and p is true in some state previous to the first state in which q is true.

An expression in BTL is formed by an application of a behavior quantifier to a single one of the usual temporal operators: always, strong-until, weak-until, next, or eventually. EBTL is much more expressive because it allows boolean combinations and nestings of the behavior quantifiers and the usual temporal operators. Thus every statement in BTL is also a statement in EBTL, but "infinitely often" and "for all but finitely many" and other interesting statements can only be expressed in EBTL.

Our BTL is closely related to Emerson's CTL and our EBTL is closely related to Emerson's CTL*. The most noticeable difference is that BTL and EBTL are applicable to finite trees as well as infinite trees. Because (E)BTL is applicable to finite trees, the temporal operator next may seem ambiguous. This is so because some states do not have a successor. Therefore, we must distinguish between what is called strong-next and weak-next. The statement (strong-next p) is true of a behavior if the behavior has a second state and p is true of that state. The statement (weak-next p) is true of a behavior if the behavior has no next state or if the behavior has a second state and p is true of it. In our discussion, we consider next alone to mean weak-next. However, the language includes both terms and the user of our program may use both.

In the following two subsections we give the formal definitions of BTL and EBTL.

2.2 SYNTAX

The formal definitions of the syntax for the temporal operators and behavior quantifiers informally described above are given below. These definitions follow the treatment of CTL(*) in [Emerson, 90]. The definition of the syntax includes three state-formula generators, followed by one behavior-formula generator in the case of BTL, but followed by three behavior-formula generators in the case of EBTL. A state formula is a formula which is true or false of a state and a behavior formula is a formula which is true or false of a behavior. State formulæ in both BTL and EBTL are generated by rules (S1-S3) below. The behavior formulæ in BTL are generated by the rule (B0) below. The behavior formulæ in EBTL are generated by rules (B1-B3) below.

Definition 2 *The syntax of EBTL is defined as follows.*

(S1) *Each atomic proposition* P *is a state formula,*

(S2) *if p, q are state formulæ then so are* (and p q) *and* (not p),

(S3) *if p is a behavior formula then* (possibly p) *and* (necessarily p) *are state formulæ,*

(B0) *if p, q are state formulæ then* (next p), (strong-next p), (strong-until p q), (always p), (weak-until p q) *and* (eventually p) *are behavior formulæ.*

(B1) *each state formula is also a behavior formula,*

(B2) *if p, q are behavior formulæ then so are* (and p q) *and* (not p),

(B3) *if p, q are behavior formulæ then so are* (next p), (strong-next p), (strong-until p q), (always p), (weak-until p q) *and* (eventually p).

There are several things to notice here. First notice that (B0) is subsumed by (B1) and (B3). Therefore every expression in BTL is in EBTL. Also notice that the following formula is well-formed in both BTL and EBTL: (strong-until (possibly (next p)) (necessarily (next p))). However, EBTL is strictly more expressive because, for example, (necessarily (precedes p q)) and (possibly (not (weak-until p q))) are expressible in EBTL but not in BTL. We also allow the standard boolean abbreviations for or and implies.

2.3 SEMANTICS

The following notation is needed before the semantics of our logic can be defined. Given a behavior $x = \langle s_0, s_1, s_2, \ldots \rangle$, for $1 \leq i \leq \Lambda(x)-1$ we let x^i denote the behavior $\langle s_i, s_{i+1}, s_{i+2}, \ldots \rangle$, which is the subbehavior of x starting at s_i. I.e. it is the behavior obtained from x by deleting from x the first i states.

Notice that if $\Lambda(x)$ is finite, then x^i is not defined for $i > \Lambda(x) - 1$ and that $\Lambda(x^i) = \Lambda(x) - i$.

Now we are ready to give the semantics for the language. We write $M, s_0 \models \Phi$ (respectively $M, x \models \Phi$) to mean that state formula Φ (respectively behavior formula Φ) is true in the behavior tree M at the state s_0 (respectively of the behavior x). Each item below gives the interpretation of the corresponding item in the syntax above.

Definition 3 *If s_0 is a state in M and $x = \langle s_0, s_1, \ldots \rangle$ is a behavior in M starting at s_0, then we inductively define $\models$ as follows:*

(S1) $M, s_0 \models$ P *if and only if* P *is true in* $L(s_0)$,

(S2) $M, s_0 \models$ (and p q) *if and only if* $M, s_0 \models p$ *and* $M, s_0 \models q$,
$M, s_0 \models$ (not p) *if and only if it is not the case that* $M, s_0 \models p$,

(S3) $M, s_0 \models$ (possibly p) *if and only if there is a behavior y in M starting at s_0, such that* $M, y \models p$,
$M, s_0 \models$ (necessarily p) *if and only if for every behavior y in M starting at s_0, $M, y \models p$.*

(B1) $M, x \models p$ *if and only if* $M, s_0 \models p$,

(B2) $M, x \models$ (and p q) *if and only if* $M, x \models p$ *and* $M, x \models q$,
$M, x \models$ (not p) *if and only if it is not the case that* $M, x \models p$,

(B3) $M, x \models$ (strong-until p q) *if and only if there is a nonnegative integer $i \leq \Lambda(x) - 1$, such that $M, x^i \models q$ and for every nonnegative integer $j < i$, $M, x^j \models p$,*
$M, x \models$ (next p) *if and only if $\Lambda(x) = 1$ or $M, x^1 \models p$,*
$M, x \models$ (strong-next p) *if and only if $\Lambda(x) > 1$ and $M, x^1 \models p$,*
$M, x \models$ (weak-until p q) *if and only if for every nonnegative integer $j \leq \Lambda(x) - 1$, if for every nonnegative integer $k \leq j$ we have $M, x^k \models$ (not q), then $M, x^j \models p$,*
$M, x \models$ (always p) *if and only if for every nonnegative integer $j \leq \Lambda(x) - 1$, $M, x^j \models p$,*
$M, x \models$ (eventually p) *if and only if there is a nonnegative integer $j \leq \Lambda(x) - 1$, such that $M, x^j \models p$,*

The semantics of BTL formulæ are the same as those given above with (B3) giving the semantics of the formulæ given in (B0) of the definition of the syntax.

Now that the semantics are defined, the reader will notice that there are two definitions of the following operators: weak-until, always and eventually. We have given semantic definitions for these operators and we have also defined them as abbreviations of expressions involving strong-until and next. The proofs of the equivalence of these definitions are omitted because they are straight-forward but tedious manipulations of quantifiers, negation symbols, and boolean operators.

3 QSIM AND THE IMPLEMENTATION OF THE LOGIC

Here we consider how the logic is implemented and applied to QSIM. First, we define the relations that make finite QSIM behavior trees into possibly infinite trees. Second, we show exactly how QSIM behavior trees and the trees they represent are used as logical models for EBTL statements. Finally, we discuss the implementation of the program which checks the truth of statements in EBTL against a QSIM behavior tree. We call the program TL for "temporal logic".

3.1 QSIM AS A MODEL FOR (E)BTL

Qualitative simulation with QSIM produces a tree of *qualitative states*, linked by *successor* and *transition* relations.[1] A *QSIM behavior* is a path in the behavior tree, terminating at a leaf of the tree, but not necessarily starting at the root state. (This differs from normal usage.) Each state describes the *qualitative value* of each *variable* appearing in the QDE model. The qualitative value of a variable v over a state s is of the form $\langle qmag, qdir \rangle$, where $qmag$ describes the magnitude of v as equal to a landmark value or in an open interval defined by two landmarks, and $qdir$ is the sign of the derivative v' of v. By considering the qualitative values of the variables at s, and the constraints in the QDE, QSIM is able to derive a number of properties of the state, including quiescence, stability, cycles, etc. Please see [Kuipers, 86, 94] for more detailed information on QSIM.

A QSIM behavior tree is made a logical model for statements in EBTL in the following way. A *QSIM behavior tree M* is an ordered triple $\langle S, R, L \rangle$ where the set S of states is the set of states in the output of the QSIM algorithm, the set R is the union of the QSIM successor and transition relations, and the interpretation $L(s)$ is as follows.

For the sake of brevity, we consider only the atomic propositions associated with any QSIM state s which are of one of the following forms:

- (status *tag*) where *tag* is an element of {quiescent, stable, unstable, transition, cycle}. Such a proposition is true exactly when *tag* is a member of the QSIM structure s.status associated with the state s.

- (qval v (*qmag qdir*)) where v is a variable of the state s, *qmag* is a landmark or open interval defined by a pair of landmarks in the quantity space associated with v, and *qdir* is one of {inc, std, dec, ign}. Such a proposition is true exactly when the value of v in the state s matches the description (*qmag qdir*).

The expressiveness of the application of EBTL to QSIM could easily be increased without adding to the complexity by adding expressiveness to this propositional part of the language. In particular, we could allow propositional formulæ other than the two given above. For example, we could add the ability to compare the values of two variables, or to consider quantitative information about variable values.

By a *QSIM behavior* we mean a path in a QSIM behavior tree, not necessarily starting at the root state, such that the last node in the path has no R-successor. We call the state at which a behavior starts the *first state* of the behavior. In this paper, when we say "a QSIM behavior tree" we are referring to the finite output of the QSIM algorithm. That is to say, given a qualitative differential equation and allowed a finite amount of time to run, QSIM will return a finite tree. The finiteness of QSIM trees may seem to be a terrible limitation. For example, expressions such as "for all but finitely many" and "infinitely often" would apparently never be sensibly satisfied by a QSIM behavior tree. However, a QSIM behavior tree may *represent* an infinite behavior tree.

3.2 THE TREE REPRESENTED BY A QSIM BEHAVIOR TREE

QSIM has two ways of presenting a behavior over an infinite time-interval with a finite sequence of qualitative states. First, a fixed-point of a behavior is represented by a state with status quiescent. Second, repeated patterns in a behavior can be described by cycles. A *cycle state* in a QSIM behavior is one that matches a previously-generated state elsewhere in the behavior tree, so its successors are already represented by the successors of the previously-generated state. The user may select the state-matching criterion, and whether cycles must lie within a single behavior or may cross among behaviors. With respect to the tree $\widehat{M}$ *represented* by a QSIM behavior tree M, the expressions (infinitely-often p) and (almost-everywhere p) have exactly the desired meaning. The solution to the problem of reasoning about the infinite tree in finite time is discussed later.

Definition 4 *The ordered pair $\langle s_i, s_j \rangle$ of states is in a* status-bound *relation if either of the following two conditions holds:*

(1) The proposition (status quiescent) *is true of s_i, and $s_i = s_j$ or*
(2) the proposition (status cycle) *is true of s_i, and s_j is a successor of the previous state s' in the tree such that $s' = s_i$.*

If the ordered pair $\langle s_1, s_2 \rangle$ is an element of the set of status-bound relations, then we say that $\langle s_1, s_2 \rangle$ is a *cycle relation* if $s_1 \neq s_2$.

Definition 5 (Represented Tree) *The possibly infinite tree $\widehat{M} = \langle \widehat{S}, \widehat{R}, \widehat{L} \rangle$, represented by a QSIM behavior tree $M = \langle S, R, L \rangle$, is the tree which results by*

---
[1]There is also a *completion* relation not discussed here, that holds between an incomplete state description and a complete one consistent with it. Handling this relation is a straight-forward extension of the methods discussed here.

adding the status-bound relations to the set R. The set $\widehat{R}$ is the union of R with the set of status-bound relations. The set $\widehat{S}$ is the union of S and the new states which are generated first as second elements of status-bound relations and then by the unwinding process. (Cf. [Emerson, 90] for a precise definition of unwinding.) We will call the new states *copies of the state in S* to which they correspond. Each new state inherits the interpretation $L(s)$ of its proposition symbols from the state of which it is a copy.

3.3 CLOSED BEHAVIOR TREES

In the best case, every behavior in the tree returned by QSIM terminates with a quiescent or cycle state. We will call such a tree *closed*. There are cases, however, in which QSIM does not return a closed tree regardless of how long it is allowed to run. In cases where QSIM returns a tree which is not closed, the Guaranteed Coverage Theorem does not necessarily apply. If the behavior tree M is not closed then it is possible that the actual behavior of the system is not represented in $\widehat{M}$.

Using the normal QSIM simulation style, creating new landmarks for critical values and applying a strong cycle-match criterion (all variables have identical landmark values), certain systems such as the damped spring have infinite behavior trees. In such cases, the QSIM algorithm cannot produce a closed behavior tree in finite time. However, by applying the *envisionment* simulation style (no new landmarks and weak cycle-match criterion), every qualitative model has a finite behavior tree. [Kuipers, 94] discusses this and a variety of methods for obtaining tractable behavior trees.

3.4 THE PARTIAL EXTENSION OF A BEHAVIOR TREE

Given an EBTL statement Φ to check against a QSIM behavior tree M, we can define a *partial extension* $\overline{M}(\Phi)$ of M,

$$M \subseteq \overline{M}(\Phi) \subseteq \widehat{M}$$

that is finite (where $\widehat{M}$ might not be) and enough larger than M to make the truth value of $\widehat{M}, s_0 \models \Phi$ be the same as that of $\overline{M}(\Phi), s_0 \models \Phi$.

In section 3.6 we will prove that if the truth checker is given a QSIM behavior tree M and a statement Φ in EBTL, then it returns the truth value of Φ regarding the generally larger tree $\widehat{M}$ represented by M. As we will see, this tree can be infinite and complex. We think of a statement in EBTL as a question which the user is asking about the given behavior tree. The user expects the program to respond with the truth value of $\widehat{M}, s_0 \models \Phi$, where $\widehat{M}$ is the possibly infinite tree represented by the QSIM tree M and s_0 is the root of the tree. The program TL accomplishes this by constructing the partial extension of the given QSIM tree and checking the truth of the given expression on this larger yet still finite tree. The proof is accomplished by showing that the partial extension of the tree is large enough to decide the question Φ.

The reader may find it helpful to examine Figure 1 for a motivation of the following definitions. The partial extension $\overline{M}(\Phi)$ of M depends also on Φ. It is constructed from M and Φ by expanding M according to the structure of nestings of until and next statements in Φ.

Let us now give the needed definitions. Recall that a QSIM behavior tree M is necessarily finite. The *until extent*, $x(\text{until})$, of a behavior x in M is a set of possibly truncated behaviors in $\widehat{M}$ which extend x. The addition of these longer behaviors enlarge M exactly enough to answer properly any propositional until statement.

Definition 6 *The* until extent $x(\text{until})$ *of a finite behavior* $x = \langle s_0, s_1, \ldots, s_n \rangle$ *is the singleton set containing x unless* (status cycle) *is true of s_n in which case* $x(\text{until})$ *is the set of paths x' in $\widehat{M}$ extending x but truncated at the first state $s \in x'$ at which the following property is satisfied:*

The Until Property: *s is not in x and either* (status quiescent) *is true of s or* (status cycle) *is true of s and s is a copy of some previous state in x'.*

It is important to understand that the until extent of a behavior x in a finite QSIM tree M is a finite set of finite behaviors. To see this we need to recall two facts. First, QSIM behavior trees are finitely branching. Second, cycle states occur only at the terminal states of a QSIM behavior tree, thus there are only finitely many cycle states in a finite QSIM tree. If some $x' \in x(\text{until})$ were infinite, it would have to pass through infinitely many cycle states. Thus it would have to pass through one of them more than once, contradicting the Until Property. Since each behavior in $x(\text{until})$ is finite, and M is finitely branching, $x(\text{until})$ must be finite.

The *next extent*, $x(\text{next})$, of a behavior x in M is the set of possibly truncated behaviors in $\widehat{M}$ which are sufficiently extended to answer a propositional next question.

Definition 7 *The* next extent $x(\text{next})$ *of a finite behavior* $x = \langle s_0, s_1, \ldots, s_n \rangle$ *is the set of paths x' in $\widehat{M}$ extending x but truncated at the first state $s \in x'$ satisfying one of the following properties:* (status cycle) *is true of s_n and s satisfies the Until Property or* (status quiescent) *is true at s and s is not in x.*

A similar argument as the one given above shows that the next extent of a finite behavior in a finite behavior tree is a finite set of finite behaviors.

Reasoning in Logic about Continuous Systems 397

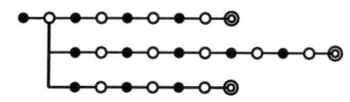

M before unwinding

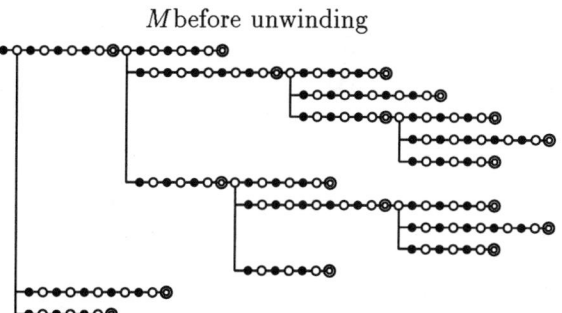

$\overline{M}(\Phi)$ after partial unwinding

Figure 1: Partial unwinding for $\Phi = $ (until p q), along first behavior only.

Each cycle state is expanded, stopping each branch at the second occurrence of a given cycle state. The double circles represent cycle states.

Definition 8 *We define the* partial extension $\overline{M}(\Phi)$ *generated by a tree M and an EBTL expression Φ recursively as follows:*

If Φ is a proposition then $\overline{M}(\Phi) = M$,
if Φ is (and p q) *then $\overline{M}(\Phi)$ is the union of $\overline{M}(p)$ and $\overline{M}(q)$.*
if Φ is (not p), (possibly p) *or* (necessarily p), *then $\overline{M}(\Phi) = \overline{M}(p)$,*
if Φ is (strong-until p q) *then $\overline{M}(\Phi)$ is the union over each behavior $x \in \overline{M}(p) \cup \overline{M}(q)$ of x(until), or*
if Φ is (next p), *or* (strong-next p), *then $\overline{M}(\Phi)$ is the union over each behavior $x \in \overline{M}(p)$ of x(next).*

Notice that the paths in the until and next extents of a behavior in M are generally not behaviors in M or $\widehat{M}$. They may, however, be behaviors in $\overline{M}(\Phi)$ for some Φ.

Our implemented prover TL, given as inputs a QSIM tree M and an EBTL expression Φ, returns true if and only if $\widehat{M}, s \models \Phi$ where s is the root state of M. We will prove that it is enough for the truth checker to examine $\overline{M}(\Phi)$, which in fact is what TL does. To be specific, we have defined the partial extension of a behavior tree generated by a QSIM behavior tree M and an EBTL statement Φ to be at least as large as the largest tree generated by TL in the process of checking

Φ on M. It, however, should be clear that this tree must be finite. This is true because each statement in EBTL is finite and each QSIM behavior tree is finite.

We will prove that given an EBTL expression Φ and a QSIM behavior tree M, TL correctly returns the truth or falsity of Φ in the behavior tree $\widehat{M}$ represented by M in finite time.

We need a way of distinguishing, for a given subexpression Φ_0 of Φ, whether Φ_0 is in the scope of a necessarily or of a possibly quantifier. The definition in the next subsection fulfills this need.

3.5 IMMEDIATE SCOPE

We recursively define an occurrence of p being in the *immediate scope* of a behavior quantifier as follows:

Definition 9 (Immediate Scope)
The occurrence of p in (possibly p) *is in the immediate scope of* possibly.
If (and p q), (not p), (strong-until p q), (next p), (strong-next p), (always p), *or* (eventually p) *occurs in the immediate scope of* possibly *then these occurrences of p and q are said to occur in the immediate scope of* possibly.
The occurrence of any EBTL expression which can not be shown to be in the immediate scope of possibly *by the above conditions is in the immediate scope of* necessarily.

Other temporal operators are treated as abbreviations of expressions involving the operators mentioned above.

Consider the following example of an EBTL expression:

(and (possibly
        (strong-until p (necessarily q)))
     (next (possibly r)))

The and and its arguments are in the immediate scope of necessarily as is the occurrence of q. Also (possibly r) is in the immediate scope of necessarily. However, the strong-until statement and its arguments are in the immediate scope of possibly.

3.6 CORRECTNESS OF THE IMPLEMENTATION

Now we come to the promised proof. Because TL examines the partial extension $\overline{M}(\Phi)$ of M, what we really need to prove is the following:

Theorem 1 *If M is a QSIM behavior tree with root s and Φ is an EBTL state expression, then*

$$\widehat{M}, s \models \Phi \Leftrightarrow \overline{M}(\Phi), s \models \Phi.$$

The proof goes by induction on the structure of Φ. If Φ is a proposition, then the theorems are obvious.

Also it is clear how to handle the booleans, i.e. we simply pass the proof on to their arguments.

If Φ is of the form (**necessarily** p) then we must really prove the following: $\widehat{M}, x \models p$ for all behaviors $x \in \widehat{M}$ if and only if $\overline{M}(p), x' \models p$ for all behaviors $x' \in \overline{M}(p)$. If Φ is of the form (**possibly** p) then we must prove the following: $\widehat{M}, x \models p$ for some behavior $x \in \widehat{M}$ if and only if $\overline{M}(p), x' \models p$ for some behavior $x' \in \overline{M}(p)$.

So the interesting parts of the proof will be when Φ begins with a temporal operator within the immediate scope of either **necessarily** or **possibly**. Theorem 2 takes care of the case when a **strong-until** statement occurs in the immediate scope of **necessarily**.

Theorem 2 *If Φ is of the form (**strong-until** p q), then $\widehat{M}, x \models \Phi$ for all rooted behaviors $x \in \widehat{M}$ if and only if $\overline{M}(\Phi), x' \models \Phi$ for every rooted behavior $x' \in \overline{M}(\Phi)$.*

Proof: ($\Rightarrow$) Suppose $\widehat{M}, x \models \Phi$ for every behavior $x \in \widehat{M}$ starting at the root. Let x' be a behavior in $\overline{M}(\Phi)$ starting at the root. Suppose for the sake of contradiction that for every nonnegative integer $k \leq \Lambda(x') - 1$, if $\overline{M}(\Phi), x'^k \models q$, then there is a number $l < k$ such that $\overline{M}(\Phi), x'^l \not\models p$. There is a behavior x in $\widehat{M}$ which extends x'. The existence of this behavior in $\widehat{M}$ contradicts our hypothesis.

($\Leftarrow$) Now suppose that for every behavior $x' \in \overline{M}(\Phi)$ starting at the root

$$\overline{M}(\Phi), x' \models \Phi \qquad (1)$$

Suppose for refutation that for every behavior x in $\widehat{M}$ starting at the root, for all $i \leq \Lambda(x) - 1$ if $\widehat{M}, x^i \models q$, then there is a nonnegative integer $j < i$ such that $\widehat{M}, x^j \not\models p$. There are two cases to consider.

First we suppose there is a rooted behavior $x \in \widehat{M}$ such that for all $i \leq \Lambda(x) - 1, \widehat{M}, x^i \not\models q$. Let x' be a behavior in $\overline{M}(\Phi)$ which x extends. (I.e. cut off x at its first state which satisfies the Until Property.) The existence of this $x' \in \overline{M}(\Phi)$ contradicts our hypothesis (1).

Now suppose that there is a rooted behavior $x \in \widehat{M}$ such that for every $i \leq \Lambda(x) - 1$ such that $\widehat{M}, x^i \models q$ there is a $j < i$ such that $\widehat{M}, x^j \not\models p$ and that such an i exists. Choose i to be the smallest number such that $\widehat{M}, x^i \models q$. Let $j < i$ be such that $\widehat{M}, x^j \not\models p$. Let y denote the path from the root to the first state, s_i in x^i. Suppose there is a state s in y which satisfies the Until Property. If such a state exists then the path $\langle s_0, s_1, \ldots, s \rangle$ is a behavior in $\overline{M}(\Phi)$. The existence of this behavior contradicts the hypothesis (1). If there is no state in y satisfying the Until Property, then there is some behavior x' in $\overline{M}(\Phi)$ which extends the path y. This behavior once again contradicts our hypothesis (1).

This completes the proof.

Theorem 3 takes care of the case when a **strong-until** statement occurs in the immediate scope of **possibly**.

Theorem 3 *If Φ is of the form (**strong-until** p q), then there is a rooted behavior $x \in \widehat{M}$ such that $\widehat{M}, x \models \Phi$ if and only if there is a rooted behavior $x' \in \overline{M}(\Phi)$ such that $\overline{M}(\Phi), x' \models \Phi$.*

Proof: ($\Rightarrow$) First, suppose there is a rooted behavior, call it x, in $\widehat{M}$ such that $\widehat{M}, x \models \Phi$. There is a path $x' \in \overline{M}(\Phi)$ which x extends. Suppose for contradiction that for all nonnegative integers $k \leq \Lambda(x') - 1$ if $\overline{M}(\Phi), x'^k \models q$ then there is a nonnegative integer $l < k$ such that $\overline{M}(\Phi), x'^l \not\models p$.

If $\overline{M}(\Phi), x'^k \models q$ for some $k \leq \Lambda(x') - 1$ and $\overline{M}(\Phi), x'^l \not\models p$ for some $l < k$ then the same is true for $x \in \widehat{M}$ which is a contradiction.

If there is no $k \leq \Lambda(x') - 1$ such that $\overline{M}(\Phi), x'^k \models q$, then it must be the case that for every state $t \in x', \overline{M}(\Phi), t \models p$. Thus far, we have assumed nothing about the behavior $x \in \widehat{M}$ except that $\widehat{M}, x \models \Phi$. We know that for any such behavior there is a smallest number $i(x)$ such that $\widehat{M}, x^{i(x)} \models q$. Let i be the smallest of all of the $i(x)$ ranging over behaviors x for which $\widehat{M}, x \models \Phi$ and let x now denote the behavior corresponding to i. If there is no state, s, in the path $y = \langle s_0, s_1, \ldots, s_i \rangle$ satisfying the Until Property, then there is a behavior $x' \in \overline{M}(\Phi)$ which extends y. In this case we are done becuase $\overline{M}(\Phi), x' \models \Phi$.

If there is a state in y which satisfies the Until Property, then we let s denote the first such state. Either (**status quiescent**) or (**status cycle**) must be true at s (or s has no successors). In the former case we are done becuase the path $\langle s_0, s_1, \ldots, s \rangle$ is a behavior in $\overline{M}(\Phi)$. In the latter case, we delete from y the state of which s is a copy and the states between it and s. What remains of the path y is again a truncated path in $\widehat{M}$, but a shorter path, and $\widehat{M}, z \models \Phi$ for any path $z \in \widehat{M}$ which extends y. But this contradicts our assumption that the state $s_i \in x$ was the nearest state to the root satisfying these conditions.

($\Leftarrow$) Now suppose there is a behavior $x' \in \overline{M}(\Phi)$ such that $\overline{M}(\Phi), x' \models \Phi$. There is a behavior $x \in \widehat{M}$ which extends x'. Thus we are done.

This completes the proof.

Similar theorems follow for **next** expressions and the other temporal operators can be treated as abbreviations of these two.

Therefore, it is enough for the truth checker to examine only $\overline{M}(\Phi)$ when trying to check $\widehat{M}, s_0 \models \Phi$. Since the until (or next) extent of a behavior in a QSIM tree starting at any state is finite and each EBTL expression is finite, the truth checker will terminate with the correct answer.

4 THE MAIN THEOREM

Our main theorem states that, under appropriate hypotheses, the answer that TL gives to an EBTL statement concerning a QSIM behavior tree will be true of the solution to any differential equation consistent with the qualitative differential equation which produced the QSIM behavior tree.

Before we state our main theorem we need some notation, definitions and a lemma. We define the parity of a position in an EBTL expression as follows:

Definition 10
The first operator in any EBTL expression given to TL is in a position of parity 0.
If (not p) occurs in a position of parity $n \in \{0, 1\}$, then p is in a position of parity $n + 1$ (mod 2).
If (O p) or (O p q) occurs in a position of parity $n \in \{0, 1\}$ and O is some temporal, boolean, or modal operator other than not, then p and q occur in positions of parity n.

Recall that (implies p q) is an abbreviation of (not (and p (not q))) so if (implies p q) occurs in a position of parity $n \in \{0, 1\}$ then p is in a position of parity $n + 1$ (mod 2) and q is in a position of parity n. This follows the use of "positive" and "negative" position in [Wang, 60].

Definition 11 An EBTL expression Φ is said to be universal if every occurence of the behavior quantifier **possibly** is in a position of parity 1 and every occurrence of the behavior quantifier **necessarily** is in a position of parity 0.

With a little thought, the reader will see that if a formula is universal, then the truth checker should examine the entire tree in order to establish the truth of the formula. This is the motivation for the definition.

If Φ is a universal formula in EBTL, then Φ' denotes the linear-time behavior formula obtained from Φ by deleting all occurrences of the behavior quantifiers. For example, if

$\Phi =$(necessarily
        (strong-until p (necessarily q))),

then

$\Phi' =$(strong-until p q).

We are now ready to proceed to the details of our main theorem. We say a real-valued function, u, satisfies a given QSIM qualitative behavior description if the qualitative description of the function matches the given qualitative behavior. The following theorem is proved in [Kuipers, 86].

Theorem 4 (Guaranteed Coverage) Let $F = 0$ be an ordinary differential equation with solution u, a real valued function. Let C be a QDE with which $F = 0$ is consistent. Let M be the QSIM behavior tree generated by the QSIM algorithm applied to C. If M is closed, then u satisfies some QSIM behavior $x = \langle s_0, s_1, s_2, \ldots \rangle$ in $\widehat{M}$ where s_0 is the root state of M.

Theorem 5 (The Main Theorem) Let Φ be a universal state formula in EBTL. Let u and M be as in the hypotheses of the Guaranteed Coverage Theorem. Let s_0 be the root state of M. If $\overline{M}(\Phi), s_0 \models \Phi$, then Φ' is true of the qualitative description of u.

Proof: Suppose $\overline{M}(\Phi), s_0 \models \Phi$, as in the hypotheses of the theorem. By definition, Φ' is a behavior formula. For simplicity, let us start by replacing every occurence of the temporal operators weak-until, always, precedes, strong-precedes, infinitely-often, almost-everywhere, and eventually with expressions involving only the temporal operator strong-until and next. (Since M is closed, it makes no difference whether we consider next to be strong or weak.) This is made possible by the abbreviations on page 3. So now Φ' is a behavior formula whose only temporal operators are next and strong-until. By the Guaranteed Coverage Theorem and the fact that Φ is universal, it is enough to show that Φ' is true of every behavior in $\widehat{M}$ starting at s_0. So, by the results in section 3.6, we need only to show that $\overline{M}(\Phi'), x \models \Phi'$ for every behavior x in $\overline{M}(\Phi')$ starting at s_0. So let x be a behavior in $\overline{M}(\Phi)$ starting at s_0. We will induct on the complexity of Φ'. Unless otherwise noted, references to (S1-S3,B1-B3) refer to the definition of the semantics.

If Φ' is an atomic proposition, then Φ' is a state formula by (S1) of the definition of the syntax of EBTL. Since Φ' is a propositional state formula, $\Phi = \Phi'$ (Cf.

(S3) of the definition of the syntax of EBTL). Therefore $\overline{M}(\Phi'), x \models \Phi'$ by hypothesis and we are done.

Suppose Φ' is of the form (and p q). Then we reduce to the case of showing $\overline{M}(p), x \models p$ and $\overline{M}(q), x \models q$.

Suppose Φ' is of the form (not p). Then we reduce to the case of showing that it is not the case that $\overline{M}(p), x \models p$.

Suppose Φ' is of the form (strong-until p q). We reduce to showing that for some nonnegative integer $j \leq \Lambda(x) - 1$ and for all nonnegative integers $k \leq j$, $\overline{M}(q), x^j \models q$ and $\overline{M}(p), x^k \models p$.

Suppose Φ' is of the form (next p) where p is a behavior formula. It must be the case that $\Lambda(x) > 1$, otherwise $M, x \models \Phi$ could not have been true (Cf. (B3)). Thus we reduce to proving $\overline{M}(p), x^1 \models p$.

In each case we have reduced Φ' to a more simple expression. The obvious induction argument on the complexity of Φ' finishes the proof.

5 APPLICATIONS OF EBTL AND QSIM

EBTL may be useful any time QSIM is used. QSIM has been used to simulate controllers, human organs and disease, abstract and real physical systems, electrical circuits, population dynamics, chemical reactions, etc.

5.1 PROVING PROPERTIES OF CONTROLLERS

Kuipers & Åström [1994] have used TL and QSIM to prove properties of heterogeneous control laws. A heterogeneous controller is a nonlinear controller created by the composition of local control laws appropriate to different operating regions. Such a controller can be created in the presence of incomplete knowledge of the structure of the system, the boundaries of the operating regions, or even the control action to take. analyzed, even in the presence of incomplete knowledge, by representing it as a qualitative differential equation and using qualitative simulation to predict the set of possible behaviors of the system. By expressing the desired guarantee as a statement in EBTL, the validity of the guarantee can be automatically checked against the set of possible behaviors. Kuipers & Åström [1994] demonstrate the design of heterogeneous controllers, and prove certain useful properties, first for a simple level controller for a water tank, and second for a highly nonlinear chemical reactor.

It should be noted that [Moon, et. al., 92] used CTL to prove a guarantee for a discrete-time control system. EBTL and QSIM make it possible to apply temporal logic to continuous-time control systems, and indeed to dynamical systems in general.

The program TL is equally easily applied to the behavior trees output by QSIM extensions such as NSIM and Q2, which use quantitative bounding information and produce quantitative bounds on the predictions. For these applications a slight extension of the propositional part of the language is helpful. We add the ability to include numerical information in the state propositions. This added expressiveness does not add to the complexity of the algorithm.

The program can be and has been used on terminals which do not support the graphics needed to see QSIM trees. In these circumstances, the user can learn everything he may need to know about a QSIM tree by evaluating a few carefully chosen EBTL statements.

5.2 TL AS A DEBUGGING TOOL FOR QSIM MODELS

Because QSIM is not complete, a QSIM tree may contain behaviors which do not correspond to real behaviors. Therefore, the truth of an EBTL statement (e.g. one beginning with the quantifier possibly), does not imply the truth of the corresponding statement in an actual behavior. This apparent limitation, however, can be and has been used as a debugging tool. For example, if the QSIM user knows that a certain sequence of events cannot occur in a real behavior, he can use TL to find out if that sequence of events occurs in any of the behaviors in the QSIM tree. The implemented program TL allows EBTL formulæ to have side effects. Therefore, it can be used to print out the undesirable behaviors or states which satisfy a certain EBTL formula. In the actual TL code, there are features which make this process very easy.

5.3 EXAMPLES

We demonstrate the use of TL to ask and answer questions about two simple models: the undamped oscillator, whose behavior tree is rooted in the initial state SS; and the damped oscillator, whose behavior tree is rooted in the state DS.

Undamped Oscillator The simple spring conserves energy, so all behaviors are cycles, as shown by the behavior tree in figure 1. The three behaviors differ according to whether the amplitude of the oscillations passes a predefined landmark value. The queries shown demonstrate that the simple spring never becomes quiescent, always reaches a cycle state, and necessarily has an infinite sequence of events crossing $x = 0$ in opposite directions.

```
(TL SS '(necessarily
          (always (not (status quiescent)))))
  => T
```

```
(TL SS '(necessarily (eventually (status cycle))))
  => T

(TL SS '(necessarily
          (and (infinitely-often (qval x (0 inc)))
               (infinitely-often (qval x (0 dec))))))
  => T

(TL SS '(necessarily
          (infinitely-often
            (precedes (qval x (0 dec))
                      (qval x (0 inc))))))
  => T
```

Damped Oscillator The damped spring loses energy. The first behavior is a cycle representing a decreasing oscillation. The second two are partial cycles followed by "nodal" convergence to quiescent states at the origin (indicated by circled dots in the behavior tree). This finite behavior tree represents an infinite family of behaviors, oscillating a finite number of half-cycles around the origin before "nodal" convergence. Each of the universal questions asked about the simple spring behavior is false of the damped spring, but the corresponding existential statements are true.

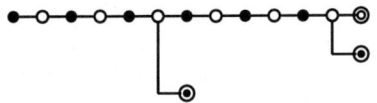

```
(TL DS '(possibly (always (not (status quiescent)))))
  => T

(TL DS '(possibly (eventually (status cycle))))
  => T

(TL DS '(possibly (eventually (status quiescent))))
  => T

(TL DS '(possibly
          (and (infinitely-often (qval x (0 inc)))
               (infinitely-often (qval x (0 dec))))))
  => T

(TL DS '(possibly
          (infinitely-often
            (precedes (qval x (0 dec))
                      (qval x (0 inc))))))
  => T
```

6 FUTURE DIRECTIONS

QSIM and EBTL can be combined to help in the design of a QDE. One possibility is to allow EBTL formulæ as part of the input to the QSIM program. In this case, QSIM would only generate those behaviors which are models for the EBTL formulæ. I.e. QSIM would test the satisfiability of the conjunction of the EBTL formulæ. This would allow a qualitative model to be described jointly by a QDE and an EBTL description of its behavior.

The limiting case, with an EBTL specification of the desired behavior and no QDE, raises an intriguing possibility. QSIM would predict all behaviors consistent with continuity and the EBTL specifications. A recently-developed program called MISQ takes as input a set of qualitative behaviors and produces the minimal QDE capable of producing that behavior [Richards, et al, 92]. This would be useful, for example, to a controller designer who knows that he wants certain qualitative events to occur, not to occur, or to occur infinitely often. By providing this specification in the form of EBTL formulæ, this combination of EBTL, QSIM, and MISQ might be able to design the appropriate QDE model.

Work is currently being done with the goal of automatically generating natural explanations of the structures associated with QSIM. This requires the detection of certain common features in physical systems, e.g. negative feed-back loops, oscillation, etc. While EBTL is useful for many parts of this process, more expressiveness is clearly required.

In particular, it will be important to compare (not just quantify over) behaviors and states, and to compare and quantify over variables in the QDE. In some cases this can be done in EBTL, though awkwardly. It would not be enough to build EBTL on a first-order logic instead of a propositional logic, since quantification to compare behaviors, states or variables must be scoped *outside* of the modal and temporal operators. This would undoubtedly have a substantial impact on complexity.

7 MISCELLANY

7.1 COMPUTATIONAL COMPLEXITY

Checking the validity of statements in BTL is polynomial, and EBTL is exponential, in the size of the statement. However, since the statements are typically not enormous, the more important constraint is that validity checking is linear in the size of the behavior tree.

7.2 CODE

The code for QSIM is available via anonymous ftp at cs.utexas.edu in the directory ftp/pub/qsim. The up-to-date version of TL will be included with the release of QSIM by KR'94.

7.3 RELATED WORK

Related work has been done in applying temporal logics to various models. Some of the logics developed have been able to express more quantitative *time* information. Since QSIM does not express information about the "real" length of time intervals, these languages are not practicable in our situation. We specifically mention for example [Jahanian, 88]. In this paper, real time systems are modeled in the Modechart language. Statements in Real Time Logic can be checked against a Modechart model. Real Time Logic is undecidable in general but certain classes of statements are shown to be decidable. These languages are suited for time-critical systems. However, if all that is important is the *order* of events, then languages such as CTL* are sufficiently expressive. In [Moon, 92], statements in CTL are checked against state transition graphs generated from programmable logic controller ladder diagrams. The specific application in [Moon, 92] is to chemical process control. Possibly the most work has been done in applications of temporal logics to computer processes such as parallel computing. [Emerson, 90] and [Lichtenstein, 84] are examples of such work. [Collins, 89] took an early step in the application of temporal logic to QSIM.

7.4 HISTORY

In 1989, Kuipers began discussing the application of branching-time temporal logic to QSIM with David W. Franke and E. Allen Emerson. In 1990, Kuipers wrote the code on which TL is based. In 1992-93, Shults added the finite unwinding of cycle states and discovered the new theorems presented in this paper.

8 CONCLUSION

This paper has presented a method using modal and temporal logic to prove properties of the behavior of a continuous physical system. If the user can describe a physical system in terms of a set of qualitative constraints, then by using QSIM and TL, he or she can prove theorems about the behavior of any real system consistent with those constraints. We therefore provide a meaningful and sound interpretation for the phrase, "proof by simulation."

We expect that this link between logic-based and simulation-based inference methods will support a variety of hybrid reasoning techniques that could be of substantial value.

Acknowledgements

We would like to thank Daniel Clancy, Sowmya Ramachandran, Rich Mallory, Jeff Rickel and Robert Schrag for fruitful discussions.

The work of Benjamin Kuipers and the Qualitative Reasoning Group at the Artificial Intelligence Laboratory, The University of Texas at Austin is supported in part by NSF grants IRI-8904454, IRI-9017047, and IRI-9216584, and by NASA contracts NCC 2-760 and NAG 9-665.

References

- Tim Collins. A Temporal Logic for QSIM. unpublished term paper. 1989.
- E. Allen Emerson. 1990. Temporal and modal logic. In *Handbook of Theoretical Computer Science*, (J. van Leeuwen, ed.), Elsevier Science Pub. B. V./MIT Press, 1990, pp. 995-1072.
- David W. Franke. 1991. Deriving and using descriptions of purpose. *IEEE Expert*, April 1991, pp. 41-47.
- Farnam Jahanian and Douglas A Stewart, A Method for Verifying Properties of Modechart Specifications. *Proceedings of the Real-time Systems Symposium*. Huntsville, AL December 1988.
- Benjamin J. Kuipers. 1986. Qualitative simulation. *Artificial Intelligence* **29**: 289 - 338.
- Benjamin J. Kuipers. Reasoning with qualitative models. 1993. *Artificial Intelligence* **59**: 125-132.
- Benjamin J. Kuipers. Qualitative simulation: then and now. 1993. *Artificial Intelligence* **59**: 133-140.
- Benjamin J. Kuipers. 1994. *Qualitative Reasoning: Modeling and Simulation with Incomplete Knowledge.* Cambridge, MA: MIT Press, in press.
- Benjamin J. Kuipers and K. Åström. 1994. The composition and validation of heterogeneous control laws. *Automatica* **30**(2), February 1994, to appear.
- O. Lichtenstein & A. Pnueli. 1984. Checking that finite state concurrent programs satisfy their linear specifications. *Twelfth Annual ACM Symposium on Principles of Programming Languages*, pp. 97-107.
- I. Moon, G. J. Powers, J. R. Burch & E. M. Clarke. 1992. Automatic verification of sequential control systems using temporal logic. *AIChE Journal* **38**(1): 67-75.
- Bradley L. Richards, Ina Kraan and Benjamin J. Kuipers. 1992. Automatic abduction of qualitative models. *Proceedings of the National Conference on Artificial Intelligence (AAAI-92)*, AAAI/MIT Press, 1992.
- Hao Wang. 1960. Toward Mechanical Mathematics. reprinted in Automation of Reasoning I. ed. Jörg Siekmann and Graham Wrightson. Springer-Verlag 1983 pp. 244-264.

Enhancing the Power of a Decidable First-Order Reasoner

Gerhard Lakemeyer and Susanne Meyer
Institute of Computer Science
University of Bonn
Römerstr. 164
53117 Bonn, Germany

gerhard@cs.uni-bonn.de

Abstract

A major challenge in knowledge representation has been to devise reasoning mechanisms that are computationally feasible. The problem is that knowledge is usually incomplete and hence calls for very expressive representation languages like that of first-order logic, yet reasoning about incomplete knowledge is undecidable when based on classical logic. Over the past decade there have been several semantic approaches defining decidable forms of first-order reasoning. The computational gain, however, came at the price of losing too many useful inferences. In this work we take one of these existing weak reasoners and extend its power without losing decidability by moving from an unsorted to a sorted logic. In contrast to similar work by Frisch, we are not limited to formulas in a certain normal form and our approach extends to introspective reasoners as well.

1 Introduction

A major challenge in knowledge representation has been to devise reasoning mechanisms that are computationally feasible. The problem is that knowledge is usually incomplete and hence calls for very expressive representation languages like that of first-order logic, yet reasoning about incomplete knowledge is undecidable when based on classical logic.

In answering this challenge, there have been proposals of weaker models of reasoning for incomplete knowledge bases which try to avoid the complexities of classical logic and still allow for useful inferences. In one line of research [Lev84b, Fri86, Pat87, Lak92a], the new forms of implication are given a model theoretic semantics, which makes them more intuitively compelling and also easier to analyze than most other approaches that are based on some form of syntactic restriction on the inference process. In a nutshell, the above semantic approaches work as follows. In classical logic, the implications of a set of assumptions are those sentences that hold in all interpretations or worlds where the assumptions are true. One way to weaken implication then is to allow more worlds than just the classical ones. The intuition is that fewer things hold in a larger set of possibilities. To introduce non-standard worlds into the picture, the above approaches use either a three-valued logic [Fri86] or a four-valued one [Lev84b, Pat87, Lak94, Lak92a], which derive from the notion of tautological entailment, a fragment of relevance logic [AB75, Dun76].

Probably the greatest pay-off of the above work has been the semantical characterization of *decidable* first-order reasoning. However, the cost of this achievement was very high in that the new forms of implication are very weak. In particular, modus ponens is thrown out altogether, which severely limits their applicability.

For example, let us consider the following KB:

$\forall x \texttt{Elephant}(x) \supset \texttt{Mammal}(x)$
$\forall x \texttt{Mammal}(x) \supset \texttt{Warm\_Blooded}(x)$
$\forall x \texttt{Warm\_Blooded}(x) \supset \texttt{Has}(x, eyes)$
$\texttt{Elephant}(clyde)$

If the predicates are given a three- or four-valued semantics according to the above approaches, neither $\texttt{Has}(clyde, eyes)$ nor even $\texttt{Mammal}(clyde)$ can be inferred from the KB. Frisch [Fri86] already realized this problem and suggested the following approach to at least handle simple taxonomic inferences as in this example, which require the use of modus ponens. His idea was to enrich the logic by switching to a *sorted* language. The sorts are unary predicates like $\texttt{Elephant}$ or $\texttt{Mammal}$, which receive a classical two-valued semantics, while the other predicates like $\texttt{has}$ are given the weaker, in his case three-valued, semantics. The KB is then divided into 2 parts, the sort theory, which contains information about sorts only, and a part which contains other assertions that may reference the sorts via restricted variables. The above example KB can then be reformulated as

$\forall x \texttt{Elephant}(x) \supset \texttt{Mammal}(x)$
$\forall x \texttt{Mammal}(x) \supset \texttt{Warm\_Blooded}(x)$
$\texttt{Elephant}(clyde)$

$\forall x{:}\texttt{Warm\_Blooded }\texttt{Has}(x, eyes)$

Here the first 3 sentences make up the sort theory, which can be reasoned about classically, and only the predicate Has is interpreted in a non-standard way, and sure enough, $\texttt{Has}(clyde, eyes)$ can now be inferred.[1] Notice that, while sorts in classical logic do not add to the expressive/deductive power of the logic, they do in this nonstandard setting.

In addition to introducing standard sorts into a nonstandard logic, Frisch also worked out restrictions on the sort theories, which allowed him to use his existing inference engine for the unsorted logic. In essence, the only upgrade necessary was a module for *sorted unification*. While sorted unification is undecidable in general, important cases of decidable sorted unification have been identified, for example [Wal88, Sch89, CD91, Uri92]. An example of a simple kind of sort theories, which subsumes our example KB and which yields decidable sorted unification can also be found in [Fri91]. Although Frisch did not elaborate on the connection with his earlier work, it does not seem hard to combine the result on decidable sorted unification with his work on non-standard sorted deduction to obtain a more powerful decidable first-order reasoner than was established previously.

So what is there left to do? A major drawback of Frisch's three-valued logic, at least from a conceptual point of view, is that the semantics is only defined for sentences in prenex normal form. Furthermore, his logic does not seem to generalize well to an epistemic logic, which would allow introspective reasoning, whose value for knowledge bases has been well established (see, for example [Lev84a]). In previous work, Lakemeyer presented an approach to unsorted decidable reasoning which avoids these shortcomings [Lak94, Lak92a]. In this paper, we demonstrate how to enhance the power of such a reasoner without sacrificing decidability by incorporating sorts into the logic. Even though Frisch's work is closely related, his results cannot be ported in a straightforward way. For one, we allow arbitrary formulas, not just formulas in prenex Skolem normal form. While this is not an issue in classical unsorted first-order logic, the situation changes both in classical sorted logic and in our nonstandard logic, where normal form transformations are no longer equivalence preserving. Furthermore, Frisch's results on sorted deduction rely heavily on applying the Herbrand Theorem, which does not hold in our case.[2] Instead we present a syntactic characterization of sorted deductive reasoning in terms of a modification of the unsorted version given in [Lak94, Lak92a]. Furthermore, these results are extended to account for sorted introspective reasoning as well.

The rest of the paper is organized as follows. In Section 2, we introduce the logic BL^q_s, which extends the logic BL^q of [Lak94] by adding sorts. Besides introducing the semantics, we also discuss various properties of the new logic. In Section 3, we show how a decidable sorted reasoner can be obtained in this framework. Section 4 extends the results to an introspective reasoner. Finally, we summarize our results in Section 5.

2 The Logic BL^q_s

The logic introduced here extends the logic BL^q of [Lak94] by introducing sorts and restricted variables into the language.

Let us begin by reviewing the main features of the old logic. BL^q is a logic of belief,[3] which models the beliefs of a deductively limited agent.[4] The question whether the agent believes a sentence α given that he believes the sentences in his KB amounts in this logic to the question whether the formula $\mathbf{B}KB \supset \mathbf{B}\beta$ is valid.[5] A key result is that these *belief implications* are decidable in BL^q. What is the semantics of the belief operator $\mathbf{B}$?

Belief is defined in a possible-world fashion.[6] Intuitively, we should think of an agent who imagines a set of states of affairs or *situations* M, which are described in more detail below. The agent is then said to believe a sentence α just in case α (or, as we will see below, a slightly modified α) holds in all situations in M.

In order to prevent beliefs from being closed under logical implication, we limit an agent's ability to reason by cases in the following ways. For one, we allow beliefs not to be closed under modus ponens. For example, if p, q, and r are atomic facts, we allow an agent to believe $(p \vee q) \wedge (\neg q \vee r)$, yet fail to believe $(p \vee r)$. Another way reasoning by cases is limited is

---

[1] To see why reasoning is still weaker than in classical logic, just add the assertions $\forall x \texttt{Has}(x, feathers) \supset \texttt{Has}(x, eyes)$, $\forall x \texttt{Has}(x, fur) \supset \texttt{Has}(x, eyes)$, and $\texttt{Has}(opus, feathers) \vee \texttt{Has}(opus, fur)$. $\texttt{Has}(opus, eyes)$ cannot be concluded.

[2] While a variant of the Herbrand Theorem may very well hold, it is likely rather unwieldy.

[3] For stylistic reasons, we will often use the terms knowledge and belief interchangeably although the logics discussed here really model beliefs that need not be true in the real world.

[4] In BL^q and BL^q_s beliefs are nonnested. This restriction is lifted in the next section.

[5] Here, KB is understood as the (finite) conjunction of the sentences in the knowledge base.

[6] Possible-world semantics is due to Kripke [Kri63] and was first introduced for epistemic logics by Hintikka [Hin62]. See also [HM85] for a brief review.

by weakening what we call *existential generalization from disjunctions* in the sense that an agent may believe $P(a) \vee P(b)$ for a predicate P and distinct terms a and b, yet fail to believe $\exists x P(x)$.

In BL^q, closure under modus ponens is avoided by decoupling the notions of truth and falsity within situations. Instead of assigning either true or false to atomic facts (predicates applied to individuals), situations are allowed to assign independent *true-support* and *false-support* to atoms. This corresponds to using four truth values $\{\}, \{\texttt{true}\}, \{\texttt{false}\}$, and $\{\texttt{true},\texttt{false}\}$, an idea originally proposed to provide a semantics for a fragment of relevance logic called *tautological entailment* [AB75, Dun76]. Note that the classical worlds of possible-world semantics are a special kind of situations, namely those where each atomic fact has either true- or false-support but not both. In BL^q, classical worlds are used to provide the standard notions of *truth* and *validity*. Non-classical situations are only allowed to be part of what agents imagine (defining their beliefs).

In order to weaken existential generalization from disjunction, BL^q restricts the interpretation of existential quantifiers within belief. Roughly, we require that an agent who believes the existence of an individual with a certain property must be able to name or give a description of that individual, although we do not require the agent to know who the individual is. More concretely, for $\exists x P(x)$ to be believed there must be a closed term t (e.g. $father(john)$) such that $P(t)$ is true in all accessible situations. In general, if the existential appears in the scope of universal quantifiers, the corresponding universals may (but need not) occur in the description chosen for the existential.

Given BL^q, the extension to a sorted logic BL^q_s is actually quite simple. We simply distinguish special unary predicates as sorts and give them the usual 2-valued instead of a 4-valued semantics. Furthermore, when choosing a term for an existential quantifier when interpreting belief we also require that the term meets the same sort restrictions as the variable which it replaces.

2.1 Syntax

The underlying language is a modal first-order dialect with countably infinite predicate and function symbols of every arity. The unary predicates are partitioned into two sets, one containing ordinary unary predicate symbols and the other containing **sort symbols**, which can also be used as restrictions of variables (see below). Furthermore, there is a countably infinite set N of standard names, which are syntactically treated like constants.[7] Given the usual definitions of **terms** and **atomic formulas**, a **primitive term (formula)** is a term (atomic formula) with only standard names as arguments.

Since we are dealing with a sorted logic, variables can occur both restricted and unrestricted. An unrestricted variable consists simply of a variable name with the usual semantics, that is, the variable ranges over all elements of the universe of discourse. A restricted variable consists of a variable followed by a colon followed by a sort symbol. An example is $x{:}\tau$. In this case, we also say that x is of type τ. Again the semantics is the obvious one, namely that the variable ranges only over individuals that are members of the sort in question.

The **formulas** of $\mathcal{L}$ are constructed in the usual way from the atomic formulas, the connectives $\neg$ and $\vee$, the quantifier $\exists$, and the modal operator **B** with the restriction that, if $\mathbf{B}\alpha$ is a formula, α may not contain any **B**.[8] To simplify the technical presentation below, we also require that no variable is bound more than once within the context of a **B**. Formulas without any occurrences of **B** are called **objective** and formulas where every predicate and sort symbol occurs within the scope of a **B** are called **subjective**. A formula α is called an **S-formula** iff α contains no restricted variables and the only predicate symbols are sort symbols. α is called an **A-formula** iff α contains no sort symbols except as part of a restricted variable. **Sentences** are formulas without free variables. Similarly, **ground terms** are terms without free variables.

Notation: To enhance readability, we often drop the restriction-part of variables when a variable is uniquely identified by its name within a formula. For example, $\forall x{:}\tau \exists y{:}\tau' P(x{:}\tau, y{:}\tau')$ is written as $\forall x{:}\tau \exists y{:}\tau' P(x, y)$.

Sequences of terms or variables are sometimes written in vector notation. E.g., a sequence of variables $\langle x_1, \ldots, x_k \rangle$ is abbreviated as $\vec{x}$ (the x_i may be either restricted or unrestricted). Also, $\exists \vec{x}$ stands for $\exists x_1 \ldots \exists x_k$. If a formula α contains the free variables $x_1, \ldots, x_k$, $\alpha[x_1/t_1, \ldots, x_k/t_k]$ denotes α with every occurrence of x_i replaced by t_i.

Definition 1 *Exist. Quantified Variables and $\alpha^{\sharp}$*
Let α be a formula. A variable x or $x{:}\tau$ is said to be **existentially (universally) quantified** in α iff the subformula $\exists x \beta$ ($\exists x{:}\tau \beta$) occurs in the scope of an **even (odd)** *number of $\neg$-operators*.

Let α be an objective sentence with existentially quantified variables $x_1, \ldots, x_k$. $\alpha^{\sharp}$ denotes α with all $\exists x_i$ ($\exists x_i{:}\tau$) removed for all $1 \leq i \leq k$.

Definition 2 *Admissible Terms*[9]

---

[7] As we will see shortly, standard names serve as our global universe of discourse for the semantics of the logic.

[8] Other logical connectives like $\wedge$, $\supset$, and $\equiv$ and the quantifiers $\forall$ and $\forall x : tau$ are used freely and are defined in the usual way in terms of $\neg$, $\vee$, and $\exists$. For example, $\forall x : \tau$ stands for $\neg \exists x : \tau \neg$.

[9] The reader should note that our use of *admissible* is

Let α be an objective formula and x $(x{:}\tau)$ an existentially quantified variable in α. A term t is said to be an **admissible** substitution for x $(x{:}\tau)$ with respect to α iff every variable y $(y{:}\tau)$ in t is universally quantified in α and x $(x{:}\tau)$ is bound within the scope of y $(y{:}\tau)$.

If the context is clear, we often say t is admissible for x $(x{:}\tau)$ or t is admissible.

To illustrate the previous definitions, let $\alpha = \exists x{:}\tau(\forall y{:}\tau'[\mathsf{P}(x{:}\tau,y{:}\tau') \lor \exists z\mathsf{Q}(z)])$. Then $\alpha^{\#}$ is simply $(\forall y{:}\tau'[\mathsf{P}(x{:}\tau,y{:}\tau') \lor \mathsf{Q}(z)])$. Note that $x{:}\tau$ and z, which are existentially bound in α, occur free in $\alpha^{\#}$. Now consider the constant a and the term $f(y{:}\tau')$, where $y{:}\tau'$ is the same variable as in α and $\alpha^{\#}$. Then a and $f(y{:}\tau')$ are admissible for $x{:}\tau$ and z, respectively, and $\alpha^{\#}[x{:}\tau/a, z/f(y{:}\tau')] = \forall y[\mathsf{P}(a,y{:}\tau') \lor \mathsf{Q}(f(y{:}\tau'))]$. Note that for the substitution to work as intended, we need the assumption that no variable within α is bound by an existentially quantifier more than once.

2.2 Semantics

For the semantics, we begin by defining situations and worlds just as in [Lak94] except that sorts are treated as 2-valued unary predicates. Note that all situations are defined over the *standard names* as the universe of discourse. Besides simplifying the technical treatment, this allows for a simple but intuitive treatment of *quantifying-in*.[10]

Definition 3 *Denotation Function*
A **denotation function** d is a mapping from closed terms into the standard names such that

1. $d(n) = n$ if $n \in N$
2. $d(f(t_1, \ldots, t_k)) = d(f(d(t_1), \ldots, d(t_k)))$ o.w.

We remark that any two denotation functions that agree on all primitive terms also agree on all other terms, that is, they are identical.

Definition 4 *First-Order Situations*
A situation s is a triple $s = \langle T, F, d \rangle$, where T and F are subsets of the set of primitive formulas and d is a denotation function. In addition, we place the following restrictions on sorts:

1. For all sort symbols τ and for all standard names n, $\tau(n)$ is a member of exactly one of T or F.
2. For all sort symbols τ there is a standard name n such that $\tau(n) \in T$.

Note that a primitive formula $\mathsf{P}(\vec{n})$, where P is *not* a sort symbol, may be in exactly one of the two sets T

---
quite different from that in [Fri91].

[10] See [Lev84a] for more details on this use of standard names and [Kap71] for a discussion of quantifying-in.

and F or in both or in neither of them, thus giving rise to a four-valued semantics. However, if P is a sort symbol, then $P(n)$ must be in *exactly* one of T and F, which gives sorts the usual two-valued semantics. Furthermore, sorts are required to be nonempty, that is, for every sort there must be at least one standard name that satisfies it at a given situation. We will see later that this restriction is significant in order to allow certain normal form transformations.

We now define worlds, where the two-valued restriction is extended to all primitive formulas.

Definition 5 *Worlds*
A situation $w = \langle T_w, F_w, d_w \rangle$ is called a **world**, iff
$\mathsf{P}(\vec{n}) \in T_w \iff \mathsf{P}(\vec{n}) \notin F_w$ for all prim. form. $\mathsf{P}(\vec{n})$.

We are now ready to define the semantic rules for the interpretation of the sentences of BL_s^q. Due to the 4-valued nature of the semantics, the following rules define independent *true*- and *false-support* denoted by $\models_T$ and $\models_F$, respectively) for sentences instead of the usual truth conditions.

Let M be a set of situations and let $s = \langle T_s, F_s, d_s \rangle$ be a situation. Let $P(\vec{t})$ be an atomic sentence and τ be a sort symbol. Let α und β be arbitrary sentences except in rule 6, where α is objective.

1. $M, s \models_T P(\vec{t}) \iff P(d_s(\vec{t})) \in T_s$.
   $M, s \models_F P(\vec{t}) \iff P(d_s(\vec{t})) \in F_s$.
2. $M, s \models_T \neg\alpha \iff M, s \models_F \alpha$.
   $M, s \models_F \neg\alpha \iff M, s \models_T \alpha$.
3. $M, s \models_T \alpha \lor \beta \iff M, s \models_T \alpha$ or $M, s \models_T \beta$.
   $M, s \models_F \alpha \lor \beta \iff M, s \models_F \alpha$ and $M, s \models_F \beta$.
4. $M, s \models_T \exists x\alpha \iff$ for some $n \in N$,
   $M, s \models_T \alpha[x/n]$.
   $M, s \models_F \exists x\alpha \iff$ for all $n \in N$,
   $M, s \models_F \alpha[x/n]$.
5. $M, s \models_T \exists x{:}\tau\, \alpha \iff$ for some $n \in N$,
   $\tau(n) \in T_s$ and $M, s \models_T \alpha[x/n]$.
   $M, s \models_F \exists x{:}\tau\, \alpha \iff$ for all $n \in N$ such that
   $\tau(n) \in T_s$, $M, s \models_F \alpha[x/n]$.

Before giving the semantic rules for **B** we need to introduce the notion of a *faithful* substitution t for a variable $x{:}\tau$ relative to a situation s, which simply means that all appropriate ground instances of that t belong to the sort τ at s.

Definition 6 *Faithful substitutions*
Given a variable $x{:}\tau$, a term t with free variables $\vec{x}$, a situation $s = \langle T_s, F_s, d_s \rangle$ and a set of situations M, t is called a **faithful** substitution of $x{:}\tau$ iff $M, s \models_T \forall \vec{x}\tau(t)$. (We apply the definition also to unrestricted variables. In this case, every substitution is faithful. Furthermore, the definition is extended in the obvious way to apply to sequences of terms as substitutions of sequences of variables.)

Let α be a sentence and $\vec{x}$ a sequence of the existentially quantified variables in α.

6. $M, s \models_\mathrm{T} \mathbf{B}\alpha \iff$ there are admissible terms $\vec{t}$ for $\vec{x}$ such that for all $s' \in M$, $\vec{t}$ is a faithful substitution of $\vec{x}$ and $M, s' \models_\mathrm{T} \alpha^{\#}[\vec{x}/\vec{t}]$.
$M, s \models_\mathrm{F} \mathbf{B}\alpha \iff M, s \not\models_\mathrm{T} \mathbf{B}\alpha$.

Note the nonstandard interpretation of existential quantifiers within belief. The rule says, intuitively, that the agent must know a term for each existentially quantified variable, and *knowing a term* means that it must be the *same* in all situations the agent considers possible. This way, the interpretation of existential quantifiers is much more restrictive than in classical modal logics and existential generalization from disjunction is no longer possible.[11]

In order to give notions such as truth and logical implication their classical meaning in BL_s^q, these are defined with respect to *worlds* only. More precisely, let M be a set of situations and w a world. A sentence α is *true* at M and w if $M, w \models_\mathrm{T} \alpha$ and *false* otherwise. α is logically implied by a set of sentences Γ ($\Gamma \models \alpha$) iff for all worlds w and for all sets of situations M, if γ is true at M and w for all $\gamma \in \Gamma$, then α is true at M and w. α is valid ($\models \alpha$) if α is implied by the empty set. Finally, α is satisfiable if $\neg \alpha$ is not valid.

Notation: If α is objective, we also write $s \models_\mathrm{T} \alpha$ ($s \models_\mathrm{F} \alpha$) instead of $M, s \models_\mathrm{T} \alpha$ ($M, s \models_\mathrm{T} \alpha$), since the true- or false-support of α depends only on s. Similarly, we write $M \models_\mathrm{T} \sigma$ ($M \models_\mathrm{F} \sigma$) if σ is subjective.

2.3 Properties of the Logic

Given that validity is defined with respect to *worlds* and sets of situations, BL_s^q if restricted to objective formulas is just an ordinary sorted first-order logic except that some additional valid sentences arise due to the fact that sorts are required to be nonempty. For example, for any sort symbol τ, $\exists x \tau(x)$ is valid. The use of standard names as the universe of discourse yields no special properties compared to classical first-order logic.[12]

The semantics of BL_s^q can easily be seen to reduce to the semantics of the unsorted logic BL^q of [Lak90] if restricted to the language of the unsorted logic. Hence the properties of sentences that contain neither restricted variables nor sort symbols are exactly the same as those of BL^q.

2.3.1 Properties of Belief

One of the peculiar properties of BL^q is that beliefs generally do not have equivalent normal forms such as prenex conjunctive normal form or PCNF (see [Lak94] for details). This is caused by the restricted interpretation of existential quantifiers within belief and hence this property carries over to BL_s^q as well. However, beliefs that do not contain existentially quantified variables can always be converted into any of the standard normal forms without losing equivalence. This fact will be very useful in the next section on decidability and its proof is completely analogous to the one in the unsorted case.

Definition 7 *An objective sentence α is said to be* **existential-free** *if α contains no existentially quantified variables.*

Theorem 1 *Normal Form Theorem*
Let α be an existential-free objective sentence and let α_PCNF be α converted into prenex conjunctive normal form. Then $\models \mathbf{B}\alpha \equiv \mathbf{B}\alpha_\mathrm{PCNF}$.

The proof is essentially as in classical logic, but relies crucially on the assumption that sorts are nonempty. To see why, assume we drop the condition of nonempty sorts and let $M = \{s\}$, where s is a situation such that $s \models_\mathrm{T} \forall x \neg \tau(x)$ for some sort symbol τ and $s \not\models_\mathrm{T} \mathsf{P}(a)$ for some predicate symbol P and constant a. Let $\alpha = (\forall x{:}\tau Q(x)) \wedge P(a)$. Then $\alpha_\mathrm{PCNF} = \forall x{:}\tau(Q(x) \wedge P(a))$. It is easy to see that s supports the truth of α_PCNF vacuously because of the empty sort, but s does not support the truth of α. Hence $\mathbf{B}\alpha$ and $\mathbf{B}\alpha_\mathrm{PCNF}$ would not be equivalent in general if we allowed empty sorts.[13]

To see what the sorted-logic approach buys us in weakening the deductive power as far as belief is concerned, let us briefly review the main limitations of the unsorted part of our logic. Let p and q be distinct primitive formulas, P a unary predicate other than a sort symbol, and a and b distinct closed terms. Then

Beliefs are not closed under modus ponens:
$\not\models (\mathbf{B}p \wedge \mathbf{B}(p \supset q)) \supset \mathbf{B}q$

A valid sentence need not be believed:
$\not\models \neg \mathbf{B}(p \vee \neg p)$

A logical equiv. of a belief need not be believed:
$\not\models \mathbf{B}p \supset \mathbf{B}(p \wedge (q \vee \neg q))$

Beliefs can be inconsistent without every sentence being believed:
$\not\models (\mathbf{B}p \wedge \mathbf{B}(\neg p)) \supset \mathbf{B}q$

---

[11] In a related semantics, Frisch [Fri86] is able to define the meaning of all logical operators and quantifiers compositionally. Unfortunately, the price of full compositionality is that the semantics is defined only for formulas in prenex normal form.

[12] However, this would change if we added = as a built-in predicate. For example, $\forall x \forall y(x = y)$ would no longer be satisfiable. See also [Lev84b] for a logic with standard names and equality, where these issues are discussed in more detail.

[13] This problem with normal form transformations in the sorted case is also noted in [Fri91]. That paper, however, side-steps the issue by considering only prenex normal form sentences in the first place.

No existential generalization from disjunction:
$\not\models \mathbf{B}(\mathrm{P}(a) \vee \mathrm{P}(b)) \supset \mathbf{B}\exists x \mathrm{P}(x)$

With S-sentences, however, we regain some of the previously lost deductive power.

Theorem 2 *Let α be an S-sentence and let β be an arbitrary sentence.*

1. $\models \mathbf{B}\alpha \wedge \mathbf{B}(\alpha \supset \beta) \supset \mathbf{B}\beta$

2. *From $\models \alpha$ infer $\models \mathbf{B}\alpha$ for all existential-free S-sentences α.*

Proof:

1. The proof is a straightforward adaptation of one for the same property of a two-valued variant of BL^q, the unsorted version of BL_s^q, and can be found in [Lak92b].

2. Let α be an existential-free S-sentence such that $\models \alpha$ and let M be a set of situations. Since α is existential-free, $M \models_T \mathbf{B}\alpha$ iff for all $s \in M$, $s \models_T \alpha$. Given an arbitrary $s \in M$, it is easy to see that there must be a world w, which agrees with s on the true- and false-support of all primitive formulas $\tau(n)$, where τ is a sort symbol. By assumption, $w \models_T \alpha$ and hence $s \models_T \alpha$. ∎

Note that for modus ponens to work only α is required to be an S-sentence. Note also that, although S-sentences have a standard two-valued interpretation at situations, the proviso for necessitation is necessary because of our non-standard interpretation of $\exists$. For example,

$\not\models \mathbf{B}\exists x\tau(x)$, where τ is a sort symbol.

To see why this is so, let M consist of two situations s and s' such that only $\tau(n)$ is true at s and only $\tau(m)$ is true at s' for different standard names n and m. Furthermore, let the denotation functions be such that no term other than n and m denotes n and m, respectively. It is easy to see that there is no admissible substitution (closed term) t such that for all $s^* \in M, s^* \models_T \tau(t)$ and, therefore, $M \not\models_T \mathbf{B}\exists x\tau(x)$, even though $\models \exists x\tau(x)$ because of the assumption of non-empty sorts.

2.3.2 Quantifying-in

With regards to quantifying-in and unrestricted variables, it is not hard to see that we obtain exactly the same properties as in the unsorted logic BL^q.

Proposition 1 *Let α be an objective formula with free variable x and let n be a standard name.*

1. $\models \exists x \mathbf{B}\alpha \supset \mathbf{B}\exists x\alpha$

2. $\models \mathbf{B}\alpha[x/n] \supset \exists x \mathbf{B}\alpha$

3. $\models \forall x \mathbf{B}\alpha \supset \mathbf{B}\forall x\alpha$ *if α is existential-free*[14]

4. $\models \mathbf{B}\forall x\alpha \supset \forall x \mathbf{B}\alpha$

With that we are able to model the distinctions between *knowing who* and *knowing that* in a simple but intuitive manner, that is, the distinction amounts to either knowing the standard name of an individual or not.

Interestingly, none of the above properties holds if x is a restricted variable. For example,

1. $\not\models \exists x{:}\tau \mathbf{B}\mathrm{P}(x) \supset \mathbf{B}\exists x{:}\tau \mathrm{P}(x)$

2. $\not\models \mathbf{B}\forall x{:}\tau \mathrm{P}(x) \supset \forall x{:}\tau \mathbf{B}\mathrm{P}(x)$

It is actually not hard to see why these properties fail. In the case of (1.), for example, let M be a set of worlds such that $M \models_T \mathbf{B}\mathrm{P}(n)$ for some standard name n and $M \not\models_T \mathbf{B}\mathrm{P}(m)$ for all $m \neq m$. Also, let w be a world such that n is of sort τ and let s be a situation in M such that n is not of sort τ. Then $M, w \models_T \exists x{:}\tau \mathbf{B}\mathrm{P}(x)$ yet $M, w \not\models_T \mathbf{B}\exists x{:}\tau \mathrm{P}(x)$. On the other hand, we do obtain the following weaker properties regarding quantifying-in.

Lemma 2.1

1. $\models \mathbf{B}\forall x{:}\tau\alpha \equiv \forall x \mathbf{B}(\tau(x) \supset \alpha)$
   if α is existential-free.

2. $\models \exists x{:}\tau \mathbf{B}\alpha \supset \mathbf{B}\exists x\alpha$

Proof: Here we only prove the second part. Let M be a set of situations and w a world such that $M, w \models_T \exists x{:}\tau \mathbf{B}\alpha$. Then there is some $n \in N$ such that $w \models_T \tau(n)$ and there are faithful and admissible terms $t_1, \ldots, t_k$ for the existentially quantified variables $x_1, \ldots, x_k$ in α such for all $s \in M$, $s \models_T \alpha^\#[x_1/t_1, \ldots, x_k/t_k, x/n]$, which is the same as $s \models_T (\exists x\alpha)^\#[x_1/t_1, \ldots, x_k/t_k, x/n]$. Notice that n is an admissible substitution of x and n is trivially faithful for x in $\exists x\alpha$ because there is no restriction. In addition, the t_i are admissible and faithful for the t_i in $\exists x\alpha$. Hence $M \models_T \mathbf{B}\exists x\alpha$. ∎

3 On Decidable Belief Implication in BL_s^q

In this section we consider the question of deciding belief implications in BL_s^q, that is, deciding the validity of formulas of the form $\mathbf{B}\alpha \supset \mathbf{B}\beta$. If α and β contain no sort symbols (and hence no restricted variables) the question was settled in [Lak94], where it was shown that belief implication for the unsorted logic BL^q reduces to Patel-Schneider's t-entailment,

---

[14] See [Lak90] for an example why the Barcan formula fails in the general case.

for which a decision procedure exists [Pat87]. It is not hard to see that, in general, belief implication in the case of BL_s^q is undecidable. This is because determining whether a belief implication holds subsumes the question whether an objective first-order formula with monadic predicates and function symbols is valid, which is known to be undecidable.[15]

The idea to obtain a decidable fragment of sorted belief implication is as follows. First, we assume that the left hand side of the belief implication is separated into two parts, one which contains the sort theory (S-sentences) and the other which is about assertions other than sorts (A-sentences). Using a restriction on sort theory introduced by Frisch, we first develop a syntactic characterization of belief implication (Theorem 9), which generalizes an analogous result for the unsorted logic in a modular way. Given this result, it follows that belief implication is decidable if we restrict ourselves to sort theories that allow sorted unification to be computable (Theorem 10). Finally, we present a restriction on sort theories borrowed from [Fri91] that actually meets this criterion.

3.1 A Syntactic Characterization of Sorted Belief Implication

Following Frisch, we use Σ to denote a finite set of S-sentences, which is called a sort theory. Abusing notation, we use Σ to denote both the set of S-sentences and the conjunction of its elements, which is no harm in the finite case.

Definition 8 $\mathcal{R}$-correspondence[16]
Let Σ be a sort theory and let $\mathcal{R}$ be the set of sort symbols occurring in Σ. A world w and Σ $\mathcal{R}$-correspond iff $w \models_T \Sigma$ and $\Sigma \models \tau(n)$ for all $\tau \in \mathcal{R}$ and for all $n \in N$ such that $w \models_T \tau(n)$.

As shown in [Fri91], $\mathcal{R}$-correspondence has the effect of banning disjunctive information from sort theories or, more precisely, such sort theories logically imply a disjunction of sort literals iff one of the disjuncts is implied. For example, while the sort theory $\{\tau(n) \lor \tau'(n)\}$ does not $\mathcal{R}$-correspond to any world, $\{\tau(n) \land \forall x \tau(x) \supset \tau'(x)\}$ does. Moreover, we obtain the following property.

Lemma 3.1 Let Σ be a sort theory which $\mathcal{R}$-corresponds to some world w^*. Then for every $\tau \in \mathcal{R}$ there is a standard name n such that $\Sigma \models \tau(n)$.

Proof : Let $\tau \in \mathcal{R}$. By assumption, sorts are nonempty and, hence, $w^* \models \tau(n)$ for some $n \in N$. By $\mathcal{R}$-correspondence, $\Sigma \models \tau(n)$. ∎

---

[15] Without function symbols, however, the monadic predicate calculus is decidable.

[16] This definition was originally proposed by Frisch [Fri91] and is presented here in a slightly modified way to suit our style of semantics.

Note: in the following, α and β always denote A-sentences. Also, let Σ denote a sort theory, where $\mathcal{R}$ is the set of sort symbols occurring in Σ, such that Σ $\mathcal{R}$-corresponds to some world and that all restrictions mentioned in A-formulas are included in $\mathcal{R}$. Further restrictions to sentences are added whenever necessary.

Theorem 3 *Skolemization Theorem*
For any objective formula, γ let $\gamma_{SK\exists}$ denote γ with all existentially quantified variables skolemized. Then
$$\models \mathbf{B}(\Sigma \land \alpha) \supset \mathbf{B}\beta \text{ iff } \models \mathbf{B}(\Sigma_{SK\exists} \land \Sigma' \land \alpha_{SK\exists}) \supset \mathbf{B}\beta,$$
where $\Sigma' = \bigwedge_{\sigma \in S} \sigma$ and $S = \{\forall \vec{y} \tau(f_x(\vec{y})) \mid x{:}\tau \text{ is an existentially quantified variable, } f_x \text{ is the corresponding Skolem function and } \vec{y} \text{ are unrestricted variables.}\}$

Lemma 3.2 Let $\Sigma_{SK\exists}$ and Σ' be as in the previous theorem. Then $\Sigma_{SK\exists} \land \Sigma'$ $\mathcal{R}$-corresponds to some world.

Proof : By assumption, Σ $\mathcal{R}$-corresponds to some world w. It is easy to see that skolemizing Σ preserves $\mathcal{R}$-correspondence. Hence let $\Sigma_{SK\exists}$ $\mathcal{R}$-correspond to some world w'.

By Lemma 3.1, for every $\tau \in \mathcal{R}$ there is some $n_\tau \in N$ such that $w' \models \tau(n_\tau)$ and $\Sigma \models \tau(n_\tau)$. Let w^* be a world just like w' except that the denotation function d^* of w^* maps the Skolem functions mentioned in Σ' as follows: for all $\vec{n} \in N^k$ $d^*(\tau(f_x(\vec{n})) = n_\tau$, where $\forall \vec{y} \tau(f_x(\vec{y}))$ occurs in Σ' and f_x is a k-ary Skolem function for the existentially quantified variable $x{:}\tau$. With that construction, it is easy to see that $\Sigma_{SK\exists} \land \Sigma'$ $\mathcal{R}$-corresponds to w^*. ∎

It should be noted that for Skolemization to work, it is essential that sorts are nonempty. To see why, assume we allow empty sorts and consider the sentence $\alpha = \forall x \neg \tau(x) \land (\exists y{:}\tau P(y) \lor Q(b))$ and $\alpha_{SK\exists} = \forall x \neg \tau(x) \land \tau(c) \land (P(c) \lor Q(b))$. $\mathbf{B}\alpha$ is satisfiable: simply let $M = \{s\}$, where $s \models_T Q(b) \land \forall x \neg \tau(x)$. $\mathbf{B}\alpha_{SK\exists}$, on the other hand, is not satisfiable. Hence $\mathbf{B}\alpha_{SK\exists}$ logically implies every formula, while $\mathbf{B}\alpha$ does not.[17]

Theorem 4 Let Σ and α be existential-free. Let $\vec{x}$ be the existentially quantified variables and $\vec{y}$ the universally quantified variables in β. Then
$$\models \mathbf{B}(\Sigma \land \alpha) \supset \mathbf{B}\beta \text{ iff } \models \mathbf{B}(\Sigma \land \alpha) \supset \mathbf{B}\beta^{\#}[\vec{x}/\vec{t}] \text{ for some admissible } \vec{t} \text{ such that } \Sigma \models \forall \vec{y} \tau_i(t_i) \text{ for all } i \text{ where } \tau_i \text{ is the restriction of the variable } x_i.$$

The following two theorems allow us to eliminate universal quantifiers on the right hand side of a belief implication assuming the right hand side is already existential-free.

---

[17] As was shown in [Fri91], if the formula is already in prenex normal form, skolemization works even if sorts are empty. Unfortunately, as we saw earlier, prenex normal form conversions are not equivalence preserving when sorts are empty.

Theorem 5 *Let β be existential-free. Then*
$\models \mathbf{B}(\Sigma \wedge \alpha) \supset \mathbf{B}(\forall x{:}\tau \beta)$ *iff*
$\models \mathbf{B}(\Sigma \wedge \alpha) \supset \forall x \mathbf{B}(\tau(x) \supset \beta)$.

Theorem 6 *Let β be existential-free and n^* a standard name which occurs nowhere in α, β, or Σ. Then*
$\models \mathbf{B}(\Sigma \wedge \alpha) \supset \forall x \mathbf{B}(\tau(x) \supset \beta)$ *iff*
$\models \mathbf{B}(\Sigma \wedge \alpha) \supset \mathbf{B}(\tau(n^*) \supset \beta[x/n^*])$.

The following theorem allows us to move the S-sentence $\tau(n^*)$ introduced in the previous theorem to the left hand side and append it to the sort theory.

Theorem 7 *Let σ be a quantifier-free S-sentence and let β be existential-free. Then*

$\models \mathbf{B}(\Sigma \wedge \alpha) \supset \mathbf{B}(\sigma \supset \beta)$ *iff* $\models \mathbf{B}(\Sigma \wedge \sigma \wedge \alpha) \supset \mathbf{B}\beta$.

Theorem 8 *Let Σ be an existential-free sort theory, $\forall \vec{z} \bigwedge \alpha_i$ an existential-free A-sentence in PCNF, and $\bigwedge \beta_j$ a quantifier-free A-sentence in CNF. Then*

$$\mathbf{B}(\Sigma \wedge \forall \vec{z} \bigwedge \alpha_i) \supset \mathbf{B} \bigwedge \beta_j \text{ iff}$$

for every β_j there is an α_i and a substitution $\vec{u}$ for $\vec{z}$ such that $\Sigma \models \tau_k(u_k)$ (for all k where the restriction of z_k is τ_k) and every literal in $\alpha_i[\vec{z}/\vec{u}]$ occurs in β_j (denoted as $\alpha_i[\vec{z}/\vec{u}] \subseteq \beta_j$).

In the following theorem, which gives us the desired syntactic characterization of sorted belief implication, we only consider the case where the left hand side of the belief implication is already in Skolem normal form. This is done merely for convenience and simplicity. The result generalizes easily to formulas not in Skolem normal form using Theorem 1 and 3.

Theorem 9 *Let Σ be a sort theory in Skolem normal form with a set $\mathcal{R}$ of sort symbols such that Σ $\mathcal{R}$-corresponds to some world. Let α and β be A-sentences whose sort symbols are included in $\mathcal{R}$. Furthermore, let $\alpha = \forall \vec{z} \bigwedge \alpha_i$ be in Skolem PCNF. Let $\vec{x}$ be a sequence of the existentially quantified variables of β and $\vec{y}$ a sequence of the universally quantified variables of β, and let $\bigwedge \beta_j$ be the matrix of $\beta^{\#}$ converted into PCNF. Let $\vec{n}^*$ be a substitution for $\vec{y}$ consisting of distinct standard names occurring nowhere in Σ, α, and β. Finally, let $\Sigma' = \Sigma \cup \{\tau(n) \mid y{:}\tau$ is the i-the variable in $\vec{y}$ and n is the i-th standard name in $\vec{n}^*\}$*

Then $\models \mathbf{B}(\Sigma \wedge \alpha) \supset \mathbf{B}\beta$ iff there are admissible substitutions $\vec{t}$ for $\vec{x}$ not containing any standard names of $\vec{n}^*$ and $\Sigma' \models \forall \vec{y} \tau_k(t_k)$ (for all k where τ_k is the restriction of variable x_k) such that for every β_j there are α_i and closed terms $\vec{u}$ for $\vec{z}$ with $\Sigma' \models \tau_k(u_k)$ (for all k where τ_k is the restriction of variable z_k) such that

$$\alpha_i[\vec{z}/\vec{u}] \subseteq (\beta_j[\vec{x}/\vec{t}])[\vec{y}/\vec{n}^*].$$

Proof: (Sketch) $\models \mathbf{B}(\Sigma \wedge \alpha) \supset \mathbf{B}\beta$ iff (by Theorem 4) there are admissible $\vec{t}$ such that $\Sigma \models \forall \vec{y} \tau_k(t_k)$ (for all k where τ_k is the restriction of variable x_k) and $\models \mathbf{B}(\Sigma \wedge \alpha) \supset \mathbf{B}\beta^{\#}[\vec{x}/\vec{t}]$ iff (by Theorem 1) $\models \mathbf{B}(\Sigma \wedge \alpha) \supset \mathbf{B}\forall \vec{y} \bigwedge \beta_j^{\#}[\vec{x}/\vec{t}]$. As in the unsorted case [Lak94], it can be shown that such admissible terms $\vec{t}$, if they exist, can be chosen such that none of the standard names of $\vec{n}^*$ occurs in $\vec{t}$. By successive applications of Theorems 5, 6, and 7 we obtain $\models \mathbf{B}(\Sigma \wedge \alpha) \supset \mathbf{B} \forall \vec{y} \bigwedge \beta_j^{\#}[\vec{x}/\vec{t}]$ iff $\models \mathbf{B}(\Sigma' \wedge \alpha) \supset \mathbf{B}(\bigwedge \beta_j^{\#}[\vec{x}/\vec{t}])[\vec{y}/\vec{n}^*]$ iff (by Theorem 8) for every β_j there are α_i and closed terms $\vec{u}$ for $\vec{z}$ with $\Sigma' \models \tau_k(u_k)$ (for all k where τ_k is the restriction of variable z_k) such that $\alpha_i[\vec{z}/\vec{u}] \subseteq (\beta_j[\vec{x}/\vec{t}])[\vec{y}/\vec{n}^*]$. ∎

The reader should note that the theorem reduces to an analogous result in the unsorted case [Lak94] if the sort theory is empty and, hence, the A-sentences contain no restricted variables. However, proving the sorted version turned out to be a rather delicate matter. For example, note that the sort theory Σ is required to $\mathcal{R}$-correspond to some world. In the course of the various transformations, the sort theory is extended according to Theorem 7 and, in the general case, also due to Skolemization (Theorem 3). Luckily, all these transformations preserve $\mathcal{R}$-correspondence. It is also worth pointing out that Theorem 7 does not hold for arbitrary S-sentences σ and A-sentences β. Again, luckily, its application in Theorem 9 only requires the restricted versions of σ and β.

In the following, we discuss under what conditions this syntactic characterization of belief implication leads to a decision procedure.

3.2 When is Belief Implication Decidable?

In the unsorted logic BL^q, testing for belief implication reduces, roughly, to finding most general unifiers of certain expressions, which are sets of literals corresponding to (sub-)clauses of the sentences in question (see [Lak92a, Pat87]). Since unification is called only a finite number of times and since unification is computable in the unsorted case, then so is belief implication.

The same idea applies in the sorted case except that instead of most general unifiers we need to compute what is called *most general well-sorted unifiers (ΣMGU's)* [Fri91]. Given a sort theory Σ, a well-sorted unifier of a set of expressions is a unifier such that every substitution t of a variable $x{:}\tau$ has the property that $\Sigma \models \forall \vec{y} \tau(t)$, where $\vec{y}$ is a sequence of the free variables in t. As pointed out in [Fri91], finding a most general well-sorted unifier may be undecidable depending on the form of the sort theory Σ. For one, two expressions may have infinitely many ΣMGU's and even finding one may be hard because it requires testing whether Σ logically implies other sentences, a problem that is undecidable for arbitrary sort theories with function symbols.

However, if we assume that sort theories are of a form such that all ΣMGU's of a set of expressions can be computed, then it is not hard to see that Theorem 9 specifies an algorithm to compute belief implication.

Theorem 10 *Let Γ be a class of sort theories satisfying the conditions of Theorem 9 such that sorted unification is computable and there are at most finitely many most general well-sorted unifiers of a set of expressions.*

Then the problem of determining the validity of belief implications of the form $\mathbf{B}(\Sigma \wedge \alpha) \supset \mathbf{B}\beta$, where $\Sigma \in \Gamma$ and α and β are A-sentences whose restrictions occur in Σ, is decidable.

Proof : (Idea) Without loss of generality, let us assume that Σ and α are both in Skolem normal form and that $\alpha = \forall \vec{z} \bigwedge \alpha_i$ is, in addition, in prenex conjunctive normal form. Furthermore, let $\bigwedge \beta_j$ be the matrix of β.

First, compute all most general well-sorted substitutions $\langle \vec{z}/\vec{u}, \vec{x}, \vec{t}\rangle$ such that $\alpha_i[\vec{z}/\vec{u}] \subseteq \beta_j[\vec{x}/\vec{t}]$ for every α_i and β_j. Given our assumptions, there are only finitely many such substitutions. On the basis of these substitutions determine, again by well-sorted unification, whether there are substitutions $\vec{t}$ for $\vec{x}$ that work for all β_j and whether these can be turned into admissible terms. Since admissibility is a simple syntactic criterion, this can be done effectively. ■

Finding decidable forms of sorted unification has been an active area of research, which can be applied to define different classes of decidable belief implication in light of Theorem 10. Early work on decidable sorted unification includes [Wal88, Sch89]. More recent developments are reported in [CD91, Uri92], for example. Frisch and Cohn [FC92] present a general criterion under which sorted unification is computable.

We end this section with a concrete example taken from [Fri91] of a class of sort theories with decidable sorted unification.

Definition 9 (Frisch) *Monomorphic Tree Restriction*
A sort theory Σ over the set of sort symbols $\mathcal{R}$ satisfies the monomorphic tree restriction iff the following conditions are met.

1. *Σ contains only S-sentences of the form*

   (a) *$\forall x \tau(x) \supset \tau'(x)$, where τ and τ' are distinct sort symbols and*

   (b) *$\forall \vec{x} \tau(t)$, where τ is a sort symbol and t is either a standard name, a constant, or a function symbol with only variables ($\vec{x}$) as arguments.*

2. *For any τ and τ' in $\mathcal{R}$ there is at most 1 sentence of the form (a).*

3. *There are no two sentences $\forall \vec{x} \tau(t)$ and $\forall \vec{y} \tau'(t')$ such that t and t' unify.*

4. *For all τ in $\mathcal{R}$ there is some $n \in N$ such that $\Sigma \models \tau(n)$.*[18]

It is straightforward to show that a sort theory that satisfies the monomorphic tree restriction also satisfies $\mathcal{R}$-correspondence (Definition 8). Also note that in Theorem 9, if Σ satisfies the monomorphic tree restriction, then so does Σ'. Frisch showed that for sort theories which satisfy the monomorphic tree restriction most general well-sorted unifiers are unique and computable. Hence, together with Theorem 10 we immediately obtain the following result.

Theorem 11 *Let Σ be a sort theory that satisfies the monomorphic tree restriction, $\mathcal{R}$ the set of sort symbols in Σ, and let α and β be A-sentences whose variable restrictions are included in $\mathcal{R}$. Then the validity problem for $\mathbf{B}(\Sigma \wedge \alpha) \supset \mathbf{B}\beta$ is decidable.*

As a final remark, we note that belief implication in the unsorted case was shown to be equivalent to Patel-Schneider's t-entailment [Pat87, Lak94]. Hence our notion of sorted belief implication can be regarded as an approach to sorted t-entailment as well. Patel-Schneider actually extended t-entailment himself, but in a very different way. Instead of moving to a sorted language, he coupled his four-valued base logic with a four-valued terminological logic to reason about taxonomic information. How the two approaches compare needs further investigation.

4 Sorted Introspective Reasoning

So far we confined our attention to deductive reasoning. However, having adopted a modal approach with an explicit model of an agent's beliefs, it is not too difficult to extend our results to agents who can reason introspectively about their own beliefs. In [Lak90], an introspective extension of the unsorted logic BL^q was presented. Here we sketch how these results can be carried over to the sorted case in a fairly straightforward way. As in [Lak90], we allow nested beliefs from now on, but disallow quantifying-in.[19]

In order to properly model introspective agents who know about what they know and do not know, it is not sufficient to allow nested formulas such as $\mathbf{B}\neg\mathbf{B}\alpha$, but we also need to model the concept that a sentence (or set of sentences) is *all* that is known [Lev90].

---

[18]This condition is absent in Frisch's definition since he allows nonempty sorts.

[19]Quantifying-in together with nested beliefs gives rise to a host of complications already in the unsorted case [Lak91].

Intuitively, if a knowledge base KB contains only the primitive formula p, then in order to conclude that a different fact q is not known, one needs the assumption that p is *all* KB knows.[20] Thus we extend our language by adding a new operator **O**, where **O**α is read as "α is all that is known/believed" or, for short, "α is only-known/believed." Note that the operators **B** and **O** can be arbitrarily nested.

Following [Lev90, Lak90], the semantics of **O** is fairly straightforward. Recall that for existential-free α, believing α means that α holds in all situations of a given set M. To convey that α is all that is known, we require that α is not only believed at M, but that M is as large as possible, that is, we require that any situation that satisfies α must be in M. As explained in more detail in [Lak90], a minor complication arises with respect to only-believing formulas with existential quantifiers. For example, since $\mathbf{O}\exists x \mathbf{P}(x)$ implies $\mathbf{B}\exists x \mathbf{P}(x)$, any set of situations M that satisfies $\mathbf{O}\exists x \mathbf{P}(x)$ must be such that $M \models_T \mathbf{B P}(t)$ for some closed term t. Intuitively, this term should act like a Skolem function, since nothing concrete is known about it. For that reason, we add a set $\mathcal{F}_{SK}$ of function symbols of every arity to the language with exactly that purpose, that is, when only-believing a sentence α, the terms (called sk-terms) that replace the existential quantifiers must be constructed from this set of "generic" function symbols.

We are now ready to extend the semantics of BL_s^q to nested **B**'s and **O**.

Definition 10 *A quantifier within a formula α occurs at the* **objective level** *of α if it does not occur within the scope of a modal operator.*

Definition 11 *Sk-terms*

Let α be a sentence and x an existentially quantified variable bound at the objective level of α. Let $U(x)$ be a sequence of the universally quantified variables in whose scope x is bound. Let $f \in \mathcal{F}_{SK}$ be a function symbol of arity $|U(x)|$ occurring nowhere else in α. Then $f(U(x))$ is called an **sk-term** *(for x).*

For the following rules, let $\vec{x} = \langle x_1, \ldots, x_k \rangle$ be a sequence of the existentially quantified variables bound at the objective level of α.

6. $M, s \models_T \mathbf{B}\alpha \iff$ there are admissible terms $\vec{t}$ for $\vec{x}$ such that for all s', if $s' \in M$ then $\vec{t}$ is a faithful substitution of $\vec{x}$ and $M, s' \models_T \alpha^\#[\vec{x}/\vec{t}]$. $M, s \models_F \mathbf{B}\alpha \iff M, s \not\models_T \mathbf{B}\alpha$.

7. $M, s \models_T \mathbf{O}\alpha \iff$ there is a sequence of distinct sk-terms $\vec{t}_{SK}$ such that for all s', $s' \in M$ iff $\vec{t}_{SK}$ is a faithful substitution of $\vec{x}$ and $M, s' \models_T \alpha^\#[\vec{x}/\vec{t}_{SK}]$. $M, s \models_F \mathbf{O}\alpha \iff M, s \not\models_T \mathbf{O}\alpha$.

[20] Note that **B**p means that *at least* α is believed and we obtain $\not\models \mathbf{B}p \supset \neg \mathbf{B}q$. Hence **B** is too weak to model introspective KB's.

Notice that the semantic rule for **B** has not changed at all. Also note that besides the use of sk-terms instead of arbitrary admissible terms, the main difference between **B** and **O** is the replacement of "then" by "iff."

Truth, logical implication etc. are defined the same way as for BL_s^q.

4.1 Some Properties

Here we confine ourselves to some of the main properties that result from the new features of the language, **O** and nested modalities. Let α and β be arbitrary sentences and let ρ and σ be subjective sentences. Let `false` denote the unsatisfiable S-sentence $\tau(n) \wedge \neg \tau(n)$ for some sort symbol τ and standard name n.

O implies **B**:
$\models \mathbf{O}\alpha \supset \mathbf{B}\alpha$

Perfect introspection:
$\models \mathbf{B}\alpha \supset \mathbf{BB}\alpha$ and $\models \neg \mathbf{B}\alpha \supset \mathbf{B}\neg \mathbf{B}\alpha$

Self-knowledge is (mostly) accurate:
$\models \mathbf{B}\sigma \wedge \neg \mathbf{B}\mathtt{false} \supset \sigma$
(Accuracy fails only in the case of the empty set of situations.)

Self-knowledge is complete:
$\models \sigma \supset \mathbf{B}\sigma$

Self-knowledge is closed under MP:
$\models \mathbf{B}(\rho \wedge (\neg \rho \vee \sigma)) \supset \mathbf{B}\sigma$

The above results show that agents with this model of belief have *perfect* knowledge about their own beliefs even if their beliefs about the world are limited. Note that these properties are exactly the same in the unsorted and sorted case.

4.2 Decidable Introspective Reasoning: the Sorted Case

A formula is called **basic** if it does not contain any occurrences of the operator **O**. In the following we are interested in the question which basic beliefs follow from an objective knowledge base. More precisely, we identify the epistemic state of an objective introspective objective KB with the set $\{\text{basic } \alpha \mid \models \mathbf{O}\text{KB} \supset \mathbf{B}\alpha$ and α does not contain sk-terms.$\}$. The motivation behind banning sk-terms from the epistemic state is that, intuitively, these should be thought of as internal identifiers used by the KB and not visible to a user who is querying the KB. (See [Lak90] for a more detailed discussion.)

In [Lak90] it was shown that for the unsorted language, membership in the epistemic states of objective KB's is decidable. The key to the proof of this theorem is the reduction of the problem to the nonintrospective case. It turns out that an exactly analogous reduction works for the sorted logic, as the following theorems show.

Theorem 12
Let α and β be objective sentences such that β does not contain sk-terms. Then $\models \mathbf{O}\alpha \supset \mathbf{B}\beta$ iff $\mathbf{B}\alpha \supset \mathbf{B}\beta$.

Theorem 13 Let the problem of determining the validity of $\mathbf{B}\alpha \supset \mathbf{B}\beta$ be decidable, where α and β are objective and where β is an A-sentence not containing sk-terms.[21]

Then the problem of determining the validity of $\mathbf{O}\alpha \supset \mathbf{B}\gamma$ is decidable, where α is objective and γ is a basic A-sentence not containing sk-terms.

The proof is a straightforward adaptation of the proof of the corresponding result in the unsorted case in [Lak90].

We conclude this section with a (very) small example. Let us go back to our initial KB about animals. Let

$$\Sigma = \left\{ \begin{array}{l} \forall x \mathtt{Elephant}(x) \supset \mathtt{Mammal}(x), \\ \forall x \mathtt{Mammal}(x) \supset \mathtt{Warm\_Blooded}(x), \\ \mathtt{Elephant}(clyde) \end{array} \right\}$$

be the sort theory and let

$$\alpha = \forall x{:}\mathtt{Warm\_Blooded}\ \mathtt{Has}(x, eyes).$$

Then

$$\models \mathbf{O}(\Sigma \wedge \alpha) \supset \mathbf{B}(\exists x{:}\mathtt{Elephant}\ \mathtt{has}(x, eyes)$$
$$\wedge \neg \mathbf{B}\mathtt{has}(dumbo, eyes)).$$

The query (the R.H.S. of the belief implication) is evaluated recursively by first determining whether $\models \mathbf{B}(\Sigma \wedge \alpha) \supset \mathbf{B}\mathtt{has}(dumbo, eyes))$ holds, which fails because the KB has no information about Dumbo, and then determining whether $\models \mathbf{B}(\Sigma \wedge \alpha) \supset \mathbf{B}\exists x{:}\mathtt{Elephant}\ \mathtt{has}(x, eyes)$ holds, which succeeds with Clyde substituting for x.

5 Conclusion

In this paper we extended a logic of limited belief that is based on a four-valued semantics by introducing sorts into the language. By giving sorts a classical two-valued semantics, we obtained a more powerful reasoner and by imposing various restrictions on the sort theories, we were able to show that the reasoning power can be increased without sacrificing decidability. In contrast to similar work by Frisch, we are not limiting ourselves to sentences in prenex normal form and our results generalize to introspective reasoners as well. Finally, since the unsorted part of the logic subsumes Patel-Schneider's t-entailment, our work also provides a generalization of t-entailment to the sorted case.

Since the decidability of reasoning in this framework hinges only on the decidability of sorted unification,

---
[21] Note that the decidability results considered in the last section are special cases.

new developments in this area seem readily applicable. However, the framework itself leaves room for improvement. For example, a truly useful KR language requires the use of equality. Furthermore, quantifying-in greatly enhances the expressive power in the introspective case. While these features have been included in the unsorted case, it is an open problem how this can be accomplished in a sorted logic.

Acknowledgements

We would like to thank an anonymous referee for valuable suggestions, which, among other things, led to the formulation of Theorem 10.

References

[AB75] Anderson, A. R. and Belnap, N. D., *Entailment, The Logic of Relevance and Necessity*, Princeton University Press, 1975.

[CD91] Common, H. and Delor, C, *Equational Formulae with Membership Constraints*, Rapport de Recherche 649, LRI, Université de Paris Sud, Orsay, France, 1991.

[Dun76] Dunn, J. M., Intuitive Semantics for First-Degree Entailments and Coupled Trees, *Philosophical Studies* **29**, 1976, pp. 149–168.

[Fri86] Frisch, A. M., *Knowledge Retrieval as Specialized Inference*, Ph.D. Thesis, University of Rochester, Department of Computer Science, 1986.

[Fri91] Frisch, A. M., The Substitutional Framework for Sorted Deduction: Fundamental Results on Hybrid Reasoning, *Artificial Intelligence* **49**, 1991, pp. 161–198.

[FC92] Frisch, A. M. and Cohn, A. G., An Abstract View of Sorted Unification, *Proc. of the 11th International Conference on Automated Deduction (CADE-11)*, Springer-Verlag LNCS, 1992, pp. 178–192.

[HM85] Halpern, J. Y. and Moses, Y. O., A Guide to the Modal Logics of Knowledge and Belief, in *Proc. of the Ninth International Joint Conference on Artificial Intelligence*, Los Angeles, CA, 1985, pp. 480–490.

[Kap71] Kaplan, D., Quantifying In, in L. Linsky (ed.), *Reference and Modality*, Oxford University Press, Oxford, 1971.

[Hin62] Hintikka, J., *Knowledge and Belief: An Introduction to the Logic of the Two Notions*, Cornell University Press, 1962.

[Kri63] Kripke, S. A., Semantical Considerations on Modal Logic, *Acta Philosophica Fennica* **16**, 1963, pp. 83–94.

[Lak90] Lakemeyer, G., Decidable Reasoning in First-Order Knowledge Bases with Perfect Introspection, *Proc. of the National Conference on Artificial Intelligence* (AAAI-90), Boston, MA, 1990, pp. 531–537. An extended version is available as: KRR Technical Report, Department of Computer Science, University of Toronto, 1990.

[Lak91] Lakemeyer, G., A Model of Decidable Introspective Reasoning with Quantifying-In, *Proc. of the 12th International Joint Conference on Artificial Intelligence*, Morgan Kaufmann, San Mateo, 1991, pp. 492–497.

[Lak92a] Lakemeyer, G., *Models of Belief for Decidable Reasoning in Incomplete Knowledge Bases*, Technical Report, Department of Computer Science, University of Toronto, Toronto, Ontario, 1992. (This is a revised version of the author's Ph.D. thesis.)

[Lak92b] Lakemeyer, G., On Perfect Introspection with Quantifying-in, *Fundamenta Informaticae*, **17**(1,2), 1992, pp. 75–98.

[Lak94] Lakemeyer, G., Limited Reasoning in First-Order Knowledge Bases, to appear in *Artificial Intelligence*. (A short version of this paper appeared also as: Lakemeyer, G., A Computationally Attractive First-Order Logic of Belief, in *Proc. of the European Workshop on Logics in AI (JELIA'90)*, Lecture Notes in Artificial Intelligence, Springer-Verlag, 1991, pp. 333–347.)

[Lev84a] Levesque, H. J., Foundations of a Functional Approach to Knowledge Representation, *Artificial Intelligence*, **23**, 1984, pp. 155-212.

[Lev84b] Levesque, H. J., A Logic of Implicit and Explicit Belief, Tech. Rep. No. 32, Fairchild Lab. for AI Research, Palo Alto, 1984.

[Lev90] Levesque, H. J., All I Know: A Study in Autoepistemic Logic, *Artificial Intelligence*, North Holland, **42**, 1990, pp. 263–309.

[Pat87] Patel-Schneider, P. F., *Decidable, Logic-Based Knowledge Representation*, Ph.D thesis, University of Toronto, 1987.

[Sch89] Schmidt-Schauß, M., *Computational Aspects of an Order-Sorted Logic with Term Declarations*, Springer-Verlag LNCS 395, New York, 1989.

[Uri92] Uribe, T. E., Sorted Unification Using Set Constraints, *Proc. of the 11th International Conference on Automated Deduction (CADE-11)*, Springer-Verlag LNCS, 1992, pp. 163–177.

[Wal88] Walther, Ch., Many-Sorted Unification, *Journal of the ACM*, **35**(1), 1988, pp. 1–17.

Knowledge, Certainty, Belief, and Conditionalisation
(abbreviated version)

Philippe Lamarre*
IRIN - Université de Nantes
2, rue de la Houssinière
44072 Nantes Cedex
France
lamarre@irin.univ-nantes.fr

Yoav Shoham[†]
Robotics Laboratory
Department of Computer Science
Stanford University
Stanford, CA. 94305
shoham@flamingo.stanford.edu

Abstract

We offer a system to capture the relationship between knowledge and belief, which also sheds new light on each of them in isolation. In the case of knowledge, we strongly reject the property of negative introspection. In the case of belief, we propose a distinction between belief (whose defeasibility is recognized by the agent) and certainty (whose defeasibility is not). The relationship between the three notions – knowledge, certainty, and belief – goes far beyond mere hierarchy. In particular, knowledge has the flavor of belief that is stable under incorporation of correct facts. We explore these first through a model theory, which is based on the notions of the agent's subconscious biases and its conscious preferences (or plausibility measure). We then provide a sound and complete axiomatic system, and point to some of its illuminating properties. We compare our construction to previous ones in AI and philosophy, and in particular point to connections with recent work in AI based on conditionals. (Proofs of our theorems are omitted from this version of the article, hence the subtitle.)

1 Introduction

In recent years there has been a great deal of interest in formal reasoning about knowledge and belief within AI and distributed computing; we will assume familiarity with this area of research and not repeat its history or philosophical origins. The aim of the work reported here has been to clarify the relationship between knowledge and belief, which have received the most detailed independent treatment in these two fields. However, although the goal has been to clarify the relationship between the two rather than studied either of them further in isolation, in pursuit of our goal we were forced to re-examine some conventional wisdom about each one. In particular, we were led to distinguish between two senses of 'belief,' reject the standard notion of idealized 'knowledge,' and propose an alternative.

1.1 Main highlights

The message of our research can be summarized in the following items:

1. One should distinguish between 'knowing,' 'being certain that,' and 'believing.' Knowledge entails certainty which entails belief, but there is more structure to the three notions than mere hierarchy. The intuition behind 'certainty' is that, to the agent, the facts of which he is certain appear to be knowledge; there is no such connection between certainty and belief. Thus, 'John is certain that' is equivalent to 'John is certain that John knows that,' but 'John believes that' is not equivalent to 'John believes that John is certain that,' and definitely not to 'John believes that John knows that.' (In fact, in our system 'John believes that John knows that' will turn out to be equivalent to 'John is certain that.')

2. Negative introspection – e.g., "if John does not believe then he believes that he does not believe" – is an acceptable idealization for belief and certainty, but not for knowledge. We therefore accept the standard system for belief (KD45), apply it to certainty as well, but reject the standard system for idealized knowledge (S5); instead we adopt a weaker system (S4.3).

3. Certainty and belief can be related semantically to knowledge via two partial orders on possible worlds, one a refinement of the other. These par-

---
*This author thanks the French Ministry of Foreign Affairs for the Lavoisier Fellowship during 1993 for his work at Stanford Unviversity.

[†]The work of this author was supported in part by grants from the National Science Foundation, Advanced Research Projects Agency, and the Air Force Office of Scientific Research.

tial orders have intuitive interpretations – one describes an agent's subconscious prejudice, and the other describes his conscious measure of plausibility, or preferences.

4. We provide sound and complete axiomatic systems for these semantics; from the mathematical point of view, these are the deepest results.

5. Our constructions can be understood as shedding light on an intriguing informal slogan, put forward in philosophy, according to which knowledge is 'belief that is stable with respect to the truth.'

6. The partial-order-based construction creates a tie with work on preference-based nonmonotonic logics [Sho88, KLM90], conditional logics [Lew73, Del87, Bou92a, KS91], and belief revision [KM91]. In particular, we are able to show that our construction strictly generalizes a Boutilier's conditional-based construction.

A couple of our insights turn out to be rediscovery of ideas already published in philosophy (but which are new to computer science and AI); this is true mostly of item 1 above somewhat of item 2, to which Lenzen's work [Len78b] is the most relevant. Other insights, and all technical results, are novel.

1.2 Some intuitions about knowledge, certainty, and belief

Before we start a technical construction, let us explicate some of our intuitions which led to it. Similar intuitions have appeared already in the philosophical literature, but we feel that it is important to articulate them here since they are crucial to understanding our formal construction, and have not been argued widely enough (in particular, to our knowledge they have never apeared in AI or distributed systems). We start with an observation about the commonsense term 'belief.' In everyday life this term is used in more than one way, a point well noted within philosophy (cf. [BP83], pp 214ff). Belief is usually distinguished from knowledge by its being *defeasible* (that is, the agent can believe something falsely, but not know it), but this defeasibility might exhibit different properties. In particular, on different readings of the term, the believing agent may or may not be aware of this defeasibility. Thus, on one reading of belief, the agent can believe something and admit that he might be wrong, as in "the robot believes there is an obstacle in front of it but it is not absolutely certain" (perhaps because it knows that its sensors occasionally malfunction). On other readings, this is not the case, as in "The robot firmly believes that there is an obstacle in front of it, but in fact there is none." The difference between these two senses of belief is manifested in a number of properties, which hold in one version but not the other. For example, the statement "if the agent believes something then he believes that he knows it" is valid in the second version but not in the first. From here on we will use the term 'belief' to refer to the belief of the first kind (in which the agent is aware of the defeasibility), and 'certainty' to refer to the other kind.[1]

Next we make an observation about knowledge. It has become routine in AI and computer science to capture an idealized version of this notion by the S5 system.[2] Formal definition of S5 is not needed at this point; suffice it to say that properties of the resulting formal notion of knowledge differ significantly from properties of its commonsense counterparts. This is in principle acceptable, the formal notion being an idealization to begin with. However, one property of the formal notion is particularly troubling, namely, negative introspection: If the agent does not know a fact, then he knows that he does not know it. Past objections in AI and computer science to this property – for example, by Vardi [Var85] and Levesque (personal communication) – tended to be brushed aside. And indeed, when knowledge is studied in isolation from any other attitude, it is hard to fully expose the unreasonableness of the negative introspection property.

However, when one considers the notion of certainty in conjunction with knowledge, the problem becomes apparent. Recall that the notions of knowledge and certainty we are after are typified by the sentence "the robot is certain that there is an obstacle in front of it, but in fact the way is clear." Consider this example further. On the one hand, since to the robot its certainties seem like knowledge, the robot is certain that it knows that there is an obstacle in front of it. On the other hand, since in reality there is no obstacle, the robot does not *know* that there is an obstacle (since by definition knowledge must be correct). If knowledge had the negative introspection property, the robot would then know that it does not know it, and thus also be certain that it does not know it. But surely the robot cannot simultaneously be certain that it knows a fact and certain that he does not know it?

Indeed, the reader who has not been subjected to indoctrination in one of the disciplines mentioned may wonder why we belabor an obvious point. Be that as it may, we will definitely reject S5 as a reasonable basis for defining knowledge. Instead, we will start with a weaker system. This system will be stronger than S4, and hence will still embody substantial idealization (in particular, closure of knowledge under tautological consequence and positive introspection; see below), but none as deadly as negative introspection.

---

[1] It may be argued that there is a single coherent abstraction spanning both senses of belief discussed here; we will not take a stance on this, as it does not impact the discussion in the paper.

[2] In economics a standard model of knowledge is that based on *partitions* [Aum76]; this turns out to be equivalent to the S5 system.

Armed with these intuitions about knowledge, certainty, and belief, we can begin the formal development. The rest of the paper is organized as follows. In section 3 we develop the model theory for knowledge, certainty, and belief, preceding the technical definitions with intuitive explanations. In the section following that, we present a sound and complete axiomatic system, and point to some facts about the three mental attitudes that are illuminated by the axioms. We end with discussion of related work and a brief summary.

2 Belief, certainty, and knowledge: the language

In this article we restrict the discussion to the single agent, propositional case. We start with a classical propositional language, and augment it with three modal operators, one 'absolute' and two 'relativized': If α and φ are any (possibly modal) formula, then $K\alpha$, $C^\varphi \alpha$ and $B^\varphi \alpha$ are also formulas. The intuitive readings of these operators are, respectively, 'the agent knows α,' 'the agent is certain of α, given evidence (or hypothesis) φ,' and 'the agent believes α, given evidence φ.' We also introduce two additional 'absolute' operators by definition: $C\alpha =_{def} C^{True}\alpha$ and $B\alpha =_{def} B^{True}\alpha$ (where True is any tautology).

3 Belief, certainty, and knowledge: a model theory

In this section we endow our language with formal semantics; in the next section we provide a sound and complete axiomatization relative to these semantics. Our formal construction is short and mathematically simple. We could simply present it and ask the reader to accept it on the basis of the properties of the corresponding axiomatic system (and, as we shall see in the next section, these properties are attractive indeed). However, we feel that intuitive motivation of the construction is as important as its formal properties, and hence we will precede the half-page of formal definition with several pages of explanations. Hopefully, after these explanations the definition will be well motivated, and will not seem like an artificial device engineered to achieve certain formal results.

We start with a standard possible-worlds structure, that is, a collection of models and a binary ('accessibility') relation between them.[3] Our intuitive interpretation of this relation is somewhat unique, however. The usual description of an epistemically-accessible world is a world considered possible by the agent. This is not our interpretation. Instead, we will take w_2 being accessible from w_1 to mean that w_2 is at least as easy for the agent to imagine as w_1. The worlds the agent *actually* considers possible are the worlds that are the most-easily imaginable. More generally, we are interested in the worlds actually imagined by the agent given any 'evidence' or 'assumption' formula φ. These are defined to be exactly the most-easily imagined worlds among the worlds that satisfy φ (that is, the most-easily imagined among the φ-worlds, not the φ-worlds among the most-easily imagined; the latter intersection could be empty). When we speak simply of the most easily imagined worlds, without mention of any evidence, we will mean the worlds most easily imagined given the tautological evidence.

The accessibility relation describes a certain *bias* or *prejudice* of the agent. This prejudice plays a role similar to that of *preference* in nonmonotonic logics [Sho88, KLM90], in that it leads agents towards some worlds and away from others. In our case, an important ingredient in the intuitive interpretation is that the agent is completely unaware of its prejudice, and hence also of the non-most-easily-imagined worlds.[4]

We will impose some requirements on the prejudice relation (denoted R_K). First, we require it to be reflexive and transitive. In addition, we require it to be *connected*: For any worlds w_1, w_2, and w_3, if ($w_1 R_K w_2$ and $w_1 R_K w_3$) then ($w_2 R_K w_3$ or $w_3 R_K w_2$). Those familiar with modal logics will recognize that these three conditions define an S4.3 accessibility relation. The motivation behind the first two requirements is presumably clear, given the intuitive reading of R_K. The third property is less obvious, but can be motivated by appealing to the distinction between equivalence and noncomparability. The "prejudice" R_K encodes nature's way of guiding the agent, revealing some possibilities and hiding others. Nature is deterministic: There is a unique collection of possible worlds that it reveals, by making them easiest to imagine. If among the R_K-minimal worlds there were two that were noncomparable, that would mean that we simply do not have the information about how easy nature has made them to imagine relative to one another, and that further information about nature might eliminate one from the most-easily-imagined set.

Our third property amounts to demanding full disclosure on the part of nature, but there is a subtlety. We have said that the set most-easily-imagined of worlds must form a cluster of mutually R_K-connected worlds, but that does not require the full connectedness property. In fact, if all we cared about were connectedness of the minimal R_K set then we could do with only the S4.2 system. However, as we shall see, we will be interested in not only the initial most-easily-imagined

---
[3]Although the development here is self-contained, we do assume familiarity with basic modal logic, possible-worlds- or Kripke-semantics, and the standard Hintikka-style application of modal logic to reasoning about mental attitudes.

[4]It is possible to generalize the construction and assign a separate prejudice relation to each world, but we do not pursue this further in this article.

worlds, but more generally in the most-easily-imagined worlds *given any particular evidence.* Each particular evidence will eliminate some subset of the possible worlds, and we will require that most-easily-imagined worlds among the remainder also all be R_K-equivalent. The full connectedness requirement provides us with just this property. (As we will mention later, previous work that ignored the notion of evidence, for example by Voorbrak [Voo90], indeed ended up with the S4.2 logic.)

We now have all the ingredients necessary to define both knowledge and certainty: Given the structure and a world w in the structure, the agent is said to *know* φ in w iff φ holds in all worlds that are as easy to imagine as w, and to be *certain* of α (given evidence φ) iff α holds in the most easily imaginable φ-worlds in the structure.[5] Certainty thus depends on the structure as a whole, but not on the particular 'real' world; the same property will be true of belief (see below). Knowledge, in contrast, may vary among worlds in the structure.

A minor technical comment: In the following, we will assume that no two worlds in the structure satisfy exactly the same set of formulas (though they may agree on all the propositional ones). This is a harmless assumption, since if two worlds do agree on all formulas in a model this model can be replaced by one in which these two worlds are merged, without affecting the truth value of any formula in any world.

What then is the intuition behind these two definitions? The intuition behind the definition of certainty has already been given: The agent is aware of only the most easily imagined among those that are compatible with the evidence, and thus is certain of a fact if and only if it holds in all of those. The definition of knowledge, however, while very standard from the technical point of view, is supported by a somewhat more involved intuition. In fact, it turns out that this intuition is closely linked with a certain informal view on knowledge and belief, namely that knowledge is belief that is 'stable with respect to the truth'; that is, the agent is said to know a fact if he believes it, and will continue to believe it no matter what true facts he might learn in the future. We find this view quite appealing. It is apparently an old one within philosophy (cf. [Sta93, PS78]); we ourselves learned it from John McCarthy (personal communication), who had come up with it independently.

One way to understand our definition of knowledge is as a formal embodiment of this informal view (except that we appeal to the 'certainty' version of belief). The intuition is that as the agent is supplied additional information true about that real world, the set of most-easily imagined worlds moves up the prejudice order, without ever moving beyond the real world. Given complete information about the real world, and given the assumption that no two worlds in the structure agree on all formulas, the agent will consider the real world and only it. Of course, any particular language may not be sufficiently expressive to completely characterize a world; in particular, our language with only finite formulas isn't. However this shouldn't stop us from using more expressive languages in our semantic definitions; in particular, we may use infinitary logic. And indeed, one way to capture the informal philosophical slogan is to define knowledge in a world w to consist of the facts that hold in all the most easily imagined Σ-worlds, for any (possibly infinite) Σ true in w. It turns out that this definition coincides with our definition of knowledge. It is obvious that our definition is at least as strong as this one, since no (finite or infinite) evidence true at w will compel the agent to consider worlds that are not at least as easy to imagine as w. To see the other direction of the equivalence, assume that α is known in w under the new definition, and let w' be any world that is as easy to imagine as w. Denote by Σ the conjunction of all (propositional and modal) formulas true in w, and by Σ' the conjunction of all formulas true in w'. Since by assumption all worlds in the structure are pairwise distinguishable by some formula, clearly the most easily imagined $\Sigma_1 \vee \Sigma_2$-worlds consist of either w and w' or of w' alone. Therefore α is true at w'.

Belief is now the last notion to be explained. It will be relatively straightforward. Here we introduce a new ordering on worlds (denoted R_B), representing the agent's ranking of plausibility (or preferences, if you will): $w_1 R_B w_2$ will be interpreted to mean that w_2 is at least as plausible as w_1. R_B will be required to be a preorder (that is, reflexive and transitive), which accords well with this intuitive interpretation[6] Given this relation, the beliefs of the agent given evidence φ are defined as the facts that holds in all the most-plausible φ-worlds. Unlike the intuitive interpretation of prejudice, the agent is assumed to be aware of the preference ordering; if the agent chooses to concentrate on some worlds as a result of this preference it does so consciously, and recognizes the risk incurred.

The prejudice ordering and the plausibility ordering of any given agent are not independent relations. Intuitively, the agent's subconscious bias leads him to consider certain possibilities, and among those the agent consciously makes finer distinctions. Informally, one can think of R_B as identical to R_K, except that when

---

[5]This latter definition requires some care, since in infinite structures the 'more easily imagined' relation need not be well founded, and hence the 'most easily imagined worlds' may not exist. Our formal definition will be a bit more complicated because of this fact.

[6]In contrast with the deterministic effect of nature, the preferences of the agent may well leave him with noncomparable possibilities. The property of connectedness is thus not imposed on the R_B relation.

two worlds are mutually R_K-accessible then their R_B-relationship is completely unconstrained. Formally, we impose two conditions to capture this intuition. First, if a two worlds are ordered by plausibility, they must be ordered the same way by prejudice (if $w_1 R_B w_2$ then $w_1 R_K w_2$). In other words, the prejudice ordering is a refinement of the plausibility ordering. However, this is not an arbitrary refinement; if one world is strictly higher than another in the prejudice ordering, the conscious preference must reflect this fact. Formally: if $w_1 R_K w_2$ and not $w_2 R_K w_1$ then $w_1 R_B w_2$.

This concludes the informal introduction. As we have mentioned, the formal definition is short and relatively simple.

Definition 1 *KCB-structure*

A KCB-structure is a tuple $M = \langle \mathcal{W}, R_K, R_B, v \rangle$ such that:
- $\mathcal{W}$ is a non empty set of world.
- $R_K \subseteq \mathcal{W} \times \mathcal{W}$ is a reflexive, transitive, and connected relation.
- $R_B \subseteq \mathcal{W} \times \mathcal{W}$ is a reflexive and transitive relation.
- These two relations satisfy the following conditions:
  - if $w_1 R_B w_2$ then $w_1 R_K w_2$
  - if $w_1 R_K w_2$ then either $w_2 R_K w_1$ or $w_1 R_B w_2$
- v is a valuation function.

The satisfiability relation is then defined in the standard fashion (in the following, $\| \varphi \|_w^{M, R_K} = \{w' \mid w R_K w'$ and $M, w' \models \varphi\}$, that is, the set of φ-worlds that are at least as easy to imagine as w):

Definition 2 *Satisfiability relation*

Let p be a propositional variable and α, β, be some formulas.
Let M be a structure and w a world of this structure.
- $M, w \models p$ iff $w \in v(p)$.
- $M, w \models \alpha \wedge \beta$ iff $M, w \models \alpha$ and $M, w \models \beta$.
- $M, w \models \neg \alpha$ iff not $M, w \models \alpha$.
- $M, w \models K\alpha$ iff for all w' if $w R_K w'$ then $M, w' \models \alpha$.
- $M, w \models C^\varphi \alpha$ iff for all w_1 [if $w_1 \in \| \varphi \|_w^{M, R_K}$ then there is a w_2 such that $\{w_2 \in \| \varphi \|_{w_1}^{M, R_K}$ and for all w_3 (if $w_3 \in \| \varphi \|_{w_2}^{M, R_K}$ then $M, w_3 \models \alpha)\}$].
- $M, w \models B^\varphi \alpha$ iff for all w_1 [if $w_1 \in \| \varphi \|_w^{M, R_K}$ then there is a w_2 such that $\{w_2 \in \| \varphi \|_w^{M, R_K}$ and $w_1 R_B w_2$ and for all w_3 (if $w_3 \in \| \varphi \|_w^{M, R_K}$ and $w_2 R_B w_3$ then $M, w_3 \models \alpha)\}$].

Unlike the definition of the operator K, which is standard, the definitions of C and B are perhaps a little hard to grasp. If the relation R_K does not induce any infinite descending chain then our definition of $C^\varphi \alpha$ exactly and simply states that α is true in all the most-easily-imagined φ-worlds. However, our definition is not restricted to the bounded case, but for infinite descending chains more subtlety is required: We require that φ be false everywhere in the chain, or else that the chain contain a world w_1 satisfying φ such that α is true in all the φ-worlds following w_1 in the chain (including w_1 itself since R_K is reflexive). This construction has already been used, for example to prove some connections between modal logics, conditional logics and non-monotonic preference inference relations in [Lam91]. Similar considerations on R_B support the definition of B^φ.

4 Belief, certainty, and knowledge: an axiomatic system

Consider the following axiomatic system:

Definition 3 *Axiomatic system*

The system contains the axioms of the propositional calculus plus:
- knowledge
  $K(\alpha \to \beta) \to (K\alpha \to K\beta)$
  $K\alpha \to \alpha$
  $K\alpha \to KK\alpha$
- belief
  $B^\varphi \varphi$
  $B^\varphi \alpha \wedge B^\varphi \beta \to B^\varphi(\alpha \wedge \beta)$
  $B^\varphi \alpha \wedge B^\psi \alpha \to B^{\varphi \vee \psi} \alpha$
  $B^\varphi \psi \wedge B^\varphi \alpha \to B^{\varphi \wedge \psi} \alpha$
- knowledge and belief
  $K(\varphi \leftrightarrow \psi) \to (B^\varphi \alpha \leftrightarrow B^\psi \alpha)$
  $K(\alpha \to \beta) \to (B^\varphi \alpha \to B^\varphi \beta)$
  $K\alpha \to B^\varphi \alpha$
  $\neg K \neg \alpha \to (B^\alpha \beta \to \neg B^\alpha \neg \beta)$
  $B^\varphi \alpha \to K B^\varphi \alpha$
  $\neg B^\varphi \alpha \to K(K \neg \varphi \vee \neg B^\varphi \alpha)$
- certainty
  $C^\varphi \alpha \leftrightarrow B^\varphi K(\varphi \to \alpha)$

The system is closed by the propositional inference rules plus:
$$\frac{\vdash \alpha}{\vdash K\alpha}$$
We also define two 'absolute' versions of the C and B operators:
$B\alpha =_{def} B^{True}\alpha$
$C\alpha =_{def} C^{True}\alpha$

The system is surprising in a number of ways, so let us first assure the reader of its relevance:

Theorem 1 *Soundness and Completeness*

For any formula α, $\vdash \alpha$ iff $\models \alpha$

A few comments about this system. First, note that the modal axioms K, T, and 4 appear in the axiomatization of the operator K, but axiom 5 (negative introspection) does not; recall the discussion in the introduction in which we argued that this is a feature, not a bug. And if our informal arguments were not enough, here is an additional formal one: Adding negative introspection to our system is equivalent to adding the axiom $K\alpha \leftrightarrow C\alpha$ (in the sense that, adding either of them to the system enables the derivation of the other one).

Another feature may be surprising: It may at first seem that there is no axiom on K to ensure the connected property required for relation R_K. In fact standard axiom for connectedness is a theorem of the system, by virtue of the links between knowledge and belief.

The belief-related axioms may be also surprising in at least two ways. First, they might seem weak; for example, no mention is made of positive or negative introspection properties. In fact, all the KD45 properties hold for belief, but they follow from the other axioms and need not be postulated. The proposition below underscores this fact. Second, the reader might notice an uncanny resemblance between these axioms and the some axioms suggested in the context of consequence relations. In particular, these axioms are a simple adaptation of the axiom and the rules proposed by Kraus, Lehmann, and Magidor in [KLM90] for preferential inference relations. This is not that surprising, however, since the notion of preference has been used to give an intuitive underlying explanation of belief. The links between these inference relations and S4 are now well known (see, for example, [Lam91]).

The axioms linking knowledge and belief are perhaps the most interesting. Among them, the first two are also simple adaptation of rules used by Kraus, Lehman, and Magidor to characterize preference inference relations. The third one is probably the most intuitive; we know of almost no approach to knowledge and belief that denies this connection between them at least in the special case in which $\varphi =$ True.[7] The fourth axiom is a generalized D axiom for belief (the special case, in which $\alpha =$ True, is yields D). The last two axioms reflect the intuition that an agent, while perhaps being wrong about what it knows and what it does not, is the best judge of what it currently believes. Indeed, it is a widely accepted epistemological view that we have 'privileged access' to our own doxastic states (cf. [Len78b]). The last axiom corresponds to the application of the same intuition to negative beliefs. It is perhaps the hardest to understand, since the naive way to capture the intuition might have been by $\neg B^\varphi \alpha \to K(\neg B^\varphi \alpha)$. However, this simpler axiom ignores the possibility of assumptions that are known to be false, and is valid only for the case of $\varphi =$ True.

We have already mentioned that the system, while perhaps appearing somewhat weak at first glance, in fact is quite powerful. Here are some of its consequences:

Proposition 1 *Some theorems*

The following formulas are theorems of the previous axiomatic system:
- Belief
  intramodal
  $B\alpha \to \neg B \neg \alpha$
  $B^\varphi(\alpha \to \beta) \to (B^\varphi \alpha \to B^\varphi \beta)$
  $B^\varphi \alpha \to B^\psi B^\varphi \alpha$
  $\neg B^\varphi \alpha \to B^\varphi \neg B^\varphi \alpha$
  $\neg B\alpha \to B^\varphi \neg B\alpha$
  intermodal
  $\neg K \neg \varphi \to (B^\varphi \alpha \to \neg B^\varphi \neg \alpha)$
  $C(\varphi \to \alpha) \to B^\varphi \alpha$
  $C^\varphi \alpha \to B^\varphi \alpha$
  $\neg B^\varphi \alpha \to B^\varphi \neg K(\varphi \to \alpha)$
  introspection
  $K\alpha \to B^\psi K\alpha$
  $B^\varphi \alpha \to KB^\varphi \alpha$ (axiom)
  $\neg B^\varphi \alpha \to K(K \neg \varphi \vee \neg B^\varphi \alpha)$ (axiom)
  $\neg B^\varphi \alpha \to K(\varphi \to \neg B^\varphi \alpha)$
- Certainty
  intramodal
  $C\alpha \to \neg C \neg \alpha$
  $C^\varphi(\alpha \to \beta) \to (C^\varphi \alpha \to C^\varphi \beta)$
  $C^\varphi \alpha \to C^\psi C^\varphi \alpha$
  $\neg C^\varphi \alpha \to C^\varphi \neg C^\varphi \alpha$
  $\neg C\alpha \to C^\varphi \neg C\alpha$
  intermodal
  $\neg K \neg \varphi \to (C^\varphi \alpha \to \neg C^\varphi \neg \alpha)$
  $K(\varphi \to \alpha) \to C^\varphi \alpha$
  $K\alpha \to C^\varphi \alpha$
  $\neg C^\varphi \alpha \to C^\varphi \neg K(\varphi \to \alpha)$
  introspection
  $K\alpha \to C^\psi K\alpha$
  $C^\varphi \alpha \to KC^\varphi \alpha$
  $\neg C^\varphi \alpha \to K(K \neg \varphi \vee \neg C^\varphi \alpha)$
  $\neg C^\varphi \alpha \to K(\varphi \to \neg C^\varphi \alpha)$
- Knowledge
  $K(K\alpha \to \beta) \vee K(K\beta \to \alpha)$
- of special note
  $C\alpha \leftrightarrow BK\alpha \leftrightarrow \neg K \neg K\alpha \leftrightarrow CK\alpha$
  $K\alpha \leftrightarrow B^{\neg \alpha} \alpha$

---
[7]One exception of which we are aware is Voorbrak's formulation [Voo90] which distinguishes between 'objective' and 'subjective' knowledge; the former does not have the K→B connection. However, in our view the usual reading of 'know' corresponds to what he calls subjective knowledge.

Also, the following inference rules are valid:

$$\frac{\vdash \alpha}{\vdash B^\varphi \alpha} \qquad \frac{\vdash \alpha}{\vdash C^\varphi \alpha}$$

Many more properties of the system could be discussed, but we will focus on only three points. The two first ones are related to the formula $\neg K \neg K \alpha$.

First, note in the above proposition that we could have introduced this formula as the definition of certainty. In some sense this would have been more elegant, in that only a single modality is involved. And indeed, this was exactly Lenzen's definition of 'conviction' [Len78b]. It is also a construct that has been mentioned in connection with nonmonotonic logics, first by Siegel [Sie90] and more recently by Schwarz and Truszczyński [ST94]. However, while we consider the coincidence of definitions further validation of our own, we find our definition (enabled by the introduction of a second operator, B) possibly more intuitive.

Second, consider the formula $\neg K \neg K \alpha \rightarrow K \neg K \neg \alpha$, which, when added to the S4 system, defines the system S4.2 (equivalently, consider the semantic property of convergence: If two worlds w_1 and w_2 are accessible from a third, then there is a fourth model accessible from both w_1 and w_2). Although many authors have proposed it as an interesting property (including all those mentioned in the above paragraph), it is quite hard to make intuitive sense of it. However, when we rewrite it using the operator C it becomes $C \alpha \rightarrow \neg C \neg \alpha$ which is our first theorem and simply the standard requirement that beliefs be consistent. Lenzen [Len78b] observed this fact before us. He defined the dual operator P ('the agent considers it possible that') by $P\alpha \leftrightarrow \neg C \neg \alpha$, and used the form $C\alpha \rightarrow P\alpha$ to argue that '... "the" logic of knowledge most probably is S4.2' and certainly that ' [this logic] must be at least as strong as the system S4.2 ... [and] at most the system S4.4 which is S4 plus $\alpha \rightarrow (C\alpha \rightarrow K\alpha)$.' We will return to discussion of S4.2 and S4.3 in the Section 5.

Finally, let us consider the last equivalence: $K\alpha \leftrightarrow B^{\neg \alpha} \alpha$. It suggest that it is possible to find an axiomatization in which only the operator B appears, all the others operators being introduced by definition. We do not claim that such an axiomatic system would illuminate these operators; in fact we would find it rather opaque. But it is interesting to note that as, suggested in the introduction, knowledge can be defined in terms of belief. In our semantic development we interpreted this reduction according by appealing to the notion of knowledge as belief that is stable given any true evidence. This alternative definition of knowledge suggestions a different intuitive reduction: $B^{\neg \alpha} \alpha$ says that the beliefs under the hypothesis $\neg \alpha$ are not consistent (because of the axiom $B^\alpha \alpha$), which together with axiom $(\neg K \neg \alpha \rightarrow (B^\alpha \beta \rightarrow \neg B^\alpha \neg \beta))$ says that α is known iff the beliefs relative to its negation are inconsistent. It is interesting that these two conceptually quite different reductions of knowledge to belief end up coinciding.

5 Related work

Philosophers have been interested in the notions of knowing and believing for a long time, and obviously we cannot do the literature justice here. A good overview can be found in Lenzen's [Len78a]. Of that literature, we single out two references. One is Hintikka's foundational work on applying possible-worlds semantics to knowledge and belief [Hin62], on which most work in the area, including our own, builds. The other is Lenzen's own recent work [Len78b], with which our work has many ties. Like him, we introduce the three operators K, B, and C, having the same intuitive interpretations. Lenzen puts forward a collection of axioms regarding the various modalities, all of which are valid in our framework. Like us, Lenzen accepts the KD45 system for certainty (or conviction). From this point on our work extends that of Lenzen.

First, Lenzen is less specific about the properties of the knowledge operator; his conclusions are that "[the logic of knowledge] must be at least as strong as the system S4.2 ... [and] at most the system S4.4 which is S4 plus $\alpha \rightarrow (C\alpha \rightarrow K\alpha)$." (In contrast, Voorbrak [Voo90] is more decisive; he argues for S4.2 as "the" logic of knowledge.) To understand our take on this, it is useful to consider three modal systems: S4.2, S4.3, and S4F (also known sometimes as S4.3.2). Although the differences between them might at first seem like obscure mathematical trivia, in fact these differences expose interesting conceptual issues. Semantically, in S4.2 the accessibility relation is a convergent preorder, in S4.3 a total preorder, and in S4F a total preorder with at most two distinct equivalence classes. We have explained why, when considering the notion of certainty and belief under evidence, the S4.3 structure is the sensible choice. It also follows from our explanation that if one does not care about such relativized notions, and thus only about the single set of most-easily-imagined worlds, the properties of S4.2 are sufficient. On the other hand, if *all* one cares about are knowledge and the unrelativized notion of certainty, then one does not need the full generality of S4.2; in this case all that is needed is a binary distinction between most-easily imagined worlds and non-most-easily imagined worlds, as captured in the S4F system. Interestingly, the system S4F was recently shown by Schwarz and Truszczyński [ST94] to have an intimate connection with nonmonotonic logic; in light of the similarity between our construction and elements in nonmonotonic logics this is perhaps not that surprising.

Thus one dimension in which we extend Lenzen's work is in shedding further light on the particular properties of knowledge, and another related one is our introduction of the notion of evidence. Most importantly, however, Lenzen does not give a complete formal system, either semantic or syntactic, for the three notions. He lists many of the syntactic properties of these three notions, but does not provide semantics and thus cannot prove soundness and completeness. We not only provide a model theory and prove soundness and completeness, but in fact are able to give intuitive motivation for the model theory and relate it to philosophical intuitions.

Artificial Intelligence is another field in which these notions have been used, and, again, we do not aim to discuss here all the relevant work. As we have mentioned, generally (though not universally) the notion of knowledge in AI includes the negative introspection, which we explicitly reject. It appears that in most of AI work no distinction is made between certainty and knowledge. In fact, sometimes the notion of knowledge is explicitly equated with certainty; this may help explain the presence of the negative introspection axiom. From the technical standpoint we can easily endow the operator K with S5 properties by adding the axiom $C^\varphi \alpha \leftrightarrow K\alpha$ to our system (or, in the special case of unrelativized certainty, we would add the axiom $C\alpha \rightarrow K\alpha$); however, as we explained, we object to S5 in the first place.

A previous attempt to link the notions of knowledge and belief within AI was made by Moses and Shoham [MS93], which had a very similar notion of relativized belief. An interesting connection between belief and nonmonotonic inference relation was noted there. Specifically, the authors presented three definitions, in some of which the belief was nonmonotonic: Just as in our system, increasing the strength of the hypothesis could reduce the set of beliefs. However this nonmonotonic behavior held only when the hypotheses were strengthened to the point of contradicting the agent's knowledge; in all other circumstances, the belief operators presented in [MS93] were monotonic. Another major element is that Moses and Shoham's work is centered on an attempt to reduce belief to knowledge. In contrast, here we argue that belief involves an extra ingredient, namely preference (or plausibility). This notion of preference crystalizes the relationship between belief and commonsense reasoning; indeed, the notion of preference has been borrowed directly from the study of nonmonotonic inference relations, see [Sho88, KLM90]. It is precisely this notion of preference that gives rise to the nonmonotonic behavior of the belief operator presented here.

This connection between the belief operator and the nonmonotonic inference relations makes for a perfect transition to another connection, this time with conditional logics. There are now well known connections between conditional logics and nonmonotonic inference relations (see [Bel91, CS92, CL92]). Indeed, one may well read the $B^\varphi \alpha$ construct as a kind of conditional, $\varphi \Rightarrow \alpha$. There have been several attempt recently to relate conditionals to the notion of knowledge and belief. Of these we will discuss two, the one by Boutilier and the other by Friedman and Halpern. (However, let us at least mention another paper published in the proceedings of KR94, by Brafman and Tennenholtz [BT94]; the main thrust of that paper is unrelated to the present article, but when they address the issue of belief change they offer two models of belief – one based on a total order on worlds, the other based on a partial order.)

In the long version of this article we will discuss the connection Boutilier's work [Bou92a, Bou92b] in more detail. Here we will have to be brief; in particular we will mention only the aspect of his system that are the most relevant to ours, which will not reflect the full power of his formalism. Like us, Boutilier introduces a Kripke structure with a reflexive, transitive and connected accessibility relation. One originality of his work is that two modal operators are defined: the usual necessity operator (noted $\Box$), and another one which corresponds to truth in all the structures. Intuitively, this last operator (denoted $\overleftrightarrow{\Box}$) "looks" at all the worlds connected to the actual one: the worlds which are accessible form the actual world via the accessibility relation and the ones for which the actual world is accessible. Using these two operators, a conditional operator is then defined: $\alpha \Rightarrow \beta =_{def} \overleftrightarrow{\Box} \neg \alpha \vee \overleftrightarrow{\Diamond}(\alpha \wedge \Box(\alpha \rightarrow \beta))$. Most of Boutilier's constructions are based on these three operators.

In order to make a connection between our system and his, we need to place some additional restrictions on our own. First K and C must be equated ($K\alpha \leftrightarrow C\alpha$). Second, we must add the axiom of 'rational nonmonotonicity' proposed by Kraus, Lehmann and Magidor ($\neg B^\varphi \neg \psi \wedge B^\varphi \alpha \rightarrow B^{\varphi \wedge \psi} \alpha$) to ensure a connected property for R_B. Under these two assumptions, it turns out that his operator $\overleftrightarrow{\Box}$ and our K (and C) coincide, as do his $\varphi \Rightarrow \alpha$ and our $B^\varphi \alpha$. To summarize, then, although Boutilier started with very different motivations, his system can be interpreted as a special case of our construction. We find this interesting, even though the special case is achieved by equating K and C, which clearly we oppose in principle.

The other, more recent related work is by Friedman and Halpern [FH94]. That paper covers a lot of ground; we will restrict the discussion to the part relevant to our system. Like us, they start with a Kripke structure whose necessity operator is interpreted as a knowledge operator. Unlike us, they adopt the S5 system, which we clearly reject as long as the knowledge interpretation is retained (however, there is no reason in principle why they could not develop their ideas while adopting S4.3 or any other system). Then, rather than introduce a single preorder on the structure, they assign to each world such a preorder; as we said in explaining our construction, this is an ultimately necessary degree of generality that we have chosen to avoid for now. This preorder is used to define a conditional in the standard way – $\varphi \Rightarrow \alpha$ holds iff α holds in the minimal φ worlds – and belief is defined by $B^\varphi \alpha =_{def} K(\varphi \Rightarrow \alpha)$. They then specialize the construction in a number of ways and prove properties of the resulting systems. Thus their construction contains elements missing from ours – most notably, world-dependent preorders – whereas our construction contains elements missing from theirs, such as a distinction between knowledge, certainty, and belief. In general there appear to be some important differences in the intuition behind the constructions. We have given a detailed explanation of the intuition behind our construction, but at this time have not yet developed sufficient intuition about theirs to make a more detailed comparison.

Overall, it is reassuring that many different researchers, all with different motivations, have ended up with similar formal constructs; this is a good indication that what otherwise might have seemed like esoteric formal systems, such as S4.3, are actually of some significance to AI.

6 Conclusions

We have offered a system to capture the relationship between knowledge and belief, which also sheds new light on each of them in isolation. In the case of knowledge, we strongly reject the property of negative introspection. In the case of belief, we propose a distinction between belief (whose defeasibility is recognized by the agent) and certainty (whose defeasibility is not). The relationship between the three notions – knowledge, certainty, and belief – went far beyond mere hierarchy. In particular, knowledge had the flavor of belief that is stable under incorporation of correct facts. We explored these first through a model theory, which is based on the notions of the agent's subconscious biases and its conscious preferences (or plausibility measure). We then provided a sound and complete axiomatic system, and pointed to some of its illuminating properties. We have shown that our construction produces attractive formal properties, which accord well with some previous work in philosophy, computer science, and AI. We have also attempted to provide comprehensive intuitive motivation behind the construction, so that theory need not be accepted on the basis of its formal properties alone.

In a companion paper we specialize the construction, and look at the special case in which no 'evidence' formulas appear (or, equivalently, where the only evidence is True); as we have mentioned, in that case we can restrict the attention to the S4F system. In future work we would like to extend the theory to handle relativization to arbitrary information, even incorrect one, and thus attain full integration with the notions of belief revision, update, and other forms of mental dynamism. Also, as we have mentioned, we would like to generalize the construction to account for partial orders that vary by world. Finally, in this article we have restricted the discussion to the propositional, single-agent case; clearly an extention to the multi-agent and first-order cases is called for, and the latter may prove challenging.

Acknowledgements. Thanks to various members of the Nobotics group for useful comments and discussions. Ronen Brafman provided useful comments on an earlier draft. Special thanks to Grisha Schwarz for incisive technical comments.

References

[Aum76] R. Aumann. Agreeing to disagree. *The Annals of Statistics*, 4:1236–1239, 1976.

[Bel91] J. Bell. Pragmatic logics. In *Proc. Second Conference on Knowledge Representation and Reasoning*, Boston, MA, 1991.

[Bou92a] Craig Boutilier. *Conditional Logics for Default Reasoning and Belief Revision*. Technical report 92-1, University of British Columbia, Department of Computer Science Rm 333 - 6356 Agricultural Road Vancouver, B.C. Canada V6T 1Z2, January 1992.

[Bou92b] G. Boutilier. Normative, subjunctive and autoepistemic defaults: adopting the ramsey test. In *Proc. Third Conference on Knowledge Representation and Reasoning*, Boston, MA, 1992.

[BP83] J. Barwise and J. Perry. *Situations and Attitudes*. MIT Press, Cambridge, Mass, 1983.

[BT94] R. I. Brafman and M. Tennenholtz. Belief ascription and mental-level modelling. In *Proc. Fourth Conference on Knowledge Representation and Reasoning*, Bonn, Germany, 1994.

[CL92] G. Crocco and P. Lamarre. On the connection between nonmonotonic inference systems and conditional logics. In *Proc. Third Conference on Knowledge Representation and Reasoning*, Boston, MA, 1992.

[CS92] A. Costa and H. Shapiro. Maps between nonmonotonic and conditional logics. In *Proc. Third Conference on Knowledge Representation and Reasoning*, Boston, MA, 1992.

[Del87] James P. Delgrande. A first order conditional logic for prototypical properties. *JAI*, (33):105–130, 1987.

[FH94] N. Friedman and J. Y. Halpern. A knowledge-based framework for belief change, part i: Foundations. In *Proceedings Conference on Theoretical Aspects of Reasoning about Knowledge*, pages 44–64. Morgan Kaufmann, 1994.

[Hin62] J. Hintikka. *Knowledge and Belief*. Cornell University Press, 1962.

[KLM90] S. Kraus, D. Lehmann, and M. Magidor. Nonmonotonic reasoning, preferential models and cumulative logic. *Artificial Intelligence*, 44, July 1990.

[KM91] H. Katsuno and A. O. Mendelzon. On the difference between updating a knowledge base and revising it. In *Proc. Second Conference on Knowledge Representation and Reasoning*, Boston, MA, 1991.

[KS91] H. Katsuno and K. Satoh. A unified view of consequence relations, belief revision, and consequence logic. In *Proc. IJCAI*, 1991.

[Lam91] P. Lamarre. S4 as the conditional logic of nonmonotonicity. In *Proc. Second Conference on Knowledge Representation and Reasoning*, Boston, MA, 1991.

[Len78a] Wolfgang Lenzen. *The aim of epistemic logic*, volume XXX of *Acta Philosophica Fennica*. North-Holland, Amsterdam, 1978.

[Len78b] Wolfgang Lenzen. *Recent Work in Epistemic Logic*, volume XXX of *Acta Philosophica Fennica*. North-Holland, Amsterdam, 1978.

[Lew73] David Lewis. *Counterfactuals*. Basil Blackwell Ltd, 1986 (first published 1973).

[MS93] Y. Moses and Y. Shoham. Belief as defeasible knowledge. *Artificial Intelligence*, 64(2):299–322, December 1993.

[PS78] G. Pappas and M. Swain, editors. *Essays on Knowledge and Justification*. Cornell University Press, Ithaca, NY, 1978.

[Sho88] Yoav Shoham. *Reasoning about Change*. The MIT Press, 1988.

[Sie90] Pierre Siegel. A modal language for nonmonotonic logic. In *Workshop DRUMS*, CEE Marseille, 1990.

[ST94] G. Schwarz and M. Truszczynsky. Minimal knowledge problem: a new approach. *artificial Intelligence*, to appear, 1994.

[Sta93] R. C. Stalnaker. Knowledge, belief and counterfactual reasoning in games. In C. Bicchieri B .Skryms (Eds.), editor, *Proceedings of conference on game theory (to appear)*. Cambridge University Press, 1993.

[Var85] M. Vardi. A model theoretic model of monotonic knowledge. In *Proceedings of 9th IJCAI*, pages 509–512, 1985.

[Voo90] F. Voorbrak. Generalized Kripke models for epistemic logic. In *Proceedings Conference on Theoretical Aspects of Reasoning about Knowledge*, pages 214–228. Morgan Kaufmann, 1990.

How to Progress a Database (and Why)
I. Logical Foundations

Fangzhen Lin and Ray Reiter*
Department of Computer Science
University of Toronto
Toronto, Canada M5S 1A4
email: fl@ai.toronto.edu reiter@ai.toronto.edu

Abstract

One way to think about STRIPS is as a mapping from databases to databases, in the following sense: Suppose we want to know what the world would be like if an action, represented by the STRIPS operator α, were done in some world, represented by the STRIPS database $\mathcal{D}_0$. To find out, simply perform the operator α on $\mathcal{D}_0$ (by applying α's elementary *add* and *delete* revision operators to $\mathcal{D}_0$). We describe this process as *progressing the database* $\mathcal{D}_0$ in response to the action α. In this paper, we consider the general problem of progressing an initial database in response to a given sequence of actions. We appeal to the situation calculus and an axiomatization of actions which addresses the frame problem (Reiter [14], Lin and Reiter [7]). This setting is considerably more general than STRIPS. Our results concerning progression are mixed. The (surprising) bad news is that, in general, to characterize a progressed database we must appeal to second order logic. The good news is that there are many useful special cases for which we can compute the progressed database in first order logic; not only that, we can do so efficiently.

1 INTRODUCTION

One way to think about STRIPS is as a mapping from databases to databases, in the following sense: Suppose we want to know what the world would be like if an action, represented by the STRIPS operator α, were done in some world, represented by the STRIPS database $\mathcal{D}_0$. To find out, simply perform the operator α on $\mathcal{D}_0$ (by applying α's elementary *add* and *delete* revision operators to $\mathcal{D}_0$). We describe this process as

---
*Fellow of the Canadian Institute for Advanced Research

progressing the database $\mathcal{D}_0$ in response to the action α (cf. Rosenschein [15] and Pednault [9]). The resulting database describes the effects of the action on the world represented by the initial database.[1] However, it may not always be convenient or even possible to describe the effects of actions as a simple process of progressing an initial world description. As we shall see in this paper, once we go beyond STRIPS-like systems, progression becomes surprisingly complicated.

In this paper, we consider the general problem of progressing an initial database in response to a given sequence of actions. We appeal to the situation calculus and an axiomatization of actions which addresses the frame problem (Reiter [14], Lin and Reiter [7]). This setting is considerably more general than STRIPS. Our results concerning progression are mixed. The (surprising) bad news is that, in general, to characterize a progressed database we must appeal to second order logic. The good news is that there are many useful special cases for which we can compute the progressed database in first order logic; not only that, we can do so efficiently.

The need to progress a database arises for us in a robotics setting. In our approach to controlling a robot,[2] we must address the so-called *projection problem*: Answer the query $Q(do(\mathbf{A}, S_0))$, where $do(\mathbf{A}, S_0)$ denotes the situation resulting from performing the sequence of actions $\mathbf{A}$ beginning with the initial situation S_0. This can be done using regression (cf. Waldinger [17], Pednault [10], and Reiter [13]) to reduce the projection problem to one of entailment from the *initial* database, consisting of sentences about the initial situation S_0. Unfortunately, regression suffers from a number of drawbacks in this application:

---
[1]This is also the way that database practitioners think about database updates (Abiteboul [1]). In fact, the STRIPS action and database update paradigms are essentially the same. Accordingly, this paper is as much about database updates as it is about STRIPS actions and their generalizations.

[2]Joint work with Yves Lespérance, Hector Levesque, Bill Millar and Richard Scherl.

1. After the robot has been functioning for a long time, the sequence **A**, consisting of all the actions it has performed since the initial situation, is extremely long, and regressing over such a long sequence becomes a computational burden.
2. Similarly, after a long while, the world state often becomes so rearranged that significantly many final steps of the regression become entirely unnecessary.
3. Most significantly, for robotics, *perceptual actions* (Scherl and Levesque [16]) lead to new facts being added to the database. But such facts are true in the current situation – the one immediately following the perceptual action – whereas the other (old) database facts are true in S_0. Reasoning about databases containing mixed facts – facts about the current and initial situations – is very complicated, and we know of no satisfactory way to do this.

Our way of addressing these problems with regression is to to periodically progress the robot's database. In particular, every perceptual action is accompanied by a progression of the database, coupled with the addition of the perceived fact to the resulting database. We envisage that these database progression computations can be done off-line, during the time when the robot is busy performing physical actions, like moving about.

2 LOGICAL PRELIMINARIES

The language $\mathcal{L}$ of the situation calculus is a many-sorted first-order one with the sorts *state* for situations, *action* for actions, and *object* for anything else. We have the following domain independent predicates and functions: a unique constant S_0 of sort *state*; a binary function $do(a,s)$ that denotes the state resulting from performing the action a in the state s; a binary predicate $Poss(a,s)$ that expresses the conditions for the action a to be executable in the state s; and a binary predicate $<: state \times state$. We shall follow convention, and write $<$ in infix form. By $s < s'$ we mean that s' can be obtained from s by a sequence of executable actions. As usual, $s \leq s'$ will be a shorthand for $s < s' \vee s = s'$. We assume a finite number of *state independent* predicates which are the ones with arity $object^n$, $n \geq 0$, a finite number of *state independent* functions which are the ones with arity $object^n \rightarrow object$, $n \geq 0$, and a finite number of *fluents* which are predicate symbols of arity $object^n \times state$, $n \geq 0$.

We shall denote by $\mathcal{L}^2$ the second-order extension of $\mathcal{L}$. Our foundational axioms for the situation calculus will be in $\mathcal{L}^2$ (Lin and Reiter [7]), because we need induction on situations (Reiter [12]).

We shall frequently need to restrict the situation calculus to a particular situation. For instance, the initial database is defined to be a finite set of sentences in $\mathcal{L}$ that do not mention any state terms except S_0, and do not mention $Poss$ and $<$. For this purpose, for any state term st, we shall define $\mathcal{L}_{st}$ to be the subset of $\mathcal{L}$ that does not mention any other state terms except st, does not quantify over state variables, and does not mention $Poss$ and $<$. Formally, it is the smallest set satisfying

1. $\varphi \in \mathcal{L}_{st}$ provided $\varphi \in \mathcal{L}$ does not mention any state term.
2. $F(t_1,...,t_n,st) \in \mathcal{L}_{st}$ provided F is a fluent of the right arity, and $t_1,...,t_n$ are terms of the right sort.
3. If φ and φ' are in $\mathcal{L}_{st}$, so are $\neg\varphi$, $\varphi \vee \varphi'$, $\varphi \wedge \varphi'$, $\varphi \supset \varphi'$, $\varphi \equiv \varphi'$, $(\forall x)\varphi$, $(\exists x)\varphi$, $(\forall a)\varphi$, and $(\exists a)\varphi$, where x and a are variables of sort *object* and *action*, respectively.

We remark here that according to this definition, $(\forall a)F(do(a,S_0))$ will be in $\mathcal{L}_{do(a,S_0)}$. This may seem odd when we want sentences in $\mathcal{L}_{st}$ to be propositions about situation st. Fortunately, we shall use $\mathcal{L}_{st}$ only when st is either a ground term or a simple variable of sort *state*.

We shall use $\mathcal{L}^2_{st}$ to denote the second-order extension of $\mathcal{L}_{st}$ by predicate variables of arity $object^n$, $n \geq 0$. So the second-order sentence $(\exists p)(\forall x).p(x) \equiv F(x,S_0)$ is in $\mathcal{L}^2_{S_0}$, but $(\exists p)(\forall x)(\exists s).p(x,s) \equiv F(x,S_0)$ is not, since the latter quantifies over a predicate variable of arity $object \times state$. Formally, $\mathcal{L}^2_{st}$ is the smallest set satisfying

1. Every formula in $\mathcal{L}_{st}$ is also in $\mathcal{L}^2_{st}$.
2. $p(t_1,...,t_n) \in \mathcal{L}^2_{st}$ provided p is a predicate variable of arity $object^n$, $n \geq 0$, and $t_1,...,t_n$ are terms of sort *object*.
3. If φ and φ' are in $\mathcal{L}^2_{st}$, so are $\neg\varphi$, $\varphi \vee \varphi'$, $\varphi \wedge \varphi'$, $\varphi \supset \varphi'$, $\varphi \equiv \varphi'$, $(\forall x)\varphi$, $(\exists x)\varphi$, $(\forall a)\varphi$, $(\exists a)\varphi$, $(\forall p)\varphi$, and $(\exists p)\varphi$, where x and a are variables of sort *object* and *action*, respectively, and p is a predicate variable of arity $object^n$, $n \geq 0$.

3 BASIC ACTION THEORIES

We assume that our action theory $\mathcal{D}$ has the following form (cf. Reiter [14] and Lin and Reiter [7]):

$$\mathcal{D} = \Sigma \cup \mathcal{D}_{ss} \cup \mathcal{D}_{ap} \cup \mathcal{D}_{una} \cup \mathcal{D}_{S_0},$$

where

- Σ, given below, is the set of the foundational axioms for situations.

- $\mathcal{D}_{ss}$ is a set of successor state axioms of the form:[3]
$$Poss(a,s) \supset F(\vec{x}, do(a,s)) \equiv \Phi_F(\vec{x}, a, s),$$
where F is a fluent, and $\Phi_F(\vec{x}, a, s)$ is in $\mathcal{L}_s$.

- $\mathcal{D}_{ap}$ is a set of action precondition axioms of the form:
$$Poss(A(\vec{x}), s) \equiv \Psi_A(\vec{x}, s),$$
where A is an action, and $\Psi_A(\vec{x}, s)$ is in $\mathcal{L}_s$.

- $\mathcal{D}_{una}$ is the set of unique names axioms for actions: For any two different actions $A(\vec{x})$ and $A'(\vec{y})$, we have
$$A(\vec{x}) \neq A'(\vec{y}),$$
and for any action $A(x_1, ..., x_n)$, we have
$$A(x_1, ..., x_n) = A(y_1, ..., y_n) \supset$$
$$x_1 = y_1 \wedge \cdots \wedge x_n = y_n.$$

- $\mathcal{D}_{S_0}$, the initial database, is a finite set of first-order sentences in $\mathcal{L}_{S_0}$.

We shall give an example of our action theory in a moment. First, we briefly explain our foundational axioms Σ since they are independent of particular applications. Σ contains axioms about the structure of situations. Formally, Σ is the following set of axioms:
$$S_0 \neq do(a,s),$$
$$do(a_1, s_1) = do(a_2, s_2) \supset (a_1 = a_2 \wedge s_1 = s_2),$$
$$(\forall P)[P(S_0) \wedge (\forall a, s)(P(s) \supset P(do(a,s))) \supset (\forall s)P(s)],$$
$$\neg s < S_0,$$
$$s < do(a, s') \equiv (Poss(a, s') \wedge s \leq s').$$

Notice the similarity between Σ and Peano Arithmetic. The first two axioms are unique names assumptions. They eliminate finite cycles, and merging. The third axiom is second-order induction. It amounts to the domain closure axiom which says that every situation has to be obtained from repeatedly applying do to S_0.[4] The last two axioms define $<$ inductively.

Σ is the only place where axioms about the structure of situations can appear. It is needed only if we want to show, usually by induction, that a state constraint of the form $(\forall s).C(s)$ is entailed by an action theory. For the purpose of temporal projection, in particular progression as we shall see, $\mathcal{D}$ has exactly the same effect as $\mathcal{D} - \Sigma$: For any formula $\varphi(s)$ in $\mathcal{L}_s$, and any sequence $\mathbf{A}$ of actions,
$$\mathcal{D} \models \varphi(do(\mathbf{A}, S_0))$$

iff
$$\mathcal{D}_{ss} \cup \mathcal{D}_{ap} \cup \mathcal{D}_{una} \cup \mathcal{D}_{S_0} \models \varphi(do(\mathbf{A}, S_0)).$$

This follows directly from the following proposition which will be used throughout this paper.

Proposition 3.1 *Given any model M of $\mathcal{D}_{ss} \cup \mathcal{D}_{ap} \cup \mathcal{D}_{una} \cup \mathcal{D}_{S_0}$, there is a model M' of $\mathcal{D}$ such that:*

1. *M' and M have the same domains for sorts action and object, and interpret all state independent predicates and functions the same;*

2. *For any sequence $\mathbf{A}$ of actions, any fluent F, and any variable assignment σ:*
$$M', \sigma \models F(\vec{x}, do(\mathbf{A}, S_0))$$
iff
$$M, \sigma \models F(\vec{x}, do(\mathbf{A}, S_0)).$$

Example 3.1 An educational database (Reiter [14]). There are two fluents:

- $enrolled(st, course, s)$: student st is enrolled in course $course$ in state s.

- $grade(st, course, grade, s)$: the grade of st in course is $grade$ in state s.

There are two state independent predicates:

- $prerequ(pre, course)$: pre is a prerequisite course for course $course$.

- $better(grade1, grade2)$: grade $grade1$ is better than grade $grade2$.

There are three database transactions:

- $register(st, course)$: register the student st into course $course$.

- $change(st, course, grade)$: change the grade of the student st in course $course$ to $grade$.

- $drop(st, course)$: drop the student st from course $course$.

This setting can be axiomatized as follows.

$\mathcal{D}_{ss}$ is the set of following successor state axioms:
$$Poss(a, s) \supset$$
$$enrolled(st, c, do(a, s)) \equiv$$
$$a = register(st, c) \vee$$
$$enrolled(st, c, s) \wedge a \neq drop(st, c),$$

$$Poss(a, s) \supset$$
$$grade(st, c, g, do(a, s)) \equiv$$
$$a = change(st, c) \vee$$
$$grade(st, c, g, s) \wedge (\forall g')a \neq change(st, c, g').$$

---

[3] In the following, unless otherwise stated, all free variables in a formula are assumed to be universally quantified from the outside.

[4] For a discussion of the use of induction in the situation calculus, see (Reiter [12]).

$\mathcal{D}_{ap}$ is the set of following action precondition axioms:

$Poss(register(st, c), s) \equiv (\forall pr).prerequ(pr, c) \supset$
$\quad (\exists g).grade(st, pr, g, s) \wedge better(g, 50),$

$Poss(change(st, c, g), s) \equiv True,$

$Poss(drop(st, c), s) \equiv enrolled(st, c, s).$

$\mathcal{D}_{S_0}$, the initial database, can be any finite set of axioms about the initial state, for example, the following ones:

$John \neq Sue \neq C100 \neq C200 \wedge prerequ(C100, C200),$

$enrolled(Sue, C100, S_0),$

$enrolled(John, C100, S_0) \vee enrolled(John, C200, S_0).$

∎

4 FORMAL FOUNDATIONS

Let α be a ground simple action, e.g. $enroll(Sue, C100)$, and let S_α denote the state term $do(\alpha, S_0)$. A progression $\mathcal{D}_{S_\alpha}$ of $\mathcal{D}_{S_0}$ in response to α should have the following properties:

1. $\mathcal{D}_{S_\alpha}$ is a set of sentences about state S_α only, i.e., in $\mathcal{L}_{S_\alpha}$ or in $\mathcal{L}^2_{S_\alpha}$.
2. For all queries about the future of S_α, $\mathcal{D}$ is equivalent (in a suitable formal sense) to
$$\Sigma \cup \mathcal{D}_{ss} \cup \mathcal{D}_{ap} \cup \mathcal{D}_{una} \cup \mathcal{D}_{S_\alpha}$$

In other words, $\mathcal{D}_{S_\alpha}$ acts like the new initial database wrt all possible future evolutions of the theory following α.

To define progression, we first introduce an equivalence relation over structures. Let M and M' be structures (for our language) with the same domains for sorts *action* and *object*. Define $M' \sim_{S_\alpha} M$ iff the following two conditions hold:

1. M' and M interpret all predicate and function symbols which do not take any arguments of sort *state* identically.
2. M and M' agree on all fluents at S_α: For every predicate fluent F, and every variable assignment σ,
$$M', \sigma \models F(\vec{x}, do(\alpha, S_0)) \text{ iff } M, \sigma \models F(\vec{x}, do(\alpha, S_0)).$$

It is clear that $\sim_{S_\alpha}$ is an equivalence relation. If $M' \sim_{S_\alpha} M$, then M' agrees with M on S_α on fluents and state independent predicates and functions, but is free to vary its interpretation of everything else on all other states. In particular, they can interpret *Poss* and *do* differently. We have the following simple lemma.

Lemma 4.1 *If $M \sim_{S_\alpha} M'$, then for any formula φ in $\mathcal{L}^2_{S_\alpha}$, and any variable assignment σ, $M, \sigma \models \varphi$ iff $M', \sigma \models \varphi$.*

So we define

Definition 4.1 *A set of sentences $\mathcal{D}_{S_\alpha}$ in $\mathcal{L}^2_{S_\alpha}$ is a progression of the initial database $\mathcal{D}_{S_0}$ to S_α (wrt $\mathcal{D}$) iff for any structure M, M is a model of $\mathcal{D}_{S_\alpha}$ iff there is a model M' of $\mathcal{D}$ such that $M \sim_{S_\alpha} M'$.*

Notice that we define the new database only up to logical equivalence. We allow the new database to contain second-order sentences because, as we shall see later, first-order logic is not expressive enough for our purposes.

Proposition 4.1 *Let $\mathcal{D}_{S_\alpha}$ be a progression of the initial database to S_α. Then*
$$models(\mathcal{D}) \subseteq models(\Sigma \cup \mathcal{D}_{ss} \cup \mathcal{D}_{ap} \cup \mathcal{D}_{una} \cup \mathcal{D}_{S_\alpha}).$$

Proposition 4.2 *Let $\mathcal{D}_{S_\alpha}$ be a progression of the initial database to S_α. Then for every model M of*
$$\Sigma \cup \mathcal{D}_{ss} \cup \mathcal{D}_{ap} \cup \mathcal{D}_{una} \cup \mathcal{D}_{S_\alpha},$$
there exists a model M' of $\mathcal{D}$ such that:

1. *M' and M interpret all state independent predicate and function symbols identically.*
2. *For every variable assignment σ, and every predicate fluent F,*
$$M', \sigma \models S_\alpha \leq s \wedge F(\vec{x}, s) \text{ iff } M, \sigma \models S_\alpha \leq s \wedge F(\vec{x}, s).$$

Proof: Let M be a model of
$$\Sigma \cup \mathcal{D}_{ss} \cup \mathcal{D}_{ap} \cup \mathcal{D}_{una} \cup \mathcal{D}_{S_\alpha}.$$
Since M is a model of $\mathcal{D}_{S_\alpha}$, there is a model M' of
$$\Sigma \cup \mathcal{D}_{ss} \cup \mathcal{D}_{ap} \cup \mathcal{D}_{una} \cup \mathcal{D}_{S_0}$$
such that $M' \sim_{S_\alpha} M$. It can be easily seen that M' satisfies the desired properties. ∎

From these two propositions, we conclude that $\mathcal{D}$ and $\Sigma \cup \mathcal{D}_{ss} \cup \mathcal{D}_{ap} \cup \mathcal{D}_{una} \cup \mathcal{D}_{S_\alpha}$ agree on all states $\geq S_\alpha$. So $\mathcal{D}_{S_\alpha}$ really does characterize the result of progressing the initial database in response to the action α. Furthermore, the following theorem says that the new database, when it exists, entails the same set of sentences in $\mathcal{L}^2_{S_\alpha}$ as $\mathcal{D}$:

Theorem 1 *Let $\mathcal{D}_{S_\alpha}$ be a progression of the initial database to S_α. For any sentence $\varphi \in \mathcal{L}^2_{S_\alpha}$, $\mathcal{D}_{S_\alpha} \models \varphi$ iff $\mathcal{D} \models \varphi$.*

Proof: If $\mathcal{D} \models \varphi$, then by Lemma 4.1, we have $\mathcal{D}_{S_\alpha} \models \varphi$. If $\mathcal{D}_{S_\alpha} \models \varphi$, then $\mathcal{D} \models \varphi$ by Proposition 4.1. ∎

From this theorem, we see that if $\mathcal{D}_{S_\alpha}$ is a progression, then it is a *strongest post-condition* (cf. Pednault [9], Dijkstra and Scholten [3], and others) of the precondition $\mathcal{D}_{S_0}$ wrt the action α. A result by Pednault [9] shows that $\mathcal{D}_{S_\alpha}$ cannot in general be a finite set of first-order sentences in $\mathcal{L}_{S_\alpha}$. In the following, we shall extend this result, and show that $\mathcal{D}_{S_\alpha}$ cannot in general be a set of first-order sentences in $\mathcal{L}_{S_\alpha}$.

4.1 Progression Is Not Always First-Order Definable

At first glance, the fact that progression cannot always be done in first-order logic may seem obvious in light of Theorem 1, and the fact that $\mathcal{D}$ includes a second-order induction axiom. However, as we mentioned in section 3, for the purpose of progression, $\mathcal{D}$ is equivalent to $\mathcal{D} - \Sigma$, which is a finite set of first-order sentences.

We shall construct a basic action theory $\mathcal{D}$ and two structures M_1 and M_2 with the following properties:

1. $M_1 \models \mathcal{D}$.
2. M_1 and M_2 satisfy the exactly same set of sentences in $\mathcal{L}_{S_\alpha}$.
3. There is no model M' of $\mathcal{D}$ such that $M' \sim_{S_\alpha} M_2$.

It will then follow from our definition that for $\mathcal{D}$, the progression of the initial database to S_α cannot be in $\mathcal{L}_{S_\alpha}$. This is possible because for $M \sim_{S_\alpha} M'$ to hold, M and M' must be isomorphic with respect to sort *object*; but in number theory, there are nonstandard models that satisfy exactly the same set of first-order sentences as the standard model, and it is this property which we now use to show that progression is not always first-order definable.

We now proceed to construct a such basic action thery.

Consider the following theory $\mathcal{D}$ with a unary fluent F_1, and a binary fluent F_2, one action constant symbol A, one constant symbol 0, and one unary function symbol $succ$:

$\mathcal{D}_{S_0} = \emptyset$. $\mathcal{D}_{una} = \emptyset$.

$\mathcal{D}_{ap} = \{(\forall s).Poss(A, s) \equiv True\}$.

$\mathcal{D}_{ss}$ is the following pair of axioms:

$Poss(a, s) \supset [F_1(do(a, s)) \equiv (\exists x)\neg F_2(x, s)]$,

$Poss(a, s) \supset (\forall x).F_2(x, do(a, s)) \equiv$
$\quad x = 0 \land F_2(0, s) \lor$
$\quad F_2(x, s) \land (\exists y).x = succ(y) \land F_2(y, s) \lor$
$\quad \neg F_2(x, s) \land x \neq 0 \land$
$\quad\quad (\forall y)(x = succ(y) \supset \neg F_2(y, s))$.

To understand the successor state axioms, think of the constant symbol 0 as the number 0, and the unary function $succ$ as the successor function. F_1 simply keeps track of the truth value of F_2 in the previous state, and for $F_2(x, do(a, s))$ to be true, either $x = 0$ and $F_2(x, s)$, or both $F_2(x, s)$ and $F_2(predecessor(x), s)$ have the same truth values.

Consider a structure M such that:

1. M is a standard model of arithmetic with respect to sort *object*. Thus the domain for *object* in M is the set of nonnegative numbers, 0 is mapped to the number 0, and $succ$ is mapped to the successor function.

2. $M \models F_1(do(A, S_0)) \land (\forall x).F_2(x, do(A, S_0))$.

Our first observation is that there cannot be a model M' of $\mathcal{D}$ such that $M \sim_{S_A} M'$. Suppose otherwise. Then M' also satisfies the above two properties 1 and 2. From $M' \models \mathcal{D}_{ss}$, and $M' \models F_1(do(A, S_0))$, we have $M' \models (\exists x)\neg F_2(x, S_0)$. Similarly, from $M' \models (\forall x).F_2(x, do(A, S_0))$, by the successor state axiom for F_2, we have $M' \models F_2(0, S_0) \land F_2(succ(0), S_0) \land \cdots$. Thus $M' \models (\forall x).F_2(x, S_0)$, a contradiction. Therefore there is not a model M' of $\mathcal{D}$ such that $M \sim_{S_\alpha} M'$.

We now show that there is a model M' of $\mathcal{D}$ such that for any sentence φ in $\mathcal{L}_{S_A}$, $M \models \varphi$ iff $M' \models \varphi$. By Skolem's theorem (cf. Kleene [5], page 326), there is a first-order structure M^* such that for any sentence φ in $\mathcal{L}_{S_A}$, $M \models \varphi$ iff $M^* \models \varphi$, and $(M, 0, succ)$ and $(M^*, 0, succ)$ are not isomorphic, i.e., M and M^* are not isomorphic on sort *object*. In particular, $M^* \models F_1(do(A, S_0)) \land (\forall x).F_2(x, do(A, S_0))$. Now revise M^* into a structure M' such that:

1. M' and M^* have the same domains for sorts *action* and *object*, and interpret state independent predicates and functions the same.

2. $M' \models (\forall a, s)Poss(a, s)$.

3. $M' \models \Sigma \cup \mathcal{D}_{una} \cup \mathcal{D}_{S_0}$.

4. For the truth values of the fluents on S_0: $M' \models F_1(S_0)$, and for the truth values of $F_2(x, S_0)$, we have that for any variable assignment σ:

    (a) If $\sigma(x)$ is a standard number, i.e., there is a $n \geq 0$ such that $M', \sigma \models x = succ^n(0)$, then $M', \sigma \models F_2(x, S_0)$.

    (b) If $\sigma(x)$ is a nonstandard number, i.e., there is no $n \geq 0$ such that $M', \sigma(x) \models x = succ^n(0)$, then $M', \sigma \models \neg F_2(x, S_0)$. Notice that since M^* and M are not isomorphic on sort *object* with respect to Peano arithmetic, there must be a nonstandard number in the domain of M^*, and thus in the domain of M'.

5. For the truth values of the fluents on $do(A, S_0)$: For any fluent F, and any variable assignment σ, $M', \sigma \models F(\vec{x}, do(A, S_0))$ iff $M^*, \sigma \models F(\vec{x}, do(A, S_0))$.

6. Inductively, for any variable assignment σ, if
$$M', \sigma \models do(A, S_0) < s,$$
then the truth values of the fluents on s will be determined according to the successor state axioms and the truth values of the fluents on $do(A, S_0)$; if
$$M', \sigma \models S_0 < s \wedge \neg do(A, S_0) < s,$$
then the truth values of the fluents on s will be determined according to the successor state axioms and the truth values of the fluents on S_0. This will define the truth values of the fluents on every state because $M' \models (\forall s).S_0 \leq s$, which follows from the fact that $M' \models (\forall a, s) Poss(a, s)$.

It is clear that $M' \sim_{S_A} M^*$. It follows that M' and M satisfy the same set of sentences in $\mathcal{L}_{S_A}$. We now show that M' satisfies the successor state axioms. By the construction of M', we only need to prove that it satisfies the successor state axioms instantiated to S_0 and action A, i.e.
$$M' \models Poss(A, S_0) \supset [F_1(do(A, S_0)) \equiv (\exists x)\neg F_2(x, S_0)],$$
and
$$M' \models Poss(A, S_0) \supset (\forall x).F_2(x, do(A, S_0)) \equiv$$
$$x = 0 \wedge F_2(0, S_0) \vee$$
$$F_2(x, S_0) \wedge (\exists y).x = succ(y) \wedge F_2(y, S_0) \vee$$
$$\neg F_2(x, S_0) \wedge x \neq 0 \wedge$$
$$(\forall y)(x = succ(y) \supset \neg F_2(y, S_0)).$$

To show the first one, we need to prove that $M' \models (\exists x).\neg F_2(s, S_0)$. This follows from our construction of M' and the existence of nonstandard numbers in the domain of M'. To show the second one, we need to prove that
$$M' \models (\forall x).x = 0 \wedge F_2(0, S_0) \vee$$
$$F_2(x, S_0) \wedge (\exists y).x = succ(y) \wedge F_2(y, S_0) \vee$$
$$\neg F_2(x, S_0) \wedge x \neq 0 \wedge$$
$$(\forall y)(x = succ(y) \supset \neg F_2(y, S_0)).$$

There are three cases:

1. If $x = 0$, then $F_2(0, S_0)$ follows from our construction.

2. If $x = succ^n(0)$ for some $n > 0$, then both $F_2(succ^n(0), S_0)$ and $F_2(succ^{n-1}(0), S_0)$ hold. Thus $F_2(x, S_0) \wedge (\exists y).x = succ(y) \wedge F_2(y, S_0)$ holds;

3. If x is a nonstandard number, then $F_2(x, S_0)$ does not hold. Furthermore, for any y such that $x = succ(y)$, y is also a nonstandard number, so $F_2(y, S_0)$ does not hold either. Thus $\neg F_2(x, S_0) \wedge x \neq 0 \wedge (\forall y)(x = succ(y) \supset \neg F_2(y, S_0))$ holds.

Therefore, M' satisfies the successor state axioms instantiated to S_0 and A. So $M' \models \mathcal{D}_{ss}$. This means that $M' \models \mathcal{D}$, and M' and M satisfy the same sentences in $\mathcal{L}_{S_A}$. Following the discussion at the beginning of the example, we see that the new database at S_A for $\mathcal{D}$ cannot be captured by a set of first-order sentences.

4.2 Progression Is Always Second-Order Definable

We now show that, by appealing to second-order logic, progression always exists. We shall first introduce some notation.

Given a finite set $\mathcal{D}_{ss}$ of successor state axioms, we define the *instantiation* of $\mathcal{D}_{ss}$ on an action term at and a state term st, written $\mathcal{D}_{ss}[at, st]$, to be the sentence:

$$\bigwedge_{F \text{ is a fluent}} \begin{array}{l} Poss(at, st) \supset \\ (\forall \vec{x}).F(\vec{x}, do(at, st)) \equiv \Phi_F(\vec{x}, at, st), \end{array}$$

where
$$(\forall a, s).Poss(a, s) \supset (\forall \vec{x})[F(\vec{x}, do(a, s)) \equiv \Phi_F(\vec{x}, a, s)]$$
is the successor state axiom for F in $\mathcal{D}_{ss}$.

Given a formula φ in $\mathcal{L}^2$, the *lifting* of φ on the state st, written $\varphi \uparrow st$, is the result of replacing every fluent atom of the form $F(t_1, ..., t_n, st)$ by a new predicate variable $p(t_1, ..., t_n)$ of arity $object^n$. For instance,
$$enrolled(John, C200, S_0) \wedge enrolled(John, C100, S_0) \uparrow S_0$$
is $p(John, C200) \wedge p(John, C100)$.[5]

Lemma 4.2 *The following are some simple properties of lifting:*

1. *If φ is a sentence that does not mention st, then $\varphi \uparrow st$ is φ.*

2. *If φ is a sentence in $\mathcal{L}^2_{st}$, then $\varphi \uparrow st$ is a state independent sentence.*

3. *If φ does not contain quantifiers over states, then $\varphi \models \varphi \uparrow st$.*

Now we can state the main theorem of this section:

Theorem 2 *Let $\mathcal{D}_{S_\alpha}$ be the union of $\mathcal{D}_{una}$ together with the sentence:*
$$(\exists p_1, ..., p_k)\{\bigwedge_{\varphi \in \mathcal{D}_{S_0}} \varphi \wedge \mathcal{D}_{ss}[\alpha, S_0](Poss/\Psi_\alpha)\} \uparrow S_0,$$
where

1. *$p_1, ..., p_k$ are the new predicate variables introduced during the lifting.*

---
[5]Lifting as we have defined it does not generally preserve logical equivalence. For instance, $[(\forall s).F(s)] \uparrow S_0$ is $(\forall s).F(s)$, but the logically equivalent $[F(S_0) \wedge (\forall s).F(s)] \uparrow S_0$ is $p \wedge (\forall s).F(s)$. Fortunately, we shall only be lifting those sentences that do preserve logical equivalence.

2. Ψ_α is a sentence in $\mathcal{L}_{S_0}$ such that
$$Poss(\alpha, S_0) \equiv \Psi_\alpha$$
is an instance of the the axiom in $\mathcal{D}_{ap}$ corresponding to the action of α.

3. $\mathcal{D}_{ss}[\alpha, S_0](Poss/\Psi_\alpha)$ is the result of replacing $Poss(\alpha, S_0)$ by Ψ_α in $\mathcal{D}_{ss}[\alpha, S_0]$.

Then $\mathcal{D}_{S_\alpha}$ is a progression of $\mathcal{D}_{S_0}$ to S_α wrt $\mathcal{D}$:

Proof: First, it is clear that the sentences in $\mathcal{D}_{S_\alpha}$ are in $\mathcal{L}^2_{S_\alpha}$.

Let M be a structure. We need to show that $M \models \mathcal{D}_{S_\alpha}$ iff there is a model M' of $\mathcal{D}$ such that $M \sim_{S_\alpha} M'$.

Suppose that there is a model M' of $\mathcal{D}$ such that $M \sim_{S_\alpha} M'$. By Lemma 4.2, $\mathcal{D} \models \mathcal{D}_{S_\alpha}$, thus $M' \models \mathcal{D}_{S_\alpha}$. Therefore by Lemma 4.1, $M \models \mathcal{D}_{S_\alpha}$.

Now suppose that $M \models \mathcal{D}_{S_\alpha}$. Then there is a variable assignment σ such that
$$M, \sigma \models \bigwedge_{\varphi \in \mathcal{D}_{S_0}} \varphi \wedge \mathcal{D}_{ss}[\alpha, S_0](Poss/\Psi_\alpha) \uparrow S_0.$$

Now construct a structure M' such that

1. M and M' have the same universe, and interpret all state independent function and predicate symbols identically.

2. For every fluent F, if $F(\vec{x}, S_0)$ is lifted in $\mathcal{D}_{S_\alpha}$ as p, then
$$M', \sigma \models F(\vec{x}, S_0) \text{ iff } M, \sigma \models p(\vec{x}).$$

3. $M' \models \mathcal{D}_{ss} \cup \mathcal{D}_{ap}$.

4. If $M' \models \neg\Psi_\alpha$, then for any fluent F, and any variable assignment σ',
$$M', \sigma' \models F(\vec{x}, S_\alpha) \text{ iff } M, \sigma' \models F(\vec{x}, S_\alpha).$$

It is clear that such a M' exists. We claim that $M \sim_{S_\alpha} M'$. There are two cases:

1. If $M' \models \neg\Psi_\alpha$, then it follows from our construction that for any fluent F, and any variable assignment σ',
$$M', \sigma' \models F(\vec{x}, S_\alpha) \text{ iff } M, \sigma' \models F(\vec{x}, S_\alpha).$$

2. If $M' \models \Psi_\alpha$, then since $M' \models \mathcal{D}_{ap}$, and $\mathcal{D}_{ap} \models Poss(\alpha, S_0) \equiv \Psi_\alpha$, therefore $M' \models Poss(\alpha, S_0)$. But $M' \models \mathcal{D}_{ss}$. Thus for any fluent F, and any variable assignment σ',
$$M', \sigma' \models F(\vec{x}, S_\alpha) \text{ iff } M', \sigma' \models \Phi_F(\vec{x}, \alpha, S_0), \quad (1)$$
where Φ_F is as in the successor state axiom for F in $\mathcal{D}_{ss}$. Now since $M' \models \Psi_\alpha$, by our construction of M', we have that $M, \sigma \models \Psi_\alpha \uparrow S_0$. But
$$M, \sigma \models \mathcal{D}_{ss}[\alpha, S_0](Poss/\Psi_\alpha) \uparrow S_0.$$

Therefore for any fluent F, and any variable assignment σ' such that $\sigma'(p) = \sigma(p)$ for any predicate variable p,
$$M, \sigma' \models F(\vec{x}, S_\alpha) \text{ iff } M', \sigma' \models \Phi_F(\vec{x}, \alpha, S_0) \uparrow S_0. \quad (2)$$

But for any variable assignment σ' such that $\sigma'(p) = \sigma(p)$ for any predicate variable p, since $\Phi_F(\vec{x}, \alpha, S_0)$ is in $\mathcal{L}_{S_0}$, by our construction of M',
$$M, \sigma' \models \Phi_F(\vec{x}, \alpha, S_0) \uparrow S_0 \text{ iff } M', \sigma' \models \Phi_F(\vec{x}, \alpha, S_0),$$

Therefore from (1) and (2), we see that for any fluent F, and any variable assignment σ',
$$M', \sigma' \models F(\vec{x}, S_\alpha) \text{ iff } M, \sigma' \models F(\vec{x}, S_\alpha).$$

It follows then that $M \sim_{S_\alpha} M'$. By the construction of M' and the fact that $M \models \mathcal{D}_{una}$, we have that $M' \models \mathcal{D}_{ss} \cup \mathcal{D}_{ap} \cup \mathcal{D}_{una}$. Thus from Proposition 3.1, there is a model M'' of $\mathcal{D}$ such that $M' \sim_{S_\alpha} M''$. Then by the transitivity of $\sim_{S_\alpha}$, we have that $M \sim_{S_\alpha} M''$. This concludes the proof that $\mathcal{D}_{S_\alpha}$ as defined is progressed database. ∎

It is clear that the theorem still holds when the initial database $\mathcal{D}_{S_0}$ is a finite set of second-order sentences in $\mathcal{L}^2_{S_0}$. Therefore, at least in principle, the theorem can be repeatedly applied to progress the initial database in response to a sequence of actions.

The new database $\mathcal{D}_{S_\alpha}$ as defined in the theorem can be unwieldy. However, it can often be simplified by using the unique names axioms in $\mathcal{D}_{una}$, as we shall see in the following example.

Example 4.1 Consider our educational database. The instantiation of the successor state axioms on $drop(Sue, C100)$ and S_0, $\mathcal{D}_{ss}[drop(Sue, C100), S_0]$, is the conjunction of the following two sentences, where $\alpha = drop(Sue, C100)$ and $S_\alpha = do(\alpha, S_0)$:

$$Poss(\alpha, S_0) \supset enrolled(st, c, S_\alpha) \equiv$$
$$\alpha = register(st, c) \vee$$
$$enrolled(st, c, S_0) \wedge \alpha \neq drop(st, c),$$

$$Poss(\alpha, S_0) \supset grade(st, c, g, S_\alpha) \equiv$$
$$\alpha = change(st, c) \vee$$
$$grade(st, c, g, s) \wedge (\forall g')\alpha \neq change(st, c, g').$$

By unique names axioms, these two sentences can be simplified to

$$Poss(\alpha, S_0) \supset enrolled(st, c, S_\alpha) \equiv$$
$$enrolled(st, c, S_0) \wedge (Sue \neq st \vee C100 \neq c),$$

$$Poss(\alpha, S_0) \supset grade(st, c, g, S_\alpha) \equiv grade(st, c, g, s).$$

By $\mathcal{D}_{ap}$,

$$Poss(\alpha, S_0) \equiv enrolled(Sue, C100, S_0).$$

Thus $\mathcal{D}_{ss}[\alpha, S_0](Poss/\Psi_\alpha)$ is the conjunction of the following two sentences:

$enrolled(Sue, C100, S_0) \supset enrolled(st, c, S_\alpha) \equiv$
$\quad enrolled(st, c, S_0) \wedge (Sue \neq st \vee C100 \neq c),$

$enrolled(Sue, C100, S_0) \supset$
$\quad grade(st, c, g, S_\alpha) \equiv grade(st, c, g, s).$

Thus $(\exists p_1, p_2)[\bigwedge_{\varphi \in \mathcal{D}_{S_0}} \varphi \wedge \mathcal{D}_{ss}[\alpha, S_0](Poss/\Psi_\alpha)] \uparrow S_0$ is

$(\exists p_1, p_2).John \neq Sue \neq C100 \neq C200 \wedge$
$\quad p_1(John, C100) \vee p_1(John, C200) \wedge$
$\quad p_1(Sue, C100) \wedge prerequ(C100, C200) \wedge$
$\quad p_1(Sue, C100) \supset enrolled(st, c, S_\alpha) \equiv$
$\qquad p_1(st, c) \wedge (Sue \neq st \vee C100 \neq c) \wedge$
$\quad p_1(Sue, C100) \supset grade(st, c, g, S_\alpha) \equiv$
$\qquad p_2(st, c, g).$

This is equivalent to

$John \neq Sue \neq C100 \neq C200 \wedge$
$prerequ(C100, C200) \wedge$
$(\exists p_1, p_2).p_1(John, C100) \vee p_1(John, C200) \wedge$
$\quad p_1(Sue, C100) \wedge$
$\quad enrolled(st, c, S_\alpha) \equiv$
$\qquad p_1(st, c) \wedge (Sue \neq st \vee C100 \neq c) \wedge$
$\quad grade(st, c, g, S_\alpha) \equiv p_2(st, c, g),$

which is equivalent to

$John \neq Sue \neq C100 \neq C200 \wedge$
$prerequ(C100, C200) \wedge$
$(\exists p_1).p_1(John, C100) \vee p_1(John, C200) \wedge$
$\quad p_1(Sue, C100) \wedge$
$\quad enrolled(st, c, S_\alpha) \equiv$
$\qquad p_1(st, c) \wedge (Sue \neq st \vee C100 \neq c),$

which is equivalent to

$John \neq Sue \neq C100 \neq C200 \wedge$
$prerequ(C100, C200) \wedge$
$enrolled(John, C100, S_\alpha) \vee$
$\quad enrolled(John, C200, S_\alpha) \wedge$
$\neg enrolled(Sue, C100, S_\alpha) \wedge$
$(\exists p_1).enrolled(st, c, S_\alpha) \equiv p_1(st, c).$

Finally, we have a first-order representation for $\mathcal{D}_{S_\alpha}$, which is $\mathcal{D}_{una}$ together with the following sentences:

$John \neq Sue \neq C100 \neq C200,$

$prerequ(C100, C200),$

$enrolled(John, C100, S_\alpha) \vee enrolled(John, C200, S_\alpha),$

$\neg enrolled(Sue, C100, S_\alpha).$

■

To summarize, we have shown that in general, progression is definable only in second-order logic. However, there are some interesting special cases for which progression can be done in first-order logic. We shall give two such special cases.

5 PROGRESSION WITH RELATIVELY COMPLETE INITIAL DATABASES

We say $\mathcal{D}_{S_0}$ is *relatively complete (wrt state independent propositions)* if it is a set of state independent sentences together with a set of sentences, one for each fluent F, of the form:

$$(\forall \vec{x}).F(\vec{x}, S_0) \equiv \Pi_F(\vec{x}),$$

where $\Pi_F(\vec{x})$ is a state independent formula whose free variables are among $\vec{x}$. Clearly, for relatively complete $\mathcal{D}_{S_0}$, if it is complete about the state independent sentences: For any state independent sentence Π,

either $\mathcal{D}_{S_0} \models \Pi$ or $\mathcal{D}_{S_0} \models \neg \Pi$,

then it is also complete about S_0: For any sentence φ in $\mathcal{L}_{S_0}$,

either $\mathcal{D}_{S_0} \models \varphi$ or $\mathcal{D}_{S_0} \models \neg \varphi$.

Theorem 3 *Let $\mathcal{D}$ be an action theory with a relatively complete initial database $\mathcal{D}_{S_0}$, and let α be a ground action term such that $\mathcal{D} \models Poss(\alpha, S_0)$. Then the following set:*

$\mathcal{D}_{una} \cup \{\varphi \mid \varphi \in \mathcal{D}_{S_0} \text{ is state independent}\} \cup$
$\{(\forall \vec{x}).F(\vec{x}, do(\alpha, S_0)) \equiv \Phi_F(\vec{x}, \alpha, S_0)[S_0] \mid$
$\quad F \text{ is a fluent}\}$

is a progression of $\mathcal{D}_{S_0}$ to S_α, where

1. *$\Phi_F(\vec{x}, \alpha, S_0)$ is as in the successor state axiom for F in $\mathcal{D}_{ss}$;*

2. *$\Phi_F(\vec{x}, \alpha, S_0)[S_0]$ is the result of replacing, in $\Phi_F(\vec{x}, \alpha, S_0)$, every occurrence of $F'(\vec{t}, S_0)$ by $\Pi_{F'}(\vec{t})$, where $\Pi_{F'}$ is as in the corresponding axiom for F' in $\mathcal{D}_{S_0}$, and this replacement is performed for every fluent F' mentioned in $\Phi_F(\vec{x}, \alpha, S_0)$.*

Proof: Denote the set of the sentences of the theorem by $\mathcal{S}$. Clearly, $\mathcal{S}$ is a set of first-order sentences in $\mathcal{L}_{S_\alpha}$. It is easy to see that $\mathcal{S} \models \mathcal{D}_{S_\alpha}$. Conversely, it is clear that $\mathcal{D} \models \mathcal{S}$. Thus by Theorem 1, $\mathcal{D}_{S_\alpha} \models \mathcal{S}$. ■

Clearly, the progressed database at S_α as given by the theorem is also relatively complete. Thus the theorem can be repeatedly applied to progress a relatively complete initial database in response to a sequence of executable actions. Notice that the new database will include $\mathcal{D}_{una}$ and the state independent axioms in $\mathcal{D}_{S_0}$; therefore we can use these axioms to simplify $\Phi_F(\vec{x}, \alpha, S_0)[S_0]$.

Example 5.1 Consider again our educational database example. Suppose now that the initial database $\mathcal{D}_{S_0}$ consists of the following axioms:

$$John \neq Sue \neq C100 \neq C200,$$

$$better(70, 50),$$

$$prerequ(C100, C200),$$

$$enrolled(st, c, S_0) \equiv$$
$$(st = John \land c = C100) \lor (st = Sue \land c = C200),$$

$$grade(st, c, g, S_0) \equiv$$
$$st = Sue \land c = C100 \land g = 70.$$

Clearly $\mathcal{D}_{S_0}$ is relatively complete, and $\mathcal{D} \models Poss(\alpha, S_0)$, where $\alpha = drop(John, C100)$. From the axiom for *enrolled* in $\mathcal{D}_{S_0}$, we see that $\Pi_{enrolled}(st, c)$ is the formula:

$$(st = John \land c = C100) \lor (st = Sue \land c = C200).$$

Now from the successor state axiom for *enrolled* in Example 3.1, we see that $\Phi_{enrolled}(st, c, a, s)$, the condition under which $enrolled(st, c, do(a, s))$ will be true, is the formula:

$$a = register(st, c) \lor (enrolled(st, c, s) \land a \neq drop(st, c)).$$

Therefore $\Phi_{enrolled}(st, c, \alpha, S_0)[S_0]$ is the formula:

$$drop(John, C100) = register(st, c) \lor$$
$$\{[(st = John \land c = C100) \lor (st = Sue \land c = C200)] \land$$
$$drop(John, C100) \neq drop(st, c))\}.$$

By the unique names axioms in $\mathcal{D}_{una}$, this can be simplified to

$$(st = John \land c = C100) \lor (st = Sue \land c = C200) \land$$
$$(John \neq st \lor C100 \neq c).$$

By the unique names axioms in $\mathcal{D}_{S_0}$, this can be further simplified to

$$st = Sue \land c = C200.$$

Therefore we obtain the following axiom about $do(\alpha, S_0)$:

$$enrolled(st, c, do(\alpha, S_0)) \equiv st = Sue \land c = C200.$$

Similarly, we have:

$$grade(st, c, g, do(\alpha, S_0)) \equiv st = Sue \land c = C100 \land g = 70.$$

Therefore a progression to $do(drop(John, C100), S_0)$ is $\mathcal{D}_{una}$ together with the following sentences:

$$John \neq Sue \neq C100 \neq C200,$$
$$better(70, 50),$$
$$prerequ(C100, C200),$$
$$enrolled(st, c, do(\alpha, S_0)) \equiv st = Sue \land c = C200,$$
$$grade(st, c, g, do(\alpha, S_0)) \equiv st = Sue \land c = C100 \land g = 70.$$

∎

6 PROGRESSION IN THE CONTEXT FREE CASE

In this section we consider progression wrt context-free action theories. A successor state axiom for F is *context free* iff it has the form:

$$Poss(a, s) \supset F(\vec{x}, do(a, s)) \equiv$$
$$(\exists \vec{u})(a = A_1(\vec{\xi_1}, \vec{u}) \land E_1) \lor \cdots \lor$$
$$(\exists \vec{v})(a = A_m(\vec{\xi_m}, \vec{v}) \land E_m) \lor$$
$$F(\vec{x}, s) \land \neg(\exists \vec{w})(a = B_1(\vec{\chi_1}, \vec{w}) \land E_{m+1}) \land \cdots \land$$
$$\neg(\exists \vec{r})(a = B_n(\vec{\chi_n}, \vec{r}) \land E_{m+n}),$$

where $\vec{\xi_i}$ and $\vec{\chi_j}$ denote sequences of all, or just some (including none) of the $\vec{x}$, the A's and B's are actions, and $E_1, ..., E_{m+n}$ are propositional formulas constructed from equality literals over the domain objects, i.e., they are quantifier free, and do not mention terms of sort *state* and *action*. The successor state axioms in our educational database are all context free. So are the following successor state axioms:

$$Poss(a, s) \supset holding(x, do(a, s)) \equiv a = pickup(x) \lor$$
$$holding(x, s) \land a \neq drop(x) \land \neg(\exists u)a = put(x, u).$$

$$Poss(a, s) \supset on(x, y, do(a, s)) \equiv a = move(x, y) \lor$$
$$on(x, y, s) \land \neg(\exists z)(a = move(x, z) \land z \neq y).$$

The following successor state axiom is not context-free:

$$Poss(a, s) \supset dead(x, do(a, s)) \equiv$$
$$(\exists y).a = explode\_bomb\_at(y) \land close(x, y, s) \lor$$
$$dead(x, s).$$

Given any action terms $A_1(\vec{t_1})$ and $A_2(\vec{t_2})$, by the unique names axioms, the equality $A_1(\vec{t_1}) = A_2(\vec{t_2})$ is either equivalent to *false* or, when A_1 and A_2 are the same, equivalent to $\vec{t_1} = \vec{t_2}$.[6] Thus, given any action term $A(\vec{t})$, the instantiation of a context-free successor state axiom on $A(\vec{t})$ is equivalent to

$$Poss(A(\vec{t}), s) \supset$$
$$F(\vec{x}, do(A(\vec{t}), s)) \equiv [E_F \lor (F(\vec{x}, s) \land \neg E_{\neg F})],$$

where E_F and $E_{\neg F}$ are propositional formulas constructed from equality literals over the domain objects. This is logically equivalent to

$$Poss(A(\vec{t}), s) \supset$$
$$[E_F \lor (F(\vec{x}, s) \land \neg E_{\neg F})] \supset$$
$$F(\vec{x}, do(A(\vec{t}), s)), \quad (3)$$

---

[6] $\vec{x} = \vec{y}$ is an abbreviation for $x_1 = y_1 \land \cdots \land x_n = y_n$. Notice that when both $\vec{x}$ and $\vec{y}$ are the empty sequence, $\vec{x} = \vec{y}$ is logically equivalent to *true*. It is equivalent to *false* when $\vec{x}$ and $\vec{y}$ have different length.

$$Poss(A(\vec{t}), s) \supset$$
$$[\neg E_F \wedge (\neg F(\vec{x}, s) \vee E_{\neg F})] \supset$$
$$\neg F(\vec{x}, do(A(\vec{t}), s)). \quad (4)$$

For instance, by the above successor state axiom for *holding*, we have

$$Poss(drop(x), s) \supset holding(y, do(drop(x), s)) \equiv$$
$$holding(y, s) \wedge y \neq x.$$

Here $E_{holding}$ is $false$, and $E_{\neg holding}$ is $x = y$.

Now assume that:

1. $\mathcal{D}_{S_0}$ is a set of state independent sentences, and sentences of the form

$$E \supset \pm F(x_1, \ldots, x_n, S_0), \quad (5)$$

where E is a propositional formula constructed from equality literals over the domain objects. For example,

$$ontable(x, S_0),$$
$$x \neq A \supset \neg ontable(x, S_0),$$
$$x = A \wedge y = B \supset on(x, y, S_0),$$

are all of this form.

2. $\mathcal{D}_{S_0}$ is *coherent* in the sense that for every fluent F, whenever $(\forall \vec{x}).E_1 \supset F(\vec{x}, S_0)$ and $(\forall \vec{x}).E_2 \supset \neg F(\vec{x}, S_0)$ are in $\mathcal{D}_{S_0}$, then

$$\{\varphi | \varphi \in \mathcal{D}_{S_0} \text{ is state independent}\} \models (\forall \vec{x}).\neg(E_1 \wedge E_2).$$

This means that $\mathcal{D}_{S_0}$ cannot use axioms of the form (5) to encode state independent sentences: For any state independent sentence ϕ, $\mathcal{D}_{S_0} \models \phi$ iff

$$\{\varphi \mid \varphi \in \mathcal{D}_{S_0} \text{ is state independent}\} \models \phi.$$

3. $\mathcal{D}_{ss}$ is a set of context-free successor state axioms.
4. α is a ground action term, say $A(\vec{t})$.
5. α is possible initially: $\mathcal{D} \models Poss(\alpha, S_0)$.

For example, our educational database in Example 3.1 with the following initial database:

$$Sue \neq John \neq C100 \neq C200 \neq 50,$$
$$st = Sue \wedge c = C100 \supset enrolled(st, c, S_0),$$
$$st = Sue \wedge c = C200 \supset \neg enrolled(st, c, S_0),$$
$$st = Sue \wedge c = C100 \wedge g = 50 \supset grade(st, c, g, S_0),$$

satisfies the above conditions for $\alpha = drop(Sue, C100)$.

To compute $\mathcal{D}_{S_\alpha}$, use Theorem 1 to construct a set $\mathcal{S}$, initially empty, of sentences as follows:

1. If $\varphi \in \mathcal{D}_{S_0}$ is state independent, then $\varphi \in \mathcal{S}$.

2. For any fluent F, by (3) and (4), the coherence assumption, and the assumption that $\mathcal{D} \models Poss(\alpha, S_0)$, add to $\mathcal{S}$ the sentences

$$E_F \supset F(\vec{x}, do(\alpha, S_0)),$$
$$E_{\neg F} \supset \neg F(\vec{x}, do(\alpha, S_0)).$$

3. For any fluent F, if $(\forall \vec{x}).E \supset F(\vec{x}, S_0)$ is in $\mathcal{D}_{S_0}$, then, by (3) and the assumption that $\mathcal{D} \models Poss(\alpha, S_0)$, add to $\mathcal{S}$ the sentence

$$E \wedge \neg E_{\neg F} \supset F(\vec{x}, do(\alpha, S_0)).$$

4. For any fluent F, if $(\forall \vec{x}).E \supset \neg F(\vec{x}, S_0)$ is in $\mathcal{D}_{S_0}$, then, by (4) and the assumption that $\mathcal{D} \models Poss(\alpha, S_0)$, add to $\mathcal{S}$ the sentence

$$\neg E_F \wedge E \supset \neg F(\vec{x}, do(\alpha, S_0)).$$

For example, consider again our educational database with the above initial database, and

$$\alpha = drop(Sue, C100),$$

we have

$$Poss(\alpha, s) \supset enrolled(st, c, do(\alpha, s)) \equiv$$
$$enrolled(st, c, s) \wedge \neg(st = Sue \wedge c = C100),$$

$$Poss(\alpha, s) \supset grade(st, c, g, do(\alpha, s)) \equiv$$
$$grade(st, c, g, s).$$

Thus $E_{enrolled}$ is $False$, $E_{\neg enrolled}$ is

$$st = Sue \wedge c = C100,$$

and E_{grade} and $E_{\neg grade}$ are both $False$. Then the above procedure will give us the following set $\mathcal{S}$:

$$John \neq Sue \neq C100 \neq C200 \neq 50,$$
$$(st = Sue \wedge c = C100) \supset \neg enrolled(st, c, S_\alpha),$$
$$(st = Sue \wedge c = C200) \supset \neg enrolled(st, c, S_\alpha),$$
$$st = Sue \wedge c = C100 \wedge g = 50 \supset grade(st, c, g, S_\alpha).$$

As we show in the following theorem, together with $\mathcal{D}_{una}$, this is a progression of $\mathcal{D}_{S_0}$ to S_α,

Theorem 4 *Under the afore-mentioned assumptions, $\mathcal{S} \cup \mathcal{D}_{una}$ is a progression of $\mathcal{D}_{S_0}$ to S_α.*

Proof: It is clear that $\mathcal{D} \models \mathcal{S} \cup \mathcal{D}_{una}$, and $\mathcal{S}$ is a set of sentences in $\mathcal{L}_{S_\alpha}$. Therefore by Theorem 1, $\mathcal{D}_{S_\alpha} \models \mathcal{S} \cup \mathcal{D}_{una}$. To prove the converse, we show that for any model M of $\mathcal{S} \cup \mathcal{D}_{una}$, there is a model M' of $\mathcal{D}$ such that $M \sim_{S_\alpha} M'$. Suppose now that M is a model of $\mathcal{S} \cup \mathcal{D}_{una}$. We construct M' as follows:

1. M' and M have the same domains for sorts *action* and *object*, and interpret all state independent predicates and functions the same.

2. For each fluent F, M' interprets it on S_0 as follows:

(a) For every variable assignment σ, if $(\forall \vec{x}).E \supset F(\vec{x}, S_0)$ is in $\mathcal{D}_{S_0}$, and $M, \sigma \models E$ (thus $M', \sigma \models E$ as well), then $M', \sigma \models F(\vec{x}, S_0)$.

(b) Similarly, for every variable assignment, if $(\forall \vec{x}).E \supset \neg F(\vec{x}, S_0)$ is in $\mathcal{D}_{S_0}$, and $M, \sigma \models E$ (thus $M', \sigma \models E$ as well), then $M', \sigma \models \neg F(\vec{x}, S_0)$.

(c) For every variable assignment σ, if $F(\vec{x}, S_0)$ has not been assigned a truth value by one of the above two steps, then $M', \sigma \models F(\vec{x}, S_0)$ iff $M, \sigma \models F(\vec{x}, do(\alpha, S_0))$.

Notice that by the coherence assumption for $\mathcal{D}_{S_0}$, our construction is well-defined.

3. M' interprets $Poss$ according to $\mathcal{D}_{ap}$, and interprets the truth values of the fluents on reachable states according to $\mathcal{D}_{ss}$.

4. $M' \models \Sigma$. This can be done according to Proposition 3.1.

Clearly $M' \models \mathcal{D}$. We show now that $M \sim_{S_\alpha} M'$. For any fluent F, suppose the successor state axiom for it is

$$Poss(\alpha, s) \supset F(\vec{x}, do(\alpha, s)) \equiv E_F \vee (F(\vec{x}, s) \wedge \neg E_{\neg F}).$$

Given a variable assignment σ, suppose $M', \sigma \models F(\vec{x}, do(\alpha, S_0))$. Since $\mathcal{D} \models Poss(\alpha, S_0)$, by the above successor state axiom, there are two cases:

1. $M', \sigma \models E_F$. This implies $M, \sigma \models E_F$. Now since $E_F \supset F(\vec{x}, do(\alpha, S_0)) \in \mathcal{S}$, and M is a model of $\mathcal{S}$, thus $M, \sigma \models F(\vec{x}, do(\alpha, S_0))$ as well.

2. $M', \sigma \models \neg E_F \wedge F(\vec{x}, S_0) \wedge \neg E_{\neg F}$. From $M', \sigma \models F(\vec{x}, S_0)$, by our construction, either $M, \sigma \models F(\vec{x}, do(\alpha, S_0))$, or there is a sentence $E \supset F(\vec{x}, S_0)$ in $\mathcal{D}_{S_0}$ such that $M, \sigma \models E$. Suppose it is the latter. Then by our construction of $\mathcal{S}$, it contains $E \wedge \neg E_{\neg F} \supset F(\vec{x}, do(\alpha, S_0))$. Thus $M, \sigma \models F(\vec{x}, do(\alpha, S_0))$ as well.

Similarly, if $M', \sigma \models \neg F(\vec{x}, do(\alpha, S_0))$, then $M, \sigma \models \neg F(\vec{x}, do(\alpha, S_0))$ as well. Therefore $M \sim_{S_\alpha} M'$. ■

We have some remarks:

1. The new database $\mathcal{S}$ has the same form as $\mathcal{D}_{S_0}$, so this process can be iterated.

2. The generation of $\mathcal{S}$ is very fast, and the size of $\mathcal{S}$ is bounded by the sum of the size of $\mathcal{D}_{S_0}$ and the twice the number of fluents.

3. The E's in context free successor state axioms can be any state independent formulas. Thus a limited context dependency can be handled.

We emphasize that the results of this section depend on the fact that the initial database has a certain specific form. In fact, a result by Pednault [9] shows that for context-free actions and arbitrary $\mathcal{D}_{S_0}$, progression is not always guaranteed to yield finite first-order theories.

7 SUMMARY

1. We have argued the need for progressing a database.

2. We have defined a formal notion of progression, and showed that in general, to capture it we need second-order logic.

3. We have studied two special cases for which progression is first order definable, and which can be done efficiently.

4. Although we don't discuss them here, there are other cases for which progression can be done in first order logic. One such case concerns actions with finitary effects, i.e. for any fluent, the action changes the truth values of the fluent at only a finite number of instances.

5. The complexity of progression depends on both the form of the initial database, and the form of the action theory. A relatively complete initial database can be progressed efficiently wrt any successor state axioms. On the other hand, even for context free successor state axioms, progression is not guaranteed to yield finite first-order theories.

6. In a companion paper (Lin and Reiter [8]) we explore the consequences of our results on progression for the semantics of STRIPS-like systems. Ever since STRIPS was first introduced (Fikes and Nilsson [4]), its logical semantics has been problematic. There have been many proposals in the literature (e.g. Lifschitz [6], Pednault [11], Bacchus and Yang [2]). These all have in common a reliance on meta-theoretic operations on logical theories in order to capture the add and delete lists of STRIPS operators, but it has never been clear exactly what these operations correspond to declaratively, especially when they are applied to logically incomplete theories. In the companion to this paper, we provide a semantics for STRIPS-like systems in terms of basic theories of actions in the situation calculus. On our view, STRIPS is a *mechanism* for computing the progression of an initial situation calculus database under the effects of an action. We illustrate this idea by specifying two different versions of STRIPS in the situation calculus as well as a generalization of STRIPS that appeals to relational database theory.

Acknowledgements

For their generous advice and feedback, we wish to thank the other members of the University of Toronto Cognitive Robotics Group: Yves Lespérance, Hector Levesque, Bill Millar, Daniel Marcu, and Richard Scherl. This research was funded by the Government of Canada National Sciences and Engineering Research Council, and the Institute for Robotics and Intelligent Systems.

References

[1] S. Abiteboul. Updates, a new frontier. In *Second International Conference on Database Theory*, pages 1–18. Springer, 1988.

[2] F. Bacchus and Q. Yang. Downward refinement and the efficiency of hierarchical problem solving. *Artificial Intelligence*. To appear.

[3] E. W. Dijkstra and C. S. Scholten. *Predicate Calculus and Program Semantics*. Springer-Verlag, New York, 1990.

[4] R. E. Fikes and N. J. Nilsson. STRIPS: A new approach to theorem proving in problem solving. *Artificial Intelligence*, 2:189–208, 1971.

[5] S. C. Kleene. *Mathematical Logic*. John Wiley & Sons, Inc., 1967.

[6] V. Lifschitz. On the semantics of STRIPS. In *Reasoning about Actions and Plans: Proceedings of the 1986 Workshop*, pages 1–9. Morgan Kauffmann Publishers, Inc., 1986. June 30–July 2, Timberline, Oregon.

[7] F. Lin and R. Reiter. State constraints revisited. *Journal of Logic and Computation*. Special Issue on Actions and Processes. To Appear.

[8] F. Lin and R. Reiter. How to progress a database II: The STRIPS connection. 1994. Submitted.

[9] E. P. Pednault. *Toward a Mathematical Theory of Plan Synthesis*. PhD thesis, Department of Electrical Engineering, Stanford University, Stanford, CA, 1986.

[10] E. P. Pednault. Synthesizing plans that contain actions with context-dependent effects. *Computational Intelligence*, 4:356–372, 1988.

[11] E. P. Pednault. ADL: Exploring the middle ground between STRIPS and the situation calculus. In *Proceedings of the First International Conference on Principles of Knowledge Representation and Reasoning (KR'89)*, pages 324–332. Morgan Kaufmann Publishers, Inc., 1989.

[12] R. Reiter. Proving properties of states in the situation calculus. *Artificial Intelligence*. To appear.

[13] R. Reiter. The frame problem in the situation calculus: a simple solution (sometimes) and a completeness result for goal regression. In V. Lifschitz, editor, *Artificial Intelligence and Mathematical Theory of Computation: Papers in Honor of John McCarthy*, pages 418–420. Academic Press, San Diego, CA, 1991.

[14] R. Reiter. On specifying database updates. Technical report, Department of Computer Science, University of Toronto, 1992. KRR-TR-92-3.

[15] S. J. Rosenschein. Plan synthesis: A logical perspective. In *Proceedings of IJCAI 7*, pages 331–337, 1981.

[16] R. Scherl and H. Levesque. The frame problem and knowledge-producing actions. In *Proceedings of the Eleventh National Conference on Artificial Intelligence (AAAI-93)*, 1993.

[17] R. Waldinger. Achieving several goals simultaneously. In E. Elcock and D. Michie, editors, *Machine Intelligence*, pages 94–136. Ellis Horwood. Edinburgh, Scotland, 1977.

Modalities Over Actions, I. Model Theory

L. Thorne McCarty
Computer Science Department
Rutgers University
New Brunswick, NJ 08903, USA

Abstract

This paper analyzes a language for actions and the deontic modalities over actions — i.e., the modalities *permitted*, *forbidden* and *obligatory*. The work is based on: (1) an action language that allows the representation of concurrent and repetitive events; (2) a deontic language that allows the representation of "free choice permissions"; (3) a proof procedure that admits a logic programming style of computation; and (4) a facility for nonmonotonic inference based on negation-as-failure. Applications of the language to several problems of common sense reasoning are also discussed. In particular, by imposing a "causal assumption" on the deontic modalities, we obtain an interesting solution to the frame problem and the ramification problem. This first part of the paper includes a model theory, and a sequel will include a proof theory, with soundness and completeness results for various fragments of the language.

1 Introduction

A standard approach to the representation of actions is to take the *state* of the world as primary, and to encode actions as *transformations* on states. McCarthy's situation calculus [15] is the best known historical example, but classical dynamic logic [33, 10] adopts essentially the same ontology. There are several problems with this approach, not the least of which is the difficulty of extending the formalism to complex actions. To be sure, recent work has shown how to extend the situation calculus to represent continuous and partially ordered events [9], and concurrent, possibly conflicting, actions [14, 3]. But these are heroic efforts, and the complex machinery that seems to be required for these extensions is strong evidence of a recalcitrant ontology.

An alternative approach is to take actions as primary, and to treat the state of the world as a derivative notion. The event calculus of Kowalski and Sergot [11] is one example of this approach, as is the work of Allen, *et al.* [2, 1] on action and time. Within the framework of dynamic logic, Pratt's early work on process logic [34] and his more recent work on action logic [35] reflect a similar shift in perspective from a world consisting of a sequence of states to a world consisting of a set of actions. One justification for this shift in perspective is the fact that the most important properties of ordinary actions — e.g., concurrency and nondeterminism — are easier to express in a language in which actions are first-class objects.

But let us look more closely at the concept of an action. In our ordinary experience, actions have *agents*, and agents have *choices*. Are there constraints on the choices of agents? Indeed, there are, and in common sense reasoning these constraints are often expressed by the *deontic* modalities: We say that actions are either *permitted* (**P**), *forbidden* (**F**), or *obligatory* (**O**). Shouldn't these modalities also be incorporated into our representation language?

In this paper, we investigate a language for actions and the deontic modalities over actions, and we show how this language can be used to model various aspects of common sense reasoning. Our work is related to recent work on the relationship between deontic logic and dynamic logic [30, 42, 27, 28], but it is based on the following developments:

1: The action language is based on [25]. In [25], McCarty and van der Meyden treat actions as predicates over a linear temporal order, and draw a distinction between *basic* actions and *defined* actions. Defined actions are represented by Horn clauses with (optional) linear order constraints, and the defined predicates are *circumscribed* to capture the intended interpretation of these Horn clauses as definitions. With this device, it is easy to represent concurrent and repetitive events, and to construct partially ordered plans. It is also easy to select an appropriate temporal ontology for a particular application, since discrete time and continuous time are just minor variations of a single logical language.

2: The deontic language is based on much earlier work in [16, 17]. In fact, the deontic modalities in the present paper are essentially the same as the deontic modalities in [16, 17], but applied to the action language in [25]. One significant feature of this early work is the fact that **P** is a "free choice permission", and this interpretation is carried forth into the present paper, with one modification (see Definition 4.2 and related text). Another modification in the present paper involves the deontic conditional. The system in [16, 17] was a *dyadic* deontic logic, with a counterfactual conditional, whereas the present paper uses *intuitionistic implication* [39] for the deontic conditional. This change was motivated by a desire to be able to answer queries in the deontic language and the action language, uniformly, in the style of a logic program [18, 19], particularly where negation is involved.

3: Since the action definitions in [25] make use of circumscription, entailment in the action language is not recursively enumerable, and this property is inherited by the deontic language. Nevertheless, there are proof methods for important special cases. If the definitions are nonrecursive, then circumscription is equivalent to predicate completion [6, 37, 12]: A PROLOG-style interpreter for this case is discussed in [23]. If the definitions are linear recursive, then a special inductive proof method based on second-order intuitionistic logic may be applicable: A PROLOG-style interpreter for this case is discussed in [22]. The combination of these two special cases is illustrated in [24] for a first-order language without a linear temporal order, and in [25] for the action language. Also, for yet another special case, circumscriptive inference in the action language is actually decidable [29]. One of the objectives of the present work is to extend these special proof techniques from the first-order language and the action language to the full deontic language.

4: Finally, since deontic rules take the form of Horn clause logic programs, we can represent nonmonotonicity by negation-as-failure. There are numerous proposals for the semantics of negation-as-failure, of course, but the approach that works best in our system is based on *partial intuitionistic circumscription* [26], or *PIC*, for short. The *PIC* semantics agrees with the perfect model semantics [36] for stratified rules, and for unstratified rules it is strictly stronger than the well-founded semantics [41] and strictly weaker than the stable model semantics [8]. Most importantly, the *PIC* semantics is based on a version of circumscription that can be immediately generalized to the present system of deontic logic. This means that we can apply negation-as-failure directly to the deontic modalities, **P**, **F** and **O**, with interesting consequences. For example, we can say that the actions of a particular agent are permitted unless they are explicitly forbidden; or, conversely, we can say that the actions of a particular agent are forbidden unless they are explicitly permitted.

This first part of the paper analyzes our action language and develops a model theory for the deontic language, essentially covering points (**1**) and (**2**) above. A discussion of the proof theory and the semantics of negation-as-failure is reserved for a sequel.

One of the main features of deontic logic is the fact that actors do not always obey the law. Indeed, it is precisely when a forbidden action occurs, or an obligatory action does not occur, that we need the machinery of deontic logic, to detect a violation and to take appropriate action. On the other hand, for purposes of planning, it is often useful to assume that actors *do* obey the law. We call this the *causal assumption*, since it enables us to predict the actions that *will* occur by reasoning about the actions that *ought* to occur. As we will see, it is straightforward to incorporate the causal assumption as an additional constraint in the deontic semantics.

Moreover, if we adopt the causal assumption, we can use the machinery of deontic logic to reason about the physical world. The slogan is simple:

Causation is Divine Obligation.

Coupled with negation-as-failure, this principle provides an interesting solution to both the *frame problem* and the *ramification problem*. The basic idea is to posit an actor named 'nature', who always obeys the law, but can be overridden in particular situations by the actions of other agents. We will see how this works in Section 2.

Following an informal exposition and several examples in Section 2, we discuss events and actions in Section 3, and then develop a semantics for the deontic modalities in Section 4. Several properties of the semantics are established in this section, including two theorems that will be needed in the proof theory. Section 5 then concludes with a discussion of related work.

2 Intuitions and Applications

The fundamental assumption underlying the action language in [25] is the idea that, at some level of detail, we can identify a set of *basic events*. This level of detail might be quite coarse in a particular application. For example, we could take 'SwimLap$(x, t_1, t_2) \wedge t_1 < t_2$' to be a basic event in which the actor x swims one lap of the pool between the time t_1 and the time t_2, ignoring the finer details about how this action is accomplished. We can then define more complex events by a set of Horn clauses. For example, the event in which x swims some finite number of laps between t_1 and t_2 could be defined by the recursive Horn clauses:

SwimLaps$(x, t_1, t_2) \Leftarrow$ SwimLap$(x, t_1, t_2) \wedge t_1 < t_2$,

SwimLaps$(x, t_1, t_2) \Leftarrow$
  SwimLap$(x, t_1, t_3) \wedge$ SwimLaps$(x, t_3, t_2) \wedge$
  $t_1 < t_3 < t_2$,

and the event in which x and y each swim some finite number of laps, with x finishing first, could be defined by the conjunction:

SwimLaps$(x, t_1, t_2) \wedge$ SwimLaps$(y, t_1, t_3) \wedge$
  $t_1 < t_2 < t_3$.

In principle, if this representation turns out to be too coarse for a particular application, we can increase the level of detail, and define 'SwimLap' itself in terms of more basic predicates, such as the position of the swimmer over time, or even the movement of the swimmer's arms and legs.

An important property of basic events is that they are *definite* relative to the chosen level of detail, whereas a defined event could be *indefinite*. If we only know 'SwimLaps(a_1, t_1, t_2)' for a particular actor a_1 and the particular times t_1 and t_2, then we don't know how many laps a_1 swam, or how fast she swam them. But basic events should not have this kind of ambiguity. Formally, basic events should have the *disjunctive* and *existential* properties, that is, a disjunction $A \vee B$ should be entailed by a basic event only if either A is entailed or B is entailed, and an existentially quantified proposition $(\exists x)P(x)$ should be entailed by a basic event only if $P(x)\theta$ is entailed for some substitution θ. (See Section 3 below for a more detailed discussion of this requirement.)

Now, there is one important class of basic events that involve changes in the state of the world, and this fact has consequences for our choice of a logic. Suppose B is a first-order predicate with a single argument. We might want to define an event in which the state of the world changes from a time t_1 at which $B(x)$ is true to a time t_2 at which $\neg B(x)$ is true. As a convenient notation for such an event, we write: $B(x)[t_1] \circ \neg B(x)[t_2] \wedge t_1 < t_2$. For this event to be basic, however, we require: (i) that B is itself a base (i.e., undefined) predicate in the first-order language, and (ii) that the overall logic is *intuitionistic* rather than classical. These two conditions will guarantee that basic events generate only definite changes in the state of the world [18]. Similarly, suppose C is a first-order predicate with two arguments. We might want to define an event: $C(x, y)[t_1] \circ (\forall w)\neg C(w, y)[t_2] \wedge t_1 < t_2$. The same conditions will guarantee that this event, too, generates only definite changes in the state of the world. (Note also that $B(x)$ and $C(x, y)$ are neither true nor false in this example when t is between t_1 and t_2, as long as we use intuitionistic rather than classical logic.) Finally, a useful class of events consists of the *nonevents*, such as $B(x)[t_1, t_2]$ or $\neg B(x)[t_1, t_2]$, which assert that $B(x)$ remains true, or remains false, respectively, over the interval from t_1 to t_2. Again, our conditions guarantee that these are definite events.

The concept of an event does not itself include the concept of agency, but if we pair an event $\alpha(t_1, t_2)$ with an agent x we have an *action*. We write $\mathbf{DO}\langle\alpha(t_1, t_2), x\rangle$ to say that x is (somehow) responsible for the occurrence of $\alpha(t_1, t_2)$, or that $\alpha(t_1, t_2)$ is (somehow) carried out by the agent x. Such statements are *veridical*. That is, if x does $\alpha(t_1, t_2)$, then $\alpha(t_1, t_2)$ is true. The converse does not hold, of course. We can observe an event $\alpha(t_1, t_2)$ without deducing $\mathbf{DO}\langle\alpha(t_1, t_2), x\rangle$ for any x. (If we wanted to make such an inference, and ascribe responsibility to a particular agent, we would have to do so by abduction [31], not by deduction.)

In our language, the deontic modalities have a syntax similar to the syntax of $\mathbf{DO}$. We write: $\mathbf{P}\langle\alpha(t_1, t_2), x\rangle$, $\mathbf{F}\langle\alpha(t_1, t_2), x\rangle$ and $\mathbf{O}\langle\alpha(t_1, t_2), x\rangle$, where $\alpha(t_1, t_2)$ is an event and x is an agent. The intuitive reading of $\mathbf{O}\langle\alpha(t_1, t_2), x\rangle$ is straightforward. It means: "The actor x is obligated to perform the action $\alpha(t_1, t_2)$." The intuitive reading of $\mathbf{F}$ and $\mathbf{P}$ is more subtle, since actions can be indefinite. To say that x is forbidden, $\mathbf{F}$, to perform the action $\alpha(t_1, t_2)$ means that *all* the ways of performing $\alpha(t_1, t_2)$ are forbidden. Analogously, $\mathbf{P}$ is a "free choice permission". To say that x is permitted, $\mathbf{P}$, to perform the action $\alpha(t_1, t_2)$ means that *all* the ways of performing $\alpha(t_1, t_2)$ are permitted. This is different from the weaker form of permission, $\neg\mathbf{F}$, that is usually studied in deontic logic. To say that x is not forbidden, $\neg\mathbf{F}$, to perform the action $\alpha(t_1, t_2)$ means simply that there is *some* way of performing $\alpha(t_1, t_2)$ that is permitted. These distinctions are difficult to express in standard deontic logic, but they are easy to express in our language because of the sharp contrast between definite and indefinite actions.

Finally, to complete the system, we write deontic conditionals as Horn clause logic programs, using any formulae we want from the action language, including the constraints on time. We also allow negation-as-failure to appear in the deontic conditionals, so that the following expressions are possible:

$$\mathbf{F}\langle\alpha(t_1, t_2), x\rangle \Leftarrow \gamma(x, t_1) \wedge {\sim}\beta(x, t_1, t_2) \wedge t_1 < t_2,$$

$$\mathbf{O}\langle\alpha(t_1, t_2), x\rangle \Leftarrow {\sim}\mathbf{F}\langle\alpha(t_1, t_2), x\rangle \wedge t_1 < t_2,$$

where α, β and γ are events, and the symbol '$\sim$' denotes negation-as-failure. Notice that the first rule here applies negation-as-failure to β, an expression in the action language, while the second rule applies negation-as-failure to an expression in the deontic language. The second rule says, intuitively, that α is obligatory if it is not forbidden.

There are obvious applications of these ideas in legal domains [20]. For example, an adequate representation of the concept of a corporation requires a representation of the "bundle of rights" available to the corporation's creditors and the owners of its stock. Here is a simplified illustration:

Example 2.1: Consider a closely held corporation, c, with three stockholders, a_1, a_2 and a_3, and a bank, b, as its sole creditor. The corporation is obligated to pay interest to the bank, in some fixed amount of dollars, d, per month. Assuming that we have properly defined the action 'TransferDollars(x, y, n, t)', we could write this obligation as follows:

$$\mathbf{O}\langle\text{TransferDollars}(c, b, d, t), c\rangle \Leftarrow \text{Month}(t),$$

where the predicate 'Month' simply tests that t is the beginning of the month. This is what we mean when we say that the bank has a "right" to receive 'd' dollars in interest from the corporation each month. The stockholders might also have a "right" to receive dividends each quarter, but the specification of this right would be quite different. First, we would write the following free choice permission:

$\mathbf{P}\langle(\exists n)\text{TransferDollars}(c, a_i, n, t), c\rangle \Leftarrow \text{Quarter}(t),$

for $i = 1, \ldots, 3$. By itself, this rule allows the corporation to select a stockholder, a_i, and a dollar amount, n, in making the transfer, but such a completely free choice would then be constrained by the following obligation:

$\mathbf{O}\langle\text{TransferDollars}(c, a_i, n_i, t), c\rangle \Leftarrow$
$\qquad \text{TransferDollars}(c, a_j, n_j, t) \wedge n_i \times r_j = n_j \times r_i,$

for $i \neq j$. Here, r_i is the fraction of total stock owned by a_i, so this rule expresses the fact that a dividend must be a *pro rata* distribution of assets to all stockholders. □

The deontic modalities are also useful for expressing planning problems. The following example is adapted from [25].

Example 2.2: Imagine two actors, a_1 and a_2, moving around in a suite of rooms, $r_1, \ldots, r_n$. We define an action '$\text{Move}(x, y, z, t_1, t_2)$' as follows:

$\text{Move}(x, y, z, t_1, t_2) \Leftarrow$
$\qquad \text{In}(x, y)[t_1, t] \wedge \text{In}(x, z)[t, t_2] \wedge$
$\qquad \text{Connected}(y, z) \wedge t_1 < t < t_2,$

$\text{Move}(x, y, z, t_1, t_2) \Leftarrow$
$\qquad \text{In}(x, y)[t_1, t] \wedge \text{Move}(x, u, z, t, t_2) \wedge$
$\qquad \text{Connected}(y, u) \wedge t_1 < t < t_2,$

where '$\text{In}(x, y)$' asserts that actor x is in room y, and '$\text{Connected}(y, z)$' asserts that room y is connected by a doorway to room z. Suppose the actors a_1 and a_2 are forbidden to be in the same room at the same time. We could represent this forbidden event by:

$\text{InSameRoom}(t_0, t_3) \Leftarrow$
$\qquad \text{In}(a_1, y)[t_1, t_2] \wedge t_0 \leq t_1 \leq t \leq t_2 \leq t_3 \wedge$
$\qquad \text{In}(a_2, y)[t'_1, t'_2] \wedge t_0 \leq t'_1 \leq t \leq t'_2 \leq t_3,$

and then assert:

$\mathbf{F}\langle\text{InSameRoom}(t_0, t_3), a_1 \& a_2\rangle \qquad (1)$

to represent the prohibition itself. (In this encoding, we are treating $a_1 \& a_2$ as a single agent, and ignoring the difficult problems of joint agency.) Given (1), we would like to know if the following action is also forbidden:

$\text{Swap}(t_0, t_3) \Leftarrow \text{Move}(a_1, r_i, r_j, t_0, t_3) \wedge$
$\qquad \text{Move}(a_2, r_j, r_i, t_0, t_3),$

where r_i and r_j are any two arbitrary rooms. In other words, we would like to know whether (1) implies:

$\mathbf{F}\langle\text{Swap}(t_0, t_3), a_1 \& a_2\rangle, \qquad (2)$

taking the universal closure over t_0 and t_3. The answer depends on the connectivity of the rooms, and the solutions are discussed in [25]. Semantically, however, if (1) does *not* imply (2), then there exists *some* way to swap the positions of the two actors without violating the deontic constraints — i.e., there exists a permitted *plan*. □

In the previous example, we were able to formulate a planning problem without reference to the frame problem because our two agents controlled all the actions relevant to the plan. We can use the same idea to formulate a classical STRIPS planning problem. In this case, however, it is necessary to modify the representation somewhat. In Example 2.2, we specified all possible actions by definitions, and then asserted that certain actions were forbidden. We assumed, in effect, that all actions are permitted unless they are explicitly forbidden. In the blocks world, we will turn this around, and assume that actions are forbidden unless they are explicitly permitted. (Think of this modality as "can do" rather than "may do".) Here is a simple example:

Example 2.3: Consider a blocks world with a base predicate '$\text{On}(x, y)$', in which x is a block and y is either another block or a location on the table. Define the following action:

$\text{Move}(x, y, z, t_1, t_2) \Leftarrow$
$\qquad (\forall w)\neg\text{On}(w, x)[t_1, t_2] \wedge$
$\qquad \text{On}(x, y)[t_1] \circ (\forall w)\neg\text{On}(w, y)[t_2] \wedge$
$\qquad (\forall w)\neg\text{On}(w, z)[t_1] \circ \text{On}(x, z)[t_2] \wedge t_1 < t_2$

This action simultaneously (i) maintains the fact that there is nothing on x, (ii) clears x from its location on y, and (iii) puts x on z. To handle the frame problem, we also define the following actions:

$\text{HoldOn}(x, y, t_1, t_2) \Leftarrow \text{On}(x, y)[t_1, t_2] \wedge t_1 < t_2,$

which maintains the fact that x is on y, and

$\text{HoldClear}(x, t_1, t_2) \Leftarrow (\forall w)\neg\text{On}(w, x)[t_1, t_2] \wedge t_1 < t_2,$

which maintains the fact that there is nothing on x. We now assert that a particular actor, a_1, is permitted to perform any bounded set of these actions *concurrently*, as long as the preconditions are satisfied:

$\mathbf{P}\langle\text{Move}(x, y, z, t_1, t_2) \wedge$
$\qquad \bigwedge_{i=1}^{m} \text{HoldOn}(u_{i1}, u_{i2}, t_1, t_2) \wedge$
$\qquad \bigwedge_{j=1}^{n} \text{HoldClear}(u_j, t_1, t_2), a_1\rangle \Leftarrow$
$\qquad (\forall w)\neg\text{On}(w, x)[t_1] \wedge \text{On}(x, y)[t_1] \wedge$
$\qquad (\forall w)\neg\text{On}(w, z)[t_1] \wedge$
$\qquad \bigwedge_{i=1}^{m} \text{On}(u_{i1}, u_{i2})[t_1] \wedge \bigwedge_{j=1}^{n} (\forall w)\neg\text{On}(w, u_j)[t_1] \wedge$
$\qquad t_1 < t_2$

This is a free choice permission, and if we assert this permission for all $m \leq M$ and $n \leq N$, then a_1 is allowed to select any blocks that it wants to 'HoldOn' and 'HoldClear'. To turn this into a planning problem, assume that we have also specified a 'Start' condition and a 'Goal' condition. To show that there is *no* way for a_1 to get from 'Start' to 'Goal', we try to prove:

$\mathbf{F}\langle \text{Start}[t_0] \circ \text{Goal}[t_k], a_1\rangle \Leftarrow t_0 < t_k,$

under the assumption that all actions are forbidden unless they are explicitly permitted. If this proof fails, we will have a sequence of permitted actions that achieves the goal. □

Notice that this is a "monotonic" solution to the frame problem, in the spirit of [13]. There are no frame axioms, just a collection of actions that explicitly change the state of the world. Unlike the solution in [13], however, our solution does not require us to update the *complete* state of the world, since the robot only needs to "hold onto" those blocks that are relevant to the planning problem. This may seem unrealistic (for example, it requires the robot to have $N + M + 1$ arms!), but this is just the first step in our analysis. It is easy to modify the example so that the inertial actions occur by default:

Example 2.4: Let 'Move', 'HoldOn' and 'HoldClear' be defined as in Example 2.3. For convenience, we define the following actions as the *opposites* of 'HoldOn' and 'HoldClear', respectively:

ChangeOn$(x, y, t_3) \Leftarrow$
 On$(x, y)[t_3] \circ (\forall w)\neg \text{On}(w, y)[t_4] \wedge t_3 < t_4$

ChangeClear$(x, t_3) \Leftarrow$
 $(\forall w)\neg \text{On}(w, x)[t_3] \circ \text{On}(z, x)[t_4] \wedge t_3 < t_4$

Intuitively, we want to assert that 'On' and 'Clear' persist unless some specific action changes them. We can write this as follows:

$\mathbf{O}\langle \text{HoldOn}(x, y, t_1, t_2), \text{nature}\rangle \Leftarrow$
 On$(x, y)[t_1] \wedge t_1 < t_2 \wedge$
 $\sim (\exists a, t_3)$
 $[\mathbf{DO}\langle \text{ChangeOn}(x, y, t_3), a\rangle \wedge t_1 \le t_3 < t_2],$

$\mathbf{O}\langle \text{HoldClear}(x, t_1, t_2), \text{nature}\rangle \Leftarrow$
 $(\forall w)\neg \text{On}(w, x)[t_1] \wedge t_1 < t_2 \wedge$
 $\sim(\exists a, t_3)$
 $[\mathbf{DO}\langle \text{ChangeClear}(x, t_3), a\rangle \wedge t_1 \le t_3 < t_2],$

where the symbol '$\sim$' denotes negation-as-failure. We thus postulate an actor named 'nature' who is obligated to perform the actions 'HoldOn' and 'HoldClear' unless some other action intervenes. (Remember: 'nature' always obeys the law!) We can now simplify the free choice permission for a_1:

$\mathbf{P}\langle \text{Move}(x, y, z, t_1, t_2), a_1\rangle \Leftarrow$
 $(\forall w)\neg \text{On}(w, x)[t_1] \wedge \text{On}(x, y)[t_1] \wedge$
 $(\forall w)\neg \text{On}(w, z)[t_1] \wedge t_1 < t_2,$

and let 'nature' do some of the work. □

The encoding in Example 2.4 suggests that we might encounter problems with the *ramifications* of an action, but these problems can also be solved using deontic modalities. Here is a standard example, from [38]:

Example 2.5: Imagine a university database system, in which the relation 'In(s, c)' means that student s is enrolled in course c. The possible actions are 'Add' and 'Drop', which are defined as follows:

Add$(s, c, t_1, t_2) \Leftarrow \neg \text{In}(s, c)[t_1] \circ \text{In}(s, c)[t_2] \wedge t_1 < t_2$

Drop$(s, c, t_1, t_2) \Leftarrow \text{In}(s, c)[t_1] \circ \neg \text{In}(s, c)[t_2] \wedge t_1 < t_2$

(In this example, time is usually discrete, and t_2 is usually the immediate successor of t_1.) Assume the existence of two deontic rules that permit (**P**) a student to add a course if she is not already enrolled in it, and to drop any course in which she is currently enrolled. There are also two deontic rules that obligate (**O**) the university to maintain a student's enrollment status unless the student herself adds or drops a course. These rules are similar to the inertial rules in Example 2.4. Finally, assume that a student is required to take 'chem120', a laboratory course, whenever she takes 'chem110'. We could represent this requirement as follows:

$\mathbf{O}\langle \text{In}(s, \text{chem120})[t_1, t_2] \vee \text{Add}(s, \text{chem120}, t_1, t_2), s\rangle$
 $\Leftarrow \text{Add}(s, \text{chem110}, t_1, t_2),$

$\mathbf{O}\langle \neg \text{In}(s, \text{chem110})[t_1, t_2] \vee \text{Drop}(s, \text{chem110}, t_1, t_2), s\rangle$
 $\Leftarrow \text{Drop}(s, \text{chem120}, t_1, t_2),$

Thus, if a student always obeys the law and is initially enrolled in no courses at all, she will always satisfy the university regulations governing enrollment in 'chem110' and 'chem120'. □

We now discuss the logic that makes these representations possible.

3 Events and Actions

This section develops a language for events and actions, and thus establishes a foundation for the deontic language in Section 4. In particular, we discuss here the concept of a *basic event*, and we clarify the distinction between *definite* and *indefinite* actions. Our logic is *intuitionistic*, rather than classical, and we show that this choice is dictated by a desire to include statechanges in the class of basic events. Most of the technical results in this section are borrowed from [21], where they are developed for a one-sorted (atemporal) language. To save space, we will not recapitulate this material here, but simply indicate how the definitions and theorems can be modified to apply to a two-sorted (temporal) language. The reader is urged to consult [21] for a more thorough analysis of circumscription in intuitionistic logic, and to consult [29] for a further discussion of indefinite actions.

Let $\mathcal{L}$ be a function-free first-order language with two sorts: an *object sort* and an *order sort*. The object sort includes constants and variables, written $x_1, x_2, \ldots$, but the order sort includes only variables, written $t_1, t_2, \ldots$. We will assume that the object arguments always precede the order arguments in the signature of the language, so that the predicate $P(x_1, \ldots, x_n, t_1, \ldots, t_m)$ has arity $\langle n, m\rangle$. A common device in the interpretation of intuitionistic logic (see, e.g., [7]) is to extend the original language by a new set of constants, which can then be used to specify a total domain for a Kripke structure. Accordingly, let $\mathcal{L}(\mathbf{c},\mathbf{t})$ be the language $\mathcal{L}$ augmented by an arbitrary set of constants $\mathbf{c}$ for the object sort, and an arbitrary (but disjoint) set of constants $\mathbf{t}$ for the order sort. We asssume that $\mathbf{t}$ is isomorphic to the rational numbers, and therefore countable, and for simplicity we assume that $\mathbf{c}$ is countable as well. Moreover, we will use the natural order on the rationals to interpret the special *order atoms* in $\mathcal{L}$, i.e., the atoms $t_1 < t_2$. Thus the total domain $\mathbf{t}$ is a dense linear order.

The main idea underlying the Kripke semantics of intuitionistic logic, however, is that we should work with partial domains and partial models. We thus write a Kripke structure for $\mathcal{L}$ as a quintuple $\langle W, \sqsubseteq, \mathbf{h}, \mathbf{u}, \mathbf{o} \rangle$, where W is a nonempty set of *worlds*, $\sqsubseteq$ is a partial order on W, $\mathbf{u}$ is a monotonic mapping from the worlds of W to nonempty sets of object constants in $\mathcal{L}(\mathbf{c},\mathbf{t})$, and $\mathbf{o}$ is a monotonic mapping from the worlds of W to nonempty sets of order constants in $\mathcal{L}(\mathbf{c},\mathbf{t})$. (Note that $\mathbf{o}(w)$, for a particular world $w \in W$, could be a finite linear order, or a singleton, or an infinite linear order that is not dense.) Intuitively, the third component of the Kripke structure, $\mathbf{h}$, tells us the ground atomic formulae that are true at each $w \in W$. Formally, we first define an *intuitionistic relation* R of arity $\langle n, m \rangle$ to be a function that assigns to every world $w \in W$ a subset of the Cartesian product $\mathbf{u}(w)^n \times \mathbf{o}(w)^m$, subject to the requirement that $R(w_1) \subseteq R(w_2)$ whenever $w_1 \sqsubseteq w_2$. We then define the mapping from the predicate constants in $\mathcal{L}$ to the set of intuitionistic relations on W. The atomic clause of the "forcing" relation [7] is thus: $w, W \models P(c_1,\ldots,c_n,t_1,\ldots,t_m)$ if and only if $\langle c_1,\ldots,c_n,t_1,\ldots,t_m \rangle \in \mathbf{h}(P)(w)$, for P a predicate constant of arity $\langle n, m \rangle$. For the order atoms: $w, W \models t_1 < t_2$ if and only if t_1 and t_2 are both in $\mathbf{o}(w)$ and t_1 is less than t_2 in the natural order on the rationals. Among the compound formulae, the definitions of forcing for conjunction, disjunction and existential quantification depend only on a single world, w, as in classical logic, but the definitions for implication and universal quantification are nonclassical:

$w, W \models \mathcal{B} \Leftarrow \mathcal{A}$ iff

$w', W \models \mathcal{A}$ implies $w', W \models \mathcal{B}$ for every $w' \sqsupseteq w$ in W, and the constants in $\mathcal{A}$ and $\mathcal{B}$ are in $\mathbf{u}(w)$ or $\mathbf{o}(w)$,

$w, W \models (\forall x)\mathcal{A}(x)$ iff

$w', W \models \mathcal{A}(c)$ for every $w' \sqsupseteq w$ in W, and for all object constants c in $\mathbf{u}(w')$,

$w, W \models (\forall t)\mathcal{A}(t)$ iff

$w', W \models \mathcal{A}(t)$ for every $w' \sqsupseteq w$ in W, and for all order constants t in $\mathbf{o}(w')$.

Now let $\mathcal{A}$ be a closed sentence in $\mathcal{L}$. If $w, W \models \mathcal{A}$ for every $w \in W$, we say that $\langle W, \sqsubseteq, \mathbf{h}, \mathbf{u}, \mathbf{o} \rangle$ *satisfies* $\mathcal{A}$. If $w, W \models \mathcal{A}$ for every $w \in W$ such that the constants in $\mathcal{A}$ are in $\mathbf{u}(w)$, then we say that $\mathcal{A}$ is *true* in $\langle W, \sqsubseteq, \mathbf{h}, \mathbf{u}, \mathbf{o} \rangle$. Finally, if ϕ is a set of sentences and ψ is a sentence, we write $\phi \models \psi$ if and only if ψ is true in every Kripke structure that satisfies ϕ.

We now apply the machinery of [21], which was developed for a one-sorted (atemporal) language, to the two-sorted language $\mathcal{L}$. First, to state the circumscription axiom, we need to extend $\mathcal{L}$ to include (at least) the second-order universal quantifier, but this works in the two-sorted case exactly as it does in the one-sorted case. If $\mathcal{R}$ is a finite set of Horn clauses, including order constraints, and if $\boldsymbol{P}$ is a tuple consisting of the *defined predicates* in $\mathcal{R}$, i.e., the predicates that appear somewhere on the "left-hand side" of $\mathcal{R}$, then we are interested in "the circumscription of $\boldsymbol{P}$ in $\mathcal{R}(\boldsymbol{P})$," which is denoted by $Circ(\mathcal{R}(\boldsymbol{P});\boldsymbol{P})$. Second, to analyze this circumscription, we need the concept of a *final Kripke model*. Let $\boldsymbol{J}_1 = \langle W_1, \sqsubseteq_1, \mathbf{h}_1, \mathbf{u}_1, \mathbf{o}_1 \rangle$ and $\boldsymbol{J}_2 = \langle W_2, \sqsubseteq_2, \mathbf{h}_2, \mathbf{u}_2, \mathbf{o}_2 \rangle$ be two Kripke structures for $\mathcal{L}$. We say that a mapping $\tau: W_1 \to W_2$ is a *homomorphism* from $\boldsymbol{J}_1$ into $\boldsymbol{J}_2$ if and only if (i) it preserves $\sqsubseteq$, and (ii) it preserves $\mathbf{h}$, $\mathbf{u}$ and $\mathbf{o}$ relative to some fixed (but arbitrary) domain isomorphism ι. (Note that this is possible only because we have assumed that the total domains $\mathbf{c}$ and $\mathbf{t}$ are countable.) Now let $\mathcal{K}$ be an arbitrary class of Kripke structures and assume that $\boldsymbol{K} = \langle W, \sqsubseteq, \mathbf{h}, \mathbf{u}, \mathbf{o} \rangle$ is a member of $\mathcal{K}$.

Definition 3.1 $\boldsymbol{K}$ *is a final Kripke structure for $\mathcal{K}$ if and only if, for every $\boldsymbol{J} \in \mathcal{K}$ and every domain isomorphism ι, there exists a unique homomorphism from $\boldsymbol{J}$ into $\boldsymbol{K}$.*

It is easy to see that two final Kripke structures for $\mathcal{K}$ are isomorphic, and thus either one could be designated as "the" final Kripke structure for $\mathcal{K}$.

We typically use Definition 3.1 as follows: We take $\mathcal{K}$ to be the class of Kripke structures that satisfy some set of first-order rules $\mathcal{R}$, and we try to find a final Kripke structure, $\boldsymbol{K}$, for $\mathcal{K}$. If such a $\boldsymbol{K}$ exists, we call it the *final Kripke model* for $\mathcal{R}$. It then turns out (see Proposition 3.7 in [21]) that a universally quantified implication is entailed by $\mathcal{R}$ if and only if it is true in $\boldsymbol{K}$. Notice, however, that Definition 3.1 is not restricted to first-order theories, and could apply equally well to second-order theories, such as the circumscription axiom. On the other hand, not every instance of the circumscription axiom has a final Kripke model (see Section 5 of [21] for the discussion of a counterexample). In fact, the existence of a final Kripke model seems to be one measure of the *coherence* of a circumscribed theory in intuitionistic logic.

It is thus of some interest that we can always construct a final Kripke model for $Circ(\mathcal{R}(\boldsymbol{P});\boldsymbol{P})$ when $\mathcal{R}$ determines the class of events discussed in Section 2. These rules look like Horn clauses, but they include special expressions like: $B(x)[t_1] \circ \neg B(x)[t_2]$ and $(\forall w)\neg C(w,y)[t_1,t_2]$. Our approach is to treat these special expressions as atomic predicates in an extended language $\mathcal{L}'$, and to define their meaning by a set of rules outside the scope of the circumscription axiom. Thus, if $B(x,t)$ and $C(x,y,t)$ are *base predicates* in $\mathcal{L}$, i.e., predicates in $\mathcal{L}$ that are not defined in $\mathcal{R}$, we would adopt the following definitions:

Definition 3.2

$B(x)[t_1] \circ \neg B(x)[t_2] \Leftrightarrow B(x, t_1) \wedge [\bot \Leftarrow B(x, t_2)]$

$\neg B(x)[t_1] \circ B(x)[t_2] \Leftrightarrow [\bot \Leftarrow B(x, t_1)] \wedge B(x, t_2)$

$C(x, y)[t_1] \circ (\forall w)\neg C(w, y)[t_2] \Leftrightarrow$
$\quad C(x, y, t_1) \wedge (\forall w)[\bot \Leftarrow C(w, y, t_2)]$

$(\forall w)\neg C(w, y)[t_1] \circ C(x, y)[t_2] \Leftrightarrow$
$\quad (\forall w)[\bot \Leftarrow C(w, y, t_1)] \wedge C(x, y, t_2)$

$B(x)[t_1, t_2] \Leftrightarrow B(x, t_1) \wedge B(x, t_2) \wedge$
$\quad\quad\quad\quad (\forall t)[B(x, t) \Leftarrow t_1 < t < t_2]$

$\neg B(x)[t_1, t_2] \Leftrightarrow \neg B(x, t_1) \wedge \neg B(x, t_2) \wedge$
$\quad\quad\quad\quad (\forall t)[\bot \Leftarrow B(x, t) \wedge t_1 < t < t_2]$

$C(x, y)[t_1, t_2] \Leftrightarrow C(x, y, t_1) \wedge C(x, y, t_2) \wedge$
$\quad\quad\quad\quad (\forall t)[C(x, y, t) \Leftarrow t_1 < t < t_2]$

$(\forall w)\neg C(w, y)[t_1, t_2] \Leftrightarrow$
$\quad (\forall w)\neg C(w, y, t_1) \wedge (\forall w)\neg C(w, y, t_2) \wedge$
$\quad (\forall w, t)[\bot \Leftarrow C(w, y, t) \wedge t_1 < t < t_2]$

(We could extend this list in obvious ways, but this is sufficient for the examples in Section 2.) Let $\mathcal{D}$ be the set of all such definitions. Even though our special expressions are "defined" in $\mathcal{D}$, we will treat them as base predicates in $\mathcal{L}'$, since they are not defined in $\mathcal{R}$. We now proceed to the construction of the final Kripke model.

Let **c** be any countable set of object constants distinct from the constants in $\mathcal{L}$, and let the total order domain, **t**, be the rational numbers. Let H be the set of all triples $\langle B, U, Q \rangle$, where U is any nonempty set of object constants in $\mathcal{L}$ or **c** that includes the constants in $\mathcal{R}$, Q is any nonempty set of rational numbers, and B is any Herbrand interpretation for the base predicates in $\mathcal{L}'$ over the universes U and Q. Set $\langle B_1, U_1, Q_1 \rangle \sqsubseteq \langle B_2, U_2, Q_2 \rangle$ if and only if $B_1 \subseteq B_2$ and $U_1 \subseteq U_2$ and $Q_1 \subseteq Q_2$. We note that $H \cup \{\langle \emptyset, \emptyset, \emptyset \rangle\}$ is a complete lattice under this order, and we use '⊓' and '⊔' to denote the *meet* and *join*, respectively, in this lattice. It is obvious that any subset of H could be interpreted as a Kripke structure for the base predicates in $\mathcal{L}'$. Simply define $\mathbf{u}(\langle B, U, Q \rangle) = U$ and $\mathbf{o}(\langle B, U, Q \rangle) = Q$, and define:

$\mathbf{h}(P)(\langle B, U, Q \rangle) = \{\langle \mathbf{c}^n, \mathbf{t}^m \rangle \mid P(\mathbf{c}^n, \mathbf{t}^m) \in B\}$

for every base predicate P in $\mathcal{L}'$. Now, using the techniques in [18], let W^* be the largest subset of H such that $\langle W^*, \sqsubseteq, \mathbf{h}, \mathbf{u}, \mathbf{o} \rangle$ satisfies the definitions in $\mathcal{D}$. (This set can always be constructed as the greatest fixed point of the "deletion" transformation associated with $\mathcal{D}$.) For the defined predicates in $\mathcal{L}$, let $S^\omega_{U,Q} \uparrow (B)$ be the least fixed point of the van Emden-Kowalski "one-step consequence" operator for $\mathcal{R}$ [40] over the universes U and Q that includes B. (For the details of this construction, see [21].) We can now define:

$\mathbf{h}^*(P)(\langle B, U, Q \rangle) =$
$\quad \{\langle \mathbf{c}^n, \mathbf{t}^m \rangle \mid P(\mathbf{c}^n, \mathbf{t}^m) \in S^\omega_{U,Q} \uparrow (B)\}$

for every predicate P in $\mathcal{L}'$. Note that $\mathbf{h}^*(P) = \mathbf{h}(P)$ whenever P is a base predicate. Our main result is:

Theorem 3.3 *Let $\mathcal{R}$ be a set of Horn clauses in $\mathcal{L}'$ with defined predicates $\mathbf{P}$, and let $\mathcal{D}$ be given by Definition 3.2. Then $\langle W^*, \sqsubseteq, \mathbf{h}^*, \mathbf{u}, \mathbf{o} \rangle$ is the final Kripke model for $Circ(\mathcal{R}(\mathbf{P}); \mathbf{P}) \cup \mathcal{D}$.*

This result follows by a minor modification of Theorem 4.7 in [21].

Now that we have constructed the final Kripke model for $Circ(\mathcal{R}(\mathbf{P}); \mathbf{P}) \cup \mathcal{D}$, we can discuss the concept of definite and indefinite events. Consider the following:

Definition 3.4 *Let $\mathcal{T}$ be a theory in a language $\mathcal{L}$, and let A, B and $A(x)$ be atomic formulae in $\mathcal{L}$. We say that $\mathcal{T}$ has the disjunctive property if:*

$\mathcal{T} \models A \vee B$ *iff* $\mathcal{T} \models A$ *or* $\mathcal{T} \models B$.

We say that $\mathcal{T}$ has the existential property if:

$\mathcal{T} \models (\exists x) A(x)$ *iff* $\mathcal{T} \models A(x)\theta$ *for some θ.*

It should be apparent that $\mathcal{R} \cup \mathcal{D}$ would not have these properties if entailment were interpreted classically, even in a simple language without linear order constraints. For example, if 'Q(a)⇐¬B(b)' is in $\mathcal{D}$, then Q(a)∨B(b) is entailed in classical logic, but neither atom is entailed by itself. If 'P(x)⇐Q(x)' and 'P(x)⇐B(x)' are also in $\mathcal{R}$, then $(\exists x)$P(x) is entailed in classical logic, but there is no substitution θ such that P(x)θ is entailed. However, in intuitionistic logic, the disjunctive and existential properties would hold. In fact, we can make a stronger statement. Let $\mathcal{R}$ be a set of Horn clauses and let $\mathcal{D}$ be a set of definitions including "embedded implications" and "embedded negations," as in Definition 3.2. Let ϕ be a conjunction of atomic formulae, and assume that ψ_1, ψ_2 and $\psi(x)$ are also atomic. Then:

$\mathcal{R} \cup \mathcal{D} \models \psi_1 \vee \psi_2 \Leftarrow \phi$ iff $\quad\quad\quad(3)$
$\quad \mathcal{R} \cup \mathcal{D} \models \psi_1 \Leftarrow \phi$ or $\mathcal{R} \cup \mathcal{D} \models \psi_2 \Leftarrow \phi$,

and

$\mathcal{R} \cup \mathcal{D} \models (\exists x)\psi(x) \Leftarrow \phi$ iff $\quad\quad\quad(4)$
$\quad \mathcal{R} \cup \mathcal{D} \models \psi(x)\theta \Leftarrow \phi$ for some θ,

as long as entailment is interpreted intuitionistically. (If ϕ or ψ, or both, have free variables in these entailments, we simply take the universal closure on the right-hand side.) These results follow from the fact that the final Kripke model for $\mathcal{R} \cup \mathcal{D}$ has an intersection property analogous to the *model intersection property* of Horn clause logic (see [18]). Intuitively, (3) and (4) show that we can assert the conjunction ϕ in the context of a theory $\mathcal{R} \cup \mathcal{D}$ and the disjunctive and existential properties will still hold.

However, the situation becomes more complicated when we add circumscription and an order sort. Let us say that ϕ is a *definite event* if (3) and (4) still hold for the two-sorted language $\mathcal{L}'$ when the theory $\mathcal{R} \cup \mathcal{D}$ is strengthened to the theory $Circ(\mathcal{R}(\boldsymbol{P});\boldsymbol{P}) \cup \mathcal{D}$. It is now insufficient that ϕ is a conjunction of atomic formulae. For example, if $\mathcal{R}$ includes:

$$P \Leftarrow Q(a) \quad \text{and} \quad P \Leftarrow Q(b),$$

then $Q(a) \vee Q(b) \Leftarrow P$ is entailed by $Circ(\mathcal{R}(\boldsymbol{P});\boldsymbol{P})$, but neither $Q(a) \Leftarrow P$ nor $Q(b) \Leftarrow P$ is entailed. In general, the disjunctive and existential properties will not hold in the context of a circumscribed theory if defined predicates are included in ϕ. Even if ϕ consists entirely of base predicates, the disjunctive and existential properties are not guaranteed. For example, suppose $B(t_1, t_2)$ is a base predicate and $\mathcal{R}$ includes the rules:

$$P \Leftarrow B(t_1, t_2) \wedge t_1 < t_2,$$
$$Q \Leftarrow B(t_1, t_2) \wedge t_1 \geq t_2.$$

Then, because t_1 and t_2 are interpreted over a linear order, the universal closure of $P \vee Q \Leftarrow B(t_1, t_2)$ is entailed by $\mathcal{R}$, but neither $P \Leftarrow B(t_1, t_2)$ nor $Q \Leftarrow B(t_1, t_2)$ is entailed.

Obviously, we can correct this problem if we specifically assert the order relations on t_1 and t_2. This will give us the class of *basic events*. If $B(x_1, \ldots, x_n, t)$ is a base predicate with only one order argument, then $B(x_1, \ldots, x_n, t)$ is a basic event. If $B(x_1, \ldots, x_n, t_1, t_2)$ is a base predicate with two order arguments, including the predicates in Definition 3.2, then

$$B(x_1, \ldots, x_n, t, t),$$
$$B(x_1, \ldots, x_n, t_1, t_2) \wedge t_1 < t_2,$$
$$B(x_1, \ldots, x_n, t_1, t_2) \wedge t_1 > t_2,$$

are all basic events. (Again, these definitions, as well as Definition 3.2, could be extended, but this is sufficient for the examples in Section 2.) The following proposition now follows easily from an analysis of the final Kripke model for $Circ(\mathcal{R}(\boldsymbol{P}); \boldsymbol{P}) \cup \mathcal{D}$:

Proposition 3.5 *If ϕ is a basic event, then the disjunctive and existential properties stated in (3) and (4) hold for the strengthened theory $Circ(\mathcal{R}(\boldsymbol{P});\boldsymbol{P}) \cup \mathcal{D}$ in the two-sorted language $\mathcal{L}'$ with linear order constraints.*

Intuitively, basic events are the minimal (nonempty) definite events, and they correspond to the minimal (nonempty) worlds of $\langle W^*, \sqsubseteq, \mathbf{h}^*, \mathbf{u}, \mathbf{o}\rangle$. We will use this fact in the following section.

4 Deontic Modalities

This section develops the semantics of $\mathbf{P}\langle\alpha, x\rangle$, $\mathbf{F}\langle\alpha, x\rangle$ and $\mathbf{O}\langle\alpha, x\rangle$, as well as the semantics of $\mathbf{DO}\langle\alpha, x\rangle$. The basic idea is to use the final Kripke model $\langle W^*, \sqsubseteq, \mathbf{h}^*, \mathbf{u}, \mathbf{o}\rangle$ to define two concepts: (i) the denotation of an action α, written $\lceil \alpha \rceil$; and (ii) the Grand Permitted Set, written $\mathcal{P}$.

The deontic modalities are then interpreted as statements about the possible relationships between $\lceil \alpha \rceil$ and $\mathcal{P}$. This is a variant of the deontic semantics first presented in [16, 17].

Consider a basic event, such as 'SwimLap$(x, t_1, t_2) \wedge t_1 < t_2$'. To assert that a particular agent, $c_0 = x\theta$, performs this event at the particular times $t_1 = t_1\theta < t_2\theta = t_2$ is to assert that c_0 determines the evolution of a very small piece of the world between t_1 and t_2. A natural way to represent this fact in W^* is to point to the set:

$$V = \{w \mid w, W^* \models \text{SwimLap}(x, t_1, t_2)\theta\}.$$

This set has a least element, $\sqcap V$, corresponding to the small piece of the world controlled by c_0, but it also includes all possible completions of $\sqcap V$, corresponding to the myriad ways that other agents (as well as c_0 herself, wearing a different hat!) could determine the evolution of the world, at t_1 and t_2, and at all other times t. When we associate such a set with a particular agent, we think of it as a *basic action*. Since all actions are defined by Horn clauses from basic actions, we adopt the following:

Definition 4.1 *The denotation of a ground action α, written $\lceil \alpha \rceil$, is defined recursively as follows:*

- *If $\alpha = B\theta$ for some base predicate B and some ground substitution θ, then*

$$\{w \mid w, W^* \models B\theta\} \in \lceil \alpha \rceil$$

- *If $\alpha = R\theta$ for some ground substitution θ, where R is defined by the rule*

$$R \Leftarrow Q_1 \wedge \ldots \wedge Q_k \wedge O,$$

and if $V_i \in \lceil Q_i\theta \rceil$ for $i = 1, \ldots, k$, and if the order constraints $O\theta$ are satisfied in the natural order on the rationals, then

$$V_1 \cap \ldots \cap V_k \in \lceil \alpha \rceil.$$

Because of the way $\langle W^*, \sqsubseteq, \mathbf{h}^*, \mathbf{u}, \mathbf{o}\rangle$ is constructed, every $V \in \lceil \alpha \rceil$ is a *principal filter* in W^*, i.e., it is an upward closed subset with a least element. We want the Grand Permitted Set, $\mathcal{P}$, to have the same property, so we simply define $\mathcal{P}$ for the agent c_0 to be any arbitrary set of principal filters in W^*. Intuitively, $\mathcal{P}$ represents the *permissible* ways that c_0 can determine the evolution of the world.

We are now ready to define the modalities, **P**, **F** and **O**. Given a Kripke structure $\langle W, \sqsubseteq, \mathbf{h}, \mathbf{u}, \mathbf{o}\rangle$ for the action language, we extend it to a *deontic structure* $\langle W, \mathcal{P}, \sqsubseteq, \mathbf{h}, \mathbf{u}, \mathbf{o}\rangle$ by adding a specification of the Grand Permitted Set. More precisely, there may be many Grand Permitted Sets, at least one for each actor, c, and each of these may vary with w in W, since we are still working with intuitionistic logic. Let us denote these sets by $\mathcal{P}_c(w)$, and include them all in the specification $\mathcal{P}$. In general, the domains of $\langle W, \sqsubseteq, \mathbf{h}, \mathbf{u}, \mathbf{o}\rangle$ may be different from the domains of $\langle W^*, \sqsubseteq, \mathbf{h}^*, \mathbf{u}, \mathbf{o}\rangle$, but they are isomorphic, and it simplifies our notation if we assume that they are identical. Thus, although $\lceil \alpha \rceil$ and $\mathcal{P}$ are actually defined on W^*, we will write them as if they used the constants in $\langle W, \sqsubseteq, \mathbf{h}, \mathbf{u}, \mathbf{o} \rangle$.

Definition 4.2 *Let $\langle W, \mathcal{P}, \sqsubseteq, \mathbf{h}, \mathbf{u}, \mathbf{o} \rangle$ be a deontic structure, and let α be a ground event. The forcing conditions for* **P, F, O** *are:*

- $w, W \models \mathbf{P}\langle \alpha, \mathbf{c} \rangle$ *iff, for all $w' \sqsupseteq w$ in W, the following condition holds:*

$$\forall V : V \in \lceil \alpha \rceil \longrightarrow \qquad (5)$$
$$\exists V' : V' \subseteq V \wedge V' \in \mathcal{P}_\mathbf{c}(w').$$

- $w, W \models \mathbf{F}\langle \alpha, \mathbf{c} \rangle$ *iff, for all $w' \sqsupseteq w$ in W, the following condition holds:*

$$\forall V, V' : V \in \lceil \alpha \rceil \wedge V' \subseteq V \longrightarrow \qquad (6)$$
$$V' \notin \mathcal{P}_\mathbf{c}(w').$$

- $w, W \models \mathbf{O}\langle \alpha, \mathbf{c} \rangle$ *iff, for all $w' \sqsupseteq w$ in W, the following condition holds:*

$$\forall V' : V' \in \mathcal{P}_\mathbf{c}(w') \longrightarrow \qquad (7)$$
$$\exists V : V' \subseteq V \wedge V \in \lceil \alpha \rceil.$$

To understand these definitions, recall that $V' \subseteq V$ means that V' says *more* about the world than V, since $\sqcap V' \sqsupseteq \sqcap V$. Also note that $\mathcal{P}_\mathbf{c}(w)$ is allowed to vary arbitrarily, i.e., nonmonotonically, over $\sqsubseteq$, but the deontic atoms $\mathbf{P}\langle \alpha, \mathbf{c} \rangle$, $\mathbf{F}\langle \alpha, \mathbf{c} \rangle$ and $\mathbf{O}\langle \alpha, \mathbf{c} \rangle$ increase only monotonically over $\sqsubseteq$ by virtue of the definition of forcing. (This will turn out to be a useful feature when we subsequently investigate negation-as-failure.)

Definition 4.2 can be simplified in the case of **F** and **O**, as shown by the following:

Lemma 4.3 *Condition (6) in Definition 4.2 is equivalent to:*

$$\forall w : w, W^* \models \alpha \longrightarrow \{w' \in W^* \mid w' \sqsupseteq w\} \notin \mathcal{P}, \quad (8)$$

and condition (7) in Definition 4.2 is equivalent to:

$$\forall w : \{w' \in W^* \mid w' \sqsupseteq w\} \in \mathcal{P} \longrightarrow w, W^* \models \alpha. \quad (9)$$

Proof: We outline the proof for $\mathbf{F}\langle \alpha, \mathbf{c}, \mathbf{t} \rangle$. Assume (6), and choose a w such that $w, W^* \models \alpha$. Since $\langle W^*, \sqsubseteq, \mathbf{h}^*, \mathbf{u}, \mathbf{o} \rangle$ is the final Kripke model for $Circ(\mathcal{R}(P); P) \cup \mathcal{D}$, this means that $\alpha \in S_{U,Q}^\omega \uparrow (B)$ for some $\langle B, U, Q \rangle$. Thus there exists a $V \in \lceil \alpha \rceil$ such that $\{w' \in W^* \mid w' \sqsupseteq w\} \subseteq V$, and from (6) we conclude that $\{w' \in W^* \mid w' \sqsupseteq w\} \notin \mathcal{P}$. Conversely, assume (8) and choose any $V \in \lceil \alpha \rceil$ and any $V' \subseteq V$. If $V' \in \mathcal{P}$, then V' has a least element w_0, and $V' = \{w' \in W^* \mid w' \sqsupseteq w_0\}$. But then $w_0, W^* \models \alpha$, and (8) implies that $V' \notin \mathcal{P}$, a contradiction. Thus $V' \notin \mathcal{P}$. The proof for $\mathbf{O}\langle \alpha, \mathbf{c}, \mathbf{t} \rangle$ is similar. $\square$

This result shows that our definition of **F** and **O** is basically the same as the definition in [16, 17]. The differences are minor: $\mathcal{P}$ was defined in [16, 17] on the least elements of the principal filters in W^*, whereas here it is defined on the principal filters themselves. With this translation, all of the results in [16, 17] for **F** and **O** carry over to the present work. Note also the rough intuitive reading of (9): "α is obligatory if it is true in all permitted worlds." This means that our logic, for **F** and **O**, is similar to standard deontic logic [5].

However, for **P**, Definition 4.2 differs both from standard deontic logic and from the logic presented in [16, 17]. The contrast with standard deontic logic has already been discussed: It should be clear from condition (5) that **P** is a "free choice permission." The other difference is more subtle. The definition of **P** in [16, 17] would be translated as follows:

$$\forall V : V \in \lceil \alpha \rceil \longrightarrow V \in \mathcal{P}_\mathbf{c}(w'). \qquad (10)$$

This is a plausible definition, but it has a curious consequence: $\mathbf{P}\langle \alpha, \mathbf{c} \rangle \Rightarrow \neg \mathbf{O}\langle \beta, \mathbf{c} \rangle$ when α and β are disjoint actions. (This fact was first pointed out by Ron van der Meyden.) For example: "If you are permitted to sell your house this year, then you are not obligated to pay your taxes." If **P** is defined using condition (5), however, permission and obligation are independent (see Theorem 4.8, below). Under the current interpretation, it is possible to say that you are "permitted to sell your house this year" if, in fact, you are "permitted to sell your house and pay your taxes this year." Moreover, that would be a necessary implication, since $\mathbf{P}\langle \alpha \wedge \beta, \mathbf{c} \rangle \Rightarrow \mathbf{P}\langle \alpha, \mathbf{c} \rangle$ becomes a valid formula when **P** is defined using condition (5). Although there are situations in which condition (10) seems appropriate (for example, if we wanted to focus very narrowly on a specific planning problem, and ignore all extraneous obligations), the current version of Definition 4.2 seems closer to our common sense intuitions about permission and obligation.

Now that we understand the semantics of **P, F** and **O**, it is simple to define a compatible semantics for **DO**. Since the permissible actions available to an agent, $\mathbf{c}$, are represented in our system by $\mathcal{P}_\mathbf{c}(w)$, which is a *set* of principal filters in W^*, the action actually taken by an agent, $\mathbf{c}$, should be represented by a single principal filter in W^*. Let us write this as $D_\mathbf{c}(w)$. We need a *veridicality* assumption, of course, and this can be conveniently encoded by the unique homomorphism τ from $\langle W, \sqsubseteq, \mathbf{h}, \mathbf{u}, \mathbf{o} \rangle$ into $\langle W^*, \sqsubseteq, \mathbf{h}^*, \mathbf{u}, \mathbf{o} \rangle$. We thus stipulate that

$$\tau(\{w' \in W \mid w' \sqsupseteq w\}) \subseteq D_\mathbf{c}(w),$$

for all $w \in W$, which implies that $\tau(w) \sqsupseteq \sqcap D_\mathbf{c}(w)$. Finally, we include the sets $D_\mathbf{c}(w)$ in a new component, D, of our deontic structure:

Definition 4.4 *Let $\langle W, D, \mathcal{P}, \sqsubseteq, \mathbf{h}, \mathbf{u}, \mathbf{o} \rangle$ be a deontic structure, and let α be a ground action. The forcing condition for* **DO** *is:*

- $w, W \models \mathbf{DO}\langle \alpha, \mathbf{c} \rangle$ *iff, for all $w' \sqsupseteq w$ in W,*

$$\exists V : D_\mathbf{c}(w') \subseteq V \wedge V \in \lceil \alpha \rceil.$$

It should now be clear what it means to say that an agent always "obeys the law", namely: $D_c(w)$ must be an element of the Grand Permitted Set!

Definition 4.5 $\langle W, D, \mathcal{P}, \sqsubseteq, \mathbf{h}, \mathbf{u}, \mathbf{o} \rangle$ *is causal for the agent* c *iff* $D_c(w) \in \mathcal{P}_c(w)$ *for all* $w \in W$.

Proposition 4.6 *If* $\langle W, D, \mathcal{P}, \sqsubseteq, \mathbf{h}, \mathbf{u}, \mathbf{o} \rangle$ *is causal for the agent* c, *then*

$$\models \bot \Leftarrow \mathbf{DO}\langle \alpha, c \rangle \wedge \mathbf{F}\langle \alpha, c \rangle,$$

$$\models \mathbf{DO}\langle \alpha, c \rangle \Leftarrow \mathbf{O}\langle \alpha, c \rangle.$$

Proof: Immediate, from Definitions 4.2, 4.4 and 4.5. □

We conclude this section with two theorems that are useful for the development of a proof theory. The first theorem states that certain inferences involving **O** and **F** can be reduced to inferences in the action language.

Theorem 4.7 *Assume that* $\mathbf{O}\langle \alpha_i \rangle$, $\mathbf{F}\langle \beta_i \rangle$, $\mathbf{O}\langle \gamma \rangle$ *and* $\mathbf{F}\langle \gamma \rangle$ *are deontic atoms with identical agents,* x, *and let* **f** *denote a special nullary predicate that does not appear in* $\mathcal{R}$ *or* $\mathcal{D}$. *Then*

$$\models \mathbf{O}\langle \gamma \rangle \Leftarrow \bigwedge_{i=1}^{n} \mathbf{O}\langle \alpha_i \rangle \wedge \bigwedge_{i=1}^{m} \mathbf{F}\langle \beta_i \rangle \quad (11)$$

iff

$$Circ(\mathcal{R}(P);P) \cup \mathcal{D} \models \gamma \vee \mathbf{f} \Leftarrow \bigwedge_{i=1}^{n} \alpha_i \wedge \bigwedge_{i=1}^{m} \mathbf{f} \Leftarrow \beta_i. \quad (12)$$

Similarly,

$$\models \mathbf{F}\langle \gamma \rangle \Leftarrow \bigwedge_{i=1}^{n} \mathbf{O}\langle \alpha_i \rangle \wedge \bigwedge_{i=1}^{m} \mathbf{F}\langle \beta_i \rangle \quad (13)$$

iff

$$Circ(\mathcal{R}(P);P) \cup \mathcal{D} \models \mathbf{f} \Leftarrow \gamma \wedge \bigwedge_{i=1}^{n} \alpha_i \wedge \bigwedge_{i=1}^{m} \mathbf{f} \Leftarrow \beta_i. \quad (14)$$

Proof: We outline the proof for (11), and note that the proof for (13) is similar. Assume that (11) is false. Then, by Definition 4.2 and Lemma 4.3, there exists a Grand Permitted Set $\mathcal{P}$ such that condition (8) holds for all β_i, and condition (9) holds for all α_i but fails for γ. Thus, for γ, there exists some w_0 such that $\{w' \in W^* \mid w' \sqsupseteq w_0\} \in \mathcal{P}$ but $w_0, W^* \not\models \gamma$. Suppose we add the special nullary predicate **f** to the worlds of W^*, so that

$$\mathbf{h}^*(\mathbf{f})(w) = \{\langle \rangle\} \text{ iff } \{w' \in W^* \mid w' \sqsupseteq w\} \notin \mathcal{P}.$$

Then $w_0, W^* \models \alpha_i$ by (9), and $w_0, W^* \models \mathbf{f} \Leftarrow \beta_i$ by (8), but $w_0, W^* \not\models \gamma \vee \mathbf{f}$. Since **f** does not appear in $\mathcal{R}$ or $\mathcal{D}$, however, we still have a Kripke model for $Circ(\mathcal{R}(P);P) \cup \mathcal{D}$, and hence a countermodel to (12).

Conversely, assume that (12) is false. Then there exists a Kripke structure, J, in a language including **f** that satisfies $Circ(\mathcal{R}(P);P) \cup \mathcal{D}$ but falsifies the implication in (12) at some world w_0. Let τ be the unique homomorphism from J, with the **f**'s removed, into $\langle W^*, \sqsubseteq, \mathbf{h}^*, \mathbf{u}, \mathbf{o} \rangle$, and then add the **f**'s back to the worlds of W^* so that τ preserves $\mathbf{h}(\mathbf{f})$ as well. In addition, for those worlds of W^* that are not in the image of τ, add **f** to w whenever $w, W^* \models \beta_i$ for some i. (Note that this cannot affect $\tau(w_0)$, since $\tau(w_0), W^* \not\models \mathbf{f}$ and $\tau(w_0), W^* \not\models \beta_i$ for all i.) Now define a Grand Permitted Set $\mathcal{P}$ on W^* by setting

$$\{w' \in W^* \mid w' \sqsupseteq w\} \in \mathcal{P} \text{ iff}$$
$$w, W^* \models \alpha_i \text{ for } i = 1, \ldots, n, \text{ and } w, W^* \not\models \mathbf{f}.$$

It is straightforward to verify that this $\mathcal{P}$ provides a countermodel to (11) at $\tau(w_0)$. In particular, we have $\{w' \in W^* \mid w' \sqsupseteq \tau(w_0)\} \in \mathcal{P}$ by construction but $\tau(w_0), W^* \not\models \gamma$, and thus condition (9) fails for γ. □

The second theorem states that inferences about **O** are independent from inferences about **P**.

Theorem 4.8 *Assume that* $\mathbf{O}\langle \alpha_i \rangle$, $\mathbf{P}\langle \beta_i \rangle$ *and* $\mathbf{O}\langle \gamma \rangle$ *are deontic atoms with identical agents,* x. *Then*

$$\models \mathbf{O}\langle \gamma \rangle \Leftarrow \bigwedge_{i=1}^{n} \mathbf{O}\langle \alpha_i \rangle \wedge \bigwedge_{i=1}^{m} \mathbf{P}\langle \beta_i \rangle \quad (15)$$

iff

$$\models \mathbf{O}\langle \gamma \rangle \Leftarrow \bigwedge_{i=1}^{n} \mathbf{O}\langle \alpha_i \rangle. \quad (16)$$

Proof: It is obvious that (16) implies (15). For the converse, assume that (16) is false. Then there exists a Grand Permitted Set $\mathcal{P}_1$ such that condition (7) in Definition 4.2 holds for all α_i but fails for γ. Thus, for γ we have:

$$\exists V' : V' \in \mathcal{P}_1 \wedge \forall V : V' \subseteq V \longrightarrow V \notin \lceil \gamma \rceil. \quad (17)$$

Construct a new Grand Permitted Set by defining

$$\mathcal{P}_2 = \{V_1 \cap V_2 \mid V_1 \in \mathcal{P}_1, V_2 \in \lceil \beta_i \rceil \text{ for some } i\},$$

and then setting $\mathcal{P} = \mathcal{P}_1 \cup \mathcal{P}_2$. (Note: It is necessary to verify that $\mathcal{P}_2$ is a set of principal filters in W^*.) Using this new $\mathcal{P}$, we note that condition (5) in Definition 4.2 now holds for all β_i, and condition (7) still holds for all α_i. Moreover, condition (7) still fails for γ, since (17) obviously remains true when we replace $\mathcal{P}_1$ by $\mathcal{P}_1 \cup \mathcal{P}_2$. We have thus shown that (15) is false. □

These two theorems show that it is possible to construct a simplified proof theory for certain fragments of our language. If we use **O** and **F**, but not **P**, Theorem 4.7 shows that the most important inferences in the deontic language can be reduced to inferences in the action language, which can then be solved using the techniques of intuitionistic logic programming, as in [22, 23]. If we use **O** and **P**, but not **F**, Theorem 4.8 shows that we can compute the obligations first, and then compute the permissions independently, which turns out to be very simple. On the other hand, if we mix all three modalities in a single system, the situation is more complex. It is interesting to note that all the examples in Section 2 fall into one category or another, and there may be cognitive (and computational!) reasons why this is so. We will discuss these observations on the proof theory in the second part of this paper.

5 Discussion

In standard deontic logic [5], modalities are applied to propositions, but there have been several attempts to develop a deontic logic in which modalities are applied to actions, as in the present work. A natural approach is to combine deontic logic with dynamic logic [33, 10] or process logic [34], and the earliest example of this approach seems to be [16, 17]. Meyer, *et al.*, have investigated a variant of dynamic logic in which a special atom, **v**, is added to the language to denote a violation of the norms [30, 42], and they have shown that this system has some attractive properties as a deontic logic. A system proposed by van der Meyden, and shown to have a sound and complete proof theory in [27], is interesting because of the way it combines weak permission with free choice permission, but it does not seem to offer a natural concept of obligation. Another system, proposed by van der Meyden in [28], applies the techniques of logic programming to a deontic specification language, including the idea of a minimal model semantics and a least fixed-point operator.

An alternative approach, which is prominent in the philosophical literature, is to add the deontic operators to a language that already includes the modal action operator "see to it that," or *stit* [32, 4]. In such a language, we can say things like "the agent x is obligated to see to it that p," where p is any arbitrary proposition. The intuitions underlying such a modality are very different from the intuitions underlying dynamic logic, and even further removed from the intuitions underlying process logic. The focus, in *stit* theory, is on the goals that an agent is trying to achieve, whereas the focus in dynamic logic and process logic is on the trajectories of possible actions. The present paper clearly belongs in the latter camp: We can talk about agents achieving goals in our language, as in Examples 2.3 and 2.4, but these are derived concepts, not primitives.

It is unlikely that the merits of the various proposals for deontic logic will be judged on their semantics alone. More likely is an evaluation based on the utility of a particular formalism for the pragmatic tasks of common sense reasoning. For this, at a minimum, we need to look at the proof theory, and at the facilities for drawing nonmonotonic inferences. These topics will be discussed in the sequel.

References

[1] J. F. Allen and J. A. Koomen. Planning using a temporal world model. In *Proceedings, International Joint Conference on Artificial Intelligence*, pages 741–747, 1983.

[2] J.F. Allen. Towards a general theory of action and time. *Artificial Intelligence*, 23(2):123–154, 1984.

[3] C. Baral and M. Gelfond. Representing concurrent actions in extended logic programming. In *Proceedings of the Thirteenth International Joint Conference on Artificial Intelligence*, pages 866–871, 1993.

[4] N. Belnap and M. Perloff. Seeing to it that: A canonical form for agentives. *Theoria*, 54:175–199, 1988.

[5] B.F. Chellas. *Modal Logic: An Introduction*. Cambridge University Press, 1980.

[6] K.L. Clark. Negation as failure. In H. Gallaire and J. Minker, editors, *Logic and Data Bases*, pages 293–322. Plenum, 1978.

[7] M.C. Fitting. *Intuitionistic Logic, Model Theory and Forcing*. North-Holland, 1969.

[8] M. Gelfond and V. Lifschitz. The stable model semantics for logic programming. In *Proceedings, Fifth International Conference and Symposium on Logic Programming*, pages 1070–1080, 1988.

[9] M. Gelfond, V. Lifschitz, and A. Rabinov. What are the limitations of the situation calculus? In R. Boyer, editor, *Automated Reasoning: Essays in Honor of Woody Bledsoe*. Kluwer, 1991.

[10] D. Harel. *First-Order Dynamic Logic*. Springer-Verlag, 1979. LNCS No. 68.

[11] R.A. Kowalski and M.J. Sergot. A logic-based calculus of events. *New Generation Computing*, 4(1):67–95, 1986.

[12] V. Lifschitz. Computing circumscription. In *Proceedings of the Ninth International Joint Conference on Artificial Intelligence*, pages 121–127, 1985.

[13] F. Lin and Y. Shoham. Provably correct theories of actions (preliminary report). In *Proceedings of AAAI-91*, pages 349–354, 1991.

[14] F. Lin and Y. Shoham. Concurrent actions in the situation calculus. In *Proceedings of AAAI-92*, pages 590–595, 1992.

[15] J. McCarthy. Programs with common sense. In M. Minsky, editor, *Semantic Information Processing*, pages 403–418. MIT Press, 1968.

[16] L.T. McCarty. Permissions and obligations. In *Proceedings of the Eighth International Joint Conference on Artificial Intelligence*, pages 287–294, 1983.

[17] L.T. McCarty. Permissions and obligations: An informal introduction. In A.A. Martino and F. Socci Natali, editors, *Automated Analysis of Legal Texts: Logic, Informatics, Law*, pages 307–337. Elsevier North-Holland, 1986. Also available as Rutgers Technical Report LRP-TR-19.

[18] L.T. McCarty. Clausal intuitionistic logic. I. Fixed-point semantics. *Journal of Logic Programming*, 5(1):1–31, 1988.

[19] L.T. McCarty. Clausal intuitionistic logic. II. Tableau proof procedures. *Journal of Logic Programming*, 5(2):93–132, 1988.

[20] L.T. McCarty. A language for legal discourse. I. Basic features. In *Proceedings of the Second International Conference on Artificial Intelligence and Law*, pages 180–189. ACM Press, June 1989.

[21] L.T. McCarty. Circumscribing embedded implications (without stratifications). *Journal of Logic Programming*, 17:323–364, 1993.

[22] L.T. McCarty. Proving inductive properties of PROLOG programs in second-order intuitionistic logic. In *Proceedings, Tenth International Conference on Logic Programming*, pages 44–63. MIT Press, 1993.

[23] L.T. McCarty and L. Shklar. A PROLOG interpreter for first-order intuitionistic logic. Draft, 1993.

[24] L.T. McCarty and R. van der Meyden. Indefinite reasoning with definite rules. In *Proceedings of the Twelfth International Joint Conference on Artificial Intelligence*, pages 890–896, 1991.

[25] L.T. McCarty and R. van der Meyden. Reasoning about indefinite actions. In *Principles of Knowledge Representation and Reasoning: Proceedings of the Third International Conference (KR92)*, pages 59–70. Morgan Kaufmann, 1992.

[26] L.T. McCarty and R. van der Meyden. An intuitionistic interpretation of finite and infinite failure. In A. Nerode, editor, *Logic Programming and Non-Monotonic Reasoning: Proceedings of the Second International Workshop*, pages 417–436. MIT Press, 1993.

[27] R. van der Meyden. The dynamic logic of permission. In *Proceedings of the Symposium on Logic in Computer Science*, pages 72–78, Philadelphia, 1990.

[28] R. van der Meyden. A clausal logic for deontic action specification. In *Proceedings of the International Logic Programming Symposium*, pages 221–238, San Diego, 1991.

[29] R. van der Meyden. *The Complexity of Querying Indefinite Information: Defined relations, Recursion and Linear Order*. PhD thesis, Rutgers University, 1992.

[30] J.-J. Meyer. A different approach to deontic logic: Deontic logic viewed as a variant of dynamic logic. *Notre Dame Journal of Formal Logic*, 29:109–136, 1988.

[31] C.S. Peirce. *Collected Papers of Charles Sanders Peirce*, volume 6:522-528. Harvard University Press, 1931.

[32] I. Pörn. *Action Theory and Social Science: Some Formal Models*, volume 120 of *Synthese Library*. D. Reidel, 1977.

[33] V. Pratt. Semantical considerations on Floyd-Hoare logic. In *Proceedings, 17th IEEE Symposium on Foundations of Computer Science*, pages 109–121, 1976.

[34] V. Pratt. Process logic. In *Proceedings, 6th ACM Symposium on Principles of Programming Languages*, pages 93–100, 1979.

[35] V.R. Pratt. Action logic and pure induction. In *Workshop on Logics in AI*, pages 97–120. Springer LNCS No. 478, 1990.

[36] T.C. Przymusinski. Perfect model semantics. In *Proceedings, Fifth International Conference and Symposium on Logic Programming*, pages 1081–1096, 1988.

[37] R. Reiter. Circumscription implies predicate completion (sometimes). In *Proceedings of the Second National Conference on Artificial Intelligence*, pages 418–420, 1982.

[38] R. Reiter. On formalizing database updates: Preliminary report. In *Proceedings of the Third International Conference on Extending Database Technology*, 1992.

[39] A. Troelstra and D. van Dalen. *Constructivism in Mathematics: An Introduction*. North-Holland, 1988.

[40] M.H. van Emden and R.A. Kowalski. The semantics of predicate logic as a programming language. *Journal of the ACM*, 23(4):733–742, 1976.

[41] A. Van Gelder, K.A. Ross, and J.S. Schlipf. The well-founded semantics for general logic programs. *Journal of the ACM*, 38:620–650, 1991.

[42] R. Wieringa, J.-J. Meyer, and H. Wiegand. Specifying dynamic and deontic integrity constraints. *Data and Knowledge Engineering*, 4:157–189, 1989.

Generating Tests using Abduction

Sheila McIlraith
Department of Computer Science
University of Toronto
Toronto, M5S 1A4 Canada

Abstract

Suppose we are given a theory of system behavior and a set of candidate hypotheses. Our concern is with generating tests which will discriminate these hypotheses in some fashion. We logically characterize test generation as abductive reasoning. Aside from defining the theoretical principles underlying test generation, we are able to bring to bear the abundant research on abduction to show how test generation can be embodied in working systems. Furthermore, we address the issue of computational complexity. It has long been known that test generation is NP-complete. This is consistent with complexity results on the generation of abductive explanations. By syntactically restricting the description of our theory of system behavior or by limiting the completeness of our abductive reasoning, we are able to gain insight into tractable test generation problems.

1 INTRODUCTION

Diagnostic reasoning is often viewed as an iterative generate-and-test process. Given a description of a system together with observations of system behavior, a set of candidate diagnoses is produced which account for the observed behavior. From the set of candidate diagnoses, one or more tests is generated, executed and the observed behavior fed back into the diagnostic problem solver to determine a new set of candidate diagnoses. In this paper we specifically examine the task of test generation as it applies to hypothetical reasoning, and in particular to diagnosis.

Consider a set of hypotheses HYP which we entertain about some state of affairs represented by a first-order sentence Σ. We are concerned with generating tests to discriminate these hypotheses relative to some hypothetical reasoning goal. In a diagnosis setting, the hypotheses could represent potential diseases, the diagnostic goal, to eliminate a particular disease candidate from consideration and the tests, observations of symptoms or medical test results. In an active vision setting, the hypotheses could represent candidate interpretations for an object in a scene, the goal, to uniquely identify the object by candidate elimination and the tests, observation of new visual features resulting from a camera movement. Hypothetical reasoning covers a range of AI applications, all characterized by the objective of generating hypotheses and then distinguishing these hypotheses relative to some theory through the use of testing. Diagnosis, plan recognition, image understanding and aspects of natural language understanding are all instances of hypothetical reasoning problems.

Hardware designers have examined the problem of test generation for years. It is acknowledged to be computationally costly; even the problem of generating tests for simple combinational Boolean circuits is NP-complete (Ibarra and Sahni, 1975). Much of what is found in the traditional design literature is test generation algorithms for specific classes of digital circuits. These algorithms are not directly applicable to the diversity of test generation problems in hypothetical reasoning domains. In the AI test generation literature, the emphasis has also been on diagnosis of digital circuits. DART (Genesereth, 1984) and GDE (de Kleer and Williams, 1987) for example, both provide mechanisms for rudimentary test generation within their diagnostic frameworks. Much of the AI literature focuses on strategies to deal with complexity, such as the use of hierarchical designs (Shirley and Davis, 1983), (Genesereth, 1984), probabilities (de Kleer, 1991) and look-up tables (Meerwijk and Preist, 1992). Computational architectures have been proposed for generating tests for circuits (Shirley, 1986). Interestingly, there has been little to no formal analysis of the problem of test generation in the AI literature. Our objective is to move beyond the specific problem of testing digital circuits and to examine the general problem of test generation for hypothetical reasoning, including diagnosis.

In an earlier paper, McIlraith and Reiter (McIlraith and Reiter, 1992) provided a logical characterization of testing for hypothetical reasoning. They characterized tests in terms of the prime implicates $PI(\Sigma)$ of Σ. Since the ATMS computes (many) $PI(\Sigma)$ in generating diagnoses, it was shown that some propositional tests could simply be "read off" from $PI(\Sigma)$ with no further computation necessary. Many tests are thus generated *for free*. While a nice result for ATMS-based problem solvers, it is of limited use for hypothetical reasoning problem solvers that do not compute the prime implicates of Σ.

In this paper we take the logical characterization of tests introduced in (McIlraith and Reiter, 1992) and use it as a basis for examining the task of test generation. We augment and extend the framework to a first-order characterization. Then we recast test generation as abduction. In so doing, we are able to apply the abundant research on abduction to gain insight into the generation of tests. Specifically, we show how the theoretical characterization can be embodied in a variety of a different computational mechanisms. Finally, we examine the issue of complexity, gaining insight into tractable and intractable test generation problems.

2 PRELIMINARIES

We review and expand upon the testing framework provided in (McIlraith and Reiter, 1992). A fixed first-order language is assumed throughout. Σ will be a fixed sentence of the language, and will serve as the relevant background knowledge describing the system under analysis. For example, in the case of circuits, Σ might describe the individual circuit components, their normal input/output behavior, their fault models, the topology of their interconnections, and the legal combinations of circuit inputs (e.g. (de Kleer and Williams, 1987), (Reiter, 1987)). We also assume a fixed set HYP of hypotheses. In the case where Σ describes a circuit, HYP might be the set of diagnoses which we currently hold for this device. How we arrived at the set HYP will be largely irrelevant for our purposes. HYP could be a set of abductive hypotheses (Poole, 1989), the result of a consistency-based diagnostic procedure (de Kleer et al., 1992), or any other conceivable form of hypothesis generation. We make two assumptions about $H \in HYP$. The first assumption is that H be a conjunction of distinguished ground literals of the language. The second assumption is that the truth status of the hypotheses is unknown, i.e., $\forall H \in HYP, \Sigma \not\models H$ and $\Sigma \not\models \neg H$.

A test specifies certain initial conditions which may be established by the tester, together with an observation whose outcome in the physical world determines the test conclusions. The initial conditions must be consistent with the theory and with the current hypotheses being entertained. For example, in circuit diagnosis the initial conditions of a test might be the provision of certain fixed circuit inputs, and the observation might be the resulting value of a circuit output, or the value of an internal probe. In the medical setting, the initial conditions might involve performing a laboratory procedure like a blood test, and the observation might be the white cell count. In an active vision setting, the initial conditions might involve changing the camera angle or moving objects in the scene, and the observation might be some aspect of the corresponding image. Some tests do not dictate initial conditions. Such is the case when the test involves simply reading a sensor value or querying a user.

To provide a formal definition of a test, we distinguish a subset of ground literals of our language, called the *achievable literals*. These will specify the initial conditions for a test. In addition, we define a distinguished subset of the literals of our language called the *observables*. Thus, a test specifies some initial condition A which the tester establishes, and an observable o whose truth or instantiated value the tester is to determine from the physical world.

Definition 1 (Test) *A test is a pair (A, o) where A is a conjunction of achievable literals and o is an observable.*

We distinguish between two types of tests, **truth tests**, which tell us *whether* the observable is true in the physical world, and **value tests**, which tell us *what* instance of the observable is true in the physical world.

Definition 2 (Truth Test) *Let the observable o be a ground literal. A truth test is a test (A, o), whose outcome α is one of o, $\neg o$.*

$(blood\_test, hepatitis\_A\_virus)$ is an example of a truth test. As a result of performing $(blood\_test, hepatitis\_A\_virus)$ in the physical world, the truth value of $hepatitis\_A\_virus$ is established; the outcome of the test is either $hepatitis\_A\_virus$, otherwise $\neg hepatitis\_A\_virus$.

In contrast, a value test establishes the existence and truth status of an instance of the observable in the physical world.

Definition 3 (Value Test) *Let the observable o contain at least one uninstantiated variable. A value test is a test (A, o) whose outcome α is a ground literal o', the instantiation of the observable o, or its negation.*

An example of a value test would be $(\{\}, colour(object, X))$, where X is an uninstantiated variable. As a result of performing $(\{\}, colour(object, X))$ in the physical world, the outcome might be $colour(object, red)$, establishing the existence and truth value of a particular instance of the observable.

Definition 4 (Confirmation, Refutation) *The outcome α of the test (A, o) confirms $H \in HYP$ iff $\Sigma \wedge A \wedge H$ is satisfiable, and $\Sigma \wedge A \models H \supset \alpha$. α refutes H iff $\Sigma \wedge A \wedge H$ is satisfiable, and $\Sigma \wedge A \models H \supset \neg \alpha$.*

Not all conjunctions A of achievable literals will be legal initial conditions, for example simultaneously making a digital circuit input 0 and 1. Since Σ will encode constraints determining the legal initial conditions, we require that $\Sigma \wedge A$ be satisfiable. Moreover, hypothesis H could conceivably further constrain the possible initial conditions A permitted in a test. For example, the hypothesis that a patient is pregnant would prevent a test in which an x-ray is performed. In such a case, Σ would include a formula of the form $pregnant \supset \neg x\_ray$ so that $\Sigma \wedge pregnant \wedge x\_ray$ would be unsatisfiable, in which case the very idea of a confirming or refuting outcome of such a test would be meaningless.

(McIlraith and Reiter, 1992) show that a refuting test outcome allows us to reject H as a possible hypothesis, regardless of how we arrived at our space of hypotheses, HYP. A confirming test outcome is generally of no deterministic value except in the case where our space of hypotheses is defined abductively and HYP is comprised of all and only the hypotheses being considered. In such a case, it was shown that there is a duality between confirming and refuting tests and that a confirming test outcome has discriminatory power, eliminating hypotheses which do not explain it, by virtue of the definition of abductive hypothesis.

Discriminating tests are characterized as those tests (A, o) which are guaranteed to discriminate an hypothesis space HYP, i.e., which will refute at least one hypothesis in HYP, regardless of the test outcome.

Definition 5 (Discriminating Tests) *A test (A, o) is a discriminating test for the hypothesis space HYP iff $\Sigma \wedge A \wedge H$ is satisfiable for all $H \in HYP$ and there exists $H_i, H_j \in HYP$ such that the outcome α of test (A, o) refutes either H_i or H_j, no matter what that outcome might be.*

By definition, a discriminating test must refute at least one hypothesis in the hypothesis space.

Definition 6 (Minimal Discriminating Tests)
A discriminating test (A, o) for the hypothesis space HYP is minimal iff for no proper subconjunct A' of A is (A', o) a discriminating test for HYP.

Minimal discriminating tests preclude unnecessary initial conditions, for example unnecessary medical tests, camera movement, etc. Only those conditions necessary for producing the test outcome are invoked.

In many instances our theory will not provide us with discriminating tests. Relevant tests are those tests (A, o) which have the *potential* to discriminate an hypothesis space HYP, but which cannot be guaranteed to do so. Given a particular outcome α, a relevant test may refute a subset of the hypotheses in the hypothesis space HYP, but may not refute any hypotheses if $\neg \alpha$ is observed. Since there is no guarantee a priori of the outcome of a test, these tests are not guaranteed to discriminate an hypothesis space.

Definition 7 (Relevant Tests) *A test (A, o) is a relevant test for the hypothesis space HYP iff $\Sigma \wedge A \wedge H$ is satisfiable for all $H \in HYP$ and the outcome α of test (A, o) either confirms a subset of the hypotheses in HYP or refutes a subset.*

By definition, a relevant test confirms or refutes at least one hypothesis in HYP.

Definition 8 (Minimal Relevant Tests)
A relevant test (A, o) for the hypothesis space HYP is minimal iff for no proper subconjunct A' of A is (A', o) a relevant test for HYP.

Example 1. To illustrate, consider a simple medical diagnosis problem where we suspect that a patient is suffering from either mumps, measles, chicken pox or flu.

$HYP = \{mumps, measles, chicken\_pox, flu\}$
$\Sigma =$
$(measles \supset red\_spots) \wedge (chicken\_pox \supset red\_spots)$
$\wedge (mumps \supset swollen\_glands) \wedge (flu \supset fever)$

Both the hypothesis that the patient has measles and the hypothesis that the patient has chicken pox, infer the observation of red spots. However, neither the hypothesis that the patient has mumps or the hypothesis that the patient has the flu infer anything about the existence or lack of existence of red spots. As a result, the outcome of a test to observe red spots will only provide discriminatory information if we observe red_spots to be false. In such a case we can refute both $chicken\_pox$ and $measles$. However, if we observe red_spots to be true, we are unable to reject any of the four hypotheses. Thus, the test $(\{\}, red\_spots)$ is an example of a minimal relevant test. No discriminating test exists for our theory Σ and hypothesis space HYP.

(McIlraith and Reiter, 1992) further showed that if HYP contains all and only the hypotheses to be considered, and if the space of hypotheses is defined abductively, then every relevant test acts as a discriminating test. In our example above, if these conditions are met, then the outcome red_spots of the relevant test $(\{\}, red\_spots)$ would eliminate flu and $mumps$ since neither hypothesis abductively explains red_spots.

Example 2. Consider a bin-picking problem where a smart computer vision system is trying to identify fruit coming down a conveyor belt. The fruit is limited to apples, lemons, limes and bananas. Hypotheses are defined abductively.

$HYP =$
$\{is(object, apple), is(object, lemon), is(object, lime),$
$is(object, banana)\}$
$\Sigma =$
$(is(object, apple) \supset colour(object, red)) \wedge$
$(is(object, lemon) \supset colour(object, yellow)) \wedge$
$(is(object, lime) \supset colour(object, green)) \wedge$
$(is(object, banana) \supset colour(object, yellow)) \wedge$
$(is(object, apple) \oplus^1 is(object, lemon) \oplus$
$is(object, lime) \oplus is(object, banana))$

By performing the value test $colour(object, X)$ with outcome $colour(object, red)$, that one test would allow us to uniquely identify the object on the conveyor belt as an apple. In contrast, we might have had to perform a number of truth tests before arriving at the same hypothesis space.

Finally, there is an even weaker notion of a test which has the potential to provide further information about the hypothesis space, but which generally does not uniquely discriminate hypotheses.

Definition 9 (Constraining Test) *A test (A, o) is a constraining test for the hypothesis space HYP iff $\Sigma \wedge A \wedge H$ is satisfiable for all $H \in HYP$ and the outcome α of test (A, o) either confirms or refutes a conjunction of hypotheses drawn from HYP.*

A constraining test has the potential to further constrain or limit the hypothesis space, but not in itself eliminate any hypotheses, except in the limiting case. The limiting case occurs when the conjunction of hypotheses contains only one hypothesis. In such a case, a constraining test becomes a relevant test.

To illustrate the notion of a constraining test, consider $\Sigma \models H_1 \wedge H_2 \supset b$, and consider the test (A, b). If the outcome α of test (A, b) is $\neg b$, then $\Sigma \wedge A \wedge \neg b \models \neg H_1 \vee \neg H_2$. The outcome of the test constrains the hypothesis space and refutes the *conjunction* of hypotheses $H_1 \wedge H_2$. Although the test did not refute an individual hypothesis, it has provided further discriminatory information. Given this test outcome, if another test results in the refutation of $\neg H_1$ (i.e., the entailment of H_1), then the additional information from the constraining test (A, b) enables refutation of H_2 (i.e., the entailment of $\neg H_2$).

Proposition 1 (Test Relationships) *Every discriminating test is a relevant test. Every relevant test is a constraining test.*

---

[1] The connective $\oplus$ is used for notational brevity to indicate exclusive-or

3 TEST GENERATION AS ABDUCTION

Suppose we are given a theory of system behavior, a set of hypotheses, a set of achievables and a set of observables. The task is to generate a test, drawn from the set of achievables and observables which will meet some hypothetical reasoning objective. The objective could be to refute a particular hypothesis, to confirm a particular hypothesis, or simply to discriminate the space.

Intuitively, the generation of tests, particularly the generation of observable outcomes seems to be deductive in nature. Given a theory Σ and achievable A, conjoin the hypothesis H and predict observations. Test whether those observations are indeed true, and if they are false, refute H.

There are several problems with using deduction to generate tests. Theorem provers generally use resolution refutation to deduce whether or not a particular proposition is true, not to deduce what is true (i.e., all logical consequences of a theory). Furthermore, deduction alone does not resolve the problem of identifying both the achievables and the observables of a test.

A better formulation of test generation is as *theory formation*. Given Σ and the objective of generating a test to attempt to eliminate $H \in HYP$, what test could be conjoined to Σ to potentially refute H? (i.e., Find a test (A, o) with outcome α such that $\Sigma \wedge A \wedge \alpha \models \neg H$.)

The pattern of inference is easily recognized as **abduction**.
It is logically equivalent to finding a test (A, o) with outcome α such that $\Sigma \wedge A \wedge H \models \neg \alpha$.

In this section, we characterize test generation as abduction (Cox and Pietrzykowski, 1986), (Poole et al., 1987). We limit ourselves to the examination of truth tests, but the generation of value tests are a simple extension of these results. The sections to follow examine some practical benefits of this theoretical characterization.

Definition 10 (Abductive Explanation) *Given a first-order theory Σ and a ground literal obs, E, a conjunction of literals is an abductive explanation for obs iff $\Sigma \wedge E \models obs$ and $\Sigma \wedge E$ is satisfiable.*

Definition 11 (Min. Abductive Explanation)
E is a minimal abductive explanation for obs iff no proper subconjunct of E is an abductive explanation for obs.

Testing is performed to meet some hypothetical reasoning objective. Often the objective is simply to perform tests which will eliminate the maximum number of hypotheses. In other instances, it may be desirable to confirm a particular hypothesis, to refute a particular hypothesis or to discriminate (and thus eliminate) some subset of hypotheses in the hypothesis space HYP. The strategy for selecting the type of test to generate may depend on the user's or system's goals and objectives. It may be influenced by decision theoretic measures of utility such as the cost (in dollars, time or human terms) of computing or executing a test, the criticality of a particular hypothesis being true or false, information gain etc. Strategies for generating tests may also depend on probabilities relating to the expected outcome of a particular test or the probability that a particular hypothesis is true or false. We do not address these issues in this paper, but rather focus on the underlying task of test generation. We characterize the notion of confirmation and refutation in terms of abductive explanations. Further, we demonstrate how a variety of tests may be characterized and hence generated abductively. The following proposition is a direct result of Definition 4.

Proposition 2 (Confirmation, Refutation) *The outcome α of the test (A, o) confirms $H \in HYP$ iff $\Sigma \wedge A \wedge H$ is satisfiable, and $A \wedge \neg \alpha$ is an abductive explanation for $\neg H$. α refutes H iff $\Sigma \wedge A \wedge H$ is satisfiable, and $A \wedge \alpha$ is an abductive explanation for $\neg H$.*

Example 3. Returning to the axioms provided in Example 1, the outcome *red_spots* of the test $(\{\}, red\_spots)$ confirms *measles* and *chicken_pox* since $\neg red\_spots$ is an abductive explanation for both $\neg measles$ and $\neg chicken\_pox$. Similarly, the outcome $\neg swollen\_glands$ of the test $(\{\}, swollen\_glands)$ would refute *mumps* since $\neg swollen\_glands$ is an abductive explanation for $\neg mumps$.

If our objective is to establish the truth or falsity of a particular hypothesis $H_i \in HYP$, we ideally want to generate and perform a minimal individual discriminating tests. As a result of this test, we will know either H_i or $\neg H_i$. For example, we may want to establish whether or not a patient is suffering from the particularly virulent hepatitis A. In a vision application, we may want to pick out all the apples from a bowl of fruit. Both examples may be addressed by performing individual discriminating tests.

Theorem 1 (Individual Discriminating Tests)
(A, o) is an individual discriminating test for $H_i \in HYP$ iff

1. *$\Sigma \wedge A \wedge H$ is satisfiable $\forall H \in HYP$;*

2. *$A \wedge o$ is an abductive explanation for $\neg H_i$; $\Sigma \wedge A \not\models \neg H_i$;*

3. *$A \wedge \neg o$ is an abductive explanation for H_i; $\Sigma \wedge A \not\models H_i$.*

The condition that $\Sigma \wedge A \not\models \neg H_i$ and $\Sigma \wedge A \not\models H_i$

ensure that it is the observable and not the achievable which is refuting the hypotheses. Note that this condition is addressed through the use of minimal abductive explanations in every minimal test defined in this section.

Corollary 1 (Min. Ind. Discriminating Tests)
(A, o) is a minimal individual discriminating test for $H_i \in HYP$ iff

1. *$\Sigma \wedge A \wedge H$ is satisfiable $\forall H \in HYP$;*

2. *$A' \wedge o$ is a minimal abductive explanation for $\neg H_i$;*

3. *$A'' \wedge \neg o$ is a minimal abductive explanation for H_i;*

4. *$A = A' \wedge A''$.*

The following corollary also pertains to minimal individual discriminating tests.

Corollary 2 (Min. Ind. Discriminating Tests)
(A, o) is a minimal individual discriminating test for $H_i \in HYP$ iff

1. *$\Sigma \wedge A \wedge H$ is satisfiable $\forall H \in HYP$;*

2. *$A \wedge o \wedge \neg o$ is a minimal abductive explanation for $H_i \vee \neg H_i$.*

Condition 2 of Corollary 2 is trivial in the sense that $o \wedge \neg o$ is vacuously *false*, $H_i \vee \neg H_i$ is vacuously *true* and *false* $\supset$ *true*. However, this corollary will still be of assistance in computing minimal individual discriminating tests in the sections to follow.

Example 4. To illustrate the concepts in this section, we take liberties with our domain and extend the Σ described in Example 1 by conjoining the following three axioms:
$(hepatitis\_A \wedge blood\_test \supset hepatitis\_A\_virus) \wedge (\neg hepatitis\_A \wedge blood\_test \supset \neg hepatitis\_A\_virus) \wedge (mumps \supset \neg red\_spots) \wedge (hepatitis\_A \supset jaundice)$

$HYP = \{mumps, measles, chicken\_pox, flu, hepatitis\_A\}$

$(blood\_test, hepatitis\_A\_virus)$ is a minimal individual discriminating test for *hepatitis_A* since $blood\_test \wedge hepatitis\_A\_virus$ is a minimal abductive explanation for *hepatitis_A*, and $blood\_test \wedge \neg hepatitis\_A\_virus$ is a minimal abductive explanation for $\neg hepatitis\_A$.

As noted previously, many domains do not provide discriminating tests. In such cases, we must settle for a relevant test in order to attempt to eliminate hypotheses. Relevant tests are those tests which have the potential to discriminate an hypothesis space, but which cannot be guaranteed to do so since they only discriminate if α is observed, but not if $\neg \alpha$ is observed. In this instance we want to generate and perform an individual relevant test.

Theorem 2 (Individual Relevant Tests)
(A, o) is an individual relevant test for the hypothesis space HYP iff

1. $\Sigma \wedge A \wedge H$ is satisfiable $\forall H \in HYP$;

2. $A \wedge o$ is an abductive explanation for $\neg H_i$;
   $\Sigma \wedge A \not\models \neg H_i$.

Corollary 3 (Min. Ind. Relevant Tests)
(A, o) is a minimal individual relevant test for the hypothesis space HYP iff

1. $\Sigma \wedge A \wedge H$ is satisfiable $\forall H \in HYP$;

2. $A \wedge o$ is a minimal abductive explanation for $\neg H_i$.

Further to Example 4., $(\{\}, jaundice)$ is a minimal individual relevant test for the hypothesis $hepatitis\_A$, since $\neg jaundice$ is a minimal abductive explanation for $\neg hepatitis\_A$. A test outcome of $jaundice$ provides no discriminatory information. Recall again that when the space of hypotheses is defined abductively and when HYP represents all the hypotheses to be considered, then the observation of $jaundice$ would result in the elimination of all hypotheses in HYP except $hepatitis\_A$, since it is the only hypothesis which explains the observation of $jaundice$.

Unless we are interested in focusing on a particular hypothesis, our testing objective will likely be to perform tests which refute a maximum number of hypotheses in the hypothesis space. Ideally we want to generate minimal discriminating tests because they guarantee that the outcome, when conjoined to Σ will refute at least one hypothesis in HYP.

Theorem 3 (Discriminating Tests)
(A, o) is a discriminating test for the hypothesis space HYP iff

1. $\Sigma \wedge A \wedge H$ is satisfiable $\forall H \in HYP$;

2. $\exists H_i \in HYP$ such that $A \wedge o$ is an abductive explanation for $\neg H_i$; $\Sigma \wedge A \not\models \neg H_i$;

3. $\exists H_j \in HYP$ such that $A \wedge \neg o$ is an abductive explanation for $\neg H_j$; $\Sigma \wedge A \not\models \neg H_j$.

Corollary 4 (Minimal Discriminating Tests)
(A, o) is a minimal discriminating test for the hypothesis space HYP iff

1. $\Sigma \wedge A \wedge H$ is satisfiable $\forall H \in HYP$;

2. $\exists H_i \in HYP$ such that $A' \wedge o$ is a minimal abductive explanation for $\neg H_i$;

3. $\exists H_j \in HYP$ such that $A'' \wedge \neg o$ is a minimal abductive explanation for $\neg H_j$;

4. $A = A' \wedge A''$.

Again, when discriminating tests do not exist or are not achievable, relevant tests are the next best alternative.

Theorem 4 (Relevant Tests)
(A, o) is a relevant test for the hypothesis space HYP iff

1. $\Sigma \wedge A \wedge H$ is satisfiable $\forall H \in HYP$;

2. $\exists H_i \in HYP$ such that $A \wedge o$ is an abductive explanation for $\neg H_i$; $\Sigma \wedge A \not\models \neg H_i$.

The definition of minimal relevant test follows from the theorem above, as per Corollary 2.

Finally, if no relevant test exists or is unachievable, a constraining test may be desirable.

Theorem 5 (Constraining Tests)
(A, o) is a constraining test for the hypothesis space HYP iff

1. $\Sigma \wedge A \wedge H$ is satisfiable $\forall H \in HYP$;

2. $A \wedge o$ is an abductive explanation for $\bigvee_{H_i \in HYP} \neg H_i$;

3. $\Sigma \wedge A \not\models \bigvee_{H_i \in HYP} \neg H_i$.

We add the third condition to eliminate both the case where the test achievable alone causes the conjunction of hypotheses to be refuted and the case where the conjunction of hypotheses is already refuted by Σ. For example, if our theory states that H_i and H_j are mutually exclusive (i.e., $\neg(H_i \wedge H_j)$) then no test is needed to discriminate them. If condition 3 is violated, then a constraining test must be designed using a subset of HYP for which condition 3 holds.

Corollary 5 (Minimal Constraining Tests)
(A, o) is a minimal constraining test for the hypothesis space HYP iff

1. $\Sigma \wedge A \wedge H$ is satisfiable $\forall H \in HYP$;

2. $A \wedge o$ is a minimal abductive explanation for $\bigvee_{H_i \in HYP} \neg H_i$.

4 PRACTICAL BENEFITS

There are many benefits to formal specification of a reasoning task. Primarily, it provides a non-procedural specification of the task from which meta-theoretic properties may be proven. From it, we are able to assess the impact of assumptions, of syntactic restrictions etc. Furthermore, it enables us to realize the task relative to the specification and to establish correctness proofs for our algorithms. In this particular instance, we are fortunate that we have characterized test generation in terms of abduction, an inference procedure that boasts a large body of research. As a result, we are able to immediately exploit research in abduction to gain valuable insight into test generation.

Here, we examine two issues: the mechanization of test generation and tractable abductive test generation.

4.1 MECHANIZING TEST GENERATION

By characterizing test generation as abduction we may employ existing abductive reasoning mechanisms to generate tests. In this section we propose several different approaches for generating tests abductively using theorem proving techniques. Some of the mechanisms are propositional, while others are first order. Recall that a first-order theory of finite domain can be transformed into a propositional theory; thus enabling the use of propositional machinery.

The general problem of abductive test generation is to find a test (A, o) satisfying a logical formula of the form $\Sigma \wedge A \wedge O \vdash X$, where O represents o or $\neg o$ and X represents an individual (negated) hypothesis or a disjunction of negated hypotheses. O and X are determined by the type of test and are specified in Theorems 1-5 and Corollaries 1-5 of the previous section. For example, when generating an individual relevant test, as specified in Theorem 2, O would be o and X would be $\neg H_i$.

By Proposition 1, we know that every discriminating test is a relevant test and that every relevant test is a constraining test. Thus, the various tests can be generated from a basic core. If we are interested in individual tests to refute H_i, then we can try to find a minimal individual relevant test which provides an abductive explanation for $\neg H_i$, as per Corollary 3. The resulting test (A, o) may then be examined to see whether it can satisfy the further requirements of a minimal individual discriminating test. Alternatively, we can use Corollary 2 to attempt to generate an individual discriminating test which provides an abductive explanation for $H_i \vee \neg H_i$, but unlike the previous strategy, if this attempt fails we have no test to fall back on.

To eliminate random hypotheses drawn from HYP, a strategy which minimizes the possibility of producing no test is to employ the criteria of Corollary 5 to generate a minimal constraining test and then examine whether it fulfills the more stringent requirements of a minimal relevant test or a minimal discriminating test (Corollary 4).

In order to compute tests, we must perform both consistency testing and actual generation of the abductive explanations. For formula F, $\Sigma \cup F$ is consistent iff $\Sigma \not\vdash \neg F$. First-order logic is semi-decidable. (i.e., Given first-order proof theory and a closed formula, a proof will be found if the formula is valid, but the proof procedure may not terminate if the formula is not valid.) Consequently, there is no decision procedure for determining the consistency of first-order formulae in general. Fortunately, there are decidable first-order theories. In particular, first-order Horn theories without function symbols are decidable. Similarly, some applications with finite domains may be rewritten as propositional theories, which are decidable. If all else fails, consistency checking can be approximated. For example, if after a certain outlay of resources the formulae have not been proven to be inconsistent, then assume that they are consistent. It is up to the developer of an individual application to ensure that consistency checking is decidable either by syntactic restrictions on Σ or by using some reasonable approximation of consistency checking.

The problem of finding an abductive explanation $A \wedge O$ for X may be computed in several different ways. By recasting the problem $\Sigma \wedge A \wedge O \vdash X$ using the deduction theorem, we can categorize the different approaches to generating abductive explanations.

- Proof-tree completion
  - $\Sigma \wedge A \wedge O \wedge \neg X \vdash \bot$,
- Direct-proof method
  - $\Sigma \vdash A \wedge O \supset X$,
  - $\Sigma \wedge \neg X \vdash \neg A \vee \neg O$,
- Model Generation[2]
  - $\Sigma^* \wedge X \vdash \bigvee_i O_i$.

Recall that X and O are defined as per Theorems 1–5 and Corollaries 1–5, and are limited by the restrictions of the specific computational machinery.

4.1.1 Proof-tree Completion

$\Sigma \wedge A \wedge O \vdash X$ is equivalent to $\Sigma \wedge A \wedge O \wedge \neg X \vdash \bot$. As such, the problem of generating an abductive explanation for X may be recast as finding a refutation proof for X which employs literals drawn from a distinguished set of achievables and observables. Currently the most popular mechanism for computing abductive explanations, this technique is often referred to as *proof-tree completion*.

To generate tests, Σ and $\neg X$ may be conjoined and converted to clausal form. Linear resolution may be used to attempt to derive $\bot$. The proof will fail, but will result in so-called *dead ends*. If these dead ends can resolve with achievables and observables to derive $\bot$ then the minimal achievables and observables required for the proof constitute an abductive explanation for X and may constitute a test if they adhere to the specific test criteria defined in Theorems 1-5 or Corollaries 1-5.

Example 5. Returning to Example 4, in order to find at least a minimal constraining test

---
[2]Severe restriciotns apply. See Section 4.1.3.

for HYP given Σ, we must convert Σ to clausal form and conjoin $\neg \bigvee_{H_i \in HYP} \neg H_i$. Thus, we conjoin $\neg(\neg mumps \vee \neg measles \vee \neg chicken\_pox \vee \neg flu \vee \neg hepatitis\_A)$ (which is equivalent to $mumps \wedge measles \wedge chicken\_pox \wedge flu \wedge hepatitis\_A$) to Σ. The proof will terminate at several dead ends including red_spots, $\neg red\_spots$, $swollen\_glands$ etc. The addition of any of these observables would complete the proof, but only the observable red_spots will fulfill the criteria for a minimal discriminating test defined in Corollary 4. Thus, $(\{\}, red\_spots)$ is a minimal discriminating test for Σ and HYP.

There are several proof-tree-completion-style abductive inference engines (e.g., (Pople, 1973), (Cox and Pietrzykowski, 1986), (Cox and Pietrzykowski, 1987), (Poole, 1988), (Poole et al., 1987)). The Theorist framework (Poole, 1989) is one such engine, but the implementation differs slightly in that the distinguished explanation literals (achievables and observables, in our case) are added to Σ a priori and rather than deriving dead ends, Theorist merely notes the distinguished explanation literals which were employed in the refutation proof.

The available implementation of Theorist provides a more sophisticated development environment for users to perform both abductive explanation and prediction. The prediction facilities, like our deductive theorem provers tell us whether or not a particular formula is true, not *what* formulae are true. Theorist classifies user-provided formulae as *Facts*, *Defaults*, *Conjectures* and *Observations*. Both *Defaults* and *Conjectures* are used to generate abductive *Explanations* for *Observations*. *Defaults* are also used for prediction.

There are several ways in which the Theorist development environment may be employed to generate tests. The simplest way is to define achievables and observables as *Conjectures* and to use them to generate abductive explanations for a user-supplied X as per Theorems 1–5 and Corollaries 1–5. Alternatively, the Theorist environment could be modified to enable test generation to occur in conjunction with hypothesis generation. It would require the creation of a new set of user-provided formulae called *Conjecturable-tests*, which would contain either achievables and observables, or predefined tests. Taking advantage of the abductive explanation generation machinery already in place, Theorist could take the set of *Explanations* (hypotheses equivalent to HYP) and generate abductive explanations drawn from *Conjecturable-tests* as per Theorems 1–5 and Corollaries 1–5. This would provide the tests to discriminate the original hypothesis space *Explanations* and enable hypothesis generation and test generation to be performed simultaneously.

Finally, off related interest, Sattar and Goebel (Sattar and Goebel, 1991) provided a mechanism within the Theorist system for recognizing so-called *crucial literals* which provides a basis for identifying discriminating tests of the form $(\{\}, o)$. They compute the crucial literals using consistency trees.

4.1.2 Direct-proof Method

Aside from proof-tree completion, there are several ways of generating tests using a direct proof method. The term *direct proof method* is often used to refer to the task of *consequence finding* – finding the consequences of a theory. $\Sigma \wedge A \wedge O \vdash X$ may be recast as both $\Sigma \vdash A \wedge O \supset X$ and $\Sigma \wedge \neg X \vdash \neg A \vee \neg O$ (assuming $\Sigma \wedge \neg X$ is consistent). In both cases, tests may be found from the logical consequences of Σ and $\Sigma \wedge \neg X$, respectively. Unfortunately, while resolution is refutation complete (complete for proof-finding), it is not deductively complete and so does not find all the logical consequences of a theory.

Fortunately, in the case of test generation, we are only interested in a subset of the logical consequences of our theories. Specifically, we want the minimal[3] clauses of the form $\neg A \vee \neg O \vee X$ and $\neg A \vee \neg O$ respectively, and we don't need them all, unless we want to select the *best* tests. Recent advances have been made in developing complete consequence-finding theorem provers for first-order and propositional theories. In particular, Inoue (Inoue, 1991) has developed a complete resolution procedure for consequence-finding, generalized to finding only interesting clauses having certain properties. A set of so-called *characteristic clauses* can be defined to specify both a set of distinguished literals from which the characteristic clauses must be drawn and any other conditions to be satisfied. In our case, the characteristic clauses would be of the form $\neg A \vee \neg O \vee X$ and $\neg A \vee \neg O$ respectively. The augmentation of the theorem prover with a skip rule allows it to focus on generating only the characteristic clauses, rather than generating all minimal logical consequences and further pruning to retrieve the desired subset of clauses. Following Theorems 1–5 and Corollaries 1–5, we can then use such a consequence-finding system to generate tests.

The RESIDUE system (Finger and Genesereth, 1985) used in the implementation of Genesereth's well-known Design Automated Reasoning Tool (DART) is also a first-order consequence-finding procedure; however, RESIDUE does not focus search as extensively as Inoue's system (Inoue, 1991). RESIDUE was employed in DART to generate potential diagnosis candidates by direct proof, and was also used for rudimentary test generation.

When dealing with propositional theories, the task of finding the minimal logical consequences of a theory is by definition equivalent to computing the prime implicates of that theory.

---
[3] We use the term minimal as per Definition 11.

Definition 12 (Prime implicates) C is a prime implicate for Σ iff $\Sigma \models C$, and for no proper subset C' of C does $\Sigma \models C'$

At the core of the well-known assumption-based truth maintenance system (ATMS) (de Kleer, 1986) is the computation of certain prime implicates of a propositional Horn theory, Σ (Reiter and de Kleer, 1987). Thus, the ATMS contains a propositional consequence-finding procedure for Σ. In this discussion, we refer to the ATMS in the broadest context, to include its extensions beyond Horn theories, to include probabilistic focusing and to include those systems which compute prime implicates incrementally (Kean and Tsiknis, 1990).

The ATMS identifies a distinguished set of literals called *assumptions* which act as the primitive abducible literals for production of abductive explanations. (McIlraith and Reiter, 1992) identified one way of acquiring certain tests from the side effects of the ATMS's computations for generating diagnoses, H_i. Since the ATMS calculates prime implicates of Σ of the form $H_i \supset o$, some tests of the form $(\{\}, o)$ would be generated *for free* through the normal operation of the ATMS. In order to actually *generate* tests using the ATMS, we take advantage of the fact that the ATMS is an abduction engine and make the achievables and observables *assumptions*. This is almost like operating the ATMS backwards. Rather than diagnostic candidates being the abductive explanations for observations, the tests are the abductive explanations for refutable hypotheses. Tests are those (A, o) for which $A \wedge O \supset X$ is a prime implicate of Σ and (A, o) satisfies all other criteria specified for the test.

Depending upon the application, there may be many achievables and observables and this may not be the most efficient mode of test generation. On a positive note, tests are generally composed of one observable and a minimal number of achievables, so the potential for an exponential number of environments is limited. This, along with probabilistic focusing of the ATMS may make the ATMS or one its generalizations a viable mechanism for test generation.

4.1.3 Model Generation

We mention this last approach to abductive test generation only to be thorough, because it is of very limited use in practical test generation applications. Model generation (e.g., Satchmo (Manthey and Bry, 1988),(Denecker and de Schreye, 1992)) and model finding techniques (e.g., GSAT (Selman et al., 1992) may be used to generate abductive hypotheses in limited cases. Console et al. (Console et al., 1991) showed that abductive explanations could be generated deductively from the Clark's completion Σ^* of a causal Horn theory Σ. By augmenting a causal Horn theory with completion axioms, we explicitly provide that a particular effect, e entails a disjunction of possible causes, c_i, i.e., $\Sigma^* \wedge e \vdash \bigvee_i c_i$. The causes, c_i can be determined by generating the minimal models of $\Sigma^* \wedge e$.

These results may be applied to a very restricted class of test generation problems. In particular, those problems for which tests are restricted to $(\{\}, o)$ and for which completion of the theory can be computed with respect to the refutation of causes, not with respect to the potential effects. Specifically, the completion axioms would state that a particular refuted hypothesis (not_H_i) implied a disjunction of possible test outcomes $o_1 \vee not\_o_2 \vee \ldots o_n$. In order to compute a test to refute the hypothesis H_i, the set of minimal models for $\Sigma^* \wedge not\_H_i$ would be computed using a model generator. The tests $(\{\}, o)$ would be the distinguished literals o_i retrieved from the minimal models.

This approach seems both awkward and impractical. A better proposal for producing tests via model generation is to generate the model for Horn theory $\Sigma \wedge \neg X$. Tests of the form $(\{\}, o)$ could then be retrieved as the distinguished observables of the minimal Herbrand model.

4.2 TRACTABLE TEST GENERATION

From the computer hardware literature, we know that the general problem of test generation, even for simple combinational Boolean circuits is NP-complete (Ibarra and Sahni, 1975). Similarly, we know that finding an abductive explanation in the general case is NP-hard (Selman, 1990). The challenge with computationally hard problems is either to attempt to deal with the worst-case complexity by employing problem-specific strategies such as probabilistic focusing of algorithms or alternatively to define tractable classes of the problem. Tractable classes may often be achieved by limiting the expressive power of a theory, or by limiting the completeness of reasoning. In the abduction research, there are a few simple classes of tractable abduction problems. In this section, we examine the complexity results on abduction to attempt to provide insight into classes of tractable tests generation problems.

In defining tractable abductive test generation problems, we may avail ourselves of certain properties of test generation that occur generally or in certain hypothetical reasoning domains. They are as follows:

1. **There is no need to generate all tests**
   In generating tests, there is always a trade-off between the cost of computing tests and the cost of performing tests. In many instances, the cost of performing a test is cheap while the generation of tests is expensive. Consequently, we need not calculate *all* tests or even the best test. Computing any relevant test is generally of value.

2. **Some application tests are limited to $(\{\}, o)$**
   There are many application domains for which

tests require no achievable literals. This issue was discussed in (McIlraith and Reiter, 1992). For example, some applications have a great deal of sensor data available. It is the job of test generation to select which sensor data to "observe"; no achievable preconditions are required. In other domains, tests of the form $(\{\}, o)$ may be performed by simply querying the user as to the truth value of the test proposition o. This may be the case for certain medical diagnosis problems or when performing certain natural language understanding tasks.

3. **An exponential number of tests is unlikely**
   Many tests are composed of one observable literal and few if any achievable literals. As such, the number of minimal tests generated as abductive explanations is unlikely to be exponential in the number of observables and achievables.

Selman (Selman, 1990), Levesque (Levesque, 1989) and Bylander et al. (Bylander et al., 1991) have all defined classes of tractable abductive reasoning problems. There are some gaps in the complexity results that need to be filled in to deal fully with test generation, however from the existing results we can gain some insight into what makes test generation problems tractable, or for that matter, intractable.

Complexity results for abduction are often based on the ATMS. Consequently, the term *assumption* refers to the distinguished set of literals from which explanations are composed. It is equivalent to our set of observable and achievable literals when abduction is applied to test generation.

It has long been known that there may be exponentially many abductive explanations for a given literal ((McAllester, 1985), (de Kleer, 1986)) and so listing them all would take exponential time. For test generation, we are often uninterested in listing all tests as explained by Property 1 above. Even if we were, by Property 3, we would be unlikely to have an exponential number of tests. Assuming, there are not an exponential number of tests, we proceed to define certain complexity results for test generation, viewed as an abductive task.

Selman (Selman, 1990) states that the problem of generating abductive explanations for theories composed of arbitrary clauses is NP-hard, because of the consistency check on Σ. Consequently it follows directly from (Selman, 1990) that:

Proposition 3 *If Σ is a conjunction of arbitrary clauses, the problem of generating a test is NP-hard.*

We would hope that the story would be better for Horn clause theories. Selman further shows that even when Σ is composed of Horn clauses, that finding an abductive explanation for a letter q, where the explanation must be derived from a set of assumptions, is NP-hard. This seems discouraging, but upon analysis of the complexity proof, we see some hope. The proof is based upon a reduction from the NP-complete decision problem "path with forbidden pairs." In this instance, the forbidden pairs are mutually incompatible assumptions drawn from our assumption set. It would appear that if we got rid of the problem of forbidden pairs, that the complexity problem would be resolved. This indeed appears to be the case.

Bylander et al. (Bylander et al., 1991) define the class of *independent abduction problems*. This class of problems has a polynomial time algorithm for finding an explanation, if one exists. The trick is to get rid of Selman's forbidden pairs – to ensure that no assumptions are mutually incompatible in the one instance and to then additionally ensure that there are no cancellation interactions among the assumptions.

If our tests are composed of single literals, then we don't have to concern ourselves with the compatibility of achievables/observables. Property 2 shows that this is a reasonable assumption for tests in certain application domains. Following (Bylander et al., 1991), we show that:

Proposition 4 *If Σ is a conjunction of Horn clauses and tests are of the form $(\{\}, o)$, then a test may be generated in polynomial time, if such a test exists*

This follows directly from the results in (Bylander et al., 1991).

For the general case, the question remains as to whether it seems reasonable to assume that no achievables/observables are mutually incompatible. Note that achievables/observables S_1 and S_2 are defined to be mutually incompatible iff $\Sigma \models \neg (S_1 \wedge S_2)$.

To be able to assume no mutually incompatible achievables/observables, we would have to assume that for every achievable A_i and observable o_i that $\Sigma \not\models \neg (A_1 \wedge A_2)$, $\Sigma \not\models \neg (o_1 \wedge o_2)$ and $\Sigma \not\models \neg (A_1 \wedge o_1)$. While it may be possible to make this assumption in specific instances, it is unlikely to be true in the general case. In circuit diagnosis for example, let A_1 be *input = 1*, A_2 be *input = 0*, obviously $\Sigma \models \neg(A_1 \wedge A_2)$. Similarly, since observations can generally be positive and negative literals, if we let $o_1 = \neg o_2$ then $\Sigma \models \neg (o_1 \wedge o_2)$. We state the following proposition for those situations where there are no mutually incompatible achievables/observables.

Proposition 5 *If Σ is a conjunction of Horn clauses and no two literals drawn from the set of achievable and observable literals are mutually incompatible with respect to Σ, then a test may be generated in polynomial time, if such a test exists.*

Finally, Levesque (Levesque, 1989) and Selman (Selman, 1990) define a linear time algorithm for finding certain explanations of a literal from Horn clause theories. Although motivated by different concerns, their algorithm and results are virtually the same. The explanations produced are those that are *explicitly* represented (Levesque, 1989) in Σ. Further, it is not required that they be drawn from a set of distinguished literals.

The algorithm searches through the clauses of Σ to find clauses containing the literal q, the literal to be explained. The negation of the other literals in the clause form the explanations. For example, if $\neg H$ is to be explained and $x \vee y \vee \neg H$ is a clause in Σ, then the abductive explanation $\neg x \wedge \neg y$ would be found in linear time. Levesque proposes using this algorithm to define a form of limited abductive reasoning in which explicit explanations are determined first, followed by a chaining process to find implicit explanations.

These results tell us that if we have tests (A, o) explicitly represented in Σ as $\neg A \vee \neg o \vee \neg H_i$, then they can be found in linear time, (along with other extraneous explanations that do not contain the desired distinguished literals and thus are not tests per se). Simple *causal theories* where clauses in Σ are of the form *hypothesis* $\supset$ *observable* (e.g., *disease* $\supset$ *symptom*) would contain such explicit tests. This is an argument in favor of encoding or even caching tests explicitly in a theory to make them computationally easy to generate (Meerwijk and Preist, 1992).

Definition 13 (Explicit test) (A, o) *is an explicit test to potentially refute* $H \in HYP$ *if* $\neg A \vee \neg o \vee \neg H$ *is a clause in* Σ.

Proposition 6 *If* Σ *is a conjunction of Horn clauses, an explicit test may be generated in linear time, if such a test exists.*

This follows from results in (Levesque, 1989) and (Selman, 1990).

5 SUMMARY

We provide three main contributions towards research in test generation. First, we characterize test generation as abductive reasoning. As a consequence, we are able to define the notions of discriminating tests, relevant tests, individual discriminating and relevant tests, and constraining tests all in terms of abductive explanation. We then outline a variety of approaches to abductive reasoning which can be modified and employed to perform test generation. Finally, we examine the research on tractable abductive reasoning to gain insight into tractable and intractable test generation problems.

This paper provides both a theoretical and computational framework for test generation, which is lacking in the test generation literature. From this framework and some of the proposed procedures for test generation, there is opportunity for experimental work to analyze the efficacy in practice of some of these alternative approaches to test generation.

Acknowledgements

We would like to thank the following people who contributed towards the development or improvement of this work: Ray Reiter, Chris Preist, David Poole, Mike Gruninger and Javier Pinto. We also acknowledge the generous support of Alberta Research Council and the Natural Science and Engineering Research Council.

References

T. Bylander, D. Allemang, M. Tanner and J. Josephson (1991). The computational complexity of abduction, *Artificial Intelligence Journal* **49**:25–60.

L. Console, D. Theseider Dupre and P. Torasso (1991). On the relationship between abduction and deduction, *Journal of Logic and Computation* **1**(5):661–690.

P. Cox and T. Pietrzykowski (1986). Causes for events: their computation and applications, *Eighth International Conference on Automated Deduction*, 608–621.

P. Cox and T. Pietrzykowski (1987). General diagnosis by abductive inference, in *Proceedings of the IEEE Symposium on Logic Programming*, 183–189.

J. de Kleer (1986). An assumption-based TMS, in *Artificial Intelligence Journal* **28**:127–162.

J. de Kleer (1991). Focusing on probable diagnoses, in *Proceedings of the National Conference on Artificial Intelligence (AAAI-91)*, 842–848.

J. de Kleer and A. Mackworth and R. Reiter (1992). Characterizing diagnoses and systems, in *Artificial Intelligence Journal* **56**:197–222.

J. de Kleer and B. Williams (1987). Diagnosing multiple faults, in *Artificial Intelligence Journal* **32**:97–130.

M. Denecker and D. de Schreye (1992). On the duality of abduction and model generation, in *Proceedings of the Fifth Generation Computer Systems Conference (FGCS-92)*, 650–657.

J. Finger and M. Genesereth (1985). RESIDUE: a deductive approach to design synthesis, Technical Report No. HPP-85-5, Department of Computer Science, Stanford University, CA.

M. Genesereth (1984). The use of design descriptions in automated diagnosis, in *Artificial Intelligence Journal* **24**:411–436.

O. Ibarra and S. Sahni (1975). Polynomially complete fault detection problems, in *IEEE Transactions on Computers* **24**(3):242–249.

K. Inoue (1991). Consequence-finding based on ordered linear resolution, in *Proceedings of the Twelfth International Joint Conference on Artificial Intelligence (IJCAI-91)*, 158–164.

A. Kean and G. Tsiknis (1990). An incremental method of generating prime implicants/implicates, in *Journal of Symbolic Computing* **9**:185–206.

H. Levesque (1989). A knowledge-level account of abduction, in *Proceedings of the Eleventh International Joint Conference on Artificial Intelligence* 1061–1067.

R. Manthey and F. Bry (1988). SATCHMO: a theorem prover implemented in Prolog, in *Ninth International Conference on Automated Deduction*.

D. McAllester (1985). A widely used truth-maintenance system, AI-lab Memo Department of Computer Science, MIT Cambridge, MA.

S. McIlraith and R. Reiter (1992). On tests for hypothetical reasoning, in W. Hamscher, L. Console and J. de Kleer, editors, *Readings in model-based diagnosis*, 89–96. Morgan Kaufmann Publishers, San Mateo, CA.

A. Meerwijk and C. Preist (1992). Using multiple tests for model-based diagnosis, in *Proceedings of the Third International Workshop on Principles of Diagnosis*, 30–39, Orcas Island, Washington, USA.

D. Poole (1988). A logical framework for default reasoning, in *Artificial Intelligence Journal* **36**(1):27–47.

D. Poole (1989). Explanation and prediction: an architecture for default and abductive Reasoning, in *Computational Intelligence* **5**:97–110.

D. Poole and R. Goebel and R. Aleliunas (1987). Theorist: a logical reasoning system for defaults and diagnosis, in N. Cercone and G. McCalla, editors, *The Knowledge Frontier: Essays in the Representation of Knowledge*, 331–352, Springer Verlag.

H. Pople (1973). On the mechanization of abductive logic, in *Proceedings of the Third International Joint Conference on Artificial Intelligence (IJCAI-73)*, 147–152.

R. Reiter (1987). A theory of diagnosis from first principles. *Artificial Intelligence Journal* **32**:57–95.

R. Reiter and J. de Kleer (1987). Foundations for assumption-based truth maintenance systems: preliminary report, *Proceedings of the National Conference on Artificial Intelligence (AAAI-87)*,183–188.

A. Sattar and R. Goebel (1991). Using crucial literals to select better theories, in *Computational Intelligence* **7**(1):11–22.

B. Selman (1990). Tractable default reasoning. Ph.D. Thesis, Department of Computer Science, University of Toronto, Canada.

M. Shirley (1986). Generating tests by exploiting designed behavior, in *Proceedings of the National Conference on Artificial Intelligence (AAAI-86)* 884–890.

M. Shirley and R. Davis (1983). Generating distinguishing tests based on hierarchical models and symptom information. in *Proceedings International Conference on Computer Design*.

Preferential entailments for circumscriptions

Yves Moinard
IRISA, Campus de Beaulieu
35042 RENNES-Cedex FRANCE
tel.: (33) 99 84 73 13
E-mail: moinard@irisa.fr

Raymond Rolland
IRMAR, Campus de Beaulieu
35042 RENNES-Cedex FRANCE
tel.: (33) 99 28 60 19
E-mail: Raymond.Rolland@univ-rennes1.fr

Abstract

The notion of preferential entailment has emerged as a generalization of circumscription. The important properties of this notion are investigated, and they are applied to various "concrete" examples of circumscription. We study only "classical" preferential entailment, i.e. the underlying logic is classical. The equivalence between the two notions of preferential entailment and of circumscription is made precise. The two other main contributions of this text are a complete study of cumulativity with respect to well-foundedness, even for preferential entailments based on non transitive preference relations, and the description of "reverse monotony", which is a fundamental property of circumscriptions.

1 Introduction

We begin with a reminder about preferential entailment. We need preference relations which enjoy none of the properties which are generally considerered as necessary. For example, we need to consider relations which are not transitive or which are neither antireflexive nor antisymetrical if we want to encompass the various existing circumscriptions. However, all the preference relations examined in this text are natural and simple, besides of being useful in artificial intelligence. We precise the results about cumulativity, reasoning by cases, contraposition and related matters. Circumscriptions are "syntactic" by nature, even if they do posess a semantics, which is precisely given by preferential entailment. Thus, a preference relation naturally associated to a circumscription cannot be defined from any relation between models: it must be somehow coherent with the syntax.

We show that a powerful property, reverse monotony, is verified by any of the circumscriptions considered here. Then, we are able to apply our general results to all these circumscriptions. Among the various examples given, we show that there are not easy connections between the classical second order well-foundedness and its first order counterpart, one consequence being that there are cases where the first order circumscription is cumulative while the second order version is not, and conversely. Also, we provide examples (with pointwise circumscription and with strong circumscription) illustrating the utility of our definitions for non transitive preference relations

In section 2, we remind the definitions of preferential entailment and of the preference relations associated, extending the notion of well-foundedness to preference relations which are not transitive. In section 3, we show precisely how circumscriptions can be considered as preferential entailments, and conversely. Section 4 gives the relevant properties of preferential entailment. Section 5 gives some concrete examples of circumscriptions, together with their "natural" preference relations. Several examples are provided, chosen to give examples and counter-examples to some properties examined in the preceding sections.

2 Preferential entailment

We refer the reader to [BS88], [Sho88], [Mak88] and [KLM90], but we provide complete definitions, as these texts need some adaptations in order to deal with circumscriptions. We start from a standard logical notion of inference.

Notations 2.1 $\mathcal{L}$ denotes a first order language, $\mathcal{T}$ is a theory (i.e. a set of formulas) in $\mathcal{L}$. If Φ is a formula (resp. $\mathcal{T}'$ a theory) in $\mathcal{L}$, and μ an interpretation over $\mathcal{L}$, we note as usual $\mu \models \mathcal{T}$ if μ is a model of $\mathcal{T}$ and $\mathcal{T} \models \Phi$ (resp. $\mathcal{T} \models \mathcal{T}'$) if any model of $\mathcal{T}$ is a model of Φ (resp. $\mathcal{T}'$). $Th(\mathcal{T})$ denotes the entailment closure of $\mathcal{T}$. $\mathcal{L}$ also contains "=" and an infinite number of individual variables. $\equiv$ is a metasymbol meaning "equivalent to". If μ is an interpretation over $\mathcal{L}$, if P is a predicate symbol, Φ a formula, f a function symbol, all of arity k, in $\mathcal{L}$, then:

- The set D_μ denotes the domain of μ.
- The subset $|P|_\mu$ (or $|\Phi|_\mu$) of D_μ^k denotes the extension of P (or Φ) in μ.
- The application f_μ from D_μ^k to D_μ denotes the interpretation of f in μ. If $k = 0$, f_μ is assimilated to its own image.

Our models and interpretations are *normal* (= interpreted as identity). $\mathcal{L}_\mu$, the *language of* μ, adds to $\mathcal{L}$ a name for each element in D_μ. □

Considering some *preferred* models among the models of a theory $\mathcal{T}$ is useful in knowledge representation if we want to deal with incomplete information or rules with exceptions. Here are the precise definitions involved:

Definitions 2.2 A binary relation $\prec$ among the interpretations over $\mathcal{L}$ is a *preference relation*. A model μ of a theory $\mathcal{T}$ is *a model of $\mathcal{T}$ minimal for $\prec$* (or *is minimal for $(\mathcal{T}, \prec)$*) iff there exists no model ν of $\mathcal{T}$ with $\nu \prec \mu$; in this case we note $\mu \models_\prec \mathcal{T}$. If any model of $\mathcal{T}$ minimal for $\prec$ is a model of ϕ (resp. $\mathcal{T}'$), we note $\mathcal{T} \models_\prec \phi$ (resp. $\mathcal{T} \models_\prec \mathcal{T}'$).
The relation $\models_\prec$ between a theory $\mathcal{T}$ and a formula ϕ is a *preferential entailment*. Each preference relation $\prec$ gives rise to one preferential entailment $\models_\prec$, but each preferential entailment may be associated to various preference relations. If some preference relation $\prec$ associated to $\models_\prec$ is antireflexive, antisymmetrical and transitive, $\models_\prec$ is an *ordered preferential entailment*. □

If a preference relation $\prec$ is not transitive, we may cautiously use its transitive closure:

Notations 2.3 Let $\prec$ be a preference relation, we note $\overline{\prec}$ for its transitive closure, and $\prec_\mathcal{T}$ for the restriction of $\prec$ to the class of the models of a theory $\mathcal{T}$.

A model is minimal for $(\mathcal{T}, \prec)$ iff it is minimal for $(\mathcal{T}, \prec_\mathcal{T})$ iff it is minimal for $(\mathcal{T}, \overline{\prec_\mathcal{T}})$. However, generally $\overline{\prec_\mathcal{T}}$ does *not* coincide with $(\overline{\prec})_\mathcal{T}$: if $\mu \overline{\prec_\mathcal{T}} \nu$ then $\mu \overline{\prec} \nu$ but the converse is not guaranteed, even if μ and ν are models of $\mathcal{T}$, as $\mu \overline{\prec} \nu$ may be true thanks to interpretations which are not models of $\mathcal{T}$. Thus we may not restrict our attention to transitive preference relations without loss of generality: a model of $\mathcal{T}$ may be minimal for $\prec$ and not for $\overline{\prec}$.

The important notion of *well-foundedness* appears under various forms in the literature. The following definitions give the notions useful for circumscriptions.

Definition 2.4 $\mathcal{T}$ is *well-founded for a preference relation* $\prec$ iff for any model μ of $\mathcal{T}$ not minimal for $\prec$, there exists ν minimal for $(\mathcal{T}, \prec)$ with $\nu \prec \mu$. If any theory $\mathcal{T}$ in $\mathcal{L}$ is well-founded for $\prec$, *the preference relation $\prec$ is well-founded* (this is *global* well-foundedness).

It is rare that a theory is well-founded for a non transitive $\prec$. Several important circumscriptions give naturally rise to non transitive relations, e.g. strong circumscription. The preference relation naturally associated to pointwise circumscription is *anti-transitive*: if $\mu_1 \prec \mu_2$ and $\mu_2 \prec \mu_3$ then $\mu_1 \not\prec \mu_3$. Also, some notions of common sense reasoning can be rendered by a preferential entailment only if the associated preference relation is not transitive [Ryc90]. Thus it is important to give a milder definition in this case. Before that, we need a preliminary result.

Theorem 2.1 If $\mathcal{T}$ is well-founded for $\prec$ and if $\mathcal{T} \models_\prec \phi$, then $\mathcal{T} \cup \{\phi\}$ is well-founded for $\prec$.

For a general ϕ, $\mathcal{T}$ may be well-founded while $\mathcal{T} \cup \{\phi\}$ is not (see example 5.1). Theorem 2.1 explains why so many results given in [Mak88] or [KLM90] for their strong notion of *global* well-foundedness are also true with the more reasonable condition of well-foundedness of a given $\mathcal{T}$. We must keep this result in mind when defining the useful notion for a non transitive preference relation. The proof is easy, but it is convenient in this text to give a preliminary lemma.

Definition 2.5 A theory $\mathcal{T}$ is *well-behaved for* $\prec$ iff for any sentence ϕ we have: if $\mathcal{T} \models_\prec \phi$, then the models minimal for $(\mathcal{T} \cup \{\phi\}, \prec)$ are the models minimal for $(\mathcal{T}, \prec)$.

Lemma 2.2 If $\mathcal{T}$ is well-founded for $\prec$, then $\mathcal{T}$ is well-behaved for $\prec$.

Proof: For any $\mathcal{T}, \phi$, a model minimal for $(\mathcal{T}, \prec)$ which happens to be also a model of ϕ, is minimal for $(\mathcal{T} \cup \{\phi\}, \prec)$. Thus, if $\mathcal{T} \models_\prec \phi$, a model minimal for $(\mathcal{T}, \prec)$ is minimal for $(\mathcal{T} \cup \{\phi\}, \prec)$.
Now, let us suppose that $\mathcal{T} \models_\prec \phi$, and that μ is minimal for $(\mathcal{T} \cup \{\phi\}, \prec)$. As $\mathcal{T}$ is well-founded, either $\mu \models_\prec \mathcal{T}$ or there exists ν with $\nu \models_\prec \mathcal{T}$ and $\nu \prec \mu$. As $\nu \models_\prec \mathcal{T}$, ν is a model of $\mathcal{T} \cup \{\phi\}$, which contradicts $\mu \models_\prec (\mathcal{T} \cup \{\phi\})$, thus $\mu \models_\prec \mathcal{T}$. The proof of theorem 2.1 follows easily. □

We need two new definitions for non transitive relations as the most natural one (the first one) does not satisfy theorems 2.1 and 4.8:

Definition 2.6 A theory $\mathcal{T}$ is *weakly well-founded for a preference relation* $\prec$ iff for any model μ of $\mathcal{T}$ not minimal for $(\mathcal{T}, \prec)$, there exists ν minimal for $(\mathcal{T}, \prec)$ with $\nu \overline{\prec_\mathcal{T}} \mu$.

Definition 2.7 A theory $\mathcal{T}$ is *mildly well-founded for a preference relation* $\prec$ iff it is weakly well-founded and for any sentence ϕ such that $\mathcal{T} \models_\prec \phi$ and any models μ and ν minimal for $(\mathcal{T} \cup \{\phi\}, \prec)$ we do *not* have $\nu \overline{\prec_\mathcal{T}} \mu$.

Property 2.3 $\mathcal{T}$ is mildly well-founded iff $\mathcal{T}$ is weakly well-founded and well-behaved.

Proof: $\Rightarrow$: $\mathcal{T}$ is mildly well-founded. Let us suppose $\mathcal{T} \models_\prec \phi$ and ν minimal for $(\mathcal{T} \cup \{\phi\}, \prec)$. If $\nu \not\models_\prec \mathcal{T}$, there exists μ with $\mu \models_\prec \mathcal{T}$ and $\mu \overline{\prec_\mathcal{T}} \nu$ (definition 2.6). As $\mathcal{T} \models_\prec \phi$, μ is a model of ϕ, and $\mu \models_\prec \mathcal{T}$ gives $\mu \models_\prec (\mathcal{T} \cup \{\phi\})$, which contradicts mild well-foundedness.

$\Leftarrow$: Let us suppose $\mathcal{T}$ is weakly well-founded and well-behaved, $\mathcal{T} \models_\prec \phi$ and μ is minimal for $(\mathcal{T} \cup \{\phi\}, \prec)$. As $\mathcal{T}$ is well-behaved, μ is minimal for $(\mathcal{T}, \prec)$. Thus, it cannot exist a model ν of $\mathcal{T}$, and a fortiori of $\mathcal{T} \cup \{\phi\}$, such that $\nu \overline{\prec_\mathcal{T}} \mu$. □

Note that we have given a "unitary version", we could also give the "general – or infinitary – version" of well-behaveness (in the finite propositionnal case, these two notions coincide):

Theorem 2.4 . Let $\mathcal{T}$ be a theory such that for any theory $\mathcal{T}'$ in the language $\mathcal{L}$, we have: if ($\mathcal{T} \models_\prec \mathcal{T}'$ and $\mathcal{T}' \models \mathcal{T}$) then a model is minimal for $(\mathcal{T}, \prec)$ iff it is minimal for $(\mathcal{T}', \prec)$.

If $\mathcal{T}$ has this property ("*general version of well-behaveness*"), then $\mathcal{T}$ is well-behaved for $\prec$.

Proof: Clear, just take $\mathcal{T}'$ to be $\mathcal{T} \cup \{\phi\}$.

Remarks 2.1 1) Contrarily to definition 2.6, definition 2.7 is an acceptable candidate which respects theorem 2.1: if $\mathcal{T}$ is mildly well-founded for $\prec$ and if $\mathcal{T} \models_\prec \phi$, then $\mathcal{T} \cup \{\phi\}$ is mildly well-founded for $\prec$ (proof: use property 2.3).

2) If $\prec$ is transitive then the three kinds of well-foundedness coincide.

3) Any well-founded theory is mildly well-founded, and any mildly well-founded theory is weakly well-founded, but the converses are not guaranteed (see examples 5.4, and 5.5 or 5.6). □

Definition 2.4 is the classical meaning of the expression "well-founded" in the literature about circumscription (see e.g. [BS85, EMR85, Lif86]). In mathematical texts, "well-founded" (cf e.g. [CK73, p.150]), prevents the existence of infinitely decreasing chains, which is not the case with definitions 2.4, 2.6, 2.7. *Bounded* in [Sho88] corresponds to this "mathematical meaning". If $\prec$ is transitive, boundedness implies well-foundedness but a condition so strong is not necessary to get the theorems 4.2 and 4.8 . If the relation is not transitive, boundedness only implies weak well-foundedness (converse false, see example 5.5); boundedness implies neither well-foundedness nor mild well-foundedness (see example 5.4), and thus it is not really interesting.

Definition 2.4 corresponds roughly to what is called *stoppered relation* in [Mak88] or *smoothness condition* in [KLM90]. The differences are:

1) Only the "*global*" notion of $\prec$-well-founded-ness is defined in these texts. It is more frequent that some theory $\mathcal{T}$ is well-founded for $\prec$.

2) None of these texts examine what happens with non transitive preference relations.

3) In [KLM90], the preference relation $\prec$ is defined between sets of models.

4) In [Mak88], the notion of models is not necessarily the classical one.

These last two complications are unnecessary for all the circumscriptions studied in this text.

Note that if $\prec_\mathcal{T}$ or $\overline{\prec_\mathcal{T}}$ is reflexive, $\mathcal{T}$ cannot be (weakly) well-founded for $\prec$ (see example 5.7).

3 Circumscriptions

We generalise the notion of *circumscription*, introduced [McC80, McC86] in order to express some commonsense problems formally.

Definitions 3.1 A process which, to any $\mathcal{T}$ closed for entailment, associates a new theory $\overline{\mathcal{T}} = Th(\mathcal{T} \cup \mathcal{T}^c)$ for some theory $\mathcal{T}^c$, is a *pre-circumscription*.

A great number of the "circumscriptions" which have been introduced in the literature are particular cases of preferential entailment. Thus, we call "*circumscription*" a pre-circumscription for which there is an associated preference relation $\prec$, such that, for any theory $\mathcal{T}$ and any formula Φ in $\mathcal{L}$, we have: $\overline{\mathcal{T}} \models \Phi$ iff $\mathcal{T} \models_\prec \Phi$. We use the notation $\mathbf{Circ_g}(\mathcal{T})$ to denote a (particular but unprecised) circumscription of $\mathcal{T}$. □

Thus, for any circumscription $\mathbf{Circ_g}$, there exists a preference relation $\prec$ such that for any theory $\mathcal{T}$ and any formula Φ in $\mathcal{L}$: $\mathbf{Circ_g}(\mathcal{T}) \models \Phi$ iff $\mathcal{T} \models_\prec \Phi$. Note that generally we may associate many preference relations to one given circumscription.

Conversely, to any preference relation $\prec$ we may associate one (and only one) circumscription. Indeed, to any theory $\mathcal{T}$, we may associate the set $\mathcal{T}'$ whose elements are all the formulas ϕ which are true in all the models of $\mathcal{T}$ minimal for $\prec$.

Thus, with our definitions, the two notions of preferential entailment and of circumscription are equivalent. We choose to keep the two expressions, using the former ($\mathcal{T} \models_\prec \cdots$) when focusing on a preference relation and the latter ($\mathbf{Circ_g}(\mathcal{T}) \models \cdots$) when the emphasis is put on the formulas $\mathcal{T}^c$ added to $\mathcal{T}$. See also in subsection 5.2, describing two "concrete examples" of circumscription, a comment about the utility of keeping the two points of view in mind.

Note that any model minimal for $(\mathcal{T}, \prec)$ is a model of $\mathbf{Circ_g}(\mathcal{T})$, but that the converse is not guaranteed, i.e., a preference relation $\prec$ is not necessarily "coherent" with respect to the syntax:

Definition 3.2 A preference relation $\prec$ is *coherent* iff for any first order theory $\mathcal{T}$, the class $\mathcal{M}_\prec(\mathcal{T})$ of all the models minimal for $(\mathcal{T}, \prec)$ is the class of all the models of some theory $\mathcal{T}'$ in $\mathcal{L}$ (clearly $\mathcal{T} \subseteq \mathcal{T}'$).

The preference relations $\prec$ "naturally associated" to all the circumscriptions defined in the litterature and respecting definition 3.1 are coherent, but it seems likely that they have also some other properties. Till now, we are unable to characterize these properties. One could think that the seemingly benign following property would be a good candidate:

"For any interpretations μ, ν and μ', if $\nu \prec \mu$ and if μ and μ' are elementarily equivalent, (i.e. for any formula ϕ in $\mathcal{L}$, $\mu \models \phi$ iff $\mu' \models \phi$), then there exists ν' elementarily equivalent to ν and such that $\nu' \prec \mu'$."

Unfortunately, there are counter-examples showing that the preference relation naturally associated to the classical first order predicate circumscription does not necessarily respect this property. Here we mean the "naturally associated" preference relation $\prec$ (see section 5). When any preference relation is allowed, [Moi94] shows that for any circumscription, we can find some $\prec$ associated to it which respects the following property, which implies the preceding property and also coherence:

Definition 3.3 A relation $\prec$ is *compatible with elementary equivalence* iff for any interpretations μ, μ', ν and ν', if μ and μ' are elementarily equivalent and if ν and ν' are elementarily equivalent, then $\mu \prec \nu$ iff $\mu' \prec \nu'$.

Now, we examine briefly the other way: we start from a pre-circumscription, is it a "circumscription", i.e. does it exist a preference relation $\prec$ such that for any theory $\mathcal{T}$, the models minimal for $(\mathcal{T}, \prec)$ are exactly the models of $\overline{\mathcal{T}}$? This is not always the case as a simple example in propositional logic shows:

Example 3.1 $\mathcal{L}$ is a propositional language with only one proposition symbol A. Thus, we have only four theories in $\mathcal{L}$, closed for entailment, which simplifies the definition of the operation $\overline{}$. We take as definition: $\overline{Th(A \vee \neg A)} = Th(A)$, $\overline{Th(A)} = Th(A \wedge \neg A)$, $\overline{Th(\neg A)} = Th(\neg A)$, $\overline{Th(A \wedge \neg A)} = Th(A \wedge \neg A)$.

It is impossible to find any $\prec$ corresponding to this pre-circumscription. This is easy to verify as there are only here two propositionnal interpretations (one with A, one with $\neg A$), thus only $2^{(2^2)} = 16$ possible $\prec$ (see also example 4.1). □

We end our general presentation by two ways of combining relations. $\mathbf{Circ_{g1}}(\mathcal{T})$ and $\mathbf{Circ_{g2}}(\mathcal{T})$ are two circumscriptions associated to $\prec_1$ and $\prec_2$ respectively.

Their union gives a circumscription, associated to the relation $\prec_1 \oplus \prec_2$ ($\mu \prec_1 \oplus \prec_2 \nu$ iff $\mu \prec_1 \nu$ or $\mu \prec_2 \nu$). Their intersection gives the circumscription associated to $\prec_1 \otimes \prec_2$ ($\mu \prec_1 \otimes \prec_2 \nu$ iff $\mu \prec_1 \nu$ and $\mu \prec_2 \nu$). If $\models_{\prec_1}$ and $\models_{\prec_2}$ are ordered preferential entailments, so is $\models_{\prec_1 \otimes \prec_2}$. All what we will say about "circumscriptions" apply to these unions (this includes priority circumscription) and intersections.

4 General properties

We make now a survey of the main properties of preferential entailment (i.e. of circumscription). Let us first give a well-known obvious result:

Theorem 4.1 For any formula ϕ in $\mathcal{L}$, if $\mathcal{T} \models \phi$ then $\mathcal{T} \models_\prec \phi$, i.e.: $\mathcal{T} \models_\prec \mathcal{T}$. In terms of circumscription: $\mathbf{Circ_g}(\mathcal{T}) \models \mathcal{T}$. This is called *"reflexivity"* e.g. in [KLM90].

Here is one partial converse very useful for standard circumscription.

Definition 4.1 A formula Φ in $\mathcal{L}$ is *positive for* $(\mathcal{T}, \prec)$ iff $\mu \overline{\prec_\mathcal{T}} \nu$ implies $|\Phi|_\mu \subseteq |\Phi|_\nu$.
A formula Φ is *negative for* $(\mathcal{T}, \prec)$ iff $\neg\Phi$ is positive for $(\mathcal{T}, \prec)$.

Theorem 4.2 $\mathcal{T}$ is a theory (weakly) well-founded for $\prec$. For any sentence ϕ in $\mathcal{L}$ positive for $(\mathcal{T}, \prec)$, we have $\mathcal{T} \models_\prec \phi$ only if $\mathcal{T} \models \phi$.

We cannot get any new positive sentence by circumscription of a (weakly) well-founded theory (note that the notions of positiveness and well-foundedness depend on the circumscription considered). This fact, which encompasses two results in [EMR85] and [Jae86], is well known for standard circumscriptions [Moi88a]. This is one of the few properties which require only *weak* well-foundedness.

Proof: We suppose ϕ positive for $(\mathcal{T}, \prec)$, $\mathcal{T} \models_\prec \phi$ and $\mathcal{T}$ weakly well-founded for $\prec$. Let μ be a model of $\mathcal{T}$. As $\mathcal{T}$ is weakly well-founded, there exists ν model of $\mathcal{T}$ minimal for $\prec$ and such that either $\nu = \mu$ or $\nu \overline{\prec_\mathcal{T}} \mu$. ν is minimal for $(\mathcal{T}, \prec)$, so it is a model of ϕ. Moreover, as ϕ is positive for $(\mathcal{T}, \prec)$ and as $\nu \models \phi$, we get $\mu \models \phi$. □

Here is another well-known property, easy corollary of theorem 4.2 (indeed, the false formula $\bot$ is positive for $(\mathcal{T}, \prec)$ for any $\mathcal{T}$ and any $\prec$):

Theorem 4.3 If $\mathcal{T} \models \bot$ then $\mathcal{T} \models_\prec \bot$. If $\mathcal{T}$ is (weakly) well-founded for $\prec$, then $\mathcal{T} \models_\prec \bot$ only if $\mathcal{T} \models \bot$.

The interest of this result is that for some circumscriptions, we know wide classes of theories which are well-founded. For these theories, circumscription cannot provoque inconsistency.

Here are two other obvious results. Firstly, circumscribing a circumscribed theory does not add anything: $\mathbf{Circg}(\mathbf{Circg}(T)) \equiv \mathbf{Circg}(T)$ (*idempotence* of circumscription [Mak88]).

Secondly, if $T \models_\prec \phi$ and $T \models_\prec \psi$ then $T \models_\prec \phi \wedge \psi$. This is sometimes called *"and rule"*. (obvious: if any model minimal for $(T, \prec)$ is a model of ϕ and of ψ, then it is a model of $\phi \wedge \psi$).

The following result is more or less folklore in circumscription literature (see e.g. [Moi88a], [Som90] or [KLM90]). [Mak88] gives it also but requests the unnecessary condition that $\prec$ must be well-founded.

Theorem 4.4 Any preferential entailment *allows to reason by cases*: for any theory T and any sentences ϕ_1, ϕ_2 and ψ in $\mathcal{L}$, if $T \cup \{\phi_1\} \models_\prec \psi$ and $T \cup \{\phi_2\} \models_\prec \psi$, then $T \cup \{\phi_1 \vee \phi_2\} \models_\prec \psi$.

Proof: Let us suppose that $T \cup \{\phi_1\} \models_\prec \psi$ and that $T \cup \{\phi_2\} \models_\prec \psi$, and let μ be a model minimal for $(T \cup \{\phi_1 \vee \phi_2\}, \prec)$. Then, μ is a model of $T \cup \{\phi_1\}$ or of $T \cup \{\phi_2\}$. If μ is a model of $T \cup \{\phi_1\}$, then it is minimal for $((T \cup \{\phi_1\}), \prec)$. Otherwise, there would exist ν model of $T \cup \{\phi_1\}$, thus of $T \cup \{\phi_1 \vee \phi_2\}$, such that $\nu \prec \mu$, which would contradict the fact that μ is minimal for $(T \cup \{\phi_1 \vee \phi_2\}, \prec)$. □

Corollary 4.5 [Mak88] If $(T \cup \{\phi\}) \models_\prec \psi$ and $(T \cup \{\neg\phi\}) \models_\prec \psi$ then $T \models_\prec \psi$.

Also, if $T \equiv T'$ then $T \models_\prec \psi$ iff $T' \models_\prec \psi$ (this is called *"left logical equivalence"* in [KLM90]).

Here is another easy result:

If $T \models_\prec \phi$ and $T \models \phi \Rightarrow \psi$, then $T \models_\prec \psi$.

As left logical equivalence, this result is trivial for preferential entailments. It has been introduced (in another context) in [Bes88] under the name *"compound modus ponens"* and is generally now referred to as *"right weakening"* [KLM90].

Theorem 4.6 (cf *observation 5* in [Mak88]) Any preferential entailment is *transitivitively cumulative*: for any theory T and sentences ϕ, ψ in $\mathcal{L}$, $T \models_\prec \phi$ and $T \cup \{\phi\} \models_\prec \psi$ imply $T \models_\prec \psi$.

It is well known that the inference defined by circumscription is *non monotonic for some* T, i.e.:
generally, $\mathbf{Circg}(T \cup \{\psi\}) \not\models \mathbf{Circg}(T)$.

In terms of preferential entailment: for some sentences ϕ and ψ, we may have $T \models_\prec \phi$ and $T \cup \{\psi\} \not\models_\prec \phi$.

One weakening of monotony remains true:

Definitions 4.2 A preferential entailment has the property of *cumulative monotony for* T iff, for any sentences ψ, ϕ in $\mathcal{L}$: if $T \models_\prec \phi$ and $T \models_\prec \psi$ then $(T \cup \{\phi\}) \models_\prec \psi$.

This is called *"restricted"* or *"cautious" monotony* in [Gab85] or [KLM90], sometimes it is also called *"triangulation"*.

An inference relation is *cumulative* iff it is transitively *and* monotonically cumulative: for preferential entailments, cumulative monotony and cumulativity are synonymous (theorem 4.6). □

Clearly, well-behaveness is the semantical counterpart of cumulativity:

Theorem 4.7 A preferential entailment is cumulative for T iff T is well-behaved for $\prec$.

Theorem 4.8 (cf *observation 6* in [Mak88]) If T is (mildly) well-founded for $\prec$, then $\models_\prec$ is cumulative for T.

The proof is an adaptation of Makinson's proof which uses only global and standard well-foundedness and global cumulativity. It suffices to use property 2.3 or lemma 2.2, and then theorem 4.7. This result is not true with the *weak* version of well-foundedness (see example 5.4).

The general converse is false (see example 5.3): cumulativity may hold while T is not (weakly) well-founded for $\prec$.

Generally contraposition does *not* hold:

Definition 4.3 A preferential entailment *allows the contraposition for* T iff for any sentences ϕ and ψ, if $T \cup \{\phi\} \models_\prec \psi$ then $T \cup \{\neg\psi\} \models_\prec \neg\phi$.

Theorem 4.9 A preferential entailment allows the contraposition for T iff it is monotonic for T.

For a proof, see [Moi92]. This does not contradict a different affirmation in [KLM90] which does not deal only with preferential entailment. In [KLM90]'s formalism, only one way is true, the other way being false. Note also that [KLM90] defines contraposition only for an empty T; however, as noted in [FLM91], for preferential entailment this is not a real difference, at least as far as T can be finitely axiomatized.

Some restricted contraposition remains:

Theorem 4.10 [Moi92] If ψ is positive for $(T, \prec)$ we have: if $T \cup \{\phi\} \models_\prec \psi$ then $T \cup \{\neg\psi\} \models_\prec \neg\phi$.

Concerning general formulas, it is known that standard circumscription may or may not allow the contraposition with some formulas ϕ and ψ, depending of the policy of circumscription, that is which predicates are to be ciscumscribed or are allowed to vary. However, the problem of choosing a policy of circumscription corresponding to the expected behavior is not a trivial one and does not have yet a general solution.

Another interesting feature of preferential entailment is that it respects the deduction principle, also called e.g. in [KLM90], the "hard part" of the deduction theorem:

Theorem 4.11 (e.g. [Sho88]) For any sentences ϕ and ψ, if $T \cup \{\phi\} \models_\prec \psi$ then $T \models_\prec (\phi \Rightarrow \psi)$.

For circumscriptions, thanks to the full deduction theorem for classical entailment, we may give a useful form to theorem 4.11 and provide a "general version":

Theorem 4.12 For any theory T and any sentence ϕ we have:
- $(\mathbf{Circg}(T) \cup \{\phi\}) \models \mathbf{Circg}(T \cup \{\phi\})$.
 We also have, for any theories T and T':
- $(\mathbf{Circg}(T) \cup T') \models \mathbf{Circg}(T \cup T')$.
 One extreme case is when T is empty:
- $\mathbf{Circg}(\emptyset) \cup T \models \mathbf{Circg}(T)$.

Proof: Let μ be a model of $(\mathbf{Circg}(T) \cup T')$, i.e. a model minimal for $(T, \prec)$ which happens to be a model of T'. If μ is not minimal for $(T \cup T', \prec)$, then there exists a model ν of $T \cup T'$ such that $\nu \prec \mu$. ν is a model of T, which contradicts the fact that μ is minimal for $(T, \prec)$. Thus μ is minimal for $(T \cup T', \prec)$, i.e. μ is a model of $\mathbf{Circg}(T \cup T')$. □

With $\mathbf{Circg}(T) \models T$, this result puts limits to the circumscription. We call this property *"reverse monotony"* (RM for short). Indeed, monotony (plus reflexivity) is $\mathbf{Circg}(T \cup \{\phi\}) \models (\mathbf{Circg}(T) \cup \{\phi\})$. RM shows that the more axioms are introduced into the circumscribed theory, the less new results (besides the original axioms) the circumscription produces. As this property is important, here is another form:

RM1: Let T_1 and T_2 be two theories, then (renaming T as T_1 and $T \cup T'$ as T_2), we get :
if $T_2 \models T_1$, then $\mathbf{Circg}(T_1) \cup T_2 \models \mathbf{Circg}(T_2)$.

Example 4.1 We examine example 3.1 again. We had the pre-circumscription: $\overline{Th(A \vee \neg A)} = Th(A)$, $\overline{Th(A)} = Th(A \wedge \neg A)$, $\overline{Th(\neg A)} = Th(\neg A)$, $\overline{Th(A \wedge \neg A)} = Th(A \wedge \neg A)$.
The property RM is violated: $\overline{Th(\emptyset)} \cup \{A\} \not\models \overline{Th(\emptyset \cup \{A\})}$. Indeed, $Th(\emptyset) = Th(A \vee \neg A)$, $Th(\emptyset \cup \{A\}) = Th(A)$, $\overline{Th(A)}$ is inconsistent while $\overline{Th(\emptyset)} \cup \{A\}$ is equivalent to $Th(A)$.
Any circumscription satisfies RM, so this is another way of proving that this pre-circumscription is not a circumscription.
Note that RM alone would not suffice: [Moi94] gives an example of a pre-circumscription verifying RM which is not a circumscription. □

RM is fundamental because a lot of the properties of circumscriptions may be considered as corollaries of RM. This has already been noted for theorem 4.11, and it is easy to verify also for idempotence and for theorems 4.4 and 4.6.

The converse of theorem 4.11 (the "right detachment" rule, also called the "easy part" of the deduction theorem because it is trivial for ordinary logic) is interesting also. As [Sho88] has noted, it is equivalent to monotony: no "interesting" preferential entailment respects fully this converse. However, a partial converse holds, which may help the automatization of circumscription: when a new negative sentence comes, we need not to recalculate the circumscription from scratch, all we need is to add this sentence to the previously calculated circumscription. This result is well known for standard circumscriptions (cf e.g. [Moi88a]).

Theorem 4.13 If ϕ is negative for $(T, \prec)$ then $(\mathbf{Circg}(T) \cup \{\phi\}) \equiv \mathbf{Circg}(T \cup \{\phi\})$.
[in terms of preferential entailment: for any sentence ψ, $T \cup \{\phi\} \models_\prec \psi$ iff $T \models_\prec \phi \Rightarrow \psi$].

We define now the relations associated to various kinds of circumscriptions. As this has already been detailed [MR91, Moi92], we give only the main lines, with representative examples.

5 Some circumscriptions viewed as preferential entailment

T is now a finitely axiomatizable theory in $\mathcal{L}$.

5.1 Domain circumscription

In many situations only the objects named, directly or not, are supposed to exist. Domain circumscription ([McC80] amended by [Mor85, EM87]) noted $\mathbf{Circd}_1$, formalizes this idea. In the lines of [McC86] for predicate circumscription, we may also define a second order domain circumscription $\mathbf{Circd}_2$.

Definition 5.1 μ and ν are interpretations over $\mathcal{L}$. We denote $\nu < \mu$, iff: $D_\nu \subset D_\mu$, and
- for each function f in $\mathcal{L}$, if $e \in D_\nu^k$, then $f_\mu(e) = f_\nu(e)$,
- for each predicate P in $\mathcal{L}$, $|P|_\mu \cap D_\nu^k = |P|_\nu$.
This is the classical notion of sub-interpretation in logic, see e.g. [End72, p.90–1].

Theorem 5.1 [Dav80] Any model of T minimal for $<$ is a model of $\mathbf{Circd}_1(T)$ and of $\mathbf{Circd}_2(T)$.

The converse is true for $\mathbf{Circd}_2(T)$ (adapt [Lif86] for domain circumscription, e.g. using [McC80] or [MR91] which relate domain circumscription to predicate circumscription), but for $\mathbf{Circd}_1(T)$ we need a more sophisticated relation.

Theorem 5.2 The models of $\mathbf{Circd}_2(T)$ are the models of T minimal for $<$.

Definition 5.2 (e.g. [KK71, p.115–135]) A subset S of D_μ^k is *definable with parameters in* μ when there exists a formula Φ in $\mathcal{L}_\mu$, of arity k, such that $S = |\Phi|_\mu$. If Φ is in $\mathcal{L}$, S is *definable in* μ.

Definition 5.3 If $\nu < \mu$ and if D_ν is definable with parameters in μ, we note $\nu <^\delta \mu$.

Theorem 5.3 [Mor85, MR91] The models of $\mathbf{Circd}_1(T)$ are the models of T minimal for $<^\delta$.

$\models_<$ and $\models_{<^\delta}$ are ordered preferential entailments. Domain circumscription minimises the domain, while predicate circumscription minimises some relations. There are ways to express the former in terms of the latter, so we will not elaborate further here.

5.2 Predicate circumscription

Definition 5.4 [McC80, PM86] The *first order circumscription of* $\mathbf{P}$ *in* T *with* $\mathbf{Q}$ *varying*, noted $\mathbf{Circ}_1(T : \mathbf{P}; \mathbf{Q})$, adds the following axiom schema to T: (SAC)
$\{T[\mathbf{p}, \mathbf{q}] \wedge \forall \mathbf{x} \, (\mathbf{p}[\mathbf{x}] \Rightarrow \mathbf{P}(\mathbf{x}))\} \Rightarrow \forall \mathbf{x} \, (\mathbf{P}(\mathbf{x}) \Rightarrow \mathbf{p}[\mathbf{x}])$,
for every lists $\mathbf{p} = (p_1, \ldots, p_m)$, $\mathbf{q} = (q_1, \ldots, q_n)$ of formulas in $\mathcal{L}$.
$T[\mathbf{p}, \mathbf{q}]$ is T except that each occurrence of P_i and Q_j is replaced by p_i and q_j, respectively.
$\forall x(\mathbf{p}[\mathbf{x}] \Rightarrow \mathbf{P}(\mathbf{x}))$ stands for: $\forall \mathbf{x}_1 \ldots \mathbf{x}_m (p_1[\mathbf{x}_1] \Rightarrow P_1(\mathbf{x}_1)) \wedge \ldots \wedge (p_m[\mathbf{x}_m] \Rightarrow P_m(\mathbf{x}_m))$.
The square braquets in $p_i[\mathbf{x}_i]$ mean that p_i may have free variables other than $\mathbf{x}_i = (x_{i1}, \ldots, x_{ik_i})$, where k_i is the arity of P_i (see [BMM89] for the need of extra free variables in first order circumscriptions).

Definition 5.5 (see [McC86, Lif86]) The *second order circumscription of* $\mathbf{P}$ *in* T, *with* $\mathbf{Q}$ *varying*, noted $\mathbf{Circ}_2(T : \mathbf{P}; \mathbf{Q})$, adds the following axiom to T:

(AC) $\forall \mathbf{p} \forall \mathbf{q} \, \{[T[\mathbf{p}, \mathbf{q}] \wedge \forall \mathbf{x} \, (\mathbf{p}(\mathbf{x}) \Rightarrow \mathbf{P}(\mathbf{x}))] \Rightarrow \forall \mathbf{x} \, (\mathbf{P}(\mathbf{x}) \Rightarrow \mathbf{p}(\mathbf{x}))\}$.
$\mathbf{p}$ and $\mathbf{q}$ are sequences of predicate variables p_i or q_j, having the same arity as P_i or Q_j.

Circ denotes indifferently $\mathbf{Circ}_1$ or $\mathbf{Circ}_2$.

Definitions 5.6 • Let μ and ν be two interpretations over $\mathcal{L}$. We write $\mu =_{\mathbf{P}; \mathbf{Q}} \nu$ when μ and ν are identical except that there is no condition on the extensions of the P_i's and of the Q_j's.
• If moreover each $|P_i|_\mu$ and $|Q_j|_\mu$ is definable with parameters in ν, we write $\mu =^\delta_{\mathbf{P}; \mathbf{Q}} \nu$.
• If $\mu =_{\mathbf{P}; \mathbf{Q}} \nu$ (resp. $\mu =^\delta_{\mathbf{P}; \mathbf{Q}} \nu$) and also $|P_i|_\mu \subseteq |P_i|_\nu$ for $1 \leq i \leq n$, with some $|P_i|_\mu \subset |P_i|_\nu$, we note $\mu <_{\mathbf{P}; \mathbf{Q}} \nu$ (resp. $\mu <^\delta_{\mathbf{P}; \mathbf{Q}} \nu$).

Theorem 5.4 [McC80] Every model of T minimal for $<_{\mathbf{P}; \mathbf{Q}}$ is a model of $\mathbf{Circ}(T : \mathbf{P}; \mathbf{Q})$.

This is the *soundness of circumscription*. $<_{\mathbf{P}; \mathbf{Q}}$ induces the "intended semantics" of circumscription. $<^\delta_{\mathbf{P}; \mathbf{Q}}$ gives the precise semantical characterization for first order circumscription:

Theorem 5.5 • [BHR88, Bes89] The models of $\mathbf{Circ}_1(T : \mathbf{P}; \mathbf{Q})$ are the models of T minimal for $<^\delta_{\mathbf{P}; \mathbf{Q}}$.
• [Lif86] The models of $\mathbf{Circ}_2(T : \mathbf{P}; \mathbf{Q})$ are the models of T minimal for $<_{\mathbf{P}; \mathbf{Q}}$.

As with domain circumscription, a model minimal for $<_{\mathbf{P}; \mathbf{Q}}$ is minimal for $<^\delta_{\mathbf{P}; \mathbf{Q}}$. If T is such that the converse is also true, we have the *completeness of first order circumscription* [PM86]. The second order version simplifies the notations (superficially) and the semantics. But it makes things harder when it comes to automatization. That is why the two versions are useful.

In "second order circumscriptions" as they are defined and used in the literature, we start from a first order theory T anyway, and we are interested by the first order formulas that the circumscription entails. Thus, definition 3.1 is respected. This is clear from the "preferential entailment point of view" of definition 2.2: $<_{\mathbf{P}; \mathbf{Q}}$ is the preference relation naturally associated.

From the "circumscription point of view" of definition 3.1, it is not so obvious. However T^c does exist: for instance take the set $\mathbf{Circ}_2(T : P; Q)$ of all the formulas in $\mathcal{L}$ true in all the models minimal for $(T, <_{\mathbf{P}; \mathbf{Q}})$, less T. Generally, there is no easy way to describe such a T^c without leaving first order logic. The simplest way, suggested in definition 5.5, uses second order logic: $\mathbf{Circ}_2(T : P; Q) = \mathcal{L} \cap Th_2(T \cup \{AC\})$, Th_2 denoting the second order entailment closure.
With the first order circumscription, it suffices to take $T^c = SAC$ which is an infinite but easily described set of formulas in $\mathcal{L}$.

So, for first order circumscriptions, a T^c such as in definition 3.1 is easy to describe, while a $\prec$ conforming to definition 2.2 is harder to describe; for second order circumscriptions, it is the opposite. Anyway, the two versions are particular cases of our general definitions.

Definitions 5.7 • [Lif86] A theory T is *(**P**;**Q**)-well-founded* iff it is well-founded for $<_{\mathbf{P}; \mathbf{Q}}$.

• [Moi88a] T is *definably (**P**;**Q**)-well-founded* iff it is well-founded for $<^\delta_{\mathbf{P}; \mathbf{Q}}$.

Universal (thus Horn) theories are always (**P**;**Q**)-well-founded [BS85, EMR85, Lif86]. There is no simple relationship between these two notions (see examples 5.2 and 5.3), and universal theories are not guaranteed to be definably well-founded (see example 5.2).
It is easy to find examples showing the importance of well-foundedness in theorem 4.8:

Example 5.1 $\mathcal{T}$ is $\mathcal{T}'$, $\mathcal{S}$, where
$\mathcal{T}' \equiv \exists x \forall y \ (P(x) \wedge (P(y) \Rightarrow x \neq f(y)))$,
$\quad \forall x \ [P(x) \Rightarrow P(f(x))]$, $0=0$; and
$\mathcal{S} \equiv \forall x \ x \neq f(x), \ \forall x \forall y \ [(f(x)=f(y)) \Rightarrow (x=y)]$
($\mathcal{S}$: Separation axioms).

$\mathbf{Circ}(\mathcal{T} : P) \models \bot$, thus e.g.: $\mathbf{Circ}(\mathcal{T} : P) \models \phi$, where $\phi \equiv P(0)$ (this is a well-known example of inconsistent circumscription, see e.g. [EMR85]).

However $\mathbf{Circ}(\mathcal{T} \wedge \phi : P)$ is consistent so $\mathbf{Circ}(\mathcal{T} : P)$ is not cumulative. Indeed, here is a model μ of $\mathcal{T} \cup \{\phi\}$ minimal for $<_P$ (thus also minimal for $<_P^\delta$): take $D_\mu = |P|_\mu = \mathbb{N}$ the set of natural integers, $0_\mu = 0 \in \mathbb{N}$ and f_μ being the successor function in $\mathbb{N}$.
$\mathcal{T}$ is not well-founded, neither for $<_P$ nor for $<_P^\delta$.

Also, this is an example of a theory $\mathcal{S}$ which is well-founded for $<_P$ (being universal), while some $\mathcal{S} \wedge \mathcal{T}'$, i.e. $\mathcal{T}$, is not (cf theorem 2.1). □

In example 5.2, the first order circumscription is cumulative while the second order one is not. In example 5.3, the opposite situation occurs:

Example 5.2 (cf example 4.6.1 in [Moi88a])
$\mathcal{T} : \ P(0), \ \forall x \ (P(x) \Rightarrow P(f(x)))$
$\left. \begin{array}{l} 0 \neq 0', \ \forall x \ x \neq f(x) \\ \forall x \forall y \ (f(x)=f(y)) \Rightarrow (x=y) \\ \forall x \ (0 \neq f(x) \ \wedge \ 0' \neq f(x)). \end{array} \right] (\mathcal{S})$

$\mathbf{Circ}_1(\mathcal{T} : P) \models \neg P(0')$ (take $p[x] \equiv P(x) \wedge x \neq 0'$ in the circumscription axiom schema).
Now, choose $\phi \equiv \forall x \ (P(f(x)) \Rightarrow P(x))$. $\mathbf{Circ}_1(\mathcal{T} : P) \models \phi$ (take $p[x] \equiv \forall x \ \{P(x) \Rightarrow [x=0 \vee \exists y \ (x=f(y) \wedge P(y))]\}$ which gives $\mathbf{Circ}_1(\mathcal{T} : P) \models \forall x \ \{P(x) \Rightarrow [x=0 \vee \exists y \ (x=f(y) \wedge P(y))]\}$, then use $(\mathcal{S})$).
$\mathcal{T} \wedge \phi$ is: $P(0) \wedge \forall x \ (P(x) \Leftrightarrow P(f(x))) \wedge (\mathcal{S})$.

This is Kueker's example of incompleteness of first order circumscription.

$\mathbf{Circ}_1(\mathcal{T} \wedge \phi : P) \not\models \neg P(0')$ (see [PM86]). A short proof of this fact uses the following model ν of $\mathcal{T} \wedge \phi \wedge P(0')$: $D_\nu = |P|_\nu = \mathbb{N} \cup \mathbb{Z}'$, where $\mathbb{N} = \{0, 1, \cdots\}$ and $\mathbb{Z}' = \{\cdots, -1', 0', 1', \cdots\}$ are copies of the sets of natural and relative integers respectively; $0_\nu = 0 \in \mathbb{N}$, $0'_\nu = 0' \in \mathbb{Z}'$. $\mathbb{N}$ is not definable with parameters in ν (see [BMM89]), so with $\mu =_P \nu$ and $|P|_\mu = \mathbb{N}$, we do not have $\mu =_P^\delta \nu$, thus we do not have $\mu <_P^\delta \nu$. The axioms of $\mathcal{T} \wedge \phi$ make that ν is a model of $\mathcal{T} \wedge \phi$ minimal for $<_P^\delta$.

• The first order circumscription is not cumulative: $\mathbf{Circ}_1(\mathcal{T} : P) \models \phi$, $\mathbf{Circ}_1(\mathcal{T} \wedge \phi : P) \not\models \mathbf{Circ}_1(\mathcal{T} : P)$. $\mathcal{T}$ is *not definably well-founded* (see [Moi88a], or use theorem 4.8).

Note that $\mathbf{Circ}_1(\mathcal{T} : P)$ is consistent.

• The second order circumscription is cumulative, as $\mathcal{T}$ is P–well-founded, being universal. □

Example 5.3 (see [MR90]). $\mathcal{L}$ contains the symbols: 0, 1 (constants), $\oplus$, $\otimes$ (binary functions), the predicates P (unary) and $<$ (binary). We use the infix notations $x < y$, $x \oplus y$ and $x \otimes y$. $\mathcal{T}$ contains the axioms of real closed field (see [KK71] p.60: it is an ordered field in which every element is a square or the opposite of a square, and every polynom with an odd degree has a zero) with the following axiom, stating that the extension of P is the whole domain, or an additive subgroup with a smallest positive element:
$\forall x \ P(x) \vee \{\forall x \forall y \ [(P(x) \wedge P(y)) \Rightarrow P(x \oplus y)] \wedge \forall x \forall y \ [(P(x) \wedge x \oplus y = 0) \Rightarrow P(y)] \wedge \exists x \ [P(x) \wedge 0 < x \wedge \forall y \ ((P(y) \wedge 0 < y) \Rightarrow (x < y \vee x=y))]\}$.

• Let μ be a model of $\mathcal{T}$ such that $|P|_\mu \neq D_\mu$. Such models exist: take $D_\mu = \mathbb{R}$ (real numbers), $|P|_\mu = \mathbb{Z}$ (relative integers).
We define ν such that $\nu <_P \mu$ and $|P|_\nu = (1 \oplus 1) \otimes |P|_\mu$ $(= \{y / \exists x \in |P|_\mu, y = x \oplus x\})$. ν is a model of $\mathcal{T}$ and $\nu <_P^\delta \mu$.

• Let μ' be a model of $\mathcal{T} \wedge \forall x \ P(x)$. The only definable subsets of $D_{\mu'}$ are finite unions of intervals, as the theory of real closed fields allows the elimination of quantifiers (see [KK71, p.59–64]). So, there is no model of $\mathcal{T}$ such that $\nu <_P^\delta \mu'$.

• For every model μ'' of $\mathcal{T}$, there exists ν such that $\nu (<_P)_\mathcal{T} \mu''$ (we can always find a subgroup).

We have proved: $\mathbf{Circ}_1(\mathcal{T} : P) \equiv \mathcal{T} \wedge \forall x \ P(x)$,
$\quad \mathbf{Circ}_2(\mathcal{T} : P)$ is inconsistent.

Also from these results it is easy to show that:

• The first order circumscription is cumulative. Indeed, for any formula ϕ such that $\mathcal{T} \wedge \forall x \ P(x) \models \phi$, we have $\mathbf{Circ}_1(\mathcal{T} \wedge \phi : P) \equiv \mathcal{T} \wedge \forall x \ P(x) \equiv \mathbf{Circ}_1(\mathcal{T} : P)$. However $\mathcal{T}$ is not definably P-well-founded: this condition is sufficient for cumulativity, but it is not necessary. As $\prec$, which is $<_P^\delta$ here, is transitive, $\mathcal{T}$ is not weakly well-founded for $\prec$. This is a counter-example to the full converse of theorem 4.8.

• The second order circumscription is not cumulative. With $\phi' \equiv P(1) \wedge \forall y \ ((P(y) \wedge 0 < y) \Rightarrow (1 < y \vee 1 = y))$ we have: $\mathbf{Circ}_2(\mathcal{T} : P) \models \phi'$ and $\mathbf{Circ}_2(\mathcal{T} \wedge \phi' : P) \not\models \mathbf{Circ}_2(\mathcal{T} : P)$. Indeed $\mathbf{Circ}_2(\mathcal{T} \wedge \phi' : P)$ is consistent as the model μ given above is minimal for $(\mathcal{T} \cup \{\phi'\}, <_P)$.

• Finally let us remind two results of [MR90]:

1) This example shows that theorems 4.9 and 4.11 in [PM86] are false if the theory is not well-founded.

2) $\mathbf{Circ}_1(\mathcal{T} : P)$ gives the most unexpected result of a circumscription: $\forall x \ P(x)$. □

To conclude on the subject, note that there exist also examples where $\mathcal{T}$ is definably well-founded (which is not the case in example 5.3) without being well-founded (example 5.2 in [MR90]).

5.3 Pointwise circumscription

Definition 5.8 [Lif88] P being a predicate, $P_{/\mathbf{y}}$ is defined by: $P_{/\mathbf{y}}(\mathbf{x}) \equiv (P(\mathbf{x}) \wedge \mathbf{x} \neq \mathbf{y})$. The *pointwise circumscription of P in $\mathcal{T}$*, noted $\mathbf{Cppp}(\mathcal{T}:P)$ adds to $\mathcal{T}$ the axiom $\mathcal{T}[P_{/\mathbf{y}}] \Rightarrow \neg P(\mathbf{y})$, which is one instance of the circumscription axiom schema of $\mathbf{Circ}_1(\mathcal{T}:P)$.

Pointwise circumscription is important for at least two reasons:

- As we add one formula only, we do not have to guess which instances of a possibly infinite axiom schema are useful, as with standard circumscription. And for some theories we have equivalence between $\mathbf{Circ}_1(\mathcal{T}:P)$ and $\mathbf{Cppp}(\mathcal{T}:P)$ [Lif88].

- This circumscription simulates and generalizes the notion of predicate completion [Moi88b].

Definition 5.9 If $\mu =_P \nu$ and if $|P|_\mu$ is $|P|_\nu$ less exactly one element, we note $\mu <_{1:P} \nu$
(we may indifferently write $\mu =_P \nu$ or $\mu =_P^\delta \nu$ here, as $|P|_\mu$ is definable with one parameter in ν).

Theorem 5.6 A model of $\mathbf{Cppp}(\mathcal{T}:P)$ is a model of $\mathcal{T}$ minimal for $<_{1:P}$.

(For a proof, straightforward, see [MR91]).

Example 5.4 $\mathcal{T}$: $P(a) \wedge \forall x\,(x=a \vee x=b \vee x=c)$.

Let μ, ν and ν' be three particular models of $\mathcal{T}$:
$D_\mu = D_\nu = D_{\nu'} = |P|_\mu = \{a,b,c\}$; $|P|_\nu = \{a,b\}$; $|P|_{\nu'} = \{a\}$.
ν' is minimal for $(\mathcal{T}, <_{1:P})$, $\nu' \overline{<_{1:P}} \mu$, but we do not have $\nu' <_{1:P} \mu$.

The models of $\mathbf{Cppp}(\mathcal{T}:P)$ are the models of $\mathcal{T}$ in which $|P|_\mu = \{a_\mu\}$.

$\mathbf{Cppp}(\mathcal{T}:P) \equiv \mathcal{T} \cup \{\forall x\,(P(x) \Rightarrow (x=a))\}$. $\mathcal{T}$ has ten models (up to isomorphism): it is easy to verify that $<_{1:P}$ is weakly well-founded (it is even "bounded" in Shoham's meaning), while it is neither well-founded nor mildly well-founded.

$\mathbf{Cppp}(\mathcal{T}:P)$ is not cumulative: it entails $\phi \equiv (a \neq b \wedge a \neq c) \Rightarrow (P(b) \Leftrightarrow P(c))$ and $\psi \equiv (a \neq b \wedge a \neq c) \Rightarrow \neg P(b)$ while $\mathbf{Cppp}(\mathcal{T} \wedge \phi : P)$ does not entail ψ. □

Now comes a second example, where $\prec$ is mildly well-founded without being well-founded.

Example 5.5 $\mathcal{L}$ contains five predicate symbols E, E_1, E_2, P (unary) and $<$ (binary, we note $x < y$), the symbol $=$ and one unary function symbol f. We describe $\mathcal{T}$ informally, as a complete list of axioms would not be readable. Any x verifies one and only one formula among $E(x)$, $E_1(x)$ and $E_2(x)$. $<$ is a discrete and total order, defined only on E, without smallest or greatest element. f is a mapping from E_2 onto E_1, from E_1 onto E, and from E onto E_2 which satisfies $\forall x\,(f^3(x) = x)$. $P \cap E$ is a final interval of E (i.e: $\forall x\,(P(x) \wedge x < y) \Rightarrow P(y))$ which has a smallest element for $<$. For the sake of brevity, let us note e this element (e is a new symbol, but any formula containing e may be translated into a formula in $\mathcal{L}$). We have also: $\forall x\,((E_1(x) \wedge x \neq f^2(e)) \Rightarrow P(x))$, $\forall x\,(E_2(x) \wedge x \neq f(e)) \Rightarrow P(x))$, and $P(f(e)) \Rightarrow P(f^2(e))$. We have described all the axioms of $\mathcal{T}$, which is finitely axiomatizable.

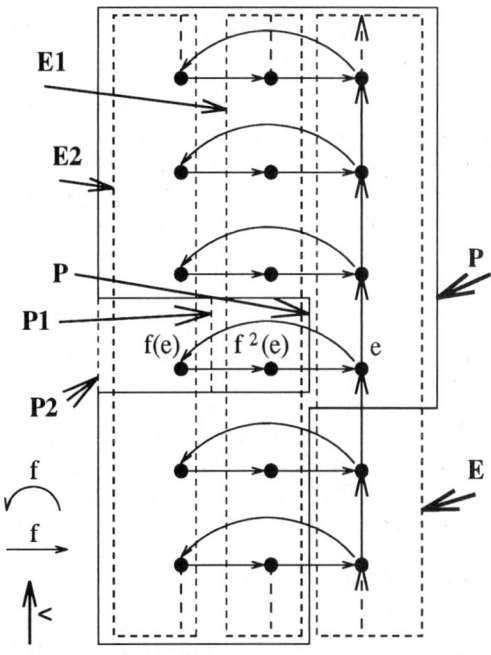

$\mathcal{T}$ has only three kinds of models: those verifying $\phi_0 = \neg P(f^2(e))$, (resp. $\phi_1 = P(f^2(e)) \wedge \neg P(f(e))$ and $\phi_2 = P(f(e))$) which have an extension for P which is like "**P**" (resp. "**P1**" and "**P2**") on the drawing. $\mathcal{T}_0 = Th(\mathcal{T} \cup \{\phi_0\})$, $\mathcal{T}_1 = Th(\mathcal{T} \cup \{\phi_1\})$ and $\mathcal{T}_2 = Th(\mathcal{T} \cup \{\phi_2\})$ are complete theories. The complete proof is tedious but not very hard, once we recall that the theory of total discrete order without endpoints is complete, and that the elements of this theory are undiscernible (no first order formula using only $<$ and $=$, with one free variable, can be true for some elements in a model and false for other elements, cf e.g [CK73, p.101, 147–150]) and once we remark that the interpretation of f is completely defined in any model of $\mathcal{T}$.

The models of $\mathcal{T}$ minimal for $<_{1:P}$ are the models of $\mathcal{T}_0$. Indeed, if μ is a model of $\mathcal{T}_0$, we cannot remove one single element in $|P|_\mu$ without contradicting some axioms in $\mathcal{T}$. If μ is a model of $\mathcal{T}_1$, we can remove $f^2_\mu(e)$ from $|P|_\mu$ (this gives a model μ' of $\mathcal{T}_0$). If μ is a model of $\mathcal{T}_2$, we can remove $f_\mu(e)$ from $|P|_\mu$ (this gives a model μ' of $\mathcal{T}_1$), and also we could remove e (this giving a model μ'' of T_2). This describes all the possibilities, thus T is weakly well-founded for $<_{1:P}$ but it is not well-founded (note that T is not "bounded" in Shoham's meaning).

T is well-behaved. Indeed, let ϕ be a formula true in all the models minimal for $(T, <_{1:P})$, and T' be $T \cup \{\phi\}$. $T_0 \models T'$ and $T' \models T$, thus as T_0, T_1 and T_2 are complete theories, T' is equivalent either to T_0, or to $T_0 \cap T_1$, or to $T_0 \cap T_2$, or to $T_0 \cap T_1 \cap T_2$, i.e T (the intersection of theories closed for entailment is the theory having for models the union of the classes of models of each theory). In each case, the models minimal for $(T', <_{1:P})$ are exactly the models of T_0.

Note that the drawing of a model of T above is also a good illustration of the relation $<_{1:P}$ among models of T, once we remove the curved arrows. The straight arrows representing f or $<$ correspond now to $<_{1:P}$. The points representing elements in E (respectively E_1, E_2) correspond now to models of T_2 (respectively T_1, T_0).

It can be shown that there are no examples of this kind with pointwise circumscription without an infinite sequence of models. □

We give now an example of the same kind with a "compound" circumscription, involving the less classical circumscription $\mathbf{Circ_{nonuniv}}(T:P)$ which adds $\neg \forall x\, P(x)$ to any theory T:

Example 5.6 T is $\forall x\, (x = a \vee x = b)$, $a \neq b$, $P(a) \vee \neg P(b)$.

We use: $\mathbf{Circg}(T : P) \equiv \mathbf{Cppp}(T : P) \cup \mathbf{Circ_{nonuniv}}(T : P)$.

T has only three models (up to isomorphism): $D_\mu = D_\nu = D_\lambda = \{a, b\}$, $|P|_\lambda = \emptyset$, $|P|_\mu = \{a\}$, $|P|_\nu = \{a, b\}$. The relation $\prec$ naturally associated to this circumscription is: $\lambda \prec \mu$, $\mu \prec \nu$, and $\nu \prec \nu$. The only minimal model is λ. T is not well-founded for $\prec$: there exists no ν' minimal for $(T, \prec)$ with $\nu' \prec \nu$; however, $\prec$ is weakly well-founded for $\prec$. Now, there are only two non trivial T' such that $T \models_\prec T'$ and $T' \models T$ (T_λ denotes the theory of λ): $T_\lambda \cap T_\mu$ and $T_\lambda \cap T_\nu$. In each case the only minimal model is λ, thus T is well-behaved (theorem 2.4). Here is an illustration of the relation $\prec$ in this case:

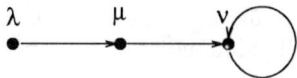

Note the analogies with the preceding example: we get here a preference relation which is the "quotient" of the relation $<_P$ of example 5.5 by elementary equivalence.

It is another example of a relation which is mildly well-founded without being well-founded (T is cumulative for the "circumscription" considered here). □

Note that $\overline{<_{1:P}}$ is antisymmetric and antireflexive. However, pointwise circumscription is not an ordered preferential entailment notion, contrarily to domain and predicate circumscriptions.

5.4 Strong circumscription

This circumscription is introduced in [Lif88] under the name *strong pointwise circumscription*. It is useful because the axiom is simpler than the standard circumscription axiom, and it is equivalent to standard circumscription for Horn theories and well-founded logic programs [Moi90]. Also it is a simulation of the "Closed World Assumption" (CWA) as defined in [Rei78]. It is a kind of CWA not restricted to ground terms.

Definition 5.10 The *second order strong circumscription of* $\mathbf{P}$ *in* T, *with* $\mathbf{Q}$ *as varying*, noted $\mathbf{Circf_2}(T : \mathbf{P}; \mathbf{Q})$, is accomplished by adding the following axiom to T: $\forall \mathbf{p} \forall \mathbf{q}\, \{T[\mathbf{p}, \mathbf{q}] \Rightarrow \forall \mathbf{x}\, (\mathbf{P}(\mathbf{x}) \Rightarrow \mathbf{p}(\mathbf{x}))\}$.

There is also a first order version $\mathbf{Circf_1}(T:\mathbf{P};\mathbf{Q})$.

$\mathbf{Circf}(T:\mathbf{P};\mathbf{Q})$ refers to any version.

Definition 5.11 [Moi90] We write $\nu \prec_{\mathbf{P};\mathbf{Q}} \mu$ (respectively $\nu \prec^\delta_{\mathbf{P};\mathbf{Q}} \mu$) when $\nu =_{\mathbf{P};\mathbf{Q}} \mu$ (respectively $\nu =^\delta_{\mathbf{P};\mathbf{Q}} \mu$) and $|P_i|_\mu - |P_i|_\nu \neq \emptyset$ for at least one i ($1 \leq i \leq n$).

Theorem 5.7 [Moi90] • The models of $\mathbf{Circf_2}(T:\mathbf{P};\mathbf{Q})$ are the models of T minimal for $\prec_{\mathbf{P};\mathbf{Q}}$.
• The models of $\mathbf{Circf_1}(T:\mathbf{P};\mathbf{Q})$ are the models of T minimal for $\prec^\delta_{\mathbf{P};\mathbf{Q}}$.

Remarks 5.1 a) If $\nu <_{\mathbf{P};\mathbf{Q}} \mu$, then $\nu \prec_{\mathbf{P};\mathbf{Q}} \mu$, the converse is false. Thus, a model minimal for $\prec_{\mathbf{P};\mathbf{Q}}$ is minimal for $<_{\mathbf{P};\mathbf{Q}}$ (i.e. $\mathbf{Circf}(T:\mathbf{P};\mathbf{Q})$ entails $\mathbf{Circ}(T:\mathbf{P};\mathbf{Q})$), the general converse is false, although it is true for some classes of theories including Horn theories.

b) The relation $\prec_{\mathbf{P};\mathbf{Q}}$ is not transitive.

c) $\nu \prec_{\mathbf{P};\mathbf{Q}} \mu$ means that in the extension of $\mathbf{P}$ in μ, we remove at least one element, even at the price of adding other elements in this extension.

a), b) and c) hold with $^\delta$-relations.

Example 5.7 $T: (P(a) \vee P(b)) \wedge a \neq b$
T is is well-founded for $<_P$, the relation naturally associated to standard circumscription $\mathbf{Circ}(T:P)$.

With strong circumscription (first order or second order versions are equivalent here) the situation is different. $\mathbf{Circf}(T:P)$ is inconsistent: from $\mathbf{Circf}(T:P)$, $\neg P(a)$ can be proved (choose $x = b$ as $p[x]$), as can $\neg P(b)$ (choose $x = a$ as $p[x]$). No model of T is minimal for $\prec_P$.

Here are two models of $\mathcal{T}$: $D_\mu = D_\nu = \{a,b\}$, $|P|_\mu = \{a\}$, $|P|_\nu = \{b\}$. We get $\nu \prec_P \mu$, as $a \in |P|_\mu$, $a \notin |P|_\nu$ and $\mu \prec_P \nu$. Thus, we have $\mu \; \overline{(\prec_P)_\mathcal{T}} \; \mu$ and $\nu \; \overline{(\prec_P)_\mathcal{T}} \; \nu$.
In fact $\overline{\prec_{P_\mathcal{T}}}$ is reflexive here. □

$\prec_{P;Q}$ is antireflexive but this is not very interesting as it is not transitive and as $\overline{\prec_{P;Q}}$ is not antireflexive. Neither $\prec_{P;Q}$ nor $\overline{\prec_{P;Q}}$ are antisymmetrical. Strong circumscription is our second example of a not ordered preferential entailment, and its preference relation $\prec_{P;Q}$ has yet less properties than $<_{1:P}$. However, the results of sections 2, 3 and 4 apply.

6 Conclusion

Our goal was to unify all the results about various kinds of circumscriptions, including domain, predicate and formula circumscriptions. To that purpose, we used a notion which in fact originated from the studies about circumscription: preferential entailment. We have made precise the equivalence between the two notions of circumscription and of preferential entailment. We have exhibited one important property of all the preferential entailments naturally associated to a circumscription: coherence with respect to the syntax. We have studied the unavoidable case of a preferential entailment corresponding to a non transitive relation. Also, we have isolated a powerful property of circumscriptions: reverse monotony, which implies most of the previously known properties of circumscriptions.

Several examples have been given, in order to illustrate the utility of an appropriate preferential entailment approach and of our definitions of well-foundedness in the non transitive case. Two examples show that the first order and the second order versions of predicate circumscription do not behave in the same way with respect to the important property of cumulativity.

The results of this paper apply also to more exotic circumscriptions, including all kinds of pointwise circumscription of [Lif88], closed or non recursive circumscriptions of [BMM89], or definabilization of [MR91].

Acknowledgements

We gratefully thank Philippe Besnard who initiated this work.

References

[Bes88] P. Besnard. Axiomatizations in the metatheory of nonmonotonic inference systems. *CSCSI*, p. 117–124, 1988.

[Bes89] P. Besnard.. *An Introduction to Default Logic*. Springer Verlag, Heidelberg, 1989.

[BHR88] P. Besnard, J. Houdebine, and R. Rolland. A formula circumscriptively both valid and unprovable. *ECAI*, p. 516–518, 1988.

[BMM89] P. Besnard, R. Mercer, and Y. Moinard. The importance of open and recursive circumscription. *Artificial Intelligence*, 39:251–262, 1989.

[BS88] P. Besnard and P. Siegel. The preferential-models approach to non-monotonic logics. In *Non-Standard Logics for Automated Reasoning*, p. 137–161. Academic Press, 1988.

[BS85] G. Bossu and P. Siegel. Saturation, nonmonotonic reasoning and the closed-world assumption. *Artificial Intelligence*, 25:13–63, 1985.

[CK73] C.C. Chang and H.J. Keisler. *Model Theory*. North-Holland, Amsterdam, 1973.

[Dav80] M. Davis. The mathematics of non-monotonic reasoning. *Artificial Intelligence*, 13:73–80, 1980.

[Doy85] J. Doyle. Circumscription and implicit definability. *Automated Reasoning*, 1:391–405, 1985.

[EM87] D.W. Etherington and R.E. Mercer. Domain circumscription: a reevaluation. *Computational Intelligence*, 3:94–99, 1987.

[EMR85] D. W. Etherington, R. E. Mercer, and R. Reiter. On the adequacy of predicate circumscription for closed-world reasoning. *Computational Intelligence*, 1:11–15, 1985.

[End72] H. B. Enderton. *A Mathematical introduction to logic*. Academic Press, 1972.

[FLM91] M. Freund, D. Lehmann, and P. Morris. Rationality, Transitivity, and Contraposition. *Artificial Intelligence*, 52:191–203, 1991.

[Gab85] D.M. Gabbay. Theoretical foundations for nonmonotonic reasoning in expert systems. In *Proc. Logics and Models of Concurrent Systems, NATO ASI Series F*, vol.13. Springer Verlag, 1985.

[Jae86] G. Jaeger. Some contributions to the logical analysis of circumscription. In *CADE-8, in LNCS-230*, p. 154–171. 1986.

[KK71] G. Kreisel and J-L. Krivine. *Elements of Mathematical Logic: Model Theory*. North Holland, 1971.

[KLM90] S. Kraus, D. Lehmann, and M. Magidor. Nonmonotonic reasoning, preferential models and cumulative logics. *Artificial Intelligence*, 44:167–207, 1990.

[Lif86] V. Lifschitz. On the satisfiability of circumscription. *Artificial Intelligence*, 28:17–27, 1986.

[Lif88] V. Lifschitz. Pointwise circumscription. In *Readings in Nonmonotonic Reasoning*, p. 179–193. Morgan Kaufmann, 1988.

[Mak88] D. Makinson. General theory of cumulative inference. In *LNAI-346*, pages 1–18. 1988.

[McC80] J. McCarthy. Circumscription–a form of non-monotonic reasoning. *Artificial Intelligence*, 13:27–39, 1980.

[McC86] J. McCarthy. Application of circumscription to formalizing common sense knowledge. *Artificial Intelligence*, 28:89–116, 1986.

[Moi88a] Y. Moinard. Contribution à l'étude de la circonscription. Thèse, Rennes, 1988.

[Moi88b] Y. Moinard. Pointwise circumscription is equivalent to predicate completion (sometimes). In *Logic Programming*, p. 1097–1105, MIT Press, 1988.

[Moi90] Y. Moinard. Circumscription and Horn theories. In *ECAI*, p. 449–454, 1990.

[Moi92] Y. Moinard. Circumscriptions as preferential entailments. In *ECAI*, p. 329–333, 1992.

[Moi94] Y. Moinard. Circumscriptions for preferential entailments. *Submitted*, 1994.

[Mor85] M.P. Morreau. Circumscription: A sound and complete form of non-monotonic reasoning. T. R. 15, University, Amsterdam, 1985.

[MR90] Y. Moinard and R. Rolland. Unexpected and unwanted results of circumscription. In *AIMSA*, p. 61–70, North-Holland, 1990.

[MR91] Y. Moinard and R. Rolland. Circumscription and definability. In *IJCAI*, p. 432–437, 1991.

[PM86] D. Perlis and J. Minker. Completeness results for circumscription. *Artificial Intelligence*, 28:29–42, 1986.

[Rei78] R. Reiter. On closed world data bases. In *Logic and Data Bases*, p. 55–76. Plenum, 1978.

[Ryc90] P. Rychlick. The Generalized Theory of Model Preference. In *AAAI*, p. 615–620, 1990.

[Sho88] Y. Shoham. *Reasoning about change*. MIT Press, Cambridge, 1988.

[Som90] Léa Sombé. *Reasoning under Incomplete Information in Artificial Intelligence*. Wiley, 1990.

A Decision Method for Nonmonotonic Reasoning Based on Autoepistemic Reasoning

Ilkka Niemelä
Department of Computer Science
Helsinki University of Technology
Otakaari 1, FIN–02150 Espoo, Finland
Ilkka.Niemela@hut.fi

Abstract

A novel decision method for autoepistemic reasoning is developed and proved correct. The method is applicable in a general setting, i.e. for an autoepistemic logic based on a given classical logic. It provides a decision procedure for a tightly grounded form of autoepistemic reasoning based on L-hierarchic expansions as well as for autoepistemic reasoning based on Moore style expansions and N-expansions. Prominent formalizations of nonmonotonic reasoning, such as default logic and circumscription, can be embedded into autoepistemic logic based on L-hierarchic expansions using simple local translations. Hence, the method can serve as a unified reasoning tool for a wide range of forms of nonmonotonic reasoning. The method is conceptually simple and the inherent sources of complexity and targets for optimization are clearly identifiable. As an example of exploiting optimization possibilities a new decision method for Reiter's default logic is developed where ideas from autoepistemic reasoning are used to efficiently prune the search space of applying default rules when constructing extensions of a default theory.

1 INTRODUCTION

We study the problem of automating nonmonotonic reasoning. Several forms of nonmonotonic reasoning have been proposed and in recent years research has been focused on relationships between different formalizations. Despite of different starting points and underlying intuitions, leading approaches to nonmonotonic reasoning have turned out to be closely related. Our aim is to exploit the close connections so that a single theorem prover could be used as a unified reasoning tool for a wide range of forms of nonmonotonic reasoning. An interesting approach is to choose some formalization of nonmonotonic reasoning as a basic system and develop a theorem prover for it. Decision procedures for other forms of nonmonotonic reasoning can then be realized by reducing decision problems in a given formalization to decision problems in the basic system. In this paper we consider the possibility of using autoepistemic logic, originally introduced by Moore (1985), as the basic system and we develop a novel decision method for autoepistemic reasoning which can serve as a basis for a unified reasoning tool for nonmonotonic reasoning.

Besides autoepistemic logic, there are many other interesting alternatives to be used as a basic system including logic programming, default logic (Reiter 1980), McDermott and Doyle style nonmonotonic modal logics (Marek, Shvarts and Truszczyński 1991), and systems based on two modalities (Lifschitz 1991). Autoepistemic logic provides a rather expressive basic language. This implies that other general approaches to nonmonotonic reasoning such as default logic can be captured using simple local translations. When using a basic language with limited expressivity such as that of logic programs more complicated translations are needed. Autoepistemic logic has a uniform syntax unlike default logic. This enables a unified treatment of default rules, queries and integrity constraints. As opposed to other approaches to formalizing nonmonotonic reasoning based on modal logic, autoepistemic logic is rather uncomplicated. It is a direct extension of the underlying classical logic where only straightforward principles of positive and negative introspection are added but no modal axioms are needed. Moreover, recent results show that autoepistemic logic covers a range of prominent forms of nonmonotonic reasoning (Konolige 1988, Marek and Truszczyński 1989, Konolige 1989, Marek et al. 1991, Elkan 1990). However, some of the embeddings are rather complicated because the original autoepistemic logic allows weakly grounded conclusions which have to be eliminated in the embeddings using extra conditions (Konolige 1988, Marek and Truszczyński 1989) or complicated translations (Gottlob 1993). In this paper we adopt a tightly grounded form of autoepistemic logic based on L-hierarchic expansions (Niemelä 1991) as the basic system. In L-hierarchic expansions the troublesome weakly grounded conclusions are excluded but without introducing any dependence on the syntactic representation of the premises. Furthermore, simple local translations can be used to reduce decision problems in other forms of nonmonotonic reasoning to decision problems in autoepistemic logic based on L-hierarchic expansions (Niemelä 1992b).

Several decision methods have been proposed for autoepistemic reasoning. Some of these (Moore 1988, Stärk 1990, Marek et al. 1991) are straightforward applications of a particular finitary characterization of autoepistemic reasoning, some (Niemelä 1988) use extensively a specific underlying proof method and some (Marek and Truszczyński 1991a, Junker and Konolige 1990, Marek and Truszczyński 1991b) are based on the idea of mapping a decision problem in autoepistemic logic into another problem. In this work we develop a decision method for autoepistemic logic in a general setting, i.e. for an autoepistemic logic based on a given classical logic. At this stage we do not want to commit to a particular underlying proof method and we aim at a conceptually clear method where the sources of complexity and targets for optimization are clearly identifiable. Furthermore, we try to avoid exponential worst-case space requirements which seem to be inherent in the more advanced methods (Niemelä 1988, Marek and Truszczyński 1991a, Junker and Konolige 1990, Marek and Truszczyński 1991b). This aspect is further discussed in Section 4.

2 AUTOEPISTEMIC LOGIC

Autoepistemic logic is a modal logic with an operator L which is interpreted as "is believed". Autoepistemic logic models the beliefs of an ideally rational fully introspective agent. The main object of interest in autoepistemic logic is the set of beliefs of the agent given a set of sentences as the initial premises of the agent. The agent's ideal rationality implies that the agent believes exactly every logical consequence of the initial assumptions and her/his beliefs. Full introspection entails that the agent is capable of using both positive introspection (if χ is a belief, so is $L\chi$) and negative introspection (if χ is not a belief, then $\neg L\chi$ is).

We consider a general setting where a classical calculus CL is given and an autoepistemic logic CL_{ae} is built on top of that. This kind of a general setting has already been studied (Niemelä 1992a). Let $\mathcal{L}$ be the language of CL. We extend $\mathcal{L}$ by adding a monadic operator L not appearing in $\mathcal{L}$ and obtain an autoepistemic language $\mathcal{L}_{ae}$ which is the language of CL_{ae}. The language $\mathcal{L}_{ae}$ is defined recursively as $\mathcal{L}$ but with an extra formation rule: if $\phi \in \mathcal{L}_{ae}$ is a sentence, then $L\phi \in \mathcal{L}_{ae}$.

Thus we consider autoepistemic logics where quantification into a modal context is not allowed even if $\mathcal{L}$ contains quantifiers (e.g. formulae of the form $\forall x L P(x)$ are not allowed). To simplify the treatment we consider only closed formulae. So from here on we let $\mathcal{L}$ and $\mathcal{L}_{ae}$ contain only closed formulae. In the general setting an ideally rational agent believes the logical consequences given by a consequence relation $\models_{ae}$ which is a simple extension of the consequence relation $\models_{cl}$ of CL where the $L\phi$ formulae are treated like atomic formulae in the propositional calculus.

To formalize a tight notion of autoepistemic reasoning Niemelä (1991) has proposed an enumeration-based method where autoepistemic reasoning is defined as a sequence of introspection steps of an ideally rational agent. The idea is to build a set of beliefs from premises Σ by applying introspection to sentences in the order given by an enumeration ε. A set $\mathbf{B}^{\varepsilon}(\Sigma)$ is constructed which contains all the results of introspection. The set $\mathbf{B}^{\varepsilon}(\Sigma)$ together with Σ induces the set of beliefs $\mathbf{SE}^{\varepsilon}(\Sigma)$ of an agent having initial assumptions Σ after introspecting sentences in the order ε.

Definition 2.1 *Let* $\Sigma \subseteq \mathcal{L}_{ae}$. *Let* $\varepsilon = \psi_1, \psi_2, \ldots$ *be an enumeration of sentences in* $\mathcal{L}_{ae}$. *Let* $\mathbf{B}_0^{\varepsilon}(\Sigma) = \emptyset$ *and define* $\mathbf{B}_{i+1}^{\varepsilon}(\Sigma)$ *for* $i = 0, 1, \ldots$ *as follows:*

$$\mathbf{B}_{i+1}^{\varepsilon}(\Sigma) = \begin{cases} \mathbf{B}_i^{\varepsilon}(\Sigma) \cup \{L\psi_{i+1}\} & \text{if } \Sigma \cup \mathbf{B}_i^{\varepsilon}(\Sigma) \models_{ae} \psi_{i+1} \\ \mathbf{B}_i^{\varepsilon}(\Sigma) \cup \{\neg L\psi_{i+1}\} & \text{otherwise} \end{cases}$$

Finally let

$$\mathbf{B}^{\varepsilon}(\Sigma) = \bigcup_{i=0}^{\infty} \mathbf{B}_i^{\varepsilon}(\Sigma)$$
$$\mathbf{SE}^{\varepsilon}(\Sigma) = \{\phi \in \mathcal{L}_{ae} \mid \Sigma \cup \mathbf{B}^{\varepsilon}(\Sigma) \models_{ae} \phi\}.$$

To guarantee that the introspection principles of autoepistemic reasoning are respected the enumeration ε is required to be acceptable with respect to the set of premises.

Definition 2.2 *An enumeration* ε *is* Σ-*acceptable if there is no i and no formula ϕ such that* $\neg L\phi \in \mathbf{B}_i^{\varepsilon}(\Sigma)$ *but* $\Sigma \cup \mathbf{B}_i^{\varepsilon}(\Sigma) \models_{ae} \phi$.

Example 1 Consider the propositional case, a set of premises $\Sigma = \{\neg Lp \to q\}$ and an enumeration $\varepsilon = q, p, \ldots$ Then $\mathbf{B}_1^{\varepsilon}(\Sigma) = \{\neg Lq\}$ as $\Sigma \not\models_{ae} q$ and $\mathbf{B}_2^{\varepsilon}(\Sigma) = \{\neg Lq, \neg Lp\}$ as $\Sigma \cup \mathbf{B}_1^{\varepsilon}(\Sigma) \not\models_{ae} p$. This enumeration is not Σ-acceptable because $\neg Lq \in \mathbf{B}_2^{\varepsilon}(\Sigma)$ but $\Sigma \cup \mathbf{B}_2^{\varepsilon}(\Sigma) \models_{ae} q$. ∎

We assume that the underlying consequence relation $\models_{ae}$ is compact, i.e., if $\Sigma \models_{ae} \phi$, there exists a finite subset Σ' of Σ such that $\Sigma' \models_{ae} \phi$. For compact logics the acceptability condition implies that the introspection principles are not violated and the resulting set of beliefs is a Moore style expansion (Moore 1985).

Theorem 2.3 (Niemelä (1992a)) *For every Σ-acceptable enumeration ε of $\mathcal{L}_{\text{ae}}$, $\mathbf{SE}^\varepsilon(\Sigma)$ is a Moore style stable expansion of Σ, i.e.*

$$\mathbf{SE}^\varepsilon(\Sigma) = \{\phi \mid \Sigma \cup L\mathbf{SE}^\varepsilon(\Sigma) \cup \neg L\overline{\mathbf{SE}^\varepsilon(\Sigma)} \models_{\text{ae}} \phi\}$$

holds where $L\Delta = \{L\phi \mid \phi \in \Delta\}$, $\neg\Delta = \{\neg\phi \mid \phi \in \Delta\}$, and $\overline{\Delta} = \mathcal{L}_{\text{ae}} - \Delta$.

Enumeration-based expansions, i.e. sets of beliefs induced by acceptable enumerations, are a proper subclass of Moore style expansions. In the propositional case they coincide with the N-expansions (Marek et al. 1991) which are the same as iterative expansions (Marek and Truszczyński 1989) (see (Niemelä 1991)). The weakly grounded beliefs in N-expansions can be eliminated by requiring enumerations to be *L-hierarchic*. The resulting L-hierarchic expansions provide an interesting tightly grounded form of autoepistemic reasoning.

Definition 2.4 *Let ε be an enumeration $\psi_1, \psi_2, \ldots$ of sentences in $\mathcal{L}_{\text{ae}}$. The enumeration ε is L-hierarchic iff for all ψ_i, ψ_j in ε holds that if $L\psi_i$ is a subformula of ψ_j, then $i < j$.*

A set of sentences Δ is an L-hierarchic expansion of Σ iff $\Delta = \mathbf{SE}^\varepsilon(\Sigma)$ for some Σ-acceptable L-hierarchic enumeration ε of $\mathcal{L}_{\text{ae}}$.

Example 2 Consider the propositional case, a set of premises

$$\Sigma = \{\neg L \neg L p \to p\} \tag{1}$$

where p is an atomic formula and an enumeration $\varepsilon = \neg Lp, p, \ldots$ Now ε leads to an enumeration-based expansion containing an ungrounded belief p (see also (Niemelä 1991)). However, ε is not L-hierarchic. ∎

An expansion of premises is a possible set of conclusions derivable from the premises. But as there are premises with multiple expansions, the concepts of cautious and brave reasoning are introduced. Given a class of expansions, a formula is derivable from a set of premises in the *cautious* sense iff it is in every expansion of the premises and in the *brave* sense iff it is at least in one of the expansions. We denote the derivability relations with respect to L-hierarchic, enumeration-based and Moore style expansions by $\vdash_{c(LE)}$, $\vdash_{b(LE)}$, $\vdash_{c(E)}$, $\vdash_{b(E)}$, $\vdash_c$, $\vdash_b$, respectively.

Expansions are infinite sets of sentences and a finitary characterization is needed to enable a computational treatment of autoepistemic reasoning. We use a characterization based on full sets (Niemelä 1990, Niemelä 1992a). The notion of full sets provides a simple and compact representation of expansions which is straightforwardly applicable in the general setting considered here. An overview of other approaches to characterizing expansions can be found in (Niemelä 1992a).

First we introduce some notation. For an $L\chi$ formula, q-atom$(L\chi)$ = q-atom$(\neg L\chi) = L\chi$ and for a set Λ, q-atom$(\Lambda) = \{$q-atom$(\phi) \mid \phi \in \Lambda\}$. The set of all subformulae of the form $L\chi$ of a formula ϕ is denoted by $\text{Sf}^L(\phi)$ and $\text{Sf}^{qL}(\phi)$ is the set of all subformulae of the form $L\chi$ of ϕ which are not in the scope of another L operator in ϕ. We define a simple consequence relation $\models_L$ which is given recursively on top of the underlying consequence relation $\models_{\text{ae}}$.

Definition 2.5 *Given a set of sentences Σ and a sentence ϕ,*

$$\Sigma \models_L \phi \text{ iff } \Sigma \cup \text{SB}_\Sigma(\phi) \models_{\text{ae}} \phi$$

where $\text{SB}_\Sigma(\phi) = \{L\chi \in \text{Sf}^{qL}(\phi) \mid \Sigma \models_L \chi\} \cup \{\neg L\chi \in \neg\text{Sf}^{qL}(\phi) \mid \Sigma \not\models_L \chi\}$.

A finitary characterization for Moore style expansions can be provided in terms of sets of sentences constructed from the $L\chi$ and $\neg L\chi$ subformulae of the premises satisfying a special fullness condition. A full set serves as the kernel of a stable expansion; it uniquely characterizes the stable expansion. In fact there is a one-to-one correspondence between full sets and expansions.

Definition 2.6 *For a set of sentences Σ, a set $\Lambda \subseteq \text{Sf}^L(\Sigma) \cup \neg\text{Sf}^L(\Sigma)$ is Σ-full iff the following two conditions hold for every $L\chi \in \text{Sf}^L(\Sigma)$:*

1. $\Sigma \cup \Lambda \models_{\text{ae}} \chi$ iff $L\chi \in \Lambda$.

2. $\Sigma \cup \Lambda \not\models_{\text{ae}} \chi$ iff $\neg L\chi \in \Lambda$.

Theorem 2.7 (Niemelä (1992a)) *Let Σ be a set of sentences of $\mathcal{L}_{\text{ae}}$. Then a function SE_Σ defined as*

$$\text{SE}_\Sigma(\Lambda) = \{\phi \in \mathcal{L}_{\text{ae}} \mid \Sigma \cup \Lambda \models_L \phi\}$$

gives a bijective mapping from the set of Σ-full sets to the set of Moore style stable expansions of Σ and $\text{SE}_\Sigma(\Lambda)$ is the unique stable expansion Δ of Σ such that $\Lambda \subseteq L\Delta \cup \neg L\overline{\Delta}$.

Example 3 The premise (1) has two Σ-full sets $\Lambda_1 = \{L\neg Lp, \neg Lp\}$ and $\Lambda_2 = \{\neg L\neg Lp, Lp\}$. For example, Λ_1 is Σ-full as $\Sigma \cup \Lambda_1 \models_{\text{ae}} \neg Lp$ and $\Sigma \cup \Lambda_1 \not\models_{\text{ae}} p$. This implies that Σ has exactly two Moore style expansions $\text{SE}_\Sigma(\Lambda_1)$ and $\text{SE}_\Sigma(\Lambda_2)$. As $\Sigma \cup \Lambda_1 \not\models_L p$, $p \notin \text{SE}_\Sigma(\Lambda_1)$. However, $\neg LLp \in \text{SE}_\Sigma(\Lambda_1)$ as $\Sigma \cup \Lambda_1 \models_L \neg LLp$. ∎

A finitary characterization for enumeration-based expansions is obtained by observing that full sets corresponding to enumeration-based (L-hierarchic) expansions are exactly those generated by acceptable (L-hierarchic) enumerations. First we note that for a finite enumeration the test for acceptability can be stated in the following simple form.

Proposition 2.8 (Niemelä (1992a))
Let $\varepsilon_n = \psi_1, \ldots, \psi_n$ be an enumeration of a finite set.

Then ε_n is Σ-acceptable iff ε_n satisfies the condition: for all $\neg L\phi \in \mathbf{B}_n^{\varepsilon_n}(\Sigma), \Sigma \cup \mathbf{B}_n^{\varepsilon_n}(\Sigma) \not\models_{ae} \phi$.

Theorem 2.9 (Niemelä (1992a)) *Let $\Sigma \subseteq \mathcal{L}_{ae}$ be a set of sentences such that $\mathrm{Sf}^L(\Sigma)$ is finite. If an enumeration $\varepsilon_n = \psi_1, \ldots, \psi_n$ of $\{\phi \mid L\phi \in \mathrm{Sf}^L(\Sigma)\}$ is Σ-acceptable, then $\mathbf{B}_n^{\varepsilon_n}(\Sigma)$ is a Σ-full set and there exists a Σ-acceptable enumeration ε of $\mathcal{L}_{ae}$ such that $\mathbf{SE}^\varepsilon(\Sigma)$ is the unique stable expansion Δ of Σ for which $\mathbf{B}_n^{\varepsilon_n}(\Sigma) \subseteq L\Delta \cup \neg L\overline{\Delta}$ (i.e. $\mathbf{SE}^\varepsilon(\Sigma) = \mathrm{SE}_\Sigma(\mathbf{B}_n^{\varepsilon_n}(\Sigma)))$. Furthermore, if ε_n is L-hierarchic, then ε is also.*

Theorem 2.10 (Niemelä (1992a)) *Let $\Sigma \subseteq \mathcal{L}_{ae}$ be a set of sentences. For every Σ-acceptable (L-hierarchic) enumeration ε of $\mathcal{L}_{ae}$, there exists a Σ-acceptable (L-hierarchic) enumeration ε_L of $\{\phi \mid L\phi \in \mathrm{Sf}^L(\Sigma)\}$ such that $\mathbf{B}^{\varepsilon_L}(\Sigma)$ is the unique Σ-full set Λ for which $\Lambda \subseteq L\mathbf{SE}^\varepsilon(\Sigma) \cup \neg L\overline{\mathbf{SE}^\varepsilon(\Sigma)}$ holds and thus $\mathbf{SE}^\varepsilon(\Sigma) = \mathrm{SE}_\Sigma(\mathbf{B}^{\varepsilon_L}(\Sigma))$.*

Example 4 The Moore style expansions in Example 3 are both characterizable using enumerations of $\{\phi \mid L\phi \in \mathrm{Sf}^L(\Sigma)\} = \{p, \neg Lp\}$: $\mathrm{SE}_\Sigma(\Lambda_1)$ by the enumeration $\varepsilon_2 = p, \neg Lp$ and $\mathrm{SE}_\Sigma(\Lambda_2)$ by the enumeration $\varepsilon'_2 = \neg Lp, p$, i.e. $\Lambda_1 = \mathbf{B}_2^{\varepsilon_2}(\Sigma)$ and $\Lambda_2 = \mathbf{B}_2^{\varepsilon'_2}(\Sigma)$. This implies that Σ has exactly two enumeration-based expansions but only one L-hierarchic expansion, i.e. $\mathrm{SE}_\Sigma(\mathbf{B}_2^{\varepsilon_2}(\Sigma))$. ∎

3 OTHER FORMS OF NONMONOTONIC REASONING

Autoepistemic logic based on L-hierarchic expansions provides an interesting unified basis for a wide range of forms of nonmonotonic reasoning. Leading formalizations such as default logic, circumscription, logic programs, justification-based truth maintenance systems and forms of abduction can be embedded into this variant of autoepistemic logic using simple local translations and without extra conditions or restriction (Niemelä 1992b). This implies that decision problems in these approaches can be reduced to decision problems in autoepistemic logic based on L-hierarchic expansions without introducing additional computational overhead.

Default logic (Reiter 1980) can be embedded into autoepistemic logic based on L-hierarchic expansions using the following translation.

$$\mathrm{AE_{DL}}(\frac{a : b_1, \ldots, b_n}{c}) =$$
$$(La \wedge L\neg L\neg b_1 \wedge \cdots \wedge L\neg L\neg b_n) \rightarrow c \quad (2)$$
$$\mathrm{AE_{DL}}(D, W) = W \cup \{\mathrm{AE_{DL}}(d) \mid d \in D\} \quad (3)$$

Theorem 3.1 (Niemelä (1992b)) *Let (D, W) be a default theory where D is finite. Then a set $E \subseteq \mathcal{L}$ is an extension of (D, W) iff $E = \Delta \cap \mathcal{L}$ for an L-hierarchic expansion Δ of $\mathrm{AE_{DL}}(D, W)$.*

Default logic is closely related to the answer set semantics (Gelfond and Lifschitz 1990) of extended logic programs, i.e. logic programs where classical negation ($\neg$) is allowed even in the scope of the negation-as-failure operator (*not*). Consequently, it is not surprising that answer set semantics can be embedded into autoepistemic logic using the following mapping.

$$\mathrm{LP_{AE}}(l_0 \leftarrow l_1, \ldots, l_m, not\ l_{m+1}, \ldots, not\ l_n) =$$
$$Ll_1 \wedge \ldots \wedge Ll_m \wedge L\neg Ll_{m+1} \wedge \ldots \wedge L\neg Ll_n \rightarrow l_0 \quad (4)$$

Theorem 3.2 (Niemelä (1992b)) *Let P be a finite extended logic program. S is an answer set of P iff S is the set of literals in an L-hierarchic expansion of $\mathrm{LP_{AE}}(P)$.*

When considering logic programs where classical negation is not allowed, i.e. general logic programs, the answer set semantics coincides with the stable model semantics (Gelfond and Lifschitz 1990).

Corollary 3.3 *Let P be a finite general logic program. S is a stable model of P iff S is the set of atomic sentences in an L-hierarchic expansion of $\mathrm{LP_{AE}}(P)$.*

Elkan (1990) has shown that given a set of justifications J the grounded model of J computed by a truth maintenance system is just a stable model of J when J is seen as a propositional logic program.

Corollary 3.4 *Let J be a finite set of justifications. M is a grounded model of J iff M is the set of atomic sentences in an L-hierarchic expansion of $\mathrm{LP_{AE}}(J)$.*

4 AUTOMATING NONMONOTONIC REASONING

In the general setting autoepistemic reasoning is decidable if the underlying consequence relation $\models_{ae}$ is decidable (Niemelä 1992a). Moreover, decision procedures can be obtained from the finitary characterization based on full sets in a very straightforward fashion. For brave reasoning an expansion containing a given formula must be found and for cautious reasoning it must be verified that a given formula is in all the expansions. This can be achieved by constructing the characterizing full set for each of the expansions and performing the membership test on the basis of the full set as implied by Theorem 2.7 using the consequence relation $\models_L$ (see (Niemelä 1992a) for details). However, a decision procedure which is based directly on the finitary characterization is not very practical because to construct the full sets using a direct approach it is necessary to iterate over every subset of the set of $L\chi$ subformulae of the premises. If the cardinality of a set is n, it has 2^n subsets. Moreover, each iteration might be computationally costly, i.e. involve a number of calls to a theorem prover for the underlying consequence relation $\models_{ae}$.

Decision problems in propositional autoepistemic reasoning are complete problems with respect to the second level of the polynomial time hierarchy (Niemelä 1992a) which implies that any general decision method for autoepistemic reasoning most likely has an exponential worst-case *time* complexity. However, a practically oriented decision method should be able to take advantage of possible regularities in a given set of premises. For example, consider a set of premises

$$\Sigma = \{p_0, Lp_0 \to p_1, Lp_1 \to p_2, \ldots, Lp_{n-1} \to p_n\}. \quad (5)$$

A straightforward approach would examine the 2^n subsets of $\{Lp_0, \ldots, Lp_{n-1}\}$ to find the unique Σ-full set $\Lambda = \{Lp_0, \ldots, Lp_{n-1}\}$. However, by carefully exploiting the monotonicity of the underlying consequence relation $\models_{ae}$ it is possible to find the full set without iterating over the subsets: for any Σ-full set Λ, $\Sigma \cup \Lambda \models_{ae} p_0$ holds and thus $Lp_0 \in \Lambda$ must hold which in turn implies $Lp_1 \in \Lambda$ and so on.

We develop first a decision method for autoepistemic reasoning based on L-hierarchic expansions. The decision method builds Σ-full sets for L-hierarchic expansions of Σ. The Σ-full sets can be found by examining the enumerations of the set $\{\phi \mid L\phi \in \mathrm{Sf}^L(\Sigma)\}$. However, the enumerations are not important but the sets of beliefs induced by the enumerations. This observation cuts the combinatorial explosion considerably as typically there is a large number of enumerations inducing the same Σ-full set. The full sets are developed together as far as possible so that the same computation is not repeated by exploiting the monotonicity of the underlying consequence relation $\models_{ae}$. The novel decision method for autoepistemic reasoning needs only a theorem prover for the underlying monotonic consequence relation $\models_{ae}$ as a subroutine.

The approach differs from techniques where nonmonotonic reasoning is reduced to another problem such as a truth maintenance problem (Junker and Konolige 1990), a theorem proving problem (Marek and Truszczyński 1991b), or a constraint satisfaction problem (Ben-Eliyahu and Dechter 1991). These reductions provide valuable insights to the relationships between the corresponding problems and enable new techniques to be used for solving nonmonotonic reasoning problems. However, while there are interesting subclasses of nonmonotonic reasoning problems where the problem size increases only polynomially as a result of the reduction mapping (see, e.g. (Marek and Truszczyński 1991b, Ben-Eliyahu and Dechter 1991)), in the general case the reductions can lead to an exponential increase in the problem size. Hence the worst case *space* complexity becomes exponential. Moreover, the reductions are computationally complex.

As an example we consider the approach of Junker and Konolige (1990). In this approach the premises are required to be in a normal form with no nested L operators. In the worst case, if a set of premises is transformed into the normal form, its size might increase exponentially. Then the premises are mapped to a set of justifications in a truth maintenance system. The size of the resulting set of justifications can be exponential with respect to the size of the premises and the mapping is computationally rather complex. This is because the set of justifications corresponding to premises Σ includes all monotonic justifications $\phi \leftarrow \omega_1, \ldots, \omega_n$ where $L\phi \in \mathrm{Sf}^L(\Sigma)$ and $\{\omega_1, \ldots, \omega_n\}$ is a minimal *proof* of ϕ from $H = \{\omega \mid \neg L\alpha \vee L\beta_1 \vee \ldots \vee L\beta_m \vee \omega \in \Sigma - \mathcal{L}\}$, i.e. a minimal subset of H such that $(\Sigma \cap \mathcal{L}) \cup \{\omega_1, \ldots, \omega_n\} \models_{cl} \phi$ holds. For an $L\phi$ subformula of the premises, ϕ can possess a very large number of minimal proofs. The problem of finding a proof of ϕ from a hypothesis set H given a background theory Σ, i.e. finding a set of $H' \subseteq H$ such that $\Sigma \cup H' \models_{cl} \phi$, is closely related to logic-based abduction (Eiter and Gottlob 1992). If the background theory is a set of clauses, then deciding whether there is a consistent proof of an atom from a set of atoms is Σ_2^p-complete in the propositional case (Eiter and Gottlob 1992). As propositional brave autoepistemic reasoning is also Σ_2^p-complete (Niemelä 1992a), the search problem of finding a consistent proof of an atom is at least as hard as brave autoepistemic reasoning.

In Junker and Konolige's approach an expansion corresponds to a suitable model of the justifications. For example, strongly grounded expansions correspond to grounded models but deciding whether there is a grounded model is **NP**-complete (Elkan 1990). The exponential worst case space complexity and the high time complexity of the reductions raise questions about the usability of the reduction approaches as general decision methods for nonmonotonic reasoning.

4.1 A NOVEL DECISION METHOD FOR AUTOEPISTEMIC REASONING

Figure 1 presents the function $\mathbf{der}_{\mathrm{LE}}$ which is the key part of the novel decision method. The function $\mathbf{der}_{\mathrm{LE}}$ is a skeleton for the decision procedures for brave and cautious reasoning as well as for checking the existence of expansions. For that purpose it contains an unspecified function **test**. By changing this function the various decision procedures are obtained. The function $\mathbf{der}_{\mathrm{LE}}$ takes as input a set of premises Σ, sets B and F which give the common part of the Σ-full sets to be considered and a sentence ϕ which is just passed as an argument to the function **test**.

The purpose of $\mathbf{der}_{\mathrm{LE}}$ is to return true iff there exists an L-hierarchic expansion Δ of Σ containing $B \cup F$ such that $\mathbf{test}(\Sigma, \Lambda, \phi)$ returns true where Λ is the Σ-full set corresponding Δ, i.e. $\Delta = \mathrm{SE}_\Sigma(\Lambda)$. This is achieved by constructing Σ-full sets which contain $B \cup F$ and correspond to L-hierarchic expansions until a full set Λ is found for which $\mathbf{test}(\Sigma, \Lambda, \phi)$ returns true.

In the correctness proof of $\mathbf{der}_{\mathrm{LE}}$ we use the following

FUNCTION $\text{der}_{\text{LE}}(\Sigma, B, F, \phi)$
INPUT: Finite sets of sentences Σ, B, and F and a sentence ϕ.

$\langle B, F \rangle := \text{pos}_{\text{LE}}(\Sigma, B, F);$
IF for some $\neg L\chi \in B$, $\Sigma \cup B \cup F \models_{ae} \chi$ **THEN**
  return false
ELSE IF $\text{Sf}^L(\Sigma) \subseteq \text{q-atom}(B) \cup F$ **THEN**
  IF $F \subseteq B$ **THEN**
    return $\text{test}(\Sigma, B, \phi)$
  ELSE
    return false
ELSE IF for some $L\chi \in \text{Sf}^L(\Sigma) - (\text{q-atom}(B) \cup F)$
    $\text{Sf}^L(\chi) \subseteq \text{q-atom}(B)$ **THEN**
  IF $\text{der}_{\text{LE}}(\Sigma, B \cup \{\neg L\chi\}, F, \phi)$ returns false **THEN**
    return $\text{der}_{\text{LE}}(\Sigma, B, F \cup \{L\chi\}, \phi)$
  ELSE
    return true
ELSE
  return false.

Figure 1: A Skeleton for the Decision Procedures for Autoepistemic Reasoning Based on L-hierarchic Expansions

two notions. An enumeration ε is *fully L-hierarchic* if for every formula ϕ in ε for each subformula $L\chi$ of ϕ, χ appears before ϕ in ε. The set B is *generated* by some enumeration ε if $B = \mathbf{B}^\varepsilon(\Sigma)$.

In the decision method the idea is to expand the set B so that finally it contains every formula in a full set. By Theorem 2.10 for every L-hierarchic expansion, the corresponding full set is generated by some fully L-hierarchic enumeration from Σ. This implies that when deciding how to extend B the number of possibilities can be reduced by considering only those extensions which are generated by some fully L-hierarchic enumeration. Hence in the decision method B is extended only if the resulting set B' is generated by some fully L-hierarchic enumeration ε_m of a subset of $\{\phi \mid L\phi \in \text{Sf}^L(\Sigma)\}$ from Σ, i.e. $B' = \mathbf{B}^{\varepsilon_m}_m(\Sigma)$. The set F contains $L\chi$ sentences which should be included in the full set to be constructed but are "frozen": a sentence $L\chi \in F$ is added to B only after B covers all $L\chi'$ subformulae of χ, i.e. $\text{Sf}^L(\chi) \subseteq \text{q-atom}(B)$, and $\Sigma \cup B \models_{ae} \chi$ holds. This ensures that B remains generatable from Σ by a fully L-hierarchic enumeration.

In der_{LE} the results of positive introspection are first propagated as far as possible using the function pos_{LE} presented in Figure 2. The function exploits the monotonicity of the underlying consequence relation $\models_{ae}$ and expands the sets B and F, i.e. if B is included in a full set and $\Sigma \cup B \models_{ae} \phi$, then $L\phi$ belongs to the full set provided it exists. It is straightforward to verify that pos_{LE} has the following properties.

Proposition 4.1 *Let* $\langle B', F' \rangle = \text{pos}_{\text{LE}}(\Sigma, B, F)$.

FUNCTION $\text{pos}_{\text{LE}}(\Sigma, B, F)$
INPUT: Finite sets of sentences Σ, B, and F.

REPEAT
  $B' := B;$
  FOR every $L\chi \in \text{Sf}^L(\Sigma) - \text{q-atom}(B')$ **DO**
    IF $\Sigma \cup B \models_{ae} \chi$ **THEN**
      IF $\text{Sf}^L(\chi) \subseteq \text{q-atom}(B)$ **THEN**
        $B := B \cup \{L\chi\}$
      ELSE
        $F := F \cup \{L\chi\}$
UNTIL $B = B';$
return $\langle B, F \rangle$.

Figure 2: The Function pos_{LE} for Positive Introspection Based on L-hierarchic Enumerations

(I1) $B \subseteq B'$ *and* $F \subseteq F'$ *and if* $\text{q-atom}(B) \cup F \subseteq \text{Sf}^L(\Sigma)$, *then* $\text{q-atom}(B') \cup F' \subseteq \text{Sf}^L(\Sigma)$.

(I2) *If there is some fully L-hierarchic enumeration generating B from Σ, then there is a fully L-hierarchic enumeration generating B' from Σ.*

(I3) *If* $B \cup F \subseteq \mathbf{B}^{\varepsilon_n}_n(\Sigma)$ *for some Σ-acceptable L-hierarchic enumeration ε_n of $\{\chi \mid L\chi \in \text{Sf}^L(\Sigma)\}$, then* $B' \cup F' \subseteq \mathbf{B}^{\varepsilon_n}_n(\Sigma)$.

(I4) *For all $L\chi \in \text{Sf}^L(\Sigma)$, if $\text{Sf}^L(\chi) \subseteq \text{q-atom}(B')$ and $\Sigma \cup B' \models_{ae} \chi$, then $L\chi \in \text{q-atom}(B')$.*

Example 5 Consider the premises Σ in (5). Then $\text{pos}_{\text{LE}}(\Sigma, \emptyset, \emptyset)$ returns $\langle \{Lp_0, Lp_1, \ldots, Lp_{n-1}\}, \emptyset \rangle$. ∎

After positive introspection if there is a *conflict*, i.e. if some $\neg L\chi$ has been included in the full to be constructed ($\neg L\chi \in B$) but χ becomes a consequence of the premises Σ and the full set under construction ($\Sigma \cup B \cup F \models_{ae} \chi$), there is no full set containing $B \cup F$ and false is returned. If there are no conflicts, $B \cup F$ covers the $L\chi$ subformulae of Σ and all the frozen beliefs F have been included in B, B is a full set corresponding to an L-hierarchic expansion and der_{LE} returns what $\text{test}(\Sigma, B, \phi)$ returns.

If there is some $L\chi \in \text{Sf}^L(\Sigma)$ not covered by $B \cup F$, $L\chi$ or $\neg L\chi$ should be included in the full set. To ensure that B extended by $\neg L\chi$ is generated by some fully L-hierarchic enumeration, only $L\chi$ formulae for which $\text{Sf}^L(\chi) \subseteq \text{q-atom}(B)$ are considered. Then we know that if B is generated by a fully L-hierarchic enumeration ε, then $B \cup \{\neg L\chi\}$ is generated by a fully L-hierarchic enumeration, i.e. ε extended by χ. This is because $\Sigma \cup B \not\models_{ae} \chi$ holds as otherwise $L\chi$ would have been added to B in the function pos_{LE}.

There are two possibilities for such a formula $L\chi$: either $\neg L\chi$ is in the full set or $L\chi$ is in the full set. The two alternatives are handled by backtracking. First B is extended by $\neg L\chi$ and if $\text{der}_{\text{LE}}(\Sigma, B \cup \{\neg L\chi\}, F, \phi)$

returns false, $L\chi$ is taken as a frozen belief and $\mathbf{der}_{\mathrm{LE}}$ returns what $\mathbf{der}_{\mathrm{LE}}(\Sigma, B, F \cup \{L\chi\}, \phi)$ returns.

Example 6 (i) Consider the propositional case and the execution of $\mathbf{der}_{\mathrm{LE}}(\Sigma, \emptyset, \emptyset, \phi)$ where the premises Σ are given in (5). As $\mathbf{pos}_{\mathrm{LE}}(\Sigma, \emptyset, \emptyset)$ returns $\langle\{Lp_0, Lp_1, \ldots, Lp_{n-1}\}, \emptyset\rangle$, backtracking is not needed at all and the return value of $\mathbf{der}_{\mathrm{LE}}(\Sigma, \emptyset, \emptyset, \phi)$ is that of

$$\mathbf{test}(\Sigma, \{Lp_0, Lp_1, \ldots, Lp_{n-1}\}, \phi).$$

(ii) Consider the premises $\Sigma = \{\neg Lp \to q, \neg Lq \to p\}$ and the execution of $\mathbf{der}_{\mathrm{LE}}(\Sigma, \emptyset, \emptyset, \phi)$. Here then $\mathbf{pos}_{\mathrm{LE}}(\Sigma, \emptyset, \emptyset)$ returns $\langle\emptyset, \emptyset\rangle$. As Lp and Lq are not covered by $\emptyset$ and p and q have no $L\chi$ subformulae, we can choose either of them. Let us choose Lp. Hence $\mathbf{der}_{\mathrm{LE}}(\Sigma, \{\neg Lp\}, \emptyset, \phi)$ is executed next. Now $\mathbf{pos}_{\mathrm{LE}}(\Sigma, \{\neg Lp\}, \emptyset)$ returns $\langle\{\neg Lp, Lq\}, \emptyset\rangle$ and

$$\mathbf{test}(\Sigma, \{\neg Lp, Lq\}, \phi)$$

is executed. If this test returns true, $\mathbf{der}_{\mathrm{LE}}(\Sigma, \emptyset, \emptyset, \phi)$ returns true. Otherwise $\mathbf{der}_{\mathrm{LE}}(\Sigma, \emptyset, \{Lp\}, \phi)$ is executed. Because $\mathbf{pos}_{\mathrm{LE}}(\Sigma, \emptyset, \{Lp\})$ returns $\langle\emptyset, \{Lp\}\rangle$, $\mathbf{der}_{\mathrm{LE}}(\Sigma, \{\neg Lq\}, \{Lp\}, \phi)$ is executed. Since now $\mathbf{pos}_{\mathrm{LE}}(\Sigma, \{\neg Lq\}, \{Lp\})$ returns $\langle\{\neg Lq, Lp\}, \{Lp\}\rangle$,

$$\mathbf{test}(\Sigma, \{\neg Lq, Lp\}, \phi)$$

is executed. If this returns true, then $\mathbf{der}_{\mathrm{LE}}(\Sigma, \emptyset, \emptyset, \phi)$ returns true. Otherwise $\mathbf{der}_{\mathrm{LE}}(\Sigma, \emptyset, \{Lp, Lq\}, \phi)$ is executed and because $\mathbf{pos}_{\mathrm{LE}}(\Sigma, \emptyset, \{Lp, Lq\})$ returns $\langle\emptyset, \{Lp, Lq\}\rangle$, $\mathbf{der}_{\mathrm{LE}}(\Sigma, \emptyset, \emptyset, \phi)$ returns false. ∎

We aim to show that the function $\mathbf{der}_{\mathrm{LE}}$ is sound and complete. For the proof it is sufficient that the function $\mathbf{pos}_{\mathrm{LE}}$ which is used in $\mathbf{der}_{\mathrm{LE}}$ satisfies the four conditions in Proposition 4.1. The next lemma shows that the function $\mathbf{der}_{\mathrm{LE}}$ is *sound*, i.e. if it returns true, there is a full set for which $\mathbf{test}$ succeeds.

Lemma 4.2 *Let Σ be a finite set of sentences. If B and F are sets of sentences such that* q-atom$(B) \cup F \subseteq \mathrm{Sf}^{\mathrm{L}}(\Sigma)$, *there is a fully L-hierarchic enumeration generating B from Σ and $\mathbf{der}_{\mathrm{LE}}(\Sigma, B, F, \phi)$ returns true, then there exists an L-hierarchic Σ-acceptable enumeration ε_n of the set $\{\chi \mid L\chi \in \mathrm{Sf}^{\mathrm{L}}(\Sigma)\}$ such that $B \cup F \subseteq \mathbf{B}_n^{\varepsilon_n}(\Sigma)$ and $\mathbf{test}(\Sigma, \mathbf{B}_n^{\varepsilon_n}(\Sigma), \phi)$ returns true.*

Proof. We prove the lemma by induction on the cardinality of the set

$$\mathrm{SL}(\Sigma, B, F) = \mathrm{Sf}^{\mathrm{L}}(\Sigma) - (\text{q-atom}(B) \cup F).$$

Let q-atom$(B) \cup F \subseteq \mathrm{Sf}^{\mathrm{L}}(\Sigma)$, let there exist a fully L-hierarchic enumeration generating B from Σ and let $\mathbf{der}_{\mathrm{LE}}(\Sigma, B, F, \phi)$ return true.

The function $\mathbf{der}_{\mathrm{LE}}$ starts by introspection. Using Proposition 2.8 and Proposition 4.1 (I1, I2) the following basic result can be established which shows that if $\mathrm{Sf}^{\mathrm{L}}(\Sigma) \subseteq$ q-atom$(B) \cup F$ after introspection, an acceptable enumeration exists.

(B) *If* $\mathrm{SL}(\Sigma, B', F') = \emptyset$ *holds where* $\langle B', F'\rangle = \mathbf{pos}_{\mathrm{LE}}(\Sigma, B, F)$, *then there exists an L-hierarchic Σ-acceptable enumeration ε_n of the set $\{\chi \mid L\chi \in \mathrm{Sf}^{\mathrm{L}}(\Sigma)\}$ such that $B \cup F \subseteq \mathbf{B}_n^{\varepsilon_n}(\Sigma)$ and $\mathbf{test}(\Sigma, \mathbf{B}_n^{\varepsilon_n}(\Sigma), \phi)$ returns true.*

Let $\mathrm{SL}(\Sigma, B, F) = \emptyset$ hold. Then also $\mathrm{SL}(\Sigma, B', F') = \emptyset$ holds where $\langle B', F'\rangle = \mathbf{pos}_{\mathrm{LE}}(\Sigma, B, F)$ as $B \subseteq B'$ and $F \subseteq F'$ by Proposition 4.1 (I1). By **(B)** there exists an acceptable enumeration for which **test** succeeds.

Let the cardinality of $\mathrm{SL}(\Sigma, B, F)$ be i. Let $\langle B', F'\rangle = \mathbf{pos}_{\mathrm{LE}}(\Sigma, B, F)$. If $\mathrm{SL}(\Sigma, B', F') = \emptyset$, then **(B)** implies that there exists an acceptable enumeration for which **test** succeeds.

Assume then that $\mathrm{SL}(\Sigma, B', F') \neq \emptyset$ holds. Because $\mathbf{der}_{\mathrm{LE}}(\Sigma, B, F, \phi)$ returns true, there is $L\chi \in \mathrm{SL}(\Sigma, B', F')$ such that $\mathrm{Sf}^{\mathrm{L}}(\chi) \subseteq$ q-atom(B') and either $\mathbf{der}_{\mathrm{LE}}(\Sigma, B' \cup \{\neg L\chi\}, F', \phi)$ returns true or $\mathbf{der}_{\mathrm{LE}}(\Sigma, B', F' \cup \{L\chi\}, \phi)$ returns true.

Assume that $\mathbf{der}_{\mathrm{LE}}(\Sigma, B', F' \cup \{L\chi\}, \phi)$ returns true. The cardinality of $\mathrm{SL}(\Sigma, B', F' \cup \{L\chi\})$ is less than i and q-atom$(B') \cup F' \cup \{L\chi\} \subseteq \mathrm{Sf}^{\mathrm{L}}(\Sigma)$. As B is generated by a fully L-hierarchic enumeration, by Proposition 4.1 (I2) there is a fully L-hierarchic enumeration $\varepsilon_{m'}$ generating B'. Hence by the inductive hypothesis there exists an L-hierarchic Σ-acceptable enumeration ε_n of $\{\chi \mid L\chi \in \mathrm{Sf}^{\mathrm{L}}(\Sigma)\}$ such that $B' \cup F' \cup \{L\chi\} \subseteq \mathbf{B}_n^{\varepsilon_n}(\Sigma)$ and $\mathbf{test}(\Sigma, \mathbf{B}_n^{\varepsilon_n}(\Sigma), \phi)$ returns true. By Proposition 4.1 (I1) $B \subseteq B'$ and $F \subseteq F'$ which implies $B \cup F \subseteq \mathbf{B}_n^{\varepsilon_n}(\Sigma)$.

On the other hand, consider now the case where $\mathbf{der}_{\mathrm{LE}}(\Sigma, B' \cup \{\neg L\chi\}, F', \phi)$ returns true. The cardinality of $\mathrm{SL}(\Sigma, B' \cup \{\neg L\chi\}, F')$ less than i and q-atom$(B' \cup \{\neg L\chi\}) \cup F' \subseteq \mathrm{Sf}^{\mathrm{L}}(\Sigma)$. Let $\varepsilon_{m'+1}$ be $\varepsilon_{m'}$ extended by χ. Hence $B' = \mathbf{B}_{m'}^{\varepsilon_{m'}}(\Sigma) = \mathbf{B}_{m'+1}^{\varepsilon_{m'+1}}(\Sigma)$. As $\mathrm{Sf}^{\mathrm{L}}(\chi) \subseteq$ q-atom$(B') =$ q-atom$(\mathbf{B}_{m'}^{\varepsilon_{m'}}(\Sigma))$ and as $\varepsilon_{m'}$ is fully L-hierarchic, $\varepsilon_{m'+1}$ is fully L-hierarchic. As $L\chi \notin$ q-atom(B'), by Proposition 4.1 (I4) $\Sigma \cup \mathbf{B}_{m'+1}^{\varepsilon_{m'+1}}(\Sigma) \not\models_{\mathrm{ae}} \chi$. Hence $B' \cup \{\neg L\chi\} = \mathbf{B}_{m'+1}^{\varepsilon_{m'+1}}(\Sigma)$. Thus $B' \cup \{\neg L\chi\}$ is generated by the fully L-hierarchic enumeration $\varepsilon_{m'+1}$. By the inductive hypothesis there exists an L-hierarchic Σ-acceptable enumeration ε_n of $\{\chi \mid L\chi \in \mathrm{Sf}^{\mathrm{L}}(\Sigma)\}$ such that $B' \cup \{\neg L\chi\} \cup F' \subseteq \mathbf{B}_n^{\varepsilon_n}(\Sigma)$ and $\mathbf{test}(\Sigma, \mathbf{B}_n^{\varepsilon_n}(\Sigma), \phi)$ returns true. By Proposition 4.1 (I1) $B \cup F \subseteq \mathbf{B}_n^{\varepsilon_n}(\Sigma)$. □

The next lemma shows that the function $\mathbf{der}_{\mathrm{LE}}$ is *complete*, i.e. if there is a full set for which the function **test** succeeds, then $\mathbf{der}_{\mathrm{LE}}$ returns true.

Lemma 4.3 *Let Σ be a finite set of sentences. Let ε_n be an L-hierarchic Σ-acceptable enumeration of $\{\chi \mid L\chi \in \mathrm{Sf}^{\mathrm{L}}(\Sigma)\}$ such that $\mathbf{test}(\Sigma, \mathbf{B}_n^{\varepsilon_n}(\Sigma), \phi)$ returns true. Then for every set B of sentences and F of $L\chi$ sentences such that $B \cup F \subseteq \mathbf{B}_n^{\varepsilon_n}(\Sigma)$, $\mathbf{der}_{\mathrm{LE}}(\Sigma, B, F, \phi)$ returns true.*

Proof. We prove the lemma by induction on the cardinality of $\mathrm{SL}(\Sigma, B, F) = \mathrm{Sf}^{\mathrm{L}}(\Sigma) - (\text{q-atom}(B) \cup F)$. Let there exist an L-hierarchic Σ-acceptable enumeration ε_n of $\{\chi \mid L\chi \in \mathrm{Sf}^{\mathrm{L}}(\Sigma)\}$ such that $\mathbf{test}(\Sigma, \mathbf{B}_n^{\varepsilon_n}(\Sigma), \phi)$ returns true. Let B be a set of sentences and let F be a set of $L\chi$ sentences such that $B \cup F \subseteq \mathbf{B}_n^{\varepsilon_n}(\Sigma)$.

Using Proposition 4.1 (I3, I4) and Proposition 2.8 it is straightforward to establish a result showing that if $\mathrm{SL}(\Sigma, B, F) = \emptyset$ after introspection, the function $\mathbf{der}_{\mathrm{LE}}$ returns true.

(B) $\mathrm{SL}(\Sigma, B', F') = \emptyset$ implies that $\mathbf{der}_{\mathrm{LE}}(\Sigma, B, F, \phi)$ returns true where $\langle B', F' \rangle = \mathbf{pos}_{\mathrm{LE}}(\Sigma, B, F)$.

Let $\mathrm{SL}(\Sigma, B, F) = \emptyset$. Then by Proposition 4.1 (I1) $\mathrm{SL}(\Sigma, B', F') = \emptyset$ where $\langle B', F' \rangle = \mathbf{pos}_{\mathrm{LE}}(\Sigma, B, F)$. Then by (B) $\mathbf{der}_{\mathrm{LE}}(\Sigma, B, F, \phi)$ returns true.

Let the cardinality of $\mathrm{SL}(\Sigma, B, F)$ be i and let $B \cup F \subseteq \mathbf{B}_n^{\varepsilon_n}(\Sigma)$. Let $\langle B', F' \rangle = \mathbf{pos}_{\mathrm{LE}}(\Sigma, B, F)$. If $\mathrm{SL}(\Sigma, B', F') = \emptyset$, then by (B) $\mathbf{der}_{\mathrm{LE}}(\Sigma, B, F, \phi)$ returns true.

Assume that $\mathrm{SL}(\Sigma, B', F') \neq \emptyset$. First we show that there exists a formula $L\chi \in \mathrm{SL}(\Sigma, B', F')$ such that $\mathrm{Sf}^{\mathrm{L}}(\chi) \subseteq \text{q-atom}(B')$. Consider a sentence ψ_i which is the sentence with the smallest index (in ε_n) such that $L\psi_i \in \mathrm{SL}(\Sigma, B', F')$. We show that $\mathrm{Sf}^{\mathrm{L}}(\psi_i) \subseteq \text{q-atom}(B')$. Let $L\psi_j \in \mathrm{Sf}^{\mathrm{L}}(\psi_i)$. As ε_n is L-hierarchic, $j < i$. Therefore $L\psi_j \in \text{q-atom}(B') \cup F'$ by the minimality requirement for i. It sufficient to show that $L\psi_j \in F'$ implies $L\psi_j \in \text{q-atom}(B')$ because this implies $L\psi_j \in \text{q-atom}(B')$ and thus $\mathrm{Sf}^{\mathrm{L}}(\psi_i) \subseteq \text{q-atom}(B')$. Let $L\psi_j \in F'$. By Proposition 4.1 (I3) $L\psi_j \in \mathbf{B}_n^{\varepsilon_n}(\Sigma)$ and $\Sigma \cup \mathbf{B}_{j-1}^{\varepsilon_n}(\Sigma) \models_{\mathrm{ae}} \psi_j$ holds. Using Proposition 4.1 (I3, I4) it can proved that

$$\mathbf{B}_{j-1}^{\varepsilon_n}(\Sigma) \subseteq B' \qquad (6)$$

holds by showing by induction on l that for all $l = 0, 1, \ldots, j - i$, $\mathbf{B}_l^{\varepsilon_n}(\Sigma) \subseteq B'$ holds.

As the enumeration ε_n is L-hierarchic, then by (6) $\mathrm{Sf}^{\mathrm{L}}(\psi_j) \subseteq \text{q-atom}(\mathbf{B}_{j-1}^{\varepsilon_n}(\Sigma)) \subseteq \text{q-atom}(B')$ and $\Sigma \cup B' \models_{\mathrm{ae}} \psi_j$ holds. By Proposition 4.1 (I4) $L\psi_j \in \text{q-atom}(B')$. Hence $\mathrm{Sf}^{\mathrm{L}}(\psi_i) \subseteq \text{q-atom}(B')$. So there is $L\chi (= L\psi_i) \in \mathrm{SL}(\Sigma, B', F')$ such that $\mathrm{Sf}^{\mathrm{L}}(\chi) \subseteq \text{q-atom}(B')$.

If $\neg L\chi \in \mathbf{B}_n^{\varepsilon_n}(\Sigma)$ holds, then $B' \cup \{\neg L\chi\} \cup F' \subseteq \mathbf{B}_n^{\varepsilon_n}(\Sigma)$ holds as well. As the cardinality of $\mathrm{SL}(\Sigma, B' \cup \{\neg L\chi\}, F')$ is less than i, by the inductive hypothesis $\mathbf{der}_{\mathrm{LE}}(\Sigma, B' \cup \{\neg L\chi\}, F', \phi)$ returns true which implies that $\mathbf{der}_{\mathrm{LE}}(\Sigma, B, F, \phi)$ returns true. If $\neg L\chi \notin \mathbf{B}_n^{\varepsilon_n}(\Sigma)$, then $L\chi \in \mathbf{B}_n^{\varepsilon_n}(\Sigma)$ and $B' \cup F' \cup \{L\chi\} \subseteq \mathbf{B}_n^{\varepsilon_n}(\Sigma)$. As the cardinality of $\mathrm{SL}(\Sigma, B', F' \cup \{L\chi\})$ is less than i, by the inductive hypothesis $\mathbf{der}_{\mathrm{LE}}(\Sigma, B', F' \cup \{L\chi\}, \phi)$ returns true which implies that $\mathbf{der}_{\mathrm{LE}}(\Sigma, B, F, \phi)$ returns true. □

As a direct consequence of Lemmata 4.2 and 4.3 we have a soundness and completeness theorem for $\mathbf{der}_{\mathrm{LE}}$.

Theorem 4.4 *Let Σ be a finite set of sentences. Let B and F be sets for which $\text{q-atom}(B) \cup F \subseteq \mathrm{Sf}^{\mathrm{L}}(\Sigma)$ and let there be a fully L-hierarchic enumeration generating B from Σ. Then $\mathbf{der}_{\mathrm{LE}}(\Sigma, B, F, \phi)$ returns true iff there exists an L-hierarchic Σ-acceptable enumeration ε_n of the set $\{\chi \mid L\chi \in \mathrm{Sf}^{\mathrm{L}}(\Sigma)\}$ such that $B \cup F \subseteq \mathbf{B}_n^{\varepsilon_n}(\Sigma)$ and $\mathbf{test}(\Sigma, \mathbf{B}_n^{\varepsilon_n}(\Sigma), \phi)$ returns true.*

The theorem implies that if the underlying consequence relation $\models_{\mathrm{ae}}$ is decidable, decision procedures for $\hspace{0.2em}\sim\hspace{-0.9em}\mid\hspace{0.4em}_{\mathrm{c(LE)}}$, $\hspace{0.2em}\sim\hspace{-0.9em}\mid\hspace{0.4em}_{\mathrm{b(LE)}}$, and the L-hierarchic expansion existence problem can be obtained by employing an appropriate function $\mathbf{test}$ and taking the empty set as the initial common part of the full sets. These $\mathbf{test}$ functions are straightforward to devise because membership in an expansion is captured by the consequence relation $\models_{\mathrm{L}}$, i.e. given a Σ-full set Λ, ϕ is in the corresponding unique expansion iff $\Sigma \cup \Lambda \models_{\mathrm{L}} \phi$.

Theorem 4.5 *Let $\Sigma \subseteq \mathcal{L}_{\mathrm{ae}}$ be a finite set of sentences and $\phi \in \mathcal{L}_{\mathrm{ae}}$ a sentence.*

1. If $\mathbf{test}(\Sigma, \Lambda, \phi)$ returns true, then $\mathbf{der}_{\mathrm{LE}}(\Sigma, \emptyset, \emptyset, \phi)$ returns true iff Σ has an L-hierarchic expansion.

2. If $\mathbf{test}(\Sigma, \Lambda, \phi)$ returns true iff $\Sigma \cup \Lambda \models_{\mathrm{L}} \phi$, then $\mathbf{der}_{\mathrm{LE}}(\Sigma, \emptyset, \emptyset, \phi)$ returns true iff $\Sigma \hspace{0.2em}\sim\hspace{-0.9em}\mid\hspace{0.4em}_{\mathrm{b(LE)}} \phi$.

3. If $\mathbf{test}(\Sigma, \Lambda, \phi)$ returns true iff $\Sigma \cup \Lambda \not\models_{\mathrm{L}} \phi$, then $\mathbf{der}_{\mathrm{LE}}(\Sigma, \emptyset, \emptyset, \phi)$ returns true iff $\Sigma \hspace{0.2em}\not\sim\hspace{-0.9em}\mid\hspace{0.4em}_{\mathrm{c(LE)}} \phi$.

Proof. Clearly, $\text{q-atom}(\emptyset) \cup \emptyset \subseteq \mathrm{Sf}^{\mathrm{L}}(\Sigma)$ and $\emptyset$ is generated from Σ by the empty enumeration which is fully L-hierarchic, of course. Then by Theorem 4.4 $\mathbf{der}_{\mathrm{LE}}(\Sigma, \emptyset, \emptyset, \phi)$ returns true iff there exists an L-hierarchic Σ-acceptable enumeration ε_n of $\{\chi \mid L\chi \in \mathrm{Sf}^{\mathrm{L}}(\Sigma)\}$ such that $\mathbf{test}(\Sigma, \mathbf{B}_n^{\varepsilon_n}(\Sigma), \phi)$ returns true.

(1) Let $\mathbf{test}(\Sigma, \Lambda, \phi)$ return true for every input. Then by Theorems 2.9 and 2.10 $\mathbf{der}_{\mathrm{LE}}(\Sigma, \emptyset, \emptyset, \phi)$ returns true iff Σ has an L-hierarchic expansion.

(2) Let $\mathbf{test}(\Sigma, \Lambda, \phi)$ return true iff $\Sigma \cup \Lambda \models_{\mathrm{L}} \phi$. ($\Rightarrow$) Let $\mathbf{der}_{\mathrm{LE}}(\Sigma, \emptyset, \emptyset, \phi)$ return true. Then there exists an L-hierarchic Σ-acceptable enumeration ε_n of $\{\chi \mid L\chi \in \mathrm{Sf}^{\mathrm{L}}(\Sigma)\}$ and $\Sigma \cup \mathbf{B}_n^{\varepsilon_n}(\Sigma) \models_{\mathrm{L}} \phi$. By Theorem 2.9 there is an L-hierarchic expansion Δ of Σ such that

$$\begin{aligned} \Delta &= \mathrm{SE}_\Sigma(\mathbf{B}_n^{\varepsilon_n}(\Sigma)) \\ &= \{\phi \in \mathcal{L}_{\mathrm{ae}} \mid \Sigma \cup \mathbf{B}_n^{\varepsilon_n}(\Sigma) \models_{\mathrm{L}} \phi\}. \end{aligned} \qquad (7)$$

Thus $\phi \in \Delta$ and $\Sigma \hspace{0.2em}\sim\hspace{-0.9em}\mid\hspace{0.4em}_{\mathrm{b(LE)}} \phi$. ($\Leftarrow$) Let $\Sigma \hspace{0.2em}\sim\hspace{-0.9em}\mid\hspace{0.4em}_{\mathrm{b(LE)}} \phi$ hold. Then there exists an L-hierarchic expansion Δ of Σ containing ϕ. By Theorem 2.10 there exists an L-hierarchic Σ-acceptable enumeration ε_n of $\{\chi \mid L\chi \in \mathrm{Sf}^{\mathrm{L}}(\Sigma)\}$ such that Δ is given by (7). Thus $\Sigma \cup \mathbf{B}_n^{\varepsilon_n}(\Sigma) \models_{\mathrm{L}} \phi$ and $\mathbf{test}(\Sigma, \mathbf{B}_n^{\varepsilon_n}(\Sigma), \phi)$ returns true. Hence $\mathbf{der}_{\mathrm{LE}}(\Sigma, \emptyset, \emptyset, \phi)$ returns true.

(3) Let $\mathbf{test}(\Sigma, \Lambda, \phi)$ return true iff $\Sigma \cup \Lambda \not\models_{\mathrm{L}} \phi$. Similarly, by Theorems 2.9 and 2.10 it can be shown

that $\mathbf{der}_{LE}(\Sigma, \emptyset, \emptyset, \phi)$ returns true iff there is an L-hierarchic expansion of Σ not containing ϕ. □

The completeness results with respect to the second level of the polynomial time hierarchy (Gottlob 1992, Niemelä 1992a) imply that there are two independent sources of complexity in nonmonotonic reasoning:

- required monotonic reasoning and
- conflict resolution.

In the decision method the two sources are clearly identifiable. In the autoepistemic framework required monotonic reasoning is given by the underlying consequence relation $\models_{ae}$ and in the decision method this task can be handled by a separate theorem prover. The conflict resolution task emerges when deciding which formula is included in the full set from the available $L\chi$ subformulae of the premises. In the decision method the conflict resolution task is solved by a simple backtracking scheme. If there is a conflict for some $\neg L\chi'$ included in the full to be constructed, the method backtracks to the last choice point where some $\neg L\chi$ was added and retracts this choice. The other alternative is explored by putting $L\chi$ as a "frozen" belief to be included in the full set later. The same backtracking mechanism can be exploited when searching for an expansion containing a given sentence (brave derivability) or an expansion not containing a given sentence (cautious derivability). Notice that the decision method can be implemented to run in polynomial space provided that the theorem prover of $\models_{ae}$ runs in polynomial space.

The decision procedures for $\vdash_{c(E)}$, $\vdash_{b(E)}$, and the enumeration-based expansion existence problem can be obtained easily by modifying the functions $\mathbf{pos}_{LE}$ and $\mathbf{der}_{LE}$ slightly. The only change is that there is no need to require that $\mathrm{Sf}^L(\chi) \subseteq \mathrm{q\text{-}atom}(B)$ for the new $(\neg)L\chi$ formulae to be added to B. The decision procedures for $\vdash_c$, $\vdash_b$, and the Moore style expansion existence problem can be devised by further modifying the function $\mathbf{pos}_{LE}$. Now the frozen beliefs can be used in positive introspection because the groundedness requirement for Moore style expansions is not as strict as for enumeration-based expansions.

The decision method described above is completely general. It does not rely on any additional assumptions about the underlying logic which determines the consequence relation $\models_{ae}$. For example, no normal form transformation of the premises is required. Properties of the underlying logic as well as possible regularities of the sets of premises can be utilized to optimize the computationally costly subtasks in the decision method: required monotonic reasoning and conflict resolution. The theorem prover for $\models_{ae}$ can exploit any special properties of the underlying logic or restricted form of the premises to achieve highest possible performance. An interesting topic of further research is to study possibilities of exploiting the regular pattern in which the theorem prover for $\models_{ae}$ is used and make use of previous computations when deciding $\models_{ae}$.

Optimization of conflict resolution is also a challenging area of further research. An interesting approach is to investigate the notion of safe disbeliefs. The idea is to identify disbeliefs $\neg L\chi$ such that χ does not follow from Σ and any possible extension of $B \cup \{\neg L\chi\} \cup F$. This reduces backtracking as then B can be extended safely by $\neg L\chi$ since for $\neg L\chi$ a conflict is not possible.

4.2 A DECISION METHOD FOR DEFAULT LOGIC

As an example of developing optimization techniques we derive a new complete decision method for Reiter's default logic. By Theorem 3.1 default logic can be seen as a special case of autoepistemic logic based on L-hierarchic expansions. The simple logical character of the $L\chi$ sentences can be exploited when deciding $\models_{ae}$ and the set of premises can be reduced considerably when the premises are restricted to the form resulting from the translation (2).

Proposition 4.6 (Niemelä(1992a)) *Let the underlying logic be a first-order calculus. Let $\Sigma \subseteq \mathcal{L}_{ae}$ be a set of sentences of the form $(Lb_1 \wedge \cdots \wedge Lb_n) \to c$ where $c \in \mathcal{L}$ and $n \geq 0$ and Λ is a consistent set of $L\psi$ sentences and their negations. Then for all $\phi \in \mathcal{L}$,*

$$\Sigma \cup \Lambda \models_{ae} \phi \text{ iff } \mathrm{Hds}(\Sigma, \Lambda) \models_{cl} \phi$$

where $\mathrm{Hds}(\Sigma, \Lambda) = \{c \mid (Lb_1 \wedge \cdots \wedge Lb_n) \to c \in \Sigma \text{ and } Lb_i \in \Lambda \text{ for all } i = 1, \ldots, n\}$.

An interesting notion of safe disbeliefs can be developed for the subclass of autoepistemic sentences resulting from the translation (2). The idea is to strengthen the premises Σ by "assuming" $\neg L\phi$ for every $L\phi \notin B \cup F$ in addition to those $\neg L\phi$ already in B. It turns out that a disbelief $\neg L\psi$ is safe if ψ does not follow from the strengthened premises Σ^* and B using positive introspection. The function $\mathbf{safeneg}_{LE}$ in Figure 3 computes these safe disbeliefs

It is easy to exploit safe disbeliefs in the decision method. Instead of propagating positive introspection by using $\mathbf{pos}_{LE}$, both positive and safe negative introspection are propagated. This means that the function $\mathbf{intro}_{LE}$ in Figure 3 is used instead of $\mathbf{pos}_{LE}$ in the beginning of $\mathbf{der}_{LE}$. Notice that $\mathbf{intro}_{LE}$ also computes safe disbeliefs which are based on the fact that $\neg L \neg L\psi$ belongs to every consistent L-hierarchic expansion containing $L\psi$. We call the resulting function $\mathbf{der}_{DL}$. The function $\mathbf{der}_{DL}$ is sound and complete when given premises of the form resulting from the translation (2).

Example 7 Consider the propositional case, the premises $\Sigma = \{L\neg Lp \to q, L\neg Lq \to p\}$ and the ex-

FUNCTION $\text{safeneg}_{\text{LE}}(\Sigma, B, F)$
INPUT: Finite sets of sentences Σ, B, and F.

$\Sigma^* := \{La \to c \mid La \wedge L\neg Lb_1 \wedge \cdots \wedge L\neg Lb_n \to c \in \Sigma,$
$\quad \text{for all } i = 1, \ldots, n, \neg Lb_i \in B \text{ or } Lb_i \notin B \cup F\};$
$\langle B^*, F^* \rangle := \text{pos}_{\text{LE}}(\Sigma^*, B, F);$
return $\{\neg L\psi \in \neg(\text{Sf}^{\text{L}}(\Sigma) - \text{q-atom}(B)) \mid \psi \in \mathcal{L},$
$\quad \Sigma^* \cup B^* \not\models_{\text{ae}} \psi\}.$

FUNCTION $\text{intro}_{\text{LE}}(\Sigma, B, F)$
INPUT: Finite sets of sentences Σ, B, and F.

REPEAT
$\quad B' := B;$
$\quad \langle B, F \rangle := \text{pos}_{\text{LE}}(\Sigma, B, F);$
$\quad B := B \cup \text{safeneg}_{\text{LE}}(\Sigma, B, F);$
$\quad$ **IF** $\Sigma \cup B$ is consistent and
$\quad\quad$ there exist $\neg L\chi \in B$ **THEN**
$\quad\quad B := B \cup \{\neg L\neg L\psi \in \neg(\text{Sf}^{\text{L}}(\Sigma) - \text{q-atom}(B)) \mid$
$\quad\quad\quad L\psi \in B\}$
UNTIL $B = B';$
return $\langle B, F \rangle.$

Figure 3: Functions for Safe Negative Introspection and Propagation of Introspection

ecution of $\text{der}_{\text{DL}}(\Sigma, \emptyset, \emptyset, \phi)$. Compare this to Example 6 where safe negative introspection is not used. First $\text{intro}_{\text{LE}}(\Sigma, \emptyset, \emptyset)$ returns $\langle \emptyset, \emptyset \rangle$. Here we can extend the full set by $(\neg)Lp$ or $(\neg)Lq$. We choose Lp. Hence first $\text{der}_{\text{DL}}(\Sigma, \{\neg Lp\}, \emptyset, \phi)$ is executed. Because $\langle \{\neg Lp, L\neg Lp, Lq, \neg L\neg Lq\}, \emptyset \rangle$ is returned by $\text{intro}_{\text{LE}}(\Sigma, \{\neg Lp\}, \emptyset)$,

$$\text{test}(\Sigma, \{\neg Lp, L\neg Lp, Lq, \neg L\neg Lq\}, \phi)$$

is executed. If this test returns true, $\text{der}_{\text{DL}}(\Sigma, \emptyset, \emptyset, \phi)$ returns true. Otherwise $\text{der}_{\text{DL}}(\Sigma, \emptyset, \{Lp\}, \phi)$ is executed. As $\langle \{Lp, \neg L\neg Lp, \neg Lq, L\neg Lq\}, \emptyset \rangle$ is returned by $\text{intro}_{\text{LE}}(\Sigma, \emptyset, \{Lp\})$, $\text{der}_{\text{DL}}(\Sigma, \emptyset, \emptyset, \phi)$ returns what $\text{test}(\Sigma, \{Lp, \neg L\neg Lp, \neg Lq, L\neg Lq\}, \phi)$ returns. ∎

Theorem 4.7 *Let Σ be a finite set of sentences of the form $(La \wedge L\neg L\neg b_1 \wedge \cdots \wedge L\neg L\neg b_n) \to c$. Let B and F be sets of sentences such that $\text{q-atom}(B) \cup F \subseteq \text{Sf}^{\text{L}}(\Sigma)$ and let there be a fully L-hierarchic enumeration generating B from Σ. Then $\text{der}_{\text{DL}}(\Sigma, B, F, \phi)$ returns true iff there exists an L-hierarchic Σ-acceptable enumeration ε_n of the set $\{\chi \mid L\chi \in \text{Sf}^{\text{L}}(\Sigma)\}$ such that $B \cup F \subseteq \mathbf{B}_n^{\varepsilon_n}(\Sigma)$ and $\text{test}(\Sigma, \mathbf{B}_n^{\varepsilon_n}(\Sigma), \phi)$ returns true.*

Proof. This is Theorem 4.4 except that the form of the premises is restricted and the function intro_{LE} is employed instead of just pos_{LE} in der_{DL}. To prove Theorem 4.4 it was sufficient that pos_{LE} satisfied the four conditions in Proposition 4.1. Hence to prove Theorem 4.7 it is sufficient to show that intro_{LE} satisfies the same four conditions (I1–I4):

Let $\langle B', F' \rangle = \text{intro}_{\text{LE}}(\Sigma, B, F)$.

(I1) $B \subseteq B'$ and $F \subseteq F'$ and if $\text{q-atom}(B) \cup F \subseteq \text{Sf}^{\text{L}}(\Sigma)$, then $\text{q-atom}(B') \cup F' \subseteq \text{Sf}^{\text{L}}(\Sigma)$.

(I2) If there is some fully L-hierarchic enumeration generating B from Σ, then there is a fully L-hierarchic enumeration generating B' from Σ.

(I3) If $B \cup F \subseteq \mathbf{B}_n^{\varepsilon_n}(\Sigma)$ for some Σ-acceptable L-hierarchic enumeration ε_n of $\{\chi \mid L\chi \in \text{Sf}^{\text{L}}(\Sigma)\}$, then $B' \cup F' \subseteq \mathbf{B}_n^{\varepsilon_n}(\Sigma)$.

(I4) For all $L\chi \in \text{Sf}^{\text{L}}(\Sigma)$, if $\text{Sf}^{\text{L}}(\chi) \subseteq \text{q-atom}(B')$ and $\Sigma \cup B' \models_{\text{ae}} \chi$, then $L\chi \in \text{q-atom}(B')$.

We prove that each condition is satisfied by showing for every step in the body of the repeat loop in intro_{LE} that if the condition holds before the step, then it holds after the step. By Proposition 4.1 the conditions hold for pos_{LE} and it remains to show that the conditions are satisfied by the two other steps where B and F are modified in intro_{LE}.

(I1) This clearly holds for intro_{LE}.

(I2) Let B be generated by a fully L-hierarchic enumeration from Σ.

($\text{safeneg}_{\text{LE}}$) Let $B_{\text{sn}} = \text{safeneg}_{\text{LE}}(\Sigma, B, F)$. We establish that there exists a fully L-hierarchic enumeration generating $B \cup B_{\text{sn}}$ from Σ. We show that for all $\neg L\psi \in B_{\text{sn}}$,

$$\Sigma \cup B \cup B_{\text{sn}} \not\models_{\text{ae}} \psi. \tag{8}$$

Now $B \cup B_{\text{sn}}$ is generated by an enumeration $\varepsilon_{m'}$ which is obtained by extending ε_m with formulae $\{\psi \mid \neg L\psi \in B_{\text{sn}}\}$ in some order. This is because it can be shown that for every i, $m < i \leq m'$, $\mathbf{B}_{i-1}^{\varepsilon_{m'}}(\Sigma) \subseteq B \cup B_{\text{sn}}$ which by (8) implies $\Sigma \cup \mathbf{B}_{i-1}^{\varepsilon_{m'}}(\Sigma) \not\models_{\text{ae}} \psi_i$ and thus $\neg L\psi_i \in \mathbf{B}_{m'}^{\varepsilon_{m'}}(\Sigma)$.

So it remains to show that (8) holds. We use the following two results in the proof. The results are straightforward to establish.

NegBels: *Let B be generated by some fully L-hierarchic enumeration from Σ. If $L\neg Lb \in B$ and $\Sigma \cup B$ is consistent, then $\neg Lb \in B$.*

Incons: *Let B be generated by some fully L-hierarchic enumeration from Σ. If $\Sigma \cup B$ is inconsistent, then $\Sigma^* \cup \{L\phi \in B \mid \phi \in \mathcal{L}\}$ is inconsistent.*

As for all $\neg L\psi \in B_{\text{sn}}$, $\Sigma^* \cup B^* \not\models_{\text{ae}} \psi$, (8) can be proved by showing that for all $\neg L\psi \in B_{\text{sn}}$,

$$\Sigma^* \cup B^* \not\models_{\text{ae}} \psi \text{ implies } \Sigma \cup B \cup B_{\text{sn}} \not\models_{\text{ae}} \psi. \tag{9}$$

If $\Sigma \cup B$ is inconsistent, then by (**Incons**) $\Sigma^* \cup \{L\phi \in B \mid \phi \in \mathcal{L}\}$ is inconsistent. By Proposition 4.1 (I1) $B \subseteq B^*$. Then also $\Sigma^* \cup B^*$ is inconsistent. This implies $B_{\text{sn}} = \emptyset$.

Let $\Sigma \cup B$ be consistent. Let $\Sigma \cup B \cup B_{\text{sn}} \models_{\text{ae}} \psi$ hold. Then by Proposition 4.6 $\text{Hds}(\Sigma, B \cup B_{\text{sn}}) \models_{\text{cl}} \psi$ holds. By Proposition 4.1 (I1) $B \subseteq B^*$. Using this and (**NegBels**) we can show

$$\text{Hds}(\Sigma, B \cup B_{\text{sn}}) \subseteq \text{Hds}(\Sigma^*, B^*). \quad (10)$$

By (10) $\text{Hds}(\Sigma^*, B^*) \models_{\text{cl}} \psi$ holds and by Proposition 4.6 $\Sigma^* \cup B^* \models_{\text{ae}} \psi$ holds. Hence (8) holds.

($\neg L \neg L \psi$) Let $\Sigma \cup B$ be consistent and there exist $\neg L \chi \in B$. Let $\neg L \neg L \psi \in B_{\text{sn}'} = \{\neg L \neg L \psi \in \neg(\text{Sf}^L(\Sigma) - \text{q-atom}(B)) \mid L\psi \in B\}$ but assume $\Sigma \cup B \cup B_{\text{sn}'} \models_{\text{ae}} \neg L \psi$. As $L\psi \in B$, $\Sigma \cup B \cup B_{\text{sn}'}$ is inconsistent. As $\text{Hds}(\Sigma, B \cup B_{\text{sn}'}) = \text{Hds}(\Sigma, B)$, by Proposition 4.6 $\Sigma \cup B$ is inconsistent, a contradiction. Hence for every $\neg L \neg L \psi \in B_{\text{sn}'}$, $\Sigma \cup B \cup B_{\text{sn}'} \not\models_{\text{ae}} \neg L \psi$ which implies that there is a fully L-hierarchic enumeration generating $B \cup B_{\text{sn}'}$ from Σ. Thus we have shown (I2).

(I3) Let there be a Σ-acceptable L-hierarchic enumeration $\varepsilon_n = \psi_1, \ldots, \psi_n$ of $\{\chi \mid L\chi \in \text{Sf}^L(\Sigma)\}$ such that $B \cup F \subseteq \mathbf{B}_n^{\varepsilon_n}(\Sigma)$ holds.

(**safeneg**$_{\text{LE}}$) Let $B_{\text{sn}} = \textbf{safeneg}_{\text{LE}}(\Sigma, B, F)$ and we prove

$$B_{\text{sn}} \subseteq \mathbf{B}_n^{\varepsilon_n}(\Sigma). \quad (11)$$

Using Proposition 4.6, (**NegBels**), (**Incons**), and Proposition 4.1 (I4) for B^* we can show by induction on i that for all $i = 1, \ldots, n$,

$$\psi_i \in \mathcal{L} \text{ and } L\psi_i \in \mathbf{B}_i^{\varepsilon_n}(\Sigma) \text{ implies}$$
$$\Sigma^* \cup B^* \models_{\text{ae}} \psi_i. \quad (12)$$

Using (12) it is straightforward to establish (11). Let $\neg L\psi \in B_{\text{sn}}$. Then $\Sigma^* \cup B^* \not\models_{\text{ae}} \psi$ holds, $L\psi \in \text{Sf}^L(\Sigma)$ and $\psi \in \mathcal{L}$. Hence ψ is some ψ_i in the enumeration ε_n. By (12) $L\psi_i \notin \mathbf{B}_i^{\varepsilon_n}(\Sigma)$ which implies that $\neg L\psi_i \in \mathbf{B}_n^{\varepsilon_n}(\Sigma)$. Hence (11) holds.

($\neg L \neg L \psi$) Let there exist $\neg L \chi \in B$. Let $\neg L \neg L \psi \in B_{\text{sn}'} = \{\neg L \neg L \psi \in \neg(\text{Sf}^L(\Sigma) - \text{q-atom}(B)) \mid L\psi \in B\}$. As $\neg L \chi \in B \subseteq \mathbf{B}_n^{\varepsilon_n}(\Sigma)$, $\Sigma \cup \mathbf{B}_n^{\varepsilon_n}(\Sigma)$ is consistent. As $L\psi \in B \subseteq \mathbf{B}_n^{\varepsilon_n}(\Sigma)$, by (**NegBels**) $\neg L \neg L \psi \in \mathbf{B}_n^{\varepsilon_n}(\Sigma)$. Hence $B_{\text{sn}'} \subseteq \mathbf{B}_n^{\varepsilon_n}(\Sigma)$. Thus we have established (I3).

(I4) By Proposition 4.1 (I4) holds for B_1 where $\langle B_1, F_1 \rangle = \textbf{pos}_{\text{LE}}(\Sigma, B, F)$ and this implies that (I4) holds for B'. □

The resulting decision method does not use the obvious idea of building an extension of a default theory by trying to find a suitable order of applying the default rules but it constructs the set of applicable rules by cautiously building a set representing the valid premises of the rules, i.e. the set B. Autoepistemic logic offers a convenient language for this as it easy to represent the fact that a prerequisite a of a rule holds (La) and that it holds that a justification b is consistent ($L\neg L\neg b$). Every time a choice is made an approximation of the intersection of the possible extensions is constructed using safe disbeliefs and propagation of positive introspection in a way which is closely related to stationary default extensions (Przymusinska and Przymusinski 1992). This can reduce the number of choice points in backtracking considerably. However, here we have integrated the approximation method efficiently in the backtracking search: not only the partially constructed set of valid premises (B) is used but also the information from the backtracking search, i.e. the frozen beliefs F, are employed when constructing the next approximation.

5 CONCLUSIONS

We have developed a novel decision method for autoepistemic reasoning which is applicable in a general setting, i.e. for an autoepistemic logic defined on top of a given classical logic. The aim has been to devise a conceptually clear method where sources of complexity and targets for further optimization are clearly identifiable. Two orthogonal sources can be identified: classical reasoning and conflict resolution. The classical reasoning task can be handled using a separate theorem prover. The decision method imposes no additional requirements leaving abundant room for optimizations of the theorem prover. The conflict resolution task is solved by employing a simple backtracking scheme. The method exploits efficiently the monotonicity of the underlying consequence relation to reduce choice points in backtracking.

The method provides a direct decision procedure for tightly grounded autoepistemic reasoning based on L-hierarchic expansions and no additional groundedness tests are needed. Decision methods for more weakly grounded forms of autoepistemic reasoning based on Moore style expansions and **N**-expansions are obtained by minor adjustments. The method can be implemented to run in polynomial space in the propositional case. Leading forms of nonmonotonic reasoning, such as default logic and circumscription, can be embedded into autoepistemic logic based on L-hierarchic expansions using simple local translations. Thus the method can be used as a unified decision method for a large range of forms of nonmonotonic reasoning. As an example of the optimization possibilities we develop a new complete decision method for default logic where the search space of applying default rules is pruned efficiently by using ideas from autoepistemic reasoning. The method provides an interesting approach to implementing truth maintenance systems as well as stable model semantics and answer set semantics of logic programs.

References

Ben-Eliyahu, R. and Dechter, R. (1991). Default logic, propositional logic and constraints, *Proceedings of the 9th National Conference on Artificial Intelligence*, The MIT Press, pp. 370–385.

Eiter, T. and Gottlob, G. (1992). The complexity of logic-based abduction, *Technical Report CD-TR 92/35*, Christian Doppler Labor für Expertensysteme, Institut für Informationssysteme, Technische Universität Wien, Vienna, Austria.

Elkan, C. (1990). A rational reconstruction of nonmonotonic truth maintenance systems, *Artificial Intelligence* **43**: 219–234.

Gelfond, M. and Lifschitz, V. (1990). Logic programs with classical negation., *Proceedings of the 7th International Conference on Logic Programming*, The MIT Press, Jerusalem, Israel, pp. 579–597.

Gottlob, G. (1992). Complexity results for nonmonotonic logics, *Journal of Logic and Computation* **2**(3): 397–425.

Gottlob, G. (1993). The power of beliefs or translating default logic into standard autoepistemic logic, *Proceedings of the 13th International Joint Conference on Artificial Intelligence*, Morgan Kaufmann Publishers, Chambéry, France, pp. 570–575.

Junker, U. and Konolige, K. (1990). Computing the extensions of autoepistemic and default logics with a truth maintenance system, *Proceedings of the 8th National Conference on Artificial Intelligence*, The MIT Press, Boston, MA, USA, pp. 278–283.

Konolige, K. (1988). On the relation between default and autoepistemic logic, *Artificial Intelligence* **35**: 343–382.

Konolige, K. (1989). On the relation between autoepistemic logic and circumscription, *Proceedings of the 11th International Joint Conference on Artificial Intelligence*, Morgan Kaufmann Publishers, Detroit, Michigan, USA, pp. 1213–1218.

Lifschitz, V. (1991). Nonmonotonic databases and epistemic queries, *Proceedings of the 12th International Joint Conference on Artificial Intelligence*, Morgan Kaufmann Publishers, Sydney, Australia, pp. 381–386.

Marek, W. and Truszczyński, M. (1989). Relating autoepistemic and default logics, *Proceedings of the 1st International Conference on Principles of Knowledge Representation and Reasoning*, Toronto, Canada, pp. 276–288.

Marek, W. and Truszczyński, M. (1991a). Autoepistemic logic, *Journal of the ACM* **38**: 588–619.

Marek, W. and Truszczyński, M. (1991b). Computing intersection of autoepistemic expansions, *Proceedings of the 1st International Workshop on Logic Programming and Non-monotonic Reasoning*, The MIT Press, Washington, D.C., USA, pp. 37–50.

Marek, W., Shvarts, G. and Truszczyński, M. (1991). Modal nonmonotonic logics: Ranges, characterization, computation, *Proceedings of the 2nd International Conference on Principles of Knowledge Representation and Reasoning*, Morgan Kaufmann Publishers, Cambridge, MA, USA, pp. 395–404.

Moore, R. (1985). Semantical considerations on nonmonotonic logic, *Artificial Intelligence* **25**: 75–94.

Moore, R. (1988). Autoepistemic logic, *in* P. Smets, E. Mamdani and D. Dubois (eds), *Non-Standard Logics for Automated Reasoning*, Academic Press, London, pp. 105–136.

Niemelä, I. (1988). Decision procedure for autoepistemic logic, *Proceedings of the 9th International Conference on Automated Deduction*, Springer-Verlag, Argonne, USA, pp. 675–684.

Niemelä, I. (1990). Towards automatic autoepistemic reasoning, *Proceedings of the European Workshop on Logics in Artificial Intelligence—JELIA'90*, Springer-Verlag, Amsterdam, The Netherlands, pp. 428–443.

Niemelä, I. (1991). Constructive tightly grounded autoepistemic reasoning, *Proceedings of the 12th International Joint Conference on Artificial Intelligence*, Morgan Kaufmann Publishers, Sydney, Australia, pp. 399–404.

Niemelä, I. (1992a). On the decidability and complexity of autoepistemic reasoning, *Fundamenta Informaticae* **17**(1,2): 117–155.

Niemelä, I. (1992b). A unifying framework for nonmonotonic reasoning, *Proceedings of the 10th European Conference on Artificial Intelligence*, John Wiley, Vienna, Austria, pp. 334–338.

Przymusinska, H. and Przymusinski, T. (1992). Stationary default extensions, *Working Notes of the 4th International Workshop on on Nonmonotonic Reasoning*, Plymouth, Vermont, USA, pp. 179–193.

Reiter, R. (1980). A logic for default reasoning, *Artificial Intelligence* **13**: 81–132.

Stärk, R. (1990). On the existence of fixpoints in Moore's autoepistemic logic and the nonmonotonic logic of McDermott and Doyle, *Proceedings of the 4th Workshop on Computer Science Logic*, Springer-Verlag, Heidelberg, Germany, pp. 354–365.

A Framework for Part-of Hierarchies in Terminological Logics

Lin Padgham*   **Patrick Lambrix**
Department of Computer and Information Science
Linköping University, S-581 83 Linköping, Sweden
email: {lin,patla}@ida.liu.se

Abstract

There is a growing recognition that part-whole hierarchies are a very general form of representation, widely used by humans in commonsense reasoning. This paper develops a terminological logic, and related inference mechanisms for representing and reasoning about composite concepts and individuals. A basic terminological logic language is extended with constructs for describing composite concepts in terms of their parts and the relationships between them. A part-of hierarchy is defined, based on the relationship of *compositional inclusion*. This part-of hierarchy is analogous to, but different from, the "is-a" hierarchy. Compositional inferencing is defined as a process which infers the existence of a whole, based on the existence of the required parts, where the parts are in the necessary relationship to each other. Three stable states are defined with respect to compositional inferencing - compositional extensions, credulous compositional extensions and skeptical compositional conclusions. This framework significantly enhances and is complementary to, knowledge representation and reasoning based on is-a hierarchies.

1 INTRODUCTION

In this paper we first motivate the importance developing a logical system for reasoning about parts and wholes. We then define the language we will use giving syntax, semantics, completion rules and subsumption definitions. We define the key relationships, builds and compositional inclusion, on which we base our part-of hierarchy, and explain the process of compositional classification which allows us to build and maintain

---
*This author is currently visiting at The University of Melbourne, Australia.

this hierarchy. We then define some notions of compositional extensions where inferences are made about the existence of compositions, based on the existence of suitable parts in the correct relationships to each other.

1.1 MOTIVATION

Part-whole hierarchies are a natural way for humans to organise and represent objects in order to manage and reason about the world, much of which can be seen in terms of objects composed of other objects in a hierarchical fashion. There have been some efforts to represent and manage composite objects in e.g. object oriented database systems [BeechMahbod 1988, KimBertinoGarza 1989, Lambrix 1992] and this is even regarded as a necessary facility for more complex database systems such as engineering databases [Stonebraker et al. 1990, Atkinson et al. 1989]. There is also an awareness that part-whole relationships may be important for knowledge representation (KR), but so far there has been very little done in this field. The sort of reasoning we may hope to do in a KR system supporting part-whole relations includes such things as inferring the existence of composite objects based on the existence of their parts, answering questions such as whether a particular object is a part of some other object, and determining whether one class is a possible building block of another class. Determination of attribute or role values based on propagation or inheritance between part and whole is also an important aspect.[1]

In this paper we propose a framework, based on terminological logics, for representing and reasoning about this kind of part-whole relation. The addition of this component significantly increases the general purpose inferencing ability of the KR system and complements the traditional is-a hierarchy on which such systems are based.

---
[1] Value propagation is not actually addressed in this paper, but is an obvious extension to the framework presented.

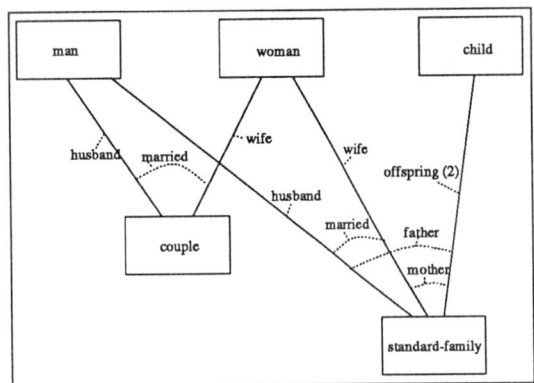

Figure 1: couple and standard family

1.2 EXAMPLE

Imagine that we have a knowledge base that defines the two concepts *couple* and *standard family*. A *couple* is defined as being composed of a part, husband, (which belongs to the concept *man*,) and a part, wife, (that belongs to the concept *woman*), with the constraint[2] that the wife is married to the husband:

couple ::=
   (**and** (**part** *husband man*) (**part** *wife woman*)
   (**pp-constraint** *married wife husband*))

A standard family is then defined as:

standard-family ::=
   (**and** (**part** *husband man*) (**part** *wife woman*)
   (**part** *offspring child*) (**parts** *2 offspring*)
   (**pp-constraint** *married husband wife*)
   (**pp-constraint** *mother wife offspring*)
   (**pp-constraint** *father husband offspring*))

meaning that a *standard family* is made up of a wife, a husband and two offspring, where the wife is a *woman*, the husband is a *man* and the offspring belong to the concept *child*. In addition there are the constraints that the wife is married to the husband, the wife is mother to the offspring, and the husband is father to the offspring. (See figure 1.)

If we are now given individuals a man, a woman and two children who are in the appropriate relationships to each other, we would like to conclude that we have a *standard family*. Similarly we would like to observe that *couple* is a module, or building block, of a *standard family*.

The framework defined in the following sections aims to support the above kind of reasoning in the context of a terminological logic.

---

[2]pp-constraint below stands for part-part-constraint, i.e. a constraint between parts of a composition.

2 LANGUAGE

In our initial work we take a relatively simple terminological logic with only unstructured roles and a limited number of constructs. We expect to be able to extend this later to include a greater number of constructs commonly found in terminological logics. We also begin with a limited representational capacity with respect to parts, choosing, in the terminology of [HalperGellerPerl 1992], to support only essential parts of fixed cardinality in concept descriptions. In common with [HalperGellerPerl 1992] we observe that it is important to allow for a mechanism to distinguish different kinds of parts - here we use a part name[3]. We also consider it important to have the ability to prescribe relationships between parts of a whole, and thus introduce the notion of part-part constraints, or necessary roles between parts.

2.1 SYNTAX

The language we will use is defined as follows:

```
concept          ::=
                 ⊤
                 | ⊥
                 | atomic-concept
                 | (and concept+)
                 | (all role concept)
                 | (atleast number role)
                 | (atmost number role)
                 | (part part-name atomic-concept)
                 | (parts number part-name)
                 | (pp-constraint role part-name part-name)
role             ::=  identifier
atomic-concept   ::=  identifier
part-name        ::=  identifier
number           ::=  non-negative-integer
```

Terminological axioms are used to introduce names for concepts, and definitions of those concepts. Let A be a concept name (*identifier*) and C be a concept description, (*concept*), then terminological axioms can be of the form:
A $\leq$ C for introducing necessary conditions (primitive concepts), or
A $\doteq$ C for introducing necessary and sufficient conditions (defined concepts).

A *terminology (Tbox) T* is a finite set of terminological axioms with the additional restrictions that (i) every concept name used must appear exactly once on the left hand side of a terminological axiom, (ii) all concepts must be defined (appear on the LHS) before

---

[3]We assume the following properties for the part-whole relation: (i) a part cannot be a part of itself and (ii) there are no cycles in the part hierarchy. We incorporate these properties in the definition of the *Tbox* (section 2.1) and *Abox* (section 4).

they are used, and (iii) T must not contain cyclic definitions directly or indirectly, via either $\doteq$, $\dot{\leq}$, or a **part** construct or any combination of these.

In the following we will use capital letters to denote concepts (with the exception of T which will be used for Tbox, $\mathcal{N}$, $\mathcal{R}$ which will be used for sets of part and role names, $\mathcal{C}$ which will be used for the set of atomic concepts, and N which will be used for a number function). Small letters will denote individuals, roles and part-names, capital greek letters denote Aboxes or extensions, and small greek letters denote sets of individuals (except for ε which denotes an extension function). Where relevant the concept an individual belongs to will be indicated by using the small letter corresponding to the capital letter used for the concept. In that case an individual a is understood to belong to concept A.

2.2 SEMANTICS

An interpretation of the language consists of a tuple $<\mathcal{D},\varepsilon>$, where $\mathcal{D}$ is the domain of individuals (which can be standard individuals, compositions and parts), and ε the extension function. The extension function is defined in the standard way for terminological logics, but extended to deal also with part names. Let $\mathcal{N}$ be the set of part names, $\mathcal{C}$ be the set of atomic concepts, and $\mathcal{R}$ the set of role names. Then,
$\varepsilon: (\mathcal{N} \to 2^{\mathcal{D}\times\mathcal{D}}) \cup (\mathcal{R} \to 2^{\mathcal{D}\times\mathcal{D}}) \cup (\mathcal{C} \to 2^{\mathcal{D}})$.
For convenience we write $x \triangleleft_n y$ for $<x,y> \in \varepsilon[n]$ where $n \in \mathcal{N}$.

We have a standard semantics for that part of our language which is common to most terminological logics (e.g. [Nebel 1990]). We give the semantics only for the new constructs.

$\varepsilon[(\textbf{part } n \; A)] =$
$\{\; x \in \mathcal{D} \;|\; \forall\, y \in \mathcal{D}\colon y \triangleleft_n x \to y \in \varepsilon[A]\}$

$\varepsilon[(\textbf{parts } m \; n)] =$
$\{\; x \in \mathcal{D} \;|\; \sharp\, \{\; y \in \mathcal{D} \;|\; y \triangleleft_n x \;\} = m \;\}$

$\varepsilon[(\textbf{pp-constraint } r \; n1 \; n2)] =$
$\{\; x \in \mathcal{D} \;|\; \forall\, y1,y2 \in \mathcal{D}\colon$
$(y1 \triangleleft_{n1} x \land y2 \triangleleft_{n2} x) \to <y1,y2> \in \varepsilon[r]\}$

Part names are really very similar to roles in standard terminological logics. In our example of figure 1, a usual way to define couple would be as having roles husband and wife, where all the fillers of the wife role belonged to the concept woman, and all those of the husband role to the concept man. Additional **atleast** and **atmost** declarations would be equivalent to the **parts** construct. A significant difference however, is that we are able to describe necessary relationships between parts as well. In addition the 'roles' defined by the **part** construct can be treated in a special way, allowing us to make inferences about composition of wholes. Essentially, part-of can be seen as a labeling on certain roles, giving them a more specific semantics than other roles.

2.3 SUBSUMPTION

Subsumption is defined as usual. C1 subsumes C2 iff $\varepsilon[C2] \subseteq \varepsilon[C1]$ for every interpretation $<\mathcal{D},\varepsilon>$. We give the relevant structural subsumption rule in the style used by [Borgida 1993].

$$\frac{\vdash\; C1 \;\Rightarrow\; C2}{\vdash\; (\textbf{part } n \; C1) \;\Rightarrow\; (\textbf{part } n \; C2)}$$

We obtain the semantics that if A subsumes B, then B may have additional kinds of parts, or more specialised parts than A, and the constraints between the parts of B may be stronger than those between the parts of A. If A has m_1 n-parts, B has m_2 n-parts and $m1 \neq m2$, then there is no subsumption relationship between A and B. We believe this semantics to be intuitive on the basis that if one has defined certain parts to be essential for individuals of a given concept, then all individuals of more specialised concepts must also contain such parts. It could be argued that one would prefer a more complex semantics, allowing for specialisations of a concept to have different parts than the more general concept. However we believe that this should be addressed eventually by the introduction of 'possible parts' into the language.

The subsumption algorithm for our language belongs to the same complexity class as the subsumption algorithm for the standard part of our language. This can be easily seen by mapping part names to roles, the **part** construct to the **all** construct and the **parts** construct to the **and** of the **atleast** construct and the **atmost** construct.

2.3.1 Normalisation and Completion

The algorithm for calculating the subsumption relationships requires that expressions are first normalised. The standard part of the language is normalised in a standard manner e.g. [Nebel 1990]. The relevant new normalisation rules are the following:

$\vdash\; (\textbf{and } (\textbf{part } n \; C1) \; (\textbf{part } n \; C2)) \equiv$
$\;\;\;\;(\textbf{part } n \; (\textbf{and } C1 \; C2))$

$\vdash\; (\textbf{part } n \; \bot) \equiv (\textbf{parts } 0 \; n)$

$$\frac{m1 \;\neq\; m2}{\vdash\; (\textbf{and } (\textbf{parts } m1 \; n) \; (\textbf{parts } m2 \; n)) \;\equiv\; \bot}$$

For the purpose of our reasoning mechanism we also *complete* the concept definitions by means of completion rules which add a $(\textbf{part } n \; \top)$ or $(\textbf{parts } 1 \; n)$ to a definition in some cases. These rules enforce a more complete specification and it is for this completed form of the language that the defined relationships apply. Completion is carried out as soon as a concept is defined, and the completed definition is used at all times. The essence of these rules is that if the number of parts is not given for a part named in a **part** or **pp-constraint** clause, then the number of parts is assumed to be one. If a concept is not given for a part named in a **pp-constraint** or **parts** clause, the concept is assumed to be $\top$[4].

For convenience we introduce some notation. If, after normalisation and completion we have that (**part** n A) occurs in the definition of B, then we say that A is a *direct n-part* of B. We define A' as an n-part of B for all A' subsumed by A.

Definition 1 A' *is a n-part of B (written $A' \triangleleft_n B$) iff*
$(\exists A : (A \text{ is a direct n-part of } B) \wedge (A \text{ subsumes } A'))$.

Definition 2 A *is a part of B (written $A \triangleleft B$) iff* $\exists n : A \triangleleft_n B$.

If for a part name n, (**part** m n) occurs in the definition of A, then we write that $N(n,A) = m$, otherwise $N(n,A) = 0$. $N(n,A)$ represents the number of n-parts which occur in the definition of A. The total number of defined parts for a concept A, denoted $N(A)$, is $\sum_n N(n,A)$.

If (**pp-constraint** r $n1$ $n2$) occurs in the definition of A, then we write $A_{n1}r_{n2}$.

3 KEY RELATIONS

The aim of our formalism and system is to be able to discuss and reason about parts and wholes, or compositions. We have already defined the notion of one concept being a part of another. We now introduce also the notion of *module*.

Definition 3 A *is a module of B*
(written $A \triangleleft_{mod} B$) iff
(i) $((N(A) < N(B))$
(ii) $\wedge \ (\forall \ n : N(n,A) \leq N(n,B))$
(iii) $\wedge \ (\forall \ n, C : C \text{ is a direct n-part of } A \rightarrow (C \triangleleft_n B))$
(iv) $\wedge \ (\forall \ n1, n2, r : (B_{n1}r_{n2} \wedge N(n1,A) > 0 \wedge N(n2,A) > 0) \rightarrow A_{n1}r_{n2}))$

In order for A to be a *module* for B we require that (i) the number of defined parts in A is strictly less than the number of defined parts in B; (ii) that all part names defined for A are also defined for B, with the number of each such defined part being at least as many for B as for A; (iii) that the domains for part names in A are included in the domains of those part names for B; and finally (iv) that all constraints defined between part names are at least as strong for A as for B. A module is essentially a collection of parts, such that none are redundant and the appropriate pp-constraints required by the composition are fulfilled.

Individuals belonging to concepts representing parts or modules of a concept C may be usable in building individuals of concept C.

We define a relationship *builds* which is a combination of *part* and *module*, and which will form the basis of our part-of hierarchy.

Definition 4 A builds B *(written $A \mathbin{\widehat{\triangleleft}} B$) iff* $(A \triangleleft B) \vee (A \triangleleft_{mod} B)$

In the example in figure 1 we have that *man* and *woman* (as parts) build *couple*, while *man*, *woman*, *child* (as parts) and *couple* (as a module) build *standard-family*.

We note that the builds relationship is not transitive. For example assume:

A ::= (**and** (**part** n_1 B) (**part** n_2 D)
             (**parts** 1 n_1) (**parts** 1 n_2))
and
B ::= (**and** (**part** n_3 C) (**part** n_4 E)
             (**parts** 1 n_3) (**parts** 1 n_4))

then C builds B, B builds A, but C does not build A.

We also define the relation of *compositional inclusion* which is the transitive closure of the inverse of *builds*.

Definition 5 B compositionally includes A
(written $B \mathbin{\widehat{\triangleright}}^* A$) iff $(A,B) \in Anc(builds)$
where $Anc(builds)$ is the transitive closure of *builds*.

Lemma 1 $\neg(A \mathbin{\widehat{\triangleleft}} A)$

Lemma 2 $(A \triangleleft_n B) \wedge (B \triangleleft_{mod} C) \rightarrow (A \triangleleft_n C)$

Lemma 3 $(A \triangleleft_{mod} B) \wedge (B \triangleleft_{mod} C) \rightarrow (A \triangleleft_{mod} C)$

Theorem 1 *Compositional inclusion is a partial order.*

Proof

(i) $\neg (A \mathbin{\widehat{\triangleright}}^* A)$.
Assume that $A \mathbin{\widehat{\triangleright}}^* A$. Then we would have that $(A,A) \in \bigcup_{i=1}^{\infty} (\mathbin{\widehat{\triangleleft}})^i$.
a) By lemma 1 $A \mathbin{\widehat{\triangleleft}} A$ is not possible.

---

[4] Observe that the addition of a (**part** n $\top$) actually does not change anything to the definition of the concept as (**part** n $\top$) $\equiv \top$. The addition of (**parts** 1 n) terms allows us to know the number of parts for each occurring part name and thus gives us the case of essential parts of fixed cardinality. Another way to obtain this case would have been to require that each concept definition is required to have a **parts** construct for each occurring part name.

b) Assume there is a sequence $(B_i)_{i=0}^{k}$ of concepts such that $A \mathbin{\widehat{\triangleleft}} B_1 \mathbin{\widehat{\triangleleft}} B_2 ... \mathbin{\widehat{\triangleleft}} B_k \mathbin{\widehat{\triangleleft}} A$.
1st case: All $\mathbin{\widehat{\triangleleft}}$ are actually modules. By lemma 3 we would have that A is a module of itself which gives us a contradiction.
2nd case: In the other case we construct a new sequence which does not contain any $\mathbin{\widehat{\triangleleft}}$ which are modules. This can be done using lemma 2. (E.g. $A \mathbin{\widehat{\triangleleft}} B_1 \mathbin{\widehat{\triangleleft}} B_2 \mathbin{\widehat{\triangleleft}} B_3 \mathbin{\widehat{\triangleleft}} C$ where the first and the last $\mathbin{\widehat{\triangleleft}}$ are parts is contracted to $A \mathbin{\widehat{\triangleleft}} B_3 \mathbin{\widehat{\triangleleft}} C$.) This shows us then that we have a cyclic definition and thus we have a contradiction.

(ii) By definition, compositional inclusion is transitive.

□

3.1 THE PART-OF HIERARCHY

Compositional inclusion is clearly a central relationship for discussing and reasoning about relationships between parts and compositions. If, given an individual, we wanted to consider what types of compositions it could be 'part of', we would look at the concepts which compositionally include the concept the individual belongs to. If we wanted to see what types of parts may be used to build an individual belonging to a composite concept A, we would look at the concepts compositionally included in A.

The is-a hierarchy in terminological logic systems can be seen as a data structure which is built and maintained to give an efficient representation of the subsumption relationship. We propose an analogous structure for keeping track of the relationship of compositional inclusion. We call this structure the *part-of hierarchy*.

The notion of *most specific subsumer* allows an efficient representation of the is-a hierarchy, as concepts are only directly linked to their most specific subsumer. This makes for a structure which is efficient to traverse when, for example, reasoning about what concepts an individual belongs to. Similarly we define the notion of *most composite includee*, to allow a minimal representation of the part-of hierarchy.

Definition 6 *A is a* **most composite includee** *of B iff*
(i) $B \mathbin{\widehat{\triangleright}}^{*} A$, ∧
(ii) $\neg(\exists A' : (B \mathbin{\widehat{\triangleright}}^{*} A') \wedge (A' \mathbin{\widehat{\triangleright}}^{*} A))$

In the example in figure 1 *couple* and *child* are most composite includees of *standard-family*.

Least composite includer is the inverse of *most composite includee*.

As new concepts are added into the hierarchy it may be necessary to remove links, as well as to add new links from and to the concept being added. This is analogous to the way links are revised when building the is-a hierarchy. Although compositional inclusion seems similar to subsumption at first glance, it is not merely a subrelation of subsumption as can be seen by the following example:

$A ::= $ (**and** (**part** n_1 $C1$) (**part** n_2 $C2$)
$\qquad\qquad$ (**parts** 2 n_1) (**parts** 1 n_2)
$\qquad\qquad$ (**pp** − **constraint** n_1 n_2 $r1$)
$\qquad\qquad$ (**pp** − **constraint** n_1 n_2 $r2$))
and
$B ::= $ (**and** (**part** n_1 $C3$) (**part** n_2 $C2$) (**part** n_3 $C4$)
$\qquad\qquad$ (**parts** 3 n_1) (**parts** 1 n_2) (**parts** 4 n_3)
$\qquad\qquad$ (**pp** − **constraint** n_1 n_2 $r1$))

where $C3$ subsumes $C1$.

A builds B and thus B compositionally includes A, but A does not subsume B and B does not subsume A. Thus the part-of hierarchy, while similar in nature to the is-a hierarchy, is in fact different and separate from it.

4 COMPOSITIONAL EXTENSIONS

In our compositional terminological logic we wish to extend our normal *Abox* inferencing to include what we will call *compositional inferencing*. (We assume in this section that we have a given *Tbox*.) Compositional inferencing is based on the notion that (in certain circumstances) we can infer compositions on the basis of existence of their parts. This will amount to adding inferred sentences in the *Abox* to obtain an *extended Abox*. In inferring a composition we can look for two different kinds of building blocks; *parts*, which are the analogy on the individual level of the parts required by the concept definitions, and *modules*, which are compositions of parts, and also analogous to modules at the concept level.

To assist in our definition of module (defined on individuals) we introduce some notation for counting parts of individuals, similar to that used for counting defined parts of concepts. N(n,x) denotes $\sharp\{\, y \mid y \triangleleft_n x \,\}$ and the total number of parts for individual x, denoted N(x), is $\sum_n$ N(n,x). We then define the notion of *module* as follows:

Definition 7 *y is a* **module** *of x,*
(written $y \triangleleft_{\mathbf{mod}} x$) iff
$(\forall\, z, n : z \triangleleft_n y \rightarrow z \triangleleft_n x) \wedge (N(y) < N(x))$.

The language of the *Abox*, in which we can add our inferences regarding compositions is as follows:

statement $\quad\quad ::=$
$\quad$ (**concept-filler** *individual concept*)
$\quad$ | (**role-fillers** *individual role individual*)
$\quad$ | (**part-fillers** *individual part-name individual*)
$\quad$ | (**module-fillers** *individual individual*)

$$individual \quad ::= \quad identifier$$

The terms *concept*, *part-name* and *role* are defined as for the *Tbox* syntax. If (**concept-filler** x C) appears in an *Abox*, then this means that $x \in \varepsilon[C]$. Similarly, (**role-fillers** x r y) means that $<x,y> \in \varepsilon[r]$, (**part-fillers** y n x) means that $y \triangleleft_n x$, and (**module-fillers** y x) means that $y \triangleleft_{mod} x$.

An *Abox* is a finite set of statements in the above language such that there are no cycles of parts. We say that an individual is defined in an *Abox* if it appears in one of the statements in the *Abox*. We will assume that within one *Abox* an individual has a unique name. We also make use of the following lemmas.

Lemma 4 $(x \triangleleft_n y) \land (y \triangleleft_{mod} z) \rightarrow (x \triangleleft_n z)$

Lemma 5 $(x \triangleleft_{mod} y) \land (y \triangleleft_{mod} z) \rightarrow (x \triangleleft_{mod} z)$

It will be useful to have the analogue of compositional inclusion for individuals.

Definition 8 x builds y (written $x \mathrel{\widehat{\triangleleft}} y$) iff
$(\exists\, n: x \triangleleft_n y) \lor x \triangleleft_{mod} y$

Definition 9 y compositionally includes x
(written $y \mathrel{\widehat{\triangleright}^*} x$) iff $(x,y) \in Anc(builds)$
where $Anc(builds)$ is the transitive closure of *builds*.

In order to discuss compositional inferencing we first define a relationship *composes*, between a set of potential parts and modules, and a concept. The intuition behind this relationship is that if we have all the pieces to form a composition of a given concept, and those pieces are in the relationship to each other expected in a composition of that concept, then the pieces can be said to compose that concept.

Definition 10 If $\alpha = \{<a_i, n_i>\}_{i=1}^k$ and $\beta = \{b_j\}_{j=1}^l$ then $<\alpha, \beta>$ **composes** C with respect to Abox Δ iff the following conditions hold in Δ:
1) $\forall n, C' : C'$ is a direct n-part of $C \rightarrow$
$((\forall a_i : (<a_i, n> \in \alpha) \rightarrow a_i \in \varepsilon[C'])$
$\land\ (\forall b_j, b_{jj} : b_j \in \beta \land b_{jj} \triangleleft_n b_j \rightarrow b_{jj} \in \varepsilon[C']))$
2) $(\forall a_i, n :\, <a_i, n> \in \alpha \rightarrow \exists C' : C' \triangleleft_n C)$
$\land\ (\forall b_j, b_{jj}, n : (b_j \in \beta \land b_{jj} \triangleleft_n b_j) \rightarrow \exists C' : C' \triangleleft_n C)$
3) $\forall n_1, n_2 : C_{n_1} r_{n_2} \rightarrow$
$((\forall a_i, a_j : (<a_i, n_1> \in \alpha \land <a_j, n_2> \in \alpha)$
$\rightarrow <a_i, a_j> \in \varepsilon[r])$
$\land\ (\forall a_i, b_j, b_{jj} : (<a_i, n_1> \in \alpha \land b_j \in \beta \land b_{jj} \triangleleft_{n_2} b_j)$
$\rightarrow <a_i, b_{jj}> \in \varepsilon[r])$
$\land\ (\forall a_i, b_j, b_{jj} : (<a_i, n_2> \in \alpha \land b_j \in \beta \land b_{jj} \triangleleft_{n_1} b_j)$
$\rightarrow <b_{jj}, a_i> \in \varepsilon[r])$
$\land\ (\forall b_i, b_{ii}, b_j, b_{jj} : (b_i \in \beta \land b_j \in \beta \land b_{ii} \triangleleft_{n_1} b_i$
$\land\ b_{jj} \triangleleft_{n_2} b_j) \rightarrow <b_{ii}, b_{jj}> \in \varepsilon[r]))$
4) $\forall n : N(n, C) = \#\{a_i\, |<a_i, n> \in \alpha\} + \Sigma_{b_j \in \beta} N(n, b_j)$
5) $(\#\,\alpha + \#\,\beta \geq 2)$

The first condition required in the above is that all n-parts in α and indirectly in β do belong to the concept required for that part by the definition of the concept being composed. The second condition ensures that every member of α and every part of every member of β is motivated by a requirement for such a part in the definition of the concept being composed. The third condition ensures that the constraints required by the definition of the concept being composed, do hold between the composing individuals. The fourth condition ensures that the number of parts of a given name in the set of composing individuals is exactly equal to the number of parts of that name required by the concept definition. The fifth condition ensures that an individual belonging to a concept does not compose this concept by requiring at least two individuals to compose. We note that the definition does not allow the composing set of modules and parts to contain any extra parts not required by the definition of the concept being composed.

We define *compositional instantiation* to be a mapping from a tuple in the composes relationship plus a system-generated unique identifier, to a set of *Abox* sentences, thus allowing a composition to be realised.

Definition 11 If $<\{<a_i, n_i>\}_{i=1}^k, \{b_j\}_{j=1}^l>$ composes C with respect to Abox Δ and x is a system-generated identifier then
$Inst(<\{<a_i, n_i>\}_{i=1}^k, \{b_j\}_{j=1}^l>, C, x) =$
$\{$ (**concept-filler** x C),
(**part-fillers** a_1 n_1 x),...,(**part-fillers** a_k n_k x),
(**module-fillers** b_1 x),...,(**module-fillers** b_l x)$\}$

We make the assumption that it is only reasonable to infer a composition in those cases where the composition is able to exclusively own its parts. To justify this assumption, suppose we had a car defined as consisting of the parts car-body, gearbox and engine, and a motor bike as consisting of parts bike-frame, gearbox and engine. Suppose also we had an *Abox* with a car-body c, two gearboxes $g1$ and $g2$, an engine e, and a bike-frame b. We would not want our compositional inferencing mechanism to infer that we had both a car and a motor bike, but that these two shared the same engine. We, along with other investigators [HalperGellerPerl 1992], consider this case of exclusive ownership of parts, to be the most common situation. Thus our *Abox* language allows a user to state explicitly that parts are shared, but we do not infer composites which are obliged to share their parts.[5] One could envisage extending the language to allow discrimination between sharable and exclusively owned parts.

We define the notion of an instantiation being *disallowed* in those cases where it would result in failure of the instantiated individual to exclusively own its parts.

---
[5] Parts are shared between a composition and its own modules - it is sharing outside of the modular structure which disqualifies compositional inference.

Definition 12 $Inst(<\alpha,\beta>,C,x)$ *is* **disallowed** *in* Δ *iff* (i) $(<\alpha,\beta>$ *composes* C) *with respect to* $\Delta \wedge$
$(\ (ii)\ (\exists a_i, n_i, y, n : (<a_i, n_i> \in \alpha) \wedge ((a_i \triangleleft_n y)\ in\ \Delta)$
$\wedge \neg((y \triangleleft_{mod} x)\ in\ \Delta \cup Inst(<\alpha,\beta>,C,x))$
$\wedge \neg((x \triangleleft_{mod} y)\ in\ \Delta \cup Inst(<\alpha,\beta>,C,x))) \vee$
(iii) $(\exists a_i, n_i, y : (<a_i, n_i> \in \alpha) \wedge ((a_i \triangleleft_{mod} y)\ in\ \Delta)$
$\wedge \neg((y \triangleleft_{mod} x)\ in\ \Delta \cup Inst(<\alpha,\beta>,C,x))$
$\wedge \neg((x \triangleleft_{mod} y)\ in\ \Delta \cup Inst(<\alpha,\beta>,C,x))) \vee$
(iv) $(\exists b_j, n, y : (b_j \in \beta) \wedge ((b_j \triangleleft_n y)\ in\ \Delta)$
$\wedge \neg((y \triangleleft_{mod} x)\ in\ \Delta \cup Inst(<\alpha,\beta>,C,x))$
$\wedge \neg((x \triangleleft_{mod} y)\ in\ \Delta \cup Inst(<\alpha,\beta>,C,x))) \vee$
(v) $(\exists b_j, y : (b_j \in \beta) \wedge ((b_j \triangleleft_{mod} y)\ in\ \Delta)$
$\wedge \neg((y \triangleleft_{mod} x)\ in\ \Delta \cup Inst(<\alpha,\beta>,C,x))$
$\wedge \neg((x \triangleleft_{mod} y)\ in\ \Delta \cup Inst(<\alpha,\beta>,C,x))))$

Thus a disallowed instantiation w.r.t. Δ is one which (i) can be composed in Δ but would result in either (ii) one of the *parts* of the new individual being a *part* of some separate[6] individual in the new Δ, (iii) one of the *parts* in the new individual being a *module* of some separate individual in the new Δ, (iv) one of the *modules* in the new individual being a *part* of some separate individual in the new Δ, or (v) one of the *modules* of the new individual being a *module* of some separate individual in the new Δ.

A *compositional extension*, where no further inferences can be made regarding the existence of compositions, is then defined as follows:

Definition 13 *An Abox* Σ *is a* **compositional extension** *of* Δ *under* T *iff it is the smallest Abox which satisfies the following conditions:*

1) $\Delta \subseteq \Sigma$;
2) $(<\alpha,\beta>$ *composes* C) *with respect to* $\Sigma \rightarrow$
$\exists\ x : ((Inst(<\alpha,\beta>,C,x) \subseteq \Sigma) \vee$
$(Inst(<\alpha,\beta>,\ C,\ x)$ *is disallowed in* $\Sigma))$
3) $\forall a, b, c, n_1, n_2 : ((a \triangleleft_{n_1} b)\ in\ \Sigma \wedge (a \triangleleft_{n_2} c)\ in\ \Sigma) \rightarrow$
$((c \triangleleft_{mod} b)\ in\ \Sigma \vee (b \triangleleft_{mod} c)\ in\ \Sigma \vee$
$((a \triangleleft_{n_1} b)\ in\ \Delta \wedge (a \triangleleft_{n_2} c)\ in\ \Delta))$

Thus (1) the original *Abox* is always part of a *compositional extension*, (2) if it is possible to find individuals (parts and modules) to compose a concept, then they will be used to instantiate an individual of that concept in the compositional extension, unless this would result in a disallowed sharing of parts,[7] and (3) any sharing of parts between individuals is either a result of a situation given in the original *Abox*, or of sharing between a module and a 'larger' composition using that module.

---

[6] With separate individuals we mean that none of the individuals participates in the other individual as a module.

[7] Sharing of parts is allowed between a module and a composition using that module.

A compositional extension is then an *Abox* where we can build no more compositions.

The outline of an algorithm for finding a compositional extension is as follows:

Let Δ be the original *Abox*. The preprocessing step generates new individuals for the parts of given individuals in Δ which are not explicitly given and initialises Σ to be this new *Abox*. This is done to easily check the composes relation. The set $Used$ is the set of the individuals which have been used already to compose other individuals. The *instantiate-intermediate-modules* step makes sure that when we instantiate an individual we also instantiate as many as possible of its potential modules and add these intermediate modules to $Used$.

begin
  Preprocess(Δ,Used,Σ);
  repeat
    if *possible* **then**
      begin
        choose α, β, C such that
          (i) $\alpha = \{<a_1,n_1>,...,<a_k,n_k>\}$ such that
          each a_i is defined in Σ,
          (ii) $\beta = \{b_1,...,b_m\}$ such that
          each b_j is defined in Σ,
          (iii) $<\alpha,\beta>$ composes C with respect to Σ,
          (iv) none of the a_i in α is in Used,
          (v) none of the b_j in β is in Used;
        generate-unique-individual-name(x);
        instantiate-intermediate-modules(α,β);
        $\Sigma \leftarrow \Sigma \cup Inst(<\alpha,\beta>,C,x)$;
        Used $\leftarrow$ Used $\cup$ { $a_1,...,a_k$ } $\cup$ { $b_1,...,b_m$ }
      end
    else break
    endif
  endrepeat
end

It is in the process of choosing a suitable α, β and C, that the part-of hierarchy helps structure the search space. A non-used individual can first be placed with respect to the part-of hierarchy. Each of the concepts immediately below the individual (i.e. concepts which compositionally include the concept representing the given individual), are then candidates for the C parameter in *composes*.

If there is some part(s) lacking[8] in each *least composite includer* of an individual, then that individual cannot be used in any *composes*. Similarly, if there is some part(s) lacking in each *most composite includee* of a concept, then neither that concept, nor any concept which *compositionally includes* that concept can be formed.

---

[8] Lacking implies not available and not able to be composed.

The part-of hierarchy can also be used to facilitate instantiation of the intermediate modules. The search for such an intermediate module is limited to concepts which are *compositionally included* by the C under consideration and which themselves can be composed by a combination of elements in the candidate α or β.

We illustrate a simplified view of the algorithm outlined using the example part-of hierarchy shown in figure 2. For simplicity we assume that there are no constraints between parts.

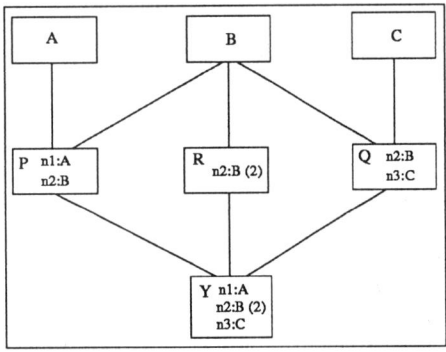

Figure 2: part-of hierarchy

P ::= (and (parts 1 n1) (part n1 A)
           (parts 1 n2) (part n2 B))
Q ::= (and (parts 1 n2) (part n2 B)
           (parts 1 n3) (part n3 C))
R ::= (and (parts 2 n2) (part n2 B))
Y ::= (and (parts 1 n1) (part n1 A)
           (parts 2 n2) (part n2 B)
           (parts 1 n3) (part n3 C))

Assume an original Abox Δ as follows:
{(concept-filler a A), (concept-filler b1 B), (concept-filler b2 B), (concept-filler c C) }

Preprocessing sets $\Sigma = \Delta$, $Used = \emptyset$. We first take a, and match to A in the part-of hierarchy. We investigate a concept immediately below A, P, as a candidate for composes. We find $b1$ and verify that
$< \{< a, n1 >, < b1, n2 >\}, \emptyset >$ composes P and fulfills the conditions required in choose. We instantiate a new individual p and see that there are no intermediate modules possible. We add a and $b1$ to $Used$ and add $\mathsf{Inst}(< \{< a, n1 >, < b1, n2 >\}, \emptyset >, P, p)$ to Σ. We take p, and investigate one of the concepts immediately below P, namely Y, as a candidate for composes. We find $b2$ and c such that
$< \{< c, n3 >, < b2, n2 >\}, \{p\} >$ composes Y. We see that we can instantiate an intermediate module q as $< \{< c, n3 >, < b2, n2 >\}, \emptyset >$ composes Q. There are no other intermediate modules to be instantiated and thus we instantiate y using
$< \{< c, n3 >, < b2, n2 >\}, \{p\} >$. We add p, q, c and $b2$ to $Used$ and add $\mathsf{Inst}(< \emptyset, \{p, q\} >, Y, y)$ to Σ. We cannot find any composes using y. As y is the only non-used individual in Σ we are finished. Σ defines the individuals $a, b1, b2, c, p, q, y$.

Theorem 2 *For a given Abox Δ, there always exists at least one compositional extension Σ.*

We prove this by showing that the above algorithm terminates, and that on termination, the final Σ is a compositional extension.

(i) This algorithm terminates.

The initial *Abox* Δ contains a finite number of individuals. The preprocessing step may introduce new individuals. As the number of defined parts for a concept is finite and we have only a finite number of concepts and we have no cycles, the number of newly introduced individuals is also finite. This also means that we have a finite number of non-used individuals. In each step in the algorithm we generate one new non-used individual. (The intermediate modules are added to $Used$.) However, to do this we need at least two old individuals which participate in the composes relation. This means that the number of non-used individuals in each step reduces by at least one. As we started out with a finite number of non-used individuals the algorithm must terminate.

(ii) The final Σ is a compositional extension.

1) $\Delta \subseteq \Sigma$;
2) Assume $< \alpha, \beta >$ composes C with respect to Σ and $\neg((\mathsf{Inst}(< \alpha, \beta >, C, x) \subseteq \Sigma)$ and all y which would share with x in $\Sigma \cup \mathsf{Inst}(< \alpha, \beta >, C, x)$ would do this module-wise. Then we have the following.
(a) If x would be a module of $y1$ then x would have been an intermediate module and thus instantiated.
(b) If x would have sharing modules then we could use the highest level modules among these to form a new $< \alpha', \beta' >$. These highest level modules would then be non-used individuals and thus the algorithm would have instantiated x.
(c) If x would not share at all then the algorithm would have instantiated x.
3) No sharing (except the allowed module-wise sharing) is introduced by the algorithm as only non-used individuals are used in each step to compose the non-used new individuals. The other new individuals are intermediate modules and sharing is allowed here.

□

In cases where it would be possible to use parts for building different composites, there will be a number of compositional extensions, with no preferences between them.

We wish to define preferences which, in the absence of application specific preferences, we believe should always be applied when inferring composites from parts.

We have identified two such general purpose preferences. We state these briefly, informally, then define them formally and give examples to clarify our intuitions.

1. Inferred composite individuals should make use of given information at the most specific level possible.
2. When inferring composite individuals on the basis of their parts, we should infer as little additional information as possible.

The application of these preferences will give what we call *credulous compositional extensions*[9].

In the compositional extensions which we generate, we will have a number of individuals with system-generated names. In order to be able to compare extensions we need to define a notion of equivalent individuals, which are the same except for differences in system-generated names.

Definition 14 *Given an original Abox Δ, compositional extensions Σ_1 and Σ_2 of Δ under T, an individual $x1$ defined in Σ_1 and an individual $x2$ defined in Σ_2, then we define* **same**$(x1, x2, \Sigma_1, \Sigma_2)$ *as follows:*
1) If $x1$ is defined in $\Delta \vee x2$ is defined in Δ then $(same(x1, x2, \Sigma_1, \Sigma_2)$ iff $x1 = x2))$
2) If $x1$ is not defined in $\Delta \wedge x2$ is not defined in Δ then $(same(x1, x2, \Sigma_1, \Sigma_2)$ iff [10]
(i) $((\forall C : x1 \in \varepsilon_{\Sigma_1}[C] \leftrightarrow x2 \in \varepsilon_{\Sigma_2}[C]) \wedge$
(ii)$(\alpha_1 = \{<a, n> | a \triangleleft_{n \Sigma_1} x1\}$
$\wedge \alpha_2 = \{<b, n> | b \triangleleft_{n \Sigma_2} x2\} \rightarrow$
$\exists f : \alpha_1 \rightarrow \alpha_2 : ((a) f : \alpha_1 \rightarrow \alpha_2$ is $1-1 \wedge$
(b)$\forall a, b, n_1, n_2 : f(<a, n_1>) = <b, n_2> \rightarrow$
$n_1 = n_2 \wedge same(a, b, \Sigma_1, \Sigma_2)))))$

This definition states that an individual in the original *Abox* can only be the same as itself and an individual inferred by compositional inferencing (i.e. did not exist in the original *Abox*) can only be the same as another inferred individual. In the latter case we must have (i) that they belong to the same concept, (ii) there is a (a) one to one mapping between the parts of the individuals, and that (b) corresponding parts are the same according to this definition - i.e. non-inferred parts are identical, while inferred parts are identical except for name.

In order to capture preferences between individuals which are not equivalent, we define two further relations.

---
[9]The analogy is to credulous extensions in defeasible inheritance, where these represent extensions where some relatively indisputable preferences (specificity in the inheritance case) have been applied, but there is still potential for multiple extensions.

[10]The symbol ε_{Σ_1} means the extension function mapping from the *Tbox* to the individuals in Σ_1. Similarly $\triangleleft_{n \Sigma_1}$ means n-part in Σ_1.

The first of these is something which we will call *more specific w.r.t. parts*. The intuition motivating this definition is that if we are going to infer an individual on the basis of the existence of the parts, we will prefer to infer an individual belonging to a concept which makes use of the specific nature of the parts or the constraints between them. For example, assume that we build on our original example[11] (figure 1), by adding a definition for the concept of *young standard family*, which is made up of a *young couple* with two children, where *young couple* is a specialisation of *couple*. Given a *young couple* and two children, with the appropriate constraints holding, we would prefer to infer a *young standard family*, rather than simply a *family*, though both would be correct. We define this relation as follows:

Definition 15 *With respect to a particular Tbox T, an individual i_1 defined in Σ_1 is* **more specific w.r.t. parts** *than an individual i_2 defined in Σ_2, written* $s_T(i_1, i_2, \Sigma_1, \Sigma_2)$ *iff* $(\exists C1, C2 :$
(i) $C1$ is a most specific concept defined in T such that $i_1 \in \varepsilon_{\Sigma_1}[C1] \wedge$
(ii) $C2$ is a most specific concept defined in T such that $i_2 \in \varepsilon_{\Sigma_2}[C2] \wedge$
(iii) $(\forall n : N(n, C1) = N(n, C2)) \wedge$
(iv) $\forall n, A : A$ is a direct part of $C1 \rightarrow A \triangleleft_n C2 \wedge$
(v) $\forall n1, n2, r : C2_{n1} r_{n2} \rightarrow C1_{n1} r_{n2} \wedge$
(vi) (a) $((\exists n, A, A' : ((A$ is a direct n-part of $C1)$
$\wedge (A'$ is a direct n-part of $C2)$
$\wedge (A'$ subsumes $A) \wedge \neg(A$ subsumes $A')))$
$\vee (b)(\exists n1, n2, r : C1_{n1} r_{n2} \wedge \neg C2_{n1} r_{n2})))$

This definition specifies that for i_1 to be *more specific w.r.t. parts* than i_2, there must be most specific concepts, $C1$ for i_1 and $C2$ for i_2, (i,ii) such that (iii) both concepts define the same part names and the same number of parts for each part name; (iv) the domains for the part names in $C1$ are included in the domains of those part names in $C2$; (v) all the constraints between part names occurring in $C2$ also occur in $C1$; and finally (v) (a) there is a part name which has a strictly more specific domain in $C1$ than in $C2$ or (b) there is a constraint between part names which appears in the definition of $C1$ but not in the definition of $C2$.

In the above case our intuition is that we prefer to compose the more specific individual, because it is making use of a more specific part, or constraint between parts. However when specificity is based on aspects other than specificity of parts, we intuitively prefer to infer individuals which are as general as possible. Assume again that we build on our original example by adding a definition for a *rich standard family*, which is the same as *standard family* except that it has an additional feature (all *bank-account large-*

---
[11]The additions to the example here are not intended as a full specification of the concepts involved.

positive-accounts). Given now that we have a couple and two children in the appropriate relationships, we would prefer to infer a *standard family* rather than a *rich standard family*. We thus define the relationship *more general*, which actually means more general, providing that there is not already a relationship of *more specific w.r.t. parts*.

Definition 16 *With respect to a particular Tbox T, an individual i_1 defined in Σ_1 is* more general *than an individual i_2 defined in Σ_2, written $g_T(i_1, i_2, \Sigma_1, \Sigma_2)$ iff*
(i) $\neg\; s_T(i_2, i_1, \Sigma_2, \Sigma_1) \wedge$
(ii) $((\alpha_1 = \{<a,n>|\; a \triangleleft_{n\Sigma_1} i_1\} \wedge$
$\alpha_2 = \{<a,n>|\; a \triangleleft_{n\Sigma_2} i_2\}) \rightarrow$
$\exists f : \alpha_1 \rightarrow \alpha_2 : (f \text{ is a } 1-1 \text{ mapping} \wedge$
$(\forall a_1, a_2, n_1, n_2 : f(<a_1, n_1>) = <a_2, n_2> \rightarrow$
$(n_1 = n_2 \wedge \forall C : a_1 \in \varepsilon_{\Sigma_1}[C] \leftrightarrow a_2 \in \varepsilon_{\Sigma_2}[C]))) \wedge$
(iii)$(\forall C : i_1 \in \varepsilon_{\Sigma_1}[C] \rightarrow i_2 \in \varepsilon_{\Sigma_2}[C]) \wedge$
$(\exists C : i_2 \in \varepsilon_{\Sigma_2}[C] \wedge \neg(i_1 \in \varepsilon_{\Sigma_1}[C]))$

Thus for i_1 to be *more general* than i_2, (i) i_2 may not be *more specific w.r.t. parts* than i_1, (ii) the parts in i_1 and i_2 must belong to the same concepts, and (iii) i_1 must be strictly more specific than i_2.

We are now ready to define a preference relation over extensions, based on the above relations between individuals.

Definition 17 Σ_2 *is preferred over* Σ_1
(written $\Sigma_2 \ll_T \Sigma_1$) iff
$\exists \Sigma_{11}, \Sigma_{12}, \Sigma_{21}, \Sigma_{22} :$
(i) $\Sigma_{11} \bigcup \Sigma_{12} = \Sigma_1 \wedge \Sigma_{11} \cap \Sigma_{12} = \emptyset$
$\wedge\; \Sigma_{21} \bigcup \Sigma_{22} = \Sigma_2 \wedge \Sigma_{21} \cap \Sigma_{22} = \emptyset$
(ii) $\wedge\; \exists$ *mapping* $f : \Sigma_1 \rightarrow \Sigma_2 :$
((a) $f : \Sigma_{11} \rightarrow \Sigma_{21}$ *is 1-1* $\wedge$
(b)$f : \Sigma_{12} \rightarrow \Sigma_{22}$ *is 1-1* $\wedge$
(c)$\forall x \in \Sigma_{11} : same(x, f(x), \Sigma_1, \Sigma_2) \wedge$
(d)$(\forall x \in \Sigma_{12} : (d1)\; s_T(f(x), x, \Sigma_2, \Sigma_1)$
$\vee\; (d2)\; g_T(f(x), x, \Sigma_2, \Sigma_1)$
$\vee\; (d3)\; \exists x' \in \Sigma_{12} : (x \,\widehat{\triangleright}^*_{\Sigma_1} x' \wedge$
$(s_T(f(x'), x', \Sigma_2, \Sigma_1) \vee g_T(f(x'), x', \Sigma_2, \Sigma_1)))) \wedge$
(e)$(\forall x, y \in \Sigma_1 : x \,\widehat{\triangleright}^*_{\Sigma_1} y \leftrightarrow f(x) \,\widehat{\triangleright}^*_{\Sigma_2} f(y)))$

This definition states that we compare two extensions by partitioning each extension into two disjoint parts (i). The individuals in the first of these partitions can be mapped directly to *same* individuals in the corresponding partition of the other extension (a,c). In the remaining partition, in order for Σ_2 to be preferred over Σ_1, there must be a 1-1 mapping (b) between the individuals in the second partition of each extension such that (d) each individual in Σ_2 is preferred to its corresponding individual in Σ_1 by a (d1) s_T or (d2) g_T preference; or (d3) there is a s_T or g_T preference between compositionally included individuals. The intuition for the latter case is that the earlier decisions in the building process are the most important. If we make a 'wrong' choice earlier on, then we cannot trust preferences based on individuals built from these less preferred building blocks. Finally, (e) the mapping requires that for composite individuals compositionally included individuals are mapped to compositionally included individuals of the corresponding individual in the other extension.

We give the following small example to illustrate this preference procedure.

P::= (and (parts 1 n1) (part n1 A)
           (parts 1 n2) (part n2 B))
P'::= (and (parts 1 n1) (part n1 A)
           (parts 1 n2) (part n2 B)
           (all colour light-colour))
Q::= (and (parts 1 n3) (part n3 P)
           (parts 1 n4) (part n4 C))
Q'::= (and (parts 1 n3) (part n3 P')
           (parts 1 n4) (part n4 C))

If we are given an *Abox* defining a, b, and c, then two of the compositional extensions, and the mappings between their individuals will then be as follows:

Σ_1		Σ_2
a	same	a
b	same	b
c	same	c
p	$g_T(p, p', \Sigma_1, \Sigma_2)$	p'
q	$s_T(q', q, \Sigma_2, \Sigma_1)$	q'

We have a g_T preference (between the p's) favouring Σ_1 and a s_T preference (between the q's) favouring Σ_2. However the s_T preference is allowed to be overridden due to the fact that the p's are compositionally included in the q's. Thus Σ_1 is preferred to Σ_2.

A credulous compositional extension is then defined as follows:

Definition 18 *A compositional extension Σ of Δ under T is a* **credulous compositional extension** *of Δ under T iff*
$\forall \Sigma' : (\Sigma' \text{ is a compositional extension of } \Delta \text{ under } T$
$\wedge\; \Sigma' \ll_T \Sigma) \rightarrow \Sigma \ll_T \Sigma'$

We also have the following theorem.

Theorem 3 *For a given Abox Δ, there always exists at least one credulous compositional extension.*

Due to space limitations we do not show the proof. It builds a.o. on the transitivity of $\ll_T$ and the fact that there are only a finite number of compositional extensions for a given *Abox* Δ.

□

Although credulous compositional extensions may allow significant pruning in the space of all possible compositional extensions, there are many situations where we will have multiple credulous compositional extensions. It is often not practical in real systems to maintain multiple extensions. Thus we also define the notion of a *skeptical compositional conclusion*, which infers compositions only where there is no ambiguity remaining after applying the preferences inherent in a credulous extension.

Definition 19 Δ^s *is a* **skeptical compositional conclusion** *of Δ under T iff*
it is the largest Abox such that ($\forall a : a$ defined in $\Delta^s \rightarrow$ ($\forall \Sigma : \Sigma$ is a credulous compositional extension of Δ under $T \rightarrow \exists a' : a'$ defined in $\Sigma \wedge same(a, a', \Delta^s, \Sigma)))$

Thus a *skeptical compositional conclusion* is in essence the intersection of the *credulous compositional extensions*, but with allowance made for the arbitrary names of system-generated compositions.

Theorem 4 *For a given Abox Δ, there always exists exactly one skeptical compositional conclusion (with allowance made for the arbitrary names of system-generated compositions).*

This follows from the definition and theorem 3.

□

We observe that a skeptical compositional conclusion is not necessarily a compositional extension, and illustrate this with the following example:

```
P::=  (and (parts 1 n1) (part n1 A)
           (parts 1 n2) (part n2 B))
Q::=  (and (parts 1 n2) (part n2 B)
           (parts 1 n3) (part n3 C))
Z::=  (and (parts 1 n1) (part n1 A)
           (parts 1 n2) (part n2 B)
           (parts 1 n3) (part n3 C))
```

Assume we have an original *Abox*:
{(concept-filler a A), (concept-filler b B), (concept-filler c C) }

We can build then two compositional extensions: Σ_1 defining a, b, c, p (with parts a and b), $z1$ (with parts a, b and c) and Σ_2 defining a, b, c, q (with parts b and c), $z2$ (with parts a, b and c). Both compositional extensions are credulous compositional extensions. We can see also that $same(z1,z2)$. The compositional conclusion defines then a, b, c, z with $same(z,z1)$ and $same(z,z2)$. This is not a compositional extension as it is possible to compose both p and q, and to instantiate one of them according to the definition of compositional extension.

5 DISCUSSION AND CONCLUSIONS

In this paper we have defined a language for describing compositional concepts and a relationship which allows us to maintain a compositional hierarchy, analogous to, but differing from the subsumption hierarchy. This part-of hierarchy supports reasoning about compositions, just as the subsumption hierarchy supports reasoning about concept membership.

We have defined and discussed a process of compositional inference - the inferring of wholes from the existence of their parts - and have defined three kinds of stable states with respect to compositional inferencing; compositional extensions, credulous compositional extensions and skeptical compositional conclusions.

We have identified two preferences which should be considered when comparing extensions - one for *specificity w.r.t. parts* and one for *generality* when the *specificity w.r.t. parts* is not present. We expect that there are also further general purpose preferences which should eventually be incorporated into the choice of credulous extension. In particular it seems intuitively that one would wish to have a preference for building a single more complex individual, rather than a number of disjoint, simpler individuals. However, definition and exploration of this type of preference is the subject of further work, and will probably require experimentation in application domains, prior to definition. It is also possible that further exploration, both theoretical and practical will lead to changes in the preferences defined in this paper. However this work is an initial step in defining a framework which can be further refined and developed.

In this paper we have not considered a number of types of questions whose answers can also be facilitated by the representation described here. However it is clear that questions like *"I want to build an individual belonging to concept Z, what building blocks do I have available?"*, or *"We have a surplus of individuals belonging to concept X, in what way could we use them?"* could be answered using reasoning mechanisms based on the framework described here. Simpler queries regarding whether one individual is a part of another can of course also be supported, as can queries regarding whether an individual belonging to one concept may be a part of an individual belonging to another concept.

Most of the work that has been done in the area of part-whole relations to date has been on one of two subjects: (1) exploring the different styles of part-of relationships (e.g. [WinstonChaffinHerrmann 1987, IrisLitowitzEvens 1988]); and (2) allowing for representation of various part-of relationships in object oriented databases, with support for some limited sorts of behaviour based on these relationships (e.g.

deletion of a part when a whole is deleted as in [KimBertinoGarza 1989]).

Franconi [Franconi 1993] has suggested an extension to terminological logics which allows for treatment of collections as individuals. However his approach is oriented towards natural language systems, whereas ours is oriented more to description of physical systems. The KOLA system [JangPatil 1989] also incorporated some aspects of part-whole relations. The emphasis here was to allow classification of a concept as a specialisation of some other concept in cases where some role filler was a part of the role filler of the parent concept, as opposed to a specialisation of the role filler (which is the normal subsumption case). This issue is not addressed in our work, but would be a natural area for further development. Napoli [Napoli 1992] defines *co-subsumption* as a special case of *object-based subsumption* and uses this to manage a particular part-whole relation, namely subgraph/graph inclusion. The graphs are maintained in a hierarchy which is called the *reactive partonomy* and is used in an application for planning the synthesis of organic molecules. His work tries to introduce reasoning about partial orders (where part-of could be a special case) in object-based systems, whereas our approach gives part-of a special status with specific reasoning mechanisms.

An important area for future work in the framework developed here is the extension to allow specification of possible, but not necessary parts, and a more flexible approach to the specification of number of parts. Mechanisms for inferring attributes of wholes from attributes of the parts, and vice versa is also an important area for continued work.

We consider the part-of relationship to be a central mechanism for representation of and reasoning about composite concepts and individuals, analogous to the is-a relationship for representing and reasoning about class organisation and membership. Inclusion of part-whole representation and inferencing significantly enhances the representation based on is-a hierarchies, central to many knowledge representation systems.

Acknowledgements

Most of this work was done while the first author was on sabbatical at The University of Melbourne, Australia, partially supported by the Swedish Institute. This work has also been partially supported by funding from the Swedish National Board for Technical Development under grant 5321-93-3263.

References

[Atkinson et al. 1989] Atkinson, M., Bancilhon, F., DeWitt, D., Dittrich, K., Maier, D., Zdonik, S., 'The Object-Oriented Database System Manifesto', *Technical Report*, GIP-ALTAIR, No. 30-89, LeChesnay, France, 1989.

[BeechMahbod 1988] Beech, D., Mahbod, B., 'Generalized Version Control in an Object-Oriented Database', *Proceedings of the 4th IEEE Conference on Data Engineering*, pp 14-22, 1988.

[Borgida 1993] Borgida, A., 'From Type Systems to Knowledge Representation: Natural Semantics Specifications for Description Logics', *International Journal of Intelligent and Cooperative Information Systems*, Vol 1(1), pp 93-126, 1993.

[Franconi 1993] Franconi, E., 'A Treatment of Plurals and Plural Qualifications based on a Theory of Collections', *Minds and Machines*, Vol 3(4), pp 453-474, November 1993.

[HalperGellerPerl 1992] Halper, M., Geller, J., Perl, Y., 'An OODB "Part" Relationship Model', *Proceedings of the 1st International Conference on Information and Knowledge Management - CIKM'92*, pp 602-611, 1992.

[IrisLitowitzEvens 1988] Iris, M.A., Litowitz, B.E., Evens, M., 'Problems with the part-whole relation', *Relational Models of the Lexicon*, ed. Evens, pp 261-288, 1988.

[JangPatil 1989] Jang, Y., Patil, R., 'KOLA: A knowledge organization language', *Proceedings of the 13th Symposium on Computer Applications in Medical Care*, 1989.

[KimBertinoGarza 1989] Kim, W., Bertino, E., Garza, J.F., 'Composite Objects Revisited', *Proceedings of the Conference on Management of Data - SIGMOD'89*, SIGMOD Rec., Vol 18(2), pp 337-347, 1989.

[Lambrix 1992] Lambrix, P., *Aspects of Version Management of Composite Objects*, Lic. Thesis 328, Department of Computer and Information Science, Linköping University, 1992.

[Napoli 1992] Napoli, A., 'Subsumption and Classification-Based Reasoning in Object-Based Representations', *Proceedings of the 10th European Conference on Artificial Intelligence - ECAI'92*, pp 425-429, 1992.

[Nebel 1990] Nebel, B., *Reasoning and Revision in Hybrid Representation Systems*, Lecture Notes in Artificial Intelligence, 422, Springer-Verlag, 1990.

[Stonebraker et al. 1990] Stonebraker, M., Rowe, L.A., Lindsay, B., Gray, J., Carey, M., Brodie, M., Bernstein, P., Beech, D., 'Third-Generation Database System Manifesto', *SIGMOD RECORD*, Vol 19(3), pp 31-43, 1990.

[WinstonChaffinHerrmann 1987] Winston, M.E., Chaffin, R., Herrmann, D., 'A taxonomy of part-whole relations', *Cognitive Science*, Vol 11(4), pp 417-444, 1987.

Means-End Plan Recognition – Towards a Theory of Reactive Recognition

Anand S. Rao
Australian Artificial Intelligence Institute
1 Grattan Street
Carlton 3053, Australia
anand@aaii.oz.au

Abstract

This paper draws its inspiration from current work in reactive planning to guide plan recognition using "plans as recipes". The plan recognition process guided by such a library of plans is called *means-end plan recognition*. An extension of dynamic logic, called *dynamic agent logic*, is introduced to provide a formal semantics for means-end plan recognition and its counterpart, means-end plan execution. The operational semantics, given by algorithms for means-end plan recognition, are then related to the provability of formulas in the dynamic agent logic. This establishes the relative soundness and completeness of the algorithms with respect to a given library of plans. Some of the restrictive assumptions underlying means-end plan recognition are then relaxed to provide a theory of *reactive recognition* that allows for changes in the external world during the recognition process. Reactive recognition, when embedded with the mental attitudes of belief, desire, and intention, leads to a powerful theory of integrated reactive planning and recognition. The primary contribution of this paper is in laying the foundations for such an integrated theory.

1 INTRODUCTION

Classical planning and plan recognition have received a great deal of attention within the Artificial Intelligence (AI) community. Classical planning deals with reaching a desired state of affairs from the current state by chaining through a given set of plan operators. Plan recognition, usually treated as the reverse process of planning, is concerned with inferring these operators based on observations.

Over the past decade the focus of research in planning has shifted from classical planning to reactive or situated planning [6]. Reactive planning is based on two premises: (a) the environment in which an agent is situated is continuously changing; and (b) agents situated in such environments have limited resources. This has led to the development of various architectures and techniques for guiding the agent in its decision-making process, for making agents commit to their decisions as late as possible and, once committed, to stay committed as long as possible, within rational bounds.

Research in reactive planning has led to the redefinition of the notion of plans. Plans are used in two different contexts: (a) plans as abstract structures or recipes for achieving certain states of the world; and (b) plans as complex mental attitudes intertwined in a complex web of relationships with the other mental attitudes of belief and desire [15]. Plans as recipes *guide* a resource-bounded agent in its decision-making process, thereby short-circuiting the time-consuming search through a possible space of solutions as done by classical planning. Plans as mental attitudes *constrain* the agent in its future decision-making by committing it to previously-made decisions. The latter are called *intentions*.

As noted by others[1] this renaissance in planning, has had very little impact on plan recognition. A majority of the work within plan recognition [1, 9, 13] is still addressing the general problem of unconstrained plan recognition. Although some of these approaches use background knowledge (in terms of event hierarchies [9] and plans [13]) as heuristics to guide the general recognition problem, they have not attempted to use plans in the above sense to guide or constrain the recognition process of resource-bounded agents in a dynamic world.

The use of plans as recipes and as mental attitudes, to guide and constrain the recognition process, respectively, will be called *reactive recognition*.

---
[1] Pollack [16] writes: "Yet, most research on plan recognition has taken place in isolation from the AI planning renaissance. Could a marriage of these two research projects bear any fruit?"

Reactive recognition is applicable to a broad class of problems where agents have limited resources and the environment may change *while* the agents are doing their recognition. However, it makes two important assumptions: (a) the recognizing agent has complete knowledge of the plans of other agents that it is trying to recognize; and (b) under any given situation the recognizing agent has a small set of plans (i.e., hypotheses) that it is trying to recognize.

In this paper, we address a part of the reactive recognition process, namely the use plans as recipes to guide the recognition process and call it *means-end plan recognition*[2]. In addition to the two assumptions (a) and (b) of reactive recognition, means-end recognition also makes the following assumptions: (c) the occurrence of events in the external world is synchronous with the recognition of events by the agent, i.e., the agent cannot wait for an event to occur and there is no memory of all the past events that have occurred; and (d) the world is not changing while the agent is performing the recognition.

Due to its restrictive assumptions means-end plan recognition is of limited applicability. However, it lays the foundation on which to build a theory of reactive recognition. We present simple algorithms for means-end plan recognition that make use of plans, similar to those used in reactive planning systems, to determine what means must be observed in order to recognize certain ends. We introduce a dynamic agent logic that provides a logical semantics for means-end plan recognition and means-end plan execution. In this paper, we are predominantly concerned with the theoretical principles of means-end plan recognition and its relationship to the algorithmic operational semantics. While we do not envisage the use of means-end plan recognition in practical applications, we do see it as an important first step towards reactive plan recognition. Extensions of the means-end plan recognition algorithms to reactive recognition can be found elsewhere [19].

In spite of the initial skepticism towards reactive planning, the approach has been quite successful compared to classical planning. This is due to the fact that, in a substantial class of problem domains (such as road-traffic management [3], space shuttle diagnosis [8], air-traffic management [14], and air-combat modelling [18]) execution of actions and decision-making tasks can be analyzed and codified as plans, in a relatively simple manner. These domain-dependent plans can then be effectively used by an agent to react in dynamic domains under resource constraints. The need for reactive recognition was motivated by the fact that plan recognition in these domains is simpler than the more general problem. In particular, an agent in these domains is not attempting to recognize any arbitrary plan, but instead knows that it is attempting to recognize one out of a small set of plans. As a result, we believe that there is a substantial class of problems (i.e., those addressed by reactive planning) that are amenable to techniques of reactive recognition.

2 MEANS-END PLAN EXECUTION AND RECOGNITION

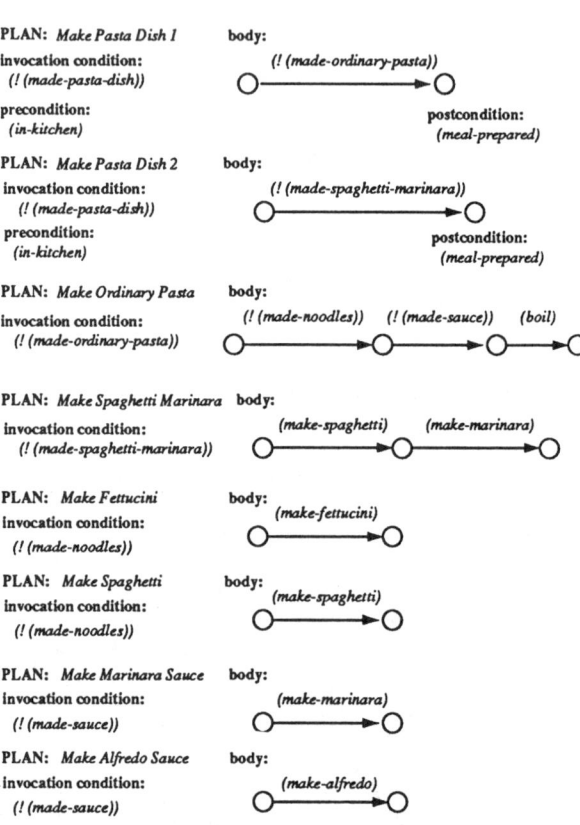

Figure 1: Plan library for making pastas

In this section, we illustrate informally our approach to the processes of plan execution and plan recognition using a well known example from the literature [9]. Figure 1 shows a number of plans, at different levels of granularity, to make two types of pasta dish. The BNF syntax of the plans is a simplified form of what is described in the Procedural Reasoning System (PRS) [5, 8] and is given in Figure 2.

A plan has a name, an invocation condition that can trigger the plan, a precondition that needs to be true before the plan body is started, a postcondition that is true after the plan body is finished successfully and the body of a plan which is an AND-OR acyclic graph with the edges labelled with certain plan expressions. Furthermore, we assume that the plans are non-recursive. In the BNF syntax an OR-node is represented as

---

[2] Analogously, we shall refer to the usage of plans to guide the planning process as *means-end plan execution*.

```
<plan>          ::= <name> <invocation> <precond>
                    <postcond> <body>
<name>          ::= string
<invocation>    ::= !α
<precond>, <postcond> ::= α
<body>          ::= <node> {- (<label>) →}+ <body> |
                    <node> {+ (<label>) →}+ <body> |
                    <node>
<label>         ::= e | !α
<node>          ::= symbol
{a}+ stands for one or more a's.
```

Figure 2: BNF syntax for Plans

$-(\text{<label>}) \rightarrow$ and an AND-node as $+(\text{<label>}) \rightarrow$ [3]. For a given proposition α, the expression $(!\ \alpha)$ means *achieve* (or recognize the achievement of) a state of the world where α is true. The expression (e) means execute (or observe) the primitive plan or action e.

Consider first the process of plan execution where the agent initially wants is in the kitchen and wants to achieve a state in which it has made a pasta dish. To achieve this end, the agent will perform means-end reasoning and determine that two plans – namely, *Make Pasta Dish 1* and *Make Pasta Dish 2* – are applicable. If the agent adopts the first plan, it will want to achieve a state in which it has made ordinary pasta. To achieve this it has to adopt *Make Ordinary Pasta*, resulting in the agent wanting to achieve a state where it has made noodles, and so on. This process continues till the making of a pasta dish is completed or the execution fails as the agent was unable to complete one of the steps successfully.

Now consider the process of means-end plan execution in conjunction with means-end recognition. When an executing agent executes a primitive plan, the observer agent observes the (execution of the) primitive plan. While the executing agent can choose an applicable plan, one after the other, until one of them succeeds, the observing agent should attempt to recognize all the applicable plans simultaneously. Otherwise, both the executing and observing agents are performing identical operations. The correspondence between execution and recognition and the conditions under which they succeed are shown in Table 1. In this table, $p_1, \ldots p_n$ refer to the plans that can achieve α; and $l_1, \ldots, l_n$ refer to the labels appearing on the outgoing edges of an OR-node or AND-node.

Now with this operational semantics let us run the example with the observer and executing agents having the same library of plans and both in the kitchen. Assume that the executing agent wants to make a pasta dish and the observer agent wants to recognize this. The executing agent can fulfill its desire by adopting either the plan *Make Pasta Dish 1* or the plan *Make Pasta Dish 2*. However, the observer agent in order to recognize this has to adopt both these plans for recognition. This would result in the observer wanting to recognize whether ordinary pasta was being made or whether spaghetti marinara was being made. This in turn would result in the observer adopting the plans *Make Ordinary Pasta* and *Make Spaghetti Marinara* in the recognition mode. The adoption of *Make Ordinary Pasta* would result in the observer agent wanting to recognize the making of noodles and in turn the adoption of the plans *Make Fettucini* and *Make Spaghetti* in the recognition mode. Assume that the executing agent adopts the plan to make ordinary pasta by first making fettucini and executes the action *make-fettucini*. The recognition plans *Make Spaghetti Marinara* and *Make Pasta Dish 2* of the observer agent fail. Instead, the observer agent observes the primitive action of making fettucini and recognizes that this results in the achievement of the desire to make noodles. Also, the observer now knows that the executing agent is making an ordinary pasta (not a spaghetti marinara) and that the next step would be to make a sauce. Thus the observer decides to recognize the making of a sauce and adopts the plans of recognizing the making of alfredo sauce and the making of marinara sauce. This process continues till the entire *Make Pasta Dish 1* plan is recognized.

3 ALGORITHMS

In this section, we present algorithms for means-end plan execution and recognition. We present simplified propositional versions of the algorithms without taking into account the mental attitudes (such as beliefs, desires, and intentions) of agents. We extend these algorithms to reactive planning and recognition and embed them into a BDI-interpreter [21] elsewhere [19].

The algorithm **means-end-recognition** (see Figure 3) takes as input a plan library given by P, a set of propositions S, and an expression E, which could be either a primitive plan or an achievement expression. The algorithm then returns a "success" or "failure" result and a set of propositions T that are true after the recognition.

If the expression we are trying to recognize is a primitive plan or action, we invoke the function **observe**. If the expression is an achievement expression, the Set Of Applicable Plans (or SOAP) is computed from the given plan library P. A plan is said to be applicable if its invocation condition matches the incoming expression and its precondition is contained in the set S. Each plan in the set of applicable plans is recognized in parallel by running **recognize-plan** until one of them succeeds. The union of the postcondition of the plan

---

[3] When displayed graphically all edges from an OR-node are shown as arrows and all edges from an AND-node are shown as arrows with has an arc connecting all the arrows.

Plan Entity	Execution	Recognition	Success Condition
(e)	execute	observe	if e succeeds
$(!\alpha)$ with $p_1 \ldots p_n$	sequentially run p_1 to p_n	in parallel run p_1 to p_n	if one of p_i succeeds
OR-node with $l_1 \ldots l_n$	in parallel run l_1 to l_n	in parallel run l_1 to l_n	if one of l_i succeeds
AND-node with $l_1 \ldots l_n$	in parallel run l_1 to l_n	in parallel run l_1 to l_n	if all of l_i succeeds

Table 1: Comparison of Execution and Recognition

that succeeded and the final state of the succeeding plan is given as the set of propositions T.

procedure means-end-recognition(P, S, E, T)
case type-of(E) is
  primitive-action:
    result = observe(E);
    return(result);
  achievement:
    soap := {};
    for p_i in P do
      if ((E = invocation-condition(p_i) and
        (precondition(p_i) $\subseteq$ S)) then
        SOAP := SOAP $\cup$ p_i;
    in parallel for each p_i in SOAP do
      result$_i$ = recognize-plan(P, S, body(p_i), T_i);
      if (result$_i$ = success) then
        T := T_i $\cup$ postcondition(p_i);
        return(success)
    return(failure).

Figure 3: Algorithm for means-end recognition

The algorithm `means-end-execution` is similar to the algorithm `means-end-recognition` except that `observe` and `recognize-plan` are replaced by `execute` and `execute-plan`, respectively. Furthermore, the applicable plans are run sequentially, one by one, until one of them succeeds. If all of them fail the execution process is said to have failed.

The functions `observe` and `execute` are primitives that return "success" or "failure" depending on the successful or failed observation or execution of an event, respectively. The assumption that the observation of events happen synchronously with the execution of actions by other agents is built into the function `observe`. In other words, if the event occurs before or after the agent runs `observe` the event will not be observed.

The algorithm for `recognize-plan` (see Figure 4), given a plan body, repeatedly recognizes the OR-nodes and AND-nodes of the plan body until the END node is reached or one of the nodes fails. The initial state S gets continuously updated during the recognition of OR-nodes and AND-nodes.

Given a node, the algorithm for recognizing an OR-node performs `means-end-recognition` in parallel on

procedure recognize-plan(P, S, plan-body, T)
n := start-node(plan-body); S_i := S;
while (not (end-node(n))) do
  case type-of(n) is
    OR:
      result := recognize-OR-node(P, S_i, n, T_i, next);
    AND:
      result := recognize-AND-node(P, S_i, n, T_i, next);
  if (result = success) then
    n := next-node;
    S_i := T_i;
  else return(failure);
T := T_i;
return(success).

Figure 4: Algorithm for recognizing a plan body

procedure recognize-OR-node(P, S, n, T, next)
in parallel for i = 1 to |out-arcs(n)| do
  e_i = out-arcs$_i$(n);
  result$_i$:= means-end-recognition(P, S, label(e_i), T_i);
  if (result$_i$ = success) then
    next := dest-node(e_i);
    T := T_i;
    return(success);
return(failure).

Figure 5: Algorithm for recognizing OR nodes

all the plan expressions labelling the out-going arcs of the OR-node (see Figure 5). As soon as one of these recognitions is successful it returns with the next node to recognize. The algorithm for recognizing an AND-node performs `means-end-recognition` in parallel for each out-going arc (see Figure 6). If any one of these recognitions fail, the algorithm returns a failure. If all these recognitions succeed, the algorithm returns with the union of all the output sets T_i.

The algorithm for executing a plan is very similar, except that the recognitions of OR-nodes and AND-nodes is replaced by the execution of OR-nodes and AND-nodes. Algorithms for executing OR-nodes and AND-nodes are similar to the algorithms for recognizing OR-nodes and AND-nodes, except that `means-end-execution` replaces `means-end-recognition`.

procedure recognize-AND-node(P, S, n, T, next)
  in parallel for i = 1 to |out-arcs(n)| do
    e_i = out-arcs$_i$(n);
    result$_i$:= means-end-recognition(P, S, label(e_i), T_i);
    if (result$_i$ = failure) then return(failure)
  T := $\bigcup_{i=1}^{|out-arcs(n)|} T_i$;
  next := dest-node(e_i);
  return(failure).

Figure 6: Algorithms for recognizing AND nodes

Now let us go back to the example considered earlier. Let us assume that the observing agent wants to recognize the making of a pasta dish. This corresponds to the `means-end recognition` algorithm being called with the expression: (! (*made-pasta-dish*)). This results in the plans *Make Pasta Dish 1* and *Make Pasta Dish 2* being added to the SOAP. Two instances of the algorithm `recognize-plan` with the plan bodies of *Make Pasta Dish 1* and *Make Pasta Dish 2* are set up in parallel. The plan for recognizing *Make Pasta Dish 1* results in the `means-end recognition` algorithm being invoked with the expression: (! (*made-ordinary-pasta*)), and so on. The calling of the various algorithms can be drawn graphically as shown in Figure 7, which shows the state of the agent just before the observation of events.

Now, if the agent observes (*make-fettucini*), i.e., the `observe` function succeeds with the (*make-fettucini*) event, the nodes marked (*make-spaghetti*) under *Make Spaghetti* and *Make Spaghetti Marinara* will fail. The expression (! (*made-noodles*)) will succeed because it is sufficient for one of the plans to succeed for the achievement expression to succeed. This will result in the next step of the plan *Make Ordinary Pasta* being invoked resulting in the achievement expression (! (*made-sauce*)). This will result in the two plans *Make Marinara Sauce* and *Make Alfredo* being called resulting in calls to observe *make-marinara* and *make-alfredo*. As the (*make-spaghetti*) under *Make Spaghetti Marinara* failed, the expression (! (*made-spaghetti-marinara*)) and the plan *Make Pasta Dish 2* will fail. This will result in the observing agent inferring that the agent is not making a spaghetti marinara and is possibly making a fettucini alfredo. If the agent subsequently observes *make-alfredo* and the act *boil* it can conclude that the agent used the plan *Make Pasta Dish 1* to make an ordinary pasta; namely, a fettucini alfredo.

4 DYNAMIC AGENT LOGIC

There are two main approaches to reasoning about programs using modal logics in the Theoretical Computer Science literature: the *exogenous* and *endogenous* approaches [12]. Dynamic logic is an *exogenous*

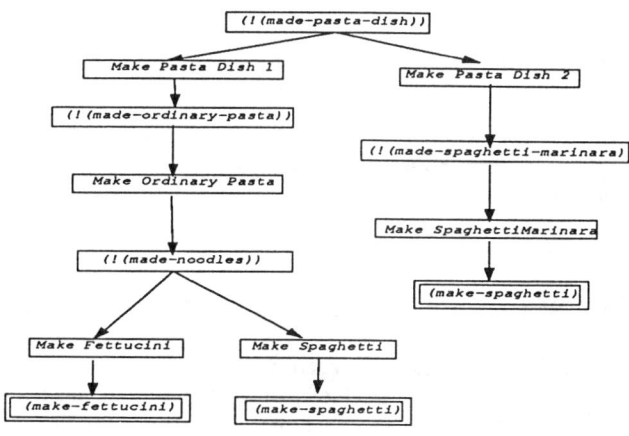

Figure 7: Call Graph for making pastas (just before the first observation)

logic as it explicitly represents programs in the language. As opposed to this, *endogenous* logics such as Computation Tree Logic (CTL) and CTL* [4] do not represent programs explicitly but consider them as part of the structure over which the logic is interpreted. In theoretical computer science, dynamic logic has essentially been superseded by the endogenous logics (particularly CTL* and a number of variants of it).

We have chosen an exogenous logic (i.e., dynamic logic) to represent the plans of an agent as it fits naturally with the compositional nature of plans. When one reasons about the mental state of an agent during the execution/recognition of a plan, an endogenous logic is more appropriate. Elsewhere [22] we have developed endogenous logics CTL$_{BDI}$ and CTL$^*_{BDI}$ to represent the mental state of an agent that captures the agent's beliefs, desires, and intentions. Rational agents have to deal with mental states as well as plans and a combination of exogenous and endogenous logics would be ideal for these purposes. Mu-calculus [11], a generalization of CTL* and Dynamic logic, could serve this purpose.

Dynamic Logic (DL) first used for providing semantics for programming languages [17] has also been used as the basis for a logic of action [23]. We extend dynamic logic in three ways. First, we provide the semantics of plans from an internal agent viewpoint rather than from an external observer viewpoint as is usually done with dynamic logic. Second, we introduce the notion of recognition as a first class entity. As a result, agents not only have the choice to *execute* an action, they also have the choice to *observe* an action. Third, we allow the indirect call of plans facilitating means-end reasoning — a notion central to means-end plan execution and recognition. Agents must be capable of reasoning about the achievement of certain states of the world (ends) without necessarily reasoning about the programs (means) that achieve these states of the world.

In the following, we extend dynamic logic by explicitly introducing agents and providing a semantics based on an internal agent viewpoint. This logic, called *Dynamic Agent Logic (DAL)*, is better suited to reasoning about plans than dynamic logic.

4.1 SYNTAX

Consider a language $\mathcal{L}_0$ with a set of primitive propositions *PrimProp*, a set of primitive plans or actions *PrimPlans* and a set of agents A. The propositional operators $\vee$ and $\neg$ are used to form *propositions*, denoted by $\alpha, \alpha_1, \ldots, \beta, \beta_1, \ldots$. The plan operators ; (sequence), | (non-deterministic or), and || (parallel), are used to form *plan expressions*, denoted by $\pi, \pi_1, \ldots$. The mixed operator ! (achieve) is used to convert propositions into plan expressions. The mixed operators $\langle\rangle$ (there exists an execution), $[]$ (for all executions), $\langle\langle\rangle\rangle$ (there exists a recognition), $[[]]$ (for all recognitions), are used to form *dynamic propositions*, denoted by $\phi, \phi_1, \ldots$.

The set of well-formed propositions, plan expressions, and dynamic propositions are defined by the following BNF notation:

$\alpha ::= p \mid \alpha_1 \vee \alpha_2 \mid \neg \alpha$.

$\pi ::= a{:}e \mid !\alpha \mid (\pi_1 \mid \pi_2) \mid (\pi_1 \parallel \pi_2) \mid (\pi_1 \,;\, \pi_2)$.

$\phi ::= \alpha \mid \phi_1 \langle \pi \rangle \phi_2 \mid \phi_1 [\pi] \phi_2 \mid \phi_1 \langle\langle \pi \rangle\rangle \phi_2 \mid \phi_1 [[\pi]] \phi_2$

In the above notation p is a primitive proposition, e is an action, and a is an agent.[4]

In Section 2, we saw that a plan involved a name, an invocation condition, a precondition, a postcondition, and a body, which was an AND-OR graph with the edges of the graph labelled with simple plan expressions. Formally, we define a *plan* to be a tuple of the form $(!\alpha, \alpha_1, \pi, \beta_1)$ where $!\alpha$ is the invocation condition, α_1 is the precondition, π is the body of a plan expressed as a plan expression, and β_1 is a postcondition.

4.2 SEMANTICS

The semantics of dynamic logic is defined in terms of a set of states, say S, and a state transition function that maps programs (both primitive and non-primitive) to a set of pairs of states, i.e., $\mathcal{R}{:}\phi \rightarrow 2^{S \times S}$ and a truth assignment function, say L. The formula $\langle \pi \rangle \phi_2$ is satisfiable in a state t iff there exists $(t\ u) \in \mathcal{R}(\pi)$ and ϕ_2 is true in u. Treating π as a program (rather than as a

---
[4]The formula $\phi_1 \langle \pi \rangle \phi_2$ (and other variants) are similar to Hoare triples and is merely a syntactic sugar for testing for the truth of ϕ_1 followed by $\langle \pi \rangle \phi_2$ as in normal dynamic logics. For convenience we shall abbreviate $true\langle \pi \rangle \phi_2$ to $\langle \pi \rangle \phi_2$, $\phi_1 \langle \pi \rangle true$ to $\phi_1 \langle \pi \rangle$, and $true\langle \pi \rangle true$ to $\langle \pi \rangle$.

plan), this semantics is reasonable as no matter which process executes the program π the result should be the same. However, in the case of plans, the notion of agency — that is, which agent executes the plan — can make an important difference. Although the plans may be identical the capabilities [24] of agents may vary significantly leading to different end results.

Unlike the semantics of dynamic logic, we introduce a *subjective* view of the world by adopting a possible worlds semantics.[5] Under this view there are multiple worlds each consisting of a set of states. The actions executed by an agent in a world at a particular state is given by a *choice* relation. A composition of such choice relations results in the execution of a plan by an agent. The actions observable by an agent in a world at a particular state is given by an *observe* relation. A composition of such observe relations results in the recognition of a plan by an agent.

More formally we define a possible-worlds structure M to be a tuple, $M = (W, P, \{S_w : w \in W\}, A, \{\mathcal{C}_w^a(e) : w \in W, a \in A, \text{ and } e \in PrimPlans\}, \{\mathcal{O}_w^a(e) : w \in W, a \in A, \text{ and } e \in PrimPlans\}, L)$ where W is a set of worlds; P is a set of plans; A is a set of agents; for each world w, S_w is a set of states; for each world w, each agent a, and each primitive plan e is a choice (observe) relation $\mathcal{C}_w^a(e)$ ($\mathcal{O}_w^a(e)$)$\subseteq S_w \times S_w$; and L_w is the truth assignment function that assigns to each state in w a set of propositional formulas, i.e., $L_w: S_w \rightarrow 2^{PrimProp}$. Associated with each world w and plan π we also define the derived relations $\mathcal{E}_w(\pi) \subseteq S_w \times S_w$ and $\mathcal{R}_w(\pi) \subseteq S_w \times S_w$. These transition relations correspond to executions and recognitions which are a composition of various choice and observe relations, respectively.

With these preliminaries we are now in a position to define the semantics of DAL. We define the semantics only for execution and recognition formulas. The semantics of other propositional formulas is straightforward.

$M, w_t \models \phi_1 \langle \pi \rangle \phi_2$ iff if $M, w_t \models \phi_1$ then there exists $u \in S_w$ such that $t\mathcal{E}_w(\pi)u$ and $M, w_u \models \phi_2$.

$M, w_t \models \phi_1 \langle\langle \pi \rangle\rangle \phi_2$ iff
 (a) $M, w_t \models \phi_1 \langle \pi \rangle \phi_2$; and
 (b) if $M, w_t \models \phi_1$ then
  there exists $u \in S_w$ such that $t\mathcal{R}_w(\pi)u$.

$M, w_t \models \phi_1 [\pi] \phi_2$ iff if $M, w_t \models \phi_1$ then for all $u \in S_w$ such that $t\mathcal{E}_w(\pi)u$, $M, w_u \models \phi_2$.

In dynamic logic $[\pi]\phi$ is usually defined as $\neg \langle \pi \rangle \neg \phi$. As a result, unlike $\langle \pi \rangle \phi$, $[\pi]\phi$ does not imply that π terminates. We avoid this complication by defining $[\pi]$ independently and by requiring that all computations of π terminate.

---
[5]This view is more important when we discuss the mental attitudes of agents performing executions and recognitions (see Section 5).

Recognition of a plan can take place only if someone is executing a plan — in a world devoid of any event occurrences there is nothing to observe or recognize. Also there needs to be an agent who is observing the events for recognition to take place. The semantic definition of $\phi_1 \langle\!\langle \pi \rangle\!\rangle \phi_2$ captures these two conditions. The formula $\phi_1 [\![\pi]\!] \phi_2$ is defined analogously.

The semantics of the various plan expressions are given by defining the transition relations $\mathcal{E}_w$ and $\mathcal{R}_w$. For primitive plans or actions the transition relations are directly given by the choice and observe functions. For plan expressions of the form $!\alpha$ we first look for all plans in P whose invocation condition is $!\alpha$. The transition relations for $!\alpha$ is the set of all transitions such that the precondition of such a plan is satisfied in the initial state, there is a transition for the body of the plan expression, and at the end of such a transition the postcondition is satisfied. The transition relation for sequences is the concatenation of the transition relations for the individual plan expressions. The transition relation for non-deterministic OR is the union of the transition relations for the individual plan expressions. The transition relation for the parallel operator is the intersection of the transition relations of the individual plan expressions, if the intersection is non-null; otherwise it is undefined.

More formally, we have the following definitions for the transition relations. In the following definitions $\mathcal{T}_w$ stands for either $\mathcal{E}_w$ or $\mathcal{R}_w$.

$\mathcal{E}_w(a{:}e) = \mathcal{C}_w^a(e)$ for a primitive plan e.
$\mathcal{R}_w(a{:}e) = \mathcal{O}_w^a(e)$ for a primitive plan e.
$\mathcal{T}_w(!\alpha) = \{(s\ t)\ |\ $ (a) $(!\alpha\ \alpha_i\ \delta_i\ \beta_i) \in P$;
    (b) $M, w_s \models \alpha_i$;
    (c) there exists $t \in S_w$ such that $s\mathcal{T}_w(\delta_i)t$ and
    (d) $M, w_t \models \beta_i$.$\}$
$\mathcal{T}_w(\pi_1\ ;\ \pi_2) = \mathcal{T}_w(\pi_1).\mathcal{T}_w(\pi_2) = \{(s\ u)\ |\ $ there exists $t \in S_w$ such that $s\mathcal{T}_w(\pi_1)t$ and there exists $u \in S_w$ such that $t\mathcal{T}_w(\pi_2)u$.
$\mathcal{T}_w(\pi_1\ |\ \pi_2) = \mathcal{T}_w(\pi_1) \cup \mathcal{T}_w(\pi_2)$.

$\mathcal{T}_w(\pi_1\|\pi_2) = $
$\begin{cases} \mathcal{T}_w(\pi_1) \cap \mathcal{T}_w(\pi_2) & \text{if } \mathcal{T}_w(\pi_1) \cap \mathcal{T}_w(\pi_2) \neq \emptyset \\ \Lambda & \text{otherwise} \end{cases}$

The model-theoretic semantics of execution and recognition is identical except for primitive plans. This is because, except for the primitive plans, there is no difference in the way the plans are used by an agent. The semantics of $|$ and $\|$ reflect the operational semantics (given by the algorithms) for OR-nodes and AND-nodes. Note that the success condition for OR-nodes is identical for both execution and recognition, and similarly for AND-nodes.

The axiomatization[6] for DAL is given below with the

[6] The axiom and inference rules are not the minimal set; we have included some of the theorems of the system

modal operator M denoting $[\![\ ]\!]$, $\langle\!\langle\ \rangle\!\rangle$, $[\ ]$, and $\langle\ \rangle$:

1. $\phi_1 \mathsf{M}(\pi) \phi_2 \equiv \phi_1 \supset (\mathsf{M}(\pi) \wedge \phi_2)$;
2. $\mathsf{M}(\pi)\phi \wedge \mathsf{M}(\pi)\psi \supset \mathsf{M}(\pi)(\phi \wedge \psi)$;
3. $\mathsf{M}(\pi)(\phi \vee \psi) \equiv \mathsf{M}(\pi)\phi \vee \mathsf{M}(\pi)\psi$;
4. $\mathsf{M}(\pi_1\ |\ \pi_2)\phi \equiv \mathsf{M}(\pi_1)\phi \vee \mathsf{M}(\pi_2)\phi$;
5. $\mathsf{M}(\pi_1\ \|\ \pi_2)\phi \equiv \mathsf{M}(\pi_1)\phi \wedge \mathsf{M}(\pi_2)\phi$;
6. $\mathsf{M}(\pi_1\ ;\ \pi_2)\phi \equiv \mathsf{M}(\pi_1)\mathsf{M}(\pi_2)\phi$;
7. $\phi_1 [\![\pi]\!] \phi_2 \supset \phi_1 \langle\!\langle \pi \rangle\!\rangle \phi_2$;
8. $\phi_1 [\![\pi]\!] \phi_2 \supset \phi_1 \langle \pi \rangle \phi_2$;
9. $\phi_1 [\![\pi]\!] \phi_2 \supset \phi_1 [\pi] \phi_2$;
10. $\phi_1 \langle\!\langle \pi \rangle\!\rangle \phi_2 \supset \phi_1 \langle \pi \rangle \phi_2$;
11. Modus Ponens.
12. Modal Generalization: From $\vdash \phi$ infer $\vdash \mathsf{M}(\pi)\phi$.
13. Achievement Plans (1&2): From a given set of plans P infer $P \vdash [\![!\alpha]\!] \equiv \bigwedge_{(!\alpha,\alpha_i,\delta_i,\beta_i) \in P} \alpha_i [\![\delta_i]\!] \beta_i$ and similarly for $[\ ]$.
14. Achievement Plans (3&4): From a given set of plans P infer $P \vdash \langle\!\langle !\alpha \rangle\!\rangle \equiv \bigvee_{(!\alpha,\alpha_i,\delta_i,\beta_i) \in P} \alpha_i \langle\!\langle \delta_i \rangle\!\rangle \beta_i$ and similarly for $\langle\ \rangle$.

The first six axioms and the inference rule Modal Generalization are common to all the four modal operators. Except for $\|$, the axioms are similar to those of dynamic logic. Dynamic logic does not have the $\|$ operator. However, dynamic logic has a test operator (?) and an iteration operator (*) which we have omitted here for simplicity.[7]

Axioms (7)-(10) are multi-modal axioms that link the various execution and recognition operators. The inference rules for achievement of states connects the achievement expression with a plan that achieves the state. In the case of all recognitions (executions) we require that all the plans that achieve the state be recognized (executed) and in the case of a single recognition (execution) we just require one of the plans that achieve the state to be recognized.

Note that we have associated agency only with respect to an agent's actions (i.e., primitive plans). Extending the syntax and semantics so as to associate the notion of agency to non-primitive plans is trivial, if all the actions are performed by the same agent. However, extending this choice to plans which involve actions by other agents is a non-trivial task. This is because it is not clear what it means for an agent a to have the choice of executing a plan that involves some other agent b executing an action. One possible

as axioms for the purposes of clarity.

[7] Introducing the iteration operator will allow us to permit cyclic and recursive AND-OR graphs as plan bodies. As the iteration operator π^* is a nondeterministically chosen finite number of iterations of π we cannot have infinite loops in the plan.

interpretation is for agent a to send a message to b to execute its action and wait for a successful completion of that action. An operational semantics along these lines was discussed elsewhere [10]. However, giving a formal account of such a theory would involve extending dynamic logic with the message passing paradigm of CSP [7] and is beyond the scope of this paper.

4.3 RELATIONSHIP BETWEEN THE ALGORITHMS AND THE LOGIC

Now we consider the relationship between the algorithms for plan execution and recognition introduced in Section 2 and the dynamic agent logic. In particular, we want to establish the relationship between the successful running of the algorithm **means-end-recognition** and the provability of recognition formulas in the dynamic agent logic. As a corollary, we get the corresponding relationship for means-end plan execution.

First, we convert the AND-OR plan graphs discussed in Section 2 into DAL expressions. The primitive plan (e) is equivalent to $(a{:}e)$ with a being the agent executing/observing e. The plan fragment with two adjacent arcs labelled l_1 and l_2 is equivalent to $l_1;l_2$. If $l_1 \ldots l_n$ are the labels on outgoing edges of an OR-node, they are equivalent to $l_1 \mid l_2 \mid \ldots \mid l_n$. Similarly, if $l_1 \ldots l_n$ are the labels on outgoing edges of an AND-node, they are equivalent to $l_1 \parallel l_2 \parallel \ldots \parallel l_n$. From these basic transformations one can easily convert the body of a plan into a single plan expression δ. A plan with invocation condition $(!\alpha)$, precondition α_1, postcondition β_1, and a body whose equivalent plan expression is δ, is treated as a formal plan $(!\alpha, \alpha_1, \delta, \beta_1)$. For example, the plan *Make Ordinary Pasta* is formally equivalent to $((!\ (made\text{-}ordinary\text{-}pasta)),\ true,\ ((!\ (made\text{-}noodles));(!\ (made\text{-}sauce));(a{:}boil)),\ true)$.

Having converted AND-OR plan executions/recognitions into equivalent DAL formulas we now examine the successful running of the algorithms with the provability of certain formulas.

Consider the simple case where the means-end-recognition algorithm for agent a is given a set of plans Π, a set of propositions Γ, and an expression of the form e where e is a primitive plan. If the algorithm returns successfully with a set of propositions Λ, it would be reasonable for us to assume that the equivalent recognition expression $\gamma \langle\!\langle a{:}e \rangle\!\rangle \lambda$ is valid in the dynamic agent logic, where γ and λ are conjunctions of propositions in Γ and Λ. Note that a successful run of the algorithm corresponds to there being at least one recognition path (rather than all recognition paths) where e is observed. If in fact the stronger recognition formula, namely $\gamma [\![a{:}e]\!] \lambda$ is valid in the dynamic agent logic we can state that the means-end recognition algorithm *will* succeed with the input set of propositions Γ and output set of propositions Λ. Formally, we have the following proposition:

Proposition 1 *(a) If means-end-recognition(Π, Γ, e, Λ) returns "success" for agent a then $\vdash \gamma \langle\!\langle a{:}e \rangle\!\rangle \lambda$.*

(b) If $\vdash \gamma [\![a{:}e]\!] \lambda$ then means-end-recognition(Π, Γ, e, Λ) returns "success" for agent a.

In the above cases γ and λ are the conjunction of all propositions in Γ and Λ, respectively.

From the above proposition we can show that similar results hold for executions.

Now let us consider expressions of the form $(!\ \phi)$. We want to show that if the means-end-recognition algorithm is called with a set of plans Π, set of input propositions Γ and the expression $(!\ \phi)$, and succeeds with the output set of propositions Λ then the corresponding recognition formula $\gamma \langle\!\langle !\ \phi \rangle\!\rangle \lambda$ is provable with respect to the set of plans Π.

The first step in this proof involves transforming each plan in the plan library into its formal equivalent as detailed above. This step also converts the body of plans into an equivalent plan expression. Next we need to show that each step of the algorithm (i.e., observing actions, recognizing plans, recognizing OR-nodes, and recognizing AND-nodes), corresponds to the axioms (or semantic definitions) of DAL; that is, observing primitive actions (Proposition 1 above), axiom for ;, and inference rule for $!\alpha$, axiom for $\mid$, and axiom for $\parallel$, respectively. More formally we can state the following theorem:

Theorem 1 *If running means-end-recognition(Π, Γ, $(!\ \alpha)$, Λ) by agent a returns "success" then $\Pi \vdash \gamma \langle\!\langle !\ \alpha \rangle\!\rangle \lambda$, where γ and λ are conjunctions of propositions in Γ and Λ, respectively.*

Proof: The proof involves a case by case analysis of all the algorithms.

means-end-recognition: If the input expression is an achievement expression of the form $!\alpha$ then this algorithm first computes the set of applicable plans. The invocation condition of plans of this set is $!\alpha$ and the precondition of these plans is contained in the input set of formulas Γ. This is equivalent to stating that $\Pi \vdash \gamma \supset \alpha_1$ and so on till $\Pi \vdash \gamma \supset \alpha_n$, where $\alpha_1 \ldots \alpha_n$ are such that they are the preconditions of formal plans whose invocation is $!\alpha$.

Next the algorithm calls **recognize-plan** for each one of the plan bodies of the set of applicable plans. Let the plan expressions corresponding to these plan bodies be $\delta_1 \ldots \delta_n$. As the entire **means-end-recognition** algorithm succeeds (by the premise of the theorem) at least one of these plan bodies, say δ_i will succeed. Assuming that recognizing the plan body is equivalent to $\gamma \langle\!\langle \delta_i \rangle\!\rangle \tau_i$ where τ_i is the conjunction of T_i, at the end of recognizing the plan we have $\Pi \vdash$

$\gamma \supset \alpha_i \supset \langle\!\langle \delta_i \rangle\!\rangle \tau_i$. Note that we have written $\gamma \supset \alpha_i \supset \ldots$ because, if the precondition is not satisfied the plan body cannot be run.

The step that adds the postcondition of the plan results in $\Pi \vdash \lambda \equiv \tau_i \wedge \beta_i$. Continuing on from the previous paragraph we also have $\Pi \vdash \gamma \supset \alpha_i \supset \langle\!\langle \delta_i \rangle\!\rangle (\beta_i \wedge \tau_i)$. From the inference rule for Achievement Plans 3 we have $\Pi \vdash \langle\!\langle !\alpha \rangle\!\rangle \equiv \alpha_i \supset \langle\!\langle \delta_i \rangle\!\rangle \beta_i$. Hence, we have $\Pi \vdash \gamma \supset \langle\!\langle !\alpha \rangle\!\rangle \lambda$. This is equivalent to $\Pi \vdash \gamma \langle\!\langle !\alpha \rangle\!\rangle \lambda$.

Now we prove our assumption that recognizing the plan body is equivalent to $\gamma \langle\!\langle \delta_i \rangle\!\rangle \tau_i$.

recognize-plan: Let the plan expression corresponding to a plan body δ_i be a sequence of $\delta_{i1} \ldots \delta_{ij}$ plan expressions, i.e., $\delta_i \equiv \delta_{i1}; \ldots; \delta_{ij}$. Each one of the δ_{im} where m = 1 to j corresponds to a plan expression equivalent to the labelling of the outgoing arcs of the node m. The node can either be an OR-node or an AND node. Let us assume that recognizing an OR-node or AND-node, m, is equivalent to $\Pi \vdash \sigma_{im} \langle\!\langle \delta_{im} \rangle\!\rangle \sigma_{im+1}$, where σ_{im} is the state of the world before recognizing δ_{im} and σ_{im+1} is the state of the world after the recognition.

By the first step of the plan $\gamma \equiv \sigma_{i1}$. By our assumption above we have $\Pi \vdash \sigma_{i1} \langle\!\langle \delta_{i1} \rangle\!\rangle \sigma_{i2}$, when the OR-node or AND-node corresponding to δ_{i1} succeeds. When we go through the loop in the **recognize-plan** for the second time S_i now is σ_{i2}. By assumption above we have $\Pi \vdash \sigma_{i2} \langle\!\langle \delta_{i2} \rangle\!\rangle \sigma_{i3}$. Combining these two, we have $\Pi \vdash \sigma_{i1} \langle\!\langle \delta_{i1} \rangle\!\rangle \sigma_{i2} \wedge \sigma_{i2} \langle\!\langle \delta_{i2} \rangle\!\rangle \sigma_{i3}$. From Axiom 1 for $\langle\!\langle \rangle\!\rangle$ and propositional axioms we have $\Pi \vdash \sigma_{i1} \langle\!\langle \delta_{i1} \rangle\!\rangle \langle\!\langle \delta_{i2} \rangle\!\rangle \sigma_{i3}$. From the axiom for sequencing (Axiom 6) we have $\Pi \vdash \sigma_{i1} \langle\!\langle \delta_{i1}; \delta_{i2} \rangle\!\rangle \sigma_{i3}$. This process can be continued for j steps of the loop, where j+1 is the number of nodes of the plan. At the end of this we will have $\Pi \vdash \sigma_{i1} \langle\!\langle \delta_{i1}; \ldots; \delta_{ij} \rangle\!\rangle \sigma_{ij+1}$. Given that the sequence of $\delta_{i1}, \ldots, \delta_{ij}$ was equivalent to δ_i we have $\Pi \vdash \sigma_{i1} \langle\!\langle \delta_i \rangle\!\rangle \sigma_{ij+1}$. From the equivalences $\gamma \equiv \sigma_{i1}$ and $\tau_i \equiv \sigma_{ij+1}$, we have $\Pi \vdash \gamma \langle\!\langle \delta_i \rangle\!\rangle \tau_i$.

Now we prove that recognizing an OR-node, m, is equivalent to $\Pi \vdash \sigma_{im} \langle\!\langle \delta_{im} \rangle\!\rangle \sigma_{im+1}$, where σ_{im} is the state of the world before recognizing δ_{im} and σ_{im+1} is the state of the world after the recognition.

recognize-OR-node: Let plan expression $\delta_{im} \equiv \delta_{im1} | \ldots | \delta_{imk}$, where k is the number of outgoing arcs from node m. Each one of δ_{im1} to δ_{imk} is either a primitive action or an achievement formula of the form !α. The call to the **means-end-recognition** results in checking the provability or otherwise of $\sigma_{im} \langle\!\langle \delta_{im1} \rangle\!\rangle \sigma_{i(m+1)1}$, $\ldots, \sigma_{im} \langle\!\langle \delta_{imk} \rangle\!\rangle \sigma_{i(m+1)k}$. As the algorithm **recognize-OR-node** succeeds, at least one of the arcs, say δ_{imn} where n is one of 1..k should succeed.

If $\delta_{imn} \equiv e$ then by Proposition 1 we have $\Pi \vdash \sigma_{im} \langle\!\langle e \rangle\!\rangle \sigma_{i(m+1)n}$ and $\sigma_{i(m+1)n} \equiv \sigma_{im+1}$. If $\delta_{imn} \equiv !\alpha'$ then invoking the current theorem for !α' results in $\Pi \vdash \sigma_{im} \langle\!\langle !\alpha' \rangle\!\rangle \sigma_{i(m+1)n}$ and $\sigma_{i(m+1)n} \equiv \sigma_{im+1}$. In either case, we have $\Pi \vdash \sigma_{im} \langle\!\langle \delta_{imn} \rangle\!\rangle \sigma_{i(m+1)n}$. We can replace $\sigma_{i(m+1)n}$ by $\sigma_{i(m+1)1} \vee \ldots \sigma_{i(m+1)n} \vee \ldots \sigma_{i(m+1)k}$ and add disjuncts for all the other plan expressions to obtain $\Pi \vdash \sigma_{im} \langle\!\langle \delta_{im1} \rangle\!\rangle (\sigma_{i(m+1)1} \ldots \sigma_{i(m+1)k}) \vee \ldots \vee \sigma_{im} \langle\!\langle \delta_{imn} \rangle\!\rangle (\sigma_{i(m+1)1} \ldots \sigma_{i(m+1)k}) \vee \ldots \vee \sigma_{im} \langle\!\langle \delta_{imk} \rangle\!\rangle (\sigma_{i(m+1)1} \ldots \sigma_{i(m+1)k})$. From the axiom for non-deterministic or recognition (Axiom 4) we have, $\Pi \vdash \sigma_{im} \langle\!\langle \delta_{im1} | \ldots | \delta_{imk} \rangle\!\rangle \sigma_{im+1}$, where $\sigma_{im+1} \equiv \sigma_{i(m+1)1} \vee \ldots \vee \sigma_{i(m+1)k}$. This is equivalent to $\Pi \vdash \sigma_{im} \langle\!\langle \delta_{im} \rangle\!\rangle \sigma_{im+1}$.

recognize-AND-node: The reasoning for the AND-node proceeds in a similar manner to that of **recognize-OR-node**, except that all the out-going arcs of the AND node succeed. Hence we have $\Pi \vdash \sigma_{im} \langle\!\langle \delta_{im1} \rangle\!\rangle \sigma_{i(m+1)1}$ and so on until $\Pi \vdash \sigma_{im} \langle\!\langle \delta_{imk} \rangle\!\rangle \sigma_{i(m+1)k}$. By the axiom for $\langle\!\langle \rangle\!\rangle$ and propositional axioms we can write this as $\Pi \vdash \sigma_{im} \supset (\langle\!\langle \delta_{im1} \rangle\!\rangle \wedge \sigma_{i(m+1)1} \wedge \ldots \wedge \langle\!\langle \delta_{imk} \rangle\!\rangle \wedge \sigma_{i(m+1)k})$. Once again by propositional rearrangement this is equivalent to $\Pi \vdash \sigma_{im} \supset ((\langle\!\langle \delta_{im1} \rangle\!\rangle \wedge (\sigma_{i(m+1)1} \wedge \ldots \wedge \sigma_{i(m+1)k}) \wedge \ldots \wedge (\langle\!\langle \delta_{imk} \rangle\!\rangle \wedge (\sigma_{i(m+1)1} \wedge \ldots \wedge \sigma_{i(m+1)k}))$. From the axiom for $\|$ for recognition (Axiom 5) we have $\Pi \vdash \sigma_{im} \supset ((\langle\!\langle \delta_{im1} \| \ldots \| \delta_{imk} \rangle\!\rangle \wedge (\sigma_{i(m+1)1} \wedge \ldots \wedge \sigma_{i(m+1)k})$. Replacing δ_{im} and from the axiom for $\langle\!\langle \rangle\!\rangle$ (Axiom 1), we finally have $\Pi \vdash \sigma_{im} \langle\!\langle \delta_{im1} \rangle\!\rangle \sigma_{im+1}$, where $\sigma_{im+1} \equiv \sigma_{i(m+1)1} \wedge \ldots \wedge \sigma_{i(m+1)k}$. ♣

The converse of Theorem 1 is false because there can be recognition paths that fail to recognize α from the given set of formulas Γ. However, strengthening the consequent of the above theorem we can state that if it is provable from Π that (! α) succeeds in *all* recognition paths then **means-end-recognition** will return "success". More formally we have the following theorem:

Theorem 2 *If $\Pi \vdash \gamma [\![! \alpha]\!] \lambda$, then running means-end-recognition$(\Pi, \Gamma, (! \alpha), \Lambda)$ by agent a will return "success", where γ and λ are conjunctions of propositions in Γ and Λ, respectively.*

Proof: The proof of this theorem is similar to that of Theorem 1 except for two major differences:

- all the axioms used are that of $[\![ ]\!]$, rather than $\langle\!\langle \rangle\!\rangle$; and
- the proof proceeds in a bottom-up fashion, i.e., we first show that if $\Pi \vdash \gamma [\![\delta_{im}]\!] \lambda$, where δ_{im} is a plan expression with all parallel operators then an AND-node that is labelled by the same expression should succeed with the correct input and output arguments. We progressively work ourselves from recognizing OR and AND-nodes, to recognizing a plan, to a means-end reasoner. ♣

These two theorems establish a strong relationship between the means-end-recognition algorithm and the recognition formulas of DAL. They provide the relative soundness and completeness of the means-end recognition algorithms with respect to a given set of plans Π.

As corollaries of these two theorems we also obtain similar relationships between running the algorithm means-end-execution and the execution formulas of DAL.

Going back to our example consider the state of the world where the executing agent has just executed the primitive plan *make-fettucini*. The means-end-recognition for the observer would succeed for *make-fettucini*. The corresponding recognition formula, *in-kitchen*⟪*make-fettucini*⟫ will be true in DAL. Now from the inference rule for achievement plans, given the set of plans Π, for making and recognizing pastas we know that *make-fettucini* is one way of achieving *made-noodles*. Therefore the agent would recognize the achievement of *made-noodles* and hence the formula *in-kitchen*⟪⟪(!(*made-noodles*))⟫⟫ will be true in DAL.

Independent of the algorithms for means-end recognition and the above theorems we can prove from the axioms and inference rules of DAL that given a set of plans P (as in Figure 1), a set of observations O, which includes the dynamic formula ⟪⟪*make-fettucini*⟫⟫, and a set of propositions Γ that includes *in-kitchen*, we can prove in DAL that ⟪⟪(!(*made-noodles*))⟫⟫. In other words, $P \cup O \cup \Gamma \vdash$ ⟪⟪(!(*made-noodles*))⟫⟫.

5 REACTIVE RECOGNITION

As discussed earlier, means-end plan recognition is based on two restrictive assumptions, namely, the world does not change during recognition, and the occurrence of events in the external world is synchronous with the recognition of events by the agent. Now we discuss modifications required to the algorithms for removing these assumptions.

To notice changes occurring in the environment during the process of recognition, the recognition algorithm has to return control to the main loop after every step of the plan. The main loop can then decide based on the new information from the environment if it is rational to proceed with the plan it is currently running or change its focus and invoke a new plan. This can be done only if the run state of the plan is captured from one step of the plan to the other, i.e., between the interrupts from the environment.

Capturing the state of a plan which is partially run and continuing to run it as long as there is no significant change in the environment introduces the notion of a *commitment* towards a plan. Such a commitment by an agent towards a plan is called an *intention*. The agent invokes a plan to satisfy a certain *desire*, i.e., the invocation condition of the plan. The precondition of the plan are what the agent should *believe* to be true before running the plan. Thus, we end up with a belief, desire, intention (or for short mental-state) interpretation of plan execution.

This mental-state interpretation of reactive plan execution is well known within the community [2, 21, 24]. One can provide an analogous mental-state interpretation of reactive plan recognition: if the agent acquires a desire to recognize the achievement of a certain state of the world it adopts all plans and intends to recognize all such plans; intending to recognize a plan will result in the agent adopting a desire to recognize the first arc in the body of the plan; this will in turn result in the agent adopting further intentions towards all plans that can recognize the desire. At any point in time the current recognition trace will enable the agent to infer the beliefs, desires, and intentions of other agents.

Having inferred the mental state of other agents, the agent can then base its future executions and recognitions on such inferred mental states. In other words, one can write plans whose precondition involves the beliefs, desires, and intentions of other agents, which have been inferred by the above process. This leads to a powerful model of interleaved reactive plan execution and recognition.

Also one can modify the syntax and semantics of plans so that the invocation condition captures the achievement or the recognition of the achievement of certain states explicitly. Similarly, the plan expressions labelling the edges can explicitly capture the execution/observation of primitive plans and the execution/recognition of the achievement of certain states. This would then provide a resource-bounded agent to balance its observation acts and recognition desires, with its execution acts and executional desires. In other words, the agent can deliberate on whether to sense or act and how long to sense before acting and how long to act before sensing.

We get rid of the other assumption of synchronized occurrence of events in the external world and the observation of events by making agents wait indefinitely to observe an event by suspending the corresponding intention. This models an agent with fanatical or blind commitment towards its recognition desires. A more reasonable model for an agent would be to have an open-minded or single-minded commitment [20]).

While the above commitment is the commitment of the observing agent towards its own recognitions, the observing agent may also need to assume (or better still, recognize) the type of commitment adopted by executing agents. This leads to interesting possibilities in terms of agents trying to recognize how other agents are attempting to recognize their own actions. This information can then lead to some agents trying to deceive other agents (e.g., their opponents in adversarial domains) into believing that they are fulfilling certain desires, while in fact they are actually attempting to thwart the recognition desires of the other agents.

6 COMPARISON AND CONCLUSIONS

Regular and Context-free Languages: It is well known that a Propositional Dynamic Logic (PDL) program can be viewed as a regular expression denoting the set of its computation sequences [12]. In its simplest form the plans introduced in this paper can be viewed likewise. However, the presence of preconditions, postconditions, and the indirect call of plans (as done by the achievement operator) make the plans less like a regular expression. In reactive recognition when the preconditions can be complex modal formulas of beliefs, desires, or intentions, the plans can no longer be viewed as simple grammars for regular languages.

Allowing recursive calls of plans results in a context-free grammar. This would correspond to *context-free PDL* [12]. Once again with more complex preconditions these plans would no longer be equivalent to context-free grammars.

Plan Recognition: Early work by Allen and Perrault [1] and more recently by Litman and Allen [13] treat plan recognition as the reverse process of planning (in the classical sense). Litman and Allen's work make use of a plan library with a rich hierarchical structure. However, unlike the theory outlined here, these plans are used in a bottom-up fashion to construct an explanation of observed behaviour on the basis of observed actions, rather than running the plans in a top-down fashion as done in this paper.

Kautz [9] presents a formal approach to plan recognition which makes use of an *event hierarchy* to guide the recognition process. An explanation (c-entailment) is constructed for each observation using the event hierarchy. Different possible explanations are combined by selecting covering models that minimize the number of events. This is done by circumscription. Kautz also provides graph-based algorithms for plan recognition.

While Kautz's approach proceeds bottom-up, creating an explanation for each observation and then merging these explanations, the *means-end plan recognition* proceeds top-down by requiring the agent to specify what top-level states of the world it is expecting to recognize and then constructing the explanation incrementally guided by the plans and the observation of events. For example, in our approach the agent needs to invoke the means-end recognition algorithm with an expression such as (!*made-pasta-dish*) before the making of a pasta dish; otherwise the agent will not be able to recognize the making of a pasta dish, even if it had such a plan. This is not the case in Kautz's approach.

Kautz deals with a more powerful underlying interval temporal logic compared to our state-based dynamic logic. Also, when an observation does not match what the function **observe** is expecting to observe the recognition plan fails. Thus, when extraneous events (i.e., events which are not associated with the current input expression) occur the means-end recognition will fail to recognize the plan, while Kautz's algorithm is robust enough to infer such plans. The reactive recognition algorithm discussed elsewhere [19] will recognize such plans.

In spite of the above differences, our approach gives the same result as Kautz, in limited cases, provided the following assumptions are true: (a) events are observed in the order in which they are specified in the plan with no extraneous events; and (b) the agent chooses a subset of plans from its plan library to recognize and the final recognized plans fall within this subset. For reactive recognition assumption (a) is not required. Assumption (b) results in a loss of generality, but increases efficiency, thereby making the approach feasible for resource-bounded agents situated in dynamic worlds.

Means-end plan recognition is fairly constrained compared to general plan recognition. However, when embedded within the other mental attitudes of an agent and combined with reactive planning it leads to a more powerful theory. This paper lays the foundation for such an integrated theory of reactive planning and recognition by providing theoretical principles of means-end recognition and analyzing its relationship to means-end execution. It also discusses how these principles can be embodied within existing reactive planning systems. Although a number of issues remain to be addressed within this form of reactive recognition and are the subject of future work, we feel that the approach shows promise in a large number of application domains where reactive planning has been used successfully [8, 14, 18].

In summary, the primary thrust of this paper is to shift (at least partially) the focus of attention within the plan recognition community towards reactive recognition.

Acknowledgements

I would like to thank Mike Georgeff for valuable comments on earlier drafts of this paper and the the anonymous reviewers for their useful suggestions. This research was supported by the Cooperative Research Centre for Intelligent Decision Systems under the Australian Government's Cooperative Research Centres Program.

References

[1] J. F. Allen and C. R. Perrault. Analyzing intention in utterances. *Artificial Intelligence*, 15:143–178, 1980.

[2] M. E. Bratman, D. Israel, and M. E. Pollack. Plans and resource-bounded practical reasoning. *Computational Intelligence*, 4:349–355, 1988.

[3] B. Burmeister and K. Sundermeyer. Cooperative problem-solving guided by intentions and perception. In E. Werner and Y. Demazeau, editors, *Decentralized A.I. – Proceedings of the Third European Workshop on Modelling Autonomous Agents and Multi-Agent Worlds*, Amsterdam, The Netherlands, 1992. Elsevier Science Publishers.

[4] E. A. Emerson. Temporal and modal logic. In J. van Leeuwen, editor, *Handbook of Theoretical Computer Science: Volume B, Formal Models and Semantics*, pages 995–1072. Elsevier Science Publishers and MIT Press, Amsterdam and Cambridge, MA, 1990.

[5] M. P. Georgeff and A. L. Lansky. Procedural knowledge. In *Proceedings of the IEEE Special Issue on Knowledge Representation*, volume 74, pages 1383–1398, 1986.

[6] M.P. Georgeff. *Planning*. Annual Reviews, Inc., Palo Alto, California, 1987.

[7] C. A. R. Hoare. *Communicating Sequential Processes*. Prentice-Hall, Englewood Cliffs, NJ, 1985.

[8] F. F. Ingrand, M. P. Georgeff, and A. S. Rao. An architecture for real-time reasoning and system control. *IEEE Expert*, 7(6), 1992.

[9] H. Kautz. A circumscriptive theory of plan recognition. In P. R. Cohen, J. Morgan, and M. E. Pollack, editors, *Intentions in Communication*. MIT Press, Cambridge, MA, 1990.

[10] David Kinny, Magnus Ljungberg, Anand Rao, Elizabeth Sonenberg, Gil Tidhar, and Eric Werner. Planned team activity. In *Proceedings of the Fourth European Workshop on Modelling Autonomous Agents in a Multi-Agent World, MAAMAW '92*, Viterbo, Italy, 1992. Also appears as Australian Artificial Intelligence Institute Technical Note 31, Melbourne, Australia.

[11] D. Kozen. Results on the propositional mu-calculus. *Theoretical Computer Science*, 27:333–354, 1983.

[12] D. Kozen and J. Tiuryn. Logics of programs. In J. van Leeuwen, editor, *Handbook of Theoretical Computer Science: Volume B, Formal Models and Semantics*, pages 791–840. Elsevier Science Publishers and MIT Press, Amsterdam and Cambridge, MA, 1990.

[13] D. J. Litman and J. Allen. Discourse processing and commonsense plans. In P. R. Cohen, J. Morgan, and M. E. Pollack, editors, *Intentions in Communication*. MIT Press, Cambridge, MA, 1990.

[14] Magnus Ljungberg and Andrew Lucas. The oasis air-traffic management system. In *Proceedings of the Second Pacific Rim International Conference on Artificial Intelligence, PRICAI '92*, Seoul, Korea, 1992.

[15] M. E. Pollack. Plans as complex mental attitudes. In P. R. Cohen, J. Morgan, and M. E. Pollack, editors, *Intentions in Communication*. MIT Press, Cambridge, MA, 1990.

[16] M. E. Pollack. The uses of plans. *Artificial Intelligence*, 57(1):43–68, 1992.

[17] V. R. Pratt. Semantical considerations on floyd-hoare logic. In *Proceedings of the 18th Annual Symposium on Foundations of Computer Science*, pages 109–121, 1976.

[18] A. Rao, D. Morley, M. Selvestrel, and G. Murray. Representation, selection, and execution of team tactics in air combat modelling. In *Proceedings of the Australian Joint Conference on Artificial Intelligence, AI'92*, 1992.

[19] A. S. Rao. Reactive plan recognition. Technical Report 46, Australian Artificial Intelligence Institute, Carlton, Australia, 1993.

[20] A. S. Rao and M. P. Georgeff. Modeling rational agents within a BDI-architecture. In J. Allen, R. Fikes, and E. Sandewall, editors, *Proceedings of the Second International Conference on Principles of Knowledge Representation and Reasoning*. Morgan Kaufmann Publishers, San Mateo, CA, 1991.

[21] A. S. Rao and M. P. Georgeff. An abstract architecture for rational agents. In C. Rich, W. Swartout, and B. Nebel, editors, *Proceedings of the Third International Conference on Principles of Knowledge Representation and Reasoning*. Morgan Kaufmann Publishers, San Mateo, CA, 1992.

[22] A. S. Rao and M. P. Georgeff. A model-theoretic approach to the verification of situated reasoning systems. In *Proceedings of the Thirteenth International Joint Conference on Artificial Intelligence (IJCAI-93)*, Chamberey, France, 1993.

[23] K. Segerberg. Getting started: Beginnings in the logic of action. *Studia Logica*, 51(3/4):347–378, 1992.

[24] Y. Shoham. Agent0: A simple agent language and its interpreter. In *Proceedings of the Ninth National Conference on Artificial Intelligence (AAAI-91)*, pages 704–709, 1991.

Terminological Cycles and the Propositional μ-Calculus*

Klaus Schild
German Research Center for Artificial Intelligence
Stuhlsatzenhausweg 3, D-66123 Saarbrücken, FRG
e-mail: schild@dfki.uni-sb.de

Abstract

We investigate terminological cycles in the terminological standard logic $\mathcal{ALC}$ with the only restriction that recursively defined concepts must occur in their definition positively. This restriction, called syntactic monotonicity, ensures the existence of least and greatest fixpoint models. This is the most general setting in which terminological cycles have ever been considered. It turns out that as far as syntactically monotone terminologies of $\mathcal{ALC}$ are concerned, the descriptive semantics as well as the least and greatest fixpoint semantics do not differ in the computational complexity of the corresponding subsumption relation. In fact, we prove that in each case subsumption is complete for deterministic exponential time. We then investigate thoroughly the expressive power of the least and the greatest fixpoint semantics of syntactically monotone terminologies of $\mathcal{ALC}$. In particular, we prove a *strict* lower bound of their expressive power in terms of $\mathcal{ALC}$ augmented by regular role expressions. These results are obtained by a direct correspondence to the so-called propositional μ-calculus, which allows to express least and greatest fixpoints explicitly. We propose $\mathcal{ALC}$ augmented by the fixpoint operators of the μ-calculus as a unifying framework for all three kinds of semantics.

1 Introduction

Terminological logics (also called *concept languages*) have been designed for the logical reconstruction and specification of knowledge representation systems descending from KL-ONE such as BACK, CLASSIC, $\mathcal{KRIS}$, and LOOM.[1] These systems are able to represent dictionary-like definitions, and their main task is to classify these definitions into a hierarchy according to semantic relations like subsumption and equivalence. The dictionary-like definitions these systems are able to represent are formulated in terms of two syntactic categories, called *concepts* and *roles*. These two categories correspond to unary and binary predicates respectively. Roles are often taken to be atomic, while concepts can be built up from the universal concept ⊤ and concept names by applying logical connectives as well as quantification over roles. A typical example of a definition of this kind is the following defining leaves as nodes which do not have any branch:

$$Leaf \doteq Node \sqcap \neg \exists branch : \top$$

It is perfectly straightforward to state the meaning of such *concept introductions* in set-theoretical terms. As usual, the meaning of concepts and concept introductions is given in terms of *interpretations* and *models*. An *interpretation* $\mathcal{I}$ over a *domain* $\Delta^\mathcal{I}$ maps the universal concept ⊤ to $\Delta^\mathcal{I}$, each concept name CN to an arbitrary subset $CN^\mathcal{I}$ of $\Delta^\mathcal{I}$, and each role name RN to a binary relation $RN^\mathcal{I}$ over $\Delta^\mathcal{I}$. Moreover, the logical connectives ⊓, ⊔ and ¬ are interpreted as the corresponding set operations on $\Delta^\mathcal{I}$, whereas $\exists RN:$ and $\forall RN:$ represent existential and universal quantification over the relation $RN^\mathcal{I}$. The meaning of a concept introduction is then given by requiring that an interpretation is a *model* of $C \doteq D$ iff the interpretation maps C and D to exactly the same subset of the domain. In the case of the concept introduction given above, this means that each model has to satisfy the following equation:

$$Leaf^\mathcal{I} = Node^\mathcal{I} \cap \{d \in \Delta^\mathcal{I} : \neg \exists e, \langle d, e \rangle \in branch^\mathcal{I}\}$$

There are also algorithms to compute both the subsumption and the equivalence relation between concepts, even with respect to finite sets of concept introductions similar to the one just considered [14].

---

*This work was supported by a grant from the *Deutsche Forschungsgemeinschaft* (DFG).

[1] For a good overview of the so-called KL-ONE family the reader is referred to [19].

Problems arise, however, when cyclic or recursive concept introductions enter the picture. It is entirely natural to define, for example, a tree recursively as a node which has only trees as branches:[2]

$$Tree \doteq Node \sqcap \forall branch{:}Tree \qquad (1)$$

The models of this cyclic concept introduction are characterized by obeying the following equation:

$$Tree^{\mathcal{I}} = Node^{\mathcal{I}} \cap$$
$$\{d \in \Delta^{\mathcal{I}} : \forall e(\langle d,e\rangle \in branch^{\mathcal{I}}), e \in Tree^{\mathcal{I}}\}$$

Unfortunately, such recursive equations do not always have unique solutions, even when the interpretation of all undefined concept and role names is fixed. Take, for instance, an interpretation $\mathcal{I}$ the domain of which is $\mathbb{N}$, the set of all natural numbers. Suppose, moreover, $Node^{\mathcal{I}}$ is $\mathbb{N}$, while $branch^{\mathcal{I}}$ is the successor relation on $\mathbb{N}$. Such an interpretation is a model of (1) just in case the following equation is satisfied:

$$Tree^{\mathcal{I}} = \mathbb{N} \cap \{n \in \mathbb{N} : \forall\, m(m = n+1), m \in Tree^{\mathcal{I}}\}$$
$$= \{n \in \mathbb{N} : n+1 \in Tree^{\mathcal{I}}\}$$

The question, then, is whether in all these models the nodes are actually trees or not. However, the recursive equation above does not tell us anything about that since it has two conflicting solutions, viz. one in which $Tree^{\mathcal{I}}$ is $\mathbb{N}$, and one in which it is the empty set. This gives rise to the question whether any of these conflicting solutions should be preferred or not. In fact, there is an ongoing discussion on which kind of solution generally accords best with our intuition.[3] In essence, there are three rivals which should be taken into consideration. First of all, simply allowing *all* solutions results in what Nebel [7, Chapter 5.2.3] called *descriptive semantics*. The remaining two alternatives allow only those solutions which are the least or greatest ones with respect to the interpretation of all *defined* concepts (i.e., those concept names which appear on the left-hand side of a concept introduction). The terms *least* and *greatest*, however, apply only to solutions which agree in the interpretation of all undefined concept and role names. Nebel [7, Chapter 5.2.2] called solutions of this kind *least* and *greatest fixpoint models*. The previously mentioned model which interprets *Tree* as the empty set is, therefore, a least fixpoint model of (1), whereas the other one interpreting *Tree* as $\mathbb{N}$ is a greatest fixpoint model. But even if we stick to one of these alternatives, it is not clear at all how to obtain the corresponding inference algorithms, except for very small languages [1].

In some cases, the consequences of choosing one of these semantics can be clarified in terms of the

---

[2] If this definition were intended to represent trees *accurately*, the concept *Node* would have to be defined properly, i.e., it would have to be defined in such a way that each *Node* has at most one *branch*-predecessor.

[3] Among others, Nebel [7, 8] as well as Baader [1] have contributed to this discussion.

reflexive-transitive closure R^* of a role. Baader [1, Theorem 4.3.1] showed that the greatest fixpoint semantics forces the recursive definition of a tree (1) to be equivalent to $Tree \doteq \forall branch^*{:}Node$, which is neither the case for the descriptive nor for the least fixpoint semantics. For this reason, Baader claimed the greatest fixpoint semantics to come off best [1, page 626]. However, least fixpoint semantics can express quantification over $branch^*$ just as well. To see this, take the following definition of a non-tree in contrary to the one of a tree:

$$NonTree \doteq \neg Node \sqcup \exists branch{:}NonTree \qquad (2)$$

That is to say, a non-tree is something which is either no node or which has some branch being a non-tree. We shall see below that in this case only the *least* fixpoint semantics forces (2) to be equivalent to $NonTree \doteq \exists branch^*{:}\neg Node$. As $\exists branch^*{:}\neg Node$ is equivalent to $\neg \forall branch^*{:}Node$, this means that the least fixpoint semantics of (2) expresses the very contrary of the greatest fixpoint semantics of (1). Anyway, insofar as solely finite trees are concerned, the least fixpoint semantics seems to be more adequate in that it excludes infinite chains of the role *branch*. In fact, we shall see that it forces (1) to be equivalent to $Tree \doteq (\forall branch^*{:}Node) \sqcap \neg \exists branch^\omega$, where the concept $\exists branch^\omega$ stipulates the existence of some infinite chain of the role *branch*. We thus allow only acyclic structures of finite depth, which is clearly a necessary condition for being a finite tree.

It should be stressed that even though both (1) and (2) alone have least and greatest fixpoint models, neither $\{(1), NonTree \doteq \neg Tree\}$ nor $\{(2), Tree \doteq \neg NonTree\}$ have any. This is due to the fact that no model can be a least or greatest one with respect to the denotation of a concept and its complement, unless the domain of the model is empty. For instance, the interpretation over $\mathbb{N}$ considered above is a model of the terminology $\{(1), NonTree \doteq \neg Tree\}$ just in case the following two equations are satisfied:

$$Tree^{\mathcal{I}} = \{n \in \mathbb{N} : n+1 \in Tree^{\mathcal{I}}\} \qquad (3)$$
$$NonTree^{\mathcal{I}} = \mathbb{N} \setminus Tree^{\mathcal{I}} \qquad (4)$$

These equations have exactly two solutions in common, namely one in which $Tree^{\mathcal{I}}$ is $\mathbb{N}$ and $NonTree^{\mathcal{I}}$ is the empty set, while in the second it is the other way around. Of course, neither solution is a least or greatest one with respect to both $Tree^{\mathcal{I}}$ and $NonTree^{\mathcal{I}}$. It seems to be counterintuitive that (1) alone has least and greatest fixpoint models, whereas the terminology $\{(1), NonTree \doteq \neg Tree\}$ does not have any. Not only that (1) alone has a least fixpoint model, but there is also a least fixpoint model of (1) which is a least fixpoint model of $NonTree \doteq \neg Tree$ as well. To see this, consider some least fixpoint model of (1). In such a model *Tree* denotes a certain subset of the domain. Now, with the interpretation of *Tree* being fixed, there remains only one single model of

$NonTree \doteq \neg Tree$, viz. the one in which $NonTree$ is interpreted as the complement of the denotation of $Tree$. This model is therefore also a least fixpoint model of $NonTree \doteq \neg Tree$. In other words, an interpretation which is a least fixpoint model of (1) and which at the same time is a least fixpoint model of (2) is not necessarily also a least fixpoint model of (1) *together with* $NonTree \doteq \neg Tree$.

The notion of least and greatest fixpoint semantics as considered in the terminological logics literature cannot tell these different situations apart. To overcome this deficiency, we introduce prefixes μ and ν as explicit references to least and a greatest fixpoint semantics. In doing so, we can simply state that $\mu\{(1), NonTree \doteq \neg Tree\}$ does not have any model, while $\{\mu\{(1)\}, \mu\{NonTree \doteq \neg Tree\}\}$ does have one. Terminologies of the former kind are called *least fixpoint terminology*, whereas terminologies of the latter kind are called *complex fixpoint terminologies*. Complex fixpoint terminologies, however, may contain not only least, but also greatest fixpoint terminologies. Having complex fixpoint terminologies at our disposal, we can even reason about the different kinds semantics. For instance, we can conclude that the greatest fixpoint semantics of (1) in fact expresses the very contrary of the least fixpoint semantics of (2):

$$\nu\{(1)\}, \mu\{(2)\} \models NonTree \doteq \neg Tree$$

But what is perhaps most important is that it has been overlooked in the whole terminological logics literature that terminological cycles can be analyzed in terms of the well-investigated *propositional μ-calculus* in a perfectly straightforward way. The propositional μ-calculus is an extension of propositional multi-modal logic to reason about (concurrent) programs, proposed by Kozen [6]. It extends the propositional multi-modal logic **K** by fixpoint operators of the form $\mu x.\alpha$ and $\nu x.\alpha$ where α can be an arbitrary formula of the propositional μ-calculus. However, a restriction, called *syntactic monotonicity*, is imposed on α which requires that the variable x may occur in α only positively. The formulae $\mu x.\alpha$ and $\nu x.\alpha$ explicitly represent the least and the greatest fixpoints of a function loosely associated with the lambda-expression $\lambda x.\alpha$. As x may occur in α only positively, this function is known to be monotone. According to the well-known Tarski-Knaster Theorem, this function therefore has both a unique least as well as a unique greatest fixpoint [17].

It will turn out that least and greatest fixpoint terminologies can be represented straightforwardly in terms of such explicit fixpoint operators. The only prerequisite will be that recursively defined concepts may occur in their definition only positively. This correspondence will not only be easy to establish, but it will also provide deep insights into the computational complexity and the expressive power of least and greatest fixpoint semantics, and moreover, in the most general setting ever considered.

The remainder of the paper is devoted to exactly these issues, but before we should give some principles of standard terminological logics. The interested reader can find omitted proofs in [13].

2 The Terminological Logic $\mathcal{ALC}$

As a starting point, we fix the basic concept language in terms of which terminologies will be formed. We decided to take the standard terminological logic $\mathcal{ALC}$, investigated by Schmidt-Schauß and Smolka [14] in their seminal paper. We did so because $\mathcal{ALC}$ is a well-known concept language which has been investigated thoroughly, and, in spite of its elegance, is quite strong in expressive power.

Definition 1. Assume $\mathcal{N}$ is the union of two disjoint, infinite sets, called $\mathcal{N_C}$ and $\mathcal{N_R}$, which contain neither $\top$ nor $\bot$.[4] The elements of these sets are called **concept names** and **role names** respectively. The concepts of $\mathcal{ALC}$ are inductively defined as follows:

1. Every concept name, $\top$, and $\bot$ are concepts of $\mathcal{ALC}$.

2. If C and D are concepts of $\mathcal{ALC}$ and RN is a role name, then $C \sqcap D$, $C \sqcup D$, $\neg C$, $\forall RN{:}C$ and $\exists RN{:}C$ are all concepts of $\mathcal{ALC}$.

Of course, we may use parentheses to resolve ambiguities.

As already mentioned in the introduction, concept names are interpreted as arbitrary subsets of some domain, while role names are interpreted as binary relations over the domain. For this very purpose, so-called $\mathcal{L}$-*valuations* are introduced, which fix the interpretation of all elements of a set $\mathcal{L}$ of concept and role names.

Definition 2. Assume $\mathcal{L}$ is a set of concept and role names and assume Δ is an arbitrary set. A $\mathcal{L}$-**valuation** $\mathcal{V}$ over Δ is a function which maps each concept name of $\mathcal{L}$ to a subset of Δ and each role name of $\mathcal{L}$ to a binary relation over Δ.

We shall frequently make use of the fact that each $\mathcal{L}$-valuation $\mathcal{V}$ over Δ can be viewed as a subset of $\mathcal{L} \times \Delta$, i.e., it can be viewed as the set $\{\langle TN, \mathcal{V}(TN)\rangle : TN \in \mathcal{L}\}$.

Before specifying how arbitrary concepts of $\mathcal{ALC}$ are interpreted, we introduce a useful projection operation on binary relations.

Notation 1. Assume $r \subseteq \Delta \times \Delta$ is an arbitrary binary relation over Δ and $d \in \Delta$. Then $\boldsymbol{r}(\boldsymbol{d})$ is defined to be $\{e \in \Delta : \langle d, e\rangle \in r\}$.

---
[4] Clearly, for both sets there should exist a deterministic acceptor running in at most polynomial time.

Definition 3. An **interpretation** $\mathcal{I}$ is a triple $\langle \Delta^{\mathcal{I}}, \cdot^{\mathcal{I}}, \mathcal{V} \rangle$, where $\Delta^{\mathcal{I}}$ is a set, called the **domain** of $\mathcal{I}$, and $\mathcal{V}$ is a $\mathcal{N}$-valuation over $\Delta^{\mathcal{I}}$. Moreover, $\cdot^{\mathcal{I}}$ is a function, called the **interpretation function** of $\mathcal{I}$, which maps concepts of $\mathcal{ALC}$ to subsets of $\Delta^{\mathcal{I}}$ and role names to binary relations over $\Delta^{\mathcal{I}}$. It extends $\mathcal{V}$ to deal with arbitrary concepts of $\mathcal{ALC}$ and is inductively defined as follows: $\top^{\mathcal{I}}$ is $\Delta^{\mathcal{I}}$, $\bot^{\mathcal{I}}$ is $\emptyset$, and $TN^{\mathcal{I}}$ is $\mathcal{V}(TN)$ whenever $TN \in \mathcal{N}$. Now, suppose $C^{\mathcal{I}}$ as well as $D^{\mathcal{I}}$ have already been defined, where C and D are concepts of $\mathcal{ALC}$. Then $\cdot^{\mathcal{I}}$ is defined as follows:

$$\begin{aligned}
(C \sqcap D)^{\mathcal{I}} &= C^{\mathcal{I}} \cap D^{\mathcal{I}} \\
(C \sqcup D)^{\mathcal{I}} &= C^{\mathcal{I}} \cup D^{\mathcal{I}} \\
(\neg C)^{\mathcal{I}} &= \Delta^{\mathcal{I}} \setminus C^{\mathcal{I}} \\
(\forall RN{:}C)^{\mathcal{I}} &= \{d \in \Delta^{\mathcal{I}} : RN^{\mathcal{I}}(d) \subseteq C^{\mathcal{I}}\} \\
(\exists RN{:}C)^{\mathcal{I}} &= \{d \in \Delta^{\mathcal{I}} : RN^{\mathcal{I}}(d) \cap C^{\mathcal{I}} \neq \emptyset\}
\end{aligned}$$

It can easily be verified that the interpretation function $\cdot^{\mathcal{I}}$ of every interpretation $\langle \Delta^{\mathcal{I}}, \cdot^{\mathcal{I}}, \mathcal{V} \rangle$ is uniquely determined by $\Delta^{\mathcal{I}}$ together with the $\mathcal{N}$-valuation $\mathcal{V}$.

Having specified the syntax and the meaning of the basic expressions in terms of which terminologies can be formed, it remains to define what exactly constitutes a terminology and what its meaning is.

Definition 4. Assume $\mathcal{L}$ is a set of concepts and assume C and D are elements of $\mathcal{L}$. Then $C \doteq D$ is called **axiom** of $\mathcal{L}$ and it is a **concept introduction** of $\mathcal{L}$ whenever C is a concept name. Axioms of the form $C \doteq C \sqcap D$ are called **primitive** and are abbreviated by $C \sqsubseteq D$. A **terminology** of $\mathcal{L}$ is a finite set $\mathcal{T}$ of concept introductions of $\mathcal{L}$ such that for every concept name CN there is at most one concept C such that $CN \doteq C$ is an element of $\mathcal{T}$.

Definition 5. A concept or role name $TN \in \mathcal{N}$ is called to be **defined** in the terminology $\mathcal{T}$ iff there is a concept or role T such that $TN \doteq T$ is an element of $\mathcal{T}$. We denote with $def(\mathcal{T})$ the set of all concept and role names which are defined in $\mathcal{T}$, whereas $undef(\mathcal{T})$ is $\mathcal{N} \setminus def(\mathcal{T})$.

Please bear in mind that $undef(\mathcal{T})$ comprises *all* concept and role names which are not defined in $\mathcal{T}$, no matter whether they occur in $\mathcal{T}$ or not.

In order to state the meaning of terminologies we have to specify their models. As usual, models are interpretations forcing something to hold. In case of terminologies, a model is simply an interpretation respecting every concept introduction of the terminology in the sense that the left-hand side of the concept introduction must denote the same set as the right-hand side. As terminologies such as $\{CN \doteq \neg CN\}$ should not have any model, the domain of an model is required to be nonempty.

Definition 6. An interpretation $\langle \Delta^{\mathcal{I}}, \cdot^{\mathcal{I}}, \mathcal{V} \rangle$ with a nonempty domain $\Delta^{\mathcal{I}}$ is a **model** of an axiom $C \doteq D$ iff $C^{\mathcal{I}} = D^{\mathcal{I}}$, and it is a **model** of a set of axioms iff it is a model of each axiom of the set.

Recall that a primitive axiom $C \sqsubseteq D$ is treated as an abbreviation of $C \doteq C \sqcap D$. It should be stressed that the models of $C \sqsubseteq D$ are exactly those interpretations which interpret C and D according to the intended subset relation. That is, an interpretation $\langle \Delta^{\mathcal{I}}, \cdot^{\mathcal{I}}, \mathcal{V} \rangle$ is a model of $C \sqsubseteq D$ iff $C^{\mathcal{I}} \subseteq D^{\mathcal{I}}$.

Having the notion of a model on hand, we can easily define semantic relations such as subsumption and equivalence.

Definition 7. Suppose $\mathcal{A} \cup \{C \doteq D\}$ is an arbitrary set of axioms. Then $\mathcal{A}$ is said to **entail** $C \doteq D$ iff every model of $\mathcal{A}$ is also a model of $C \doteq D$. Whenever this is the case, we write $\mathcal{A} \models C \doteq D$, possibly omitting the curly brackets of $\mathcal{A}$ and $\mathcal{A}$ altogether if it is the empty set. We say that D **subsumes** C with respect to $\mathcal{A}$ iff $\mathcal{A} \models C \sqsubseteq D$. Moreover, C and D are **equivalent** iff $\models C \doteq D$, and a concept is **coherent** iff it is not equivalent to $\bot$.

We close this section with a formal definition of cyclic and acyclic terminologies.

Definition 8. Assume $\mathcal{T}$ is some terminology and assume $CN \doteq C$ and $CN' \doteq C'$ are concept introductions of $\mathcal{T}$. We say that $CN \doteq C$ **directly uses** $CN' \doteq C'$ iff C involves an occurrence of CN'. If $\mathcal{T}$-*uses* denotes the transitive closure of *directly uses* over $\mathcal{T}$, then two concept introductions are defined to be **mutually dependent** within $\mathcal{T}$ iff they $\mathcal{T}$-use each other.

The reader may check that the relation *mutually dependent within $\mathcal{T}$* is always transitive as well as symmetric, but it is not necessarily reflexive.

Definition 9. A terminology $\mathcal{T}$ is **cyclic** iff it contains concept introductions which are mutually dependent within $\mathcal{T}$; otherwise it is **acyclic**.

It can easily be seen that as far as acyclic terminologies $\mathcal{T}$ of $\mathcal{ALC}$ are concerned every $undef(\mathcal{T})$-valuation $\mathcal{V}_u$ can uniquely be extended to a model of $\mathcal{T}$. That is to say, there is exactly one model of $\mathcal{T}$ which *extends* $\mathcal{V}_u$ in the sense that an interpretation $\langle \Delta^{\mathcal{I}}, \cdot^{\mathcal{I}}, \mathcal{V} \rangle$ is defined to **extend** a $\mathcal{L}$-valuation $\mathcal{V}_u$ over Δ iff $\Delta^{\mathcal{I}} = \Delta$ and $\mathcal{V}_u \subseteq \mathcal{V}$. However, we have already seen in the introduction that this does not apply to *cyclic* terminologies.

3 Syntactically Monotone Fixpoint Terminologies

So far, we regarded simply all models of terminologies as admissible. We now introduce prefixes μ and ν to distinguish terminologies for which any model is admissible from those for which only least and greatest fixpoint models are taken into account.

Definition 10. Assume $\mathcal{L}$ is a set of concepts and $\mathcal{T}$ is an arbitrary terminology of $\mathcal{L}$. Then $\mu\mathcal{T}$ is called **least fixpoint terminology** of $\mathcal{L}$, whereas $\nu\mathcal{T}$ is a **greatest fixpoint terminology** of $\mathcal{L}$.

In order to state the meaning of such least and greatest fixpoint terminologies, $\mu\mathcal{T}$ and $\nu\mathcal{T}$, all models of $\mathcal{T}$ which agree in the interpretation of all undefined concept and role names of $\mathcal{T}$ must be compared to each other, hence the following definition:

Definition 11. Suppose $\mathcal{I} = \langle \Delta^{\mathcal{I}}, \cdot^{\mathcal{I}}, \mathcal{V} \rangle$ and $\mathcal{J} = \langle \Delta^{\mathcal{J}}, \cdot^{\mathcal{J}}, \mathcal{W} \rangle$ are arbitrary interpretations with $\Delta^{\mathcal{J}} = \Delta^{\mathcal{I}}$. If $\mathcal{L}$ is a set of concept and role names, then $\mathcal{J}$ is said to be $\mathcal{L}$-**compatible** with $\mathcal{I}$ iff for every $TN \in \mathcal{L}$, $TN^{\mathcal{J}}$ is $TN^{\mathcal{I}}$.

Definition 12. Assume $\mathcal{T}$ is some terminology and assume $\mathcal{I} = \langle \Delta^{\mathcal{I}}, \cdot^{\mathcal{I}}, \mathcal{V} \rangle$ is an arbitrary interpretation. Then $\mathcal{I}$ is a **least fixpoint model** of $\mathcal{T}$ iff it is a model of $\mathcal{T}$ and, additionally, for each other model $\langle \Delta^{\mathcal{I}}, \cdot^{\mathcal{J}}, \mathcal{W} \rangle$ of $\mathcal{T}$ which is $undef(\mathcal{T})$-compatible with $\mathcal{I}$, it holds that $CN^{\mathcal{I}} \subseteq CN^{\mathcal{J}}$, for every CN defined in $\mathcal{T}$. The **greatest fixpoint models** of $\mathcal{T}$ are defined correspondingly by requiring $CN^{\mathcal{I}} \supseteq CN^{\mathcal{J}}$ instead of $CN^{\mathcal{I}} \subseteq CN^{\mathcal{J}}$. Furthermore, $\mathcal{I}$ is defined to be a **model** of $\mu\mathcal{T}$ (resp., $\nu\mathcal{T}$) iff it is a least (resp., greatest) fixpoint model of $\mathcal{T}$.

The motivation of the notion of a *fixpoint* model is the observation that a terminology $\mathcal{T}$ together with an $undef(\mathcal{T})$-valuation $\mathcal{V}_u$ over Δ induces a n-ary function $f : (2^{\Delta})^n \to (2^{\Delta})^n$, provided that $\mathcal{T}$ comprises exactly n concept introductions. Consider, for instance, the terminology $\{Tree \doteq Node \sqcap \forall branch\!:\!Tree\}$. This terminology together with an $undef(\mathcal{T})$-valuation $\mathcal{V}_u$ over Δ induces a function $nb : 2^{\Delta} \to 2^{\Delta}$ which can be thought of as mapping each subset S of Δ to all those *n*odes the only *b*ranches of which are among S. Formally, this function is defined for each $S \subseteq \Delta$ as follows:

$$nb(S) = \mathcal{V}_u(Node) \cap \{d \in \Delta : \mathcal{V}_u(branch)(d) \subseteq S\}$$

In the general case, this function will be defined in terms of an interpretation $\mathcal{I} = \langle \Delta, \cdot^{\mathcal{I}}, \mathcal{V} \rangle$ which extends $\mathcal{V}_u$ in such a way that $Tree^{\mathcal{I}}$ is S, i.e., $\mathcal{I}$ extends the $\mathcal{N}$-valuation $\mathcal{V}_u \cup \{\langle Tree, S \rangle\}$. Resorting to this interpretation, $nb(S)$ can simply be defined to be $(Node \sqcap \forall branch\!:\!Tree)^{\mathcal{I}}$. This definition yields the intended function:

$$\begin{aligned} nb(S) &= (Node \sqcap \forall branch\!:\!Tree)^{\mathcal{I}} \\ &= Node^{\mathcal{I}} \cap \{d \in \Delta^{\mathcal{I}} : branch^{\mathcal{I}}(d) \subseteq Tree^{\mathcal{I}}\} \\ &= \mathcal{V}_u(Node) \cap \{d \in \Delta : \mathcal{V}_u(branch)(d) \subseteq S\} \end{aligned}$$

Next we give the general definition of the function induced by $\mathcal{T}$ and an $undef(\mathcal{T})$-valuation.

Definition 13. Suppose $\mathcal{T}$ is a terminology of the form $\{CN_i \doteq C_i : 1 \leq i \leq n\}$, where $CN_1, ..., CN_n$ are ordered by some fixed total ordering on $\mathcal{N}_C$. Suppose, furthermore, $\mathcal{V}_u$ is an $undef(\mathcal{T})$-valuation over Δ. Then the **function induced by** $\mathcal{T}$ and $\mathcal{V}_u$ is the function $f : (2^{\Delta})^n \to (2^{\Delta})^n$ defined as follows: Assume $S_1, ..., S_n$ are arbitrary subsets of Δ and $\langle \Delta, \cdot^{\mathcal{I}}, \mathcal{V} \rangle$ is the interpretation which extends the $\mathcal{N}$-valuation $\mathcal{V}_u \cup \mathcal{V}_d$ over Δ, where $\mathcal{V}_d$ is $\{\langle CN_i, S_i \rangle : 1 \leq i \leq n\}$. Then $f(S_1, ..., S_n)$ is $\langle C_1^{\mathcal{I}}, ..., C_n^{\mathcal{I}} \rangle$.

It should be clear that $\mathcal{V}_u \cup \mathcal{V}_d$ is in fact a $\mathcal{N}$-valuation because it combines an $undef(\mathcal{T})$-valuation with a $def(\mathcal{T})$-valuation, so that each concept and role name is handled either by the former or by the latter. In the previous section, it has already been noted that the interpretation function $\cdot^{\mathcal{I}}$ of every interpretation $\langle \Delta^{\mathcal{I}}, \cdot^{\mathcal{I}}, \mathcal{V} \rangle$ is uniquely determined by the $\mathcal{N}$-valuation $\mathcal{V}$. The $C_i^{\mathcal{I}}$'s of the definition immediately given above are, therefore, uniquely defined.

Definition 14. Assume Δ is an arbitrary set and f is some n-ary function mapping $(2^{\Delta})^n$ into $(2^{\Delta})^n$. An element $\langle S_1, ..., S_n \rangle$ of $(2^{\Delta})^n$ is called **fixpoint** of f iff $f(S_1, ..., S_n)$ is $\langle S_1, ..., S_n \rangle$, and such a fixpoint is a **least fixpoint** of f iff for each other fixpoint $\langle S'_1, ..., S'_n \rangle$ of f, it holds that $S_i \subseteq S'_i$, for every i ($1 \leq i \leq n$). The **greatest fixpoints** of f are defined correspondingly by requiring $S_i \supseteq S'_i$ instead of $S_i \subseteq S'_i$.

A moment's thought should convince the reader that there is a close connection between the fixpoints of the function induced by a terminology and an $undef(\mathcal{T})$-valuation $\mathcal{V}_u$ on the one hand, and models of $\mathcal{T}$ on the other hand. Take, for instance, the already familiar terminology $\mathcal{T} = \{Tree \doteq Node \sqcap \forall branch\!:\!Tree\}$ and the function nb induced by $\mathcal{T}$ and an arbitrary $undef(\mathcal{T})$-valuation $\mathcal{V}_u$. Every model $\langle \Delta^{\mathcal{I}}, \cdot^{\mathcal{I}}, \mathcal{V} \rangle$ extending $\mathcal{V}_u$ is a model of $\mathcal{T}$ iff $Tree^{\mathcal{I}}$ is a fixpoint of the function nb. Clearly, exactly the same close relationship exists between the least and greatest fixpoints of nb on the one hand, and the least and greatest fixpoint models of $\mathcal{T}$ on the other.

Lemma 1. *Suppose $\mathcal{T}$ is some terminology, $\mathcal{V}_u$ is an $undef(\mathcal{T})$-valuation over Δ, $\langle \Delta^{\mathcal{I}}, \cdot^{\mathcal{I}}, \mathcal{V} \rangle$ is an arbitrary interpretation extending $\mathcal{V}_u$, and f is the function induced by $\mathcal{T}$ and $\mathcal{V}_u$. Assume, moreover, $def(\mathcal{T})$ is $\{CN_1, ..., CN_n\}$, where $CN_1, ..., CN_n$ are ordered by the same ordering as in the definition of f. Then $\mathcal{I}$ is a least (resp., greatest) fixpoint model of $\mathcal{T}$ iff $\langle CN_1^{\mathcal{I}}, ..., CN_n^{\mathcal{I}} \rangle$ is the least (resp., greatest) fixpoint of the function f.*

To ensure the existence of least and greatest fixpoint models of a terminology $\mathcal{T}$ the function induced by $\mathcal{T}$ and an arbitrary $undef(\mathcal{T})$-valuation $\mathcal{V}_u$ should be monotonically increasing. As customary, a n-ary function $f : (2^{\Delta})^n \to (2^{\Delta})^n$ is said to be **monotonically** increasing (or **monotone**, for short) iff for every two elements $\overline{S}$ and $\overline{S'}$ of $(2^\Delta)^n$, it holds that $f(\overline{S}) \subseteq \overline{S'}$ whenever $\overline{S} \subseteq \overline{S'}$. It should be clear that in this case $\subseteq$ indicates component-wise subset relation rather than ordinary subset relation.

The monotonicity of the function induced by $\mathcal{T}$ and $\mathcal{V}_u$ can be achieved by requiring all occurrences of concept names which are defined in $\mathcal{T}$ to be positive, i.e., they must occur in the scope of an even number of negations. This restriction is called syntactic monotonicity.

Definition 15. A terminology $\mathcal{T}$ is **syntactically monotone** iff all occurrences of concept names which are defined in $\mathcal{T}$ are **positive**, i.e., they are in the scope of an even number of negation signs $\neg$. Clearly, $\mu\mathcal{T}$ and $\nu\mathcal{T}$ are defined to be syntactically monotone iff $\mathcal{T}$ is syntactically monotone.

An immediate consequence of Theorem 3.2 of [9] is the fact that for each syntactically monotone terminology $\mathcal{T}$ and for each $undef(\mathcal{T})$-valuation $\mathcal{V}_u$, the function induced by $\mathcal{T}$ and $\mathcal{V}_u$ is actually monotone. Apart from the syntactic monotonicity, $\mathcal{T}$ is only required to be equivalent to some first-order formula. It is folklore that this is the case for all terminologies of $\mathcal{ALC}$.

Lemma 2. *Assume $\mathcal{T}$ is some syntactically monotone terminology of $\mathcal{ALC}$ and $\mathcal{V}_u$ is an arbitrary $undef(\mathcal{T})$-valuation over Δ. Then the function induced by $\mathcal{T}$ and $\mathcal{V}_u$ is monotone.*

According to the well-known Knaster-Tarski Theorem, monotone functions always have least and greatest fixpoints [17]. In addition, this theorem states that the least and greatest fixpoints of every monotone function f are unique, and, in particular, the least fixpoint of f is the intersection of all its fixpoints, while the greatest fixpoint of f is their union [17]. Whenever $\mathcal{T}$ is a *syntactically monotone* terminology of $\mathcal{ALC}$, the Knaster-Tarski Theorem can be applied to the function induced by $\mathcal{T}$ and an arbitrary $undef(\mathcal{T})$-valuation in that the previous lemma assures the monotonicity of this function. According to Lemma 1 this result can be carried over to the corresponding least and greatest fixpoint models of $\mathcal{T}$:

Proposition 1. *Suppose $\mathcal{T}$ is some syntactically monotone terminology of $\mathcal{ALC}$. Then $\mathcal{T}$ has both a least as well as a greatest fixpoint model. In particular, an arbitrary interpretation $\langle \Delta^{\mathcal{I}}, \cdot^{\mathcal{I}}, \mathcal{V} \rangle$ is a least (resp., greatest) fixpoint model of $\mathcal{T}$ iff for each CN which is defined in $\mathcal{T}$, $CN^{\mathcal{I}}$ is the intersection (resp., union) of all $CN^{\mathcal{J}}$ where $\cdot^{\mathcal{J}}$ ranges over the interpretation functions of all models of $\mathcal{T}$ which are $undef(\mathcal{T})$-compatible with $\mathcal{I}$.*

In a nutshell, this means that the least and greatest fixpoint terminologies of a syntactically monotone terminology can be characterized in terms of its ordinary models.

In the introduction we argued that *single* least and greatest fixpoint terminologies are too limited in at least two respects. First of all, they do not allow for reasoning about different kinds of semantics. Second, we do need both least as well as greatest fixpoint terminologies of $\mathcal{ALC}$ whenever we want to express not only universal, but also existential quantification over the reflexive-transitive closure R^* of a role. In fact, we shall see in Section 5 that as far as syntactically monotone terminologies of $\mathcal{ALC}$ are concerned concepts like $\exists R^*{:}C$ can be defined solely by least fixpoint terminologies, while $\forall R^*{:}C$ can be defined solely by greatest fixpoint terminologies. At this very point it should be stressed again that in this context it is not possible to resort to the duality $\models \forall R^*{:}C \doteq \neg \exists R^*{:} \neg C$. To see this recall that $\nu\{A \doteq C \sqcap \forall R{:}A\}$ defines $\forall R^*{:}C$, but $\nu\{A \doteq C \sqcap \forall R{:}A, \overline{A} \doteq \neg A\}$ is neither syntactically monotone nor does it have any model.

We introduce complex fixpoint terminologies just to overcome these deficiencies. To do so, however, we have to extend the notion of mutual dependence to apply to terminologies rather than concept introductions.

Definition 16. Let $\mathcal{T}_1, .., \mathcal{T}_n$ be terminologies the union of which is $\mathcal{T}$. Then $\mathcal{T}_1, .., \mathcal{T}_n$ are called to be **mutually dependent** iff there exist two terminologies $\mathcal{T}_i$ and $\mathcal{T}_j$ ($1 \leq i, j \leq n, i \neq j$) and two concept introductions which are mutually dependent within $\mathcal{T}$ such that one is an element of $\mathcal{T}_i$, while the other is an element of $\mathcal{T}_j$.

Definition 17. Assume $\mathcal{L}$ is a set of concepts. A finite set $\{\sigma_i \mathcal{T}_i : 1 \leq i \leq n, \sigma_i \in \{\mu, \nu\}\}$ of least and greatest fixpoint terminologies of $\mathcal{L}$ is called **complex fixpoint terminology** of $\mathcal{L}$ iff $def(\mathcal{T}_1), ..., def(\mathcal{T}_n)$ are pairwise disjoint, and $\mathcal{T}_1, .., \mathcal{T}_n$ are not mutually dependent.

Such a complex fixpoint terminology Γ is said to be **syntactically monotone** iff all least and greatest fixpoint terminologies of Γ are syntactically monotone. Notably, the syntactic monotonicity is required for each *single* fixpoint terminology of Γ rather than for the union of all involved terminologies.

Not very surprisingly, an interpretation is defined to be a **model** of a complex fixpoint terminology Γ iff it is a model of each least and greatest fixpoint terminology of Γ. The straightforward generalization of the notion of a *defined* concept as well as semantic relations such as subsumption and equivalence to deal with complex fixpoint terminologies is left to the reader.

We have already seen that every syntactically monotone terminology of $\mathcal{ALC}$ does have both a least as well as a greatest fixpoint model. The question arises, however, whether this result also applies to an arbitrary syntactically monotone complex fixpoint terminology $\Gamma = \{\sigma_i \mathcal{T}_i : 1 \leq i \leq n, \sigma_i \in \{\mu, \nu\}\}$ of $\mathcal{ALC}$. According to the definition of complex fixpoint terminologies, the terminologies $T_1, ..., T_n$ must not be mutually dependent, so that there is at least one terminology T_i ($1 \leq i \leq n$) which does not involve any occurrence of a concept name defined in any other terminology T_j with $j \neq i$. Moreover, T_i is syntactically monotone since so is Γ. According to Proposition 1, T_i does have a least as well as a greatest fixpoint model. Induction on n then proves that Γ has in fact a model as well.

Proposition 2. *Each syntactically monotone complex fixpoint terminology of $\mathcal{ALC}$ has a model.*

4 The Terminological Logic $\mathcal{ALC}\mu$

So far, we dealt with least and greatest fixpoints on the metalevel rather than on the concept level. In what follows, we shall introduce an extension of $\mathcal{ALC}$, called $\mathcal{ALC}\mu$, which comprises explicit least as well as greatest fixpoint operators. $\mathcal{ALC}\mu$ additionally comprises concepts of the form $\mu CN.T$ and $\nu CN.T$, where T stands for an arbitrary syntactically monotone terminology of $\mathcal{ALC}\mu$, i.e., T may involve not only concepts of $\mathcal{ALC}$, but also least and greatest fixpoint operators. The meaning of these concepts is given in terms of the function induced by T and an $undef(T)$-valuation $\mathcal{V}_u$. If T is a terminology such that $def(T)$ is $\{CN_1, ..., CN_n\}$ and $\langle \Delta^\mathcal{I}, .^\mathcal{I}, \mathcal{V}\rangle$ is an interpretation extending $\mathcal{V}_u$, then $(\mu CN_j.T)^\mathcal{I}$ and $(\nu CN_j.T)^\mathcal{I}$ represent the jth component of the least and the greatest fixpoint of the function induced by T and $\mathcal{V}_u$. However, this is only the case if CN_j is actually defined in T; otherwise $\mu CN_j.T$ is equivalent to $\bot$, whereas $\nu CN_j.T$ is equivalent to $\top$.

We consider this extension of $\mathcal{ALC}$ for various reasons. First of all, it is a rather natural extension to cope with least and greatest fixpoints explicitly, and therefore it provides a unifying framework for all three kinds of semantics. Second, $\mathcal{ALC}\mu$ will turn out to be a notational variant of the so-called propositional μ-calculus. This is of great benefit because the latter is already well-understood in terms of its expressive power and computational complexity. Last but not least, a certain fragment of $\mathcal{ALC}\mu$ will turn out to be a suitable framework for analyzing the expressive power and computational complexity of syntactically monotone complex fixpoint terminologies of $\mathcal{ALC}$.

Definition 18. The concepts of $\mathcal{ALC}\mu$ are inductively defined as follows:

1. Every concept name, $\bot$ and $\top$ are a concepts of $\mathcal{ALC}\mu$.

2. If C and D are concepts of $\mathcal{ALC}\mu$ and RN is a role name, then $C \sqcap D$, $C \sqcup D$, $\neg C$, $\forall RN{:}C$ and $\exists RN{:}C$ are all concepts of $\mathcal{ALC}\mu$.

3. If CN is a concept name and T is some syntactically monotone terminology of $\mathcal{ALC}\mu$, then both $\mu CN.T$ and $\nu CN.T$ are concepts of $\mathcal{ALC}\mu$. Concepts of this form are called **least** and **greatest fixpoint operators** respectively.

We next extent the notion of an **interpretation** $\langle \Delta^\mathcal{I}, .^\mathcal{I}, \mathcal{V}\rangle$ to cope with least and greatest fixpoint operators. We do so by additionally requiring that $(\mu CN.T)^\mathcal{I}$ is the intersection and $(\nu CN.T)^\mathcal{I}$ is the union of all $CN^\mathcal{J}$ where $.^\mathcal{J}$ ranges over the interpretation functions of all models of T which are $undef(T)$-compatible with $\mathcal{I}$. According to Proposition 1, this amounts to requiring that $(\mu CN_j.T)^\mathcal{I}$ denotes the jth component of the least fixpoint of the function f induced by T and $\mathcal{V}_u$, provided that $\langle \Delta^\mathcal{I}, .^\mathcal{I}, \mathcal{V}\rangle$ is an interpretation extending the $undef(T)$-valuation $\mathcal{V}_u$, $def(T)$ is $\{CN_1, ..., CN_n\}$, and $1 \leq j \leq n$. Similarly, $(\nu CN_j.T)^\mathcal{I}$ denotes the jth component of the greatest fixpoint of the function f.

In [12], we have shown that $\mathcal{ALC}$ is a notational variant of the propositional multi-modal logic **K**. The main observation is that the elements of the domain of an interpretation can be thought of as *worlds* or *states* rather than objects. Consequently, concept names can be viewed as propositional variables denoting the set of worlds in which they hold, and $\top$, $\bot$, $\sqcap$, $\sqcup$ and $\neg$ naturally correspond to the logical connectives *true*, *false*, $\wedge$, $\vee$ and to $\neg$. But then $\forall RN{:}$ and $\exists RN{:}$ become RN-indexed modalities of necessity $[RN]$ and of possibility $\langle RN \rangle$ respectively. In a nutshell, this explains why $\mathcal{ALC}$ is a notational variant of the propositional multi-modal logic **K**. For details, the reader is referred to [12]. The *propositional μ-calculus* extends **K** by explicit least and greatest fixpoint operators to reason about concurrent programs. The propositional version of the μ-calculus has been proposed by Kozen [6], while Vardi and Wolper [18] investigated the propositional μ-calculus with multiple fixpoints. The fixpoint operators of the latter directly correspond to those of $\mathcal{ALC}\mu$. The only difference is that $\mu CN_j.T$ and $\nu CN_j.T$ are written as $\mu CN_j(CN_1, ..., CN_n){:}(C_1, ..., C_n)$ and as $\nu CN_j(CN_1, ..., CN_n){:}(C_1, ..., C_n)$, provided that T is of the form $\{CN_i \doteq C_i : 1 \leq i \leq n\}$.

Correspondence Theorem 1. *$\mathcal{ALC}\mu$ is a notational variant of the propositional μ-calculus with multiple fixpoints.*

In view of of this correspondence, we assume henceforth that all results shown for the propositional μ-calculus and its variants are also shown for $\mathcal{ALC}\mu$ and the corresponding variants.

It is worth mentioning that the meaning of the concepts $\mu CN.T$ and $\nu CN.T$ is preserved by renaming each concept name which is defined in T, so that those concept names which are defined in T behave like quantified variables in $\mu CN.T$ and in $\nu CN.T$, where the notion of a *variable* is the very same as in classical logic when viewing μCN and νCN as (second-order) quantifiers. The following lemma, due to Kozen [6, Proposition 5.7(i)], is devoted to this renaming.

Lemma 3. *Assume $\mathcal{T}$ is an arbitrary terminology such that CN_i is defined in this terminology, but there is no occurrence of the concept name A_i in $\mathcal{T}$. Suppose, moreover, $(\mu CN_j.\mathcal{T})_{CN_i/A_i}$ and $(\nu CN_j.\mathcal{T})_{CN_i/A_i}$ are obtained from $\mu CN_j.\mathcal{T}$ and from $\nu CN_j.\mathcal{T}$ by replacing each occurrence of CN_i with A_i. Then the following equivalences hold, even when i and j are not distinct:*

$$\models \mu CN_j.\mathcal{T} \doteq (\mu CN_j.\mathcal{T})_{CN_i/A_i}$$
$$\models \nu CN_j.\mathcal{T} \doteq (\nu CN_j.\mathcal{T})_{CN_i/A_i}$$

In view of this Lemma, we henceforth assume that no concept name is quantified twice.

The reader may have wondered why there is only an indication of the least fixpoint operator in the name '$\mathcal{ALC}\mu$' although it extends $\mathcal{ALC}$ not only by least, but also by greatest fixpoint operators. The reason for this is that we can eliminate greatest fixpoint operators in favor of least fixpoint operators and vice versa. For instance, the least fixpoint operator $\mu A.\{A \doteq C \sqcup \exists R:A\}$ is equivalent to the negated greatest fixpoint operator $\neg\nu A.\{A \doteq \neg(C \sqcup \exists R:\neg A)\}$. It is important to realize that the terminology $\{A \doteq \neg(C \sqcup \exists R:\neg A)\}$ is syntactically monotone iff so is $\{A \doteq C \sqcup \exists R:A\}$. Park [9] showed that this equivalence can be generalized as follows: Suppose $\tilde{C}_i$ is obtained from C_i by replacing all occurrences of concept names defined in $\mathcal{T}$ with their negation. According to Theorem 2.3 of [9], the following equivalences then hold:

$$\models \neg\mu CN.\mathcal{T} \doteq \nu CN.\{CN_i \doteq \neg\tilde{C}_i : (CN_i \doteq C_i) \in \mathcal{T}\}$$
$$\models \neg\nu CN.\mathcal{T} \doteq \mu CN.\{CN_i \doteq \neg\tilde{C}_i : (CN_i \doteq C_i) \in \mathcal{T}\}$$

As $\neg\tilde{C}_i$ adds exactly two negations to the scope of each occurrence of a concept name which is defined in $\mathcal{T}$, the terminology $\{CN_i \doteq \neg\tilde{C}_i : (CN_i \doteq C_i) \in \mathcal{T}\}$ is clearly syntactically monotone iff $\mathcal{T}$ is syntactically monotone.

These equivalences are crucial to obtain the so-called negation normal form. As usual, the negation normal form of a concept is an equivalent concept involving no negated compound concepts. In case of $\mathcal{ALC}$, it can be obtained by exploiting de Morgan's laws as well as the equivalences $\models \neg\forall R:C \doteq \exists R:\neg C$ and $\models \neg\exists R:C \doteq \forall R:\neg C$. In case of $\mathcal{ALC}\mu$, however, we additionally have to exploit the dualities for least and greatest fixpoint operators given immediately above.

Definition 19. The function nnf maps concepts of $\mathcal{ALC}\mu$ to concepts of $\mathcal{ALC}\mu$. Applied to an arbitrary concept, nnf yields the concept obtained from the original one by repeatedly applying the following substitution rules:

$$\begin{array}{lcl}
\neg\neg C & \rightsquigarrow & C \\
\neg(C \sqcap D) & \rightsquigarrow & \neg C \sqcup \neg D \\
\neg(C \sqcup D) & \rightsquigarrow & \neg C \sqcap \neg D \\
\neg(\forall R:C) & \rightsquigarrow & \exists R:\neg C \\
\neg(\exists R:C) & \rightsquigarrow & \forall R:\neg C \\
\neg\mu CN.\mathcal{T} & \rightsquigarrow & \nu CN.\{CN_i \doteq \neg\tilde{C}_i : (CN_i \doteq C_i) \in \mathcal{T}\} \\
\neg\nu CN.\mathcal{T} & \rightsquigarrow & \mu CN.\{CN_i \doteq \neg\tilde{C}_i : (CN_i \doteq C_i) \in \mathcal{T}\}
\end{array}$$

As above, $\tilde{C}_i$ denotes the concept obtained from C by simultaneously replacing each occurrence of $CN_1, ..., CN_n$ with its negated form. We call $\mathit{nnf}(T)$ to be the **negation normal form** of T.

Lemma 4. *Every concept of $\mathcal{ALC}\mu$ is equivalent to its negation normal form.*

In view of the fact that many μ-calculi considered in the literature do not allow for mutual fixpoints, we should clarify the actual role of multiple fixpoints. By *mutual fixpoints* we mean least or greatest fixpoint operators applied to terminologies comprising more than one concept introduction. It turns out that we can eliminate mutual fixpoints in favor of nested ones. Consider, for instance, the mutual fixpoint $\nu A.\{A \doteq \forall R:B, B \doteq \forall S:(A \sqcap B)\}$. This concept is in fact equivalent to $\nu A.\{A \doteq \forall R:\nu B.\{B \doteq \forall S:(A \sqcap B)\}\}$, which obviously does not contain any mutual fixpoint. The following lemma just generalizes this observation.

Lemma 5. *Assume $\mathcal{T}$ is a syntactically monotone terminology of $\mathcal{ALC}\mu$ which is of the form $\{CN_i \doteq C_i : 1 \leq i \leq n\}$. Assume, moreover, $\hat{C}_j$ and $\check{C}_j$ are obtained from C_j by simultaneously replacing all occurrences of every CN_l ($l \neq j$) with $\mu CN_l.\{CN_l \doteq C_l\}$ and with $\nu CN_l.\{CN_l \doteq C_l\}$ respectively. Then $\mu CN_j.\mathcal{T}$ is equivalent to $\mu CN_j.\{CN_j \doteq \hat{C}_j\}$ and $\nu CN_j.\mathcal{T}$ is equivalent to $\nu CN_j.\{CN_j \doteq \check{C}_j\}$.*

A proof of this lemma is given by, e.g., De Bakker [3, Theorem 5.14.e]. Of course, a finite number of applications of the last lemma eliminates all mutual fixpoints. Remarkably, this works also for concepts of $\mathcal{ALC}\mu^-$ as this language restricts only the interaction of nested *alternating* least and greatest fixpoints operators which are not used in this lemma.

Corollary 1. *Every concept of $\mathcal{ALC}\mu$ is equivalent to a concept of $\mathcal{ALC}\mu$ which involves solely terminologies which contain at most one concept introduction. The corresponding statement holds for $\mathcal{ALC}\mu^-$ as well.*

Unfortunately, the size of equivalent concept is not always bounded polynomially in the size of the original concept.

As Proposition 1 suggests, there exists a close relationship between syntactically monotone least and greatest fixpoint terminologies on the one hand, and least and greatest fixpoint operators of $\mathcal{ALC}\mu$ on the other hand. The least fixpoint terminology $\mu\{CN \doteq C\}$, for instance, has exactly the same models as the concept introduction $CN \doteq \mu A.\{A \doteq C_{CN/A}\}$. As usual, $C_{CN/A}$ is obtained from C by replacing all occurrences of CN with A. Note, however, that the concept names which are defined in $\mathcal{T}$ behave like quantified variables in $\mu A.\mathcal{T}$ and in $\nu A.\mathcal{T}$ in that they have *local* meaning, whereas those defined in fixpoint terminologies have *global* meaning. This is due to the fact that according to Lemma 3 the meaning of the concepts $\mu A.\mathcal{T}$ and $\nu A.\mathcal{T}$ is preserved by *renaming* each concept name which is defined in $\mathcal{T}$. In contrast to this, renaming defined concepts does change the meaning of least and greatest fixpoint terminologies. Therefore, for *each* concept introduction $CN_i \doteq C_i$ of the least fixpoint terminology $\mu\mathcal{T}$, a concept introduction $CN_i \doteq \mu A_i.\mathcal{T}_{CN_i/A_i}$ is needed.

Proposition 3. *Assume $\mathcal{T}$ is some syntactically monotone terminology of $\mathcal{ALC}$ which is of the form $\{CN_i \doteq C_i : 1 \leq i \leq n\}$ and which does not contain any of the (pairwise distinct) concept names $A_1, ..., A_n$. Suppose, furthermore, $\mathcal{T}_A$ is obtained from $\mathcal{T}$ by replacing each occurrence of $CN_1, ..., CN_n$ with $A_1, ..., A_n$ respectively. Then $\mu\mathcal{T}$ has the same models as $\{CN_i \doteq \mu A_i.\mathcal{T}_A : 1 \leq i \leq n\}$ and $\nu\mathcal{T}$ has the same models as $\{CN_i \doteq \nu A_i.\mathcal{T}_A : 1 \leq i \leq n\}$.*

This proposition describes how to represent syntactically monotone least and greatest fixpoint terminologies of $\mathcal{ALC}$ by terminologies of $\mathcal{ALC}\mu$. It should be remarked that we could have taken also $\mu CN_i.\mathcal{T}$ and $\nu CN_i.\mathcal{T}$ instead of $\mu A_i.\mathcal{T}_A$ and $\nu A_i.\mathcal{T}_A$ because renaming defined concepts does not change the meaning of least and greatest fixpoint operators. However, we have taken the other ones because they end up with *acyclic* terminologies. Let us take a closer look at these terminologies. $\mathcal{T}_A$ is clearly a terminology of $\mathcal{ALC}$ since $\mathcal{T}$ is assumed to be a terminology of $\mathcal{ALC}$. This means neither $\mu A_i.\mathcal{T}_A$ nor $\nu A_i.\mathcal{T}_A$ involve any nested fixpoint operators. In fact, we shall see that we do not need the full power of $\mathcal{ALC}\mu$ to represent syntactically monotone fixpoint terminologies of $\mathcal{ALC}$. In particular, we do not need nested *alternating* least and greatest fixpoints interacting via a defined concept, which are rather involved.

Definition 20. A concept C of $\mathcal{ALC}\mu$ is called **restricted** iff its negation normal form does not contain any least fixpoint operator $\mu CN.\mathcal{T}$ (resp., greatest fixpoint operator $\nu CN.\mathcal{T}$) which involves some greatest (resp., least) fixpoint operator in which a concept defined in $\mathcal{T}$ occurs. We denote with $\boldsymbol{\mathcal{ALC}\mu^-}$ the set of all restricted concepts of $\mathcal{ALC}\mu$.

Consider, for instance, the concept $\mu \boldsymbol{A}.\{\boldsymbol{A} \doteq \forall R{:}\nu B.\{B \doteq \boldsymbol{A} \sqcap \forall S{:}B\}\}$. First of all, it is already in negation normal form. Second, it comprises a greatest fixpoint operator, viz. $\nu B.\{B \doteq \boldsymbol{A} \sqcap \forall S{:}B\}$, which is nested in a least fixpoint operator of the form $\mu A.\mathcal{T}$. As there is an occurrence of $\boldsymbol{A}$ in the greatest fixpoint operator $\nu B.\{B \doteq \boldsymbol{A} \sqcap \forall S{:}B\}$, the concept above is not restricted and is therefore no concept of $\mathcal{ALC}\mu^-$. Observe, however, that $\mu A.\{A \doteq \forall R{:}\mu B.\{B \doteq A \sqcap \forall S{:}B\}\}$ *is* restricted.

Representation Theorem 1. *There is a function π which maps an arbitrary syntactically monotone complex fixpoint terminology Γ of $\mathcal{ALC}$ to some acyclic terminology $\pi(\Gamma)$ of $\mathcal{ALC}\mu^-$ in such a way that Γ and $\pi(\Gamma)$ have exactly the same models. Additionally, π is computable in polynomial time and the size of $\pi(\Gamma)$ is linearly bounded in the size of Γ.*

5 Expressive Power

In this section we shall investigate the expressive power of fixpoint terminologies. In particular, we shall see that the concepts definable by syntactically monotone complex fixpoint terminologies of $\mathcal{ALC}$ are exactly those concepts which are equivalent to concepts of $\mathcal{ALC}\mu^-$. We then give a strict lower bound of the expressive power of $\mathcal{ALC}\mu^-$ and of full $\mathcal{ALC}\mu$ in terms of $\mathcal{ALC}$ augmented by regular and ω-regular role expressions. Of course, before engaging into details, we have to clarify what exactly is meant by *expressive power* and *definability*.

Definition 21. Suppose $\mathcal{L}$ and $\mathcal{L}'$ are two sets of concepts. Then $\mathcal{L}$ is **at least as strong in expressive power** as $\mathcal{L}'$, $\mathcal{L}' \leq \mathcal{L}$ for short, iff for each concept in $\mathcal{L}'$ there is at least one equivalent concept in $\mathcal{L}$, and $\mathcal{L}$ is **strictly stronger in expressive power** than $\mathcal{L}'$ iff $\mathcal{L}' \leq \mathcal{L}$, but it is not the case that $\mathcal{L} \leq \mathcal{L}'$. Furthermore, a concept C is **definable** by a set of complex fixpoint terminologies of $\mathcal{L}$ iff there is an element Γ of the set and there is a concept name CN which is defined in Γ such that $\Gamma \models CN \doteq C$.

That is to say, $\mathcal{L}$ is at least as strong in expressive power as $\mathcal{L}'$ just in case that for each concept in $\mathcal{L}'$ there is a concept in $\mathcal{L}$ which has exactly the same meaning, though the two concepts may differ in their syntax. If there is additionally a concept in $\mathcal{L}$ which is not equivalent to any concept of $\mathcal{L}'$, $\mathcal{L}$ is said to be strictly stronger in expressive power than $\mathcal{L}'$. For example, it can be shown that $\mathcal{ALC}$ augmented by the reflexive-transitive closure RN^* of a role name is strictly stronger in expressive power than $\mathcal{ALC}$. The definition of definability of concepts takes into account the fact that the definitional power of terminologies consists in the concept names which they define. The concept $\exists RN^*{:}C$, for instance, is definable by syntactically monotone complex fixpoint terminologies of $\mathcal{ALC}$ since $\mu\{A \doteq C \sqcup \exists RN{:}A\} \models A \doteq \exists RN^*{:}C$, provided that A is a concept name not occurring in C.

Expressiveness Theorem 1. *The concepts definable by syntactically monotone complex fixpoint terminologies of $\mathcal{ALC}$ are exactly those concepts equivalent to concepts of $\mathcal{ALC}\mu^-$.*

This result is of great importance in that it justifies to take $\mathcal{ALC}\mu^-$ (rather than full $\mathcal{ALC}\mu$) as a unifying framework for the least and the greatest fixpoint semantics. The proof of the theorem is based on Proposition 3 which can be used to prove that every least fixpoint operator $\mu CN_i.\mathcal{T}$ of $\mathcal{ALC}\mu^-$ can be replaced with some fresh concept name A_i, at least if the least fixpoint terminology $\mu \mathcal{T}_A$ is added where $\mathcal{T}_A$ is defined as in Proposition 3. Of course, the corresponding statement holds for greatest fixpoint operators as well. However, nested fixpoints interacting via defined concepts may cause problems. For instance, the nested fixpoint in $\mu A.\{A \doteq \forall R:\mu B.\{B \doteq A \sqcap \forall S:B\}\}$ cannot be eliminated in the described way in that this would involve two terminologies which are not mutually dependent. Such a concept must be replaced by the equivalent concept $\mu A.\{A \doteq \forall R:B, B \doteq A \sqcap \forall S:B\}$, which contains no nested fixpoint any more. Note, for *restricted* concepts there are always equivalent concepts of this kind. Equivalences of the latter kind are also the basis for the next theorem; however, in this case they have to be used the other way around.

Expressiveness Theorem 2. *$\mathcal{ALC}\mu$ involving solely terminologies comprising at most one concept introduction is at least as strong in expressive power as $\mathcal{ALC}\mu$. This holds for $\mathcal{ALC}\mu^-$ as well.*

We next compare both $\mathcal{ALC}\mu^-$ and full $\mathcal{ALC}\mu$ with the regular and the ω-regular extension of $\mathcal{ALC}$ in their expressive power. For the **regular extension** of $\mathcal{ALC}$ see [2] or [12]. It additionally comprises the reflexive-transitive closure R^* of a role, the composition $R \circ S$ and union $R \sqcup S$ of two roles, the identity role ϵ, as well as the role $R|C$ restricting the range of a role to a concept. The **ω-regular extension** of $\mathcal{ALC}$ extends its regular extension by the additional concept $\exists R^\omega$, which stipulates the existence of an infinite chain of the role R.

It is worth mentioning that this language can sometimes be used to clarify the actual meaning of fixpoint terminologies. For instance, Streett [15, page 364] mentioned the following equivalences:

$$\models \mu A.\{A \doteq C \sqcap \forall R:A\} \doteq (\forall R^*:C) \sqcap \neg \exists R^\omega$$
$$\models \nu A.\{A \doteq C \sqcup \exists R:A\} \doteq (\exists R^*:C) \sqcup \exists R^\omega$$

Of course, A has to be some concept name not appearing in C. According to Proposition 3, both equivalences can be carried over directly to the corresponding fixpoint terminologies:

$$\mu\{A \doteq C \sqcap \forall R:A\} \models A \doteq (\forall R^*:C) \sqcap \neg \exists R^\omega$$
$$\nu\{A \doteq C \sqcup \exists R:A\} \models A \doteq (\exists R^*:C) \sqcup \exists R^\omega$$

This indicates that *some* concepts of the ω-regular extension of $\mathcal{ALC}$ are definable by syntactically monotone complex fixpoint terminologies of $\mathcal{ALC}$. The next theorem together with Expressiveness Theorem 1 implies that they are in fact able to define *all* concepts of the *regular* extension of $\mathcal{ALC}$. They are even able to define concepts which are not equivalent to any concept of the regular extension of $\mathcal{ALC}$.

Expressiveness Theorem 3.
$\mathcal{ALC}\mu^-$ is strictly stronger in expressive power than the regular extension of $\mathcal{ALC}$, while $\mathcal{ALC}\mu$ is strictly stronger in expressive power than the ω-regular extension of $\mathcal{ALC}$.

Proof. Consider the following equivalences, due to Kozen [6], which presuppose that A is some concept name not occurring in C:

$$\models \forall R:C \doteq \neg \exists R:\neg C$$
$$\models \exists R^*:C \doteq \mu A.\{A \doteq C \sqcup \exists R:A\}$$
$$\models \exists (R \circ S):C \doteq \exists R:\exists S:C$$
$$\models \exists (R \sqcup S):C \doteq (\exists R:C) \sqcup (\exists S:C)^5$$
$$\models \exists (R|C):D \doteq \exists R:(C \sqcap D)$$
$$\models \exists \epsilon:C \doteq C$$
$$\models \exists R^\omega \doteq \nu A.\{A \doteq \exists R:A\}$$

These equivalences can be used directly to prove by induction on the structure of concepts of the ω-regular extension of $\mathcal{ALC}$ that $\mathcal{ALC}\mu$ is at least as strong in expressive power as the ω-regular extension of $\mathcal{ALC}$. As A does not occur in C, all but the last equivalence yield restricted concepts in case that C and D are restricted. The last equivalence, however, may yield concepts which are not restricted. For instance, $\exists (R \circ S^*)^\omega$ is equivalent to $\nu A.\{A \doteq \exists R:\mu B.\{B \doteq A \sqcup \exists S:B\}\}$, which is obviously not restricted. This concerns, however, solely the last of the above equivalences, so that $\mathcal{ALC}\mu^-$ is yet at least as strong in expressive power as the *regular* extension of $\mathcal{ALC}$. Now, according to Kozen [6, Proposition 4.1], there is at least one concept of $\mathcal{ALC}\mu^-$ which is not equivalent to any concept of the regular extension of $\mathcal{ALC}$, viz. $\nu A.\{A \doteq \exists RN:A\}$. Despite the fact that the latter concept is yet equivalent to a concept of the ω-regular extension of $\mathcal{ALC}$, Niwinsky has shown that this does not apply to $\nu A.\{A \doteq \exists RN_1:A \sqcap \exists RN_2:A\}$ (see [15, Theorem 2.7]). □

6 Computational Complexity

In what follows we shall see that as far as syntactically monotone terminologies of $\mathcal{ALC}$ are concerned all three kinds of semantics do not differ essentially in the computational complexity of the corresponding subsumption relation. In each case subsumption turns

---
[5] If we were concerned with linear length-boundedness, we could have taken the equivalent concept $\mu A.\{A \doteq (\exists R:B) \sqcup (\exists S:B), B \doteq C\}$ instead.

out to be complete for deterministic exponential time. To be more accurate, we investigate the computational complexity of the following three problems: For an arbitrary syntactically monotone terminology $\mathcal{T}$ of $\mathcal{ALC}$ and for an arbitrary primitive concept introduction $CN \sqsubseteq C$ of $\mathcal{ALC}$ decide whether (a) $\mathcal{T} \models CN \sqsubseteq C$, (b) $\mu\mathcal{T} \models CN \sqsubseteq C$, and (c) $\nu\mathcal{T} \models CN \sqsubseteq C$. It turns out that all three problems are hard for deterministic exponential time, even if $\mathcal{T}$ is restricted to contain at most one concept introduction. All these lower complexity bounds are obtained by utilizing a result, due to Fischer and Ladner [4], proving that the set of coherent concepts of the regular extension of $\mathcal{ALC}$ is hard for deterministic exponential time. Inspection of their proof immediately reveals that the syntactic form of the concepts can be restricted considerably. In fact, the set of all coherent concepts of the form $C \sqcap \forall RN^*{:}D$ such that both C and D are concepts of $\mathcal{ALC}$ and RN is a role name is hard for deterministic exponential time as well. We have shown this set to be polynomial time (many-one) reducible to each of the three problems mentioned above. The proof involves the following reductions:

$$\models C \sqcap \forall RN^*{:}D \doteq \bot$$
$$\textit{iff} \quad A \sqsubseteq D \sqcap \forall RN{:}A \quad \models \quad A \sqsubseteq \neg C$$
$$\textit{iff} \quad \nu\{A \doteq D \sqcap \forall RN{:}A\} \quad \models \quad A \sqsubseteq \neg C$$
$$\textit{iff} \quad \mu\{A \doteq \neg D \sqcup \exists RN{:}A\} \quad \models \quad \neg A \sqsubseteq \neg C$$

The last two reductions are immediate consequences of the fact that the corresponding fixpoint terminologies entail $A \doteq \forall RN^*{:}D$ and $A \doteq \exists RN^*{:}\neg D$ respectively. The first reduction, however, is more involved. Anyway, Fischer and Ladner's result holds even if C is of the form $CN \sqcap C'$, where CN is a concept name, so that the axiom $\neg A \sqsubseteq \neg C$ can be shown to be equivalent to some *primitive* concept introduction, viz. $CN \sqsubseteq A \sqcup \neg C'$.

Complexity Theorem 1. *The set of all $\langle \mathcal{T}, CN \sqsubseteq C \rangle$ such that $\mathcal{T}$ ranges over all syntactically monotone terminologies of $\mathcal{ALC}$ and $CN \sqsubseteq C$ ranges over all concept introductions of $\mathcal{ALC}$ with $\mathcal{T} \models CN \sqsubseteq C$ is hard for deterministic exponential time. This holds even if $\mathcal{T}$ may contain at most one concept introduction. Corresponding statements hold for syntactically least and greatest fixpoint terminologies of $\mathcal{ALC}$ as well.*

We have also shown that the entailment relation integrating all three kinds of semantics is computable in deterministic exponential time. By that we mean the problem to decide whether $\mathcal{A} \cup \Gamma \models C \doteq D$, for arbitrary syntactically monotone complex fixpoint terminologies Γ of $\mathcal{ALC}$ and arbitrary finite sets $\mathcal{A} \cup \{C \doteq D\}$ of axioms of $\mathcal{ALC}\mu^-$. According to Proposition 3, all fixpoint terminologies of Γ can be represented by acyclic terminologies of $\mathcal{ALC}\mu^-$, so that we may assume Γ to be empty. Now, Vardi and Wolper [18] showed the set of coherent concepts of $\mathcal{ALC}\mu^-$ to be computable in deterministic exponential time.[6] In the same paper Vardi and Wolper also showed that each concept C of $\mathcal{ALC}\mu^-$ is coherent iff there is a *tree-like* interpretation $\langle \Delta^\mathcal{I}, \cdot^\mathcal{I}, \mathcal{V} \rangle$ such that the empty word is a element of $C^\mathcal{I}$. This ensures that any axiom $C \doteq D$ can be internalized within $\mathcal{ALC}\mu^-$ using the technique introduced independently by Baader [2] and Schild [12]. This means Vardi and Wolper's result can be shown to hold also for subsumption with respect to finite sets of axioms of $\mathcal{ALC}\mu^-$.

Complexity Theorem 2. *The set of all $\langle \mathcal{A} \cup \Gamma, C \doteq D \rangle$ such that Γ ranges over all syntactically monotone complex fixpoint terminologies of $\mathcal{ALC}$ and $\mathcal{A} \cup \{C \doteq D\}$ ranges over all finite sets of axioms of $\mathcal{ALC}\mu^-$ with $\mathcal{A} \cup \Gamma \models C \doteq D$ is computable in deterministic exponential time.*

7 Conclusion

We investigated terminological cycles in the terminological standard logic $\mathcal{ALC}$ with the only restriction that recursively defined concepts must occur in their definition positively. This restriction, called syntactic monotonicity, ensures the existence of least and greatest fixpoint models. It turned out that as far as syntactically monotone terminologies of $\mathcal{ALC}$ are concerned the descriptive semantics as well as the least and greatest fixpoint semantics do not differ in the computational complexity of the corresponding subsumption relation. In fact, in each case subsumption is complete for deterministic exponential time. These results significantly improve those of Baader [1] in the sense that he investigated only syntactically monotone terminologies in a very small sublanguage of ours. The concept language he considered comprises neither concept disjunction $\sqcup$, concept negation $\neg$, nor existential quantification $\exists R{:}$ over a role.

In addition, we saw that in our setting not only the greatest, but also the least fixpoint semantics is capable of expressing the reflexive-transitive closure R^* of a role. While the former is able to express universal quantification over R^*, the latter can express existential quantification over R^*. There are, however, also concepts which are in our setting definable with respect to one of the fixpoint semantics, but which are provably *not* expressible within $\mathcal{ALC}$ augmented by regular role expressions. This contrasts a result of Baader [1] who proved that in his restricted language least and greatest fixpoint semantics can define solely concepts of the regular extension of $\mathcal{ALC}$ [1].

---

[6]Concerning the computational complexity of full $\mathcal{ALC}\mu$, the following is known: Streett and Emerson [16] gave an elementary upper time bound for accepting the set of coherent concepts of $\mathcal{ALC}\mu$, while Safra [11] proved that this set is even computable in deterministic exponential time, at least when no mutual fixpoints are involved.

Our results clarify the ongoing discussion on the adequate semantics for terminological cycles. They show that none of the three kinds of semantics is preferable in terms of computational complexity of the corresponding subsumption relation. Moreover, our results show that neither the least nor the greatest fixpoint semantics is preferable in terms of expressive power and, actually, we do need both to express the reflexive-transitive closure of roles.

Especially our results on the expressive power of least and greatest fixpoint semantics are obtained by a direct correspondence to the so-called propositional μ-calculus, which allows to express least and greatest fixpoints explicitly. It turned out that $\mathcal{ALC}$ augmented by these fixpoint operators provides a unifying framework for all three kinds of semantics.

The pursued approach, however, is not restricted to capture purely terminological reasoning only. Many propositional modal logics have been extended successfully to deal with constructs corresponding to *individual concepts* and the *universal role*, as they are called in the context of concept languages [10]. It is not hard to see that *assertional axioms* such as $a{:}C$ and $(a,b){:}R$ can be expressed in such extensions in a straightforward manner. An extension of exactly this kind has already been considered for the propositional μ-calculus [5], so that the presented results can be extended to deal with assertional axioms too.

Acknowledgements

I would like to thank Franz Baader, Bernhard Nebel, and Albrecht Schmiedel for several valuable comments on earlier drafts of the paper.

References

[1] F. Baader. Terminological cycles in KL-ONE-based knowledge represenation languages. In *Proceedings of the 9th National Conference of the American Association for Artificial Intelligence*, pages 621–626, Boston, Mass., 1990.

[2] F. Baader. Augmenting concept languages by the transitive closure: An alternative to terminological cycles. In *Proceedings of the 12th International Joint Conference on Artificial Intelligence*, pages 446–451, Sydney, Australia, 1991.

[3] J. de Bakker. *Mathematical Theory of Program Correctness*. Prentice-Hall, 1980.

[4] M. J. Fischer and R. E. Ladner. Propositional dynamic logic of regular programs. *Journal of Computer and System Science*, 18:194–211, 1979.

[5] G. Gargov and S. Passy. A μ-calculus based on combinatory PDL. Manuscript, 1985.

[6] D. Kozen. Results on the propositional μ-calculus. *Theoretical Computer Science*, 27:333–354, 1983.

[7] B. Nebel. *Reasoning and Revision in Hybrid Representation Systems*. Lecture Notes in Computer Science. Springer-Verlag, Berlin, FRG, 1990.

[8] B. Nebel. Terminological cycles: Semantics and computational properties. In J. Sowa, editor, *Formal Aspects of Semantic Networks*, pages 331–361. Morgan Kaufmann, San Mateo, Cal., 1991.

[9] D. Park. Fixpoint induction and proofs of program properties. In B. Meltzer and D. Michie, editors, *Machine Intelligence*, volume 5, pages 59–78. Edinburgh University Press, Edinburgh, Scotland, 1970.

[10] S. Passy and T. Tinchev. An essay in combinatory dynamic logic. *Information & Computation*, 93(2):263–332, 1991.

[11] S. Safra. On the complexity of ω-automata. In *Proceedings of the 29th Annual Symposium on Foundations of Computer Science*, pages 319–327, 1988.

[12] K. Schild. A correspondence theory for terminological logics: Preliminary report. In *Proceedings of the 12th International Joint Conference on Artificial Intelligence*, pages 466–471, Sydney, Australia, 1991.

[13] K. Schild. Terminological cycles and the propositional μ-calculus. DFKI Research Report RR-93-18, German Research Center for Artificial Intelligence (DFKI), Saarbrücken, FRG, April 1993.

[14] M. Schmidt-Schauß and G. Smolka. Attributive concept descriptions with complements. *Artificial Intelligence*, 48(1):1–26, 1991.

[15] R. S. Streett. Fixpoints and program looping: Reductions from the propositional mu-calculus into propositional dynamic logics of looping. In *Proceedings of the Workshop on Logics of Programs*, pages 359–372, Brooklyn, 1985.

[16] R. S. Streett and E. A. Emerson. An automata theoretic decision procedure for the propositional mu-calculus. *Information & Computation*, 81:249–264, 1989.

[17] A. Tarski. A lattice-theoretical fixpoint theorem and its applications. *Pacific Journal of Mathematics*, 5:285–309, 1955.

[18] M. Y. Vardi and P. Wolper. Automata theoretic techniques for modal logics of programs (extended abstract). In *Proceedings of the 16th ACM Annual Symposium on Theory of Computing*, pages 446–456, Washington, D.C., 1984.

[19] W. A. Woods and J. G. Schmolze. The KL-ONE family. In F. Lehmann, editor, *Semantic Networks in Artificial Intelligence*, pages 133–178. Pergamon Press, 1992.

Near-Optimal Plans, Tractability, and Reactivity

Bart Selman
AT&T Bell Laboratories
Murray Hill, NJ 07974
selman@research.att.com

Abstract

Many planning problems have recently been shown to be inherently intractable. For example, finding the shortest plan in the blocks-world domain is NP-hard, and so is planning in even some of the most limited STRIPS-style planning formalisms. We explore the question as to what extent these negative results can be attributed to the insistence on finding plans of *minimal* length.

Using recent results form the theory of combinatorial optimization, we show that for domain-independent planning, one cannot efficiently generate *any* reasonable approximation of the optimal plan. Our result holds for a very restricted form of STRIPS. So, the negative complexity results for domain-independent planning are *not* just a consequence of searching for the optimal plans, because even finding reasonable approximations is hard.

Next we consider domain-dependent planning. For blocks-world planning one can generate in polynomial time good approximations of the minimal plan — within a factor of two of optimal. We show, however, that one cannot efficiently generate *arbitrarily* good approximations. This result places a limit on the usefulness of certain anytime approximation algorithms for generating better and better plans in the basic blocks-world domain.

Finally, we consider further several examples of tractable domain-dependent planning. We show how they can be solved using reactive style plans. Our analysis reveals a surprisingly close connection between tractable domain-dependent planning (optimal and near-optimal) and reactive style planning.

1 INTRODUCTION

Recent complexity results formally establish the inherent intractability of many basic planning problems. In particular, finding the shortest plan in the familiar blocks-world domain is NP-hard, and so is finding minimal plans in STRIPS-style planning formalisms, even with very restricted planning operators (Gupta and Nau 1991; Chenoweth 1991; Bylander 1991; and Erol *et al.* 1992). A further analysis of the basic blocks-world planning domain shows, however, that plans that are at most twice the length of the optimal plan can be generated efficiently. This suggests that perhaps the negative complexity results are at least partly due to the insistence on finding minimal length plans. We explore this issue by studying the complexity of finding plans that are not much longer than the shortest possible ones. Our results are based on recent developments in the theory of approximating optimization problems (Arora *et al.* 1992; Johnson 1992).

We first examine the complexity of domain-independent planning. Bylander (1991) studied a series of syntactic restrictions on the planning operators in STRIPS (Fikes and Nilsson 1971). Erol *et al.* (1992) discuss how one can encode the blocks-world problem using a slight extension of one of Bylander's most restricted classes. This class has the interesting property that one can determine whether some plan exists in polynomial time, but finding the shortest plan is NP-complete. So, the natural question to ask is whether one can efficiently compute reasonable approximations of the optimal plan (*e.g.*, within some constant factor, as can be done in the basic blocks-world domain). Unfortunately, we have a strong negative result in this case: For domain-independent planning, there does not exist a polynomial algorithm that can produce a plan that is within *any* constant factor of the minimal length plan. This result shows that the many negative complexity results for domain-independent planning formalisms are not just because one wants to find the shortest possible plan: even reasonable approximations of the optimal plan cannot be generated efficiently.

Next we consider the complexity of finding near-optimal plans in a domain-dependent setting. We first discuss whether we can efficiently generate better and better approximations of the optimal plan in the basic blocks-world domain. More specifically, for any constant $c > 1$, does there exist a polynomial time algorithm that finds plans with length within a factor c of optimal? We are able to show that, unfortunately, such algorithms do not exist (provided P$\neq$NP). So, although we can get a reasonably good approximation (within a factor of two) efficiently, there will be no way to generate efficiently arbitrarily good approximations. Note that such algorithms do exist for other optimization problems, such as the knapsack problem (Garey and Johnson 1979).

In the basic blocks-world domain, one assumes that each block has a unique name. In a somewhat more general setting, one allows for several different blocks to have the same name ("type" or "color"). Clearly, finding the minimal length plan is also NP-hard in this setting (Chenoweth 1991). What is surprising, however, is that the two planning problems behave very differently with respect to finding near-optimal plans: While with unique names we can efficiently generate plans within a factor two of optimal, we will show that without the unique name guarantee, one cannot efficiently generate plans within any constant factor of optimal. So, planning problems that look the same from the standard worst-case complexity point of view, may behave very differently when it comes to approximation results. It may thus be useful to search for appropriate restrictions on domain-dependent planning tasks that allow for efficient approximate planning, even if finding the optimal plan is still intractable.

Our aim in the final part of this paper is to show that in a domain-dependent setting there are still many interesting tractable planning problems. We also show that there is a close connection between such tractable domain-dependent planning and reactive planning (Agre and Chapman 1987). For example, the algorithm that can generate a factor of two approximation of the minimal blocks-world plan can be cast in terms of a set of reactive planning rules. We study this issue by considering the notion of universal plans, which are one way of formalizing some of the main intuitions behind reactive planning (Schoppers 1987).

There has been a lively debate on the pros and cons of universal plans (Ginsberg 1989; Chapman 1989; and Schoppers 1989). Ginsberg argues against such plans, by suggesting that they will generally be much too large to be feasible in practice. Using recent results for non-uniform circuit complexity, we will show formally that there are indeed no feasible universal plans for certain specific blocks-world planning problems. On the other hand, we also identify interesting cases where short universal plans do exist. Those cases lie within the scope of tractable classical planning. In fact, we will see that tractable, classical planning implies the existence of reasonable size universal plans.

2 DOMAIN-INDEPENDENT PLANNING

Domain-independent planning formalisms provide the user with a general framework for encoding planning problems. STRIPS is the canonical example of such a formalism (Fikes and Nilsson 1971). In STRIPS, states are represented as a set of ground atomic facts, and actions by operators that map states into states. A STRIPS planner takes as input an initial state, a goal state, and a set of operators. Its task is to determine whether there exists some plan that leads from initial state to goal state, and if so, to find the minimal length plan.

Bylander (1991; 1992) and Erol et al. (1992) provide complexity results for propositional STRIPS planning. In its full generality, such planning is easily shown to be intractable. They therefore explore various syntactic restrictions on the operators in search of tractable subclasses.

One of the most interesting restricted classes studied by Bylander involves restricting the pre-condition of each STRIPS operator to positive atoms only, and having at most one atom on either the delete or the add list.[1] Let's call this class STRIPS$^-$. Finding an optimal plan in STRIPS$^-$ is intractable. However, determining whether some plan *exists* is still tractable. This raises the question as to whether we can efficiently generate plans of reasonable size. Unfortunately, as the following theorem shows, one cannot efficiently generate *any* reasonable approximations to the optimal plan in this formalism.

Theorem 1 *There does not exist a constant c such that one can generate in polynomial time plans in STRIPS$^-$ that are within a factor c of optimal (provided P$\neq$NP).*

Proof: Our proof is based on an *approximation preserving* reduction from HITTING SET. The HITTING SET problem is defined as follows. Given a collection S of subsets of a finite set U, find a minimum cardinality subset of U that intersects every set in S. Lund and Yannakakis (1993) show that the HITTING SET problem cannot be approximated efficiently within *any* constant factor (unless P=NP). We show that if we could find STRIPS$^-$ plans within some constant factor c of optimal, we then could generate minimum

---
[1] A STRIPS operator consists of a pre-condition, and an add and delete list. In order for a operator to be applicable in a certain state, the pre-condition has to be satisfied in the state. The effect of the operator is modeled by adding the atoms on the add list to the current state while deleting those on the delete list.

hitting sets within a factor $2c$ of optimal. Suppose we are given an instance of the HITTING SET problem. Assume that the elements of U are numbered from 1 to n, and and the subsets in collection S are named $s_1, s_2, \ldots, s_k$. Now construct the following instance of a STRIPS$^-$ planning problem. The operators are defined as follows. For each element i of U, we introduce $2(k+1)$ rules: $\to i_1$, $i_1 \to i_2$, $\ldots$, $i_k \to i$, and $\to \bar{i}_1$, $\to \bar{i}_2$, $\ldots$, $\to \bar{i}_k$, $\to \bar{i}$. (The rule $x \to y$ ($x \to \bar{y}$) denotes the operator with precondition x, and y on the add list (delete list).) So, starting from the empty initial state these rules allow us to "turn on" various elements of U. Note that we use a series of $k+1$ steps to turn on an element of U instead of a single rule; such a long series is necessary in order to preserve the relative distances between solutions and near-solutions in our reduction. Also, note that we have rules for turning things off again. Then, for each set s in S, we introduce for each element i in set s a rule $i \to \bar{s}$. Let $\{s_1, s_2, \ldots, s_k\}$ be the initial state, and the empty set be the goal state.

It is not difficult to verify that any minimal length plan for this planning problem correspond to some minimum hitting set and vice versa. Let L_{opt} be the length of the minimal plan, and V_{opt} the cardinality of the minimum hitting set. We have $L_{opt} = 2(|S|+1)V_{opt} + |S|$ (1). In general, from a plan of length L, we can obtain a hitting set of size V with $V \leq (L-|S|)/2(|S|+1)$ (2). Assume we can generate a plan with length L in polynomial time such that $L \leq c \cdot L_{opt}$ for some constant $c > 1$. From (2), it follows that we can obtain from this plan a hitting set with cardinality $V \leq (c \cdot L_{opt} - |S|)/2(|S|+1)$. By (1), we have $V \leq [c(2(|S|+1)V_{opt} + |S|) - |S|]/2(|S|+1)$. And thus, $V \leq cV_{opt} + c|S|/2(|S|+1)$, which gives $V \leq 2cV_{opt}$. So, we can obtain an approximation of the minimum hitting set within a factor of $2c$, contradicting the result by Lund and Yannakakis. ∎

Given the restricted form of the planning operators, STRIPS$^-$ is clearly a quite limited formalism. Erol et al. are able to encode standard blocks-world planning in this formalism, but only after extending it by allowing compositions of pairs of operators. In this extended class, one can still determine plan existence efficiently, but of course our negative results also applies here, i.e., one cannot efficiently generate a reasonable approximation of the optimal plan.

Our approximation result strengthens Bylander's observation that there do not appear to be reasonable syntactic restrictions on STRIPS operators that would allow for efficient planning. Our result shows that this observation remains true even if one would only require the planner to generate plans of reasonable size (compared to optimal). This situation should be contrasted with that for basic blocks-world planning, where we can easily generate approximations within a factor of two, as we will see below. This suggests that in order to obtain efficient planning systems, one should concentrate on domain-dependent planning, where one can often identify special domain features that lead to tractable planning.[2] Recent work by Agre and Hor-

---

[2]Chapman (1987) already argued a similar point, us-

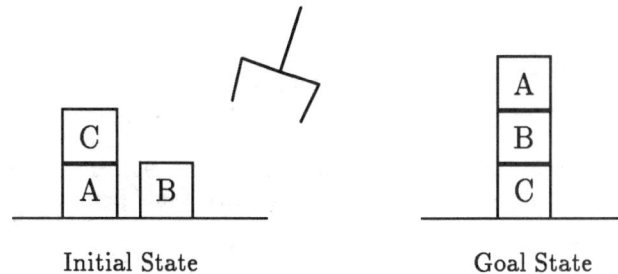

Initial State   Goal State

Figure 1: An example blocks-world planning problem.

swill (1992) supports this view. They argue that the ontology of the world is such that it facilitates efficient domain-dependent planning.

3 DOMAIN-DEPENDENT PLANNING

We now consider the complexity of near-optimal planning in the standard blocks-world domain. We first briefly review the recent complexity results by Gupta and Nau (1991). Fig. 1 gives an example of a typical blocks-world planning problem. The domain consists of a collection of blocks placed in various stacks on a table top. A robot arm can move blocks around, but only one block at a time.

More formally, a planning problem $P = (I,G)$ is defined by an initial state I and a goal state G. A state is described by a series of atomic facts, such as on(x,y) which denotes that block x is on block y; clear(x) which denotes that there is nothing on top of block x; and ontable(x) which says that block x is on the table. For example, in Fig. 1, we have an initial state I= {on(C,A), ontable(A), clear(C), clear(B), ontable(B)}. A move action by the robot arm is given by move(x,y,z), for moving block x from on top of block y onto block z. (The second and third argument can also refer to the table T.) It is assumed that before one can execute a move operation, the block that is to be moved is clear (i.e., there is no block on top of it); if the block is to be placed on top of another block, the other block should be clear also. There is always space on the table to place blocks. A plan consists of a sequence of actions, to be carried out by the robot arm, leading from the initial state to the goal state. For example, the sequence move(C,A,T), move(B,T,C), and move(A,T,B) leads from the initial state to the goal state as given in Fig. 1.

---

ing negative complexity results for quite general planning systems. Our new results show that those negative results were not simply due to the choice of an overly general planning formalism: domain-independent planning is hard even in very restricted formalisms and when allowing for approximate solutions. An interesting exception can be found in the work by Bäckström and Klein (1991; Bäckström 1992; Bäckström and Nebel 1993). They propose a different planning formalism, and identify *global* restrictions on the set of operators, which lead to a tractable subformalism — its practical applicability is currently being studied.

The blocks-world planning problem can now be stated as follows: Given an initial state I and a goal state G what is the shortest possible sequence of moves that leads from I to G? Gupta and Nau (1991) show that finding such a sequence is an intractable problem.

Theorem 2 (Gupta and Nau 1991) *Given a blocks-world planning problem (I, G), finding a minimal length sequence of moves that leads from I to G is NP-hard.*

Can we relax the requirement that the plans should be optimal and obtain tractability? The answer is yes. Not only can we generate some plan in polynomial time, we can even generate a plan that is of reasonable size. More specifically, Gupta and Nau discuss a polynomial time algorithm that generates plans that are at most twice as long as the shortest possible one. We reformulate their approach into the following surprisingly simple strategy for obtaining such near-optimal plans: repeatedly execute the following rules in random order until the goal state is reached. (To execute a rule one finds a block that matches the if-part.)

1. If block is not in final position, not on table and clear, then move it to table.
2. If block is on table, not in final position, and final position is free, then move it to final position.

A block is "in final position" iff the stack of blocks below it is as specified by the goal state.[3] Clearly, this condition can be checked efficiently for each block. Note that this set of planning rules has a "reactive flavor," i.e., the rules simply suggest the next action to take based on the current state.[4] The fact that the length K of the plan generated in this manner is at most twice the length OPT of the optimal plan follows from the observation that rule 1 only moves blocks that will need to be moved in any valid plan, and rule 2 will move each block directly into place. One can obtain a shorter plan by merging a rule 1 move and a rule 2 move into one single move. If one could merge all pairs of rule 1 and rule 2 moves, one would get a plan of length $K/2$. In this situation, no blocks are moved unnecessarily; it follows that there does not exist a shorter plan. However, one might not be able to merge all pairs of rule 1 and rule 2 moves, so $K \leq 2 \cdot OPT$. It follows that the NP-hardness of the blocks-world planning problem, stems from the problem of how to merge *in an optimal manner* the various rule 1 and rule 2 ('via-the-table' moves) moves into direct stack-to-stack moves.

The fact that we can generate plans that are at most a factor of 2 of optimal, raises the question as to whether we can do even better. The following theorem shows that there exists a hard limit on how much better one could possibly do.[5]

Theorem 3 *There exists a constant c $(1 < c < 2)$ such that there is no polynomial time algorithm that generates plans with length of at most $c \cdot OPT$ (provided P$\neq$NP).*

Proof: The proof is based on an L−reduction from MAXIMUM SUBDAG. Papadimitriou and Yannakakis (1991) introduce L−reductions to preserve the notion of closeness between solutions and near-solutions in reductions between optimization problems. (Standard polynomial time reductions do not preserve closeness.)

The proof by Gupta and Nau (1992) of Theorem 2 is based on a reduction from FEEDBACK ARC SET. We have to modify their approach to obtain an L-reduction for preserving approximability. In our reduction, we use MAXIMUM SUBDAG: Given a directed graph $G = (V, E)$, find an acyclic subgraph $G' = (V, E')$, with E' as large as possible.

Consider an instances $G = (V, E)$ of MAXIMUM SUBDAG. Assume the vertices are numbered from 1 to n. We will transform this into a planning problem. As our initial state and goal state, we use modifications of the states given by Gupta and Nau. In the initial state, we have n stacks of blocks, one for each vertex. Gupta and Nau define for vertex i a stack of $2n + 3$ blocks (from top to bottom): $[i, O, n], [i, O, n - 1], \ldots, [i, O, 0], [i, I, 0], \ldots, [i, I, n], [i, I, n + 1]$. In our initial state, we remove the blocks that do not correspond to actual edges, i.e., if edge (i, j) is not in E, then remove block $[i, O, j]$ and $[j, I, i]$. (We eliminate any unnecessary moves. This is necessary to maintain approximability.) Blocks with 0 or $n+1$ as the third element in their name should not be removed. Our goal state is given by $|E|$ stacks each of two blocks: for edge (x, y) in E we have the block $[x, O, y]$ on $[y, I, x]$; the remaining blocks are placed on the table. Now, given a plan leading from the initial state to the goal, we can obtain an acyclic subdag of G, by eliminating all edges that correspond to blocks that are moved via the table. Moreover, our reduction satisfies the constraints on L−reductions: (1) we have that $L_{OPT} \leq \alpha S_{OPT}$, where L_{OPT} is the length of the minimal plan, S_{OPT} is the size (number of edges) of the minimum acyclic subdag, and α is a constant; (2) a plan of length L corresponds to a acyclic subdag of size S, where $|S - S_{OPT}| \leq \beta |L - L_{OPT}|$ (β is a constant). (Proving these properties is tedious but fairly

---

[3] We assume a completely specified goal state. Alternatively, one can add a condition to handle those blocks not mentioned in the goal: If a block is not specified in the goal state, it is in the final position iff there are no blocks below it that are mentioned in the goal state and that are not in their final positions, and it is not in place of another block mentioned in the goal. I would like to thank Lynn Stein for this observation.

[4] One might be concerned that the rules implicitly refer to the goal state. This is not an issue, because, as we will see later on, in reactive planning the goal is (generally) considered predefined. So, given a particular goal state, one would generate rules with the goal compiled in.

[5] Note that there are optimization problems, such as the knapsack problem, where for each $c > 1$ there is a polytime algorithm, which generates a solution within a factor c of optimal.

straightforward.)

Since MAXIMUM SUBDAG is a MAX SNP[π] complete problem (Yannakakis and Papadimitriou 1991), and our reduction is an L−reduction, it follows that blocks-world planning problem is a MAX SNP[π] hard problem. This hardness result combined with the recent results by Arora et al. (1992) implies that there does *not* exist a Polynomial Time Approximation Scheme (PTAS) for the blocks-world planning problem. (A PTAS is a family of polynomial time algorithms, one for each $\epsilon > 0$, that each achieve an approximation ratio of $1 + \epsilon$.) The theorem follows. (We already know that we can obtain a ratio of 2 efficiently.) ∎

Theorem 3 places the blocks-world planning problems among a class of optimization problems that have relatively simple approximation algorithms which generate solutions within some constant factor of optimal (*e.g.*, 3/4 for maximum satisfiability), but where no algorithms are known that produce better ratios. Moreover, even if one could achieve a better ratio, it is now known that there exists some fixed ratio within which one *cannot* efficiently approximate.[6]

As an example of a practical consequence of Theorem 3 consider an anytime planner that runs a series of efficient better and better approximation algorithms to obtain increasingly better plans until time runs out. (We assume of course that the better the approximation, the longer it takes. For example, getting within a factor of five of optimal may take linear time in the size of the planning problem, whereas getting within a factor of three may take quadratic time.) Theorem 3 shows that there is a hard limit on how effective such an approach can be: beyond a certain ratio there are no efficient approximation algorithms, and one has to fall back to an inherently inefficient algorithm for generating the optimal solution.

Finally, let us now consider the slightly more general setting in which several blocks can have the same name. Finding the optimal plan is again NP-hard (Chenoweth 1991), but we have the following surprising result.

Theorem 4 *For blocks-world planning problems where several blocks can have the same name, there does not exist a constant c such that one can generate in polynomial time plans that are within a factor c of optimal (provided P≠NP).*

Because of space limitations, we moved the proof to the appendix. (Note that the strategy for finding a near-optimal solution in the basic blocks-world domain

---

[6]It would of course be nice to know the absolute best possible ratio for which one can still obtain approximations efficiently, but the theory of approximation algorithms does not yet provide such ratios, *i.e.*, there is a gap between the ratio achieved by the known best approximation algorithms and the ratio for which one can *prove* that it cannot be achieved by any efficient approximation method.

does not work here because now we do not know exactly which blocks from the initial state to move to a goal position.) So, when it comes to finding reasonable size plans, we see a remarkable difference between planning in the basic blocks-world domain and in the somewhat more general setting, even though these problems are equally hard from the perspective of standard worst-case complexity. Considering approximation results may thus prove useful in finding restrictions on domain-dependent planning problems that allow for approximately optimal planning, even if optimal planning is still intractable.

4 TRACTABILITY: REACTIVE PLANNING AND UNIVERSAL PLANS

In this section, we explore further the possibilities for tractable planning, both optimal and near-optimal. Because of our strong negative results for domain-independent planning (Theorem 1), we will concentrate on domain-dependent planning. We saw how basic blocks-world plans within a factor of two of optimal can be generated using a strategy that can be viewed as a form of *reactive* planning. Reactive planning has been proposed as an alternative planning paradigm, largely in response to negative complexity results for traditional domain-independent planning systems (Chapman 1987; Agre and Chapman 1987; Georgeff and Lansky 1987). The underlying assumption in reactive planning is that an agent can achieve its goals — at least to a large extent — by simply reacting to its current environment, as opposed to planning an elaborate sequence of actions. There are a number of papers describing particular applications of such planning, but little is known, in general, about the class of planning problems that can be solved using it. In this section, we show how complexity theoretic-tools can be used to provide some insight into this issue. In the process, we will uncover an interesting relation to tractable, domain-dependent planning (both optimal and near-optimal).

One impediment to a rigorous analysis is that there does not exist a formal definition of what constitutes reactive planning. We therefore restrict our attention to the well-defined notion of *universal plans*, which formally captures some of the main intuitions behind reactive planning (Schoppers 1987). Ginsberg (1989) gives the following definition.

Definition: A universal plan is an arbitrary function from the set of possible situations S into the set of primitive actions A.

The basic idea is that an agent works towards a general goal by simply looking up in some large table what primitive action to take next based on its current situation, *i.e.*, given universal plan u, when in situation s, take action $u(s)$. Representing the universal plan explicitly in a lookup table generally leads to infeasibly large tables because of the large number of possible states. More efficient representations can be obtained by using decision trees (Schoppers 1987) or Boolean circuits (Nilsson 1989; Rosenschein and Kaebling 1986). To keep our analysis as general as possible, we will assume the latter. Since $u(s)$ must be efficiently computable, the Boolean circuit representing u can be at most of polynomial size.[7]

Note that in contrast with classical planning, the agent does not plan an explicit *sequence* of steps, but rather decides after each step what to do next based on the current situation.[8] This makes the approach quite robust with respect to unexpected changes in the environment. Another distinguishing feature of universal plans is that the goal is part of the universal plan: the planning task is "compiled" with a certain goal in mind.

There has been much debate on the usefulness of universal plans (Ginsberg 1989; Chapman 1989; and Schoppers 1989). Ginsberg conjectured that such plans would be infeasibly large for almost any interesting planning task. We reconsider this issue by studying universal planning in the blocks-world setting. One of the main differences from our previous description of blocks-world planning is that we now have to take the goal as fixed. Our universal plan will tell us "what to do next" for each state. We will find that the fact that our goal is fixed can make a significant difference in the complexity of the task of computing what to do next.

For a basic example, consider the goal state "all blocks on the table." Repeatedly executing the rule "If block is not on table and clear, then move block to table," will establish this goal in polynomial time, in the *minimum* number of steps. Pippenger and Fischer (1979) have shown how to construct a small (*i.e.*, polysize) Boolean circuit for each polynomial time computable function. It follows that there is a compact (polysize) universal plan for achieving the goal of putting all blocks on the table. More generally, we have:

Proposition 1 *If there exists a polynomial time planning algorithm that given as input an initial state I can generate a plan for achieving a fixed goal G, then there exists a polysize universal plan for achieving G.*

This proposition follows by considering how the polysize universal plan can be obtained from the polynomial time planning algorithm. First, we modify the planning algorithm to output, in polynomial time, only the first step of the plan that leads from an initial state to the (fixed) goal state. (Note that we end up with an algorithm that takes as input an initial state. In the reactive view, this becomes the current state.) Using Pippenger and Fischer's result we can construct from this modified algorithm a polynomial size circuit giving the universal plan for the planning problem.

The approach of running a classical planner to generate the next step may not appear to be very informative from the perspective of reactive planning. However, in determining the computational cost of finding the next step, we can of course consider any algorithm for obtaining the result, including a classical planner.

Let us consider another example of tractable domain-dependent planning: *near-optimal* planning in the basic blocks-world. Given any goal state, one can use the strategy discussed in section 3 to obtain a near-optimal plan (within a factor of two) starting from any initial state. From Proposition 1, it follows that there is a compact universal plan for each goal state. In this case the plan will generate a near-optimal sequence of moves.

We consider one more example of a feasible universal plan. Assume that each block is assigned a unique name and let the goal be to stack all blocks in a single, alphabetically ordered stack. Consider the following strategy. Search for the block that needs to be placed next on the goal stack. If that block is clear, then move it to the goal. Otherwise, move the blocks on top of it to the table (one by one, starting with the block at the top of the stack). This polynomial time strategy will generate a *minimal* plan for this goal. So, again, from Proposition 1, we know that there exists a compact universal plan.

A similar strategy can be used to solve the 'spell fruitcake problem' and, more general, the 'stack copying problem,' as discussed in Ginsberg (1989) and Chapman (1989). Interestingly, Ginsberg conjectured that no feasible universal plan would exist for the fruitcake problem, but Chapman showed this conjecture to be false, by giving a universal plan for solving it. Chapman's solution follows a strategy very similar to our alphabetical stacking approach.[9] Our analysis illustrates that it should not come as a surprise that there exists such a compact universal plan for the 'fruitcake' problem. The reason is simple: the problem is a polynomial time planning task, and by Proposition 1, it follows that there exists a compact universal plan.

---

[7] Further restrictions such as logarithmic depth would also be interesting to pursue, especially in exploring parallel complexity issues.

[8] It is a form of "one-step planning." One might argue whether this should still be called "planning." Here, we simply view universal plans as a way to solve planning problems.

[9] Chapman makes elaborate use of specialized visual routines. Such routines determine various properties of the scene, for example, finding a block with a certain label. From a computational complexity point of view, the key aspect of the routines is that they compute properties of the scene efficiently (*i.e.*, in polynomial time).

This leads us to the issue of whether there are planning problems for which no reasonable size universal plans exist. One might think that given the intractability of optimal blocks-world planning, it would follow immediately that there are no feasible universal plans for this form of planning. However, the argument is not as simple as that, because in the NP-completeness proof for the blocks-world, both the initial state *and* the goal state are taken to be inputs to the problem. For universal plans we take the goal state as fixed, which may very well reduce the complexity. Nevertheless, we can still formally show that there does exist a blocks-world planning task for which there is no compact universal plan that leads us to the goal in a minimal number of steps (unless NP $\subseteq$ non-uniform P, *i.e.*, the polynomial-time hierarchy collapses to the second level, which is considered very unlikely (Boppana and Sipser 1990)).

Theorem 5 *Unless NP $\subseteq$ non-uniform P, there exists a blocks-world planning goal for which there is no polynomial size universal plan for generating the minimal sequence of moves leading to the goal.*

See the appendix for the proof. We would like to stress the generality of this negative results. We use *non-uniform* circuit complexity theory because the universal plans are Boolean circuits, handcrafted to deal with fixed size domains (*e.g.*, domains with up to a certain number of blocks). So, we can have different circuits for different size input domains. Non-uniform circuits are surprisingly powerful. For example, they can compute certain undecidable functions. Consider the function that returns "1" on inputs of length n iff Turing Machine number n halts on all inputs. For any n, the circuit is simply fixed to return 1 or 0. As a consequence of the very powerful nature of non-uniform circuits as computational devices, our negative result extends to other known representations of universal plans, such as, for example, finite state automata (even if the automaton keeps state information around, such information can be added to the Boolean circuit). To get better understanding as to why the negative result extends to reactive planners which can maintain state information, let us briefly consider the main idea behind the proof of Theorem 5.

In the proof, we show how to reduce an NP-complete problem (FEEDBACK ARC SET) to a planning problem with a fixed goal state. We do this by identifying a generic fixed goal state and encoding all the the complexity of the FEEDBACK ARC SET problem into the initial (the input) state of the planning problem. If there would exist a (reactive) planning system that could *efficiently* generate the optimal next step towards the goal given any initial state, such a planner could be used to solve efficiently the NP-complete FEEDBACK ARC SET problem. So, in effect, we have shown that the intractability of certain planning tasks does not necessarily depend on a subtle interplay between initial state and goal state; even for certain fixed goal states the planning problem can be NP-complete.

To summarize, Theorem 5 shows that there are concrete blocks-world planning problems that do not have reasonable size universal plans. However, as we discussed earlier, there are many other goal states that do allow for compact universal plans. This shows that the reactive view of planning with the fixed goal state can indeed lead to certain computational advantages. We are dealing here with an interesting, general progression: in domain-independent planning, the initial state, goal state and operators are all inputs to the planner; in domain-dependent planning systems, only the initial state and the goal state is part of the input; finally, in universal planning, only the current state is part of the input. So, we have more and more restrictive systems, thereby gaining computational efficiency.

5 CONCLUSIONS

We considered the computational complexity of finding plans that are of reasonable, but not necessarily optimal, size. For domain-independent planning, we showed that it is just as difficult to find plans within any constant factor as it is to find optimal ones. This result holds for a very restricted form of STRIPS. So, even the most restricted forms of domain-independent planning are too general to allow for efficient approximately optimal planning. This strong negative result suggests that in order to obtain efficient (near-optimal) planning systems, one will generally need to exploit certain domain-specific properties.

In the basic blocks-world domain, one can efficiently generate plans that are at most twice as long as optimal. We did show, however, that one cannot generate *arbitrarily* good approximations efficiently. In other words, there is a hard limit on how well one can approximate the optimal plans efficiently. This places a limit on the effectiveness of certain anytime procedures for generating better and better plans. We also showed that a somewhat more general setting (several blocks can have the same name), one again cannot efficiently generate plans within any constant factor of optimal. Thus, even when planning problems look the same from a standard worst-case complexity point of view, they may have very different approximation properties. It therefore is useful to study restrictions that allow for efficient approximate planning, even if finding the optimal plan is still intractable.

Finally, we considered reactive style planning, and, in particular, universal plans. We gave several examples of blocks-world planning problems that have feasible universal plans. We also showed some of the limitations of universal planning, by showing that there are certain goals in the blocks-world domain that cannot be achieved by *any* reasonably sized universal plan.

Our analysis shows that tractable classical planning and reactive style planning lead to a very similar set of planning tasks. For future research, it would be interesting to recast other forms of reactive planning as studied by, for example, Brooks (1990), in terms of classical domain-dependent planning. Such a reformulation may give us new insights into the class of planning problems that can be solved by those systems.

Acknowledgments

I would like to thank Christer Bäckström, Ron Brachman, Henry Kautz, Carsten Lund, Bernhard Nebel, Stuart Russell, and Lynn Stein for many useful discussions and comments.

References

Agre, P. and Chapman, D. (1987). Pengi: An implementation of a theory of activity. *Proc. AAAI87*, Seattle, 268-272.

Agre, P. and Horswill, I. (1992). Cultural support for improvisation. *Proc. AAAI92*, San Jose, 363-368.

Arora, S., Lund, C., Motwani, R., Sudan, M., and Szegedy, M. (1992). Proof verification and intractability of approximation problems. *Proc. STOC92*.

Bäckström, C. (1992). *Computational complexity of reasoning about plans.* Ph.D. thesis, Linkoping University, Linkoping, Sweden.

Bäckström, C. and Klein, I. (1991). Parallel non-binary planning in polynomial time. *Proc. IJCAI91*, Sidney, Australia, 268-273.

Bäckström, C. and Nebel, B. (1993). Complexity results for SAS+ planning. *Proc. IJCAI-93*, Chambery, France, 1430-1435.

Boppana, R.B. and Sipser, M. (1990). The complexity of finite functions. In *Handbook of Theoretical Computer Science*, Vol. A, J. van Leeuwen (Ed.), The MIT Press/Elsevier.

Brooks, R.A. (1990). Elephants don't play chess. In *Designing Autonomous Agents: Theory and Practice*, P. Maes (Ed.), MIT Press, 1990.

Bylander, T (1991). Complexity results for planning. *Proceedings of IJCAI91*, Sidney, Australia, 274-279.

Bylander, T (1992). The computational complexity of propositional STRIPS planning. Submitted for publication.

Chapman, D. (1987). Planning for conjunctive goals. *Artificial Intelligence*, 32(3), 333-377.

Chapman, D. (1989). Penguins can make cake. *AI Magazine*, Winter 1989, 45-50.

Chenoweth, S.V. (1991). On the NP-hardness of the blocks world. *Proceedings AAAI91*, Anaheim, CA, 623-628.

Erol, K., Nau, D.S., and Subrahmanian, V.S. (1991). On the complexity of domain-independent planning. *Proceedings AAAI92*, 381-386.

Fikes, R.E. and Nilsson, N.J. (1971). STRIPS: A new approach to the application of theorem proving to problem solving. *Artificial Intelligence*, 2(3/4), 189-208.

Garey, M.R. and Johnson, D.S. (1979). *Computers and Intractability, A Guide to the Theory of NP-Completeness.* New York, NY: W.H. Freeman, 1979.

Georgeff, M. and Lansky, A. (1987). Reactive reasoning and planning. *Proceedings AAAI87*, 677-682.

Ginsberg, M.L. (1989). Universal planning: An (almost) universally bad idea. *AI Magazine*, Winter 1989, 40-44.

Gupta and Nau (1991). Complexity results for blocks-world planning. *Proceedings AAAI91*, Anaheim, CA, 629-633.

Gupta and Nau (1992). On the complexity of blocks-world planning. *Artificial Intelligence*, 56, 139-403.

Johnson, D.S. (1992). The NP-Completeness Column: An Ongoing Guide. 23rd column. *J. of Algorithms*.

Kolata, G. (1992). New short cut found for mathematical proofs, *New York Times*, Science Section, April 7, 1992.

Lund, C., and Yannakakis, M. (1993). On the hardness of approximating minimization problems. *Proc. STOC93*, May 1993.

Nilsson, N.J. (1989) Action networks. Technical Report, Dept. of Computer Science, Stanford University.

Papadimitriou, C.H. and Yannakakis, M. (1991). Optimization, Approximation, and Complexity Classes. *J. of Computer and System Sciences*, Vol. 43, no. 3, 425-440.

Pippenger, N. and Fischer, M.J. (1979). Relations among complexity measures, *JACM*, 26, 361-381.

Rosenschein, S.J., and Kaebling, L.P. (1986). The synthesis of machines with provable epistemic properties. *Proceedings of the 1986 Conference on Theoretical Aspects of Reasoning about Knowledge*, 83-98.

Schoppers, M.J. (1987). Universal plans for reactive robots in unpredictable domains. *Proceedings IJCAI87*, Italy, 1039-1046.

Schoppers, M.J. (1989). In defense of reaction plans as caches. *AI Magazine*, Winter 1989, 51-60.

Appendix

Proof of theorem 4

Proof: We use an approximation preserving reduction from HITTING SET. See the proof of Theorem 1 for the definition on the HITTING SET problem and its approximation properties. Given an instance of the HITTING

SET problem, we will define a initial and a goal state such that any plan within a constant factor of optimal would give us a hitting set within a constant factor of optimal. Lund and Yannakakis (1993) show that the latter cannot be found polynomial time, so neither can the near-optimal plan.

Let the HITTING SET instance consist of a collection of subsets, $s_1, s_2, ..., s_k$, of a finite set U. Assume that the elements of U are numbered 1 through n. The initial state consists of a n piles of blocks. At the bottom of each pile is a block labeled "-1". The rest of each pile is constructed as follows. Consider the jth pile. On top of the "-1" block we place blocks labeled with the names of the subsets in which j occurs. On top of those blocks, we place k blocks with the label "0". As the goal state, we have k blocks, labeled s_1 though s_k on the table, each is clear (no block on top). In order to achieve this goal, we will have to unstack at least some of the initial piles. Using a calculation similar to the one used in the proof of Theorem 1, we can show that generating a plan within a factor c of optimal, would give us a hitting set within a factor of $2c$ of optimal. From the result by Yannakakis and Lund it follows that one cannot generate a plan within a constant factor of optimal in polynomial time because there does not exist (unless $P = NP$) no polynomial algorithm for finding a hitting set within a constant factor of optimal. ∎

Proof of theorem 5

Proof: We consider the reduction by Gupta and Nau (1992) from FEEDBACK ARC SET to blocks-world planning. In this reduction, the goal state contains most of the information about the feedback arcs set instance under consideration. So, the goal state varies with each problem instance, and cannot be taken as fixed. Fortunately, in blocks-world planning, the initial state and goal-state are interchangeable with a straightforward one-to-one correspondence between plans (simply reverse the sequence of actions). The initial state in Gupta and Nau's reduction is quite regular. From this state, we can derive a *fixed* goal for our planning problem. More specifically, the goal G^* is defined as follows. Let N be the number of blocks. If N is equal to $2p^2 + 3p$ for some integer $p > 0$, put the blocks in p stacks of $2p+3$ blocks each (this state was also described in the proof of theorem 3); otherwise, have all blocks on the table. (We assume that each block has a unique label.)

Now, we can still reduce an instance (V, E) of the FEEDBACK ARC SET to an instance of the minimum blocks-world planning problem with the fixed goal G^*. Basically, we encode all the information from the instance (V, E) in the initial state I. We do this by using for I the goal state as used by Gupta and Nau in their reduction. More specifically, for every edge (x,y) in E, the state I contains the atom on([x,0,y],[y,1,x]). For every other block b, we have ontable(b). (We use the naming of the blocks as defined by Gupta and Nau.) Given the reversability of the blocks-world planning task, it follows that an optimal plan in this setting corresponds to a minimum feedback arc set. So far, we have in effect shown that optimal blocks-world planning remains NP-complete even if we use the fixed goal state G^* and take the initial state I as only input.

Given this NP-completeness result it follows that there cannot exist a non-uniform family of polynomial size circuits for solving the optimal blocks-world planning problem with fixed goal G^* (unless NP $\subseteq$ non-uniform P). See also Boppana and Sipser (1990). And, therefore, there does not exist a compact universal plan for this task. ∎

Specification and Evaluation of Preferences under Uncertainty

Sek-Wah Tan and Judea Pearl
< tan@cs.ucla.edu > < judea@cs.ucla.edu >
Cognitive Systems Lab, Computer Science Department
University of California, Los Angeles, CA 90024
United States of America

Abstract

This paper describes a framework for specifying preferences in terms of conditional desires of the form "α is desirable if β", to be interpreted as "α is preferred to $\neg\alpha$ other things being equal in any β world". We demonstrate how such preference sentences may be interpreted as constraints on admissible preference rankings of worlds and how they, together with normality defaults, allow a reasoning agent to evaluate queries of the form "would you prefer σ_1 over σ_2 given ϕ" where σ_1 and σ_2 are action sequences. We also prove that by extending the syntax to allow for importance-rating of preference sentences, we obtain a language that is powerful enough to represent all possible preferences among worlds.

1 Introduction

This paper describes a framework for specifying planning goals in terms of preference sentences of the form "prefer α to $\neg\alpha$ if γ". Consider an agent deciding if she should carry an umbrella, given that it is cloudy. Naturally, she will have to consider the prospect of getting wet $\neg d$ (not dry), the possibility of rain r, that it is cloudy c, and so on. Some of the beliefs and knowledge that will influence her decision may be expressed in conditional sentences such as: "if I have the umbrella then I will be dry", $u \to d$, "if it rains and I do not have the umbrella then I will be wet", $r \wedge \neg u \to \neg d$ and "typically if it is cloudy, it will rain", $c \to r$. She may also have preferences like "I prefer to be dry", $d \succ \neg d$ and "I prefer not to carry an umbrella", $\neg u \succ u$. From the beliefs and preferences above, we should be able to infer whether to carry an umbrella if she observes that it is cloudy, assuming that keeping dry is more important to her than not carrying an umbrella.

The research reported in this paper concerns such decisions. Our aim is to eventually equip an intelligent

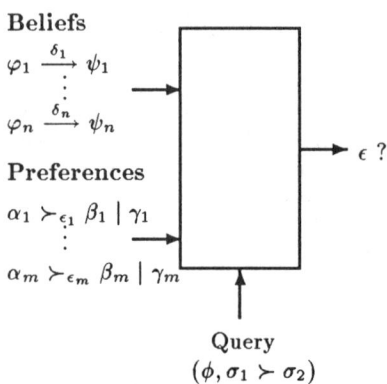

Figure 1: Schematic of the proposed system

autonomous artificial agent with decision making capabilities, based on two types of inputs: beliefs and preferences. Beliefs, some of which may be defeasible, will be specified by normality defaults like "if you run across the freeway then you are likely to die", written $run \to die$. Preferences may be encoded in conditional sentences such as "if it is morning then I prefer coffee to tea", written $coffee \succ tea \mid morning$. Figure 1 shows a schematic of the program. Each normality default $\varphi_i \xrightarrow{\delta_i} \psi_i$ and preference sentence $\alpha_i \succ_{\epsilon_i} \beta_i \mid \gamma_i$ will be quantified by an integer δ_i or ϵ_i which indicates the *degree* of the corresponding belief or preference. A larger degree implies a stronger belief or preference. The program will also accept queries in the form of $(\phi, \sigma_1 \succ \sigma_2)$, which stands for "would you prefer σ_1 over σ_2 given ϕ?". The output of the program is the degree ϵ to which the preference $\sigma_1 \succ \sigma_2$ holds in the context ϕ.

We take Bayesian decision theory and maximum expected utility [von Neumann and Morgenstern, 1947, Pearl, 1988, Keeney and Raiffa, 1976] as ideal norms for decision making. The problems with the theory are that it requires complete specifications of a probability distribution and a utility function and that the specifications are numeric. The problems with the complete specification of numeric probabilities had been considered and partly resolved in [Goldszmidt, 1992, Goldszmidt and Pearl, 1992]. The approach is to move from numeric probabilities to qualitative, order-of-magnitude abstractions and to use conditional statements of the form $\varphi \stackrel{\delta}{\rightarrow} \psi$ as a specification language that constrains qualitative probabilities. These constraints translate to a unique belief ranking $\kappa(\omega)$ on worlds that permits the reasoning agent to economically maintain and update a set of deductively closed beliefs. Pearl in [Pearl, 1993] addressed the problem of numeric utilities. Paralleling the order-of-magnitude abstraction of probabilities, he introduced an integer-valued utility ranking $\mu(\omega)$ on worlds that, combined with the belief ranking $\kappa(\omega)$, scores qualitative preferences of actions and their consequences. However, the requirement for the complete specification of the utility ranking remains problematic.

Here we propose a specification language which accepts conditional preferences of the form "if β then α is preferred to $\neg\alpha$", $\alpha \succ \neg\alpha \mid \beta$. A conditional preference of this form will also be referred to as a *conditional desire*, written $D(\alpha|\beta)$, which represents the sentence "if β then α is desirable". The output is the evaluation of a preference query of the form $(\phi, \sigma_1 \succ \sigma_2)$ where ϕ is any general formula while σ_1 and σ_2 may either be formulas or action sequences. The intended meaning of such query is "is σ_1 preferred to σ_2 given ϕ"? Our program is as follows. Each conditional desire $D(\alpha|\beta)$ is given *ceteris paribum* (CP) semantics; "α is preferred to $\neg\alpha$ other things being equal in any β-world". A collection of such expressions imposes constraints over *admissible* preference rankings $\pi(\omega)$. From the set of admissible rankings we select a subset of the most *compact* rankings $\pi^+(\omega)$, each reflecting maximal indifference. At the same time we use the normality defaults to compute the set of *believable* worlds $\{\omega \mid \kappa(\omega) = 0\}$ that may result after the execution of σ_i given ϕ. One way of computing the beliefs prevailing after an action is through the use of causal networks, as described in [Pearl, 1993]. To compare sets of believable worlds we introduce a preference relation between sets of worlds, called preferential dominance, that is derived from a given preference ranking $\pi(\omega)$. To confirm the preference query $(\phi, \sigma_1 \succ \sigma_2)$, we compare the set of believable worlds[1] resulting from executing σ_1 given ϕ to those resulting from executing σ_2 given ϕ, and test if the former *preferentially dominates* the latter in all the most compact preference rankings. A set of worlds W preferentially dominates V if and only if:

1. W provides more and better possibilities,
2. W provides less possibilities but excludes poorer possibilities or
3. W provides better alternative possibilities

when compared with V.

So far we have described the *flat* version of our language, where a degree is not associated with each conditional desire sentence $D(\alpha|\beta)$. We will show that the flat language is not sufficient for specifying all preference rankings. In particular we exhibit a preference ranking that is not the most compact admissible ranking with respect to any set of conditional desires. Also, by not specifying the relative importance of conditional desires, the flat language does not allow us to decide among preferences resulting from conflicting goals. To alleviate these problems we allow conditional desires to be quantified by a integer indicating the degree or strength of the desire. We prove that this quantified language is expressive enough to represent all preference rankings.

In the next section, we describe the language and the semantics for conditional desires. In section 3, we introduce preferential dominance between sets and show how a preference query may be evaluated. Quantified conditional desires are introduced in section 4 together with the sufficiency theorem. Related work is compared in section 5 and we conclude with a summary of the contributions of this paper.

2 Preference Specification

2.1 The Context

In this section we consider conditional desires of the form $D(\alpha|\beta)$ where α and β are well-formed formulas obtained from a finite set of atomic propositions $X = \{X_1, X_2, \ldots, X_n\}$ with the usual truth functionals $\wedge, \vee$ and $\neg$. Consider the desire sentence "I prefer to be dry", $D(d)$. This sentence may mean that

1. "d is preferred to $\neg d$ regardless of other things", or that
2. "d is preferred to $\neg d$ other things being equal" or
3. some intermediate reading.

In this paper we take the *ceteris paribum* (CP) reading which is "d is preferred to $\neg d$ other things being equal". Similarly, the interpretation for a conditional desire $D(\alpha|\beta)$ is "α is preferred to $\neg\alpha$ other things being equal in any β-world".

The first interpretation is not very useful, as shown by von Wright in [von Wright, 1963], in that it does not allow for two or more unconditional preference statements to exist consistently together. For example, the desire to be rich, $D(r)$ and the desire to be healthy,

---

[1] In general, "surprising worlds" should be considered as well, in case they carry extremely positive or negative utilities (e.g. getting hit by a car). But, to simplify the exposition, we consider only believable worlds. A system combining both likelihood and utility considerations, reflecting a qualitative version of the expected utility criterion, is described in [Pearl, 1993].

$D(h)$ will quickly run in to a conflict when considering the worlds $r\overline{h}$ and $\overline{r}h$. This is because the world $r\overline{h}$ is preferred to $\overline{r}h$ by virtue of $D(r)$ and $\overline{r}h$ is preferred to $r\overline{h}$ by virtue of $D(h)$. The CP interpretation becomes reasonable in the light of this. Now we are going to question the CP interpretation.

Our first task is to explicate the meaning of $D(\alpha|\beta)$ in terms of preference constraints on pairs of worlds. Given the statement $D(\alpha)$, the CP interpretation imposes constraints only between worlds that agree on propositions that are not part of α. However to explicate what it means to be "part of α" it is insufficient to examine α syntactically, a semantic definition is required. For example, if $\omega = X_1 \wedge X_2 \wedge (\bigwedge_3^n X_i)$, $\nu = \neg X_1 \wedge \neg X_2 \wedge (\bigwedge_3^n X_i)$ and $\alpha = X_1$ we will conclude that $\omega \succ \nu$ is not sanctioned by CP, but if we were to write alpha as $X_1 \wedge (X_2 \vee \neg X_2)$ one might conclude that the preference above holds, because X_2 appears to be part of α and every thing else seems to be equal. To explicate this notion we say that a wff α *depends on* a proposition X_i if all wffs that are logically equivalent to α contain the symbol X_i. The set of propositions that α depends on is represented by $S(\alpha)$. This set is referred to as the *support* of α, written $support(\alpha)$ in [Doyle et al., 1991]. The set of propositions that α does not depend on is represented by $\overline{S}(\alpha) = X \setminus S(\alpha)$. To explicate the notion of "other things being equal in any β-world", we say that two worlds *agree* on a proposition if they assign the same truth value to the proposition. Two worlds *agree* on a set of propositions if they agree on all the propositions in the set. We say that ω and ν are *S-equivalent*, written $\omega \sim_S \nu$ if ω and ν agree on the set $S \subseteq X$. Given a conditional desire $D(\alpha|\beta)$ and a β-world, ω, the worlds that have "other things being equal" in ω are those that are $\overline{S}(\alpha)$-equivalent to ω. We call $D(\alpha|\omega)$ a *specific* conditional desire if ω is a wff of the form $\bigwedge_1^n x_i$, where $x_i = X_i$ or $\neg X_i$. (As a convention we will use the same symbol ω to refer to the unique model of the wff ω.)

Every specific conditional desire imposes constraints on some set of worlds; we call that set the context.

Definition 1 (Context) *Let $D(\alpha|\omega)$ be a specific conditional desire. The* **context** *of $D(\alpha|\omega)$, $C(\alpha, \omega)$ is defined as*

$$C(\alpha, \omega) = \{\nu \mid \nu \sim_{\overline{S}(\alpha)} \omega\}. \tag{1}$$

We write $C_\gamma(\alpha, \omega)$ for $\{\nu \models \gamma \mid \nu \in C(\alpha, \omega)\}$ where γ is a wff.

In the umbrella example the support of $u \vee d$ is, $S(u \vee d) = \{u, d\}$ and the context of the specific conditional desire $D(u \vee d|udcr)$ is $\{udcr, \overline{u}dcr, u\overline{d}cr, \overline{u}\overline{d}cr\}$, the set of worlds which agree with $\omega = udcr$ on all propositions except for u and d. The constraints imposed by $D(u \vee d|udcr)$ are shown in figure 2, where

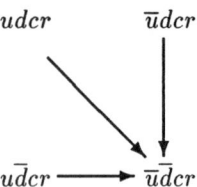

Figure 2: Constraints imposed by $D(u \vee d|udcr)$

the existence of an arrow $\omega \to \nu$ represents a preference constraint between ω and ν. The meaning of the direction of the arrow will be explained later.

Going from specific conditional desires to conditional desires, a conditional desire $D(\alpha|\beta)$ is interpreted as a conjunction of specific conditional desires $D(\alpha|\omega)$ over all models ω of β, $\bigwedge_{\omega \models \beta} D(\alpha|\omega)$. We note that $D(\alpha|\beta)$ may impose constraints on worlds that do not satisfy the condition β which may sound paradoxical. The reason being that each world fixes only $\overline{S}(\alpha)$, the atomic propositions which are not in α; however not all worlds that are constrained by $D(\alpha|\beta)$ are models of β; $\nu \in C(\alpha, \omega) \not\Rightarrow \nu \models \beta$. This stands contrary to [Doyle et al., 1991] where conditional desires were restricted to apply only to the models of β. Consider the sentence, "I desire the light to be ON if it is night and the light is OFF", $D(l|n \wedge \neg l)$. Clearly such a sentence compares *night*-worlds in which the light is ON to those in which the light is OFF. The former does not satisfy the condition $\beta = \neg l$. Such a reasonable sentence would be deemed meaningless in a restricted interpretation such as [Doyle et al., 1991]. β does not act as a filter for selecting worlds to which the desired constraints apply, instead it identifies worlds in which the desires are satisfied.

2.2 Admissible Rankings

A preference ranking π is an integer-valued function on the set of worlds Ω. The intended meaning of a ranking is that the world ω is no less preferred than the world ν if $\pi(\omega) \geq \pi(\nu)$. Given a non-empty set of worlds, W, we write $\pi_*(W)$ for $\min_{\omega \in W} \pi(\omega)$ and $\pi^*(W)$ for $\max_{\omega \in W} \pi(\omega)$. If W is empty then we adopt the convention that $\pi_*(W) = \infty$ and $\pi^*(W) = -\infty$. The constraints imposed by a specific conditional desire $D(\alpha|\omega)$ translates into constraints over admissible preference rankings. The constraints are that every α-world in the context $C(\alpha, \omega)$ has a higher rank (is preferred) than any $\neg \alpha$-world in the same context.

Definition 2 (Admissibility of rankings) *Let D be a set of conditional desires. A preference ranking π is* **admissible** *with respect to a conditional desire $D(\alpha|\beta)$ if for all $\omega \models \beta$, $\nu \in C_\alpha(\alpha, \omega)$ and $\nu' \in C_{\neg\alpha}(\alpha, \omega)$ implies*

$$\pi(\nu) > \pi(\nu'). \tag{2}$$

A preference ranking π is **admissible** *with respect to D if it is admissible with respect to all conditional desires in D.*

If there exist a ranking that is admissible with respect to a set of conditional desires, D then we say that D is *consistent*. A trivial example of an inconsistent set is $\{D(u), D(\neg u)\}$. Another example of an inconsistent set is $\{D(\alpha), D(\neg\alpha|\beta)\}$. The proof will be given later. Figure 2 shows the three constraints imposed by the conditional desire $D(u \vee d|udcr)$. An arrow $\omega \to \nu$ represents the constraint $\pi(\omega) > \pi(\nu)$.

The principle of CP, though simple and reasonable, is still insufficient for drawing some conclusions we would normally draw from conditional desire sentences. Consider the sentence $D(d)$ "I desire to remain dry" in the original umbrella story. If this were truly the only desire we have, we should prefer every situation in which we are dry to any in which we are wet. No other consideration can get into conflict with this ramification. This conclusion is not sanctioned in the semantics considered thus far. For example we would not be able to deduce that the situation in which we are dry with the umbrella is preferred to the situation in which we are wet without the umbrella. The reason is that $D(d)$ does not impose any constraints between worlds that do not agree on any of the other propositions u, c or r. Although we do not want to deduce constraints between u and $\neg u$ worlds from the sole expression of the desirability of d, we would still want to be able to deduce a preference for d-worlds over $\neg d$-worlds by default if it is consistent to do so. This discussion suggests that in normal discourse we enforce additional constraints which are implicit in our reasoning. One such constraint is the principle of *maximal indifference*.

2.3 The Principle of Maximal Indifference

In [Goldszmidt, 1992] a distinguished ranking, the κ^+ ranking, was selected from among the admissible belief rankings. The κ^+ belief ranking assumes that every situation is as normal as possible, reflecting the principle of maximal ignorance. In the case of preferences the principle that we want to adopt is the principle of maximal indifference. We want to assume that there is no preference between two worlds unless compelled to be so by preferences that are explicated by the reasoning agent. From the set of admissible preference rankings we want to select a distinguished ranking which best capture the essence of the principle of maximal indifference. This ranking, the π^+ preference ranking, will minimize the difference in the preference ranks.

Definition 3 (The π^+ ranking) *Let D be a set of consistent set of conditional desires and let Π be the set of admissible rankings relative to D. A π^+ ranking is an admissible ranking that is **most compact**, that is*

Table 1: Two most compact rankings

Worlds	π_1	π_2
abc	$m+2$	$m+2$
$\bar{a}bc$	$m+1$	$m+1$
$a\bar{b}c$	$m+1$	$m+1$
$\bar{a}\bar{b}c$	m	m
$ab\bar{c}$	$m+3$	$m+2$
$\bar{a}b\bar{c}$	$m+2$	$m+1$
$a\bar{b}\bar{c}$	$m+1$	m
$\bar{a}\bar{b}\bar{c}$	m	$m-1$

$$\sum_{\omega,\nu \in \Omega} |\pi^+(\omega) - \pi^+(\nu)| \leq \sum_{\omega,\nu \in \Omega} |\pi(\omega) - \pi(\nu)| \quad (3)$$

for all $\pi \in \Pi$.

The π^+ rankings reflects maximal indifference[2] in the reasoning agent. Consider the extreme case where the set of desires D is empty. Without compactness, all preference rankings are admissible and no conclusions can be drawn. However with compactness we will select the "unique" ranking that ranks all worlds the same. In this way we make definite conclusions about the reasoning agent's lack of preferences among worlds.

In the umbrella example, if we have the sole desire $D(d)$ then the π^+ rankings are

$$\pi^+(\omega) = \begin{cases} m+1 & \text{if } \omega \models d \text{ and} \\ m & \text{otherwise.} \end{cases} \quad (4)$$

where m is an integer. These preference rankings allow us to conclude that all worlds that satisfy d are preferred over all worlds that do not.

Although the π^+ ranking is unique in the above umbrella example it is not so in general. Consider the set $D = \{D(a|c), D(b|c), D(a|\neg c), D(a \wedge b|\neg c), D(a \vee \neg b|\neg c)\}$. The first two conditional desires impose the constraints

$$\pi(abc) > \pi(\bar{a}bc) > \pi(\bar{a}\bar{b}c)$$
$$\pi(abc) > \pi(\bar{a}bc) > \pi(\bar{a}\bar{b}c)$$

and the last three conditional desires dictate

$$\pi(ab\bar{c}) > \pi(a\bar{b}\bar{c}) > \pi(\bar{a}b\bar{c}) > \pi(\bar{a}\bar{b}\bar{c}).$$

Table 1 shows two admissible preference rankings of D. The sum of difference in ranks for both π_1 ad π_2 is 68 and that is the minimum sum achievable subject to the constraints. Therefore both π_1 ad π_2 are π^+ preference rankings of D.

---
[2] An alternative interpretation of maximal indifference can be developed whereby the distance $\pi(\omega) - \pi(\nu)$ cannot be reduced without either violating admissibility or increasing the difference between some other pair of worlds.

This is a simple and small example and the π^+ ranking can be easily computed. In the general case the conditional desires introduce a set of linear constraints between worlds of the form $\pi(\omega) - \pi(\nu) > 0$. The problem of finding the most compact preference ranking can be modeled as a nonlinear programming programming problem; minimizing

$$\sum_{\omega,\nu \in \Omega} |\pi(\omega) - \pi(\nu)|$$

subject to linear constraints of the form

$$\pi(\omega) - \pi(\nu) > 0.$$

There is no known efficient algorithm for solving the general nonlinear programming problem. However it is quite possible that this optimization problem is tractable for a restricted sublanguage of conditional preferences.

3 Evaluation of Preferences

3.1 The Role of Normality Defaults

So far we have paid no attention to normality defaults and this might lead us to counterintuitive behavior. Consider the preference query, "given that it is cloudy and raining, would you prefer to have an umbrella", $(cr, u \succ \neg u)$? If we have the sole desire $D(d)$ then we will certainly want to confirm the query despite the unlikely possibilities of remaining dry without the umbrella or being wet with the umbrella. Unless the knowledge base categorically excludes such scenarios as impossible, the semantics thus far will prevent us from the commonsensical conclusion to carry an umbrella. The purpose of normality defaults in the knowledge base is to identify such scenarios as unlikely. What we need is a system that on the one hand will keep esoteric situations as possibilities (just in case they become a reality) and on the other hand not let them interfere with mundane decision making. To disregard the unlikely scenarios, we compute the "believability" or likelihood of the worlds after the execution of actions, σ_i (u and $\neg u$ in this example) given some context, ϕ (cr in this example) and focus only on the worlds that are believable. An example of such a belief model is described in [Pearl, 1993][3]. We will assume that the output of this model is a belief ranking κ on worlds. We will write $\kappa(\phi; \sigma_i)$ to represent the ranking that results after the executing σ_i given context, ϕ. $\kappa^0(\phi; \sigma_i)$ will represent the set of believable worlds, namely the set of worlds for which $\kappa(\phi; \sigma_i) = 0$.

3.2 From Preferences on Worlds to Preferences on Sets

In a framework that tolerates imprecision and uncertainty, the consequence of the execution of an action

---

[3] In [Pearl, 1993] the computation of the post-action beliefs requires the use of a causal model.

may not be a specific world but a set of believable worlds. Thus to confirm a preference query we will need to define a preference relation between sets of worlds for example worlds in which we have an umbrella and worlds in which we do not have an umbrella. The straightforward approach would be to say that a set W (of believable worlds) is preferred over another set V if every world in W is preferred over any world in V. This criterion however is too restrictive. Consider the case where we have worlds u, v and w with ranks 0, 1 and 2 respectively. Let $W = \{u, v, w\}$ and $V = \{u, v\}$. In this example, the common possibilities u and v ensure that there is at least a world (u) in W that is not strictly preferred to a world (v) in V and vice versa. Therefore we are unable to determine any preference between the two sets because of the common possibility. However W offers all the possibilities that are available in V and in addition provides an additional possibility that is "better" than what is currently available in V. Intuitively we ought to prefer W to V.

Another consideration in determining the preferences between sets of worlds is the likelihoods of the worlds. This is the theme in Bayesian decision theory where the expected utilities, the sum of the utilities weighted by their corresponding probabilities, are compared and the set with the largest expected utility is preferred. Unfortunately the basic assumption of this paper was that the numeric probabilities and utilities are not available; what we have are order-of-magnitude approximations of probabilities and utilities which are expressed as normality defaults and conditional desires. Pearl in [Pearl, 1993] proposed an order of magnitude of abstraction of the maximum expected utility criterion. There are two problems with the proposal. An assumption in the proposal is that the scale of the abstraction of preferences is the same as the scale of the abstraction of beliefs. While this assumption could conceivably be valid when the utility ranks are explicitly specified, it is not justifiable when beliefs and preferences are specified in terms of normality defaults and conditional desires. The other problem is that the conclusions of the system are not invariant under a lateral shift of worlds along the preference scale (a linear translation of the utility ranking). The utility rankings, π and $\pi + 1$ may admit different conclusions in the system. This is problematic in our framework because lateral shifts of admissible preference rankings are always admissible since conditional desires impose only interval constraints among worlds. In this paper we take into account the likelihoods of the worlds by comparing worlds only when they have the same belief ranks of 0. All worlds of the same degree are considered to be equally believable.

In summary, when determining the preference between two sets, we will assume that the worlds in both sets are equally believable and will consider separately three types of worlds characterizing the compared set:

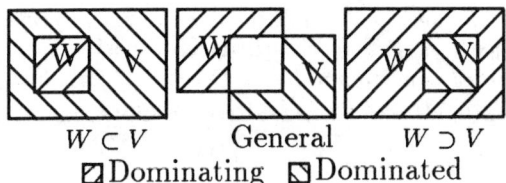

$W \subset V$ General $W \supset V$
⊡ Dominating ⊠ Dominated

Figure 3: Interesting cases for $W \succ_\pi V$

Table 2: Rankings in the umbrella example

Worlds ω	Preference ranking $\pi^+(\omega)$	Belief ranking $\kappa(\omega)$
$udcr$	$m+1$	0
$\bar{u}dcr$	$m+1$	>0
$u\bar{d}cr$	m	>0
$\bar{u}\bar{d}cr$	m	0
$udc\bar{r}$	$m+1$	>0
$\bar{u}dc\bar{r}$	$m+1$	>0
$u\bar{d}c\bar{r}$	m	>0
$\bar{u}\bar{d}c\bar{r}$	m	>0

the common possibilities, the additional possibilities and the excluded possibilities. Let us consider when we will prefer the set W over the set V (see figure 3) by imagining that the set V represents the possibilities that are currently available to us and the set W represents the set of new possibilities. Let us consider the case when $W \subset V$. Since W excludes some possibilities from V we have to compare these excluded possibilities (in $V \setminus W$) with the new possibilities offered by W. If the excluded possibilities are ranked lower than those that remain then W protects us from those excluded possibilities and we should prefer W to V. In the case when $V \subset W$, W provides more possibilities. If these additional possibilities (in $W \setminus V$) are ranked higher than the current possibilities, W provides an opportunity for improvement over the situation in V and again we should prefer W to V. In the general case, if W and V have some possibilities in common, then these common possibilities (in $W \cap V$) can be disregarded from consideration. If the additional possibilities (in $W \setminus V$) are ranked higher than the excluded possibilities (in $V \setminus W$) then we will prefer W to V. This motivates the definition of *preferential dominance*, a preference criterion between sets that depends on whether one set includes or overlaps the other.

Definition 4 (Preferential Dominance) *Let W and V be two subsets of Ω and let π be a preference ranking. We say that W π-dominates V, written $W \succ_\pi V$, if and only if $W \neq V$ and*

1. $\pi_*(W) > \pi^*(V \setminus W)$ *when* $W \subset V$ *or*

2. $\pi_*(W \setminus V) > \pi^*(V)$ *when* $W \supset V$ *or*

3. $\pi_*(W \setminus V) > \pi^*(V \setminus W)$ *otherwise.*

In figure 3, W π-dominates V, (written $W \succ_\pi V$), if the worlds in the dominating set are preferred over the worlds in the dominated set. Consider the example where we have the worlds u, v and w with preference ranks 0, 1 and 2 respectively. Let $W = \{u, w\}$ and $V = \{u, v\}$. In determining the preference between W and V, the common possibility u is disregarded and $\pi_*(W \setminus V) = 2 > \pi^*(V \setminus W) = 1$. Therefore $W \succ_\pi V$.

3.3 Preferential Entailment

Let us consider the preference query "would you prefer σ_1 over σ_2 given ϕ?". In evaluating this query, we condition our beliefs on the context ϕ and compute the rankings that result after executing σ_i. To confirm the preference query $(\phi, \sigma_1 \succ \sigma_2)$, we compare the set of believable worlds resulting from executing σ_1 given ϕ with those resulting from executing σ_2 given ϕ, and test if the former *preferentially dominates* the latter in all the most compact preference rankings.

Definition 5 (Preferential Entailment) *Let D be a set of conditional desires and κ be some belief ranking on Ω. ϕ preferentially entails $\sigma_1 \succ \sigma_2$ given $\langle D, \kappa \rangle$, written $\phi \hspace{0.2em}\mid\hspace{-0.5em}\sim (\sigma_1 \succ \sigma_2)$, if and only if*

$$\kappa^0(\phi; \sigma_1) \succ_{\pi^+} \kappa^0(\phi; \sigma_2)$$

for all π^+ rankings of D.

Example
Let us reconsider the umbrella story where we need to verify the preference query "would you prefer to have the umbrella given that it is cloudy", $(c; u \succ \neg u)$? We have four atomic propositions, u - have umbrella, d - dry, c - cloudy and r - rain. Let us assume that we have the normality defaults, $\Delta = \{u \to d, r \wedge \neg u \to \neg d, c \to r\}$ and one unconditional desire, $D = \{D(d)\}$. For this example we will adopt the belief model in [Goldszmidt, 1992, Pearl, 1993]. First we process the defaults set Δ to get the resulting belief rankings $\kappa(\omega)$. Next, table 2 lists the possible worlds, given that it is cloudy, and gives the belief ranking $\kappa(\omega)$ and the π^+ preference ranking, where m is some fixed integer. $\kappa^0(c; u) = \{udcr\}$ and has rank $m+1$ while $\kappa^0(c; \neg u) = \{\bar{u}\bar{d}cr\}$ with rank m. Therefore the preference query $(c; u \succ \neg u)$ is confirmed.

4 Quantified Conditional Desires

A typical reasoning agent may have many desires. She may desire to be alive, $D(a)$, desire to be dry, $D(d)$ and also desire not to carry an umbrella, $D(\neg u)$. These

Table 3: Preference Rankings, π_1 and π_2

Worlds, ω	$\pi_1(\omega)$	$\pi_2(\omega)$
ab	2	2
$\bar{a}b$	0	1
$a\bar{b}$	1	1
$\bar{a}\bar{b}$	0	0

desires are not perceived as being equally important; being alive is more important than being dry and being dry is probably more important than not carrying an umbrella. In the specification language described so far there is no mechanism for indicating the varying degrees of preference. Let us examine the importance of having such degrees.

Suppose, in the umbrella example, that we have the desire $D_1(\neg u)$ in addition to the desire $D_2(d)$. These desires are quantified by a number indicating the strength of the preference. The strength of the desire to be dry is 2 which is stronger than the strength of the desire not to have the umbrella. In this case we will still expect the reasoning agent to confirm the preference query $(c; u \succ \neg u)$ as before. However, in the flat system where there is no consideration for the strength of the preferences, the constraints imposed by the two desires would yield

$$\pi^+(\omega) = \begin{cases} m+1 & \text{if } \omega \models d \wedge \neg u \text{ and} \\ m-1 & \text{if } \omega \models \neg d \wedge u \text{ and} \\ m & \text{otherwise} \end{cases}$$

as the most compact ranking. Now $\kappa^0(c; u)$ has the single world $udcr$ while $\kappa^0(c; \neg u)$ has the single world $\bar{u}dcr$, both of rank m. This means that we are unable to confirm the obvious fact that one should carry an umbrella on a cloudy day, $(c; u \succ \neg u)$.

The unquantified specification language is also not expressive enough to express all possible preferences. Consider the preference rankings, π_1 and π_2, shown in table 3. For any set of conditional desires, π_2 is admissible whenever π_1 is admissible because the language does not allow us to impose a constraint between $a\bar{b}$ and $\bar{a}b$. Furthermore π_2 is more compact than π_1 because $\sum |\pi_1(\omega) - \pi_1(\nu)| = 7 > \sum |\pi_2(\omega) - \pi_2(\nu)| = 6$. Therefore π_1 cannot be the π^+ ranking for any set of conditional desires. This means that if π_1 represents our preferences among worlds, there is no way we can express these preferences exactly in terms of conditional desires alone.

To alleviate these weaknesses we extend the syntax of the specification language by quantifying a conditional desire with an integer ϵ which indicates the strength of the desire. A *quantified* conditional desire is a preference expression of the form $D_\epsilon(\alpha|\beta)$, where ϵ is an integer, read: "Given β, α is preferred to $\neg\alpha$ by ϵ".

Definition 6 (Quantified Admissibility) *Let D be a set of quantified conditional desires. A preference ranking π is said to be* **admissible** *with respect to a quantified conditional desire $D_\epsilon(\alpha|\beta)$ if for all $\omega \models \beta$, $\nu \in C_\alpha(\alpha, \omega)$ and $\nu' \in C_{\neg\alpha}(\alpha, \omega)$ implies*

$$\pi(\nu) \geq \pi(\nu') + \epsilon. \qquad (5)$$

A preference ranking is **admissible** *with respect to D if it is admissible with respect to all desires in D.*

An unquantified conditional desire is assumed to have a default degree of $\epsilon = 1$.

Example with multiple desires

Let us reconsider the umbrella example assuming that we have two desires $D_2(d)$ and $D_1(\neg u)$. The degrees of these desires indicate that the desire to remain dry is more important by an order of magnitude than the discomfort of carrying an umbrella. The most compact preference ranking in this case is

$$\pi^+(\omega) = \begin{cases} m+3 & \text{if } \omega \models d \wedge \neg u \text{ and} \\ m+2 & \text{if } \omega \models d \wedge u \text{ and} \\ m+1 & \text{if } \omega \models \neg d \wedge \neg u \text{ and} \\ m & \text{otherwise} \end{cases}$$

The believable worlds are $\kappa^0(c; u) = \{udcr\}$ with rank $m + 2$ and $\kappa^0(c; \neg u) = \{\bar{u}dcr\}$ with rank $m + 1$. This confirms the obvious conclusion $(c; u \succ \neg u)$ (with degree 1) which remain unsettled in the flat system.

Now we want to show that the quantified language is powerful enough to express all possible preference ranking.

Definition 7 (Conditional Desires of π) *Given a preference ranking π, the* **conditional desires** *entailed by π is the set $D^\pi = \{D(\alpha|\beta) \mid \pi \text{ is admissible with respect to } D(\alpha|\beta)\}$.*

We note that if a preference ranking π is admissible with respect to D_1 and D_2 then π is admissible with respect to $D_1 \cup D_2$. This means that π is admissible with respect to D^π and D^π is the largest set that has π as an admissible preference ranking.

Theorem 1 (Uniqueness) *Let π and μ be preference rankings. If μ is admissible with respect to D^π then*

$$\mu = \pi + k$$

for some constant integer k.

In other words two preference rankings entail the same set of conditional desires if and only if one is a lateral shift of the other.

Corollary 1 (Sufficiency of the Language) *For all preference rankings, π, there exists a set of quantified conditional desires, Π, such that π is the most compact ranking admissible with respect to Π. In fact π is unique up to a linear translation.*

If our preferences among worlds are represented by a preference ranking, then the sufficiency corollary tells us that our preferences may be completely specified by a set of quantified conditional desires.

One significant point to note is that the proof of the sufficiency corollary makes use of conditional desires that have negative degrees. This is somewhat unfortunate as conditional desires with negative degrees are not particularly intuitive. Another way of augmenting the expressiveness of the specification language is to allow for conditional preferences of the form $\alpha \succ \beta \mid \gamma$, "if γ then α is preferred to β". This will not be considered here.

Another problem with the ceteris paribum semantics is that it does not handle specificity of conditional preferences very well. For example the conditional desires $\{D(\alpha|\beta), D(\neg\alpha|\beta')\}$ is inconsistent whenever $\beta \supset \beta'$.

Theorem 2 (Specificity) *If α, β and β' are wffs and $\beta \supset \beta'$ then $\{D(\alpha|\beta), D(\neg\alpha|\beta')\}$ is inconsistent.*

In normal discourse, we have no difficulty accommodating general expressions of preferences which are subsequently qualified in more specific scenarios. For example I desire to be alive, $D(a)$, yet I am willing to die for some noble cause, $D(\neg a|c)$. In such a situation $D(\neg a|c)$, having a more specific condition, overrides the former unconditional desire, $D(a)$. Such other desirable behavior is sanctioned by a more recent interpretation of conditional desires which further weakens the CP semantics [Tan and Pearl, 1994].

5 Comparison with Related Work

Verification of the assertability of conditional ought statements of the form "you ought to do A if C" is considered in [Pearl, 1993]. The conditional ought statement is interpreted as "if you observe, believe or know C then the expected utility resulting from doing A is much higher than that resulting from not doing A". The treatment in [Pearl, 1993] assumed that a complete specification of a utility ranking on worlds is available and that the scale of the abstraction of preferences is the same as the scale of the abstraction of beliefs. Another problem is that the conclusions of the system is not invariant under a lateral shift of the utility ranking; for example utility rankings π_1 and π_2, where $\pi_2(\omega) = \pi_1(\omega) + 1$, may admit different conclusions; which endows special status to worlds toward which one is indifferent.

Goal expressions were given preference semantics in [Wellman and Doyle, 1991] while relative desires were considered in [Doyle et al., 1991]. These accounts are similar to our semantics for unquantified unconditional desires. However their treatment of conditional preferences (called restricted relative desires) of the form "given γ, α is preferred over β" is problematic. In particular the semantics forces us to conclude that we must be indifferent[4] to the inevitable. This fatalistic view shows itself in a theorem: "you must be indifferent to α, given α". Thus if you discovered that your car has been stolen then you must be indifferent to it. While some may subscribe to such a fatalistic attitude, our semantics here is more optimistic.

In [Boutilier, 1993], expressions of conditional preferences of the form "$I(\alpha|\beta)$ - if β then ideally α", are given modal logic semantics in terms of a preference ordering on possible worlds. $I(\alpha|\beta)$ is interpreted as "in the most preferred worlds where β holds, α holds as well". This interpretation places constraints *only* on the most preferred β-worlds, allowing only β-worlds that also satisfy α to have the same "rank". This contrasts with our ceteris paribum semantics which places constraints between pairs of worlds. In discussing the reasoning from preference expressions to actual preferences (preference query in our paper) Boutilier [Boutilier, 1993] suggests that the techniques in default reasoning (for handling irrelevance in particular) could be similarly applied to preferential reasoning. For example he suggests that worlds could be assumed to be as preferred or as ideal as possible which parallels the assumption made in computing the κ^+ belief ranking [Goldszmidt, 1992], that worlds are as normal as possible. While it is intuitive to assume that worlds would gravitate towards normality because abnormality is a monopolar scale, it is not at all clear that worlds ought to be as preferred as possible since preference is a bipolar scale. In our proposal there is no preference for either end of the bipolar preference scale. The π^+ rankings actually compacts the worlds away from the extremes thus minimizing unjustified preferences. The difference can be seen in the example shown in table 1. The compactness criterion selects two distinguished compact preference rankings π_1 and π_2. If worlds are assumed to be as preferred as possible then π_1 would be the sole distinguished preference ranking. It remains to be seen if the I operator corresponds closely with the common linguistic use of the word "ideally".

In [Pinkas and Loui, 1992] consequence relations are classified according to their boldness (or cautiousness). We may also employ a bolder (or more cautious) entailment principle which would correspond to a risk seeking (or risk averse) disposition.

6 Conclusion

In this paper we describe a framework for specifying preferences in terms of conditional desires of the form "α is desirable if β", to be interpreted as "α is preferred to $\neg\alpha$ when all else is fixed in any β world". We demonstrate how such preference sentences may be in-

---

[4]You are indifferent to α if you desire both α and $\neg\alpha$.

terpreted as constraints on admissible preference rankings of worlds and how they, together with normality defaults, allow a reasoning agent to evaluate queries of the form "would you prefer σ_1 over σ_2 given ϕ" where σ_1 and σ_2 could be either action sequences or observational propositions. We also prove that by extending the syntax to allow for importance-rating of preference sentences, we obtain a language that is powerful enough to represent all possible preferences among worlds. This work is an extension of [Pearl, 1993] and [Doyle et al., 1991].

A Proofs

Lemma 1 (Common Contexts) $\nu \in C(\alpha, \omega) \Rightarrow C(\alpha, \omega) = C(\alpha, \nu)$.

Lemma 2 (Extreme worlds) Let π be a preference ranking and let μ be admissible with respect to D^π. For all contexts C,

$$\pi(\omega) = \max_{\nu \in C} \pi(\nu) \Rightarrow \mu(\omega) = \max_{\nu \in C} \mu(\nu)$$

and

$$\pi(\omega) = \min_{\nu \in C} \pi(\nu) \Rightarrow \mu(\omega) = \min_{\nu \in C} \mu(\nu)$$

Proof: Let $\omega \in C$ and x_i be X_i if $\omega \models X_i$ and $\neg X_i$ otherwise. By lemma 1 we may assume that $C = C(\alpha, \omega)$ for some wff α. Consider $\beta = \bigwedge_{X_i \in S(\alpha)} x_i$. If $\pi(\omega) = \max_{\nu \in C} \pi(\nu)$ then $D_0(\beta|\omega) \in D^\pi$. This implies that $\mu(\omega) \geq \mu(\nu)$ for all $\nu \in C$. Therefore $\pi(\omega) = \max_{\nu \in C} \pi(\nu) \Rightarrow \mu(\omega) = \max_{\nu \in C} \mu(\nu)$. If $\pi(\omega) = \min_{\nu \in C} \pi(\nu)$ then $D_0(\neg\beta|\omega) \in D^\pi$. This implies that $\mu(\omega) \leq \mu(\nu)$ for all $\nu \in C$. So $\pi(\omega) = \min_{\nu \in C} \pi(\nu) \Rightarrow \mu(\omega) = \min_{\nu \in C} \mu(\nu)$. □

Corollary 2 (Extreme worlds) Let π be a preference ranking and let μ be admissible with respect to D^π.

$$\pi(\omega) = \max_{\nu \in \Omega} \pi(\nu) \Rightarrow \mu(\omega) = \max_{\nu \in \Omega} \mu(\nu)$$

and

$$\pi(\omega) = \min_{\nu \in \Omega} \pi(\nu) \Rightarrow \mu(\omega) = \min_{\nu \in \Omega} \mu(\nu)$$

Given a preference ranking, we write ω_* for a world that has the minimum rank and ω^* for a world that has maximum rank.

Lemma 3 (Larger Admissible Differences) Let π be a preference ranking and let μ be admissible with respect to D^π. For all $\omega \in \Omega$,

$$\mu(\omega) - \mu(\omega_*) \geq \pi(\omega) - \pi(\omega_*).$$

Proof: We will prove by induction on m, the number of variables ω and ω_* disagree on. In the base case, if $m = 0$ then $\omega = \omega_*$. Therefore the lemma holds trivially. Let us assume that the lemma holds for $m = 0, \ldots, k-1$. Without loss of generality, we may assume that ω and ω_* disagree on $Y = \{X_1, \ldots, X_k\}$ and that $\omega \models x_i$ for $i = 1, \ldots, m$. If $\pi(\omega) = \pi(\omega_*)$ then the theorem holds by corollary 2. Therefore we may assume that $\pi(\omega) - \pi(\omega_*) > 0$. We consider the context, $C = C(\bigwedge_1^k x_i|\omega)$.

If we can find a world $\nu \sim_{X \setminus X_i} \omega$, $\nu \models \neg x_i$ such that $\pi(\omega) \geq \pi(\nu)$ then let $d = D_{\pi(\omega)-\pi(\nu)}(x_i|\omega) \in D^\pi$ and we also have d implies $\mu(\omega) - \mu(\nu) \geq \pi(\omega) - \pi(\nu)$. Otherwise, let ν be such that $\pi(\nu) = \max_{\nu' \in C} \pi(\nu')$ and $d = D_{\pi(\omega)-\pi(\nu)}(\bigwedge_1^k x_i|\omega) \in D^\pi$. In this case, by lemma 2, we also have d implies $\mu(\omega) - \mu(\nu) \geq \pi(\omega) - \pi(\nu)$. Now clearly, in both cases, $\nu \neq \omega$. This implies, by the induction hypothesis, that $\mu(\nu) - \mu(\omega_*) \geq \pi(\nu) - \pi(\omega_*)$. By adding the two inequalities, we get the desired inequality $\mu(\omega) - \mu(\omega_*) \geq \pi(\omega) - \pi(\omega_*)$. □

Lemma 4 (Smaller Admissible Differences) Let π be a preference ranking and let μ be admissible with respect to D^π. For all $\omega \in \Omega$,

$$\mu(\omega) - \mu(\omega_*) \leq \pi(\omega) - \pi(\omega_*).$$

Proof: For all worlds ω, $D_{\pi(\omega_*)-\pi(\omega)}(\neg\omega) \in D^\pi$. This implies $\mu(\omega) - \mu(\omega_*) \leq \pi(\omega) - \pi(\omega_*)$. □

Theorem 1 (Uniqueness) Let π be a preference ranking. If μ is admissible with respect to D^π then

$$\mu = \pi + k$$

for some constant integer k.

Proof: Lemmas 3 and 4 imply that $\mu = \pi + \mu(\omega_*) - \pi(\omega_*)$. □

Corollary 1 (Sufficiency of the Language) For all preference rankings, π, there exists a set of quantified conditional desires, Π, such that π is the most compact ranking admissible with respect to Π. In fact π is unique up to a linear translation.

Proof: The proof follows when we set Π to be D^π. □

Theorem 2 (Specificity) If α, β and β' are wffs and $\beta \supset \beta'$ then $\{D(\alpha|\beta), D(\neg\alpha|\beta')\}$ is inconsistent.

Proof: (By contradiction) Let us assume that $\{D(\alpha|\beta), D(\neg\alpha|\beta')\}$ is consistent. Let π be an admissible preference ranking, the world ω be such that $\omega \models \beta$ (note that $\omega \models \beta'$ as well since $\beta \supset \beta'$) and $C = C(\neg\alpha, \omega) = C(\alpha, \omega)$. By $D(\alpha|\beta)$ we have $C_\alpha \succ_\pi C_{\neg\alpha}$ and by $D(\neg\alpha|\beta')$ we have $C_{\alpha} \succ_\pi C_{\neg\alpha}$. This is a contradiction. □

Acknowledgements

We would like to thank two anonymous reviewers for their constructive comments and suggestions. The first author is supported in part by a scholarship from the National Computer Board, Singapore. The research was partially supported by Air Force grant #AFOSR 90 0136, NSF grant #IRI-9200918, Northrop Micro grant #92-123, and Rockwell Micro grant #92-122.

References

[Boutilier, 1993] Craig Boutilier. A modal characterization of defeasible deontic conditionals and conditional goals. In *Working Notes of the AAAI Spring Symposium Series*, pages 30–39, Stanford, CA, March 1993.

[Doyle et al., 1991] John Doyle, Yoav Shoham, and Michael P. Wellman. The logic of relative desires. In *Sixth International Symposium on Methodologies for Intelligent Systems*, Charlotte, North Carolina, October 1991.

[Goldszmidt and Pearl, 1992] Moisés Goldszmidt and Judea Pearl. Reasoning with qualitative probabilities can be tractable. In *Proceedings of the 8th Conference on Uncertainty in AI*, pages 112–120, Stanford, 1992.

[Goldszmidt, 1992] Moisés Goldszmidt. *Qualitative Probabilities: A Normative Framework for Commonsense Reasoning*. PhD thesis, University of California Los Angeles, Cognitive Systems Lab., Los Angeles, October 1992. Available as Technical Report (R-190).

[Keeney and Raiffa, 1976] Ralph L. Keeney and Howard Raiffa. *Decisions with Multiple Objectives: Preferences and Value Tradeoffs*. John Wiley, New York, 1976.

[Pearl, 1988] Judea Pearl. *Probabilistic Reasoning in Intelligent Systems*. Morgan Kaufmann, 1988.

[Pearl, 1993] Judea Pearl. From conditional oughts to qualitative decision theory. In *Proceedings of the Ninth Conference on Uncertainty in Artificial Intelligence*, Washington DC, July 1993.

[Pinkas and Loui, 1992] Gadi Pinkas and Ronald P. Loui. Reasoning from inconsistency: A taxonomy of principles for resolving conflict. In *Proceedings of the Third International Conference on Knowledge Representation and Reasoning*, pages 709–719, Cambridge, MA, October 1992.

[Tan and Pearl, 1994] Sek-Wah Tan and Judea Pearl. Specification and evaluation of preferences for planning under uncertainty. In J. Doyle, E. Sandewall, and P. Torasso, editors, *Principles of Knowledge Representation and Reasoning: Proceedings of the Fourth International Conference (KR94)*, Bonn, Germany, 1994. Morgan Kaufmann.

[von Neumann and Morgenstern, 1947] J. von Neumann and O. Morgenstern. *Theory of Games and Economic Behaviour*. Princeton University Press, second edition, 1947.

[von Wright, 1963] Georg Henrik von Wright. *The Logic of Preference*. Edinburgh, 1963.

[Wellman and Doyle, 1991] Michael P. Wellman and Jon Doyle. Preferential semantics for goals. In *Proceedings of the Ninth National Conference on AI*, pages 698–703, Anaheim, CA, 1991.

Making the Difference: A Subtraction Operation for Description Logics

Gunnar Teege
Institut für Informatik, TU München
80290 München, Germany
Email: teege@informatik.tu-muenchen.de

Abstract

We define a new operation in description logics, the difference operation or subtraction operation. This operation allows to remove from a description as much as possible of the information contained in another description. We define the operation independently of a specific description logic. Then we consider its implementation in several specific logics. Finally we describe practical applications of the operation.

1 INTRODUCTION

Description Logics, also called Terminological Logics are a popular formalism for knowledge representation and reasoning. They allow the formation of terms denoting descriptions. A term describes a set of individuals by restricting their properties. Terms are formed using atomic descriptions and a fixed set of term constructors. Usually, the meaning of the terms is given by a denotational semantics. A typical example of a description logic is the concept language of $\mathcal{KRIS}$ [Baader and Hollunder, 1992].

In addition to the constructors, a description logic usually defines a number of basic operations on the terms. The most important operation is the subsumption test which determines whether a description is more general than another one. The conjunction operation returns a description containing the information of all argument terms. It usually corresponds directly to the conjunction constructor. The least common subsumer (lcs) operation, as it is defined by Cohen et. al. [Cohen et al., 1992], returns the most specific description containing information which is common to all argument terms. If the logic includes the disjunction constructor the lcs operation corresponds directly to this constructor.

This paper introduces a new operation on descriptions, the *difference* or *subtraction* operation. Informally, the difference of two descriptions is a description containing all information which is a part of one argument but not a part of the other argument. Although many description logics support the construction of this kind of descriptions, the difference operation has not yet been considered for description logics in general. Exceptions are logics with negation and disjunction, where the difference can be easily defined by the logical complement. Another exception is the BACK language [Peltason et al., 1989]. However, no algorithm is given there.

A related approach is that of distinction measures and commonality measures. These were already investigated for frame-based descriptions and were mainly used to conduct the classification of descriptions into concepts [Tversky, 1988; Ben-Bassat and Zaidenberg, 1984; Moneta et al., 1990]. However, a measure can only give the *size* of the difference between two descriptions (usually in the form of a number), not the difference itself.

In our case, the difference of two descriptions is a description as well. Thus, it can be used in the same way in which any other description is used in the system, e.g., for indexing other information or as argument in subsequent operations. A distinction measure can easily be defined with the help of some information measure on descriptions, by applying this measure to the difference of two descriptions. However, the most interesting application of the description difference is that of removing information from descriptions. For this reason we also call the operation a subtraction operation.

We will consider the application of the difference operation in more detail in Section 4, after investigating the operation itself. In Section 2 we give a formal definition for the difference operation. This definition is applicable to all description logics. In Section 3 we consider the actual construction of the difference, depending on the constructors present in several description logics. Section 5 summarizes our results.

2 THE DIFFERENCE OPERATION IN DESCRIPTION LOGICS

For our formal definition of the difference operation we consider a wide range of description logics. For every description logic we assume a denotational semantics S. Usually, there are three kinds of terms for descriptions.

Concepts are descriptions of objects. The denotational semantics S maps every concept C to a domain subset $S(C)$. *Roles* are descriptions of relations between objects. Semantically, a role R corresponds to a relation $S(R)$ on the domain. Finally, *features* are descriptions of functions between objects. Semantically, a feature f corresponds to a partial function $S(f)$ on the domain. Description logics differ mainly in what kinds of terms they include and in the constructors they allow for each kind.

We do not consider the definition of names for descriptions. The corresponding constructors are often called "terminological axioms". Instead, we define the difference operation as a purely structural operation on two given description terms of the same kind without using any additional context. Unlike a distinction measure, the difference operation returns a term of the description logic. However, the difference is not itself a constructor. It does not add new terms or "completes" the term language in any way. It simply constructs a term using the constructors which are defined in the chosen logic.

2.1 DEFINING THE DIFFERENCE OPERATION

Of course, the expressiveness and usefulness of the difference operation thus depends on the respective description logic. If the term constructors do not allow the expression of subtle differences, the operation will construct only rather coarse difference descriptions. Nevertheless, we give a common formal definition of the difference operation. The definition is independent of the actual description logic. It uses only two properties of the logic: the conjunction operation "$\sqcap$" and the subsumption test "$\sqsupseteq$". These are common to all description logics, at least for concept terms. Semantically, concept conjunction corresponds to set intersection, and concept subsumption, on the other hand, corresponds to the superset relation. Finally, we use the relation "$\equiv$" of semantical equivalence, defined by $D_1 \equiv D_2 :\Leftrightarrow S(D_1) = S(D_2)$.

We now give the definition for the difference operation and afterwards consider some properties which immediately follow from the definition.

Definition 2.1 (Description difference)
*Let $\mathcal{L}$ be a description logic. Let $\sqcap$ denote the conjunction operation in $\mathcal{L}$, let $\sqsupseteq$ denote the subsumption relation in $\mathcal{L}$, and let $\equiv$ denote semantical equivalence in $\mathcal{L}$. Let $A, B \in \mathcal{L}$ be two descriptions in the logic with $A \sqsupseteq B$. Then the **difference** $B - A$ of A and B is defined by*

$$B - A := \max_{\sqsupseteq} \{C \in \mathcal{L} : A \sqcap C \equiv B\}.$$

*We call the set $\{C \in \mathcal{L} : A \sqcap C \equiv B\}$ the **difference candidates** and denote it by $B \ominus A$.*

We define the difference to be the set of most general descriptions in the set $B \ominus A$ of difference candidates. Since $B \in B \ominus A$ holds true for all $A \sqsupseteq B$, there is at least one difference candidate in any case. If the set $B \ominus A$ is finite maximal elements exist and hence the set $B - A$ is never empty. If the number of difference candidates is infinite the set $B \ominus A$ may contain an infinite ascending sequence and there may be no maximal element. However, although it is possible to construct infinite ascending sequences in several description logics, they usually cannot occur as difference candidates for two finite descriptions $A \sqsupseteq B$. Hence we will ignore this case and assume nonempty differences in the rest of the paper.

If in a logic $\mathcal{L}$, all descriptions in $B - A$ are semantically equivalent, the difference is semantically unique and can be implemented as an operation on descriptions. In this case we also write $B - A = C$ for any member C of $B - A$. Since the set $B \ominus A$ is closed with respect to disjunction, the difference is always semantically unique provided the logic $\mathcal{L}$ includes the disjunction constructor and every set of difference candidates contains only finitely many non-equivalent members.

If in a logic $\mathcal{L}$, $B - A$ may contain descriptions which are not semantically equivalent, the difference is not a true operation on descriptions but only a relation. In many practical applications any single maximal description from the set is equally useful as a description of the difference. This is due to the fact that every member of $B - A$ covers in some way the information difference between A and B. If this is sufficient in the application, the difference operation may be implemented as a nondeterministic operation on descriptions. Otherwise the difference operation must be implemented as a set-valued operation. We will address this topic in more detail in the Sections 3 and 4.

Note that $A \sqsupseteq B$ implies A and B to be of the same kind. Since the conjunction is only defined for descriptions of the same kind, the result C must be of this kind as well. Thus, the difference of two concepts is a set of concepts, and that of two features is a set of features.

A simple example of a logic $\mathcal{L}$ is the logic $\mathcal{L}_0$ with only atomic concepts and the conjunction constructor. The terms of this logic are equivalent to atom sets, the conjunction operation is the set union, subsumption is the subset relation, and semantic equivalence is the set equality. It is easy to see that in this logic the difference is semantically unique and a member of $B - A$ is always given by the atom set difference $B \setminus A$. The difference of A and B contains exactly those atoms of B which are missing in A.

2.2 ADDITIONAL REMARKS

2.2.1 Semantics

The definition 2.1 can be motivated as follows. First, every description C in the result contains enough information to yield the information in B if added to A, i.e., it contains all information from B which is missing in A. Second, C is maximally general, i.e., it does not contain any additional unnecessary information.

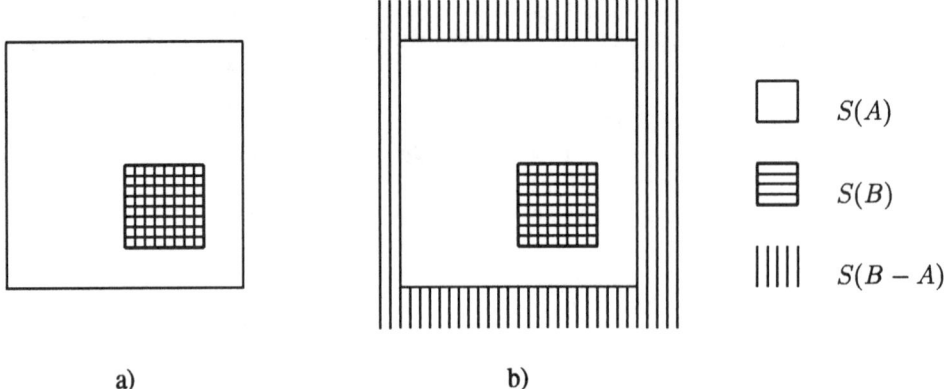

Figure 1: Extreme Cases of the Difference Operation

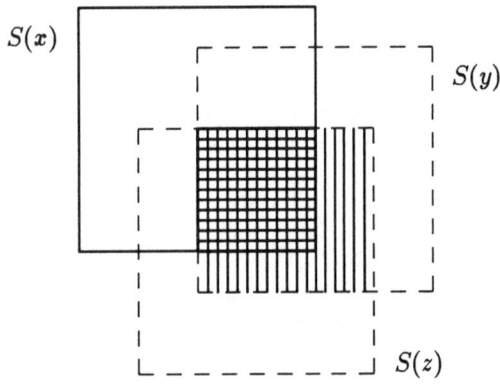

Figure 2: Difference of Concept Atoms

Semantically, the description difference $S(B-A)$ is a maximal domain subset that contains every individual in $S(B)$ and no individual in $S(A) \setminus S(B)$. Thus, there are two extreme possibilities for $S(B-A)$. It may be identical to $S(B)$ or it may be identical to $S(B) \cup (\mathcal{D} \setminus S(A))$, where $\mathcal{D}$ is the domain (see Figure 1). In most description logics, the description difference lies somewhere in between these extremes. Figure 2 depicts the situation in logic $\mathcal{L}_0$ when A is a single atom x and B is the conjunction of three atoms x, y, z.

2.2.2 Roles and Features

Several logics restrict the constructors for roles and features in such a way that a role or feature never subsumes a different one, e.g., the logic allows only atomic roles. In this case our definition only yields the trivial case $A - A := \{A\}$ for roles and features. If, however, the logic allows nontrivial conjunction and subsumption for roles or features the definition yields nontrivial differences for them as well. Semantically, role conjunction and subsumption correspond to the usual set intersection and superset of relations. Feature subsumption corresponds to the "weaker defined" relation of partial functions. Feature conjunction corresponds to the restriction of two partial functions to that part of their common domain where they have identical values.

Since the semantics of the difference for concepts, roles, and features depends on the constructors used in a specific logics, no definitive way of interaction among these three cases can be given in general. Even in specific description logics the interaction is only rather weak. As an example consider the constructor of value-restriction. The term $\forall (R_1 - R_2) : C$ is not equivalent to any term using a difference of concepts. Only the relation $(\forall R_1 : C) - (\forall R_2 : C) \sqsupseteq \forall (R_1 - R_2) : C$ is valid. However, a similar situation arises for other description operations, such as the conjunction. If a role conjunction appears in a value-restriction it cannot be replaced by concept conjunction. Only the relation $\forall (R_1 \sqcap R_2) : C \sqsupseteq (\forall R_1 : C) \sqcap (\forall R_2 : C)$ is valid.

2.2.3 Difference and Lattice Complement

In some description logics, the terms of the same kind form a lattice with respect to subsumption. Whenever this lattice is a *complementary* lattice, our definition of the difference $B - A$ is identical to the definition of the singleton set containing the complement of A relative to B and the top element $\top$, i.e., the unique element C with $\inf(C, A) = B$ and $\sup(C, A) = \top$. This situation is depicted in Figure 3. An example of this case is the logic $\mathcal{L}_0$.

If the lattice is not complementary there may either be no complement of A relative to B and $\top$, or it may not be unique. In the first case our definition of the difference operation implies the use of best approximations to the complement, since it uses the maximality condition in the place of the condition $\sup(C, A) = \top$. In the second case our definition implies the use of all maximal complements.

2.2.4 Difference of Uncomparable Descriptions

Our definition of difference requires that the second argument subsumes the first one. Thus the difference is not defined for arbitrary description pairs. In general, the difference between two incomparable descriptions A and B cannot be given in the form of a single description. A possible solution for this case is to construct a common subsuming description D of A and B, such as a least common subsumer or a disjunction. Then the difference may be given by the two single differences $A - D$ and $B - D$. A similar approach using two descriptions to define the difference between arbitrary descriptions can be found in BACK [Peltason et al., 1989].

3 THE DIFFERENCE OPERATION IN SPECIFIC DESCRIPTION LOGICS

We will now investigate the difference operation in more detail in specific description logics. As usual, we characterize these logics by the set of constructors they allow for descriptions. In Figure 3 we list all constructors we consider besides atomic descriptions. For every constructor its semantics is specified. We use C, C_i for denoting concepts, R, R_i for denoting roles, and f, f_i for denoting features. The domain of the corresponding interpretation is denoted by $\mathcal{D}$. The set of images $\{y \in \mathcal{D} : (x, y) \in S(R)\}$ of a domain element x under a role is denoted by $S(R)(x)$. Analogously $S(f)(x)$ denotes the set of images of x under a feature f. Since features corresponds to partial functions $S(f)(x)$ may either be a singleton or it may be empty.

We assume that every description logic uses at least the concept conjunction constructor.

3.1 NEGATION

Whenever the negation constructor "$\neg$" is part of the logic we can construct the term $\neg(A \sqcap \neg B)$ for arbitrary given terms A, B. Its semantics $S(\neg(A \sqcap \neg B))$ is $(\mathcal{D} \setminus S(A)) \cup S(B)$. This is the extreme case depicted in Figure 1b for the difference $B - A$. Since it is semantically the maximal possible description, it always meets the definition of $B - A$. Furthermore, it is unique up to semantical equivalence. Thus in every logic with the negation constructor we have

$$B - A = \neg(A \sqcap \neg B).$$

However, this case is not very useful in practice. Consider the descriptions "red thing" and "big red car". Using negation, the difference would be equivalent to "big red car or not red" which is mainly a simple repetition of the original descriptions. It cannot be used to remove information syntactically from the more specific one of the two descriptions, since it simply negates the information and hence still contains it syntactically.

For this pragmatic reason, our definition of the difference operation is not suitable in description logics with negation, if we consider the applications described in Section 4. However, the definition can easily be adapted by not using the negation constructor for constructing the result. Formally, this corresponds to the replacement of the semantic equivalence relation "$\equiv$" used in definition 2.1. Instead, the coarser relation has to be used which results from "$\equiv$" by ignoring the semantics of "$\neg$".

3.2 STRUCTURAL DIFFERENCE

In the logic $\mathcal{L}_0$ the difference operation can be implemented in a simple syntactical way by constructing the set difference of subterms (atoms) in a conjunction. We will now generalize this case and give a sufficient condition for logics where the difference operation is always semantically unique and can be implemented in a similar way.

3.2.1 Reduced Clause Form

We can always write a description as a conjunction of clauses. A *clause* is a description which may not be further decomposed into a conjunction in a nontrivial way.

Definition 3.1 (Clause)
Let $\mathcal{L}$ be a description logic. A **clause** in $\mathcal{L}$ is a description A with the following property:

$$A \equiv B \sqcap A' \Rightarrow B \equiv \top \lor B \equiv A$$

Every conjunction $A_1 \sqcap \ldots \sqcap A_n$ of clauses can be represented by the clause set $\{A_1, \ldots, A_n\}$. We call a clause set *reduced* if it does not contain "unnecessary" clauses.

Definition 3.2 (Reduced Clause Form)
Let $\mathcal{L}$ be a description logic and let $A = \{A_1, \ldots, A_n\}$ be a set of clauses in $\mathcal{L}$. The clause set A is **reduced** if either $n = 1$, or no clause subsumes the conjunction of the other clauses:

$$\forall 1 \leq i \leq n : A_i \not\sqsupseteq A \setminus \{A_i\}$$

We call the set A a **reduced clause form** (RCF) of every description $B \equiv A_1 \sqcap \ldots \sqcap A_n$.

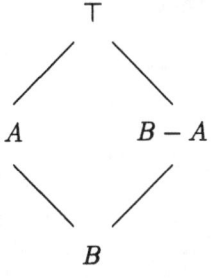

Figure 3: The Difference as Lattice Complement

$$
\begin{array}{ll}
\textbf{Concepts:} & \\
S(C_1 \sqcap \ldots \sqcap C_n) = S(C_1) \cap \ldots \cap S(C_n) & \text{(conjunction)} \\
S(C_1 \sqcup \ldots \sqcup C_n) = S(C_1) \cup \ldots \cup S(C_n) & \text{(disjunction)} \\
S(\neg C) = \mathcal{D} \setminus S(C) & \text{(negation)} \\
S(\top) = \mathcal{D}, S(\bot) = \{\} & \text{(top, bottom)} \\
S(\forall f : C) = \{x \in \mathcal{D} : S(f)(x) \subseteq S(C)\} & \text{(value-restriction)} \\
S(\forall R : C) = \{x \in \mathcal{D} : S(R)(x) \subseteq S(C)\} & \text{(value-restriction)} \\
S(\exists f : C) = \{x \in \mathcal{D} : S(C) \cap S(f)(x) \neq \{\}\} & \text{(exists-restriction)} \\
S(\exists R : C) = \{x \in \mathcal{D} : S(C) \cap S(R)(x) \neq \{\}\} & \text{(exists-restriction)} \\
S(\leq nR) = \{x \in \mathcal{D} : |S(R)(x)| \leq n\} & \text{(atmost-restriction)} \\
S(\geq nR) = \{x \in \mathcal{D} : |S(R)(x)| \geq n\} & \text{(atleast-restriction)} \\
S(f_1 \downarrow f_2) = \{x \in \mathcal{D} : S(f_1)(x) = S(f_2)(x) \neq \{\}\} & \text{(agreement)} \\
S(R_1 \downarrow R_2) = \{x \in \mathcal{D} : S(R_1)(x) = S(R_2)(x)\}\} & \text{(role value map)} \\
\textbf{Roles:} & \\
S(\bot) = \{\} & \text{(bottom)} \\
S(R|C) = \{(x,y) \in S(R) : y \in S(C)\} & \text{(role differentiation)} \\
S(R_1 \circ R_2) = \{(x,y) \in \mathcal{D}^2 : \exists z \in S(R_1)(x) : y \in S(R_2)(z)\} & \text{(role composition)} \\
\textbf{Features:} & \\
S(\bot) = \{\} & \text{(bottom)} \\
S(f_1 \sqcap f_2) = S(f_1) \cap S(f_2) & \text{(conjunction)} \\
S(f_1 \circ f_2) = \{(x,y) \in \mathcal{D}^2 : \exists z \in S(f_1)(x) : y \in S(f_2)(z)\} & \text{(feature composition)}
\end{array}
$$

Figure 4: Usual Constructors in Description Logics and their Semantics

In a reduced clause set no clause can be omitted without changing the semantics of the set, i.e., reduced clause sets do not contain redundant clauses. In particular, no clause may subsume another clause or may be equivalent to another clause. It is easy to see that every description in a description logic is equivalent to at least one reduced clause set. Hence, every description has at least one RCF. However, RCFs are usually not unique.

In the simplest case of two different RCFs for a description A there is a one-to-one mapping of the clauses in one RCF onto equivalent clauses in the other RCF. In this case we call the two clause sets to be *structure equivalent*.

Definition 3.3 (Structure Equivalence)
Let $A = \{A_1, \ldots, A_n\}$ and $B = \{B_1, \ldots, B_m\}$ be reduced clause sets in a description logic $\mathcal{L}$. We say that A and B are **structure equivalent** (denoted by $A \cong B$) iff the following condition is satisfied:

$$n = m \land$$
$$\forall 1 \leq i \leq n \exists 1 \leq j, k \leq n : A_i \equiv B_j \land B_i \equiv A_k$$

If in a description logic for every description all its RCFs are structure equivalent, we say that RCFs are *structurally unique* in that logic.

In many description logics the reduced clause form is a first step for defining a canonical form of descriptions. In a logic with structurally unique RCFs it is often possible to make RCFs unique by eliminating certain kinds of clauses. Typically, this is done by eliminating certain term constructors and by replacing all clauses which use a corresponding outermost constructor by an equivalent clause using a different outermost constructor. In this way a canonical form is defined, e.g., in [Patel-Schneider, 1989].

3.2.2 An Implementation of the Difference Operation

In a description logic with structurally unique RCFs it is relatively straightforward to calculate the difference operation, as it is defined in Definition 2.1. The difference $B - A$ can be calculated by removing all clauses from an RCF for B which are semantically equivalent to a clause in an RCF for A. By "$\setminus_\equiv$" we denote the set difference of clause sets where clauses are compared with the help of the relation "$\equiv$". We call the operation $B \setminus_\equiv A$ the *structural difference* operation.

Theorem 3.1
Let $\mathcal{L}$ be a description logic with structurally unique RCFs. Let $A, B \in \mathcal{L}$ be descriptions given by their RCFs with $A \sqsupseteq B$. Then the difference $B - A$ is semantically unique and is given by the structural difference:

$$B - A = B \setminus_\equiv A.$$

Proof:
Let $B' := B \setminus_\equiv A$ be the set of clauses in B for which there is no semantically equivalent clause in A. B' is a difference candidate in $B \ominus A$, since the union of the clause sets B' and A is an RCF of $A \sqcap B'$ and it is structure equivalent to B. Hence we have to prove that B' is maximal in $B \ominus A$.

Let $C \in B - A$ be a member of the difference $B - A$ such that C is in RCF. The conjunction $A \sqcap C$ must be equivalent to B. We can construct a reduced clause set $B'' \equiv A \sqcap C$ by uniting the clause sets A and C and by eliminating all redundant clauses from this union. Since RCFs are structurally unique, B'' is an RCF of $A \sqcap C$, and B'' must be structure equivalent to B. Accordingly, for every clause in B' there must be an equivalent clause in B''. Since no clause in B' has an equivalent clause in A, all these clauses must have been in C. Since C is a maximal member in $B \ominus A$ it may not contain any additional clauses for which there is no equivalent clause in B'. Thus we have $C \cong B'$, i.e., B' is maximal in $B \ominus A$ and every maximal element of $B \ominus A$ is structure equivalent to B'. □

Note that the implementation of the difference operation by the structural difference directly depends on an implementation of the semantic equivalence relation "$\equiv$". In general, the semantic equivalence in description logics can be intractable or it can even be undecidable [Donini et al., 1991b; Donini et al., 1991a; Schmidt-Schauß, 1989]. If, on the other hand, the subsumption in a description logic is tractable or decidable, the same holds true for the structural difference, respectively. Here, however, we do not investigate the complexity of the difference operation any further.

3.2.3 Structural Subsumption

Next we will show that the property of a "structural subsumption" is a sufficient condition for a description logic to have structurally unique RCFs. This will provide us with a number of examples of logics which have this property.

Whenever two descriptions A, B are given by their RCFs, the subsumption $A \sqsupseteq B$ may be tested by testing the clauses of A separately:

$$\{A_1, \ldots, A_n\} \sqsupseteq \{B_1, \ldots, B_m\} \Leftrightarrow$$
$$\forall 1 \leq i \leq n : A_i \sqsupseteq \{B_1, \ldots, B_m\}$$

However, in general it is not possible to test the clauses of B separately. A logic in which it is possible to determine subsumption by testing the clauses of B separately is said to have a *structural subsumption*.

Definition 3.4 (Structural Subsumption)
Let $\mathcal{L}$ be a description logic. We say that the subsumption relation in $\mathcal{L}$ is **structural** iff for any clause $A \in \mathcal{L}$ and any description $B = B_1 \sqcap \ldots \sqcap B_m \in \mathcal{L}$ which is given by its RCF the following is valid:

$$A \sqsupseteq B \Leftrightarrow \exists 1 \leq i \leq m : A \sqsupseteq B_i$$

Informally, in a logic with structural subsumption, the subsumption test can always be reduced to subsumption tests of single clauses. The term "structural subsumption" has been introduced informally by Patel-Schneider in [Patel-Schneider, 1989]. A formal definition has been given in [Cohen et al., 1992]. However, there it was defined in respect to a canonical form and it was formulated with the help of outermost constructors. Our definition with the help of RCFs is more general, since it does not require the existence of a canonical form.

Logics with a structural subsumption have several interesting properties. In [Patel-Schneider, 1989] the structural subsumption was an important basis for proving that calculating the subsumption relation was tractable in that logic. However, a structural subsumption does not necessary imply tractability. Either the tractability can be prevented by the complexity of the clauses, or the canonization procedure may exponentially increase the size of the descriptions.

In [Cohen et al., 1992] it was shown that the least common subsumer operation can be calculated in an easy "structural" way in a logic with structural subsumption. With the help of the next theorem we get a similar result for the difference operation. The theorem states that every description logic with a structural subsumption has structurally unique RCFs.

Theorem 3.2
Let $\mathcal{L}$ be a description logic with a structural subsumption. Let A and B be two reduced clause sets in $\mathcal{L}$. Then the following property holds true:

$$A \equiv B \Rightarrow A \cong B$$

Proof:
As usual, semantic equivalence can be expressed with the help of two subsumption relations: $A \equiv B \Leftrightarrow A \sqsupseteq B \wedge B \sqsupseteq A$. The structuralness of the subsumption relation implies that every clause in A subsumes a clause in B and vice versa. Additionally, the fact that A and B are RCFs implies that a clause B_i always subsumes the same clause A_j by which it is subsumed, and hence it is equivalent to it. Otherwise we had $A_k \sqsupseteq B_i \sqsupseteq A_j$, i.e., the clause set A is not reduced since the clause A_k subsumes the clause A_j. Analogously we can show that for every clause in A there must be an equivalent clause in B. □

Cohen et. al. give several examples of description logics with a structural subsumption. These are Krypton [Brachman et al., 1983], Kandor [Patel-Schneider, 1984], Meson [Edelman and Owsnicki, 1986], Entity-Situation [Bergamaschi et al., 1988], CLASSIC (without the SAME-AS constructor) [Borgida et al., 1989], and the logic of [Patel-Schneider, 1989].

We give another example of a description logic with structurally unique RCFs. We denote it by $\mathcal{L}_1$. The logic $\mathcal{L}_1$ allows atoms for concepts, roles, and features, together with the following constructors:

- $\sqcap, \sqcup, \top, \bot, (\exists R : C), (\exists f : C), (\geq nR)$ for concepts,
- $\bot, \circ, |$ for roles,
- $\bot, \circ$ for features.

Theorem 3.3
Subsumption in the logic $\mathcal{L}_1$ is structural.

Proof:
We give only a shortened proof which uses several state-

ments of equivalence and non-decomposability of terms. All these statements, however, can easily be proved with the help of the semantics of the term constructors as it is specified in Figure 3.

The case for roles and features is trivial, since $\mathcal{L}_1$ does not include conjunction constructors for them.

For concepts, we can use the equivalences $(\exists R : C) \equiv (\geq 1R|C)$ and $(\exists f_1 \circ f_2 : C) \equiv (\exists f_1 : \exists f_2 : C)$ to eliminate exists-restriction for roles and composition for features. Additionally we can eliminate some cases of the disjunction, of the exists-restriction for features and of the atleast-restriction for roles with the help of the equivalences $C \sqcup \top \equiv \top$, $C \sqcup \bot \equiv C$, $\exists \bot : C \equiv \exists f : \bot \equiv \bot$, $\geq n\bot \equiv \bot$ and $\geq 0R \equiv \top$.

Next we characterize clauses among the remaining terms. $\top$ is always a clause. In $\mathcal{L}_1$ there is no incoherent concept besides $\bot$, hence $\bot$ is a clause. Since there is no negation in $\mathcal{L}_1$ all atomic concepts are clauses. A disjunction can be decomposed with the help of the equivalence $C_1 \sqcup (C_2 \sqcap C_3) \equiv (C_1 \sqcup C_2) \sqcap (C_1 \sqcup C_3)$ if one of its arguments is a conjunction. No decomposition is possible in the remaining cases of the arguments, hence $C_1 \sqcup C_2$ is a clause if C_1 and C_2 are clauses. An exists-restriction of an atomic feature can be decomposed with the help of the equivalence $\exists f : C_1 \sqcap C_2 \equiv (\exists f : C_1) \sqcap (\exists f : C_2)$ if the concept argument is a conjunction. No decomposition is possible in the remaining cases of the concept argument, hence $\exists f : C$ is a clause if f is an atom and C is a clause. An atleast-restriction $\geq nR$ cannot be decomposed.

For characterizing the subsumption relation between atleast-restrictions we use the following form of roles. Using the equivalences $(R_1 \circ R_2)|C \equiv R_1 \circ (R_2|C)$, $(R|C_1)|C_2 \equiv R|(C_1 \sqcap C_2)$, and the associativity of the role composition, every role which is not equivalent to $\bot$ can be represented by a term of the form $(R_1|C_1) \circ \ldots \circ (R_n|C_n)$ where the R_i are role atoms and the C_i are coherent concepts.

Let A be a concept clause and let $B = \{B_1, \ldots, B_n\}$ be a reduced clause set with $A \sqsupseteq B$. We prove

$(*) \quad \exists 1 \leq i \leq n : A \sqsupseteq B_i$

by induction over the structure of A and B.

If $n = 1$ we have nothing to prove. If any B_i is equivalent to $\top$ or $\bot$ the clause set B must be a singleton for being reduced, hence these cases are included. If $A \equiv \top$ then A subsumes every clause, in particular those in B.

Let $A = C_1 \sqcup C_2$. Then $A \sqsupseteq B \Leftrightarrow C_1 \sqsupseteq B \lor C_2 \sqsupseteq B$. By induction we get $\exists 1 \leq i,j \leq n : C_1 \sqsupseteq B_i \lor C_2 \sqsupseteq B_j$ which implies $(*)$ since $A \sqsupseteq C_1 \land A \sqsupseteq C_2$.

Let $i \leq n$ be an index such that $B_i = B' \sqcup B''$ and let $\hat{B} := B \setminus \{B_i\}$. Then $A \sqsupseteq B \Leftrightarrow A \sqsupseteq (\{B'\} \cup \hat{B}) \sqcup (\{B''\} \sqcap \hat{B}) \Leftrightarrow A \sqsupseteq (\{B'\} \sqcap \hat{B}) \land A \sqsupseteq (\{B''\} \sqcap \hat{B})$. By induction we get $(A \sqsupseteq B' \land A \sqsupseteq B'') \lor \exists b \in \hat{B} : A \sqsupseteq b$ which implies $(*)$ since $(A \sqsupseteq B' \land A \sqsupseteq B'') \Leftrightarrow A \sqsupseteq B_i$.

In the remaining cases all clauses must be concept atoms, exists-restrictions, or atleast-restrictions. Hence, every clause is characterized by a distinct concept atom or feature atom or by a sequence of distinct role atoms. Since in $\mathcal{L}_1$ there are no constructs for defining concepts, all atoms are primitive and can be interpreted arbitrarily by the semantics. This implies $A \sqsupseteq B \Leftrightarrow A \sqsupseteq B \setminus \{B_i\}$ for every B_i which is characterized by other atoms than A. Hence in the remaining cases all clauses in B are characterized by the same atoms which characterize A.

Let A be a concept atom. Then B may contain only this atom and we have nothing to prove. Let $A = \exists f : C$. Then $B_i = \exists f : C_i$ for all clauses in B, $B \equiv \exists f : C_1 \sqcap \ldots \sqcap C_n$, and $A \sqsupseteq B \Leftrightarrow C \sqsupseteq C_1 \sqcap \ldots \sqcap C_n$. By induction we get $\exists 1 \leq i \leq n : C \sqsupseteq C_i$ which implies $(*)$. Let $A = (\geq p(R_1|\bar{C_1}) \circ \ldots \circ (R_m|C_m))$. Then $B_i = (\geq p_i(R_{i1}|C_{i1}) \circ \ldots \circ (R_{im}|C_{im}))$ for all clauses in B. The semantics implies that $A \sqsupseteq B \Leftrightarrow \exists 1 \leq i \leq n : p \leq p_i \land C_1 \sqsupseteq C_{i1} \land \ldots \land C_m \sqsupseteq C_{im}$ which implies $(*)$. □

Since in $\mathcal{L}_1$ RCFs are structurally unique, the same holds true for every sublogic of $\mathcal{L}_1$, such as $\mathcal{L}_0$. Hence the difference operation in all sublogics of $\mathcal{L}_1$ can be implemented by the structural difference. In particular, if the agreement constructor is omitted, "feature terms" [Nebel and Smolka, 1990; Dörre and Rounds, 1992; Carpenter, 1992] are a sublogic of $\mathcal{L}_1$.

In logics with structurally unique RCFs, the difference operation yields most detailed results when the terms can be decomposed in a large number of clauses. For example, in $\mathcal{L}_1$ it is crucial whether a description uses features or roles. An exists-restriction $\exists f : C_1 \sqcap \ldots \sqcap C_n$ for a feature with concept atoms C_i can be decomposed in the clauses $\exists f : C_1 \sqcap \ldots \sqcap \exists f : C_n$. Consequently, the difference $(\exists f : C_0 \sqcap \ldots \sqcap C_n) - (\exists f : C_1 \sqcap \ldots \sqcap C_n)$ is equivalent to $\exists f : C_0$. If the feature f is replaced by a role R, the term $\exists R : C_1 \sqcap \ldots \sqcap C_n$ is already a clause and cannot be decomposed. Hence the difference $(\exists R : C_0 \sqcap \ldots \sqcap C_n) - (\exists R : C_1 \sqcap \ldots \sqcap C_n)$ is equivalent to the full first argument $(\exists R : C_0 \sqcap \ldots \sqcap C_n)$.

3.3 LOGICS WITH A NON-STRUCTURAL DIFFERENCE

In this section we will investigate cases where the simple structural difference is no solution for the description difference $B - A$. We will call this situation a *non-structural difference*. We will show that non-structural differences evolve whenever a description has RCFs which are not structure equivalent. Thus, the property of having structurally unique RCFs is not only sufficient but also necessary for implementing the difference operation by the structural difference.

Theorem 3.4
Let $\mathcal{L}$ be a description logic. Let $A \in \mathcal{L}$ be a description in RCF and let $B \in \mathcal{L}$ be another RCF of A with $A \equiv B \land A \not\equiv B$. Then there is a description $C \in \mathcal{L}$ in RCF

with

$$A - C \neq A \setminus_\equiv C.$$

Proof:
Let $x \in B$ be a clause such that there is no equivalent clause in A. Without loss of generality, a clause of this kind must exist in the clause set B if $A \not\equiv B$. Let $C := \{x\}$ be the singleton RCF which contains only this clause. We have to show that there is no description in $A - C$ which is equivalent to $A \setminus_\equiv C$.

Since x is not equivalent to any member of A, $A \setminus_\equiv \{x\}$ is identical with A. On the other hand, $A - \{x\} \equiv B - \{x\}$, since $A \equiv B$. Let $B' := B \setminus \{x\}$. Since $(C \sqcap B') = (\{x\} \cup B') \equiv B$, B' is a difference candidate in $B \ominus C$. Since the set $B - C$ contains all maximal elements of $B \ominus C$ there must be a description B'' in $B - C$ which subsumes the clause set B'. This clause set strictly subsumes B. Since $A - C \equiv B - C$ the description B'' must be a member of $A - C$ as well. Together we have $B'' \sqsupseteq B' \sqsupset B \equiv A \equiv A \setminus_\equiv C$. Hence $A \setminus_\equiv C$ is always strictly subsumed by a member B'' in $A - C$. Since $A - C$ only contains the maximal elements of $A \ominus C$, $A \setminus_\equiv C$ cannot be a member of $A - C$. □

Structurally non-unique RCFs may additionally give rise to non-unique differences. Consider again the two RCFs A and B in Theorem 3.4. There must be a clause $y \in A$ such that there is no equivalent clause in B. Otherwise, the clause x would be redundant. Let $A' := A \setminus \{y\}$ and let $C := \{x, y\}$. Then both A' and B' are difference candidates in $A \ominus C$. Whenever A' and B' have no common subsumer in $A \ominus C$ there must be at least two non-equivalent descriptions in $A - C$, one of them subsuming A' and the other one subsuming B'.

We will now investigate three concrete cases in which structurally non-unique RCFs appear in description logics. The cases are characterized by using certain constructors from the list given in Figure 3 or combinations thereof. Since the cases cover all constructors in the list which are not used in the logic $\mathcal{L}_1$, we thus demonstrate that the constructor set used by $\mathcal{L}_1$ is a maximal set supporting structurally unique RCFs. Any other constructor from the list will introduce structurally non-unique RCFs if it is added to $\mathcal{L}_1$.

3.3.1 Decompositions of $\bot$.

One source of structurally non-unique RCFs are nontrivial decompositions of $\bot$, i.e., incoherent conjunctions of coherent clauses. Whenever there are clauses $A \not\equiv \bot$ and $B \not\equiv \bot$ with $A \sqcap B \equiv \bot$, then $\bot$ is not a clause. In this case there are typically other pairs of coherent clauses A', B' with $A' \sqcap B' \equiv \bot$ which are otherwise unrelated with A and B, i.e., $\{A, B\} \not\equiv \{A', B'\}$. As a consequence there are RCFs for $\bot$ which are not structure equivalent.

The simplest way of decomposing $\bot$ is that using negation. For every coherent clause A which is not equivalent to $\top$ the description $\neg A$ is coherent as well, and the conjunction of both is equivalent to $\bot$. However, we already treated the specific situation in description logics with negation in Section 3.1. Without using negation, the constructors in Figure 3 provide two possibilities of a nontrivial decomposition of $\bot$: combining $\exists$ and $\forall$ and combining $\leq$ and $\geq$.

For features the following equivalence is valid:

$$(\forall f : \bot \sqcap \exists f : \top) \equiv \bot$$

Hence $\bot$ is not a clause in logics which allow both exists-restrictions and value-restrictions for features. If f is a feature atom, the left side of the equivalence is an RCF for $\bot$. If there are arbitrary many feature atoms, $\bot$ has arbitrary many structurally non-equivalent RCFs.

Using this property we can construct differences which are non-structural, and, if the logic does not include disjunction, non-unique. The following case gives an example. Let f_1, f_2, f_3 be distinct feature atoms.

$$(\exists f_3 : \top \sqcap \forall f_3 : \bot) - (\exists f_1 : \top \sqcap \exists f_2 : \top)$$
$$= \{\forall f_1 : \bot, \forall f_2 : \bot\}$$

For roles the following equivalence is valid:

$$(\geq (n+1)R) \sqcap (\leq nR) \equiv \bot$$

If R is a role atom, the left side is an RCF for $\bot$. Note that this equivalence includes cases of exists-restriction and value-restriction for roles, since the following equivalences are valid: $(\exists R : \top) \equiv (\geq 1R)$ and $(\forall R : \bot) \equiv (\leq 0R)$.

Analogous to the case for features we can construct the following situation for a non-structural difference in a logic without disjunction. Let R_1, R_2, R_3 be distinct role atoms and let $n, m, p \geq 0$.

$$(\geq (p+1)R_3) \sqcap (\leq pR_3)$$
$$-(\geq (n+1)R_1) \sqcap (\geq (m+1)R_2)$$
$$= \{(\leq nR_1), (\leq mR_2)\}$$

An informal example of this situation is the difference between "person with at least tree children and at least five friends" and "person with and without a hobby" (or some other incoherent description). This difference is either "person with at most two children" or "person with at most four friends".

Altogether these examples show that none of the constructors $(\forall f : C)$, $(\forall R : C)$, and $(\leq nR)$ can be added to the logic $\mathcal{L}_1$ without the appearance of structurally non-unique RCFs.

Note, however, that the situations described so far can easily be detected, since they always involve a difference $B - A$ where B is an incoherent description equivalent to $\bot$. Hence an algorithm which computes the structural difference can easily be extended to handle these cases as well by testing the coherence of the first argument.

If the first argument of $B - A$ is incoherent the result of the difference operation is the set of all maximally general descriptions which are incoherent in conjunction with A. It depends on the application whether it is interested in an arbitrary description from this set or whether it needs all these descriptions. Accordingly, the difference operation can either be implemented as a nondeterministic operation or as a set-valued operation.

The remaining two cases of structurally non-unique RCFs do not involve incoherent descriptions.

3.3.2 Roles with a Fixed Number of Images

The first case arises from roles with a fixed number of images, if combined with value-restriction. The following equivalence is valid:

$$(\leq n(R|C)) \sqcap (\geq nR) \sqcap (\forall R : C)$$
$$\equiv (\leq nR) \sqcap (\geq n(R|C))$$

If R and C are atoms, both sides are RCFs. Informally, both sides describe all domain elements which have exactly n R-images, and all R-images have the property C. If we set $n = 1$ we have the special case of a functional role. A corresponding example of a non-structural difference is the following.

$$(\leq nR) \sqcap (\geq nR|C) - (\leq nR|C) \sqcap (\geq nR)$$
$$= \{\forall R : C\}$$

An informal example is the difference between "person with at most two children and at least two sons" and "person with at most two sons and at least two children" which is given by "person where all children are sons".

3.3.3 Feature Agreement and Role Value Map

The second case arises from the use of feature agreement or role value map. The following equivalence is valid for roles or features:

$$(RF_1 \downarrow RF_2) \sqcap (RF_2 \downarrow RF_3)$$
$$\equiv (RF_1 \downarrow RF_2) \sqcap (RF_1 \downarrow RF_3)$$

If either all the RF_i are feature atoms, or all the RF_i are role atoms, both sides are RCFs. This equivalence is due to the transitivity of feature agreement and role value map. If the logic does not include disjunction we get the following example of a non-unique and non-structural difference. Let f_1, f_2, f_3 be feature atoms.

$$(f_1 \downarrow f_2) \sqcap (f_2 \downarrow f_3) - (f_1 \downarrow f_3)$$
$$= \{(f_1 \downarrow f_2), (f_2 \downarrow f_3)\}$$

As an informal example, consider the descriptions "man who's father is his boss and his best friend" and "man who's father is his best friend". The difference can be either described by "man who's father is his boss" or by "man who's best friend is his boss". It is evident that these descriptions have different semantics.

Note that feature agreement can be reduced to feature conjunction and exists-restriction using the equivalence $f_1 \downarrow f_2 \equiv \exists (f_1 \sqcap f_2) : \top$. Thus, when adding feature conjunction to $\mathcal{L}_1$, the difference operation becomes non-structural. In particular, we can conclude that the difference in the usual feature term languages is non-structural. If the feature term language does not allow to express disjunction the difference operation is even non-unique.

Altogether these examples show that none of the constructors $(f_1 \downarrow f_2)$, $(R_1 \downarrow R_2)$, and $(f_1 \sqcap f_2)$ can be added to the logic $\mathcal{L}_1$ without the appearance of structurally non-unique RCFs.

We suppose that the three cases presented here are the only sources of structurally non-unique RCFs which occur in description logics using the constructors given in Figure 3. If this is true it would be possible to implement the difference operation in all these logics based on an implementation of the structural difference by detecting these cases and handling them separately. In a similar way it should be possible to implement the difference operation in logics using additional constructors. This is an area for future work.

4 APPLICATIONS

There are two general kinds of applications of the difference operation. It can be used for removing specific information from a description and it can be used for description decomposition. In the second case a given description D is decomposed by determining a subsuming description D_1 and then calculating the difference $D - D_1$. This either yields a single description D_2 which can be further decomposed in the same way, or it yields a set of descriptions which are components of D. Since each single description in the set fully covers the difference any of them may be selected as second component D_2. Hence, for description decomposition the nondeterministic version of the difference operation is appropriate. The specific way of the decomposition mainly depends on how the description D_1 is selected.

As an example consider a description such as "big red car" and a subsuming description such as "red thing". The difference operation determines the rest "big car" which remains after subtracting the information in the subsuming description. This rest may be further decomposed into "big thing" and "car". Hence we have decomposed the given description into three single descriptions each of which covers a single aspect of the original description.

Description decomposition has several practical applications. In systems which teach or explain concepts, such as in intelligent help systems or in intelligent tutoring systems, it can be used as follows. If the system has to explain a certain concept it may try and decompose it into components which are explained separately. In current tutoring systems no general method for concept decomposition exists. If a complex concept is to be explained by a system, the knowledge engineer has to decompose it manually.

On the other hand, if a tutoring system inquires the learner, concept composition can be applied for determining errors in the answer given by the learner and for explaining and correcting these errors. Consider the situation in which the learner is asked by the system to explain a concept. The system compares the description given by the learner with the correct description in its knowledge base. If both descriptions are equivalent, the learner knows the concept. If the learner's description subsumes the correct description the learner does not know all aspects of the concept. If the learner's description is subsumed by the correct description the learner has a concept in mind which is too specific. In both cases the system may construct the difference of both descriptions. Then the learner can be corrected by explaining the kind of the error and explaining the difference. If the learner's description is incomparable with the correct description the system may construct the least common subsumer (lcs) of both and the two differences between the lcs and the descriptions. It may then use these three descriptions for explaining the learner's error.

As an example consider the concept "interprocess communication", defined by the description "communication between processes". If the user defines the concept by "communication between processes by message passing", the system constructs the difference "something done by message passing". It may then tell the user that interprocess communication does not necessarily imply message passing.

The use of the difference operation for removing information from descriptions has several applications too. If descriptions are used in automatic reasoning it can be useful to remove unnecessary information from a description before it is involved in a complex reasoning step. A simple example is the subsumption test itself. Suppose it has to be determined whether a given description B subsumes a description D. If there is a description $A \sqsupseteq B$ of which it is known that A subsumes D, we can subtract A from B and perform the subsumption test for $B - A$ instead of B. Again, the nondeterministic version of the difference operation is appropriate, since the subsumption test will yield the same result for all members of $B - A$.

Another practical application of removing unnecessary information appears as a form of user modeling. If the system is informed about the user's knowledge, it may tailor its answers by omitting those parts of the information the user already knows. The difference operation can be used for subtracting the redundant information from descriptions before they are displayed to the user. In this case it may be interesting to calculate the full set of all alternative descriptions by the difference operation. Then the system may select among them with the help of additional conditions.

Finally, description logics can be used as query languages for retrieving sets of individuals matching a description from knowledge bases [Lenzerini and Schaerf, 1991; Schaerf, 1993]. Since the result of the difference operation is a description or a set of descriptions, the same mechanisms can be used for retrieving sets of individuals matching the difference between two descriptions.

5 CONCLUSION

In the paper we defined a difference operation for descriptions. The difference of a description and a more specific description is a description containing at least the information which "makes the difference" between the two descriptions. It can be used to decompose descriptions or to subtract a given information from a description.

The definition was based on conjunction and subsumption alone, and was thus independent from the actual description logic. It was applicable to concepts as well as to roles and features. We then characterized description logics where the calculation of the difference can be reduced to calculating a reduced clause form and testing clauses for equivalence.

Finally we presented typical cases where the difference cannot be calculated in this way and cases where the difference operation does not yield a unique result. However, since any result meets the definition of the difference, the operation is still useful if it is implemented by returning one of the possible results.

The difference operation will be implemented in the $\mathcal{RICE}$ system, which is currently under development at our institute. The $\mathcal{RICE}$ description logic [Teege, 1994] is a generalization of feature term logics. It includes feature agreement but no disjunction, hence the difference operation is non-unique and it will be implemented as a nondeterministic operation. The system uses a graph representation for description terms and calculates the difference on these graphs.

Additional work remains to be done for logics which are more expressive. Two interesting points are the complexity of the difference operation and algorithms for computing the description difference. A good starting point for a difference algorithm is the structural difference which works in logics with structurally unique RCFs. By identifying the sources of structurally non-unique RCFs and handling these cases separately it should be possible to implement the difference operation in more expressive description logics.

Acknowledgments

I would like to thank Uwe Borghoff for useful comments on an early version of this paper and to thank two anonymous referees for pointing out interesting improvements. I also would like to thank Alex Borgida for an email discussion about earlier concepts of the difference operation.

References

[Baader and Hollunder, 1992]
Baader, F., Hollunder, B.: A Terminological Knowledge Representation System with Complete Inference Algorithm. In: Boley, H., Richter, M. (eds.): Processing Declarative Knowledge: Proceedings of Int. Workshop PDK'91, number 567 in Lecture Notes in Computer Science, Berlin: Springer, 1992, pp. 67–86

[Ben-Bassat and Zaidenberg, 1984]
Ben-Bassat, M., Zaidenberg, L.: Contextual Template Matching: A Distance Measure for Patterns with Hierarchically Dependent Features. IEEE Transactions on Pattern Analysis and Machine Intelligence **PAMI-6**:2, 201–211 (March 1984)

[Bergamaschi et al., 1988]
Bergamaschi, S., et al.: Entity-Situation: A Model for the Knowledge Representation Module of a KBMS. In: Schmidt, J. W., et al. (eds.): Advances in Database Technology: Proceedings of 1st Internat. Conference on Extending Database Technology EDBT'88, Venice, Italy, number 303 in Lecture Notes in Computer Science, Berlin et. al.: Springer, 1988

[Borgida et al., 1989]
Borgida, A., et al.: CLASSIC: A Structural Data Model for Objects. In: Proceedings of SIGMOD'89, Vol. 18 of SIGMOD record, jun 1989, pp. 58–67

[Brachman et al., 1983]
Brachman, R. J., Fikes, R. E., Levesque, H.: Krypton: A Functional Approach to Knowledge Representation. IEEE Computer, pp. 67–73 (Oct. 1983)

[Carpenter, 1992]
Carpenter, B.: The Logic of Typed Feature Structures. Cambridge University Press, 1992

[Cohen et al., 1992]
Cohen, W. W., Borgida, A., Hirsh, H.: Computing Least Common Subsumers in Description Logics. In: Proceedings of the AAAI Conference. MIT Press, 1992, pp. 754–760

[Donini et al., 1991a]
Donini, F. M., et al.: The Complexity of Concept Languages. In: Allen, J., et al. (eds.): Proceedings of the 2nd International Conference on Principles of Knowledge Representation and Reasoning KR'91, San Mateo, Calif.: Morgan Kaufmann, 1991, pp. 151–162

[Donini et al., 1991b]
Donini, F. M., et al.: Tractable Concept Languages. In: Proceedings of the International Joint Conference on Artificial Intelligence, 1991, pp. 458–463

[Dörre and Rounds, 1992]
Dörre, J., Rounds, W. C.: On Subsumption and Semiunification In Feature Algebras. Journal of Symbolic Computation **13**, 441–461 (1992)

[Edelman and Owsnicki, 1986]
Edelman, J., Owsnicki, B.: Data Models in Knowledge Representation Systems. In: Rollinger, C.-R., et al. (eds.): Proceedings of GWAI'86, number 124 in Informatik-Fachberichte, Berlin et. al.: Springer, 1986, pp. 69–74

[Lenzerini and Schaerf, 1991]
Lenzerini, M., Schaerf, A.: Concept Languages as Query Languages. In: Proceedings of the AAAI Conference, 1991, pp. 471–476

[Moneta et al., 1990]
Moneta, C., Vernazza, G., Zunino, R.: A Vectorial Definition of Conceptual Distance for Prototype Acquisition and Refinement. In: Advanced Matching in Vision and AI; Proceedings of ESPRIT Workshop; Report TUM-I-9019. Technical University Munich, 1990, pp. 95–105

[Nebel and Smolka, 1990]
Nebel, B., Smolka, G.: Representation and Reasoning with Attributive Descriptions. In: Bläsius, K.-H., Hedtstück, U., Rollinger, C.-R. (eds.): Sorts and Types in Artificial Intelligence. Lecture Notes in Artificial Intelligence 418, Berlin: Springer, 1990, pp. 112–139

[Patel-Schneider, 1984]
Patel-Schneider, P. F.: Small can be Beautiful in Knowledge Representation. In: Proceedings of the IEEE Workshop on Principles of Knowledge-Based Systems, 1984, pp. 11–16

[Patel-Schneider, 1989]
Patel-Schneider, P. F.: A Four-Valued Semantics for Terminological Logics. Artificial Intelligence **38**, 319–351 (1989)

[Peltason et al., 1989]
Peltason, C., Schmiedel, A., Kindermann, C., Quantz, J.: The BACK System Revisited. Technische Universität Berlin, KIT-Report 75, Sep. 1989

[Schaerf, 1993]
Schaerf, A.: Reasoning with Individuals in Concept Languages. In: Torasso, P. (ed.): Advances in Artificial Intelligence: Proceedings of the 3rd Congress of the Italian Association for Artificial Intelligence, AI*IA'93, Torino, Italy, number 728 in Lecture Notes in AI, Berlin et. al.: Springer, 1993, pp. 108–119

[Schmidt-Schauß, 1989]
Schmidt-Schauß, M.: Subsumption in KL-ONE is Undecidable. In: Brachman, R. J., Levesque, H. J., Reiter, R. (eds.): Proceedings of the 1st International Conference on Principles of Knowledge Representation and Reasoning KR'89, San Mateo, Calif.: Morgan Kaufmann, 1989, pp. 421–431

[Teege, 1994]
Teege, G.: Abstract Descriptions in the RICE Knowledge Representation Formalism. Inst. für Informatik, Technische Universität München, Munich, Germany, Technical Report I9407, Feb. 1994

[Tversky, 1988]
Tversky, A.: Features of Similarity. In: Collins, A., Smith, E. E. (eds.): Readings in Cognitive Science, Chap. 3.1, pp. 290–302, San Mateo, Calif.: Morgan Kaufmann, 1988

Tractable Databases: How to Make Propositional Unit Resolution Complete through Compilation

Alvaro del Val
Robotics Lab
Computer Science Department
Stanford University
Stanford, CA 94035
delval@cs.stanford.edu

Abstract

We present procedures to compile any propositional clausal database Σ into a logically equivalent "compiled" database $\Sigma^\star$ such that, for any clause C, $\Sigma \models C$ if and only if there is a unit refutation of $\Sigma^\star \cup \neg C$. It follows that once the compilation process is complete any query about the logical consequences of Σ can be correctly answered in time linear in the sum of the sizes of $\Sigma^\star$ and the query. The compiled database $\Sigma^\star$ is for all but one of the procedures a subset of the set $PI(\Sigma)$ of prime implicates of Σ, but $\Sigma^\star$ can be exponentially smaller than $PI(\Sigma)$.

Of independent interest, we prove the equivalence of unit-refutability with two restrictions of resolution, and provide a new sufficient condition for unit refutation completeness, thus identifying a new class of tractable theories, one which is of interest to abduction problems as well. Finally, we apply the results to the design of a complete LTMS.

1 INTRODUCTION

The problem of propositional entailment is central to AI, and various approaches have been devised to circumvent its intractability. In this paper, we will be interested in what we may call equivalence preserving logical compilation. By this we mean a process of mapping a propositional database or theory[1] into another logically equivalent database, so that query answering with respect to the resulting database is tractable. We speak of "compilation," because of the resulting speed up in query answering, and because computation of the mapping is intended to be an offline process, since propositional entailment is co-NP-complete. We speak of "logical" compilation because

[1]The terms "theory" and "database" will be used interchangeably.

the target is another logical theory, rather than, say, some special data structures. Finally, the compilation is "equivalence preserving" because source and target are logically equivalent.

Equivalence preserving logical compilation is only one of the possible ways of circumventing the intractability of propositional entailment. Most approaches to this problem typically involve one or more of the following dimensions:

- expressiveness restrictions that make the problem of inference tractable (e.g. Horn theories, terminological logics);

- tractable but incomplete inference procedures (e.g. restriction to unit resolution);

- approximation schemes that allow efficient processing of some subset of the possible queries (e.g. [Cadoli and Schaerf, 1991], the "vivid" knowledge bases of [Levesque, 1986], and the Horn approximations of [Selman and Kautz, 1991]);

- off-line preprocessing of the database, so that query answering becomes tractable after the compilation phase has been completed (e.g. computation of prime implicates [Reiter and de Kleer, 1987], off-line query answering [Tennenholtz and Moses, 1993], and again Horn approximations).

Each of these dimensions involves some kind of sacrifice, but equivalence preserving logical compilation is the only one that trades off only preprocessing time, but neither expressiveness, soundness, or completeness. As long as compilation time is reasonable for offline computation (which it will not always be), the attractiveness of this approach as a way to speed up online response time is clear, as the cost of compilation can be amortized over many queries to the database. With an all-important caveat: Whereas query answering may be tractable with respect to the compiled database, if the compilation process produces an exponential growth in the database then all potential efficiency gains achieved through tractability are wiped out. This is the problem faced by the best known approach to equivalence preserving logical compilation, namely, the computation of the set $PI(\Sigma)$ of prime implicates of the database Σ [Reiter and de Kleer, 1987; de Kleer, 1992]. This computation can be seen as an equivalence preserving logical compilation, since for any non-tautologous clause C, Σ entails C iff there exists $C' \in PI(\Sigma)$ such that $C' \subseteq C$, which can be checked in time polynomial in the size of $PI(\Sigma)$. However, not only is the compilation process very costly, $PI(\Sigma)$ may easily be exponentially larger in size than Σ; in this case, query answering is tractable with respect to $PI(\Sigma)$, but still exponential in the size of Σ.

In this paper we present a novel approach to equivalence preserving logical compilation. Analysis of the compilation procedures, furthermore, allows us to identify a new class of theories for which query answering is tractable. We begin by identifying some restrictions of resolution that are refutationally equivalent to unit resolution, a well known tractable but incomplete restriction of resolution. These restrictions, together with what can be seen as an exhaustive exploration of the search space of resolution derivations from the database Σ, can be used to identify clauses that need to be added to Σ in order to ensure that unit resolution can answer all queries correctly. In this way, we map Σ into an equivalent database $\Sigma^\star$ with the property that, for any clause C, $\Sigma \models C$ iff there is a unit refutation of $\Sigma^\star \cup \neg C$. After the compilation is complete, therefore, any query whether $\Sigma \models C$ can be answered in time linear in the size of $\Sigma^\star \cup \neg C$.

As said, the compilation process involves an exhaustive search of the space of possible resolution derivations. We find it convenient to use a resolution-based prime implicate (PI) algorithm as the basis of this search. Because any non-tautologous clause entailed by Σ must be subsumed by a prime implicate of Σ, PI algorithms perform all resolutions "of interest," which makes them a suitable tool for exploring the resolution search space. As an additional benefit of this choice, the compiled database $\Sigma^\star$ is a subset of the set $PI(\Sigma)$ of prime implicates of Σ. This guarantees that $\Sigma^\star$ is no larger than $PI(\Sigma)$; as we will see, the former can in fact be exponentially smaller than the latter, and even can beat Horn approximations by an exponential factor.

This is then our way of addressing the main obstacle to tractable query answering through compilation. Though we have no guarantee that $\Sigma^\star$ will not be, under any of the proposed procedures, exponentially larger than Σ, we know at least that the procedures will consistently be no worse than PI compilation, and that they can yield much better results.

The structure of this paper is as follows. In the next section, we introduce two restrictions of resolution, and establish their relation with unit resolution. In section 3 we present a number of compilation procedures based on these results. Section 4 looks at the sources of unit refutation incompleteness in order to assess the effect of ordering strategies on these compilation procedures, and presents a new sufficient condition for unit refutation completeness which allows us to identify new classes of tractable theories, and which has implications on the tractability of certain abduction problems. In section 5 we show the compiled databases can be used as the basis of a complete LTMS (logical truth maintenance system) that uses only unit propagation. Section 6 presents some experimental results, providing evidence for the substantial space savings achievable with our compilation procedures.

2 NO-MERGE RESOLUTION AND ITS RELATION TO UNIT RESOLUTION

In this section, we introduce two restricted versions of resolution and prove their (refutation) equivalence with unit resolution. The first restriction can be seen as a dual of P.B. Andrews' "resolution with merging" [Andrews, 1968], from which we take much of the terminology; the second one is again some sort of dual of a restriction of resolution found e.g. in [Reiter, 1971]. Note that these restrictions are introduced only as a way to analyze resolution deductions; they are not intended for actual use.

We assume some propositional language $\mathcal{L}$ obtained by closing off a set of symbols $\mathcal{P}$ under the usual boolean connectives. We write $\Sigma \models C$ to denote that C is a propositional consequence of Σ. For $p \in \mathcal{P}$, p is a (positive) literal and $\neg p$ is a (negative) literal; p and $\neg p$ are said to be complementary literals. A clause is a set of literals, representing their disjunction; we will switch between set and disjunctive notation whenever convenient. The empty clause is denoted with the special symbol $\bot$, which is not satisfied by any interpretation. A unit clause is a singleton clause. A tautologous clause is a clause containing complementary literals. A clause C_1 (strictly) subsumes a clause C_2 iff C_1 is a (proper) subset of C_2. Given a clause $C = \{l_1, \ldots, l_k\}$, we denote with $\neg C$ the set of unit clauses $\{\{\neg l_1\}, \ldots, \{\neg l_k\}\}$. A clausal database is a set of clauses, representing the conjunction of the clauses. We will only consider clausal databases in this paper.

Definition 1 *A clause C is said to be obtained by* resolution *from two clauses C_1 and C_2 iff there exists a literal $l \in C_1$ such that $\neg l \in C_2$ and $C = (C_1 \setminus \{l\}) \cup (C_2 \setminus \{\neg l\})$. C is said to be the* resolvent *of C_1 and C_2, with l and $\neg l$ being the literals resolved upon. Furthermore:*

- *If either C_1 or C_2 are unit clauses, C is said to be obtained from C_1 and C_2 by* unit resolution.

- *If the set $M = (C_1 \setminus \{l\}) \cap (C_2 \setminus \{\neg l\})$ is not empty,* *then C is obtained by* merge resolution *from, and is a* merge resolvent *of C_1 and C_2, with M being the set of* merge literals *of C.*

- *If l' is a literal in $C_1 \setminus \{l\}$ then the occurrence of l' in C is an* immediate descendant *of its occurrence in C_1, and the latter is an* immediate ancestor *of the former; and similarly with C_1 replaced by C_2.*

Definition 2 *A* resolution deduction *of a clause C from a set of clauses Σ is a sequence $C_1, \ldots, C_k$ of clauses such that $C_k = C$, and each C_i either is in Σ, or is a resolvent of clauses preceding C_i. Furthermore:*

- *A* unit resolution deduction *is a resolution deduction in which every resolvent has been obtained by unit resolution.*

- *A* weak no-merge (wnm) resolution deduction *is a resolution deduction in which no resolvent is a merge resolvent.*

For the next definition, let *descendant* be the reflexive and transitive closure (wrt. a given resolution deduction) of the relation "immediate descendant" introduced in definition 1.

Definition 3 *A* no-merge (nm) resolution deduction *of a clause C from a set of clauses Σ is a resolution deduction of C from Σ in which no merge resolvent has any descendants of its merge literals resolved upon.*

Thus, wnm-resolution rules out merges, while nm-resolution allows merges as long as no merge literal (or more exactly, no descendant of a merge literal) is resolved upon later in the deduction. Note that unit resolution involves no merges, and is thus a special case of both types of no-merge resolution. We write $\Sigma \vdash_r C$ (respectively, $\Sigma \vdash_{wnm} C$, $\Sigma \vdash_{nm} C$, $\Sigma \vdash_u C$) to indicate that there is a resolution deduction of clause C from the set of clauses Σ (respectively, a wnm, nm, or unit resolution deduction of C from Σ).

The following theorem is the key to the compilation procedures presented later:

Theorem 1 *Let Σ be a set of clauses, C a clause. The following two statements are equivalent:*

1. *$\Sigma \vdash_{nm} D$ for some $D \subseteq C$.*

2. *$\Sigma \cup \neg C \vdash_u \bot$.*

Note that every wnm-deduction is also an nm-deduction, and thus the (1 ⇒ 2) direction of this theorem, the crucial one for compilation, applies to wnm resolution as well. The fact that the other direction also holds suggests that resolution upon descendants of merge literals is a key source of the incompleteness of unit resolution. To put it in a different way, suppose $\Sigma \models C$. Then we know that there exists a resolution deduction of some $D \subseteq C$ from Σ [Lee, 1993]; theorem 1 tells us that in this case, if $\Sigma \cup \neg C$ is not unit refutable, then *every* such resolution deduction must involve at least one resolution upon a descendant of a merge literal.

We end this section with the concepts of refutation and refutation completeness.

Definition 4 *A* unit (nm, wnm) resolution refutation *of a set of clauses Σ is a unit (nm, wnm) deduction of $\bot$ from Σ. If this is the case, Σ is said to be* unit (nm, wnm) refutable.

Definition 5 *A set of clauses Σ is* unit (nm, wnm) refutation complete *iff for any clause C: $\Sigma \models C$ iff $\Sigma \cup \neg C$ is unit (nm, wnm) refutable.*

Checking whether $\Sigma \cup \neg C$ is unit refutable can be done in time linear in the size of $\Sigma \cup \neg C$. Thus, unit refutation completeness ensures tractable query answering. Note:

Corollary 2 *A set of clauses Σ is wnm-refutable iff it is nm-refutable iff it is unit refutable. Similarly, the notions of unit, wnm, and nm refutation completeness are equivalent.*

In [Henschen and Wos, 1974] it is shown that a minimally unsatisfiable set of clauses Σ is unit refutable iff Σ is in the class "renamable Horn," i.e. it can be converted into a Horn database by an uniform renaming of symbols. The class of unit refutation complete databases is however much more general than the class renamable Horn, and involves, unlike the latter, no loss of expressive power. This follows from the fact that *every* theory can be converted into an equivalent unit refutation complete theory, but not into an equivalent renamable Horn theory. The connection between both classes is as follows: a unit refutation complete database has the property that if $\Sigma \models C$ then there exists a *minimally unsatisfiable* subset Σ_C of $\Sigma \cup \neg C$ such that Σ_C is renamable Horn. The minimality requirement, however, is crucial; furthermore, if D is some other clause entailed by Σ, for all we know the renaming functions associated with the sets Σ_C and Σ_D may well be incompatible.

3 COMPILATION

3.1 PROCEDURES

The goal of the compilation procedures we are about to propose is to map the database Σ into a logically equivalent, unit refutation complete database $\Sigma^\star$. In order to do this, as anticipated, we exhaustively explore the space of resolution derivations from Σ, using some resolution-based prime implicate algorithm. The key idea is to add to Σ *only* those clauses obtained by this procedure in violation of the wnm or nm restrictions. We thus ensure wnm or nm refutation completeness, and therefore unit refutation completeness.

3.1.1 Compilation based on weak no merge resolution

Recall that a non-tautologous clause C is an *implicate* of a set of clauses Σ iff $\Sigma \models C$, and it is a *prime implicate* of Σ iff no other implicate of Σ strictly subsumes it. We denote the set of prime implicates of Σ by $PI(\Sigma)$. Our first compilation procedure ensures that every prime implicate can be derived by wnm-resolution, and is independent of the prime implicate (PI) algorithm used. We call it FPI_0 because the database it returns is a "filtered" set of prime implicates.

Procedure $FPI_0(\Sigma)$

1. Initialize variables FPI and PI to the set of clauses Σ.
2. Compute a new implicate C of Σ using some resolution-based PI algorithm. If no new implicate is generated, then return FPI. If C is subsumed by some clause in PI, then repeat this step, ignoring C.
3. Delete from PI and from FPI any clause subsumed by C and add C to PI.
4. If C is a merge resolvent, or a clause in FPI was subsumed by C, then add C to FPI.
5. Go back to step 2.

Theorem 3 $FPI_0(\Sigma)$ *is unit refutation complete and logically equivalent to* Σ.

In particular, therefore, for any clause C, $\Sigma \models C$ iff $FPI_0(\Sigma) \land \neg C \vdash_u \bot$.

3.1.2 Compilation based on no merge resolution

The next compilation procedure, FPI_1, is based on nm-resolution, and it is guaranteed to produce a database no larger than the one returned by FPI_0 when the same PI algorithm is used. While FPI_0 keeps all merge resolvents, FPI_1 tries to use the fact that using merges does not destroy the unit refutability of $\Sigma \cup \neg C$, as long as no merge literal is resolved upon. One way to use this fact would be to record the ancestry of every merge literal generated by the PI algorithm, storing the merge resolvent only if some descendant of its merge literals is resolved upon. The overhead produced by this approach can be significant, however. A much simpler solution exploits the ordering of symbols used by Tison's PI algorithm [Tison, 1967]. Briefly, Tison's method initializes PI to Σ, and iterates over the set of propositional symbols $\mathcal{P}$, in some fixed order. For each $p \in \mathcal{P}$, it computes all (non-tautologous) resolvents that can be obtained from two clauses in PI by resolving them on p; each new resolvent C, if not subsumed by some other clause in PI, is added to PI after deleting every clause in PI subsumed by C. The key observation is that once a given symbol has been processed, it will never again be resolved upon. Our next compilation procedure uses this information to prune merges when all merge literals have already been processed by Tison's method.

Procedure $FPI_1(\Sigma)$ As $FPI_0(\Sigma)$, with the following changes:

- The PI algorithm of line 2 is Tison's method, with some fixed ordering of all symbols.
- Line 4 should read: If C is a merge resolvent and some merge literal in C is later in the ordering than the symbol currently being resolved upon, or if some clause in FPI was subsumed by C, then add C to FPI.

Theorem 4 $FPI_1(\Sigma)$ *is unit refutation complete and logically equivalent to* Σ.

To obtain a rough idea of how much can FPI_1 save over FPI_0 in database growth, consider the case in which every merge resolvent generated by Tison's method contains exactly one merge literal. Assuming merge literals have, on average, about an equal chance of being earlier or later in the ordering than the symbol being resolved upon, FPI_1 would store only about half the merge clauses stored by FPI_0, thus halving database growth as well.[2] Note that the same argument gives us a rough estimate of *minimum* savings with respect to $PI(\Sigma)$, an estimate that is confirmed by our experiments so far.

Example 1 Let $\Sigma = \{\{p,q,s\}, \{p, \neg q, r\}, \{\neg p, q, t\}, \{\neg p, \neg q, u\}, \{\neg t, v, w\}, \{\neg v, x\}\}$. Table 1 gives the results of using Tison's method with the ordering $p, q, r, s, t, u, v, w, x$. The middle columns contain non-subsumed resolvents obtained by resolving on the leftmost symbol in the row, with merge literals indicated on the rightmost column (brackets and commas in clauses are omitted). The sets $PI(\Sigma)$, $FPI_0(\Sigma)$ and $FPI_1(\Sigma)$ can be obtained by unioning together the corresponding columns. $PI(\Sigma)$ adds fourteen clauses, $FPI_0(\Sigma)$ four, and $FPI_1(\Sigma)$ only two.

More generally, it is easily seen that the set of filtered prime implicates (under either procedure) is a subset of the prime implicates. The compiled database is therefore in either case no larger than $PI(\Sigma)$. In fact, it can be exponentially smaller:

---

[2] FPI_0 is nevertheless analytically interesting, because of its relative independence from the PI algorithm used, and for reasons given in section 5.

Table 1: Prime Implicates, Example 1

Symbol	Prime implicates Σ	FPI_0 Σ	FPI_1 Σ	Merge literals
p	$qst, \neg qru$	$qst, \neg qru$	$qst, \neg qru$	$q, \neg q$
q	$prs, \neg ptu, rstu$	$prs, \neg ptu$		$p, \neg p$
t	$\neg pqvw, qsvw, \neg puvw, rsuvw$			
v	$\neg twx, \neg pqwx, qswx, \neg puwx, rsuwx$			

Example 2 Let $\Sigma = \{\{p_1, q_1^1\}, \ldots, \{p_1, q_1^m\}, \ldots, \{p_k, q_k^1\}, \ldots, \{p_k, q_k^m\}, \{\neg p_1, \ldots, \neg p_k\}\}$. $PI(\Sigma)$ has $(m+1)^k + mk$ prime implicates [Kean and Tsiknis, 1990]. Using results from section 4, it is easily shown that $FPI_0(\Sigma) = FPI_1(\Sigma) = \Sigma$. In section 6 we also present some experimental results for some k-clause databases shown in [Chandra and Markowsky, 1978] to have at least $3^{\lfloor k/3 \rfloor}$ prime implicates.

FPI_1 can produce exponential savings even with respect to the "Horn approximation" compilation procedure of [Selman and Kautz, 1991], which does *not* preserve logical equivalence.

Example 3 Let $\Sigma_n = \{\{\neg p_1, \neg p_2, \ldots, \neg p_n, s\}, \{\neg q_1, p_1, s\}, \{\neg q_2, p_2, s\}, \ldots, \{\neg q_n, p_n, s\}\}$. In [Kautz and Selman, 1992] it is shown that the LUB Horn approximation of Σ_n contains 2^n clauses. Using results from section 4 one can show that $FPI_1(\Sigma_n) = \Sigma_n$, for some easily found orderings of symbols.

This comparison applies only to the LUB; the size of the Horn GLB approximation is guaranteed to be linear in the size of the original database. Note however that it is only the LUB that allows us to derive consequences of the database; the GLB, in contrast, only allows us to reject non-consequences. Thus, it is comparison with the LUB that is most relevant.

3.1.3 Avoiding resolutions between Horn clauses

There is however an important insight in the Generate_LUB algorithm of [Selman and Kautz, 1991] that can be useful for our purposes. The Horn LUB is equivalent to the set of Horn prime implicates, so one could compute it by using a prime implicate algorithm. Selman and Kautz observed, however, that any resolution tree with a Horn clause at the root can be transformed into a tree where all resolutions between two Horn clauses are at the bottom, an observation that allowed them to avoid all resolutions between two Horn clauses. The algorithm that generates the LUB is in essence the so-called "consensus method" for generating prime implicates modified to incorporate this restriction.[3]

[3] The LUB algorithm can however be improved by banning resolutions between two non-Horn clauses as well

Can this observation be incorporated into our procedures? The answer is a qualified yes. Adding the resolvent of two Horn clauses to a Horn database Σ clearly cannot improve the ability of unit resolution to answer queries by indirect proof, but this is no longer true if Σ contains at least one non-Horn clause. Indeed, it can be shown that FPI_1 cannot guarantee unit refutation completeness if the restriction against resolving two Horn clauses is incorporated in the procedure in an straightforward way. There may be other more sophisticated ways of incorporating it into no merge compilation procedures, but the question is open at this point. Nevertheless, the following procedure, directly based on the Generate_LUB algorithm of [Selman and Kautz, 1991], shows that the restriction can be incorporated at least for procedures based on wnm-resolution.

Procedure $FPI_2(\Sigma)$
$H :=$ Horn clauses of Σ; $FPI_H := H$;
$N :=$ non-Horn clauses of Σ; $FPI_N := N$;
loop
   try to choose $B \in H \cup N$, $C \in N$ with resolvent A
     s.t. A is not subsumed by any $D \in H \cup N$;
   If no such choice is possible then exit loop;
   If A is Horn
   then delete from H, N, FPI_H, and FPI_N any clauses
     subsumed by A and set $H := H \cup \{A\}$;
     If A is a merge clause,
     or some $D \in FPI_H \cup FPI_N$ was subsumed by A
     then $FPI_H := FPI_H \cup \{A\}$;
     end if
   else delete from N and FPI_N any clauses
     subsumed by A and set $N := N \cup \{A\}$
     If A is a merge clause,
     or some $D \in FPI_N$ was subsumed by A
     then $FPI_N := FPI_N \cup \{A\}$;
     end if
   end if
end loop
return $FPI_H \cup FPI_N$.

Theorem 5 $FPI_2(\Sigma)$ *is unit refutation complete and logically equivalent to* Σ.

Banning resolutions between Horn clauses has two huge potential advantages. First, it may result in much

[Kautz, 1994].

fewer resolvents being generated, so the compilation can be much faster. Second, and equally importantly, resolvents that are not generated could well be *merge* resolvents, which would have been stored without this restriction.

The procedure has a number of drawbacks, though. First, it is based on wnm resolution instead of nm resolution, something which may wipe out the space advantages of not resolving Horn clauses, in particular given that the algorithm does compute all non-Horn prime implicates. Second, the underlying prime implicate algorithm behind the procedure is, as mentioned, the consensus method, that is, in essence a brute force algorithm that performs a huge number of redundant derivations; this makes the procedure quite inefficient, and redundant derivations may result in more merges being added to the compiled database. In fact, the procedure is not even *guaranteed* to be more space or time efficient than the underlying brute force prime implicate algorithm.[4]

While the advantages may well be weightier than the disadvantages, specially for databases most of whose clauses are Horn, it would still be desirable to be able to incorporate the restriction against resolving Horn clauses into more efficient prime implicate algorithms, and even better (but less likely), to be able to base the compilation on nm rather than wnm resolution.

3.1.4 Compilation based on linear resolution

There is another important family of prime implicate algorithms, namely, those based on some variant of linear resolution. The reader is referred to [Chang and Lee, 1973] for a general description of linear resolution, and to [Inoue, 1991; Minicozzi and Reiter, 1972] for a discussion of the completeness of various variants of linear resolution for prime implicate computation (or consequence-finding, as it used to be called). As mentioned, FPI_0 is independent of the prime implicate algorithm used, so a linear resolution prime implicate algorithm could be used for this purpose. There are other ways in which linear resolution can be interesting for compilation. First, a compilation procedure can be devised by storing "side clauses" of the deduction that are not input clauses. By adding such clauses to the database any linear deduction becomes an input deduction, which allows us to achieve unit refutation completeness. This can be combined with restrictions on merges. Furthermore, the stack based

---

[4]For example, by not resolving two Horn clauses $\neg p \vee \neg q$ and $\neg p \vee q$, we fail to derive the unit clause $\neg p$ (though it may perhaps be derived later); but adding this clause could greatly cut the search space and thus improve efficiency. Furthermore, if the database consists of only these two clauses, the algorithm would leave it untouched, rather than replace it by the smaller database consisting of the single unit clause $\neg p$. (Which shows, incidentally, that $FPI_2(\Sigma)$ can be a strict *superset* of the prime implicates.)

discipline of linear resolution, combined with the way that information about literals resolved upon is kept around in ordered linear resolutions, may allow for an easy recognition of when descendants of merge literals are resolved upon. Finally, [Inoue, 1991] provides procedures that allow us to focus on certain "interesting" implicates. The idea of using these procedures in order to focus the compilation process will be discussed in the extended version of this paper.

3.2 INCREMENTAL COMPILATION

Given the cost of compilation, one may wonder about the utility of these procedures in situations in which the database is often subject to change. Small changes in the database, in particular, should not require the recompilation of the database from the scratch. In general, compilation procedures based on wnm resolution are fully incremental, since the question of whether a clause is a merge is independent of the order in which resolutions are performed. Thus, any incremental prime implicate algorithm can be used in FPI_0 to make compilation incremental; similarly, FPI_2 is easily seen to be incremental. The question is more complicated in the case of compilation procedures based on nm-resolution, since whether a merge literal will later be resolved upon obviously depends on which clauses are later added.

3.3 COMPILATION AS CONVERGENT, ANYTIME APPROXIMATION

All the compilation procedures we have described are "anytime." The database can be queried before completion of compilation. As time passes, the number of queries that can be answered successfully by unit indirect proof increases, and after execution is completed every query can be answered by unit resolution. This suggests that there is a sense in which the compilation process can be seen as a form of anytime "approximation," with the crucial property that the approximation *converges* towards the correct result.

To make this idea precise, let $FPI_t(\Sigma)$ be the set of clauses stored in the variable FPI at time t by any given compilation procedure, let $Cl(\Sigma,t) = \{C \mid \Sigma \models C$ and $FPI_t(\Sigma) \cup \neg C \vdash_u \bot\}$ be the set of (clausal) consequences of Σ derivable by (indirect proof) unit resolution at time t, and let $Cl(\Sigma)$ be the set of all clausal consequences of Σ. Clearly, $Cl(\Sigma,t) \subseteq Cl(\Sigma)$ for any t. $Cl(\Sigma,t)$ monotonically grows with time, and eventually converges towards $Cl(\Sigma)$. Thus, $Cl(\Sigma,t)$ can be seen as an anytime, convergent approximation "from below" to $Cl(\Sigma)$. At time t, before completion of the algorithm, we know that if $C \in Cl(\Sigma,t)$ then $\Sigma \models C$, but we cannot reach any conclusion from the fact that $C \notin Cl(\Sigma,t)$; in particular, we cannot conclude that $\Sigma \not\models C$. Thus, $Cl(\Sigma,t)$ plays the same role as, for example, the Horn upper bounds defined in [Selman and

Kautz, 1991], with the crucial difference that when the algorithm is completed at time t_e, $Cl(\Sigma, t_e)$ equals $Cl(\Sigma)$, the clausal closure under logical consequence of Σ; i.e. for any clause C, $\Sigma \models C$ if and only if $C \in Cl(\Sigma, t_e)$. In contrast, the set of clauses derivable by unit resolution from Horn upper and lower bounds does not converge towards this logical closure for any Σ that is not expressible (possibly after removal of redundant clauses and renaming) as a Horn theory.

There is no analogous in our compilation procedures to Horn lower bounds; this suggest using Horn lower bounds (or some other approximation "from above") in order to rule out a positive answer to certain queries before the compilation is completed. After completion of the compilation procedure, on the other hand, the question of whether keeping the Horn bounds is worthwhile reduces to the question of whether the fully compiled database is deemed too large, and furthermore, the Horn bounds are *substantially* smaller than the compiled database (so as to justify the loss of completeness). As shown in example 3 this is by no means always the case. Nevertheless, approximation schemes are useful as a fallback approach when the compilation procedures of this paper do not yield satisfactory results.

In principle, the interest of this "convergent approximation" view of compilation is that it has the potential to greatly decrease the inconvenience of using off-line computation: since compilation can take forever, it is clearly desirable to be able to process queries before completion. Carried to the extreme, one could think of compilation as a process of increasing the efficiency and quality of query answering over the life cycle of the database. A more realistic view is, we believe, that compilation that takes "too" long is also likely to be too space demanding.

4 TIED CHAINS, MERGES, AND ORDERING STRATEGIES

We suggested in section 2 that resolutions upon descendants of merge literals are a crucial source of incompleteness of unit resolution for indirect proof purposes. In this section, we carry the analysis further by asking about the properties of the database from which such resolutions can arise. Our immediate motivation for this analysis is to improve the compilation procedures based on nm resolution, since, as the following example shows, FPI_1 is very sensible to the chosen ordering of symbols. As we will see, a by-product of the analysis is the identification of a new class of tractable theories.

Example 4 Let Σ be as in example 2, except that every clause contains an additional literal r. Every resolvent will now be a merge resolvent. If r is earlier in the ordering than every p_i, then $FPI_1(\Sigma) = \Sigma$, but if it is later than every p_i then $FPI_1(\Sigma) = PI(\Sigma)$.

One simple solution is to observe that r is a "pure literal" in Σ, *i.e.* its complementary literal $\neg r$ never occurs in Σ. Because pure literals will never be resolved upon, they can be put first in the ordering for the purposes of the FPI_1 procedure.[5] What other ordering strategies are available to reduce the number of merges stored by FPI_1? A promising concept is that of a "tied chain," introduced in [Esghi, 1993].

Definition 6 *A tied chain in a set of clauses Σ is a sequence of triples $(x_1, C_1, y_1), \ldots, (x_n, C_n, y_n)$ such that:*

- *For $1 \leq i \leq n$: $C_i \in \Sigma$, $x_i, y_i \in C_i$, and $x_i \neq y_i$;*
- *For $1 \leq i < n$: y_i and x_{i+1} (the link literals of the chain) are complementary literals;*
- *$x_1 = y_n$, called the tied literal of the chain.*

For example, $\Sigma = \{p \vee q \vee r, \neg r \vee s, \neg s \vee p\}$ contains a tied chain with p as tied literal and r and s as link symbols. In [Esghi, 1993] it is shown that the absence of tied chains is a sufficient condition for unit refutation completeness. This result can be rederived (and, in a sense, explained) using the concept of merges, as an easy consequence of the next lemma and theorem 1.

Lemma 6 *Suppose there is a resolution deduction D of a merge resolvent C from a set of clauses Σ. Then Σ contains, for each merge literal l of C, a tied chain T_l with l as its tied literal. Furthermore, each link literal in T_l has a descendant in D which is resolved upon.*

If there are no tied chains, therefore, there are no merges, so $FPI_1(\Sigma) = FPI_0(\Sigma) = \Sigma$, and thus Σ must be unit refutation complete. More significantly for our purposes, we can use the ordering restrictions imposed on resolution by Tison's method in combination with the second part of the theorem to obtain a much weaker sufficient condition for unit refutation completeness, and, possibly, to reduce the number of merges stored by FPI_1. In what follows, we let $<$ be some total ordering of the propositional symbols, which we extend to an ordering over literals in the obvious way. We adopt the convention that Tison's method resolves upon "smaller" symbols earlier than upon "larger" symbols.

Definition 7 *A tied chain T in Σ with tied literal l is free wrt $<$ iff $l < l'$ for some link literal l' of T*

Definition 8 *A literal l is a free literal wrt $<$ iff every tied chain with l as tied literal is free wrt $<$. A symbol*

---

[5] Note also that placing pure literals first in the ordering also ensures that FPI_1 will store exactly as many merges as if we had recorded the ancestry of merge literals as suggested before introducing FPI_1.

$p \in \mathcal{P}$ is a free symbol wrt $<$ iff both p and $\neg p$ are free literals wrt $<$.

The idea behind these definitions is as follows. Since *all* literals in a chain have to be resolved upon in order to obtain a merge resolvent, if l is a free literal wrt $<$ then FPI_1, using $<$ as ordering, will generate a merge resolvent C with l as merge literal only when l has already been processed by Tison's method. Hence, l will never be resolved upon after C is generated, and thus if C contains no other merge literal then it will not be stored by FPI_1. More generally:

Lemma 7 *Let $<$ be any total ordering of the symbols in Σ, and let F be the set of free literals wrt $<$. $FPI_1(\Sigma)$ will not store any merge clause whose set M of merge literals is such that $M \subseteq F$.*

Note that this lemma is compatible with the requirement that pure symbols (the symbols of pure literals) are placed as a prefix of the ordering, as this ensures that they are free symbols. Note also that the lemma has as an immediate consequence a new, much more general sufficient condition for unit refutation completeness:

Theorem 8 *Suppose there exists an ordering $<$ of the symbols in a set of clauses Σ such that every tied chain (and thus every symbol) in Σ is free wrt $<$. Then Σ is unit refutation complete.*

This theorem also has consequences in abduction. [Esghi, 1993] showed that certain class of abduction problems (involving acyclic Horn theories) is tractable whenever certain extended theory is unit refutation complete. Thus, we are now able to verify membership into this tractable class for a much wider class of problems. Furthermore, we can compile abduction problems based on acyclic Horn theories so as to make them tractable.

The question whether an ordering with the properties required by this corollary exists can be seen as a constraint satisfaction problem (CSP). Namely, a tied chain having the symbol p or $\neg p$ as tied literal, and having $p_1, \ldots, p_k$ as link symbols, will be free wrt any total ordering satisfying the $(k+1)$-ary constraint $(p < p_1) \vee \ldots \vee (p < p_k)$. Each tied chain generates one such constraint, and thus the set of tied chains of Σ defines a CSP with the property that, if it has a solution, then Σ is unit refutation complete —every tied chain will be free with respect to the total ordering determined by this solution.

An equivalent, graph-theoretic view of this CSP is as follows. Let $\mathcal{C}$ be any set containing at least one disjunct from each constraint generated from some tied chain of Σ. Let $G_\mathcal{C}(\Sigma)$ be the directed graph whose nodes are the symbols of the language, with a directed edge from node p to node q iff $(p < q) \in \mathcal{C}$. If $G_\mathcal{C}(\Sigma)$ is acyclic for *some* choice $\mathcal{C}$ of disjuncts, then Σ is unit refutation complete (and a topological sort of the nodes of $G_\mathcal{C}$ will provide the required ordering).

As these formulations suggest, the problem of verifying whether the condition of theorem 8 holds is likely to be intractable in general. It is however possible to identify classes of theories for which the condition can be verified in polynomial time. One such class is presented next.

Definition 9 *The* tied chain graph $G_T(\Sigma)$ *of a set of clauses Σ is the directed graph whose nodes are all literals whose symbol occurs in Σ, and such that there is an edge from l to l' iff $\{l, \neg l'\} \subseteq C$ for some clause $C \in \Sigma$.*

It can be shown that Σ contains a tied chain with tied literal l iff there is a path in $G_T(\Sigma)$ from l to $\neg l$ [Esghi, 1993], in which case the link literals can be directly read off the path. The following theorem uses theorem 8 to identify a class of unit refutation complete theories, a class which includes in particular the theories of example 3. Clearly, membership in this class can be determined in polynomial time.

Theorem 9 *If $G_T(\Sigma)$ is acyclic then Σ is unit refutation complete.*[6]

Our main goal is not however to identify tractable classes of theories, but to *make* theories tractable through compilation. Coming back to the constraint satisfaction perspective, it is important to note that the CSP defined by the tied chains of Σ (that we can read off $G_T(\Sigma)$) will often be overconstrained, and have no solution. For our purposes it would suffice to find an ordering $<$ that makes $FPI_1(\Sigma)$ "sufficiently" small when computed using $<$. This is true even when a solution exists, as it may be too costly to find it. In either case, we enter the realm of constraint relaxation techniques, in which the goal is to minimize constraint violations.

Is there any guarantee that such an approach will reduce the size of $FPI_1(\Sigma)$? In order to measure the effects of ordering strategies in a general way, it is useful to think of them in terms of *re*-ordering steps, steps that modify an initial ordering by changing the position of a single symbol. Under this perspective, moving a pure symbol from its initial position to the front of the ordering is *safe*, in the sense that it can only reduce, but never increase, the number of merges stored by FPI_1, in comparison with those that would be stored under the initial ordering. The reason is that the space of resolutions explored by Tison's method is unaffected by the position of pure literals. Another reordering strategy that can be proved to be safe is a

---

[6] Note on the other hand that $G_T(\Sigma)$ can contain cycles even if Σ contains no tied chains.

simple form of dynamic reordering: as soon as a unit clause is derived, its symbol should be placed immediately after the current symbol being processed in the ordering, performing all unit resolutions immediately. This shortens some clauses and deletes others, which will generally reduce the number of stored merges; and it can be shown that it will not add any merge that would not have been added anyway with the original ordering.

We believe most other reordering strategies are likely to be unsafe, due to the somewhat unpredictable effects of reordering in Tison's method. Consider the simple strategy of moving a symbol p, such that neither p nor $\neg p$ are the tied literal of some chain, to the end of the ordering. Any tied chain free under the initial ordering will still be free after this single reordering operation, and others may become free as a result. Yet it can be shown that this can actually increase the number of merges stored by $FPI_1(\Sigma)$. Thus, whereas the investigation of ordering strategies that decrease the size of $FPI_1(\Sigma)$ is important, the status of these strategies is most likely to be purely heuristic, to be validated mostly by experimental rather than analytical means.

5 A COMPLETE LTMS

As mentioned in section 3.2, it would be desirable for small changes in the database not to require the recompilation of the database from the scratch. In this section, we will focus on a particularly simple, but also very common, form of database change. Very often, a database can be partitioned into a highly stable and a highly changing set of clauses. For example, the first set of clauses may capture the behavior of a device with arbitrary inputs, while the second set, typically consisting of unit clauses, represents various assumptions about the inputs of this device.

For this purpose, a logical truth maintenance system (LTMS) is often used [McAllester, 1990]. The task of a LTMS is, given a set of clauses Σ, to produce a labeling L_Σ for all the symbols in the language, $L_\Sigma : \mathcal{P} \to \{true, false, unknown\}$, when Σ is consistent, and to detect a contradiction otherwise. For consistent Σ, the labeling is *sound* with respect to Σ iff $\Sigma \models p$ whenever $L_\Sigma(p) = true$, and $\Sigma \models \neg p$ whenever $L_\Sigma(p) = false$; and it is *complete*[7] iff $L_\Sigma(p) = true$ whenever $\Sigma \models p$, and $L_\Sigma(p) = false$ whenever $\Sigma \models \neg p$. The method used by an LTMS, variously called "unit propagation" or "boolean constraint propagation" (BCP), is logically equivalent to unit resolution, differing from it mostly in that resolvents are never explicitly generated. In particular, if Σ is consistent, $L_\Sigma(p) = true$ iff $\Sigma \vdash_u p$, and $L_\Sigma(p) = false$ iff $\Sigma \vdash_u \neg p$. Furthermore, BCP signals a contradiction iff $\Sigma \vdash_u \bot$.

[7]Note that our terminology differs from that of [de Kleer, 1990].

For the purposes of an LTMS, it is often useful to partition the database into a set of "assumption literals" $\mathcal{A}$, treated as unit clauses, and a set of clauses Σ. An LTMS supports very efficient addition and retraction of assumptions, which makes it an ideal tool for managing database changes restricted to these two operations. But because BCP is equivalent to unit resolution, an LTMS will in general produce sound but incomplete labelings. This deficiency can easily be fixed by using the procedures developed in this paper.

Lemma 10 *If Σ is unit refutation complete and $\mathcal{A}$ is a set of unit clauses then $\Sigma \cup \mathcal{A}$ is unit refutation complete.*

Theorem 11 *$BCP(FPI_0(\Sigma) \cup \mathcal{A})$ produces a sound and complete labeling with respect to $\Sigma \cup \mathcal{A}$ whenever the latter is consistent, and signals a contradiction otherwise.*

This theorem unfortunately does not hold for $FPI_1(\Sigma)$. We can use instead the following "indirect boolean constraint propagation" procedure:

Procedure $IBCP(\Sigma \cup \mathcal{A})$

1. Run BCP on $\Sigma \cup \mathcal{A}$.

2. While there exists an unprocessed symbol p such that $L(p) = unknown$, do:
   - If $\Sigma \cup \mathcal{A} \cup \{p\} \vdash_u \bot$ then set $L(p) = false$ and propagate the new label with BCP.
   - Otherwise, if $\Sigma \cup \mathcal{A} \cup \{\neg p\} \vdash_u \bot$ then set $L(p) = true$ and propagate the new label with BCP.
   - If neither test succeeds, mark p as processed.

The idea behind this procedure is very simple: if BCP on the initial input fails to produce a *true* or *false* label for a given symbol, IBCP tries to produce such a label by indirect proof, using standard LTMS mechanisms for addition and retraction of assumptions (BCP to add the negation of the desired conclusion to the set of assumptions, and roughly the reverse process to later retract it). Needless to say, one may want to attempt the indirect proof only for certain literals of interest. Note that when both tests for a given symbol p fail, BCP can ignore clauses with p or $\neg p$ in the future, as those clauses cannot be the source of new labels.

Theorem 12 *If Σ is unit refutation complete then $IBCP(\Sigma \cup \mathcal{A})$ produces a sound and complete labeling with respect to $\Sigma \cup \mathcal{A}$ whenever the latter is consistent, and signals a contradiction otherwise.*

This theorem is interesting because we know how to obtain unit refutation complete databases. If we do not know whether Σ satisfies the conditions of the theorem, we can replace it by $FPI_1(\Sigma)$, and the condition will be automatically satisfied. Note that $IBCP$ runs in time polynomial in the size of its input, as any symbol is considered only once.

$IBCP$ is compatible with an efficient implementation of assumption retraction. It suffices to keep track, for any symbol p whose label was derived by indirect proof, of the assumptions used in the derivation of the label. If one such assumption is retracted, we must attempt to rederive the label for p; if this fails, we treat the literal corresponding to the label for p (e.g. $\neg p$ if the label is $false$) as an additional assumption to retract.

6 EXPERIMENTAL RESULTS

We implemented the procedures FPI_0 and FPI_1 by adapting the code from [Forbus and de Kleer, 1993], and tested them on several databases drawn from qualitative physics and diagnosis, most of which are either provided with this code or are variants of databases provided with it. We have not tested FPI_2 yet, but plan to do so in the future. The table below includes results for the largest databases tested among these, and for C&M21 and C&M24, the databases from [Chandra and Markowsky, 1978] mentioned in example 2, for k=21 and k=24. Given the importance of the ordering, we experimented with a number of ordering heuristics, involving criteria such as frequency of symbol occurrence, estimated number of tied chains associated to each symbol, a greedy approach to maximizing the number of satisfied ordering constraints, and various combinations thereof. We have not reached any firm conclusion on the effects of the various heuristics, which often vary widely with the problem, and thus we can only present preliminary experimental results. In spite of our very limited understanding of how to obtain good orderings, the results clearly show that our procedures can result in huge savings in the growth of the database by comparison with compilation into the set of prime implicates.

Table 2 gives the size $|\Sigma|$ of the initial database, the number PI of prime implicates, and the sizes FPI_0 and FPI_1 of the corresponding compiled databases for the ordering which gave the smallest $FPI_1(\Sigma)$ in each case. The rightmost columns, $Growth$ and $Savings$, respectively measure the growth of FPI_1 with respect to Σ (FPI_1 divided by $|\Sigma|$), and the reduction in growth with respect to prime implicate compilation, $(PI - |\Sigma|)/(FPI_1 - |\Sigma|)$. For example, in the Adder database, PI grows almost 40 times as much as FPI_1. Though other results are not as impressive, they still produce significant savings. In all examples tested, furthermore, the absolute growth of FPI_1 is at most around an order of magnitude, which will often be a quite reasonable price to pay in exchange for tractable query answering.[8] Of course, a much more compre-

---
[8]The Adder database is the same tested in [de Kleer,

Table 2: Experimental Results

Problem	$|\Sigma|$	PI	FPI_0	FPI_1	G	S
3 pipes	82	2360	1741	545	6.6	4.9
4 pipes	110	6208	4416	1328	12.1	5.0
Regulator	106	2814	2125	829	7.8	3.7
Adder	50	9700	2342	294	5.9	39.5
C&M21	21	2685	498	192	9.1	15.6
C&M24	24	7179	618	258	10.7	30.6

hensive experimental evaluation would be needed to see whether this order of growth can be reasonably expected in interesting cases.

7 DISCUSSION

In this paper, we have introduced a new approach to equivalence preserving logical compilation, which makes query answering tractable with respect to the compiled database. We also have analytically and experimentally demonstrated that the approach can lead to substantial space savings with respect to the compilation of the database into its prime implicates. Given the central role of propositional entailment in AI, it is easy to see that these results can have wide application. We have discussed in some detail one such application, a complete LTMS, and briefly mentioned the increased ability to recognize tractable abduction problems derivable from some of our results.

We have not yet addressed the question of worst case growth in the size of the database as a result of compilation. Using almost identical arguments to those of [Kautz and Selman, 1992], it is easily shown that a polynomial worst case bound on growth would imply $NP \subseteq non\text{-}uniform\ P$, something which is considered very unlikely, and that would imply the collapse of the polynomial hierarchy to Σ_2. (The notion of "non-uniform P" arises from work in circuit complexity [Boppana and Sipser, 1990].)

There are many questions that remain to be answered. The effect of ordering strategies needs to be examined more closely, both analytically and experimentally. Incremental compilation, and the ability to focus compilation on certain interesting clauses (such as the "characteristic clauses" of [Inoue, 1991] are also topics for further research. Finally, an important question is the extent to which these results can be lifted to predicate calculus.

1992]; the divergence in the number of prime implicates arises from a Lisp reader related error in the encoding of the database in [de Kleer, 1992]. Note that many of the databases tested in [de Kleer, 1992] are those of example 2, which we now know need not be compiled.

Acknowledgements

Thanks to Henry Kautz and Bart Selman for sending me the proof of correctness of the Generate-LUB algorithm.

References

[Andrews, 1968] Andrews, Peter B. 1968. Resolution with merging. *Journal of the ACM* 15:367–381.

[Boppana and Sipser, 1990] Boppana, R.B. and Sipser, M. 1990. The complexity of finite functions. In Leeuwen, Jan, editor 1990, *Handbook of Theoretical Computer Science, Volume A: Algorithms and Complexity*. Elsevier.

[Cadoli and Schaerf, 1991] Cadoli, Marco and Schaerf, Marco 1991. Approximate entailment. In *Proceedings of the Second Conference of the Italian Association for Artificial Intelligence*.

[Chandra and Markowsky, 1978] Chandra, Ashok K. and Markowsky, George 1978. On the number of prime implicants. *Discrete Mathematics* 24:7–11.

[Chang and Lee, 1973] Chang, Chin-Liang and Lee, Richard Char-Tung 1973. *Symbolic Logic and Mechanical Theorem Proving*. Academic Press, Inc.

[de Kleer, 1990] de Kleer, Johan 1990. Exploting locality in a TMS. In *Proceedings of the Eight Conference of the AAAI*.

[de Kleer, 1992] de Kleer, Johan 1992. An improved incremental algorithm for generating prime implicates. In *Proceedings of the Tenth Conference of the AAAI*.

[Esghi, 1993] Esghi, Kave 1993. A tractable class of abduction problems. In *Proceedings of the Thirteenth International Joint Conference on Artificial Intelligence*.

[Forbus and de Kleer, 1993] Forbus, Ken and Kleer, Johande 1993. *Building Problem Solvers*. The MIT Press.

[Henschen and Wos, 1974] Henschen, L. and Wos, L. 1974. Unit refutations and horn sets. *Journal of the ACM* 21:590–605.

[Inoue, 1991] Inoue, Katsumi 1991. Consequence-finding based on ordered linear resolution. In *Proceedings of the Twelfth International Joint Conference on Artificial Intelligence*.

[Kautz and Selman, 1992] Kautz, Henry and Selman, Bart 1992. Forming concepts for fast inference. In *Proceedings of the Tenth Conference of the AAAI*.

[Kautz, 1994] Kautz, Henry 1994. Personal communication.

[Kean and Tsiknis, 1990] Kean, Alex and Tsiknis, George 1990. An incremental method for generating prime implicants/implicates. *Journal of Symbolic Computation* 9:185–206.

[Lee, 1993] Lee, R.C.T. 1993. *A Completeness Theorem and a Computer Program for Finding Theorems Derivable from Given Axioms*. Ph.D. Dissertation, University of California at Berkeley.

[Levesque, 1986] Levesque, Hector J. 1986. Making believers out of computers. *Artificial Intelligence* 30:81–108.

[McAllester, 1990] McAllester, David 1990. Truth maintenance. In *Proceedings of the Ninth Conference of the AAAI*.

[Minicozzi and Reiter, 1972] Minicozzi, Eliana and Reiter, Raymond 1972. A note on linear resolution strategies in consequence-finding. *Artificial Intelligence* 3:175–180.

[Reiter and de Kleer, 1987] Reiter, Raymond and Kleer, Johannde 1987. Foundations of assumption-based truth maintenance systems. In *Proceedings of the Sixth Conference of the AAAI*.

[Reiter, 1971] Reiter, Raymond 1971. Two results on ordering for resolution with merging and linear format. *Journal of the ACM* 18:630–646.

[Selman and Kautz, 1991] Selman, Bart and Kautz, Henry 1991. Knowledge compilation using Horn approximations. In *Proceedings of the Ninth Conference of the AAAI*.

[Tennenholtz and Moses, 1993] Tennenholtz, Moshe and Moses, Yoram 1993. Off-line reasoning for on-line efficiency. In *Proceedings of the Thirteenth International Joint Conference on Artificial Intelligence*.

[Tison, 1967] Tison, P. 1967. Generalized consensus theory and application to the minimization of boolean circuits. *IEEE Transactions on Computers* EC-16:446–456.

The Role of Reversible Grammars in Translating Between Representation Languages

Jeffrey Van Baalen
Computer Science Department
P.O.Box 3682
University of Wyoming
Laramie, WY 82071
jvb@uwyo.edu

Richard E. Fikes
Knowledge Systems Laboratory
Stanford University
701 Welch Rd., Bldg. C
Stanford, CA 94304
fikes@ksl.stanford.edu

Abstract

A capability for translating between representation languages is critical for effective knowledge base reuse. We describe a translation technology for knowledge representation languages based on the use of an *interlingua* for communicating knowledge. The interlingua-based translation process can be thought of as consisting of three major steps: (1) translation from the source language into a subset of the interlingua, (2) translation between subsets of the interlingua, and (3) translation from a subset of the interlingua into the target language. The first translation step into the interlingua can typically be specified in the form of a grammar that describes how each top-level form in the source language translates into the interlingua. We observe that in cases where the source language does not have a declarative semantics, such a grammar is also a specification of a declarative semantics for the language. We describe the conditions under which such a grammar is *reversible* so that the grammar can also be used to translate out of the interlingua. In particular, we formally describe the translation process into and out of an interlingua, present a method for determining whether a given grammar in fact specifies how to construct a translation for every top-level form in a given source language; and present a method for determining whether a given grammar is reversible so that it can be used to translate both into and out of an interlingua.

1 Introduction

Acquiring and representing knowledge is the key to building large and powerful AI systems. Unfortunately, knowledge base construction is difficult and time consuming. The development of most systems requires a new knowledge base to be constructed from scratch. As a result, most systems remain small to medium in size. The cost of this duplication of effort has been high and will become prohibitive as attempts are made to build larger systems. A promising approach to removing this barrier to the building of large scale AI systems is to develop techniques for encoding knowledge in a reusable form so that large portions of a knowledge base for a given application can be *assembled* from knowledge repositories and other systems.

For encoded knowledge to be incorporated into a system's knowledge base or interchanged among interoperating systems, the knowledge must either be represented in the receiving system's representation language or be translatable in some practical way into that language. Since an important means of achieving efficiency in application systems is to use specialized representation languages that directly support the knowledge processing requirements of the application, we cannot expect a standard knowledge representation language to emerge that would be used generally in application systems. Thus, we are confronted with a *heterogeneous language problem* whose solution requires a capability for translating encoded knowledge among specialized representation languages.

We are addressing the heterogeneous language problem by developing a translation technology for knowledge representation languages based on the use of an *interlingua* for communicating knowledge among systems. Given such an interlingua, a sending system would translate knowledge from its application-specific representation into the interlingua for communication purposes and a receiving system would translate knowledge from the interlingua into its application-specific representation before use. In addition, the interlingua could be the language in which libraries would provide reusable knowledge bases. An interlingua eases the translation problem in that to communicate knowledge to and from N languages without an interlingua, one must write $(N-1)^2$ translators into and out of the languages. With an interlingua, one need only write 2N translators into and out of the interlingua.

We consider in this paper the problem of translating declarative knowledge among representation languages using an interlingua with the following properties:

- A formally defined declarative semantics;
- Sufficient expressive power to represent any theory that is representable in the languages for which translators are to be built.

In practice, one cannot expect any given interlingua to have sufficient expressive power to support usable representations of *any* theory that is representable in *any* language. However, an interlingua with the expressive power of first-order logic, such as the Knowledge Interchange Format (KIF) being developed in the ARPA Knowledge Sharing Effort [Genesereth & Fikes 92], can provide that support for a broad spectrum of theories and languages. For our purposes in this paper, we will assume an interlingua and a set of languages for which the properties listed above hold.

The interlingua-based translation process can be thought of as consisting of three major steps:

- Translation from the source language into a subset of the interlingua;
- Translation between subsets of the interlingua; and
- Translation from a subset of the interlingua into the target language.

Since the interlingua is assumed to be at least as expressive as the source language, the first translation step into the interlingua can typically be specified in the form of a grammar that describes how each *top-level form* (e.g., sentence, definition, rule) in the source language translates into the interlingua. In this paper we specify the conditions under which such a grammar is *reversible* so that the grammar can also be used to translate out of the interlingua. If one has such a reversible grammar for the target language, then step 2 involves translating from the subset of the interlingua produced by the source language grammar to the subset of the interlingua that is translated (i.e., recognized) by the reverse of the target language grammar. For any given top-level form F_s in the source subset, translation step 2 involves determining a top-level form F_t in the target subset such that F_s is logically equivalent to F_t. Thus, formally, step 2 requires hypothesizing an equivalent form in the target subset and then proving the equivalence.

Step 2 of the translation process is the difficult one for most languages. However, steps 1 and 3 are far from trivial. In this paper, we present formal languages and methods that are adequate for doing steps 1 and 3. In particular, we:

- Formally describe the translation process into and out of an interlingua;
- Present a method for determining whether a given grammar in fact specifies how to construct a translation for every top level form in a given source language; and
- Present a method for determining whether a given grammar is reversible so that it can be used to translate both into and out of an interlingua.

These languages and methods have been incorporated into a "translator shell" system that provides facilities for specifying interlingua-based translation using KIF as the interlingua. The system has been used to build translators for multiple representation languages and those translators have successfully translated non-trivial knowledge bases. The examples in this paper are taken from two of these grammars: a CLASSIC [Borgida, et al 89] to KIF grammar and a LOOM [MacGregor 91] to KIF grammar. The CLASSIC to KIF grammar is used in a bi-directional translator [Fikes, et al 91], and the LOOM to KIF grammar is used in a bi-directional translator currently under development.

2 Interlingua-Based Translations and Semantics

We consider here *equivalence preserving translations* [Buvac and Fikes 93] in which the translation of an axiomatization of a logical theory is an axiomatization of an equivalent logical theory. To make such a requirement on translators meaningful, a declarative semantics including logical entailment needs to be formally specified for both the source and target languages. We are assuming such a declarative semantics for the interlingua. In cases where a language does not have such a declarative semantics, specifying a translation of that language into the interlingua provides a declarative semantics for the language. Thus, another advantage of using an interlingua is that it offers a relatively easy way to specify a semantics for new representation languages. This use of an interlingua for specifying the semantics of representation languages may turn out to be at least as important as its role in facilitating translation among representation languages. This method of semantics specification is based on the following definition:

Definition 2.1 (interlingua-based semantics)
Let L be a language, L_i be an interlingua language with a formally defined declarative semantics, $TRANS_{L,L_i}$ be a binary relation between top-level forms of L and top-level forms of L_i, and BT_L be a set of top-level forms in L_i. The pair $\langle TRANS_{L,L_i}, BT_L \rangle$

is called an L_i-based semantics for L when for every set T_L of top-level forms in L, there is a set T_{L_i} of top-level forms in L_i such that

$$\forall s_1 \in T_L \exists s_2 \in T_{L_i} \; TRANS_{L,L_i}(s_1, s_2)$$
$$\forall s_2 \in T_{L_i} \exists s_1 \in T_L \; TRANS_{L,L_i}(s_1, s_2)$$

and the theory of $T_{L_i} \cup BT_L$ is equivalent to the theory represented by T_L.

Hence, $TRANS_{L,L_i}$ specifies translations of top-level forms in L to top-level forms in L_i. Roughly speaking, BT_L is the set of axioms that are included in the semantics of L expressed in L_i. For example, a device modeling language might have a vocabulary of measures (e.g., inch, foot) and include in its semantics the axioms that relate those measures.

If $\langle TRANS_{L,L_i}, BT_L \rangle$ is being used to define the semantics of L, then "the theory represented by T_L" is equivalent to "the theory of $T_{L_i} \cup BT_L$" by definition. If L has an independently defined semantics, then the equivalence of the two theories is a requirement on the definition of $TRANS_{L,L_i}$.

TRANS is defined as a relation rather than a function because we allow there to be more than one translation of a top-level form in L so long as it does not matter which translation is picked. Thus, TRANS can be viewed as a function into equivalence classes of interlingua top-level forms. Note also that TRANS defines what it means for two sentences in L to be equivalent, namely that their translations are equivalent sentences in L_i.

An additional advantage of the interlingua-based approach to semantics is that if such a semantics is given in a machine executable form, it can be used to automatically translate a new language into the interlingua. Hence, with a single effort, one can give both a semantics for a new language and a procedure for translating it into the interlingua.

In this paper, we describe a language translation methodology in which one specifies the semantics of a new representation language using a special kind of definite clause grammar [Pereira & Warren 80] that we call a *definite clause translation grammar* (DCTG). This grammar can be used to translate top-level forms in the new language into an interlingua. A DCTG is a set of Horn clauses that has a distinguished binary predicate symbol TRANS such that if s_1 is a top-level form in the new language and s_2 is a top-level form in the interlingua, $TRANS(s_1, s_2)$ follows from the grammar just in case s_2 is a translation of s_1. Our methodology is related to that reported in [Strzalkowski 91] in which the notion of reversible definite clause grammars is informally developed for use in the context of producing generators from parsers for natural languages.

3 Definite Clause Translation Grammars

We now discuss the role of DCTGs in the language translation task. Given an interlingua-based semantics for a language L_1 that is written as a DCTG, we show how to check whether or not it can be used to translate sets of top-level forms in L_1 into the interlingua. Perhaps, by itself, this is not particularly significant since one normally writes a DCTG so that it has this property. However, we show how to use the same techniques to check a much more obscure property, whether or not a DCTG can be used to translate in the other direction, i.e., to translate sets of top-level forms from a subset of the interlingua into sets of top-level forms in L_1. Such a "reverse" translator defines a subset of the interlingua that can be directly translated into a specialized language.

The formalism that follows is generalized to two arbitrary languages, rather than requiring one of the languages to be an interlingua, since all of our results apply to this more general case. We begin by defining what it means for a DCTG to be a translator. Several preliminary notions are required. The first is the notion of a set of first-order Horn clauses *implementing* a relation.

Definition 3.1 (implements) Let $\vdash_p$ be the reflexive, transitive closure of the PROLOG inference relation; i.e., $\Gamma \vdash_p \delta$ just in case there is an SLD refutation of $\{\neg \delta\} \cup \Gamma$ [Loyd 87]. A set of first-order Horn clauses G is said to *implement* a relation R if

$$\forall x_1, \ldots, x_n \{R(x_1, \ldots, x_n) \Leftrightarrow [G \vdash_p R(x_1, \ldots, x_n)]\}$$

Definition 3.2 (verifier) Let $\langle TRANS_{L_1,L_2}, BT_{L_1} \rangle$ be an L_2-based semantics for L_1. A set of Horn clauses G is said to be an L_1,L_2-*verifier* when G implements $TRANS_{L_1,L_2}$. The predicate symbol $TRANS_{L_1,L_2}$ is called the *goal symbol* of G.

A set of Horn clauses G can implement a relation R in such a way that G can be used only to check whether R is true of some tuple of constants. We distinguish sets of Horn clauses for which this is the case from sets which implement R in such a manner as to enable R to be used like a function; i.e., given values for some of the arguments of R, the Horn clauses can be used to derive the remaining arguments. We call such implementations *constructive*.

Definition 3.3 (constructively implements) Let R be an n-ary relation symbol and G be a set of Horn clauses that implements R. G is said to *constructively implement* R in arguments $i_1, \ldots, i_m$, where $1 \leq i_j \leq n$, for all $j = 1, \ldots, m$, if

$$\forall x_1, \ldots, x_n \{[G \vdash_p R(x_1, \ldots, x_n)] \Rightarrow$$
$$[G \vdash_p \exists x_{i_1}, \ldots, x_{i_m} R(x_1, \ldots, x_n)]\}$$

and the terms $x_{i_1}, \ldots, x_{i_m}$ are extractable from the above existence proof.

Hence, if G constructively implements R in some subset of its arguments $i_1, \ldots, i_m$, whenever G can be used to verify that R is true of some n-tuple $\langle x_1, \ldots, x_n \rangle$, then given the values for all the $x_i, i \neq i_1, \ldots, i_m$, G can also be used to derive the other values in the n-tuple $x_{i_1}, \ldots, x_{i_m}$. This notion is similar to "in" and "out" arguments as reported in [Strzalkowski 90]. Note that, it is possible for $m = 0$ or $m = n$. In other words, it is possible for the implementations of some relations to construct all of their arguments or none of them.

If G constructively implements an n-ary predicate R in arguments $i_1, \ldots, i_m$, we write

$$G : R[(\{1, \ldots, n\} - \{i_1, \ldots, i_m\}) \rightarrow \{i_1, \ldots, i_m\}]$$

For example, if G constructively implements a 3-ary predicate R such that given values for R's first and second argument, G can be used to construct values for R's third argument, we write $G : R[\{1, 2\} \rightarrow \{3\}]$, or just $G : R[1, 2 \rightarrow 3]$.

When an n-ary predicate R occurs positively in a Horn clause C, we will say that the clause C (rather than a set of clauses) *constructively implements* R if for all n-tuples of terms $\langle t_1, \ldots, t_n \rangle$ for which there is a refutation proof of $R(t_1, \ldots, t_n)$ in which C occurs, it is the case that given just the terms $t_{i_1}, \ldots, t_{i_m}$, there exists a refutation proof in which C occurs that constructs the terms $t_{i_{m+1}}, \ldots, t_{i_n}$. We will use the same notation for constructive implementation by a single clause C as we do for constructive implementation by a set of clauses, namely $C : R[i_1, \ldots, i_m \rightarrow i_{m+1}, \ldots, i_n]$.

If, in addition to being a verifier, a set of Horn clauses G can be used to construct sentences in L_2 that are the translations of sentences in L_1, G is called a translator.

Definition 3.4 (translator) A set of Horn clauses G that is an L_1, L_2-verifier is called a *translator from L_1 to L_2* when G's goal symbol $TRANS_{L_1,L_2}$ is constructive in its second argument, i.e., $G : TRANS_{L_1,L_2}[1 \rightarrow 2]$.

3.1 Showing that a set of Horn clauses is a translator

Given a set of Horn clauses G with goal symbol $TRANS$, we show how to prove that G is a translator. The proof involves showing that G has the property $G : TRANS[1 \rightarrow 2]$, which is done by showing that each clause C in G in which $TRANS$ occurs positively has the property $C : TRANS[1 \rightarrow 2]$. This, in turn, requires showing that the predicate symbols in each of those clauses construct values for certain of their arguments.

The results in this section give a method of checking whether a DCTG can be used as a translator. The technique has been used successfully on DCTGs for CLASSIC to KIF, LOOM to KIF, and EXPRESS [Spiby, et al ?] to KIF. We have found that the technique is very effective not only for showing that a DCTG can be used as a translator, but also for identifying where the problems are in a DCTG that is not a translator.

The key notion used in the technique, which we now define, is called a *constructive chain*.

Definition 3.5 (definition) Let G be a set of Horn clauses that implements the predicate P. The set of clauses in G in which P occurs positively is called the *definition* of P.

Definition 3.6 (constructive chain) Let G be a set of Horn clauses, C be a clause in G of the following form:

```
(<- (P e_1 e_2 ...)
    (Q_1 e_1,1 e_1,2 ...) ... (Q_n e_n,1 e_n,2 ...)),
```

and $\{x_1, \ldots, x_r\}$ be a subset of the variables occurring in C. We say that C contains a *constructive chain* ending in its head from $\{x_1, \ldots, x_r\}$ to every variable $x_i, i = 1, \ldots, r$ that occurs in the head. Moreover, if y is a variable occurring in term $e_{i,j}$ (i.e., in the jth argument of the ith literal of the tail of C), we say that C contains a *constructive chain* ending in i from $\{x_1, \ldots, x_r\}$ to y when $G : Q_i[k_1, \ldots, k_m \rightarrow \ldots, j]$ and for each variable z occurring in expressions $e_{i,k_1}, \ldots, e_{i,k_m}$ either there is a constructive chain ending in the head of C from $\{x_1, \ldots, x_r\}$ to z or there is some $1 \leq l < i$ such that there is a constructive chain ending in l from $\{x_1, \ldots, x_r\}$ to z.

The definition of a constructive chain from a given set of variables $\{x_1, \ldots, x_r\}$ to a given variable y occurring in a clause is recursive. The base case for the recursion is when y occurs in the head of the clause. The recursive case is when y occurs in the jth argument of the ith literal of the tail of the clause. In that case, the grammar G must constructively implement argument j of the predicate in the ith literal given arguments $k_1, \ldots, k_m$, and there must be a constructive chain from $\{x_1, \ldots, x_r\}$ to every variable occurring in arguments $k_1, \ldots, k_m$.

Example: Constructive chain.

Consider the following clause from the grammar $G_{CL,KIF}$:

```
(<- (TRANS_CL,KIF
     (cl-define-concept ?Con-name ?Expr)
     (defrelation ?Con-Name (?Cl-Var) := ?New))
    (var ?CL-Var)
```

```
(relation-symbol ?Con-Name)
(newexpr ?Expr ?New ?Cl-Var))
```

Suppose that var constructs an instantiation for its argument (i.e., $G_{CL,KIF}$: var$[\to 1]$), relation-symbol is not constructive (i.e., $G_{CL,KIF}$: relation-symbol $[1 \to]$), and grammar $G_{CL,KIF}$ constructively implements the second and third arguments of newexpr given the first argument (i.e., $G_{CL,KIF}$: newexpr$[1 \to 2,3]$). Then, there is a constructive chain ending in 3 (i.e., ending in the third literal in the tail) from {?Con-name, ?Expr} to ?New because there is a constructive chain to ?Expr ending in the head of the clause and newexpr has the property $[1 \to 2, 3]$.

More generally, in order to prove that the above clause has the property $TRANS_{CL,KIF}[1 \to 2]$, we must show that there is a constructive chain from the variables occurring in the first argument of $TRANS_{CL,KIF}$ (i.e., {?Con-name, ?Expr}) to each variable occurring in the second argument of $TRANS_{CL,KIF}$, (i.e., ?Con-Name, ?Cl-Var, and ?New). There is a trivial chain to ?Con-Name, there is a chain ending in 1 to ?CL-Var, and we have just shown that there is a chain to ?New.

For purposes of exposition, if there is a constructive chain in the head of a clause from $\{x_1, \ldots, x_r\}$ to a variable y or a constructive chain in some $i \leq n$ from $\{x_1, \ldots, x_r\}$ to y, then we say that there is a *constructive chain in the clause* from $\{x_1, \ldots, x_r\}$ to y, i.e., we drop the reference to where the chain ends.

We now state and prove the main results of the paper. The following theorem and corollary tell us that we can prove a predicate is constructive in some subset of its arguments by showing that there are constructive chains to certain of the variables occurring in each clause in the predicate's definition.

Theorem 3.1 *Let G implement P, the definition of P contain the clause*

```
C = (<- (P e1 e2 ... ek)
        (Q1 e1,1 e1,2 ...) ... (Qn en,1 en,2 ...)),
```

G implement each of the Q_i in C, and $\{x_1, \ldots, x_r\}$ be the variables occurring in the expressions $e_{i_1}, \ldots, e_{i_m}$, $1 \leq i_i \leq k, i = i_1, \ldots, i_m$. If there is a constructive chain from $\{x_1, \ldots, x_r\}$ ending in the left most occurrence of every variable in the tail of C and there is a constructive chain to every variable occurring in $e_{i_{m+1}}, \ldots, e_{i_k}$, then $C : P[i_1, \ldots, i_m \to i_{m+1}, \ldots, i_k]$.

Proof: Let $\langle t_1, \ldots, t_k \rangle$ be a k-tuple of values such that $G \vdash_p P(t_1, \ldots, t_k)$ and without loss of generality, suppose that $P : [1, \ldots, m \to m+1, \ldots, n]$. We show that, given an SLD refutation of $\{\neg P(t_1, \ldots, t_k)\} \cup G$ in which $\neg P(t_1, \ldots, t_k)$ is resolved with C, we can construct a refutation of

$$\{\neg P(t_1, \ldots, t_m, y_{m+1}, \ldots, y_n)\} \cup G$$

, where the variables $y_{m+1}, \ldots, y_n$ are bound to $t_{m+1}, \ldots, t_n$, respectively, in the refutation.

First, suppose the refutation is of length 1. Then C has an empty tail and, by assumption, there must be a constructive chain ending in the head to each of the variables occurring in $e_{m+1}, \ldots, e_k$; i.e., the variables occurring in $e_{m+1}, \ldots, e_k$ must be a subset of those occurring in $e_1, \ldots, e_m$. Hence, since the $e_1, \ldots, e_m$ must unify with $t_1, \ldots, t_m$, the single step refutation of

$$\{\neg P(t_1, \ldots, t_m, y_{m+1}, \ldots, y_k)\} \cup G$$

results in bindings for all of the variables occurring in $e_{m+1}, \ldots, e_k$, so that each of the $y_{m+1}, \ldots, y_k$ is bound to $t_{m+1}, \ldots, t_k$ respectively.

Now, we suppose there is a refutation of

$$\{\neg P(t_1, \ldots, t_k)\} \cup G$$

of length greater than one and show how to construct a refutation of

$$\{\neg P(t_1, \ldots, t_m, y_{m+1}, \ldots, y_k)\} \cup G$$

resulting in each of $y_{m+1}, \ldots, y_k$ being bound to $t_{m+1}, \ldots, t_k$. The first step in the refutation being constructed is to resolve $\neg P(t_1, \ldots, t_m, y_{m+1}, \ldots, y_k)$ with C. As in the one step case above, the $t_1, \ldots, t_m$ must unify with $e_1, \ldots, e_m$, resulting in a unifier σ containing bindings for each of the variables in those expressions.

Now suppose that in the refutation of

$$\{\neg P(t_1, \ldots, t_k)\} \cup G,$$

the step that eliminates the ith literal in the tail of C yields a unifier σ_1 such that $e_{i,1}\sigma_1 = t_{i_1}, \ldots, e_{i,r}\sigma_1 = t_{i_r}$, and suppose that Q_i has the property $[j_1, \ldots, j_l \to j_{l+1}, \ldots, j_r]$. Suppose further that we have constructed a refutation of

$$\{\neg P(t_1, \ldots, t_m, y_{m+1}, \ldots, y_k)\} \cup G$$

up to the point where the next step is to eliminate the ith literal in the tail of C. Since the left most occurrence of every variable in the tail of C is constructive, the refutation to this step must have yielded a unifier σ_2 in which the variables occurring in $e_{i,j_1}, \ldots, e_{i,j_l}$ are all bound. Suppose that $e_{i,j_1}\sigma_2 = t_{i_1}, \ldots, e_{i,j_l}\sigma_2 = t_{i_l}$. Since there is a refutation of $\{\neg P(t_1, \ldots, t_k)\} \cup G$, it must be the case that $G \vdash_p Q_i(t_{i_1}, \ldots, t_{i_r})$, and since Q_i has the property $[j_1, \ldots, j_l \to j_{l+1}, \ldots, j_r]$, it must be the case that $G \vdash_p \exists z_{l+1}, \ldots, z_r Q_i(t_{i_1}, \ldots, t_l, z_{l+1}, \ldots, z_r)$ and that the terms $t_{l+1}, \ldots, t_r$ are constructed in that proof. Hence, the resolution step that eliminates the ith literal will produce a unifier σ_3 such that $e_{i,j_{l+1}}\sigma_3 = t_{i_{j_{l+1}}}, \ldots, e_{i,j_r}\sigma_3 = t_{i_r}$.

Hence given a refutation of $\{\neg P(t_1, \ldots, t_k)\} \cup G$, it is possible to construct a refutation of
$$\{\neg P(t_1, \ldots, t_m, y_{m+1}, \ldots, y_k)\} \cup G$$
in which every variable is bound to the value it has in the refutation of $\{\neg P(t_1, \ldots, t_k)\} \cup G$ Since there is a constructive chain in C to every variable occurring in the expressions $\mathbf{e_{m+1}}, \ldots, \mathbf{e_k}$, and we can construct values for these variables that are the same as those occurring in a refutation of $\{\neg P(t_1, \ldots, t_k)\} \cup G$, it must be the case that the refutation produces a unifier σ such that $\mathbf{e_{m+1}}\sigma = t_{m+1}, \ldots, \mathbf{e_k}\sigma = t_k$. Therefore, it must be the case that $y_{m+1} = t_{m+1}, \ldots, y_n = t_k$. □

It is interesting to note that for most "reasonable grammars," the converse of this theorem is also true. That is, if for a clause C, $C : P[i_1, \ldots, i_m \rightarrow i_{m+1}, \ldots, i_n]$, there are constructive chains from the variables in arguments $i_1, \ldots, i_m$ of the head to the left most occurrence of every variable in the tail of C and to the variables in the arguments $i_{m+1}, \ldots, i_n$ of the head. However, it is possible to write "weird" grammars for which this is not the case. For example, if a predicate has extra arguments that it ignores, then the converse of the theorem will not hold.

Corollary 3.1 Let G implement P. If $C : P[i_1, \ldots, i_m \rightarrow i_{m+1}, \ldots, i_n]$ for all C in P's definition, then $G : P[i_1, \ldots, i_m \rightarrow i_{m+1}, \ldots, i_n]$.

Proof: Consider an n-tuple $\langle t_1, \ldots, t_n \rangle$ such that $G \vdash_p P(t_1, \ldots, t_n)$. $P(t_1, \ldots, t_n)$ must be established by an SLD refutation involving one or more clauses in the definition of P. Since every such clause has the property $[i_1, \ldots, i_m \rightarrow i_{m+1}, \ldots, i_n]$, there must also be a refutation of $P(t_{i_1}, \ldots, t_{i_m}, y_{i_{m+1}}, \ldots, y_{i_n})$ yielding a unifier σ such that $y_{i_{m+1}}\sigma = t_{i_{m+1}}, \ldots, y_{i_n}\sigma = t_{i_n}$. □

Here again, for most reasonable grammars the converse of this corollary is true. In the proof of theorem 3.1, we used the fact that if $G \vdash_p P(t_1, \ldots, t_n)$ and $G : P[i_1, \ldots, i_m \rightarrow i_{m+1} \ldots, i_n]$, then there exists a proof from G that constructs $t_{i_{m+1}}, \ldots, t_{i_n}$ from $t_{i_1}, \ldots, t_{i_m}$. A question that arises is whether or not this is the first proof that PROLOG finds. Because we assume in the definition of interlingua-based semantics that all translations of a given sentence are equivalent, if $G \vdash_p TRANS_{L_1,L_2}(l_1, l_2)$ and a proof of $G \vdash_p \exists x \, TRANS_{L_1,L_2}(l_1, x)$ produces a sentence l'_2, then it must be the case that l'_2 is equivalent to l_2. Hence, the first sentence constructed in the proof of $G \vdash_p \exists x \, TRANS_{L_1,L_2}(l_1, x)$ can be used whether or not it is l_2.

Example: Proving that a predicate is constructive.

To show that a given DCTG is a translator, we must show that its goal symbol has the property $[1 \rightarrow 2]$. The method of proving Theorem 3.1 can be used directly to show that a DCTG has that property or to identify the clauses in a grammar that must be modified in order to obtain that property (and therefore to produce a translator from a verifier that is not a translator). For example, as with all the grammars we have developed, we have verified that our CLASSIC to KIF grammar is indeed a translator. This was done by showing that its goal symbol $TRANS_{CL,KIF}$ has the property $[1 \rightarrow 2]$. To accomplish this, we showed that the predicate **newexpr**, which occurs in the definition of $TRANS_{CL,KIF}$, has the property $[1 \rightarrow 2, 3]$. Below is the definition of **newexpr** from the grammar.

```
(<- (newexpr host-thing (host-thing ?Cl-Var)
             ?Cl-Var)
    (var ?Cl-Var))

(<- (newexpr (and ?Expr1 ?Expr2)
             (and ?New1 ?New2)
             ?Cl-Var)
    (newexpr ?Expr1 ?New1 ?Cl-Var)
    (newexpr ?Expr2 ?New2 ?Cl-Var))

(<- (newexpr (and ?Expr1 ?Expr2 .  ?Rest)
             (and ?New1 .   ?RNEW)
             ?Cl-Var)
    (newexpr ?Expr1 ?New1 ?Cl-Var)
    (newexpr (and ?Expr2 .  ?Cl-Rest)
             (and .  ?RNEW)
             ?Cl-Var))

(<- (newexpr (all ?Role-Name ?Expr)
             (=> (?Role-Name ?Cl-Var ?New-Var)
                 ?New)
             ?Cl-Var)
    (var ?Cl-Var) (relation-symbol ?Role-Name)
    (newexpr ?Expr ?New ?New-Var))
```

To show that **newexpr** has the property $[1 \rightarrow 2, 3]$, we must show that it has this property in each of the above clauses. To do this, we must show two things: that there are constructive chains from the variables occurring in the first argument of the clause's head to the left most occurrence of every variable that occurs in the tail, and that there are constructive chains from the variables in the first argument to the variables in the other arguments.

As before, assume that $G_{CL,KIF} : \mathtt{var}[\rightarrow 1]$ and that $G_{CL,KIF} : \mathtt{relation\text{-}symbol}[1 \rightarrow]$. The proof is done for the first clause as follows. There are no variables in the first argument in the head, so we must show that there is a constructive chain from $\{\}$ to the left most occurrence of ?Cl-Var in the clause. This is straightforward because $\mathtt{var}[\rightarrow 1]$.

The property $[1 \rightarrow 2, 3]$ is more difficult to establish in the subsequent clauses of **newexpr**'s definition because they define **newexpr** recursively. An inductive argument is required to show the property in these clauses. The basis step in the inductive argument requires showing that the predicate has the property in each clause in which it is not defined in terms of itself. For example, we must show (as we have) that `newexpr` is $[1 \to 2, 3]$ in the first clause above. In each clause in which a predicate is defined recursively, we assume that the predicate has the property in each of its occurrences in the tail of the clause and show that, under this assumption, the predicate has the property in the clause. For example, we assume in the second clause above that `newexpr` has the property $[1 \to 2, 3]$ in both of its occurrences in the tail, and we must show that there are constructive chains from {?Expr1, ?Expr2} to the left most occurrences of ?New1, ?New2, and ?Cl-Var. There is a constructive chain from {?Expr1, ?Expr2} to ?Cl-Var ending in 1, a constructive chain from {?Expr1, ?Expr2} to ?New1 ending in 1, and a constructive chain from {?Expr1, ?Expr2} to ?New2 ending in 2. Therefore, `newexpr` has the property $[1 \to 2, 3]$ in this clause.

A property of $\to$ that is often useful when proving that predicates are constructive is that if a predicate is constructive in some subset of its arguments then it is constructive in any smaller subset of its arguments. For example, the predicate `member` has the property $[2 \to 1]$. Therefore, it is also $[2, 1 \to]$.

Lemma 3.1 *Let G be a set of horn clauses and P be an n-ary predicate symbol such that*

$$G : P[\{i_1, \ldots, i_m\} \to \{i_{m+1}, \ldots, i_n\}], m < n$$

. Then,

$$G : P[\{i_1, \ldots, i_m, i\} \to (\{i_{m+1}, \ldots, i_n\} - \{i\})]$$

for every $i \in \{i_m + 1, \ldots, i_n\}$.

Proof: Suppose that $G \vdash_p P(t_1, \ldots, t_n)$ and, without loss of generality, that $G : P[1, \ldots, m \to m+1, \ldots, n]$. Then, $G \vdash_p \exists x_{m+1}, \ldots, x_n P(t_1, \ldots, t_m, x_{m+1}, \ldots, x_n)$, and the terms $t_{m+1}, \ldots, t_n$ are extractable from the proof; i.e., there exists a refutation of $G \cup \{\neg P(t_1, \ldots, t_m, x_{m+1}, \ldots, x_n)\}$ that yields a most general unifier σ such that $x_{m+1}\sigma = t_{m+1}, \ldots, x_n\sigma = t_n$.

We must show that for any of the variables x_i, where $m + 1 \leq i \leq n$, that there is a refutation of the new goal that results from replacing x_i with t_i in $\neg P(t_1, \ldots, t_m, x_{m+1}, \ldots, x_n)$. So, we arbitrarily choose x_n, replace it with t_n, and show that there exists a refutation of $G \cup \{\neg P(t_1, \ldots, t_m, x_{m+1}, \ldots, x_{n-1}, t_n)\}$. This is done by showing how to transform the refutation of $G \cup \{\neg P(t_1, \ldots, t_m, x_{m+1}, \ldots, x_n)\}$ into the desired refutation.

The refutation of $G \cup \{\neg P(t_1, \ldots, t_m, x_{m+1}, \ldots, x_n)\}$ is a finite sequence

$$g_0 = \neg P(x_1, \ldots, t_m, x_{m+1}, \ldots, x_n)$$
$$\vdots$$
$$g_k = \square$$

of goals, a sequence $c_1, \ldots, c_k$ of variants of clauses of G, and a sequence $\sigma_1, \ldots, \sigma_k$ of most general unifiers such that each g_{i+1} is derived by resolving $g_i \sigma_{i+1}$ with $c_{i+1}\sigma_{i+1}$. Note that, by assumption, $x_n \sigma_k = t_n$.

Now, consider the unifier σ_{t_n} whose only substitution is t_n for x_n. We transform the above refutation by replacing each σ_i with $\sigma_i \sigma_{t_n}$. Since each of the new unifiers is a specialization of the original, each resolution step must still be correct. Furthermore, $\sigma_k \sigma_{t_n} = \sigma_k$, so the final bindings for all of the x_i remain the same.

But now we can replace x_n in g_0 with t_n without effecting the first step of the refutation, and so this new refutation is a refutation of $G \cup \{\neg P(t_1, \ldots, t_m, x_{m+1}, \ldots, x_{n-1}, t_n)\}$ that yields a unifier σ_k such that $x_{m+1}\sigma_k = t_{m+1}, \ldots, x_{n-1}\sigma_k = t_{n-1}$.
$\square$

We have found this result to be useful in proving predicates constructive because it allows us to "short circuit" some required steps. Often we show that some predicate is constructive in some subset of its arguments and then later need to show that it is constructive in a smaller subset. Using this lemma, the needed result is immediate.

4 Reversible Definite Clause Translation Grammars

Now, we are in a position to specify when a DCTG can be used not only to translate from L_1 to L_2, but also from L_2 to L_1, a property we term *reversible in place*.

Definition 4.1 (reversible in place) Let G be a translator from L_1 to L_2. If G can also be used as a translator from a subset of L_2 to L_1, we call G reversible in place.

Lemma 4.1 *Let G be a translator from L_1 to L_2. If G's goal symbol $TRANS_{L_1,L_2}$ has the property $[2 \to 1]$, then G is reversible in place.*

This result is obvious since given a value s_2 for $TRANS_{L_1,L_2}$'s second argument, for any value s_1 that the DCTG constructs for its first argument, it must be the case that $TRANS_{L_1,L_2}(s_1, s_2)$.

Translators that are reversible in place have some useful properties that follow from our assumptions about an interlingua-based semantics, as follows. Given languages L_1 and L_2, a DCTG with goal predicate $TRANS_{L_1,L_2}$, and equivalence relations $\equiv_1$ and $\equiv_2$ on top-level forms in L_1 and L_2 respectively:

$\forall x_1 y_1 x_2 y_2$
$[TRANS_{L_1,L_2}(x_1, y_1) \wedge TRANS_{L_1,L_2}(x_2, y_2) \wedge$
$x_1 \equiv_1 x_2 \Rightarrow y_1 \equiv_2 y_2]$
$\forall x_1 y_1 x_2 y_2$
$[TRANS_{L_1,L_2}(x_1, y_1) \wedge TRANS_{L_1,L_2}(x_2, y_2) \wedge$
$x_1 \not\equiv_1 x_2 \Rightarrow y_1 \not\equiv_2 y_2]$

These properties imply that any sentence s_1 in L_1 can be translated to a sentence s_2 in L_2, and s_2 can be translated back into a sentence in L_1 that is equivalent to s_1. Hence, $TRANS_{L_1,L_2}$ can be used as its own inverse with respect to the equivalence classes $\equiv_1$ and $\equiv_2$.

5 Showing that a Translator is Reversible

In our methodology, the developer of a specialized representation language who wishes to build a translator from his or her language to an interlingua, first writes a DCTG G that is an interlingua-based semantics for the language. The developer then shows that G's goal symbol is $[1 \rightarrow 2]$, yielding a translator from the specialized language to the interlingua. The developer then shows that G's goal symbol is $[2 \rightarrow 1]$, yielding a reverse translator to be used as a first approximation of a translator from the interlingua to the specialized language.

Example: A DCTG that is a translator and reversible in place.

We have shown that our CLASSIC to KIF translator is reversible in place by showing $TRANS_{CL,KIF}[2 \rightarrow 1]$. Doing that requires showing that **newexpr** has the property $[2 \rightarrow 1, 3]$, which is done using an inductive argument structurally identical to the argument that **newexpr** has the property $[1 \rightarrow 2]$.

Example: A DCTG that is a translator, but not reversible in place.

Another DCTG that we have worked on is a KIF-based semantics for LOOM. We have shown that this DCTG is a translator. However, it is not reversible in place. One difficulty can be illustrated by the following clause from the DCTG:

```
(<- (TRANS_LOOM,KIF
        (defconcept ?name ?key1 . ?rest) ?new)
    (member :is ?rest)
    (translate-condef
        (defconcept ?name ?key1 . ?rest) ?new))
```

The predicate **translate-condef** has the properties $[1 \rightarrow 2]$ and $[2 \rightarrow 1]$ in the grammar. The predicate **member** has the property $[2 \rightarrow 1]$, although in its normal use, it is $[1, 2 \rightarrow]$. $TRANS_{LOOM,KIF}$ has the property $[1 \rightarrow 2]$ because there is a constructive chain ending in 2 from {?name, ?key1, ?rest} to ?new and

the left most occurrence of every variable in the tail of the clause is constructive. However, $TRANS_{LOOM,KIF}$ is not $[2 \rightarrow 1]$ because, while there is a constructive chain from {?new} to each of the variables ?name, ?key1, and ?rest, the left most occurrence of ?rest in the tail is not constructive. As a result, if one attempts to use this DCTG in reverse, it does not halt.

The purpose of the **member** literal in the above clause is to speed the translation from LOOM to KIF by performing a quick check on the form of ?rest to determine if **translate-condef** is the right way to translate it. Removing the **member** literal does not effect correctness when translating from LOOM to KIF and, in addition, $TRANS_{LOOM,KIF}$ becomes $[2 \rightarrow 1]$ in the clause. Hence, this example clause can be made reversible in place simply by removing the **member** literal.

When a DCTG is reversible in place, the sense of the variables in the head of the clauses that define the goal symbol must be reversible, from input to output and vice versa. When translating in one direction, the input variables are in the first argument and the constructed variables are in the second argument. When translating in the other direction, the input variables are in the second argument and the constructed variables are in the first.

This phenomenon of reversing the sense of variables "trickles down" to other predicates in a grammar that is reversible in place. The sense of some nonempty subset of the variables in these "supporting" predicates must be reversible. For example, in order for $TRANS_{CL,KIF}$ to have both the properties $[1 \rightarrow 2]$ and $[2 \rightarrow 1]$, **newexpr** must have the properties $[1 \rightarrow 2, 3]$ and $[2 \rightarrow 3, 1]$; i.e., the sense of the variables in arguments 1 and 2 must be reversible.

The above property, along with the linearity of SLD resolution, implies that a DCTG can be reversible in place only if every constructive chain has a length no greater than 1. To see this, consider **newexpr** and suppose the constructive chain from the variables in argument 1 to some variable in argument 2 is of length greater than 1. Then, when the sense of the variables in these arguments is reversed, the direction of the chain is reversed, i.e., it is right-to-left instead of left-to-right.

Hence, there are some grammars that would be reversible if it were not for the linearity of SLD resolution. Given such a grammar, it is straightforward to produce another grammar that performs the reverse translations. To obtain the reverse grammar from the original, the order of the literals in constructive chains is reversed.

A *reversed constructive chain* is defined exactly as is constructive chain, except that the direction in which the chain is constructed through the tail is from right to left. We use the notation $C : P[i_1, \ldots, i_m \leftarrow$

$i_{m+1}, \ldots, i_n], 1 \leq i_i \leq n, i = 1, \ldots, n$, when P is the predicate symbol of the head of C and there is a reversed constructive chain from every variable occurring in arguments $i_1, \ldots, i_m$ of the head to the right most occurrence of every variable in the tail and to every variable occurring in arguments $i_{m+1}, \ldots, i_n$ of the head.

Definition 5.1 (simply reversible) A DCTG G that is a translator from languages L_1 to L_2 is *simply reversible* if $G : TRANS_{L_1, L_2}[2 \leftarrow 1]$.

6 Ongoing Work

Our ongoing work falls into three categories: extending our results on reversible grammars, translation between subsets of the interlingua, and applications.

The results in this paper apply to DCTGs that are context free. Such grammars require a knowledge base in a specialized representation to be a set of independent top-level forms. Unfortunately, knowledge bases in many representation languages contain context sensitivities where the presence of one top-level form affects the meaning of other top-level forms. To circumvent this limitation, our work on grammars is currently focused on extending our results to context sensitive grammars.

Because of the expressive power of first-order horn logic, it is not difficult to write DCTGs that are context sensitive. However, techniques must be developed for writing context sensitive DCTGs that are provably constructive and reversible. The approach we are pursuing is to allow the input argument of the goal symbol in a DCTG to be a set of top-level forms rather than a single form. Then, a grammar can specify a translation for a set of sentences that is different from the translation of the individual sentences.

It appears that our techniques for proving that a DCTG is constructive and reversible extend in a straightforward manner to grammars of this new form. However, there is at least one unresolved issue. The interpretation is unclear when a grammar contains a rule for translating a set of sentences and also contains rules for translating subsets of that set. In some cases, the interpretation should be that the translations of supersets should always supersede the translations of subsets. Unfortunately, this is not always the case, and further research is required to develop a complete understanding and formal analysis of this situation.

Thus far, our work on translation between subsets of the interlingua has been focused on building systems. For example, we have built a system that translates between LOOM and CLASSIC. When translating from LOOM to CLASSIC, the steps are: (1) a grammar is used to translate from LOOM into a subset of KIF, (2) this subset of KIF is translated into another subset of KIF, and (3) this latter subset translates via a KIF to CLASSIC grammar into CLASSIC. Examples from both of these grammars have appeared in this paper. The fact that these grammars are reversible plays a key role in this system's ability to also translate from CLASSIC to LOOM.

Translation between the "LOOM recognizable" subset of KIF and the "CLASSIC recognizable" subset of KIF requires determining, for any given top-level form F_{LOOM} in the LOOM subset, a top-level form F_{CL} in the CLASSIC subset such that F_{LOOM} is logically equivalent to F_{CL}. We have developed a number of heuristic techniques for finding such equivalent forms. These are rewriting techniques that often involve the introduction of new nonlogical symbols (many of these techniques are enhancements to those discussed in [Van Baalen92]). We are in the process of performing a formal analysis of these techniques.

Our work on applications falls into two categories. First, we continue to construct grammars for additional knowledge representation languages and to construct systems that translate these languages into and out of KIF. Second, we are working on applying our translation techniques to translating between databases in different database languages. It appears that our techniques apply to this problem as well.

7 Summary

We have described a methodology for translating knowledge representation languages based on the use of an *interlingua* for communicating knowledge. The interlingua-based translation process can be thought of as consisting of three major steps: (1) translation from the source language into a subset of the interlingua, (2) translation between subsets of the interlingua, and (3) translation from a subset of the interlingua into the target language. The methodology advocates that the first translation step into the interlingua be specified by a grammar consisting of a set of Horn clauses (called a Definite Clause Translation Grammar) that constructively implements a translation predicate relating top-level forms in a source language to their translations in an interlingua. We observed that in cases where the source language does not have a declarative semantics, specifying a translation of that language into the interlingua provides a declarative semantics for the language. Thus, another advantage of using an interlingua is that it offers a relatively easy way to specify a semantics for new representation languages.

We specified and proved the correctness of a set of conditions under which such a DCTG is reversible so that the grammar can also be used to translate out of the interlingua. The proof provides a method that can be used directly to show that a DCTG is constructive and reversible or to identify the clauses in a grammar that must be modified in order to obtain those properties. Given these techniques, a developer of a specialized representation language that desires to build a translator from the specialized language to an interlingua first writes a DCTG G that is an interlingua-based semantics for the language. The developer then uses the methods we have provided to show that G constructs a translation in the interlingua for any top-level form in the specialized language and therefore that G is a translator from the specialized language to the interlingua. The developer then again uses the methods we have provided to show that G also is a translator out of the interlingua in that it constructs a top-level form in the specialized language as a translation for any top-level form in the subset of the interlingua that could be produced by G when it is being used as a translator from the specialized language. Such a reverse translator provides a first approximation of a translator from the interlingua to the specialized language.

These languages and methods have been incorporated into a "translator shell" system that provides facilities for specifying interlingua-based translators using KIF as the interlingua. The system has been used to build translators for multiple representation languages and those translators have successfully translated nontrivial knowledge bases.

Our ongoing work falls into three categories: extending our results on reversible grammars to context sensitive grammars, translation between subsets of the interlingua, and the development of grammars for additional representation languages as well as for database languages.

Acknowledgments

Ramesh Patil assisted with the LOOM to KIF grammar. Sasa Buvac and John Cowles participated in helpful discussions with the authors. This work is supported in part by AFOSR under contract number F49620-92-J-0434, by the Advanced Research Projects Agency, ARPA Order 8607, monitored by NASA Ames Research Center under grant NAG 2-581, and by NASA Ames Research Center under grant NCC 2-537.

References

[Borgida, et al 89] A. Borgida, R.J. Brachman, D.L. McGuinness, and L.A.Resnick; "CLASSIC: A Structural Data Model for Objects"; Proceedings of the1989 ACM SIGMOD International Conference on Management of Data; Portland, Oregon; May-June, 1989.

[Buvac and Fikes 93] S. Buvac and R. Fikes; "Semantics of Translation"; Proceedings of the workshop on Knowledge Sharing and Information Interchange at the 13th International Joint Conference on Artificial Intelligence; Chambery, France; August 1993.

[Fikes, et al 91] R. Fikes, M. Cutkosky, T. Gruber, and J. Van Baalen; "Knowledge Sharing Technology Project Overview"; Stanford University Report KSL 91-71, 1991.

[Genesereth & Fikes 92] M. Genesereth and R. Fikes; "Knowledge Interchange Format Version 3.0 Reference Manual"; Logic Group Report Logic-92-1; Computer Science Department, Stanford University; June 92.

[Loyd 87] J. W. Loyd; "Foundations of Logic Programming," 2nd edition, Springer Verlag, pp. 40-41, 1987.

[MacGregor 91] R. MacGregor; LOOM Users Manual, USC/Information Sciences Institute; Technical Report Working Paper ISI/WP-22; 1990.

[Pereira & Warren 80] F. C. N. Pereira and D. H. D. Warren; "Definite Clause Grammars for Language Analysis – A Survey of the Formalism and a Comparison with Augmented Transition Networks," Artificial Intelligence, 13, pp. 231-278, 1980.

[Spiby, et al ?] P. Spiby; "EXPRESS language reference manual," ISO TC184/SC4/WG 5.

[Strzalkowski 90] T. Strzalkowski, "Reversible Logic Grammars for Natural Language Parsing and Generation," Computational Intelligence, 6(3), pp. 145-171, 1990.

[Strzalkowski 91] T. Strzalkowski, "A General Computational Method for Grammar Inversion," Proceedings of the workshop Reversible Grammar in Natural Language Processing, UC Berkeley, 1991.

[Van Baalen92] Van Baalen, J., "Automated Design of Specialized Representations," *Artificial Intelligence*, 54, pp. 121-198, 1992.

Constraint Tightness versus Global Consistency

Peter van Beek
Department of Computing Science
University of Alberta
Edmonton, Alberta, Canada   T6G 2H1
vanbeek@cs.ualberta.ca

Rina Dechter
Department of Computer and Information Science
University of California, Irvine
Irvine, California, USA   92717
dechter@ics.uci.edu

Abstract

Constraint networks are a simple representation and reasoning framework with diverse applications. In this paper, we present a new property called *constraint tightness* that can be used for characterizing the difficulty of problems formulated as constraint networks. Specifically, we show that when the constraints are tight they may require less preprocessing in order to guarantee a backtrack-free solution. This suggests, for example, that many instances of crossword puzzles are relatively easy while scheduling problems involving resource constraints are quite hard. Formally, we present a relationship between the tightness or restrictiveness of the constraints, and the level of local consistency sufficient to ensure global consistency, thus ensuring backtrack-freeness. Two definitions of local consistency are employed. The traditional variable-based notion leads to a condition involving the tightness of the constraints, the level of local consistency, and the arity of the constraints, while a new definition of *relational* consistency leads to a condition expressed in terms of tightness and local-consistency level, alone. New algorithms for enforcing relational consistency are introduced and analyzed.

1 Introduction

Constraint networks are a simple representation and reasoning framework. A problem is represented as a set of variables, a domain of values for each variable, and a set of constraints between the variables, and the reasoning task is to find an instantiation of the variables that satisfies the constraints. In spite of the simplicity of the framework, many interesting problems can be formulated as constraint networks, including graph coloring [Montanari, 1974], scene labeling [Waltz, 1975], natural language parsing [Maruyama, 1990], and temporal reasoning [Allen, 1983; Dechter et al., 1991; Meiri, 1991; van Beek, 1992].

Constraint networks are often solved using a backtracking algorithm. However, backtracking algorithms are susceptible to "thrashing:" discovering over and over again the same reason for reaching a dead end in the search for a solution. To ameliorate this thrashing behavior, algorithms for preprocessing a constraint network by removing local inconsistencies have been proposed and studied (e.g., [Dechter and Meiri, 1989; Mackworth, 1977; Montanari, 1974]). Sometimes a certain level of local consistency is enough to guarantee that the network is globally consistent. A network is globally consistent if any solution for a subnetwork can always be extended to a solution for the entire network. Hence, if a network is globally consistent, a solution can be found in a backtrack-free manner.

In this paper, we present a relationship between the tightness or restrictiveness of the constraints, the arity of the constraints, and the level of local consistency sufficient to ensure global consistency. Specifically, in any constraint network where the constraints have arity r or less and the constraints have tightness of m or less, if the network is strongly $((m+1)(r-1)+1)$-consistent, then the network is globally consistent. Informally, a network is strongly k-consistent if any consistent instantiation of any $k-1$ or fewer variables can be extended consistently to any additional variable. Also informally, given an r-ary constraint and an instantiation of $r-1$ of the variables that participate in the constraint, the parameter m is an upper bound on the number of instantiations of the rth variable that satisfy the constraint.

We also present a new definition of local consistency called *relational m-consistency*. The virtue of this definition is that, firstly, it allows expressing the relationship between tightness and local consistency in a way that avoids an explicit reference to the arity of the constraints. Secondly, it is operational, thus generalizing the concept of the composition operation defined for binary constraints, and can be incorporated naturally in algorithms for enforcing desired levels of relational consistency. Thirdly, it unifies known operators such as resolution in theorem proving, joins in relational databases, and variable elimination for solving equations and inequalities. Finally, it allows identifying those formalisms for which consistency can be decided by enforcing pairwise consistency, like propositional databases and linear equalities and inequalities, from general databases requiring higher levels of local consistency.

The results we present are particularly useful in applications where a knowledge base will be queried over and over and we desire that queries be answered quickly. In such applications the preprocessing time to enforce local consistency is of less importance. What is of importance is knowing what level of local consistency will guarantee that queries can be answered quickly.

2 Background

We begin with some needed definitions and describe related work.

Definition 1 (binary constraint network; Montanari [1974])
A binary constraint network consists of a set X of n variables $\{x_1, x_2, \ldots, x_n\}$, a domain D_i of possible values for each variable, and a set of binary constraints between variables. A binary constraint or relation, R_{ij}, between variables x_i and x_j, is any subset of the product of their domains (i.e., $R_{ij} \subseteq D_i \times D_j$). An instantiation of the variables in X is an n-tuple $(X_1, X_2, \ldots, X_n)$, representing an assignment of $X_i \in D_i$ to x_i. A consistent instantiation of a network is an instantiation of the variables such that the constraints between variables are satisfied. A consistent instantiation is also called a solution.

Mackworth [1977] defines three properties of networks that characterize local consistency of networks: *node*, *arc*, and *path consistency*. Freuder [1978] generalizes this to k-consistency.

Definition 2 (k-consistency; Freuder [1978])
A network is k-consistent if and only if given any instantiation of any $k-1$ variables satisfying all the direct relations among those variables, there exists an instantiation of any kth variable such that the k values taken together satisfy all the relations among the k variables. A network is strongly k-consistent if and only if it is j-consistent for all $j \leq k$.

Node, arc, and path consistency correspond to strongly one-, two-, and three-consistent, respectively. A strongly n-consistent network is called *globally consistent*. Globally consistent networks have the property that any consistent instantiation of a subset of the variables can be extended to a consistent instantiation of all the variables without backtracking [Dechter, 1992b].

Following Montanari [1974], a binary relation R_{ij} between variables x_i and x_j is represented as a (0,1)-matrix with $|D_i|$ rows and $|D_j|$ columns by imposing an ordering on the domains of the variables. A zero entry at row a, column b means that the pair consisting of the ath element of D_i and the bth element of D_j is not permitted; a one entry means the pair is permitted. A concept central to this paper is the tightness of constraints.

Definition 3 (m-tight)
A binary constraint is m-tight if every row and every column of the (0,1)-matrix that defines the constraint has at most m ones, where $0 \leq m \leq |D| - 1$. Rows and columns with exactly $|D|$ ones are ignored in determining m. A binary constraint network is m-tight if all its binary constraints are m-tight.

Example 1. We illustrate some of the definitions using a variant of n-queens proposed by Nadel [1989] called confused n-queens. The problem is to find all ways to place n-queens on an $n \times n$ chess board, one queen per column, so that each pair of queens *does* attack each other. One possible constraint network formulation of the problem is as follows: there is a variable for each column of the chess board, $x_1, \ldots, x_n$; the domains of the variables are the possible row positions, $D_i = \{1, \ldots, n\}$; and the binary constraints are that two queens should attack each other. The (0,1)-matrix representation of the constraints between two variables x_i and x_j is given by,

$$R_{ij,ab} = \begin{cases} 1 & \text{if } a = b \lor |a - b| = |i - j| \\ 0 & \text{otherwise,} \end{cases}$$

for $a, b = 1, \ldots, n$. For example, consider the constraint R_{12} between x_1 and x_2: $R_{12,34} = 1$, which states that putting a queen in column 1, row 3 and a queen in column 2, row 4 is allowed by the constraint since the queens attack each other.

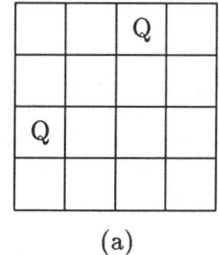 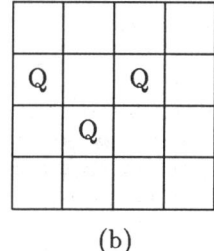

Figure 1: (a) not 3-consistent; (b) not 4-consistent

It can be seen that the networks for the confused n-queens problem are 2-consistent since, given that we have placed a single queen on the board, we can always place a second queen such that the queens attack each other. However, the networks are not 3-consistent. For example, for the confused 4-queens problem shown in Fig. 1a, there is no way to place a queen in the last column that is consistent with the previously placed queens. Similarly the networks are not 4-consistent (see Fig. 1b). Finally, every row and every column of the (0,1)-matrices that define the constraints has at most 3 ones. Hence, the networks are 3-tight.

2.1 Related work

Much work has been done on identifying relationships between properties of constraint networks and the level of local consistency sufficient to ensure global consistency. This work falls into two classes: identifying topological properties of the underlying graph of the network and identifying properties of the constraints. Here we review only the literature for constraint networks with finite domains.

For work that falls into the class of identifying topological properties, Freuder [1982; 1985] identifies a relationship between the *width* of a constraint graph and the level of local consistency needed to ensure a solution can be found without backtracking. As a special case, if the constraint graph is a tree, arc consistency is sufficient to ensure a solution can be found without backtracking. Dechter and Pearl [1988] provide an adaptive scheme where the level of local consistency is adjusted on a node-by-node basis. Dechter and Pearl [1989] generalize the results on trees to hyper-trees which are called acyclic databases in the database community [Beeri et al., 1983].

For work that falls into the class of identifying properties of the constraints (the class into which the present work falls), Montanari [1974] shows that path consistency is sufficient to guarantee that a binary network is globally consistent if the relations are monotone. Van Beek and Dechter [1994] show that path consistency is sufficient if the relations are row convex. Dechter [1992b] identifies a relationship between the size of the domains of the variables, the arity of the constraints, and the level of local consistency sufficient to ensure the network is globally consistent. She proves the following result.

Theorem 1 (Dechter [1992b]) *Any $|D|$-valued r-ary constraint network that is strongly $(|D|(r-1)+1)$-consistent is globally consistent. In particular, any $|D|$-valued binary constraint network that is strongly $(|D|+1)$-consistent is globally consistent.*

For some networks, Dechter's theorem is tight in that the level of local consistency specified by the theorem is really required (graph coloring problems formulated as constraint networks are an example). For other networks, Dechter's theorem overestimates. Our results should be viewed as an improvement on Dechter's theorem. In particular, our main theorem, by taking into account the tightness of the constraints, always specifies a level of strong consistency that is less than or equal to the level of strong consistency required by Dechter's theorem.

3 Binary constraint networks

In this section we restrict our attention to binary constraint networks and present a relationship between the tightness of the constraints and the level of local consistency sufficient to ensure a network is globally consistent. The results are generalized to constraint networks with constraints of arbitrary arity in the next section.

The following lemma is needed in the proof of the main result for constraint networks with binary constraints and in a later proof of the result generalized to constraint networks with constraints of arbitrary arity. The lemma is really about the "tightness" of constraints and the sufficiency of a certain level of consistency. We state the lemma in more colloquial terms to make the proof more understandable.

Lemma 1 *Suppose there are fan clubs that like to meet and talk about famous people, and the following conditions.*

1. *There are n fan clubs and d famous people.*

2. *Each fan club meets and talks about at most m, $m < d$, famous people.*

3. *For every set of $m + 1$ or fewer fan clubs, there exists at least one famous person that every club in the set talks about.*

Then, there must exist at least one famous person that every fan club talks about.

Proof. The proof is by contradiction and uses a proof technique discovered by Dechter for Theorem 1. Assume to the contrary that no such famous person exists. Then, for each famous person, f_i, there must exist at least one fan club that does not talk about f_i. Let c_i denote one of the fan clubs that does not talk about f_i. By construction, the set $c = \{c_1, c_2, \ldots, c_d\}$ is a set of fan clubs for which there does not exist a famous person that every club in the set talks about (every candidate f_i is ruled out since c_i does not talk about f_i). For every possible value of m, this leads to a contradiction.

Case 1 ($m = d - 1$): The contradiction is immediate as $c = \{c_1, c_2, \ldots, c_d\}$ is a set of fan clubs of size $m + 1$ for which there does not exist a famous person that every club in the set talks about. This contradicts condition (3).

Case 2 ($m = d - 2$): The nominal size of the set $c = \{c_1, c_2, \ldots, c_d\}$ is $m + 2$. We claim, however, that there is a repetition in c and that the true size of the set is $m + 1$. Assume to the contrary that $c_i \neq c_j$ for $i \neq j$. Recall c_i is a club that does not talk about f_i, $i = 1, \ldots, d$ and consider $\{c_1, c_2, \ldots, c_{d-1}\}$. This is a set of $m + 1$ fan clubs so by condition (3) there must exist an f_i that every club in the set talks about. The only possibility is f_d. Now consider $\{c_1, \ldots, c_{d-2}, c_d\}$. Again, this is a set of $m+1$ fan clubs so there must exist an f_i that every club in the set talks about. This time the only possibility is f_{d-1}. Continuing in this manner, we can show that fan club c_1 must talk about exactly $m + 1$ famous people. This contradicts condition (2). Therefore, it must be the case that $c_i = c_j$ for some $i \neq j$. Thus, the set c is of size $m + 1$ and this contradicts condition (3).

Case 3 ($m = d - 3$), ..., **Case d-1** ($m = 1$): The remaining cases are similar. In each case we argue that (i) there are repetitions in the set $c = \{c_1, c_2, \ldots, c_d\}$, (ii) the true size of the set c is $m + 1$, and (iii) a contradiction is derived by appealing to condition (3).

Thus, there exists at least one famous person that every fan club talks about. □

We now state the theorem for binary constraint networks.

Theorem 2 *If a binary constraint network, R, is m-tight, and if the network is strongly $(m+2)$-consistent, then the network is globally consistent.*

Proof. We show that any network with $\leq m$ ones in every row that is strongly $(m + 2)$-consistent is $(m + 2 + i)$-consistent for any $i \geq 1$. Suppose that variables $x_1, \ldots, x_{m+1+i}$ can be consistently instantiated with values $X_1, \ldots, X_{m+1+i}$. To show that the network is $(m + 2 + i)$-consistent, we must show that there exists at least one instantiation, X_{m+2+i}, of variable x_{m+2+i} such that

$$(X_j, X_{m+2+i}) \in R_{j,m+2+i} \qquad j = 1, \ldots, m+1+i$$

is satisfied. Let v_j be the (0,1)-vector given by row X_j of the (0,1)-matrix $R_{j,m+2+i}$, $j = 1, \ldots, m+1+i$ (see Figure 2 for an illustration; the v_j are shown boxed). The one entries in the v_j are the allowed instantiations of x_{m+2+i}, given the instantiations $X_1, \ldots, X_{m+1+i}$. That there exists a consistent instantiation of x_{m+2+i} follows from Lemma 1 where (i) $X_1, \ldots, X_{m+1+i}$ are the fan clubs, (ii) $1, \ldots, d$, the domain elements of x_{m+2+i}, are the famous people, (iii) the one entries in the v_j's are the famous people that fan club X_j talks about, and (iv) condition (3) of Lemma 1 follows from the assumption of strong $(m + 2)$ consistency. Therefore, from Lemma 1 it follows that there exists at least one instantiation of x_{m+2+i} that satisfies all the constraints simultaneously. Hence, the network is $(m + 2 + i)$-consistent. □

Theorem 2 always specifies a level of strong consistency

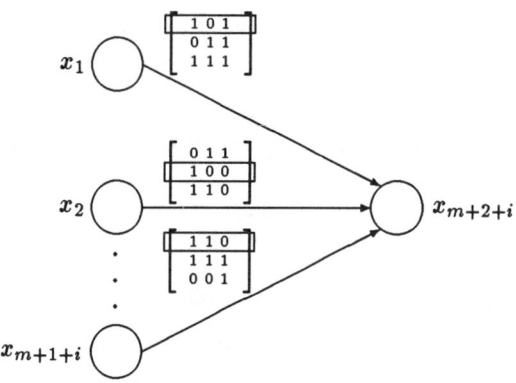

Figure 2: Instantiating x_{m+2+i}

that is less than or equal to the level of strong consistency required by Dechter's theorem (Theorem 1). The level of required consistency is equal only when $m = |D| - 1$ and is less when $m < |D| - 1$. As well, the theorem can sometimes be usefully applied if $|D| \geq n - 1$, whereas Dechter's theorem cannot.

As the following example illustrates, both r, the arity of the constraints, and m can change if the level of consistency required by the theorem is not present and must be enforced. The parameter r can only increase; m can decrease, as shown below, but also increase. The parameter m will increase if all of the following hold: (i) there previously was no constraint between a set of variables, (ii) enforcing a certain level of consistency results in a new constraint being recorded between those variables, and (iii) the new constraint has a larger m value than the previous constraints.

Example 2. Consider again the confused n-queens problem introduced in Example 1. The problem is worth considering, as Nadel [1989] uses confused n-queens in an empirical comparison of backtracking algorithms for solving constraint networks. Thus it is important to analyze the difficulty of the problems to set the empirical results in context. As well, the problem is interesting in that it provides an example where Theorem 2 can be applied but Dechter's theorem can not (since $|D| \geq n - 1$). Independently of n, each row of the constraints has ≤ 3 ones. Hence, the networks are 3-tight and the theorem guarantees that if the network for the confused n-queens problem is strongly 5-consistent, the network is globally consistent.

First, suppose that n is even and we attempt to either verify or achieve this level of strong consistency by applying successively stronger local consistency algorithms. Kondrak [1993] has shown that the following analysis holds for all n, n even.

1. Applying an arc consistency algorithm results in no changes as the network is already arc consistent.

2. Applying a path consistency algorithm does tighten the constraints between the variables. Once the network is made path consistent, each row has ≤ 2 ones. Now the theorem guarantees that if the constraint network is strongly 4-consistent, the network is globally consistent.

3. Applying a 4-consistency algorithm results in no changes as the network is already 4-consistent. Thus, the network is strongly 4-consistent and therefore also globally consistent.

Second, suppose that n is odd. This time, after applying path consistency, the networks are still 3-tight and it can be verified that the networks are not 4-consistent. Enforcing 4-consistency would require non-binary constraints, hence Theorem 2 no longer applies. We take this example up again in the next section where the results are generalized to non-binary constraints. There we show that recording 3-ary constraints is sufficient.

Recall that Nadel [1989] uses confused n-queens problems to empirically compare backtracking algorithms for finding all solutions to constraint networks. Nadel states that these problems provide a "non-trivial testbed" [1989, p.190]. We believe the above analysis indicates that these problems are quite easy and that any empirical results on these problems should be interpreted in this light. Easy problems potentially make even naive algorithms for solving constraint networks look promising. To avoid this potential pitfall, backtracking algorithms should be tested on problems that range from easy to hard. In general, hard problems are those that require a high level of local consistency to ensure global consistency. Note also that these problems are trivially satisfiable.

Example 3. The graph k-colorability problem can be viewed as a problem on constraint networks: there is a variable for each node in the graph; the domains of the variables are the possible colors, $D = \{1,\ldots,k\}$; and the binary constraints are that two adjacent nodes must be assigned different colors. Graph k-colorability provides examples of networks where both Theorems 1 and 2 give the same bound on the sufficient level of local consistency (since $|D| = k$ and $m = |D| - 1$). Further, as Dechter [1992b] shows, the bound is tight. For example, consider coloring a complete graph on five nodes with four colors. The network is 3-tight and strongly 4-consistent, but not strongly 5-consistent and not globally consistent. Hence, when $m = |D|-1$, the level of local consistency specified by Theorem 2 is as strong as possible and cannot be lowered.

We can also construct examples to show that Theorem 2 is as strong as possible for all $m < |D| - 1$. This can be done by "embedding" graph coloring constraints into the constraints for the new network. For example, consider the network where the domains are $D = \{1,\ldots,5\}$ and the constraints between all variables is given by,

$$R_{ij} = \begin{bmatrix} 1 & 0 & 0 & 0 & 1 \\ 0 & 0 & 1 & 1 & 0 \\ 0 & 1 & 0 & 1 & 0 \\ 0 & 1 & 1 & 0 & 0 \\ 1 & 0 & 0 & 0 & 1 \end{bmatrix}.$$

The inner 3×3 matrix is the 3-coloring constraint. The network is 2-tight and strongly 3-consistent, but not strongly 4-consistent and not globally consistent.

4 R-ary constraint networks

In this section we generalize the results of the previous section to networks with constraints of arbitrary arity. We will define m-tightness of r-ary relations, namely relations having r variables. We use the following notations and definitions.

Definition 4 (Relations)
Given a set of variables $X = \{x_1,\ldots,x_n\}$, each associated with a domain of discrete values $D_1,\ldots,D_n$, respectively, a relation (or, alternatively, a constraint) ρ over X is any subset

$$\rho \subseteq D_1 \times D_2 \times \cdots \times D_n.$$

Given a relation ρ on a set X of variables and a subset $Y \subseteq X$, we denote by $Y = y$ or by y an instantiation of the variables in Y, called a subtuple and by $\sigma_{Y=y}(\rho)$ the selection of those tuples in ρ that agree with $Y = y$. We denote by $\Pi_Y(\rho)$ the projection of relation ρ on the subset Y. Namely, a tuple over Y appears in $\Pi_Y(\rho)$ if and only if it can be extended to a full tuple in ρ. If Y is not a subset of ρ's variables the projection is over the subset of variables that appear both in Y and in X. The operator $\bowtie$ is the join operator in relational databases.

Definition 5 (Constraint networks)
A constraint network R over a set X of variables $\{x_1, x_2, \ldots, x_n\}$, is a set of relations $R_1, \ldots, R_t$, each defined on a subset of variables $S_1, \ldots, S_t$ respectively. A relation in R specified over $Y \subseteq X$ is also denoted R_Y. The set of subsets $S = \{S_1, \ldots, S_t\}$ on which constraints are specified is called the scheme of R. The network R represents its set of all consistent solutions over X, denoted $\rho(R)$ or $\rho(X)$, namely,

$$\rho(R) = \{x = (X_1, \ldots, X_n) \mid \forall S_i \in S, \Pi_{S_i}(x) \in R_i\}.$$

For non-binary networks the notion of *consistency of a subtuple* can be defined in several ways. We will use the following definition. A subtuple over Y is consistent if it satisfies all the constraints defined over Y including all R's constraints obtained by projection over Y.

Definition 6 (Consistency of a subtuple)
A subtuple $Y = y$ is consistent relative to R iff, for all $S_i \in S$,

$$\Pi_{S_i \cap Y}(y) \in \Pi_{S_i \cap Y}(R_i).$$

$\rho(Y)$ is the set of all consistent instantiations of the variables in Y. One can view $\rho(Y)$ as the set of all solutions of the subnetwork defined by Y.

Informally, an r-ary relation is m-tight if every tuple of $r-1$ values can be extended in at most m ways.

Definition 7 *An r-ary relation is m-tight if and only if all of its binary projections (projections on pairs of variables) are m-tight.*

Example 4. We illustrate some of the definitions using the following network, R, over the set of variables, $\{x_1, x_2, x_3, x_4\}$. The relations are given by,

$$R_{S_1} = \{(1,4,2), (2,4,1), (3,1,4), (4,1,3)\},$$
$$R_{S_2} = \{(1,4,2), (2,1,3), (2,1,4), (2,3,1),$$
$$(3,2,4), (3,4,1), (3,4,2), (4,1,3)\},$$

where $S_1 = \{x_1, x_2, x_3\}$ and $S_2 = \{x_1, x_3, x_4\}$. The set of all solutions of the network is given by,

$$\rho(R) = \{(2,4,1,3), (2,4,1,4), (3,1,4,1), (3,1,4,2)\}.$$

Let $Y = \{x_1, x_3\}$ be a subset of the variables and let the subtuple $y = (2, 1)$ be an instantiation of the variables in Y. Then, $\sigma_{Y=y}(R_{S_2}) = \{(2,1,3), (2,1,4)\}$ and, $\Pi_Y(R_{S_1}) = \{(1,2), (2,1), (3,4), (4,3)\}$. It can be verified that the subtuple $y = (2, 1)$ is consistent relative to R and that the subtuple $y = (1, 2)$ is not consistent relative to R (since $\Pi_{S_2 \cap Y}(y) \notin \Pi_{S_2 \cap Y}(R_{S_2})$). Finally, the network is 3-tight since projecting the relation R_{S_2} onto $\{x_1, x_4\}$ results in a binary relation that is 3-tight, and this is the maximum of all the binary projections.

We now state the general theorem.

Theorem 3 *If an r-ary network, R, is m-tight, and if the network is strongly $((m+1)(r-1)+1)$-consistent, then the network is globally consistent.*

Proof. Let $k = (m+1)(r-1) + 1$. We show that any network with relations that are m-tight that is strongly k-consistent is $(k + i)$-consistent for any $i \geq 1$.

Let $X' = (X_1, X_2, \ldots, X_{k+i-1})$ be a consistent instantiation of $k + i - 1$ variables[1] and let x_{k+i} be an arbitrary new variable. We will show that there exists an instantiation X_{k+i} of x_{k+i} such that the extended tuple $(X_1, X_2, \ldots, X_{k+i-1}, X_{k+i})$ is consistent. This means that any relation $R_Y \in R$ involving variable x_{k+i}, and a non-empty subset of variables from $\{x_1, \ldots, x_{k+i-1}\}$ should be satisfied. Let X'_Y be the partial tuple of X' that is restricted to the set Y over which R_Y is defined. We call this tuple a *constraint-tuple*. Since all the constraints and their

[1] Note that according to the definition of consistency this means that X' satisfies all the constraints defined on its own subset of variables as well as those obtained by projection.

projections are m-tight, constraint R_Y will allow X'_Y to be extended by at most m values of x_{k+i}. Each such constraint-tuple, X'_Y can be regarded as a fan club, with its allowed values in x_{k+i} relative to R_Y as the discussed famous people. Therefore, condition (2) of Lemma 1 is satisfied. Also, condition (3) of Lemma 1 is satisfied, since the length of each constraint-tuple is $r-1$ or less, the requirement of strong $(m+1)(r-1)+1$-consistency, ensures that any set of up to $(m + 1)$ constraint-tuples (overlapping or not), has a consistent extension in x_{k+i}. Therefore, from Lemma 1 it follows that there is a common value of x_{k+i} that satisfies all the constraints simultaneously. □

Example 5. Consider again the confused n-queens problem discussed in Example 2. There we saw that, after enforcing path consistency, the networks are 3-tight, for n odd. Enforcing 4-consistency requires 3-ary constraints. Adding the necessary 3-ary constraints does not change the value of m; the networks are still 3-tight. Hence, by Theorem 3, if the networks are strongly 9-consistent, the networks are globally consistent. Kondrak [1993] has shown that recording 3-ary constraints is sufficient to guarantee the networks are strongly 9-consistent for all n, n odd. Hence, independently of n, the networks are globally consistent once strong 4-consistency is enforced.

Example 6. Constraint networks have proven fruitful in representing and reasoning about temporal information. We use an example from Allen's [1983] framework for reasoning about temporal relations between intervals or events to illustrate the application of Theorem 3. Allen identifies thirteen *basic* relations that can hold between two intervals. In order to represent indefinite information, the relation between two intervals is allowed to be a disjunction of the basic relations. For example, the relation {b,bi} between events A and D in Figure 3 represents the disjunction, (A before D) ∨ (A after D). Allen provides a transitivity table for propagating the temporal information.

Allen's framework can be formulated as a constraint network with finite domains as follows: there is a variable for each pair of intervals, the domains of the variables are the possible basic relations, and there are ternary constraints defined by the transitivity table. For example, consider the temporal information given by,

A {oi,m} B   A {b,o} C_i A {b,bi} D_i
B {b,d} C_i B {bi,o} D_i D_i {b,oi} C_i

for $i = 1, \ldots, (n-2)/2$. Formulating this temporal information as a constraint network with finite domains, we can show that enforcing strong 4-consistency is sufficient to ensure the network is globally consistent, for all $n \geq 4$. Below we show the analysis for the simple case of $n = 4$. The general case is similar, just notationally more complicated. Figure 3 shows the six

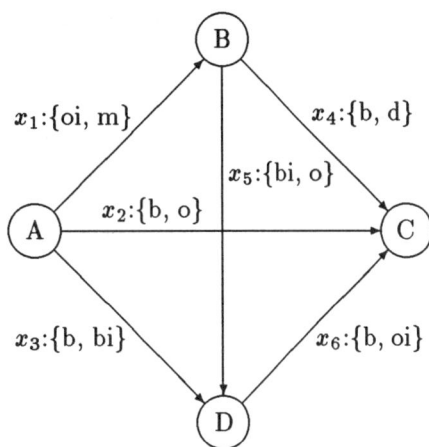

Figure 3: Example temporal network

variables and their associated domains for our example. The ternary constraints for our example are given by,

$R_{124} = \{(\text{oi,b,b}), (\text{oi,o,b}), (\text{m,b,b}), (\text{m,o,d})\}$,
$R_{135} = \{(\text{oi,bi,bi}), (\text{m,bi,bi}), (\text{m,b,o})\}$,
$R_{236} = \{(\text{b,b,b}), (\text{b,b,oi}), (\text{b,bi,b}), (\text{o,b,oi}), (\text{o,bi,b})\}$,
$R_{456} = \{(\text{b,bi,b}), (\text{b,o,b}), (\text{d,bi,b}), (\text{d,o,oi})\}$.

It can be shown that the network is 1-tight. Therefore, by Theorem 3, if the network is strongly 5-consistent, then the network is globally consistent. Suppose that we attempt to either verify or achieve this level of strong consistency. The network is strongly 3-consistent, but not 4-consistent. For example, (b,b,oi) is a consistent instantiation of (x_2, x_3, x_6), since it satisfies the constraint R_{236} as well as all the constraints obtained by projection. However, there is no way to extend the instantiation to x_4: (i) $x_4 \leftarrow$ b is inconsistent by the constraint R_{46} obtained by projecting R_{456} on $\{x_4, x_6\}$, and (ii) $x_4 \leftarrow$ d is inconsistent by the constraint R_{24} obtained by projecting R_{124} on $\{x_2, x_4\}$. The modified constraint R'_{236} is given by,

$R'_{236} = \{(\text{b,b,b}), (\text{b,bi,b}), (\text{o,b,oi}), (\text{o,bi,b})\}$.

As well, some 3-ary constraints between previously unconstrained triples of variables need to be introduced. For example, (oi,o,oi) is a consistent instantiation of (x_1, x_2, x_6), since it satisfies all the constraints obtained by projection. However, there is no way to extend the instantiation to x_3: (i) $x_3 \leftarrow$ b is inconsistent by the constraint R_{13} obtained by projecting R_{135} on $\{x_1, x_3\}$, and (ii) $x_3 \leftarrow$ bi is inconsistent by the constraint R'_{236}. Once the following 3-ary relations are added, the network is strongly 4-consistent:

$R_{126} = \{(\text{oi,b,b}), (\text{oi,o,b}), (\text{m,b,b}), (\text{m,o,b}), (\text{m,o,oi})\}$,
$R_{234} = \{(\text{b,b,b}), (\text{b,bi,b}), (\text{o,b,d}), (\text{o,bi,b}), (\text{o,bi,d})\}$,
$R_{256} = \{(\text{b,bi,b}), (\text{b,o,b}), (\text{o,bi,b}), (\text{o,o,oi})\}$,
$R_{346} = \{(\text{b,b,b}), (\text{b,d,oi}), (\text{bi,b,b}), (\text{bi,d,b})\}$.

It can now be verified that the network is also strongly 5-consistent. Therefore, by Theorem 3, the network is globally consistent. The network is also minimal. A network of r-ary relations is minimal if each tuple in the relations participates in at least one consistent instantiation of the network. These two properties, global consistency and minimality, ensure that we can efficiently answer some important classes of temporal queries.

4.1 Relational local consistency

In [van Beek and Dechter, 1994] we extended the notion of path-consistency to non-binary relations, and used it to specify an alternative condition under which row-convex non-binary networks of relations are globally consistent. This definition, since it considers the relations rather than the variables as the primitive entities, does not mention the arity of the constraint explicitly. We now extend this definition even further and show how it can be used to alternatively describe Theorem 3.

Definition 8 (Relational m-consistency)
Let R be a network of relations over a set of variables X, let $R_{S_1}, \ldots, R_{S_{m-1}}$ be $m-1$, $m \geq 3$, relations in R, where $S_i \subseteq X$. We say that $R_{S_1}, \ldots, R_{S_{m-1}}$ are relational m-consistent relative to variable x iff any consistent instantiation of the variables in A, where $A = \bigcup_{i=1}^{m-1} S_i - \{x\}$, has an extension to x that satisfies $R_{S_1}, \ldots, R_{S_{m-1}}$ simultaneously. Namely, if and only if

$$\rho(A) \subseteq \Pi_A(\bowtie_{i=1}^{m-1} R_{S_i}).$$

(Recall that $\rho(A)$ is the set of all consistent instantiations of the variables in A). A set of relations $R_{S_1}, \ldots, R_{S_{m-1}}$ are relational m-consistent iff they are relational m-consistent relative to each variable in $\bigcap_{i=1}^{m-1} S_i$. A network of relations is said to be relational m-consistent iff every set of $m-1$ relations is relational m-consistent. Relational 3-consistency is also called relational path-consistency. A network is strongly relational m-consistent if it is relational i-consistent for every $i \leq m$.

Note that we do not need to define relational 2-consistency since our definition of consistency of a subtuple, which takes into account all the networks' projections, guarantees that any notion of relational 2-consistency is redundant.

Example 7. Consider the following network of relations. The domains of the variables are all $D = \{0, 1, 2\}$ and the relations are given by,

(1) $R_{fxyz} = \{0000, 1000, 0100, 0010, 0001\}$,

(2) $R_{fzs} = \{011, 122, 021\}$.

The constraints are not relational path-consistent. For example, the instantiation $f = 0, x = 1, y = 0$ satisfies all the constraints, (namely all the projections of

(1) and (2) on $\{f,x,y\}$ and $\{f\}$ respectively), but it cannot be consistently extended to a legal value of z. If we add the constraint $(3) R_{fxy} = \{000\}$, the first two constraints will become relational path-consistent relative to z since constraint (3) will disallow the partial assignments $f = 0, x = 1, y = 0$. Constraints (1) and (2) are relational path-consistent relative to f since any consistent instantiation of x, y, z will have to satisfy the two constraints $R_{xyz} = \{000, 100, 010, 001\}$ and $R_z = \{1,2\}$ obtained by projecting constraints (1) and (2) over x, y, z, respectively. Remember that consistency of a subtuple needs to obey all the projected constraints. Once these constraints are obeyed there is an extension to $f = 0$ that satisfies (1) and (2) simultaneously.

We now show that strong relational $(m+2)$-consistency is sufficient to ensure globally consistency when the relations are m-tight.

Theorem 4 *Let R be a network of relations that is strongly relational $(m+2)$-consistent. If the relations are m-tight, then the network is globally consistent.*

Proof. Assume that the network is relational $(m+2)$-consistent. Let $X' = (X_1, X_2, \ldots, X_{i-1})$ be a consistent instantiation of $i-1$ variables, $i > m+2$. We will show that for any x_i, there exists an instantiation X_i of x_i such that the extended tuple $(X_1, X_2, \ldots, X_{i-1}, X_i)$ is consistent. This means that any relevant relation $R_Y \in R$ or any of its projections, that are defined over x_i should be satisfied by such an extension. Since all constraints and all their projections are m-tight, all the values of x_i that together with X'_Y are allowed by R_Y do not exceed m. Also, strong relational $(m+2)$-consistency implies that any subset of $m+1$ or fewer constraints can be consistently extended by x_i. Consequently, due to Lemma 1 there is a value X_i such that the tuple $(X_1, X_2, \ldots, X_{i-1}, X_i)$ satisfies all the constraints simultaneously. □

When all the constraints are binary, relational m-consistency is identical (up to minor preprocessing) to variable-based m-consistency. Otherwise the conditions are different. In general, the definition of relational m-consistency is similar but not identical to that of m-consistency over the dual representation of the problem in which the constraints are the variables, their allowed tuples are their respective domains and two such constraint-variables are constrained if they have variables in common. The virtue in this new explicit definition (relative to the one based on the dual graph) is that it is simpler to work with, it uses known notations from relational databases, and it immediately translates to consistency enforcing algorithms.

Relational m-consistency can be enforced on a network that does not possess this level of consistency. Below we present algorithm RC_m, a brute-force algorithm for enforcing strong relational m-consistency on a network R. The algorithm seems to enforce relational m-consistency only (joining every set of $m - 1$ relations), however due to our convention of testing all projections when verifying consistency, strong m-consistency results as well.

$RC_m(R)$
1. **repeat**
2. $Q \leftarrow R$
3.   **for** every $m - 1$ relations $R_{S_1}, \ldots, R_{S_{m-1}} \in Q$ and every $x \in \bigcap_{i=1}^{m-1} S_i$
4.   **do** $A \leftarrow \bigcup_{i=1}^{m-1} S_i - \{x\}$
5. $R_A \leftarrow R_A \cap \Pi_A(\bowtie_{i=1}^{m-1} R_{S_i})$
6. **until** $Q = R$

Note that R_Y stands for the current unique constraint specified over a subset of variables Y. If no constraint exists, then R_Y is the universal relation over Y. The algorithm takes any $m - 1$ relations that may or may not be relational m-consistent and enforces relational m-consistency by tightening the relation among the appropriate subsets of variables. We call the operation in Step 5 of the algorithm *extended m-composition*, since it generalizes the composition operation defined on binary relations. Algorithm RC_m computes the closure of R with respect to extended m-composition. We can conclude that:

Theorem 5 *For any network, R, whose closure under extended i-composition, for $i = 3, \ldots, m$, is an $(m-2)$-tight network, $m \geq 3$, algorithm RC_m computes an equivalent globally consistent network.*

Proof. Follows immediately from Theorem 4 and from the fact that RC_m generates a strong relational m-consistent network. □.

While enforcing *variable-based* m-consistency can be done in polynomial time, it is unlikely that relational m-consistency can be achieved tractably, since, as we will shortly see, even for $m = 3$ it solves the NP-complete problem of propositional satisfiability. A more direct argument suggesting an increase in time and space complexity is the fact that the algorithm may need to record relations of arbitrary arity and also that the constraints' tightness may increase.

Example 8. Bi-valued relations are 1-tight and closed under extended 3-composition. Thus, by Theorem 5, bi-valued networks can be solved by algorithm RC_3. In particular, the satisfiability of propositional $CNFs$ can be decided by RC_3. Here the extended composition operation (Step 5 of algorithm RC_m) takes the form of pair-wise resolution [Dechter and Rish, 1994]. A different derivation of the same result is already given by [Dechter, 1992b; van Beek and Dechter, 1994].

As with variable-based local-consistency, we can improve the efficiency of enforcing relational consistency by enforcing it only along a certain direction. Below we present algorithm *Directional Relational m-Consistency (DRC_m)* that enforces strong relational m-consistency on a network R, relative to a given ordering, d, of the variables $x_1, x_2, \ldots, x_n$. We denote as $DRC_m(R, d)$, a network that is strongly relational m-consistent relative to an ordering d.

$DRC_m(R, d)$
1. *Initialize*: generate an ordered partition of the constraints, $bucket_1, \ldots, bucket_n$, where $bucket_i$ contains all the constraints whose highest variable is x_i.
2. **for** $i \leftarrow n$ **downto** 1
3.   **do for** every set of $m-1$ relations $R_{S_1}, \ldots, R_{S_{m-1}}$ in $bucket_i$ (if $bucket_i$ contains fewer than $m-1$ relations, then take all the relations in the bucket).
4.   **do** $A \leftarrow \bigcup_{i=1}^{m-1} S_i - \{x_i\}$
5. $R_A \leftarrow R_A \cap \Pi_A(\bowtie_{i=1}^{m-1} R_{S_i})$
6.   Add R_A to its appropriate bucket.

While the algorithm is incomplete for deciding consistency in general, it is complete for $(m-2)$-tight relations that are closed under extended m-composition. In fact, it is sufficient to require directional $(m-2)$-tightness relative to the ordering used. Namely, requiring that if x_i appears before x_j in the ordering then any value of x_i will be $(m-2)$-tight relative to x_j but not vice-versa. For example, functional relations are always 1-tight from input to outputs but not for any ordering.

Definition 9 (directionally m-tight)
A binary constraint, R_{ij}, is directionally m-tight with respect to an ordering of the variables, $d = (x_1, \ldots, x_n)$, if x_i appears before x_j in the ordering and every row of the (0,1)-matrix that defines the constraint has at most m ones. An r-ary relation is directionally m-tight with respect to an ordering of the variables if and only if all of its binary projections are directionally m-tight with respect to the ordering.

The following theorems will be stated without proofs. Their correctness can be verified using similar theorems on directional consistency algorithms reported earlier [Dechter and Pearl, 1989].

Theorem 6 (Completeness)
If a network $DRC_m(R, d)$ is directionally $(m-2)$-tight relative to d, then $DRC_m(R, d)$ is backtrack-free along d.

Like similar algorithms for imposing directional consistency, DRC_m's worst-case complexity can be bounded as a function of the topological structure of the problem via parameters like the *induced width* of the graph [Dechter and Pearl, 1988].

A network of constraints R can be associated with a constraint graph, where each node is a variable and two variables that appear in one constraint are connected. A general graph can be embedded in a *clique-tree* namely, in a graph whose cliques form a tree-structure. The induced width, $W*$, of such an embedding is its maximal clique size and the induced width $W*$ of an arbitrary graph is the minimum induced width over all its tree-embeddings. For more details see [Dechter and Pearl, 1989]. The complexity of DRC_m can be bounded as a function of the $W*$ of its constraint graph.

Theorem 7 (Complexity) *Given a network of relations R, the complexity of algorithm DRC_m along ordering d is $O(exp(mW^*(d)))$ where $W^*(d)$ is the induced width of the constraint graph of R along d.*

Example 9. Crossword puzzles have been used in experimentally evaluating backtracking algorithms for solving constraint networks [Ginsberg et al., 1990]. We use an example puzzle (taken from [Dechter, 1992a]) to illustrate algorithm DRC_m (see Figure 4).

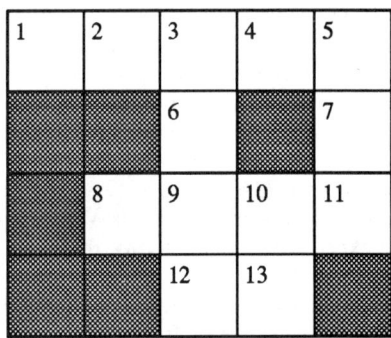

Figure 4: A crossword puzzle

We can formulate this problem as a constraint problem as follows, each possible slot holding a character will be a variable, and the possible words are relations over the variables. Therefore, we have $x_1, \ldots, x_{13}$ variables as marked in the figure. Their domains are the alphabet letters and the constraints are the following relations:

$R_{1,2,3,4,5}$ = {(H,O,S,E,S), (L,A,S,E,R), (S,H,E,E,T), (S,N,A,I,L), (S,T,E,E,R)}

$R_{3,6,9,12}$ = {(H,I,K,E), (A,R,O,N), (K,E,E,T), (E,A,R,N), (S,A,M,E)}

$R_{8,9,10,11}$ = $R_{3,6,9,12}$

$R_{5,7,11}$ = {(R,U,N), (S,U,N), (L,E,T), (Y,E,S), (E,A,T), (T,E,N)}

$R_{10,13}$ = {(N,O), (B,E), (U,S), (I,T)}

$R_{12,13}$ = $R_{10,13}$

We see that constraints $R_{10,13}$ and $R_{12,13}$ are 1-tight, however all the rest have higher tightness. For example, the tightness of $R_{5,7,11}$ is 3 due to words like RUN, SUN, and TEN. Constraint $R_{1,2,3,4,5}$ is also 3-tight since its binary projection on $\{x_1, x_5\}$ contains the three pairs $\{(S,L), (S,T), (S,R)\}$. For the ordering $d = x_5, x_4, ..., x_1$, however, the constraint is only 2-tight. The tightness of all constraints does not go beyond 3. According to Theorem 6, enforcing relational 5-consistency, if not increasing the tightness, will generate a globally consistent network relative to the ordering used.

Applying DRC_5 to this problem using the ordering $d = x_{13}, x_{12}, x_{11}, x_{10}, x_9, x_5, x_3$ (we disregard the rest of the letters since they appear in just one word), gives the following: Initially the bucket for x_3 contains two relations $R_{3,9,12}$ and $R_{3,5}$ (resulting from projecting away x_6 from $R_{3,6,9,12}$ and x_1, x_2, x_4 from $R_{1,2,3,4,5}$, respectively). Processing variable x_3 adds the relation $R_{5,9,12}$ to the bucket of variable x_5 that is processed next. The relation is:

$$R_{5,9,12} = \Pi_{5,9,12}(R_{3,9,12} \bowtie R_{3,5})$$
$$= \{(S,M,E), (R,M,E), (T,R,N),$$
$$(R,R,N), (L,O,N)\}.$$

Next, processing of x_5 adds the relation $R_{9,11,12}$ to the bucket of variable x_9. The relation is:

$$R_{9,11,12} = \Pi_{9,11,12}(R_{5,9,12} \bowtie R_{5,11})$$
$$= \{(M,N,E), (R,N,R), (O,T,N), (R,N,N)\}.$$

Next, processing x_9 adds the relation $R_{10,11,12}$ to the bucket of variable x_{10}. The relation is:

$$R_{10,11,12} = \Pi_{10,11,12}(R_{9,10,11} \bowtie R_{9,11,12})$$
$$= \{(O,N,R)\}.$$

Next, processing x_{10} adds $R_{11,12,13}$ to the bucket of variable x_{11}. The relation is:

$$R_{11,12,13} = \Pi_{11,12,13}(R_{10,11,12} \bowtie R_{10,13})$$
$$= \{\ \}.$$

Namely, resulting in an empty relation. At this point the algorithm stops and determines that the problem is inconsistent.

It turns out, however, that cross-word puzzles have a special property that makes them solvable by relational 3-consistency only.

Lemma 2 *When processing a crossword problem by DRC_m for any m, the resulting buckets contain at most two constraints.*

Proof: Let us annotate each variable in a constraint by a + if it appears in a horizontal word and by a − if it appears in a vertical word. Clearly, in the initial specification each variable appears in at most two constraints and each annotated variable appears in just one constraint (with that annotation). We show that this property is maintained throughout the algorithm's performance. The argument can be proved by induction on the processed buckets. Assume that after processing buckets $x_n, ..., x_i$ all the constraints appearing in the union of all $bucket_{i-1}$ to $bucket_1$ satisfy that each annotated variable appears in at most one constraint. When processing $bucket_{i-1}$, since it contains only two constraints (otherwise it will contain multiple annotations of variable x_{i-1}), it generates a single new constraint. Assume that the constraint is added to the bucket of x_j.

Clearly, if x_j is annotated positively in the added constraint, $bucket_j$ cannot contain already a constraint with a positive annotation of x_j. Otherwise, it means that before processing bucket $i - 1$, there were two constraints with positive annotation of x_j, one in the bucket of x_{i-1} and one in the bucket of x_j, which contradicts the induction hypothesis. Therefore, the rest of the buckets still obey the claimed property. □

Consequently, applying DRC_3 to a cross-word puzzle along any ordering enforces global consistency along that ordering.

Theorem 8 *Given a cross-word puzzle of size n, and for any ordering d, algorithms DRC_3 enforces directional global-consistency along d.*

Note, that it does not mean that cross-word puzzles are tractable. The size of the constraints in the bucket may be exponential. Nevertheless, if the size of the constraints is bounded somehow—by the width, for example—the problem becomes tractable.

5 Conclusions

In this paper, we have identified a sufficient condition based on the tightness of the constraints, the arity of the constraints, and the level of local consistency, that guarantees that a solution can be found in a backtrack-free manner. The results will be useful in applications where a knowledge base will be queried over and over and the preprocessing costs can be amortized over many queries. As well, we believe our results may have significant explanatory value. In recent computational experiments we discovered that the parameter m, which measures the tightness of the constraints, is a good predictor of the amount of time needed by backtracking algorithms to solve particular constraint networks. A goal in our work is to discover parameters of constraint networks that will allow us to predict how a backtracking algorithm will perform on a given problem.

Acknowledgements

This work was supported in part by the Natural Sciences and Engineering Research Council of Canada, by the NSF under grant IRI-9157636, by the Air Force Office of Scientific Research under grant AFOSR 900136, by Toshiba of America, and by a Xerox grant.

References

[Allen, 1983] J. F. Allen. Maintaining knowledge about temporal intervals. *Comm. ACM*, 26:832–843, 1983.

[Beeri et al., 1983] C. Beeri, R. Fagin, D. Maier, and M. Yannakakis. On the desirability of acyclic database schemes. *J. ACM*, 30:479–513, 1983.

[Dechter and Meiri, 1989] R. Dechter and I. Meiri. Experimental evaluation of preprocessing techniques in constraint satisfaction problems. In *Proceedings of the Eleventh International Joint Conference on Artificial Intelligence*, pages 271–277, Detroit, Mich., 1989.

[Dechter and Pearl, 1988] R. Dechter and J. Pearl. Network-based heuristics for constraint satisfaction problems. *Artificial Intelligence*, 34:1–38, 1988.

[Dechter and Pearl, 1989] R. Dechter and J. Pearl. Tree clustering for constraint networks. *Artificial Intelligence*, 38:353–366, 1989.

[Dechter and Rish, 1994] R. Dechter and I. Rish. Directional resolution: The Davis-Putnam procedure, revisited. In *Proceedings of the Fourth International Conference on Principles of Knowledge Representation and Reasoning*, Bonn, Germany, 1994.

[Dechter et al., 1991] R. Dechter, I. Meiri, and J. Pearl. Temporal constraint networks. *Artificial Intelligence*, 49:61–95, 1991.

[Dechter, 1992a] R. Dechter. Constraint networks. In S. C. Shapiro, editor, *Encyclopedia of Artificial Intelligence, Second Edition*, pages 276–285. John Wiley & Sons, 1992.

[Dechter, 1992b] R. Dechter. From local to global consistency. *Artificial Intelligence*, 55:87–107, 1992.

[Freuder, 1978] E. C. Freuder. Synthesizing constraint expressions. *Comm. ACM*, 21:958–966, 1978.

[Freuder, 1982] E. C. Freuder. A sufficient condition for backtrack-free search. *J. ACM*, 29:24–32, 1982.

[Freuder, 1985] E. C. Freuder. A sufficient condition for backtrack-bounded search. *J. ACM*, 32:755–761, 1985.

[Ginsberg et al., 1990] M. L. Ginsberg, M. Frank, M. P. Halpin, and M. C. Torrance. Search lessons learned from crossword puzzles. In *Proceedings of the Eighth National Conference on Artificial Intelligence*, pages 210–215, Boston, Mass., 1990.

[Kondrak, 1993] G. Kondrak, 1993. Personal Communication.

[Mackworth, 1977] A. K. Mackworth. Consistency in networks of relations. *Artificial Intelligence*, 8:99–118, 1977.

[Maruyama, 1990] H. Maruyama. Structural disambiguation with constraint propagation. In *Proceedings of the 28th Conference of the Association for Computational Linguistics*, pages 31–38, Pittsburgh, Pennsylvania, 1990.

[Meiri, 1991] I. Meiri. Combining qualitative and quantitative constraints in temporal reasoning. In *Proceedings of the Ninth National Conference on Artificial Intelligence*, pages 260–267, Anaheim, Calif., 1991. An expanded version is available as: Department of Computer Science Technical Report R-160, University of California, Los Angeles.

[Montanari, 1974] U. Montanari. Networks of constraints: Fundamental properties and applications to picture processing. *Inform. Sci.*, 7:95–132, 1974.

[Nadel, 1989] B. A. Nadel. Constraint satisfaction algorithms. *Computational Intelligence*, 5:188–224, 1989.

[van Beek and Dechter, 1994] P. van Beek and R. Dechter. On the minimality and decomposability of row-convex constraint networks. *Accepted for publication in J. ACM*, 1994.

[van Beek, 1992] P. van Beek. Reasoning about qualitative temporal information. *Artificial Intelligence*, 58:297–326, 1992.

[Waltz, 1975] D. Waltz. Understanding line drawings of scenes with shadows. In P. H. Winston, editor, *The Psychology of Computer Vision*, pages 19–91. McGraw-Hill, 1975.

Honesty in Partial Logic

Wiebe van der Hoek
Dept. of Computer Science
Utrecht University
P.O. Box 80089
3508 TB Utrecht
the Netherlands

Jan Jaspars
Software Engineering
CWI
P.O. Box 4079
1009 AB Amsterdam
the Netherlands

Elias Thijsse
ITK
Tilburg University
P.O. Box 90153
5000 LE Tilburg
the Netherlands

Abstract

We propose a new logic in which knowledge is fully introspective and implies truth, although truth need not imply epistemic possibility. The logic is interpreted in a natural class of partial models. Then we examine the notions of honesty and minimal knowledge in this logic: Which so-called *honest* φ can be 'all that is known' and what is the state of the agent that only knows φ? Redefining *stable sets* enables us to provide suitable syntactic and semantic criteria for honesty. The rough syntactic definition of honesty is the existence of a minimal stable expansion, so the problem resides in the ordering relation underlying minimality. We discuss three different proposals for this ordering, together with their semantic counterparts, and show their effects on the induced notions of honesty. We then show that each of the three obtained kinds of honesty allows for its own disjunction property. Previous accounts of honesty and minimizing knowledge, most of them based on the modal system **S5** and classical possible world semantics, were only partly successful. We conclude that our final proposal, which uses the effects of the weakened logic and its partial semantics as well as the strengthened notion of honesty, improves upon this: it captures the right intuitions and produces satisfactory results.

1 INTRODUCTION

We argue that honesty in knowledge representation calls for a *partial* approach, for reasons of adequacy and efficiency. Let us first (re)introduce the central concepts, honesty and partiality.

Honesty is the quality of a proposition which can be said to be *only* known, i.e. knowing that fact and its consequences, but not knowing more than that. For example, you may only know that Pat will come tomorrow, without knowing anything at all about, say, Sue. Also, you may only know that either Pat or Sue will come tomorrow, which implies you do not know which one of the two will come. These are examples of honest knowledge. By contrast, you cannot honestly say you only know (that you know) *whether* Pat will come, for then you would either know that Pat will come or know that she won't come, both options being logically stronger than what is supposed to be known.

Partiality is the idea of not giving a truth value to every proposition: in a given situation the truth of a formula may be undefined, for example due to lack of information. Such undefinedness may even occur for classical tautologies, such as the well-known 'law of excluded middle' (*tertium non datur*) $\varphi \vee \neg\varphi$, which is therefore not valid in the partial semantics we advocate.

Partiality and honesty may seem totally unrelated themes, but in fact we argue that they are closely related. Let us reinspect the case in which you only know that Pat will come tomorrow. This, we claim, does not involve any knowledge about Sue or some other part of the universe. For example, it does not even imply that you know the possibility that Sue will come too: you may not be acquainted with her, or just not consider her possible arrival. In a straightforward total semantics ignorance leads to wide knowledge of possibilities, which, however, contradicts the initial idea of *only* knowing some honest formula. The proliferation problem simply does not occur in our partial semantics, since facts unrelated to some honest formula can be left undefined.

This, in a nutshell, is our prime motivation for 'going partial': it provides a more adequate and natural account of minimizing one's knowledge (i.e. describing what you *only* know). But there is more to it. One of the other advantages of partial semantics is its efficiency, which is reflected in the much smaller size of the characterizing models. Classical possible world semantics leads to a combinatorial explosion: the less one knows, the bigger the model. For example, honest knowledge of p and complete ignorance of n other propositional variables leads to 2^n worlds in a model that represents what one only knows. This may be contrasted to a partial model for only knowing p that uses but one or two worlds. Moreover, addition of information may lead to growth of the partial model, unlike the elimination usual in possible worlds models — again the partial approach seems more natural and intuitive.

Partial semantics also allows for a greater flexibility with respect to the epistemic background logic. For the case study presented in this paper this is revealed in adopting the veridicality principle of knowledge $\Box \varphi \Rightarrow \varphi$ ('if you know something, it must be true'), without being forced to accept its contrapositive $\varphi \Rightarrow \Diamond \varphi$ ('if something is true, you must consider it possible'). Moreover, knowledge will be fully introspective: both positive introspection and negative introspection as well as their contrapositives are properties our logic embraces. In all, the logic resembles a weak variant of the classical system **S5**, although its epistemic properties are stronger than so-called *weak* **S5** (which has $\Box \varphi \Rightarrow \Diamond \varphi$, $\Box \varphi \Rightarrow \Box \Box \varphi$ and $\Diamond \varphi \Rightarrow \Box \Diamond \varphi$ but not $\Box \varphi \Rightarrow \varphi$). Apart from fitting our intuitions about (strong) knowledge, this logic enables us to simplify the partial models needed, essentially omitting most of the relational structure.

Apart from the fact that our partial semantics both allows for a greater flexibility of the underlying epistemic background logic, and elegantly solves the proliferation problem, let us try and indicate how we think our approach to honesty improves upon 'classical' treatments. A first difference deals with the *logical omniscience* of a — possibly totally ignorant — agent, and is related to the proliferation problem.

In the classical approach of Halpern and Moses (1985) for instance, the formula $\top$ ('always true') is perfectly honest, doing justice to the fact that it makes sense to claim that one 'knows nothing'. We agree with the designation of $\top$ being honest, but we depart from Halpern and Moses (1985) when determining the *consequences* of such an observation. To make our point clear, let us write, for any honest formula φ and epistemic formula ψ,

$$\varphi \hspace{0.2em}\vert\hspace{-0.3em}\sim \psi$$

for 'the agent knows ψ, if he claims to only know φ'.

Then, in the framework of Halpern & Moses (1985) one obtains $\top \hspace{0.2em}\vert\hspace{-0.3em}\sim \psi$ when ψ is an **S5**-tautology, implying that the agent who claims to only know $\top$, also knows that he is fully introspective ($\top \hspace{0.2em}\vert\hspace{-0.3em}\sim \Box \chi \to \Box \Box \chi$, $\top \hspace{0.2em}\vert\hspace{-0.3em}\sim \neg \Box \chi \to \Box \neg \Box \chi$), and one also obtains that possibly the Queen of Holland is on strike ($\top \hspace{0.2em}\vert\hspace{-0.3em}\sim \Diamond s$). However, we prefer the ignorant agent who only knows $\top$, to really let him know no more than that; in our set-up, we have $\top \hspace{0.2em}\vert\hspace{-0.3em}\sim \psi$ iff ψ is a tautology. Fortunately, there are relatively few tautologies in partial logic: all of them contain $\top$.

More generally, we agree with the analysis of Halpern & Moses (1985) that objective (propositional) formulas should be rendered honest, but we depart from Halpern & Moses when it comes to the $\hspace{0.2em}\vert\hspace{-0.3em}\sim$-consequences of such formulas. Generalizing the situation we gave above, one may say that our $\hspace{0.2em}\vert\hspace{-0.3em}\sim$ gives a serious account of *relevance*: if φ and ψ have no proposition symbol in common, and do not contain $\top$, then $\varphi \hspace{0.2em}\vert\hspace{-0.3em}\not\sim \psi$. Thus, e.g. $p \hspace{0.2em}\vert\hspace{-0.3em}\not\sim (q \vee \neg q)$.

Moving up in the hierarchy from objective formulas to epistemic statements, our classification of honest formulas is starting to diverge from the classical analysis. We agree with that analysis that disjunctive epistemic assertions often are problematic with regard to honesty. The argument runs like this: the formula $\varphi = \Box p \vee \Box q$ is dishonest; only knowing φ implies not knowing any stronger formula, in particular, one obtains not knowing p ($\neg \Box p$) and not knowing q ($\neg \Box q$), but the latter two conclusions are easily seen to be inconsistent with φ.

However, where the framework of Halpern & Moses (1985) does indeed label the disjunctive epistemic formula ($\Box p \vee \Box q$) dishonest, we think their set-up still yields some counterintuitive results. For instance, their definitions are such that the disjunctive epistemic formula $\psi = (\Diamond p \vee \Diamond q)$ is still honest! But here, we think a similar argument as for ($\Box p \vee \Box q$) can be given to account for ψ's dishonesty: if you only know that you either consider p to be possible, or q (to be possible), then you must know which of the two.

Here is a good point to emphasize that in our framework, compared to those based on classical logic, it would even be worse to consider ψ honest, because our interpretation of $\Diamond \chi$ is a rather strong one: it means that the agent has decided to assign 'true' to the formula χ in one of his epistemic alternatives (rather than expressing that it is not the case that he knows $\neg \chi$). This also supports our $p \hspace{0.2em}\vert\hspace{-0.3em}\not\sim \Diamond q$: if the agent only knows p, he has no reason yet to assign the value 'true' to q in one of his epistemic alternatives. The reader may compare this to the situation in which we have an even weaker premiss: $(p \vee q) \hspace{0.2em}\vert\hspace{-0.3em}\sim \Diamond q$! This seems intuitively correct: if the agent only knows $p \vee q$ then he must consider at least some state to be possible in which he assigned 'true' to q. (By comparing the latter two assertions about $\hspace{0.2em}\vert\hspace{-0.3em}\sim$ in our system, the reader of course recognizes the non-monotonic flavour of this consequence relation.)

What about disjunctions of objective formulas with epistemic ones? Quite surprisingly, although we think one's intuitions should not be too far apart from those explained above, the analysis made in systems based on classical logic yields different outcomes. To wit, Schwarz and Truszczyński (1992) propose a treatment in which $\varphi = (\neg \Box p \to q)$ is considered honest, in contrast with Halpern and Moses. At this point, we agree with the latter approach: only knowing φ implies not knowing p, and thus, by φ, knowing q, which is stronger than φ itself. Our accounts thus judges φ dishonest.

Before starting off, we make one more preliminary remark here. Clearly, determining whether φ is honest, and, if so, what exactly are its $\hspace{0.2em}\vert\hspace{-0.3em}\sim$-consequences involves 'minimizing' one's knowledge. In the formal language, this is tied up with minimizing sets of formulas, and semantically, with somehow minimizing our models — we argued above that the latter is a typical offspring of 'going partial'. However, speaking mathematically, we misuse the word 'minimal' [1] in many places: where this predicate usually means 'noth-

---

[1] We thank one of the referees for making our small entanglement with these terms — which is the least we were aiming for — minimal.

ing is smaller', we rather use it to denote 'smaller than everything else'. The alternative 'least' would be misleading since it wrongly suggests that we would have unique minima — this is not the case since most of the underlying orders are pre-orders, not partial orders.

The rest of the paper is organized as follows. In the next section we introduce the epistemic logic, presenting its language, semantics and inference system, and state its completeness. Then, in section 3, we study ways to minimize knowledge for this logic, discussing different notions of honesty, both from a deductive (minimal stable sets) and from a model-theoretical perspective (minimal models). We round off by providing a syntactic perspective on honesty (disjunction properties). Proofs are often omitted: they are found in van der Hoek, Jaspars and Thijsse (1993).

2 THE LOGIC

In this section we introduce a partial modal logic **L** of which we will investigate the notions of stability, honesty and several disjunction properties in subsequent sections. We present our logic following a common pattern: we first give its language and a partial semantics, and then we provide a deductive system for **L**. Finally we mention a completeness result connecting them.

2.1 LANGUAGE AND SEMANTICS

Definition 2.1 Let $\mathcal{P}$ be a non-empty finite set of propositional variables. The *language* $\mathcal{L}$ is the smallest superset of $\mathcal{P}$ such that

$$\varphi, \psi \in \mathcal{L} \Rightarrow \neg\varphi, (\varphi \wedge \psi), \bot, \Box\varphi \in \mathcal{L}.$$

$\mathcal{L}_0$ is the subset of $\mathcal{L}$ of all formulas which do not contain $\Box$-operators. For any $\Gamma \subseteq \mathcal{L}$, we write Γ_0 for $\Gamma \cap \mathcal{L}_0$ and $\overline{\Gamma}$ for $\{\varphi \in \mathcal{L} \mid \varphi \notin \Gamma\}$. Moreover, for any $\Gamma \subseteq \mathcal{L}$ and any $\odot \in \{\neg, \Box, \Diamond\}$, we define $\odot\Gamma = \{\odot\gamma \mid \gamma \in \Gamma\}$ and $\odot^-\Gamma = \{\gamma \mid \odot\gamma \in \Gamma\}$.

Here, the intended meaning of $\bot$ is 'always false', and that of $\Box\varphi$ is 'φ is known'. We write $\top$ for $\neg\bot$, $\varphi \vee \psi$ for $\neg(\neg\varphi \wedge \neg\psi)$ and $\Diamond\varphi$ for $\neg\Box\neg\varphi$.

Definition 2.2 Let Γ and Σ be sets of formulas of $\mathcal{L}$. Then:

- $\Gamma \subseteq_0 \Sigma \Leftrightarrow \Gamma_0 \subseteq \Sigma_0$
- $\Gamma \subseteq_\Box \Sigma \Leftrightarrow \Box^-\Gamma \subseteq \Box^-\Sigma$
- $\Gamma \subseteq_\Diamond \Sigma \Leftrightarrow \Diamond^-\Gamma \subseteq \Diamond^-\Sigma$

Let Π be some subset of $\wp(\mathcal{L})$, the powerset of $\mathcal{L}$. For any $\star \in \{0, \Box, \Diamond\}$, we say that $\Gamma \in \Pi$ is $\subseteq_\star$-*minimal in* Π if $\Gamma \subseteq_\star \Sigma$ for all $\Sigma \in \Pi$, and similarly for $\subseteq$-minimality in Π.

The mathematical structure for the interpretation of $\mathcal{L}$ is that of a Kripke model with partial worlds. Here, instead of considering arbitrary partial Kripke models[2], we restrict attention to what we call 'balloon models', which are somewhat reminiscent of the standard **KD45**-Kripke models.

Definition 2.3 A *partial valuation* V is a partial function which assigns truth-values to a given set of propositional variables $\mathcal{P}$. The collection of all partial valuations is denoted by VAL. $V' \in$ VAL is said to be an *extension* of $V \in$ VAL if $V(p) = V'(p)$ for all p such that $V(p) \in \{0, 1\}$. We abbreviate the extension relation by $V \sqsubseteq V'$.

Definition 2.4 A *balloon model* is a triple $M = \langle W, g, V \rangle$ with W a non-empty finite set of worlds, called the *balloon*, g the *root* or *generator* of the model, and V a global valuation function such that $V : W \cup \{g\} \to$ VAL. We require that M satisfies the *root condition*:

$$V(w) \sqsubseteq V(g) \text{ for some } w \in W.$$

We also write M_g for such a model: note that any $w \in W$ and $V : W \to$ VAL give rise to a model $M_w = \langle W, w, V \rangle$. The *truth* and *falsity* of a formula $\varphi \in \mathcal{L}$ in a balloon model $M = \langle W, g, V \rangle$, written as $M \models \varphi$ and $M =\!\!| \varphi$, respectively, are defined by induction

$$
\begin{array}{lcl}
M \not\models \bot & & \\
M =\!\!| \bot & & \\
M \models p & \Leftrightarrow & V(g)(p) = 1 \ (p \in \mathcal{P}) \\
M =\!\!| p & \Leftrightarrow & V(g)(p) = 0 \ (p \in \mathcal{P}) \\
M \models \neg\varphi & \Leftrightarrow & M =\!\!| \varphi \\
M =\!\!| \neg\varphi & \Leftrightarrow & M \models \varphi \\
M \models \varphi \wedge \psi & \Leftrightarrow & M \models \varphi \text{ and } M \models \varphi \\
M =\!\!| \varphi \wedge \psi & \Leftrightarrow & M =\!\!| \varphi \text{ or } M =\!\!| \psi \\
M \models \Box\varphi & \Leftrightarrow & M_w \models \varphi \text{ for all } w \in W \\
M =\!\!| \Box\varphi & \Leftrightarrow & M_w =\!\!| \varphi \text{ for some } w \in W
\end{array}
$$

A balloon model for epistemic formulas may be conceived as just a collection of epistemic alternatives for an agent relative to some 'real world' g: for each alternative, the agent has decided to make some propositional atoms true, and some others false (and leave yet others undefined). At the propositional level, our definitions induce a so-called *strong Kleene* semantics (the reader may consult Langholm (1988) for a thorough introduction into partial semantics for the propositional and first-order language). Furthermore, the truth and falsity conditions yield the intended effect for $\Diamond$-formulas: we have $M \models \Diamond\varphi \Leftrightarrow M_w \models \varphi$ for some $w \in W$. In particular, our partial semantics makes $(\Box\varphi \vee \neg\Box\varphi)$, and hence $(\Box\neg\varphi \vee \Diamond\varphi)$ invalid. This reflects the idea that, in our opinion, $\Diamond\varphi$ should express some positive evidence about φ, not just lack of knowledge of $\neg\varphi$. Finally, the root condition expresses that the agent has at least one alternative that can be extended to the real world. This effects veridicality, as is guaranteed by lemma 2.6. The first model in figure 1 shows that the dual of veridicality is not valid: $M \models r$, but $M \not\models \Diamond r$.

---

[2] For a general approach, see Thijsse (1992) or Jaspars & Thijsse (1993).

Lemma 2.5 (Propositional Persistence)
Let $M = \langle W, g, V \rangle$ and $M' = \langle W', g', V' \rangle$ be two balloon models. Then, for all $w \in W \cup \{g\}$ and all $w' \in W' \cup \{g'\}$:

$$V(w) \sqsubseteq V'(w') \Leftrightarrow \forall \pi \in \mathcal{L}_0 : (M_w \models \pi \Rightarrow M'_{w'} \models \pi)$$

Lemma 2.6 (Internal Persistence)
For every balloon model $M = \langle W, g, V \rangle$ and all worlds $w, w' \in W \cup \{g\}$:

$$V(w) \sqsubseteq V(w') \Leftrightarrow \forall \varphi \in \mathcal{L} : (M_w \models \varphi \Rightarrow M'_{w'} \models \varphi)$$

Example 2.7 Figure 1 denotes two typical balloon models. We call a world in which no atom is true or false an *empty world*; note that M' has such a world. Moreover note that $M \models \Box p \wedge \Diamond q$, $M \not\models \Diamond \neg q$ and $M \not\models \Box q$. For M', we have $M' \models \Box \top$, but at the same time $M' \not\models \Box(\neg p \vee p)$, $M' \not\dashv \Box(\neg p \vee p)$.

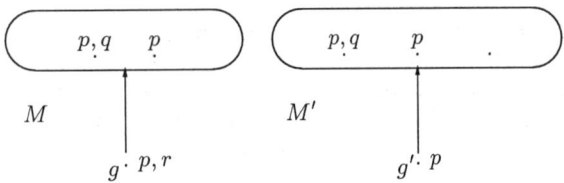

Figure 1: two balloon models M and M'

For any $M = \langle W, g, V \rangle$ we define the *theory* $Th(M)$ of M as $\{\varphi \in \mathcal{L} \mid M \models \varphi\}$, the *knowledge* $\kappa(M)$ in M as $\{\varphi \in \mathcal{L} \mid M \models \Box\varphi\}$ and the *possibilities* $\pi(M)$ as $\pi(M) = \{\varphi \in \mathcal{L} \mid M \models \Diamond\varphi\}$. Let Γ and Δ be sets of formulas; $M \models \Gamma$ means $\Gamma \subseteq Th(M)$ and the consequence relation $\Gamma \models \Delta$ is defined by: $M \models \Gamma \Rightarrow \Delta \cap Th(M) \neq \emptyset$ for all M, i.e. all balloon models which verify all members of Γ also verify at least one element of Δ.

2.2 DEDUCTIONS IN L

We now formally define the deductive machinery of our logic. The sequent $\Gamma \vdash \Delta$ should be understood as: 'the disjunction of the members of Δ follows from the conjunction of the formulas in Γ'. Instead of $\Gamma \cup \{\varphi\}$ and $\Gamma \cup \Delta$ we write Γ, φ and Γ, Δ respectively.

Definition 2.8 To start with, we distinguish the following *structural rules*:

- $\Gamma \cap \Delta \neq \emptyset \Rightarrow \Gamma \vdash \Delta$ START

- $\dfrac{\Gamma \vdash \Delta \quad \Delta \subseteq \Delta' \quad \Gamma \subseteq \Gamma'}{\Gamma' \vdash \Delta'}$ MON

- $\dfrac{\Gamma \vdash \varphi, \Delta \quad \Gamma', \varphi \vdash \Delta'}{\Gamma, \Gamma' \vdash \Delta, \Delta'}$ CUT

If we add to those structural rules the following *propositional rules*, we obtain the partial propositional logic $\mathbf{rL}^+$.[3]

---
[3] Without the rule for $\bot$. Cf. Urquhart (1986) and Thijsse (1992) for natural deduction type systems.

Those propositional rules explain how the logical connectives are introduced on the left (L-TRUE) and right hand side (R-TRUE) of the '$\vdash$', respectively; possibly accompanied with a negation sign (L-FALSE or R-FALSE).

- $\Gamma \vdash \neg\bot, \Delta$ R-FALSE $\bot$

- $\dfrac{\Gamma \vdash \varphi, \Delta}{\Gamma, \neg\varphi \vdash \Delta}$ L-TRUE $\neg$

- $\dfrac{\Gamma, \varphi \vdash \Delta}{\Gamma, \neg\neg\varphi \vdash \Delta}$ L-FALSE $\neg$

- $\dfrac{\Gamma \vdash \varphi, \Delta}{\Gamma \vdash \neg\neg\varphi, \Delta}$ R-FALSE $\neg$

- $\dfrac{\Gamma, \varphi, \psi \vdash \Delta}{\Gamma, \varphi \wedge \psi \vdash \Delta}$ L-TRUE $\wedge$

- $\dfrac{\Gamma \vdash \varphi, \Delta \quad \Gamma' \vdash \psi, \Delta'}{\Gamma, \Gamma' \vdash \varphi \wedge \psi, \Delta, \Delta'}$ R-TRUE $\wedge$

- $\dfrac{\Gamma, \neg\varphi \vdash \Delta \quad \Gamma', \neg\psi \vdash \Delta'}{\Gamma, \Gamma', \neg(\varphi \wedge \psi) \vdash \Delta, \Delta'}$ L-FALSE $\wedge$

- $\dfrac{\Gamma \vdash \neg\varphi, \neg\psi, \Delta}{\Gamma \vdash \neg(\varphi \wedge \psi), \Delta}$ R-FALSE $\wedge$

Finally, we add to $\mathbf{rL}^+$ the following epistemic rules:

- $\dfrac{\Gamma, \varphi \vdash \Delta}{\Gamma, \Box\varphi \vdash \Delta}$ L-TRUE $\Box$

- $\dfrac{\Gamma \vdash \varphi, \neg\Delta}{\Box\Gamma \vdash \Box\varphi, \neg\Box\Delta}$ R-TRUE $\Box$

- $\dfrac{\Gamma, \neg\varphi \vdash \neg\Delta}{\Box\Gamma, \neg\Box\varphi \vdash \neg\Box\Delta}$ L-FALSE $\Box$

- $\dfrac{\Gamma \vdash \Box\varphi, \Delta}{\Gamma \vdash \Box\Box\varphi, \Delta}$ 4$_\Box$

- $\dfrac{\Gamma, \Box\varphi \vdash \Delta}{\Gamma, \neg\Box\neg\Box\varphi \vdash \Delta}$ 5$_\Diamond$

- $\dfrac{\Gamma \vdash \neg\Box\varphi, \Delta}{\Gamma \vdash \Box\neg\Box\varphi, \Delta}$ 5$_\Box$

The rule L-TRUE $\bot$ ($\Gamma, \bot \vdash \Delta$) is derivable in $\mathbf{L}$. On the other hand, the rule R-TRUE $\neg$

$$\dfrac{\Gamma, \varphi \vdash \Delta}{\Gamma \vdash \neg\varphi, \Delta}$$

is not derivable: adding R-TRUE $\neg$ to $\mathbf{rL}^+$ would even yield a sequent system for classical propositional logic! (cf. Thijsse (1992)).

Definition 2.9 The rules above are called **L**-rules. A sequence $\Delta \subseteq \mathcal{L}$ is said to be **L**-derivable from another sequence $\Gamma \subseteq \mathcal{L}$, $\Gamma \vdash_\mathbf{L} \Delta$, if $\Gamma \vdash \Delta$ can be derived by a finite number of applications of the rules above. We usually drop the subscript '**L**' in the sequel. Then, two formulas

$\varphi, \psi \in \mathcal{L}$ are said to be equivalent, $\varphi \dashv\vdash \psi$, if $\varphi \vdash \psi$ and $\psi \vdash \varphi$.

Lemma 2.10 (Soundness)
For all $\Gamma, \Delta \subseteq \mathcal{L}$: $\Gamma \vdash \Delta \Rightarrow \Gamma \models \Delta$.

Let us pause for a moment and reflect on our basic logic. Claims below that some sequents are not derivable, are now easily verified semantically, as is justified by lemma 2.10.

- The first thing to note about the logic is that it is indeed partial, which is mirrored by the fact that we do not have the *law of excluded middle*:

$$\not\vdash \varphi, \neg\varphi$$

In fact, as is shown in Thijsse (1992), there is not any theorem of **L** in the $\{\bot, \top\}$-free language.

- Moreover, we do not have *contraposition*:

$$\Gamma \vdash \Delta \not\Rightarrow \neg\Delta \vdash \neg\Gamma$$

- Although **L** lacks contraposition and does not have any $\{\bot, \top\}$-free theorems, there are the following *propositional equivalences*:

  De Morgan:
  $\neg(\varphi \wedge \psi) \dashv\vdash \neg\varphi \vee \neg\psi$
  $\neg(\varphi \vee \psi) \dashv\vdash \neg\varphi \wedge \neg\psi$

  Double negation: $\neg\neg\varphi \dashv\vdash \varphi$

  Distribution:
  $\varphi \wedge (\psi \vee \chi) \dashv\vdash (\varphi \wedge \psi) \vee (\varphi \wedge \chi)$
  $\varphi \vee (\psi \wedge \chi) \dashv\vdash (\varphi \vee \psi) \wedge (\varphi \vee \chi)$

  Associativity:
  $\varphi \wedge (\psi \wedge \chi) \dashv\vdash (\varphi \wedge \psi) \wedge \chi$
  $\varphi \vee (\psi \vee \chi) \dashv\vdash (\varphi \vee \psi) \vee \chi$

  Idempotence:
  $\varphi \wedge \varphi \dashv\vdash \varphi$
  $\varphi \vee \varphi \dashv\vdash \varphi$

  Commutativity:
  $\varphi \wedge \psi \dashv\vdash \psi \wedge \varphi$
  $\varphi \vee \psi \dashv\vdash \psi \vee \varphi$

  Absorption:
  $\varphi \vee (\varphi \wedge \psi) \dashv\vdash \varphi$
  $\varphi \wedge (\varphi \vee \psi) \dashv\vdash \varphi$

- For the defined symbols one can easily prove *derived rules* such as the rules for $\vee$ below, or *reformulate* rules such as R-TRUE $\Box$ (by means of double negation, CUT, and the definition of $\Diamond$).

  - $\dfrac{\Gamma, \varphi \vdash \Delta \quad \Gamma', \psi \vdash \Delta'}{\Gamma, \Gamma', \varphi \vee \psi \vdash \Delta, \Delta'}$ L-TRUE $\vee$

  - $\dfrac{\Gamma \vdash \varphi, \psi, \Delta}{\Gamma \vdash \varphi \vee \psi, \Delta}$ R-TRUE $\vee$

  - $\dfrac{\Gamma \vdash \varphi, \Delta}{\Box\Gamma \vdash \Box\varphi, \Diamond\Delta}$ R-TRUE $\Box$

- **L** has the following distribution property:

$$\Box\varphi \wedge \Box\psi \dashv\vdash \Box(\varphi \wedge \psi)$$

- For the *epistemic part*, we have the following:

  Positive introspection:
  $\Box\varphi \vdash \Box\Box\varphi \quad \Diamond\Diamond\varphi \vdash \Diamond\varphi$

  Negative introspection:
  $\neg\Box\varphi \vdash \Box\neg\Box\varphi \quad \Diamond\Box\varphi \vdash \Box\varphi$

  Veridicality: $\Box\varphi \vdash \varphi \quad \varphi \not\vdash \Diamond\varphi$!

Note that, although we *do* have veridicality of knowledge ('known facts are true') we got rid of its contrapositive ('true facts are considered to be possible'). In the sequel, we will denote a property like positive introspection by '$\Box \Rightarrow \Box\Box$' or '$\Diamond\Diamond \Rightarrow \Diamond$'.

To see the system **L** at work, we will provide a proof of a lemma that is crucial for proving that nestings of operators are in fact superfluous. The *modal depth* $md(\varphi)$ of a formula φ is defined straightforwardly, being 0 for $\bot$ and propositional atoms, $md(\neg\varphi) = md(\varphi)$; $md(\varphi \wedge \psi) = \max(md(\varphi), md(\psi))$; $md(\Box\varphi) = 1 + md(\varphi)$.

Proposition 2.11 (reduction properties)

1. $\Box(\Box\alpha \vee \psi) \dashv\vdash \Box\alpha \vee \Box\psi$

2. $\Diamond(\Box\alpha \wedge \psi) \dashv\vdash \Box\alpha \wedge \Diamond\psi$

Proof: We only prove the first equivalence.

($\vdash$)

1.	$\Box\alpha \vdash \Box\alpha$	START
2.	$\psi \vdash \psi$	START
3.	$\Box\alpha \vee \psi \vdash \Box\alpha, \psi$	L-TRUE $\vee$ (1,2)
4.	$\Box(\Box\alpha \vee \psi) \vdash \Diamond\Box\alpha, \Box\psi$	R-TRUE $\Box$ (3)
5.	$\Diamond\Box\alpha \vdash \Box\alpha$	$\Diamond\Box \Rightarrow \Box$
6.	$\Box(\Box\alpha \vee \psi) \vdash \Box\alpha, \Box\psi$	CUT (4,5)
7.	$\Box(\Box\alpha \vee \psi) \vdash \Box\alpha \vee \Box\psi$	R-TRUE $\vee$ (6)

($\dashv$)

1.	$\psi \vdash \Box\alpha, \psi$	START
2.	$\psi \vdash \Box\alpha \vee \psi$	R-TRUE $\vee$ (1)
3.	$\Box\psi \vdash \Box(\Box\alpha \vee \psi)$	R-TRUE $\Box$ (2)
4.	$\Box\alpha \vdash \Box\alpha, \psi$	START
5.	$\Box\alpha \vdash \Box\alpha \vee \psi$	R-TRUE $\vee$ (4)
6.	$\Box\Box\alpha \vdash \Box(\Box\alpha \vee \psi)$	R-TRUE $\Box$ (5)
7.	$\Box\alpha \vdash \Box\Box\alpha$	$\Box \Rightarrow \Box\Box$
8.	$\Box\alpha \vdash \Box(\Box\alpha \vee \psi)$	CUT (6,7)
9.	$\Box\alpha \vee \Box\psi \vdash \Box(\Box\alpha \vee \psi)$	L-TRUE $\vee$ (3,8)

∎

Theorem 2.12 Every $\varphi \in \mathcal{L}$ is equivalent with a formula φ' with $md(\varphi') \leq 1$.

We refer to van der Hoek, Japars and Thijsse (1993) for the full proof that **L** is complete for the class of balloon models. By definition 2.4 our models are *finite*; as a consequence, not all consistent sets would be satisfiable, if we had not chosen $\mathcal{P}$ to be finite. Our completeness proof uses a Henkin-type construction of a canonical balloon model, based on consistent sets of formulas.

However, instead of working with *maximally consistent sets*, we build such a model out of *consistent, disjunction-saturated, deductively closed theories*.

Definition 2.13 Let $\Sigma \subseteq \mathcal{L}$. Then:

- Σ is *consistent* iff $\Sigma \not\vdash \varphi \wedge \neg\varphi$ for all φ.

- Σ is a (deductively closed) *theory* iff
  $\Sigma \vdash \varphi \Rightarrow \varphi \in \Sigma$ for all φ.

- Σ is *disjunction-saturated* iff
  $\Sigma \vdash \varphi \vee \psi \Rightarrow \Sigma \vdash \varphi$ or $\Sigma \vdash \psi$ for all φ and ψ.

- $\Sigma \subseteq \mathcal{L}$ is *saturated* iff for every Δ:
  $\Sigma \vdash \Delta \Rightarrow \Sigma \cap \Delta \neq \emptyset$.

It can be shown that saturated sets are precisely the consistent, disjunction-saturated theories. Now, we have the apparatus to define canonical models for **L**. Whereas in classical modal logic the canonical worlds are maximally consistent sets, in partial logic this role is taken over by saturated sets.

Definition 2.14 (Canonical Model)
Let Γ be a saturated set. We define the canonical model for Γ as $\mathcal{M}_\Gamma = \langle \mathcal{W}_\Gamma, \Gamma, \mathcal{V} \rangle$, where

- $\mathcal{W}_\Gamma = \{\Sigma \mid \Sigma \text{ is saturated and } \Box^-\Gamma \subseteq \Sigma \subseteq \Diamond^-\Gamma\}$

- For all $\Sigma \in \mathcal{W}_\Gamma \cup \{\Gamma\}$ and $p \in \mathcal{P}$:
  $$\mathcal{V}(\Sigma)(p) = \begin{cases} 1 & \text{if } p \in \Sigma \\ 0 & \text{if } \neg p \in \Sigma \end{cases}$$

Then we can prove what are essentially the counterparts of the Lindenbaum lemma and the truth lemma for partial logic.

Lemma 2.15 (Separation Lemma)
If $\Sigma \not\vdash \Delta$ then there exists a saturated set Γ such that $\Sigma \subseteq \Gamma$ and $\Delta \cap \Gamma = \emptyset$.

Lemma 2.16

- The canonical model $\mathcal{M}_\Gamma$ is a balloon model.

- For all formulas $\varphi \in \mathcal{L}$, and all saturated sets Γ and each canonical model $\mathcal{M}_\Gamma$:

  $\mathcal{M}_\Gamma \models \varphi \Leftrightarrow \varphi \in \Gamma$ $\quad \mathcal{M}_\Gamma \dashv \varphi \Leftrightarrow \neg\varphi \in \Gamma$

Combining the results of Lemmas 2.10, 2.15 and 2.16, we obtain a completeness result for **L** with respect to balloon models.[4]

Theorem 2.17 For all Σ and Δ, $\Sigma \vdash \Delta \Leftrightarrow \Sigma \models \Delta$

3 HONESTY

This section concerns both the 'syntactic' and 'semantic' view on *honesty* and *minimal knowledge*. The idea is to minimize the knowledge expressed by, say, φ, i.e. to characterize what a rational agent knows when he or she *only* knows φ (together with its logical consequences). If such minimization is possible, φ is called 'honest' by Halpern & Moses (1985). Though it may seem, *prima facie*, that such characterization is always possible (by taking, say, the deductive closure of $\Box\varphi$), this need not be the case. For example, the formula $\varphi = \Box p \vee \Box \neg p$ does not express minimal knowledge (and is, hence, *dishonest*): only knowing φ implies not knowing more than that, in particular, not knowing p and not knowing $\neg p$. However, the latter two conclusions, combined with φ, lead to an inconsistency.

The main issue we want to address is the problem of deciding which formulas can be rendered honest. Using minimal stable sets we will in fact present several notions of honesty and illustrate them by means of a number of examples. Most of the technical justification for the examples, in particular when the formula is honest, is provided after we have given semantic characterizations of the various notions of honesty in terms of minimal models. We also supply inferential tests (disjunction properties) which are convenient for demonstrating that a formula is dishonest.

3.1 STABLE SETS AND HONESTY

We start out by investigating the deductive view on honesty. Which criteria does the set $C_{\Box\varphi}$ consisting of consequences of $\Box\varphi$ have to meet for φ to be honest? The crucial notion here is that of a *stable set*.[5] Although stability can be defined in many ways, the notion itself is stable, since various definitions turn out to be equivalent.

Thinking of $C_{\Box\varphi} = \{\psi \mid \Box\varphi \vdash \psi\}$ as the 'epistemic state' of a rational agent knowing only φ, it is clear that a stable set at least has to be a *consistent theory* (Cf. definition 2.13). In addition, we want a stable set to have the property that the ignorance of non-consequences is compatible with the knowledge of consequences. In Moore (1985) and Jaspars (1991) this leads to the following requirements for a stable set: (recall that $\overline{S} = \{\varphi \in \mathcal{L} \mid \varphi \notin S\}$)

- S is a theory

- $\Box S \cup \neg \Box \overline{S}$ is consistent

---

[4] For a general procedure to prove completeness in this sequential style, see Jaspars (1994).

[5] See Stalnaker, Moore (1985) and Halpern & Moses (1985) for **S5** stability. Jaspars (1991) defines stability for arbitrary normal systems. Our text definition is from Thijsse (1992).

Though correct for normal systems, the latter requirement is too strong for the partial logic we advocate. Recall that our logic does not have any $\{\top, \bot\}$-free theorems. Yet we want to allow $S = C_{\Box\top}$ to be stable, characterizing the epistemic state of an agent knowing nothing. However, S is unstable by the second requirement: since $\Box\top \not\vdash (p \vee \neg p)$, we have $(p \vee \neg p) \in \overline{S}$, and therefore $\{\Box\top, \neg\Box(p \vee \neg p)\}$ would be consistent, which it is not. So we propose replacing the requirement above by the more general condition that knowledge of non-consequences does not follow from the initial knowledge.

Definition 3.1 A theory S is *stable* iff $\Box S \not\vdash \Box\overline{S}$

This definition can be recast in a format which is closer to Stalnaker's original formulation.

Proposition 3.2 S is a stable set of formulas iff

1. S is a theory
2. if $\varphi \in S$ then $\Box\varphi \in S$ (positive introspection)
3. if $\Box\varphi \vee \Box\psi \in S$ then $\varphi \in S$ or $\psi \in S$ (modal saturation)[6]
4. $\varphi \notin S$ for some φ (consistency)

Proof: This is rather straightforward. To illustrate this we prove consistency, assuming S is stable. Suppose (4) does not hold, then $S = \mathcal{L}$, hence $\Box\overline{S} = \emptyset$. Yet by the rules START and L-TRUE $\Box$, $\Box\bot \vdash \bot$ and so by monotonicity $\Box S \vdash \bot$. The derived rule L-TRUE $\bot$ shows $\bot \vdash \emptyset$ and thus by CUT $\Box S \vdash \emptyset$. In total this yields $\Box S \vdash \Box\overline{S}$, contradicting stability. ∎

Although the characterization of stability given by proposition 3.2 is useful, sometimes another concise requirement is more convenient. Since saturated sets are the possible worlds in the canonical model, the proposition essentially means that a stable set consists of all and only formulas known in some world.

Proposition 3.3
S is stable iff $S = \Box^-\Gamma$ for some saturated set Γ.

Proof: ($\Rightarrow$) Let S be stable, then $\Box S \not\vdash \Box\overline{S}$. By our separation lemma there is a saturated set Γ such that (i) $\Box S \subseteq \Gamma$ and (ii) $\Gamma \cap \Box\overline{S} = \emptyset$. Then $\varphi \in S \Rightarrow$ (by i) $\Box\varphi \in \Gamma \Rightarrow \varphi \in \Box^-\Gamma$ and $\varphi \notin S \Rightarrow \Box\varphi \in \Box\overline{S} \Rightarrow$ (by ii) $\Box\varphi \notin \Gamma \Rightarrow \varphi \notin \Box^-\Gamma$. Hence $S = \Box^-\Gamma$. ($\Leftarrow$) Suppose $S = \Box^-\Gamma$ for some saturated set Γ, and also that $\Box S \vdash \Box\overline{S}$. Since $\Box S \subseteq \Gamma$, and using L-MON we have $\Gamma \vdash \Box\overline{S}$. Γ is saturated, and hence there is some $\psi \notin S$ with $\Gamma \vdash \Box\psi$. But then, since Γ is deductively closed, we have $\Box\psi \in \Gamma$ and hence $\psi \in S$, a contradiction. ∎

Having characterized stability in different ways, we are ready for a formal account of honesty. Writing $\mathcal{ST}(\varphi)$

---
[6]For consistent theories S modal saturation is equivalent to $S \vdash \Box\Gamma \Rightarrow S \cap \Gamma \neq \emptyset$ for all $\Gamma \subseteq \mathcal{L}$.

for $\{S \subseteq \mathcal{L} \mid \varphi \in S \ \& \ S \text{ is stable}\}$, minimization of knowledge φ involves finding a minimal element in $\mathcal{ST}(\varphi)$, the set of stable expansions of φ. If there is a stable set which is minimum, according to some order on sets of formulas, the knowledge is honest. What is this ordering relation? In the paradigm case of the (total) system **S5**, different stable sets are incomparable, so set inclusion does not work. This is not the case for the present (partial) system, basically because the notorious Stalnaker condition $\varphi \notin S \Rightarrow \neg\Box\varphi \in S$ does not hold for stable sets in partial logic. The invalidity of the latter condition implies that in **L** a stable set is not determined by its propositional content (the purely propositional formulas in it), although a stable set is determined by its formulas of degree 1 (i.e. of modal depth less than or equal to 1, or equivalently, without nested boxes). This might suggest set inclusion as the ordering relation of the stable sets, and a notion of honesty induced by $\subseteq$: basically existence of a smallest stable expansion.

Definition 3.4 φ is called *naïvely honest* iff there is a $\subseteq$-minimal element in $\mathcal{ST}(\varphi)$.

Example 3.5 The formulas p, $p \wedge q$, $\Box p$, $\Box(p \wedge q)$, $\Diamond p$ and $\Diamond(p \wedge q)$ are naïvely honest.

In order to prove the correctness of these examples, we would like to dispose of other conditions for establishing naïve honesty. To this purpose reinspect $C_{\Box\varphi}$. Observe that

- $C_{\Box\varphi}$ is a *theory*, since $\vdash$ is transitive for single formulas;
- $C_{\Box\varphi}$ is contained in every stable set containing φ: by proposition 3.2(2) if $\varphi \in$ some stable S, then $\Box\varphi \in S$, so, by proposition 3.2(1) S contains all the consequences of $\Box\varphi$, i.e. $C_{\Box\varphi} \subseteq S$.

As an easy result, we now present a necessary and sufficient condition for a stable set to be $\subseteq$-minimal.

Theorem 3.6
A set S is $\subseteq$-minimal in $\mathcal{ST}(\varphi)$ iff $S = C_{\Box\varphi}$ is stable.

Proof: ($\Rightarrow$) Suppose S is $\subseteq$-minimal for φ. By definition $\varphi \in S$, and, by the remark above, $C_{\Box\varphi} \subseteq S$. Now suppose that $S \not\subseteq C_{\Box\varphi}$, then we have a ψ with $\psi \in S$ and $\Box\varphi \not\vdash \psi$. The separation lemma then provides a saturated set Γ for which $\Box\varphi \in \Gamma, \psi \notin \Gamma$. Since $\Box\psi \vdash \psi$ and Γ is a theory, we also have $\Box\psi \notin \Gamma$. By proposition 3.3, $\Box^-\Gamma$ is a stable set containing φ, contradicting the $\subseteq$-minimality of S. ($\Leftarrow$) If $C_{\Box\varphi}$ is a stable set, then, by the remarks above, it must be $\subseteq$-minimal. ∎

The theorem above immediately provides a necessary and sufficient condition for naïve honesty.

Corollary 3.7 φ is naïvely honest iff $C_{\Box\varphi}$ is stable.

Proof: Let $C_{\Box\varphi}$ be stable. By L-TRUE $\Box$, $\varphi \in C_{\Box\varphi}$. By theorem 3.6, $C_{\Box\varphi}$ is also $\subseteq$-minimal for φ, implying that φ is naïvely honest. The other direction is obvious. ∎

Intuition says that *objective* (i.e. propositional, without boxes) formulas should be rendered honest, for it seems to be perfectly sensible to claim to only know some objective information. This is why naïve honesty is too strong and too naïve:

Observation 3.8
The objective formula $(p \vee q)$ is not naïvely honest.

Proof: Suppose that S would be $\subseteq$-minimal in $\mathcal{ST}(p \vee q)$, then $(p \vee q) \in S$, and, by proposition 3.2(2), also $\Box(p \vee q) \in S$. Since (by R-TRUE and $\Diamond \Rightarrow \Box\Diamond$)), we have $\Box(p \vee q) \vdash \Box p \vee \Box\Diamond q$, we use proposition 3.2(3) to conclude that either $p \in S$ or $\Diamond q \in S$ (*). Now, let $\Sigma_1 = \{\Box p\}$ and $\Sigma_2 = \{\Box q\}$. Using completeness, we immediately see that $\Sigma_1 \not\vdash \Box\Diamond q$ and $\Sigma_2 \not\vdash \Box p$. The separation lemma then guarantees the existence of saturated sets Γ_1, Γ_2 for which $\Sigma_i \subseteq \Gamma_i (i = 1, 2), \Box\Diamond q \notin \Gamma_1$ and $\Box p \notin \Gamma_2$. By proposition 3.3 we find two stable sets $S_i = \Box^-\Gamma_i, (i = 1, 2), S_i \in \mathcal{ST}(p \vee q)$, for which $\Diamond q \notin S_1$ and $p \notin S_2$. Since S is $\subseteq$-minimal in $\mathcal{ST}(p \vee q)$ we find $p \notin S, \Diamond q \notin S$, contradicting (*). ∎

Therefore, though the set inclusion ordering of stable sets is (non-trivially) possible, it produces incorrect results as far as honesty is concerned. Now one alternative is to replace ordinary set inclusion by the relation of epistemic inclusion $\subseteq_\Box$. This, however, will not produce any new results, due to the following observation.

Observation 3.9
For all stable sets Γ, Δ: $\Gamma \subseteq_\Box \Delta \Leftrightarrow \Gamma \subseteq \Delta$.

Somewhat surprisingly, since its propositional content does not determine the stable set, minimality of propositional content of a stable expansion produces a more adequate notion of honesty.

Definition 3.10 φ is *weakly honest* iff there is a $\subseteq_0$-minimal element in $\mathcal{ST}(\varphi)$.

This is in fact the same definition of honesty that was proposed by Halpern & Moses (1985). However, in **L** one can generally derive less conclusions from the minimal description of a weakly honest formula than in the **S5** case. For example, $\Diamond p$ is honest for **S5**, and also weakly honest for **L**, but 'knowing only $\Diamond p$' entails different conclusions in both set-ups. Also notice that all naïvely honest formulas are weakly honest.

Example 3.11 The disjunction $(p \vee q)$ is weakly honest: more generally, for each consistent objective formula π, π itself, $\Box\pi$ and $\Diamond\pi$ are weakly honest. Other examples of weakly honest formulas are $(\Box p \wedge \Diamond q)$, and disjunctions such as $(\Box p \vee \neg\Box p)$ and $(p \vee \neg\Box p)$. The formula $(\Box p \vee \Box q)$ is not weakly honest, nor are $(\Box p \vee \neg p)$, or $(\Box p \vee q)$. (This will be proved in section 3.3.)

Notice that a propositionally smallest stable expansion for some formula need not be unique: $S \cap \mathcal{L}_0$ does not determine S. For example with $p \vee q$, S may or may not contain $\Diamond(p \wedge q)$.

Proving weak honesty may be facilitated somewhat by a characterization similar to theorem 3.6: a stable expansion of $\Box\varphi$ is $\subseteq_0$-minimal if all its propositional elements are consequences of $\Box\varphi$.

Theorem 3.12 A set S is $\subseteq_0$-minimal in $\mathcal{ST}(\varphi)$ iff $S \in \mathcal{ST}(\varphi)$ and $S_0 = (C_{\Box\varphi})_0 = \{\mu \in \mathcal{L}_0 \mid \Box\varphi \vdash \mu\}$.

We have already explained why $(\Box p \vee \Box q)$ should not be rendered honest: although it makes perfect sense for an agent to claim that he knows that he either knows p or q, it is absurd for an agent to claim that *all* he knows is that he either knows p or q, because it would imply that he does not know p ($\Box p$ being stronger than $(\Box p \vee \Box q)$), nor q. As we noticed in the introduction, a similar analysis can be made for the agent who is supposed to only know $(\Diamond p \vee \Diamond q)$: this formula should not be honest either. This is why the current notion of honesty is too weak:

Observation 3.13
The formula $(\Diamond p \vee \Diamond q)$ is weakly honest.

Proof: It is easily seen that $\Diamond p \vee \Diamond q \not\vdash \Box\mathcal{L}_0$. By the separation lemma, there is a saturated set Γ for which $\Diamond p \vee \Diamond q \in \Gamma$, and $\Gamma \cap \Box\mathcal{L}_0 = \emptyset$. By proposition 3.3, $\Box^-\Gamma$ is a stable set, which moreover contains $\Diamond p \vee \Diamond q$ (the latter is true by $\Diamond p \vee \Diamond q \vdash \Box(\Diamond p \vee \Diamond q)$). Since $\Box^-\Gamma \cap \mathcal{L}_0 = \emptyset$, $\Box^-\Gamma$ is obviously a $\subseteq_0$-minimal set for $\Diamond p \vee \Diamond q$. ∎

Analyzing the reason for this observation, we note that for weak honesty, we did minimize the *objective* formulas in the stable set for φ, but not the *possibilities* contained in it. In fact, $\subseteq_0$-minimality is insufficiently restrictive: among the $\subseteq_0$-minimal stable sets, we want to single out those containing the smallest number of epistemic possibilities. This is achieved in our last notion of honesty:

Definition 3.14 A formula φ is called *strongly honest* iff there is a $\subseteq_\Diamond$-minimal element in

$$\{S \subseteq \mathcal{L} \mid S \text{ is } \subseteq_0 \text{-minimal in } \mathcal{ST}(\varphi)\}.$$

Such an S is called *strongly minimal* for φ.

Example 3.15 $(\Diamond p \vee \Diamond q)$ is not strongly honest. As with weak honesty, for each objective formula $\pi \in \mathcal{L}_0$, the formulas π and $\Box\pi$ are strongly honest, but now, $\Diamond(p \vee q)$ is not strongly honest.[7]

Can we give other sufficient and necessary conditions for strong honesty? To give this characterization we need one more definition. For a formula ψ we define its *diamond remainder* $R^\Diamond_{\Box\varphi}$ as

$$R^\Diamond_{\Box\varphi} = \{\Diamond\mu \in \Diamond(\mathcal{L}_0) \mid \Box\varphi \vdash \Box(\overline{C_{\Box\varphi}})_0, \Diamond\mu\}.$$

In words, $R^\Diamond_{\Box\varphi}$ contains the $\Diamond$-formulas with a propositional argument that are derivable from $\Box\varphi$, in disjunction with

---
[7]Cf. section 3.2 for a proof.

those □-formulas of which the argument is propositional and not a consequence of $\Box \varphi$.

Theorem 3.16 A set S is strongly minimal for φ iff $S_0 = (C_{\Box\varphi})_0$, $S \cap \Diamond \mathcal{L}_0 = R^{\Diamond}_{\Box\varphi}$ and $S \in \mathcal{ST}(\varphi)$.

3.2 MINIMAL MODELS

Proposition 3.3 ties up the notion of stable set with a major semantic notion: recall that in the canonical model saturated sets correspond to partial worlds. The following corollary of proposition 3.3 relates stability directly to the knowledge in a balloon model.

Corollary 3.17
S is stable iff $S = \kappa(M)$ for some balloon model M.

To decide whether some formula is honest, we considered stable sets that were minimal in some sense. Combined with corollary 3.17 the following orders on models emerge.

Definition 3.18 For any two models $M = \langle W, g, V \rangle$ and $M' = \langle W', g', V' \rangle$ we define:

- (Smyth order)
  $M \sqsubseteq_\Box M' \Leftrightarrow \forall w' \in W' \exists w \in W : V(w) \sqsubseteq V'(w')$

- (Hoare order)
  $M \sqsubseteq_\Diamond M' \Leftrightarrow \forall w \in W \exists w' \in W' : V(w) \sqsubseteq V'(w')$

- (Egli-Milner order)
  $M \sqsubseteq M' \Leftrightarrow M \sqsubseteq_\Box M' \ \& \ M \sqsubseteq_\Diamond M'$

- For any $\preceq \in \{\sqsubseteq_\Box, \sqsubseteq_\Diamond, \sqsubseteq\}$, we say that a model M is $\preceq$-minimal for φ if $\varphi \in \kappa(M)$ and for all M' with $\varphi \in \kappa(M')$ it holds that $M \preceq M'$. We then say that φ has a $\preceq$-minimal model.

The above orders are familiar from *domain theory*; see e.g. Stoy (1977). The orders do not specify anything about the root g of a model $M = \langle W, g, V \rangle$. Recall that $Th(M) = \{ \varphi \in \mathcal{L} \mid M \models \varphi \}$, that $\kappa(M) = \Box^-Th(M)$ and $\pi(M) = \Diamond^- Th(M)$. A second step towards linking the semantic and the syntactic approach to minimal knowledge is to compare the relations $\subseteq_\star$ and $\sqsubseteq_\star$. This is how $\subseteq_\star$ and $\sqsubseteq_\star$ are related:

Theorem 3.19 Consider two models $M = \langle W, g, V \rangle$ and $M' = \langle W', g', V' \rangle$. Then:

- $M \sqsubseteq_\Box M' \Leftrightarrow Th(M) \cap \Box \mathcal{L}_0 \subseteq_\Box Th(M') \Leftrightarrow \kappa(M) \subseteq_0 \kappa(M')$

- $M \sqsubseteq_\Diamond M' \Leftrightarrow Th(M) \cap \Diamond \mathcal{L}_0 \subseteq_\Diamond Th(M') \Leftrightarrow \pi(M) \subseteq_0 \pi(M')$

- $M \sqsubseteq M' \Leftrightarrow \kappa(M) \subseteq \kappa(M')$

- $M \sqsubseteq M' \ \& \ V(g) \sqsubseteq V'(g') \Leftrightarrow Th(M) \subseteq Th(M')$

Proof: We only prove the first item *in extenso*; the second is proven similarly, whereas the third can be deduced from the others, using the degree 1 normal forms from the proof of theorem 2.12 for the first equivalence.

So, suppose that $M \sqsubseteq_\Box M'$ and let μ be some propositional formula for which $M \models \Box \mu$, i.e. for all $w \in W : M_w \models \mu$. Choose any $v' \in W'$. Since $M \sqsubseteq_\Box M'$ there is a $v \in W$ such that $V(v) \sqsubseteq V'(v')$, and so, since $\mu \in \mathcal{L}_0$ we use propositional persistence (lemma 2.5) to conclude $M'_{v'} \models \mu$. Since v' was arbitrary, we have $M' \models \Box \mu$. The opposite direction is proven using contraposition: if $M \not\sqsubseteq_\Box M'$, then there is some $w' \in W'$ such that for all $w \in W: V(w) \not\sqsubseteq V'(w')$. So, for each $w \in W$ there is a literal $\alpha_w \in \mathcal{P} \cup \neg\mathcal{P}$ such that $M_w \models \alpha_w$ and $M'_{w'} \not\models \alpha_w$. Now if $\alpha = \bigvee_{w \in W} \alpha_w$, obviously $\alpha \in \mathcal{L}_0$ and $M_w \models \alpha$ for all $w \in W$, so $M \models \Box \alpha$, yet $M'_{w'} \not\models \alpha$, so $M' \not\models \Box\alpha$. Therefore $\kappa(M) \cap \mathcal{L}_0 \not\subseteq \kappa(M')$, i.e. $\kappa(M) \not\subseteq_0 \kappa(M')$. ∎

It is not hard to see that the restrictions on $\mathcal{L}_0$ in the theorem are necessary. In the case of $\sqsubseteq_\Box$ for instance, let $M' = \langle W', g', V' \rangle$ such that $V'(w')(p) = 0$ for all $w' \in W'$. Consider $M = \langle W, g, V \rangle$ with $W = W' \cup \{x\}$ for some $x \notin W'$, $V(x)(p) = 1$ and $V(w') = V'(w')$ for all $w' \in W'$. Although $M \sqsubseteq_\Box M'$, we have $M \models \Box\Diamond p$, but at the same time $M' \not\models \Box\Diamond p$.

Switching to the semantic view may help to provide proofs for simple facts about stable sets and their ordering relations. In its turn the following result is needed to prove theorem 3.16:

Corollary 3.20 Let S and S' be two stable sets such that $\Box^-S \subseteq_0 \Box^-S'$ and $\Diamond^-S \subseteq_0 \Diamond^-S'$. Then $S \subseteq S'$.

Proof: Let M and M' be such that $S = \kappa(M), S' = \kappa(M')$. Applying the first two items of theorem 3.19, we obtain $M \sqsubseteq_\Box M'$ and $M \sqsubseteq_\Diamond M$, hence $M \sqsubseteq M'$ and thus, by the last item of the same theorem, $S \subseteq S'$. ∎

Now we can characterize our different notions of honesty in semantic terms.

Theorem 3.21
φ is naïvely honest iff $\Box\varphi$ has a $\sqsubseteq$-minimal model.

Proof: Using corollary 3.17 and theorem 3.19, the argument is straightforward:

φ is naïvely honest
$\Leftrightarrow$ (def. naïve honesty)
$\exists S \in \mathcal{ST}(\varphi) \ \forall S' \in \mathcal{ST}(\varphi) : S \subseteq S'$
$\Leftrightarrow$ (cor. 3.17)
$\exists M : \varphi \in \kappa(M) \ \& \ \forall M'(\varphi \in \kappa(M') \Rightarrow \kappa(M) \subseteq \kappa(M'))$
$\Leftrightarrow$ (def. κ, thm 3.19)
$\exists M : M \models \Box\varphi \ \& \ \forall M'(M' \models \Box\varphi \Rightarrow M \sqsubseteq M')$
$\Leftrightarrow$ (def. 3.18)
$\exists M$ which is $\sqsubseteq$-minimal for $\Box\varphi$

Example 3.5 (continued) Figure 2 gives $\sqsubseteq$-minimal models for $(p \wedge q)$, $\Diamond(p \wedge q)$ and $\Box(p \wedge q)$, respectively. Let us prove that M' is $\sqsubseteq$-minimal for $\Diamond(p \wedge q)$: suppose N is an arbitrary model for $\Diamond(p \wedge q)$. Since M' has an empty world, we immediately obtain $M' \sqsubseteq_\Box N$; moreover, since $N \models \Diamond(p \wedge q)$, there must be some world u in N verifying both p and q, and this world obviously extends the two balloon worlds of M', so $M' \sqsubseteq_\Diamond N$. ∎

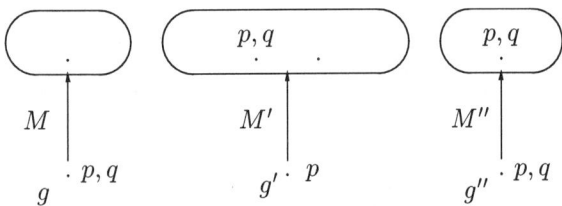

Figure 2: Three $\sqsubseteq$-minimal models

Theorem 3.22
φ is weakly honest iff $\Box\varphi$ has a $\sqsubseteq_\Box$-minimal model.

Proof: Again a direct argument is possible:

φ is weakly honest
$\Leftrightarrow$ (def. weak honesty)
$\exists S \in \mathcal{ST}(\varphi) \, \forall S' \in \mathcal{ST}(\varphi) : S \subseteq_0 S'$
$\Leftrightarrow$ (cor. 3.17)
$\exists M : \varphi \in \kappa(M) \, \& \, \forall M'(\varphi \in \kappa(M') \Rightarrow \kappa(M) \subseteq_0 \kappa(M'))$
$\Leftrightarrow$ (def. κ, thm 3.19)
$\exists M : M \models \Box\varphi \, \& \, \forall M'(M' \models \Box\varphi \Rightarrow M \sqsubseteq_\Box M')$
$\Leftrightarrow$ (def. 3.18)
$\exists M$ which is $\sqsubseteq_\Box$-minimal for $\Box\varphi$
∎

Example 3.11 (continued)
The models M and M' of figure 3 are $\sqsubseteq_\Box$-minimal for $\Box(p \vee q)$ and $\Box p \vee \neg\Box p$, respectively. To see the latter, note first that M' is a model for $\neg\Box p$, and hence for $\Box p \vee \neg\Box p$. Moreover, $M' \sqsubseteq_\Box N$ for any N, due to the empty world in M'; thus M' is $\sqsubseteq_\Box$-minimal amongst the models for $\Box(\Box p \vee \neg\Box p)$. Connecting strong honesty with a semantic

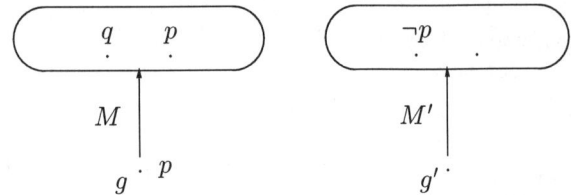

Figure 3: Two $\sqsubseteq_\Box$-minimal models

notion requires one more definition.

Definition 3.23 A model M is called *strongly minimal* for φ iff M is $\sqsubseteq_\Diamond$-minimal in the set

$$\{M' \mid M' \text{ is } \sqsubseteq_\Box \text{-minimal for } \varphi \}.$$

Note that strongly minimal models for φ are by definition $\sqsubseteq_\Box$-minimal for φ. Also note, however, that a strongly minimal model need not be $\sqsubseteq_\Diamond$-minimal.

Theorem 3.24
φ is strongly honest iff $\Box\varphi$ has a strongly minimal model.

Proof: Similar to theorems 3.21 and 3.22, though more laborious. ∎

Example 3.15 (continued) We argue that $(\Diamond p \vee \Diamond q)$ is not strongly honest: consider the two models M and M' of figure 4. Both models verify $\Box(\Diamond p \vee \Diamond q)$ and contain an empty balloon world, hence both are $\sqsubseteq_\Box$-minimal for $\Box(\Diamond p \vee \Diamond q)$. But then we also see that there can be no model N for $\Box(\Diamond p \vee \Diamond q)$ for which both $N \sqsubseteq_\Diamond M$ and $N \sqsubseteq_\Diamond M'$: such a model N has to contain at least a p- or a q-world, if it has a p-world then $N \not\sqsubseteq_\Diamond M'$, if it has a q-world, then $N \not\sqsubseteq_\Diamond M$.

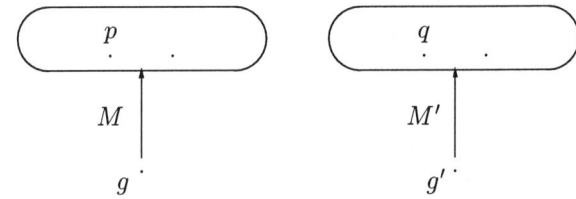

Figure 4: Two $\sqsubseteq_\Box$-minimal models for $(\Diamond p \vee \Diamond q)$

The last example shows that the model-theoretical approach may also be a convenient tool for proving dishonesty. The following subsection contain tests that are particularly useful for this goal.

3.3 DISJUNCTION PROPERTIES

One might want to have an even more direct condition providing honesty, without interference of the notion of stability. Here, we will provide several syntactic, or perhaps rather deductive characterizations for honesty.[8] Inspecting the properties of saturated and stable sets, one good candidate for this is the *disjunction property*, defined below. In fact, this property is already mentioned by Hughes & Cresswell (1984), albeit that there it is a property of logical systems, rather than of formulas. In partial logic the property should be slightly reformulated, and adapted to the different notions of honesty.

Definition 3.25 Let $\varphi \in \mathcal{L}$. The following conditions determine when φ has the *disjunction property* (DP), the *propositional disjunction property* (PDP) or the *propositional disjunction diamond property* (PDDP), respectively.

---

[8] In fact, it is highly questionable whether a fully syntactic (i.e. morphological) criterion for minimal knowledge exists.

DP $\forall \Sigma \subseteq \mathcal{L}: \Box\varphi \vdash \Box\Sigma \Rightarrow \exists \sigma \in \Sigma: \Box\varphi \vdash \sigma$

PDP $\forall \Pi \subseteq \mathcal{L}_0: \Box\varphi \vdash \Box\Pi \Rightarrow \exists \pi \in \Pi: \Box\varphi \vdash \pi$

PDDP $\forall \Pi \subseteq \mathcal{L}_0: \Box\varphi \vdash \Box(\overline{C_{\Box\varphi}})_0, \Diamond\Pi \Rightarrow$
$\exists \pi \in \Pi: \Box\varphi \vdash \Box(\overline{C_{\Box\varphi}})_0, \Diamond\pi$

Note that all disjunction properties imply consistency: take $\Pi, \Sigma = \emptyset$ for the arguments Π, Σ in the rules of the definition above. But we can show a much stronger result:

Theorem 3.26

φ has the DP $\Leftrightarrow$ φ is naïvely honest

φ has the PDP $\Leftrightarrow$ φ is weakly honest

φ has the PDDP $\Leftrightarrow$ φ is strongly honest

Proof: We only demonstrate the easiest equivalence, i.e. the first. First, let φ be naïvely honest. This means it has a $\subseteq$-minimal stable set S. Now suppose $\Box\varphi \vdash \Box\Sigma$, then $S \vdash \Box\Sigma$. By proposition 3.2(3), we know $S \cap \Sigma \neq \emptyset$. According to theorem 3.6 $S = C_{\Box\varphi}$, so there is a consequence of $\Box\varphi$ in Σ, i.e., for some $\sigma \in \Sigma$, $\Box\varphi \vdash \sigma$. In short, φ has the disjunction property.

For the other direction, suppose that φ satisfies DP. In order to apply the separation lemma, we take $\Sigma = \{\Box\varphi\}$ and $\Delta = \Box\overline{C_{\Box\varphi}}$. In order to show that $\Box\varphi \not\vdash \Box\overline{C_{\Box\varphi}}$, suppose to the contrary that $\Box\varphi \vdash \Box\overline{C_{\Box\varphi}}$. The disjunction property DP implies that for some $\psi \in \overline{C_{\Box\varphi}}$, $\Box\varphi \vdash \psi$, i.e. $\psi \in C_{\Box\varphi}$, a contradiction. Thus, by the separation lemma, there is a saturated set Γ, with $\Box\varphi \in \Gamma$ and $\Gamma \cup \Box\overline{C_{\Box\varphi}} = \emptyset$. This implies that

$$\{\Box\varphi\} \subseteq \Gamma \subseteq \Box C_{\Box\varphi} \cup \overline{\Box\mathcal{L}} \quad (*)$$

Now, take $S = \Box^-\Gamma$. By proposition 3.3, S is stable. Moreover, (*) above guarantees that $S = C_{\Box\varphi}$. To see '$\supseteq$', note that $\varphi \in S$ and apply the remark that we made about theorem 3.6 saying that $C_{\Box\varphi}$ is contained in every stable set containing φ. For '$\subseteq$', consider any $\sigma \in S$. Then $\Box\sigma \in \Gamma$. If $\Box\sigma \notin \Box C_{\Box\varphi}$, then, by (*), $\Box\sigma \in \overline{\Box\mathcal{L}}$, which is impossible. So $\Box\sigma \in \Box C_{\Box\varphi}$ and hence $\sigma \in C_{\Box\varphi}$. But if S is stable and equal to $C_{\Box\varphi}$, we have stability of $C_{\Box\varphi}$ and may use corollary 3.7 to conclude that φ is naïvely honest. ∎

Since the disjunction properties are purely inferential and strictly related to the possibly honest formula under inspection, and neither involves extension to a stable set that is minimal in some sense, or minimization in a class of models, they provide a very convenient tool for testing honesty. Disjunction properties are particularly useful for proving that some formula is *dishonest*, as is illustrated below.

Example 3.11 (continued)

Using the PDP we can easily conclude that $(\Box p \vee \Box q)$ is not weakly honest: $\Box(\Box p \vee \Box q) \vdash \Box p \vee \Box q$, so $\Box(\Box p \vee \Box q) \vdash \Box\{p, q\}$, yet $\Box(\Box p \vee \Box q) \not\vdash p$ and $\Box(\Box p \vee \Box q) \not\vdash q$ (where non-derivability is shown by providing a counter-model, as usual). That $(\Box p \vee \neg p)$ and $(\Box p \vee q)$ are not weakly honest can be shown by taking $\Pi = \{p, \neg p\}$ and $\Pi = \{p, q\}$, respectively, thus contradicting the PDP.

By means of theorem 3.21 some of the earlier proofs can now be simplified. For example, observation 3.8 now has a very easy proof:
$\Box(p \vee q) \vdash \Box p \vee \Box\Diamond q$, yet $\Box(p \vee q) \not\vdash p$ and $\Box(p \vee q) \not\vdash \Diamond q$, and thus DP shows that $p \vee q$ is not naïvely honest.

4 CONCLUSION

We have described a new epistemic logic with the remarkable feature that on the one hand knowledge implies truth, yet on the other hand truth does not imply epistemic possibility, thus avoiding at least one type of logical omniscience. The logic can be shown to be sound and complete for so-called balloon models with a partial interpretation.

This logic is then used as a vehicle to study minimization of knowledge. We have introduced different notions of honesty, each of which can be equivalently described in a number of ways. We summarize our notions of honesty and their various characterizations in the following list.

- φ is *naïvely honest* iff
  there is a $\subseteq$-minimal stable expansion of φ iff
  the set of consequences of $\Box\varphi$ is stable iff
  φ has the disjunction property iff
  $\Box\varphi$ has a $\sqsubseteq$-minimal model.

- φ is *weakly honest* iff
  there is a $\subseteq_0$-minimal stable expansion of φ iff
  φ has a stable expansion of which the propositional (i.e. objective) elements are consequences of $\Box\varphi$ iff
  φ has the propositional disjunction property iff
  $\Box\varphi$ has a $\sqsubseteq_\Box$-minimal model.

- φ is *strongly honest* iff
  there is a $\subseteq_\Diamond$-minimum (called strongly minimal for φ) in the set of $\subseteq_0$-minimal stable expansions of φ iff
  φ has a stable expansion S of which the propositional elements are consequences of $\Box\varphi$ and for all objective formulas π, π': $\Diamond\pi \in S \Leftrightarrow \Box\varphi$ implies $\Diamond\pi$ in disjunction with the formulas $\Box\pi'$ which are not consequences of $\Box\varphi$ iff
  φ has the propositional diamond disjunction property iff
  $\Box\varphi$ has a model which is $\sqsubseteq_\Diamond$-minimal with respect to its $\sqsubseteq_\Box$-minimal models.

Whereas the stable expansion criteria makes a comparison to 'classical' definitions of honesty[9] possible, the disjunction properties provide viable tests for honesty, and the model-theoretical treatment shows one of the main advantages of our partial semantics: the minimal models are really quite small.

---

[9] We prefer our formulation of stable expansion to the much less perspicuous fixed–point definitions that are still common in much work on honesty and autoepistemic logic.

Comparing the different notions above, we arrive at a hierarchy of honesty, since we can easily prove

φ is naïvely honest $\Rightarrow$ φ is strongly honest $\Rightarrow$ φ is weakly honest.

As we have illustrated on a number of examples, naïve honesty is too strong (i.e. it yields too many dishonest formulas), whereas weak honesty is indeed too weak — *strong honesty* is the preferable option. By means of honesty we can also define the semantics of the operator 'Agent only knows'.[10]

Evidently, we can define a non-monotonic preferential entailment relation $\mathrel{\smash{\vert\mkern-4mu\sim}}$ by:

$\varphi \mathrel{\smash{\vert\mkern-4mu\sim}} \psi \Leftrightarrow \varphi$ is strongly honest and for all strongly minimal stable expansions S of $\varphi : \psi \in S$

This relation intuitively means that, if φ is only known, then ψ is also known. Then, due to the partial background logic, we find no entailment of irrelevant possibilities, e.g.:

$$p \not\mathrel{\smash{\vert\mkern-4mu\sim}} \Diamond q.$$

Notice that though many non-monotonic entailments that were valid for the classical system **S5** do not qualify for our partial system **L**, such entailment still differs from (partial) consequence and derivability: we have, for example

$$(p \vee q) \not\vdash \Diamond p \ \& \ (p \vee q) \mathrel{\smash{\vert\mkern-4mu\sim}} \Diamond p$$

A systematic study of the properties of $\mathrel{\smash{\vert\mkern-4mu\sim}}$ will be the subject of future research.

Acknowledgements

We thank the audiences of the Seminar on Intensional Logic (Amsterdam) and the ESPRIT workshop on Partiality, Dynamics and Non-monotonicity (Blanes) for their comments on earlier presentations about the subject in 1993. The KR referees also provided valuable suggestions on how to improve the abstract. Piero d'Altan and Thomas A Pieter Niewint kindly provided a last minute correction of the English. The first author is partially supported by ESPRIT Basic Research Action No. 6156 (DRUMS).

References

Halpern, J. & Y. Moses (1985), 'Towards a theory of knowledge and ignorance', in Kr. Apt (ed.) *Logics and Models of Concurrent Systems*, Berlin: Springer–Verlag

van der Hoek, W., J. Jaspars & E. Thijsse (1993), *Honesty in Partial Logic*, Technical Report RUU-CS-93-32, Utrecht University

Hughes, G. & M. Cresswell (1984), *A Companion to Modal Logic*, London: Methuen

Jaspars, J. (1991), 'A generalization of stability and its application to circumscription of positive introspective knowledge', *Proceedings of the Ninth Workshop on Computer Science Logic* (CSL'90), Berlin: Springer–Verlag

Jaspars, J. (1994), *Calculi of Constructive Communication*, dissertation, University of Tilburg.

Jaspars, J. & E. Thijsse (1993), 'Fundamentals of Partial Modal Logic', in P. Doherty & D. Driankov (eds.), *Partial Semantics and Non-monotonic Reasoning for Knowledge Representation* (provisional title). Also as ITK Research Report 47, Tilburg University, 1994

Lakemeyer, G. (1992), 'All you ever wanted to know about Tweety', in *Proceedings of the 3rd International Conference on Knowledge Representation and Reasoning*, San Mateo CA: Morgan Kaufmann, pp. 639–648

Langholm, T. (1988), *Partiality, Truth and Persistence*, Stanford CA: CSLI Lecture Notes No. 15

Levesque, H. (1990), 'All I know: a study in autoepistemic logic', *Artificial Intelligence* 42, pp. 263–309

Moore, R. (1985), 'Semantical considerations on non-monotonic logic', *Artificial Intelligence* 25, pp. 75–94

Schwarz, G. & M. Truszczyński (1992), 'Modal logic S4F and the minimal knowledge paradigm', in Y. Moses (ed.), *Proceedings of* TARK *4*, Palo Alto CA: Morgan Kaufmann

Stalnaker, R., *A note on non-monotonic modal logic*, unpublished manuscript, Department of Philosophy, Cornell University

Stoy, J. (1977), *Denotational Semantics: The Scott-Strachey Approach to Programming Language Theory*, The M.I.T. Series in Computer Science, Cambridge MA: M.I.T. Press

Thijsse, E. (1992), *Partial logic and knowledge representation*, dissertation, Delft: Eburon Publishers

Urquhart, A. (1986), 'Many valued logic', in Gabbay and Günthner (eds.) *Handbook of Philosophical Logic*, volume 3, Dordrecht: Reidel

---

[10]Cf. Levesque (1990) and Lakemeyer (1992).

Mutual Belief Revision (Preliminary Report)

Ron van der Meyden
NTT Basic Research Labs
3-1 Wakamiya Morinosato Atsugi-shi
Kanagawa 243-01, Japan

Abstract

A semantical theory of belief revision in synchronous multi-agent systems is presented. The theory assumes that the world is static, and that the belief revision methods used by the agents are common knowledge. It is shown that the theory has as a special case the revision of knowledge in a broadcast variant of Fagin and Vardi's *communicating scientists* model, in which knowledge is defined in terms of an equivalence relation on runs in a distributed system. Next, the theory is applied to give a semantic reconstruction of a default logic theory of speech acts proposed by Perrault. This reconstruction characterizes the way the speech act transforms an *only knowing* representation of the agent's belief states. The results are shown to differ from those obtained by Perrault. In particular, it is argued that a sincere assertion does not necessarily lead to mutual belief of the proposition asserted, even when the hearer does not initially have any beliefs about this proposition.

1 INTRODUCTION

The question of how an agent should maintain its epistemic state has long been a subject of interest in the areas of artificial intelligence, databases and philosophy, and the literature on this topic is extensive. In particular, there has been a considerable amount of work on the semantics of single agent belief revision [Gärdenfors, 1986; Katsuno and Mendelzon, 1991]. In multiple agent situations, belief revision is more complex, since an agent must revise not just its own beliefs about the world, but also its beliefs about other agents' beliefs about the world. Moreover, an agent must also revise its beliefs about other agents' beliefs about its own beliefs, and so on. We may call this iterated process *mutual belief revision*. The extant theories treating the dynamics of belief in multiple agent environments are primarily syntactical [Appelt and Konolige, 1988; Cohen and Levesque, 1990; Isozaki and Shoham, 1992; Morgenstern, 1990; Perrault, 1990; Thomason, 1990]. In this paper we develop a semantic theory of mutual belief revision.

Among the domains of application of such a theory is a strand in natural language pragmatics that seeks to characterize the meaning of a speech act by describing the effect it has on the mental states of the participants of the conversation [Allen and Perrault, 1980; Cohen and Levesque, 1990; Cohen and Perrault, 1979; Perrault, 1990]. Another potential application is the semantics of agent/knowledge oriented programming languages [Fagin et al., 1994; Moses and Kislev, 1993; Shoham, 1993], which include as primitive constructs modal operators for knowledge and belief.

One can study the dynamics of belief under a variety of assumptions about the nature of agents and their environment. We work in this paper with a very specific set of assumptions. Prototypical of the situations to which our theory is intended to apply are face to face communication, mutual observation of a set of circumstances, and broadcast in synchronous systems with guaranteed message delivery. Thus, we assume agents revise their beliefs synchronously, in response to an event whose occurrence is common knowledge. Each agent is assumed to employ an individual belief revision method, which is common knowledge to the other agents.

In addition, we assume that the world is static - it is only the beliefs of the agents that change. In the terminology of [Katsuno and Mendelzon, 1991], we deal with the *revision* of belief, occasioned when additional information is obtained, or some existing beliefs are are found to be false. This is opposed to the notion of *update*, applicable when a change of belief is required because of a change in the state of the world.[1]

---

[1] For an investigation of update in multi-agent environments see [Meyden, 1994].

The theory we develop represents mutual belief revision as an operator on certain sets of Kripke structures that are canonical for the multi-agent version of the perfect introspection logic K45. However, because our theory is semantical it applies also to logics stronger than K45, such as KD45 and S5. The mutual belief revision process is factored into two stages. In the first stage, agents revise their individual beliefs, ignoring the fact that other agents are also revising their beliefs. In the second stage, the other agents are taken into account. The main concern of the paper is with the relationship between the individual belief revision methods and the agents' mutual belief revision.

The model of individual belief revision used in this paper is very general, and does not satisfy the postulates for rational belief revision recommended by [Alchourrón et al., 1985], commonly referred to as the *AGM postulates*. This is in part because our focus is on the issue of mutuality rather than rationality, and we prefer to cast the theory at the most general possible level. However, we would also argue that the AGM postulates, and others like them, are too restrictive. Indeed, we present an example of interest in mutual belief revision (derived in essence from work of Perrault) in which the AGM postulates are not satisfied by the revision method of the individual agents. Nevertheless, one could restrict our theory by adding the AGM postulates as constraints on the agents' individual belief revision methods. One of the merits of our theory is that it allows for the incorporation of such assumptions in a very natural way.

In Section 3 capture the above assumptions on agents and their environment by formalizing the relationship between mutual belief revision and individual belief revision. We show that for each assignment of agents' individual belief revision methods there is a unique mutual belief revision operator satisfying this formalization. The remainder of the paper is devoted to justifying this theory by studying its consequences in two special cases.

First, we consider knowledge, a special case of belief. The dynamics of knowledge are better understood than those of belief: there exists an independently motivated account of the revision of knowledge, arising directly from the semantics of knowledge in distributed systems [Halpern and Moses, 1990]. We consider a particular distributed system, the *scientists in conference* model, which satisfies the assumptions above. This system is a modification of the *communicating scientists* model of [Fagin et al., 1994; Fagin and Vardi, 1986], which was based on message passing. We show that when our theory of mutual belief revision is applied to the states of knowledge arising in the scientists in conference system, the results are identical to those implied by the semantics of knowledge. We take this to be strong evidence for the reasonableness of our approach.

As a second application, we consider the implications of the theory for an account of speech acts proposed by Perrault. Perrault's work was syntactical, being cast in terms of an extension of default logic [Reiter, 1980]. In order to give a semantic reconstruction, we use the notion of *only knowing* [Levesque, 1990] to represent the agents' initial state of knowledge. We then study the prediction of our theory for the state of knowledge after an assertion. The results turn out to differ from those obtained by Perrault. In particular, our theory entails that a sincere assertion does not necessarily lead to mutual belief of the proposition asserted, even when the hearer does not initially have any beliefs about this proposition. However, a weaker proposition does become mutual knowledge, and we argue that this is an appropriate result, that again supports the reasonableness of our theory.

The structure of the paper is as follows. The preliminary Section 2 introduces a particular class of canonical Kripke structures for $K45_n$. Section 3 describes our theory of mutual belief revision. Section 4 shows that the theory correctly describes the revision of knowledge in the scientists in conference model. In Section 5 we apply the theory to model Perrault's default logic theory of speech acts. Section 6 concludes.

2 PRELIMINARIES

We work with a propositional modal language $\mathcal{L}_n$ generated over the set of propositional constants Φ. The language contains a modal operator B_i for each agent $i = 1 \ldots n$, representing the belief of agent i. The set of formulae is the smallest set containing Φ such that if φ and ψ are formulae then $\neg \varphi$, $\varphi \wedge \psi$ and $B_i \varphi$ are formulae. A formula is said to be *i-objective* if it is a boolean combination of atomic formulae and formulae of the form $B_j \varphi$ where $j \neq i$.

The class of semantic structures used to interpret this language will be the $K45_n$ structures, defined as follows. A *propositional assignment* is a function $\alpha : \Phi \to \{0, 1\}$. A *valuation* on a set X is a function V mapping each element of X to a propositional assignment. A $K45_n$ structure is a tuple $M = \langle W, R_1, \ldots, R_n, V \rangle$ where W is a set of worlds, the R_i are binary relations on W, and V is a valuation on W. The relations R_i are required to be *transitive* and *euclidean* [Chellas, 1980]. An alternate way to understand these conditions is as follows. Given a world w and agent i, define the *possibilities of i at w* to be the set $poss_i(w) = \{v \in W \mid wR_i v\}$. Then R_i is transitive and euclidean just when for all worlds w and all $v \in poss_i(w)$, we have $poss_i(v) = poss_i(w)$. In particular, note that this means that R_i restricted to $poss_i(w)$ is an equivalence relation.

A $K45_n$ *situation* is a pair (M, w) where M is a $K45_n$ structure and w is a world of M. Satisfaction of formulae of $\mathcal{L}_n$ in situations is denoted by a binary relation symbol '$\models$', and defined along the usual lines:

$(M,w) \models p$ if $V(w)(p) = 1$, where $p \in \Phi$,

$(M,w) \models \varphi \wedge \psi$ if $(M,w) \models \varphi$ and $(M,w) \models \psi$,

$(M,w) \models \neg\varphi$ if not $(M,w) \models \varphi$,

$(M,w) \models B_i\varphi$ if $(M,w') \models \varphi$ for all $w' \in W$ such that wR_iw'.

Intuitively, a situation describes a particular state of the world, the agents' beliefs about the world, their beliefs about each others beliefs, etc. It is well-known that requiring the relations R_i to be transitive and euclidean results in the validity of the formulae $B_i\varphi \to B_iB_i\varphi$ and $\neg B_i\varphi \to B_i\neg B_i\varphi$, known respectively as the *positive* and *negative introspection* rules.

We will, in the next section, seek to represent mutual belief revision by means of an operator mapping situations to situations. Since the set of worlds of a Kripke structure may have arbitrarily large cardinality, the class of all situations does not form a set, which means that a function from all situations to situations cannot be formulated within set theory. To get around this problem, and to enable explicit description of the revision operators, we will use certain canonical structures. These will be infinite tree-like structures, in which the degree of branching is bounded.

It is convenient to represent these structures using a generalization of the notion of tree domain. Let L be a set of *labels*, equipped with a valuation V. Define an (L,n)-*sequence of length* m to be a sequence of the form $l_0i_1l_1i_2l_2\ldots i_ml_m$ where $m \geq 0$, the l_j are labels in L, the i_j are agents in $\{1\ldots n\}$ and $i_j \neq i_{j+1}$ for each $j = 1\ldots m-1$. A set T of (L,n)-sequences is said to be *closed under prefixes* if whenever $l_0i_1l_1i_2l_2\ldots i_ml_m \in T$ we have $l_0i_1l_1i_2l_2\ldots i_kl_k \in T$ for all $k \leq m$. An (L,n)-*labelled tree* is a possibly infinite set T of (L,n)-sequences that is closed under prefixes and contains a unique (L,n)-sequence of length 0, i.e. a label l_0 in L. In this case we define $root(T) = l_0$. We write $\mathcal{T}(L,n)$ for the set of (L,n)-labelled trees on L. When L and n are clear from the context we will refer simply to "labelled trees".

We call the elements of a labelled tree T the *vertices* of T. If v is a vertex of T and the sequence[2] $w = v \cdot il$ is also a vertex of T, where $i \in \{1\ldots n\}$ and $l \in L$, then we say that w is an i-*successor* of v. An (L,n)-labelled tree T has an obvious interpretation as a tree with edges labelled by elements of $\{1\ldots n\}$, vertices labelled by elements of L. We define the labelling function lab from n-sequences to L by $lab(l_0i_1l_1i_2l_2\ldots i_ml_m) = l_m$. Note that no two distinct i-successors of any vertex have the same label. Thus, the cardinality of branching is bounded by the cardinality of the set L. Additionally, note that the requirement that $i_j \neq i_{j+1}$

---

[2]The operator '$\cdot$' denotes concatenation of sequences.

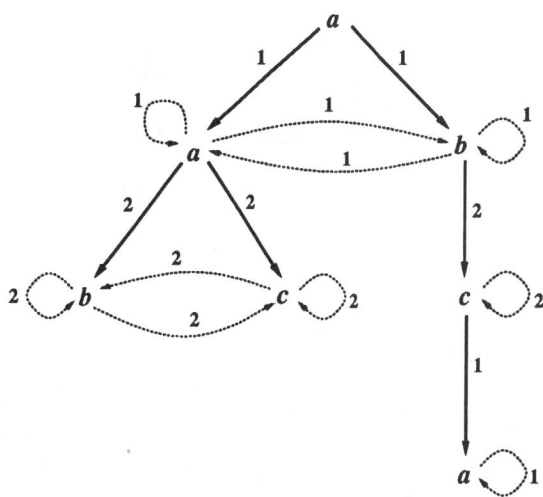

Figure 1: A labelled tree

in the definition of (L,n)-sequences implies that an i-successor of any vertex can have no i-successors itself, though it may have j-successors for $j \neq i$. The reason for this will become apparent below.

A labelled tree in which the root has no i-successors will be called an i-*objective tree*. We write $\mathcal{T}_i(L,n)$ for the set of i-objective (L,n)-labelled trees. An (L,n)-*labelled forest* is a set F of (L,n)-labelled trees such that when T and T' are distinct trees in F we have $root(T) \neq root(T')$. We say that the forest F is i-objective if every tree in F is i-objective, and write $\mathcal{F}_i(L,n)$ for the set of i-objective (L,n)-labelled forests.

If T is a labelled tree and v is a vertex of T with $lab(v) = l_0$ then we define the *subtree of T rooted at* v, denoted by $T \uparrow v$, to be the tree containing the sequences $l_0i_1l_1i_2l_2\ldots i_ml_m$ such that T contains the sequence $v \cdot i_1l_1i_2l_2\ldots i_ml_m$. An i-*child* of a vertex v in a labelled tree T is a labelled tree $T \uparrow w$ where w is an i-successor of v. We write $child_i(T)$ for the set of all i-children of the root of T. Note that $child_i(T)$ is an i-objective forest for all trees T.

Example 2.1: Suppose $L = \{a,b,c\}$. Then

$T = \{a,\ a1a,\ a1a2b,\ a1a2c,\ a1b,\ a1b2c,\ a1b2c1a\}$

is an $(L,2)$-labelled tree, depicted in Figure 1. Here the solid edges represent the tree structure - the meaning of the broken edges will be explained below. If $v = a1a$ then $T \uparrow v = \{a,\ a2b,\ a2c\}$. Note that T is a 2-objective tree. The set of 1-children of T is the 1-objective forest $child_1(T) = \{\{a,\ a2b,\ a2c\},\ \{b,\ b2c,\ b2c1a\}\}$.

An (L,n)-labelled tree T may be regarded as a K45$_n$ structure $M(T) = \langle W, R_1, \ldots, R_n, V_M \rangle$. The worlds

W of this structure are just the vertices of T, and the valuation V_M is given by $V_M(v) = V(lab(v))$, where v is a vertex of T and V is the valuation on L. The accessibility relations R_i are not the i-successor relations, however, but the larger relations given by vR_iv' if and only if v' is an i-successor of v or there exists a vertex $w \in T$ such that v and v' are both i-successors of w. Note that because no i-successor of a vertex has an i-successor, these relations are transitive and euclidean, so $M(T)$ is indeed a K45$_n$ structure.

By adding to $M(T)$ the world represented by root of the tree T, we also obtain a K45$_n$ situation $(M(T), root(T))$. We write $T \models \varphi$ when $(M(T), root(T)) \models \varphi$. Note that under this interpretation of T the i-objective forest $child_i(T)$ constitutes a set of situations representing agent i's state of belief.

Example 2.2: Consider the tree of example 2.1. The broken edges in Figure 1 represent the additional tuples added to the tree edges to construct the relations R_i. If Φ contains a single proposition p and the valuation V on L is given by $V(a)(p) = V(b)(p) = 0$ and $V(c)(p) = 1$, then $T \models B_1 \neg B_1 B_2 p$.

Conversely, the class of all labelled trees is able to represent all K45$_n$ situations by a construction similar to a well known 'unravelling' construction [Bull and Segerberg, 1984]. Suppose we are given a structure $M = \langle W, R_1, \ldots, R_n, V \rangle$ and a world w of M. Let the set L of labels be the set W of worlds of M, equipped with the valuation V of M. Take $T(M,w)$ to be the (L,n)-labelled tree containing a vertex $wi_1 u_1 i_2 u_2 \ldots i_m u_m$ for every sequence of worlds $u_1 \ldots u_m$ and every sequence of indices $i_1 \ldots i_m$ without consecutive repetitions such that $wR_{i_1} u_1 R_{i_2} u_2 \ldots R_{i_m} u_m$.

This construction is unlike the standard one in that it deals with multi-agent structures, but the main difference is the condition that there be no consecutive repetitions of agent indices. Intuitively, the reason for this is that, because we are dealing with K45$_n$ structures, allowing agent repetitions yields trees with a great deal of redundancy, satisfying certain constraints related to the positive and negative introspection conditions. We could formulate our work in this paper in terms of such trees, but find it more convenient to eliminate the need to deal explicitly with the additional constraints by factoring out the redundant parts of the tree. The following result shows that, with respect to the language $\mathcal{L}_n$, the tree $T(M,w)$ expresses the same information as the situation (M,w).

Proposition 2.3: If $\varphi \in \mathcal{L}_n$ then $(M,w) \models \varphi$ iff $T(M,w) \models \varphi$.

This result shows that labelled trees are canonical in that they are able to represent all situations. In some respects the labelled trees form too large a class of structures, however. Suppose the tree T' is obtained from the tree T by replacing the label l at the root by another label l' associated with the same assignment, i.e. for which $V(l) = V(l')$. Since the vertex labelling is opaque to the language $\mathcal{L}_n$, these trees satisfy the same formulae, and intuitively represent the same information about the state of the world and the beliefs of the agents. Further, suppose that T_1 and T_1' are trees identical except in that the 1-children of T_1 are T and T', whereas T_1' has only the 1-child T. Then the trees T_1 and T_1' again satisfy the same formulae: intuitively, the fact that the situation corresponding to T is a possibility for agent 1 is redundantly represented in the tree T_1.

A general notion that captures this sort of invariance is the following. We say that two trees $T, T' \in \mathcal{T}(L,n)$ are *congruent*, and write $T \cong T'$, if there exists a binary relation R on $T \times T'$ such that $root(T)Rroot(T')$ and for all vertices $u \in T$ and $v \in T'$, and all agents $i = 1 \ldots n$,

1. if uRv then $V(lab(u)) = V(lab(v))$, and
2. if uRv and u' is an i-successor of u in T then there exists an i-successor v' of v in T' such that $u'Rv'$, and
3. if uRv and v' is an i-successor of v in T' then there exists an i-successor u' of u in T such that $u'Rv'$.

If the relation R is additionally a one-to-one correspondence, then we say that the trees T, T' are *isomorphic*. We say that two forests F and F' are congruent if for all trees $T \in F$ there exists a tree $T' \in F'$ with $T \cong T'$, and vice versa.

Example 2.4: Suppose that the valuation V on the set L of Example 2.1 satisfies $V(b) = V(c)$. Then the tree

$$T' = \{a, a1a, a1a2b, a1c, a1c2b, a1c2b1a\}$$

is congruent to the tree T of Example 2.1 by means of the relation R consisting of the tuples

$\langle a, a \rangle$
$\langle a1a, a1a \rangle$ $\quad$ $\langle a1b, a1c \rangle$
$\langle a1a2b, a1a2b \rangle$ $\quad$ $\langle a1b2c, a1c2b \rangle$
$\langle a1a2c, a1a2b \rangle$ $\quad$ $\langle a1b2c1a, a1c2b1a \rangle$.

Conditions 1-3 of the definition of congruence generalize the notion of a *zig-zag connection* [Benthem, 1984] between Kripke structures to the multi-agent case, and are also related to the *bisimulations* [Hennessy and Milner, 1985] used in the theory of concurrency. The first part of the following proposition, which is similar to known results for these related notions, may be interpreted as stating that congruent trees represent the same state of mutual belief.

Proposition 2.5:

1. If $T \cong T'$ then for all formulae $\varphi \in \mathcal{L}_n$ we have $T \models \varphi$ iff $T' \models \varphi$.

2. If $T \cong T'$ then $child_i(T) \cong child_i(T')$ for each agent i.

We will take the point of view in what follows that congruent trees should be revised in a similar fashion.

3 A Theory of Mutual Belief Revision

We now present our theory of mutual belief revision. Our approach will be indirect. Instead of explicitly describing the operator representing the mutual belief revision process, we begin by stating a number of constraints on this operator. We then derive the operator from these constraints, by showing that they have an essentially unique solution.

Prototypical of the sort of situation we wish to model is an utterance made in a face-to-face conversation, where all agents hear the utterance, each observes that the others are in a position to hear the utterance, and each observes the others making this observation. Informally, in such situations agents simultaneously revise their beliefs, and the fact that belief revision is taking place is common knowledge. The cause of belief revision need not be an utterance, but could be any occurrence that provides the agents with some information about the world, such as switching on the lights, observing the outcome of an experiment, or even the failure of some event to occur. Nor do the agents need to be in a face-to-face position: they could, for example, be processes in a distributed system with synchronous broadcast as the communication medium.

Thus, we will not go into any detailed description of the event causing belief revision. What will be important is that each agent has a specific way of revising its beliefs when this event occurs. Intuitively, this individual revision method is determined by the informational content that the event has for the agent. It represents how the actuating event causes the agent revise its beliefs *about the situation in which the event occurred*. The objective of the present section is to describe how these individual revision methods determine the agents' mutual belief revision.

We now set out to formalize these ideas, stating along the way a number of the assumptions implicit in the formalization. These assumptions are meant to motivate the theory only - they are not intended to entail the formalization.

Assumption I. Agents have perfect introspection, but may be inconsistent.

This assumption may be made precise by taking the logic of agents to be $K45_n$. We showed in the previous section that labelled trees are a canonical class of $K45_n$ structures. Accordingly, we suppose that the class of situations of interest is represented by the set $\mathcal{T} = \mathcal{T}(L,n)$ of labelled trees, where we fix the set L of labels, its associated valuation V, and the number of agents n. The use of $K45_n$ semantic structures does not prevent the theory being applicable in situations where a stronger logic is appropriate as a model of the agents' reasoning powers. All that is required for such an application is to restrict attention to the appropriate subset of trees. We will present an application in the next section based on the logic $S5_n$, which models knowledge rather than belief.

Assumption II. The agents revise their beliefs synchronously, in response to an event ϵ whose occurrence is common knowledge.

If the agents are in an initial state of belief at time t_0, then the assumption of synchronicity means that the belief revision process is complete by some time $t_1 > t_0$, and this fact is common knowledge. In particular, all agents know at time t_1 that the others have completed revising their beliefs.

Let $g : \mathcal{T} \rightarrow \mathcal{T}$ be an operator on $\mathcal{T}$ that represents the relationship between the agents' initial and final states of belief. This operator is specific to the event ϵ under consideration: the mutual belief revision caused by different actuating events will be represented by different operators. Suppose that the initial situation, before occurrence of the event, is represented by a labelled tree $T \in \mathcal{T}$, which describes the facts about the world at time t_0, as well as the agents' mutual beliefs about these facts at time t_0. Then the tree $g(T)$ represents the situation resulting at time t_1 when the agents mutually revise their beliefs because of the occurrence of event ϵ. That is, $g(T)$ represents the facts about the world at time t_1, and the agents' mutual beliefs about these facts at time t_1. Thus, in each case the belief operators B_i are to be interpreted as referring to the current time.

Assumption III. The world is static - it is only the beliefs of the agents that change.

Of course, if an event has occurred then something has changed, but we assume that the truth value of the objective propositions of interest to the agents remains invariant during the belief revision episode. Since these objective propositions are represented by the root of a labelled tree, we may capture part of this assumption by requiring that

$$V(root(g(T))) = V(root(T)) \qquad (1)$$

for each tree $T \in \mathcal{T}$.

Next, let us consider the individual belief revision method of the agents. The intuitive interpretation of these methods is that they capture the agents' revision of belief *about time* t_0. Upon observing the event ϵ each agent asks itself "given what I believe about time t_0, what should have been true at that time for it to be possible (or likely) for ϵ to have occurred." This leads the agent to a new set of beliefs about time t_0.

Since we represent a situation as a labelled tree in $\mathcal{T}(L,n)$, agent i's epistemic state is represented by means of an i-objective forest in $\mathcal{F}_i(L,n)$. Thus, the method used by agent i to revise its beliefs may be represented by a function $\rho_i : \mathcal{F}_i(L,n) \to \mathcal{F}_i(L,n)$ which maps a state of belief to a new state of belief. Like the mutual belief revision operator g, these individual revision functions are specific to the event ϵ under consideration: different actuating events will lead agents to revise their beliefs in different ways.

If the forest F represents the agent i's initial beliefs about time t_0, then the forest $\rho_i(F)$ represents the agent's beliefs about time t_0 after the actuating event has occurred. In particular, in the situation T agent i's beliefs are represented by the forest $child_i(T)$. Thus, if the initial situation is T then agent i's revised state of belief about the initial situation is represented by the forest $\rho_i(child_i(T))$.

However, this forest does not represent agent i's state of belief in the final situation. Since the occurrence of the event ϵ is common knowledge, the agent is aware that other agents are also revising their beliefs. While an agent, after performing individual belief revision, will believe its beliefs about other agents' beliefs at time t_0 to be accurate,[3] it knows that the other agents' beliefs will have changed by time t_1. What it seeks is an accurate state of belief not about time t_0, but about time t_1. How should an agent take other agents' belief revision into account? Clearly, if it does not know how the actuating event will be interpreted by other agents, there is little an agent can say about the other agents' beliefs in the final situation. We therefore make the following (strong) assumption.

Assumption IV. Each agent's revision method is common knowledge.

We now make an intuitive leap in the justification of our theory of mutual belief revision: we claim that if assumptions I-IV are common knowledge then not just the individual belief revision functions, but also the mutual belief revision process itself is known to each agent. The results below will provide some support for this step in the justification, but this argument is, admittedly, circular. As remarked above, our theory consists in the formal definitions, not in the informal assumptions.

Since we have represented the mutual belief revision process by the operator g, the assumption that an agent knows that g is the mutual belief revision operator being applied means that it knows for each situation T' that if T' were the initial situation, then $g(T')$ would be the final situation. Since agent i, after individual belief revision, considers each situation T' in $\rho_i(child_i(T))$ to be a possibility for the situation obtaining at time t_0, it should consider $g(T')$ a possibility for the situation obtaining at time t_1. This suggests the following condition on the function g:

$$child_i(g(T)) = \{g(T') \mid T' \in \rho_i(child_i(T))\} \quad (2)$$

for all trees $T \in \mathcal{T}$. Intuitively, equation (2) states that the mutual belief revision process operates in two steps: first the agents revise their beliefs about time t_0, then they propagate the resulting state of belief to apply to time t_1, by reasoning about how other agents are modifying their beliefs.

If g is an operator satisfying equations (1) and (2) for all trees $T \in \mathcal{T}$ and all agents i, then we say that g is *compatible* with the revision functions $\rho_1 \ldots \rho_n$. In addition to compatibility, we add some further constraints arising from the slack in our semantic structures. As we argued in Section 2, it is possible for distinct trees to represent what is intuitively the same situation, and for distinct forests to represent what is intuitively the same state of belief. The remedy proposed was the notion of congruence. This motivates the following definitions. Say that the revision function ρ_i is *proper* if $F_1 \cong F_2$ implies that $\rho_i(F_1) \cong \rho_i(F_2)$ for all i-objective forests F_1, F_2. Similarly, say that the operator g is proper if $T_1 \cong T_2$ implies $g(T_1) \cong g(T_2)$ for all trees T_1, T_2. We add to the compatibility condition the requirement that both the revision functions and the operator g be proper.

Do there exist any operators satisfying all these conditions? Note that together with equation (1), equation (2) yields a complete description of the tree $g(T)$, since a tree is determined by its root and its children. Of course, this description is circular, since the children are described in terms of the operator g itself. It is therefore tempting to view equations (1) and (2) as a recursive definition of g. Unfortunately, the standard fixpoint semantics for recursion yields an unsatisfactory answer in this case, because labelled trees are not in general finite, so the recursion never bottoms out and g remains undefined on infinite trees.

However, these intuitions do lead us to a solution. Given the revision functions $\rho_1, \ldots, \rho_n$, define the operator $g = g[\rho_1, \ldots, \rho_n]$ on $\mathcal{T}$ as follows. For each tree $T \in \mathcal{T}$ let $g(T)$ be the set of (L,n)-sequences $l_0 i_1 l_1 i_2 \ldots i_m l_m$ such that there exists a sequence of trees $T_0 T_1 \ldots T_m$ with $T_0 = T$ and

1. $T_j \in \rho_{i_j}(child_{i_j}(T_{j-1}))$ for $j = 1 \ldots m$, and
2. $l_j = root(T_j)$ for $j = 0 \ldots m$.

It is clear from the definition that $g(T)$ is closed under prefixes, and contains a unique (L,n)-sequence of

---

[3] Note that the formula $B_i(B_i\varphi \to \varphi)$ is valid in $K45_n$ structures.

length zero. Thus $g(T)$ is an (L,n)-labelled tree, and g is a mapping from $\mathcal{T}$ to $\mathcal{T}$. The following result shows that g is a candidate for the mutual belief revision operator.

Theorem 3.1: Let $\rho_i : \mathcal{F}_i(L,n) \to \mathcal{F}_i(L,n)$ be a proper revision function for each agent i. Then $g[\rho_1,\ldots,\rho_n]$ is proper, and compatible with $\rho_1\ldots\rho_n$.

Because of this result, we will call $g[\rho_1,\ldots,\rho_n]$ the *canonical operator compatible with* $\rho_1,\ldots,\rho_n$. In general, this operator is not the only one compatible with the revision functions - others can be constructed by systematically relabelling the vertices of the values $g(T)$, or by identifying isomorphic subtrees. However, these are essentially the only dimensions of flexibility: as the following result shows, there is a unique solution up to congruence.

Theorem 3.2: If g_1 and g_2 are two operators on $\mathcal{T}$ compatible with $\rho_1\ldots\rho_n$ then $g_1(T) \cong g_2(T)$ for all $T \in \mathcal{T}$.

Our claim about mutual belief revision, then, is that the mutual belief revision operator g applied when an event occurs should be the canonical operator compatible with the functions ρ_i used by the agents to revise their beliefs about the situation in which the event occurred.

Is this a reasonable account of mutual belief revision? Theorem 3.1 and Theorem 3.2 show that, up to congruence, the canonical operator is the *only* operator compatible with the revision functions. Thus, our theory is reasonable to the extent that it is reasonable to require that mutual belief revision be compatible with individual belief revision. We have informally argued for such a requirement by motivating it from Assumptions I-IV. However, we have not provided a rigorous proof that compatibility is entailed by these assumptions. It may be possible to close this gap by means of a more detailed formalization of the assumptions, but we will not pursue this course here. Instead, in the remainder of the paper we will seek to garner some further support for our claims by presenting two applications of the theory. We will argue that it yields the appropriate answers in both cases. These applications will also serve to illustrate the theory and should help to clarify the intended interpretation of the individual belief revision functions.

4 Scientists in Conference

As a first application of our theory we consider its consequences when the operators B_i are interpreted to refer not to belief, but to the stronger notion of knowledge. There is an independently motivated theory of the dynamics of knowledge in distributed systems [Halpern and Moses, 1990]. This theory gives a very natural semantics to knowledge operators, and has the benefit that it is not necessary to give a separate account of the revision of knowledge. Instead, such an account follows directly from the semantics. In this section we introduce a particular distributed system, and show that states of knowledge in this system are revised in a way corresponding precisely to the theory of the previous section. This gives strong support to the claim that our theory is a reasonable one.

The system we consider is an example of the notion of *knowledge based protocol* [Halpern and Fagin, 1989], in which actions taken depend on the state of knowledge of the agents. In particular, it is a variant of the *communicating scientists* model of [Fagin et al., 1994; Fagin and Vardi, 1986]. In this model a group of scientists, each member of which has made an initial observation of the world, communicate by sending messages in a synchronous system. The world remains static during the communication. We will adapt model this by changing the communication medium from message passing to synchronous broadcast, since this better fits the intended applications of our theory. Accordingly, we refer to our variant of the communicating scientists as the *scientists in conference* model.

We suppose that there are n scientists, and that Φ is a set of atomic propositions, representing objective facts about the world. A state of the world will be an assignment α on Φ. An *initial state* s will be a tuple $(\alpha, S_1, \ldots, S_n)$ where α is an assignment and, for each scientist i, S_i is a set of assignments, intended to represent the set of world states consistent with scientist i's observation. We assume that the observations are accurate, so we require that $\alpha \in S_i$ for each $i = 1 \ldots n$. We also suppose that the scientists have a complete and correct theory of their instruments, so that they know what observations are possible in each state of the world. Semantically, we take I to be a set of initial states, such that an initial state $s = (\alpha, S_1, \ldots, S_n)$ is in I just when the observations S_i are in accordance with the theory, given that the state of the world is described by the assignment α.

Given the set I, we construct the $K45_n$ Kripke structure $SC_n(I) = \langle W, R_1, \ldots, R_n, V \rangle$ representing n scientists in conference with initial observations described by I. The worlds, also called *runs*, of this structure will be certain sequences of the form $s \cdot \sigma$, where s is an initial state and σ is a sequence of tuples of the form (i, φ), in which i is an scientist and φ is a formula in $\mathcal{L}_n$. Intuitively, in such a run s describes the objective facts about the state of the world and the scientists' observations of this state, and σ represents a sequence of assertions made by the scientists during the conference. The world is assumed to be static, so the truth value of the atomic propositions at $s \cdot \sigma$ is determined by the assignment in s. Formally, we define the valuation V by letting $V(s \cdot \sigma)$ be the assignment α of the initial state s.

For each scientist i, let the equivalence relation R_i^0 on initial states be given by

$$(\alpha, S_1, \ldots, S_n) R_i^0 (\alpha', S_1', \ldots, S_n')$$

if and only if $S_i = S_i'$. Intuitively, if he makes the same observation in two initial states, the scientist cannot, without obtaining further information, distinguish these states. This relation may be extended to the equivalence relation R_i on the runs of $\mathrm{SC}_n(I)$ by letting $(s \cdot \sigma) R_i (t \cdot \tau)$ just when $s R_i^0 t$ and $\sigma = \tau$. Intuitively, this definition reflects the fact that the scientist is able to observe (and recall) all the assertions made during the conference.

This completes the description of $\mathrm{SC}_n(I)$, except that we have not yet described which sequences are included in the set of runs W. Not every sequence of assertions will yield a valid run. We require that the scientists be *honest*: they should assert φ only if they know φ to be true. More precisely, if $s \cdot \sigma$ is a run then $s \cdot \sigma \cdot (i, \varphi)$ is a run if and only if $\mathrm{SC}_n(I), s \cdot \sigma \models B_i \varphi$. This leads to what at first appears to be a circularity in the definition of $\mathrm{SC}_n(I)$: in order to determine a scientist's knowledge we need to know the set of runs, which in turn depends on the scientists' knowledge.

This sort of circularity is characteristic of the notion of knowledge based protocol, and it has a standard resolution. Intuitively, before any communication has taken place the scientists' states of knowledge are determined by their observations. These states of knowledge then determine what assertions are possible in the first round, and this in turn determines the scientists' state of knowledge after the first round. More generally, the scientists' state of knowledge after k rounds of communication determines what assertions are possible in the next round, and this in turn determines the scientists' knowledge after round $k+1$.

To make these intuitions precise, we define the runs W of $\mathrm{SC}_n(I)$ inductively using a sequence of M_k of Kripke structures. The structure M_k will represent the fragment of $\mathrm{SC}_n(I)$ consisting of the runs of length k. The valuation V and accessibility relations R_i of these structures are defined exactly as for $\mathrm{SC}_n(I)$. The structure M_0 has as its set of worlds W_0 the set I of initial states. Given the structure M_k, we then define the structure M_{k+1} by taking its set of worlds W_{k+1} to contain just those sequences $s \cdot \sigma \cdot (i, \varphi)$ such that $s \cdot \sigma$ is a world of M_k, and $M_k, s \cdot \sigma \models B_i \varphi$. This completes the description of the structures M_k.

The definition of the structure $\mathrm{SC}_n(I)$ is now completed by taking its runs to consist of the worlds $s \cdot \sigma$ contained in W_k for some $k \geq 0$. Because the R_i are defined to be equivalence relations, the structure $\mathrm{SC}_n(I)$ is in fact an $S5_n$ structure [Halpern and Moses, 1992], so the modal operator B_i may be interpreted as referring to the *knowledge* of scientist i.

Example 4.1: Mathematician P knows the product $N1 \times N2$ of two numbers $N1, N2$ in the range 2 to 100; mathematician S knows the sum $N1 + N2$. They have the following conversation:

S: I don't know what the numbers are, but I know that you don't know either.
P: Now I know the numbers!
S: Aha! Now I also know them!.

We leave it to the reader to verify that this well known example [Gardner, 1979] can be formalized as a run in a certain model of the form $\mathrm{SC}_2(I)$.

Using the unravelling construction of Proposition 2.3, we may associate with any run $s \cdot \sigma$ of $\mathrm{SC}_n(I)$ a tree $T(\mathrm{SC}_n(I), s \cdot \sigma)$ over the set of labels consisting of all runs of $\mathrm{SC}_n(I)$. However, a consideration of the nature of the accessibility relations in $\mathrm{SC}_n(I)$ shows that this set of labels may be simplified. It is readily seen from the definition of the relations R_i that if $t \cdot \tau$ labels a vertex of the tree $T(\mathrm{SC}_n(I), s \cdot \sigma)$ then $\tau = \sigma$, hence all but the initial state t is redundant. This means that the tree associated with a given run may be represented using the set of labels consisting of the initial states I only. Given a run $w = s \cdot \sigma$, define $rep(w)$ to be the (I, n)-labelled tree consisting of the (I, n)-sequences $s_0 i_1 s_1 \ldots i_m s_m$ such that

$$(s_0 \cdot \sigma) i_1 (s_1 \cdot \sigma) \ldots i_m (s_m \cdot \sigma)$$

is in $T(\mathrm{SC}_n(I), s \cdot \sigma)$. Clearly $rep(w)$ is an (I, n)-labelled tree. The considerations above then yield the following result.

Lemma 4.2: For all runs w of $\mathrm{SC}_n(I)$, the tree $rep(w)$ is isomorphic to the tree $T(\mathrm{SC}_n(I), w)$.

This result justifies the use of the tree $rep(w)$ to represent the situation $(\mathrm{SC}_n(I), w)$. We now establish that the theory of belief revision of the previous section can express in a natural way the knowledge revision of scientists in $\mathrm{SC}_n(I)$. We represent situations as trees in $\mathcal{T}(I, n)$. Consequently, a state of belief for scientist i corresponds to a forest in $\mathcal{F}_i(I, n)$, and we require for each scientist a belief revision function $\rho_i : \mathcal{F}_i(I, n) \to \mathcal{F}_i(I, n)$.

Suppose we wish to represent the belief revision process when scientist S, the *speaker*, asserts the formula φ in $\mathcal{L}_n$. Recall that the intended interpretation of the belief revision functions is that they capture the agents' revision of belief about the initial situation. What information does a scientist gain about the situation corresponding to $s \cdot \sigma$ when the speaker asserts in this situation the formula φ? One way to characterize this information is as being that the run $s \cdot \sigma$

may be extended by the assertion (S, φ). But this is possible just when $SC_n(I), s \cdot \sigma \models B_S \varphi$. Intuitively, the information gained is that the speaker knows φ.

Thus, when $i \neq S$, we define $\rho_i(F) = \{T \in F \mid T \models B_S \varphi\}$ for all i-objective forests F. Intuitively, this simply adds to scientist i's knowledge about the initial situation the fact that the speaker knows φ. We could define the revision function similarly for the speaker, but note that when the speaker asserts φ, he already knows that he knows φ. Hence when $i = S$, we put $\rho_i(F) = F$ for all $F \in \mathcal{F}_i(I, n)$. It follows from Proposition 2.5(1) that these revision functions are proper.

Our theory of mutual belief revision now states that the mutual belief revision process is represented by $g = g[\rho_1, \ldots, \rho_n]$, the canonical operator on $\mathcal{T}(I, n)$ compatible with $\rho_1, \ldots, \rho_n$. Thus, if the initial situation, corresponding to the run w, is represented by the tree $rep(w)$, our theory predicts that after mutual belief revision actuated by the assertion of φ by S, the scientists' epistemic state is represented by $g(rep(w))$. How does this compare with the revision of knowledge obtained directly from the structure $SC_n(I)$ itself, which predicts the state $rep(w \cdot (i_S, \varphi))$? The following result shows these predictions to be identical.

Theorem 4.3: If w is a run of $SC_n(I)$ such that $SC_n(I), w \models B_S \varphi$, then $rep(w \cdot (S, \varphi)) = g(rep(w))$.

Thus, the theory of mutual belief revision of the previous section accurately describes the mutual *knowledge* revision process of the scientists in conference. Moreover, note that the choice of revision functions needed to obtain this result is very natural. We take this to be strong evidence that our theory is an appropriate model for more the general problem of revision of mutual *belief*.

5 Speech Act Semantics

Speech acts [Austin, 1962] are linguistic actions such as assertions, requests and promises, having an explicit propositional content. One strand in the theory of speech acts, [Allen and Perrault, 1980; Cohen and Perrault, 1979; Cohen and Levesque, 1985; Cohen and Levesque, 1990; Perrault, 1990], seeks to characterize the semantics of a speech act by describing the effect it has on the mental states of the participants of the conversation. In this section we apply our theory of mutual belief revision to give a semantic reconstruction of one such theory, that of [Perrault, 1990], for the simplest type of speech act, assertions.

Perrault observes that the beliefs of the participants after an utterance depend in a complicated way on their beliefs before the utterance. For example, if the speaker sincerely asserts a proposition p and the hearer has no beliefs that would lead him[4] to doubt this assertion, then the hearer should come to believe p also. However, if the speaker lied, or was mistaken, in uttering p, and the hearer knew that p was false when the utterance was made, the hearer does not come to believe p, although he may come to believe that the speaker believes p. Even this latter conclusion does not hold in the situation where it is mutually believed that p is false, and the speaker utters p ironically.

The difficulties pointed out by Perrault may be characterized by saying that in describing how a speech act changes states of belief one faces a (particularly severe) form of the *qualification problem*. Even in simpler domains not involving epistemic states it is often difficult to give a complete set of necessary and sufficient conditions for an action to bring about a given state of affairs. The solution advocated by Perrault is one that has also been proposed as an approach to the qualification problem in other contexts: the use of nonmonotonic logic.

In particular, Perrault uses a modal extension of Reiter's [Reiter, 1980] default logic. The most important operators in this extension[5] are the time-stamped belief operators $B_{x,t}$, referring to the belief of agent x at time t. Each of these operators is assumed to satisfy the axioms and inference rules of the logic KD45 [Chellas, 1980]. Furthermore, these operators satisfy the two axioms

$\vdash B_{x,t} \varphi \supset B_{x,t+1} B_{x,t} \varphi$ Memory
$\vdash B_{x,t+1} B_{x,t} \varphi \supset B_{x,t+1} \varphi$ Persistence

whose combined effect is that agents maintain their objective and positive beliefs. There is also a construct $Do_{x,t}(p)$, which represents that agent x utters the proposition p at time t, and an action of observation.

Perrault assumes two basic default rules. One of these is the *declarative rule*[6] $Do_{x,t}(p) \Rightarrow B_{x,t} p$, which authorizes the conclusion, if it is consistent to do so, that the speaker believes the proposition she utters. Secondly, there is the *belief transfer rule* $B_{x,t} B_{y,t} \varphi \Rightarrow B_{x,t} \varphi$, which allows an agent to adopt another agent's beliefs. In order to make the applicability of these two default rules common knowledge, there is also a closure condition, stating that for all agents x and all times t, if $\varphi \Rightarrow \psi$ is a default rule, then so is $B_{x,t} \varphi \Rightarrow B_{x,t} \psi$. Note that in this system we obtain the following chain of logical and default inferences:

$$B_{H,1} Do_{S,0}(p) \Rightarrow B_{H,1} B_{S,0} p$$
$$\supset B_{H,1} B_{S,1} p$$
$$\Rightarrow B_{H,1} p$$

---

[4] We will use the masculine pronoun for the hearer and the feminine pronoun for the speaker.

[5] We confine our discussion to the simplest version of the theory: a more elaborate variant also includes operators for intention.

[6] The notation $p \Rightarrow q$ denotes the normal default rule $p : q/q$.

That is, if the hearer believes the speaker to have uttered p then he will first adopt the belief that the speaker believes p, provided this is consistent. If, having done so, it is consistent with his beliefs that p, he will also come to believe p himself.

Perrault works out a number of examples in his theory: sincere assertion, lie, unsuccessful lie, and irony. Here we study the consequences of our theory of mutual belief revision for the first of these examples, the sincere assertion.[7] To do so, we must formulate his assumptions in our framework.

We defer for the moment the question of the appropriate set of trees, and begin with a specification of the revision functions applied when the speaker S asserts p. For the hearer H we define $\rho_H(F)$ to be

$$\begin{cases} \{T \in F \mid T \models p \wedge B_S p\} & \text{if this set} \neq \emptyset, \text{else} \\ \{T \in F \mid T \models B_S p\} & \text{if this set} \neq \emptyset, \text{and} \\ F & \text{otherwise.} \end{cases}$$

for all H-objective forests F. Intuitively, this revision function captures the two-step operation of the defaults noted above. Observe that in each case $\rho_H(F)$ is a subforest of the forest F. This reflects the effect of the persistence and memory axioms.

Perrault's default rules are symmetrical with respect to the speaker and hearer, which suggests that we define an identical revision function for the speaker. However, this aspect of Perrault's theory has been criticised by Appelt and Konolige [Appelt and Konolige, 1988]. They point out that this symmetry implies that if the speaker originally does not believe p, then she will become convinced that p is true merely because she asserted it! Since this is counter-intuitive (albeit not unheard of), we assume instead that the speaker's beliefs are not changed by making an utterance, and put $\rho_S(F) = F$ for all S-objective forests F. There is a close correspondence between these revision functions and those we used for the scientists in conference, and indeed our work in this section in the present section may be shown to generalize that of the previous section.

As the next step in formulating Perrault's examples in our model, we need to choose a tree to represent the initial situation. It is not immediately clear what this tree should be, because there is a difference in kind between Perrault's theory and ours. Perrault views his defaults as being applied by an external observer who is reasoning about the beliefs of the participants of the conversation, rather than being applied by the agents themselves. Thus, the formulae in his logic represent the observer's knowledge of the beliefs of the agents. This knowledge, he allows, may be incomplete. But if it is the case that the observer does not know whether an agent x believes φ, what justifies his application of

---

[7] The results for the others, to be presented in the final version of this paper, are similar.

the rule $B_{x,t} B_{y,t} \varphi \Rightarrow B_{x,t} \varphi$, which surely is meant to reflect a default inference performed by agent x when φ is consistent with the latter's beliefs.

One plausible construal of Perrault's approach that would make the observer's application of this rule valid is to interpret the observer as implicitly applying some additional defaults: if he does not know that an agent believes φ, then he assumes that the agent does not believe φ. In other words, the observer presumes he has complete knowledge of the agent's beliefs. This suggests an *only knowing* formulation [Levesque, 1990] of the initial states of belief of the agents. A number of accounts of only knowing in a multiple agent setting have recently been developed [Halpern, 1993; Lakemeyer, 1993]. The account we sketch here is closely related to these works: we will elaborate on this in the full paper.

Say that a function $f : \mathcal{L}_n \rightarrow \{0, 1\}$ is a *satisfiable truth assignment* on $\mathcal{L}_n$ if there exists a K45$_n$ structure M with a world w such that for all formulae $\varphi \in \mathcal{L}_n$ we have $f(\varphi) = 1$ if and only if $M, w \models \varphi$. Take the set of labels L to be the set consisting of all satisfiable truth assignments on $\mathcal{L}_n$, with the associated valuation V defined by $V(f)(p) = f(p)$. We will work with the set of labelled trees $\mathcal{T}(L, n)$. If f is a satisfiable truth assignment, we define the tree $\tau(f)$ to consist of all n-sequences $f_0 i_1 f_1 \ldots i_m f_m$ such that $f_0 = f$ and for all $j = 1 \ldots m$ and all $\varphi \in \mathcal{L}_n$, if $f_{j-1}(B_{i_j}\varphi) = 1$ then $f_j(\varphi) = 1$. The *i-objectification* $\tau_i(f)$ of $\tau(f)$ is defined to be the tree obtained from $\tau(f)$ by removing all n-sequences with $i_1 = i$.

Proposition 5.1: For all $f \in L$, and all $\varphi \in \mathcal{L}_n$ satisfying $f(\varphi) = 1$, we have $\tau(f) \models \varphi$.

Suppose we are given a tuple $(\Gamma_1, \ldots, \Gamma_n)$ such that Γ_i is a set of i-objective formulae for each $i = 1 \ldots n$. Let f_0 be an arbitrary label. We now define the *only believing tree* $T(\Gamma_1, \ldots, \Gamma_n)$ to be the tree consisting of the n-sequences $f_0 i \cdot \sigma$ for which there exists a label $f \in L$ such that σ is an n-sequence in $\tau_i(f)$ and $f(\varphi) = 1$ for all $\varphi \in \Gamma_i$. This tree is intended to represent a situation in which all that agent i believes is Γ_i, for each $i = 1 \ldots n$. Notice that the i-children of the root are precisely the trees $\tau_i(f)$, where $f(\varphi) = 1$ for all $\varphi \in \Gamma_i$. Our claim that this tree models only believing is supported by the following:

Proposition 5.2: Let φ be an i-objective formula. Then $T(\Gamma_1, \ldots, \Gamma_n) \models B_i \varphi$ if and only if φ is a K45$_n$ logical consequence of Γ_i.

We are now ready to consider the revision of belief in a sincere assertion Specialize to $n = 2$, for agent 1 (the speaker) write S and for agent 2 (the hearer) write H. In the case of a sincere assertion of proposition p, Perrault begins with the theory containing only the formula $B_{S,0}\, p$, together with some formulae representing that S utters p and that the agents are observing each other, so that the fact of utterance becomes common knowledge. Accordingly, we take our initial situation to be the tree $T_0 = T(\{p\}, \emptyset)$, in which the speaker believes only p, and the hearer believes only the vacuous proposition *true*. Letting g be the canonical operator compatible with the belief revision functions ρ_H, ρ_S defined above, our theory predicts the tree $g(T_0)$ as the situation after the speech act.

What do the agents believe in this situation? Perrault argues that there exists a default extension of the original theory that is generated by the original formulae together with the infinite set of formulae

$$B_{S,1}p,\ B_{H,1}p,\ B_{S,1}B_{H,1}p,\ B_{H,1}B_{S,1}p, \ldots$$

He conjectures that this is the only default extension of the theory, and hence an appropriate description of the agent's beliefs after the utterance. That is, according to Perrault, after the utterance it is mutually believed that p. Does the same hold in the tree $g(T_0)$ obtained from our theory? It does not: in fact, even the formula $B_S B_H p$ does not hold in this tree! The reason for this, intuitively, is that the speaker considers it possible that the hearer takes her to be lying, in which case mutual belief is not established by the utterance. More precisely, since all that the speaker believes in T_0 is p, she considers possible a situation T' in which $B_H(\neg p \wedge \neg B_S p)$ holds. In this situation the hearer will not be persuaded to change his beliefs: $\rho_H(child_H(T')) = child_H(T')$. Furthermore, T' has an H-child T'' in which p is false. Thus $g(T'')$ is an H-child of $g(T')$, and since g preserves the valuation at the root we see that $g(T')$ does not satisfy $B_H p$. Because $g(T')$ is an S-child of $g(T_0)$, we obtain that the latter does not satisfy $B_S B_H p$.

If mutual belief of p is not established by the utterance, then what state of belief does our theory predict instead? In order to characterize this state of belief, let ψ be the formula

$$B_H(p \wedge B_S p) \vee B_H(\neg p \wedge B_S p) \vee B_H \neg B_S p$$

Note the correspondence between the disjuncts of this formula and the three cases of the hearer's revision function. Write $M(H, \psi)$ for the infinite set of formulae

$$B_H \psi,\ B_H B_S \psi,\ B_H B_S B_H \psi, \ldots$$

which intuitively corresponds to the hearer believing that ψ is mutually believed. Note that these formulae are S-objective. Similarly, write $M(S, \psi)$ for the corresponding set of H-objective formulae in which the leading modality is B_S. Then following result characterizes the belief state reached after the speech act.

Theorem 5.3:
$$g(T_0) \cong T(\ \{p\} \cup M(H, \psi)\ ,\ \{p, B_S p\} \cup M(S, \psi)\ )$$

That is, in $g(T_0)$, all that the speaker believes is p and that ψ is mutually believed, and all that the hearer believes is p, that the speaker believes p, and that ψ is mutually believed. In particular, it follows from this that after the assertion the formula ψ is mutually believed[8].

Perault's theory predicts that p is mutually believed after a sincere assertion; our theory predicts that it is not. Which is right? We will not offer any answer to this question. Perrault's formalization is itself only a rough approximation to reality, and in modelling it in our framework we made a number of assumptions and modifications. It would be interesting to investigate alternative choices of revision function and initial state to determine precisely under what conditions the proposition asserted does come to be mutually believed. However, we would argue that given the assumptions we have made in the present section, it is very reasonable that the formula ψ should become mutual belief, and that this supports the appropriateness of our account of mutual belief revision.

6 Conclusion

What we hope to have achieved in this paper is the introduction of a semantic framework and to have demonstrated by means of the examples that it is worthy of further study. Much remains to be done. It would be interesting if the circularity in our justification of the framework could be removed. Additionally, we would like to have a general formalism in which the revision functions ρ_i can be defined, and construct for this formalism a calculus that generalizes Theorem 5.3. Such a calculus would facilitate the determination of under what conditions mutual belief is a consequence of a speech act. One could also study the consequences of assuming that the agents' individual belief revision functions satisfy AGM-like postulates. An interesting question would then be to determine how the postulates are reflected in the mutual belief revision process.

Due to space limitations we defer to the full version of the paper a discussion of the related literature, on syntactic accounts of multi-agent belief revision, and on semantic accounts of the revision of knowledge

Acknowledgements

Thanks to Hirofumi Katsuno for comments on earlier versions of this paper. I have also benefited from discussions with Joe Halpern and Gerhard Lakemeyer on only knowing.

---

[8]It has to be shown that the speaker and hearer both believe ψ. Observe that $B_H(B_H \varphi_1 \vee B_H \varphi_2) \supset (B_H \varphi_1 \vee B_H \varphi_2)$ is valid, which implies that $g(T_0) \models B_S \psi$. That $g(T_0) \models B_H \psi$ follows directly from the fact that $B_H(p \wedge B_S p) \supset B_H \psi$ is valid.

References

[Alchourrón et al., 1985] C.E. Alchourrón, P. Gärdenfors, and D. Makinson. On the logic of theory change: partial meet contraction and revision functions. *Journal of Symbolic Logic*, 50:510–530, 1985.

[Allen and Perrault, 1980] J. F. Allen and C. R. Perrault. Analyzing intention in utterances. *Artificial Intelligence*, 15:143–178, 1980.

[Appelt and Konolige, 1988] D. Appelt and K. Konolige. A practical nonmonotonic theory for reasoning about speech acts. In *Proc. Annual Meeting of the ACL*, pages 170–178, Chicago, IL, 1988. Association for Computational Linguistics.

[Austin, 1962] J. L. Austin. *How To Do Things with Words*. Oxford University Press, Oxford, 1962.

[Benthem, 1984] J. van Benthem. Correspondence theory. In D. Gabbay and F. Guenthner, editors, *Handbook of Philosophical Logic II: Extensions of Classical Logic*, pages 167–247. D. Reidel, Dordrecht, 1984.

[Bull and Segerberg, 1984] R. A. Bull and K. Segerberg. Basic modal logic. In D. Gabbay and F. Guenthner, editors, *Handbook of Philosophical Logic II: Extensions of Classical Logic*, pages 1–88. D. Reidel, Dordrecht, 1984.

[Chellas, 1980] B. Chellas. *Modal Logic*. Cambridge University Press, Cambridge, 1980.

[Cohen and Levesque, 1985] P. R. Cohen and H. J. Levesque. Speech acts and rationality. In *Proc. 23rd Annual Meeting of the ACL*, pages 49–59, Chicago, IL, 1985. Association for Computational Linguistics.

[Cohen and Levesque, 1990] P. R. Cohen and H. J. Levesque. Rational interactions as the basis for communication. In *Intentions in Communication*. Bradford Boooks, Cambridge, MA, 1990.

[Cohen and Perrault, 1979] P. R. Cohen and C. R. Perrault. Elements of a plan based theory of speech acts. *Cognitive Science*, 3:177–212, 1979.

[Fagin and Vardi, 1986] R. Fagin and M.Y. Vardi. Knowledge and implicit knowledge in a distributed environment. In *Theoretical Aspects of Reasoning about Knowledge: Proc. 1986 Conf.*, pages 187–206. Morgan Kaufmann, 1986.

[Fagin et al., 1994] R. Fagin, J. Halpern, Y. Moses, and M. Y. Vardi. *Reasoning about Knowledge*. MIT Press, Cambridge, MA, 1994.

[Gärdenfors, 1986] P. Gärdenfors. *Knowledge in Flux: Modelling the Dynamics of Epistemic States*. MIT Press, Cambridge, Mass., 1986.

[Gardner, 1979] M. Gardner. Mathematical games. *Scientific American*, pages 20–24, December 1979.

[Halpern and Fagin, 1989] J. Halpern and R. Fagin. Modelling knowledge and action in distributed systems. *Distributed Computing*, 3(4):159–179, 1989.

[Halpern and Moses, 1990] J. Halpern and Y. Moses. Knowledge and common knowledge in a distributed environment. *Journal of the ACM*, 37(3):549–587, 1990.

[Halpern and Moses, 1992] J. Halpern and Y. Moses. A guide to completeness and complexity for modal logics of knowledge and belief. *Artificial Intelligence*, 54:319–379, 1992.

[Halpern, 1993] J. Halpern. Reasoning about only knowing with many agents. In *Proc. National Conf. on AI*, pages 655–661, 1993.

[Hennessy and Milner, 1985] M. Hennessy and R. Milner. Algebraic laws for non-determinism and concurrency. *Journal of the ACM*, 32(1):137–161, 1985.

[Isozaki and Shoham, 1992] H. Isozaki and Y. Shoham. A mechanism for reasoning about time and belief. In *Proc. Int. Conf. on Fifth Generation Computer Systems*, pages 694–701, 1992.

[Katsuno and Mendelzon, 1991] H. Katsuno and A. Mendelzon. Propositional knowledge base revision and minimal change. *Artificial Intelligence*, 52:263–294, 1991.

[Lakemeyer, 1993] G. Lakemeyer. All they know: A study in multi-agent autoepistemic reasoning. In *Proc. Int. Joint Conf. on AI*, 1993.

[Levesque, 1990] H.J. Levesque. All I know: A study in autoepistemic logic. *Artificial Intelligence*, 42:263–309, 1990.

[Meyden, 1994] R. van der Meyden. Common knowledge and update in finite environments I. In *Proc. 5th Conf. on Theoretical Aspects of Reasoning about Knowledge*, 1994.

[Morgenstern, 1990] L. Morgenstern. A formal theory of multiple agent nonmonotonic reasoning. In *Proc. National Conf. on AI.*, pages 538–544, 1990.

[Moses and Kislev, 1993] Y. Moses and O. Kislev. Knowledge oriented programming. In *Proc. Symp. on Principles of Distributed Computing*, 1993.

[Perrault, 1990] C. R. Perrault. An application of default logic to speech act theory. In *Intentions in Communication*, pages 161–185. Bradford Books, Cambridge, MA, 1990.

[Reiter, 1980] R. Reiter. A logic for default reasoning. *Artificial Intelligence*, 13:81–132, 1980.

[Shoham, 1993] Y. Shoham. Agent oriented programming. *Artificial Intelligence*, 60(1):51–92, 1993.

[Thomason, 1990] R. H. Thomason. Propagating epistemic coordination through mutual defaults I. In *Theoretical Aspects of Reasoning about Knowledge: Proc. Third Conf.*, pages 29–39. Morgan Kaufmann, 1990.

REVISE: An Extended Logic Programming System for Revising Knowledge Bases

Carlos Viegas Damásio
CRIA, Uninova and DCS
U. Nova de Lisboa
2825 Monte da Caparica, Portugal

Wolfgang Nejdl
Informatik V
RWTH Aachen
D-52056 Aachen, Germany

Luís Moniz Pereira
CRIA, Uninova and DCS
U. Nova de Lisboa
2825 Monte da Caparica, Portugal

Abstract

In this paper we describe REVISE, an extended logic programming system for revising knowledge bases. REVISE is based on logic programming with explicit negation, plus a two-valued assumption revision to face contradiction, encompasses the notion of preference levels. Its reliance on logic programming allows efficient computation and declarativity, whilst its use of explicit negation, revision and preference levels enables modeling of a variety of problems including default reasoning, belief revision and modelbased reasoning. It has been implemented as a Prolog-meta interpreter and tested on a spate of examples, namely the representation of diagnosis strategies in modelbased reasoning systems.

1 INTRODUCTION

While a lot of research has been done in the area of nonmonotonic reasoning during the last decade, relatively few systems have been built which actually reason nonmonotonically. This paper describes the semantics and core algorithm of REVISE, a system based on an extended logic programming framework. It is powerful enough to express a wide variety of problems including various nonmonotonic reasoning and belief revision strategies and more application oriented knowledge such as diagnostic strategies in modelbased reasoning systems ([de Kleer, 1991, Friedrich and Nejdl, 1992, Lackinger and Nejdl, 1993, Dressler and Bottcher, 1992]).

We start, in Section 2, by reviewing the well founded semantics with explicit negation and two valued contradiction removal [Pereira et al., 1993b], which supplies the basic semantics for REVISE. We then introduce in Section 3 the concept of preference levels amongst sets of assumptions and discuss how it integrates into the basic semantics. Section 4 gives examples of application of REVISE for describing diagnostic strategies in modelbased reasoning systems. Section 5 describes the core algorithm of REVISE, which is an extension of Reiter's algorithm, in [Reiter, 1987],

for computing diagnoses in modelbased reasoning systems, corrected in [Greiner et al., 1989]. Finally, Section 6 contains comparisons with related work and conclusions.

2 REVIEW OF THE LOGIC PROGRAMMING BASIS

In this section we review WFSX, the Well Founded Semantics of logic programs with eXplicit negation and its paraconsistent version. We focus the presentation on the latter. Basically, WFSX follows from WFS [Gelder et al., 1991] plus one basic "coherence" requirement relating the two negations: $\neg L$ entails $\sim L$ for any literal L. We also present its two-valued contradiction removal version [Pereira et al., 1993b]. For details refer to [Pereira and Alferes, 1992, Alferes, 1993].

Given a first order language $Lang$, an extended logic program (ELP) is a set of rules and integrity rules of the form

$$H \leftarrow B_1, \ldots, B_n, \sim C_1, \ldots, \sim C_m \ (m \geq 0, n \geq 0)$$

where $H, B_1, \ldots, B_n, C_1, \ldots, C_m$ are objective literals, and in integrity rules H is $\bot$ (contradiction). An objective literal is either an atom A or its explicit negation $\neg A$, where $\neg\neg A = A$. $\sim L$ is called a default or negative literal. Literals are either objective or default ones. The default complement of objective literal L is $\sim L$, and of default literal $\sim L$ is L. A rule stands for all its ground instances wrt $Lang$. A set of literals S is non-contradictory iff there is no $L \in S$ such that $\sim L \in S$. For every pair of objective literals $\{L, \neg L\}$ in $Lang$ we implicitly assume the integrity rule $\bot \leftarrow L, \neg L$.

In order to revise possible contradictions we need first to identify those contradictory sets implied by a program under the paraconsistent WFSX. The main idea here is to compute all consequences of the program, even those leading to contradiction, as well as those arising from contradiction. The following example provides an intuitive preview of what we mean to capture:

Example 1 *Consider program P*:

$$a \leftarrow \sim b \quad (i) \qquad d \leftarrow \sim a \quad (iii)$$
$$\neg a \leftarrow \sim c \quad (ii) \qquad e \leftarrow \sim \neg a \quad (iv)$$

1. $\sim b$ and $\sim c$ hold since there are no rules for either b or c
2. $\neg a$ and a hold from 1 and rules (i) and (ii)
3. $\sim a$ and $\sim \neg a$ hold from 2 and the coherence principle relating the two negations
4. d and e hold from 3 and rules (iii) and (iv)
5. $\sim d$ and $\sim e$ hold from 2 and rules (iii) and (iv), as they are the only rules for d and e.
6. $\sim\neg d$ and $\sim\neg e$ hold from 4 and the coherence principle.

The whole set of literal consequences is then:

$$\{\sim b, \sim c, \neg a, a, \sim a, \sim \neg a, d, e, \sim d, \sim e, \sim \neg d, \sim \neg e\}.$$

For the purpose of defining WFSX and its paraconsistent extension we begin by defining paraconsistent interpretation.

Definition 2.1 *A p–interpretation I is any set $T \cup \sim F$, such that if $\neg L \in T$ then $L \in F$ (coherence).*

The definition of WFSX (in [Pereira and Alferes, 1992]) is based on a modulo transformation and a monotonic operator. On first reading the reader may now skip to definition 2.5.

Without loss of generality, and for the sake of technical simplicity, we consider that programs are always in their canonical form, i.e. for each rule of the program and any objective literal, if L is in the body then $\sim\neg L$ also belongs to the body of that rule[1].

Definition 2.2 *Let P be an canonical extended logic program and let I be a p–interpretation. By a $\frac{P}{I}p$ program we mean any program obtained from P by first non-deterministically applying the operations until they are no longer applicable:*

- *Remove all rules containing a default literal $L = \sim A$ such that $A \in I$;*
- *Remove from rules their default literals $L = \sim A$ such that $\sim A \in I$;*

and by next replacing all remaining default literals by proposition **u.**

---

[1] When the coherence principle is adopted, the truth value of L coincides with that of $(L, \sim \neg L)$. Taking programs in canonical form simplifies the techniques since we don't need to concern ourselves with objective literals in bodies in the modulo transformation, but only with default literals, just as for non-extended programs. The proof that generality is not lost can be found in [Alferes, 1993].

Programs $\frac{P}{I}p$ are by definition non–negative, and thus always has a unique Fitting–least 3-valued model, $least(\frac{P}{I}p)$, obtainable via a generalization of the van Emden–Kowalski least model operator Ψ [Przymusinska and Przymusinski, 1990]. In order to obtain all consequences of the program, even those leading to contradictions, as well as those arising from contradictions, we consider the consequences of all such possible $\frac{P}{I}p$ programs.

Definition 2.3 *Let $QI = QT \cup \sim QF$ be a set of literals. We define $Coh^p(QI)$ as the p–interpretation $T \cup \sim F$ such that $T = QT$ and $F = QF \cup \{\neg L \mid L \in T\}$.*

Definition 2.4 *Let P be an canonical extended logic program, I a p–interpretation, and let $P_1, \ldots, P_i, \ldots$ be all the permissible results of $\frac{P}{I}p$. Then:*

$$\Phi^p{}_P(I) = \bigcup_i Coh^p(least(P_i))$$

Definition 2.5 *The paraconsistent WFSX of an extended logic program P, denoted by $WFSX_p(P)$, is the least fixpoint of Φ^p applied to P. If some literal L belongs to $WFSX_p(P)$ we write $P \models_p L$.*

Indeed, it can be shown that Φ^p is monotonic, and therefore for every program it always has a least fixpoint, which can be obtained by iterating Φ^p starting from the empty set. It also can be shown that for a non–contradictory program P the paraconsistent WFSX coincides with WFSX.

Definition 2.6 *A program P is contradictory iff $P \models_p \bot$.*

To remove contradiction the first issue is defining which default literals $\sim A$ without rules, and so true by Closed World Assumption (CWA), may be **revised** to false, i.e. by adding A.

Example 2 *Consider $P = \{a \leftarrow \sim b; \bot \leftarrow a\}$. $\sim b$ is true by CWA on b. Hence, by the second rule, we have a contradiction. We argue the CWA may not be held of atom b as it leads to contradiction.*

Contradiction removal is achieved by adding to the original program P the complements of revisable literals:

Definition 2.7 (Revisables) *Let $\mathcal{R}_P$ be the set of all default literals $\sim A$ with no rules for A in an ELP P. The revisable literals of P are a subset of $\mathcal{R}_P$. A subset S of $\sim \mathcal{R}_P$ is a set of positive assumptions.*

Definition 2.8 (Revision of a program) *A set of positive assumptions A of P is a revision of P iff $(P \cup A) \not\models_p \bot$*

Example 3 *Consider the wobbly wheel problem:*

$$wobbly\_wheel \leftarrow flat\_tyre$$
$$wobbly\_wheel \leftarrow broken\_spokes$$
$$flat\_tyre \leftarrow punctured\_tube$$
$$flat\_tyre \leftarrow leaky\_valve$$
$$\bot \leftarrow \sim wobbly\_wheel$$

Using as revisables the literals $\sim broken\_spokes$, $\sim punctured\_tube$, and $\sim leaky\_valve$, there are 7 possible revisions, corresponding to the non-empty subsets of $\{punctured\_tube, broken\_spokes, leaky\_valve\}$.

Without loss of generality, as recognized in [Kakas and Mancarella, 1991], we can restrict ourselves to consider as revisables default literals for which there are no rules in the program; objective literals can always be made to depend on a default literal by adding a new rule or new literals in existing rules:

First, consider the case where a given literal is to be assumed true. For instance, in a diagnosis setting it may be wished to assume all components are ok unless it originates a contradiction. This is simply done, by introducing the rule $ok(X) \leftarrow \sim ab(X)$. Because $\sim ab(X)$ is true then $ok(X)$ also is. If $\sim ab(X)$ is revised $ok(X)$ becomes false, i.e. $ok(X)$ is revised from true to false.

Suppose now it is desirable to consider revisable an objective literal, say L, for which there are rules in the program. Let $\{L \leftarrow Body_1; \ldots; L \leftarrow Body_n\}$ be the rules in the definition of L. To make this literal "revisable" replace the rules for L by $\{L \leftarrow Body_1, \sim rev\_false(L,1); \ldots; L \leftarrow Body_n, \sim rev\_false(L,n); L \leftarrow rev\_true(L)\}$, with $\sim rev\_false(L,i)$ and $\sim rev\_true(L)$ being revisables. If L was initially false or undefined then to make it true it is enough to revise $\sim rev\_true(L)$. If L was true or undefined then to make it false it is sufficient to revise to false the literals $\sim rev\_false(L,i)$ in the bodies for L that are true or undefined.

In order to define the revision algorithm we'll need the concept of contradiction support. This notion will link the semantics' procedural and declarative aspects.

Definition 2.9 (Support set of a literal) *Support sets of any literal $L \in WFSX_p(P)$ of an ELP P, denoted by $SS(L)$, and are obtained as follows:*

1. *If L is a positive literal, then for each rule $L \leftarrow B_1, \ldots, B_n$ in P such that $P \models_p B_1, \ldots, B_n$, each $SS(L)$ is formed by the union of $\{L\}$ with some $SS(B_i)$ for each B_i.*

2. *If L is a default literal $\sim A$:*

    (a) *If no rules exist for A in P then $SS(L) = \{\sim A\}$.*

    (b) *If rules for A exist in P then choose from each rule with non-empty body a single literal whose complement belongs to $WFSX_p(P)$. For each such multiple choice there are several $SS(\sim A)$, each formed by the union of $\{\sim A\}$ with a SS of the complement of every chosen literal.*

    (c) *If $P \models_p \neg A$ then there exist, additionally, support sets SS of $\sim A$ equal to each $SS(\neg A)$.*

We are particularly interested in the supports of $\bot$, where the causes of contradiction can be found. The supports of $\bot$ in example 1 are $\{\sim b\}$ and $\{\sim c\}$. In examples 2 and 3 we have the single $SS(\bot) = \{\sim b\}$ and $SS(\bot) = \{\sim punctured\_tube, \sim broken\_spokes, \sim leaky\_valve\}$, respectively.

3 PREFERENCE LANGUAGE AND SEMANTICS

We have shown how to express nonmonotonic reasoning patterns using extended logic programming such as default reasoning and inheritance in [Pereira *et al.*, 1993a]. Additionally, we have discussed the relationship of our contradiction removal semantics to modelbased diagnosis and debugging in [Pereira *et al.*, 1993b, Pereira *et al.*, 1993c, Pereira *et al.*, 1993d]. However, while in these works we could easily express certain preference criteria (similar to those used in default reasoning) in our framework, other preference relations (as discussed for example in [Nejdl, 1991b, Nejdl and Banagl, 1992]) could not easily be represented.

To illustrate this, let us use an example from [Dressler and Bottcher, 1992]. We want to encode that we prefer a diagnosis including $mode_i(C)$ to one including $mode_{i+1}(C)$, where C is a component of the system to be diagnosed. The coding in default logic is a set of default rules of the form $\neg mode_1 \wedge \ldots \wedge \neg mode_i : mode_{i+1}/mode_{i+1}$, which can easily be translated into a logic program using WFSX semantics by including rules of the form $b_i(C) \leftarrow ab_1(C), \ldots, ab_{i-1}(C), \sim ab_i(C)$, where the b_i stand for the behaviour predicted by $mode_i$, and ab_i stands for the assumption that $mode_i$ has lead to a contradiction.

However, if we want to encode the slightly generalized preference relation, that prefers a diagnosis including $mode_i(C1)$ to one including $mode_{i+1}(C2)$ for any C1 and C2, this is no longer possible without enumerating all possible combinations of modes and components, which is not feasible in practice. Because of their declarative nature, logic programming and default logic give us a mechanism for prefering to include in an extension one fact over another (what we call *local preferences*), but not a mechanism for expressing *global preferences* stating we should only generate extensions including a certain fact after finding that no extensions including another fact exist, i.e. to attain sequencing of solutions.

To express global preferences, i.e. preferences over the order of revisions, we use a labeled directed acyclic and/or graph defined by rules of the form:

$$Level_0 \ll Level_1 \wedge Level_2 \wedge \ldots \wedge Level_n \quad (n \geq 1) \quad (1)$$

$Level_i$ nodes in the graph are preference level identifiers. To each preference level node is associated a set of revisables denoted by $\mathcal{R}(Level_i)$. The meaning of a set of preference rules like (1) for some $Level_0$ is "I'm willing to consider the $Level_0$ revisions as "good" solutions (i.e the revisions of the original program using as revisables

$\mathcal{R}(Level_0))$ only if for some rule body its levels have been considered and there are no revisions at any of those levels." The root of the preference graph is the node denoted by **bottom**, the bottom preference level. Thus, **bottom** cannot appear in the heads of preference rules. Additionally, there cannot exist a level identifier in the graph without an edge entering the node. This guarantees all the nodes are accessible from **bottom**.

The revisions of the **bottom** preference level are (transitively) preferred to all other ones. Formally:

Definition 3.1 (Preferred Revisions) Let P be an ELP, and Π a preference graph containing a preference level Lev. The revision R is preferred wrt Π iff R is a minimal revision of P (in the sense of set inclusion), using revisables $\mathcal{R}(Lev)$, and there is an and-tree $\mathcal{T}$ embedded in Π, with root Lev, such that all leaves of $\mathcal{T}$ are **bottom** and no other preference levels in $\mathcal{T}$ have revisions.

Example 4 *Consider the following program P:*

$have\_fun \leftarrow go(theater) \qquad watch\_tv \leftarrow tv\_movie$
$have\_fun \leftarrow watch\_tv \qquad watch\_tv \leftarrow tv\_show$
$have\_fun \leftarrow go(cinema) \qquad \bot \leftarrow \sim have\_fun$
$\neg go(theater) \leftarrow sold\_out(theater)$
$\neg go(cinema) \leftarrow sold\_out(cinema)$

P is contradictory because $\sim have\_fun$ *is true. Its minimal revisions are* $\{go(theater)\}$, $\{go(cinema)\}$, $\{tv\_movie\}$ *and* $\{tv\_show\}$ *expressing have fun if I go to the theater or to the cinema, or stay at home watching a movie or tv show. If the next preference graph with associated revisables is added:*

$1 \ll \textbf{bottom} \qquad 2 \ll \textbf{bottom} \qquad 3 \ll 1 \wedge 2$
$\mathcal{R}(\textbf{bottom}) = \{\sim go(theater)\} \quad \mathcal{R}(2) = \{\sim tv\_movie\}$
$\mathcal{R}(1) \quad = \{\sim go(cinema)\} \quad \mathcal{R}(3) = \{\sim tv\_show\}$

then there is a unique preferred revision, namely $\{go(theater)\}$. *Assume now the theater tickets sold out. We represent this situation by adding to the original program the fact* $sold\_out(theater)$. *Now the preferred revisions are* $\{go(cinema)\}$ *and* $\{tv\_movie\}$. *If the cinema tickets are also sold out the preferred revision will be* $\{tv\_movie\}$.

I'll only stay at home watching the TV show if the cinema and theater tickets are sold out and there is no TV movie. If there is no TV show then I cannot remove contradiction, and cannot have fun. This constraint can be relaxed by replacing the integrity rule by $\bot \leftarrow \sim have\_fun, \sim sleep$ *and adding an additional preference level with revisables* $\{\sim sleep\}$ *on top of 3. With this new encoding the preferred revision* $\{sleep\}$ *is produced.*

Similarly, coming back to our example on preferences in a diagnosis system, we can encode the preference relation preferring diagnoses including a certain mode to ones not including it, by defining a linear order of levels where level i includes the set $\{ab_1(\_), \ldots ab_i(\_)\}$ as revisable literals in addition to the set of rules $b_i(C) \leftarrow$ $ab_1(C), \ldots, ab_{i-1}(C), \sim ab_i(C)$.

This simple but quite general representation can capture the preference orderings among revisions described in the literature: minimal cardinality, most probable, minimal sets, circumscription, etc. Any of these preference orderings can be "compiled" to our framework. Furthermore, we can represent any preference based reasoning or revision strategy, starting from preferences which are just binary relations to preference relations, which are transitive, modular and/or linear ([Nejdl, 1991b, Kraus et al., 1990]). Preferred revisions specified declaratively by preference level statements can be computed as follows:

Algorithm 3.1 (Preferred Revisions)
Input: An extended logic program P and a preference graph Π.
Output: The set of preferred revisions $PrefRev$.

$Explored = \{\}; ToExpl = \{\textbf{bottom}\};$
$PrefRev = \{\}; ContrLevels = \{\};$
repeat
  Let $lev \in ToExpl; Explored = Explored \cup \{lev\};$
  $ToExpl = ToExpl - \{lev\};$
  $LevelRev = MinRevisions(P, \mathcal{R}(lev));$
  if $LevelRev \neq \{\}$ then
    $PrefRev = PrefRev \cup LevelRev$
  else $ContrLevels = ContrLevels \cup \{lev\}$
  $Applicable = \{l_0 \mid l_0 \ll l_1 \wedge \ldots \wedge l_n \in \Pi$ and
               $l_1, \ldots, l_n \in ContrLevels\}$
  $ToExpl = ToExpl \cup (Applicable - Explored)$
until $ToExpl = \{\}$

Algorithm 3.1 assumes the existence of a "magic" subroutine that given the program and the revisables returns the minimal revisions.

The computation of preferred revisions evaluates the preference rules in a bottom–up fashion, starting from the **bottom** level, activating the head of preference rule when all the levels in the body were unsuccessfully tried. At each new activated level the revision algorithm is called. If there are revisions then they are preferred ones, but further ones can be obtained. If there are no revisions, we have to check if new preference rules are applicable, by generating new active levels. This process is iterated till all active levels are exhausted.

4 EXAMPLES OF APPLICATION

We've tested REVISE on several examples, including the important problem of representing diagnostic strategies in a modelbased reasoning system. Below are two examples.

4.1 Two Inverter Circuit

In this example we present two extended diagnosis cases which illustrate the use of the preference graph to capture diagnosis strategies. Consider the simple two inverter circuit in figure 1.

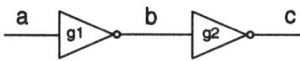

Figure 1: Two Inverter Circuit

The normal and abnormal behaviour of the inverter gate is modelled by the rules below. We assume that our inverter gates have two known modes of erroneous comportment, either the output is always "0" (mode "stuck at 0") or is always "1" (mode "stuck at 1"). The fault mode "unknown" describes unknown faults, with no predicted behaviour. The last argument, T, is a time-stamp that permits the modelling of distinct observations in time. It is also implicit that an abnormality is permanent.

$inv(G, I, 1, T) \leftarrow \sim ab(G), node(I, 0, T)$
$inv(G, I, 0, T) \leftarrow \sim ab(G), node(I, 1, T)$

$inv(G, \_, 0,) \leftarrow ab(G), s\_at\_0(G)$
$inv(G, \_, 1,) \leftarrow ab(G), s\_at\_1(G)$

$s\_at\_0(G) \leftarrow fault\_mode(G, s0)$
$s\_at\_1(G) \leftarrow fault\_mode(G, s1)$
$unknown(G) \leftarrow fault\_mode(G, unknown)$

The connections among components and nodes are described by:

$node(b, B, T) \leftarrow inv(g1, a, B, T)$
$node(c, C, T) \leftarrow inv(g2, b, C, T)$

The first integrity rule below ensures that the fault modes are exclusive, i.e. to an abnormal gate at most one fault mode can be assigned. The second one enforces the assignment of at least one fault mode to anomalous components. The last integrity rule expresses the fact that to each node only one value can be predicted or observed at a given time.

$\perp \leftarrow fault\_mode(G, S1), fault\_mode(G, S2), S1 \neq S2$
$\perp \leftarrow ab(G),$
  $\sim fault\_mode(G, s0),$
  $\sim fault\_mode(G, s1),$
  $\sim fault\_mode(G, unknown)$
$\perp \leftarrow node(X, V1, T), node(X, V2, T), V1 \neq V2$

Now we show how the preference graph can be used to implement distinct reasoning modes. The basic idea is to focus reasoning by concentrating on probable failures first (simple views, high abstraction level, etc...), to avoid reasoning in too large a detail. In this example, we'll prefer single faults to multiple faults (i.e. more than one component is abnormal), fault mode "stuck at 0" to "stuck at 1" and the latter to the "unknown" fault mode. One possible combination of these two preferences is expressed using the following integrity rules and preference graph. This graph and its associated revisables are depicted in figure 2.

$\perp \leftarrow fault\_mode(\_, s1), \sim s0\_impossible$
$\perp \leftarrow fault\_mode(\_, unknown), \sim s0\_impossible$
$\perp \leftarrow fault\_mode(\_, unknown), \sim s1\_impossible$
$\perp \leftarrow fault\_mode(G1, \_), fault\_mode(G2, \_)$
  $G2 \neq G1, \sim single\_fault\_impossible$

$1 \ll \text{bottom} \quad 2 \ll \text{bottom}$
$3 \ll 1 \quad 4 \ll 1 \wedge 2$
$5 \ll 3 \wedge 4$

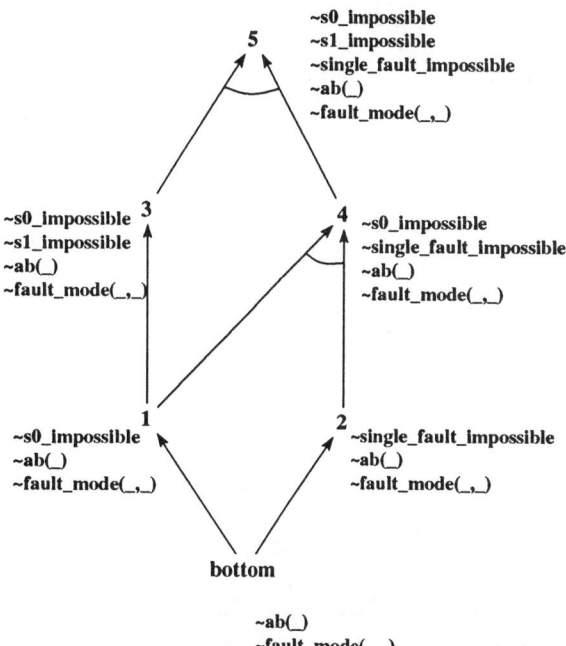

Figure 2: Reasoning Modes Preference Graph

In the bottom level only $\sim ab(\_)$ and $\sim fault\_mode(\_, \_)$ are revisables. Because neither of $\sim s0\_impossible$, $\sim s1\_impossible$ and $\sim single\_fault\_impossible$ are revisables, the integrity rules enforce single "stuck at 0" faults. Level 1 and level 3 correspond to single "stuck at 1" faults and single "unknown faults." Level 2 express possible multiple "stuck at 0" faults. Level 4 captures multiple "stuck at 0" or "stuck at 1" faults. Finally, all kind of faults, single or multiple, are dealt with in level 5.

We could migrate the knowledge embedded in the last four previous integrity rules to the preference graph. This preference graph is more elaborate (but probably more intuitive) as shown in figure 3. The dashed boxes correspond to the levels of the previous preference graph and are labeled accordingly. This demonstrates how the meta-knowledge represented in the preference graph could move to the program, with a substancial reduction of the preference relation. If instead of 2 components we had 100, the extended graph we will have about 304 nodes and the smaller one is identical to the one of figure 2. The general conditions of the preference graph that allow this transference of information are the subject of further investigation.

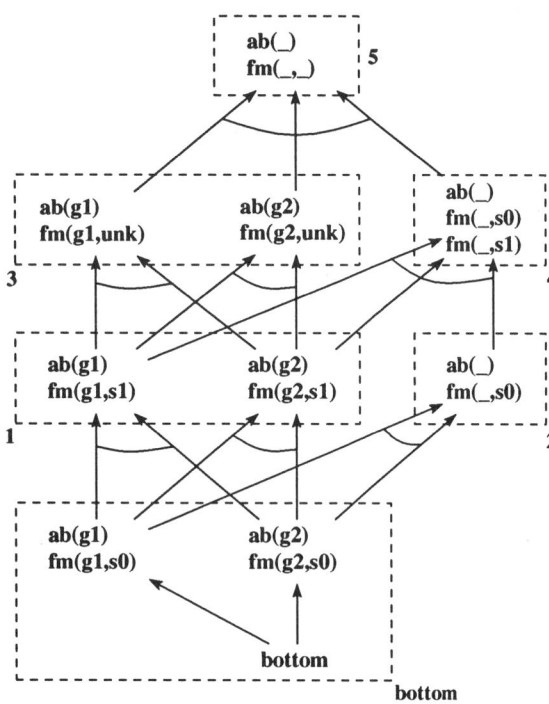

Figure 3: Extended Preference Graph

Suppose that in the first experiment made the input is 0 and the values at nodes b and c are also 0 (see figure 4). These observations are modelled by the facts:

$$node(a,0,t0) \quad node(b,0,t0) \quad node(c,0,t0)$$

Figure 4: First Experiment

This program is contradictory with the following single preferred revision obtained at level 2:

$$\{ab(g1), ab(g2), fault\_mode(g1, s0),\\ fault\_mode(g2, s0), single\_fault\_impossible\}$$

The facts $\{node(a,0,t1), node(b,1,t1), node(c,0,t1)\}$ describe the results of a second experiment made in the circuit. The above two experiments together generate, at level 5, the revisions below. Notice that the second one is at first sight non intuitive. We formulated the problem employing the consistency–based approach to diagnosis, therefore it is consistent with the observations to have both gates abnormal with "unknown" faults.

$$\{\; s0\_impossible, s1\_impossible,\\ single\_fault\_impossible,\\ ab(g1), fault\_mode(g1, unknown),\\ ab(g2), fault\_mode(g2, s0) \;\}$$

$$\{\; s0\_impossible, s1\_impossible,\\ single\_fault\_impossible,\\ ab(g1), fault\_mode(g1, unknown),\\ ab(g2), fault\_mode(g2, unknown) \;\}$$

4.2 MULTIPLE MODELS AND HIERARCHY

In the rest of this section we will consider a small abstract device. We will focus on the use of different abstraction and diagnosis strategies and leave out the actual details of the models.

This device is built from chips and wires and has a certain behaviour. If it does not show that behaviour, then we consider one of its parts abnormal.

% concept: structural hierarchy,
% axiom: some part is defect, iff one its subparts is defect,
% strategy: decompose the system into its subcomponents

$$\neg a(device) \leftarrow \sim a(chips), \sim a(wires)\\ behaviour(device) \leftarrow \sim a(device)$$

% first observation
% contradiction found at highest level

$$\neg behaviour(device)$$

In our case, either the chips can be faulty or the wires can be faulty. To check that, we use a functional model if available (in the case of the chips) or a physical model. As we will see later, our specified preference order leads us to suspect the chips first.

% concept: functional/physical hierarchy.
% a contradiction is found, if the functional model leads to
% contradiction. If this is the case, check the physical models
% of the suspected component (these axioms come later)

$$\neg a(chips) \leftarrow \sim a(functionalChipModel)\\ assump(ChipModel) \leftarrow a(FunctionalChipModel)$$

% no functional model for wires,
% directly start with the physical model

$$\neg a(wires) \leftarrow \sim a(physicalWireModel)$$

When testing the chips, we use the functional hierarchy and get three function blocks fc1, fc2 and fc3.

% enumeration of possible abnormal
% components (functional decomposition)

$$\neg a(functionalChipModel) \leftarrow \sim af(fc1), \sim af(fc2),\\ \sim af(fc3)$$

The functions of these blocks and their interdependencies are described in an arbitrary way, below we show a very simple sequential relationship.

% behaviour of single components in one model view
% simple kind of sequential propagation, model valid
% only if we just use chip model (no faulty wires)

$$fb(fc1) \leftarrow \sim af(fc1), assump(ChipModel)$$
$$fb(fc2) \leftarrow \sim af(fc2), fb(fc1),$$
$$assump(ChipModel)$$
$$fb(fc3) \leftarrow \sim af(fc3), fb(fc2),$$
$$assump(ChipModel)$$
$$behaviour(device) \leftarrow fb(fc3), assump(ChipModel)$$

We really find out, that the functional block fc1 malfunctions. Now we have to check, which physical components compose that functional block and which one of them is faulty. As functional block fc1 consists of two physical components c1 and c4, these two are our suspects after the first two observations.

% second observation, restricts the found diagnoses to fc1

$\neg fb(fc1)$

% concept: multiple models.
% When a fault is found using the functional model, check the
% physical chip models, prefer physical chip model 1 over
% physical chip model 2.

type(c1,chip)type(c2,chip)
type(c3,chip)type(c4,chip)

The functional decomposition need not be the same as the physical composition, functional component c1 consists of physical components c1 and c4), physical model 2 (ap2) corresponds to the unknown failure mode, we prefer physical mode 1, if it resolves the contradiction.

$$\neg af(fc1) \leftarrow \sim ap(c1), \sim ap2(c1), \sim ap(c4), \sim ap2(c4)$$
$$\neg af(fc2) \leftarrow \sim ap(c2), \sim ap2(c2)$$
$$\neg af(fc3) \leftarrow \sim ap(c3), \sim ap2(c3)$$

On the level of physical components we have descriptions of behavioural models, in our case models of the correct mode and two fault modes. We further have the assumption, that there is no other unknown fault mode.

% behavioue single components in the physical model 1

$$pb(c1) \leftarrow \sim ap(c1), \sim ap2(c1), assump(ChipModel)$$
$$pb(c2) \leftarrow \sim ap(c2), \sim ap2(c2), assump(ChipModel)$$
$$pb(c3) \leftarrow \sim ap(c3), \sim ap2(c3), assump(ChipModel)$$
$$pb(c4) \leftarrow \sim ap(c4), \sim ap2(c4), assump(ChipModel)$$

% exclusive failure modes for chips in physical model 1

$$\neg ap(C) \leftarrow \sim f1(C), \sim f2(C), type(C, chip)$$

% behaviour of components with fault mode 1

$$faultb1(C) \leftarrow f1(C)$$

% behaviour of components with fault mode 2

$$faultb2(C) \leftarrow f2(C)$$

Now, we have two more observations, which tell us, that c1 is not functioning according to its fault mode 1 and c4 is not either. So, as we prefer fault mode 1 to fault mode 2 (as specified later in the preference ordering) the effect of the third observation is to focus on c4 in fault mode 1, while the effect of the fourth observation is to reconsider both c4 and c1 in fault mode 2.

% third observation

$\neg faultb1(c1)$

% fourth observation

$\neg faultb1(c4)$

Finally, with a last observation, we restrict our suspect list again to c4 in fault mode 2. Finally, observation 6 leads us to consider unknown faults.

% fifth observation

$\neg faultb2(c1)$

% sixth observation

$\neg faultb2(c4)$

For the wires, we just have a physical model:

% types

$$type(w1, wire)$$
$$type(w2, wire)$$

$$\neg a(physicalWireModel) \leftarrow \sim ap(w1), \sim ap(w2)$$

$$pb(w1) \leftarrow \sim ap(w1)$$
$$pb(w2) \leftarrow \sim ap(w2)$$

Finally, we specify a specific diagnosis strategy by using the preference order of revisables. The preference graph below starts to tes the most abstract hierarchy level (**bottom**). If something is wrong, then go to the next hierarchy level (chips and wires) on this level, first consider chip faults with fault mode 1 first (level 1). Otherwise try single fault with fault mode 2 (level 2). If this doesn't explain the behaviour try a double fault with fault mode 1 or a single unknown fault (3,4). Otherwise suspect faulty wires (level 5). If this does not work then everything is possible in the last level (6).

$$1 \ll \textbf{bottom} \quad 2 \ll 1$$
$$3 \ll 2 \quad 4 \ll 2$$
$$5 \ll 3 \wedge 4 \quad 5 \ll 6$$

The sequence of revisions and the revisable levels are listed below:

Level	Revisions
bottom	$\{a(device)\}$
1	$\{a(device), a(chips), ab(\_), af(\_),$ $ap(\_), f1(\_), a(functionalChipModel)\}$
2	$\{a(device), a(chips), ab(\_), af(\_),$ $ap(\_), f2(\_), a(functionalChipModel)\}$
3	$\{a(device), a(chips), ab(\_), af(\_),$ $ap(\_), ap2(\_), a(functionalChipModel)\}$
4	$\{a(device), a(chips), ab(\_),$ $a(functionalChipModel), af(\_),$ $not\_single\_fault, ap(\_), f1(\_)\}$
5	$\{a(device), a(wires), ab(\_)), af(\_),$ $ap(\_), a(physicalWireModel)\}$
6	$\{a(device), a(chips),$ $a(functionalChipModel), ab(\_)),$ $af(\_), ap(\_), ap2(\_), f1(\_), f2(\_),$ $a(wires), a(physicalWireModel)\}$

Table 1: Levels and Revisables

Observation 1, Revisions at level 1:

$\{a(chips), a(device), a(functionalChipModel),$
$af(fc1), ap(c4), f1(c4)\}$
$\{a(chips), a(device), a(functionalChipModel),$
$af(fc1), ap(c1), f1(c1)\}$
$\{a(chips), a(device), a(functionalChipModel),$
$af(fc2), ap(c2), f1(c2)\}$
$\{a(chips), a(device), a(functionalChipModel),$
$af(fc3), ap(c3), f1(c3)\}$

Observation 2, Revisions at level 1:

$\{a(chips), a(device), a(functionalChipModel),$
$af(fc1), ap(c4), f1(c4)\}$
$\{a(chips), a(device), a(functionalChipModel),$
$af(fc1), ap(c1), f1(c1)\}$

Observation 3, Revisions at level 1:

$\{a(chips), a(device), a(functionalChipModel),$
$af(fc1), ap(c4), f1(c4)\}$

Observation 4, Revisions at level 2:

$\{a(chips), a(device), a(functionalChipModel),$
$af(fc1), ap(c4), f2(c4)\}$
$\{a(chips), a(device), a(functionalChipModel),$
$af(fc1), ap(c1), f2(c1)\}$

Observation 5, Revisions at level 2:

$\{a(chips), a(device), a(functionalChipModel),$
$af(fc1), ap(c4), f2(c4)\}$

Observation 6, Revisions at level 3:

$\{a(chips), a(device), a(functionalChipModel),$
$af(fc1), ap2(c1)\}$
$\{a(chips), a(device), a(functionalChipModel),$
$af(fc1), ap2(c4)\}$

5 REVISION ALGORITHM

The main motivation for this algorithm is that at distinct preference levels the set of revisables may differ, but it is necessary to reuse work as much as possible, or otherwise the preferred revisions algorithm will be prohibitively inefficient. We do so by presenting an extension to Reiter's algorithm [Reiter, 1987], corrected in [Greiner et al., 1989], that fully complies with this goal. The preference revision process can be built upon this algorithm simply by calling it with the current set of revisables, as shown in section 3. This permits the reuse of the previous computations that matter to the current set of revisables. The algorithm handles arbitrary sets of assumptions, handles different sets of revisables at different levels, and provides a general caching mechanism for the computation of minimal "hitting sets" obtained at previous levels.

The main data structure is a DAG constructed from a set $\mathcal{C}$ of conflict sets (all the inconsistencies) and a non-contradictory initial context Cx which expresses what are the initial truth values of the revisables. An inconsistency is a support of contradiction. In our setting, these conflict sets are the intersection of a support set of $\bot$ with the set of revisables and their negations. Thus, a conflict set contains only literals that were already revised and literals that can be revised, which jointly lend support ot contradiction.

Remark that the next algorithm is described independently of the initial context and of the type of revisable literals (they may be true positive literals that are allowed to become false through revision).

A generalized–hitting–set directed–acyclic–graph (GHS-DAG) is a DAG where nodes are labeled with sets of conflict sets. Edges are labeled with negations of revisables. In the basic algorithm (without pruning) the need for labeling nodes with sets of conflict sets is not evident. For clarity we'll describe the basic algorithm assuming that there is only one conflict set in the label. After introducing pruning we'll slightly revise the basic algorithm to cope with the more general case.

In the following, D_{new}, is used to build the level specific GHS–DAG using the conflict sets stored in the GHS–DAG D (used as the global cache). While computing the level specific DAG the global cache is updated accordingly. This latter GHS–DAG will be fed into the next iteration of algorithm 3.1 to minimize computation effort in less preferred levels. The minimal, level specific, revisions for a given set of revisables are obtained from D_{new}. Conflict sets are returned by a theorem prover; as in [Reiter, 1987, Greiner et al., 1989] the algorithm tries to minimize the number of calls to the theorem prover.

The set of all revisables is a non-contradictory set of literals denoted by $\mathcal{R}$. Intuitively, if a literal L (resp. $\sim L$) belongs to $\mathcal{R}$ then we allow L to change its truth-value to false (resp. to true). A conflict set CS is a subset of $\mathcal{R}$. A conflict set contains literals that cannot be simultaneously true (similar to the definition of NOGOOD [McDermott,

1991]). A context is a subset of $\mathcal{R} \cup \sim\mathcal{R}$.

The reader is urged to recourse to figure 5 when reading the basic algorithm below, where the initial context is $\{a, b, c, d\}$ and $Rev = \{\sim a, \sim b, \sim c, \sim d\}$. The set of inconsistencies, $\mathcal{C}$, contains the sets appearing in the figure. We assume, for simplicity, that the global GHS–DAG is empty and therefore in every step D and D_{new} are equal. The nodes are numbered by order of creation.

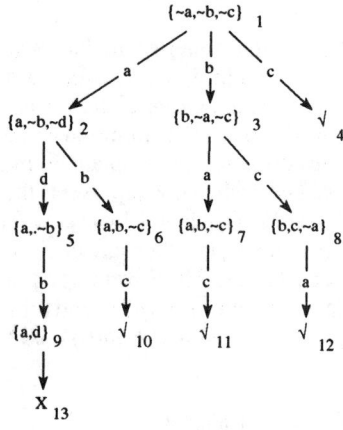

Figure 5: Basic Algorithm

0. Let $\mathcal{C}$ be a set of conflict sets and Cx context. The first time this algorithm is called GHS–DAG D is empty.

1. Let $Rev \subseteq \mathcal{R}$ be a set of revisables, D a GHS–DAG and D_{new} an empty GHS–DAG. If D is not empty then insert a clone of its root node in D_{new}. Otherwise, insert in D_{new} an unlabeled node and a clone node in D.

2. Process the nodes in D_{new} in breadth–first order. Let n be a node. The set $H(n)$ contains the revisions of literals in the path from the root to the node and $M(n)$ is the context at node n. To process node n :

    (a) Define $H(n)$ to be the set of edge labels on the path in D_{new} from the root down to node n (empty if n is the root). Let $M(n) = [Cx - \sim H(n)] \cup H(n)$.

    (b) If n is not labeled then if for all $X \in \mathcal{C}$, $X \not\subseteq M(n)$ then label n and its clone with the special symbol $\sqrt{}$. Otherwise, label the node with one arbitrary X such that $X \subseteq M(n)$. Copy the label to its clone in D.
    If n is already labeled denote its label by X.
    If $X \cap Rev = \{\}$ then mark the node in D_{new} as closed.

    (c) If n is labeled by a set $X \in \mathcal{C}$, then for each $l_i \in X \cap Rev$, generate a new outgoing arc labeled by $\sim l_i$ leading to a new node m_i. If an arc already exists in D, from a clone of n and label $\sim l_i$ to some node r_i, then copy the label of r_i to m_i in D_{new}. Node r_i becomes the clone of m_i.

    Otherwise m_i remains unlabeled and a clone arc is created in D.

3. Return the resulting GHS–DAGs, D_{new} and D.

If the node is not labeled in step 2b then it was unexplored. The algorithm attempts to find a conflict set compatible with the current context. If there is no conflict then a revision is found (possibly not minimal) and it is marked with $\sqrt{}$. If a conflict set is found then it is intersected with the current revisables. If the intersection is empty a non-revisable contradiction was found. Otherwise, the node must be expanded in order to restore consistency. This is accomplished by complementing a single revisable literal in the conflict set. This process is iterated till there are no more nodes to expand.

An access to the set of inconsistencies in step 2b can be regarded has a request to the theorem prover to compute another conflict set. Also, notice in the end D_{new} will be contained in D. All the revisions wrt the specified set of revisables can be obtained from D_{new}. We now define pruning enhancements to D_{new} such that, in the end, the minimal revisions can be obtained from this new DAG.

The result of the application of the next optimizations to the problem described in figure 5 is shown in figure 6. Node 5 is obtained by application of pruning step 3a. Node 6 is reused by node 3 and nodes 7 and 8 were closed by node 4.

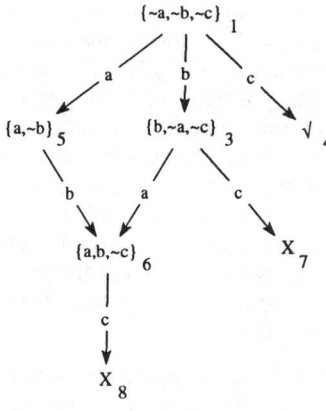

Figure 6: Pruning Enhancements

1. Reusing nodes: this algorithm will not always generate a new node m_i as a descendant of node n in step 2c:

    (a) If there is a node n' in D_{new} such that $H(n') = H(n) \cup \{l\}$, then let the l–arc under n point to this existing node n', and reflect this in its clone in D. Thus, these nodes will have more than one parent.

    (b) Otherwise generate m_i as described in the basic algorithm.

2. **Closing:** If there is a node m in D_{new} labeled with $\sqrt{}$ and $H(m) \subseteq H(n)$, then close node n and its clone in D.

3. **Pruning:** Let X be the label of node n in step 2b, and m be another node in D_{new} labeled with conflict set Y. Attempt to prune D_{new} and D as follows:

    (a) Pruning D_{new} : If $X \cap Rev \subseteq Y \cap Rev$ and $X \cap H(n) \subseteq H(m)$, then relabel m with X. For any $\sim l_i$ in $(Y - X) \cap Rev$ the l_i–arc under m is no longer allowed. The node connected by this arc and all of its descendants are removed, except for those nodes with another ancestor which is not being removed. This step may eliminate the node currently being processed.

    (b) Pruning D : Let n' and m' be the clones of n and m in D, respectively.

    i. If $X \cap \mathcal{R} \subseteq Y \cap \mathcal{R}$ and $X \cap H(n') \subseteq H(m')$, for some Y in m'. Apply the procedure in 3a) to D, taking into account that more than one set may label the node: remove all the Ys that verify the condition, insert X in the label and retain l–edges and descendant nodes such that $\sim l$ belongs to some of the remaining sets. Notice this procedure was already applied to D_{new}.

    ii. If the condition in 3a) was verified by n and m then insert in the label of m' the set X.

The reuse and closing of nodes avoids redundant computations of conflict sets. The closing rule also ensures that in the end the nodes labeled with $\sqrt{}$ are the minimal revisions. The pruning strategy is based on subset tests, as in Reiter's original algorithm, but extended to take into account the contexts and revisables. The principle is simply that given two conflict sets one contained in the other, the bigger one can be discarded when computing minimal revisions. The algorithm handles the case when a conflict set is a subset of another wrt the revisables, but not if the revisables are not considered. Also notice that condition 3(b)ii is redundant if step 3(b)i was applied.

The need to consider nodes labeled by several conflict sets is justified by the pruning step 3(b)ii: the set X is minimal wrt the current set of revisables. We store this set in the global cache D for later use by the algorithm. To reap the most benefit from this improvement it is necessary to change step 2b) by introducing the following test:

> "If n is labeled by conflict sets, i.e. it was previously computed, then intersect these sets with Rev. Select from the obtained sets a minimal one such that the number of nodes below this node, wrt Rev, is maximum. Relabel n with this set."

The heuristic in the modified step is to use a minimal set wrt to the current set of revisables having the most of search space explored. This has two main advantages: first, the new algorithm can ignore redundant branches (the minimal set condition); second it directs the search to the sub-DAG with less nodes remaining to be explored, reusing maximally work done before.

It can be shown that if the number of conflict sets is finite, and they themselves are finite, then this algorithm computes the minimal revisions and stops. It is known this problem is NP-Hard: an exponential number of minimal revisions can be generated. Under the previous conditions algorithm 3.1 is sound and complete, if it has a finite number of preference rules (wrt def. 3.1).

The computation of the preferred revisions of example in section 4.1 is portrayed in figure 7, with the obvious abreviations for the literals appearing. The whole example has 25 minimal inconsistencies, i.e. minimal support sets of $\bot$. The computations done at each level are bounded by the labeled bold lines. The dashed line represents the bound of the level specific GHS–DAG at levels **bottom**, 2 and 4. These leves all nodes are closed, i.e. there are no revisions. Notice that pruning steps 3a) and 3(b)ii were applied between the node initially labeled with $\{\sim ab(g2)\}$ and the nodes labeled with $\{\sim fm(g1, uk), \sim s0i\}$ and $\{fm(g1, uk), \sim s1i\}$.

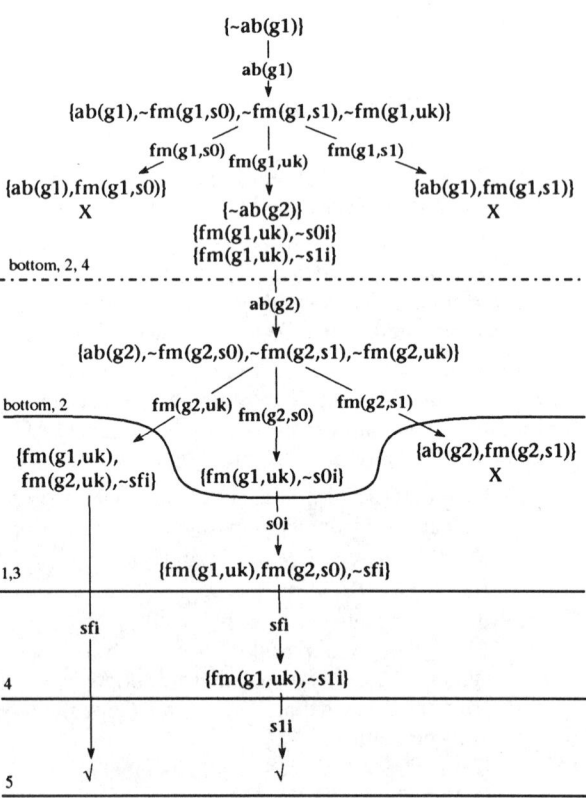

Figure 7: Preferred Revisions Computation

As the reader may notice, the higher the level is in the preference graph the deeper is the GHS–DAG generated. This corresponds to what is desired: preferred revisons should be obtained with less theorem proving costs.

The efficiency of the algorithm is highly dependent on the order in which conflict sets are generated. It is possible to devise very nasty examples having $n+1$ conflict sets with a single revision of cardinality 1, where the above algorithm has to explore and generate an exponential GHS–DAG. One possible solution to this problem is to guarantee that the theorem prover only returns minimal sets of inconsistencies. This can be done by an intelligent search strategy used by the theorem prover. This topic will be the subject of a future paper.

6 COMPARISONS AND CONCLUSIONS

We start by concentrating on diagnosis strategies, only recently approached in [Struss, 1989, Dressler and Bottcher, 1992, Böttcher and Dressler, 1994], where they discuss the necessity of including diagnostic strategies in a modelbased reasoning system such as when to use structural refinement, behavioural refinement, how to switch to different models, and when to use which simplifying assumptions. [Dressler and Bottcher, 1992] also gives an encoding of these preferences on top of an NM-ATMS, using both default rules of the form discussed earlier for local preferences and meta-level rules for explicitly specifying global preference during the revision process.

The disadvantage of the implementation discussed in [Dressler and Bottcher, 1992] and its extended version is that the specification of these preferences is too closely intertwined with their implementation (NM-ATMS plus belief revision system on top) and that different preferences must be specified with distinct formalisms. Default logic allows a rather declarative preferences specification, while the metarules of [Dressler and Bottcher, 1992] for specifying global preferences have a too procedural flavour.

In contrast, REVISE builds upon a standard logic programming framework extended with the explicit specification of an arbitrary (customizable) preference relation (including standard properties ([Kraus et al., 1990, Nejdl, 1991b]) as needed). Expression of preferences is as declarative as expressing diagnosis models, uses basically the same, formalism and is quite easy to employ according to our experience.

In our diagnosis applications, although our implementation still has some efficiency problems due to being implemented as a meta-interpreter in Prolog (a problem which can be solved without big conceptual difficulties), we are very satisfied with the expressiveness of REVISE and how easy it is to express in it a range of important diagnosis strategies.

We are currently investigating how to extend our formalism for using an order on sets of diagnoses/sets of worlds/sets of sets of assumption sets, instead of the current order on diagnoses/worlds (or assumption sets). Without this greater expressive power we are not able to spell out strategies depending on some property out of the whole set of diagnoses (two or three of such strategies are discussed in a belief revision framework in [Böttcher and Dressler, 1994]).

Revising a knowledge base has been the main topic for belief revision systems and it is quite interesting to compare REVISE to a system like IMMORTAL [Chou and Winslett, 1991]. IMMORTAL starts from a consistent knowledge base (not required by our algorithm) and then allows updating it. These updates can lead to inconsistencies and therefore to revisions of the knowledge base. In contrast to our approach, all inconsistencies are computed statically before any update is done, which for larger examples is not feasible, in our opinion. Also, due to their depth-first construction of hitting sets, they generate non-minimal ones, which have to be thrown away later. (This could be changed by employing a breadth-first strategy.)

Priority levels in IMMORTAL are a special kind of our preference levels, where all levels contain disjoint literals and the levels are modular, both of which properties can be relaxed in REVISE (and have to be in some of our examples). Accordingly, IMMORTAL does not need anything like our DAG global data structure for caching results between levels.

Additionally, IMMORTAL computes all conflict sets and then removes non-updateable literals, in general leading to duplicates; therefore, in our approach, we have less conflict sets and so a faster hitting sets procedure (and less theorem prover costs).

Comparing our work to database updates and inconsistency repairing in knowledge bases, we note that most of this work takes some kind of implicit or explicit abductive approach to database updates, and inconsistency repairs are often handled as a special case of database update from the violated constraints (such as in [Wüthrich, 1993]). If more than one constraint is violated this leads to a depth-first approach to revising inconsistencies which does not guarantee minimal changes. Moreover, we do not know of any other work using general preference levels. All work which uses some kind of priority levels at all uses disjoint priority levels similar to the IMMORTAL system.

Compared to other approaches, which are based on specific systems and specific extensions of these systems such as [Dressler and Bottcher, 1992], REVISE has big advantages in the declarativity, and is built upon a sound formal logic framework.

We therefore believe the REVISE system is an appropriate tool for coding a large range of problems involving revision of knowledge bases and preference relations over them. REVISE is based on sound logic programming semantics, described in this paper, and includes some interesting implementation concepts exploiting relationships between belief revision and diagnosis already discussed in very preliminary form in [Nejdl, 1991a]. While REVISE is still a prototype, we are currently working on further improving its efficiency, and are confident the basic implementation structure of the current system provides an easily extensible backbone for efficient declarative knowledge base revision systems.

Acknowledgements

We thank project ESPRIT Compulog 2, JNICT Portugal and the Portugal/Germany INIDA program for their support.

References

[Alferes, 1993] José Júlio Alferes. *Semantics of Logic Programs with Explicit Negation*. PhD thesis, Universidade Nova de Lisboa, October 1993.

[Böttcher and Dressler, 1994] Claudia Böttcher and Oskar Dressler. Diagnosis process dynamics: Putting diagnosis on the right track. *Annals of Mathematics and Artificial Intelligence*, 11(1–4), 1994. Special Issue on Principles of Model-Based Diagnosis. To appear.

[Chou and Winslett, 1991] Timothy S-C Chou and Marianne Winslett. Immortal: A model-based belief revision system. In *In Proc. KR'91*, pages 99–110, Cambridge, April 1991. Morgan Kaufmann Publishers, Inc.

[de Kleer, 1991] Johan de Kleer. Focusing on probable diagnoses. In *Proceedings of the National Conference on Artificial Intelligence (AAAI)*, pages 842–848, Anaheim, July 1991. Morgan Kaufmann Publishers, Inc.

[Dressler and Bottcher, 1992] O. Dressler and C. Bottcher. Diagnosis process dynamics: Putting diagnosis on the right track. In *Proc. 3nd Int. Workshop on Principles of Diagnosis*, 1992.

[Friedrich and Nejdl, 1992] Gerhard Friedrich and Wolfgang Nejdl. Choosing observations and actions in model-based diagnosis-repair systems. In *In Proc. KR'92*, pages 489–498, Cambridge, MA, October 1992. Morgan Kaufmann Publishers, Inc.

[Gelder et al., 1991] A. Van Gelder, K. A. Ross, and J. S. Schlipf. The well-founded semantics for general logic programs. *Journal of the ACM*, 38(3):620–650, 1991.

[Greiner et al., 1989] Russell Greiner, Barbara A. Smith, and Ralph W. Wilkerson. A correction to the algorithm in Reiter's theory of diagnosis. *Artificial Intelligence*, 41(1):79–88, 1989.

[Hamscher et al., 1992] W. Hamscher, L. Console, and J. de Kleer. *Readings in Model-Based Diagnosis*. Morgan Kaufmann, 1992.

[Kakas and Mancarella, 1991] A.C. Kakas and P. Mancarella. Generalized stable models: A semantics for abduction. In *Proc. ECAI'90*, pages 385–391, 1991.

[Kraus et al., 1990] Sarit Kraus, Daniel Lehmann, and Menachem Magidor. Nonmonotonic reasoning, preferential models and cumulative logics. *Artificial Intelligence*, 44(1–2):167–207, 1990.

[Lackinger and Nejdl, 1993] Franz Lackinger and Wolfgang Nejdl. DIAMON: A model-based troubleshooter based on qualitative reasoning. *IEEE Expert*, February 1993.

[McDermott, 1991] Drew McDermott. A general framework for reason maintenance. *Artificial Intelligence*, 50(3):289–329, 1991.

[Nejdl and Banagl, 1992] Wolfgang Nejdl and Markus Banagl. Asking about possibilities — revision and update semantics for subjunctive queries. In *In Proc. KR'92*, Cambridge, MA, October 1992. Also appears in the ECAI-Workshop on Theoretical Foundations of Knowledge Representation and Reasoning, August 1992, Vienna.

[Nejdl, 1991a] Wolfgang Nejdl. Belief revision, diagnosis and repair. In *Proceedings of the International GI Conference on Knowledge Based Systems*, München, October 1991. Springer-Verlag.

[Nejdl, 1991b] Wolfgang Nejdl. The P-Systems: A systematic classification of logics of nonmonotonicity. In *Proceedings of the National Conference on Artificial Intelligence (AAAI)*, pages 366–372, Anaheim, CA, July 1991.

[Pereira and Alferes, 1992] L. M. Pereira and J. J. Alferes. Well founded semantics for logic programs with explicit negation. In B. Neumann, editor, *European Conference on Artificial Intelligence*, pages 102–106. John Wiley & Sons, Ltd, 1992.

[Pereira et al., 1993a] L. M. Pereira, J. N. Aparício, and J. J. Alferes. Non–monotonic reasoning with logic programming. *Journal of Logic Programming. Special issue on Nonmonotonic reasoning*, pages 227–263, 1993.

[Pereira et al., 1993b] L. M. Pereira, C. Damásio, and J. J. Alferes. Diagnosis and debugging as contradiction removal. In L. M. Pereira and A. Nerode, editors, *2nd Int. Ws. on Logic Programming and NonMonotonic Reasoning*, pages 316–330. MIT Press, 1993.

[Pereira et al., 1993c] L. M. Pereira, C. V. Damásio, and J. J. Alferes. Debugging by diagnosing assumptions. In *Automatic Algorithmic Debugging, AADEBUG'93*. Springer–Verlag, 1993.

[Pereira et al., 1993d] L. M. Pereira, C. V. Damásio, and J. J. Alferes. Diagnosis and debugging as contradiction removal in logic programs. In *Proc. 6th Portuguese Conference On Artificial Intelligence (EPIA'93)*. Springer-Verlag, LNAI 727, 1993.

[Przymusinska and Przymusinski, 1990] H. Przymusinska and T. Przymusinski. Semantic issues in deductive databases and logic programs. In R. Banerji, editor, *Formal Techniques in AI, a Sourcebook*, pages 321–367. North Holland, 1990.

[Reiter, 1987] R. Reiter. A theory of diagnosis from first principles. *AI*, 32:57–96, 1987.

[Struss, 1989] P. Struss. Diagnosis as a process. In *Working Notes of First Int. Workshop on Model-based Diagnosis*, Paris, 1989. Also in [Hamscher et al., 1992].

[Wüthrich, 1993] B. Wüthrich. On updates and inconsistency repairing in knowledge bases. In *Proceedings of the International IEEE Conference on Data Engineering*, Vienna, Austria, April 1993.

Transmutations of Knowledge Systems

Mary-Anne Williams*
maryanne@frey.newcastle.edu.au
Information Systems Group
Department of Management
University of Newcastle, NSW 2308
Australia

Abstract

Within the AGM paradigm revision and contraction operators are constrained by a set of rationality postulates. The logical properties of a set of knowledge are not strong enough to uniquely determine a revision or contraction operation, therefore constructions for these operators rely on some form of underlying preference relation, such as a systems of spheres, or an epistemic entrenchment ordering. The problem of iterated revision is determining how the underlying preference relation should change in response to the acceptance or contraction of information. We call this process a transmutation. Generalizing Spohn's approach we define a transmutation of a well-ordered system of spheres using ordinal conditional functions. Similarly, we define the transmutation of a well-ordered epistemic entrenchment using ordinal epistemic entrenchment functions. We provide several conditions which capture the relationship between an ordinal conditional function and an ordinal epistemic entrenchment function, and their corresponding transmutations. These conditions allow an ordinal epistemic entrenchment function to be explicitly constructed from an ordinal conditional function, and vice versa, in such a way that the epistemic state and its dynamic properties are preserved.

1 INTRODUCTION

The AGM paradigm is a formal approach to theory change. The logical properties of a theory are not strong enough to uniquely determine a contraction, or revision operation, therefore the constructions for these operators rely on some form of underlying preference relation, such as a system of spheres [6], a nice preorder on models [11], or an epistemic entrenchment ordering [4]. Theory change operators based on such preference relations require the relation to be predetermined or given at the outset. Although this provides desirable theoretical freedom, it leads to difficulties in designing computer-based knowledge revision systems. In order to accommodate a subsequent theory change such a system would require guidance in determining a subsequent preference relation. Revision and contraction operators result in a theory or set of knowledge and not a modified preference ordering. Hence, the problem of iterated revision is determining how the underlying preference relation should change in response to the acceptance or contraction of information. According to Schlecta [15] "...iterated revision...is a very common phenomenon for cognitive systems". We refer to the process of changing the underlying preference relation, and hence the knowledge system as a *transmutation*.

We make use of ordinal conditional functions [18], such functions can be thought of as well-ordered system of spheres, with possibly empty partitions. A conditionalization [18, 2] is a specific constructive method for modifying ordinal conditional functions in such a way as to accommodate a revision (or a contraction), and results in another ordinal conditional function. We address the problem of iterated revision by generalizing Spohn's conditionalization, in particular we define transmutations to be any modification of an ordinal conditional function, such

---

*Knowledge Systems Group, Department of Computer Science, University of Sydney, NSW 2006, Australia.

that it satisfies the revision and contraction postulates, and results in another ordinal conditional function. We show that conditionalization is a transmutation.

We introduce an ordinal epistemic entrenchment function. We define transmutations for these structures, and provide perspicuous conditions which capture the relationship between ordinal conditional functions, and ordinal epistemic entrenchment functions, such that the same knowledge set, and transmutations are obtained.

We briefly describe the AGM paradigm in Section 2. Spohn's approach is outlined and generalized in Sections 3, in particular ordinal conditional functions, together with their contraction, revision, and transmutation are described. In Section 4, we introduce ordinal epistemic entrenchment functions, and their contraction, revision, and transmutation. In Section 5 we provide conditions which capture the relationship between ordinal conditional functions and ordinal epistemic entrenchment functions, so that contractions, revisions, and certain transmutations are equivalent. These conditions provide explicit translations which allow an ordinal conditional function and an ordinal epistemic function to be constructed from one another in such a way that a knowledge system and its dynamic properties are preserved. Related work is described in Section 6, and a summary of our results is given in Section 7. Examples and proofs can be found in [22].

2 THE AGM PARADIGM

We begin with some technical preliminaries. Let $\mathbf{L}$ denote a countable language which contains a complete set of Boolean connectives. We will denote formulae in $\mathbf{L}$ by lower case Greek letters. We assume $\mathbf{L}$ is governed by a logic that is identified with its consequence relation $\vdash$. The relation $\vdash$ is assumed to satisfy the following conditions [2]:

(a) If α is a truth-functional tautology, then $\vdash \alpha$.
(b) If $\alpha \vdash \beta$ and $\vdash \alpha$, then $\vdash \beta$ (*modus ponens*).
(c) $\vdash$ is consistent, that is, $\not\vdash \bot$, where $\bot$ denotes the inconsistent theory.
(d) $\vdash$ satisfies the deduction theorem.
(e) $\vdash$ is compact.

The set of all logical consequences of a set $T \subseteq \mathbf{L}$, that is $\{\alpha : T \vdash \alpha\}$, is denoted by $\mathrm{Cn}(T)$. The set of tautologies, $\{\alpha : \vdash \alpha\}$, is denoted by $\top$, and those formulae not in $\top$ are refered to as *nontautological*. A *theory* of $\mathbf{L}$ is any subset of $\mathbf{L}$, closed under $\vdash$. A *consistent* theory of $\mathbf{L}$ is any theory of $\mathbf{L}$ that does not contain both α and $\neg \alpha$, for any formula α of $\mathbf{L}$. A *complete* theory of $\mathbf{L}$ is any theory of $\mathbf{L}$ such that for any formula α of $\mathbf{L}$, the theory contains α or $\neg\alpha$. A theory is *finite* if the consequence relation $\vdash$ partitions its elements into a finite number of equivalence classes. The *dual atoms* for a finite theory T are those nontautological elements $\alpha \in T$ such that for all $\beta \in \mathrm{Cn}(\{\alpha\})$, either $\vdash \beta$ or $\vdash \alpha \equiv \beta$ [12]. We define $\mathbf{L}^{\bowtie}$ to be the set of consistent nontautological formulae in $\mathbf{L}$.

We introduce the following notation: $\mathcal{K}_{\mathbf{L}}$ is the set of all theories of $\mathbf{L}$, and Θ_L is the set of all consistent complete theories of $\mathbf{L}$. If α is a formula of $\mathbf{L}$, define $[\alpha]$ to be the set of all consistent complete theories of $\mathbf{L}$ containing α. If α is inconsistent, then $[\alpha] = \emptyset$, and if $\vdash \alpha$, then $[\alpha] = \Theta_L$.

In the AGM paradigm knowledge sets [4] are taken to be theories, and informational changes are therefore regarded as transformations on theories. There are three principal types of AGM transformations; expansion, contraction and revision. These transformations allow us to model changes of information based on the *principle of minimal change*. Expansion is the simplest change, it models the incorporation of a formula. More formally, the *expansion* of a theory T with respect to a formula α, denoted as T_α^+, is defined to be the logical closure of T and α, that is $T_\alpha^+ = \mathrm{Cn}(T \cup \{\alpha\})$.

A *contraction* of T with respect to α, T_α^-, involves the removal of a set of formulae from T so that α is no longer implied. Formally, a *well-behaved contraction operator* $^-$ is any function from $\mathcal{K}_{\mathbf{L}} \times \mathbf{L}$ to $\mathcal{K}_{\mathbf{L}}$, mapping (T, α) to T_α^- which satisfies the postulates $(^-1)$ – $(^-9)$, below. We define a *very well-behaved contraction operator* $^-$ to be a well-behaved contraction operator that satisfies the postulate $(^-10)$, below.

($^-$1) For any $\alpha \in \mathbf{L}$ and any $T \in \mathcal{K}_{\mathbf{L}}$, $T_\alpha^- \in \mathcal{K}_{\mathbf{L}}$
($^-$2) $T_\alpha^- \subseteq T$
($^-$3) If $\alpha \notin T$ then $T_\alpha^- = T$
($^-$4) If $\not\vdash \alpha$ then $\alpha \notin T_\alpha^-$
($^-$5) $T \subseteq (T_\alpha^-)_\alpha^+$
($^-$6) If $\vdash \alpha \equiv \beta$ then $T_\alpha^- = T_\beta^-$
($^-$7) $T_\alpha^- \cap T_\beta^- \subseteq T_{\alpha \wedge \beta}^-$
($^-$8) If $\alpha \notin T_{\alpha \wedge \beta}^-$ then $T_{\alpha \wedge \beta}^- \subseteq T_\alpha^-$
($^-$9) For every nonempty set Γ of nontautological formulae, there exists a formula $\alpha \in \Gamma$ such that $\alpha \notin T_{\alpha \wedge \beta}^-$ for every $\beta \in \Gamma$.
($^-$10) For every nonempty set Γ of nontautological formulae, there exists a formula $\alpha \in \Gamma$ such that $\beta \notin T_{\alpha \wedge \beta}^-$ for every $\beta \in \Gamma$.

A *revision* attempts to transform a theory as "little as possible" in order to incorporate a formula. Formally, a *well-behaved revision operator* * is any function from

$\mathcal{K}_\mathbf{L} \times \mathbf{L}$ to $\mathcal{K}_\mathbf{L}$, mapping (T, α) to T_α^* which satisfies the postulates (*1) – (*9), below. We define a *very well-behaved revision operator* * to be well-behaved revision operator that satisfies the postulate (*10), below.

(*1) For any $\alpha \in \mathbf{L}$ and any $T \in \mathcal{K}_\mathbf{L}$, $T_\alpha^* \in \mathcal{K}_\mathbf{L}$
(*2) $\alpha \in T_\alpha^*$
(*3) $T_\alpha^* \subseteq T_\alpha^+$
(*4) If $\neg \alpha \notin T$ then $T_\alpha^+ \subseteq T_\alpha^*$
(*5) $T_\alpha^* = \perp$ if and only if $\vdash \neg \alpha$
(*6) If $\vdash \alpha \equiv \beta$ then $T_\alpha^* = T_\beta^*$
(*7) $T_{\alpha \wedge \beta}^* \subseteq (T_\alpha^*)_\beta^+$
(*8) If $\neg \beta \notin T_\alpha^*$ then $(T_\alpha^*)_\beta^+ \subseteq T_{\alpha \wedge \beta}^*$
(*9) For every nonempty set Γ of nontautological formulae, there exists a formula $\alpha \in \Gamma$ such that $\alpha \notin T_{\neg \alpha \vee \neg \beta}^*$ for every $\beta \in \Gamma$.
(*10) For every nonempty set Γ of nontautological formulae, there exists a formula $\alpha \in \Gamma$ such that $\beta \notin T_{\neg \alpha \vee \neg \beta}^*$ for every $\beta \in \Gamma$.

The class of well-behaved revision operators was identified by Peppas [10] and shown to be a proper subclass of the class of revision operators satisfying (*1) – (*8). We note that (*9) is not identical with the well-behaved postulate in [10], however the same family of revision operators is obtained.

In the next section we review Spohn's ordinal conditional functions [18] and describe definitions from [18] and Gärdenfors [2].

3 ORDINAL CONDITIONAL FUNCTIONS

Spohn [18] represents a knowledge system as an ordinal conditional function which is defined over possible worlds. We represent possible worlds by consistent complete theories, in [22] we give an analogous analysis based on models as the underlying representation. An ordinal conditional function [18] defines a ranking of its domain which provides a 'response schema for all possible consistent information' [18]. More formally, we have the following definition [18,2].

Definition: An *ordinal conditional function*, OCF, is a function $\mathbf{C}$ from Θ_L, the set of all consistent complete theories, into the class of ordinals such that there is some element of $\Theta_\mathbf{L}$ assigned the smallest ordinal 0. We denote the family of all ordinal conditional functions by $\mathcal{C}$. If $\mathbf{C}$ has a finite range, then we say $\mathbf{C}$ is finite.

Intuitively $\mathbf{C} \in \mathcal{C}$ represents not only a well-ordering, but a *plausibility* grading of possible worlds [2] or a grading of *disbelief* [18], the worlds that are assigned the smallest ordinal are the most plausible.

Definition: *The ordinal assigned to a nonempty set of consistent complete theories* $\Delta \subseteq \Theta_L$ *by an OCF is the smallest ordinal assigned to the elements of* Δ. That is, for $\mathbf{C} \in \mathcal{C}$ we have; $\mathbf{C}(\Delta) = \min(\{\mathbf{C}(K) : K \in \Delta\})$.

Definition: We define the *knowledge set* represented by $\mathbf{C} \in \mathcal{C}$ to be $\text{ks}(\mathbf{C}) = \bigcap \{K \in \Theta_\mathbf{L} : \mathbf{C}(K) = 0\}$.

It is not hard to see that, the knowledge set represented by $\mathbf{C} \in \mathcal{C}$, $\text{ks}(\mathbf{C})$, is always a consistent theory.

Definition: Given a $\mathbf{C} \in \mathcal{C}$, for any nontautological formula α, we say α is *accepted with firmness* $\mathbf{C}([\neg \alpha])$, and call $\mathbf{C}([\neg \alpha])$ the *degree of acceptance of* α. A formula α is *accepted* if and only if $\alpha \in \text{ks}(\mathbf{C})$. If α and β are both accepted then α is more *firmly accepted* than β if and only if either $\mathbf{C}([\neg \alpha]) > \mathbf{C}([\neg \beta])$, or $\vdash \alpha$ and $\nvdash \beta$. More generally, for nontautological formulae α and β not necessarily in $\text{ks}(\mathbf{C})$, α is more *plausible* than β if and only if either $\mathbf{C}([\neg \alpha]) > \mathbf{C}([\neg \beta])$, or $\mathbf{C}([\beta]) > \mathbf{C}([\alpha])$ [2].

The tautologies can be thought of as being assigned to an ordinal greater than all ordinals in the range of $\mathbf{C}$ (since $\mathbf{L}$, and consequently the range of $\mathbf{C}$, is countable such an ordinal exists). In [19] Spohn introduces a *natural conditional function* in which consistent complete theories are assigned a natural number rather than an ordinal, and $\mathbf{C}(\emptyset) = \omega$, hence the degree of acceptance of the tautologies is ω.

3.1 DYNAMICS OF ORDINAL CONDITIONAL FUNCTIONS

Revision and contraction operators take knowledge sets to knowledge sets. In this section we will see that transmutations take knowledge systems to knowledge systems, where a knowledge system is composed of a knowledge set together with a preference relation.

The relationship between Spohn's conditionalization and the AGM paradigm is identified and discussed by Gärdenfors in [2], and it is this relationship that underpins and motivates our approach.

We begin our discussion with a representation result for revision. Theorem 1, below, provides a condition which characterizes a well-behaved and a very well-behaved revision operator, using an OCF and a finite OCF, respectively. Theorems 1 and 2 are based on the work of Grove [6] and Peppas [10].

Theorem 1: Let T be a consistent theory of $\mathbf{L}$. For every well-behaved (very well-behaved) revision operator * for T, there exists a (finite) $\mathbf{C} \in \mathcal{C}$ such that $\text{ks}(\mathbf{C}) = T$, and the condition below, henceforth referred to as ($\mathbf{C}^*$), is true for every $\alpha \in \mathbf{L}$. Conversely, for every (finite) $\mathbf{C} \in \mathcal{C}$ there exists a well-behaved (very well-behaved) revision operator $*$ for ks($\mathbf{C}$) such that the ($\mathbf{C}^*$) condition is true for every $\alpha \in \mathbf{L}$.

$$(ks(\mathbf{C}))^*_\alpha = \begin{cases} \bigcap \{K \in [\alpha] : \mathbf{C}(K) = \mathbf{C}([\alpha])\} & \text{if } \not\vdash \neg\alpha \\ \bot & \text{otherwise} \end{cases}$$

Similarly, Theorem 2, below, provides a condition which captures a well-behaved and a very well-behaved contraction operator using an OCF and a finite OCF, respectively.

Theorem 2: Let T be a consistent theory of $\mathbf{L}$. For every well-behaved (very well-behaved) contraction operator $^-$ for T, there exists a (finite) $\mathbf{C} \in \mathcal{C}$ such that ks($\mathbf{C}$) $= T$, and and the condition below, henceforth referred to as ($\mathbf{C}^-$), is true for every $\alpha \in \mathbf{L}$. Conversely, for every (finite) $\mathbf{C} \in \mathcal{C}$ there exists a well-behaved (very well-behaved) contraction operator $^-$ for ks($\mathbf{C}$) such that the ($\mathbf{C}^-$) condition is true for every $\alpha \in \mathbf{L}$.

$$(ks(\mathbf{C}))^-_\alpha = \bigcap \{K \in \Theta_\mathbf{L} : \text{either } \mathbf{C}(K) = 0 \\ \text{or } K \in [\neg\alpha] \text{ with } \mathbf{C}(K) = \mathbf{C}([\neg\alpha])\}$$

For contraction and revision the informational input is a formula α. We now define a transmutation of OCF's where the informational input is composed of an ordered pair, (Δ, i), that is, a nonempty set of consistent complete theories (worlds) Δ and a degree of acceptance i. The interpretation [2] of this is that Δ is the information to be accepted by the knowledge system, and i is the degree of acceptance with which this information is incorporated into the transmuted knowledge system. Note, for $\Delta \subseteq \Theta_L$ we define $\bar{\Delta}$ to be the complement of Δ, that is $\bar{\Delta} = \Theta_\mathbf{L} \setminus \Delta$.

Definition:
We define a transmutation schema for OCF's, $*$, to be an operator from $\mathcal{C} \times \{2^{\Theta_\mathbf{L}} \setminus \{\emptyset, \Theta_\mathbf{L}\}\} \times \mathcal{O}$ to $\mathcal{C}$, where $\mathcal{O}$ is an ordinal, such that $(\mathbf{C}, \Delta, i) \mapsto \mathbf{C}^*(\Delta, i)$ which satisfies:

(i) $\mathbf{C}^*(\Delta, i)(\bar{\Delta}) = i$, and

(ii) ks($\mathbf{C}^*(\Delta, i)$) $=$
$$\begin{cases} \bigcap \{K \in \Delta : \mathbf{C}(K) = \mathbf{C}(\Delta)\} & \text{if } i > 0 \\ \bigcap \{K \in \Theta_\mathbf{L} : \text{either } \mathbf{C}(K) = 0, \\ \quad \text{or } K \in \bar{\Delta} \text{ with } \mathbf{C}(K) = \mathbf{C}(\bar{\Delta})\} & \text{otherwise.} \end{cases}$$

We say $\mathbf{C}^*(\Delta, i)$ is a (Δ, i)-transmutation of $\mathbf{C}$. The definition excludes a transmutation with respect to an empty set of worlds, hence a contradiction is not acceptable information.

It is not hard to see that, for $i > 0$ and a nontautological consistent formula α, an $([\alpha], i)$-transmutation of $\mathbf{C}$ is an OCF in which the 'smallest' worlds in $[\alpha]$ are mapped to zero and the 'smallest' world in $[\neg\alpha]$ is mapped to i. Hence the knowledge set represented by the transmuted knowledge system is equivalent to the revised knowledge set $(ks(\mathbf{C}))^*_\alpha$, via ($\mathbf{C}^*$). Similarly, in view of Theorem 2, we have that, a contraction of $(ks(\mathbf{C}))^-_\alpha$ can be modeled by an $([\alpha], 0)$-transmutation of $\mathbf{C}$, where the 'smallest' $[\neg\alpha]$ worlds are assigned zero, and hence $[\alpha]$ is no longer accepted, in other words, $[\alpha]$ is 'neutralized' [18].

Rumelhart and Norman [14] distinguish three modes of learning; accretion, tuning, and restructuring. Accretion involves the expansion of episodic memory without changing semantic memory, and tuning involves revision of semantic memory in order to accommodate new information. Restructuring involves major reorganization of semantic memory. According to Sowa [17, p331] restructuring takes place when a knowledge system attains new insight, and a 'revolution' takes place that repackages old information. In the following definition we define a restructuring of an OCF, as a reorganization of accepted information.

Definition: Let $\mathbf{C}$ be an OCF, and let Δ be a nonempty, proper subset of $\Theta_\mathbf{L}$ such that $\mathbf{C}(\bar{\Delta}) > 0$. If i is a nonzero ordinal, then we refer to a (Δ, i)-transmutation of $\mathbf{C}$ as a *restructuring*.

A restructuring is discussed by both Spohn [18] and Gärdenfors [2]. In our terminology whenever a (Δ, i)-transmutation of $\mathbf{C}$ is a restructuring, if $i > \mathbf{C}(\bar{\Delta}) > 0$, then the knowledge system has additional reason for accepting Δ, and its firmness is increased, that is, strengthened. On the other hand, if $\mathbf{C}(\bar{\Delta}) > i > 0$, then the knowledge system has reduced reason for accepting Δ, and its firmness is decreased, that is, weakened.

The imposing problem for iterated revision is; how are the worlds ordered after a revision, or a contraction. Spohn [18] considers that it might be that after information Δ is accepted, all possible worlds in Δ are less disbelieved than worlds in $\bar{\Delta}$. The result of such a transmutation would be that the knowledge system has overwhelming confidence in Δ, however knowledge systems must also be capable of accepting information with less confidence.

Spohn [18] has argued that conditionalization, defined below, is a desirable transmutation, for instance it is reversible (that is, there is an inverse conditionalization) and commutative. Intuitively, conditionalization means that becoming informed about Δ, a proper and nonempty subset of $\Theta_\mathbf{L}$, does not change the grading of disbelief restricted to either Δ or $\bar{\Delta}$, rather the worlds in Δ and $\bar{\Delta}$ are shifted in relation to one another [2], and this Spohn argues is reasonable, since becoming informed only about Δ should not change $\mathbf{C}$ restricted to Δ, or $\mathbf{C}$ restricted to $\bar{\Delta}$. The construction in Theorem 3 is based on *left-sided subtraction* of ordinals that is, for $i \leq j$; $-i + j$ is the uniquely determined ordinal k such that $i + k = j$.

Theorem 3: For $\Delta \subset \Theta_\mathbf{L}$, $\Delta \neq \emptyset$, and i an ordinal, $\mathbf{C}^*(\Delta, i)$, defined below, is a (Δ, i)-transmutation of $\mathbf{C}$. We refer to this transmutation as the (Δ, i)-conditionalization of $\mathbf{C}$.

$$\mathbf{C}^*(\Delta, i)(K) = \begin{cases} -\mathbf{C}(\Delta) + \mathbf{C}(K) & \text{if } K \in \Delta \\ -\mathbf{C}(\bar{\Delta}) + \mathbf{C}(K) + i & \text{otherwise} \end{cases}$$

The (Δ, i)-conditionalization of $\mathbf{C}$ is the combination of $\mathbf{C}$ restricted to Δ left unaltered, and $\mathbf{C}$ restricted to $\bar{\Delta}$ shifted up i grades [18].

A property enjoyed by conditionalization is that any transmutation of $\mathbf{C}$, where the underlying language is finitary, can be achieved by a finite sequence of conditionalizations. This is seen by observing, that for a $K \in \Theta_\mathbf{L}$ such that $\mathbf{C}(K) > 0$, $\mathbf{C}^*(\overline{\{K\}}, i)$ assigns the consistent complete theory K the ordinal i and assigns $\mathbf{C}(K')$ to each of the worlds $K' \in \overline{\{K\}}$.

We now explore another transmutation, an adjustment, in which only the least disbelieved worlds containing the information the knowledge system is accepting are reassigned zero. Intuitively, an adjustment is a transmutation which is commanded by the principle of minimal change, that is, an OCF is changed or disturbed 'as little as necessary' so as to accept the information with the desired degree of acceptance. In other words, as much structure of the OCF persists after the adjustment as possible.

Theorem 4: For $\Delta \subset \Theta_\mathbf{L}$, $\Delta \neq \emptyset$, and i an ordinal, $\mathbf{C}^*(\Delta, i)$, where * is defined below, is a (Δ, i)-transmutation of $\mathbf{C}$. We refer to this transmutation as the (Δ, i)-adjustment of $\mathbf{C}$.

$$\mathbf{C}^*(\Delta, i) = \begin{cases} \mathbf{C}^-(\Delta) & \text{if } i = 0 \\ (\mathbf{C}^-(\Delta))^\times(\Delta, i) & \text{if } 0 < i < \mathbf{C}(\bar{\Delta}) \\ \mathbf{C}^\times(\Delta, i) & \text{otherwise} \end{cases}$$

where

$$\mathbf{C}^-(\Delta)(K) = \begin{cases} 0 & \text{if } K \in \bar{\Delta} \text{ and } \mathbf{C}(K) = \mathbf{C}(\bar{\Delta}) \\ \mathbf{C}(K) & \text{otherwise} \end{cases}$$

$$\mathbf{C}^\times(\Delta, i)(K) = \begin{cases} 0 & \text{if } K \in \Delta \text{ and } \mathbf{C}(K) = \mathbf{C}(\Delta) \\ \mathbf{C}(K) & \text{if either } K \in \Delta \text{ and } \mathbf{C}(K) \neq \mathbf{C}(\Delta), \\ & \text{or } K \in \bar{\Delta} \text{ and } \mathbf{C}(K) > i \\ i & \text{otherwise} \end{cases}$$

Essentially, $\mathbf{C}^-(\Delta)$ models the contraction of Δ, and is used for (Δ, i)-transmutations where Δ is accepted, and $\mathbf{C}(\bar{\Delta}) > i$, that is, a restructuring where Δ's firmness is decreased.

We are not advocating that adjustment is a more desirable transmutation than conditionalization, however in [21] we have shown that it lends itself to theory base transmutations. It can also be shown that in a finitary language, we can find a sequence of adjustments which will result in an arbitrary transmutation. For instance, an adjustment can be used to reassign all but one consistent complete theory, say $K_1 \in \Theta_\mathbf{L}$ where $\mathbf{C}(\{K_1\}) = 0$ to the largest desired ordinal, say k, by $\mathbf{C}^*(\{K_1\}, k)$. Then grade by grade the remainder $\overline{\{K_1\}}$ can be assigned the desired ordinal, for instance $(\mathbf{C}^*(\{K_1\}, k))^*(\{K_1 \cup K_2\}, j)$ assigns K_1 to 0, K_2 to k, and $\Theta_\mathbf{L} \backslash \{K_1 \cup K_2\}$ to j. Continuing in this way, $((\mathbf{C}^*(\{K_1\}, k))^*(\{K_1 \cup K_2\}, j))^*(\{K_1 \cup K_2 \cup K_3\}, i)$ assigns K_1 to 0, K_2 to k, K_3 to j, and $\Theta_\mathbf{L} \backslash \{K_1 \cup K_2 \cup K_3\}$ to i. This process can be continued until all $K_i \in \Theta_\mathbf{L}$ are assigned their desired ordinal.

As noted earlier any transmutation where the underlying language is finitary can be achieved by a finite sequence of conditionalizations, therefore a sequence of conditionalizations can be used to effect an adjustment, and conversely.

One view of the difference between conditionalization and adjustment is that in order to accomodate the desired informational change, conditionalization preserves the *relative* gradings of $\mathbf{C}$ restricted to Δ and $\bar{\Delta}$, whilst adjustment minimizes changes to the *absolute* gradings $\mathbf{C}$ as a whole. Adjustments are discussed further in Section 6.

4 ORDINAL EPISTEMIC ENTRENCHMENT FUNCTIONS

Intuitively, an ordinal epistemic entrenchment function maps the formulae in a language to the ordinals, the higher the ordinal assigned the more firmly it is held. Throughout the remainder of this paper it will be understood that $\mathcal{O}$ is an ordinal chosen to be sufficiently large for the purpose of the discussion. We now formally define an ordinal epistemic entrenchment function.

Definition: An *ordinal epistemic entrenchment function*, OEF, is a function $\mathbf{E}$ from the formulae in $\mathbf{L}$ into the class of ordinals such that the following conditions are satisfied.
  (OEF1) For all $\alpha, \beta \in \mathbf{L}$, if $\alpha \vdash \beta$, then $\mathbf{E}(\alpha) \leq \mathbf{E}(\beta)$.
  (OEF2) For all $\alpha, \beta \in \mathbf{L}$, $\mathbf{E}(\alpha) \leq \mathbf{E}(\alpha \wedge \beta)$ or $\mathbf{E}(\beta) \leq \mathbf{E}(\alpha \wedge \beta)$.
  (OEF3) $\vdash \alpha$ if and only if $\mathbf{E}(\alpha) = \mathcal{O}$.
  (OEF4) If α is inconsistent, then $\mathbf{E}(\alpha) = 0$.

Intuitively, $\mathbf{E}$ represents an *epistemic entrenchment* [2,4] grading of formulae; the higher the ordinal assigned to a formula the more entrenched that formula is. Whenever the codomain of $\mathbf{E}$ is ω (c.f. Spohn's natural conditional functions [19]), then we can, and will, take $\mathbf{E}(\alpha) = \omega$ for all $\vdash \alpha$. If $\mathbf{E}$ has a finite range, then we say $\mathbf{E}$ is finite.

Definition:
We denote the family of all ordinal epistemic entrenchment functions to be $\mathcal{E}$. The *knowledge set* represented by $\mathbf{E} \in \mathcal{E}$ is $\mathrm{ks}(\mathbf{E}) = \{\alpha \in \mathbf{L} : \mathbf{E}(\alpha) > 0\}$.

Definition: Given an $\mathbf{E} \in \mathcal{E}$, for any formula α we say α is accepted with firmness $\mathbf{E}(\alpha)$, and call $\mathbf{E}(\alpha)$ the *degree of acceptance of* α. A formula α is *accepted* if and only if $\alpha \in \mathrm{ks}(\mathbf{E})$. If α and β are both accepted, then α is more *firmly accepted* than β if and only if $\mathbf{E}(\alpha) > \mathbf{E}(\beta)$. More generally, for formulae α and β not necessarily in $\mathrm{ks}(\mathbf{E})$, α is more *plausible* than β if and only if either $\mathbf{E}(\alpha) > \mathbf{E}(\beta)$, or $\mathbf{E}(\neg\beta) > \mathbf{E}(\neg\alpha)$.

A knowledge set, $\mathrm{ks}(\mathbf{E})$, is the set of accepted formulae and is always consistent. Gärdenfors and Makinson [4] have shown that for a finitary language an epistemic entrenchment ordering is determined by its dual atoms. Similarly, we can describe an OEF for a finite language by assigning an ordinal to each dual atom. The ordinal assigned to all other formulae in $\mathbf{L}$ is then uniquely determined by (OEF1) – (OEF4).

4.1 DYNAMICS OF ORDINAL EPISTEMIC ENTRENCHMENT FUNCTIONS

In this section we discuss the dynamics of ordinal epistemic entrenchment functions, in particular we discuss their revisions, contractions, and transmutations.

In Theorems 5 and 6 we establish several conditions which characterize well-behaved and very well-behaved revision and contraction operators, using OEF's and finite OEF's, respectively. These results are based on the work of Gärdenfors and Makinson in [4].

Theorem 5: Let T be a consistent theory of $\mathbf{L}$. For every well-behaved (very well-behaved) revision operator $*$ for T, there exists an (finite) $\mathbf{E} \in \mathcal{E}$, such that $\mathrm{ks}(\mathbf{E}) = T$ and the condition below, henceforth referred to as ($\mathbf{E}^*$), is true for every $\alpha \in \mathbf{L}$. Conversely, for every (finite) $\mathbf{E} \in \mathcal{E}$ there exists a well-behaved (very well-behaved) revision operator $*$ for $\mathrm{ks}(\mathbf{E})$ such that the ($\mathbf{E}^*$) condition is true for every $\alpha \in \mathbf{L}$.

$$(\mathrm{ks}(\mathbf{E}))^*_\alpha = \begin{cases} \{\beta \in \mathbf{L} : \mathbf{E}(\neg\alpha) < \mathbf{E}(\neg\alpha \vee \beta)\} & \text{if } \not\vdash \neg\alpha \\ \bot & \text{otherwise} \end{cases}$$

Theorem 6: Let T be a consistent theory of $\mathbf{L}$. For every well-behaved (very well-behaved) contraction operator $^-$ for T, there exists an (finite) $\mathbf{E} \in \mathcal{E}$ such that $\mathrm{ks}(\mathbf{E}) = T$, and the condition below, henceforth referred to as ($\mathbf{E}^-$), is true for every $\alpha \in \mathbf{L}$. Conversely, for every (finite) $\mathbf{E} \in \mathcal{E}$ there exists a well-behaved (very well-behaved) contraction operator $^-$ for $\mathrm{ks}(\mathbf{E})$ such that the ($\mathbf{E}^-$) condition is true for every $\alpha \in \mathbf{L}$.

$$(\mathrm{ks}(\mathbf{E}))^-_\alpha = \begin{cases} \{\beta \in \mathrm{ks}(\mathbf{E}) : \mathbf{E}(\alpha) < \mathbf{E}(\alpha \vee \beta)\} & \text{if } \not\vdash \alpha \\ \mathrm{ks}(\mathbf{E}) & \text{otherwise} \end{cases}$$

The conditions ($\mathbf{E}^*$), and ($\mathbf{E}^-$) determine a new knowledge set when a formula α is incorporated or removed, however these conditions do not determine another OEF, upon which a subsequent revision, or contraction could be specified. According to Rott [12] it is not theories that have to be revised but epistemic entrenchment orderings. The definition below describes a transmutation of an OEF into another OEF, such that a nontautological consistent formula α is accepted with degree i.

Definition: We define a transmutation schema for OEF's, $\star$, to be an operator from $\mathcal{E} \times \mathbf{L}^{\bowtie} \times \mathcal{O}$ to $\mathcal{E}$, where $\mathbf{L}^{\bowtie}$ is the set of consistent nontautological formulae in $\mathbf{L}$, and $i < \mathcal{O}$, such that $(\mathbf{E}, \alpha, i) \mapsto \mathbf{E}^\star(\alpha, i)$ satisfies:

(i) $\mathbf{E}^\star(\alpha, i)(\alpha) = i$, and

(ii) $\text{ks}(\mathbf{E}^\star(\alpha, i)) =$
$$\begin{cases} \{\beta \in \mathbf{L} : \mathbf{E}(\neg\alpha) < \mathbf{E}(\neg\alpha \vee \beta)\} & \text{if } i > 0 \\ \{\beta \in \text{ks}(\mathbf{E}) : \mathbf{E}(\alpha) < \mathbf{E}(\alpha \vee \beta)\} & \text{otherwise} \end{cases}$$

We say $\mathbf{E}^\star(\alpha, i)$ is an (α, i)-transmutation of $\mathbf{E}$. A transmutation is not defined with respect to tautological, or inconsistent formulae. An OEF is incapable of representing an inconsistent knowledge set, therefore we should not expect a transmutation of a knowledge system to accept inconsistent information.

Intuitively, for a nontautological consistent formula α, a transmutation $\mathbf{E}^\star(\alpha, i)$, is an OEF where $\text{ks}(\mathbf{E}^\star(\alpha, i))$ represents a 'minimal change' of the knowledge set represented by $\mathbf{E}$, that is $\text{ks}(\mathbf{E})$, and α is assigned the degree of acceptance i.

In the following definition we define a restructuring of an OEF, as a reorganization of accepted information.

Definition: Let $\alpha \in \mathbf{L}^{\bowtie}$, and let $\mathbf{E}$ be an OEF, where α is accepted, that is, $\mathbf{E}(\alpha) > 0$. If i is an ordinal such that $0 < i < \mathcal{O}$, then we refer to a (α, i)-transmutation of $\mathbf{E}$ as a *restructuring*.

Theorems 7 and 8, below, establish that conditionalization and adjustment of OEF's, respectively, are transmutations.

Theorem 7: Let $\mathbf{L}$ be a finitary language, let $\mathbf{E} \in \mathcal{E}$, let i be an ordinal such that $i < \mathcal{O}$, and let $\alpha \in \mathbf{L}^{\bowtie}$. Then $\mathbf{E}^\star(\alpha, i)$ defined below, is an (α, i)-transmutation of $\mathbf{E}$. We refer to this transmutation as the (α, i)-conditionalization of $\mathbf{E}$.

$$\mathbf{E}^\star(\alpha, i)(\beta) = \begin{cases} -\mathbf{E}(\neg\alpha) + \mathbf{E}(\beta) & \text{if } \alpha \wedge \neg\beta \not\vdash \bot \\ -\mathbf{E}(\alpha) + \mathbf{E}(\beta) + i & \text{otherwise,} \end{cases}$$

where $\beta \in \mathbf{L}$ is a dual atom.

Theorem 8: Let $\mathbf{E} \in \mathcal{E}$, let i be an ordinal such that $i < \mathcal{O}$, and let $\alpha \in \mathbf{L}^{\bowtie}$. Then $\mathbf{E}^\star(\alpha, i)$, where $\star$ is defined below, is an (α, i)-transmutation of $\mathbf{E}$. We refer to this transmutation as the (α, i)-adjustment of $\mathbf{E}$.

$$\mathbf{E}^\star(\alpha, i) = \begin{cases} \mathbf{E}^-(\alpha) & \text{if } i = 0 \\ (\mathbf{E}^-(\alpha))^\times(\alpha, i) & \text{if } 0 < i < \mathbf{E}(\alpha) \\ \mathbf{E}^\times(\alpha, i) & \text{otherwise} \end{cases}$$

where,

$$\mathbf{E}^-(\alpha)(\beta) = \begin{cases} 0 & \text{if } \mathbf{E}(\alpha) = \mathbf{E}(\alpha \vee \beta) \\ \mathbf{E}(\beta) & \text{otherwise} \end{cases}$$

$$\mathbf{E}^\times(\alpha, i)(\beta) = \begin{cases} 0 & \text{if } \mathbf{E}(\neg\alpha) = \mathbf{E}(\neg\alpha \vee \beta) \\ \mathbf{E}(\beta) & \text{if } \mathbf{E}(\neg\alpha) < \mathbf{E}(\neg\alpha \vee \beta) \\ & \text{and } \mathbf{E}(\beta) > i \\ i & \text{if } \mathbf{E}(\neg\alpha) < \mathbf{E}(\neg\alpha \vee \beta) \\ & \text{and} \\ & \mathbf{E}(\beta) \leq i < \mathbf{E}(\neg\alpha \vee \beta) \\ \mathbf{E}(\neg\alpha \vee \beta) & \text{otherwise} \end{cases}$$

Both conditionalizations and adjustments are transmutations of OEF's, however unlike a conditionalization, an adjustment does not refer to the dual atoms in the theory and is therefore more general in that it can be used on arbitrary languages rather than just finitary ones. Moreover, adjustments have been shown [21] to be very easily adapted to theory base transmutations based on ensconcements [20].

We note however, for a finitary language, as in the case of an OCF, an individual dual atom can be assigned a firmness, say i, without changing the firmness of any other dual atom using both conditionalization and adjustment. Therefore it can be shown that any transmutation of an OEF in a finitary language, can be achieved by a finite sequence of conditionalizations or adjustments.

Intuitively, an (α, i)-adjustment of $\mathbf{E}$ is a transmutation that minimizes the changes to $\mathbf{E}$ so that a formula α is accepted with firmness i. Computationally, the process of adjustment is straightforward [20], and whenever the change is not maxichoice [1,2] less explicit information is required than is the case for conditionalization.

Adjustments $\mathbf{E}^\star(\alpha, i)$ possess an interesting property in that, all the accepted formulae of $\mathbf{E}$ which are held more firmly than $\max(\{i, \mathbf{E}(\neg\alpha), \mathbf{E}(\alpha)\})$ are retained and not reassigned a different ordinal during the transmutation $\star$. This behaviour is intuitively appealing, since we would not expect a transmutation which affects weakly held information such as *a goldfish is blocking the main pump*, to change the degree of acceptance of more firmly held information, such as *if main pump is blocked, then the temperature will rise*.

In general the knowledge system will lose *granularity* during an adjustment, in the sense that the only way to increase granularity is to assign α an ordinal to which no other formula is assigned, and not merge any existing grades. The granularity can be increased at most by one grade in this manner.

In contradistinction, during a conditionalization the granularity of the knowledge system can be increased substantially, more precisely the number of grades could be doubled.

A shortcoming of adjustments is that all formulae β such that $\mathbf{E}(\beta) \leq i$, are assigned $\mathbf{E}(\neg\alpha \vee \beta)$ after an (α, i)-adjustment, which may not be desirable. If formulae are being accepted and contracted on the *fringe*, that is when i is close to zero, then this is not likely to be a significant problem. Perhaps adjustment could be used to accept and contract information until it becomes necessary for the knowledge system to reorganize its knowledge, that is undergo a restructuring, in which case a more sophisticated mechanism might be required. In the finitary case a series of conditionalizations and/or adjustments could be applied.

In the next section we formalize the relationship between OCF's and OEF's such that their adjustments and conditionalizations are equivalent.

5 TRANSLATIONS

In this section we give explicit conditions which capture the relationship between an OCF, and an OEF such that they represent the same knowledge set, and possess the same dynamic behaviour with respect to contraction, revision, and transmutation. In order to establish relationships between OCF's and OEF's we define what we mean by their similarity in the definition below.

Definition:
We say $\mathbf{E} \in \mathcal{E}$ and $\mathbf{C} \in \mathcal{C}$ are *similiar* whenever the following condition is satisfied for all nontautological formulae $\alpha, \beta \in \mathbf{L}$:

$\mathbf{E}(\alpha) \leq \mathbf{E}(\beta)$ if and only if $\mathbf{C}([\neg\alpha]) \leq \mathbf{C}([\neg\beta])$.

Intuitively, $\mathbf{E}$ and $\mathbf{C}$ are similar if and only if for all nontautological formulae α, β, it is the case that α is at least as firmly accepted as β with respect to both $\mathbf{E}$ and $\mathbf{C}$.

The following theorem follows from the work of Grove [6] and Gärdenfors [2], in particular, it is based on the relationship between an epistemic entrenchment ordering and a system of spheres. It says that, if the ordinal functions $\mathbf{C}$ and $\mathbf{E}$ are similar, then their transmuted knowledge sets are equivalent.

Theorem 9: Let $\alpha \in \mathbf{L}^{\bowtie}$ and let i be an ordinal such that $i < \mathcal{O}$. Let $\star$ be a transmutation schema for OCF's. Let $\star$ be a transmutation schema for OEF's. For $\mathbf{E} \in \mathcal{E}$ and $\mathbf{C} \in \mathcal{C}$, $\text{ks}(\mathbf{E}^\star(\alpha, i)) = \text{ks}(\mathbf{C}^*([\alpha], i))$ for all $i < \mathcal{O}$ if and only if $\mathbf{C}$ and $\mathbf{E}$ are similar.

The definition below describes when an OCF and an OEF are equivalent.

Definition: We define $\mathbf{C} \in \mathcal{C}$ and $\mathbf{E} \in \mathcal{E}$ to be *equivalent* if and only if they satisfy the following condition for all nontautological formulae α.

(**EC**) $\mathbf{E}(\alpha) = \mathbf{C}([\neg\alpha])$.

Intuitively, $\mathbf{E}$ and $\mathbf{C}$ are equivalent if and only if all nontautological formulae possesses precisely the same degree of acceptance with respect to both $\mathbf{E}$ and $\mathbf{C}$. Clearly, if $\mathbf{C}$ and $\mathbf{E}$ are equivalent then they are similar. Hence we obtain the following corollary, which says that, if the ordinal functions $\mathbf{C}$ and $\mathbf{E}$ are equivalent, then their transmuted knowledge sets are equivalent.

Corollary 10: Let $\alpha \in \mathbf{L}^{\bowtie}$ and let i be an ordinal such that $i < \mathcal{O}$. Let $\star$ be a transmutation schema for OCF's. Let $\star$ be a transmutation schema for OEF's. If (**EC**) holds for $\mathbf{E} \in \mathcal{E}$ and $\mathbf{C} \in \mathcal{C}$, then $\text{ks}(\mathbf{E}^\star(\alpha, i)) = \text{ks}(\mathbf{C}^*([\alpha], i))$.

The definition below describes when transmutations for an OCF and an OEF are equivalent.

Definition: Given a transmutation schema $\star$ on OCF's, and a transmutation schema $\star$ on OEF's, we define $\mathbf{C} \in \mathcal{C}$ and $\mathbf{E} \in \mathcal{E}$ to be *equivalent with respect to $\star$ and $\star$* if and only if they satisfy the following condition for all nontautological, consistent formulae α and β, and all ordinals $i < \mathcal{O}$.

($\mathbf{E}^\star \mathbf{C}^*$) $\mathbf{E}^\star(\alpha, i)(\beta) = \mathbf{C}^*([\alpha], i)([\neg\beta])$.

Intuitively, an OEF, $\mathbf{E}$, and an OCF, $\mathbf{C}$, are equivalent with respect to $\star$ and $\star$ if and only if all nontautological formulae possess exactly the same degree of acceptance in the ordinal functions, $\mathbf{E}^\star(\alpha, i)$ and $\mathbf{C}^*([\alpha], i)$, after every possible transmutation.

In the following theorems we show if $\mathbf{E}$ and $\mathbf{C}$ are equivalent then both their conditionalizations and their adjustments are equivalent, that is, (**EC**) implies ($\mathbf{E}^\star \mathbf{C}^*$), and conversely.

Theorem 11: Let $\mathbf{L}$ be a finitary language. Let $\mathbf{C} \in \mathcal{C}$, and $\mathbf{E} \in \mathcal{E}$. Given a conditionalization $\star$ on OCF's, and a conditionalization $\star$ on OEF's, (**EC**) holds for

C and **E** if and only if ($\mathbf{E}^\star\mathbf{C}^*$) holds for $\mathbf{E}^\star(\alpha, i)$ and $\mathbf{C}^*([\alpha], i)$, for all nontautological consistent formulae α, and all ordinals $i < \mathcal{O}$.

Theorem 12: Let $\mathbf{C} \in \mathcal{C}$, and $\mathbf{E} \in \mathcal{E}$. Given an adjustment * on OCF's, and an adjustment ⋆ on OEF's, (**EC**) holds for **C** and **E** if and only if ($\mathbf{E}^\star\mathbf{C}^*$) holds for $\mathbf{E}^\star(\alpha, i)$ and $\mathbf{C}^*([\alpha], i)$, for all nontautological consistent formulae α, and all ordinals $i < \mathcal{O}$.

6 RELATED WORK

Various approaches to the iterated revision problem other than Spohn's have been explored, we briefly compare and contrast some of them. Schlechta [15] describes a *preference relation* on **L**, from which an epistemic entrenchment can be derived for each knowledge set, he also provides a means of naturally constructing this preference relation from a probability distribution. Hansson [8], using what he calls *superselectors*, develops a more general account of the AGM paradigm. A superselector can be construed to be a function that assigns a selection function [1,2], to sets of formulae or theory bases. Rott uses a *generalized epistemic entrenchment* [13], from which a family of revision and contraction operators can be derived, one for every theory in the language.

These approaches, with the exception of Hansson's, associate a preference relation with a theory which means that the dynamical behaviour of a given theory is fixed. Therefore an informational restructure is not naturally supported. The fundamental reason for this is that in contrast to Spohn's approach, a formula is the only informational input, consequently the resulting knowledge set is constructed regardless of the evidential strength of the informational input.

Other forms of informational input have been used, in particular, Spohn [18] has described the conditionalization of an OCF by another OCF which embodies the new evidence, and Nayak [9] describes a mechanism for incorporating an epistemic entrenchment ordering representing new evidence, into another epistemic entrenchment ordering.

Spohn [18] has observed that OCF's are related to degrees of potential surprize [16], and in view of the translation conditions described in Section 5 so too are OEF's. According to Shackle [16, p80] surprize, is a function from a field of propositions into a closed interval [0, 1] such that for all propositions $\Delta, \Psi \in 2^{\Theta_\mathbf{L}}$ the following are satisfied:

- surprize($\emptyset$) = 1.
- either surprize(Δ) = 0, or surprize($\bar{\Delta}$) = 0.
- surprize($\Delta \cup \Psi$) = min({surprize(Δ), surprize(Ψ)}).

The maximal degree of potential surprize is 1. The major difference with OCF's for instance is that there is no need for a maximal degree of firmness, but recall that Spohn later used a natural conditional function whose maximal degree of firmness is ω. Spohn notes that Shackle does not present a transmutation schema for potential surprize. However it is not hard to see that the transmutations of OCF's could be used for such a purpose.

Transmutations have been used [24] to support Spohn's notion of 'reason for', which can be specified [18, 3] by:

α is a *reason for* β if and only if raising the epistemic rank of α would raise the epistemic rank of β.

Clearly, this condition can be expressed using the degree of acceptance, such a notion of 'reason for' will be dependent on the particular transmutation employed. In [24] Williams et al. have provided a simple condition which captures 'reason for' when adjustments are used as the underlying transmutation. Furthermore, they use adjustments to determine the relative plausibility of alternative explanations, based on the principle that one would expect a *best* explanation to be one that increases the degree of acceptance of the expanandum at least as much as any other explanation.

Transmutations for theory bases based on ensconcements [20] have been investigated by Williams in [21]. In particular, a *partial* OEF is used to specify a theory base and its associated preference relation. A partial OEF can be used to implicitly capture an OEF, on which theory transmutations could be used. Alternatively, one can specify transmutations for them using only the explicit information they represent. Both of these approaches are used in [21]. It turns out that adjustments are straightforward transmutations for theory bases. In addition, Williams [23] recasts Spohn's 'reason for' in a theory base setting by using adjustments of partial OEF's.

7 DISCUSSION

We have explored transmutations of knowledge systems, by considering not only how the knowledge set is revised, but how the underlying preference structure for the knowledge system is revised, or more precisely transmuted.

We have provided representation results for well-behaved and very well-behaved theory change operators. In particular, transmuted knowledge sets of OCF's, and OEF's, characterize well-behaved contraction, and well-behaved revision within the AGM paradigm. Furthermore, transmutations of finite OCF's, and finite OEF's, characterize very well-behaved contraction, and very well-behaved revision operators. For a finitary language all OCF's and OEF's will be finite and consequently the transmutations representing revision and contraction will be very well-behaved.

We have provided explicit and perspicuous conditions which capture the relationship between OCF's, and OEF's. These conditions can be used to construct each of these structures from the other, such that the knowledge set and its dynamical properties are preserved.

We have also provided an explicit condition which relates the transmutations on OCF's, and OEF's, and moreover we showed that both conditionalizations and adjustments satisfy this condition.

Since any transmutation of a knowledge system in a finitary language can be achieved by a sequence of conditionalizations or adjustments of OCF's, or OEF's, they provide a powerful mechanism for supporting the computer-based implementation of a knowledge system transmutation. With judicious modularization of suitable applications parallel processing could be adopted, since the reassignment of ordinals for each consistent complete theory (or dual atom) is determined by its compatibility with the new information, and is completely independent of the compatibility with other consistent complete theories (or dual atoms).

We would expect that for a given application, domain constraints could be used to identify consistent complete theories representing possible world states which are so inconceivable as to always be assigned very remote grades or 'large' ordinals.

If the underlying preference structure of a knowledge system is an OCF then model checking [6] can be used to implement transmutations. Alternatively, if the underlying preference structure is an OEF, then theorem proving techniques can be used to support the implementation.

Acknowledgements

The author gratefully acknowledges, Peter Gärdenfors for drawing her attention to the work of Spohn, and suggesting how it might be used, and David Makinson for pointing out other relevant results, namely those of Schlechta and Rott. The author has benefited from discussions with Norman Foo, Pavlos Peppas, Maurice Pagnucco and Brailey Sims, thanks guys!

References

1. Alchouron, C., Gärdenfors, P., Makinson, D., *On the logic of theory change: Partial meet functions for contraction and revision*, Journal of Symbolic Logic, 50: 510-530, 1985.

2. Gärdenfors, P., *Knowledge in flux: Modeling the dynamics of epistemic states*, A Bradford Book, MIT Press, Cambridge Massachusetts, 1988.

3. Gärdenfors, P., *The dynamics of belief systems: Foundations vs. coherence theories*, Revue Internationale de Philosophie 44: 24 – 46, 1990.

4. Gärdenfors, P., and Makinson, D., *Revisions of knowledge systems using epistemic entrenchment*, in the proceedings of the Second Conference on Theoretical Aspects of Reasoning about Knowledge, M. Vardi (ed), Morgan Kaufmann, 1988.

5. Gärdenfors, P., and Rott, H., *Belief revision*, Chapter 4.2 in the Handbook of Logic in AI and Logic Programming, Volume IV: Epistemic and Temporal Reasoning, D. Gabbay (ed), Oxford University Press, Oxford, to appear.

6. Grove, A, *Two modellings for theory change*, Journal of Philosophical Logic 17:157 – 170, 1988.

7. Halpern, J.Y. and Vardi, M.Y., *Model checking v.'s theorem proving: A manifesto*, Proceedings of the International Conference on Principles of Knowledge Representation and Reasoning, Morgan Kaufmann, 325 – 334, 1991.

8. Hansson, S. O., *New operators for theory change*, Theoria 55, 114 – 132, 1989.

9. Nayak, A., *Studies in belief change*, Ph. D. Dissertation, Department of Philosophy, University of Rochester, USA, 1993.

10. Peppas, P., *Belief change and reasoning about action: An axiomatic approach to modelling inert dynamic worlds and the connection to the logic of theory change*, PhD Dissertation, University of Sydney, Australia, submitted 1993.

11. Peppas, P., and Williams, M.A., *A Unified View of Constructive Modellings for Revision*, Technical Report No. 431, Department of Computer Science, University of Sydney, 1992.

12. Rott, H., *On the logic of theory change: More maps between different kinds of contraction functions*, in Gärdenfors, P., Belief Revision, Cambridge University Press, 1992.

13. Rott, H., *On the logic of theory change: Partial meet contraction and prioritized base contraction*, Report

27, Zentrum Philosophie and Wissenschaftstheorie, Universität Konstanz, 1992.

14. Rumelhart, D.E., and Norman, D.A., *Accretion, tuning and restructuring: Three modes of learning*, in Cotton, J.W., and Klatzky, R. (eds), Semantic Factors in Cognition, Lawerence Erbaum Associates, Hilldale NJ, 37 – 54.

15. Schlecta, K., *Theory revision and probability*, Notre Dame Journal of Formal Logic, 32, 2: 45 – 78, 1991.

16. Shackle, G.L.S., *Decision, order and time in human affairs*, Cambridge University Press, 1961.

17. Sowa, J.F., *Conceptual structures: Information processing in mind and machine*, The Systems Programming Series, Addison-Wesley Publishing Company, 1984.

18. Spohn, W., *Ordinal conditional functions: A dynamic theory of epistemic states*, In Harper, W.L., and Skyrms, B. (eds), Causation in decision, belief change, and statistics, II, Kluwer Academic Publishers, 105 – 134, 1988.

19. Spohn, W., *A reason for explanation: Explanations provide stable reasons*, In W. Spohn et al. (eds), Existence and Explanation, Kluwer Academic Publishers, 165 – 196, 1991.

20. Williams, M.A., *On the logic of theory change*, Information Systems Research Report, University of Newcastle, 1993. A revised version of a Technical Report, University of Sydney, 1992.

21. Williams, M.A., *Transmutations of theory bases*, Information Systems Research Report, University of Newcastle, 1993. A revised and corrected version of a paper with the same name in the Proceedings of the Australian Joint Artificial Intelligence Conference, 83 – 90, 1993.

22. Williams, M.A., *Transmutations of knowledge systems*, PhD Dissertation, University of Sydney, Australia, submitted 1993.

23. Williams, M.A., *Explanation and theory base transmutations*, Information Systems Research Report, University of Newcastle, 1994.

24. Williams, M.A., Pagnucco, M., Foo, N.Y., and Sims, B., *Determining explanations using knowledge transmutations*, Technical Report, University of Sydney, 1994.

Invited Talks

Knowledge Representation Issues in Integrated Planning and Learning Systems

Jaime G. Carbonell
School of Computer Science
Carnegie Mellon University
Pittsburgh, PA 15213
USA

Abstract

Advances in Machine Learning and in non-linear planning systems in Artificial Intelligence have proceeded somewhat independently of Knowledge Representation issues. In essence, both fields borrow from KR the very essentials (e.g. typed FOL, or simple inheritance methods), and then proceed to address other important issues. However, the increasing sophistication of integrated architectures such as SOAR. PRODIGY and THEO at CMU (that combine problem solving, planning and learning) place new demands on their KR infrastructures. These demands include reasoning about strategic knowledge as well as factual knowledge, supporting representational shifts in domain knowledge, and metareasoning about the system's own reasoning and learning processes. The presentation will focus on the PRODIGY architecture and its needs and implications for KR, especially when these may be in divergence with the primary active topics in modern KR research.

Non-Standard Theories of Uncertainty in Knowledge Representation and Reasoning

Didier Dubois – Henri Prade
Institut de Recherche en Informatique de Toulouse (I.R.I.T.) – C.N.R.S.
Université Paul Sabatier, 118 route de Narbonne
31062 Toulouse Cedex – France

INTRODUCTION

The last 15 years have witnessed a noticeable research effort towards a rational theory of exception-tolerant reasoning. However this research appears very much scattered, partially due to a clash between scientific backgrounds. While probability theory has recently blossomed in this area with the emergence of Bayesian nets, the role of logic and symbolic representations will seemingly continue to be prominent. Besides, the monopoly of probability theory as a tool for modelling uncertainty has been challenged by alternative approaches such as belief functions and possibility theory among others. Current efforts seem to be directed towards the specification of a knowledge representation framework that combines the at first glance incompatible merits of classical logic and Bayesian probability. This paper tries to provide a perspective view of uncertainty models in the scope of exception-tolerant plausible reasoning by stressing some important ideas and problems that have been laid bare, independently of the chosen approach.

1 PLAUSIBLE EXCEPTION-TOLERANT INFERENCE

The problem considered in this paper is at the core of the knowledge-based systems enterprise, namely how to handle the presence of (possibly hidden) exceptions in the rule-base of an expert system. The kind of plausible reasoning that is involved here can be summarized as follows: how to automatically derive plausible conclusions about an incompletely described situation, on the basis of generic knowledge describing what is the normal course of things. For instance, in a medical expert system, generic knowledge encodes what the physician knows about the relationships between symptoms and diseases, and the situation at hand is a given patient on which some test results are available, and plausible inference is supposed to perform a diagnosis task. More generally, this kind of problem can be cast in the setting of taxonomic reasoning, where generic knowledge describe the links between classes and subclasses, and some factual evidence provides an incomplete description of an instance to be classified. The particularity of the problem is that the generic knowledge encoded as a set of rules is pervaded with uncertainty due to the presence of exceptions. Solving this problem in a satisfactory way presupposes that three requirements be met

i) *The necessity of a clear distinction between factual evidence and generic knowledge*. This distinction is fundamental and has been explicitly acknowledged in the expert systems literature at the implementation level (facts versus rules). The generic rules encode a background knowledge that is used to jump to conclusions that the only consideration of the available factual evidence would not allow. Clearly, accounting for the arrival of a new piece of evidence does not produce the same effect as the arrival of a new rule or the mofication of a rule. The arrival of a new piece of evidence does not affect the generic knowledge, but modifies the reference class of the case under study. On the contrary the introduction of a new rule causes a revision of the generic knowledge.

ii) *The need for representing partial ignorance in an unbiased way*. There are three extreme epistemic attitudes with regard to a proposition p: on the basis of current evidence and background knowledge one can be sure that p is true, sure that p is false, or the truth-value of p can be unknown. The third situation corresponds to partial ignorance, and its representation should not depend on the count of situations in which p is true, since this count can depend on how these situations are described, i.e., is language-dependent.

iii) *The inference at work cannot be monotonic*. A plausible reasoning system is expected not to be cautious, namely to go beyond the conclusions strictly entailed by the incomplete evidence. This is done by assuming that the particular situation under study is as normal as possible, so that it is possible to jump to adventurous, but plausible conclusions. The price paid by this kind of deductive efficiency is that such conclusions may be canceled upon the arrival of new evidence, when the latter tells us that the current situation is not so normal. This is in obvious contradiction with the monotonicity property of classical logic that forbids conclusions to be retracted when new axioms come in.

The solutions proposed by the expert systems literature were either based on the propagation of certainty coefficients (like in MYCIN and PROSPECTOR), or based on an explicit handling of the reasons for uncertainty at the control level. However these solutions were partially ad hoc, and exception handling in rule-based systems has motivated further, better founded streams of work, namely Bayesian networks and nonmonotonic reasoning. While the first of these approaches could be safely developed due to the strong probabilistic tradition, the second line of research proved to be more adventurous, but eventually fruitful. In the following, limitations of classical logic and those of Bayesian nets are laid bare; but it turns out that many lessons from the Bayesian net literature are worth being learned, in order to solve the exception-tolerant inference problem while remaining in the tradition of logic.

2 LIMITATIONS OF CLASSICAL LOGIC

The problems of exception handling in classical logic are well-known (e.g., Léa Sombé, 1990). We face a dilemma due to the fact that generic knowledge expresses rules with a hidden context, while everything must be explicitly encoded in classical logic. If exceptions are not explicitly encoded, encountering exceptions leads to inconsistencies (like when encountering a penguin, given that penguins typically do not fly, birds typically fly and penguins are birds). If exceptions are explicitly encoded, then the rules will no longer be triggered in the face of incomplete information. If Tweety is only known to be a bird, we cannot conclude on its flying capabilities using the rule that says that birds that are not penguins fly. Besides, the list of exceptions is typically an ever open one, and adding an exception comes down to a non-trivial modification of a knowledge base.

Considering the three requirements of Section 1, classical logic only satisfies the second one. Indeed, if we stick to propositional logic there is no difference between factual evidence and generic knowledge. Both will be propositional formulas. If we use first order logic, factual evidence will be encoded as grounded formulas, and generic knowledge will be encoded as universally quantified formulas, that, by definition, rule out the possibility of exceptions. As for existentially quantified formulas, their expressive power looks inadequate to describe the normal course of things. So the first requirement is not met. The second requirement, namely modelling partial ignorance is basically fulfilled. If K is a set of formulas (encoding factual evidence and generic knowledge), a conclusion p is certainly true in the context of K if and only if $K \vdash p$. p is certainly false if $K \vdash \neg p$. When neither $K \vdash p$ nor $K \vdash \neg p$ hold, the truth of p is unknown, and this is precisely the definition of total ignorance about p. We can define partial ignorance as the epistemic state described by a set of formulas K such that neither $K \vdash p$ nor $K \vdash \neg p$ hold, for some p. This phenomenon occurs each time K is not complete, i.e., has more than one model. The third requirement, i.e., nonmonotonic inference, is clearly not met since

$$K \vdash p \text{ implies } \forall q, K \cup \{q\} \vdash p. \qquad (1)$$

Monotonicity is strongly similar to conditional independence in probability theory. Namely let A, B, C be events that represent the set of models of K, q and p respectively. Conditional independence of C with respect to B in the context A means

$$P(C|A \cap B) = P(C|A). \qquad (2)$$

Clearly (1) is a particular case of (2) when $P(C|A \cap B) = P(C|A) = 1$, interpreting $K \vdash p$ as $P(C|A) = 1$. The fact that classical logic is monotonic can be interpreted as systematic conditional independence. When the inference symbol no longer means deduction in the usual sense, but plausible inference that can be viewed as high probability inference, the validity of (1) looks dubious. Note that in classical logic the only available notion of independence is logical independence. In classical logic, independence is not a supplementary information which can be expressed.

An important remark is that the problem of exception-handling in classical logic is closely related to two other problems, namely inconsistency management and belief revision (Gärdenfors, 1988). Indeed encountering exceptions lead to inconsistencies, and getting rid of this inconsistency means revising the set of formulas. Makinson and Gärdenfors (1991) have pointed out that belief revision and nonmonotonic reasoning were two sides of the same coin. Indeed the claim that p is a plausible conclusion of K in the context where q is true comes down to accepting that q lies in the deductively closed belief set which is the revision of K by input p. This equivalence is important, especially at the computational level. However it is conceptually limited because in this approach, K is encoded in propositional logic, i.e., there is no clear distinction between factual evidence and generic knowledge.

3 LIMITATIONS OF BAYESIAN NETWORKS

Classical logic represents beliefs by means of a set K of formulas that implicitly point out a subset of possible states of the world (the set of models of K) one of which is the actual one. Bayesian nets encode belief in a weighted acyclic graph that represents a single probability distribution on the set of states of the world. We shall consider only Bayesian nets that carry binary variables.

Bayesian networks are the most popular and most widely implemented model of reasoning under uncertainty. From a computational point of view, Bayesian networks are nice because they are a good example of an approach where efficient local propagation algorithms succeed in properly handling complex probabilistic knowledge in a rigorous way. In some sense they make certainty factor-based expert systems obsolete. The problem with Bayesian networks is neither in their mathematical nor their algorithmic sides. The main difficulty is to grasp which kind of reasoning task they can address.

In the theory of Bayesian nets, as presented by Pearl (1988) it is not always obvious whether probabilities are subjective or objective ones. Bayesian nets look like a very powerful tool for an efficient encoding of any complex multivariate probability distribution, starting from statistical data. The problem is then how to extract the simplest acyclic graph that lays bare as many independence relationships as possible. The strength of the approach relies on the fact that any probability distribution can be encoded as an (acyclic) Bayesian net. In other words, you do not need to be a subjective Bayesian probabilist to enjoy Bayesian nets.

Now if you adopt a subjectivist Bayesian point of view, it does not look very convincing nor feasible to directly assess a complex joint probability distribution. Then the Bayesian network methodology basically runs as follows: first draw an acyclic directed graph where links express direct causation, and picture dependencies; assess conditional probabilities on the links, and a priori probabilities on the roots of the graph; these data uniquely determine a probability distribution underlying the graph, using appropriate conventions for the graphical representation of independence. Objections to this approach are as follows:

1) The results of the approach heavily rely on the independence assumptions encoded in the topology of the graph as well as the numerical values put in the network. These values must be precise numbers which in practice, and when no statistical knowledge is available, may be out of reach (for instance Prob(other symptom | other disease) when exhaustive lists of observable symptoms and diseases are not available). Invariably there is some a priori probability to be supplied. It is not clear that experts are always capable of supplying all the numbers.

2) The network building method never produces inconsistencies. The "expert" is asked exactly the amount of data required for ensuring the unicity of the underlying distribution. Hence this distribution depends upon the set of questions you ask.

3) The assumption of an acyclic network, if innocuous with statistical data, becomes very questionable with a subjectively defined Bayesian net. One of the often found justification is that arrows in the graph express causation. However a generic rule such as "most students are young" does not mean that the youth of individuals is caused by their being registered as student. It is not clear how to encode the set of two generic rules {"most student are young", "few young people are student"} under the form of an acyclic graph.

The first objection can be tackled by using sensitivity analysis techniques and more generally by admitting that knowledge can be represented by a set of conditional probability bounds that constrain a set of admissible probability distributions. For instance we know that $P(B|A) \in [0.7, 0.8]$, or that "most A's are B", where the linguistic quantifier "most" is modelled by an interval restricting the possible values of the proportion $|A \cap B| / |A|$ (where | | denotes cardinality). However it goes against the Bayesian credo that a unique probability is necessary and sufficient to encode subjective beliefs. Some Bayesian proposals that handle the lack of knowledge about probabilities come down to introducing higher-order probabilities or extra variables. These proposals basically make the picture even more complex. It is not clear that people can quantify their uncertainty about probabilities they ignore. As for the use of extra variables, it looks very efficient for the purpose of learning from cases. However, in this paper we take commonsense knowledge for granted and do not consider the learning problem.

The second objection is a significant problem. When representing knowledge in logic, inconsistency is almost unavoidable at the acquisition level and tools for detection of such inconsistencies must be used in order to improve the available pieces of information. Inconsistency handling is apparently ignored by the Bayesian network approach. This question is clearly related to the acyclicity assumption: If the network has cycles, then the risk for an inconsistent assignment of probabilities is high.

It is clear that classical logic possesses none of the above drawbacks. Now as it turns out, Bayesian nets do fulfil the two requirements of plausible reasoning that classical logic violates. First, the distinction between generic knowledge and factual evidence is carefully made by the Bayesians. Generic knowledge is encoded by probabilities, and especially conditional probabilities. Factual evidence is modelled like in propositional logic by allocating values to some variables. Plausible inference is made by focusing the generic knowledge on the factual evidence E, and this is achieved by conditioning, i.e., computing $P(C|E)$ for events C of interest. Note that finding the most plausible values of (binary) variables in the network, in the presence of evidence E is often called "revision" by some authors. The term "revision" looks more convincing when modifying the network itself.

The nonmonotonicity requirement is also met by the Bayesian approach. Namely, it is possible to have a high value for $P(C|A)$ (hence C is a plausible conclusion when only A is know) and a very low value for $P(C|A \cap B)$ when B is learned. Interestingly, the Bayesian network topology is tailored to encode the cases when nonmonotonicity phenomena do not occur, i.e., when $P(C|B) = P(C|B \cap A)$ holds.

Bayesian probability fails on requirement (ii) of plausible reasoning, i.e., contrary to classical logic, it cannot encode incomplete knowledge. This is due to the assumption that a Bayesian network encodes a single probability distribution. Let K be a propositional knowledge base on a finite language L and Ω be the set of interpretations of the language. Let M(K) be the set of models of K and assume that M(K) contains three interpretations. Then let U(K) = {p | neither K ⊢ p nor K ⊢ ¬p hold}, U(K) is the set of unknown propositions in the face of K. All these propositions are equally unknown in the sense that there is no reason to consider one to be more plausible than another. Assume you are a subjective Bayesian, and that you allocate probabilities a_1, a_2, a_3 such that $a_1 + a_2 + a_3 = 1$ to each model of K. The fact that a unique probability distribution cannot model partial ignorance is made precise by the following statement: there is no probability assignment (a_1, a_2, a_3) to M(K) that ensures that for all p ∈ U(K) and q ∈ U(K), P(p) = P(q), i.e., some equally unknown propositions must have distinct probability values.

In fact the most commonly found reason why Bayesians insist on unique probability distributions is because of the betting behavior interpretation of subjective probability. Clearly this approach models a decision problem, and betting rates depend on your degrees of belief about what is the actual world. However, partial ignorance differs from uncertainty about how to bet, as argued in Dubois et al. (1993). One may have a lot of knowledge about a (fair) die, and still be uncertain about the result of the next outcome. Uncertainty about how to act does not imply total ignorance. And if degrees of belief govern betting rates, it is not clear that the correspondence between them is one to one. Plausible reasoning is about entertaining beliefs, not about decision-making, and degrees of belief can be construed as distinct from betting rates. Especially when revising plausible conclusions upon facing new pieces of evidence, it is not clear that we should revise the prior *betting rates* (through Bayesian conditioning).

On the whole it is clear that the deficiencies of classical logic and Bayesian networks with respect to the plausible reasoning endeavor are not the same. In fact they are strikingly complementary. The ambition of knowledge representation and reasoning on plausible inference is to lay bare a logic that preserves the advantages of Bayesian nets and classical logic. Especially, there are several useful lessons to be remembered from the field of Bayesian nets, if classical logic is to be suitably augmented to capture the intuitive properties of exception-tolerant inference.

4 LESSONS FROM BAYESIAN NETWORKS

Despite their limitations regarding the representation of incomplete knowledge, the Bayesian network approach has significantly modified the notion of a knowledge base. As pointed out by Pearl (1988), an uncertain "if... then..." rule cannot be regarded as a "production rule" in the sense of expert systems, because the meaning of sentences such as "if x is A then plausibly y is B" is not "if A is in the factual base then B should be added to it", but rather "if all I know about x is A, then tentatively conclude that y is B". Hence the whole of the factual evidence should be taken into account simultaneously, in order to derive plausible conclusions.

Another lesson from the Bayesian approach is that material implication should not be used without caution to model the logical part of an uncertain rule. Material implications forget about the directedness of rules, as intended by the person that provides them, and they imbed monotonicity. The meaning of uncertain "if... then..." rules is more in accordance with conditional probability. A conditional probability is directed in the sense that P(p|q) differs from P(¬q|¬p), and in particular it differs from P(¬q ∨ p) except for very special cases. The Bayesian way of using the rule base Δ is to infer from it a rule whose antecedent exactly matches the contents of the factual base E, under the form of a conditional probability P(C|E). However, what can be done if we want to keep the idea of a directed conditional and drop the probability? One appealing answer is the use of a conditional object, denoted p|q, which is a three-valued entity. If ω is an interpretation of the language, then ω satisfies p|q if and only if ω ⊨ p ∧ q (ω is an example of p|q); ω falsifies p|q if and only if ω ⊨ ¬p ∧ q (ω is an exception to p|q); otherwise p|q does not apply to ω. This case corresponds to a third truth-value.

This notion, originally proposed by De Finetti (1936, 1937), has been rediscovered several times in the literature (see Goodman el al., 1991; Dubois and Prade, 1994), including Adams (1975), and Calabrese (1987). p|q can be viewed as a set of propositions rather than a single one, namely {r | p ∧ q ⊨ r ⊨ ¬q ∨ p}, and the probability of a conditional event p|q is indeed a conditional probability P(p|q) since the latter can be expressed in terms of P(p ∧ q) and P(¬q ∨ p) only. Conditional objects are not at the same level as formulas of propositional calculus but are constructed on top of them. Defining a body of generic knowledge Δ as a set of conditional objects Δ, while the body of evidence E is a set of propositional formulas, the first requirement of plausible reasoning as per Section 1 is potentially met. Dropping the need for assigning precise probabilities opens the door to the fulfilment of requirement (ii).

A last lesson from Bayesian network is that a knowledge base is not just a bunch of unordered well-formed formulas. For a Bayesian, a knowledge base is a directed graphical structure, which is useful to reveal conditional independence properties that are implicit in the knowledge. Graphical representations of knowledge base also pervade the literature of taxonomic reasoning, without reference to independence. However a set of exception-tolerant rules Δ once represented as a graph, will significantly differ from a Bayesian net. In a Bayesian net, nodes are (logical or n-ary) variables while a graph built from Δ will contain nodes representing literals. Moreover nothing forbids cycles in the graph while cycles are prohibited by Bayesian representations. The problem is then to become capable of "reading" independence assertions from a structured set of rules. This question may become an important issue in the future.

5 GRADED REPRESENTATIONS OF INCOMPLETE KNOWLEDGE

One obvious limitation of classical logic when representing partial ignorance is its crudeness. In the front of partial information represented by a set of propositions K, the language can be partitioned in three sets: the propositions that are certainly true, that form the set C(K) of consequences of K, the set F(K) of propositions that are certainly false and the remainder whose truth or falsity is not known, say U(K). Very naturally, one may wish to refine this classification by distinguishing in U(K) propositions that are more certainly true (or false) than others. The introduction of certainty factors in expert systems tried to achieve this purpose, and more generally all quantified theories of uncertainty. One reason why Bayesian probability theory was not the only candidate pertains to its failure to represent partial ignorance. For instance the MYCIN certainty factors were deliberately tailored to express the difference between a non-certainly true proposition and a certainly false one. However many calculi of uncertainty in expert systems were requested to be compositional. In this section we indicate why compositionality is impossible. Then we review various theories of uncertainty and discuss their relevance in the problem of exception-tolerant knowledge-based systems.

5.1 THE COMPOSITIONALITY PROBLEM

One of the main simplicity of classical logic lies in its compositionality property, i.e., the truth-value of a formula is always a function of the truth-value of the atomic propositions it involves. Many people have assumed that this property could carry over to degrees of uncertainty. Compositional quantified extensions of Boolean logic are called multiple-valued logics (Rescher, 1969). They have been developed in the early thirties, especially by Lukasiewicz. Hence the temptation to found uncertainty calculi on multiple-valued logics. Quite at the same period, fuzzy set theory (Zadeh, 1965) was construed as the set-theoretic counterpart of multiple-valued logics. Hence the often found claims that fuzzy logic is an approach to handle uncertainty in knowledge-based systems. This state of facts also caused the rejection of fuzzy set theory by people realizing the impossibility of compositionality of uncertainty coefficients in the presence of a Boolean logic. For instance, Elkan (1993) concluded that fuzzy logic collapses on two-valued logic.

This apparent state of confusion is basically due to the lack of acknowledged distinction between a degree of truth and a degree of uncertainty. One should realize that the idea of intermediary truth completely differs from the idea of not knowing if a proposition (in the classical sense) is true or false, a crucial distinction whose importance has been pointed out as early as 1936 by De Finetti. Mixing up these two situations comes down to claim that an unseen bottle which is either empty or full is actually half full. The understanding of propositions as 2-valued entities is a matter of convention, and leads to the Boolean algebra structure. Modifying this convention makes sense but affects the meaning of the word "proposition": introducing intermediary truth-values means that we use a language with entities that differ completely from what is usually understood by the term "proposition". This is what fuzzy logic, a logic of gradual properties, does. As a consequence the structure of Boolean algebra is lost. Especially what are usually considered as tautologies may no longer be so. Collapse results such as Elkan's are due to the impossible quest for compatibility of a Boolean algebra structure and intermediary truth-values that would remain compositional.

On the contrary degrees of uncertainty are not intermediary truth-values, they correspond to an epistemic attitude expressing that some individual does *not know* if a proposition (in the usual sense) is true or false. To quote De Finetti (1936): "This attitude does not correspond to a third truth-value distinct from yes or no, but to the *doubt* about yes or no". Hence the third modality expressing ignorance should not enter as a third truth-value, but should be put on top of the two values "true" and "false". Especially all tautologies of classical logic should be kept. For instance even if p and ¬p are unknown, p ∨ ¬p is still ever true as is p ↔ p ∧ p, and p ∧ ¬p is still ever false. This simple requirement breaks down the compositionality hypothesis, when uncertainty levels are more than 2 (see Dubois and Prade, 1988b). But it does not harm fuzzy logic where p ∨ ¬p, p ↔ p ∧ p are never simultaneously acknowledged as being tautologies.

Uncertainty calculi can remain partially compositional. For instance probabilities are compositional with respect to negation only. Possibility measures (Zadeh, 1978) are compositional with respect to union, as are Spohn (1988)'s disbelief functions. But Shafer's belief functions are not compositional at all.

5.2 BELIEF FUNCTIONS ON UNCERTAIN RULES

The ad hocery of compositional uncertainty calculi in the expert systems literature has been overcome by the development of Bayesian nets. However the lack of capability of the latter in representing partial ignorance has prompted some researchers to model uncertain knowledge bases in the setting of a more flexible uncertainty calculus, namely belief functions (Shenoy and Shafer, 1990). The idea is to use the hypergraph machinery underlying the local propagation of probabilities as done by Lauritzen and Spiegelhalter (1988), and extend it to belief functions.

A belief function on a set Ω is defined by a family $\mathcal{F}$ of non-empty subsets of Ω called focal elements to which positive numbers called masses $\{m_i, A_i \in \mathcal{F}\}$ are attached. The sum of the masses is one. m_i is interpreted as the probability that the available information is correctly described by A_i. In logical terms the pair $(\mathcal{F},m)$ defined on a set Ω of interpretations of a language comes down to a random propositional knowledge base K such that $A_i = M(K_i)$ and $m_i = P(K$ is semantically equivalent to $K_i)$. The belief degree $Bel(A)$ of a proposition p such that $A = M(p)$ is defined by

$$Bel(A) = \Sigma_{i: A_i \subseteq A} \, m_i = \Sigma_{i: K_i \vdash p} \, m_i$$

hence $Bel(A)$ can be viewed as the probability of provability of p (Pearl, 1988).

In the belief function approach to knowledge bases each piece of knowledge is represented as a belief function relating some variables, and is viewed as an hyperedge of the hypergraph formed by all pieces of knowledge. A global belief function is constructed using Dempster rule of combination. This combination rule is also the one used to absorb new evidence. Question-answering is achieved by projecting the global belief function over the range of the variables of interest. When the hypergraph is an hypertree, uncertainty propagation and combination can be done locally. The generic machinery that is put at work in the hypergraph approach is capable of encompassing Bayesian networks and classical constraint propagation techniques (when the masses m_i take on value 0 or 1). Yet, this approach is not well adapted to exception-tolerant plausible reasoning for several reasons

1) This approach fails to distinguish between factual evidence and generic knowledge. Indeed belief functions are construed as a theory of evidence, not as a theory of generic knowledge, and Dempster rule of combination is good at pooling independent pieces of uncertain evidence. Especially the hypergraph is supposed to encode both uncertain rules and (possibly uncertain) evidence. All pieces of information receive a uniform treatment, as in classical logic;

2) The question of how to encode an exception-prone rule in the setting of belief function has been little considered by the advocates of the hypergraph methods. Especially an uncertain rule is often encoded by putting some mass α on a material implication $\neg \psi \vee \varphi$ and the remainder $1 - \alpha$ on the tautology (e.g., Smets, 1988). If such pieces of information are combined with Dempster rule, the obtained results are often counter-intuitive because the assumption of independence between the rules in a knowledge base is seldom satisfied (Dubois and Prade, 1994a).

For instance consider the penguin example where b = bird, f = fly, p = penguin, and the following belief functions for the rules in Δ

$b \rightarrow f$: $\quad m_1(\neg b \vee f) = \alpha$; $m_1(T) = 1 - \alpha$ (T: tautology)

$p \rightarrow b$: $\quad m_2(\neg p \vee b) = 1$

$p \rightarrow \neg f$: $\quad m_3(\neg p \vee \neg f) = \alpha$; $m_3(T) = 1 - \alpha$.

Let the evidence E be another belief function saying that Tweety is a penguin, i.e., $m_4(p) = 1$. Then it can be checked that combining these pieces of information using Dempster rule leads to the counter-intuitive result that $Bel(f) = Bel(\neg f) = (\alpha(1 - \alpha) / (1 - \alpha^2))$, which is a variant of the inconsistency result one would get in pure classical logic (letting $\alpha = 1$). And indeed the presence of the normalization factor $1 - \alpha^2$ indicates that the bodies of evidence $\{m_1, m_2, m_3, m_4\}$ are partially inconsistent.

5.3 UPPER AND LOWER PROBABILITIES

Another approach to relaxing the Bayesian framework is to admit that the available knowledge does not necessarily determine a single probability distribution. We keep the idea that an uncertain rule is modeled by a conditional probability but its exact value may be ill-known.

A collection of pieces of information of this kind leads to consider a knowledge base Δ as a set of statements of the form $P(B_i|A_i) \in [\alpha_i,\beta_i]$, that form an interval-valued network. We are interested in computing the tightest bounds on the value of some other conditional probability of interest, without using systematic independence assumptions as in Bayesian networks. A missing arrow in such a network corresponds to a quantifier or a conditional probability which is completely unknown (then represented by the interval [0,1]). All probabilities that we handle are (bounds of) conditional probabilities; no prior probability information is required in order to start the inference process in this approach. Such networks do not obey the same conventions as Bayesian nets. In the latter the network is the result of a data compression procedure that accounts for a joint probability distribution. In the present approach the data consists of incomplete statistics under the form of interval-valued conditional probabilities, and a network is only a display of the raw data expressing local constraints on an unknown joint probability distribution. This approach leaves room for inconsistent specifications (which can be detected by constraint propagation), and thus addresses the other objections to Bayesian networks. In particular cycles are allowed.

The non-Bayesian view of a probabilistic knowledge base is thus a collection of general statements regarding a population X of objects; these statements express possibly in unspecific terms the proportions of objects in various subclasses of X, that belong to other subclasses. This knowledge base allows for answering queries about a given object, given a subclass E to which evidence assigns it (also called its "reference class" by Kyburg (1974)). To make an inference we just apply to this object the properties of this subclass, implicitly assuming that it is a typical element of it. That is, we compute a new rule "if E then C" and optimal bounds on P(C|E), for a class C of interest. If more information becomes available for this object, we just change its reference class accordingly. The computation of optimal bounds can be done by linear programming techniques (Amarger et al., 1991). But local techniques have been studied as well (Thöne et al., 1992; Dubois et al., 1993). The latter are interesting because more efficient and capable of handling inepencence assumptions more easily, if needed. However they are sometimes suboptimal.

This probabilistic model also maintains the difference between querying a knowledge base and revising it, what we call focusing and revision respectively. The querying problem is to ask for P(C|E) on the basis of a case belonging to class E for which we want to know its probability of belonging to C. Revision means adding a new piece of knowledge to the database, for instance the value of a new conditional probability that has become known. A particular case is when we learn that E is true for the whole concerned population. That means we add the constraint P(E) = 1 to the database. Note that the bounds on P(C) given that P(E) = 1 usually differ from the bounds on P(C|E) computed from the original database. Hence focusing differs from revision. However when the probability distribution underlying the database is uniquely determined (as in the case of Bayesian nets), the two operations yield the same result: a point-valued P(C|E) provided by Bayes rule. Clearly Bayes rule serves two purposes, and this is sometimes a source of confusion. When the assumption of a unique available probability distribution is dropped, the two tasks (focusing and revision) lead to different types of conditioning rules.

The representation of ignorance with upper and lower probabilities is unbiased. Namely, it is possible to obtain that the truth of a conclusion C is unknown, in the presence of evidence E, if all that can be obtained from the knowledge base is that P(C|E) ∈ [0,1].

Moreover the behavior of a set of conditional probabilities is nonmonotonic. Indeed, considering again the example of Section 5.2, the set Δ = {P(f|b) ≥ α, P(¬f|p) ≥ α, P(b|p) = 1}, is not at all inconsistent for α ≠ 1. However the inferential power of this probabilistic approach is low because it does not allow for systematic subclass inheritance. For instance, if the available evidence is {b,r} where r stands for red, it is not possible to conclude from Δ anything about flying, i.e., P(f|b ∧ r) ∈ [0,1]. Here classical logic is doing better since {b, r, ¬b ∨ f, ¬f ∨ ¬p, ¬p ∨ b} ⊢ f. To do so, a conditional independence assumption is needed for irrelevant properties. Again we face a case where the merits of classical logic and probability are complementary.

Belief functions are special cases of lower probabilities. Yet the approach of Section 5.2 is not a special case of the above approach to exception-tolerant rules. First, the rule of combination used in Section 5.2 is not idempotent. If you use b → f twice (i.e., m_1 twice), it affects the resulting global belief function. This is not the case here, i.e., putting P(f|b) ≥ α twice is innocuous. Another difference is that material implication is used in 5.2 for rule representation. To do the same here means using P(¬b ∨ f) ≥ α instead of P(f|b) ≥ α, as in Nilsson (1986)'s probabilistic logic. This would not be satisfactory. For instance, considering the knowledge base {P(¬b ∨ f) ≥ α, P(¬p ∨ b) = 1, P(¬p ∨ ¬f) ≥ λ}, it is easy to see that if Tweety is a penguin

- answering queries by computing conditional probabilities leads to P(¬f|p) ∈ [0,1] only
- adding P(p) = 1 to the knowledge base leads to a contradiction as soon as α + λ > 1 (which is the regular situation since birds fly and penguins don't).

5.4 ORDINAL AND SEMI-QUANTITATIVE APPROACHES TO UNCERTAINTY

Apart from full-fledged numerical methods based on additive properties, and purely symbolic representations of uncertainty, it is natural to consider ordinal methods as well. Incomplete probabilistic databases can be questioned as to their capability to model all kinds of commonsense knowledge. In many instances it is not possible to quantify the amount of exceptions to a default rule. We know that "birds usually fly", but not the proportion of flying birds. One may be tempted to change interval-valued probabilities into fuzzy probabilities (Zadeh, 1985), but that makes sense for a refined sensitivity analysis only. One may also try to devise a purely symbolic approach to probabilistic inference using linguistic probability terms referring to partially unspecified probability intervals, the inferred linguistic probabilities being linguistic approximations of the intervals obtained through numerical constraint propagation (Dubois et al., 1993). Experience shows that it results in weakening the inferential power of the reasoning system compared to the numerical setting. Moreover reasoning with linguistic probabilities does not solve the irrelevant property problem and results in more ambiguous responses than in the numerical case.

Instead of quantifying uncertainty, one might prefer to compare propositions in terms of their relative certainty. Namely consider a relation ≥ defined on a language, such that p ≥ q means that one is at least as confident in the truth of p as in the truth of q. Most quantitative approaches to uncertainty have comparative counterparts (see Dubois and Prade, 1993 for a review). It is clear that the relation ≥ should be reflexive, transitive and complete, so that the language can be partitioned into classes of propositions of equal strength, these classes being totally ordered. Certainty should go along with logical consequence in the sense that p ⊢ q ⇒ q ≥ p. The oldest kind of such comparative uncertainty relations was introduced by De Finetti (among others), namely the comparative probability, that satisfies the additivity axiom

$$p \wedge (q \vee r) = \bot \Rightarrow (q \geq r \Leftrightarrow p \vee q \geq p \vee r). \quad (A)$$

This axiom has been further on generalized by Savage to the comparison of acts under the name "sure thing principle", and is at the root of subjective expected utility theory. Unfortunately in the finite case this property does not characterize only orderings induced by probability measures (Fine, 1973). Comparative probabilities are not simple to use because, on finite sets, the ordering among propositions cannot be recovered from the knowledge of its restriction to interpretations. The situation is much simpler if we turn the additivity axiom into the following one (Dubois, 1986)

$$q \geq_\Pi r \Rightarrow p \vee q \geq_\Pi p \vee r. \qquad (\Pi)$$

This is obtained by dropping the disjointness condition and relaxing the equivalence in the additivity axiom. The obtained uncertainty relations are actually called **comparative possibility relations** by Lewis (1973). They can be represented equivalently by a function Π from the language to a (finite) totally ordered set S with top 1 and bottom 0, such that

$$\Pi(p \vee q) = \max(\Pi(p), \Pi(q)).$$

These functions are called possibility measures by Zadeh (1978) when S is the unit interval. $q \geq_\Pi r$ means that q is at least as consistent as r with the current knowledge. Dually, when $\neg r \geq_\Pi \neg q$, q is said to be at least as certain as r, which is denoted $\geq_C$. Comparative certainty relations satisfy an axiom dual to (Π), namely

$$q \geq_C r \Rightarrow p \wedge q \geq_C p \wedge r. \qquad (N)$$

$q >_C r$ (strict preference) means that in the presence of inconsistency, if dropping either q or r does restore consistency, one would rather drop r. Axiom (N) can be derived from Gärdenfors (1988) postulates of belief revision (see Dubois and Prade, 1991), and is satisfied by Gärdenfors (1988)'s epistemic entrenchment. If c denotes an order reversing map on S, $\Pi(p)$ is the degree of possibility, then certainty orderings can be equivalently represented by functions N with range S, such that $N(p) = c(\Pi(\neg p))$ which expresses that p is all the more certain as $\neg p$ is impossible, just like in modal logics. $N(p)$ is called degree of necessity of p.

A possibility (or a certainty) ordering on a finite set can be characterized by a complete preordering of the set Ω of interpretations, encoded by an assignment $\pi(\omega) \in S$ to each interpretation ω. π is called a possibility distribution, and encodes a preference relation describing the respective levels of plausibility of ω as being the actual world. $\pi(\omega) = 0$ means that ω is impossible, while $\pi(\omega) = 1$ means that ω is a most plausible world (say a most normal one). Then we have

$$\Pi(p) = \max\{\pi(\omega), \omega \models p\}$$
$$N(p) = \min\{c(\pi(\omega)), \omega \models \neg p\}.$$

This kind of uncertainty measure can be viewed as completely symbolic (S is a totally ordered set) or numerical (S is the unit interval). When numerical, $N(p)$ is a special kind of belief function, called consonant belief functions (Shafer, 1976), where focal elements are nested. Spohn (1988) has considered a very similar kind of uncertainty functions k such that $k(p \vee q) = \min(k(p), k(q))$ where $k(p)$ is a non-negative integer. $k(p) = n$ is viewed as expressing that the probability of p is of the form ε^n where ε is a very small number. If has been pointed out that the set function Π_k such that $\Pi_k(p) = a^{-k(p)}$ for $a > 1$ is a possibility measure, valued on a subset of [0,1].

6 POSSIBILISTIC LOGIC

Possibility theory enables classical logic to be extended to layered sets of formulas, where layers express certainty levels. This is possibilistic logic (Dubois et al., 1991). The encoding of the layers is simply achieved by assigning to each formula φ of K an element $\alpha \in S$, which expresses a constraint of the form $N(p) \geq \alpha$. Inference in possibilistic logic can be achieved by means of the following extension of the resolution principle

$$(\varphi, \alpha), (\psi, \beta) \vdash (\text{Res}(\varphi, \psi), \min(\alpha, \beta)) \qquad (R)$$

where $\text{Res}(\varphi, \psi)$ is the resolvent of the two clauses φ and ψ. For instance if $\varphi = \neg p \vee q$ and $\psi = p \vee r$, then $\text{Res}(\varphi, \psi) = q \vee r$. The use of this rule presupposes that a knowledge base K be put under clausal form, which turns out to be always possible. In order to prove (φ, β) from K, denoted $K \vdash (\varphi, \beta)$, one can proceed as follows:

1) add($\neg\varphi$, 1) to K (or the clauses corresponding to $\neg\varphi$); let $K' = K \cup \{(\neg\varphi, 1)\}$;
2) try to derive the contradiction $\bot$ from K' using (R) with a sufficient level α of certainty, i.e., $K' \vdash (\bot, \beta)$ with $\beta \geq \alpha$. Then, it can be proved that $N(\varphi) \geq \beta$.

A knowledge base K is said to be totally consistent if it is not true that $K \vdash (\bot, \alpha)$ for $\alpha > 0$, by successive applications of (R). More generally, $\text{Inc}(K) = \sup\{\alpha, K \vdash (\bot, \alpha)\}$ is called the degree of inconsistency of K.

The main advantage of graded inconsistency is to avoid the main drawback of classical logic inference whereby the presence of contradiction trivializes the inference notion (anything follows from an inconsistent knowledge base). Indeed non-trivial deductions can be performed from an inconsistent possibilistic knowledge base. A formula φ is called a non-trivial deduction from K, denoted $K \vdash_\pi \varphi$, if and only if

$$K \vdash (\varphi, \alpha) \text{ with } \alpha > \text{Inc}(K)$$

$K \vdash_\pi \varphi$ means that, in order to derive φ, only a consistent subpart of K has been used, namely one containing formulas of certainty higher than the inconsistency degree. The consequence relationship $\vdash_\pi$ does not obey the usual postulates of consequence relationships, especially it is not transitive; it is reflexive up to the contradiction and it is not monotonic. For instance if we consider the Tweety example, let $K = \{(\neg b \vee f, \alpha), (\neg p \vee \neg f, \beta), (\neg p \vee b, \beta)\}$ with $\beta > \alpha$. Then $K \cup \{b\} \vdash_\pi f$ while $K \cup \{b, p\} \vdash_\pi \neg f$.

In order to figure out why this is so, one must turn to the semantics of possibilistic logic, and realize that the ordering over formulas in K induces an ordering over interpretations. The latter can be obtained by first representing each uncertain assertion (φ_i, α_i) in K by means of a possibility distribution π_i over the set of interpretations, defined as

$$\pi_i(\omega) = 1 \text{ if } \omega \models \varphi_i$$
$$= 1 - \alpha_i \text{ if } \omega \models \neg\varphi_i.$$

That is, $1 - \alpha_i$ is interpreted as the degree of possibility that φ_i is false. The ordering over $M(K)$ is then defined by π_K such that

$$\pi_K = \min_{i=1,n} \pi_i.$$

The construction of π_K from K obeys the principle of minimal specificity, namely each interpretation is assigned the highest possibility degree so as not to violate any constraint of the form $N(\varphi_i) \geq \alpha_i$. The possibility distribution π_K defines the fuzzy set of models of K. The maximal possibility degree sup π turns out to be equal to $1 - \text{Inc}(K)$. The semantic entailment is then defined following Zadeh. Namely if $\pi_{(\varphi,\alpha)}$ is the possibility distribution deriving from (φ,α), $K \models (\varphi,\alpha)$ means $\pi_K \leq \pi_{(\varphi,\alpha)}$. Possibilistic logic is sound and complete in the sense that $K \models (\varphi,\alpha)$ if and only if $K \vdash (\varphi,\alpha)$ (see Dubois et al., 1991).

The non-trivial inference $\vdash_\pi$ can be expressed semantically as follows: $K \models_\pi \varphi$ if and only if all preferred interpretations of K (in the sense of π_K) are models of φ. This is clearly a kind of preferential inference which Shoham (1988) has proved to be at work in many non-monotonic logics. The absence of monotony of inference $\models_\pi$ should not be surprizing.

7 PROPERTIES OF EXCEPTION-TOLERANT INFERENCE

Possibilistic logic obeys requirements (ii) and (iii) of exception-tolerant reasoning. It models ignorance in an unbiased way: if p is ignored, $N(p) = N(\neg p) = 0$ and the proposition p is simply omitted. Moreover inference is indeed nonmonotonic. However possibilistic logic as such does not allow for a clear separation of generic knowledge from factual evidence as clear from the treatment of the Tweety example in Section 6. Especially, modelling "birds fly" as $(\neg b \vee f, \alpha)$ is not justified, since the nice treatment of the example entirely relies on the proper choice of the weight α; α must be less than β in $(\neg p \vee \neg f, \beta)$. Otherwise the expected inference will not take place. The question is then: where do the weights come from? The answer is: from a proper modeling of the generic knowledge.

One way out of this difficulty is to consider a generic rule as a constraint on the result of a plausible inference between two facts. This is the path followed by Lehmann and colleagues (Kraus et al., 1990; Lehmann and Magidor, 1992). Their idea is that the rule $b \to f$ constrains the pair (b,f) to belong to a consequence relationship denoted $\vdash\!\sim$, i.e., $b \vdash\!\sim f$. The problem is then to prescribe what the properties of this consequence relationship should be. They take the form of the following postulates:

Left logical equivalence:
    from $p \leftrightarrow p' = T$ and $p \vdash\!\sim q$ deduce $p' \vdash\!\sim q$ (LLE)

Right weakening:
    from $q \models q'$ and $p \vdash\!\sim q$ deduce $p \vdash\!\sim q'$ (RW)

Reflexivity: $p \vdash\!\sim p$

Left OR:
    from $p \vdash\!\sim r$ and $q \vdash\!\sim r$ deduce $p \vee q \vdash\!\sim r$ (LOR)

Cautious monotony:
    from $p \vdash\!\sim q$ and $p \vdash\!\sim r$ deduce $p \wedge q \vdash\!\sim r$ (CM)

Weak transitivity:
    from $p \wedge q \vdash\!\sim r$ and $p \vdash\!\sim q$ deduce $p \vdash\!\sim r$ (cut)

The three last rules already appear in Gabbay (1985). Kraus, Lehmann and Magidor (1990) call "preferential" a non-monotonic consequence relation $\vdash\!\sim$ satisfying the above postulates and name P the corresponding logic. They prove that the following rules of inference can be derived from the above set of postulates

from $p \vdash\!\sim q$ and $p \vdash\!\sim r$ deduce $p \vdash\!\sim q \wedge r$ (Right AND)
from $p \wedge q \vdash\!\sim r$ deduce $p \vdash\!\sim q \to r$ (S)

It is interesting to check the relevance of the above inference rules for plausible reasoning. CM restricts the use of monotonicity to when q is plausibly inferred from p already, i.e., property q is not exceptional for models of p. And the cut rule restricts transitivity to when models of p are normal models of q with respect to property r. LLE is only a consistency condition with respect to classical logic. The rules RAND and RW ensure that the set of plausible consequences of p is deductively closed. Property (S) looks like one half of the classical deduction theorem $p \wedge q \vdash r \Leftrightarrow p \vdash q \to r$. Kraus et al. (1990) define a syntactic deduction operation, denoted $\vdash$ in the following, acting from a set Δ of conditional assertions of the form $p_i \vdash\!\sim q_i$. Namely, $\Delta \vdash p \vdash\!\sim q$ if and only if $p \vdash\!\sim q$ can be derived from Δ using $p \vdash\!\sim p$ as an axiom schema and the inference rules LLE, RW, LOR, CM and cut of logic P. $\text{CONS}_P(\Delta)$ is the set of conditional assertions deduced from Δ in P.

Kraus et al. (1990) have proposed a semantics for $p \vdash\!\sim q$ that is based on a two level structure involving a set X of states, a mapping f from X to the set Ω of interpretations of the language and a preference relation among states which is symmetric and transitive. A state x satisfies p iff $f(x) \models p$. Then $p \vdash\!\sim q$ means that all the preferred states satisfying p satisfy q. Another semantics of $p \vdash\!\sim q$ is that $P(q|p) \geq 1 - \varepsilon$, i.e., the conditional probability $P(q|p)$ should be very close to 1. This type of conditional has been studied by Adams (1975) and revived by Pearl (1988). Probabilistic inference with infinitesimal lower probabilities does satisfy the rules of system P, hence showing the consistency of the above logical approach with the one of Section 5.3, based on upper and lower probabilities. In these proceedings, Dubois and Prade (1994b) give a simpler semantics of conditional assertions based on the three-valued conditional events of De Finetti. Lastly Fariñas del Cerro et al. (1992) have proposed another semantics of conditional assertions based on possibility theory, whereby $p \vdash\!\sim q$ is viewed as a constraint restricting a set of possibility distributions on

Ω that verify the condition $\Pi(q \wedge p) >_\Pi \Pi(\neg q \wedge p)$. It means that in the framework where p is true, q is more plausible than $\neg q$. It also means that all the most plausible worlds satisfying p satisfy q, i.e., $p \vDash_\pi q$ in the sense of possibilistic logic. Then the problem of proving $\varphi \mathrel|\!\sim \psi$ under the form $\Pi(\varphi \wedge \psi) > \Pi(\neg \psi \wedge \varphi)$ from a set of constraints of the form $\Pi(p_i \wedge q_i) > \Pi(p_i \wedge \neg q_i)$ satisfies all the properties of system P. This semantics can be interpreted in terms of a qualitative notion of conditioning in possibility theory, namely $N(q|p) > 0$ where $N(q|p) = 1 - \Pi(\neg q|p)$ and $\Pi(q|p)$ is the greatest solution of the Bayesian-like equation

$$\Pi(p \wedge q) = \min(\Pi(q|p), \Pi(p)).$$

The above approach, whatever the chosen semantics, satisfies all three requirements that an exception-tolerant logic should satisfy. Exception-handling is imbedded in the inference process. Instead of enriching the factual base by triggering the rules in order to derive conclusions, new rules are produced from the knowledge base until one rule is produced that fits the evidence as a whole. Namely if E contains the available (propositional) evidence and Δ the generic knowledge under the form of conditional assertions, then C is a plausible conclusion from (E,Δ) if and only if $E \mathrel|\!\sim C$ can be derived from Δ.

8 POSSIBILISTIC ENCODING OF RATIONAL INFERENCE

The above logic of conditional assertions is very cautious. Like the approach based on upper and lower conditional probability, it does not solve the problem of irrelevant properties. For instance, if $\Delta = \{b \mathrel|\!\sim f, p \mathrel|\!\sim \neg f, p \mathrel|\!\sim b\}$ it does not follow that red birds fly, i.e., $b \wedge r \mathrel|\!\sim f$. This is a by-product of the lack of monotony property; the cautious monotony property is too weak because in the example, we do not have that $b \mathrel|\!\sim r$. This difficulty has been solved by Lehmann by making the inference more monotonic. Namely, even if we do not have that $b \mathrel|\!\sim r$, we do not have that $b \mathrel|\!\sim \neg r$ either; this should enable us to jump to the conclusion that $b \wedge r \mathrel|\!\sim f$, and that $b \wedge \neg r \mathrel|\!\sim f$ as well, i.e., the redness of the bird is irrelevant to its flying. The idea is then to augment the preferential closure $\text{Cons}_P(\Delta)$ by other conditional assertions, and construct the so-called Rational Closure of Δ, $\text{Cons}_R(\Delta)$ which satisfies the following property called rational monotony

$$\text{if } p \mathrel|\!\sim q, \neg(p \mathrel|\!\sim \neg r) \text{ then } p \wedge r \mathrel|\!\sim q. \quad (RM)$$

Unfortunately $\text{Cons}_P(\Delta)$ cannot be defined using (RM) as an inference rule like others. There are several supersets of $\text{Cons}_P(\Delta)$ that are closed under (RM), and the intersection of two rational closures is generally not rational (Lehmann and Magidor, 1992). It can be proved (Lehmann and Magidor, 1992; Gärdenfors and Makinson, 1992; Benferhat et al., 1992) that any rational closure corresponds to a unique complete partial ordering of interpretations. In terms of possibilistic logic, the result reads: for any rational consequence relationship $\mathrel|\!\sim$, there exists a possibility distribution π on the set of interpretations such that $\mathrel|\!\sim$ coincides with $\mathrel|\!\sim_\pi$; conversely $\mathrel|\!\sim_\pi$ is rational. The problem is then to find the "best" ordering of interpretations that defines a rational closure of $\text{Cons}_P(\Delta)$. This problem has been solved by Lehmann and Magidor (1992), and Pearl (1990). The idea is to find the ranking of interpretations that agrees with Δ, where each interpretation is as normal as possible. This construction can be entirely reinterpreted in the setting of possibility theory. Namely let $PI(\Delta)$ be the set of possibility distribution π such that $\forall\ p_i \mathrel|\!\sim q_i$ in Δ, $\Pi(p_i \wedge q_i) > \Pi(p_i \wedge \neg q_i)$. A possibility distributions π is said to be less specific than π' if and only if $\pi < \pi'$. Clearly each interpretation is at least as normal in the sense of π' than in the sense of π. The ordering that determines the rational closure is defined by the least specific possibility distribution π^* in $PI(\Delta)$.

Equivalently as proposed by Pearl (1990) rational inference can be captured through an ordering of the conditional knowledge base Δ. This ordering is based on a concept of toleration of a default rule by a conditional knowledge base. If $p \mathrel|\!\sim q$ is a conditional assertion, let $\neg p \vee q$ be its material implication counterpart. Let K be the set of material implication counterparts of the conditional assertions in Δ. A rule $p \mathrel|\!\sim q$ is tolerated by Δ, if and only if $p \wedge q$ is consistent with K. In order to get a flavor of the reason for this definition consider again the penguin example. The examples to the rule $\neg f | p$ are exceptions to the two other rules $f|b$, $b|p$, i.e., $\neg f|p$ is not tolerated by them. Contrastedly, $f|b$ is tolerated by the others since this rule has examples that are not exceptions to the others (consider non-penguins). Hence using rule $f|b$ does not cause any conflict in Δ. But applying the other rules does conflict with $f|b$. Hence non-tolerated rules should be given priority over tolerated ones. An algorithm for priority ranking of objects has been proposed by Pearl (1990). It can be described as follows. If $\Delta = \{q_i \mathrel|\!\sim p_i, i = 1,n\}$, then partition Δ into $\Delta_0 \cup \Delta_1 \cup \ldots \cup \Delta_k$ where Δ_0 has the lowest priority and Δ_k has the highest one. Δ_0 is made of conditional objects $p \mathrel|\!\sim q$ tolerated by Δ, i.e., such that $p \wedge q$ is consistent with $\{\neg p_i \vee q_i, i = 1,n\}$. Δ_1 is made of the conditional objects tolerated by $\Delta - \Delta_0$, etc. This ordering respects the priority to the most specific rules (Poole, 1985).

The obtained ordering is exactly the same as the one derived by changing each conditional assertion $p_i \mathrel|\!\sim q_i$ in Δ into its material counterpart $\neg p_i \vee q_i$ and attaching to it the weight $N^*(\neg p_i \vee q_i)$ computed using π^*. Let K^* be the possibilistic knowledge base thus constructed from Δ. It can be proved that $p \mathrel|\!\sim q$ belongs to the rational closure of Δ if and only if $K^* \cup \{p\} \vdash_\pi q$. Hence plausible conclusions derived from evidence p and generic knowledge Δ can be computed via possibilistic logic proof methods of Section 6. Particularly the complexity of system P and rational inference is the same as propositional logic inference (e.g., polynomial for Horn clause-like conditional assertions).

This approach partially solves the problem of irrelevant properties. In the Tweety example the possibilistic knowledge base obtained by the ranking procedure is the one of Section 6, and it holds that $\{b,r\} \cup K^* \vdash_\pi f$. Unfortunately the rational closure still has problems when a class is exceptional for a superclass with respect to some attribute. Then the least specific ranking does not allow to conclude anything about whether this class is normal with respect to other attributes. For instance, if we add $b \hspace{2pt}\vdash\hspace{2pt} \ell$ (birds have legs) to the knowledge base of the Tweety example, then $p \hspace{2pt}\vdash\hspace{2pt} \ell$ is not in the rational closure of $\Delta \cup \{b \hspace{2pt}\vdash\hspace{2pt} \ell\}$. This problem has been solved in various ways by several authors: Geffner (1990) defines a partial ordering that comes down to checking for maximal consistent subbases of $K^* \cup E$. Goldszmidt et al. (1990) exploit the infinitesimal probability setting and apply maximal entropy methods to characterize another ranking of worlds. More recently Benferhat et al. (1993) and Lehmann (1993) have suggested an approach based on a lexicographic ordering whereby each interpretation should satisfy as little conditional assertions as possible. All these methods solve the problem of blocking of property inheritance in the Tweety example, but their motivations are unclear, and counter-examples where these techniques give counterintuitive results can be found. Moreover, all of them are syntax-dependent, and their complexity is higher than the rational closure.

CONCLUSION

Numerical and symbolic approaches to uncertainty should not be considered as competing models. It is more interesting to display their deep coherence rather than to argue in favor of one against the other. The notion of conditional assertions, or equivalently of conditional event captures the basic features of plausible reasoning, in accordance with non-monotonic logics and also with probability theory and possibility theory as well. Possibilistic logic, that can encode ordered sets of default rules, can be viewed as a logic of accepted beliefs, in full agreement with a calculus of extreme probabilities. It is a natural framework for encoding Lehmann's rational closure.

An important issue that has received little attention so far is the notion of independence. Namely it is worth investigating to what extent the probabilistic definition of independence has counterparts in other uncertainty models. The limitations of conditional event logic for dealing with property inheritance is directly linked to this question. The RM axiom expresses a default independence assumption, but is not productive enough to address all the difficulties. Note that in probability theory, independence assumptions are always made explicit, while in logic distinct propositional symbols are implicitly independent. The language of logic encodes dependencies, but there is no independence symbol. Some insights in qualitative independence can be found in Pearl (1988); these results could be usefully related to the conditional event logic. The next promising step in exception-tolerant reasoning seems to search for a new concept of independence that is less permissive than logical independence, but more flexible than probabilistic independence, in the context of ordinal uncertainty approaches like possibility theory. Our suggestion is that rational monotonicity should be augmented by conditional independence assertions whose statement is dictated by the structure of the knowledge base Δ. This is the last lesson from Bayesian nets to be taken advantage of. Preliminary steps along that line can be found in Goldszmidt and Pearl (1992), Fonck (1993), and Benferhat et al. (1994).

References

E.W. Adams (1975). *The Logic of Conditionals*. Dordrecht: D. Reidel.

S. Amarger, D. Dubois, and H. Prade (1991). Constraint propagation with imprecise conditional probabilities. *Proc. 7th Conf. on Uncertainty in AI*, 26-34.

S. Benferhat, C. Cayrol, D. Dubois, J. Lang, and H. Prade (1993). Inconsistency management and prioritized syntax-based entailment. *Proc. IJCAI'93*, 640-645.

S. Benferhat, D. Dubois, and H. Prade (1992). Representing default rules in possibilistic logic. *Proc. KR'92*, 673-684.

S. Benferhat, D. Dubois, and H. Prade (1994) Expressing independence in a possibilistic framework and its application to default reasoning. Submitted.

P. Calabrese (1987). An algebraic synthesis of the foundations of logic and probability. *Information Sciences* 42:187-237.

B. De Finetti (1936). La logique de la probabilité. *Actes du Congrès Inter. de Philosophie Scientifique*, Paris, 1935, 565-573. Hermann et Cie. Editeurs.

B. De Finetti (1937). La prévision, ses lois logiques et ses sources subjectives. Eng. trans. in *Studies in Subjective Probability* (H. Kyburg, and H.E. Smokler, eds.), 1964. New York: Wiley.

D. Dubois (1986). Belief structures, possibility theory and decomposable confidence measures on finite sets. *Computers and Artificial Intelligence* 5(5):403-416.

D. Dubois, L. Godo, R. López de Màntaras, and H. Prade (1993). Qualitative reasoning with imprecise probabilities. *J. of Intelligent Information Systems*.

D. Dubois, J. Lang, and H. Prade (1991). Possibilistic logic. Tech. Report IRIT/91-98-R. In D.M. Gabbay et al. (eds.), *Handbook of Logic in AI and Logic Programming 3*, to appear. Oxford University Press.

D. Dubois, and H. Prade (1988a). *Possibility Theory*. New York: Plenum Press.

D. Dubois, and H. Prade (1988b). An introduction to possibilistic and fuzzy logics. In P. Smets et al. (eds.),

Non-Standard Logics for Automated Reasoning, 287-326. New York: Academic Press.

D. Dubois, and H. Prade (1991). Epistemic entrenchment and possibilistic logic. *Artificial Intelligence* **50**:223-239.

D. Dubois, and H. Prade (1993). A glance at non-standard models and logics of uncertainty and vagueness. In J.P. Dubucs (ed.), *Philosophy of Probability*, 169-222. Dordrecht: Kluwer Academic Publ.

D. Dubois, and H. Prade (1994a). Focusing versus updating in belief function theory. In R.R. Yager et al. (eds.), *Advances in the Dempster-Shafer Theory of Evidence*, 71-95. New York: Wiley.

D. Dubois, and H. Prade (1994b). Conditional objects as nonmonotonic consequence relations. *Proc. KR'94*, these proceedings.

D. Dubois, H. Prade, and P. Smets (1993). Representing partial ignorance. *Post-UAI-93 Workshop on Higher Order Uncertainty*, Washington, DC.

C. Elkan (1993) The paradoxical success of fuzzy logic. *Proc. AAAI'93*, 698-703.

L. Fariñas del Cerro, A. Herzig, and J. Lang (1992). From ordering-based nonmonotonic reasoning to conditional logics. *Proc. ECAI'92*, 314-318.

T.L. Fine (1973). *Theories of Probability*. New York: Academic Press.

P. Fonck (1993). Réseaux d'inférence pour le raisonnement possibiliste. Thèse de Docteur es Sciences, Université de Liège, Belgium.

D.M. Gabbay (1985). Theoretical foundations for non-monotonic reasoning in expert systems. In K.R. Apt (ed.), *Logics and Models of Concurrent Systems*, 439-457. Berlin: Springer Verlag.

P. Gärdenfors (1988). *Knowledge in Flux*. Cambridge, MA: The MIT Press.

P. Gärdenfors, and D. Makinson (1992) Non-monotonic inference based on expectations. *Artif. Intellig.*, to appear.

H. Geffner (1992). *Default Reasoning: Causal and Conditional Theories*. Cambridge, MA: The MIT Press.

M. Goldszmidt, P. Morris, and J. Pearl (1990). A maximum entropy approach to nonmonotonic reasoning. *Proc. AAAI'90*, 646-652.

M. Goldszmidt, and J. Pearl (1992). Rank-based systems. *Proc. KR'92*, 661-672.

I.R. Goodman, H.T. Nguyen, and E.A. Walker (1991). *Conditional Inference and Logic for Intelligent Systems*. Amsterdam: North-Holland.

K. Kraus, D. Lehmann, and M. Magidor (1990). Nonmonotonic reasoning, preferential models and cumulative logics. *Artificial Intelligence* **44**:167-207.

H.E. Kyburg, Jr. (1974). *The Logical Foundations of Statistical Inference*. Dordrecht: D. Reidel.

S.L. Lauritzen, and D.J. Spiegelhalter (1988). Local computations with probabilities on graphical structures and their application to expert systems. *J. of the Royal Statist. Society* **50**(2):157-224.

Léa Sombé (1990). *Reasoning Under Incomplete Information in Artificial Intelligence*. New York: Wiley.

D. Lehmann (1993). Another perspective on default reasoning. Inst. Computer Science, Hebrew Univ., Jerusalem.

D. Lehmann, and M. Magidor (1992). What does a conditional knowledge base entail? *Artificial Intelligence* **55**:1-60.

D. Lewis (1973). *Counterfactuals*. Oxford: Basil Blackwell.

D. Makinson, and P. Gärdenfors (1991). Relations between the logic of theory change and nonmonotonic logic. In A. Furhmann, and M. Morreau (eds.), *The Logic of Theory Change*, 185-205. Berlin: Springer Verlag.

N. Nilsson (1986). Probabilistic logic. *Artificial Intelligence* **28**:71-87.

J. Pearl (1988). *Probabilistic Reasoning in Intelligent Systems*. San Mateo, CA: Morgan & Kaufmann.

J. Pearl (1990). System Z: A natural ordering of defaults with tractable aplications to default reasoning. In M. Vardi (ed.), *Proc. TARK'90*, 121-135. San Mateo, CA: Morgan & Kaufmann.

D.L. Poole (1985). On the comparison of theories: Preferring the most specific explanation. *Proc. IJCAI'85*, 144-147.

N. Rescher (1969) *Many-Valued Logic*. New York: McGraw-Hill.

G. Shafer (1976). *A Mathematical Theory of Evidence*. Princeton, New Jersey: Princeton University Press.

P.P. Shenoy, and G. Shafer (1990). Axioms for probability and belief-function propagation. In R.D. Shachter et al. (eds.), *Uncertainty in Artificial Intelligence 4*, 169-198. Amsterdam: North-Holland.

Y. Shoham (1988). *Reasoning About Change*. Cambridge, MA: The MIT Press.

P. Smets (1988). Belief functions. In P. Smets et al. (eds.), *Non-Standard Logics for Approximate Reasoning*, 253-286. New York: Academic Press.

W. Spohn (1988). Ordinal conditional functions: A dynamic theory of epistemic states. In W.L. Harper, and B. Skyrms (eds.), *Causation in Decision, Belief Change, and Statistics*, 105-134. Dordrecht: Kluwer Academic.

H. Thöne, U. Güntzer, and W. Kießling (1992). Towards precision of probabilistic bounds propagation. *Proc. 8th Conf. on Uncertainty in AI*, 315-322.

L.A. Zadeh (1965). Fuzzy sets. *Information and Control* **8**:338-353.

L.A. Zadeh (1978). Fuzzy sets as a basis for a theory of possibility. *Fuzzy Sets and Systems* **1**:3-28.

L.A. Zadeh (1985). Syllogistic reasoning in fuzzy logic and its application to usuality and reasoning with dispositions. *IEEE Trans. on S.M.C.* **15**(6):745-763.

Beyond Ignorance-Based Systems

William A. Woods
Sun Microsystems Laboratories, Inc.
2 Elizabeth Drive
Chelmsford, MA 01824-4195
USA

Abstract

The field of artificial intelligence has a long tradition of exploiting the potential of limited domains. While this is beneficial as a way to get started and has utility for applications of limited scope, these approaches will not scale to systems with more open-ended domains of knowledge. Many "knowledge-based" systems actually derive their success as much from ignorance as from the knowledge that they contain. That is, they succeed because they don't know any better. Too great a reliance on a closed-world assumption and default reasoning in a limited domain can result in a system that is fundamentally limited and cannot be extended beyond its initial domain.

If the field of knowledge-based systems is to move beyond this stage, we need to develop knowledge representation and reasoning technology that is more robust in the face of domain extensions. Non-monotonic reasoning becomes a liability if the fundamental abilities of a system can be destroyed by the addition of knowledge from a new domain. This talk will discuss some of the challenges that we must meet to develop systems that can handle diverse ranges of knowledge.

Panels

Systems vs. Theory vs. ...: KR&R Research Methodologies

Lin Padgham, Moderator
Department of Computer Science
University of Linköping
Sweden

Abstract

This panel will explore the issues regarding what research methodologies are appropriate for KR&R research and hopefully expand our awareness of how methodological issues affect and influence the usefulness and relevance of a research effort. It can be argued that it is meaningless to build research systems until one has a clear theory one is attempting to implement. It can equally well be argued that formal theory development without a grounding in application requirements is futile. Just as we do not want systems that grind to a halt while they consider all the alternatives for action, so we don't want research that sinks into the mire of formalism for its own sake.

What is the correct balance between theory and application? Is there a particular order in which the various methodological approaches of informal theory development, formal theory development, system building, implementation of applications, empirical experimentation and validation, etc. should be applied? Are all equally relevant? Is building of applications really research? If so what qualities are necessary in order for application development to be legitimate research? When is system building an important research activity? What qualities qualify or disqualify application development as a research activity? What research methodologies are currently most needed in KR&R research?

The panel members will attempt to address these and related questions from the viewpoint of both varying areas of KR research, and various methodological styles.

Exploiting Natural Language for Knowledge Representation and Reasoning

Len Schubert, Moderator
Department of Computer Science
University of Rochester
Rochester, NY 14627-0226
USA

Abstract

As the title suggests, the panel will address such questions as, "What syntactic/semantic (or other) resources does NL potentially offer that could be profitably exploited for knowledge representation and reasoning? What are the prospective benefits? How can they be realized? What's the down side?". The intention is that some sense of the state of the art, difficulties, tradeoffs, and the most promising directions for further work should emerge from the presentations and discussion.

Some specific resources suggested in advance as possible topics for discussion are:

- generalized quantifiers
- predicate and sentence nominalization
- predicate and sentence modification
- probabilistic qualification
- collections, substances, kinds, properties
- events, situations, times, locations, actions, plans
- aspectual classes (Aktionsarten)
- more generally, commonsense ontologies
- donkey anaphora and generics
- "natural" forms of inference
- language (especially narratives) as a guide to "warranted nonmonotonic inference"
- feature logics (aimed at NL syntax) as general KRs
- indexicality, context
- vagueness as a useful feature
- ambiguity as a useful feature
- theory of communication, knowledge, collaboration

One can consider the potential benefits of such resources collectively or one by one. Let us imagine that we have a formalized representation that is natural-language-like, incorporating many of the above features. One potential benefit would be the improved opportunity for "knowledge bootstrapping" via natural language, since the necessary transformations in going from NL input to the internal representation would then be minimal. Moreover, since we tend to have good intuitions about what follows from what (either deductively or defeasibly) when considering examples formulated in natural language, a language-like representation might facilitate the formulation of effective deductive and nondeductive inference mechanisms. Another significant benefit might be the *comprehensibility* of a representation parasitic on language, from the perspective of users of the KR who need to peruse, extend, and debug sizable knowledge bases.

Against such an across-the-board strategy one might argue that it would make inference intractable or at least "gappy" in unforseeable ways. Even unquantified predicate logic is intractable in a worst-case sense (if $P \neq NP$). Keeping in mind that the goals of AI are *performance* goals (or, goals of explicating human performance), we must ensure that our KR's lend themselves to fast, reliable inference. So we should move *away* from general language-like expressiveness towards collections of tractable, specialized sublanguages.

There are replies to this objection, but one can also remain agnostic about the across-the-board strategy and consider benefits obtainable by exploiting *some* of the above resources. Knowledge bootstrapping, formulation of inference rules, and knowledge base browsing may become significantly easier even with some seemingly minor, "cosmetic" changes to a representation, bringing it superficially closer to NL without increase in expressive power.

The expectation is that some panelists will be able to point to specific gains already obtained or eventually expected from language-inspired approaches to various representational issues: NL-like quantification might promote readability and effective inference; ordinary ways of talking about properties, propositions, actions, and plans (often involving phrasings that reify or nominalize these) might provide the key to a workable analysis of attitudes and actions; ontological categories derived from language (including collections, substances, time, space, events, and specific "natural taxonomies") should facilitate the encoding of at least the "commonsense core" of many applications; the form taken by generics in NL might suggest ways of formalizing defeasible generalizations; indexicality in NL (e.g., as exemplified by words like 'now', 'here', or 'I') might suggest effective ways of "situated reasoning", for instance by a planner; the ways in which language allows for vagueness and ambiguity might suggest ways of dealing effectively with imprecise or underspecified information; the conventions underlying cooperative dialogs might suggest formal protocols for arriving at mutual knowledge; the feature logics that have evolved for describing the syntactic structure of natural languages show signs of being apt for world-description as well; and so on.

No doubt there are caveats and unresolved difficulties. Language may perhaps mislead, where the devices it employs are peculiar to its communicative function and its one-dimensional acoustic form; and it may not lead to any one place, judging from the variety of theories that have been proposed for many of the linguistic phenomena mentioned above. But it is surely an invaluable source of representational ideas that should be heeded by the KR&R community.

Contributions by Topic

DEDUCTION, ABDUCTION, AND SEARCH

Proofs in Context *G. Attardi and M. Simi* **15**

Directional Resolution: The Davis-Putnam Procedure, Revisited *R. Dechter and I. Rish* **134**

GSAT and Dynamic Backtracking *M. L. Ginsberg and D. A. McAllester* **226**

Easy to be Hard: Difficult Problems for Greedy Algorithms *K. Konolige* **374**

Enhancing the Power of a Decidable First-Order Reasoner *G. Lakemeyer and S. Meyer* **403**

Generating Tests Using Abduction *S. McIlraith* **449**

Tractable Databases: How to Make Propositional Unit Resolution Complete Through Compilation *A. del Val* **551**

Constraint Tightness versus Global Consistency *P. van Beek and R. Dechter* **572**

DESCRIPTION LOGICS AND LANGUAGES

A Computational Account for a Description Logic of Time and Action *A. Artale and E. Franconi* **3**

A Unified Framework for Class-based Representation Formalisms *D. Calvanese, M. Lenzerini, and D. Nardi* **109**

Learning the Classic Description Logic: Theoretical and Experimental Results *W. W. Cohen and H. Hirsh* **121**

Action Representation for Interpreting Purpose Clauses in Natural Language Instructions *B. Di Eugenio* **158**

An Ontology of Meta-Level Categories *N. Guarino, M. Carrara, and P. Giaretta* **270**

Probabilistic Reasoning in Terminological Logics *M. Jaeger* **305**

An Application of Terminological Logics to Case-based Reasoning *J. Koehler* **351**

A Framework for Part-of Hierarchies in Terminological Logics *L. Padgham and P. Lambrix* **485**

Terminological Cycles and the Propositional μ-Calculus *K. Schild* **509**

Making the Difference: A Subtraction Operation for Description Logics *G. Teege* **540**

The Role of Reversible Grammars in Translating Between Representation Languages *J. Van Baalen and R. E. Fikes* **562**

KNOWLEDGE AND BELIEF

An Integrated Implementation of Simulative, Uncertain and Metaphorical Reasoning about Mental States *J. A. Barnden, S. Helmreich, E. Iverson, and G. C. Stein* **27**

Belief Ascription and Mental-Level Modelling *R. I. Brafman and M. Tennenholtz* **87**

Knowledge, Certainty, Belief, and Conditionalisation (Abbreviated Version) *P. Lamarre and Y. Shoham* **415**

Honesty in Partial Logic *W. van der Hoek, J. Jaspars, and E. Thijsse* **583**

NONMONOTONIC REASONING AND BELIEF REVISION

Reasoning with Minimal Models: Efficient Algorithms and Applications *R. Ben-Eliyahu and L. Palopoli* **39**

On the Relation Between Default and Modal Consequence Relations *A. Bochman* **63**

Default Logic as a Query Language *M. Cadoli, T. Eiter, and G. Gottlob* **99**

A General Approach to Specificity in Default Reasoning *J. P. Delgrande and T. H. Schaub* **146**

Conditional Objects as Nonmonotonic Consequence Relations: Main Results *D. Dubois and H. Prade* **170**

Tractable Closed World Reasoning with Updates *O. Etzioni, K. Golden, and D. Weld* **178**

A Knowledge-based Framework for Belief Change, Part II: Revision and Update *N. Friedman and J. Y. Halpern* **190**

On the Complexity of Conditional Logics *N. Friedman and J. Y. Halpern* **202**

Defeasible Reasoning with Structured Information *A. Hunter* **281**

On Positive Occurrences of Negation as Failure *K. Inoue and C. Sakama* **293**

On Multiagent Autoepistemic Logic—An Extrospective View   *Y. J. Jiang*   **317**

Preferential Entailments for Circumscriptions   *Y. Moinard and R. Rolland*   **461**

A Decision Method for Nonmomotonic Reasoning Based on Autoepistemic Reasoning   *I. Niemelä*   **473**

Mutual Belief Revision (Preliminary Report)   *R. van der Meyden*   **595**

REVISE: An Extended Logic Programming System for Revising Knowledge Bases   *C. Viegas Damásio, L. Moniz Pereira, and W. Nejdl*   **607**

Transmutations of Knowledge Systems   *M.-A. Williams*   **619**

REASONING ABOUT ACTION AND TIME

An Efficient Method for Managing Disjunctions in Qualitative Temporal Reasoning   *A. Gerevini and L. Schubert*   **214**

Actions with Indirect Effects (Preliminary Report)   *G. N. Kartha and V. Lifschitz*   **341**

Complexity Results for First-Order Theories of Temporal Constraints   *M. Koubarakis*   **379**

How to Progress a Database (and Why) I. Logical Foundations   *F. Lin and R. Reiter*   **425**

Modalities Over Actions, I. Model Theory   *L. T. McCarty*   **437**

PLANNING, PREFERENCE, AND DECISION-MAKING

Toward a Logic for Qualitative Decision Theory   *C. Boutilier*   **75**

Representing Uncertainty in Simple Planners   *R. P. Goldman and M. S. Boddy*   **238**

Refinement Search as a Unifying Framework for Analyzing Planning Algorithms   *S. Kambhampati*   **329**

Risk-Sensitive Planning with Probabilistic Decision Graphs   *S. Koenig and R. G. Simmons*   **363**

Means-End Plan Recognition—Towards a Theory of Reactive Recognition   *A. S. Rao*   **497**

Near-Optimal Plans, Tractability, and Reactivity   *B. Selman*   **521**

Specification and Evaluation of Preferences Under Uncertainty   *S.-W. Tan and J. Pearl*   **530**

REASONING ABOUT THE PHYSICAL WORLD

Spatial Reasoning with Propositional Logics   *B. Bennett*   **51**

How Far Can We 'C'? Defining a 'Doughnut' Using Connection Alone   *N. M. Gotts*   **246**

An Ontology for Engineering Mathematics   *T. R. Gruber and G. R. Olsen*   **258**

Reasoning in Logic about Continuous Systems   *B. J. Kuipers and B. Shults*   **391**

GENERAL TOPICS

Knowledge Representation Issues in Integrated Planning and Learning Systems (*Invited Talk—abstract only*)   *J. Carbonell*   **633**

Non-Standard Theories of Uncertainty in Knowledge Representation and Reasoning (*Invited Talk*)   *D. Dubois and H. Prade*   **634**

Beyond Ignorance-Based Systems (*Invited Talk—abstract only*)   *W. A. Woods*   **646**

Systems vs. Theory vs. ... : KR&R Research Methodologies (*abstract only*)   (Panel)   **649**

Exploiting Natural Language for Knowledge Representation and Reasoning (*abstract only*)   (Panel)   **650**

Author Index

Artale, A. *3*
Attardi, G. *15*

Barnden, J. A. *27*
Ben-Eliyahu, R. *39*
Bennett, B. *51*
Bochman, A. *63*
Boddy, M. S. *238*
Boutilier, C. *75*
Brafman, R. I. *87*

Cadoli, M. *99*
Calvanese, D. *109*
Carbonell, J. *633*
Carrara, M. *270*
Cohen, W. W. *121*

Dechter, R. *134, 572*
Delgrande, J. P. *146*
Di Eugenio, B. *158*
Dubois, D. *170, 634*

Eiter, T. *99*
Etzioni, O. *178*

Fikes, R. E. *562*
Franconi, E. *3*
Friedman, N. *190, 202*

Gerevini, A. *214*
Giaretta, P. *270*
Ginsberg, M. L. *226*
Golden, K. *178*
Goldman, R. P. *238*
Gottlob, G. *99*
Gotts, N. M. *246*
Gruber, T. R. *258*
Guarino, N. *270*

Halpern, J. Y. *190, 202*
Helmreich, S. *27*
Hirsh, H. *121*
Hunter, A. *281*

Inoue, K. *293*
Iverson, E. *27*

Jaeger, M. *305*
Jaspars, J. *583*
Jiang, Y. J. *317*

Kambhampati, S. *329*
Kartha, G. N. *341*
Koehler, J. *351*
Koenig, S. *363*
Konolige, K. *374*
Koubarakis, M. *379*
Kuipers, B. J. *391*

Lakemeyer, G. *403*
Lamarre, P. *415*
Lambrix, P. *485*
Lenzerini, M. *109*
Lifschitz, V. *341*
Lin, F. *425*

McAllester, D. A. *226*
McCarty, L. T. *437*
McIlraith, S. *449*
Meyer, S. *403*
Moinard, Y. *461*
Moniz Pereira, L. *607*

Nardi, D. *109*
Nejdl, W. *607*
Niemelä, I. *473*

Olsen, G. R. *258*

Padgham, L. *485*
Palopoli, L. *39*
Pearl, J. *530*
Prade, H. *170, 634*

Rao, A. S. *497*
Reiter, R. *425*
Rish, I. *134*
Rolland, R. *461*

Sakama, C. *293*
Schaub, T. H. *146*
Schild, K. *509*
Schubert, L. *214, 650*
Selman, B. *521*
Shoham, Y. *415*
Shults, B. *391*
Simi, M. *15*
Simmons, R. G. *363*
Stein, G. C. *27*

Tan, S.-W. *530*
Teege, G. *540*
Tennenholtz, M. *87*
Thijsse, E. *583*

del Val, A. *551*
Van Baalen, J. *562*
van Beek, P. *572*
van der Hoek, W. *583*
van der Meyden, R. *595*
Viegas Damásio, C. *607*

Weld, D. *178*
Williams, M.-A. *619*
Woods, W. A. *646*